# Dover:
# The Buckland Anglo-Saxon Cemetery

HISTORIC BUILDINGS AND MONUMENTS COMMISSION FOR ENGLAND
Archaeological Report No. 3

# Dover:
# The Buckland Anglo-Saxon Cemetery

Vera I Evison

LONDON: HISTORIC BUILDINGS AND
MONUMENTS COMMISSION FOR ENGLAND

© Historic Buildings & Monuments Commission for England 1987

First published 1987 by the
Historic Buildings & Monuments Commission for England,
Fortress House, 23 Savile Row,
London, W1X 2HE

Distributed by Academic Marketing Services, Alan Sutton Publishing Limited,
Brunswick Road, Gloucester, GL1 1JJ

British Library Cataloguing in Publication Data

Evison, Vera I.
   Dover: The Buckland Anglo-Saxon Cemetery—(Historic Buildings and Monuments Commission for England archaeological report; no. 3)
   1. Anglo-Saxons—England—Dover (Kent)
   2. Excavations (Archaeology)—England—Dover (Kent)
   3. Buckland Estate Site (Dover, Kent)
   4. Dover (Kent)—Antiquities
   5. England—Antiquities
   I. Title     II. English Heritage   III. Series
   942,2'352    DA690.D7

ISBN 1-85074-090-9

E/115/558–872/W/120387/520

Produced by Alan Sutton Publishing, Gloucester
Printed in Great Britain by WBC Print Ltd, Bristol

# Contents

|  | Page |
|---|---|
| List of figures | 7 |
| List of plates | 9 |
| List of tables | 9 |
| Acknowledgements | 10 |

*Chapter I* **Excavation**
- i Introduction ... 11
- ii Features other than Anglo-Saxon graves
  - a. Prehistoric barrow ... 13
  - b. Romano-British pit ... 15
  - c. Postholes ... 15
  - d. Medieval reburial ... 15
  - e. Modern disturbance ... 15
  - f. Disturbance by animals ... 16
- iii The Anglo-Saxon cemetery
  - a. Orientation of graves ... 16
  - b. The shaping of the graves ... 16
  - c. The fill in the graves ... 17
  - d. The skeletons, positions of bones ... 18
  - e. The grave furniture, positions of objects ... 18
  - f. Grouping as suggested by the plan of the cemetery ... 19
  - g. The limits of the cemetery ... 20

*Chapter II* **Grave goods: discussion of types**

WEAPONS:
- swords ... 21
- spears ... 26
- arrows ... 30
- seaxes ... 31
- shields ... 31

JEWELLERY:
- brooches, square-headed ... 35
- small-long ... 39
- Kentish disc ... 39
- Frankish disc ... 47
- saucer ... 47
- button ... 48
- annular ... 48
- Pendants, coins ... 49
- gold bracteates ... 51
- silver disc ... 55
- silver, oval and mushroom, garnet-set, shell, glass, bronze ... 56
- Beads, non-glass, amber ... 57
- amethyst quartz ... 57
- jet ... 57
- stone ... 60
- shell ... 60
- white composition ... 60
- bronze and silver ... 61
- Glass beads ... 61
- glass, monochrome ... 61
- glass, polychrome ... 63
- Discussion ... 65

|  | Page |
|---|---|
| Positions of brooches and beads | 69 |
| Analysis of the glass beads | 70 |
| Pins | 82 |
| Bracelets and finger rings | 85 |
| Buckles, belt and strap mounts | 86 |

CONTAINERS:
- pottery ... 92
- glass ... 94
- coffins ... 99
- wooden boxes with iron fittings ... 100
- bronze bowls ... 103
- buckets ... 104
- turned wooden vessels ... 105
- bone-covered boxes ... 106
- bronze workbox ... 106
- bone lid ... 108

TOOLS:
- sharpening steels ... 110
- awls ... 110
- ?mattock ... 110
- fire-steels ... 110
- hones ... 111

WEAVING EQUIPMENT:
- iron weaving battens ... 111
- bone weaving pick ... 112
- bronze needle ... 112
- spindle whorls ... 112
- shears ... 113

PERSONAL EQUIPMENT:
- knives ... 113
- keys ... 116
- girdle-hangers ... 117
- tweezers ... 118
- spoons ... 118
- iron diamonds ... 118
- ivory rings ... 118
- silver, bronze and iron rings ... 119
- combs ... 119
- bronze balance ... 120
- ?lyre ... 121

AMULETS AND KEEPSAKES:
- cowrie shell ... 121
- horse tooth ... 122
- fossils ... 122
- iron ore, pebbles, playing piece, stud, coins ... 122

*Chapter III* **Discussion**
- Determination of sex and age ... 123
- Age at death ... 127
- Skeleton positions ... 129
- Grouping according to grave finds ... 134
- Relative and absolute chronology ... 136
- Interpretation of the layout and expansion of the cemetery ... 142
- Family grouping ... 145
- Social status ... 146
- Depths of graves ... 150
- Cemetery layout and orientation ... 152

|  | | Page |
|---|---|---:|
| | Comparable cemetery plans | 162 |
| | Anglo-Saxon Dover | 168 |
| | List of graves in each plot | 175 |
| | List of graves allocated to phases | 175 |
| | List of Anglo-Saxon finds in the Dover area | 176 |
| Chapter IV | **Specialist reports** | |
| | Prehistoric pottery sherds, *P Ashbee* | 179 |
| | The petrology of the Anglo-Saxon pottery, *I C Freestone* | 179 |
| | Coins, *J P C Kent* | 180 |
| | Gold analyses, *M Cowell* | 181 |
| | Quantitative analyses of beads, *J Bayley* | 182 |
| | Textiles, *E Crowfoot* | 190 |
| | Wood, *D F Cutler* | 195 |

|  | Page |
|---|---:|
| Organic material associated with metal objects, *J Watson* | 196 |
| The wooden belt from grave 20, *K Wilson* | 196 |
| Hones, *S E Ellis* | 197 |
| Seed analysis, *G W Dimbleby* | 197 |
| Human skeletal remains, *R Powers and R Cullen* | 197 |
| Bibliography | 202 |

Chapter V

| | Page |
|---|---:|
| Catalogue of graves | 214 |
| Concordance of catalogue numbers and British Museum registration numbers | 254 |
| Table LV, Grave contents | 262 |
| Distribution map lists | 266 |
| Index | 405 |

# List of figures

*Text figures*

|  |  | Page |
|---|---|---|
| 1a,b | Site location maps | 12 |
| 2 | Plan of Anglo-Saxon cemetery, Buckland Estate, Dover | 14 |
| 3a | Sword C/1, reconstruction of leather holder | |
| b | Sword 27/3, reconstruction of button and baldric | 24 |
| 4 | Spears: a. Dover 8/1. b. Mucking 662/1 | 28 |
| 5a | Shield appliqué, Dover 93/10d | |
| b | Shield appliqué, Mucking grave 600 | |
| c | Shield appliqué, Thames at Barnes | 33 |
| 6 | Animal ornament on Dover square-headed brooches: a. 13/1, b. 13/2, c. Unassociated 9, d. 20/8 | 36 |
| 7 | Kentish disc brooches in the Dover cemetery | 40 |
| 8 | Design on disc brooch, Avent No. 20 | 42 |
| 9 | Runic inscription on the back of disc brooch 126/1 | 46 |
| 10 | Designs on gold bracteates a,b,c. Nebenstedt, Dannenberg, West Germany   d,e,f. Dover 20/4   g,h. Dover 1/1, i. Kingston, Kent   j. Dover 134/1, k. Dover 29/8, l. Bolbro, Odense, Denmark | 50 |
| 11 | Dover: Non-glass beads, monochrome glass bead forms, drawn glass bead forms | 58 |
| 12 | Dover: polychrome glass beads | 64 |
| 13 | Dover: positions of beads and brooches in the graves | 68 |
| 14a | Drawing of radiograph of pin, Dover 161/3 | |
| b | Bronze head from Gåtebo, Öland | 84 |
| 15a | Reconstruction of belt, Dover grave 56 | |
| b | Reconstruction of belt, Dover grave 98 | 88 |
| 16 | Reconstruction of lacing of wooden belt, Dover 20/19 | 91 |
| 17a | Diagram of boltplate in box lid, section of shot bolt with key inserted in lock | |
| b | View of bolt inside the box | 101 |
| 18a | Reconstruction of box, Dover grave 43 | |
| b | Reconstruction of box, Dover grave 143 | 102 |
| 19 | Reconstruction of bronze-bound bucket, Dover 28/1 | 104 |
| 20a | Bronze workbox, Dover 107/4 before later alterations | |
| b | Bronze workbox from Hawnby, North Yorkshire | |
| c | Bronze workbox from Sibertswold, grave 60 | |
| d | Bronze hinges, Dover 84/3 | 107 |
| 21a | Bone lid, Dover 157/6h | |
| b | Bone box and lid, Sainte Walburge, Liège, Belgium | 109 |
| 22 | Knife types at Dover | 113 |
| 23 | Reconstruction of knife 158/2 | 114 |
| 24 | Reconstruction of comb and case 110/9 | 120 |
| 25 | Grave good types in phases 1 and 2 | 138 |
| 26 | Grave good types in phases 3 and 4 | 139 |
| 27 | Grave good types in phases 5, 6 and 7 | 140 |
| 28 | Cemetery area with field boundaries according to the tithe map of 1842 | 144 |
| 29 | Orientation. All graves | 157 |
| 30 | Orientation. a-d. Graves influenced by barrow | 158 |
| 31 | Orientation. a-d. Graves not influenced by barrow | 159 |
| 32a | Cemetery at Lyminge, Kent: sex | |
| b | Cemetery at Lyminge, Kent: chronology | 163 |
| 33a | Cemetery at Orpington, Kent: sex | |
| b | Cemetery at Orpington, Kent: chronology | 165 |
| 34a | Cemetery at Bergh Apton, Norfolk: sex | |
| b | Cemetery at Holborough, Kent: sex | 167 |
| 35 | The Dover area in the Roman period (after Philp) | 169 |
| 36 | Anglo-Saxon sites in the Dover area | 170 |
| 37 | Plot of analytical results for monochrome beads; iron (Fe) v. manganese (Mn) | 182 |
| 38 | Histograms of analytical results for manganese (Mn) and tin (Sn) | 183 |
| 39 | Plot of analytical results for monochrome beads; tin (Sn) v. copper (Cu) | 184 |
| 40 | Plot of analytical results from monochrome beads; zinc (Zn) v. copper (Cu) | 185 |
| 41 | Plot of analytical results for monochrome beads; lead (Pb) v. copper (Cu) | 185 |
| 42 | Plot of analytical results for monochrome beads; iron (Fe) v. copper (Cu) | 186 |
| 43 | Textiles: i,a. Tabby weave, b. 2/2 (four shed) twill, c. Four-shed chevron twill  ii. Diagram of ground weave, pattern threads missing, from spearhead 4/1  iii. Diagram of broken diamond twill weave, shaded threads as preserved on 96b/7 | 194 |
| 44 | Grave 28, objects at waist | 223 |
| 45 | Grave 38, iron objects between femurs | 227 |
| 46 | Grave 48, objects at left hip | 230 |
| 47 | Grave 129, objects at right shoulder | 244 |
| 48 | Grave 134, a. objects at neck position  b. objects at left hip | 246 |
| 49 | Grave 138, objects at left hip | 247 |
| 50 | Grave 141, objects at left waist | 248 |

*Figures accompanying catalogue*

|  |  | Page |
|---|---|---|
| 1 | Objects in Graves B and C | 272 |
| 2 | Objects in Grave C continued | 273 |
| 3 | Objects in Grave C continued, grave C or D and grave D | 274 |
| 4 | Objects in Graves F and 1 | 275 |
| 5 | Objects in Grave 1 continued | 276 |
| 6 | Objects in Graves 3, 4 and 5 | 277 |
| 7 | Objects in Grave 6 | 278 |
| 8 | Objects in Graves 8, 9, 10, 11 and 12 | 279 |
| 9 | Objects in Grave 13 | 280 |
| 10 | Objects in Graves 14 and 15 | 281 |
| 11 | Objects in Grave 15 continued, graves 16, 17, 18 and 19 | 282 |
| 12 | Objects in Grave 20 | 283 |
| 13 | Objects in Grave 20 continued | 284 |
| 14 | Objects in Graves 21 and 22 | 285 |
| 15 | Objects in Graves 23 and 27 | 286 |

| | | Page | | | Page |
|---|---|---|---|---|---|
| 16 | Objects in Grave 28 | 287 | 66 | Grave plans C, F, 1, 3–6, 8 | 337 |
| 17 | Objects in Grave 29 | 288 | 67 | Grave plans 9–16 | 338 |
| 18 | Objects in Grave 30 | 289 | 68 | Grave plans 17–19, 22 | 339 |
| 19 | Objects in Grave 32 | 290 | 69 | Grave plans 20, 21, 23, 25, 27–30, 32 | 340 |
| 20 | Objects in Graves 33, 34, 36 and 37 | 291 | 70 | Grave plans 33–40 | 341 |
| 21 | Objects in Grave 35 | 292 | 71 | Grave plans 41–44, 46, 48–50, 52 | 342 |
| 22 | Objects in Grave 38 | 293 | 72 | Grave plans 53–59 | 343 |
| 23 | Objects in Grave 38 continued, graves 39 and 40 | 294 | 73 | Grave plans 60–67 | 344 |
| 24 | Objects in Graves 41 and 42 | 295 | 74 | Grave plans 68–76 | 345 |
| 25 | Objects in Grave 42 continued and grave 43 | 296 | 75 | Grave plans 77–85 | 346 |
| 26 | Objects in Graves 44 and 46 | 297 | 76 | Grave plans 87–93 | 347 |
| 27 | Objects in Grave 48 | 298 | 77 | Grave plans 94A–96B, 98–102 | 348 |
| 28 | Objects in Graves 49, 50, 52 and 53 | 299 | 78 | Grave plans 103–110 | 349 |
| 29 | Objects in Grave 53 continued and grave 54 | 300 | 79 | Grave plans 111–117, 119, 121 | 350 |
| 30 | Objects in Grave 55 | 301 | 80 | Grave plans 120, 122–125, 127–130 | 351 |
| 31 | Objects in Grave 56 | 302 | 81 | Grave plans 131–138 | 352 |
| 32 | Objects in Graves 57 and 58 | 303 | 82 | Grave plans 139–146 | 353 |
| 33 | Objects in Grave 59 | 304 | 83 | Grave plans 147–151, 155–157 | 354 |
| 34 | Objects in Grave 60 | 305 | 84 | Grave plans 158–165 | 355 |
| 35 | Objects in Graves 61 and 62 | 306 | 85 | Distribution. Weapons and weaving swords | 356 |
| 36 | Objects in Graves 63, 64 and 65 | 307 | 86 | Distribution. Shields | 357 |
| 37 | Objects in Graves 66 and 67 | 308 | 87 | Distribution. Brooches | 358 |
| 38 | Objects in Graves 71, 74 and 75 | 309 | 88 | Distribution. Pendants | 359 |
| 39 | Objects in Graves 76, 77, 78, 79, 80, 81, 82 and 83 | 310 | 89 | Distribution. Beads | 360 |
| 40 | Objects in Graves 84, 85, 87 and 90 | 311 | 90 | Distribution. Beads | 361 |
| 41 | Objects in Grave 91 | 312 | 91 | Distribution. Pins | 362 |
| 42 | Objects in Grave 92 | 313 | 92 | Distribution. Buckles, bronze or white metal | 363 |
| 43 | Objects in Grave 93 | 314 | 93 | Distribution. Glass vessels, pots, bronze bowls, buckets | 364 |
| 44 | Objects in Grave 94a, 94b and 95 | 315 | 94 | Distribution. Wooden boxes and cups. | 365 |
| 45 | Objects in Grave 96a | 316 | 95 | Distribution. Bags or pouches. Iron diamonds, fire-steels, ivory rings | 366 |
| 46 | Objects in Graves 96b, 97 and 98 | 317 | 96 | Distribution. Knives | 367 |
| 47 | Objects in Grave 98 continued | 318 | 97 | Distribution. Keys | 368 |
| 48 | Objects in Graves 100, 101, 103, 104, 105, 106, 107 and 108 | 319 | 98 | The cemetery divided into plots A-I | 369 |
| 49 | Objects in Graves 109 and 110 | 320 | 99 | Sex distribution | 370 |
| 50 | Objects in Graves 111, 113, 114, 115, 116, 117 and 119 | 321 | 100 | Skeleton positions | 371 |
| 51 | Objects in Graves 120, 121, 122, 123, 124 and 125 | 322 | 101 | Phase 1 | 372 |
| | | | 102 | Phase 2 | 373 |
| 52 | Objects in Graves 126, 127 and 128 | 323 | 103 | Phase 3 | 374 |
| 53 | Objects in Graves 129 and 130 | 324 | 104 | Phase 4 | 375 |
| 54 | Objects in Graves 131 and 132 | 325 | 105 | Phase 5 | 376 |
| 55 | Objects in Graves 133 and 134 | 326 | 106 | Phase 6 | 377 |
| 56 | Objects in Graves 135, 136 and 137 | 327 | 107 | Phase 7 | 378 |
| 57 | Objects in Graves 138, 139 and 140 | 328 | 108 | Depth of graves | 379 |
| 58 | Objects in Graves 141, 142 and 143 | 329 | 109 | Orientation of graves | 380 |
| 59 | Objects in Graves 144, 145, 146, 147 and 148 | 330 | 110 | Layout of cemetery | 381 |
| | | | 111 | Distribution of button brooches, class B | 382 |
| 60 | Objects in Graves 149, 150 and 155 | 331 | 112 | Distribution of saucer brooches decorated with five spirals | 383 |
| 61 | Objects in Graves 156 and 157 | 332 | 113 | Distribution of dolphin buckle loops with tails | 383 |
| 62 | Objects in Grave 157 continued, graves 158, 159 and 160 | 333 | 114 | Distribution of glass Kempston-type cone beakers | 384 |
| 63 | Objects in Graves 161, 162, 163 and 164 | 334 | 115a,b | Distribution of glass claw-beakers in England | 385 |
| 64 | Unassociated objects. 1–3 A reburial. 4–12 Finds made before the beginning of the excavation | 335 | 116 | Distribution of bronze bowls with beaded rim | 386 |
| 65 | Unassociated objects continued. 13–15 Finds from the area where five graves were destroyed between graves 8 and 38. 16–19 Loose finds in topsoil. 20–21 Unidentified knives | 336 | 117 | Distribution of bronze workboxes | 386 |
| | | | 118 | Distribution of ivory rings | 387 |
| | | | 119 | Distribution of bronze balances | 387 |
| | | | 120 | Distribution of cowrie shells | 388 |

# List of plates

*Colour plates*

    I  Brooches and pendant: *a* 13/1, *b* 20/8, *c* 13/2, *d* 35/3, *e* 14/1, *f* 59/1 .. .. 389
   II  Brooches: *a* 38/1, *b* 1/2, *c* 35/1, *d* 29/1, *e* 126/1 .. .. 390
  III  Non-glass beads, monochrome and polychrome glass beads .. .. .. 391
  IV  Polychrome glass beads, part necklace 59/3 in original order, glass fragments .. .. 392

*Plates*

  1  *a* Air view of cemetery site in 1947, *b* Dover harbour from cemetery site .. .. 393
  2  *a* Cemetery site from the west in 1951 *b* Excavating grave 56 .. .. 394
  3  *a* Posthole Z, *b* Grave 29, *c* Grave 20, *d* Grave 67, *e* Grave 75 .. .. 395
  4  *a* Grave 96a and b, *b* Grave 93, *c* Grave 110, *d* Grave 117, *e* Grave 148 .. .. 396
  5  Sword, buckles and pin: *a* C/1, *b* 61/3, *c* 21/1, *d* 38/5, *e* 161/3 .. .. 397
  6  Brooches: *a* Unassociated 9, *b* 13/1, *c* 13/2, *d* 20/6, *e* 20/8, *f* 32/1, *g* 30/2, *h* 92/1, *i* F/1, *j* 48/2, *k* 48/1, *l* 23/1, *m* 20/2, *n* 92/2 .. 398
  7  Pendants: *a* Unassociated 6, *b* 29/7, *c* 110/10, *d* 110/11, *e* 20/4, *f* 1/1, *g* 29/8, *h* 134/1, *i* 29/5a, *j* 29/6, *k* 67/2 .. .. 399
  8  Glass vessels: *a* 20/16, *b* 22/1, *c* 38/12 .. .. 400
  9  Glass and pottery vessels: *a* 6/1, *b* 160/8, *c* 139/4, *d* 87/3, *e* 109/3 .. .. 401
 10  Belt, bronze bowl and buckets: *a* 20/19, *b* 20/17, *c* 28/1, *d* 53/7 .. .. 402
 11  Textile impressions: *a* 96b/7, *b* 113/5, *c* Unassociated 16, *d* 4/1 .. .. 403
 12  *a* Preserved cattle horn from pommel of ring-sword C/1 *b* Copper alloy preserved wood from reverse of buckle 48/14 *c* Preserved animal fur from 'knife' blade associated with seax 93/7 *d* Preserved organic material from pommel 93/6, possibly ivory, *e* Preserved ivory from lower guard of sword hilt 93/6 .. 404

# List of tables

| | | Page |
|---|---|---|
| I | Sword measurements | 21 |
| II | Spears | 26 |
| III | Shield characteristics | 34 |
| IV | Characteristics of the disc and plated brooches | 41 |
| V | Gold, silver and copper content of Kentish bracteates | 52 |
| VI | Beads: amber | 57 |
| VII | Beads: types in graves | 59 |
| VIII | Beads: non-glass | 71 |
| IX | Beads: monochrome glass | 72 |
| X | Beads: drawn glass | 75 |
| XI | Beads: polychrome glass | 76 |
| XII | Beads: non-glass, in phases | 79 |
| XIII | Beads: monochrome, in phases | 79 |
| XIV | Beads: drawn, in phases | 81 |
| XV | Beads: polychrome, in phases | 82 |
| XVI | Iron fittings on wooden boxes | 103 |
| XVII | Knife types in relation to phases | 116 |
| XVIII | Knife types in relation to sex | 116 |
| XIX | Sex according to grave finds and bone reports | 123 |
| XX | Age at death: male | 128 |
| XXI | Age at death: female | 128 |
| XXII | Age at death: juvenile | 128 |
| XXIII | Deaths over and under 45 in the 7 phases | 129 |
| XXIV | Skeleton positions: complete | 130 |
| XXV | Skeleton positions: defective | 131 |
| XXVI | Male skeletons: supine | 133 |
| XXVII | Female skeletons: supine | 133 |
| XXVIII | Plots A-N in relation to the phases | 136 |
| XXIX | Male graves classed according to grave goods | 147 |
| XXX | Female graves classed according to grave goods | 148 |
| XXXI | Juvenile graves classed according to grave goods | 148 |
| XXXII | Unsexed adult graves classed according to grave goods | 148 |
| XXXIII | Depths of graves in relation to the contents | 151 |
| XXXIV | Dover orientations: male, female | 154 |
| XXXV | Dover orientations: juvenile, unknown sex | 155 |
| XXXVI | Dover orientations: in orientation order | 155 |

|  |  | Page |  |  | Page |
|---|---|---|---|---|---|
| XXXVII | Lyminge orientations | 162 | XLVII | Wood identifications | 196 |
| XXXVIII | Classification of graves at Lyminge | 162 | XLVIII | Age and sex distribution of adults | 200 |
| XXXIX | Orpington: contents of male graves | 164 | XLIX | Age distribution of juveniles | 200 |
| XL | Holborough orientations | 168 | L | Post-cranial means | 200 |
| XLI | XRF results for five gold bracteates | 181 | LIA | Cranial means | 200 |
| XLII | The monochrome beads | 183 | LIB | Facial and mandibular means | 200 |
| XLIII | Comparison of opacifying and decolourising agents | 186 | LII | Estimated maximum stature from long bones | 200 |
| XLIV | Beads | 187 | LIII | Dental pathology | 201 |
| XLV | Beads | 188 | LIV | Reduction of upper molars | 201 |
| XLVI | Textile Catalogue | 190 | LV | Grave contents | 261 |

# Acknowledgements

Grateful thanks must be accorded to a number of people who helped in this venture, particularly those mentioned here. The task of excavation was greatly facilitated by the generous co-operation of Dover Borough Council and the various contractors working on the housing estate. The conservation of most of the finds was expertly carried out by V Rickard. Most of the drawings are the work of Elizabeth Fry-Stone, and more recent additions are by Sue Heaser, J Thorn and C Evans, and F Gardiner contributed the paintings of beads and advice on illustrations. Administrative co-operation was readily forthcoming from staff of the Inspectorate of Ancient Monuments: John Hurst, Sarnia Butcher and Alison Cook. Valerie Cooper and Margaret Hardie provided research assistance, Valerie Cooper being especially involved with the site plan, tables of the beads, and with the bibliography. The manuscript was typed by Shireen Karanjia and Christiania Clemence. Access to the objects in the British Museum was facilitated by Leslie Webster and Katherine East. Premises and facilities for completion of the manuscript were provided by Birkbeck College. The following supplied photographs: British Museum, plates 5a–e, 6e-g, i, l, 7b-d, h-k, 8c, 9a, c, e, 10b, 11a, b, d; National Monuments Board plate 1a. Text figures 1b, 28, 36, and Figures 112, 113, 116–120 are based on Ordnance Survey maps with the permission of the Ordnance Survey.

# Chapter I

# Excavation

### i. Introduction

In 1951 a new housing estate, the Buckland Estate, was being built on Long Hill, near Buckland, Dover. (TR310430). A few interesting objects were discovered and picked up by men working on the site, but no serious attention was paid to them until human skeletons in graves began to appear under the blade of the scraper. The late Mr W P B Stebbing, FSA, who was well-known for his work in the archaeology of the area, was notified, and one grave (grave C) was excavated under his supervision. This contained the ring-sword, spearhead, shield-boss, scale and weights. This find, together with the square-headed brooch (Figure 64, 9) and other objects which had already found their way from the site to Mr F L Warner, then curator of Dover museum, was sufficient to show that this was a rich Kentish cemetery of the early Anglo-Saxon period, and the decision was taken by the Inspectorate of Ancient Monuments to mount a rescue excavation.

Accordingly, work began in September 1951, and during the first few weeks I was fortunate to have the assistance for short spells of Mr John Anstee and Mr (now Dr) David Smith. The late Dr G C Dunning undertook the surveying on the site, and his advice and encouragement were much valued. Apart from this early assistance the undertaking had all the advantages and disadvantages of a project where the duties of excavating, recording of fieldwork and small finds, drawing of grave plans, and photography all devolved on a single person. On the profit side it meant that I was able to excavate or participate in the actual excavation of almost every grave, in spite of the fact that the work had to be fitted in wherever possible with concurrent duties as a lecturer in London. Every effort was made to clear the chalk surface in order to track down all the graves amongst the activity of the building of roads, drains and houses (plate 2b) and a continued search was carried on by Mr W G K Latchem from the staff of Dover Castle until every available part of the area was covered by July 1953. During the later stages some students from Birkbeck College took part in the excavations, among whom were Miss Jean Cook, Miss June Travers, and Mr Kenneth Whitehorn.

Many years have passed between the excavation and publication. When work began, the organisation for excavation was in its formative post-war years when resources were almost non-existent. Consequently the work of conservation and drawing of the objects was not undertaken until many years later and was not nearing completion before 1963. At this time the decision was taken by the Inspectorate of Ancient Monuments to transfer the objects to the British Museum, and during the hiatus caused by the upheaval of moving all the objects to this less accessible place other commitments took precedence. Nevertheless work was begun on the dating of some of the key objects which resulted in a study of ring-swords as in grave C, of Kempston-type cone-beakers (grave 22), seaxes (graves 65 and 93), hones (grave 162), wheel-thrown pottery (graves 43, 109, 129, 137, 139, 156, 157) and glass claw-beakers (grave 20). Other items published were the brooch with the runic inscription (grave 126), the anthropomorphic pin (grave 161) and the coffin fittings (grave 41). The space needed in the present work for the discussion of these items is therefore considerably reduced, and reference is given to the more comprehensive, published discussions in the appropriate sections. The material has been available for study in the British Museum, and has been referred to or published by a number of archaeologists, notably the disc brooches[1] and spearheads[2]. From 1974–80 most of the contents of the cemetery were on exhibition as a single group in the medieval gallery of the British Museum. All finds are in the possession of the British Museum, and the human bones are in the British Museum (Natural History). The manuscript was completed in February 1984, and it has not been possible to take into consideration publications subsequent to that date.

The cemetery lay on Long Hill on the east bank of the Dour, separated from the Castle Hill, which overlooks Dover harbour, by a tributary valley on the same side. The site is on the southern slope of Long Hill and was fortunately just missed by the loop of the railway cutting connecting Dover with Deal (Text Figure 1b). It is in full view from the river valley up to the coast line. The undisturbed surfaces of the hill were covered with a thin layer of turf, scarcely anywhere deeper than 6 inches (15cm) on top of unbroken solid chalk. It is clear that the topsoil must have been considerably diminished since the time of the Anglo-Saxons by cultivation,

---

1 Avent 1975

2 Swanton 1973; Swanton 1974.

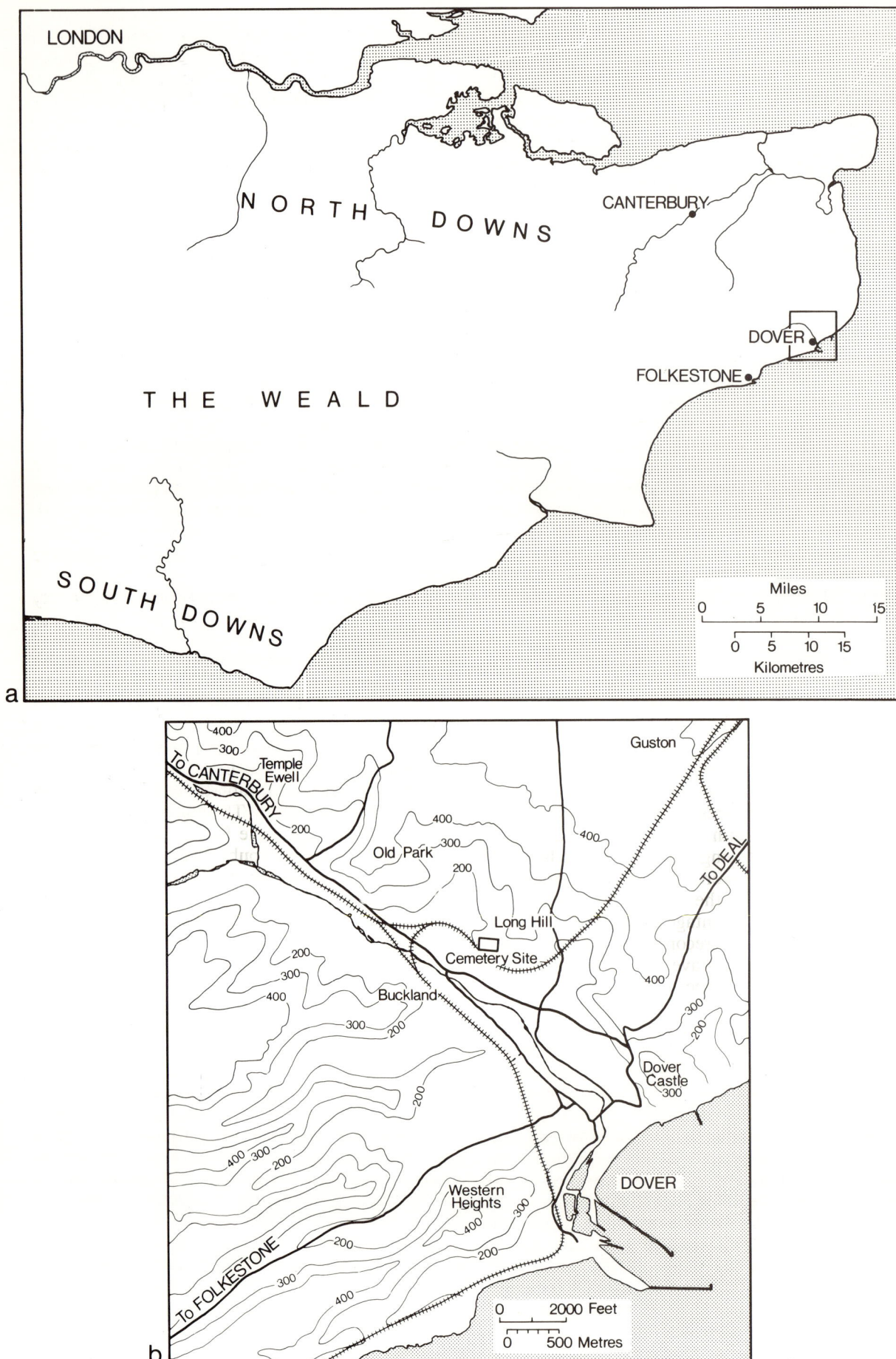

*Text Figure 1 a, b* Site location maps (Roads as before 1956)

erosion, or both, for some of the grave contents were lying on the chalk surface.

At my first visit to the site, the rock chalk of the hillside had been cut away and levelled off in certain places for the purposes of road-making and foundations of houses. The houses in the north-west of plan, Text Figure 2, were already built. To the south of them ran a strip of untouched topsoil a few feet wide, and immediately to the south of this the roadway had been excavated and was beginning to branch to the north and east into the oval loop of the new housing scheme which became Hobart Crescent and Napier Road. My attention was drawn to the area south of what was to be Napier Road which had been terraced for houses. The grave excavated by Mr Stebbing had been found here, and there were various other similar soft patches in the solid chalk. A particularly wet season had just set in, and this terrace had been denuded of topsoil, the chalk below having been churned up by machines and saturated with rain to present a very slippery surface. A certain amount of digging for loot had been going on on this terrace. The soft patches were therefore lettered A-K and investigated. Of these C proved to be the grave already excavated which had contained the ring sword, and F turned out to be a grave in which the fill had been disturbed but the contents had not been reached. A few more graves were found to the south under turf which had not been removed (6–10). Some way to the north of this group half of a grave (11) was found in the side of a deep cut made for the road, and this indicated the extension of the graveyard in this direction. Investigation revealed nothing in the immediate vicinity, but a grave (13) exposed by road cutting led us to a closely packed group of burials in the immediate path of commercial excavations in progress on the new road (Napier Crescent). Blasting of the rock chalk in the meantime dramatically apprised us of the position of grave 26 on the west side of the road by showering the site with human bones.

As the most urgent requirement of the building contractors was the construction of the road, we set to work to investigate the graves in its course, and in the meantime a scraper removed the topsoil from the rest of the loop of the road, so exposing more graves in this vital area. On occasion it was necessary to remove the contents of a grave literally under the blade of the scraper, but in every case the grave and its contents were drawn and a vertical photograph taken. This ubiquitous nature of our excavations is mirrored in the apparently erratic numbering of the graves.

By this time a large area had been denuded of topsoil, and lorries and other heavy mechanical vehicles were traversing the chalk surface, churning it up in the frequent rain storms. In this way four graves which had been detected and numbered were unavoidably obliterated – Nos. 31, 47, 51 and 86, but the exact positions of 47 and 86 were plotted before destruction. Further misfortune befell when the rain stopped and a dry season set in, for the slimy surface, a mixture of chalk, soil and water, turned into a rough-cast concrete crust over the rock chalk which demanded hard and slow work with pickaxes in the work of tracing graves. The topsoil from the road was dumped in the middle of the site so that it could later be spread into the gardens when the houses were built. A watch was kept, and when the dumps were finally removed much later further graves were found beneath them.

On the plan Text Figure 2 the areas shaded are those which were destroyed, mainly before notification of the archaeological finds, and which we had no opportunity to search. Two houses in the north-west corner had already been built, and immediately to the south of them the strip of about 15ft. wide (4.57m) which had been left untouched proved to contain graves 115, 116, 41 and 98 unmolested, as well as the remains of 26. In the area to the south which had already been terraced for road and houses one grave was preserved in the middle, grave D, as it was at the bottom of the road terrace and at the top of the terrace cut out for the houses immediately to the south. It was possible to search almost the whole of the rest of the site and pick up even outlying graves such as 151 and 152–4 so that some of the limits of the cemetery are certain, (see p 20 below).

The general method of excavation had already been followed at Holborough[3]. Each grave was excavated so that the bones and finds were exposed as far as possible but not moved. The plan of the grave was then drawn and vertical photographs taken. When the finds and bones were removed, occasionally other small objects which had been covered by the bones were revealed and added to the plan. It was always necessary to excavate a grave completely in one day because of the risk of interference at night. Some objects or groups of objects were removed in a block of earth for later excavation in a laboratory, e.g. the workbox in grave 107. On the completion of the excavation of each grave an index card was made the same day for each object found, recording the measurements and description of each find together with a measured sketch. In the various processes such as conservation which followed excavation there were many possibilities for confusion of objects to arise, and this prompt recording method proved invaluable in avoiding or disentangling subsequent confusion. Measurements at the time were taken in feet and inches, but in this report metric equivalents are also given. Present county divisions are given in accordance with the changes brought about by local government re-organisation in 1974, the earlier county names being added in brackets where necessary.

## ii. Features other than Anglo-Saxon Graves

a. *Prehistoric barrow ditch* (Text Figure 2).
This was noted in the highest part of the cemetery for a segment of its circumference, but it was not

---

3 Evison 1956, 85–6.

14 THE BUCKLAND ANGLO-SAXON CEMETERY

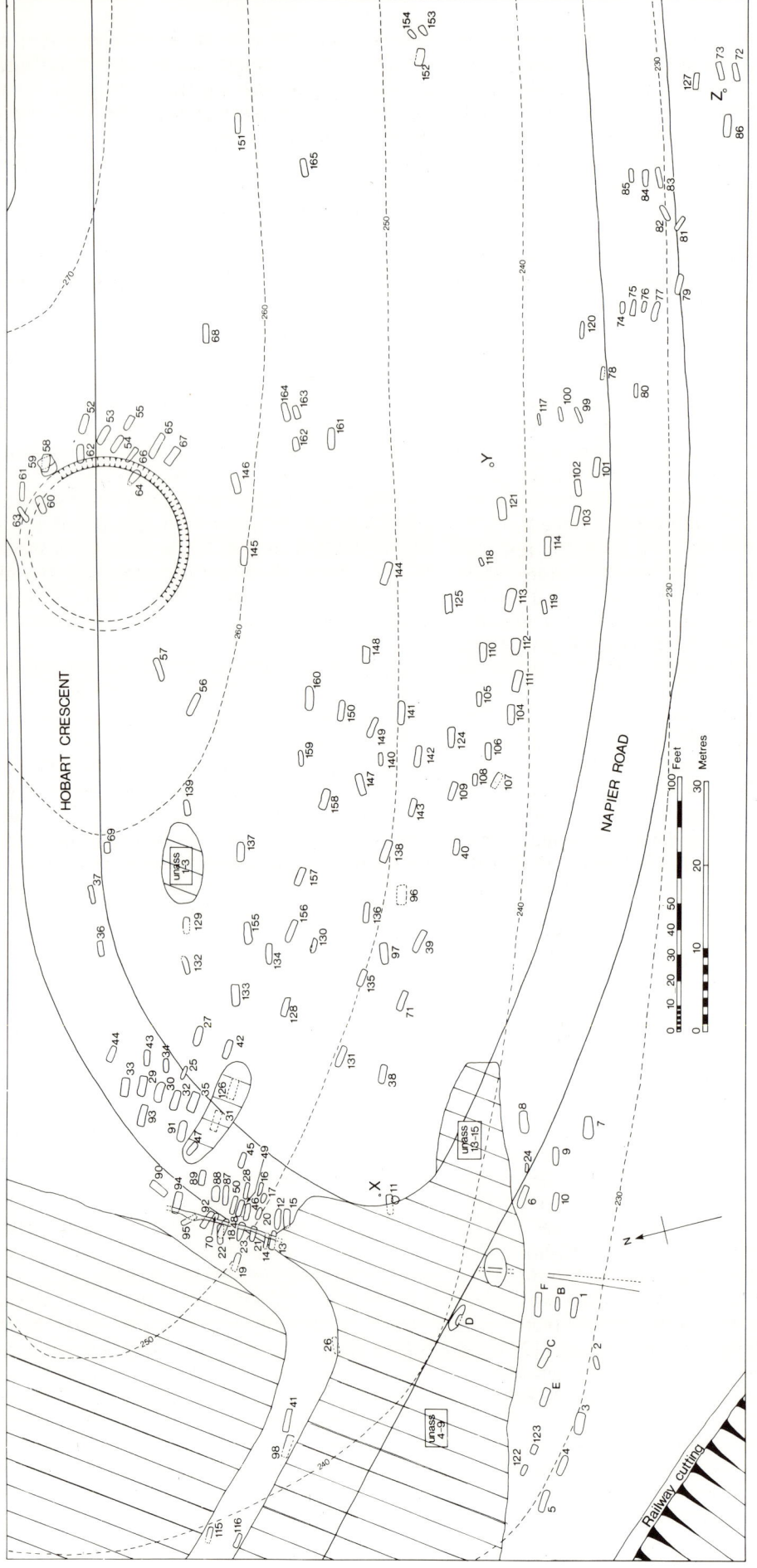

*Text Figure 2* Plan of Anglo-Saxon cemetery, Buckland Estate, Dover

excavated as our brief from the Inspectorate was limited to excavation of the Saxon cemetery. It was 3ft. 9in. (1.14m) wide and 2ft. to 2ft. 6in. (0.61m to 0.76m) deep, and the internal diameter of the circle was reckoned to be about 60ft. (18.2m). As the ditch was narrow and shallow in proportion to the diameter of the circle, it is likely that the surface of the chalk had been worn down by ploughing. The barrow was on a false crest as viewed from the valley, and was near the highest point of that part of the hill. Some Anglo-Saxon graves partly overlaid the ditch and the grave-diggers delved deeper into the soft fill than into the chalk. As a result graves 60 and 64 were deeper at the foot than at the head, and the head of grave 64 was high enough to be destroyed by ploughing. A few prehistoric sherds were found in grave fills, and one of the more distinctive sherds came from a position on the chest of the skeleton near the necklace from grave 66 actually on the barrow. The other sherds were not evenly or randomly distributed. Some came from the fills of graves 113, 114 and 125, all near together some distance south of the barrow, some from graves 128 and 156, near together and a similar distance to the south-west, and from 127 and 151 also at a distance and widely spaced but to the south-east[4].

b. *Romano-British pit*

There was a neatly shaped, circular pit (Figure 67) cut into by grave 11, measuring 2ft. 10in. (0.86m) in diameter and 2ft. (0.61m) deep in the chalk. It contained three flint flakes and a few Romano-British sherds of early date. These consisted of: rim and side of Dragendorff form 15/17 plate, cf Oswald and Pryce 1920, pl.XLIII.28 Aislingen (Knorr 1912, pl.XV.12); hand-made sherd with scored surface, cf Bushe-Fox 1926, 101, pl.XXVII.82; hand-made olla with bead rim and concave base, first century; three sherds of coarse hand-made cooking pots; one sandy wheel-thrown sherd.

c. *Post-holes*

Very near the Romano-British pit, but the other side of the head of grave 11 was a single upright post-hole, X, 9in. (22.8cm) in diameter and 9in. deep. Another post-hole, Y, was some 13ft. (3.96m) from the foot of grave 121, although not exactly in line with the grave axis. This grave was not of any obvious importance as it contained few finds, simply a knife and iron fragment. The post-hole was 1ft. 4in. to 1ft. 6in. (40.6cm to 45.7cm) in diameter and 10in. (25.4cm) deep, roughly circular with a few flints. Another single post-hole, Z (plate 3a), diameter 1ft. 8in. (50.8cm), depth 5in. (12.7cm), circular and lined with large flints, was situated in the centre of the group of graves 72, 73, 86, 27.

d. *Medieval reburial*

A shallow rough hole in the chalk was found in the area east of grave 129 which had been much churned up by machines. It contained a mixture of human bones, a knife fragment and five iron clench bolts which could be Anglo-Saxon, and a fragment of a medieval jug handle (Figure 64, 1–3). The bones are reported to represent at least six individuals from male and female adults to a newborn or full-term foetus (see p 252), so supporting to some extent our impression at the time that this was a hasty reburial of the contents of Saxon graves disturbed, perhaps by accident, in the medieval period.

Later on in the same area grave 69 was found, which was taken to be either a damaged grave or a reburial. It contained fragments of a pelvis, ribs, right hand and arm together at one end. A connection between this and the communal burial above is suggested by the bone report, for it was noticed that there was a resemblance between these two groups of bones in the state of their preservation, which differed from that of most of the bones from the Anglo-Saxon graves. Either, therefore, these two groups have no connection with the Anglo-Saxon cemetery, which is unlikely in view of their positions, or disinterment and reburial of both in the medieval period produced an effect on their state of preservation, which distinguishes them from the other skeletons (see p 127).

e. *Modern disturbance*

There was a modern trench which had cut through the rich graves 13, 14, 21, 23, 18, 92, 94a and b and 95. It was V-shaped, 3ft. 8in. (1.12m) wide at the top and 2ft. 6in. (0.76m) deep with a flat bottom 1ft (0.30m) wide. Objects such as the hilt of a sword in grave 94b which lay directly in its path had been removed, and it must be assumed that the excavation was by machine as other parts of these graves appear to have been unnoticed and were quite intact. The trench ran straight down the slope of the hillside and, although some of it was destroyed in the commercial terracing, part of it was traced as far south as to the east of grave D and grave 1 (Text Figure 2).

It is surprising that, when this trench was cut through so many well-furnished graves, the other graves which were closely packed in this area were not rifled. One in this area does seem to have been disturbed, however, grave 88, where there was only a body stain and a fragment of a humerus, and the fill was very loose.

When the railway cutting was made only a few yards to the south in the late nineteenth century it is probable that the 'navvies' of that time came upon the graves nearest to their operations, i.e. 3, 4, 5 and 7. In grave 3 they left only fragments of a shield boss and some bones, apparently mixed, male and female. In grave 4 only a part was disturbed, a spearhead and some of the bones were left *in situ*, but other bones, a buckle and part of a sword tang were amongst the loose fill returned to the grave, so showing that a sword at least had been removed. Grave 5 had similarly been partially scooped out, the right arm only being left undisturbed, and in the loose returned fill fragments of a knife, an iron

---
4 For descriptions and discussion of these sherds see p 179.

buckle and a spearhead socket. At grave 7 the search had been more thorough, the grave edges being hacked away, and the loose returned fill containing only scraps of bone, and a fragment of a clay pipe.

Graves 152 and 153 were rifled in 1953 by children on the site. They are said to have contained nothing but a few bone fragments in 152 and a few teeth in 153. This is credible as grave 154, the third of this isolated group, was undisturbed, and this contained nothing at all except two small sherds in the fill. Apart from these signs of interference, and possibly the reburials mentioned above, the graveyard has been free of disturbance since Anglo-Saxon days. There was no sign of near-contemporary robbing in the Anglo-Saxon period.

In the twentieth century the area in the west of the site was destroyed by terracing for houses. Even after the beginning of the excavation a few graves were unavoidably obliterated after detection by the passage of scrapers and lorries working on the site: 31, 47, 51, 86 and 126.

f. *Disturbance by animals*

A certain amount of movement in the grave of bones and objects can often take place as the result of decomposition of the body and other organic materials and of the subsequent natural subsidence of soil and stones. Where the direct gravitational path is obstructed by large stones, lumps of chalk or a large object such as a shield boss, objects will slip sideways and so move position. Sometimes, however, displacement is caused by the fauna of the area. In any soil a freshly-dug grave presents an area easy for burrowing compared with the surrounding undisturbed soil, but on a hill of solid chalk the advantage is even more obvious. There were signs of animal disturbance on the chest of the skeleton in grave 165, which no doubt accounts for the slight displacement of the left forearm and a few teeth near the top of the femurs. A rabbit hole in the corner of the head of grave 75 accounts for the displacement of the skull and left shoulder area. In grave 124 where only the femurs and a few other bone fragments were preserved, some teeth were found in the position of the lower legs, but there was no obvious trace of animals. Inarticulated displaced bones are often the result of the activity of nesting creatures, and traces of them may sometimes be detected. Where a small articulated limb was out of place, as in grave 135 where most of the fingers and part of the wrist of the right hand were found about 9in. (22.8cm) away from the rest of the wrist, this could have been the work of rats or some such creatures soon after burial. Further disturbances in the same grave are indicated by the separation of the left radius and ulna, and the position of the left patella under the middle of the left femur. Although the occupant was a spearman, these disarticulations could not be the result of battle amputations. In fact, it can now be seen that some romantic interpretations of the past can be rationalised in similar ways. Bones of mice and seeds have been found in Anglo-Saxon graves and have been considered part of the pagan ritual.[5] The bones of these creatures are so small, however, that they soon decay without any trace, and they are not likely to remain intact from Anglo-Saxon times. The mouse bones found in grave 121 were seen by Dr Cornwall who considered they were much too well preserved to be Anglo-Saxon. Black specks and seeds have been noticed in graves, and clusters of such black specks were retrieved from graves 13, 40, 44 and 62. Some seeds were found in the bronze bucket in grave 28 which seemed to be an appropriate container for seeds, but these seeds are not ancient and a family of some type of small creature no doubt found the bucket to be a very cosy nest. Earthworms are also quoted as being responsible for the introduction of seeds (p 197).

iii. **The Anglo-Saxon cemetery**

a. *Orientation of graves*

The orientation of most of the graves may be considered to be with head to the west, although in fact they are mostly WNW-ESE. The impression that the aim of the grave-diggers was to make a more or less W-E burial is created by variations such as 97, 121, etc which are W-E and 132, 146, etc. which are WSW-ENE. A few lie at more widely varied angles, see Text Figure 2. Only one was in the entirely opposite direction, grave 21, ESE-WNW. Some are clearly influenced by the prehistoric barrow, and orientation is fully discussed below, p 152.

b. *The shape of the graves*

The depth to which the grave was sunk in the chalk was variable, the deepest being 2ft. 6in. (0.76m) deep and the norm 1ft. 2in. (0.36m), but the fact that many were laid just under the surface of the chalk, only 6–9in. (15–23cm) below the modern surface, indicates that the topsoil must have been much deeper overall in Anglo-Saxon times. Grave 49 was only sunk about 7cm into the chalk, and it is therefore possible that other graves of similar shallowness had been lost in the erosion of the topsoil.

The shape is roughly rectangular, with rounded corners, sometimes wider at the head, sometimes wider at the foot, and always deeper on the north side than on the south because of the slope of the hill, and it is the deeper measurement which is given in the catalogue. Some of the graves, however, have rounded ends. The floor of the grave was sometimes not flat so that the depth was much greater at one end than the other. The reason for this is evident in graves 60 and 64 which were partly in the natural chalk and partly over the ditch of the prehistoric barrow, so that the grave-digger went deeper into the softer soil. There is no obvious reason, however, why grave 32, for instance, should have been 9in. (23cm) deeper at the foot than at the head.

The size varies from the largest grave, 65, 10ft. 6in. × 2ft. 10in. × 1ft. 4in. (3.2m × 0.86m ×

---

5 Smith 1908a, 344

0.41m) to the smallest grave, 118, 3ft. 4in. × 1ft. 8in. × 11in. (1.02m × 0.51m × 0.28m). The size of the grave seems generally to correspond to the size of the individual, so that a child was sometimes given a smaller grave. None was made especially large to accommodate an important personage with a great deal of grave furniture. The sizes also vary according to the area, smaller graves appearing in plot A in the north-west, and larger graves elsewhere except in the south-east, plot I, where they are small, narrow and relatively deep slot graves.

The standard of grave digging varies from expert sharply-cut sides to rather careless hacking. The blade of the ?adze used to dig grave 145 broke, and part of the tool (Figure 59) was left firmly wedged in the wall of the grave by the no doubt exasperated grave-digger. Grave 163, which was 5ft. 6in. (1.68m) long and 2ft. 6in. (0.76m) wide and 1ft. 4in. (0.41m) deep, had a rough ledge around the grave about 3in. (7cm) above the floor. The short length suggests that the occupant was not fully grown, and the ledge may have no great significance if the grave-digger began a grave for a child in this hard chalk and narrowed down the excavated hole for the last few inches on finding that even so it was unnecessarily large. The form matches the type b7 distinguished by Hogarth at St. Peter's, Kent.[6] As the depth of the ledge is only 7cm, it is hardly deep enough to function as the basis for a lid to the grave. Nor is it wide enough to function as a side-walk in the funeral ritual as seems to have happened in some inhumation graves in Jutland of the pre-invasion period.[7]

The wall at the foot of grave 57 was a gradual incline instead of the almost vertical cut which was usual. In grave 135 the floor of the grave rose slightly at the head so that the skull was tipped forward, and in grave 14 the floor was cut in a shallow step to form a pillow. Grave 125 had corners extended in a lengthwise direction, giving the impression that it had been specially enlarged to receive the supporting poles of a bier or stretcher.

As so few of the burials are superimposed there must have been some surface marking, which, in the case of the more widely spaced graves could perhaps have been small tumuli. Superimposed graves are discussed below, p 140. All are single graves, with the exception of grave 96 where an old and young warrior are carefully placed side by side in a cavity double the usual size.

The cavity of graves 58 and 59 is an amorphous shape. Grave 59, containing a woman with a necklace, brooch, etc was made first, and from the way in which the outline of the head of the grave begins to turn to the right of the skull it seems that the grave must have been dug to a usual shape, 6ft. 9in. (2.08m) long and about 3ft. 6in. (1.07m) wide. Although many of the bones between chest and knee must have been disturbed when grave 58 was laid down, the remains of one tibia was left *in situ*. The iron fittings of the wooden box could have fitted neatly into a grave of this shape and size.

Grave 58 was about 3ft. (0.91m) wide, as can be seen by the outline which joins the contour of grave 59 at the level of the left knee of 58 and continues round the feet, starting to turn towards the head again. Here, however, the limit of the grave expands far beyond the right side of skeleton 58, and also beyond its head, and this part was quite empty. An explanation which would account for this peculiar shape would be that there was originally another grave lying parallel to grave 59, that this was found and emptied by the diggers of grave 58, who removed only part of 59 (Figure 72).

The shapes of the graves at Dover have very little to compare, therefore, with the variety of structures detected at St. Peter's. Particularly noticeable by their absence are the penannular or ring ditches surrounding graves at St. Peter's, Finglesham, Kingston, etc. Some of these were as shallow as 3in. (8cm), so that it is possible that as the original topsoil was much deeper at Dover, and if some of the chalk has been ploughed away as well, there may have been such ditches which either did not reach the chalk level, or they have since been erased.

c. *The fill in the graves*
The fill of the graves often contained very little soil, consisting mainly of chalk lumps which had resulted from the digging of the grave, and loose silt. The lumpy fill was often loose, with large air pockets. There were sometimes large flints also, e.g. graves 12 and 150. In some graves these had been placed in a selected position, e.g. grave 23 along the middle part of the inside of the south wall, grave 17 along the south side of the grave outside. In graves 141, 147 and 160 they were round the edge inside. Grave 161 was entirely covered by a large number of big flints, and so was grave 10 where even the skull was squashed by flints. In grave 149 the skeleton lay on top of a few inches of fill, and there were some large flints round and underneath it. The corpse must therefore have been placed in the grave on a bed or bier which stood a few inches above the floor of the grave.

In grave 8 a line of large flints was placed along each side of the body, and, between these flints and the brown body stain with a few bone fragments, the fill was of fine, hard chalk. The rest of the fill outside and above the flints was of the normal lumpy chalk type. The spear was then put in on top of these flints. The same very hard fill was detected also in graves F and 12. The body must have been in a coffin, although there was no trace of the wood, the chalk must have filtered in as fine silt, and, combining with the decomposed body and grave goods, it would form a closely packed conglomeration before the disintegration of the coffin boards, so presenting a totally different appearance from the chalk lump fill surrounding it.

The large flints were obtainable from flint beds on the same hillside, but as there were none in the immediate vicinity of any grave they are unlikely to have been dug out of the grave cavities and must

---

6 Hogarth 1973, fig. 7

7 Neumann 1981

have been expressly carried to the graves and put in. Their function was most likely to add considerable volume to the heap of excavated chalk and soil, so providing a higher mound as a more distinctive marker. Large flints immediately above the body would sink as perishable matter below decayed in the natural course of events, and an interpretation which suggests a ritual of stoning the corpses seems unnecessarily imaginative.[8] As the remaining topsoil was so shallow, it is quite likely that all trace of some piles of flints on top of a grave has been lost, so that little significance can be attached to the distribution of those which do remain. However, there seems to be no particular pattern governing the use of large flints, as they occur in the graves of men, women and children. There were some plots in which they did not occur, but they were present in plot A (12, 17), C (6 and 8), D (F), H (140, 160) and L (161), i.e. throughout the period of use of the cemetery.

A few prehistoric sherds in grave fills have been noted on p 179. The only other type of sherd represented in the graves was one medieval example in the fill of grave 151.

d. *The skeletons, positions of bones*

The bones were not well preserved, and yet the skull and most of the sturdier bones of arms and legs, the pelvis, spine and ribs were very often present, even if in a crumbling state. The reasons for more complete decomposition of some skeletons are no doubt many, depending to a great extent on the chemical composition of the enveloping grave fill which was often greatly altered by the chemical changes taking place in the variety of possessions placed in the grave, which included many perishables such as food, wood, leather and textiles as well as other more durable objects of metal, glass, etc. However the more fragile bones of children and old people tend to disintegrate more easily than those of people in the prime of life. Where the total length of the body as indicated by the skeletal remnants was less than about 5ft. (1.52m) the surviving limb fragments were often limited to humerus, femur and tibia. The length of the grave too, was often less than usual, and the grave may be assumed to be that of a young person, although an undersized adult cannot be ruled out. In a number of the small graves (Nos. 16, 17, 85, 108, 118, 122, 123, 154, 162, 163) there was no trace of the bones at all. It is surprising, therefore, to find the bones of the unborn child in grave 110 quite well preserved.

In the double grave 96a/b it is interesting to notice the difference in the decomposition of the two bodies. The report (p 124) gives the age of 96a as over 40 and of 96b as 20–30. Of 96a most of the spine, ribs and pelvis had disappeared, as well as the smaller bones of the hands and feet. The complete decomposition of the feet may have been accelerated by the chemicals derived from the shield boss placed over them. Most of 96b was better preserved, the sacrum, pelvis and smaller bones of the extremities being present.

One body was placed on its right side (146) with the left foot on top of the right. Occasionally the position of the skeleton was influenced by the grave furniture, e.g. grave 43 where the body was placed diagonally in the grave to make room for the wooden box with iron fittings by the feet. In grave 60 the feet were crossed, presumably to make room for the box beside them. In the double grave 96 the feet of 96b were crossed to give room for the shield placed over the feet of 96a.

One skeleton was found in a quite extraordinary position (grave 67). The top part of the body was front downwards, and the skull at an extraordinary angle was facing upwards. The right arm was under the body with the right hand over the left shoulder. The left arm was bent at the elbow, with the forearm and hand under the pelvis. The left leg was extended, and the right leg was bent up underneath it with the right foot under the left knee. This peculiar position could have been caused by the body being unceremoniously bundled into the grave, but there are indications of something more gruesome. The woman was wearing a necklace with a garnet pendant and silver gilt pendants with a cruciform design, presumably of Christian significance. A lump of iron pyrites was by her left foot, but this could have been a natural element in the fill, although function as an amulet cannot be ruled out. Apart from these items there were no other grave goods with the exception of a slip-knot bronze wire bracelet in the unusual position of more than six inches to the right of the skull. The necklace was in the place it occupied in life at the woman's neck, and one would expect a bracelet to be on a forearm unless it was in a bag or box, in which case it was usually accompanied by other objects. An explanation that would account for the extraordinary position of the skeleton, and the isolated position of the bracelet, would be that the woman was alive in the grave, either interred alive or possibly reviving after burial, and in her struggles to get out she dragged her right arm under her body to lever herself up, so leaving the bracelet in the position where her wrist had been, enveloped in, and retained there by, the earth filling.

Grave 110 contained the comparatively well-preserved skeleton of a young adult female. Both arms were slightly bent with the hands on top of the femurs. The head was inclined downwards to the left. In the pelvis was the skeleton of an infant described (p 124) as newly-born or full-term foetus. The position of these bones, curled up with the head downwards, makes it certain that the child was unborn.

e. *The grave furniture: positions of objects*

Possessions placed in the grave were found usually either on the floor of the grave or on the body. With the decay of the body and clothing everything sank to the floor unless prevented from doing so by bones or other objects. The positions of brooches, pins and beads on the chest cannot always be used as an

---

8 Meaney and Hawkes 1970, 31

accurate guide to the original positions for they often fell between the bones tumbling or turning as they did so. Although the position of the necklace could be seen, therefore, the exact position of one bead in regard to another on the string could not as a rule be discovered.

Objects normally worn on the person, such as brooches, rings, buckles, etc, were usually situated as worn in life. A sword was placed along the left side of the torso pointing towards the feet, with the exception of grave 71 where it was on the right. The three weaving battens of the women were in different positions, one pointing downwards outside the right leg, one pointing to the head outside the right leg and one pointing to the head of the grave on the left side of the skull. Six of the pots were at the foot and two by the head. One bucket was by the head and one by the feet, and one bowl was by the head, one by the feet. Wooden boxes were often near the feet. In grave 81 part of an iron lock was 4in. (10cm) above the floor which may have been its original relatively elevated position on the side or lid of the box. The jawbone nearby, however, was displaced, so that there may have been disturbance by animal action in this area. Spearheads are mostly placed to one side or other of the head, but one was pointing down by the left foot. The reversed position of the ferrule in a few graves shows that the shaft was broken before burial. Sometimes the spear must have been placed on top of some piece of grave furniture as in grave 9 where it was found 5in. (13cm) above floor level, and in this grave it was possibly the pillow on which the head rested. In grave 8 the spear had been placed resting on top of the flints on the left side of the body, with the spearhead about 5in. (13cm) above the floor, and there were charcoal traces and a cylindrical space in the fill showing the place occupied by the shaft, the end resting on the floor near the foot of the grave. In grave 137 the pot at the foot of the grave was standing 2in. (5cm) above the floor, and the bronze bowl at the head had preserved traces of wood underneath[9]. This evidence suggests a wooden bier or coffin below the body. In grave 149 the skeleton was a few inches above the floor with some flints below the bones – this again suggests some sort of stretcher beneath.

Iron coffin clamps were 6in. (15cm) above the floor in grave 155 which would have been their original position on the coffin. In two graves the shield boss was placed on end, the wood of the shield presumably surviving long enough so that the boss remained 7in. (18cm) above the floor in grave 91 and 10in. (25cm) in grave 90.

Any other object not lying on the floor might therefore be suspected of being disturbed or not a part of the original grave furniture, and the horseshoe fragment in grave 139, although only 2in. (5cm) above the floor of this shallow grave, is most likely to be an intrusion. A knife was found in the fill of some graves: nos. 83, 87, 91. This phenomenon has occurred elsewhere as in grave 53 at Polhill, Dunton Green, Kent and, because of this frequency, must be assumed to be an intentional deposition[10].

f. *Grouping as suggested by the plan of the cemetery*
The plan of the cemetery[11] shows variations in size, shape and orientation of graves, and their distribution, arrangement and clustering. On this basis a segregation into separate plots suggests itself. This grouping is adopted as there are obvious advantages for reference and comprehension if distinguishable parts of the cemetery are considered separately and in turn with a view to discovering whether the individual plots are homogeneous in other respects, and whether any of the groups are related to each other. In the final discussion the relevance of these plots to the chronology of the cemetery will be considered. The plots have been given the letters A to N, as shown on plan Figure 98.

*Plot A*. There is an obvious nucleus of high density of graves in the north-western area. Here there are two main rows of graves between 13 and 92, 15 and 88, with a less regular third row to the east, two other graves, 19 and 45, on the fringe and two graves, 90 and 95, at variant angles to the north on either side of 94 which is orientated like the two main rows, but not directly in line with either. It is a group which is definitely isolated from the others by intervening spaces. The graves are rather small and very close together, and it is the only plot where more than one grave has disturbed another. Grave 18 was placed over grave 22, at a higher level and at an angle to it (Figure 68). One of the two interments in grave 94 was about one foot higher than the other, but the orientation was the same for both, and there was no noticeable variation in the grave walls.

Graves 46 and 48 were lying parallel to one another, about a foot deep in the chalk, and what was left of grave 49 was lying on the chalk surface between these two. Graves 46 and 48 must have been contemporary, and grave 49 made at a different time. It was too shallow and fragmentary to allow a decision to be made as to whether it was dug earlier or later. The space available for it between 46 and 48 was very narrow, so that the width of grave 49 must have overlapped 46 and 48 for a few inches on each side. All that remained of grave 70 was the foot end of a shallow grave which contained loose skull and pelvis fragments and articulated and undisturbed foot bones. It had been disturbed by grave 92 which had a slightly different orientation, and which was itself cut through the middle by a modern trench.

*Plot B*. To the north-east of the first group there is a fairly regular row of large graves more widely spaced, 33 to 35, which might have extended for one

---

9  Similar local preservation by metal objects (a silver bowl, etc), in their immediate vicinity only, of part of a large coffin floor seems to have taken place in the Sutton Hoo ship burial, Evison 1980b, 358.

10  Philp 1973a, 178
11  The position and orientation of grave 96 is approximate only.

or two more graves which were destroyed to the south. To the west of these there are two graves in a row, 91 and 93, to the east four small graves in a row, 25–44, and to the east of these two more side by side, 42 and 27.

*Plot C.* To the south was a wide space with no trace of graves before reaching a group of graves widely spaced. These show some inclination to align sideways also, but in the middle section about five graves were destroyed and it is not possible to know how regular this arrangement was.

*Plot D.* The space to the west of grave 10 in plot C and 19 in plot A seems to indicate that plot D may have been a separate group or groups. An unknown number of graves were destroyed here in the middle, and although the western and southern limits are certain in the southern part, neither the western nor northern limits of the northern part are known. There was, however, a graveless space between plot A and graves 26 and 41 of plot D.

*Plot E*, the furthest north, is situated on the eastern ditch of a prehistoric barrow, and it is likely that, as the topsoil here was no deeper than elsewhere at the time of the excavation, a number of other graves in this group may have been interred in the overburden of the barrow and have been lost when the topsoil was reduced by erosion or cultivation. The graves fall into two sub-groups. The northernmost are orientated in a variety of directions: 63, 61, 60, 59 and 62. Those further south are all orientated in the same direction: 58, 52, 53, 54, 55, 64, 66, 65 and 67. One grave here is superimposed on another with a different orientation – 58 on 59.

*F* is a small plot, extending east-south-eastwards, the lower edge following a more or less straight line and the alignment of graves 38 and 131 delineating a right-angled corner. These two graves and four others may be paired sideways in rows.

*G* is a plot to the north of F, and although a space divides it from Plot F, some graves seem to follow a sideways row begun by a pair of graves in plot F, i.e. 128–133–132 and even 36 further north might be following the pair 38–131, but 71–135–130–156 and 39–136–157–137 are more regular.

*H* is a larger plot, also with wide spaces between graves, which continues along the south-eastern line from plot F. Sideways alignments are discernible but not regular, and there is a posthole, Y, some distance from the foot of grave 121, but not aligned to its axis. The group ends at grave 101.

*I* is a section which differs from H which it adjoins, for, although it follows a similar border line south-eastwards, the graves are more clearly and closely grouped, partly in rows, and the shapes are smaller and narrower. The four graves at the end, 86, 72, 73 and 127, are arranged with a posthole, Z, in the middle.

The remaining plots, *J, K, L, M* and *N* are all small groups in the northern parts of the cemetery. If some of the graves were very shallow, dug only in the topsoil and not reaching down to the chalk rock, it is possible that some graves could have been lost in the erosion of the topsoil, as any graves on the central part of the barrow no doubt were. If this is so, the cemetery might have been more regularly laid out than seems from the extant plan. However, of the graves on the northern edges only two graves, 37 and 44, were less than 15cm deep, and as the particular area in the vicinity of 37 and 44 had been damaged by a scraper, it is probable that the shallowness was caused by this modern activity. All the others were between 15cm and 60cm deep, so that it appears that it may be concluded that the isolated, sporadic grouping is original.

g. *The limits of the cemetery*
With the exception of the areas to the west which were destroyed in the terracing for houses, and are indicated by shading on the plan, (Text Figure 2) the surface of the chalk was examined over almost all of the site, so that it is unlikely that features such as grave pits or postholes were missed, although it would not have been impossible as the conditions prevailing during the construction of a housing estate in alternate wet and dry conditions presented numerous difficulties. The ragged northern limit of the cemetery can, however, be accepted with reasonable confidence. Similarly, the straight line border from grave 72 in the south-east to grave 38, where it turns at right angles to grave 131 and ultimately to 36, can also be regarded as definite. The space between graves 38 and 15 and grave 11, and the destroyed patch containing graves 31 and 126, i.e. between plots A, B, C and F, was a barren area. The southern, western and eastern limits to plots C and D are definite, but the strip remaining undamaged at the north of plot D was too narrow to indicate whether the cemetery extended further north at that point. The amount of undamaged strip to the west of graves 115 and 116 in plot D suggested that the western border had been reached, but this cannot be regarded as definite. The strip left undamaged immediately to the west of plot A was also narrow, but the graves there are clustered so densely that the narrow blank strip remaining is at least sufficient to show that that was the limit of that particular plot. Other graves could, however, have extended further westwards at this point.

It is clear that there was a straight border limiting the cemetery between graves 38 and 72, and the fact that there was a blank space between grave 38 and plot C suggests that the border may have been formed by a fairly wide feature, such as a track. This blank space recurs between graves 13 and 26, plots A and D, perhaps indicating the continuance of the track. The large rectangular space west of grave 38 could have contained a building or buildings connected with the cemetery (Text Figure 2). It is interesting that the only indication in the area of Roman occupation is the Claudian pit cut by grave 11, just on the edge of this space and the track. A single posthole, X, 9in. (23cm) in diameter and 9in. (23cm) deep, was near the head of grave 11 and not far from the Roman pit. There was no trace of any other postholes in the immediate vicinity.

# Chapter II

# Grave Goods: Discussion of Types

**Weapons**

*Swords* (distribution figure 85)
The total number of swords is seventeen, but one of these is represented by a fragment of the tang only, 4/2, which was all that remained of the sword in a grave which had been plundered. Some of them consist of a blade and tang without embellishment, five have a small iron pommel of semi-circular shape (93/6, 71/1, 131/2, 33/2 and 27/3), and five have fittings of bronze or silver (98/1, 96b/10, 96a/4, 94b/1 and C/1).

All but one of the fourteen swords that were excavated and seen *in situ* (two were earlier finds), were placed along the left hand side of the body and some actually on top of it, the hilt somewhere in the region of the shoulder and the tip beside the femur. In grave 71 the sword was on the right hand side of the body. There is no indication that any sword belt or baldric with attached metal buckle and plates was wrapped round the sword, unless this might possibly be inferred from the position of the bronze buckle and shoe-shaped rivets on the forearm of the skeleton in grave 91. In four graves there was no buckle or any other metal fitting for a belt (22, 41, 94b and 96b). In eight others the man was buried wearing his belt (27, 33, 56, 71, 93, 96a, 98 and 131) for the buckle was in place at the waist. None of these belts had extravagant buckles although the buckles were of bronze in graves 56 and 96a. Buckle 56/6 had a triangular plate and matching belt plates, and 96a/4 as well as 91/5 was accompanied by shoe-shaped rivets. This means that the three distinctive buckles belonging to sword belts were Frankish in type, possibly an indication of the origin of the swords as well.

The length of the tang is about 11 to 12cm, and on most swords there are the transverse marks of the grain of an upper guard and a lower guard of organic material, both about 1.2cm in width. The length of grip in between gives space for a hand between 8.8 and 10cm wide, i.e. a single-handed grip, and not for a very large fist.

The total length of tang and blade remains of most swords (Table I), but more than half of the tang of 94b/1 is missing, and perhaps a few millimetres of the tangs of 22/3 and 41/3. This means that 94b/1 would have been about 7cm longer, and at 94.5cm would have been the longest sword in the cemetery. Five others are between 90.2 and 91.4cm (C/1, 96a/4, 96b/10, 98/1, and Unassociated 8), and the rest are between 86.8 and 89.4cm long with the exception of 27/3 which is much the shortest at 65.6cm. Nine of the blades are 5–5.1cm wide, but two are wider at 5.5 or 5.6cm (33/2 and 71/1). Narrower blades at 4.6 to 4.8cm are 131/2, 96a/4 and 94b/1), and the narrowest at 4.3cm are 93/6 and 96b/10.

There seems to be no consistent relationship between length and width of blade and importance of the owner, but the longest sword does, in fact, belong to a grave which also contained a decorated spear and, although the pommel had been lost, its high quality is indicated by the lower guard which was of silver with gold-headed rivets. The longest blade belongs to phase 2, and another long one (22/3) to phase 1, otherwise the various lengths occur indiscriminately in phases 3 and 4. The shortest blade, 27/3, 53.6cm long, is an unusually short weapon, and it is possible that a damaged point had been trimmed off.

TABLE I  SWORD MEASUREMENTS

| Grave | Total length | Width | Pommel | Phase |
| --- | --- | --- | --- | --- |
| C | 91.4 | 5.1 | x | 3 |
| 4 | Tang only | | | 3 |
| 22 | 87.6+ | 5.1 | | 1 |
| 27 | 65.6 | 5.1 | x | 4 |
| 33 | 89.4 | 5.5 | x | 3 |
| 41 | 87.7+ | 5.1 | | 3 |
| 56 | 87 | 5 | | 3 |
| 71 | 88.8 | 5.6 | x | 4 |
| 91 | 89.4 | 5.1 | | 3 |
| 93 | 86.8 | 4.3 | x | 3 |
| 94b | 87.5+ | 4.8 | | 2 |
| 96a | 90.2 | 4.8 | x | 4 |
| 96b | 91 | 4.3 | | 4 |
| 98 | 91.4 | 5.1 | x | 3 |
| 131 | 88.9 | 4.6 | x | 4 |
| Unass. 7 | 87 | 5 | | ?3 |
| Unass. 8 | 90.9 | 5 | | ?3 |

Traces of organic material with grain running lengthwise along the tangs show that the grips were encased in wood or possibly horn. A band of grain running at right angles to this at each end of the grip indicates the guards. The guards and the covering of the grip in grave C have been identified as probably horn, and the guard and grip on the sword 93/6 are possibly made of ivory (see p 196). In grave C silver gilt plates are fitted each side of the guards, the lower plates having upturned edges and the upper plates are of flat sheet, a dome-headed rivet securing each end. This form of guard occurs abroad as well as in England, and it was used by the makers of

Kentish swords during the sixth century[1]. The sword from grave 94b has a similar lower guard. The silver rivets have the additional embellishment of gold domed heads and filigree collars, and the lost pommel from this sword must also have been of Kentish manufacture and of corresponding magnificence. Comparable silver rivets occur on a Bifrons sword[2], and gold rivets on the Sutton Hoo sword[3]. A later typological step in the development of the guards[4] is illustrated by 96a/4, where the guards are of organic material and the outer edge covered with a band of iron ornamented with inlaid transverse bronze strips. The thin metal plates which were fastened together above and below by iron rivets no longer exist. Swords at Bulach in Switzerland with similar inlay[5] belong to the second half of the seventh century, but the Swiss pommels also are inlaid, and the Dover hilt with its plain pommel may be at an earlier stage in development. A sword in a grave from Mannheim-Hermsheimer Bösfeld is similar, and the grave contained a solidus of Justinian I, AD 538–565[6]. Iron guards decorated with inlaid strips are gripped between bronze plates on the sword from Vendel grave 1[7]. The type of sword in grave 96a at Dover is not known elsewhere in England and must have been imported from the Rhineland.

The only ornamented pommel was found in grave C (Plate 5a), a silver-gilt cocked-hat form with the additional feature of a moveable ring. The form of the pommel, a low, cocked-hat shape with slashes along each corner and two rivet lugs at each end, is one of the earliest in the series of Kentish cocked-hat pommels[8]. These are all in silver gilt, and production began in the first half of the sixth century. The rings are all in the stage 1b, that is, the head of one of the upper guard rivets is enlarged to become a circle segment, the free end of which rests on one end of the pommel. Into this is linked a complete ring which is free and moveable. On the Dover sword this movement was limited to rotation, and the ring could not be turned outwards away from the pommel. The ring is decorated with nielloed zig-zag and triangles and gilded beading in a style of decoration usual on later Kentish pommels and rings, and so must be a subsequent addition to an early pommel. Support for this proposition is given by the fact that the niello used on the sword and the niello used on the ring are of two quite different compositions, the niello on the ring being the same as that on the grip mounts of the sword 98/1 at Dover and on the Kells crozier (see p 45). The pommel therefore was made in Kent in the early part of the sixth century, and the ring added after the middle of the century.

A silver-gilt beaded loop (C/1f, Figure 1) is one of a pair which originally sealed the join at each end of the grip between the organic cover of the grip and the metal guards. It is more or less oval, but slight angularities suggest that the organic grip it encircled may have been rather hexagonal in shape. Other Kentish swords had comparable beaded borders in this position[9], but the wire on a sword from Gilton is grooved lengthwise instead of being beaded[10]. On the Sutton Hoo sword in these positions there are ropes of beaded gold wire twisted round a core, and the shape taken up by these ropes is a flat hexagonal as on the Dover sword[11].

As a later development the wire ring was expanded into ornamented plates or sleeve rings, narrow versions occurring on the seventh-century swords from Coombe[12] and Crundale[13]. The sleeve rings on the sword from Dover grave 98 (Figure 46) are rather wider than those two, the upper one near the pommel being plain silver, and the one near the lower guard being silver also, but with ornamental bands of niello in key pattern. Similar sleeves, in bronze and undecorated, were found on a sword hilt with bronze pommel in a seventh-century grave at Alton, Hants, grave 16[14]. Sleeve bands occur on continental and Scandinavian swords of the seventh century and later, e.g. in gold decorated with filigree on the ring sword from Nocera Umbra[15], but apparently not often before this date.

The key pattern may be compared with key patterns on late types of Kentish disc brooches where they function as a border, on either the front or the back, and one of these brooches was found in grave 29[16] (Figure 17) of the Dover cemetery. The niello in the key pattern border on the sword is jalpaite, the same type as the niello in the ring on the sword in grave C (see p 45).

Various traces of scabbards are visible on all swords. On the rust of the blades there are traces of fur or fleece and leather, with wood traces on top of these, the grain running lengthwise along the sword, showing that each blade was sheathed in its wooden scabbard lined with fur at the time of burial. The wood of the scabbard on sword C/1 has been identified as possibly field maple (p 196) or probably poplar or willow (p 196). The scabbard mouth was strengthened in various ways. On 94b/1 there are traces of four rows of twisted yarn cord immediately below the lower guard, (Figure 44). A number of rows of twisted cord also bind the top of the scabbard in grave C to a depth of 1.4cm where they

---

1  Evison 1967a, figs 4b, 7a,b, 8a,c, 9b,c, 10a,d, 11a, 12a,b, 14a
2  Ibid, fig. 8a
3  Bruce-Mitford 1979, pl.D
4  Dunning and Evison 1961, 143
5  Werner 1953, 52, Taf. XXIII.2
6  Werner 1935, Taf. 25.B
7  Stolpe and Arne 1927, pl.II
8  Evison 1967a, 72
9  Ibid, fig. 8a, 9b
10  Ibid, fig. 8c
11  Bruce-Mitford 1978, fig. 217,a and b, fig. 218i,k and l
12  Evison 1967a, fig. 12a and b
13  Behmer 1939, Taf. II.3
14  Evison 1963, 43, fig. 20m; cf also Evison 1967a, fig. 12 (Coombe)
15  Behmer 1939, Taf. XLI,7; cf. also Taf. LVI.3, Bavaria as well as Valsgärde 8, Sweden and Pappilanmäki, Finland; Evison 1967a, pls. XIII.b and XIV
16  Avent 1975 i, fig. 4, 8 and 15, fig. 28.7; ii, pl.9.52, pl.34.114

meet the top of a pair of U-sectioned silver binding strips, 16cm long, on the sides of the scabbard. On one unassociated sword, Unassociated 7, a braid about 7mm wide was wound round the mouth of the scabbard. The sword scabbards at Broomfield, Essex, and Sutton Hoo were firmly bound by tape in this way to a greater depth[17] (see p 194).

On some swords, the scabbard mouth was reinforced by metal binding. The fragment of iron bordering wood traces on sword 131/2 and the iron strip on 27/3 may have been the binding of scabbards, or they may have been frames of wooden guards as in grave 96a (Figure 45), although not, in this case, inlaid. On 96a/4 there was a plain bronze strip scabbard border 1.3cm wide. On 96b/10 the binding strip was ornamented with ribbing tooled to imitate beading. This is an Anglo-Saxon scabbard mount type, and occurs at Long Wittenham, grave 96, Linton Heath, grave 64[18], at Battle Edge, near Burford, Oxfordshire[19] and Cirencester[20]. Closely related plain ribbed scabbard mounts occur both in England and abroad, and beaded ribbing also occurs on the more splendid mount from Selmeston grave 1[21] which is further adorned with garnets and zoomorphic designs.

At the back of the scabbard top 96b/10b a small rectangle of bronze with a perforated lug was soldered over the butted join at the back. The purpose and precise position of an accompanying identical shape of rectangle and perforated lug in leather are unknown (Figure 46, 10c), and it may be that part of a larger leather object, such as a strap, was selectively preserved in this shape alone by close contact with the bronze rectangle. Other sword scabbards with this kind of bronze fixture with perforated lug at the back have been noted in England, on the Continent and in Scandinavia[22]. The English examples are from Gilton, Kent, Petersfinger, Wiltshire, Selmeston, East Sussex and Chessel Down, Isle of Wight[23]. As they have been found in association both with rings on the swords and with sword beads, the thong or cord may have been attached to either, although a suspended bead is more likely as the perforation is on the lower edge of the scabbard mount.

The custom of attaching a bead to a sword began as early as the first century BC and spread westwards across Europe, reaching this country by the beginning of the fifth century, if we are to regard as a sword bead the bone disc found in Dorchester grave 1[24]. A number of beads found with swords in Anglo-Saxon graves have been listed[25]. One sword bead was found at Dover in grave 93, a brightly-coloured cylindrical glass bead of reticella rods (Figure 43,1). It was found about 30cm away from the sword pommel. One other bead of this kind was found in this cemetery not far away in grave 42 on a woman's necklace.

Possibly functioning as a sword bead was a bronze band fastened by a rivet in a circle of 1cm diameter (71/3 Figure 38). It was found 30cm from the sword pommel, under the blade. It probably did not serve as a 'bead' on its own, but formed the core of a bead of perishable material.

Since the earlier accounts of sword beads, another sword bead has been found in a sword grave at Collingbourne Ducis, Wiltshire, although the position of finding is not recorded[26]. The bead is disc-shaped and made of bone. Although the report describes the accompanying pommel as a cocked-hat shape, the drawing shows it as a sub-triangular shape with nearly straight sides, i.e. similar to the pommel with curved sides from Chessel Down[27] or the straight-sided pommels from Petersfinger and North Luffenham[28]. These pommels all belong to the types made of bronze, which are demonstrably early, and are most likely imported. The disc-shaped bead of bone may be compared with the bone bead from Dorchester, Oxfordshire which came from a grave of about AD 400[29]. A square bead made of horn was found in grave 15 at Brighthampton, Oxfordshire[30], undateable, but, again, probably early. The material so far excavated from the Collingbourne Ducis cemetery all belongs to the fifth century, so that this sword bead in bone is similar in date to the other two known. A further sword bead is probable in cremation 1105 at Spong Hill, where an early bronze pommel with open top was found in a decorated pot with iron tweezers and a disc-shaped bone bead[31].

In regard to three of the swords at Dover the method of suspension is apparent. On C the two strips of silver binding are to strengthen the part of the scabbard which accommodated the leather baldric or straps supporting the sword from the belt. These U-sectioned mounts occurred in the fifth or sixth centuries on the Continent and in England and Scandinavia, in various lengths from 6 to 15cm[32]. On some of the swords additional mounts indicate a narrow strap passing across the middle of the area between them, sometimes fastened with rivets as on the sword from Selmeston, grave 1[33]. Where there are no rivets the leather strap was no doubt fastened by sewing (Text Figure 3a). On the sword in grave C there is no indication of a second support area lower down the scabbard, although there could have been a second strap without metal fittings. It is also possible that the strap could have been broader, in fact part of a leather baldric which passed over the

17 Bruce-Mitford 1978, fig. 213
18 Kennett 1971, 14, figs. 2d and e
19 Kennett 1969a, fig. 21b
20 Mr P D C Brown kindly drew my attention to this mount
21 Evison 1976, pl.LXV.a
22 Evison 1967a, 65–6
23 Ibid, 84, figs. 9d, 3e; Evison 1976, fig. 3a
24 Ibid, 309, pl.LXV c
25 Evison 1967a and 1976; some additions are noted in Meaney 1981, 196
26 Gingell 1975–6, 71–2, figs. 13,6 and 14,1
27 Evison 1967a, fig. 10c
28 Ibid, fig. 3c and g
29 Evison 1976, pl.LXV, c
30 Ibid, 309, pl.LXV, d
31 Hills 1977a, 43, figs. 79, 117, 122, 135
32 For a distribution map: Menghin 1973, fig. 17
33 Evison 1976, fig. 3a

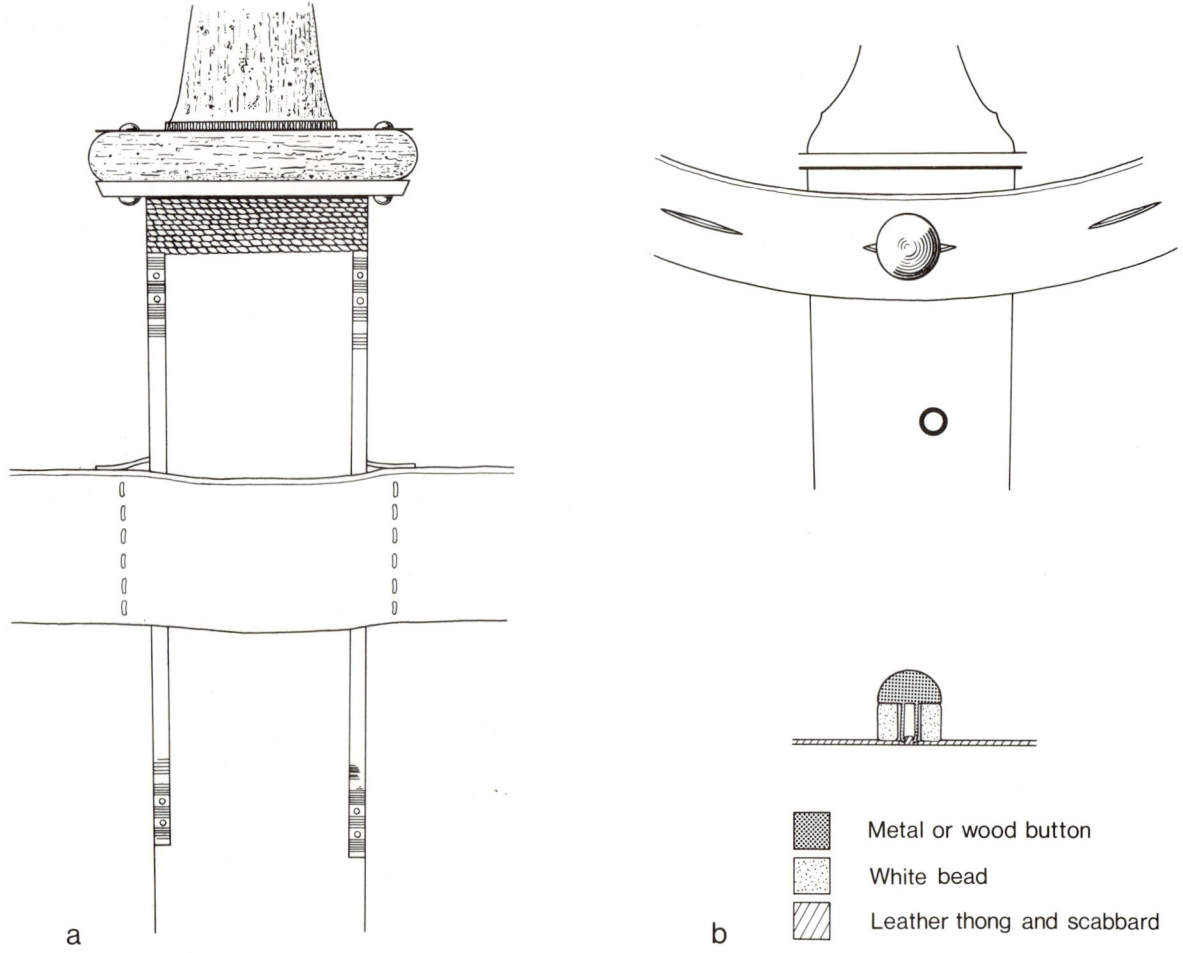

Text Figure 3  *a* Sword C/1, reconstruction of leather holder. Scale 1/2
*b* Sword 27/3, reconstruction of button and baldric. Scale 1/2

right shoulder as depicted on one of the Torslunda plates[34].

On two of the scabbards a radiograph and visual examination together faintly indicate another feature. On 27/3 a double ring mark, the outer ring 21mm and the inner ring 6mm in diameter, lies in the middle of the blade 7cm below the guard and above the inlaid ring, (Figure 15). On 22/3 a double ring mark of slightly denser material than the surrounding iron, diameter 20mm, occupies the middle of the blade 6.5cm from the tang. There are similar faint traces on 93/6. An example of this may have been noted in France as a similar double ring mark diameter 15 and 12.5mm is shown on the drawing of the pattern-welded blade just below the guard of the sword with decorated pommel and guards from grave 87 at Barbaise in the Ardennes. The well-furnished grave belongs to the end of the sixth or beginning of the seventh century. No mention is made of this ring in the description of the sword, however[35].

These single marks at Dover are very similar in size and position to the two impressions left on the Sutton Hoo scabbard by the bedding of the jewelled buttons[36], where the marks are 27.5 and 25.5mm in diameter and 10.5cm below the mouth of the scabbard. In the reconstruction proposed[37] these buttons fasten the sword to a narrow hip belt, and on this particular sword at Sutton Hoo there is a second support point lower down the scabbard in the form of a dummy buckle. No fittings of any other kind were preserved in Dover grave 22, but the man in grave 27 was wearing a belt with an iron buckle, which may have fastened a sword belt. The gold buttons at Sutton Hoo must have been set in a white bead so that the loop of the button fitted into the perforation of the bead, and thongs secured the buttons through the loops to the scabbard which was probably enveloped in a leather band at this point. The investigations into the material of the matrix of the buttons produced no definite conclusion[38].

Fortunately there are many comparable buttons

---

34  Menghin 1973, fig. 2; Bruce-Mitford 1978, fig. 41b, a and b (upper figure)
35  Chalvignac and Lemant 1978, fig. 3
36  Bruce-Mitford 1978, fig. 208
37  Ibid, fig. 425
38  Ibid, 308

and also a contemporary illustration to elucidate their function. Other jewelled buttons set in white beads have been found in association with swords, for example at Morken, Krefeld Gellep and Niederstotzingen in Germany, and at Wickhambreux in Kent[39]. The contemporary illustration is one of the repoussé plates on the helmet in Vendel grave 14, where two warriors are each wearing a sword on a baldric which appears to have slots along its length, into one of which two buttons on the scabbard are fastened[40]. The reconstruction figure[41] suggested for the Sutton Hoo buttons illustrates a white bead *en cabochon* shape, but this has no parallel, and a cylindrical shape seems to be the most usual. A reconstruction for the Dover swords (Text Figure 3b) is based on the Sutton Hoo and other known button-and-bead knobs, but as there were no metal parts at Dover they must either have been removed before burial or were in perishable material such as wood or bone. The use, in this functional position, of white beads which were made of a variety of friable comsitions, does not seem practical. The material at Niederstotzingen was magnesite, at Morken and Krefeld Gellep it is reported as meerschaum, and in Selmeston grave 1 it was cristobalite. Cylindrical white beads were also worn on necklaces, as the bead at Dover 14/2c of magnesium carbonate, and the bead 20/18 of apatite was probably used with the wooden belt. A metal button bedded in a white bead might have been used either as a scabbard button or as a pendant sword bead, and certainty on this point of function is only possible in the case of well recorded graves, where the position is precisely noted.

The evidence from the Dover cemetery regarding the method of wearing swords therefore is mainly limited to four swords where one point of suspension only is visible, a strengthened part of the scabbard for the attachment of a strap on one, and a button on three. Nine of the men with swords were wearing a belt with buckle, so that it is possible that these swords were suspended from a waist belt although none of the swords were visibly connected with the belt in the grave. Two of these belts were ornamented with metal plates. As the slots in the metal plates of graves 56 and 98 were only wide enough to accommodate straps 5mm wide, it does not seem likely that they were used to suspend something as heavy and unwieldy as a sword. In the four graves where there were no metal fittings the leather baldric or belt must have been sewn or tied.

The surfaces of the blades are obscured by rust and adhesions of fur, wood, etc, but of the extant sixteen sword blades pattern-welding is revealed by X-ray on each one. The longitudinal welding lines between the strips are sometimes clear enough to show whether the inner decorated part of the blade was made up of two or three strips side by side. The radiographs are not usually clear, however, no doubt because the strips were in double layers, and the presence of a longitudinal welding line running along the middle of a middle strip of three, as happens on 131/2, suggests that although on this blade there were three strips on one face, there were two, or even perhaps four, on the other.

The patterns visible are straight lengthwise lines where the bar was left untwisted, and short diagonal lines where the bar had been twisted. This combination occurs on C/1, 22/3, 41/3, 56/1, 91/5, 131/2, and Unassociated 8, in most of which three zones are more or less clear. On 33/2 and 94b/1 three zones of zig-zag only are visible. On 71/1 there seem to be four rows, the inner two being herringbone and the outer ones lengthwise and straight. The short sword 27/3 also appears to have four zones of straight and diagonal lines. Although the radiograph is not clear enough to be conclusive, it does appear that the pattern-welding does continue to the point, so that the blade may have been accidentally broken at the tip and reshaped to a shorter length. Two rows of herringbone fashion are visible on 93/6, 96a/4, 96b/10, 98/1 and Unassociated 7. There is no indication of the curling pattern except possibly on 96a/4.

It has been suggested that manufacture in four zones or more did not begin before the middle of the sixth century[42], and the examples of this arrangement at Dover came from graves 27 and 71, both dated to phase 4, the latest date for the deposition of swords in this cemetery. Investigations regarding the technique of pattern welding continue.

It is noteworthy that all of the swords at Dover were pattern-welded, and this result may be compared with the Schretzheim cemetery where, although the number of blades not pattern-welded is not large, there were seventeen where the technique was not detected[44]. Systematic radiography has not yet been carried out in England to an extent that yields useful figures, but it seems possible that the high proportion at Dover may well recur at other Kentish cemeteries of the same period.

The sword in grave 27 is remarkable for its very short blade, but even more remarkable for the inlaid ring of denser metal, ?silver or bronze, which was revealed by radiograph and is shown on the drawing, Figure 15. Inlaid work of this kind is liable to disintegrate as the iron surface flakes away, and a later radiograph indeed, shows no sign of this ring. In the same way loss of decoration in this technique with the passage of time after excavation has been noted on German finds[45]. A similar inlaid ring in brass occupies a comparable position, but in the middle of the blade, on a pattern-welded sword from Schretzheim grave 108[46], a grave of the early

---

39 Evison 1976, 312
40 Menghin 1973, fig. 3; Bruce-Mitford 1978, fig. 416b (lower figure)
41 Ibid, fig. 224
42 Koch 1977 1, 98

43 For recent work see Ypey 1980
44 Koch 1977 2, Taf. 254
45 Hässler 1981, 79
46 Koch 1977 1, 99; Koch 1977 2, Taf. 185.6

seventh century. Another sword with an inlaid oval ring was found in grave 7 at Mindelheim, and belongs to the middle of the seventh century[47]. Inlaid marks of other shapes are known on swords of this period, e.g. the runic cross in grave 79 at Schretzheim[48]. Another has been detected by X-ray on the sword from grave 250 at Sarre, Kent, which was found with a shield boss, and three rivets, two spears, a knife and a pottery vessel[49]. This mark also included a ring, but the ring encircled the outlined pommel of a tiny sword. Inlaid marks of this type have more often been detected on spear blades, cf Dover 93/3.

Although the number of swords found at Dover is large in proportion to the number of graves, they do not occur at all in the later phases and are limited to one in phase 1, one in phase 2, eight to ten in phase 3, and five in phase 4, all situated in the western half of the cemetery. The practice of burying a sword at Dover therefore begins with the cemetery and occurs mostly in the period AD 575–650, after which date it had ceased completely.

*Spears* (distribution Figure 85)
Some of the spearheads have deteriorated since finding, but the measured sketch on the index card made on the day of excavation is evidence of the original outline, and radiographs have been useful in distinguishing the contours.

The form of the spearheads will be considered in the order of those of Swanton's types which are present in the cemetery, beginning with type C2 (Table II), although their characteristics do not always seem to fit the type to which they were designated by Swanton. Spearhead 27/1 (Figure 15) was specified as D1 by Swanton[50]. Both C2 and D1 types have leaf-shaped blades, but the short solid neck of 27/1 would seem to put it in the C2 class. Two belong to class C3, a longer leaf-shaped blade, 10/2 and 131/1 (Figures 8 and 54), although Swanton regards 10/2 as class E3 i.e. an angular type. Slender leaf-shaped blades with a smooth curve are: 57/1 (Figure 32), the length being between types C4 and C5 (defined as E4 by Swanton[51] although it has no angle), and the shorter Kentish variety C5, 114/2 and 135/1 (Figures 1, 50 and 56), on the last of which the socket finishes in two socket extensions.

As to Swanton's D group, leaf-shaped blades on longer sockets, 41/1 and 137/3 (Figures 24 and 56) belong to type D/1, but the latter is unusual in having a solid neck of triangular section. Of the longer D2 type there are: 50/1 (Figure 28)[52], 61/1 (Figure 35), 63/1 (Figure 36), 96a/1 (Figure 45), 96b/7 (Figure 46), 128/1 (Figure 52) although nearly lozengiform, and 9/1 (Figure 8). (This last is classed as E2 by Swanton, but is definitely leaf-shaped.) Leaf-shaped with a long shank, but shorter, i.e. type D3, is 90/1 (Figure 40).

TABLE II  SPEARS

| Type | Phase 1 | 2 | 3 | 4 | 5 | 6 |
|---|---|---|---|---|---|---|
| C2 | | | | 27/1 | | |
| C3 | | | 131/1 | | 10/2 | |
| C4/C5 | | | 57/1 | | | |
| C5 | | | | 135/1 | | 114/2 |
| D1 | | | | 41/1 | 137/3 | |
| D2 | | 50/1 | 61/1 63/1 | 96a/1 96b/7 128/1 9/1 | | |
| D3 | | | | 90/1 | | |
| E2 | | | 4/1 | | | |
| E3 | | | | 39/1 65/1 71/2 91/3 56/3 | | |
| F1 | 87/1 | | | | 156/1 | |
| G2 | | | 33/1 | | | |
| H3 | | | C/2a | | | |
| L | | | 93/3 | | | |

Bold indicates a ferrule, which also occurs in graves 22, phase 1 and 94b, phase 2.

Type E2, an angular blade with short solid neck, is represented by 4/1 (Figure 6), allocated by Swanton to type E3 which is a longer-bladed type[53]. To type E3 belong 39/1 (Figure 23), 65/1 (Figure 36), 71/2 (Figure 38), 91/3 (Figure 41) and 56/3 (Figure 31) which has an unusually triangular blade with a mid rib. The mid rib is not noted by Swanton[54] but he does elsewhere draw attention to the fact that a mid rib is an ornamental form on an expensive type[55]. Another Kentish spear with mid rib was found at Holborough[56]. There is a fragmentary example of

---

47  Werner 1955b, Taf. 4
48  Koch 1977 2, Taf. 210.2
49  Brent 1868, 315; Evison 1979a, 93–4; Maidstone Museum
50  Swanton 1973, 64
51  Swanton 1974, 44

52  Swanton 1973, 67, 173, fig. 20b
53  Swanton 1974, 44
54  Swanton 1973, 85, 179
55  Ibid, 42; cf Bruce-Mitford 1978, fig. 189
56  Evison 1956, fig. 17, 2a, b

E4 in the shape of Unassociated 10 (Figure 64). Spear 39/1 is called E4 by Swanton, but the blade does not seem sufficiently slender to put it in this category, and E3 is preferred here (Figure 23).

Type F1 is represented by 87/1 (Figure 40)[57], and also by 156/1 (Figure 61), which is the same shape, (although Swanton regards this latter as a D1 shape and is not aware of the inlay on the socket[58].

Of type G2, a parallel-sided, sword-shaped blade, there is only one, 33/1 (Figure 20). Type H3 has a concave, angular blade with solid shank i.e. C/2a (Figure 1). There was only one type L, 93/3 (Figure 43), a concave angular blade with stepped section. (The angles of the original outline were lost by corrosion before drawing. The spearhead itself has since been lost.) Socket fragments only, of which the types are unidentifiable, occurred in graves 5/4 (Figure 6), 22/5 (Figure 14), 94b/2 (Figure 44) and 98/2 (Figure 46).

There are two spears which do not fall into any of Swanton's categories. One is the small spear or dart found in a child's (?small boy's) grave 139/5 (Figure 57). This is only 9cm long and has a welded socket and leaf-shaped blade, possibly identifiable with type C5. It is, however, similar in size and shape to some of the 'arrows' or darts found at Buttsole, Eastry, Kent[59]. A small spear, 10.5cm long, was found in grave 378 at Lankhills, Winchester[60], where the occupant was a child buried prone with five coins giving a date *post quem* of AD 390–410. The spear has a split socket, and the drawing shows the blade as lozenge-shaped, i.e. an angular blade, classified as E1 by Swanton. A spear, frequently a particularly small one, was often placed in the grave of a Germanic child, and a number of examples were cited by Clarke on the Continent and in this country. Small spearheads in children's graves were found in Anglo-Saxon cemeteries at Abingdon, Oxfordshire (Berkshire)[61], Alfriston, East Sussex[62], and Girton, Cambridge[63].

The other unusual spear is 8/1 (Figure 8), classified as D2 by Swanton although, in fact, its blade is asymmetrical in shape and single-edged with a crescent-shaped tip. It cannot have been used for throwing like the rest of the spears, and, if it was in fact a functional weapon, it must have been used with a slashing action in hand-to-hand combat. The man in this grave was buried in a coffin which was packed around with large flints. The spear was placed on top of the coffin and flints, the head being found 13cm higher than the floor of the grave. There was no trace of the spear shaft near the head, but about 2ft. 4ins. (0.71m) away and in line with the head there were black wood fragments, and continuing this line for 3ft. (0.91m) until it reached floor level there was a long hole in the chalk fill, oval in section 2¼in. × 1½in. (5.7cm × 3.8cm). Some distance away, near the middle of the foot of the grave, was an oval iron ring binding remains of a wooden shaft of maximum diameter 2.8cm. The measurement from the tip of the spearhead to the end of the hole in the fill was about 6ft. (1.83m). The three completely different states of preservation of the shaft, i.e. complete absence or disintegration near the spearhead, adjoined by a length of black wood remains, and then by complete disintegration with the shape preserved in the fill, suggest that the shaft was in three sections, covered perhaps by different materials such as paint which may have acted selectively as a preservative, or it consisted of three different types of wood. With a length of 6ft. in a direct line it would appear that the spear was placed complete in the grave. The iron ring was binding a wood shaft smaller, but of similar oval shape. If it was a mount on the same shaft the spear would have been over 6ft. long and must have been broken off at the end to fit in the grave.

It is usually accepted that the wood normally used for Anglo-Saxon spear shafts was ash[64], as may be deduced from a common Anglo-Saxon term for them, *aescas*, and, in fact, the wood in the ferrule of spears 41/2 and 94b/3 has been identified as 'probably ash'. However out of eight spear sockets at Polhill, three contained traces of hazel, some of oak, and only one of ash[65]. The black wood remains of the middle part of the shaft of Dover 8/1 has been identified as *acer*, maple, and the remains in the spearhead socket as *Fraxinus* sp., ash from mature timber. Fragments of one other spear shaft, 94b/2 and 3, are identified as probably of field maple, *Acer campestre*, by one expert, and as probably ash by another. It may be that more than one type of material was used for the shaft of 8/1, and the combination of a unique blade, with a shaft of unusual size, shape and material, indicates a display weapon such as a standard.

A comparable spear occurred as the only find in grave 662 at Mucking. It is in a bad state of corrosion, so that although it appears to be a single-edged weapon with the same kind of curved tip, it is not possible to be absolutely sure that this was its original shape. It is, however, clearly a class above the normal spear, for the socket was covered for most of its length by sheet bronze, and the blade is very similar in size and shape to the Dover spear (Text Figure 4).

A spear which must have functioned as some kind of ceremonial standard was found in significant circumstances at Welbeck Hill, Lincolnshire. It was angular in shape with a mid rib, and one, probably originally two, small bronze rings were inserted in the lower end of the blade. It was in the grave of an old man with knife and bucket, and a decapitated woman was lying over the skeleton in a reverse

---

57  Swanton 1973, 91, 182–3, fig. 72a–c
58  Ibid, 64, 171, fig. 18b
59  Brown 1915 III, pl. XXXII.1; cf arrows below
60  Clarke 1979, 256, 393, 398, fig. 96
61  Leeds and Harden 1936, graves 21 (pl.XVIII), 35A and 77
62  Griffith and Salzmann 1914, 28, grave 63, pl.XX.6, 6A, 6B
63  Hollingworth and O'Reilly 1925, 8, grave 58
64  Bruce-Mitford 1978, 272
65  Philp 1973a, 202

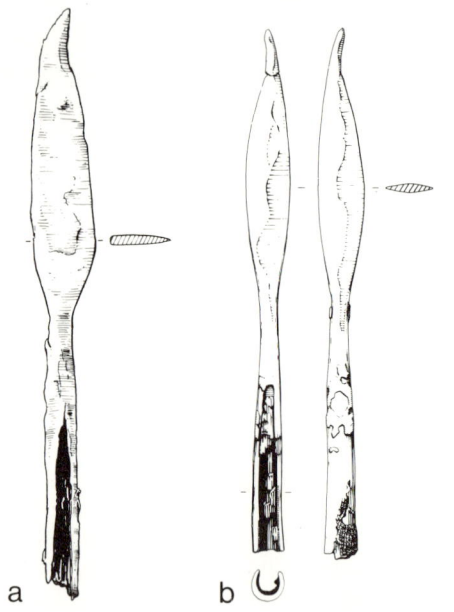

Text Figure 4  Spears, a Dover 8/1, b Mucking 662/1. Scale 1/4

direction[66]. From this we may deduce that the man had filled an important role in life, and that the ornamental spear was connected with this role.

Single-edged hafted weapons of similar size found on the Continent are mostly without context, but one grave at Hamoir, Belgium, was a typical warrior's grave. This grave 36 contained a seax, knife, shield, belt mount, pot and a cutlass with a right-angled hook on the back[67]. This cutlass and similar bill-hooks are sometimes of more practical solidity like tools and would not be suitable as show pieces. Various types of weapon, i.e. seax, cutlass, bill-hook and single-edged spear may be considered in connection with the unidentified weapon referred to in Beowulf as *haeft-mece* and in a corresponding story in Grettis-saga as *heptisax*, both unique terms indicating an unusual hewing weapon with a handle[68].

Grave 8, in which the Dover spear was found, contained a Frankish buckle and was on the edge of the cemetery in a group of five graves, of which two others contained spears, and one was a woman with a Frankish glass. The spear in grave 9 nearby is a D2 type which Swanton noted is often found with Frankish objects[69]. A Frankish connection is therefore strong.

One more spearhead from Dover was included by Swanton, as a C2 type[70], and this must be a spearhead with leaf-shaped blade and closed socket, length 28.5cm which was a casual find on a nearby hillside in Green Lane. It was brought to Dover Museum before the excavation, but is not likely to have any connection with the Buckland cemetery, and probably not even with the Saxons.

A number of spears were provided with a ferrule, all of a hollow conical type, C2b (Figure 1), 22/6 (Figure 14), 27/2 (Figure 15), 41/2 (Figure 24), 56/4 (Figure 31), 65/2 (Figure 36), 87/2 (Figure 40), 91/4 (Figure 41), 93/4 (Figure 43), 94b/3 (Figure 44), except 137/4 (Figure 56) with a solid conical type with a square-sectioned strig. Of these the following total lengths from tip of spearhead to tip of ferrule are indicated by the relative positions: C/2a–2b = 6ft. (1.83m), 22/5–6 = 5ft. 3ins. (1.6m), plus the length of the missing spear blade, 41/1–2 = 6ft. 8ins. (2.03m), 56/3–4 = 7ft. 3ins. (2.21m) (this is a long spear perhaps because the man himself was over six foot tall), 87/1–2 = 6ft. 10ins. (2.08m), 91/3–4 = 6ft. 6ins. (1.98m), 94b/2–3 = 5ft. 8ins. (1.73m) plus the length of the missing spear blade. In graves 27, 65 and 93, however, the spear-shaft had obviously been broken before burial as the ferrule was pointing the opposite way. In two of these graves the man was over 45, and in the other between 30 and 45, which gives rise to the thought that possibly this destruction of the spear indicated that the man's fighting life was over, and he was not prepared to continue in battle in the next world. The custom of breaking the spear was followed in the Sutton Hoo ship burial, where, although there were a number of spears and angons in the burial chamber, the King's personal spear was broken in half and placed one half on either side of the body just inside the coffin[71]. The contents of these three spear graves include a number of Frankish objects, however, so that the men buried may actually have been Franks: 27 buckle and inlaid sword; 65 buckle and seax, 93 inlaid spear and seax.

The spearhead was normally placed beside the man's head, on the left in graves C, 8, 9, 22, 27, 33, 39, 50, 57, 63, 71, 87, 90, 93, 96b, and on the right in graves 4, 10, 41, 56, 91, 94b, 96a, 128, 131, 135, 139. The only exceptions are grave 61 where the spearhead was to the right of the body by the top of the femur, pointing towards the head, and in grave 65 after the spear was broken, the spearhead was placed along the left humerus. In grave 114 the spearhead was placed just outside the left foot, pointing to the foot of the grave, a position more common in Frankish graves[72].

Decoration, in the form of inlaid strips of bronze or silver, occurs in horizontal bands on the sockets of spearheads 50/1 (on an iron binding ring) and 156/1. It occurs on a fragmentary spearhead socket 94b/2 as well as on its matching ferrule, and on a fragmentary socket 22/5 on an iron band with ribbing below, where the matching ferrule is not inlaid but bears a bronze disc. The missing spear blades to the sockets 94b/2 and 22/5 might have been a D2 type like 50/1 or an F1 type like 156/1. In any case there is very

66  Swanton 1973, 207, fig. 82e
67  Alénus-Lecerf 1975, 13, pl.14,1; Alénus-Lecerf 1978, 45–6; cf a *fauchard* at Nouvion-en-Ponthieu, Piton and Schuler 1981, pl.27, 26.
68  Evison 1961
69  Swanton 1974, 11
70  Ibid, 44
71  Evison 1979b, fig. 6.3
72  Joffroy 1974, 26

little difference in the shape of these two types. A fine, dense line visible on a radiograph across the socket of the spear 87/1 appears to be too thin to represent inlaid metal, although it might be a remnant of it. Spearheads with these inlaid bands were noted in England some time ago[73], and others have been found since[74]. Similar inlaid bands of another metal occur on iron binding rings on angons[75], one at least found in England at Sarre. This kind of inlay on spears has not yet been detected in any large numbers on continental spears of this date, and it is therefore not possible to be certain whether any manufacture took place in this country or whether those found in England are imports.

The same uncertainty regarding origin still applies to the inlaid spear blades. The most common are the ring-and-dot motifs which are the continuation of such ornamentation on third-century and fourth-century Scandinavian and continental spears[76] and this occurs at Great Chesterford[77]. Much finer inlay is used for the ring and swastika on the type L spearhead 93/3 at Dover, although even the swastika has a forerunner on earlier inlaid blades from Dahmsdorf, Brandenburg and Kowel, Volhynia, Poland[78]. The finer inlay seems only to be paralleled by one other spearhead which was found in grave 7 at Holborough, Kent[79], where the symbol was probably runic in origin. Although type L is often an early type, the position of grave 93 and its contents suggest a date near AD 600, and the Holborough spearhead is a later type (G2) with seventh-century associations. As there are no close continental examples known, the case for an insular origin for these two spears is stronger than for the blades with inlaid ring-and-dot.

In grave 71 an iron ring, diameter 2.8cm was lying outside the man's left femur, in line with the spearhead and $c$ 45cm from the end of the socket. As the diameter is a normal size for a spear shaft, it is likely that this ring marked the middle or grasping point of the shaft. In grave 22 an oval bronze ring, diameter 1.5cm, was lying in the same position outside the left femur, and about halfway between the spearhead and its ferrule. This ring, however, is too small in diameter to have encircled the spearshaft. In grave 93, outside the right hip, a bronze ring with an internal diameter of 2.2cm was lying in line with the ferrule and $c$ 30cm away from it. Another oval iron ring, diameter 2cm, was found by the femur in line with a spearhead at the foot of grave 114 and could have been set into the middle part of the spearshaft. It was, however, among bronze fragments of a ?lyre, and could alternatively be connected with them. The fact that a ring occurred in this position in four graves in line with the spearhead is strong evidence of connection with the shaft. In grave 94b a bronze strip, length 3.3cm, was lying in line with the spearhead and ferrule, but nearer the ferrule. It is possible that this could have been a mend or strengthening strip riveted longitudinally on the shaft. This would presumably be for burial purposes only, as it would alter the flight of the spear.

Textile impressions of various kinds have been detected on the spearheads in graves 4, 5, 10, 65, 137 and 156 (see p 190). Some of these impressions may have come from clothing or even grave or coffin lining or covering. However, in addition, a pin was found with the spearheads in graves 10, 96a and 96b. Evidently these spearheads had been wrapped in cloth, and in these three graves the wrapping had been fastened with a pin. In grave 94b the ferrule was inlaid with another metal, and it carried traces of two textiles.

Every sword grave also contained a spear. A spear occurred in association with a seax in grave 93, with a shield in 39, with arrows in 57 and 156, always with a knife, but often without other weapons.

Spearheads often lay at a higher level in the grave. In grave 8, for instance, the spear was placed on top of the coffin and surrounding flints. In graves 9, 56 and 90 the spearhead was probably resting on a cushion placed under the head of the skeleton. In grave 156 the spearhead was in an unusual position by the left hip, lying over the left arm and $c$ 11.5cm above the floor.

The allocation of these spearheads to the various types is not a great help in arriving at precision dating as most of the types were in use for a century or more, and some were in use throughout the pagan period. Amongst the latter are C2, D1, E2, F1. Probable dates for the other types according to Swanton are:−

| | |
|---|---|
| fifth century − sixth century | = H3, L |
| sixth century | = D3, E4 |
| sixth century − seventh century | = C3, D2, E3, G2 |
| seventh century | = C4, C5 |

Since the spearheads are not yet precisely dateable a reverse process has been adopted here and their relations to the seven phases distinguished in the Dover cemetery have been examined. The first two phases contain few male graves, and only one F1 and one D2 type (Table II). Spearheads occur most plentifully in the next two phases, ten in phase 3 and nine in phase 4. The varieties in both are numerous, phase 3 with C4/5, D1, D2, E2, E3, G2, H3 and L, and phase 4 with C2, C3, C5, D2, D3 and E3. Phase 5 has four, C3, D1, D2, and F1, phase 6 has one, C5, and phase 7 none. The types D2 and E3 therefore occur in phases 3 and 4, D2 also in phases 2 and 5 and D1 in both phase 3 and 5. Peculiar to phase 3 are C4/5, D1, E2, E3, G2, H3 and L, and peculiar to phase 4 is one, D3. A type C5 occurs in both phase 4 and phase 6, and an F1 occurs in both

---

73 Evison 1955, 24, figs. 1 and 2; Evison 1958
74 Swanton 1973, 109, 137, figs. 53a, 85b
75 Ibid, 33
76 Holmqvist 1951, Abb.33 and 34
77 Evison 1955, pl.IIIe
78 Krause and Jankuhn 1966 II, Taf. 16 and 17
79 Evison 1956, 97–100, figs. 7 and 15, 1, pl.IIIa

phase 1 and phase 5. These distributions exhibit no obvious significance as to form development. The spears were therefore mainly limited to phases 3 – 5, with only one each in phases 1, 2 and 6. The spears in plots C and F are all without ferrules.

*Arrows*

Apart from the dart or arrow in a child's grave, 139/5 (Figure 57) mentioned above in connection with spears, there appear to be the remains of three arrowheads in grave 57 which contained an adolescent. A small buckle was near the head and nearby three iron fragments, each of which had a square-sectioned tang which had been embedded in wood. One was a complete spike, length 6.1cm, like an awl 57/3 (Figure 32), one was broken 57/4a, and one, 57/5a, b, had a leaf-shaped blade. The grave also contained a spear and a knife, and it may be considered that in a weapon grave these three objects are more likely to be arrowheads than tools, and a position by the head is a likely one for a quiver with buckled strap for wearing over the shoulder. Arrows are frequently found in groups of three in Frankish graves, and the types are usually socketed with barbed or leaf-shaped blades[80].

A similar, single spike was found in three other graves. Grave 156 (Figure 61) also contained a spear, knife and small buckle. A spike, 149/3 (Figure 60), was associated with two buckles and a knife, and a single spike, 162/6 (Figure 63), was with knives and whetstones. In two of these three graves the spike was more likely to be an awl than an arrow as the graves belonged to old men, but 162 was the grave of a boy. Although the four graves were no great distance from each other, grave 57 probably belonged to phase 3, and the others to phases 5 and 6 when weapons were less frequent.

Records of the finding of arrowheads in Anglo-Saxon graves are fairly numerous, but there are usually no accurate measurements, descriptions or illustrations so that it is not possible to be certain whether they are arrowheads or small spears or awls. Most of those which are recognisable appear to be similar in shape and size to the dart in grave 139, i.e. leaf-shaped blade and welded socket, which is one of the six types in the Trier region[81]. The following is a list of 15 examples identifiable as arrowheads from illustrations or other information, followed by references to the mention of arrowheads of which either the date or the identification is uncertain.

*Arrowheads*

1. Bowcombe Down, Isle of Wight. No. 20. Disturbed skeletons with arrowhead, half a horseshoe, iron fragments, iron ring, bead etc. Wilkins *et al.* 1860 258; Arnold 1982, 67, 93.
2. Chalton, Hampshire. Arrowhead L 57mm. W 13.9mm. End pointed and flat in section, split socket. Addyman *et al.* 1972, 30, fig. 18, 5.
3. Chessell Down, Isle of Wight. About 24 tanged arrowheads with remains of a bow, bronze bowl, bronze pail, silver rim of a 'bucket', shield boss, grip, knife, sword, spearhead and ferrule. Lengths about 4.6–6.1cm. Hillier 1856, 30, figs. 108–11; Arnold 1982, 24, 67.
4. Buttsole (Eastry), Kent. 23 ?socketed arrowheads 8.3–13.3cm long. Payne 1893–5, 182–3; Brown 1915 III pl. XXXII.
5. Chartham Down, Kent. An arrowhead L 5.1cm, W 2.6cm, length of shank 5.1cm. Remains of two others (these may be spears). Douglas 1793, 106, 108.
6. Chatham Lines, Kent. 4 socketed iron arrowheads. Douglas 1793, 77, pl. xix, figs. 2, 3, 6, 8.
7. Garton, Humberside (Yorkshire). Iron arrowhead L 8.9cm, socketed, found with skeleton and 6 spearheads. Mortimer 1905, 237 fig. 600.
8. Empingham, Leicestershire (Rutland). Grave 96. Iron arrowhead L 8.4cm with spearhead L 26.3cm. Clough *et al.* 1975, pl. 10b. Male burial with 10 arrowheads, spearhead and pair of bronze tweezers. Wilson 1970, 162.
9. Kingston Down, Kent. Grave 111. Spear, nails, iron fragments, tanged arrowhead L 7.1cm, brass ferrule with iron spike. Faussett 1856, 60.
10. Kingston near Lewes, East Sussex. A socketed arrowhead L 3.8cm with a copper alloy ring, spearhead, shield boss and knife. Sawyer 1892, 180; Welch 1983 ii, 413, fig. 73d.
11. Maxey, Cambridgeshire (Northamptonshire). Arrowhead L *c* 7.5cm, small head, long socket. Addyman 1964, 60, fig. 16, 12.
12. North Luffenham, Leicestershire (Rutland). 2 arrowheads with spearheads and brooch. L 6.6cm, 6.4cm socketed. Meaney 1964, 215; Smith 1908b, 97, fig. 1.
13. Pewsey (Black Patch) Wiltshire, grave 16. Arnold 1982, 67.
14. Steep Lowe, Staffordshire. Iron arrowhead, no socket – ?tanged. Bateman 1861, 126.
15. Thornhill Lane, Broad Town, Clyffe Pypard, Wiltshire. Iron arrowhead, socketed, with barbs and midrib, L 6.1cm found in tumulus with amber bead and green glass bead. *Wiltshire Archaeol Natur Hist Mag* 29 (1897), 86; Cunnington and Goddard 1934, pl. lxxxi, fig. 1.

*Possible arrowheads*

16. Beddington, London (Surrey) Carpenter 1874–9.
17. Bidford-on-Avon, Warwickshire. Grave 95. Humphreys *et al.* 1923, 115.
18. Breach Downs, Kent. Croker 1844, 379.
19. Chartham Down, Kent. Grave 39. Faussett 1856, 173.
20. Cheesecake Hill, Driffield, Humberside (Yorkshire). Wright 1846, 55; Mortimer 1905, fig. 834.
21. Colchester, Essex. Smith 1854, 22–3.
22. Galley Lowe, Ballidon, Derbyshire. Bateman 1848, 37–8.

---

80 Böhner 1958 2, Taf. 29, 7–14; Breuer and Roosens 1957, 261–2

81 Böhner 1958 2, Taf. 29, 7, 8

23. Garton Slack, Humberside (Yorkshire). Mortimer 1905 268–9, fig. 734.
24. Gilton, Kent, Graves 4, 46, 65. Faussett 1856 4–5, 7, 17, 22, figs. 1 and 7 on p 10.
25. Glynde (Saxon Down) East Sussex. A socketed arrowhead near a skeleton. Horsfield 1824, 46, pl. 3, 9; Welch 1983, 402, fig. 64b.
26. Kingston Down, Kent. Graves 3, 94, 105, 113, 178, 179, 180, 213, 284. Faussett 1856 41–2, 57, 59, 61, 74–5, 80, 90.
27. Little Wilbraham, Cambridgeshire. *Cambridge Antiq Soc Rep* 14 (1854), 12.
28. Londesborough, Humberside (Yorkshire). Meaney 1964, 294.
29. Lowesby Hall, Leicestershire. Wright 1849–53b.
30. Marston St. Lawrence, Northamptonshire. Dryden 1849, 330; Dryden 1885, 330–1.
31. Saffron Walden, Essex. Smith 1884, 330.
32. St. Margaret's at Cliff, Kent. Douglas 1793, 77, pl. xix, fig. 7.
33. West Stow Heath, Suffolk. Smith 1852, 165–7.
34. Wetwang Vicarage, Humberside (Yorkshire). Mortimer 1905, 206, figs. 504a, 505.
35. Winterslow Hut, Idmiston, Wiltshire. Hutchins 1844, 157.

*Seaxes* (distribution Figure 85)
There were only two seaxes. The seax 65/3 (Figure 36), with a slightly angled back and curved cutting edge, was 41.2cm long and the blade 4cm wide. The pommel was lying in line with the blade a few centimetres away, and if its position was undisturbed, as it appeared to be, the length of the grip would have been about 18cm, making the total length of the weapon 51.5cm. The measurements are on the border line between the narrow seax and the broad seax, and the continental seax was at this stage of development at about AD 600[82]. The extra long grip and the slight angle in the back match the shape of the rather later, grooved and inlaid blade from Northolt[83]. The simple, undecorated weapon 65/3 however, must belong to an earlier date, and was no doubt imported along with the Frankish belt set in the same grave.

The other seax 93/7 (Figure 43), with a length of 39cm and a blade width of 3.5cm, is a little shorter and narrower, and the grip is only long enough for a single hand. The shape of the blade is unusual for a seax as the back is incurved at the point, but this is a shape that is fairly common in knives and is described as type 6 (p 113). A pommel slightly curved towards the blade, as this one is, has been noted on seaxes from Shudy Camps, Cambridgeshire, Winchester, Hampshire and grave 36, Sibertswold, Kent, and as continental seax pommels are usually set on a straight guard it was suggested that this might be an insular development[84]. The technique used in inlaying copper strips into the lower guard is not much in evidence either in England or abroad in the sixth century. A further peculiarity is the sheath which appears to have been made of wood, probably poplar or willow, and a shaped strip of iron was in position on each side. Although the strips are severely corroded, the 'blades' appear to be flat on the sides near the seax blade, and curved on the outside, so that identification as part of the scabbard is possible. It must be noticed, however, that sometimes a knife was inserted in a seax scabbard in this position[85], so that these could be a pair of knives or a knife and a sharpener. The absence of a knife elsewhere in this grave could be regarded as significant in this connection. Further, the traces of organic matter on the grip of the seax and on the corresponding narrow parts of the two iron strips all appear to be of horn. While there are traces of the wooden scabbard on the seax blade, the iron strips show only animal fur (p 196). It is most likely, therefore, that this is a seax in a wooden sheath covered with animal fur, the ?knives being carried in a pocket on each side. Later leather seax sheaths have been found in this country at York[86], sheath fittings of the late seventh century at Ford, Laverstock, Wiltshire[87], and Merovingian leather sheaths in Holland[88].

Many of the seaxes found in this country, including those mentioned above, belong to the second half of the seventh century, but 93/7 must belong to phase 3, and 65/3 in phase 4 is only slightly later. Both graves contain other Frankish material, and although there are a number of curved pommels in this country, it is probable that 93/7 was an import, as well as 65/3[89]. Seaxes are larger versions of the domestic knife, and intermediate examples are discussed below, p 114.

*Shields* (distribution Figure 86)
The form of the shield bosses does not vary a great deal as they are all of low to medium height, waisted, with a convex curve to the dome. Six have a flange about a centimetre wide with five disc-headed rivets, although the fragmentary C/8 (Figure 3) may only have had four. All had a small button top except 56/5a (Figure 31) which had no projection, and 71/8 (Figure 38) which had a spike.

It has been noted that there was a general tendency in the development of Anglo-Saxon shield boss forms from low, wide shapes with wide flange and disc-headed rivets and up-turned or extended grips to taller, narrower shapes with narrower flange, knob-headed rivets and strap grips, and this same tendency is illustrated by the Dover series[90]. From Table III it may be seen that the type with narrow flange and knob-headed rivets (27/7, 39/2,

---

82 Ibid 1, 130–145
83 Evison 1961, 227, fig. 58, 4
84 Ibid, 228
85 Pirling 1974 1, 138, Abb.13; Ypey 1983, fig. 2
86 MacGregor 1978, 53, fig. 35.1
87 Musty 1969, fig. 5h
88 Ypey 1980
89 A blade with back curved in near the point is illustrated in Böhner 1958 2, Taf. 25.8, but as it does not receive special comment this may be a defect of corrosion.
90 Evison 1963

71/8, 90/3, figs. 15, 23, 38 and 40) are all less than 15cm in diameter, although only one is over 8cm in height. Each has a strap grip, and three of them have medium or small disc appliqués. The earlier type with wide flange, however, (C/8, 56/5a, 91/1, 93/10a, 96a/6, 98/3, Figures 3, 31, 41, 43, 45 and 47) has a diameter over 15cm, three have an upturned or extended grip, while three have strap grips, two have large or small iron discs and two have other types of appliqué.

Decorative iron appliqués are present in seven graves. It is not certain whether the iron strips in grave C were fastened on the shield because, although they were found near the boss there are no fixing rivets visible on the fragments. Iron disc-headed rivets, usually with a slightly convex upper surface and central knob, appear in three sizes, the largest 98/3, diameter 8.6cm (Figure 47) being placed in two pairs, one on either side of the boss. At Lyminge, Kent, the shield in grave 31 was furnished with a grip 48cm long, each end of which was riveted through the shield to a large iron disc (diameter 9.2cm), beside which was a second disc. At Swaffham, Norfolk, two graves had shields with large discs. In grave 15 a man was buried prone, with a shield placed over his head and shoulders. A pair of large iron discs were lying each side of the boss. A less well preserved boss with two pairs of large discs was lying on the chest of the supine male in grave 18. Grave 25 at Orpington contained a shield with a pair of large disc rivets each side of the boss[91].

As to discs of medium size, in grave 27 (diameter 4.3cm, Figure 15), one is placed each side of the boss. In grave 39 the shield seems to have been placed at an angle over the skull because the boss was on its side above the skull together with one of the rivets, and the other two rivets were spaced each side of the boss but 15cm above the floor of the grave. On this shield it seems that the 3 discs were placed equidistantly round the boss. The two discs in grave 131 were found, together with an iron buckle, near the side of a grave only 20cm deep in the chalk. The shield must have been standing on its edge, so that the boss was ploughed away in the top soil and one pair of discs and the shield buckle only remain. Iron discs of this size (diameter 4.4cm) have been found in Humberside (Yorkshire) at Driffield[92] placed in two pairs on opposite sides of the boss, with two double crescent-shaped iron appliqués placed elsewhere on the shield. Four large iron disc-headed studs were placed singly at quarter points on the shield in grave 2 on the same barrow[93], and there were three on a shield in a grave on Cheescake Hill, Barrow C44[94].

Of the small discs three were placed together in grave 56 (Figure 31) where the shield had been deposited leaning against the side of the grave. In grave 71 (Figure 38) the four disc-headed rivets were joined as pairs, one set being found near the boss and the other pair some distance away on the other side. Although all these objects were found on the floor of the grave, the shield must have been deposited in a leaning position and one pair of discs must have become displaced as the shield collapsed.

The placing of iron disc-headed rivets on either side of the boss may be seen at the cemetery of Bergh Apton in Norfolk, where grave plans have been published showing approximate positions in the grave in schematic fashion[95]. A pair of disc-headed rivets was found each side of the boss in graves 8, 12 and 66. In grave 8 they were of tinned bronze, in grave 12 of iron, probably with additional sheet bronze decoration, in grave 66 of iron with an extra small one.

The pair of appliqués in Dover grave 93/10c,d (Figure 43) were fragmentary but more decorative, and were placed one on each side of the boss, parallel to each other and 35.5cm apart. They consist of a long diamond shape of iron bearing two rivets, one with a silver disc head and the other with a silver lozenge-shaped head. At one end is a fish-tail shape in silver plate, and part of one similar plate at the other end remains on one of the appliqués.

Useful information about decoration on Anglo-Saxon shields has been assembled[96], although not all of the appliqués mentioned can be regarded definitely as appliqués on Anglo-Saxon shields. No boss was found with the bird figures from Shelford, Kent[97], and, like the appliqués from Eastry with which they were compared, they were probably strap or harness mounts. No context is known for the bird from Ashwell, Hertfordshire[98], and as it is unlike any manufactured object of Anglo-Saxon origin it is best left out of consideration. The fish from Warren Hill, Suffolk[99] was found in a grave which was presumably female as it contained 'half a bracelet clasp' i.e. presumably part of a wrist clasp[100], and Dr Hills points out that the rivets are too small for attachment to a shield.

Comparable appliqués are therefore reduced to six examples considered below, of which four are in the form of fish. There were three mounts on the shield from Bergh Apton, Norfolk, one a bronze rosette, and the others a pair of griffin-type creatures[101], a hybrid creature which reminds one on the one hand of the bird appliqués of the Sutton Hoo and Swedish shields[102], and on the other of the riders and hunted animals on the shield from Stabio,

---

91  Hills and Wade-Martins 1976, 7, 8–9, figs. 6, 7, 9, 10; Tester 1968, pl. I
92  Mortimer 1905, Barrow C38, Driffield grave 5, 277, fig. 757
93  Ibid, 276–7, fig. 749, diam. 4.2cm
94  Ibid, pl.CV, fig. 835, diam. 'about 2in.', (5.1cm), but they appear to be larger by comparison with the boss in the illustration.
95  Green and Rogerson 1978, graves 8, 12, 66 and 73, figs. 11, 15, 55 and 61
96  Kennett 1974; Hills 1977b
97  Kennett 1974, fig. 5c, d
98  Ibid, fig. 5e
99  Ibid, fig. 5b; Brown 1915 III, pl.XXIV, 1
100 Smith 1911, 342
101 Green and Rogerson 1978, fig. 80, B–D, pl.II
102 Bruce-Mitford 1978, pl.I; 1977, Taf. 5
103 Moosbrugger-Leu 1971 B, Taf. 19, 15–17

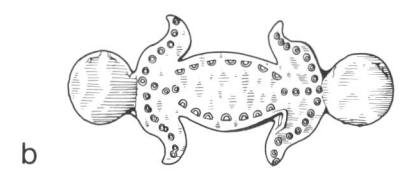

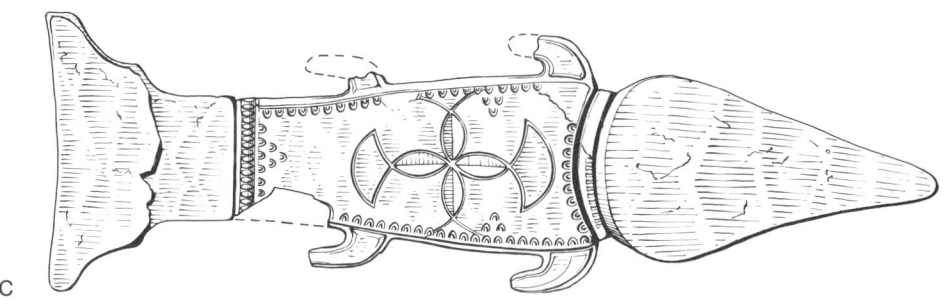

Text Figure 5  *a* Shield appliqué, Dover 93/10d
 *b* Shield appliqué, Mucking grave 600
 *c* Shield appliqué, Thames at Barnes. Scale 1/1

Italy[103]. The tinned bronze mount from Kempston grave 52[104] is crudely shaped, but might be interpreted as a fish with two pairs of fins. It is fixed by three tinned bronze disc-headed rivets which are comparable to the disc and diamond-shaped rivets on the Dover mount. The Spong fishes, however, are so accurately outlined that it has been possible to identify the species as pike or zander. They, too, have the two pairs of fins in the same position, with the addition of an extra dorsal fin in the middle. The Kenninghall mount[105] is nearer to the Dover mounts. The body part on the Kenninghall fish has only one pair of fins near the head, while the Dover fish has none, and the body is geometric, lozenge-shaped with incurving sides. On both the Dover and Kenninghall fishes the tail is silver-plated; the head of the Kenninghall fish is also silver-plated, and so is the remaining fragment of the head on the Dover fish.

Mounts on the shield in grave 600 at Mucking (Text Figure 5b) are a mixture of two types of shield appliqué, the pisciform and discoid[106]. The middle part, which is gilt as on the Kenninghall fish, is obviously derived from the body shape with two pairs of fins and it also has the stamped border and medial line. The terminals are, in contrast, silvered like the head and tail of the Kenninghall and Dover fishes, but they are shaped as discs, clearly derived from the disc appliqués applied in pairs, or even together as a single mount in Dover grave 71.

As to the contexts, the shield boss in grave 52 at Kempston has an unusually long button top and wide flange, a type which has not been closely studied, but which does not seem to occur in fifth- or seventh-century contexts. The objects associated with the shield mounts at Mucking, Spong Hill and Bergh Apton belong to the sixth century, and the end of the century is indicated by the taller type of shield boss with small button top and strap grip, and the reticella bead in Dover grave 93. This grave, like its neighbouring sword grave 91, must be connected with the row of rich women, who were Christian. The suspicion that the symbol of a fish may have a Christian meaning is thereby supported, and it should also be remarked that the fish symbol from Kenninghall is further distinguished by a cruciform motif on its body.

104 Kennett 1974, fig. 1
105 Ibid, fig. 5a
106 Evison 1973, pl.LI,b

TABLE III   SHIELD CHARACTERISTICS

| Characteristics | C5a | C/8 | 56 | 91 | 93 | 96a | 98 | 27 | 39 | 71 | 90 | 3 | 5 | 131 |
|---|---|---|---|---|---|---|---|---|---|---|---|---|---|---|
| Wide flange |  | X | X | X | X | X | X |  |  |  |  |  |  |  |
| Disc-headed rivets | X | X | X | X | X | X | X |  |  |  |  |  |  |  |
| Narrow flange |  |  |  |  |  |  |  | X | X | X | X |  |  |  |
| Knob-headed rivets |  |  |  |  |  |  |  | X | X | X | X |  |  |  |
| Diam. less than 15cm |  |  |  |  |  |  |  | X | X | X | X |  |  |  |
| Ht. over 8cm |  | X |  | X |  |  |  |  |  | X |  |  |  |  |
| Upturned grip | X |  |  | X |  | X |  |  |  |  |  | X |  |  |
| Strap grip |  |  | X |  | X |  |  | X | X | X | X |  | X |  |
| Extended grip | ? |  |  | X |  | X |  |  |  |  |  |  |  |  |
| Button top | X | X |  |  | X | X | X | ? | X |  | X |  |  |  |
| Large iron discs |  |  |  |  |  |  |  | X |  |  |  |  |  |  |
| Medium iron discs |  |  |  |  |  |  |  |  | X | X |  |  |  | X |
| Small iron discs |  |  | X |  |  |  |  |  |  |  | X |  |  |  |
| Appliqués | X |  |  |  | X |  |  |  |  |  |  |  |  |  |

Another fish appliqué, found on the foreshore of the Thames at Barnes[107], (Text Figure 5c) may be compared with the Kenninghall mount. The form of a fish has four fins and slightly different outlines to the head and tail, which are, nevertheless, plated with silver or tin. The middle part is gilded, with decoration by two stamps, of which the double-u type is similar to the stamp on the Mucking mounts. Like the Kenninghall appliqué, it also has a central faceted cross motif, the delineation of which is more clear as the circular lines are continued to form fan-shaped cross terminals. The Christian origin of this form of cross is even more definite. The general shape of these fishes has much in common with the dragons on the Sutton Hoo and Swedish shields[108], for they all have a head, a fish tail and usually wings or fins. On other metal objects a top view of a fish with two pairs of fins appears four-fold on the Hardingstone mount and on a gilt-bronze buckle from Faversham, while a fish in relief with one pair of fins decorates the panel of the Crundale buckle[109].

Another series of mounts, not apparently connected with shields, appear to be derived from the Dover-Kenninghall type of fish, and these are three of the Eastry mounts, a pair clearly representing fishes, but the other larger, with a rectangular 'head', diamond-shaped middle section and tri-partite tail[110]. Similar mounts occurred in two graves at Mucking, 639 and 767 where they may have functioned as strap or belt mounts. The contexts of the Sutton Hoo and Swedish shields and the contexts at Mucking, Dover, Spong Hill and Bergh Apton show that these particular appliqués were insignia attached to the shields of warriors of high rank, and although no doubt originally of pagan significance, some at least had assumed Christian connotations.

Silver-plated disc-headed rivets on the boss occurred in only one grave, C, and they are fitting to the high rank of the man buried with sword, spear and balance. These decorated bosses have been studied and allocated to the late fifth and first half of the sixth century[111], when they were distributed between southern England, northern France, the Rhineland, Thuringia and southern Germany. A further number which occur in this country have subsequently been listed[112]. A suggestion that the silver stud had some significance is supported by the evidence of grave 14 where a young woman carried a single one in her bag. Bronze disc-headed rivets were used on both the shield boss and grip in grave 96a, and a single one occurred in grave 3. There is no indication that the tops of these discs were originally tinned or silvered, but such a coating could have disappeared without trace. There is likely to be some relationship between these silver rivets on the bosses and the silver rivets fastening the fish appliqués to the shield in Dover grave 93, and the silver rivets on the mounts in Mucking grave 600. A significance was presumably attached to the boss rivets, and must have been retained when they were used also for the appliqués.

There are certain indications of the construction of the shield. No stains remained to give the shape, but it was presumably circular. The extended grip in grave 96a was fragmentary, but enough remained of the grip 91/1 to show that the shield was curved. The length of the rivet shanks usually gives a thickness of about 1cm, sometimes less, e.g. 6mm in graves 56 and 90. The grain of the wood traces on the inside of

107   Clark 1980, 348–9, pl.LXVI,b
108   Bruce-Mitford 1978, fig. 72
109   Speake 1980, pl.16d; Smith 1923, fig. 42; Speake 1980, pl.7d
110   Brown 1915 III, pl.XXIV,2
111   Werner 1962a, 32, distribution map Taf. 68.1
112   Kennett 1974, 62–4

the grip always runs longitudinally up to the ends where it meets transverse grain, showing that the iron grip was lined with a bar of wood and the grip was riveted to the shield board with its grain at right angles[113]. The underside of the shield in grave 39 must have been covered with leather as this material was found on the underside of the strap grip at the ends, while the middle of the grip was bound with coarse twine. The grip 98/3 shows traces of textile which may have been used as binding. The rivets frequently bear traces of having pierced leather covering wood, so that a board with leather covering on top appears to be normal.

In some graves a maximum diameter can be established by the space available in the grave, the shield sometimes being placed flat, and sometimes on its edge, leaning against the side of the grave. The minimum diameter is established by the length of the grip or spacing of the appliqués.

| Grave No. | Maximum diameter | Minimum diameter |
|---|---|---|
| 27 | 81cm | 38cm |
| 39 | 61cm | 46cm |
| 93 | 91.5cm | 38cm |
| 96a | 84cm | 43cm |
| 98 | 61cm | 48cm |

The normal diameter is therefore likely to have been between 48 and 91.5cm. In two graves, 27 and 131, a small iron buckle must have fastened a strap at the back.

There does not seem to have been any special position in the grave appointed for the shield, it was put in any place convenient for its large size: over the head (graves C, 39), at the head (grave 91), over the body (grave 98), over the legs (graves 27, 71, 93, 96a), beside the right shoulder (grave 56), beside the left elbow (grave 90) and beside the right hip (grave 131).

As to distribution in the cemetery, no shield bosses occur in the early part of plot A, although this contains one sword grave and three with spears. Instead the shield bosses are found only in later graves, in grave 90, plot A, in plots B, D, F and K, but none at all east of grave 96, not even on the barrow. They are therefore limited in this cemetery to phases 3 and 4, being completely absent from earlier or later graves. Nine of the thirteen sheilds occurred in sword graves, three were in spear graves, and one in a grave where the other objects were disturbed and lost.

## Jewellery

### Square-headed brooches

Both the square-headed brooches in grave 13 (Colour plate Ia,c; Plate 6b,c) show signs of a great deal of wear, and as the occupant was probably an old woman it is likely that she was buried with the brooches she had acquired in her youth. Although not a pair, they are sufficiently similar in size to be regarded as such, and were worn one below the other and in parallel, on the upper part of the right chest. They are very different in decoration, but have many points in common. The size and shape of the head, bow and foot are similar, they are both of silver gilt without garnet decoration. The foot is undivided with a lozenge centre and lateral roundels and downward-biting animal heads. There is extensive use of animal ornament, including marginal animals on the foot, and rows of billeting. Details of ornament, however, diverge considerably[1].

The border of the head of 13/1 consists of a row of semi-circles, a rather rare form of the shingle pattern, Haseloff's *Zangenmuster* type B1[2], which in England only occurs on a brooch from Chessel Down, and one from Stowting[3], as well as elsewhere in Thuringia, Bornholm and the upper Rhine[4]. The Bornholm example is demonstrably the earliest of the series, and the two English brooches cited are later, garnet-set Kentish brooches. Many of the characteristics of the Bornholm brooch are repeated on the Dover brooch, i.e. the proportions, panelled bow, hanging animal heads, lateral roundels, animal head finial and central diamond on the foot, but its scroll decoration has completely disappeared, to be replaced by Style I animal ornament.

13/1 has much in common with the 'Jutland group' of brooches, but the border of semi-circles is not a feature of that group unless the border of the head of the Pompey brooch[5] may be regarded as consisting of circle segments instead of the possible scrolls suggested by Haseloff. The semi-circles do occur on an early brooch of similar type from Kurtzenhausen, France[6]. The head of 13/1 has a single panel completely filled with animal ornament. The six brooches of Jutland Group C have ornamentation on the head of a mask between two animals, and this is also the basis of the 13/1 design. (The animal designs of the whole brooch are abstracted in Text Figure 6a.) The position of the centre mask, however, is occupied by a single profile eye. The replacement of the normal central mask by a single profile eye may also be found on a gold scabbard mount from Darum, Ribe, where a U-shaped eye profile and beak belong in common to the bodies of two animals[7]. The rest of the design at Dover is symmetrical, consisting of disintegrated human or animal parts. Each side of the eye is a bent arm with cuff at the wrist and outspread fingers. In each corner is a thigh and leg with curled-under claw, the two toes of which continue on the other side of the leg into the double arc line which frames the thigh. The band of parallel ribbing in the middle near the bow must represent a common body for the human-

---

113 Various methods of fitting the grip are noted in Härke 1981.

1 Many scholars have contributed to the study of square-headed brooches and zoomorphic ornament over the years. Only the last and most comprehensive work is quoted here: Haseloff 1981.

2 Haseloff 1981 II, 310ff.

3 Åberg 1926, figs. 121 and 144

4 Haseloff 1981 II, distribution map, Abb. 203b

5 Haseloff 1981 I, 34, Abb. 26, III, Taf. 21

6 Haseloff 1981 III, Taf. 51

7 Haseloff 1981 II, Abb. 295

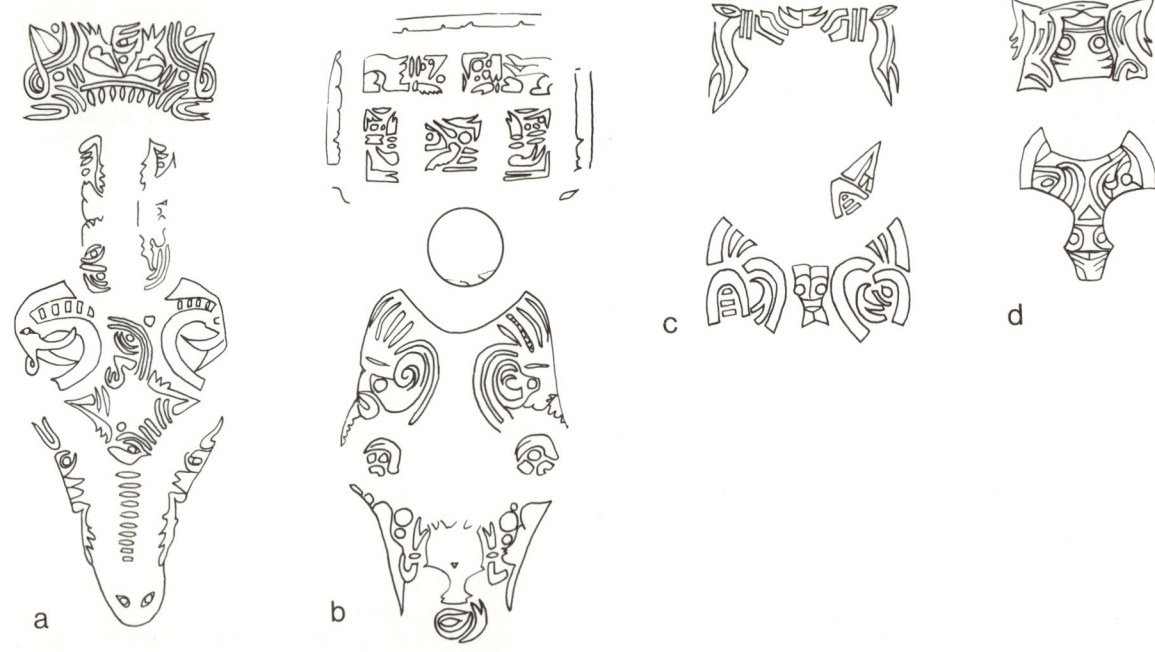

*Text Figure 6*
Animal ornament on Dover square-headed brooches.
*a* 13/1, *b* 13/2, *c* Unassociated 9, *d* 20/8. Scale 1/1

headed animals, and the remaining dot, two pairs of lines and doubled element must represent the eye, cheek and mouth of a profile human head.

The bow is divided into two panels, each occupied with animal parts. An almost identical leg and claw appears at the top of each, and two probable profile eyes at the bottom of the left-hand panel. The pattern in the middle of both sides is worn and obliterated, but at the bottom of the right-hand side there is a recognisable human foot. Some of the Jutland group have a vertically panelled bow, but zoomorphic decoration does not appear on any of them. It may be found on the brooch from Vedstrup, Seeland, and the brooch from Idstedt, near Schleswig. On the Vedstrup bow the middle of the design is interrupted by a roundel, but the animal elements relate to each other across the middle bar to form one complete animal at the top and one at the bottom. Although there is no dividing roundel on 13/1, there are indications that the constituents are separate entities, and it could be that the elements here also related across the middle bar, especially as there appears to be a profile head in the left lower segment, with a human foot in the opposite segment, juxtaposed as they are on the lower panels of the Vedstrup bow[8].

Round the diamond shape in the middle of the foot are unarticulated zoomorphic elements. There is a profile eye at the bottom, possibly another at the top, and a bent leg and claw with double arc thigh in each side corner, with a third leg with bent-over claw towards the top. Ribbing towards the terminal represents the animal body. In the Vedstrup foot panel a circular cell occupies the centre, and a pair of articulated animals are arranged around it with heads at the top and a bent leg and claw in the right and left corner as on 13/1.

The lateral pendant animal heads are partly worn away, but the left hand creature still has a curling top jaw and a tongue as well as a lower jaw. The necks are ribbed, although it is a single row instead of the more complicated pattern on the Vedstrup brooch.

The border animals on the foot are badly worn, but enough remains to show a double-barred body and a thigh, leg and claw which indicates that the animals were crawling in the direction of the mask terminal as they do on the Vedstrup brooch. This is in contrast to the Jutland group, where the border animals crawl upwards[9].

The square-headed brooch from Bifrons grave 63[10] differs from 13/1 in a number of points, such as the tongue border to the head and the scroll panel in the middle, the lateral heads on the foot and the animals and masks at the junction with the bow. A comparable element, however, is the downward direction of the one partly remaining border animal on the bottom of the foot. The centre panel to the foot is also very similar, for it also has a profile head at the bottom and a leg in each side corner. At the top is some parallel ribbing and a curved element as on 13/1 which is damaged but interpreted by Haseloff as probably a second head[11].

This brooch 13/1 is therefore related in shape, technique and decoration to the brooches made in Kent and classified as Jutland Group C, manufactured between AD 480 and 520. In view, however, of the many points on which it diverges from the Jutland Group C and is related to brooches

---

8  Haseloff 1981 I, Abb. 106 a and 106 b
9  Ibid, 50–1
10 Haseloff 1981 I, Abb. 184, III, Taf. 93
11 Haseloff 1981 II, 485, I, Abb. 184

of Scandinavian origin, particularly the Vedstrup brooch from Seeland, its origins must be regarded as east Scandinavian. Although its animal ornament shows it to be the work of Kentish craftsmen, it does betray signs of the *Stilphase B* ribbing on bodies and in the positioning of the animals. The shingle-pattern head border is also to be derived from east of Jutland in the Danish islands.

13/2 was similar enough to 13/1 to be worn with it as the second of a pair. There is a difference of only a few millimetres in the length, and it is in silver gilt with a good deal of zoomorphic ornament (Text Figure 6b). The metal is cast thin, so that there are perforations by the border animals on the foot. While on 13/1 the raised inner border of the head and foot was plain, the raised inner border on 13/2 is decorated with a black groove and is extended on the head to frame inner panels, and on the foot to frame the central diamond shape and the terminal disc.

The head has a beaded outer border on the lower edge ending in a shape at each corner. The rest of the outer borders is mostly worn away, but an irregular pattern is indicated by the remaining traces, so that it was probably zoomorphic. The inner field is divided into five rectangular panels. The two top panels are occupied by a pair of crouching animals facing each other, each having two legs, the one on the left with numerous toes on the front claw, and the one on the right with two toes. The middle panel below contains a profile head facing left, with two legs and body shapes. On each side of this is a couchant animal facing upwards with a double-cuffed foreleg and a two-toed back leg.

The bow is flattened on top and still shows the outline of a disc which could have contained a mask. There is no other decoration except for moulded lines.

The foot is basically the same shape, but there are many differences. The pendent heads by the bow have curling beaks. The eye of the bird, however, also serves as the eye of an outward-facing human profile with nose, drooping mouth and beard, the parallel lines of the bird's neck doubling as a hat or hair. The human face on the left is clearly visible, but on the right is badly worn. The central diamond is surrounded by rows of ribbing. The lateral lobes are circular and there is an animal head at the foot as on 13/1, but the lateral discs are each decorated with a profile human head, and the snout of the animal head terminal overlaps into another disc containing another profile head. A helmeted, human-headed animal with bent arm and hand crawls upwards each side on the outer border.

An animal border on the head is not very common, but a pair of animals are placed on the edge of the head of the Vedstrup brooch near the bow[12]. In the Jutland group they appear on the brooches from Agerskov, Donzdorf, Gilton and Richborough[13]. As to the panelling with animals on the head, this seems to have no close parallel, although some of the Jutland brooch heads have an internal rectangular panel in a comparable layout with geometric patterns: Agerskov, St. Martyrs Field, Engers, Finglesham, and some have zoomorphic designs: Donzdorf, Bifrons 41, Gilton, while other northern brooches also have sub-divisions into rectangles: Gummersmark, Hardenberg, Seeland, Overhornbaek Fonnås[14]. The animals on the Donzdorf head have the Vimose triangular profile snout containing two bars and dots, which appears in a simplified form on the head of 13/2.

Most of the Jutland group of brooches have a very similar bow with a roundel and grooving, and a roundel also appeared on the Vedstrup bow. Adjacent to the bow pendent birds' heads are very common, but human profiles are less frequent in this position, and Dover 13/2 may be added to the list of only five brooches known with this characteristic, i.e. Donzdorf, Gilton 48, Richborough, Pompey and Tranum Klit[15], all of the Jutland group. Some of the same group have a diamond shape with geometric ornament in the centre of the foot i.e. Donzdorf and Richborough, but Pompey is closer with a diamond shape surrounded by similar ribbing[16]. Some of the group have lateral discs and a terminal animal head on the foot, but those with a terminal animal head as well as a third roundel are few: Tranum Klit, Donzdorf and Gilton, and early Scandinavian versions are to be seen on Gummersmark, Seeland and Vedstrup[17]. This brooch, therefore, is much more firmly related to the Jutland group of brooches, and may be regarded as a fully-fledged member.

Both of these brooches 13/1 and 13/2 show extreme signs of wear, and on both the right-hand side has suffered most loss of detail in this way. On both the pin-catch is a replacement, and so, too, is the spring-holder on 13/1. There is no doubt that they underwent a great deal of wear before burial, and it has been noticed that this was the fate of most of these early square-headed brooches. The woman's other two brooches, a ring and a small long brooch, had not been subjected to this amount of wear, and were probably later acquisitions. The date of manufacture of the square-headed brooches must be similar to that of the others in the Jutland group, i.e. between AD 480–520.

The silver gilt *square-headed* brooch (Unassociated 9, Plate 6a, Figure 64, Text Figure 6c), which was found before the beginning of the excavation, is closely associated with the disc brooch Avent class 2.5 as the disc affixed to its bow takes that form. The disc compares closely with the disc brooch from Dover grave 14, although there are slight differences in the ornamental animals which are more formalised in appearance and further decorated with

---

12  Haseloff 1981 III, Taf. 26
13  Ibid, Taf. 10, 2, 15, 22, 1 and 2
14  Ibid, Taf. 23, 24, 1, 25, 28, 30
15  Haseloff 1974, 13
16  Haseloff 1981 III, Taf. 15, 22, 2, and 21
17  Ibid, Taf. 23, 25, and 26

nicked beading on the outline of the heads. The flat white centre setting has an incised ring without the centre dot present in the setting of the grave 14 brooch.

It is further interesting to note that the whole square-headed brooch is nearly a replica of one found at Howletts[18], Kent, and could perhaps have been made from the same mould. There are however, various differences of detail: the outer border of the head is a reserved silver zigzag on the Howletts brooch, and a flat surface stamped with ring-and-dot round three sides and annulets on the fourth side on the Dover brooch. The disc brooch is set at a different angle on each, and there are differences regarding some of the inlaid jewels. On the head the middle disc setting on the Howletts brooch is a flat white setting with incised ring, and the jewel on the foot terminal is a circular garnet in a flat white setting, while both of these on the Dover brooch are single disc garnets. The centre of the disc-on-bow on the Howletts brooch is also a garnet in a white ring, while the Dover setting is white only with an incised circle. The lateral foot settings on the Dover brooch are circular garnets, while on the Howletts brooch these are further inlaid with a gold ring. On the Howletts brooch the backing foil to the garnets appears to be uniformly a fine trellis, except for the central stone of the disc brooch which has no backing, while on the Dover brooch all appear to be special boxed foils, as noticed by Avent and Leigh[19]. On the head of the Howletts brooch there is extra tooling to represent beading on the animal bodies, and the double row of beading along the top border is in 'light-and-shade' arrangement. On the head of the Howletts brooch there is niello inlay in the bars above the triangles, and the border round the foot is in reserved silver zigzag and niello triangles, while the border of the Dover brooch is simplified to niello triangles only. Although the two can hardly be other than twin products of the same workshop, the work on the Howletts brooch is throughout more painstaking and complicated. The Howletts brooch has a silver pin at the back with a shield over the spring decorated with niello lines and triangles. The shield on the Dover bronze pin is not decorated, but it is interesting to note that the jeweller has copied the exact shape of the shield-on-tongue employed by the makers of Frankish buckles (cf Figure 25, 42/3), and the fact that here it occurs on a brooch of undoubted Kentish workmanship increases the probability that some of the buckles with tongue bases of this shape found in England may be the work of native jewellers.

The technique of setting a gold ring in a garnet is not common, and although it does not occur on the Dover brooch, the Dover brooch does have an incised ring in the shell of the disc-on-bow which may have contained a gold ring. In England this technique of gold ring in garnet occurs on the head and foot of a pair of square-headed brooches at Lyminge, grave 44[20].

It is clear that this type of square-headed brooch belongs to the middle part of the sixth century, if only because of its physical attachment to a disc brooch and its general technical and artistic similarities with that type. Thus it belongs to the later stage of square-headed brooch in Kent, when inset garnets and shell or white paste were used freely and animal ornament was reduced to a minimum. A number of Kentish square-headed brooches were produced in the same idiom, and, although they appear with three varieties of foot, i.e. undivided, divided vertically and divided with a cross, they are linked one to another by several characteristics.

The brooch Unassociated 9 (Figure 64) is clearly related in regard to certain elements to earlier brooches, some of which were included by Haseloff in his group of Jutlandic brooches. With a length of 9.5cm it is nearest to the size of the Finglesham brooch[21]. The design on the head consists of a pair of ascending human-headed animals (Text Figure 6c) and may be compared with the similar designs on the brooches from Donzdorf, Gilton and Richborough[22], although the central mask has been replaced on the Dover brooch by the garnet settings. Like most of this group the Dover brooch has downward-biting animal heads with curling beaks below the bow, and, like the brooch from Tranum Klit, it has a human mask at the top of the middle of the foot[23]. In spite of these elements clearly derivative from earlier brooches, the Dover brooch has taken on the unmistakeable qualities of Kentish workmanship, a neatness of pattern and execution, and its attachment of a disc brooch, certainly made in Kent with the same patterns and techniques, shows that there is no doubt of its local manufacture. It probably came from the same workshop that produced the Howletts brooch, but less expensive materials and less craftsman's time was expended on it.

The two brooches from grave 20 (Colour Plate Ib, Plate 6d,e, Figure 12, Text Figure 6d) were just over 6cm long, and they are a small and simplified version of the jewelled, Kentish square-headed brooch. Although possibly made from the same mould and worn as a pair, there are differences of detail between these two brooches. There is an inlaid disc on the bow of each, a sliced garnet surrounded by zigzag grooves on 20/6, and shell with an inset ring on 20/8. The head bears a human mask in the middle

---

18  B.M. Reg. No. 1918 7–11 1; Avent 1975 ii, pl. 5, 29
19  Avent and Leigh 1977, 25
20  Warhurst 1955, pl. XII, and Avent and Leigh 1977, pl. I, A
21  Haseloff 1981 I, 34, Abb. 12
22  Ibid, Abb. 24a, Abb. 75, 2; Abb. 27, Abb. 75, 4; Abb. 28, Abb. 75, 5. An article by D. Leigh, 1984 suggests that some human and animal designs may have been intended to be seen from more than one point of view e.g. upside down.

Such ambiguities have been noticed by others, and many are convincing, but others depend on the imagination of the viewer. In interpreting the design on the head of this Dover brooch as an animal rather than a human, he omits to point out that this necessitates disregarding entirely the part of the design that portrays the mouth of the human (his fig. 1b, f, m).

23  Haseloff 1981 I, Abb. 29

and a row of three bars between mask and animals on 20/6 only. A second mask on the foot and pendent heads with curving beaks are also familiar motifs as on other Kentish brooches, and the frames of reserved silver and niello zigzag are present as well. A single circular groove surrounds the lateral lobes of 20/6, and zigzags surround the lobes on 20/8. Only the diagonal cross centre of the lobes is unusual, but somewhat similar is the bottom lobe of the Richborough brooch[24] which is filled with a vertical cross, and this brooch has many other characteristics in common with Dover 20/6 and 8. All three give prominence to the reserved silver zigzag and niello triangles border which is a well-defined feature of Kentish square-headed and disc brooches of the sixth century. They must have been made in the first quarter of the century, and Dover grave 20 belongs to the end of phase 1.

*Small long brooch* (Figure 9)
The small long brooch in grave 13 is the same type as one said to be from Howletts, Kent, which was purchased by the British Museum in a lot with a medieval strapend and Roman bronze mount from Sotheby's in 1951[25]. The Howletts brooch has an additional ring-and-dot motif in the middle of the head, and lacks the grooves across the foot. Another has recently been found in a well-furnished grave at Broadstairs (Valetta House – Bradstow School, excavator Mrs L Webster). The foot is an unusual ovoid shape, but the way in which it is nipped in towards the terminal, and at the narrowest point on the Dover brooch is crossed by transverse grooves, shows that its origin is to be found in the form with ribbed moulding near the finial which sometimes expanded into spatulate or other shapes[26]. On the other hand, the square-head and decoration by ring-and-dot stamps links it to a series of small long brooches in Kent and Surrey.[27] There may also be some connection with a type of disc-on-bow square-headed brooch from Achlum, Frisia which bears a human mask between two animals on the head, but the foot ends in a double lobate terminal produced by a pair of birds' heads with curling beaks, this latter trait influenced by Thuringian imports[28]. Other Domburg brooches have a double-lobed head, but the bow is nearer to the Dover and Howletts brooches in being long and slightly faceted[29]. A pair of fifth-century brooches with bi-lobed foot was found at Ozingell, Kent[30], and this cemetery also produced another small long brooch of comparable type[31], i.e. a square-head, long bow, triangular foot and discoid terminal. The length of the bow in particular suggests that this and the Dover brooch belong to the fifth century.

Very little use was made of stamps to ornament the decorative metalwork found in this cemetery. The most frequently used was the ring-and-dot motif which occurred in a variety of sizes. On the small long brooch 13/5 it was used in spaced-out groups of four, three and two on the head and foot. It was used as a border on three sides of the head of the square-headed brooch Unassociated 9. It was also used as a border row on the buckles 21/1 and 158/1, and in the inner panel of a belt plate 56/8. It also appeared in rows on the girdle hangers 129/10c and 164/2, and on the tweezers 41/5. Three ornamented the pin-head 44/1, and one was used to indicate the eye of a bird on the pin 30/3. On the buckle plate 21/1 it is formed by a combination of a ring stamp and a dot stamp.

On some of these objects it was combined with rows of dotting: 21/1, 30/3, 56/8 and Unassociated 9, and rows of dotting alone decorated the other belt mounts in grave 56, the buckle and rivets 96a/3, the small pendant 30/5, and the birds' head appliqués 29/12a and b. On the hair pendant 38/13 dots were combined with a dash stamp.

Stamps which occur once only are: the arc stamps with ring-and-dot and dots on the birds' head pin 30/3, the rings and the S-stamps arranged in cable formation on the pendant 35/3, the minute triangles on the pendant 38/3, the sharp triangular indentations made by the end of a tool on the annular brooch Unassociated 16, and the triangular stamps each consisting of four tiny triangles on the tweezers 65/8.

*Kentish disc brooches* (distribution Figure 87)
In considering the chronology of Kentish jewelled disc brooches, Avent noted that there are only two graves where the contents are dated by a coin[32]. These are Gilton grave 41 with a tremissis of Justinian I dated c AD 570, and the Sarre grave which contained a composite brooch, beads and coins, of which the latest belongs to about AD 615[33]. The other contents of Gilton grave 41 included amethysts and silver wire rings, which confirm a date for the grave at the end of the sixth century or the beginning of the seventh.

Avent proposed a sequence of development for some of the brooch classes, based on a study of all the elements in their make-up. The classes which occur at Dover are as follows (Text Figure 7, Table IV).

|  | *Avent class* | *Grave/find No.* |
|---|---|---|
| disc | 2.1 | Unassociated 9, 14/1, 30/2 |
|  | 2.2 | 59/1 |
|  | 2.5 | 38/1 |
|  | 3.1 | 1/2, 35/1 |
|  | 6.1 | 29/1 |
|  | Unclassified | 32/1 |
| plated | 6 | 126/1 |
|  | 7 | F/1 |

---

24 Haseloff 1981 III, Taf. 22, 2
25 BM Reg. No. 1951 2–4 2
26 Leeds 1945, figs. 23a–f
27 Ibid, fig. 25, where he suggests that the ring-and-dot decoration on the head might imply derivation from the cross-pattée type.

28 Roes 1954a, 65–9, pl. XIXc; Werner 1955a, 75–7, pl. V, 8
29 Ibid, pl. V, 1–4; Capelle 1976 1, 9; ibid 2, Taf. 1, 1–3
30 Werner 1955a, Abb. 1, 1; Smith 1854, fig. on p 17
31 Ibid, pl. VI, 3
32 Avent 1975 1, 56
33 Ibid, 69–72

14/1    Un/9    30/2

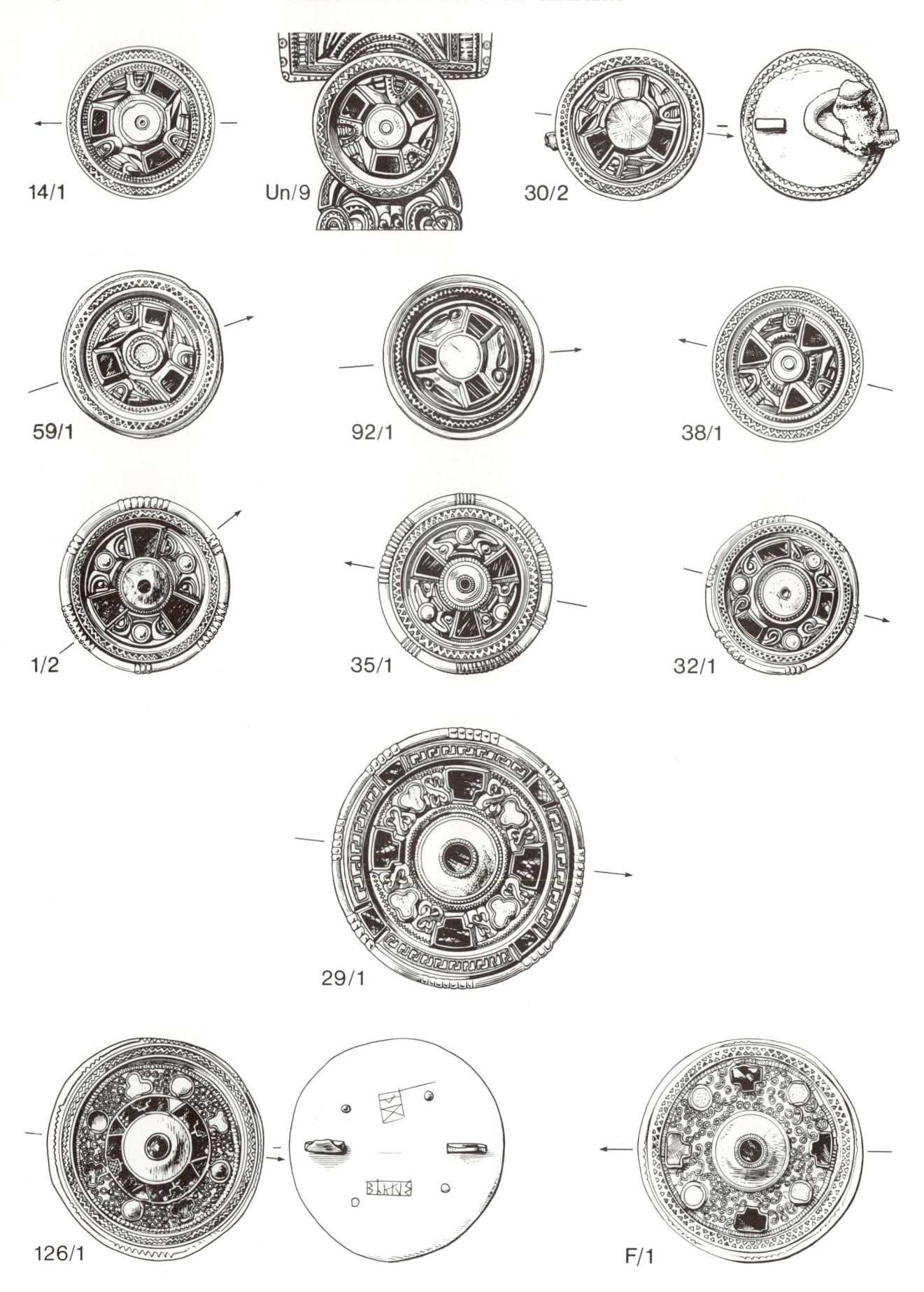

59/1    92/1    38/1

1/2    35/1    32/1

29/1

126/1    F/1

*Text Figure 7*    Kentish disc brooches in the Dover cemetery. Scale 1/1

In addition there is 92/1 (Plate 6h) which was not included in Avent's study. The typological development sequences proposed by Avent are based on types of rims, settings and diameters, but ignoring the chip-carved ornament because 'the ornament types vary from one class to another and are therefore not involved in these typological sequences[34].' Class 2.2 is said to be a development of 2.1. The two examples of class 2.1 at Dover, 14/1 (Colour Plate Ie) and 30/2 (Plate 6g), are very similar, but 30/2 has additional decoration on the back, which might indicate a later development. This would fall in with the relative position of the graves in cemetery plots A and B respectively. A third example of class 2.1 is the disc on the bow of the square-headed brooch Unassociated 9 which has a similar white material setting with ring incision to the shell setting with ring incision on 14/1. It is slightly more ornate than 14/1 and 30/2 in that the head frames of the animals are nicked to imitate beading.

Class 2.2 is represented by 59/1 (Colour Plate If) which has an additional beaded rim, giving a greater diameter, and its position is in plot E. The brooch 92/1 was not considered by Avent, and does not fit into his classes. The chip-carved animal is less accurately executed and the outer rim is plain, possibly a slightly later progression from 14/1. However, both are in plot A and belong to phase 2. An unusual characteristic shared by three of these brooches, 30/2, 59/1 and 92/1, is that there is no gold foil backing to the garnets. Many keystone garnet brooches were found at Faversham, so that a production centre is likely there, but of the fifteen class 2.1 noted by Avent not one was found at Faversham. Their occurrence further to the south-east of Kent suggests a production centre in that area.

Avent class 2.5 is represented at Dover by 38/1 (Colour Plate IIa). One noticeable characteristic which 38/1 has in common with later phase brooches such as 1/2, 32/1 and 35/1, in contrast to the early brooches 14/1, 30/2 and 59/1, is that there is a greater difference between the depth of the chip-carving and the garnets, so that the garnets stand up higher in a deeper field. Class 2.5 is considered by Avent to be developed from class 1.2, but from a stylistic point of view, the development is the opposite way round. The Style I animal, head, body and leg, appears on some of the earliest keystone brooches, as on the brooches 14/1, 30/2 and 59/1 just discussed. The profile head alone occurs on some of the later types, so that Avent's class 1.1 and 1.2 with profile heads must be typologically subsequent to his classes 2.1, 2.2, 2.3, 2.4 and 2.5 where the more complete animal is portrayed.

Further, Avent classes 1.2, 2.5 and 2.6 have triangular garnets instead of keystone shapes, prob-

TABLE IV CHARACTERISTICS OF THE DISC AND PLATED BROOCHES

| Characteristics | 14 | Unass. 9 | 30 | 59 | 92 | 38 | 1 | 35 | 32 | 29 | 126 | F |
|---|---|---|---|---|---|---|---|---|---|---|---|---|
| Plot | A | D | B | E | A | F | D | B | B | B | B | D |
| Phase | 2 | 3 | 3 | 3 | 2 | 3 | 3 | 3 | 3 | 3 | 3 | 3 |
| Avent No. | 25 | 27 | 26 | 138 | | 56 | 73 | 74 | 136 | 114 | 163 | 164 |
| Avent Class | 2.1 | 2.1 | 2.1 | 2.2 | | 2.5 | 3.1 | 3.1 | Uncl. | 6.1 | pl.6 | pl.7 |
| Disc | X | X | X | X | X | X | X | X | X | X | | |
| Plated | | | | | | | | | | | X | X |
| 3 key-stones | X | X | X | X | X | | | X | X | X | | |
| 3 triangles | | | | | | X | | | | | | |
| 4 T-shaped | | | | | | | | | | X | | X |
| 4 trefoil | | | | | | | | | | X | X | |
| Intervening cells | | | | | | | X | X | X | X | X | X |
| Foil standard | X | | | | | X | | | X | | | X |
| Foil boxed | | X | | | | | | | X | | X | |
| Foil special boxed | | X | | | | | X | | X | | | |
| Foil unusual | | | | | | | | X | | | X | |
| No foil | | | X | X | X | | | | | | | |
| Bone inlay | | | | | X | | | | | | | |
| Composition | | X | | | | | | | | | X | |
| Shell flat | X | | | ? | | X | X | | X | X | X | X |
| Shell cabochon | | | | | | | X | X | X | X | X | X |
| Glass blue, flat | | | | | | | | X | | | | |
| Glass yellow and lt. blue | | | | | | | | | | | X | |

34 Avent 1975 1, 57

ably again, a later development. This assumption is made more likely by the number of the triangular garnets set on each brooch in class 1.2, where there are four, creating a cruciform pattern. The assumption that these brooches with triangular garnets are early was first made by Leeds, for he thought that they were derived from similar Frankish brooches[35]. I am not at present aware, however, that any of these continental brooches can be dated before the Kentish series, and as there appear to be a number of indifferent Frankish copies of these good quality Kentish brooches it is probable that the influence was in the reverse direction, particularly since export of the Kentish brooches is recorded by an example at Hardenthun, North France[36] and by further more recent discoveries in Normandy. Leeds' view was followed by Bakka[37], although he was troubled by the fact that triangular cells also occur on later types of brooch. The contents of the grave at Mersham, Kent, from which he derived support for a mid sixth-century date was an early nineteenth century find, and could perhaps be doubted. On the other hand there is the Gilton grave 41 brooch, a class 1.2 type with four triangular garnets, and its association with amethysts, silver rings and a coin of AD 570. Further confirmation of a late date is provided by an unusual version from Ash, Kent[38], where a brooch, dominated by a cross, presumably Christian, in reserved silver and niello zigzag, has a garnet centre and four triangles in chip-carving instead of garnets. Another brooch with four triangular garnets is also further on in development as it possesses four intervening circular cells as well, Avent No. 135, Unclassified, from Breach Downs. Clear and competently executed Style II animal ornament adorns two other brooches with four triangles, so indicating a date near AD 600, Avent No. 130, Class 7.1, Unprovenanced, and Avent No. 131, Class 7.2, Faversham.

In fact, although the design of the disc brooches is divided sometimes into three and sometimes into four, and the two varieties are often clearly contemporary, figures derived from Avent's corpus show that it is in general the demonstrably later types which are divided into four. Avent has drawn attention to a number of brooches where the design must be interpreted as being related to a Christian cross[39], and it seems to me that it is possible to go further and suggest that most, if not all, of the Kentish disc brooches divided into four sections were produced by the jeweller with his Christian customers in mind, his output at the beginning continuing to include the triple design for pagan customers, but this line being largely discontinued as the faith and taste of his customers changed. There is even a likelihood of the portrayal of a crucifixion in a couple of the cruciform-designed class 1.2, Avent 19 (Sarre, grave 158) and 20 (Unprovenanced), where

*Text Figure 8* Design on disc brooch, Avent No. 20. Scale 1/1

the spaces usually occupied by zoomorphic patterns have become a profile head at the top, legs below, and a hand each side, (Text Figure 8). The basic shape of the chip-carved fields is a cross with straight edges and widening arms. The profile head consists of an eye with right angle behind, two straight diagonal lines above, and two curved shapes below. The side elements are divided into five finger-like segments, and in the bottom space are two inverted U-shapes with a bar in the middle, probably indicating legs or clothing. Although rudimentary, the anthropomorphic character is undeniable.

These two brooches are pertinent to the dating of 38/1 for, like 38/1, they are among the few brooches with triangular garnets, and 38/1 is the only disc brooch at Dover with garnets of this shape. The brooch in Sarre grave 158 was accompanied by amber beads, but also a Frankish garnet brooch of 525–600[40]. The quadripartite arrangement of Avent 19 and 20 and their anthropomorphic ?crucifix ornament suggest the beginning of the seventh century and a Christian context, so that Avent class 2.5 must precede his class 1.2, although the chronological divide may not be large.[41] The period AD 575–625 is likely for grave 38, i.e. later than graves in plot A, but probably not far divorced in date from graves in plot B.

Two brooches at Dover are of Avent class 3.1, i.e. 1/2 and 35/1 (Colour Plate IIb,c). They are presumably at a stage later than the triple keystone and animal type as a circular cell is interspersed between each keystone, so breaking up the animal ornament which is suitably converted into an animal head only on each side. The circular settings are of shell, flat on 1/2 and *en cabochon* on 35/1. Although not classified by Avent, 32/1, a third brooch with intervening circular cells and narrower keystone cells, is identical to class 3.1 except that the zoomorphic decoration has become a loop only. Each of these three brooches has a shell cabochon centre, and while the centre stone is garnet on 1/2 and 32/1, on 35/1 it is blue glass. Avent considers that class 3.1 continues from class 2.4.

The brooch 29/1 (Colour Plate II d) is much larger than the others examined so far, and the design is cruciform and much more complicated. The four T-shaped garnet cells combine with the cabochon

---

35 Leeds 1913, 130–1 and fig. 26 middle row left hand side
36 Avent 1975 ii, pl. 77, No. 189; Pilet *et al.* 1981, pl. 2
37 Bakka 1958, 71
38 Faussett 1856, pl. II, 5
39 Avent 1975 i, 64
40 Böhner 1958 1, Type C.7, 95; Ibid, 2 Taf. 13. 1
41 Since this was written, others have voiced their opinion of the inverted sequence of Avent's class 1 and 2, without giving reasons: Hawkes and Pollard 1981, 332

centre to make a definite Christian cross shape. However, the intervening trefoil shapes are filled with white shell, so making a colour combination with the central boss, and this white cruciform arrangement is further emphasised by the insertion of an oblong garnet in the niello rim beside each trefoil cell. Both crosses are further picked out by the placing of a run of beading in the appropriate positions on the outer border, and it is difficult to decide which was regarded as the principal design. It may be noted, however, that on the brooches with triple partition, as 1/2, 32/1, 35/1, the garnets are emphasised by a longer run of beading on the border than the intervening settings. On 29/1 it is the T-shaped garnets which are emphasised in this way, and this cross could therefore be given precedence. As Avent has remarked[42], this brooch has close affinities with plated brooches, in the stepped pattern of the inner border which is similar to cloisonné work, and the trefoil cell which only appears elsewhere on plated brooches[43]. Further, the chip-carved decoration now takes the form of a double loop, which must be related to other looped designs, some of which are zoomorphic Style II[44]. The border of nielloed lines in the shape of boxed zigzags is unique. It may be compared, however, with the border of step-pattern and zigzag lines on the back of a keystone garnet disc brooch of the same class, Avent's 6.1, from Faversham[45]. One other keystone garnet disc brooch (Avent class 2.4) has an incised border on the front of a similar step pattern[46]. A comparable pattern appears also on the border of the gold bracteate in Dover grave 134 (Figure 55), on the bow of the square-headed brooch Dover 20/8 (Figure 12), as well as in the rouletted pattern on the biconical pot in Dover grave 137, (Figure 56).

The trefoil cell reappears on the Dover plated brooch 126/1 (Colour Plate IIe), where the design is again quadripartite. As is normal in Christian jewelled crosses of the period[47] it is the cabochon settings which here probably form the main design and indicate the cross arms. Apart from the centre piece the cabochon settings are in yellow translucent and opaque light blue glass. One of the triangular cells in the cloisonné band is empty, but the opposite one is filled with white material. The other two triangular cells are lighter in colour than the garnets beside them, this difference of tone probably being caused or assisted by the different pattern of their foil backing. It is these light garnet and white triangular cells which connect the central boss to the cabochon settings, so leading the eye to distinguish the cross thus formed. The intervening trefoil cells are less noticeable, being flat and not connected by a lighter colour to the centre boss, although they do provide a secondary cross pattern. This is also supported by the adjoining step cloisons in the cloisonné zone which have the lozenge-shaped pattern foil behind them, and these garnets appear lighter in colour than those beside them.

The main cross is again emphasised by a longer run of beading on the rim by the cabochon glass settings, but the gold plate has not been set accurately on its base plate so that the runs of beading are not directly positioned in regard to these settings as they should be. The design of step pattern and triangles is obviously related to the combination of step pattern and semi-circle as on brooches from Faversham[48], but there are a number of variations on this theme, and the combination of step pattern and triangle only as on Dover 126/1 occurs occasionally on brooches[49], on a pendant decorated with birds' heads from Faversham[50], and on a stud from Wickhambreux[51].

The trefoil cell is unusual, but does occur on other plated brooches, Avent 1975, Nos. 152 and 165. It is also found on a brooch not included by Avent in his corpus[52]. This brooch was unprovenanced and in Canterbury Museum where it cannot now be traced. The shape of the cell is no doubt inspired by Frankish jewellery, where the quatrefoil cell occurred as early as the Childeric garnet work, and both quatrefoil and trefoil cells are found as centre pieces of Frankish disc brooches of the sixth century[53]. The Canterbury Museum brooch itself was probably Frankish. Avent places this Dover brooch in a class of its own, although it does conform to the general pattern of plated brooches where the central boss is surrounded by a zone of cloisons, and the outer zone, occupied by filigree annulets, is interrupted by four circular settings, and, in addition here, by the four trefoil settings.

The brooch from grave F, on the other hand, shares a place in his class 7 with a brooch from Faversham, of which only the applied gold plate and its settings remain[54]. These two are unusual in lacking the cloisonné zone surrounding the centre boss. In this they show greater affinity to the disc brooches like 29/1 above, and the relationship between the two brooches 29/1 and F/1 is pretty close in spite of differences in technique as both are set with four T-shaped cloisons with shell settings in between. Also, the same pattern of gold foil is used on both, as noted below. In F/1 the gold plate is covered with filigree ringlets set in a haphazard fashion with a few C and S scrolls, in contrast to 126/1 where the ringlets are set in not very regular rows. On stylistic grounds the three brooches 29/1, 126/1 and F/1 would appear to be contemporary, and

---

42  Avent 1975 i, 57; ii, pl. 34
43  From Faversham, Avent 1975 ii, pl. 50, No. 147 and pl. 57, No. 165, and an unprovenanced brooch once in Canterbury Museum, Avent 1975 ii, pl. 52, No. 152
44  Avent 1975 i, fig. 17, 12, 1–12. 6; cf also fig. 26, 8.1, 8.2, fig. 30, 25.1 and 25.3
45  Avent 1975 i, fig. 28, 7, ii, pl. 35, 115
46  Avent 1975 ii, pl. 9, 52

47  Evison 1977, 9, fig. 4k
48  Avent 1975 ii, pl. 55, Nos. 158 and 159
49  Ibid, pl. 51, No. 151; pl. 67, No. 178
50  Kendrick 1933a, pl. 1, 4
51  Evison 1976, pl. LXVI, a,b
52  Smith 1908a, pl 1, 11
53  Werner 1961, Taf. 37, 156–8
54  Avent 1975 ii, pl. 57, No. 165

their deposition in cemetery plots B and D support this contention. The date of late sixth century to early seventh century suggested by Leeds and Avent is acceptable in the light of information at Dover.

On the brooches set with three garnets, the line of direction of the pin runs exactly through the middle of one garnet and midway between the other two, (38/1, 32/1, 14/1, 59/1) or very near to this line. The direction of the pin is indicated on the drawings (Text Figure 7), an arrow denoting the point. In the case of the quadripartite brooches 29/1 and F/1, the line runs through the T-shaped garnets, and if the pin was horizontal on the clothing the garnet cross-design would be given maximum emphasis. The pin of F/1 is shorter than usual in relation to the size of the brooch, being only 2.5cm long. On 126/1 the line of the pin is slightly off the line of the cabochon settings. It does, however, run through the middle of opposing runs of beading on the outer edge, and, had the central gold plate been set accurately on its silver base, the line would have coincided with the cabochon cross, as must have been intended.

The varieties of pattern on the gold-foil backing to the garnets has been studied by Avent in respect of some of the Dover brooches. It has already been noticed above that three of the early disc brooches (92/1, 30/2, 59/1) have no foil backing. Four (F/1, 14/1, 29/1 (centre only), 38/1) have the standard cross-hatched pattern[55], and two have a boxed pattern (32/1, 126/1)[56]. An unusual pattern, however, occurs on Unassociated 9, 1/1 and 29/1 (in two rim and four keystone garnets), where the boxed pattern contains sixteen or twenty squares instead of the normal nine[57]. A diamond pattern (?unique) occurs on 126/1[58], and on 35/1 there is a ringed grid pattern[59] which is rare here but occurs sometimes in Rhineland jewellery, notably on a strap end in the woman's grave under Cologne cathedral[60]. Another ringed grid pattern occurs in the Dover cemetery on the bronze backing to the garnet or amber glass setting in the fragmentary pendant 6/8.

There is the minimal use of blue glass inlay in these brooches, i.e. the opaque green-blue which led earlier writers to describe it as lapis lazuli, and it was, no doubt, manufactured to imitate this stone (see p 98). Here it is restricted to the stud in the central shell boss of 35/1, and it does not even occur in the cloisonné zone of 126/1, a zone which does contain blue glass on a number of similar brooches[61]. The only other brooch with glass inlay is 126/1, where of the four circular settings in the field one is empty, the one opposite appears to be a greyish-blue cabochon and the other pair are translucent yellow glass cabochon.

The stones used in these brooches are all sliced garnets, with the exception of a small garnet *en cabochon* in the centre of 126/1. Some variation in shade is devised, from light orange to dark ruby red by various means, sometimes by varying the pattern of the gold foil backing, possibly by a foil of silver or gold with silver content, occasionally by setting the garnet without a foil backing, and probably also by varying the type or thickness of the stones. These remarks are visual notes only, and have not been verified by removing the stones from their settings.

White is the colour used for contrast with the red of the garnets, and almost all of the white settings (some of them stained green by corrosion products) can be seen to be shell as the structural lines are visible. Some of the central shell settings are flat, and these are on the early types, 14/1, 38/1 and possibly 59/1. One flat centre, 92/1, consists of bone. All the other central settings which remain are shell *en cabochon*. A white composition seems to have been used only on the central disc of Unassociated 9, and in a triangular cloison on 126/1. When materials of this type were investigated by Sir (then Dr) Frank Claringbull in 1951[62] it was suggested that the shell may have been cuttlefish bone. Before the date of publication it was realised that this tentative identification was not correct, and a note was added on the same page to that effect. Nevertheless, subsequent authors have mistakenly continued to quote the cuttlefish bone identification[63]. Retraction of the cuttlefish identification was repeated by me in 1976 when considering large shell beads[64]. The type of shell still cannot be identified with certainty, but Sir Frank Claringbull has noted that the large size of some of the pieces presupposes a large shell from tropical waters, and has further noticed that the structure is very similar to that of the chank shell (*Xancus pyrum*). The chank has been a sacred shell in India since a time earlier than the arrival of the Aryans[65]. Archaeological evidence of Roman trade is limited to the southern part of that continent[66], and there is literary evidence that some of this trade was connected with products from the chank shell[67]. Although the trade may have faltered for a while after the break-up of the Roman Empire, it must have picked up again as it was mentioned by one foreign observer in the sixth century, Cosmas Indicopleustos, and by the Arab Abouzeyd in the ninth century[68].

The chank shell has a number of ceremonial uses in its complete form, but it is also cut up to produce bracelets and beads. It is interesting to notice a report that 'Naga coolies wore necklaces formed of square concave portions of chank shell with a large cornelian set *en cabochon* in the centre', for this is

---

55  Avent and Leigh 1977, fig. 1, a
56  Ibid, fig. 1, b
57  Ibid, fig. 1, c,d
58  Ibid, fig. 1, h, pl. II, C
59  Ibid, fig. 1, g, pl. II, B
60  Rupp 1937, Taf. 1, 1 and 2; Arrhenius 1971, 117–8, fig. 21
61  Avent 1975 ii, pl. 50, Nos. 147, 148, 149, pl. 51, Nos. 150, 151, pl. 53, No. 155, pl. 54, No. 157, pl. 57, No. 162

62  Evison 1951, 199
63  Rigold and Webster 1970, 5, 15; Hawkes and Hogarth 1974, 58; Bruce-Mitford 1978, 296; Avent 1975|i, 16
64  Evison 1976, 313
65  Hornell 1942, 114
66  Wheeler, 1951, fig. 72, distribution map of Roman coins
67  Warmington 1974, 174
68  Hornell 1914, 127

how it was used by the Anglo-Saxons, as a setting and contrasting background for a garnet or stone of coloured glass. If some of the beads manufactured from the shell were spherical, they would need only to be cut in half to produce a cabochon setting with a hole in the middle suitable for a garnet. There is a strong possibility that some of the shell was imported already shaped in this way, perhaps even with a garnet already inset, because the perforated cabochon and garnet is a component of many Kentish disc brooches, and is even found as a component outside Kent, as a centre piece for Cuthbert's pectoral cross, for instance. In the Dover cemetery a hemisphere of shell is used as a bead threaded on a necklace 75/1, and may be used as a head for a pin 155/1, although the identity of the substance on this pin is not certain, and it may be an imitation in composition.

The remaining colour used on the Dover jewellery is black. Inquiry into the composition of niello on archaeological objects has had a two-fold motivation, firstly it has been an attempt to discover the method used at different periods to achieve a black inlay (apart from black enamel), and, secondly, a desire to use this knowledge, if possible, to determine the antiquity of an object. In this way, for instance, the knowledge gained of the composition of niello was used to establish the genuine antiquity of an Anglo-Saxon brooch which had been suspected of being a modern product, the Fuller brooch[69].

The examination by Dr A A Moss[70] of various nielloed objects to which a date could reasonably be assigned showed that one composition was used before the eleventh century AD and another after that date. In the earlier period, a silver sulphide (acanthite) was used, and the powdered sulphide was presumably placed in the cavity to be filled, heated gently, and rubbed in with a burnisher. In the later period sulphides of silver and copper (stromeyerite) and sometimes lead (Galena) replaced the earlier mixture, presumably because they were found to be easily fusible in a liquid form on to the silver base.

Subsequent work has shown that the division between the two methods of niello inlay is not as clear-cut as first appeared. An examination by Dr Moss of niello in the Kells Crosier discovered a 25% cuprous sulphide in the brass collar knop, and a 15% cuprous sulphide on the silver crook, of which the 25% mixture could easily have been melted in, but it is uncertain whether this mixture could have been used successfully for the 15% mixture. It was therefore concluded that these niello inlays probably represent a transitional stage between the two periods, but the archaeological dating for both of these niello inlays was considered to be the early eleventh century, i.e. no earlier than the changeover period already postulated[71].

Further investigations of black inlays on swords of the eighth and ninth centuries were made by Sir Frank Claringbull, among which the niello on the Fetter Lane sword proved to be a cuprous sulphide, and information provided by Claringbull enabled the following report to be made:

'The niello now consists of stromeyerite with silver (AgCuS), and this is interesting as no stromeyerite has been recorded earlier than the eleventh century, the bell shrine of St. Cuillean being the earliest examined so far. In fact, the stromeyerite in the niello of the Fetter Lane hilt, containing, as it does, some 40 per cent of cuprous sulphide, could have been applied by fusion more readily than the niello found in the knop of the Kells Crosier (early eleventh century), in which the proportion of cuprous sulphide is only 25 per cent. This means that the Fetter Lane hilt holds the first example traced so far of a niello which could have been applied by fusion, as opposed to the earlier silver sulphide types which had perforce to be applied by rubbing in[72].'

Since then, examination of niello on some of the brooches from the Buckland cemetery by Sir Frank Claringbull has added to the list of silver sulphide (acanthite) inlays apparently normal in the early Saxon period, i.e. disc brooches 38/1 and 1/2. On some brooches the niello had either disappeared completely or had been altered by chemical action in the course of time to a swollen inlay consisting mostly of silver, i.e. brooches F/1, 14/1, 29/1, 30/2, 59/1 and 126/1.

Further examples of copper-containing niello were found in the silver sword grip sleeve 98/1 and the ring of the ring sword C/1. These contain jalpaite ($Ag_3CuS_2$) as on the crook of the Kells Crosier, but they are some five centuries earlier in date. The niello on the pommel of the ring sword, however, was again of different composition, mostly silver, with traces of stromeyerite (AgCuS) and chalcocite (CuS). The inlay on the ring is almost certainly the original composition, but the inlay on the pommel appears to have changed since application, in that the larger proportion of it is no longer a sulphide, and it appears to have spread out of its prepared channel. This pommel was made earlier than the ring which must have been added some fifty years later, and which brings the date of the earliest niello which could have been fused in to the period AD 575–625.

On the square-headed brooch 13/2 there is a raised framework along the outer border of the head, on the inner three sides of a rectangular frame, a vertical between two top panels, the frame to the lozenge foot, the necks of downward-biting animals, and the lateral and finial lobes. A groove runs along the middle of this framework lined with a shiny black colour, as though painted, but there is no detectable trace of any actual inlay or filling such as niello or black paste. Sir Frank Claringbull reports that the black material consists of silver and cuprite,

---

69  Bruce-Mitford, 1974, 312–3, 326–7
70  Moss 1953a; Idem 1953b
71  Idem 1955
72  Dunning and Evison 1961, 144

i.e. there is no trace of anything materially different from the silver of the brooch. These framing lines, however, are clearly black in colour, and it must be assumed that some kind of black colouring was used to imitate niello. These brooch border frames are often in reserved silver and niello zigzag, as on the unassociated square-headed brooch (Figure 64). A single black niello line does occur on this kind of frame, e.g. on the Taplow horns, but I know of no other framework similar to this in appearance.

Two other circular brooches have been found in the vicinity of Dover. One, now lost, came from the cemetery on Priory Hill, which is on the opposite side of the river[73] (Text Figure 36, No. 4). It has a general resemblance to the brooch 126/1, and could be regarded as a slightly later product of the same school. The layout of the design is the same, with slight differences in the cloisonné band. The trefoil cells have been changed into three squared lobes and are connected to the cloisonné band by a triangular cloison, while the cabochon intervening settings are also connected to the cloisonné band by cloisons which emphasise the main cross design.

The other brooch was bought in Dover in 1879, but the exact provenance is unknown. Rigold pointed out that houses were being built on Priory Hill at this time, and this brooch therefore, could have come from this site[74]. He also mentioned Long Hill in this connection, for the Dover-Deal railway which cuts through the hill immediately to the south of the Buckland cemetery was opened in 1881. It was discovered in 1951 that the graves nearest to the railway, 3, 4, 5 and 7, were in a state of disturbance which did not appear to be very recent, and a fragment of a clay pipe was found in the fill of grave 7. It is therefore quite possible that the brooch came from one of these graves. The remains in graves 3, 4 and 5 were of male equipment, but grave 7 was thoroughly rifled and even enlarged, and while the male graves had only been partially investigated, it seems that the finds in grave 7 had prompted thorough and over-enthusiastic excavation. Such a fine brooch may well have been the cause. Although, therefore, the brooch could equally well have come from some early unrecorded find from Priory Hill, High Meadows or Old Park, or even from the western section of Buckland subsequently destroyed in 1950, grave 7 at Buckland would also seem to be a likely source.

There are no other composite brooches in this cemetery. The well-defined cross, marked out by five cabochon jewels, has Christian meaning. The high quality of the craftsmanship, and the fineness of the filigree work cannot be paralleled by any other work in this cemetery. In fact, this standard does not seem to be reached even elsewhere, although a plated brooch from Faversham[75] also makes use of pseudo-plait filigree for a border, and attains the nearest approach to the precision and delicacy of the filigree work. The composite brooch has a limited relationship to the plated brooch 126/1 in the step pattern and triangles of the cloisonné collar, and has the same cruciform system of cloisons joining this band to the outer cabochon settings as on the Priory Hill brooch. It is of later date than the other disc brooches in this cemetery, and belongs to the same class as the Sarre brooch (Avent class 2, No. 177) which has a *terminus post quem* of 615. If it was buried in grave 7 of plot C in phase 5 it would have been a very old brooch, surviving into a period when the practice of depositing brooches in graves had been discontinued.

*The runes on the disc brooch 126/1:*
There are two runic inscriptions on the back (Text Figure 9). The smaller one is very faintly scratched at an angle to the line of the pin, and is contained in a rectangle, one side of which is extended for some length. The opposite side of the rectangle forms one upright stroke of a ᛞ (d), and in between there is the letter ᚦ (th).[76] The symbols make no sense, even if the vowel 'i' is acquired by including in consideration the stroke of the frame by the ᚦ.

The other inscription is fairly well centred in the opposite half of the brooch, parallel to the line of the

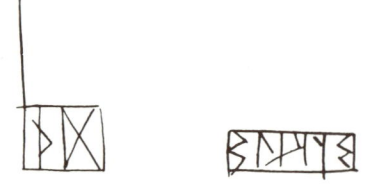

*Text Figure 9* Runic inscription on the back of disc brooch 126/1 Scale 2:1

pin. It is framed in a rectangle, the short ends of which are formed by the uprights of two letters ᛒ, one written the right way round and the other reversed. The normal ᛒ is followed by a recognisable rune ᛚ (l), then follows an upright with a diagonal line crossing it. The two following symbols are both an upright joined by a short diagonal line on the left-hand side at the top. In 1964 I attempted to make sense of this inscription[77] by regarding the final reversed ᛒ as a device for visual effect, and a rune repeated in this way could have had magical value. The other suggestions were that the cross diagonal on the third symbol could be ignored as a probable mistake resulting from a slip of the tool, and the vertical regarded as 'i', while the two identical symbols could be the reverse of ᛋ = s. In this way a reading of the word 'bliss' was achieved, and this is in the tradition of the *utere felix* inscriptions often found on gifts of an earlier period, or it could have connections with the blessing of the newly-arrived Christianity. Page resists these temp-

---

73  Rigold and Webster 1970, fig. 4; Avent 1975 ii, pl. 53, No. 154
74  Rigold and Webster 1970, 10
75  Avent 1975 ii, pl. 53, No. 155
76  Page 1973, 185, 186, fig. 38, sees this letter as ᚹ (w). Although the surface of the brooch is corroded at this point, and the scratches faint, it seems to me that a continuation of the line to form a ᚦ (th) is visible.
77  Evison 1964, 244–5

tations without any difficulty and regards the inscription as illegible.

When this brooch was first published in 1964, no other brooch bearing runes had been found in England. Since then others have been found, and are included in the list of the small number of runic objects belonging to the period before AD 650 shown on a distribution map[78]. The new inscriptions are not of much consequence and consist of 'rune-like forms' on a swastika brooch from Hunstanton, Norfolk, and a single rune scratched on a mid sixth-century brooch from Sleaford, Lincolnshire. One more has subsequently been found at Wakerley, Northamptonshire[79], where four runes are inscribed on the back of a square-headed brooch. In spite of these additional finds, runic inscriptions on the backs of brooches are still far more common on the Continent, and there are analagous garnet-encrusted disc brooches with runes on the back at Soest in Westphalia[80], Osthofen and Friedberg in the Rhine valley[81], Schretzheim, Balingen and Bülach in the area of the upper Rhine and Danube[82]. These brooches belong to the sixth and early seventh centuries, and must have provided a model for the writer of the Dover runes, particularly the Soest brooch where the main inscription is similarly placed in a centred position in relation to the pin, although nearer the rim and following its contour. Other runic symbols are placed on the opposite side of the pin, as on the Dover brooch.

The evidence for the presence of the rune-masters in England in the period before 650 remains extremely scanty, and a distribution map shows only ten runic objects for the whole of England during those 250 years[83]. Of those objects, three, the Caistor knuckle-bone, the Loveden pot, and the Sarre pommel[84] were no doubt fifth-century imports from abroad, complete with their runes. Others bear no more than a single symbol, for the writing of which it was hardly necessary to have comprehensive knowledge of the futharc[85]. With the exception of two inscriptions at Chessel Down, Isle of Wight, the evidence really rests almost completely on the Gilton sword pommel[86] and the Dover brooch, both objects of undoubted Kentish manufacture, the sword pommel belonging to the middle of the sixth century, and the brooch to the end of the century or the beginning of the next. The writer on the sword pommel scribbled some runes and a number of non-runic symbols, possibly out of ignorance[87], and the positioning of runes on the back of a brooch seems to have been derived from continental custom. They are the only examples of runic inscriptions in Kent before 650. It is not surprising, therefore, to find that rune-writing did not persist in this county, and the whole of the post 650 period can provide only one runic inscription, the grave slab[88] that also was found at Dover.

*Frankish disc brooches*
Three of the garnet disc brooches are Frankish work and imported. The rosette brooch from grave 23 (Figure 15, Plate 6l) has lost the inlay in the middle cloison, which could have contained one of many designs carried out in garnets and filigree[89]. The type belongs to Böhner's *Stufe* III, 525–600. In England one similar with a garnet centre was found at Chessell Down, Isle of Wight, and one with both garnets and filigree was found in grave 203 at Finglesham[90].

The other two brooches are similar to each other in design and construction. The brooch 20/2 (Figure 12, 2, Plate 6m) has six keystone garnets set round an elliptical centre cell, and copper strips inlaid on the edges of the iron back plate. On the brooch 92/2 (Figure 42, 2, Plate 6n) eight keystone garnets surround a circular garnet, and yellow metal strips are inlaid on the edge of the thicker iron back plate. These are common Frankish brooches[91], and one of the same type was found in a grave containing a coin of Athalaric (AD 527–34) at Samson, Belgium, grave 18[92]. Other sixth-century garnet-set objects which have striped edges achieved by this inlaid metal technique have been noted by Holmqvist[93], and include buckles with kidney-shaped plates, and also radiate brooches, i.e. *Stufe* II/III. The circular Frankish brooches have been found elsewhere in the south of England, e.g. Sarre, grave 148[94], Broadstairs and Bifrons in Kent[95], and the Isle of Wight as noted above.

These 3 graves are fairly close together in the early part of the cemetery and belong to phases 1 and 2. Associated Frankish objects in the graves are buckles in graves 20 and 92.

*Saucer brooch* (distribution Figure 87)
The saucer brooch with five chip-carved spirals (48/2, Figure 27, Plate 6j) is a type which was already firmly established on the Continent before the

---

78 Page 1973, 26, fig. 6, 28–9
79 Ibid, 37 note 4; Adams 1982
80 Krause and Jankuhn 1966 I, 279–81, Nr. 140, Ibid II, Taf. 60
81 Ibid I, 285, Nr. 145; Ibid II Taf. 62; Arntz and Zeiss 1939, 232–5, Nr. 16, Taf. XIV
82 Krause and Jankuhn 1966 I, 297–8, Nr. 156, Ibid II, Taf. 66; Nr. 160, Taf. 70; Nr. 165, Taf. 70
83 Page 1973, 28–9, fig. 6
84 Evison 1964
85 Sleaford brooch and Willoughby-on-the-Wolds copper bowl, Page 1973, 29
86 Evison 1967a, 97–102; for the more recently found inscription from Chessel Down see Arnold 1982, 27, 59–60, fig. 10

87 However, for the latest interpretation see Odenstedt 1981
88 Page 1973, fig. 7
89 Rupp 1937, Taf. I, 6, Taf. XVI, 10–14, Taf. XXVII, 6–10; Böhner 1958 2, Taf. 13, 3–6
90 Åberg 1926, fig. 166; Arnold 1982, 40, fig. 26, 24; Hawkes and Pollard 1981, 338, fig. 4, 23
91 Dasnoy 1968, fig. 18; Rupp 1937, Taf. XIV, A, 3, 8; C, 6; Böhner 1958 2, Taf. 12. 15
92 Dasnoy 1955, pl. V
93 Holmqvist 1951, 44ff, Abb. 17. 4 and 5, Abb. 20. 1 and 2
94 Brent 1866, 179, pl. VI. 8
95 Brown 1915 IV, pl. CXLV. 5 and 6

migration, and it continued in use for a while in England but went out of circulation in its homeland. A development in England was an increase in the number of spirals, from six to ten. The continental examples in cast bronze were usually decorated with five spirals, but already there was variation in the borders e.g. dotted borders at Heeslingen and Perlberg, and a notched border also from Perlberg[96]. One type of construction was composite, with a cast centre piece applied to a backing, and only one of these has been found in England, at Caistor-by-Norwich[97]. The third type of construction consisted of a back-plate with a thin repoussé sheet bearing the five-spiral design, and probably also a vertical ribbon-type rim separately applied. A silver version of this type comes from grave 131 at Issendorf, near the Elbe mouth, and there are others in bronze in Germany, Holland and Belgium[98]. In England there are seven examples[99].

The distribution of the cast form with five spirals on the Continent lies in the area between the mouths of the Elbe and Weser, mostly between the river Oste and the Elbe, while the repoussé brooches were found west of the Oste[100]. In England the distribution is in the upper and lower Thames, the Sussex coast, some in Hampshire, and some north of the Thames in the regions of the Wash and the Icknield Way. The distribution map (Figure 112) is the latest in a series[101]. The contextual dating on the Continent is about AD 400, and in England it is often in the first half of the fifth century, e.g. Alfriston, East Sussex, grave 60[102], where it is associated with a sharp-rimmed tumbler of c AD 400, and at Cassington, Oxfordshire[103], where it was accompanied by a strap end of the same date. In grave 65 at Alfriston was also a dome-headed pin of a type near its Roman forerunners[104]. The spiral-decorated saucer brooch in grave 65 has further decoration in the shape of a border of radial lines, and the brooches in grave 60 had a stamped border, so stressing the fact that there are some variations which are not exactly paralleled in north Germany, although stamping and variety were already apparent there. Some of these variations may indicate later developments for there are sixth-century contexts also. The brooch at Dover has no decorated border and no beading at the centre, only a half-hearted tooling of a bordering ridge to simulate beading. The rim is turned up at a sharp angle, nearly approaching the vertical. The other contents of grave 48 include a number of remnants of the Roman period, and support a fifth-century date. It was paired with a button brooch, and both were wanderers from a Saxon area into Kentish territory.

*Button brooch*
Although the origins of the button brooch can be traced to disc brooches of the fourth century decorated with a human mask in repoussé metal from Denmark and north Germany, and although a roundel with human mask in chip-carving appears on some Danish long brooches of the end of the fifth century, it is almost exclusively in England that the small mask-decorated disc brooches have been found. A total of 118 have been assembled and studied, of which the only examples found abroad, 15 from France, must have been exported from England, or copied from exports.

The earliest button brooches appear to have been of saucer brooch size with a vertical pin, and the distribution concentrated in the upper Thames area and the Thames estuary. The smaller size of button brooch, often with a horizontal pin, then began to appear further south as well in the periphery of Andredesweald, i.e. Kent, Sussex, Isle of Wight, Hampshire and Wiltshire, the latest and finest quality brooches being produced in Kent.

The brooch from grave 48 (Figure 27, 1, Plate 6k) at Dover was allocated to class Bii[105], and is nearest in design to the brooch from Alfriston, grave C[106]. Both have slightly off-centre faces, with the nose a little to the right. The Alfriston brooch is a shallower saucer and the pin is of bronze, while the Dover pin is of iron. The only other brooches of type Bii occur in other graves at Alfriston, at High Down and at Worthy Park, Hampshire, (Figure 111 distribution map) and none of them has been found in a definitely sixth-century context. The associations with the Alfriston brooch, iron ring fragments and a perforated Roman coin, could belong to the fifth century, and the bronze pins on this and the Worthy Park brooch, as well as the vertical position of the pins on the High Down brooches, are likely to indicate an early date. The Bii brooches are slightly larger than those of class Bi, which they must pre-date.

The alignment of the Dover pin is 270°, i.e. the pin in a horizontal position places the mask in the correct vertical position. Many of the early button brooches have a pin in a vertical position, 180° or 360°, but the Kentish and later button brooches usually have the pin in a horizontal position, 90° or 270°. This no doubt reflects a difference of function in dress fastening from one area and period to another. The Dover brooch must have been acquired from Sussex, and was one of the earliest of the button brooches to be seen in Kent.

*Annular brooches*
There were four annular brooches in the cemetery.

---

96  Roeder 1927, Taf. 3, 6, 7 and 8
97  Myres and Green 1973, 90, Text fig. 2, pl. XIX. c
98  Janssen 1972, Taf. 23, 131f, Taf. 65f; Evison 1978b, 275, and distribution map fig. 4
99  Ibid, 276, distribution map fig. 4
100  Genrich 1951, 277, Abb. 30
101  Bidder and Morris 1959, 81, 92, fig. 10; Leeds 1945, fig. 39; Myres 1969, map 8; Evison 1981a, fig. 11
102  Griffith and Salzmann 1914, 44, pl. VII, 3, 3a
103  Leeds and Riley 1942, 65, pl. Vc
104  Griffith and Salzmann 1914, 45, pl. VII, 4 and pl. VIII, 6, 6A
105  Avent and Evison 1982, 82, 93, 108, No. 12.1, pl. XV.
106  Ibid, 107, No. 2.1, pl. XV

The brooch Unassociated 16 (Figure 65) is a flat ring decorated with triangular stamps and transverse scored lines by the pin perforation and on the opposite side of the ring. It must have been used not as a brooch but for suspension, possibly of keys, because two opposing sides are worn thin as if by the rubbing of straps. This is the most common variety of annular brooch about 1cm broad, which, as Leeds noted[107], occurs mostly in Anglian areas, in the 'full Anglo-Saxon period', by which he no doubt meant the sixth century. There are a few also in the southern part of the country, e.g. at Howletts, Kent, grave 33. One of the type found in grave 8 at Caistor-by-Norwich was placed at the hip and was interpreted as part of a chatelaine[108]. A dissimilar pair of comparable types without pins were found in grave 12 at Monkton in Kent, and signs of wear from suspending cords are clear on the contours[109]. The accompanying pottery bottle suggests a seventh-century date. A series of rings and other objects hanging from the waist of a woman in grave 83 at Burwell also included a pinless annular brooch of this type[110].

The bronze ring brooch with iron pin fastened over the ring 13/6 (Figure 9) in a woman's grave may have been used as a buckle or for attaching the knife to the belt in a scabbard or purse, as it was found at the left waist by the handle of the knife. Alternatively, it may have been used, in conjunction with the small-long brooch 13/5, to fasten the edge of a garment. A cast bronze ring of this kind, with an iron pin, was found with bronze, bone and iron rings in a container by the skull of a young girl in grave 76 at Burwell, so that here even in an Anglian district, it was not being used for display or as a fastening device on the breast[111].

The smaller annular brooch from grave 127 (Figure 52) is decorated with moulded transverse ridges at intervals and was provided with a slot for the passage of the point of the pin. This is missing, but it had been fastened to the brooch by encircling a narrower part opposite the slot. The brooch falls in with the group described by Leeds as 'about 1 inch in diameter, which are unquestionably late. Uncleby and Garton Slack, Humberside (East Riding) and Camerton, Avon (Somerset), have yielded the most, but they are also known from Lincolnshire, Cambridgeshire and Kent.'[112] Grave 127 is certainly late as the occupant was wearing an amethyst bead on her necklace, and the grave is amongst the last at the east end. A similar brooch occurred in grave 35 at Howletts. The brooch in grave 127 at Dover was no doubt functioning in a suspending capacity rather than as a breast ornament, for it was found with keys, iron rings and an iron spoon at the left hip.

The bronze ring 94a/2 (Figure 44) is oval in section with decoration on one face only and has lost its pin. It was displaced at the foot of a shallow grave. A pair of similar rings, each furnished with an iron pin, functioned as a pair of annular brooches near the neck of a young girl in a richly furnished grave of the sixth century at Holywell Row[113].

None of the annular brooches at Dover were worn on the chest as a brooch, and seem to have functioned in connection with suspension at the hip, as they did in other seventh-century graves[114], but even in graves 13 and 94a, i.e. as early as between AD 475 and about 575, they fulfilled the same role. The Kentish ladies obviously were above adopting the traditions for wearing jewellery followed by their less wealthy Anglian neighbours across the Thames, but they found a use for their brooches as suspension rings.

*Pendants*

*Coin pendants*[1]

Pendants were included on a number of necklaces. In accordance with a normal practice of Anglo-Saxon women in the fifth and sixth centuries there was a perforated Roman coin on the necklace in graves 14 (14/2, Figure 10) and 129, (129/3, Figure 53) and in 141 (141/3, Figure 58) a perforated coin was with beads and other objects probably in a bag at the waist.

Four post-Roman coins were found in the cemetery, each mounted with a loop as a pendant. A find made before the beginning of the excavation was the gold Visigothic tremissis of King Leovigild (568–586), (Unassociated 6, Figure 64, Plate 7a). A three-ribbed, fluted loop was soldered to the coin so that the obverse design was right way up, and while this side bore a profile bust, the important part of the design from the point of view of the wearer was no doubt the fair-sized cross clearly visible on the clothing of the figure. It was found west of grave D in an area of disturbed graves, and gives a *terminus post quem* of AD 575 and a possible indication of Christianity for the area.

In grave 29 a gilt-bronze imitation of a tremissis with a three-ribbed silver loop, 29/7, Figure 17, Plate 7b, was worn on a woman's necklace. The obverse with profile bust was again mounted as the front of the pendant, but this time the alignment was not accurate and the human figure was a little out of the vertical. The date assigned to it is the third quarter of the sixth century.

Two silver sceattas, 110/10 and 11, Figure 49, Plate 7c, d, were each mounted with a six-ribbed silver loop. They were both fastened with an iron rivet which passed through the coin and the loop end each side, so that each side is identical and it is not obvious which face was intended for show. It does not seem likely that it was the obverse this time, for

---

107 Leeds 1945, 48–9, type (g)
108 Myres and Green 1973, 213, fig. 60
109 Hawkes and Hogarth 1974, 65, fig. 7.1 and 2
110 Lethbridge 1931, 62, fig. 32
111 Ibid, 63, fig. 33, 3

112 Leeds 1945, 49
113 Lethbridge 1931, 5, fig. 2.2
114 Myres and Green 1973, 213

1 Numismatic report p 180

*Text Figure 10* Designs on gold bracteates.
 a, b, c Nebenstedt, Dannenberg, West Germany
 d, e, f Dover 20/4
 g, h Dover 1/1, i Kingston, Kent, j Dover 134/1, k Dover 29/8, l Bolbro, Odense, Denmark

although a cross is just visible on the clothing of one of the profile busts, one coin is mounted so that the profile portrait is standing on its head and the other nearly so. On the other hand, the reverse of 110/11 has a central diagonal cross, and the beaded circle designs on both are fairly symmetrically placed in relation to the loops, so that these were probably the display sides. The date ascribed to these, 660–70, gives a *terminus post quem* for the grave and for that part of the cemetery.

The custom of depositing coins in graves was current in the pagan period, and increased after the acceptance of Christianity. Mounted coins were buried frequently in Kent and fairly frequently in the rest of the Anglo-Saxon settlement area[2].

*Gold bracteates*
The bracteate 20/4 (Figure 12, Plate 7e) is close in design to the earliest D-type, which was named Jutlandic group I by Mackeprang, a group which has been augmented by finds of bracteates published since his major work on the subject in 1952[3]. The design consists of a side view of a bird-headed animal with body and legs of double-banded elements of equal width, the curving body being crossed at different points by a fore and hind leg, a design more clearly delineated on the bracteate from Nebenstedt, Dannenberg, Niedersachsen[4]. The parts of the animal on the Dover bracteate are illustrated in Text Figure 10, d-f.

This design is a simplified version of the design on the Nebenstedt bracteate (Text Figure 10, a-c), so that it lacks the kidney shape and the detail of a human foot at the end of the two legs, and a further human foot in the middle. The legs themselves, however, are in the same position, and an element of half-moon shape represents the central human foot. On all of the examples illustrated by Mackeprang except two[5] the bird faces to the left, and on all except one there is a kidney-shaped object by its beak. The Dover bird faces right, and there is no kidney-shaped object. The only one without the kidney-shaped object illustrated by Mackeprang is from Skodborg, Haderslev[6], but its differences from the Dover bracteate are that the bird faces left, its border is of wire twisted instead of beaded, and its loop is considerably wider. Another bracteate made from the same model was found at Vester Nebel, Vejle. A series of bracteates from Jutland, Fyn and Skåne were considered by Mackeprang to be degenerate copies of his first group, and although the Dover design retains the distinct character of the body and limbs of the first group[7], it has, like the degenerate series, lost the kidney shape and prefers the right-facing stance which is more prevalent in these copies. A separate group of bracteates with similar animals but more slender bodies was named the North Jutland-West Swedish group by Mackeprang, and on a higher proportion of these also the bird is facing right[8]. The two bracteates illustrated by Mackeprang on which the bird faces right are from Vejle and Skåne, and six from the same stamp were found in the hoard at Sievern, North Germany[9]. The distribution of the Jutlandic group I bracteates and near copies is mainly confined to north and mid Jutland, north Germany, Frisia and Kent, with outliers in Fyn, northern France, the Rhineland and southern Sweden[10]. The closest relations to the design on the Dover bracteate are from the middle of the eastern coast of the Jutland peninsula, north Germany and Skåne. Although belonging to the same group as a number of other bracteates found in Kent, it differs from all of them as the bird faces in the opposite direction, and the kidney shape is missing. This kidney shape matches the shape of the ear of some of the humans portrayed on other bracteates and probably originated from that source[11], and the combination of human feet and ear with the animal suggests the possibility of a separate man and animal design origin.

The question of provenance must largely be governed by the distribution of bracteates with similar profile bird portraits which are regarded as Jutland group I. However, there is no exact parallel to the Dover design; the nearest parallels are six bracteates from north Germany, three from east mid Jutland and one from Skåne, and the right-facing position of the bird without the kidney shape is more common in degenerate copies and the north Jutland-west Sweden group I[12]. A place of origin for Jutland group I, other than Jutland, was proposed by Genrich as distribution maps based on the presence of the kidney shape in the design of Jutland group I and on published occurrences of twisted wire borders on various types of bracteate led him to suggest a north German provenance for bracteates with these two characteristics[13]. Neither of these two characteristics are to be found on the Dover example, which has no kidney shape and has a beaded border, but the presence of six right-facing birds at Sievern somewhat balances the other claims for a Jutland origin.

The dating of all types of bracteates has long been under discussion, the complexities of typology of the bracteates and the dates of associated objects now being complemented by further studies of the bracteates themselves, including analyses of the gold content and estimations of the time involved in their state of wear or preservation by hoarding. The question of the amount of wear evident on jewellery being used as an indication of its age is beset with perils as much depends on whether the object was worn everyday or on special occasions only, whether it was worn on the person in a position where there

---

2  Rigold 1975, 655, maps figs. 426 and 427
3  Hauck 1970, 31; Axboe 1981, 61ff; the bracteate from Dover 20/4 is noted on p 77, pl. IX, 314d
4  Haseloff 1981 I, 217, Abb. 123
5  Mackeprang 1952, pl. 16, 1 and 2
6  Ibid, pl. 16, 8
7  Ibid, pl. 16, 16–23
8  Ibid, pl. 16, 32–8, pl. 17, 1 and 2
9  Schröter and Gummel 1957, Taf. II
10 Hawkes and Pollard 1981, fig. 1
11 Genrich 1967, 90
12 Mackeprang 1952, pl. 16, 16–23, 32–8, pl. 17, 1 and 2
13 Genrich 1967, Abb. 4 and 5

was a great deal of friction or very little, and also on the type of metal involved. The softness of gold means that it becomes worn far more quickly than silver or bronze, and constant wear for even one year shows visible results. The problem of hoarding or heirlooms is one that is ever present in archaeological studies.

A recent study by Bakka places the Dover piece in the first division of Mackeprang's Jutlandic group I, named by Bakka variety 1. This variety is considered by him to have started just before 525[14]. The Dover bracteate, however, does not fit so indisputably into variety 1, and is at the beginning of the degeneration process, so that it is typologically between variety 1 on the one hand and the Mackeprang group I degenerate series and Bakka's variety 3 (which corresponds to Mackeprang's N. Jutland–W. Sweden group) on the other. Because of the worn condition of the Dover bracteate Sonia Hawkes considers it to be an antique piece preserved from the later fifth century[15]. Neither of these authors discusses possible implications of the right-facing aspect or the absence of the kidney shape. In any case, either view places its manufacture before 525, which is the latest date it is likely to have been buried.

The gold, silver and copper content of a number of the gold bracteates found in Kent has been established by M Pollard[16], and may be compared with the analysis of the Dover bracteate 20/4 by M Cowell (report p 181). The list of bracteates examined is given below (Table V), grouped in the three varieties suggested by Bakka, following Mackeprang, together with the gold, silver and copper content, and a reference to the relevant plates published by S Hawkes. An exceptional feature is the unusually high gold content, of 91.6%–96.8%, to be found in variety 3 and in three unusual die-linked examples of variety 1, all from Sarre grave 4. Their silver content varies from 2.7% to 7.3%, but the copper is less variable, from 0.6% to 2.1%. The figures for the bracteates with the normal variety 1 design are more homogeneous, the gold being between 88.9% and 89.9%, the silver 7.4% to 10.2% and the copper 0.8% to 2.8%. An exception is a bracteate from Finglesham D3 where the design is more jumbled, no doubt a late development, and the gold content is as low as 86.8%, the silver more normal at 9.1%, and the copper higher at 4.2%. The Dover bracteate is the nearest match to the Finglesham bracteate for gold content at 87%, with silver 11% and copper 1.8%. The lower gold content of these two bracteates in relation to that of the normal variety 1 is in accord with a later typological stage of development. The later variety 3 also has a comparatively low gold content from 84% to 88.7%. Both the design and gold content of the Dover bracteate, therefore, separate it from the Jutlandic group, so that its origin cannot be regarded as certainly from Jutland.

TABLE V  GOLD, SILVER AND COPPER CONTENT OF KENTISH BRACTEATES
*(after M Pollard and M Cowell)*

|  | Hawkes plate | Au | Ag | Cu |
|---|---|---|---|---|
| *Variety 1* | | | | |
| Bifrons 29 | IX.15 | 89.9 | 9.0 | 1.2 |
| Bifrons 29 | IX.16 | 89.9 | 9.2 | 0.9 |
| Finglesham D3 | V.6 | 89.8 | 7.4 | 2.8 |
| Finglesham D3 | V.7 | 89.1 | 9.4 | 1.5 |
| Finglesham 203 | IV.4 | 89.9 | 9.2 | 0.9 |
| Finglesham 203 | IV.5 | 88.9 | 10.2 | 0.8 |
| Sarre 90 | XIV.21 | 89.4 | 9.4 | 1.3 |
| Sarre 4 | XVIII.25 | 95.4 | 4.1 | 0.6 |
| Sarre 4 | XIX.26 | 93.2 | 4.7 | 2.1 |
| Sarre 4 | XX.27 | 93 | 4.9 | 2.1 |
| Finglesham D3 | VI.8 | 86.8 | 9.1 | 4.2 |
| Dover 20 |  | 87 | 11 | 1.8 |
| *Variety 2* | | | | |
| Bifrons 63 | XI.18 | 91.6 | 7.3 | 1.1 |
| Sarre 4 | XVI.23 | 93.2 | 6.1 | 0.8 |
| Sarre 4 | XVII.24 | 96.8 | 2.7 | 0.6 |
| *Variety 3* | | | | |
| Bifrons 29 | X.17 | 88.7 | 9.1 | 2.3 |
| Bifrons 64 | XII.19 | 84 | 10.9 | 5.1 |
| Lyminge | XIII.20 | 88.7 | 7.5 | 3.9 |
| *Degenerate* | | | | |
| Sarre 4 | XI.22 | 83 | 15.6 | 1.5 |

The bracteate design 1/1 (Figure 4, Text Figure 10g, h, Plate 7f) gives a first appearance of a meaningless jumble of interlacing double strands, all of equal width and closely interwoven. Two left-facing animal heads may be distinguished, however, consisting of a dot and semi-circle eye in a right-angle head: in front are three dots adjoining a pair of looped jaws. The neck at the back of the head extends in a figure-of-eight body loop which runs under the head and out of the design, but returns in the grip of the jaws to continue into a loop which may represent vestigial hind-quarters.

This bracteate must be a development from the D-type, but it differs from the norm in several respects. The series from which it developed is one of the sub-divisions of Mackeprang's Jutlandic group I (Bakka's variety 2) which consisted of animals with looped and interlacing jaws[17]. These are retained on the Dover bracteate, but the head profile is now a smooth right angle instead of a serrated U-shape, and three dots are placed between the eye and the jaws. A further difference is that there are two animals instead of one. The angular shape of the

---

14  Bakka 1981, 27, fig. 1
15  Hawkes and Pollard 1981, 370
16  Ibid, 363–6
17  Mackeprang, 1952, pl. 16, 24–31; Bakka 1981, fig. 1; Haseloff 1981 I, Abb. 125

heads and the symmetrical interlace are recognisable elements of Style II. Intermediate stages between this and the original Style I-type can be seen in some D bracteates in which a second animal head has been inserted into the design, e.g. at Sievern in north Germany and Sarre grave 4 in England[18]. Symmetrical interlacing composition can be seen in various other Style I D-type bracteates: with one animal only in the north Jutland-west Swedish group II[19], and with two unlike animals or two identical animals in Norwegian bracteates[20]. The tendency towards Style II can therefore be seen in Scandinavian bracteates. The Dover bracteate is in no intermediate stage, however. It is a fully developed Kentish Style II, and may be compared with other locally produced bracteates[21].

The other examples may be conveniently referred to in one work as they have recently been assembled. Although the bracteates from Dover graves 29 and 134 have been included in this survey, it is strange to find that 1/1 has not been mentioned, save in a footnote, where it is described as a D-bracteate[22]. It may be seen, on the contrary, to belong to a series of bracteates which must have been made in Kent as they are found there almost exclusively. On some the pattern consists, as here, of two interlacing animals: Wieuwerd, Frisia; Westbere, Kent; East Kent; unprovenanced, Denmark; Faversham and Kingston, Kent[23]. Of these a right-angled head profile is visible on the Westbere, Faversham, East Kent and Kingston bracteates, and all, except the Faversham bracteate[24] have the long, looped jaws as at Dover. The long, looped jaws with the lower jaw curved upwards are also to be seen in the garnet cloisonné animals on the Tongres mount[25], and on the disc brooch from Little Houghton, Northamptonshire[26]. None of the animal bodies are in double-strand interlace, although the Kingston bracteate, which is made of silver, has a body of two strands. The other bodies are beaded between limiting parallel lines, and so show some relationship to the technique of triple rows of filigree beading widely used in Kent in the late sixth and seventh centuries.

The beaded pattern of the animal bodies is to be found on the bracteate from Dover 134/1 (Figure 55, Text Figure 10j, Plate 7h), and this may be considered in relation to bracteate 1/1. After the development of patterns of two Style II animals with beaded bodies the next typological development was no doubt the patterns with four or more animals as on Dover 134/1 and others from Kent[27]. On these, too, the bodies are beaded. The animals on Dover 134/1 each have rudimentary heads, which appear to consist of a forward-pricked ear, and the upper jaw curling over the lower jaw. A border consists of zigzag and beaded elements in an angular twist pattern. Two more examples of bracteates from the same die are known from Wingham, Kent[28]. Similar interlacing animals with forward-pricked ear have been noted on a bracteate from east Kent in Canterbury Museum[29]. The stepped pattern of the border was also in use locally as it appears on disc brooches from Faversham, and in the Dover cemetery itself on a disc brooch 29/1 (Figure 17) and a square-headed brooch 20/8 (Figure 12).

The analysis of the gold content shows that there is a large drop in bracteate 1/1 of 14% from the 87% gold content of the bracteate 20/4, and an increase in the silver content from 11% to 24% and in the copper content from 1.8% to 3.1%. There is an even more spectacular difference in the drop in the gold content to 59% in the four-animal bracteate 134/1, and although the copper content remains more steady at 2.3%, the silver has risen to 39%.

In the case of the three bracteates so far considered, therefore, the fall in gold content corresponds to the sequence of typological development. Bracteate 20/4 has a slightly lower gold content than continental D-type bracteates, and has some stylistic differences. The two-animal bracteate 1/1 and the four-animal bracteate 134/1 follow in typological sequence and lower gold content. The bracteate 1/1 has a pleasing red tint, no doubt due to its higher copper content, and the bracteate 134/1 looks a particularly pale gold colour beside 20/4 and 29/8, no doubt because of its especially high silver content.

There was a considerable gap in time between grave 20 with its Frankish disc brooch, early square-headed brooches, buckle and claw-beaker of phase 1, and grave 1 in a different part of the cemetery with its late development of a keystone garnet disc brooch of phase 3. A further lapse in time is indicated by the associated objects in grave 134, where garnet pendants, a shell bead and a hipped silver pin are appropriate to phase 5.

The bracteate 29/8[30] (Figure 17, Text Figure 10k, Plate 7g) is unique in its design which is composed of three completely independent creatures placed back to back, all facing right. All other formalised zoomorphic bracteates in this country have designs based on halving or quartering of the circular field. The creature has a body of substantial size with

---

18 Schröter and Gummel 1957, Taf. I, bottom left, 16, Abb. 3; Hawkes and Pollard 1981, Taf. XVIII, XIX and XX
19 Mackeprang 1952, pl. 17, 26–30
20 Haseloff 1981 I, 222–30, Abb. 130, 132, 133, 134
21 This opinion conflicts with Axboe 1981, 76, 314c, pl. IX, who lists it as a D-bracteate
22 Speake 1980, 66 note 4
23 Ibid, pl. 13c, fig. 13n; pl. 13d, fig. 13a; pl. 13e, fig. 13d; pl. 13f, fig. 13b; pl. 13g, fig. 13c; pl. 13h, fig. 13e
24 The drawing, Speake 1980, fig. 13c, unfortunately errs in following Kendrick's drawing, Kendrick 1934, Taf. 23.11, which omitted the chequered or beaded snout which fills the space between the eye and mouth. A snout of similar shape and length occurs on the animals of one of the Torslunda plates: Bruce-Mitford 1974, pl. 58b.
25 Speake 1980, pl. 3e
26 Evison 1962, 53–6, figs. 1 and 3
27 Speake 1980, pl. 13a, b, l
28 Ibid, pl. 13a
29 Ibid, fig. 13t
30 A photograph of this bracteate is published in Ahrens 1978, 505, No. 255, but the provenance attribution to Faversham and other details given are mistaken.

curved back, a ring-and-dot eye and curling beak. The front haunch is pear-shaped, the back haunch is composed of two ring-and-dot elements with a bar in between, and both legs have 'cuffs' and frond-like claws curled under the body. Most unusual is the transverse ribbing on the body, alternately plain and beaded. The outline of the ring-and-dot eye is not quite complete and projects slightly forward, so that the head resembles the simpler heads on the animals of bracteate 134/1, where the beaks are comparable and the projection is more pronounced so that it looks like an ear. On the head of this type on a larger scale on the Taplow horns, it can be seen that the element there is a part of the helmet[31]. An obviously comparable animal is the single creature at the end of the great gold buckle plate from the Sutton Hoo ship burial[32], and the animal repeated in procession on the silver mount from Caenby, Lincolnshire[33]. One gold bracteate found in a grave at Camerton, Avon (Somerset)[34] does have a tri-partite design in the centre of three bird heads. It is surrounded by a failed attempt at interlace, and is unlikely to be the work of the Kentish bracteate goldsmiths whose competence in this regard was on a higher level.

The prototypes of the bracteate from Dover grave 29 are also to be sought in the Scandinavian bracteates. The tri-partite division of this bracteate can only be paralleled by a double bracteate from Trollhättan, Västergötland which has a design of three animals on one side[35]. Style I elements are visible on the Dover beasts in the curved outline behind the eye, curved beak, frond-like claws with cuffs, and pear-shaped hips. Frond-like claws sometimes provided with cuffs are also fairly common in Anglo-Saxon Style I ornament, but it is less often that they are curled back in this way. In England the shape does occur, without the cuff, already in the Quoit Brooch Style on the Sarre brooch[36], where only the front paw is curled. In Scandinavia the beginning of the curling of the cuffed front paw can be seen on the animals on the head of the Galsted brooch[37], the next stage in development being the half-curled claws of the rampant animals of the Engers brooch[38], and the front claw of the animals on the pendent bird heads of the Bifrons grave 41 brooch[39]. This trait occurs in Style I sixth-century products such as the rectangular plates of the Howletts buckle[40], an imported example of which was found near Neuss in the Rhineland[41].

The animal may be compared with three backward-glancing animals on the bronze mould for making repoussé bands probably for the rim of a cup or drinking horn from Salmonby, Lincolnshire[42]. These have rather angular bodies with beaded contours and feathered feet. The eyes and haunches are ring-and-dot motifs, and Vierck rightly compares these to the ring-and-dot eyes and joints on type D bracteates. On the Dover bracteate the eyes, rumps and hind haunch are also more or less ring-and-dot motifs.

The Dover design, however, does not seem to owe much to the original D-bracteates which portray animals only, and it may be that inspiration came from another source, and another type of bracteate should be considered. With this in mind, it may be remembered that the profile head of the emperor is the main motif on the A-type bracteate, but this profile head also occurs on B types where a whole man often appears, and on C types where a horse also is included.

It is possible that most, if not all, of the later Kentish bracteates with symmetrical designs were inspired by one of the varieties of Scandinavian or continental bracteates, as the following instances show. One example of the B type of bracteate has been found in England, that from Bifrons, grave 29[43] which shows the figure of a man with profile head upturned and legs bent out and up. In another type B design from Nebenstedt, Hannover, the head is still in profile and upturned, but the arms and legs are in a more natural position and there are snakes also in the design[44]. An Anglo-Saxon bracteate which has clearly devolved from this type comes from Riseley, Kent[45] and a second example of this design on a bracteate has recently come to light at Shrewton, Wiltshire[46]. A much more unusual version of the design occurs as roundel stamps on the bronze binding of a bucket from Loveden Hill[47] and the die which produced the design.

Combination of human face and animals from type C may be noted on a number. On a large bracteate from Faversham, Kent[48] a central human mask is surrounded by eight interlocked animals so that there are connections also with formal versions of type D bracteates like Dover 134/1. Grave 253 at Kingston, Kent[49] contained a bracteate with a central human mask surrounded by six animal legs each bordered by a beaded semicircle which gives a star effect to the design. This layout of human mask surrounded by animal legs is repeated on a group of saucer brooches[50]. Perhaps in this group may also be included the bracteate from Prittlewell[51] which is divided, star-like, into six triangles each containing a

---

31  Speake 1980, pl. 1b
32  Ibid, fig. 1i
33  Ibid, fig. 8i
34  Ibid, pl. 13j
35  Mackeprang 1952, pl. 5, 22b
36  Evison 1965b, fig. 30i, pl. 12c
37  Bakka 1958, fig. 21
38  Ibid, fig. 23, top left
39  Ibid, fig. 15 and 25
40  Jessup 1950, pl. XXXVII. 1
41  Haseloff 1981 I, Abb. 190
42  Capelle and Vierck 1971, 66–7, fig. 9; Speake 1980, fig. 8, 1
43  Bakka 1981, fig. 53; Hauck 1970, Abb. 14a
44  Leeds 1946, pl. VII, second row; Hauck 1970, Abb. 13, 1–2
45  Hauck 1970, Abb. 63
46  Wilson 1969, 241
47  Fennell 1969, 211 ff; Hauck 1970, Abb. 61. The die has recently been found, information from Mrs L Webster.
48  Speake 1980, fig. 13s, pl. 131
49  Ibid, pl. 13m
50  Leeds 1912, 172, fig. 11
51  Pollitt 1931, fig. 1

motif which probably represents the eyebrows and nose of a half mask. The border is decorated with a zigzag of triangular stamps like that on many of the continental bracteates[52]. A cross design on the bracteate from Ash, Kent[53] contains a quatrefoil interlace in the centre and a moustached human head in each arm, with double strand treble twists in the spaces between the heads.

On many of the three types of bracteate, A, B and C, the man's hair becomes formalised into a shape like a segment of an orange with transverse ribbing, and frequently the lower end of the segment is terminated by a bird's head with curling beak[54]. The horses on C bracteates frequently have three curled legs, the hair of the man is depicted by transverse ribbing and beading[55], and the body of the horse is often filled in with transverse ribbing and beading[56]. Even the tri-partite arrangement of the bracteate Dover 29/8 may have been inspired by the kind of C-type bracteate on which there are three items: the man's head, the horse and a bird, and in particular the Bolbro bracteate[57], Text Figure 10l, the man's hair terminating in a bird's head and with the additional two figures of an animal and bird, is a likely prototype.

The associated objects in Dover grave 29 of a late type of plated disc brooch and a garnet pendant ensure that the grave was made not long after the date of the coin it also contained, which is c 560–70[58]. The metal analysis shows a slightly higher gold content than bracteate 134/1 at 63%, and comparable silver and copper content at 34% and 2.5%. The similarity of these two results prompted M Cowell to suggest a common origin for the two bracteates. Other factors do, however, indicate a difference of date. The associated objects and position in the cemetery would put 134/1 into phase 5 as compared with phase 3 for 29/8, and this is no doubt reflected in the lower gold content for 134/1.

The results obtained here for the three Dover bracteates 1/1, 29/8 and 134/1 may be compared with earlier analyses of other examples from this Kentish series of imitation bracteates, although figures obtained cannot yet be regarded as reliable[59]. Three are all very close to the analysis of Dover 1/1: a geometric star design with boss centre from Kingston Down grave 205, a mask from Kingston Down grave 253 surrounded by six legs and a bracteate from near Canterbury with a pattern of pure interlace[60]. All contain 71–73% gold, 24–26% silver and 2–3.1% copper. The larger bracteate from Faversham decorated with central mask surrounded by eight interlocking animals has a slightly higher gold content, 80%, with silver 18% and copper 2%[61].

One matched the low gold content of Dover 134/1, a stylistically contemporary bracteate with equal-armed cross and interlacing snakes in the quadrants from Kingston Down grave 235[62]. Other objects with a similar low gold content are composite brooches with bronze cloisons, a rather plain bracteate with restrained garnet and filigree decoration and garnet or amethyst pendants, all of which are amongst some of the latest jewels found in furnished graves[63].

*Silver disc pendants*

There is a further series of disc-shaped pendants but in silver with a bossed centre, and decorated with punched designs. The design of the pendant 35/3 (Figure 21) is cruciform, with the equal-armed cross picked out in gilding on the silver background. The Christian character of the jewel is further emphasised by a cross scratched in an amateur fashion on the lowest cross arm. In the neighbouring grave 32 (Figure 19, 4p) were fragments of a similar silver pendant with punched line decoration. Three silver pendants with punched cross designs were on the necklace in grave 67 (Figure 37), and another fragmentary disc was in grave 38 (Figure 22, 3). Two comparable pendants were suspended on necklaces at Chamberlain's Barn, Leighton Buzzard, Bedfordshire, and several others were noted in the publication of that cemetery[64], but the cruciform designs present on some were not commented upon, designs which are all probably, and in some cases certainly Christian[65]. The date of production suggested, ranging from the beginning to the end of the seventh century, is not contradicted by the evidence at Dover. These silver pendants are a less expensive version of gold disc pendants with cabochon jewels in a cruciform design, e.g. Ducklington, Oxfordshire, Faversham, Kent, Compton Verney, Warwickshire, Kingston Down and Sibertswold, Kent, Uncleby, Humberside (Yorkshire)[66].

The shape of these pendants is similar to a shield with a central boss, and the possibility that this similarity was intentional on the part of the maker is rendered a certainty by a pendant on a necklace

---

52  Mackeprang 1952, C-type pl. 10, 2, 15, 2; D-type pl. 17, 3; B-type pl. 5, 16
53  Speake 1980 pl. 13o, fig. 12j
54  Mackeprang 1952, A-type pl. 3, 13; B-type pl. 5, 1; C-type pl. 8, 19–21
55  Ibid, pl. 8, 18–22
56  Ibid, pl. 11, 10–12 etc
57  Ibid, pl. 8, 19; Hauck 1970, Abb. 45c, 1
58  Unfortunately the grave number is erroneously given as 20, and the information on the grave contents is therefore incorrect in Speake 1980, 68.
59  Brown and Schweitzer 1973, 181ff
60  Hawkes *et al*. 1966, 109–10, fig. 2, L. 16 and L. 18; Brown and Schweitzer 1973, 177, plate facing page 178, AM3

61  Brown and Sweitzer 1973, 178, AM11
62  Hawkes *et al*. 1966, 112, fig. 3, L. 17
63  Brown and Schweitzer 1973, 179, AM20; 180, AM28; 178, AM14; Hawkes *et al*. 1966, 112, fig. 3, L. 25 etc
64  Hyslop 1963, 199–200, figs. 13b, 17h
65  Ibid, fig. 17h; Faussett 1856, pl. IV, 20, 22, pl. XI, 7; Lethbridge 1931, fig. 23, 1; Fox 1923, pl. 34, 8; Wilson 1955, pl. IV, m; Matthews 1962, fig. 3; Smith 1911–12, 153; *J Brit Archaeol Ass* ser. 1, 32 1876, 109
66  Brown and Schweitzer 1973, AM10, AM12, AM19; Faussett 1856, pl. IV, 11, 13; Leeds 1936, pl. XXVII, 31

from Szilagy-Samlyo, Roumania, which even has a minute hand-grip applied to the back of the boss[67]. It is therefore easy to believe that they had a protective, amuletic function, and this obviously continued as a belief when the religion changed to Christianity and the decoration became cruciform[68].

*Silver, garnet-set, shell, glass and bronze pendants*
The small oval silver pendant decorated with dots 30/5 (Figure 18) is uncommon, perhaps to be regarded as analagous to the bronze spangles on a necklace at Holywell Row[69]. Also in sheet metal, there were three silver pendants of different sizes on the necklace in grave 29 (29/5a-c, Plate 7i), each in the shape of a mushroom, the largest bearing a simple scratched design. Although not quite the same shape, they are obviously related to the mounts in the shape of double birds' heads fastened at the rim of the pair of wooden vessels in the same grave 29/12a,b (Figures 17, 5a-c, 12a,b), and were no doubt the work of the same craftsman[70]. While the details of the birds' heads are in punch marks on the Dover mounts, they are in repoussé on the silver pendant in grave 76 at St. Peter's, Kent[71]. Other examples with punched decoration came from Faversham (Ashmolean Museum 1942.217)[72] and from Kingston Down, grave 161, on a necklace[73]. A pair in gold with filigree decoration were included in the Wieuweerd hoard[74]. These pieces, as well as some of the other jewels in the hoard, may be of Kentish manufacture, and the date of deposition of the hoard is about AD 630. One other mushroom pendant was found in Holland at Wierum, Groningen[75], and one occurred in a Merovingian grave at Kirchberg in Germany of about AD 700[76]. However, this form of pendant was known much earlier and was widespread in Germanic regions by AD 400, so that it is probable that it was derived in the first place from the classical pelta[77].

Amongst the six garnet-set pendants only one was set completely in gold, 67/2, four were set in silver, 29/6 (Plate 7j), 134/3, 134/4, 160/3, one of which had a gold foil backing to the garnet, and one, 6/8, was set in bronze with an impressed bronze backing. Two sliced oval garnet pendants formed part of the necklace in grave 134 (Figure 55, 3, 4), one being cut flat at the back and the other hollow ground. Flat-topped garnets were among the pendants in Barfriston, grave 34[78]. A variant on this theme appeared in graves 6 and 29 where the oval of the pendant was divided into half, on one side a sliced garnet with a circular shell inset, and on the other an inset of light amber glass in grave 6 (Figure 7, 8) and light blue glass in grave 29 (Figure 17, 6). This division into two sections is a compromise between a single, whole inset garnet and a *cloisonné* inset such as on a pendant from Kent[79]. It does not seem to occur elsewhere, although a pendant garnet divided in two is achieved in a different technique at Barfriston Down, grave 34, where a decorated gold band crosses a cabochon garnet diagonally[80]. The backing to the garnet is unusual in both of the pendants 6/8 and 29/6. In the former it is of bronze impressed with a continental pattern of a pellet-in-grid, similar to the pattern of the backing under the keystone garnets in the disc brooch 35/1. The pattern of the backing in 29/6 is the special boxed pattern also present in the brooches Unassociated 9, 1/1 and 29/1. The pattern on the gold backing of the tiny garnet pendant 67/2 discussed below is no doubt a standard cross-hatched pattern distorted into rectangular pattern by the curved surface of the garnet.

The silver pendant 160/3 (Figure 62) was trapezoidal in shape with dog-tooth retaining collar and cabochon garnet. This dog-tooth collar is a late feature in Kentish jewellery[81]. Another pendant with toothed collar, sub-triangular in shape, was found in grave 48 at Barfriston Down[82], and one of almond shape at Chartham Down[83].

The tiny gold pendant 67/2 (Figure 37, Plate 7k), with a rectangular garnet semi-cylindrical in section, must surely represent the converted use of a garnet originally shaped for inset as one component of a complex piece of jewellery, e.g. the garnet-encrusted button from Wibtoft, Warwickshire, (Leicestershire) where the border consists of alternating gold and garnet, and where the garnets are cut with a semi-cylindrical surface[84]. The garnets in the same position on the corresponding buttons on the Sutton Hoo sword scabbard are cut to a similar shape, but with the additional detail of a curved cable surface[85]. The Dover garnet would not have been intended for a button as it is straight-sided, but it could have been part of the border of a rectangular piece of jewellery, such as the panels of the Sutton Hoo shoulder clasps.

Pendants of other materials include 129/5a and 141/5 (Figures 53 and 58) which are fashioned from

---

67  Meaney 1981, fig. III ff; cf. Vierck 1978a, Abb. 12, 7–8
68  Ibid, 159–62
69  Lethbridge 1931, fig. 1A
70  The reference to these in Meaney 1981, 191: 'some of these latter had been hung in long loops from the mountings of a drinking horn' is misinformation. Further misinformation regarding the contents of the grave and its number is contained in Hawkes 1979, 92.
71  Evison 1974, fig. 5b
72  Speake 1980, pl. 2g
73  Faussett 1856, pl. XI, 22; Speake 1980, pl. 2c and p. 42 where they are referred to as 'belt mounts'
74  Lafaurie *et al.* 1961, 101, pl. VI, K, L; pl. VII, L
75  Ibid, pl. XVII, 2
76  Göldner and Sippel 1980, front cover
77  *Van Friezen Franken en Saksen 350–750* 1959–60, 69a-c; *l'Art mérovingien* 1954, pl. 3; Forssander 1936–7, Abb. 3, Abb. 8, 4, 5 and 8; Voss 1954, 187–8, fig. 6; Gebers *et al.* 1977, 23–4, Abb. 5, 1–2, Abb. 11, 1–6
78  Hawkes *et al.* 1966, fig. 4 L29, L31, L34
79  Smith 1908a, pl. 2. 1
80  Faussett 1856, pl. IV, 18; Hawkes *et al.* 1966, 113, fig. 4. L32
81  Bruce-Mitford 1956, 321, pl. XVI, 6, 8
82  Faussett 1856, pl. IV, 5; Hawkes *et al.* 1966, 113, fig. 4 L28
83  Leeds 1936, pl. XXIXa
84  Evison 1976, pl. LXVIc
85  Bruce-Mitford 1978, pl. 21c

shell[86], rounded at one end and squared at the other, and no doubt share the same provenance as the shell beads, cf p 59. A disc-shaped pendant of light green glass 1/4r (Figure 5), may be matched from other Kentish sites.[87] A probable source for these may be indicated by the large number housed at the museum of Damascus, which are considered there to be of local origin[88] as the colours of the glass match those of vessels of Syrian origin.

The perforated coin pendants belonged to phases 2, 5 and 6, the coins fitted with loops to phases 3 and 6, and the bracteates to phases 1, 3 and 5. The silver shield discs, as befits Christian objects, did not occur before phase 3, and one belonged to phase 5. The rest of the pendants, of metal, garnet, glass and shell also began in phase 3 and occurred in phases 5 and 6, so that the period when pendants were in vogue was mainly confined to 575–700. The display of pendants on a necklace, as well as amethyst quartz beads which were probably suspended in vertical fashion, is a custom which had filtered through to the North from the Mediterranean, Byzantium and Egypt, where mosaics and splendid necklaces which survive are witnesses to the custom (see p 69)[89].

The small bronze pendant in the shape of a bar with a loop on one side, 38/13 (Figure 23), is broken off at one end, and the loop shows a great deal of wear. There is decoration on both sides, and the signs of wear must have resulted from much friction caused by swinging. These facts, together with the position in which it was found at the back of the skull, show that it was used as a hair ornament, the only certain example in the cemetery.

*Beads* (Colour Plates III, IV, distribution Figure 89, 90)
Most of the beads are made of glass in a variety of shapes and colours, the next most numerous are amber, and the remainder are of amethyst quartz, jet, shell and white composition, metal and stone.

*Non-glass beads* (Tables VIII and XII, Text Figure 11)
The amber beads (Type Nos. A01–3) are roughly shaped, none being particularly large, and those under 5mm in length are described as 'small'. Only a few take on more precise shapes, such as oval 13/3a (Figure 9) or disc 18/2a (Figure 11). They occur in twenty graves (Figure 89), the total number of 275 appearing in various size groups from one to seventy-four in any one grave. Ten of the graves contained five amber beads or under, and only five graves contained more than fifteen, as may be seen from Table VI.

In a contemporary cemetery at Schretzheim in

TABLE VI  AMBER BEADS

| Grave No. | 1–5 | 5–10 | 10–15 | Over 15 |
|---|---|---|---|---|
| F  | 5  |   |   |   |
| 1  |    | 6 |   |   |
| 13 | 3  |   |   |   |
| 14 |    |   |   | 27 |
| 18 | 1  |   |   |   |
| 20 |    |   |   | 21 |
| 23 | 1  |   |   |   |
| 29 | 3  |   |   |   |
| 30 |    |   | 14 |   |
| 35 | 2  |   |   |   |
| 38 |    |   |   | 70 |
| 42 |    |   |   | 17 |
| 48 |    | 8 |   |   |
| 49 | 1+ |   |   |   |
| 55 | 2  |   |   |   |
| 59 | 3  |   |   |   |
| 60 |    | 7 |   |   |
| 62 | 3  |   |   |   |
| 66 |    | 7 |   |   |
| 92 |    |   |   | 74+ |

+ indicates additional fragments

Germany[90] amber beads were present in low numbers in *Stufe* I and in higher numbers in *Stufe* II, after which there was a decline in numbers. With few exceptions the number of amber beads on any one necklace was between one and five, and, as at Dover, one or two graves contained larger numbers. Their period of existence at Schretzheim was from the beginning of the cemetery in AD 525 to AD 630.

At Dover they occur in association with glass, jet, stone and composition beads, but never with amethyst, shell, or metal beads (Figure 89; Table VII). Necklaces consisting of amber beads alone occurred in graves 49 and 66, although it is possible that some beads had been lost from grave 49 which was exposed in the top soil. They are mostly in well-furnished female graves, in plots A, B, D, E, and in plot F in grave 38 only.

The two graves with the highest number, 38 and 92, belong to phases 3 and 2 respectively, and the necklaces are very similar in composition in that they consist of 70 and 74 amber beads respectively, with only seven other beads in 38, of which one is of millefiori, and eleven other beads in 92, of which one

---

86  cf Sarre, Brent 1868, pl. VIII, xxxii. One of these, 141/5, is mistakenly described as being of bone, and illustrated twice as large as it, in fact, is, in Meaney 1981, 145, fig. IVjj
87  cf pendants of green and purple glass from Chatham. Douglas 1793, 86, and of green 'stone or porcelain' i.e. probably glass from Sarre, Brent 1868, pl. VII, xxiii

88  Zouhdi 1978, 52–4, fig. 1
89  Vierck 1981, Taf. 8, 9
90  Koch 1977, 1, 72

58                    THE BUCKLAND ANGLO-SAXON CEMETERY

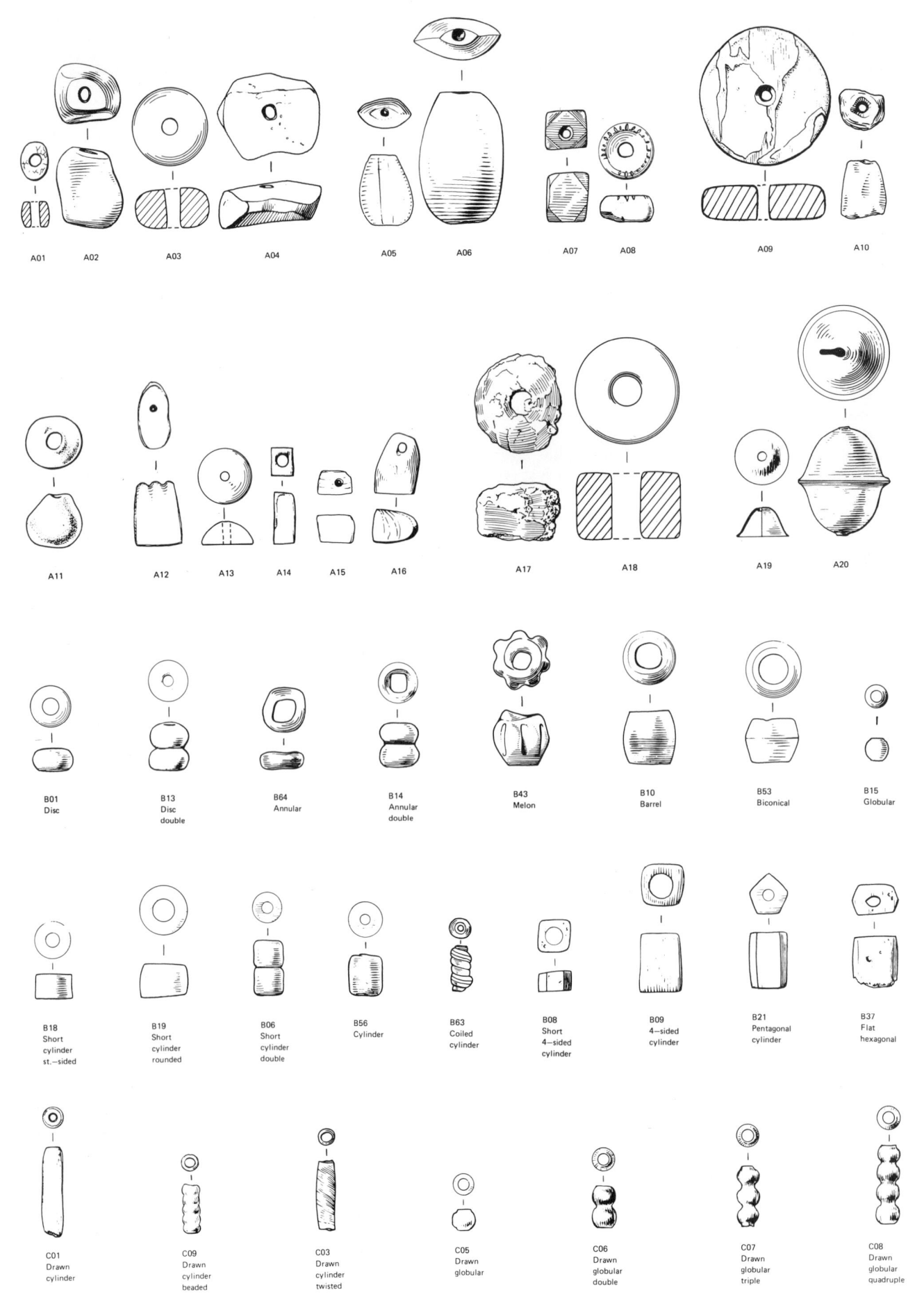

A01   A02   A03   A04   A05   A06   A07   A08   A09   A10

A11   A12   A13   A14   A15   A16   A17   A18   A19   A20

| B01 | B13 | B64 | B14 | B43 | B10 | B53 | B15 |
| Disc | Disc double | Annular | Annular double | Melon | Barrel | Biconical | Globular |

| B18 | B19 | B06 | B56 | B63 | B08 | B09 | B21 | B37 |
| Short cylinder st.–sided | Short cylinder rounded | Short cylinder double | Cylinder | Coiled cylinder | Short 4–sided cylinder | 4–sided cylinder | Pentagonal cylinder | Flat hexagonal |

| C01 | C09 | C03 | C05 | C06 | C07 | C08 |
| Drawn cylinder | Drawn cylinder beaded | Drawn cylinder twisted | Drawn globular | Drawn globular double | Drawn globular triple | Drawn globular quadruple |

*Text Figure 11*   Dover: Non-glass beads, monochrome glass bead forms, drawn glass bead forms. Scale 1/1

## TABLE VII  TYPES OF BEADS IN INDIVIDUAL GRAVES

| Grave number | Amber | Amethyst | Jet | Shell | Composition | Metal | Stone | Monochrome | Orange Barrel | Drawn Globular | Drawn Globular Gilded | Drawn Cylinder | Polychrome | Mosaic | Millefiori | Reticella | Total in Grave |
|---|---|---|---|---|---|---|---|---|---|---|---|---|---|---|---|---|---|
| B | | | | | | | | 1 | | | | | | | | | 1 |
| F | 5 | | | | | | | 1 | | | | | | | | | 6 |
| 1 | 6 | | | | | | | 83 | 1 | 13 | | | 19 | | | | 122 |
| 6 | | | | 1 | | | | 32 | | 1 | 2 | | | | | | 36 |
| 12 | | | | | | | | | | | | | 1 | | | | 1 |
| 13 | 3 | | 1 | | | | | | | | 7 | 5 | 1 | | | | 17 |
| 14 | 27 | | | | 1 | | | | | 11 | | | | | | | 39 |
| 15 | | | | | | | | 1 | | | | 7 | | | | | 8 |
| 18 | 1 | | | | | | | 7 | 2 | | | | 9 | | | | 19 |
| 20 | 21 | | | | 1 | | | 8 | | | 21 | 4 | | | | | 55 |
| 23 | 1 | | | | | | | 3 | | | | | 1 | | | | 5 |
| 29 | 3 | | | | | | | 84 | | 4 | | 1 | 3 | | | | 95 |
| 30 | 14 | | | | | | | 49 | | | | | 15 | 4 | | | 82 |
| 32 | | | | | | | | 131 | | 24 | 27 | | 11 | | | | 193 |
| 35 | 2 | | | | | | | 10 | | 22 | 30 | | 1 | | | | 65 |
| 38 | 70 | | | | | | | 4 | | | | 1 | 1 | | 1 | | 77 |
| 42 | 17 | | | | | | | 9 | | | | | 28 | | | 1 | 55 |
| 46 | | | | | | | | 141 | | 14 | 24 | | | | | | 179 |
| 48 | 8 | | | | | | | 2 | | 5 | 1 | 7 | | | | | 23 |
| 49 | 1 | | | | | | | | | | | | | | | | 1 |
| 53 | | 3 | | | | | | | 4 | | | | | | 1 | | 8 |
| 55 | 2 | | | | | | 2 | 3 | 1 | | | | 2 | | | | 10 |
| 59 | 3 | | | | | | | 28 | | | | | 12 | 1 | | | 44 |
| 60 | 7 | | | | | | | 30 | | 2 | | 2 | 7 | 2 | | | 50 |
| 62 | 3 | | | | | | | 22 | | | | | 1 | | | | 26 |
| 66 | 7 | | | | | | | | | | | | | | | | 7 |
| 67 | | 3 | | 6 | | 3 | | 5 | 4 | | | | | | | | 21 |
| 75 | | 4 | | 1 | | | | 5 | | | | | | | | | 10 |
| 76 | | | | | | | | 1 | | | | | 2 | | | | 3 |
| 83 | | | | | | | | 1 | | | | | | | | | 1 |
| 92 | 74 | | 1 | | | | | | | 6 | | 3 | | | | 1 | 85 |
| 93 | | | | | | | | | | | | | | | | 1 | 1 |
| 107 | | | | | | | | 2 | | | | | | | | | 2 |
| 110 | | | | | | | | 13 | | | | | | | | | 13 |
| 124 | | 2 | | | | | | | | | | | | | | | 2 |
| 127 | | 2 | | | | | | 5 | | | | | | | | | 7 |
| 129 | | | | 1 | | 3 | 1 | 5 | | | | | 1 | 1 | | | 12 |
| 132 | | 6 | | | | | | 2 | 2 | | | | 1 | | 2 | | 13 |
| 133 | | 2 | | | | 3 | | 2 | 5 | | | | 2 | | | | 14 |
| 134 | | | | 2 | | | | 4 | 2 | | | | 1 | | | | 9 |
| 141 | | | | 1 | | | | 2 | | | | | | | | | 3 |
| 155 | | | | | | | | 5 | | | | | | | | | 5 |
| 157 | | | | 1 | | | | 3 | 2 | | | | 1 | | | | 7 |
| 160 | | | | | | | | 6 | | | | | | | | | 6 |
| 161 | | | | | | | | 1 | | | | | | | | | 1 |
| UN | | | | | | | | 2 | | | | | 1 | | | | 3 |
| Total | 275 | 22 | 2 | 13 | 2 | 9 | 3 | 713 | 23 | 102 | 112 | 30 | 121 | 8 | 4 | 3 | 1442 |

is in reticella. The three graves with the next highest total belong to phases 1–4. Most of the graves with smaller numbers belong to phase 3, two belong to phase 1 in the fifth century, and they do not survive phase 4. Amber beads cannot, therefore, be regarded as belonging exclusively to the sixth century, although that is no doubt the period of their greatest popularity[91].

Amethyst quartz beads (Type Nos. A05–6) do not occur at all in the same graves as amber beads (Figure 89). They are much fewer in number, only twenty-two beads in all, fairly evenly spread through seven graves. Some of these graves, 132 and 133 in plot G, and 53 and 67 just outside the barrow in plot E, are fairly close to, but subsequent to, the disc-brooch graves, and 124, 127 and 75 are further east in plots H and I. None of these women was wearing brooches.

Amethyst quartz beads frequently form part of a necklace in Kentish graves e.g. Kingston Down, graves 6, 96, 103, Barfriston grave 48, Gilton grave 41 and Sibertswold grave 172[92]. Two formed part of the Sarre necklace which was accompanied by a composite disc brooch and coin pendants no earlier than $c$ AD 625[93]. They make their earliest appearance in Germanic graves on the Continent and in England in the second half of the sixth century. At Schretzheim amethysts do not appear before 565, and there are few after 600[94]. At Dover, however, they extend from phase 5 to 7, i.e. from the second half of the seventh to the eighth century.

The two jet beads in graves 13 and 92 (Types A07–8, Figures 9 and 42) are in the earliest part of the cemetery, plot A, and they are possibly of Roman origin. Jet beads are rare in Anglo-Saxon graves but three disc beads with nicked edges similar to those in grave 92 were found in a well-furnished sixth-century grave at Holywell Row[95], and a single disc came from the West Stow settlement[96]. A faceted cube like the bead in grave 13 was found in the West Stow cemetery[97].

One bead made of stone (Type A09, Figure 30) was included in the necklace in Dover grave 55. This was a flat disc attractively marbled white and grey, obviously chosen for its pretty appearance and neatly shaped as a bead. The bead 55/1c (Type A10) is probably of cup coral. One fossil *porosphaera* (Type A11) was on the necklace in grave 129/5b, and this would have been chosen, not for its appearance, which is very dull, but because of superstitions attached to a naturally perforated stone[98].

White shell beads (Types A12–6) are cut in different shapes, four are nearly rectangular and retain the natural corrugated edge of the shell along one side (6/10a, 67/1b, 157/1a Figures 7, 37, 62), four are roughly rectangular but minus the corrugated edge (67/1c Figure 37), two are four-sided cylinders (134/2a, Figure 55), and one is a cabochon jewel setting, presumably threaded as a bead through the central perforation (75/1c, Figure 38). Two have a straight, sawn edge and are perforated as pendants, 129/5a and 141/5, (Figure 53, 58). The containing graves 6, 129, 134, 141 and 157 are in plots C, G and H; one grave (67) is outside the barrow in plot E, and the grave containing the cabochon mount is further away near the east end of the cemetery in plot I. The shell beads were, therefore, fashionable between AD 650 and 700, but there is also the single later occurrence of the cabochon.

Similar shell beads with an original indented edge occurred in grave 121 at Shudy Camps, Cambridgeshire, with a silver ring, pendant fragments and glass beads[99], where Lethbridge compared them with the cowrie shell found in grave 48, and deduced that they were cut from a cowrie shell. Shell beads were amongst the finds at Valetta House, Broadstairs[100] and at Chatham, Kent[101]. A shell bead without the corrugations was found in grave 11 at Shudy Camps[102] with silver rings, other beads including silver wire beads, a Roman coin and a bronze hasp, so that here also the contexts belong to the second half of the seventh century.

In two graves large cylindrical beads of white composition were found, Types A17–8 14/3c (Figure 10) and 20/18 (Figure 13), consisting of magnesium carbonate and apatite respectively[103]. The first of these corresponds to one of the considerable variety of materials which have been identified in the white settings of Kentish jewelled disc brooches[104], compositions which were manufactured in imitation of the shell settings. Of these two beads one was included in a necklace 14/3c, and one seems to have been used for fastening a belt, 20/18, but two similar beads at Selmeston, East Sussex were attached to swords. One of the Selmeston beads has been examined and proves to be cristobalite, another of the white materials identified in Kentish jewels[105]. These white cylindrical beads do, however, occur on necklaces elsewhere, e.g. at Staxton, North Yorkshire[106]. Further examples and related beliefs are discussed by Meaney[107].

White cylindrical beads of this type also appear on the Continent, and in the descriptions it is not always indicated whether the material is identified by visual judgement or scientific examination. There are, for instance, cylindrical brownish-white beads referred

---

91 Dickinson 1979, 41, where it is stated that 'beads of amber, rock crystal and metal-in-glass were essentially sixth century'.
92 Faussett 1856, 42, 57, 59, 143, 15 and 131
93 Avent 1975 ii, 47, Corpus No. 177
94 Koch 1977 1, 71–2
95 Lethbridge 1931, fig. 3. 5
96 Evison and Cooper 1985, fig. 275.2 No. 821
97 Ibid, fig. 275, 1 (No. B16)
98 Oakley 1965, 15–16
99 Lethbridge 1936, fig. 4j. 2; fig. 9.6
100 Hurd 1913, 16
101 Douglas 1793, 86
102 Lethbridge 1936, fig. 2, C3
103 Identified by Sir Frank Claringbull, sometime Director, British Museum (Natural History)
104 Evison 1951, 198
105 Evison 1976, 311, fig. 3b
106 Sheppard 1938, 16, fig. 28
107 Meaney 1981, 96–7

to as 'Kaolinperle' at Schretzheim[108]. Cylindrical white beads which acted as a seat for jewelled sword buttons in graves 1782 and 1812 at Krefeld Gellep were identified as meerschaum[109]. One from Weimar is described as gypsum[110]. Now for the first time in England meerschaum has been identified in an Anglo-Saxon context at Fonaby, Lincolnshire, where there were two unstratified cylindrical beads in the cemetery[111]. This identification implies Mediterranean trade as the nearest sources are Asia Minor, North Africa and Spain. The material is rather friable so that sometimes complete disintegration results, as seems to have happened to the white beads under the jewelled buttons on the Sutton Hoo sword scabbard[112]. There was probably one of these buttons on two or more of the Dover swords (p 24).

Biconical bronze beads in graves 67 and 129 and silver beads in grave 133 (types A19 and A20) had fallen into pieces, but all no doubt originally consisted of an inner tube, central disc and a cone on either side, fixed together to form a bead as in the reconstruction, Figure 53, 6b. Fragments of this type of bead have been found at Burwell, Cambridgeshire[113], and also at Luton, Bedfordshire according to Lethbridge.[114] Basically, the construction is the same as used in the larger bronze-framed beads inset with shell which have been found in a few seventh-century graves in this country and in a grave of the same period in Sweden[115].

*Glass beads*

Most of the beads are made of glass, and of these, monochrome versions occur on almost every necklace. The extent of the variety of glass beads at Dover is comparable with that of other Kentish cemeteries, but it is far smaller than that of later beads of the Viking period in Scandinavia[116], or even of contemporary cemeteries in Germany such as Schretzheim. On the whole, the level of precision achieved in the manufacture, in the shaping, decorating and colouring, is not very high, with the result that it is not useful to attempt to apply an extremely systematised and rigid method of classification to such intractable material. For instance, whether a bead turned out to be discoid, globular, barrel or cylindrical in shape was sometimes a matter of chance, and often one half of the bead may differ from the other half in shape, colour and decoration. Small differences like this are usually of no significance. The descriptions of shape, therefore, are as follows, with no pretensions to mathematical precision: disc, annular, globular, barrel, biconical, cylinder, and a few less common are listed as: cylindrical pentagonal, cylindrical four-sided, hexagonal flat, melon, drawn globular, drawn cylindrical, drawn cylindrical twisted, drawn cylindrical beaded. A few are described as annular where the central hole is wider than the thickness of the bead. Many beads are described as disc-shaped where the central hole is narrower than the thickness of the bead.

The descriptions of colour also are simple. A series of beads is sometimes obviously intended to be identical, but, as the shapes may be varied and inconsistent, the colour can also vary, perhaps because of the use of a different recipe, but sometimes affected by impurities, and no doubt also by fluctuations in temperature or conditions in the furnace. The thickness of the glass also controls the depth of colour. The only qualifications noted in the text, therefore, are light or dark, and juxtaposition of colours, such as blue-green. With one exception the only reds are variations of opaque brownish, or rust red. The exception is one mosaic bead which partly consists of a translucent purple. The coloured illustrations published in the two above-mentioned works, Callmer 1977 and Koch 1977, are idealised, i.e. they presumably portray what is considered to have been the original colouring when the beads were new. The paintings by Mr F Gardiner (Colour Plates III and IV) are exact portrayals of the present condition of the beads, and show the gradations of colour which occur. The glass has been diversely affected by wear and by contact with chemicals in the grave, has sometimes deteriorated considerably and some decoration has even disappeared completely.

One bead from each type present in an individual grave is illustrated in the grave group as a black and white drawing. One colour illustration of each polychrome bead type is given on Colour Plates III and IV, as well as one colour illustration of each colour which may occur in a number of forms of monochrome beads. The complete range of types present at Dover is illustrated in Text Figures 11 and 12. The only necklace of which part of the original order of the beads is certain is illustrated on Colour plate IV. Perforations are circular unless otherwise described, glass is to be regarded as opaque unless described as translucent (but see p 183), and trails and dots are usually marvered.

*Monochrome glass beads* (Tables IX and XIII Text Figure 11): The rust red colour (types BO1-9) was popular, occurring in a number of different forms, and achieving the second highest total of 71. Beads of this colour did not appear before phase 3, continued through phases 4, 5 and 6, but only five occurred in phase 7. Type BO4, the short cylinder (straight-sided) belonged mostly to phases 3 and 4 with one in phase 6, and BO5, the version with rounded sides occurred only in phases 6 and 7.

One distinctive type is orange, barrel-shaped or biconical, with a matt, porous appearance like pottery instead of the glossy surface usual to glass beads, but one only, 1/4f, has a smooth surface

---

108 Koch 1977 1, 71
109 Pirling 1974 1, 137; 2, Taf. 45, 3a, b. Taf. 126, 2; Taf. 55, 3a-d; Taf. 118, 3
110 Pirling 1974, 1, 137
111 Cook 1981, 48, 83, fig. 19, 25 and 16, pl. VII
112 Evison 1980c, 125
113 Lethbridge 1931, fig. 23.2
114 Austin *et al.* 1928, 185, where they are described as 'two very small bronze caps'
115 Evison 1976, 313, pl. LXV, e, f
116 Callmer 1977

(types B10–1). These occur with amethyst beads 53/1b (Figure 28), 67/1f (Figure 37), 132/2b (Figure 54), 133/1b and 2b (Figure 55), as they did on the Sarre necklace dated by coins to the first quarter of the seventh century mentioned above. At Dover they also occur with shell beads, 67/1f, 134/2e and 157/1e, and they are mainly confined to phase 5, with two in phase 4, grave 55 which has two amber beads on the same necklace, and grave 18 which has one amber bead (see below p 137). The earlier occurrence in grave 1 of phase 3 is the smooth-surfaced orange bead, no doubt of different origin.

The bright yellow colour (types B12–21) was used for a number of forms which together came to the largest total of any one colour of over 308. The main concentration was in phase 3, types B12, B13, B15, B17, B18 and B20, where grave 29 contained as many as 58, and grave 32 contained 49. Type B12 also appeared in phases 1, 2, 4, 5 and 6, type B13 in phases 1 and 5, type B14 in phase 4 and type B15 in phase 1. The short cylinders (straight-sided), and type B18, were limited to phase 3, and the single short cylinder with rounded sides was in phase 7.

The rest of the colour totals, including the translucent colours, are low, none of them exceeding 28, with one exception. These types of bead are smaller than the rest (B34–6): they are opaque blue-green, cylindrical in shape, and occur in unbroken double and treble forms as well as the single form[117]. They total 191, of which 79 came from one grave, 46, and 46 came from grave 32. All of the graves with types B34–6 belong to phase 3, with the exception of grave 46 in phase 1. Beads as tiny as this may have been overlooked in early excavations. One has recently been found in a hut of c AD 700 at Swindon in Wiltshire[118].

There are only 16 of the translucent, dark blue disc or annular beads B48 and B49 which occur frequently in late Roman and early Anglo-Saxon graves. These probably form part of the long-lasting group of annular beads noted by Guido as being in use from the sixth century BC to the eighth century AD[119]. Fourteen of these occur in phase 3 with one each in phases 5 and 6 (Table XIII). Some beads of this type also occur in fifth-century graves e.g., Howletts grave 26, and Mucking grave 355[120].

There are two melon beads, both dark green-blue (type B43), 141/6b and 129/5d. This form was in existence in this country in the first and second centuries AD, but then does not reappear until after the Roman period in Germanic contexts[121]. The Germanic melon beads are usually irregularly shaped, and occur in small numbers in Anglo-Saxon graves, as at Bergh Apton[122]. At Dover they occur in plots G and H, in phases 5 and 6.

Unusual monochrome beads include the large, very light green, annular bead which occurred singly in grave 83 (Figure 39), and the large, dark blue annular bead which was the only glass bead found with five of amber, in grave F (Figure 4). There are also four-sided beads: 48/4d (Figure 27), 62/4g (Figure 35), 133/2c (Figure 55), 155/2c (Figure 60), five-sided beads: 1/4q (Figure 5), 62/4i,j,k, (Figure 35), 133/2d (Figure 55) and a flat six-sided bead: 38/4d (Figure 22), all of which are forms known on Roman necklaces[123]. At Dover, one four-sided bead does in fact, occur in one of the earliest graves, 48, which contains other Roman pieces. The others occur in plots D, E, F and G, i.e. phases 3–5.

The only graves which do not contain monochrome beads are 92, where there was a necklace consisting mostly of amber beads but with some monochrome drawn beads, graves 13 and 14 which also had monochrome drawn beads, graves 12 and 49 which only had one bead each, 53 and 124 with amethysts, and 66 with a few amber beads only. The largest number of monochrome beads, i.e. 141, occurs in grave 46 of phase 1, and the other graves which contain between 141 and 49 are 29, 30 and 32 in a row together, and grave 1, all of phase 3. No grave of a later phase, except grave 6 in phase 5, contains more than 13 monochrome beads. Of the 39 blue-white or white beads, none makes an appearance before phase 3.

Some types of monochrome beads were formed by drawing, (Tables X and XIV). Amongst them are a few dark blue, cylindrical drawn beads in phases 1–3, plain, twisted or beaded[124]. There are also colourless or very light green translucent segmented beads which sometimes possess an inner gold or silver skin (types C04–13). These beads are often iridescent and disintegrated, so that it is not possible to be certain whether there had been a metallic inner skin or not. An inner tube of glass was drawn, coated with a gold or silver skin and an outer cover of glass, and then nipped at intervals to form segments which could be broken off into individual beads. They were known in Roman Britain from the second to the fourth century[125], and continued to appear in Germanic graves both here and on the Continent in the fifth and early sixth century[126], even later versions occurring in Viking graves. The source of supply was probably Egypt, and they were traded as far as Finland[127]. At Dover they occur in twelve graves (Table VII), nine of which also contain amber beads, all except one contain monochrome beads, two contain jet beads, two contain composition beads, and one a reticella bead. With the exception of three beads in grave 6 of phase 5, all these types are confined to phases 1–3, the very light green belonging mostly to phase 3, the colourless being distributed more evenly between

---

117 cf Guido 1978, 91–3, fig. 37, 2
118 Information from the excavator, Caroline Washbourn
119 Guido 1978, group 6, iva and b, 66–8
120 Evison 1978b, 263–4, fig. 2c–j
121 Guido 1978, 100, fig. 37, 21
122 Green and Rogerson 1978, fig. 69, Jvii; fig. 74, Dii; fig. 84, Hii; fig. 96, Lii, Lv

123 Guido 1978, fig. 37, 6–8, 11.
124 Ibid, 94–5, fig. 37, 4
125 Boon 1966; Boon 1977; Guido 1978, 93–4, fig. 37.3
126 Lethbridge 1931, 14, grave 21, fig. 8, 4
127 Koch 1974b, 500, Abb. 2

phases 1, 2 and 3, and the gilt ones belonging mainly to phase 1.

Graves which contain only monochrome glass beads and no other variety are almost exclusively limited to plot H, phase 6. The only exceptions are grave 161 in plot L, also in phase 6, and 83 in plot I, phase 7, which have one each, and 155 in plot G (phase 5) which has five. The number of beads in plot H is small, and limited in types to short cylinders and two discs. The beads in plot I are also mainly of short cylinder type. The bead in grave 83, however, is a large disc, and as it was found at the neck (with a pin), it could have functioned as a fastening or toggle. Other instances of a single large bead at the neck have been noticed.

The short cylinder type with straight sides does not appear in any of the early graves, and only begins in phase 3, where there is a total of 48, to be followed by only one each in phases 4 and 5. There is an increase in numbers in phase 6 (a total of 20) and phase 7 (a total of 8) but these beads, while retaining the same colours with the addition of green, exhibit a more rounded profile, with only three exceptions. It therefore appears that the straight-sided short cylinder beads were only available during the period 575–625. There then was a hiatus before a similar set of short-cylinder beads, made mostly from the same colour recipes, but with more rounded profile, were available between 675 and 750. These occurrences probably represent two shipments from abroad with an interval between of 75 to 100 years.

*Polychrome glass beads* (Tables XI and XV Text Figure 12): The rest of the beads are of glass in two or more colours. Polychrome beads have been studied with particular attention at the cemetery of Schretzheim[128]. Most of the types present were widely distributed throughout Europe, and some of the types found in that cemetery were also brought to England and some were buried at Dover. The colour reproductions of types published by Ursula Koch provide an accurate record for comparative purposes, and correspondences between Dover and Schretzheim beads are noted below, (Table XI). Correspondences with beads from other sites are also given, where illustrations and descriptions are sufficiently detailed to allow comparisons to be made with confidence, e.g. the water-colour pages of beads from Sarre, Kent show a number of the bead types found at Dover[129]. Most of the polychrome effects are achieved by surface application of trails and dots in various patterns. The trails occur as stripes, zig-zags, arcades (combed), and crossing trails. Sometimes the crossing trails are combined with a circumference trail, and sometimes with dots. Marvered dots also appear without trails.

A flat, white, disc bead with translucent blue spiral trails, as 59/3g (type DO1, Figure 33) was illustrated by Koch and described as a late Roman type although at Schretzheim it occurred on a necklace in grave 233 of *Stufe* IV (590/600–620/30)[130]. One was found with an early fifth-century cruciform brooch, a finger-ring and other beads in Site K, Guildford Road Estate, Colchester, Essex. Some other examples, including a few from Anglo-Saxon graves, of the fifth century at Holywell Row, Cambridgeshire, grave 39 and grave 47[132]: of the fifth or sixth century at Bergh Apton, Norfolk, grave 82[133], and in later graves of the seventh century at Harrold, Bedfordshire[134], Polhill, Kent[135], and Shudy Camps, Cambridgeshire, grave 121[136]. The type therefore appears to have figured on necklaces throughout the pagan period, see below (p 70). However, the bead 59/3g contained antimony, a constituent more general in the Roman period.

The polychrome beads occur in 21 graves (Table VII) as opposed to 40 graves which contained monochrome glass beads. They are found in plots A, B, D, E, F and G, i.e. in phases 1–5, but are not present in the rest of the cemetery and later phases.

Table XV shows the occurrence of the individual types of polychrome beads in the various phases. There are sporadic single occurrences of some types in phases 1 and 2, most of the polychrome beads and some of each variety occurred in phase 3, with fewer in phase 4 and less still in phase 5, and none at all after that save for the two in child's grave in phase 7. Of the four beads in phases 1 and 2, three (12/6, 13/3h and 23/4d) are aberrant variants of the types to which they are allocated, and the fourth, 92/3d in phase 2, is probably not very far in date from grave 93 in phase 3 which contained a similar bead. However, 92/3d and possibly also 13/3h contained antimony, which appears more often in Roman beads (see p 70). At Schretzheim the polychrome beads with crossing trails or crossing trails and dots belong mainly to *Stufe* IV 590/600–625/30[137], while at Dover, as they last from phase 3 to 5 (with one exception), they have a life from 575 to 675.

The mosaic beads have much in common with the millefiori beads (Text Figure 12 D57–61, D62–65), for the design goes right through to the core on both, as opposed to the other polychrome beads where the design of trails and dots etc is laid on the surface. The mosaic beads types D57–8, 30/4s, t, Text Figure

---

128  Koch 1974a; *idem* 1977 1, 71–2, Farbtafel 1–6, 2, distribution plans Taf. 234–45
129  Brent 1868, e.g. Amber pl. VII, XX, pl. VIII, IV, CCLX. Amethyst pl. VII, XX, pl. VIII, CCXX. Shell with corrugated edge pl. VII, CXXIX. ?Shell, rectangular pl. VII, CV. Glass: brown, yellow feathered trails, Dover 42/1i cf pl. VII, LXXVI; mosaic glass like Dover 30/4s,t but of a different colour, cf pl. VII, XXVII; millefiori Dover 53/1c cf pl. VIII, XIX.
130  Koch 1977, 1, 215, R1. Mistakenly reported as coming not from a grave but from a late Roman horizon by Guido, 1981, 11–12
131  Ibid, 11–12, fig. 13, 7
132  Lethbridge 1931, 21, fig. 10, A, 5; 25, fig. 11, F, 1
133  Green and Rogerson 1978, 48, fig. 99, 82, Bii
134  Eagles and Evison 1970, fig. 13j
135  Philp 1973a, fig. 55, 526, 528 and 529
136  Lethbridge 1936, 25, fig. 4, J, 3
137  Koch 1977 2, Taf. 242

64    THE BUCKLAND ANGLO-SAXON CEMETERY

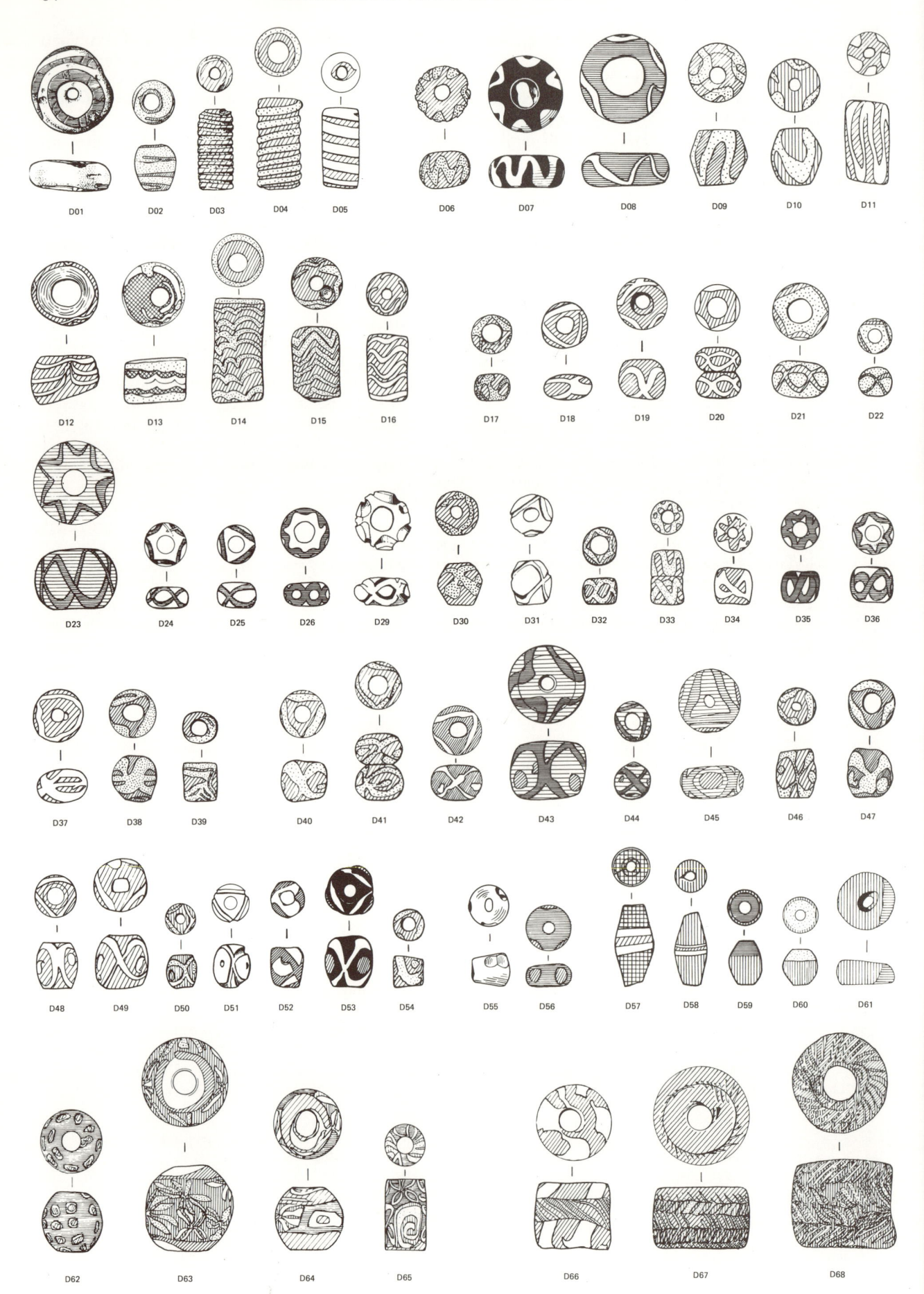

*Text Figure 12*    Dover: polychrome glass beads. Scale 1/1

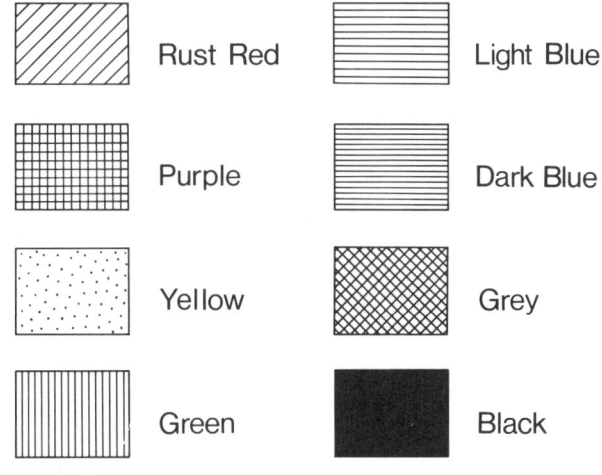

*Key to bead drawings*

- Rust Red
- Purple
- Yellow
- Green
- Light Blue
- Dark Blue
- Grey
- Black

12 are similar to a class referred to by Guido as 'Long blue biconical or square-sectioned beads with bands or chevrons in opaque white with a red line in the centre'[138], although the basic colours here are purple and green. Romano-British examples appear to belong to the third or fourth century, and Guido quotes some later Germanic examples from Stouting, Sussex and Canterbury, Kent[139] which are larger. Biconical examples of the same type at Schretzheim have different colour schemes[140]. Of the oval types of mosaic bead in two colours, D59–60, the bead illustrated by Koch[141] is green and yellow like 60/3t (Figure 34). The olive green disc bead type D61, 129/5i has an inclusion of blue glass which appears to be intentional, so that the bead is here considered to be mosaic.

The single globular translucent blue bead with white-collared red millefiori dots, type D62 (Text Figure 12), occurred in grave 38 of phase 3. The type also appears in continental contexts and continues into the Viking period. There are three other millefiori beads (Text Figure 12 D57–61, D62–65), (Figures 28, 54 and Figure 90) belonging to a fairly common and widespread basic group of high quality beads, which presumably issued from related production centres in view of similarity of shapes, and of the identity of colours and patterns used for the millefiori rods. The monochrome circumference rods are in red or colourless glass, while the millefiori rods in 53/1c (Figure 28) are of flowers, yellow on a green background and blue on white. In 132/2e (Figure 54) the yellow-on-green flowers reappear, combined with another composite rod of a red, white and blue spot, while in 132/2f (Figure 54) the blue-on-white flowers recur combined with an element of green and yellow spirals. All these elements appear on several of the beads on Koch Taf. 6.

At Schretzheim millefiori beads hardly occurred at all before AD 550, were most numerous (five or more on a necklace) in the period 565–600, and disappeared by the middle of the seventh century. At Dover they are rare, 38/4g belonging to phase 3, and the others to phase 5, i.e. 575–675.

Reticella beads appear on the necklaces of two women at Dover (types D66–7) (Figure 90). In grave 42 (Figure 24) the bead is cylindrical in form like those of Koch class 48, 5–14, and the middle red-and-yellow twist appears on the Schretzheim beads, but the two outer zones of thickly twisted pale blue and rust red do not. The bead in grave 92 (Figure 42) has twists of red and yellow, green and yellow, and red, green and yellow, all of which may be seen on the Schretzheim beads. A third example occurs in grave 93 (type D68) which is a man's grave, and as the reticella bead was not far from the sword pommel it presumably functioned as a sword bead (Figure 43)[142]. It also has red and green, and red, yellow and green twists, but the number of four bands of these contrasts with the five- or three-band composition of the Schretzheim beads. There the reticella beads occur mostly in the part of the cemetery deposited between 550 and 600[143], and this accords to a certain extent with the dating of the Dover graves between 525 and 650. Reticella beads have been found in a number of English graves, e.g. at Broadstairs[144], Bekesbourne (Canterbury Museum), and in a cremation at Sancton, Humberside (Yorkshire)[145].

Judging from the way in which identical elements of millefiori and reticella are used in varying combinations on different forms of bead, it would appear that the millefiori and reticella rods were manufactured at centres where the special techniques were practised, the finished rods then being exported to other districts where operators with less expertise were nevertheless able to make them malleable by heating and to work them up into beads.

*Discussion*

The varieties of beads found on one string were obviously limited by the types available for purchase during each ensuing period. Nevertheless, it looks as though a considerable amount of personal taste went into the selection. The woman in grave 38, for instance, selected amber for 70 of her 77 beads, and the woman in grave 92 also had a long string of amber beads. In grave 46 there was a large number of small beads, and, in contrast to most strings which consisted of beads with a miscellany of shapes and colours, these were more uniform in shape and size, and were all in greens and yellows.

Silver slip-knot rings are associated with some of the beads. The necklace in grave 29 (Figure 17) consisted of beads and pendants with a plain silver ring apparently at one end on the right shoulder and a silver slip-knot ring in the middle of the chest may

---

138 Guido 1978, 98–9, fig. 37, 15
139 Ibid, 98
140 Koch 1977 1, Farbtafel 6, M65, M66, M67
141 Ibid, Farbtafel 6, M73
142 Evison 1967a, 65, fig. 2b
143 Koch 1974a, fig. 2; Koch 1977, 1, 211
144 Hurd 1913, 16
145 Myres and Southern 1973, fig. 1. 2012; Myres 1977 2, fig. 2. 2012

have held the other end[146]. In grave 35 a silver slip-knot ring is in the middle of the beads on the chest, in grave 110 there is one with beads in a container between the knees, in grave 107 a silver ring fragment was with two beads at the neck, in grave 157 three silver slip-knot rings were with beads and an iron pin at the neck. These rings were therefore already being used in connection with necklaces about AD 600, but some are in graves about fifty years later, and only the necklace in grave 157, phase 5, consists of silver rings and a few beads in the manner noted as typical of the fashion of seventh-century graves[147].

As to the methods of wearing the necklaces, the beads were all found at the neck or on the chest, with a few exceptions where they must have been in a container, such as a purse or pocket, sometimes with other trinkets. They all seem to have been suspended in front, no beads having been found under the neck bones to indicate a continuous string round the neck. It was usually impossible to be certain of the order of stringing of the beads because the bones were partially or completely disintegrated and the beads had become displaced by falling and rolling. The method of suspension is not, however, immediately apparent as the fashion for wearing a pair of brooches, one on each shoulder, is not normal practice at Dover. A pin is frequently found among the beads on the chest, (in 19 graves) and may have a connected function, such as to fasten one end of the necklace. The positions of beads in relation to brooches are discussed below (p 69).

The distribution plans of beads (Figures 89, 90) show that necklaces were worn mainly in the sixth century. After that beads were rare, and were mainly limited to amethyst, metal, shell and monochrome glass. The wide variety of beads found at Dover is fairly well representative of the assortment usual in Anglo-Saxon graves. As to non-glass beads, amber and jet could have come from the North Sea coast and the white composition and metal beads were no doubt made by Kentish jewellers. The amethyst quartz and shell, however, came from further afield, possibly as far as India. Regarding the glass beads, it is impossible to be sure of the exact source of each kind, although probable production areas for some distinctive or complicated glass types are generally assumed: Egypt for the drawn beads, northern Italy for some polychrome, reticella and millefiori beads. Nevertheless convincing evidence for the manufacture of some glass beads has been found at several more northern places including Helgö and Birka in Sweden, Paviken in Gotland, Kaupang in Norway, Ribe in Denmark, Hedeby in Schleswig, Lagore Crannog and Garranes in Ireland, Brough of Birsay and Mote of Mark in Scotland and Dinas Powys in Wales[148]. Some of these workshops were operating at the time the Dover cemetery was in use, i.e. Lagore Crannog, Garranes, Brough of Birsay, Mote of Mark, Dinas Powys and Helgö. Some of the monochrome beads from Helgö are no doubt comparable, but most of the polychrome beads so far published[149] are not similar and probably belong to the Viking period. One exception is a type D42, a red disc with crossing white trails and dots[150].

Most important in regard to the Dover cemetery, however, is the site of Rothulfuashem in Holland, north-west of Leiden. Excavated in 1961, it has not yet been fully published, but a short mention of glass finds, accompanied by a colour photograph has appeared[151]. The photograph shows complete single and unseparated beads in the colours rust red, white, yellow and dark blue, together with partly-formed beads and rods from which they were made. The report mentions these finds, and also that pieces of the oven were found. Most of the beads are clearly types found at Dover, i.e.,

| | | | |
|---|---|---|---|
| B48 | dark blue disc | 30/4e | Colour Plate III |
| B57 | white disc | 35/5e | Figure 21 |
| B12–3 and triple | yellow disc | 46/3a | Figure 26 |
| B01 (double) | rust red disc | 29/2c | Figure 17 |
| D19, D34 | rust red, white crossing trails, disc and short cylinder | 42/1j 18/2g | Colour Plate IV |
| cf D05 cylinder | rust red, white stripes disc | 42/1g | Colour Plate III |
| D25, white | blue translucent crossing trails disc | 32/4l | Colour Plate IV |

Three beads together, apparently unseparated, are decorated with white crossing trails, and while one of them is rather disc-shaped or globular, one is cylindrical. Two others which appear to be stuck together are rust red, but each is decorated in a different pattern of a white trail. This shows how beads manufactured on the same rod were not necessarily uniform and could vary both in basic form and in decoration.

Although little has been published regarding this important site, there is enough evidence to show that beads were being fashioned there, but whether the manufacture was carried through the entire process from the raw materials, or whether imported glass rods, cullet and other ready made material only was used cannot be known until further details are available. The evidence which indicates a bead factory is the discovery of an oven, several unseparated beads, some split in half, and rods and waste fragments in the same colours as the finished beads. Beads manufactured near the Dutch coast could easily have been shipped over to England, but the movement of an itinerant bead-maker is just as likely.

Beliefs were current concerning the magical properties of most of the materials used for beads, e.g. amber, shell, fossils and semi-precious stones, and in the case of the glass beads the designs and colours were no doubt also significant, conjuring up such

---

146 cf a slip-knot ring at each end of a necklace at Holywell Row, Lethbridge 1931, fig. 1A
147 Hyslop 1963, 191, figs. 8, 9
148 Lundström 1976
149 Lundström 1961; Lundström and Lindeberg 1964; Lundström 1970; Lundström 1976; Lundström 1981
150 Ibid, fig. 12. 13022
151 Bloemers et al. 1981, 132

ideas as the 'evil eye'. Beads of various types therefore figure largely in Meaney's discussions of amulets. Regarding amber, it is suggested that its rarity in Christian period cemeteries was because ecclesiastics condemned its use as an amulet[152]. As at Dover the wearing of amber beads extended from the beginning of the cemetery up to about AD 625, and was in full force in the earliest Christian graves, if its termination was due to proscription it took a considerable time for the Christian dogma to register. There seems no reason why the subsequent beads of amethyst and shell should have been looked on with any more favour by the ecclesiastics. The reason is more likely to be, as also suggested by Meaney, that trade with the north which included amber, was losing ground to trade with the Mediterranean after the introduction of Christianity. Jet, crystal, amethyst, white material and shell beads as well as glass beads are also discussed by Meaney[153].

The positions of brooches, and of some pendants and beads are illustrated in Text Figure 13, and described below in the order of the phases to which they belong.

| Phase | Grave No. | Description |
|---|---|---|
| 1 | 13 | Square-headed brooch, nearly horizontal at mid neck, a second a few inches below and to the right. A large bead (3c) near head of upper brooch, the other beads in line between the two brooch heads. Small-long brooch on its side inside left humerus, and ring brooch at left elbow. |
| 1 | 20 | Disc brooch, pin, beads and bracteate mid neck, two square-headed brooches parallel to each other further down near the ?waist. |
| 1 | 48 | Button brooch mid neck, saucer brooch about 15cm below, a swag of iron chain and beads from one brooch to the other. |
| 2 | 14 | Disc brooch right of neck and beads between it and a perforated coin in horizontal line. |
| 2 | 92 | Disc brooch mid neck, a Frankish disc brooch six inches below: a scatter of small beads between the two brooches and a double vertical row of large amber beads pendent from the Frankish brooch, with a reticella bead at the bottom. |
| 3 | F | A pin, silver ring and bead together at mid neck, disc brooch below and beads between. |
| 3 | 1 | Disc brooch mid neck, pin and bracteate slightly towards right shoulder, beads to left and right of neck. |
| 3 | 29 | Disc brooch mid neck, silver ring at top right shoulder with gilt pendants, a garnet pendant and a coin pendant just below. A silver ring towards the middle of the chest, gold pendant by right elbow and beads between these items. The silver rings may have held the ends of the necklace, of which the gilt pendants, coin pendant and garnet pendant would have been the centre pieces of an upper string, and the gold pendant the centre piece of a lower string. |
| 3 | 30 | Disc brooch slightly left of mid neck with small silver pendant and silver pin just to right, and a swag of beads stretching from left shoulder to right shoulder. |
| 3 | 32 | Disc brooch mid neck: iron pin just below and a zone of beads, including a silver pendant, turning at right angles towards a bronze earscoop near mid waist. |
| 3 | 35 | Disc brooch and iron pin mid neck; zone of beads descending to left mid chest with silver gilt pendant and silver ring in the middle. |
| 3 | 38 | Disc brooch and pin together mid neck; beads nearby and extending to waist. |
| 3 | 59 | Disc brooch and pin mid neck, beads in a meandering line straight down to the waist. |
| 3 | 60 | Beads horizontal across neck to an iron pin on left shoulder, then beads (and a tiny bronze loop) straight down to left waist. |
| 4 | 62 | Bronze pin on right shoulder, beads in shallow swag. |
| 4 | 42 | Beads from one shoulder to the other, with a bronze pin in the middle. |
| 4 | 55 | Large bead right shoulder (1a), beads in shallow swag. |
| 5 | 129 | A bronze bracelet, perforated coin, bronze tag, beads and bronze pendant were all together on the right shoulder with a melon bead a few inches below. Presumably they were all part of a necklace. |
| 5 | 134 | Bracteate, two garnet pendants, beads and pin all together at neck. |
| 7 | 127 | Few beads together mid neck; a single red bead near mid waist. |

---

152 Meaney 1981, 70   153 Ibid, 71–82, 128, 192–210

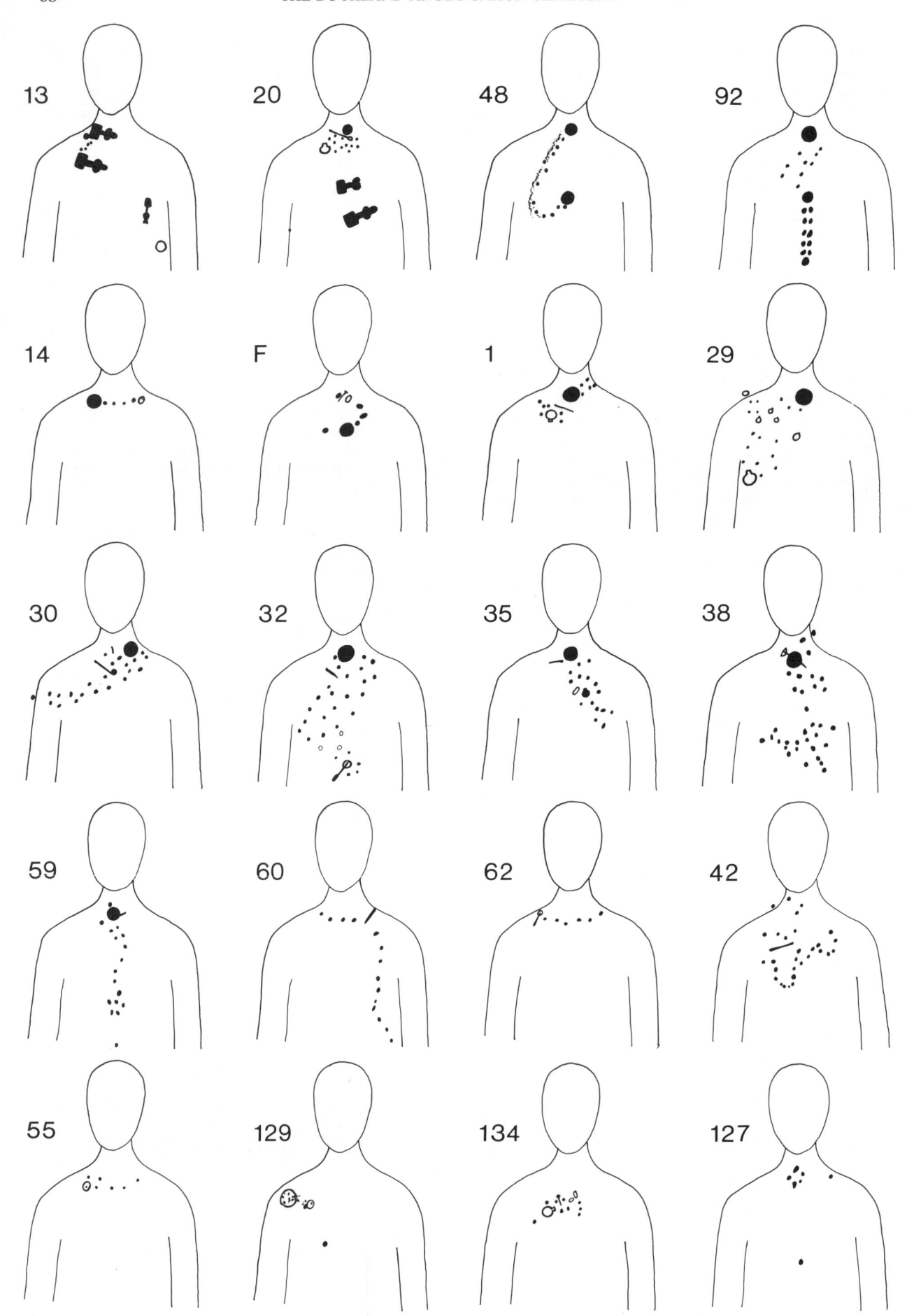

*Text Figure 13*   Dover: positions of beads and brooches in the graves

*Positions of brooches and beads*
In grave 13 a pair of square-headed brooches were pinned within a few inches of each other on the right shoulder and pointing at about 100°, a position most conveniently accomplished by a right-handed wearer (Text Figure 13). Their main function must therefore have been to fasten the edge of a garment, probably a cloak, but they also held a string of beads which extended from the head of one brooch to the other. The small-long brooch and ring brooch to the same grave were lower down on the left side of the chest, and may have been used to fasten a garment under the cloak. Traces of a fine braid or border were found under the small-long brooch (see p 190).

The child in grave 20 (Text Figure 13) was also wearing a cloak fastened by a pair of near horizontal square-headed brooches, this time without beads and lower down in the middle part of the chest. Beads and a bracteate were lying near a disc brooch and pin at the neck. In this cemetery a disc brooch is usually at the neck, and disc brooch and pin are often surrounded by beads, so that both these articles may have been used in the suspension of the necklace. The main function of the disc brooch at the neck, however, must have been to fasten a garment. In grave 13 the square-headed brooches were unconnected with the other two brooches, and in grave 20 the two square-headed brooches were some distance from the cluster of beads, disc brooch and pin, so that in both cases it is clear that the square-headed brooches would be visible on the cloak, but the other brooches, and in grave 20, the beads, were adorning the undergarment and were covered by the cloak. Both grave 13 and 20 belong to phase 1 of the cemetery.

In the same phase is grave 48, where a button brooch at the neck is connected to a saucer brooch in the middle of the chest by a swag of iron chain and beads. The garment closed by these brooches must have met in the middle.

In phase 2 the two disc brooches in grave 92 repeat this pattern, but a string of small amber and glass beads was suspended below the brooch at the neck and a double row of larger amber beads and one jet bead from the lower brooch, with a multi-coloured reticella bead at the lowest point. This seems to indicate two entirely separate strings of beads, which may have been worn one on an outer garment and one on an inner garment. In grave 14 the disc brooch is slightly to the right of the middle, and beads extend in a shallow festoon from this to a perforated coin on the left side of the neck.

In eight disc brooch graves of phase 3 the brooch is at, or very near, mid neck, (F, 1, 29, 30, 32, 35, 38, 59). Nearby, in seven of the graves, there is a pin, and the brooch and pin may have held the two ends of the string on which the beads were threaded. Candidates for this function also are two rings in 29 and one in F and 35. In 29, at the lowest point of the beads, was a gold bracteate, presumably the centre piece of the necklace. The centre piece in 32, however, was a bronze ear scoop.

The beads in grave 59 were lying undisturbed in their original sequence for part of the length of the necklace showing that, although the arrangement was not regular, the large amber and cylindrical glass beads were interspersed with a run of smaller beads (Colour Plate IV). The disc brooch, pin and large blue and white bead were at the neck, with a string of beads hanging straight down the chest in a single line. The larger beads are amber and cylindrical rust-coloured glass paste with yellow or white trails. These are placed so that three times two of them are situated together with only one bead separating them, and in between are the smaller disc beads including the blue ones. In this way a pattern or symmetry of size and colour was arrived at as far as is possible with beads which are basically not uniform in size or shape. The beads were lying in the order in which they had been strung, but it is possible that the action of the digging of grave 58 could have moved the beads, still on their original string, from a festooned or other position to the straight line. Such a theoretical explanation is unnecessary, however, for it is a style of wearing beads which does occur in other graves in the cemetery.

In graves 55 (phase 4) and 62 (phase 4) there is a short swag of beads across the neck, with possible terminal points in a large bead in 55 and a pin in 62. There is a small bead cluster in 127 (phase 7), in 129 (phase 5) it is combined with a bracelet, tag end, pendant spatula and coin, and in 134 (phase 5) with pendants and pin. A single bead separate from the bead cluster at the neck and in mid chest position in graves 127 and 129 may have acted as a button or toggle.

In an unusual arrangement in grave 60 (phase 3) a line of beads crosses the neck to a pin on the left shoulder, then falls straight down to the waist. It seems likely that most of the beads in this cemetery were worn threaded on a string, but some could have been sewn as edging on a double-breasted garment, the corner of which was fastened on the left shoulder by a pin. Support for the theory of attachment by sewing is the flat fragment of glass found among beads, 59/3q, which has no perforation for threading, and in this grave, also, the beads are in a vertical line.

It is likely that most of the beads were strung with a single thread so that the necklace hung in a swag across the chest. Alternative methods are also possible, and it is probable that the amethyst quartz beads were strung with double thread stopped at the bottom by a knot or small bead, so that they were in a vertical or pendant position. In this way they would be imitating the contemporary Byzantine court fashion for pendant amethysts and other jewels on necklaces, earrings and brooches, a fashion illustrated in mosaics, on the 'chemise' of Bathild and by extant necklaces[154]. The necklace in grave 67

---

154 Vierck 1978b, pls. I, II and III

was provided with other pendants as well as the amethysts, for there were also silver disc pendants and a garnet pendant set in gold.

Where one large bead occurs alone, it is possible that it was used as a toggle or fastening, e.g. at the neck of a woman 83/1. The large cylindrical apatite bead found with the wooden belt under the bronze bowl was probably used as a toggle to the thread lacing the belt (Text Figure 16). The cylindrical reticella bead 93/1 (Figure 43) was in a man's grave near the sword hilt, and may also have functioned as a kind of fastening as part of the 'peace strings', unless its function was purely magical.

*Analysis of the beads*

A report by Miss Justine Bayley, Ancient Monuments Laboratory, on analyses of some of the beads is fully quoted on p 182. From the monochrome beads at least one example was selected of each colour for analysis, and from the polychrome beads one of each type. No sign of antimony was detected in any of the monochrome beads, not even amongst some of the shapes which existed in the Roman period and which might have been survivals from that time.

The yellow beads were exceptional as they contained a much higher level of lead than beads of other colours. Yellow beads from Faversham and Haslingfield have been noted as having similar compositions to the yellow enamels in hanging bowl escutcheons from Northumberland, Benty Grange and Great Barton[155], and the composition of the Dover beads is also similar[156].

On the whole, the examination of the polychrome beads suggests that the compositions of the various colours in their make-up follow closely those of the same colours in the monochrome beads. Also, there is, perhaps surprisingly, no discernible difference in general between the compositions of the more simple trail-and-dot decorated polychrome beads and the more sophisticated millefiori, mosaic and reticella beads which have often been attributed to Mediterranean or Middle East sources. As might have been expected, the unique purple colour of the mosaic bead 30/4s was achieved by manganese, but in the bead of matching pattern in dark green glass instead of purple, 30/4t, the manganese content was also high.

Four polychrome beads out of a total of 37 contained antimony, and two showed possible traces of antimony. One of the reticella beads 92/3d contained antimony, but there was no trace of it in the other two reticella beads analysed, 93/1 and 42/1t, or in the mosaic or millefiori beads. The other polychrome beads containing antimony are simple types, three are decorated with trails only: 59/3g a white disc with a dark blue translucent spiral, 133/2e a black disc with a white zigzag (possible traces only), and 133/1c, annular dark blue translucent with a white zigzag. Bead 157/1f, a blue disc with rust red dots, also contained antimony. Each of these four is the only example of that particular type in the cemetery, and each one is a type which has been found in Roman contexts. The bead 59/3g has been discussed above, disc beads with zigzag trail decoration like 133/2e and 133/1c have been found in Roman graves at Krefeld-Gellep[157], and a disc bead with marvered dots like 157/1f has also appeared in a Roman grave in the same cemetery[158]. They may, therefore, very well be Roman survivals, although the graves in which they occurred at Dover are as late as phase 3 and phase 5.

The decoration of the remaining bead possibly containing antimony, 13/3h, a light blue disc, with blue translucent crossing trails and rust red dots, is a combination of the trail and dot patterns occurring separately on 133/2e, 13/1c and 157/1f, and so would have been within the normal technical range of a Roman period bead-maker, although the pattern is common in the Anglo-Saxon period. As the grave is one of the earliest in the cemetery, belonging to phase 1, the possibility that the bead might have been a Roman survival is quite strong. If it can be accepted that these beads are Roman, these findings accord with the conclusion that antimony was used as an opacifier down into the Roman period, but only exceptionally in later periods (see p 186). Miss Bayley's examination of beads in the Anglo-Saxon cemeteries at Portway, Andover, Hampshire, and Sewerby, Yorkshire, detected no antimony present in the polychrome beads, although it was present in some of the monochrome beads.

The only other trace of antimony was found in the fragment of green-blue glass 59/3q, which was further distinguished by the unique occurrence of arsenic. The presence of a probable Roman bead in the same grave, discussed above, might be regarded as increasing the probability that this fragment also was Roman. There are other possibilities, however, such as a Mediterranean centre where Roman traditions were maintained, and as the composition is so unusual, judgement should be suspended until comparable analyses are available. Moreover, as the reticella bead 92/3d contained antimony, and it does not seem to be a type which occurred in the Roman period, it provides further evidence for the continuance of the use of antimony after AD 400. Two other beads of the Merovingian period found at Cleavel Point, Dorset contained antimony, one a flower-pattern millefiori, and the other in opaque red and blue[159], so adding to the evidence which will no doubt be increased as investigations continue.

---

155 Brown 1981, 231
156 Information regarding the Faversham and Haslingfield beads from Dr Hughes, BM Research Laboratory.
157 Pirling 1966 1, Abb. 13. 25
158 Pirling 1974 1, Abb. 4, 5
159 Biek 1983, 308–9

TABLE VIII  NON-GLASS BEADS (Text Figure 11, Colour Plate III)

| Type No. | Material | Shape | Grave and catalogue number | Quantity in each grave | Totals | Figs. |
|---|---|---|---|---|---|---|
| A01 | Amber | Small roughly-shaped | 23/4a, 29/2a, 35/5a, 48/4b, 92/3e | 1 | 24 | 15, 17, 21, 27, 42 |
|  |  |  | 14/3a | 4 |  | 10 |
|  |  |  | 20/5a | 15 |  | 12 |
| A02 | Amber | Roughly-shaped | 35/5b | 1 |  | 21 |
|  |  |  | 49/1a | 1 + frags. |  | 28 |
|  |  |  | 29/2b, 55/1a | 2 |  | 17, 30 |
|  |  |  | 13/3a, 59/3a, 62/4a | 3 |  | 9, 33, 35 |
|  |  |  | 1/4b | 4 |  | 5 |
|  |  |  | F/4a | 5 |  | 4 |
|  |  |  | 20/5b, 48/4c, 12a | 6 | 247 + | 12, 27 |
|  |  |  | 66/1, 60/2a, 3a, 11 | 7 | 275 + | 37, 34 |
|  |  |  | 30/4a | 14 |  | 18 |
|  |  |  | 42/1a | 17 |  | 24 |
|  |  |  | 14/3b | 23 |  | 10 |
|  |  |  | 38/4a | 70 |  | 22 |
|  |  |  | 92/3a, f | 73 + frags. |  | 42 |
| A03 | Amber | Disc | 18/2a | 1 | 3 | 11 |
|  |  |  | 1/4a | 2 |  | 5 |
| A04 | Amber | Wedge-shaped | 48/4a | 1 | 1 | 27 |
| A05 | Amethyst | Small almond-shaped | 75/1a | 1 |  | 38 |
|  |  |  | 127/1a | 2 |  | 52 |
|  |  |  | 67/1a | 3 | 12 | 37 |
|  |  |  | 132/2a | 6 | 22 | 54 |
| A06 | Amethyst | Large almond-shaped | 124/1, 133/2a | 2 | 10 | 51, 55 |
|  |  |  | 53/1a, 75/1b | 3 |  | 28, 38 |
| A07 | Jet | Faceted | 13/3b | 1 | 1 | 2 | 9 |
| A08 | Jet | Disc with nicked decoration | 92/3b | 1 | 1 |  | 42 |
| A09 | Stone | Disc white, marbled grey | 55/1b | 1 | 1 | 1 | 30 |
| A10 | Coral | Cup coral | 55/1c | 1 | 1 | 1 | 30 |
| A11 | Fossil | Porosphaera | 129/5b | 1 | 1 | 1 | 53 |
| A12 | Shell | Corrugated edge | 6/10a | 1 |  | 7 |
|  |  |  | 157/1a | 1 + frags. | 4 + | 61 |
|  |  |  | 67/1b | 2 |  | 37 |
| A13 | Shell | Hemispherical with central perforation | 75/1c | 1 | 1 | 13 + | 38 |
| A14 | Shell | 4-sided cylinder | 134/2a | 2 | 2 |  | 55 |
| A15 | Shell | Roughly rectangular | 67/1c | 4 | 4 |  | 37 |
| A16 | Shell | Small pendant | 141/5 | 1 | 2 + | 58 |
|  |  |  | 129/5a | 1 + frag. |  | 53 |
| A17 | White composition apatite | Large short cylinder | 20/18 | 1 | 1 | 2 | 13 |
| A18 | Magnesium carbonate | Large short cylinder | 14/3c | 1 | 1 |  | 10 |
| A19 | Metal bronze | Conical halves | 67/5, 129/6, 7 | 3 | 6 | 9 | 37, 53 |
| A20 | silver | Conical halves | 133/1a | 3 | 3 |  | 55 |

TABLE IX   MONOCHROME GLASS BEADS (Text Figure 11, Colour Plate III)

| Type No. | Colour | Shape | Grave and catalogue number | Quantity in each grave | Totals | Figs. |
|---|---|---|---|---|---|---|
| B01 | Rust Red | Disc | 29/2c, 38/4b, 141/6a, UN/4 | 1 | 26 | 17, 22, 58, 64 |
| | | | 75/1d, 155/2a | 2 | | 38, 60 |
| | | | 59/3b | 6 | | 33 |
| | | | 30/4b | 12 | | 18 |
| B02 | Rust Red | Barrel | 67/1e | 3 | 8 | 37 |
| | | | 18/2b | 5 | | 11 |
| B03 | Rust Red | Biconical | 1/4g | 1 | 1 | 5 |
| B04 | Rust Red | Short cylinder (straight sided) | 107/6b | 1 | 15 | 48 |
| | | | 62/4f | 2 | | 35 |
| | | | 1/4i | 4 | | 5 |
| | | | 60/3f | 8 | | 34 |
| B05 | Rust Red | Short cylinder (rounded) | 160/2a | 1 | 10 | 62 |
| | | | 127/1b, c | 3 | | 52 |
| | | | 110/12a | 6 | | 49 |
| B06 | Rust Red | Short cylinder (double) | 29/2g | 1 | 1 | 17 |
| B07 | Rust Red | Cylinder | 6/10f | 7 | 7 | 7 |
| B08 | Rust Red | Short 4-sided cylinder | 155/2c | 1 | 1 | 60 |
| B09 | Rust Red | 4-sided cylinder | 62/4h, 133/2c | 1 | 2 | 35, 55 |
| B10 | Orange | Barrel | 1/4f | 1 | 20 | 5 |
| | | | 18/2c, 132/2b, 134/2e | 2 | | 11, 54, 55 |
| | | | 53/1b, 67/1f | | | 28, 37 |
| | | | 133/1b, 2b | 4 | | 55 |
| | | | | 5 | | |
| B11 | Orange | Biconical | 55/1e | 1 | 3 | 30 |
| | | | 157/1e | 2 | | 61 |
| B12 | Yellow | Disc | B/1, 20/5c, 55/1d, 107/6a, 134/2b | 1 | 211 + | 1, 12, 30, 48, 55 |
| | | | 23/4b | 2 | | 15 |
| | | | 62/4b | 3 + frag. | | 35 |
| | | | 35/5c | 4 | | 21 |
| | | | 60/2b, 3b | 5 + frag. | | 34 |
| | | | 42/1b | 7 | | 24 |
| | | | 59/3c | 9 | | 33 |
| | | | 30/4c | 12 | | 18 |
| | | | 6/10b | 18 | | 7 |
| | | | 46/3a | 39 | | 26 |
| | | | 32/4a | 49 | | 19 |
| | | | 29/2d | 58 | | 17 |
| B13 | Yellow | Disc (double) | 35/5d | 1 | 36 | 21 |
| | | | 6/10c | 5 | | 7 |
| | | | 32/4b | 9 | | 19 |
| | | | 46/3b | 10 | | 26 |
| | | | 29/2e | 11 | | 17 |
| B14 | Yellow | Annular (double) | 42/1c | 1 | 1 | 24 |
| B15 | Yellow | Globular | 1/4e, 46/3c | 4 | 22 | 5, 26 |
| | | | 32/4c | 14 | | 19 |
| B16 | Yellow | Barrel | 62/4e | 1 | 1 | 35 |

Totals (right column grouping): 71, 23, 308 +

# GRAVE GOODS: DISCUSSION OF TYPES

| Type No. | Colour | Shape | Grave and catalogue number | Quantity in each grave | | Totals | Figs. |
|---|---|---|---|---|---|---|---|
| B17 | Yellow | Biconical | 1/4h | 1 | 1 | | 5 |
| B18 | Yellow | Short cylinder (straight sided) | 32/4d<br>1/4j<br>29/2h, 60/3g | 1<br>2<br>4 | 11 | | 19<br>5<br>17, 34 |
| B19 | Yellow | Short cylinder (rounded) | 76/1a | 1 | 1 | | 39 |
| B20 | Yellow | Cylinder | 1/4p | 17 | 17 | | 5 |
| B21 | Yellow | Pentagonal cylinder | 62/4i | 6 | 6 | | 35 |
| B22 | Yellow translucent | Disc | 157/1b | 1 | 1 | 1 | 61 |
| B23 | Very lt. green translucent | Disc | 83/1, 134/2c, 157/1c | 1 | 3 | 5 | 39, 55, 61 |
| B24 | | 4-sided cylinder | 48/4d | 2 | 2 | | 27 |
| B25 | Lt. green | Pentagonal cylinder | 133/2d | 1 | 1 | 1 | 55 |
| B26 | Lt. green translucent | Disc | 6/10d | 1 | 1 | 1 | 7 |
| B27 | Green | Disc | 20/5d, 23/4c<br>134/2d, 155/2b | 1<br>2 | 6 | | 12, 15<br>55, 60 |
| B28 | Green | Globular | 75/1e | 1 | 1 | 19 + | 38 |
| B29 | Green | Short cylinder (rounded) | 127/1d<br>75/1f, 110/12b<br>160/2b | 1<br>2<br>3 | 8 | | 52<br>38, 49<br>62 |
| B30 | Green | Short cylinder (double) | 29/2i | 2 | 2 | | 17 |
| B31 | Green | Cylinder | 30/4i<br>20/5g | 1<br>1 + frags. | 2 + | | 18<br>12 |
| B32 | Dk. Green | Globular | 55/1e | 1 | 1 | 3 | 30 |
| B33 | Dk. green | Biconical | 30/4h, 129/5e | 1 | 2 | | 18, 53 |
| B34 | Blue-green | Small short cylinder | 35/5f<br>29/2j<br>1/4k<br>32/4e<br>46/3d | 1<br>3<br>27<br>46<br>79 | 156 | | 21<br>17<br>5<br>19<br>26 |
| B35 | Blue-green | Small short cylinder (double) | 46/3e<br>32/4f<br>1/4l | 9<br>10<br>12 | 31 | 192 | 26<br>19<br>5 |
| B36 | Blue-green | Small short cylinder (triple) | 32/4g<br>1/4m | 1<br>3 | 4 | | 19<br>5 |
| B37 | Blue-green | Flat hexagonal | 38/4d | 1 | 1 | | 22 |
| B38 | Dk. blue-green | Cylinder | 55/1g | 1 | 1 | 1 | 30 |
| B39 | Lt. green-blue | Barrel | UN/5 | 1 | 1 | 1 | 64 |
| B40 | Green-blue | Disc | 1/4 | 1 | 1 | | 5 |
| B41 | Green-blue | Barrel | 18/2d, 132/2c | 2 | 4 | 7 | 11, 54 |
| B42 | Green-blue | Short cylinder (straight sided) | 110/12c | 2 | 2 | | 49 |

| Type No. | Colour | Shape | Grave and catalogue number | Quantity in each grave | Totals | | Figs. |
|---|---|---|---|---|---|---|---|
| B43 | Dk. green-blue | Melon | 129/5d, 141/6b | 1 | 2 | 3 | 53, 58 |
| B44 | Dk. green-blue | Biconical | 129/5f | 1 | 1 | | 53 |
| B45 | Blue | Disc | 29/2f<br>30/4d<br>59/3d | 2<br>7<br>8 | 17 | | 17<br>18<br>33 |
| B46 | Blue | Short cylinder (straight sided) | 29/2k, 32/4h, 60/3h<br>1/4n | 1<br>3 | 6 | 28 | 17, 19, 34<br>5 |
| B47 | Blue | Pentagonal cylinder | 1/4q<br>62/4j | 1<br>4 | 5 | | 5<br>35 |
| B48 | Dk. blue translucent | Disc | 60/3c, 161/5<br>38/4c, 59/3e<br>30/4e | 1<br>2<br>8 | 14 | | 34, 63<br>22, 33<br>18 |
| B49 | Dk. blue translucent | Annular | F/4b, 67/1d | 1 | 2 | 22 | 4, 37 |
| B50 | Dk. blue translucent | Short cylinder (straight sided) | 60/2c, 3i | 4 | 4 | | 34 |
| B51 | | Cylinder | 20/5h, 30/4j | 1 | 2 | | 12, 18 |
| B52 | Blue-white | Disc | 60/3d, 62/4c, 129/5c<br>59/3f<br>30/4f | 1<br>3<br>6 | 12 | | 34, 35, 53<br>33<br>18 |
| B53 | Blue-white | Biconical | 129/5g | 1 | 1 | | 53 |
| B54 | Blue-white | Short cylinder (straight sided) | 35/5g, 67/1g<br>60/3j<br>1/4o | 1<br>3<br>5 | 10 | 28 | 21, 37<br>34<br>5 |
| B55 | Blue-white | Short cylinder (rounded) | 127/1e<br>110/12d | 1<br>3 | 4 | | 52<br>49 |
| B56 | Blue-white | Cylinder | 62/4g | 1 | 1 | | 35 |
| B57 | White | Disc | 1/4d, 6/10e, 35/5e | 1 | 3 | | 5, 7, 21 |
| B58 | White | Short cylinder (straight sided) | 29/2l, 42/1d<br>35/5h | 1<br>2 | 4 | 11 | 17, 24<br>21 |
| B59 | White | Short cylinder (rounded) | 160/2c | 2 | 2 | | 62 |
| B60 | White | Pentagonal cylinder | 62/4k | 2 | 2 | | 35 |
| B61 | Black | Disc | 30/4g, 62/4d, 157/1d<br>20/5e, 60/3e | 1<br>2 | 7 | | 18, 35, 61<br>12, 34 |
| B62 | Black | Cylinder | 60/3k | 1 | 1 | 9 | 34 |
| B63 | Black | Coiled cylinder | 15/7a | 1 | 1 | | 11 |
| B64 | Colourless | Annular | 20/5f | 1 | 1 | 1 | 12 |
| B65 | Colour uncertain | Cylinder | 20/5i | 1 | 1 | 1 | 12 |

TABLE X   DRAWN GLASS BEADS (Text Figure 11, Colour Plate III)

| Type No. | Colour | Shape | Grave and catalogue number | Quantity in each grave | | Totals | Figs. |
|---|---|---|---|---|---|---|---|
| C01 | Dk. blue translucent | Cylinder | 38/4e<br>60/3n, 92/3c, k<br>13/3e<br>20/5n, 48/4i, 12b<br>15/7b | 1<br>2<br>3<br>4<br>6 | 22 | 27 | 22<br>34, 42<br>9<br>12, 27<br>11 |
| C02 | Dk. blue translucent | Beaded cylinder | 13/3f, 48/4j | 1 | 2 | | 9, 27 |
| C03 | Dk. blue translucent | Twisted cylinder | 13/3g, 15/7c, 48/12c | 1 | 3 | | 9, 11, 27 |
| C04 | Very lt. green translucent | Globular | 6/10g<br>29/2m<br>1/4s<br>46/3f<br>35/5i<br>32/4i | 1<br>2<br>13<br>14<br>22<br>24 | 76 | 76 | 7<br>17<br>5<br>26<br>21<br>19 |
| C05 | Colourless | Globular | 60/3l<br>29/2n, 48/4e, 92/3g<br>14/3d | 1<br>2<br>6 | 13 | | 34<br>17, 27, 42<br>10 |
| C06 | Colourless | Globular (double) | 60/3m<br>92/3h<br>14/3e | 1<br>2<br>5 | 8 | 29 | 34<br>42<br>10 |
| C07 | Colourless | Globular (triple) | 92/3i<br>48/4f | 1<br>2 | 3 | | 42<br>27 |
| C08 | Colourless | Globular (quadruple) | 48/4g, 92/3j | 1 | 2 | | 27, 42 |
| C09 | Colourless | Beaded cylinder | 29/2o, 48/4k, 92/3l | 1 | 3 | | 17, 27, 42 |
| C10 | Colourless gilt | Globular | 6/10h<br>20/5j<br>46/3g<br>32/4j<br>35/5j | 2<br>8<br>24<br>27<br>30 | 91 | | 7<br>12<br>26<br>19<br>21 |
| C11 | Colourless gilt | Globular (double) | 13/3c, 48/4h<br>20/5k | 1<br>8 | 10 | 112 | 9, 27<br>12 |
| C12 | Colourless gilt | Globular (triple) | 20/5l<br>13/3d | 4<br>6 | 10 | | 12<br>9 |
| C13 | Colourless gilt | Globular (quadruple) | 20/5m | 1 | 1 | | 12 |

TABLE XI  POLYCHROME GLASS BEADS (Text Figure 12, Colour Plates III, IV)

| Type No. | Pattern | Colour | Decoration | Shape | Grave and catalogue number | Quantity in each grave | Total | Fig. | Parallels |
|---|---|---|---|---|---|---|---|---|---|
| D01 | Stripes | White | Dk. blue translucent | Disc | 59/3g | 1 | | 33 | K.R1; P.fig.55.526; G.fig.99. 82Bii; CR. fig. 13.7; E.fig.13j; L.fig.10A5; K.42.18* |
| D02 | | Rust red | Yellow | Barrel | 42/1e | 1 | | 24 | |
| | | | | | 59/3h | | | 33 | |
| D03 | | Rust red | Yellow | Cylinder | 42/1f | 1 | 9 | 24 | K.42.21*; S.pl.XXII.V. 65-h; G.fig.89.44Ki |
| D04 | | Rust red (Unmarvered) | Yellow | Cylinder | 62/41 | 1 | | 35 | K.42.21; S.pl.XXIII. S.1-k; G.fig.89.44Ki |
| D05 | | Rust red | White | Cylinder | 59/3i | 1 | | 33 | K.42.13*; S.pl.XXII.V. 65-h; G.fig.89.44Ki |
| | | | | | 42/1g | 3 | | 24 | |
| D06 | Zig-zag trails | Rust red | Yellow | Disc | 30/4k | 1 | | 18 | |
| D07 | | Black | White | Disc | 133/2e | 1 | | 55 | K.27.12*; G.fig.69.7.Jviii |
| D08 | | Dk. blue translucent | White | Annular | 133/1c | 1 | 11 | 55 | K.27.10 |
| D09 | | Rust red | Yellow | Biconical | UN/15 | 1 | | 65 | S.pl.XXII.V.45-c |
| D10 | | Lt. green | Yellow | Biconical | 1/4t | 2 | | 5 | |
| D11 | | Rust red | White | Cylinder | 42/1h | 5 | | 24 | K.29.4 |
| D12 | Combed trails | Rust red | White | Disc | 12/6 | 1 | | 8 | |
| D13 | | Dk. grey | Yellow trails, combed white | Short cylinder | 76/1b | 2 | | 39 | J.Gr.21 fig.51.pl.2 |
| D14 | | Rust red | Yellow | Cylinder | 42/1i | 2 | 11 | 24 | K.49.11*; S.pl.XXIII.S. 1-e |
| | | | | | 59/3j | 3 | | 33 | |
| D15 | | Rust red | Yellow | Cylinder | 59/3k | 1 | | 33 | K.50.8* |
| D16 | | Rust red | White | Cylinder | 1/4u | 2 | | 5 | K.49.8*; C.pl.8.B.2030 |
| D17 | Crossing trails | Rust red | Yellow | Disc | 32/4k | 1 | | 19 | K.34.18* |
| D18 | | Rust red | White | Disc | 1/4v | 2 | | 5 | K.33.10* and K.34.11* |
| D19 | | Rust red | White | Disc | 42/1j | 1 | | 24 | K.34.12 |
| D20 | | Rust red | White | Disc (double) | 1/4w | 1 | | 5 | K.34.11; G.fig.93.56.Avi |
| | | | | | 30/4l | 2 | | 18 | |
| D21 | | Yellow | Rust red | Disc | 30/4m | 1 | | 18 | K.34.9*; C.colour pl.I. B.2230 |
| D22 | | Yellow | Rust red | Disc | 38/4f, 60/3o | 1 | | 22, 34 | K.33.7 |
| D23 | | Lt. blue | Blue translucent | Disc | 42/1k | 2 | | 24 | K.34.5 |
| D24 | | Blue-white | Blue translucent | Disc | 60/3p | 3 | | 34 | K.34.1; G.fig.93.59.Di |
| D25 | | White | Blue translucent | Disc | 32/41 | 1 | | 19 | K.33.3* or 33.5* |
| D26 | | White | Blue translucent | Disc | 1/4x, 60/3q, 134/2f | 1 | 45 | 5, 34, 55 | K.34.1* or 34.5*; G. fig.93. 59.Di |
| | | | | | 32/4m | 4 | | 19 | |
| D27 | | White | Trails missing | Disc | 1/4y | 2 | | — | K.34.1 or 34.5 and K.33.3 or 33.5 |
| D28 | | White | Trails missing | Disc | 60/3r | 1 | | — | K.33.3 or 33.5 |
| D29 | | Blue-white | Trails missing | Annular | 42/11 | 1 | | 24 | K.34.5 |

# GRAVE GOODS: DISCUSSION OF TYPES

| Type No. | Pattern | Colour | Decoration | Shape | Grave and catalogue number | Quantity in each grave | Total | Fig. | Parallels |
|---|---|---|---|---|---|---|---|---|---|
| D30 | | Rust red | Yellow | Barrel | 30/4n | 1 | | 18 | K.33.14 |
| D31 | | Blue-white | Trails missing | Barrel | 42/1m | 2 | | 24 | |
| D32 | | Rust red | Yellow | Short cylinder | 32/4n | 3 | | 19 | K.34.20* |
| | | | | | 18/2e | 4 | | 11 | K.34.20 |
| D33 | | Rust red | Yellow | Short cylinder (double) | 18/2f | 1 | | 11 | |
| D34 | | Rust red | White | Short cylinder | 18/2g | 2 | | 11 | K.34.14* |
| D35 | | Blue-white | Green-blue translucent | Short cylinder | 18/2h | 2 | | 11 | K.34.6* |
| D36 | | White | Blue translucent | Short cylinder | 55/1h | 1 | | 30 | K.34.6 |
| | | | | | 32/4o | 2 | | 19 | |
| D37 | Crossing trails and circumference trail | Rust red | White | Disc | 1/4z | 2 | 5 | 5 | |
| D38 | | Rust red | Yellow | Barrel | 30/4o | 1 | | 18 | K.35.2* |
| | | | | | 59/3l | | | 33 | |
| D39 | | Rust red | Yellow | Short cylinder | 29/2p | 1 | | 17 | |
| D40 | Crossing trails and dots | Rust red | Yellow | Disc | 42/1n | 1 | | 24 | K.20.4 |
| | | | | | 30/4p | 3 | | 18 | |
| D41 | | Rust red | Yellow | Disc (double) | 30/4q | 4 | | 18 | K.20.4 |
| D42 | | Rust red | White | Disc | 59/3m | 2 | | 33 | |
| D43 | | Lt. blue | Blue translucent, rust red dots | Disc | 13/3h | 1 | | 9 | K.21.1 or 21.2 |
| D44 | | Lt. blue | Blue translucent, rust red dots | Disc | 29/2q | 1 | | 17 | K.21.2 |
| D45 | | Lt. blue | Blue translucent, rust red dots | Disc | 132/2d | 1 | | 54 | K. series 21 |
| D46 | | Rust red | Yellow | Barrel | 1/4z¹, 42/1o | 3 | | 5, 24 | K.20.7* |
| D47 | | Rust red | Yellow | Barrel | 59/3n | 2 | 39 | 33 | K.20.4 |
| D48 | | Rust red | White | Barrel | 42/1p | 3 | | 24 | K.20.2* |
| | | | | | 1/4z² | 4 | | 5 | |
| D49 | | Rust red | White | Barrel | 29/2r, 59/3o, 60/1 3s | 17, 33, 34 | | | K.20.1 (one with trails and dots unmarvered) |
| | | | | | 30/4r | 2 | | 18 | |
| D50 | | Dk. green | Yellow | Barrel | 35/5k | 1 | | 21 | |
| D51 | | Blue-white | Trails and dots missing | Barrel | 42/1q | 1 | | 24 | |
| D52 | | White | Rust red | Barrel | 42/1r | 1 | | 24 | |
| D53 | | Black | White, rust red dots | Barrel | 129/5h | 1 | | 53 | |
| D54 | | Rust red | Yellow | Short cylinder | 42/1s | | | 24 | |
| | | | | | 55/1i | 1 | | 30 | |
| D55 | Marvered dots | Yellow | Dots decomposed | Disc | 23/4d | 1 | 2 | 15 | |
| D56 | | Blue | Rust red | Disc | 157/1f | 1 | | 61 | K.1.2 |
| D57 | Mosaic | Purple translucent | Rust red and white band | Biconical | 30/4s | 3 | | 18 | K.M67; S.pl.XXIII.S.1-g |
| D58 | | Dk. green translucent | Rust red and white band | Biconical | 30/4t | 1 | | 18 | K.M67; S.pl.XXIII.S.1-g |
| D59 | | Green | Dk. blue translucent end | Oval | 59/3p | 1 | 8 | 33 | K.M73 |
| D60 | | Green | Yellow end | Oval | 60/3t | 2 | | 34 | K.M73* |

# THE BUCKLAND ANGLO-SAXON CEMETERY

| Type No. | Pattern | Colour | Decoration | Shape | Grave and catalogue number | Quantity in each grave | Total | Fig. | Parallels |
|---|---|---|---|---|---|---|---|---|---|
| D61 | | Lt. olive tran-slucent | Dk. blue translucent blob | Disc | 129/5i | 1 | | 53 | |
| D62 | Millefiori | Dk. blue tran-slucent | Rust red dots in white rings | Globular | 38/4g | 1 | | 22 | K.M1; C.pl.18.9012, 1–11 |
| D63 | | Colourless | Rust red border, yellow flowers on green translucent, white on dk. blue translucent | Globular | 53/1c | 1 | | 28 | K.M22* |
| D64 | | Rust red | Green translucent/yellow flowers, white ring and dk. blue translucent background and rust red dot | Globular | 132/2e | 1 | 4 | 54 | K.M27 |
| D65 | | | Green translucent and yellow spir-als, dk. blue translucent and white flowers, rust red band | Cylinder | 132/2f | 1 | | 54 | K.M54 |
| D66 | Reticella | | Blue-white and rust red, rust red and yellow twists | Short cylinder | 42/1t | 1 | | 24 | K.48 |
| D67 | | Rust red | Rust red and yellow, green and yellow, rust red, green and yellow twists | Short cylinder | 92/3d | 1 | | 42 | K.48 |
| D68 | | | Rust red, yellow and lt. green translucent, rust red and lt. green translucent twists | Short cylinder | 93/1 | 1 | 3 | 43 | A.8.4 |

*Exact parallel.

A. Arnold 1982.
C. Callmer 1977.
CR. Crummy 1981.
E. Eagles and Evison 1970.
G. Green and Rogerson 1978.
J. Joffroy 1974.
K. Koch 1977.
L. Lethbridge 1931.
P. Philp 1973a.
S. Salin 1939.

Note: 1/4u is classified with combed trails as it is visually similar, but the technique was undulation rather than combing. 29/2p, classed with crossing trails and circumference trail, has no clearly discernible pattern of trailing.

## TABLE XII  TYPES OF NON-GLASS BEADS IN PHASES

| | \multicolumn{14}{c}{PHASE} | | | | | | | | | | | | | |
|---|---|---|---|---|---|---|---|---|---|---|---|---|---|
| | 1 | | 2 | | 3 | | 4 | | 5 | | 6 | | 7 | |
| Type | Grave | Quantity | Grave | Quantity | Grave | Quantity | Grave | Quantity | Grave | Quantity | Grave | Quantity | Grave | Quantity |
| A01 | 20 | 15 | 14 | 4 | 29 | 1 | | | | | | | | |
| | 48 | 1 | 23 | 1 | 35 | 1 | | | | | | | | |
| | | | 92 | 1 | | | | | | | | | | |
| A02 | 13 | 3 | 14 | 23 | F | 5 | 42 | 17 | | | | | | |
| | 20 | 6 | 49 | 1+ | 1 | 4 | 55 | 2 | | | | | | |
| | 48 | 6 | 92 | 73+ | 29 | 2 | 62 | 3 | | | | | | |
| | | | | | 30 | 14 | 66 | 7 | | | | | | |
| | | | | | 35 | 1 | | | | | | | | |
| | | | | | 38 | 70 | | | | | | | | |
| | | | | | 59 | 3 | | | | | | | | |
| | | | | | 60 | 7 | | | | | | | | |
| A03 | | | | | 1 | 2 | 18 | 1 | | | | | | |
| A04 | 48 | 1 | | | | | | | | | | | | |
| A05 | | | | | | | | | 67 | 3 | | | 75 | 1 |
| | | | | | | | | | 132 | 6 | | | 127 | 2 |
| A06 | | | | | | | | | 53 | 3 | 124 | 2 | 75 | 3 |
| | | | | | | | | | 133 | 2 | | | | |
| A07 | 13 | 1 | | | | | | | | | | | | |
| A08 | | | 92 | 1 | | | | | | | | | | |
| A09 | | | | | | | 55 | 1 | | | | | | |
| A10 | | | | | | | 55 | 1 | | | | | | |
| A11 | | | | | | | | | 129 | 1 | | | | |
| A12 | | | | | | | | | 6 | 1 | | | | |
| | | | | | | | | | 67 | 2 | | | | |
| | | | | | | | | | 157 | 1+ | | | | |
| A13 | | | | | | | | | | | | | 75 | 1 |
| A14 | | | | | | | | | 134 | 2 | | | | |
| A15 | | | | | | | | | 67 | 4 | | | | |
| A16 | | | | | | | | | 129 | 1+ | 141 | 1 | | |
| A17 | 20 | 1 | | | | | | | | | | | | |
| A18 | | | 14 | 1 | | | | | | | | | | |
| A19 | | | | | | | | | 67 | 3 | | | | |
| | | | | | | | | | 129 | 3 | | | | |
| A20 | | | | | | | | | 133 | 3 | | | | |

## TABLE XIII  TYPES OF MONOCHROME GLASS BEADS IN PHASES

| | \multicolumn{16}{c}{PHASE} | | | | | | | | | | | | | | | |
|---|---|---|---|---|---|---|---|---|---|---|---|---|---|---|---|---|
| | 1 | | 2 | | 3 | | 4 | | 5 | | 6 | | 7 | | Unass. | |
| Type | Grave | Quantity | Grave | Quantity | Grave | Quantity | Grave | Quantity | Grave | Quantity | Grave | Quantity | Grave | Quantity | Bead | Quantity |
| B01 | | | | | 29 | 1 | | | 155 | 2 | 141 | 1 | 75 | 2 | Un 4 | 1 |
| | | | | | 30 | 12 | | | | | | | | | | |
| | | | | | 38 | 1 | | | | | | | | | | |
| | | | | | 59 | 6 | | | | | | | | | | |
| B02 | | | | | | | 18 | 5 | 67 | 3 | | | | | | |
| B03 | | | | | 1 | 1 | | | | | | | | | | |
| B04 | | | | | 1 | 4 | 62 | 2 | | | 107 | 1 | | | | |
| | | | | | 60 | 8 | | | | | | | | | | |
| B05 | | | | | | | | | | | 110 | 6 | 127 | 3 | | |
| | | | | | | | | | | | 160 | 1 | | | | |
| B06 | | | | | 29 | 1 | | | | | | | | | | |
| B07 | | | | | | | | | 6 | 7 | | | | | | |
| B08 | | | | | | | | | 155 | 1 | | | | | | |
| B09 | | | | | | | 62 | 1 | 133 | 1 | | | | | | |
| B10 | | | | | 1 | 1 | 18 | 2 | 53 | 4 | | | | | | |
| | | | | | | | | | 67 | 4 | | | | | | |

80    THE BUCKLAND ANGLO-SAXON CEMETERY

| Type | Phase 1 Grave | Quantity | Phase 2 Grave | Quantity | Phase 3 Grave | Quantity | Phase 4 Grave | Quantity | Phase 5 Grave | Quantity | Phase 6 Grave | Quantity | Phase 7 Grave | Quantity | Unass. Bead | Quantity |
|---|---|---|---|---|---|---|---|---|---|---|---|---|---|---|---|---|
| B11 | | | | | | | 55 | 1 | 132<br>133<br>134<br>157 | 2<br>5<br>2<br>2 | | | | | | |
| B12 | 20<br>46 | 1<br>39 | 23 | 2 | ?B<br>29<br>30<br>32<br>35<br>59<br>60 | 1<br>58<br>12<br>49<br>4<br>9<br>5+ | 42<br>55<br>62 | 7<br>1<br>3+ | 6<br>134 | 18<br>1 | 107 | 1 | | | | |
| B13 | 46 | 10 | | | 29<br>32<br>35 | 11<br>9<br>1 | | | 6 | 5 | | | | | | |
| B14 | | | | | | | 42 | 1 | | | | | | | | |
| B15 | 46 | 4 | | | 1<br>32 | 4<br>14 | | | | | | | | | | |
| B16 | | | | | | | 62 | 1 | | | | | | | | |
| B17 | | | | | 1 | 1 | | | | | | | | | | |
| B18 | | | | | 1<br>29<br>32<br>60 | 2<br>4<br>1<br>4 | | | | | | | | | | |
| B19 | | | | | | | | | | | | | 76 | 1 | | |
| B20 | | | | | 1 | 17 | | | | | | | | | | |
| B21 | | | | | | | 62 | 6 | | | | | | | | |
| B22 | | | | | | | | | 157 | 1 | | | | | | |
| B23 | | | | | | | | | 134<br>157 | 1<br>1 | | | 83 | 1 | | |
| B24 | 48 | 2 | | | | | | | | | | | | | | |
| B25 | | | | | | | | | 133 | 1 | | | | | | |
| B26 | | | | | | | | | 6 | 1 | | | | | | |
| B27 | 20 | 1 | 23 | 1 | | | | | 134<br>155 | 2<br>2 | | | | | | |
| B28 | | | | | | | | | | | | | 75 | 1 | | |
| B29 | | | | | | | | | | | 110<br>160 | 2<br>3 | 75<br>127 | 2<br>1 | | |
| B30 | | | | | 29 | 2 | | | | | | | | | | |
| B31 | 20 | 1+ | | | 30 | 1 | | | | | | | | | | |
| B32 | | | | | | | 55 | 1 | | | | | | | | |
| B33 | | | | | 30 | 1 | | | 129 | 1 | | | | | | |
| B34 | 46 | 79 | | | 1<br>29<br>32<br>35 | 27<br>3<br>46<br>1 | | | | | | | | | | |
| B35 | 46 | 9 | | | 1<br>32 | 12<br>10 | | | | | | | | | | |
| B36 | | | | | 1<br>32 | 3<br>1 | | | | | | | | | | |
| B37 | | | | | 38 | 1 | | | | | | | | | | |
| B38 | | | | | | | 55 | 1 | | | | | | | | |
| B39 | | | | | | | | | | | | | | | UN/5 | 1 |
| B40 | | | | | 1 | 1 | | | | | | | | | | |
| B41 | | | | | | | 18 | 2 | 132 | 2 | | | | | | |
| B42 | | | | | | | | | | | 110 | 2 | | | | |
| B43 | | | | | | | | | 129 | 1 | 141 | 1 | | | | |
| B44 | | | | | | | | | 129 | 1 | | | | | | |
| B45 | | | | | 29<br>30<br>59 | 2<br>7<br>8 | | | | | | | | | | |
| B46 | | | | | 1<br>29<br>32<br>60 | 3<br>1<br>1<br>1 | | | | | | | | | | |
| B47 | | | | | 1 | 1 | 62 | 4 | | | | | | | | |
| B48 | | | | | 30<br>38<br>59<br>60 | 8<br>2<br>2<br>1 | | | | | 161 | 1 | | | | |
| B49 | | | | | F | 1 | | | 67 | 1 | | | | | | |
| B50 | | | | | 60 | 4 | | | | | | | | | | |
| B51 | 20 | 1 | | | 30 | 1 | | | | | | | | | | |
| B52 | | | | | 30 | 6 | 62 | 1 | 129 | 1 | | | | | | |

# GRAVE GOODS: DISCUSSION OF TYPES

| Type | Phase 1 Grave | Quantity | Phase 2 Grave | Quantity | Phase 3 Grave | Quantity | Phase 4 Grave | Quantity | Phase 5 Grave | Quantity | Phase 6 Grave | Quantity | Phase 7 Grave | Quantity | Unass. Bead | Quantity |
|---|---|---|---|---|---|---|---|---|---|---|---|---|---|---|---|---|
|  |  |  |  |  | 59 | 3 |  |  |  |  |  |  |  |  |  |  |
|  |  |  |  |  | 60 | 1 |  |  |  |  |  |  |  |  |  |  |
| B53 |  |  |  |  |  |  |  |  | 129 | 1 |  |  |  |  |  |  |
| B54 |  |  |  |  | 1 | 5 |  |  | 67 | 1 |  |  |  |  |  |  |
|  |  |  |  |  | 35 | 1 |  |  |  |  |  |  |  |  |  |  |
|  |  |  |  |  | 60 | 3 |  |  |  |  |  |  |  |  |  |  |
| B55 |  |  |  |  |  |  |  |  |  |  | 110 | 3 | 127 | 1 |  |  |
| B56 |  |  |  |  |  |  | 62 | 1 |  |  |  |  |  |  |  |  |
| B57 |  |  |  |  | 1 | 1 |  |  | 6 | 1 |  |  |  |  |  |  |
|  |  |  |  |  | 35 | 1 |  |  |  |  |  |  |  |  |  |  |
| B58 |  |  |  |  | 29 | 1 | 42 | 1 |  |  |  |  |  |  |  |  |
|  |  |  |  |  | 35 | 2 |  |  |  |  |  |  |  |  |  |  |
| B59 |  |  |  |  |  |  |  |  |  |  | 160 | 2 |  |  |  |  |
| B60 |  |  |  |  |  |  | 62 | 2 |  |  |  |  |  |  |  |  |
| B61 | 20 | 2 |  |  | 30 | 1 | 62 | 1 | 157 | 1 |  |  |  |  |  |  |
|  |  |  |  |  | 60 | 2 |  |  |  |  |  |  |  |  |  |  |
| B62 |  |  |  |  | 60 | 1 |  |  |  |  |  |  |  |  |  |  |
| B63 |  |  | 15 | 1 |  |  |  |  |  |  |  |  |  |  |  |  |
| B64 | 20 | 1 |  |  |  |  |  |  |  |  |  |  |  |  |  |  |
| B65 | 20 | 1 |  |  |  |  |  |  |  |  |  |  |  |  |  |  |

TABLE XIV TYPES OF DRAWN GLASS BEADS IN PHASES

| Type | Phase 1 Grave | Quantity | Phase 2 Grave | Quantity | Phase 3 Grave | Quantity | Phase 4 Grave | Quantity | Phase 5 Grave | Quantity | Phase 6 Grave | Quantity | Phase 7 Grave | Quantity |
|---|---|---|---|---|---|---|---|---|---|---|---|---|---|---|
| C01 | 13 | 3 | 15 | 6 | 38 | 1 |  |  |  |  |  |  |  |  |
|  | 20 | 4 | 92 | 2 | 60 | 2 |  |  |  |  |  |  |  |  |
|  | 48 | 4 |  |  |  |  |  |  |  |  |  |  |  |  |
| C02 | 13 | 1 |  |  |  |  |  |  |  |  |  |  |  |  |
|  | 48 | 1 |  |  |  |  |  |  |  |  |  |  |  |  |
| C03 | 13 | 1 | 15 | 1 |  |  |  |  |  |  |  |  |  |  |
|  | 48 | 1 |  |  |  |  |  |  |  |  |  |  |  |  |
| C04 | 46 | 14 |  |  | 1 | 13 |  |  | 6 | 1 |  |  |  |  |
|  |  |  |  |  | 29 | 2 |  |  |  |  |  |  |  |  |
|  |  |  |  |  | 32 | 24 |  |  |  |  |  |  |  |  |
|  |  |  |  |  | 35 | 22 |  |  |  |  |  |  |  |  |
| C05 | 48 | 2 | 14 | 6 | 29 | 2 |  |  |  |  |  |  |  |  |
|  |  |  | 92 | 2 | 60 | 1 |  |  |  |  |  |  |  |  |
| C06 |  |  | 14 | 5 | 60 | 1 |  |  |  |  |  |  |  |  |
|  |  |  | 92 | 2 |  |  |  |  |  |  |  |  |  |  |
| C07 | 48 | 2 | 92 | 1 |  |  |  |  |  |  |  |  |  |  |
| C08 | 48 | 1 | 92 | 1 |  |  |  |  |  |  |  |  |  |  |
| C09 | 48 | 1 | 92 | 1 | 29 | 1 |  |  |  |  |  |  |  |  |
| C10 | 20 | 8 |  |  | 32 | 27 |  |  | 6 | 2 |  |  |  |  |
|  | 46 | 24 |  |  | 35 | 30 |  |  |  |  |  |  |  |  |
| C11 | 13 | 1 |  |  |  |  |  |  |  |  |  |  |  |  |
|  | 20 | 8 |  |  |  |  |  |  |  |  |  |  |  |  |
|  | 48 | 1 |  |  |  |  |  |  |  |  |  |  |  |  |
| C12 | 13 | 6 |  |  |  |  |  |  |  |  |  |  |  |  |
|  | 20 | 4 |  |  |  |  |  |  |  |  |  |  |  |  |
| C13 | 20 | 1 |  |  |  |  |  |  |  |  |  |  |  |  |

TABLE XV  TYPES OF POLYCHROME GLASS BEADS IN PHASES

| | PHASE | | | | | | | | | | | | | | |
|---|---|---|---|---|---|---|---|---|---|---|---|---|---|---|---|
| | 1 | | 2 | | 3 | | 4 | | 5 | | 6 | | 7 | | Unass. | |
| Type | Grave | Quantity | Grave | Quantity | Grave | Quantity | Grave | Quantity | Grave | Quantity | Grave | Quantity | Grave | Quantity | Bead | Quantity |
| D01–5 | | | | | 59 | 3 | 42 | 5 | | | | | | | | |
| | | | | | | | 62 | 1 | | | | | | | | |
| D06–11 | | | | | 1 | 2 | 42 | 5 | 133 | 2 | | | | | UN 15 | 1 |
| | | | | | 30 | 1 | | | | | | | | | | |
| D12–16 | 12 | 1 | | | 1 | 2 | 42 | 2 | | | | | 76 | 2 | | |
| | | | | | 59 | 4 | | | | | | | | | | |
| D17–36 | | | | | 1 | 6 | 18 | 9 | 134 | 1 | | | | | | |
| | | | | | 30 | 4 | 42 | 6 | | | | | | | | |
| | | | | | 32 | 11 | 55 | 1 | | | | | | | | |
| | | | | | 38 | 1 | | | | | | | | | | |
| | | | | | 60 | 6 | | | | | | | | | | |
| D37–39 | | | | | 1 | 2 | | | | | | | | | | |
| | | | | | 29 | 1 | | | | | | | | | | |
| | | | | | 30 | 1 | | | | | | | | | | |
| | | | | | 59 | 1 | | | | | | | | | | |
| D40–54 | 13 | 1 | | | 1 | 7 | 42 | 10 | 129 | 1 | | | | | | |
| | | | | | 29 | 2 | 55 | 1 | 132 | 1 | | | | | | |
| | | | | | 30 | 9 | | | | | | | | | | |
| | | | | | 35 | 1 | | | | | | | | | | |
| | | | | | 59 | 5 | | | | | | | | | | |
| | | | | | 60 | 1 | | | | | | | | | | |
| D55–56 | | | 23 | 1 | | | | | 157 | 1 | | | | | | |
| D57–61 | | | | | 30 | 4 | | | 129 | 1 | | | | | | |
| | | | | | 59 | 1 | | | | | | | | | | |
| | | | | | 60 | 2 | | | | | | | | | | |
| D62–65 | | | | | 38 | 1 | | | 53 | 1 | | | | | | |
| | | | | | | | | | 132 | 2 | | | | | | |
| D66–68 | | | 92 | 1 | 93 | 1 | 42 | 1 | | | | | | | | |

*Pins* (Distribution Figure 91)

There is a total of 45 pins, of which 7 are silver, 17 bronze and 21 iron. Except for five, they are in female graves or in graves where the sex is unknown. Most, too, are worn at the neck. Considering these figures, it may be that, where there are no other possessions to indicate sex, a pin at the neck may be taken as an indication that the grave belonged to a female e.g. bronze pins 78/1 and 101/1 (Figures 39, 48), iron pins 150/4 and 136/2. The latter was under the skull, but as the skull was tipped forward the pin may have been at the neck (Figure 81). Presumably in a bag at the left hip were 138/2 and 4 and 158/3 (Figures 57, 62). Pin 107/5a (Figure 48) was inside a bronze workbox.

There is no evidence that a pin was used in the hair. The function of the pin at the neck can only be guessed at, and perhaps the most likely is the fastening under the chin of a head scarf. It might have been used to fasten a shroud, but this is not possible where the positions of other pieces of jewellery show that the woman was buried fully dressed. Perhaps it might be true of the burials where a pin at the neck was the only grave furnishing i.e. 100/1, 101/1, 140/1 (Figures 48, 57). For possible use in connection with a necklace, see above p 69.

The only pins in male graves are 10/1, 33/4, 50/3, 96a/2, 96b/8 (Figures 8, 20, 28, 45, 46) of which only 10/1 is bronze, the rest iron. Pins 10/1 and 33/4 are plain disc-headed and 50/3, 96a/2 and 96b/8 are also disc-headed but the head is formed by coiling the end of the shaft. An iron pin with head similarly coiled was found in a woman's grave at Bergh Apton, Norfolk[1]. The pin 10/1 was underneath the middle of the spearhead, and pin 96a/2 was beside a spearhead. In these graves the pin may have been used to fasten some cloth covering wrapped round the spearhead – a supposition supported by traces of textile on the socket of the spearhead in grave 10 and on the pin in grave 96a. Grave 96a and b was the double burial of two men, and although the pin in 96b was on the chest of that man it was only a few inches away from his spear which was on the left shoulder. This coiled-head pin therefore, may not have been connected with clothing but could have been used to fasten a wrapping on his spearhead too. In grave 33/4 the pin was beside the knife and sword by the left forearm on the pelvis, and in grave 50/3 at the left waist beside the knife, and so presumably in the same container or sheath. Clearly, at Dover, only one type of pin was proper for use by a man. One grave, 50, was in the earliest part of the cemetery, but the others belonged to the seventh century. Similarly in grave 43 at Barfriston, Kent, which contained a spearhead and ferrule, knife,

---

1 Green and Rogerson 1978, 14, fig. 72, grave 11,F. The head is there described as '?looped', but the drawing shows a coiled head.

egg-shells and a Frankish bottle, there was also a silver pin, possibly, but not certainly, the hipped pin illustrated by Faussett[2]. In grave 1 of the mid sixth century at Lyminge, Kent a bronze pin or bodkin was found beside a spearhead[3], so that in these two graves they probably fastened a cloth wrapped round the blade.

Seven pins are of silver, and some of these are the most ornate. The head of the pin 30/3 (Figure 18) is flattened, curled round and decorated with stamps to give the impression on one face of a bird's head. A similar technique and design is used on a hook-and-eye wrist clasp from Market Overton in Rutland Museum[4] where the silver wire forming the eye half of a clasp is beaten flat and coiled round in a bird's head with stamped decoration. Bird-headed pins are also known from: Sibertswold[5], Wingham[6] and on the Continent of the period AD 525–600, from Krefeld-Gellep, Basel-Gotterbarmweg, Basel-Kleinhüningen and Böckingen[7].

In grave 155 the silver pin 155/1 has a disc head ornamented with a shell and garnet centre *cabochon*, which, together with its filigree border is a jewellery component of a type usually set in the middle of a Kentish disc brooch, although one was also used in an unusual fashion as the centre piece of St. Cuthbert's pectoral cross[8]. The silver pin 20/3 has an oval ring head surmounted by a knob.

Two smaller silver pins have knob heads set with garnets: 161/1 has a single small *cabochon* garnet on each of two opposite sides of the sperical head; on 134/5 (Figure 55) the head has a garnet in the top and a hole on each of four flattened sides which may once have held garnets. This type of head with five-stone setting occurs on a bone pin where the stones are amber at Rosemarkie, Highland (Ross and Cromarty)[9]. Another tiny pin in bronze with four holes in the head and a ring top, also with a 'hipped', faceted point, was found at Whitby[10]. Another bone pin was found in the sunken-featured building No. 3 at West Stow, Suffolk, and this is decorated by rows of dots on the shaft and on the spherical head, apparently coloured with red paint in imitation of garnets[11]. A disc-headed pin was also found in SFB 3 at West Stow. Both of these Dover silver pins have moulding at the neck and at a constriction lower down, below which the shaft swells slightly before narrowing to the point. The point on the pin 134/5 is faceted. 'Hipped' pin shafts do not appear before the second half of the seventh century, but continue into the eighth century on larger pins such as the linked series found at Witham[12]. In late furnished graves they occur at Little Wilbraham[13] and Shudy Camps, Cambridgeshire[14], Jevington, East Sussex[15] and at Chartham Down, Sibertswold, Kingston, Barfriston[16], Polhill[17] and Sarre[18] in Kent. A spatulate-headed pin of like size and shape to 138/2 (Figure 57) occurred in grave 18 at Holborough, Kent[19]. In later contexts are the pin from Whitby mentioned above, and similar pins from York[20], and from Waltham Abbey in Essex[21] and Southampton, Hampshire[22].

Among the pins with a flat disc head, five have moulding in the middle of the shaft, 44/1 (Figure 26) F/2 (Figure 4), 132/1 (Figure 54), 138/2 (Figure 57), 33/4 (Figure 20) and of these 44/1 is of silver, 33/4 of iron and 138/2 has a spatulate head. The pin 18/3 has lost its head, but as the shaft is flattening out at the top and has moulding in the middle it may be that this also was a disc-headed type of pin. In other cemeteries there was a disc-headed pin at Sarre, Kent in grave CLIV/CLV[23], and two at Kingston Down grave 6[24] and grave 119[25]. Similar disc-headed pins have been found in Scotland at the Broch of Burray and Culbin Sands[26]. A disc-headed pin in grave 10 at Winnall, Hampshire[27] had a loop at the back of the head.

Three bronze pins with disc head do not have the medial moulding in the shaft, 10/1 (Figure 8), 78/1 (Figure 39), 158/3 (Figure 62), and one, 160/1 (Figure 62) in silver has the head of a double-axe shape. Four have a perforation in the disc, and in two of these there is a bronze wire ring: 101/1 (Figure 48), 142/1 (Figure 58), 44/1 (Figure 26) 147/1 (Figure 59). A parallel to the perforated disc head with ring-and-dot decoration, 44/1, comes from Burwell, Cambridgeshire[28]. One pin with a spatulate head is also perforated, 42/2.

Amongst the other bronze pins, one, 38/2, had a scalloped setting probably intended to hold a spherical glass bead, and three had rather simple knob heads 83/2, 100/1, 107/5a (Figures 39, 48). The pin 62/5 is simply a twist of wire, and 1/3 is hollow and constructed of rolled sheet bronze.

---

2  Faussett 1856, 142, pl. XII. 24
3  Warhurst 1955, 6–8, fig. 5, 4
4  Brown 1915 III, pl. LXXVI.4; Clough *et al.* 1975, pl. 76
5  Faussett 1856, grave 18 on page 105 and grave 101 on page 118, both refer to pl. XII.19
6  Smith 1923, 58, fig. 63
7  Pirling 1966, 1, 182, 2, Taf. 71, 8
8  Battiscombe 1956, pl. XVI, fig. 7
9  Stevenson 1955, 286, fig. A. 21
10  Peers and Radford 1943, 64, fig. 14 lower row, fifth from right
11  West 1985 2, fig. 36.9
12  Wilson 1964, pl. XVIII
13  Lethbridge 1931, fig. 38.1
14  Lethbridge 1936, fig. 4.1
15  Holden 1969, fig. 3, 3
16  Faussett 1856, pl. XII, 18, 10, 22, 24 and 25,
17  Philp 1973a, fig. 54. 509
18  Brent 1866, grave CLXXIV, 184
19  Evison 1956, fig. 19
20  Waterman 1959, fig. 11, 5 and 9
21  Huggins 1976, 115, fig. 41, 1 and 2
22  Addyman and Hill 1969, fig. 26; cf also Laing 1975, fig. 124. 17
23  Brent 1866, 179
24  Faussett 1856, 43
25  Ibid, 61, fig. 3
26  Stevenson 1955, fig. A17 and 20
27  Meaney and Hawkes 1970, fig. 9
28  Lethbridge 1931, fig. 29.2

Pins of similar shape, but in a different kind of context were found in two houses lying one on top of the other in the Saxon settlement on Swindon Hill, Wiltshire, the lower one, House 4, containing fourteen bone pins, all 'hipped', seven of them disc-headed and one of a similar double-axe shape to 160/6. In House 3 above there were also some 'hipped' bone pins, one disc-headed, and one disc-headed bronze pin. One might conclude that the pins were being made on the site.[29]

Only one iron pin is decorated, 157/3 (Figure 61) and this is by means of a spherical glass head. The glass ball has a circumference groove, possibly once occupied by an inlaid trail or, alternatively, intended to facilitate engagement with the iron stem. The custom of decorating the head of a pin with a glass ball or bead was followed in the Roman period, and probably later also, for bronze pins ornamented in this way have been found at Shakenoak, Oxfordshire, and West Stow, Suffolk[30], where they could have been either of Roman or Saxon origin. A bronze pin with glass head was also found at Cheddar[31], so increasing the probability of Saxon manufacture.

The rest of the iron pins are deformed by rust, but knob heads are discernible on 6/9 (Figure 7), 35/2 (Figure 21), 43/1 (Figure 25), 136/2 (Figure 56), 138/4 (Figure 57), 147/3 (Figure 59) and the shaft of 32/2 (Figure 19) is turned over to form a head. Some heads are flattened like nail heads: 6/4 (fig. 7), 138/1 (Figure 57), 150/1 (Figure 60); other heads are lost or obscured: 59/2 (Figure 33), 60/1 (Figure 34), 140/1 (Figure 57), 141/4, 7 and 8 (Figure 58). The two pins 107/5a and 138/4, which was found with a bronze needle, are like a small, modern dressmaker's pin.

The distribution plan Figure 91 shows that pins were in use in all phases of the cemetery. Pins over 6cm in length occur in phases 1 and 3 – 6, but not in the latest phase. A shorter pin, usually in bronze, with a disc or spatulate head and moulding in the middle of the shaft to improve anchorage, occurs mainly in phases 3 to 6. The 'hipped' shaft on a silver pin is a development in phases 5 and 6, and would have performed the non-slip function even more efficiently than the moulding. This form of pin-shaft continued elsewhere into the eighth century.

*Pin with man's head*
As may be seen from the description p 251, this object (161/3, Figure 63, Text Figure 14a, Plate 5e) is now missing its tip, and a radiograph throws some doubt on its reconstruction. However, its essential characteristics are certain. It was an iron pin with a decorative bronze head designed for suspension from a strap. The bronze head was exposed to view, but the iron part, and the lowest part of the bronze shaft, were encased in wood, probably a wooden sheath. A major part of the iron pin was inlaid with two spiralling strips of a dense metal, probably either silver or bronze. The folded, replaced textile remains on the tip were of tabby weave, probably linen, no doubt part of the woman's dress on which it was resting. The remains of wood must represent a sheath and not the traces of a wooden implement such as a spoon, for there would have been no point to the decoration of the iron shaft with inlaid strips of metal if it was to be permanently covered. It was lying at the left waist with a knife, and because of this association and its obvious relationship with toilet instrument sets found at Birka[32], it must have been used for some purpose of the toilet. In view of the inlaid metal, it could not have been used as a sharpening steel[33], and this was a suggestion made before the presence of inlay was revealed by X-ray.

Pins of this type with helmeted and other heads occur in numbers at Birka as part of a set of two implements, the other item being a pair of tweezers. As metal inlay had not been detected on any of them Dr F K J Waller of the Statens Historiska Museet has kindly had the following human-headed pins and tweezers from Birka X-rayed, but none of them show any inlay of another metal.

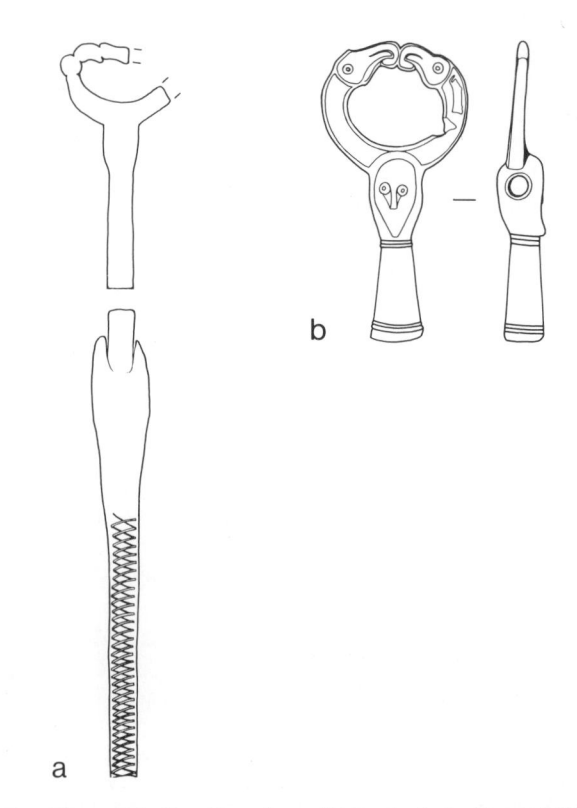

*Text Figure 14* a Drawing of a radiograph of pin, Dover 161/3
b Bronze head from Gåtebo, Öland. Scale 1/1

---

29　Information kindly supplied by Caroline Washbourne
30　Harden 1971, 106, No. 152, fig. 45, 69; Evison 1985, fig. 277, 2, 3
31　Rahtz 1979, 280, fig. 94. 81
32　Evison 1965a, 217
33　Ibid, 214; Bruce-Mitford 1971–2, 130; Bruce-Mitford 1974, 208

|  | Grave | Arbman 1943 |
|---|---|---|
| Pin | 494 | Taf. 170:5 |
| Pin | 504 | " 170:4 |
| Tweezers | 973 | " 173:3 |
| Tweezers and pin | 735 | " 172:4 |
| Pin with wooden handle (awl) | 838 | Abb. 258:b |
| Tweezers | 944 | " 321:42 |
| Tweezers | 946 | Taf. 172:1 |
| Pin | 954 | " 171:6 |
| Tweezers | 980 | " 172:2 |
| Tweezers | 1014 | Abb. 387 |
| Tweezers | 1083 | — |
| Tweezers and pin | 1084 | " 422 |
| Tweezers | 1026 | — |
| Tweezers | 1144 | " 444 |

The group selected includes pins completely of bronze, graves 494 and 504, and also others, like the Dover pin, with a bronze head and iron shaft, graves 171, 422 and 735. This type of pin with human head at Birka is found in female graves, most of which also contain tortoise brooches and therefore belong to the ninth century. The pin and tweezers are usually lying close to shears, a knife and key. One pair of shears, from the rich grave 464 allocated to the first half of the ninth century[34] is inlaid on the shafts with silver strips in a similar fashion to the inlaid spirals on the Dover pin, so that although the X-rays of the pins have produced negative results, it is evident that this type of decoration was currently used at Birka on this kind of female equipment.

This particular type of pin does not seem to be known from elsewhere, but a bronze head very close in size and appearance has been found at Gåtebo, Bredsätra, Öland (Text Figure 14b), probably from a disturbed cremation grave of the Vendel period[35]. The head is hollow and the helmet is not clearly defined, but the face and horns with bird's head terminals are present as at Dover.

Although other examples of this type of pin have not come to light, pictures of men wearing this kind of helmet have been found in England on a buckle plate from Finglesham[36], the Sutton Hoo helmet[37], and on a fragment preserved from the Caenby burial[38]. They also occur in Scandinavia on *repoussé* helmet plates from Vendel[39], Valsgärde 7[40], Valsgärde 8[41] and on one of the Torslunda dies from which such plates were made[42]. A bronze key shaft found at Gamla Uppsala[43] is about the same size and is ornamented with a head which is somewhat similar. It is double-sided, however, as befits a key shaft, and the head is surmounted by a pair of bird's heads, this time facing outwards. There are small warrior figures, one in bronze, from a cremation at Ekhammer, Kungsängen, Uppland[44] and one in silver from grave 571 at Birka[45]. There is also one on a ninth-century coin and on a wall-hanging at Oseberg[46]. Their appearances therefore extend from the Vendel period to the Viking period, about two centuries.

There has been much discussion about the personage represented by this helmeted figure[47], and the most convincing identification, in view of the fact that the Torslunda man has only one eye[48], is Odin. Their occurrence in connection with weapon-bearing men, which has been stressed[49] is therefore easy to understand, but their use as decoration on toilet implements used by women is not readily explicable. As for much of the martial equipment of the Germans, however, a Roman origin can be cited[50] for this kind of helmet. The horns on the Roman helmets were not tipped with animal heads, but this is an adaptation very likely to have been made by Germanic people, especially as many of the shield insignia of Germanic contingents in the Roman army illustrated in the *Notitia Dignitatum* consist of a pair of confronted animal heads, e.g. those of the Batavi, Cornuti and Marcomanni[51]. The tradition of a horned helmet being the attribute of a god or great commander probably started in Egypt and the Near East, became firmly established by the Roman army and was continued subsequently by the Anglo-Saxons and Scandinavians. It may first have been adopted in manuscript illumination in the Aelfric Pentateuch (BM Cotton Claudius B IV) where Moses was depicted in a horned headdress[52]. The tradition in regard to Moses has persisted to the present day, but the Dover, Finglesham and Caenby men with horned helmets are the earliest Anglo-Saxon versions traceable as they belong to the end of the seventh century.

The isolated position of grave 161 and its small *entourage* of three other graves, the large number of flints on top of the grave, the silver pin and this probable cult object, all suggest that the woman was an eminent adherent to a heathen religion.

*Bracelets and finger-rings*
Most of the bracelets are made of wire with the ends twisted over the hoop to give a sliding elasticity. Five are bronze (1/5, 15/3, 20/10, 67/6, 129/2) and one silver (20/7), (Figures 5, 11, 12, 37, 53)[53]. They belong to graves ranging from plot A to plot G, i.e. c AD 525 to 675.

34 Arbman 1937, 39
35 Hagberg 1976, 336, Taf. XI, 13. Another has recently been found at Old Ladoga in the Baltic, Vierck 1983, 13–14, Abb. 3.2
36 Hawkes *et al.* 1965
37 Bruce-Mitford 1972, fig. 8
38 Bruce-Mitford 1974, pl. 54, b
39 Stolpe and Arne 1927, VI, 1
40 Bruce-Mitford 1949–51, pl. Xa
41 Arwidsson 1954, fig. 79
42 Bruce-Mitford 1974, pl. 59a

43 Olsen 1949–51, fig. 1
44 Ringquist 1969, fig. 1
45 Arbman 1943, 185, Taf. 92:9
46 Ringquist 1969, figs. 6 and 7
47 e.g. Hawkes *et al.* 1965; Evison 1965a
48 Bruce-Mitford 1974, pl. 54c
49 Hawkes *et al.* 1965, 23,
50 Almgren 1948
51 Alföldi 1935, Taf. 46
52 Mellinkoff 1970, 13, pl. 13
53 cf Faussett 1856, pl. XVI, 12, 14 and 15

Fairly near together in plot H are two more substantial bronze bracelets with some decoration, one being a kind of snake's head type (110/1, Figure 49). This type has a long history and was particularly popular in the Roman period[54], but bracelets and rings with snake or animal heads are to be found in late Anglo-Saxon graves[55]. The other Dover bracelet was decorated with zones of transverse lines (141/1, Figure 58), and a bracelet of this type was found in grave 121 at Kingston in association with amethyst beads and other objects[56]. At Dover the decorated bracelets both belong to phase 6, AD 675–700, in a short period when the wire bracelets had gone out of use, and before bracelets ceased to be buried with their owners.

Only two finger-rings were found in the cemetery, one being a plain gold overlapping band (38/6, Figure 22). Rings of similar shape in bronze or silver occur, for example, at Chessell Down, Isle of Wight[57]. The analysis of the gold (p 182) shows it to be extraordinarily fine, i.e. 98.4% gold, 1.5% silver and 0.2% copper. If compared with the analyses of Kentish bracteates (p 52), this is approached only by one of the bracteates in Sarre grave 4[58] in which the gold content was as much as 96.8%. Amongst jewellery which has been analysed at the Ashmolean Museum, a bracteate stamped in imitation of a coin of Constantine has a gold content of 98%, and, although its frame of pseudo-plait filigree cannot have been added before $c$ 600, the bracteate itself might have been stamped much earlier[59]. The only other pendant with such a high gold content is the pseudo-imperial solidus of Maurice Tiberius, dated by Rigold to $c$ 583–7[60]. A similar gold content is normal for Byzantine and some early Germanic coins[61], and it is most likely that the Dover finger-ring was made from a coin of this kind. A date later than about 580 is therefore not likely for its manufacture.

The other finger-ring is of silver wire twisted into a disc to form a bezel (F/3, Figure 4). These wire rings are fairly common in Anglo-Saxon graves of the second half of the sixth century,[62] but they also occur earlier as in a cremation at Spong Hill, Norfolk in a plain pot with tweezers, a flint flake and an early comb[63]. Others are found abroad[64]. Further examples are listed by Meaney[65], and the suggestion made that the knot may have been regarded as protection against the Evil Eye.

As there was no skeleton remaining in grave F and the ring was amongst beads near the neck, it is not possible to know whether it was worn on one of the fingers or on the necklace. In grave 38 the ring was in the pelvic region, and although none of the bones of the hands were remaining, the position of the right radius and ulna beside the body shows that the ring could not have been worn on the right hand. The absence of the left radius and ulna leaves the probability that it was worn on the left hand.

## Buckles, belt and strap mounts

The bronze buckle in grave 48 consists of a pair of confronted dolphins, a form which recalls on the one hand a non-zoomorphic buckle form known in Germanic graves during the third and fourth centuries[66], and on the other, handles in use on boxes and helmets in the third century in the Danube region consisting of a pair of confronted dolphins biting on a mussel[67]. The dolphins on the Dover buckle have curling tails, to which are attached a pair of projecting lugs to act as hinges on a bar which also supports an iron tongue. This is a replacement, for the original tongue would have been in bronze with curling side pieces which neatly engaged with the curling tails, as on the complete example from Colchester[68] which also has an ornamental plate hinged on the same bar.

When found, a thin piece of wood (lime) was preserved by rust on the back of the loop as shown in Figure 27, 14. This cannot be an accidental position because the wood was carefully cut out in a curve to match the curve of the curling tail, and there was a straight edge coinciding with the middle of the loop. This was presumably a backing for the loop, carefully cut so that it was not visible from the front and so that it did not interfere with the movement of the tongue. A wood backing for a small bronze buckle of a later period was also found at Holborough[69].

These dolphin types in England have been considered along with the much more numerous buckle types which are decorated with animal heads at the opposite side of the loop[70]. There have also been a number of continental studies[71], and it is probable that many of the continental dolphin buckles were produced in northern France, although some were found further inland. Since then the dolphin type in England has been regarded as divided into seven variants[72], some of which were found on the Continent as well as in Britain, but three variants occurred in Britain only. Amongst these were variant $a^1$, which is the kind to which the Dover buckle belongs, and variant $a^2$ which is very similar, but there the dolphin is less realistic and the

---

54 Liversidge 1973, 141–2, figs. 54d, 55c
55 Speake 1980, fig. 11, h, j, k, l
56 Faussett 1856, fig. on p 62
57 Arnold 1982, fig. 19, 96ii and iii, and fig. 28. 55.
58 Hawkes and Pollard 1981, 360, Taf. XVII, 24
59 Brown and Schweizer 1973, AM29, 180
60 Ibid, AM2, 176–7
61 Hawkes *et al.* 1966, 117, 134
62 Hyslop 1963, 199, fig. 13h; Bakka 1958, fig. 53, Sarre 4; Douglas 1793, pl. 4, fig. 6, Chatham Lines, Tumulus IV; Smith 1923, fig. 45, Faversham; Chadwick 1958, fig. 6, Finglesham grave G1

63 Hills 1977a, 57, fig. 123, 1465
64 Genrich 1981, 61, fig. 4b
65 Meaney 1981, 170–4
66 Böhme 1974, Taf. 104. 9
67 Keller 1971, Taf. 14, 13; Robinson 1975, pl. 192, figs. 117–9
68 Hawkes and Dunning 1961, fig. 17e
69 Evison 1956, fig. 16.8, pl. IIb
70 Hawkes and Dunning 1961
71 e.g. Martin 1967 and Nowothnig 1970
72 Evison 1981a, 129–30

tail has been transformed into an animal head (Figure 113). Variant $a^1$, with the exception of the Dover buckle, has only been found on Roman sites, and the distribution is south of the Thames from Dover to Winchester, and otherwise at more distant sites in Wales, Leicester, Lincolnshire, Gloucestershire and Humberside. Four examples of variant $a^2$ were also found on Roman sites, but three of them were in Anglo-Saxon graves. The distribution is near the Thames, Winchester and a line of sites to the south-east of the distribution of variant $a^1$, near the Icknield Way in Wiltshire, Northamptonshire, Suffolk and Norfolk. Variant $a^2$ would therefore seem to be a slightly later version of $a^1$ which was produced at the end of the fourth century. The number of these dolphin buckles is not sufficiently substantial on which to base firm conclusions, but the fact that the outer distribution limit of variant $a^1$ lies far to the north and west, while the outer distribution limit of variant $a^2$ approximates to a more south-easterly line along the Icknield Way might have implications. It is already evident that a number of Germanic possessions of the years around AD 400, such as carinated pedestal bowls, vessels with faceted carination[73], supporting-arm and equal arm brooches[74] are provenanced along the Icknield Way, and one possible interpretation of the distribution of dolphin buckles variants $a^1$ and $a^2$ might be that they represent military equipment of Germanic mercenaries in a first line of defence followed by a secondary withdrawal line on the Icknield Way[75]. The Dover buckle, therefore is much older than the grave in which it was found, but it was produced in this country.

With the exception of four buckles in white metal or covered with white metal, 15/2 (Figure 10), 30/6 (Figure 18), 92/4 (Figure 42) and 96a/3 (Figure 45), the buckles discussed below are of bronze. The sword-bearer in grave 56 was wearing a belt with a silvered bronze buckle, an iron tongue replacing the original bronze tongue, which would have had a shield-shaped base. The plate is triangular with three dome-headed rivets. Six appliqués were spaced at intervals on the belt. Two appliqués are rectangular, one silvered-bronze and stamp-decorated, the other a re-used silver sheet. Three other mounts are sub-rectangular and narrower at the top, and are each perforated with a slot into which a narrow strap 5mm wide, could be fitted to suspend some light object such as a pouch or knife-sheath. The buckle was worn in the front and the rectangular silver plate may have been on the opposite end of the belt as a counterplate. Near the counterplate end were the rectangular plaque with a strap mount each side, and the mount with three slots and the zoomorphic mount were both under the knife. The straps held by the mounts 7, 9 and 11 were too narrow to have functioned as straps for supporting the sword, and presumably held the knife in a sheath at the left side,

and a pouch at the other. (Reconstruction Text Figure 15a.) Other mounts similar to the slotted sub-rectangular mounts for strap attachment in grave 56, were found in graves 103 and 113. The belt in grave 103 (male) also had a rectangular plate (103/3), and 113/2 (in a female grave) was accompanied by a bronze buckle. One more triangular mount, Unass/14, was unassociated. Similar buckles to 56/6, with rectangular, slotted and zoomorphic appliqués, are noted by Böhner in the Trier region[76] in the sixth century and the beginning of the seventh. Similar buckles and a complete set of mounts occur at Rhenen, Holland[77].

The strap end in grave 98 was a few inches below the belt mounts, as would be expected if the belt end was left hanging free. The other belt mounts in this grave consist of tinned bronze rectangular plaques ornamented with a diagonal cross. Like the mounts in grave 56 they are also of Frankish origin, but differ in that the rivets are accommodated on a plane lower than the middle panel. One was recessed at a short end (98/4c, Figure 47) to permit the passage of a buckle tongue, which together with the buckle loop, was missing at the time of burial. An identical plaque without the indentation, 98/4a, was found under the right forearm, and acted as a counterplate. A third rectangular plaque, 98/4b, lacked the ornamental beading on the other two, and was recessed in the middle of one long side to admit a strap 1cm wide. This plaque was lying face downwards at mid waist, and so was on the back of the belt. It might have suspended the knife, of which a fragment was found just below, in a leather sheath. (Reconstruction Text Figure 15b).

There are as many as ten other buckles with the shield-on-tongue which is of Frankish origin, although it was taken over by Kentish jewellers at least by the early seventh century when buckles of the Taplow type were manufactured. Plainer buckles of this type are of frequent occurrence in Kent and it is not possible to be certain how early they were made in this country. Two buckles at Dover consist of the loop and tongue only 4/3 and 42/3 (Figures 6 and 25). The other eight, however, are accompanied by one to three rivets to fasten the two layers of the belt together after it has passed over the buckle loop. All the rivets are shoe-shaped, with the exception of the two in grave 20 which are disc-headed. The method of fastening was shown by a rivet in grave 65 which had the remains of a leather thong threaded through the perforation in the lug projecting at the back. The shield-on-tongue of D/1 (Figure 3) is a different six-sided shape, and once held an inset stone. The full set of rivets was usually three but one or two inevitably were lost in wearing. The position on the belt in the grave was noted in each case and is shown in the drawings: the two rivets next to the loop always point away from it and sometimes the third also, but in three graves, 15, 65

---

73 Myres 1969, 79, maps 5a and b
74 Evison 1981a, 141 ff.
75 But see ibid, 142

76 Böhner 1958 2, Taf. 37, 3a-f; Taf. 38, 3b; Taf. 39, 1
77 Glazema and Ypey 1956, pl. 70, 72

88                    THE BUCKLAND ANGLO-SAXON CEMETERY

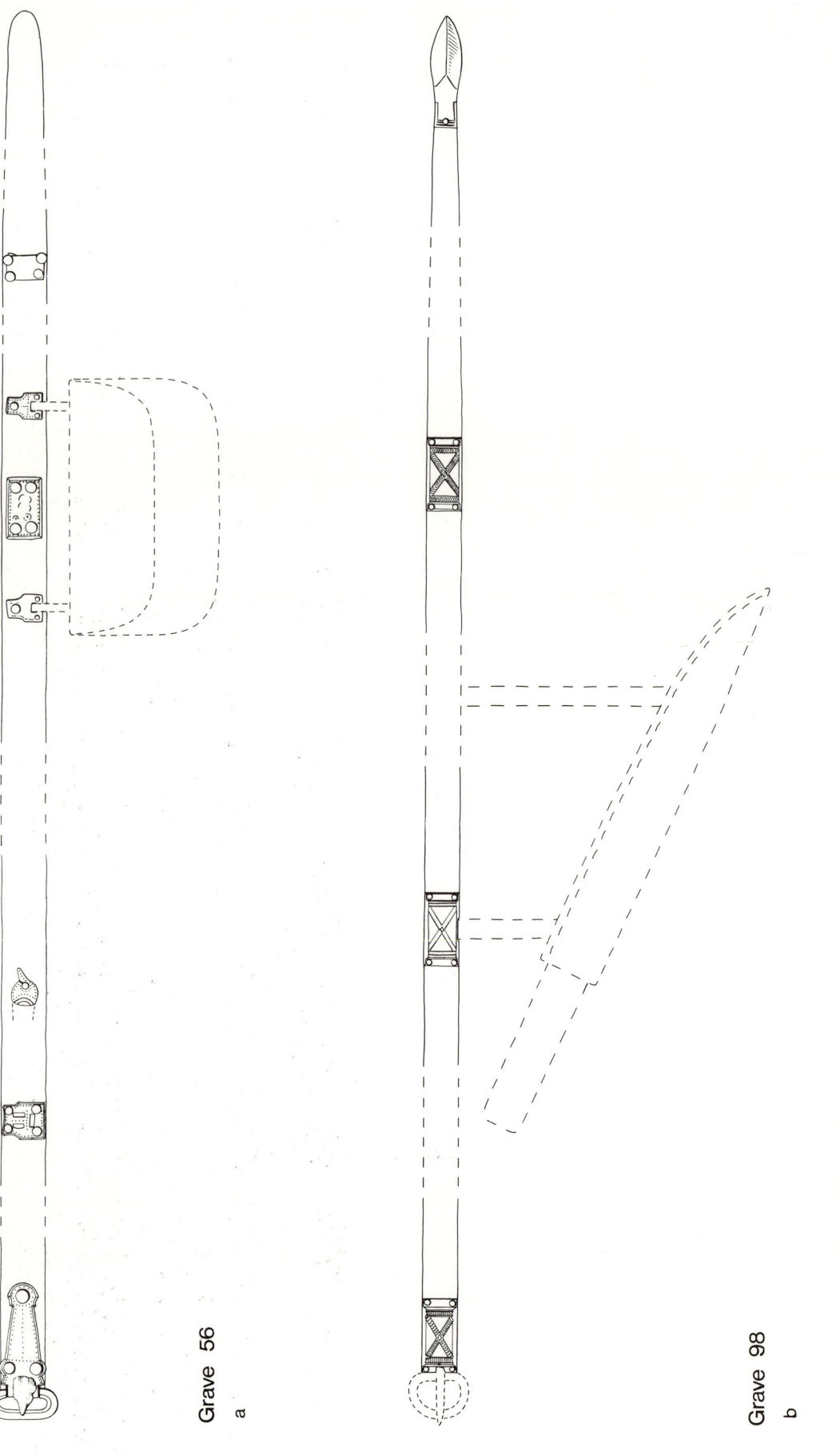

Grave 56

Grave 98

Text Figure 15 a Reconstruction of belt, Dover grave 56
b Reconstruction of belt, Dover grave 98. Scale 1/3

and 91, the third rivet further away from the loop points towards it. Of the buckles with shoe-shaped rivets 4, 50, 65, 91 and 96a are male graves, and 15, 20, 28 and 42 are female graves, although in the Trier region this type of buckle belonged mostly to men. The period during which they were in use is about AD 525–625. They are very common on the Continent, occurring frequently, for instance, in the cemetery of Lavoye[78]. There are also several in this country[79]. The disc-headed rivets as in grave 20 are less frequent[80] and appear to be earlier than the shoe-shaped rivets.

158/1 (Figure 62) is a simple type of buckle with triangular plate of the sixth or early seventh century. A rectangular loop as 30/6 (Figure 18) is not common in this country. One in the Trier region comes from a sixth century grave[81], and rectangular loops in north-east and north-west France belong mainly to the same century[82]. English examples are from Petersfinger, grave XIIIa and High Down, grave 34[83]. The Dover buckle has a replacement iron tongue, but a very similar buckle in Bifrons grave 29 still retains its original shield-on-tongue[84]. The Bifrons grave contains radiate brooches of AD 525–50, and Bakka suggests that the burial took place in the following 25 years.

The buckle in grave 21 (Plate 5c) is an early type for its tongue is constricted near the tip and expands only slightly at the base, while the plate is semi-circular in shape. Semi-circular plates are amongst fifth-century inlaid iron forms as at Petersfinger grave XXIX[85]. The terminal projection for the rivet also suggests the heart-shaped plate also of that period, as for instance, the square-looped buckle with heart-shaped plate set with a central stone from High Down grave 34[86] which also has a stamped border and belongs to the Quoit Brooch Style group. The sliced garnet, however, set without a foil backing, suggests work of the beginning of the sixth century, and it may well be a Kentish product.

The buckle in grave 38 (Plate 5d) is certainly of Kentish workmanship. Its plate is half-cylindrical with a flat terminal on a lower plane holding the rivets. The iron tongue is a replacement, for the original would have been in bronze with a half-cylindrical base to match and fit against the plate. It is a lesser bronze version of a complete silver-gilt and nielloed set found at Faversham. This consisted of a similar buckle but complete with original tongue and decorated loop, identical counterplate, and another belt mount, no doubt for the middle back, with slightly different ornamentation including sets of three ring-and-dot motifs which are echoes on the strap end also belonging to the suite[87]. The cylindrical mounts are divided into four triangular fields by a diagonal cross, only two opposing fields on each being occupied by animal ornament on the Faversham buckle, but on the Dover buckle all four have animal decoration. It is in chip-carved Style I, but not as well executed as on the Faversham mount. Two comparable semi-cylindrical plates with ring-and-dot ornament from Milton-next-Sittingbourne are in Maidstone Museum. Simpler buckles of this type, with half-cylindrical plate and tongue base have been found in Grave LI at Petersfinger[88] with a Roman coin, bracelet fragment and amber beads; at Chessell Down, Isle of Wight[89], at Herpes in France[90], and a number were forthcoming from Howletts, Kent: three were unassociated[91], and one was in grave 37 with a claw-beaker. The Petersfinger grave L1 associations suggest an early date for the simple type, the Howletts claw-beaker in grave 37 belongs to the second half of the sixth century, and the degenerate animal ornament, the associations and position of grave 38 suggest the end of the century. The manufacture must have been Kentish, centred at or near Faversham and Howletts.

There are five small bronze buckles with folded rectangular plate fastened by two or three rivets, and two loops without plates, all for straps between 0.9 to 1.2cm wide. Of these one was at the waist of a boy and one by a young man's hip, no doubt fastening narrow belts 1.2cm wide (137/2 and 146/1, Figures 56 and 59). Five, 9/5, 52/2, 144/4, 156/3 and 158/4, (Figures 8, 28, 59, 61 and 62) were near a knife on a man's skeleton, and must have been used to suspend the knife sheath from the belt, the presence of which is evident from a second and larger buckle at mid waist in three of the graves. The woman in grave 113 fastened her belt with a small buckle for a strap slightly wider, 1.6cm, and a triangular mount was slotted for a strap to hold her knife.

Turning now to buckles in iron, the buckle 8/3 (Figure 8), with oval loop and circular plate with three bronze dome-headed rivets, is clearly a Frankish type which often occurs in bronze[92]. The few that have been imported to this country were found at Ipswich in Suffolk, and the rest in Kent, at Lympne, Sittingbourne and Faversham[93]. One in the Trier region is allocated to *Stufe* III (AD 525–600) by Böhner, his type B.2.[94]

Two iron buckles have a triangular plate with

---

78 Joffroy 1974, pl. 23, 208 etc.
79 e.g. Smith 1917/18a, 104, pl. I
80 Joffroy 1974, pl. 20. 187, pl. 25. 235, pl. 26. 243, 248
81 Périn 1980, fig. 50. 54; Piton and Schuler 1981, 263, pl. 32, 24–33
82 Böhner 1958 2, Taf. 35.8
83 Leeds and Shortt 1953, pl. VII; Evison 1955, pl. VIIc
84 Godfrey-Faussett 1876, 310; Bakka 1958, 73. fig. 53
85 Leeds and Shortt 1953, pl. VI. 107
86 Evison 1955, pl. VIIc, cf. also Chatham Lines, Leeds 1913, fig. 20; Alfriston, Griffith and Salzmann 1914, pl. V.4, 4a; Petersfinger, Leeds and Shortt 1953, pl. VII.114
87 Smith 1923, 43, fig. 39; Smith 1868, 141, pl. XXIV. 2, 3, 1 and 6
88 Leeds and Shortt 1953, pl. VII. 144
89 Arnold 1982, fig. 28. 85, pl. 8g; BM Reg. No. 67 7–29 44; Hillier 1856, figs. 14, 58
90 BM Reg. No. 1905 5–20 785; also 1905 5–20 704 belt plate
91 BM Reg. Nos. 1918 7–11 3 and 1936 5–11 4 and one in private possession
92 Joffroy 1974, fig. 37
93 Brown 1915, III, 349, LXXI; Åberg 1926, 206, Nos. 80–83; Avent 1973
94 Böhner 1958 1, 184, ibid 2 Taf. 36, 8d

three bronze rivets (135/4, 149/2, Figures 56, 60). A number of small buckles have a rectangular plate fastened by rivets. Two, (18/1 and 61/3, Figures 11 and 35, Plate 5b) are unusual in that the studs are arranged in three rows of three on one and a quincunx on the other, and the rivets are of copper with tinned bronze disc heads giving a silver appearance. The buckle with three rivets, 33/5 (Figure 20), may have been of the same kind or the rivet heads may have been dome-shaped as on 128/3 (Figure 52). Except for the buckle 27/4 (Figure 15) which attached a strap at the back of a shield, all of these iron buckles were worn by men, and some of them served to fasten sword belts. One buckle, 33/5, (Figure 20) must have been worn at the back as it was found underneath the lower vertebrae.

These iron buckles just described were for belts or straps about 2cm wide. Much smaller buckles with plates for straps 1 to 1.5cm wide are 34/2, 57/4c, 108/2, 129/10b, 148/3, 149/4 and 159/2. The small size of two of these may be due to their function as belt fastening for a child's dress 34/2 (Figure 20) and 108/2 (Figure 48). Three of the others 148/3 (Figure 59), 149/4 (Figure 60), and 159/2 (Figure 62) fastened the strap to support a knife sheath; 129/10b (Figure 53) was with keys and 57/4c (Figure 32) was with awls or arrows, both articles probably held in a leather or textile container. A small iron fragment, 57/4b (Figure 32), found near the buckle 57/4c, is inlaid with two yellow metal rings, and may be part of an ornamented strap mount.

There are a number of iron buckle loops without plates, C/6, 5/1, 9/3, 12/5, 14/13, 27/6, 63/3, 85/2, 93/8, 94a/1, 131/4, 131/6 and 160/5d, and of these four were worn by a woman at waist or hip: 12/5, 14/13, 94a/1 and 160/5d (Figures 8, 10, 44 and 62), and eight by a man, two of them for a sword belt: 27/6 (Figure 15) and 131/4 (Figure 54) and one was probably at the waist of a juvenile 85/2 (Figure 40). A second buckle in grave 131/6 (Figure 54) must have been connected with strapping on the shield.

In connection with very small buckles at Polhill it was stated that 'It was only after the first decades of the seventh century, apparently, that narrow belts with this type of lightly constructed buckle became almost universal'[95]. Some of the flimsy buckles in question at Polhill were similar to these in bronze and iron discussed above which accommodated straps about 1cm wide, and which are hardly strong enough to have been used as belts. The other examples referred to in that context as being evidence for seventh-century belts were from early excavations without grave plan, so that the buckles may have there performed another function such as securing the straps at the back of the shields with which they were found[96]. At Dover it is clear that such small buckles were not used for belts, except possibly by a child or youth, but that they were generally used to fasten a knife sheath to a belt or to fasten the strap on a shield. There is therefore no evidence that in the seventh-century men took to wearing belts less than a centimetre wide.

Three strap-ends are of the pointed tongue shape with a slightly keeled upper surface which was fairly common in Kent in the sixth century[97], but only occurs infrequently abroad. In grave 14 (Figure 10) a pair of bronze strap-ends were placed on the right side of the female skeleton, apparently unconnected with the clothing on the body and so presumably mounted on straps placed separately in the grave. A single strap-end in grave 98 (Figure 47) terminated a ?sword belt bearing three rectangular plates (see below).

A child in grave 34 was dressed in a narrow belt with an iron buckle and a small but similar type of keeled strap-end with a rounded tip (Figure 20), the shape not unlike a more elaborate version with animal head from Finglesham grave 95[98]. Another from Polhill grave 28, a closer parallel by reason of the two rivets arranged longitudinally in the back section[99], was used on shoe straps.

An early stage of the pointed tongue, keeled strap-end is known from late Roman sources, e.g. in the richly furnished fourth-century graves at Leuna, Merseburg and Hassleben, Weimar[100]. The shape occurs in a later period in Sweden[101], in Gotland[102], Västergötland and Uppland[103], and in Germany, where in a seventh-century grave at Niederstotzingen three served as strap-ends on a harness[104]. Others have been found at Herbrechtingen, Heidenheim and at Planig[105]. Two of these strap-ends, one bearing Style II animal ornament, were found in a well-furnished grave of the late sixth or seventh century at Gilton, Kent[106]. The Dover graves in which they were found belong to phases 2 and 3. A similar keeled shape from Faversham, decorated with rectangular garnets without foil backing, has been assigned to the fifth century on the basis of its early type of cloisonné work[107], and if this reasoning is valid, the type must have arrived early in this country from the Continent and remained in use until the seventh century.

Metal terminals were also used on very narrow straps or thongs, and as some of these at Dover were found near the feet of the skeleton they must have been used on shoe laces or legging straps. The pair of thin bronze keyhole-shaped strap-ends in grave 156 (Figure 61) were found at the foot. A date in the

---

95 Philp 1973a, 194
96 Evison 1963, figs. 16–18, 29–30
97 Brown 1915 III, pl. LXXVI. 1, 2. Recent finds at Broadstairs, Kent excavator Mrs L Webster; cf. two from Kingston-by-Lewes, Welch 1983, fig. 70a
98 Hawkes et al. 1965, 22
99 Philp 1973a, fig. 54.506
100 Reinerth 1940, I, Taf. 150. 1, Taf. 145
101 Lindqvist 1936, 219
102 Nerman 1935, 79, Text Figure 183, figs. 482, 483
103 Ibid, 79
104 Paulsen 1967, 73, Abb. 41. 4, Abb. 45, Taf. 46, 12–14
105 Ibid, 73–4, Abb. 43. 8
106 Faussett 1856, 11–12, pl. VIII, 2, 4a, 5, 8, pl. IX, 3; Åberg 1926, 130, fig. 239
107 Smith 1923, 40, fig. 34; followed by Bruce-Mitford 1956, 318, pl. XVII, fig. 4

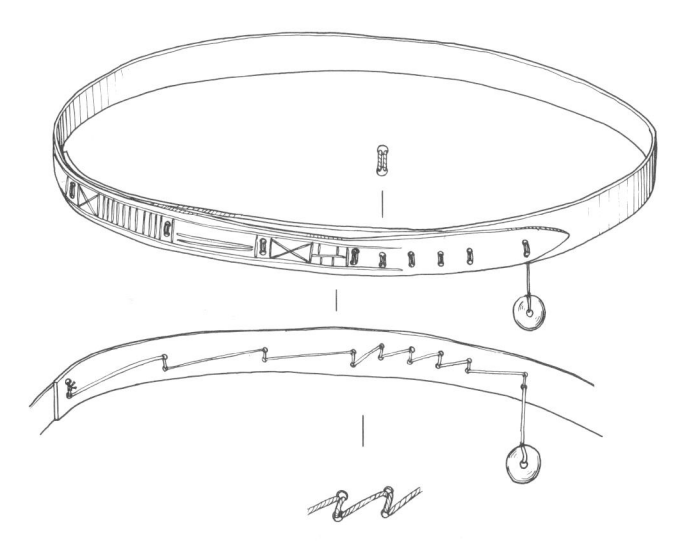

*Text Figure 16* Reconstruction of lacing of wooden belt, Dover 20/19. Scale 1/4

second half of the seventh century has already been noted for this type[108] which occurred at Rodmead Down, Wiltshire in association with a sugar-loaf shield boss, and at Shudy Camps, Cambridgeshire[109] accompanied by a seax, where they formed part of the fittings of a pouch. Pairs of cast bronze strap-tags of similar size, and accompanied by small buckles occurred at the feet in grave 28 at Polhill, Kent, and others have been noted at Finglesham[110].

A single thong terminal consisting of a hollow cone of bronze with a transverse rivet was found in grave 129 (Figure 53) at the right shoulder of a woman together with beads, a bracelet and other items which may have been strung on a necklace or contained in a bag. In grave 150 a similar bronze cone fitting (Figure 60) was at the foot so that it may have functioned as a shoe fastening, but it was also amongst fragments of a wooden bowl and wooden box, and so could have been inside one of them. A cone of this type was found at the foot of a male in grave 30 at Polhill[111] and others have been found singly at the foot at Finglesham and in a wooden casket and position unrecorded at Kingston. As shoe fastenings may be expected to occur in pairs the function of these cones is not yet established. This also holds true with two other thong tags which are made of iron and split at one end for attachment. In grave 113 a single one was at the foot and in grave 120 another single one was on the left ankle (Figures 50, 51). A single fragment of iron in grave 144, similar in size but formless, and a solid cone in grave 160 were also at the foot, and presumably performed the same unidentified function (Figures 59, 62). These thong terminals are in both male (120, 144, 150, 156) and female graves (113, 129, 160) and do not begin before phase 4.

The pieces of wooden belt in grave 20 (Figure 13, Plate 10a) owe their preservation to the bronze bowl inverted over them. The belt consists of a veneer strip of willow cut from the radial plane of the tree (p 196). One end is squared off and the other pointed, and there are pairs of perforations at regular intervals near the ends. The remains of a cord fragment in one pair of holes show that the belt was fastened by overlapping the ends, the decorated part placed over the plain, and with the pairs of perforations in each part matching. Either there is a section of belt missing which had perforations at short intervals corresponding to those on the pointed end, or the lacing was intended to miss some of the perforations at that end. The remaining cord fragment suggests that a length of cord was then attached to one end of the series of holes, drawn through to the front, back to the underside through the neighbouring matching holes, back again to the front and again through the neighbouring holes, then travelling diagonally along the underside to the next set of holes where the process was repeated (Text Figure 16). In this way only short vertical stretches of thread were visible from the front, placed at the borders of the decorative panels, and the lacing would be very firm. Loosening would not be easy, and complete unlacing would be necessary to take off the belt. As there was a large white cylindrical bead 20/18 nearby, this may have been used as a toggle for the end of the thread.

The decoration of the outer surface in panels, especially the rectangles with diagonal crosses, suggests an imitation of a belt ornamented with metal plaques as in grave 98 (Figure 47). A similar arrangement of decorative panels may be seen on a long bronze belt mount from Droxford, Hampshire[112]. This is a type of belt consisting basically of a D-shaped section of bone or wood which has also been noted from Beckford, Hereford and Worcester (Worcestershire), Riseley, Horton Kirby, Kent, Harnham Hill, Wiltshire, and Blewburton Hill, Oxfordshire (Berkshire). The wooden backing to

---

108 Evison 1963, 47, fig. 29d; Evison 1979a, 13
109 Lethbridge 1936, 14, fig. 7, 2
110 Philp 1973a, 194, fig. 54, 492, 494, 506
111 Ibid, 194–5, fig. 54.507
112 Musty 1969, 115–6, fig. 4e, f

these long belt mounts, the accidental and unique preservation of the wooden belt and traces of wood on buckles at Dover (e.g. grave 48) suggests a much more widespread use of wood for this purpose than has been suspected.

## Containers

*Pottery* (distribution plan Figure 93)
Only one hand-made pot was found, in grave 87 (Figure 40, Plate 9d). The shouldered form with decoration by bosses and horizontal and vertical lines is quite common among Anglian pots from Schleswig, Fyn, North Germany, Frisia and England. Dr Myres places the Dover pot (his Corpus fig. 221.2261) in his series II.6, 'bossed linear panel decoration on biconical and shouldered forms'[1]. The horizontal zone at the top containing diagonal lines chevron fashion in groups of three is derived from the raised, slashed neck cordons found on early fifth-century pots e.g. from Mucking (Myres fig. 181. 4130), a *Buckelurne* with bosses, swastika and *stehende Bogen* designs. (cf also other collars Myres figs. 188.1174, 189.328). Immediate predecessors to the flatter type of decoration of the Dover vessel are pots from Kettering, North Elmham and Newark (Myres figs. 126.767; 201. 3586; 229.3888) where the neck cordon is not very prominent. A close version of the Dover pot is known from Longthorpe, Cambridgeshire (Huntingdonshire) which is placed by Myres in his group II.2, 'linear zones, various patterns above bosses' (Myres fig. 126.3560). A more spherical urn, with nearly identical decoration was found at Blumental-bei-Bremen[2]. The decoration on the Dover pot therefore is derived from patterns used on fifth-century pots which have early features such as a foot, *stehende Bogen*, slashed collars and ornamented bosses, and so it should have been made at the end of that series, about the end of the century.

The excavations in the town of Dover carried out by B Philp have not produced much hand-made pottery which can be assigned to the pagan period, but there are two sherds which were parts of pots identical to this complete cemetery pot, and they must be the work of the same potter. They were found separately, one in the Market Square, and one on the bacon factory site, and so presumably belonged to two separate vessels.[3]

The bottle in grave 156, Figure 61[4], has the appearance of being made on a slow wheel although the thick walls and inelegant form may be due only to the clumsiness of the potter. It is unusual in shape, its body being spherical, the neck cylindrical and rim everted, and the fabric is grey and full of large grits or small pebbles[5], the surface patchy red and black. Only the rouletted decoration of chevron design is familiar, for this is common in Belgium and northern France where it is frequently used to ornament biconical bowls, e.g. at Harmignies and Ciply in Belgium and Seraincourt, Vexin in France[6], and some imported bowls e.g. Broomfield[7].

There is another such bottle from Margate, Kent which corresponds in every detail of form, decoration and fabric[8]. These two may represent the unprofessional efforts of a Kentish potter to copy continental bottles. It might seem just as possible that they were imported from across the Channel, for although no corresponding wares have actually been noticed they may exist amongst the numerous types produced abroad. This question will be discussed below.

The rest of the pottery found in the Dover graves is wheel-thrown in a competent fashion. Two bottles from graves 109 and 157, (Figures 49 and 61, Plate 9e)[9] are very much alike: a rather squat form, one with an incurved neck and one with a vertical neck, both rims being rounded on top and pointed at the outer edge. Girth grooves are visible on the body, and the upper part is covered with rouletting, faintly impressed and overrolled, consisting of notches in a five strand interlace pattern. The fabric is the same as other bottles at Dover and is the most usual type met with in Kentish wheel-thrown pots, i.e. it occurs in a variety of colours, red, grey or buff, with rounded sand grains fairly equal in size, some grog, fairly smooth finish, the surfaces sometimes blackened and/or burnished[10]. Of these two, 109/3 has a reddish-buff core and black surface slightly burnished, and 157/8 is red with grey surfaces. A sherd of grey ware bearing the same interlace rouletting was found in excavations in the town of Dover at site 3, Yewdens Court[11]. A number of sherds of reddish-buff similar ware with black, burnished exterior were found in the Market Street, Dover excavations in 1972 by Mr B Philp. They were also decorated with horizontal grooves and probably belonged to a biconical bowl. The five-strand interlace rouletting design has not been noted on bottles abroad. However, a biconical bowl in St. Peter's grave 382 is decorated with a three-strand interlace of the same kind, and this can be matched on a small biconical bowl in similar ware from Maroeuil in northern France[12]. A sherd only, bearing a three-strand interlace, has also been found at Nouvion-en-Ponthieu (Somme)[13].

The bottle from grave 43 (Figure 25)[14] takes the same form of body and rim, but the rouletting pattern is a zig-zag type giving the impression of a

---

1 Myres 1977 1, 38
2 Grohne 1953, Abb. 34, f.
3 I am very grateful to Mr B Philp who kindly allowed me to examine these and other sherds mentioned below. They will be published in his excavation report.
4 Evison 1979a, 1j1, fig. 11a
5 Ibid, 25, fabric group IV
6 Haigneré 1866, pl. xvii, 6; Faider-Feytmans 1970 2, pl. 91, t.107, pl. 103, t.327, pl. 121, t.918; Sirat 1967, pl. III, s.16
7 Evison 1979a, 16, fig. 16g
8 Ibid, 1j2, fig. 11b
9 Ibid, 1f1 and 1f2, figs. 7a and b
10 Ibid, 24, group I
11 Threipland 1957, 36, fig. 14. 3; Evison 1979a, 1f3
12 Evison 1979a, figs. 15g and 30e
13 Piton and Schuler 1981, pl. 22, 56
14 Evison 1979a, 1g8, fig. 8c

schematic fern-leaf design. Zig-zag rouletting patterns occur in France and Belgium in great variety, but an exact replica of this one has not been noted. The bottle from grave 137 (Figure 56)[15] has lost its neck and the body is more ovoid with a narrow base. The rouletting pattern of a band of rows of small square impressions is very common, particularly in the Rhineland[16], although it does frequently occur elsewhere as at Hantes-Wihèries, Belgium[17]. The lower half of a vessel in grave 129 (Figure 53) is also part of a bottle in grey fabric[18], and while this part is undecorated the missing top part may have borne decoration.

On a tall biconical bowl with everted neck in grave 139 (Figure 57, Plate 9c)[19] the rouletted bands of a key pattern between borders are interrupted by a break in the wall but appear to be two separate bands as opposed to the usual rouletting pattern where the wheel stamp is applied in one continuous track round the pot. The same type of roulette occurred on a sherd of a more rounded bowl from Canterbury[20]. The form of the Dover vessel is commonly found in Germany, France and Belgium in the late sixth century and in the seventh century[21].

The fabrics of wheel-thrown pots found in Anglo-Saxon graves have been studied in various ways. In the first place broad and general sub-divisions based on simple visual study and subjective judgement were suggested[22]. Most of the fabrics were of the same type, I, in a variety of colours, red, grey, buff, with rounded sand grains fairly equal in size, some grog, fairly smooth finish, surfaces sometimes blackened and burnished. This kind of fabric is not normally found in Rhineland bottles with which the Kentish bottles were compared by Leeds, but it does occur frequently in Belgium and northern France in biconical bowls as well as bottles[23]. Other types, II, III and IV and some single specimens were also distinguished. Of the Dover pots, five of the bottles belong to the most common group I, 43/4, 109/3, 129/1, 137/7, 157/8, Figures 25, 49, 53, 56, 61. The biconical bowl may also belong to this group, but as there was no exposed broken edge which could be examined visual judgement was inconclusive, (139/4, Figure 57). The bottle with globular body, 156/6, Figure 61, and its twin from Margate[24] together formed group IV, for the fabric contained large grits and the form was clumsy, so that a 'slow wheel' was suggested.

A study by atomic absorption spectroscopy was made by Mr M Cowell of the British Museum Research Laboratory[25], and this corroborated to a considerable extent the tentative results of visual typological examination. A graphic representation shows that the fabrics of type I are all clustered together with an example found at Wierre Effroy in northern France, and are near sherds from a kiln site at Huy in Belgium. Two other distinct groups were recognised, one of hand-made pots from Kent and one of wheel-thrown pots from more distant parts of France and Germany, and there were over-lap areas between. The hand-made pot from Dover 87/3 settled comfortably amongst the hand-made pots from Kent, and must therefore have been made in that county. Five of the bottles and the biconical pot were within the cluster of group I, 43/4, 109/3, 129/1, 137/7, 157/8. The fabrics of the bottle from Dover, 156/6 and its double from Margate, however, were distinct from those of imported continental pots and were closely related to the fabric group of hand-made pots produced in Kent. It seems very likely, therefore, that these two clumsily formed bottles were thrown on the wheel from Kentish clay, and so provide the earliest evidence for wheel-thrown and rouletted Kentish products as the grave belongs to the third quarter of the seventh century.

Thin sections were made of a number of the pots and were examined by Dr A C Bishop of the Department of Mineralogy, British Museum (Natural History)[26]. As a result the difficulty of different appearances of a thin section from different parts of the same pot because of imperfect mixtures of the clay and sand was stressed, and the fabric of the hand-made pot 87/3 was distinguished from the rest.

The same thin sections have more recently been examined by Dr I C Freestone, Research Laboratory, British Museum (see p 179). The inclusions in the hand-made pot are established as consistent with a derivation from Kentish sediments. For the wheel-thrown pottery a suggestion of three fabrics is made. For the globular bottle 156/6, a distinctive fabric and Kentish source already suggested is here supported by the fact that the petrology is consistent with these conclusions, based on observations of pre-Roman Iron Age Kentish pottery. The large grits or small pebbles visible in the pot were not picked up on the section which must have skirted these, showing only the fine particles.

A further observation is that the biconical bowl 139/4 has a very fine fabric lacking the quartz sand component characteristic of the bottles. This is useful additional information as it had not been possible to establish this fact visually, and as it is combined with a black, burnished surface it may be that it should be grouped with the fine ware represented by the bottle from St. Peters grave 245[27]. This

---

15 Ibid, 1h4, fig. 9d
16 Ibid, fig. 29b; Hübener 1969, maps 21–8
17 Brulet 1970, 23, fig. 9, t.9
18 Evison 1979a, 1a2, fig. 1b
19 Ibid, 3c10; fig. 15i
20 Ibid, fig. 17b. This drawing does not represent the roulette pattern accurately as it is obviously overrolled.
21 Böhner 1958 2, types B1b, C3, Taf. 1, 15, Taf. 3, 7; Hübener 1969, Taf. 75. 3, 119.5; Brulet 1970, fig. 8, t.1, fig. 14, t.70
22 Evison 1979a, 23–5
23 Ibid, 31
24 Ibid, fig. 11b
25 Ibid, 54–7, 96–9
26 Ibid, 95
27 Ibid, 1g5, fig. 8a

was earlier identified as a single specimen and compared with similar products in Belgium and northern France[28].

The conclusions resulting from these various approaches are tentative. They are the first examinations published of this imported and local pottery, and it is to be hoped that necessary cross-checking and comparative studies which have not so far been possible may be achieved in the future, both by these methods and by others.

Associated objects with the pottery provide some dating evidence e.g. the keyhole-shaped strap ends in 156 belong to the middle of the seventh century (see p 90). The silver rings in 157, worn with beads at the neck, are usual in graves of the second half of the seventh century. Amongst the associated objects in grave 137 was a small bronze buckle with plate of seventh-century type. The tall biconical shape of the pot in 139 is itself indicative of seventh-century date, as is the interlace pattern of the rouletting in 109 and 157.

Five of these pots were in graves all near each other in the middle part of the cemetery, plot G. Of the exceptions, 109/3 was further south in plot H, and 43/4 was in plot B. The sole hand-made pot was significantly in the tightly-packed early section. There was a total of only eight pots from the whole cemetery. Only one occurred in phase 1, the hand-made pot of grave 87, and none in phases 2 and 3. A single one only, 43/4, occurred in phase 4. Five belong to phase 5, only one to phase 6 and none to phase 7. This cemetery therefore demonstrates that the placing of a pot with an inhumation was rare, and that in this cemetery most belong to the period 650–675, and possibly to one family.

It must be noted that the pots are grey, buff or black, so falling in with the majority of the colouring of continental funeral pots. There are none of the red pots of which the Anglo-Saxons seemed particularly fond[29]. The pots were mostly with young people: they were buried with both males and females, of which three were children, 157 was a young female and 109 an adult or juvenile. It appears that exactly the same kinds of pots that were used for funerary purposes at Buckland were currently being used in domestic activities in the town, as there are precise parallels between both decorated hand-made and rouletted sherds. The form, fabric and decoration of the wheel-thrown pots show that they must have been imported from northern France.

The fragment of a jug handle (Figure 64, 3) was found with disturbed bones, clinch bolts and a knife fragment. This is a type which was current about the thirteenth century, and perhaps indicative of the time of disturbance of the Anglo-Saxon bones and objects with which it was buried, although it may have been lying in the topsoil at the time of a much later disturbance.

*Glass* (distribution plan Figure 93)

The cone-beaker in grave 22 (Figure 14, Plate 8b) is one of the Kempston-type cone-beakers which have been studied in detail[30]. From the evidence provided by the distribution and associated finds it was possible to draw some conclusions regarding their provenance and date of production which may be briefly summarised here. The beaker is a cone shape with everted rim, and decorated with a zone of horizontal trails below the rim and vertical looped trails on the lower part of the vessel. The earliest types were produced soon after the beginning of the fifth century. They were not very slender, with a proportion of height to diameter of mouth of 2:1, the tip was sometimes pushed in, the pontil wad was not knocked off, and the colours were olive green, brown, light green or almost completely colourless. By at least the middle of the fifth century, if not before, the true Kempston type had developed, a more slender shape of the proportions 3:1 with the colours limited mainly to light green and a number belong to the late fifth and early sixth century. Some of the beakers occur in contexts of the late sixth century, and even of the seventh century where they must be regarded as heirlooms, not only because the contexts sometimes include other earlier material, but also because it is not conceivable that the design of the vessel could have remained completely unchanged over a span of two centuries. The distribution map (Figure 114) showed a concentration in Kent with others in Sussex, the Isle of Wight, along the Thames valley and a few further north. On the Continent most were in the middle Rhine valley with more isolated find spots in France, Belgium, Holland, Germany and Czechoslovakia. One production area is suggested by a homogeneous group of cones in nearly colourless, yellowish glass at Pry and St. Gillis in Belgium and an unprovenanced one at Troyes museum in France. Three other cones of French provenance have related features, from Arras, Herpes and Marchélepot, and if a producer in France can be deduced for this group, he may also have been responsible for similar colourless cones found in England at Cassington, Oxfordshire and Alfriston, East Sussex. For the rest, particularly the normal light green Kempston type, other likely production areas are the Rhineland and Kent.

Since this survey was first made in 1972 a number of new finds have been made which have widened our knowledge of the type, as may be seen from the list p 267 and map Figure 114. A new olive green cone was found in grave 1850 at Krefeld Gellep, and fragments of another cone in the fill of grave 2528. A nearly colourless, yellowish glass from Anderlecht, Belgium was omitted from the earlier list, and may now be added to the products of the French glass-blower mentioned above, together with a colourless squat beaker with similar trail technique from

---

28 Ibid, 25, 31
29 Ibid, 21

30 Evison 1972; *idem* 1981a, 134–6, 146–7 and revised distribution map fig. 10; *idem* 1983b, p 87 map fig. 1

Pommerhof in the Rhine valley. Most spectacular, however, is the bichrome glass found at Dankirke, near Ribe in Denmark, of a bright blue glass with two zones of opaque white trails. The colouring must place it early in the period, before the Roman techniques of bright and polychrome effects were forgotten.

In England, one of the light green, slender type was found at Mucking, Essex and in the grave with it were the remains of two early applied brooches. From Lyminge, Kent, comes the earliest form yet, a light green, nearly colourless vessel, its base wide, kicked and stable, and the vertical loops rather pointed and thickening at the ends in 'merrythought' style, partially overlying the horizontal trails after the fashion of the French group. To this group it no doubt belongs, and the stable base links it closely to other beakers of this shape produced about AD 400 in the Roman tradition[31].

Important though these new finds are, they are overwhelmed by the importance of the implications of the finds at Spong Hill, Norfolk. There a large cremation cemetery was meticulously excavated, and fragments of six definite and six probable Kempston-type cones have been sifted from the urn contents. The colours are light green, light blue-green and nearly colourless. This alters the distribution considerably and the large number of fragments of glass vessels retrieved from this cremation cemetery makes it painfully clear that such evidence could have been lost in past excavations, and an assiduous study of the occurrence of glass vessels in cremation cemeteries will alter distribution maps of glass in England by filling in many of the unoccupied spaces north of the Thames.

Another particularly important find spot is Der Runde Berg bei Urach, Baden-Württemberg, where no less than twenty-three fragments of probable Kempston types have been found in five different shades of green. Eight of these are certainly Kempston types[32]. One other rim fragment is in light blue and differs from the others in being slightly cupped[33], so that its original shape when complete cannot be certain, and it might have been a claw-beaker. A large number of Kempston-type cones thereby significantly extends the southernmost group on the distribution map in south Germany.

The Dover cone is the tallest of the slender Kempston type which was mainly produced between the middle and end of the fifth century, but which may have started even earlier. The grave is one of the few disturbed by a later grave (18), which belongs to the second quarter of the seventh century (see p 137). The accompanying grave finds were a sword, knife, spear ferrule and inlaid socket of a spearhead so that a date of about 500 is likely.

The Kempston type of cone-beaker has some characteristics in common with the Scandinavian Snartemo type of beaker which does also occur on the Continent, but which is found mostly in Scandinavia and not at all in England. That is generally, but not always, a more squat vessel, with proportions of height to mouth diameter of about 2:1, like those of the earlier Kempston-type beakers, while most of the later Kempston-type beakers have proportions of 3:1. The Snartemo type, however, often has a foot, and the walls and trails are thicker and in a darker colour of olive green. Apart from that the general shape and the horizontal trail decoration with looped trails below is similar. As each Scandinavian fragment had not been closely studied in 1972 there was no published evidence as to whether they were of the Snartemo or Kempston type[34]. A general study of Scandinavian glass was subsequently made by Hunter for a thesis[35], and he has now stated that with one exception, the blue Ribe cone, there are no Kempston types in Scandinavia[36]. A distribution map of Snartemo-type beakers in Scandinavia shows them mainly concentrated in southern Norway and Gotland[37].

The theory suggested[38] that both types may have been manufactured in the Namur area, the thicker variant being more suitable for the long distance trade to Scandinavia, was not convincing as many of the Roman glass vessels exported from the Continent to Scandinavia are, on the contrary, extravagant and delicate types. Now an analytical study has shown significant chemical differences between some of the Snartemo and Kempston types, suggesting the use of geologically different raw materials from two distinct sources[39]. The possibility that the Snartemo beakers were made in Scandinavia, is quite strong, the distribution indicating a possible source in south Norway. No detailed study of the individual examples is available, however, so that a judgement cannot be made as to whether a single source or more than one is likely. The variety of the Kempston-type beakers and their distribution, however, suggests possible multiple sources for this type, the major ones being in Kent and the Rhineland, with another in northern France. It would be useful, therefore, if the analytical studies so far based solely on beakers from Helgö and Spong Hill could be extended to material from other sites, and if these could be accompanied by a typological study of the Scandinavian beakers and fragments.

The analytical study so far conducted has, however, produced a useful result in suggesting two distinct origins. The distinction between the two types is not complete however, as there is a footless beaker found in Norway with the proportions of a Kempston type, which appears to be a product of the Snartemo type of glass-blowers because of the thickness of the wall and trails and darkness of the

---

31  cf Haberey 1942, Abb. 6a, 7a, 9a, 11a, 15a etc.
32  Christlein 1979, Taf. 26, 1–11, 13–18, 20, 21, 23–7
33  Ibid, Taf. 26, 8
34  Evison 1972, 49ff
35  Hunter 1977

36  Hunter and Sanderson 1982, 25. It is to be hoped that detailed evidence on this point will be forthcoming.
37  Bakka 1970, 42, fig. 1
38  Shetelig 1925, 156; Bjørn 1929
39  Hunter and Sanderson 1982

colour[40]. Further, in a recent examination of some of the glass fragments found at Helgö I noted a thin light green fragment which has been flattened by heat, but which has horizontal trails and the top of a looped trail and should have been part of a Kempston-type beaker[41]. The analysis of the fragments from Spong Hill, No. 1911 showed a higher potassium content and other differences from the other fragments from the same site, and as the colour is a light blue-green unusual and possibly unique for the type, a connection with late Roman producers is likely.

A different type of cone-beaker with diagonal moulding, everted rim and a zone of white trails below occurred in grave 38 (Figure 23, Plate 8c). The earliest version of the type, a low, straight-walled cone with a broad and stable kicked base, occurred in a number of graves at Mayen which are dated to the period AD 400–450[42]. Later developments of the form have been studied by Rademacher and Rau[43]. Rau distinguished three types with diagonal rippling: the Mayen type of AD 400–450, the Gellep type which is taller, with straight rim and narrow base and belongs to about AD 450–500, and the Rheinsheim type which is also tall and narrow-based, but with an out-bent rim, dated to AD 500–550 by Rau. This type he compared with the cone-beaker in grave 812 at Gellep, dated to AD 525–600 by Pirling[44]. The Rheinsheim type occurs in various shades of light green, and none of the descriptions available mention use of a different colour for the trails, so that they are presumably of self-colour.

In England a cone found at Islip, Northamptonshire[45] belongs to the Gellep type as it has a straight rim. The tall, light green cone with everted rim found in cremation E.19 at Caistor-by-Norwich[46] would seem to belong to the Rheinsheim type, although allocated to the Gellep type by Rau. The base, however, is fairly wide and similar examples are also from Westbere, Kent[47] and Loveden, Lincolnshire[48], and the heights of these three cones range from 14.5cm to 15cm, the trails are self-coloured and the base only just sufficiently wide or kicked for stability. Only the cone from grave 73, Linton Heath, Cambridgeshire[49] is a close parallel to the Dover cone; it is light green with an everted rim and the trail, although decomposed, appears to have been opaque white. The base is narrow and rounded, and also retains remains of the punty knob. The Islip cone was in a well-furnished female grave of about AD 500. The Caistor-by-Norwich cone was found with fragments of an undecorated pot and fused beads. The Loveden cone was in a decorated pot of a type dated by Myres to the sixth century. Only a shell was found in the Linton Heath grave.

It was a young woman who was buried in Dover grave 38 with a Kentish brooch and buckle of the end of the sixth century. Besides the glass vessel other items which denote her high status are a gold finger ring and a weaving sword. She was also distinguished by a small bronze ornament by the skull denoting an individual style of hair ornament or headdress. The glass cone is probably an import, for the type occurs also in Belgium, Holland and Germany.[50] Except for the examples from Samson and Linton Heath, however, none appear to be decorated with white trails. These often appear on plain cone-beakers, stemmed beakers, bell-beakers and vertically moulded cone-beakers common in northern France in the fifth and sixth centuries[51], so that this area is the probable source.

Amongst the numerous possessions in grave 20 was a claw-beaker (Figure 13, Plate 8a). This was a form of glass vessel very popular in the post-Roman period, mainly in Germany and England, and the origin of the distinctive feature of hollow claws may be traced to the dolphin appliqués on a particular variety of late Roman beakers[52]. With the additional evidence provided by new finds there is no appreciable hiatus between these late Roman products and the claw-beaker from Flavion, Belgium on the Continent on the one hand and the claw-beakers from Mucking grave 843[53] and Broadstairs I, grave 42 in England on the other. The basic stemmed beaker form of the Mucking glass, and the wide-based cone of the Broadstairs glass may be recognised as types belonging to the decades around AD 400. These two vessels, and others of type 2a and b, find no parallels on the Continent, so that fifth-century production in England must be considered probable. The appearance of another example of type 2b in grave 204 at Finglesham now reinforces this likelihood[54]. Thereafter there can be no doubt about the insular production of types 3–5 of the sixth and seventh century.

Since the publication of the study of claw-beakers the glass fragments at the Runde Berg bei Urach have provided further valuable evidence as they include parts of claw-beakers[55]. There are some pieces of the foot and wall sections of stemmed

---

40 Rygh 1880, No. 337
41 Historical Museum, Stockholm
42 Haberey 1942
43 Rademacher 1942, 296–301, Taf. 50, 51, 52, 1 and 2; Rau 1976
44 Pirling 1966, 1, 150; ibid 2, Taf. 71
45 Smith 1917–18b, 115, fig. 3
46 Myres and Green 1973, pl. XIX, E.19
47 Canterbury Museum
48 Myres 1977, 1, 42–3; ibid 2, fig. 236, 1291
49 De Baye 1893, pl. XIV, 2; Neville 1854, fig. on 109; Cambridge Museum No. 48. 1599. Strangely, this one, too is allocated to the Gellep type by Rau 1976, 116

50 1. Samson, grave 12, Belgium, with sword mounts of the type found at Petersfinger and Abingdon of the first half of the fifth century, Dasnoy 1968, 305–7, fig. 12. 2. Rhenen, grave 675, Holland, Glazema and Ypey 1955, pls. 35 and 37. 3. Krefeld-Gellep, grave 812, Germany, Pirling 1966 2, Taf. 71.5 in a grave of AD 525–600. 4. Schwarzrheindorf, grave 62, Germany, with objects probably of the sixth century, Behrens 1947, 22, Abb. 56.1, Taf. 5.5.
51 Rademacher 1942, 307ff
52 Evison 1982, fig. 2, pl. Vc and d
53 Ibid, pl. IVa
54 Campbell et al. 1982, 25. fig. 4
55 Christlein 1979, Taf. 22.20, 23, 25, 26

beaker shapes which might have been claw-beakers. There are also some actual fragments of claws[56], testifying to the presence of such vessels, in the colours of green, light green, dark olive and light yellow-colourless. There are, furthermore, fragments of claws decorated with indented trails. One in brown[57] must belong to the Anglo-Saxon type 3c. This is no doubt the type also of a light green claw[58] for the only examples listed as light green which are not type 3c[59] are the claw-beaker from Mucking grave 843 which is in unusually good quality glass, and the lost beaker from Eastry for the description of which we have to rely on an early record. Another claw with trails at the Runde Berg is in light blue-green[60], a colour only found in the beakers from Castle Eden and Faversham (1336a '70) which belong to the fifth-century types 2a and 2b respectively. The fourth claw with a trail at the Runde Berg is in light blue, and so far this is a unique combination. The light blue, cupped rim with horizontal trails mentioned above[61], which does not fit in with the known colour range of Kempston cones, should perhaps be considered in connection with this claw. The shade of blue in the three Kentish claw-beakers of the sixth-century type 4c cannot be described as light, and none are decorated with indented trails on the claws. The fragments from this site, therefore, indicate a range from the fifth century, through the sixth century and possibly into the seventh century, with both Frankish and Anglo-Saxon provenances.

A distribution map of claw-beakers on the Continent[62] which closely resemble Anglo-Saxon products and may be imports, included four of type 2a and four of type 3c. To these may now be added the site furthest south in Germany at the Runde Berg, one of type 2a and two of type 3c. The unique nature of the blue claw-beaker necessitates it remaining enigmatic until explained by further finds.

Yet one more find-spot should be added to the map, for clawbeaker fragments found in a grave of the first half of the sixth century at Roma, Gotland[63]. This is in light green-brown, with a large foot and distinct stem of stemmed beaker form, and two claws remain, of which one only has a vertical tooled trail. These features belong to the fifth or early sixth century, with affinities to types 2a and 2b. This beaker is therefore the only early claw-beaker type so far detected in Sweden.

The claw-beaker 20/16 is one of a group of three, designated as type 3a[64], all from Kent, which appear to have been made by the same person. They are in olive green or brown and blown very thin. The body is a stemmed beaker, tall and slim with a sweeping S-curve to the wall, and two rows of four claws each on the lower two-thirds of the body which harmonise with the outline. No other claw-beaker is known of this type except one from Hermes, Oise, France[65]. The others in England are also from Kent, from Lyminge, grave 41[66], and Sarre, grave 60[67]. One more claw-beaker similar to the Dover glass was found in 1974 at Ozingell, Kent which has some of the characteristics of type 3a, i.e. it is brown, with a flaring rim, and claws on the lower two-thirds of the beaker following the body contour[68]. Its lower height and narrow foot, however, relate it also to the examples of type 3b.

The Ozingell beaker was associated with a mixed group of objects from two graves varying from the sixth to seventh century. In the Sarre grave was a knife, small spear, and buckle with shield-on-tongue. The Lyminge, Sarre and Dover beakers have some points in common with the claw-beaker in grave D3 at Finglesham[69], such as a similar height, although the Finglesham vessel has been classified with the shorter type 3b because of its basic conical shape and unstable foot. The contents of the Finglesham grave have frequently been scrutinised to determine its date, and the latest examination by Bakka points to just before AD 525[70]. This is the same date that has been deduced for grave 20 at Dover using all the criteria and data available, both from comparable archaeological sources and from the cemetery itself.

Types 3a and 3b must have been produced during the first quarter of the sixth century, and as the distribution, with the exception of one at Hermes, North France, is confined to Kent (Figure 115b) production must have taken place in that county. This is in direct contrast to the succeeding type 3c with indented trails, to which the majority of Anglo-Saxon claw-beakers belong, and which are mainly found in counties outside Kent (Figure 115a), with three in Kent and six in Germany and Belgium[71]. As the find spots of the later, seventh-century types 4b and 5 are once more mainly in Kent, either the producers of types 3c and 3d had moved their site of operation for a time or they had produced for distance trade. Types 3a and 3b, however, were of local manufacture for local consumption.

The glass tumbler form 6/1 (Figure 7, Plate 9a) is classified as a variant of the bell-beakers by Harden

---

56 Ibid, Taf. 22.3, 4, 5 and 9
57 Ibid, Taf. 22.2
58 Ibid, Taf. 22.6,
59 Evison 1982, Table 1
60 Christlein 1979, Taf. 22.7
61 See note 33 above
62 Evison 1982, fig. 8
63 Arwidsson 1942, 119; *Fornvännen* 1908, 290, Abb. 176
64 Evison 1982, 47–8, pl. IX, b and c. Since the publication of Evison 1982, it has been suggested that a fragment of glass found at Heybridge in Essex might be either a fragment of a Roman amphora or a Saxon claw-beaker (Harden 1982). In view of its colour which is 'bright green', the absence of traces of a claw, and the wide spaces between the trails, it seems unlikely that it was a claw-beaker.
65 Ibid, pl. VIc
66 Warhurst 1955, 27, pl. XI
67 Brent 1866, 168, pl. V, 3
68 Evison 1982, 60
69 Bakka 1958, fig. 53
70 Bakka 1981, 27
71 Evison 1982, figs. 6–8

(his class V.bi.), and is a type which is given the name *Sturzbecher* in Germany[72]. Of the types studied by Böhner in the Trier region[73], the Dover beaker falls between his forms A and D, form A belonging mostly to the sixth century and D to the sixth and seventh century. Form A has an incurved wall and form D has a nearly straight wall, while the Dover contour is a slight curve. The Dover beaker however, has another distinguishing characteristic in that the rim is rolled over to the inside. Most rims of the pagan period are simply thickened, but Böhner notes that the roll of glass at the rim is to the inside on his Type D *Sturzbecher*. From the photograph[74] the rim appears to be thickened rather than hollow-rolled as on the Dover glass. By the late sixth or early seventh century more complex rims are introduced, particularly on the palm cups where rims are often folded or rolled or both, a tubular air space being left inside the roll, and these rims continue into the eighth century and later[75]. Such a rolled rim does not occur on the other bell-beakers found in England, but it does occur on other forms such as a squat jar from Ipswich in Ipswich Museum, and on a pouch bottle from Kingston Down grave 46[76], both of these being late types.

The other glasses of this bell-beaker kind in England, in Harden's class V.b, domed with constriction in body, are decorated with vertical moulding, i.e. from Ashford, Kent,[77]. Vb1 Faversham, Kent[78], Mitcham, grave 34, London (Surrey)[79] and Breach Down, Kent[80]. As to the associated objects in grave 6 at Dover, the fragments of a pendant match one in grave 29, but a later date for grave 6 in phase 5 is indicated by the absence of a brooch. The rarity of the glass type in this country indicates that it must be an import, possibly from the Rhineland[81] or the Meuse valley[82]. Examples from the Ardennes are dated to the seventh century.

The type of palm cup found in grave 160, (Figure 62, Plate 9b), plain with an outward folded rim, is the most common variety found in England, and although many were found in Kent there are several from other parts of the country as well, from Southampton to Desborough in Northamptonshire. There is nothing particularly distinctive about the Dover vessel except the rim which is pinched to a hollow roll at the edge and then pressed to the wall in a fold. The type was noticed as being very common by Rademacher[83], and Böhner registers a *Stufe* IV dating (seventh century) for a similar palm cup from Eisenach Grave 65[84]. The cabochon pendant found in grave 160 at Dover gives a late seventh-century date.

The two Dover glasses that belong to the seventh century, therefore, the bell-beaker and the palm cup, are both common types on the Continent. The bell-beaker is no doubt an import, as the palm cup might be also, but as there are more of these in England, with a concentration in Kent and four at Faversham, it is possible that some may have been manufactured here. The cone beaker with diagonal moulding must have been imported in the sixth century, probably from northern France, but a Kentish production centre must be recognised for the Kempston-type cone-beaker in the fifth century and the claw-beaker in the early sixth century. Two of the glass vessels therefore belong to the first phase of the cemetery, and one each to phases 3, 5 and 6. There were none on the barrow or in the latest phase.

The fragment of opaque blue glass 59/3q (Figure 33, Colour Plate IV) was amongst the beads of a necklace, and, as it was not perforated, it was presumably attached to it in some way by textile or threads. The colour is the green-blue of lapis lazuli, no doubt a deliberate imitation by the glass blowers of the time, and, along with the white insets of shell and composition, this colour of glass was the other main inlaid stone which complemented the garnets in Kentish keystone garnet brooches[85], and also in the Sutton Hoo jewels, the pyramids, the purse lid and the shoulder clasps[86]. The fragment is a trapezoid shape with two damaged corners, blown glass about a millimetre thick, with a slight curvature, and blemished by sand granules. As there are few fragments of Roman glass in this cemetery, and those only in phases 1 and 2, the likelihood of this being a random fragment picked up locally in phase 3 is not very great. For analysis and further comment see p 185. It may be the remnant of a blown vessel cut up by a jeweller for use as inlay in disc brooches or other pieces of jewellery. The sand blemishes would have made this last piece unusable. The suggestion that Roman glass vessels were used for this purpose can be entertained, but if garnet-coloured glass was being produced for inlay in the Sutton Hoo jewellery[87], the blue glass may also have been an insular product. This blue glass is found only occasionally in keystone disc brooches, but more often in plated and composite brooches. In the Dover cemetery it occurs as an inlay only once, as the small disc centre piece of the disc brooch 35/1. As it is a common feature only in Kentish jewellery and in some of the Sutton Hoo pieces, it may well have been manufactured in south-east England.

A small glass fragment 48/11 (Figure 27) is part of a light green Roman vessel, and, along with some other small items, was in a purse or bag worn at the

---

72 Rademacher 1942, 307–11, Taf. 60–2
73 Böhner 1958 1, 228–31, Ibid 2 Taf. 65.4, 65.5, 65.6 and 67.1
74 Ibid, Taf. 67.1
75 e.g. Ypey 1968, 385, Afb. 11, 13, 14, 15; Besteman 1974, 97, fig. 36.2
76 Liverpool Museum M6118
77 Harden 1956a, fig. 25.Vb
78 Ibid, pl. XVII.A.d
79 *Glass in London* 1970, No. 44
80 B.M. Reg. No. 79 5–24 2; Conyngham 1844b, pl. 1
81 Rademacher 1942, 307–11, Taf. 61
82 Périn 1972, fig. 9.5b
83 Rademacher 1942, 304, Taf. 57.1
84 Böhner 1958, 227, Taf. 64.4
85 Avent 1975 i, 15
86 Bruce-Mitford 1978, 595, pls. 16, 17, 21b
87 Evison 1983a, 10

hip of a young woman. Another fragment of a light blue-green Roman vessel was found along with a Roman coin and beads at the hip of the woman in grave 15 (Figure 11). The only other glass fragment, 49/1b (Figure 28, Colour Plate IV), was with some beads at the neck of an older woman in a grave adjoining 48. Although the colouring is distinctive, colourless with a bright blue streak, it is a chip with no original surfaces remaining, so that the form of the original product cannot be deduced. These three remnants of Roman glass are in the earliest part of the cemetery. Anglo-Saxon women frequently kept a small fragment of glass, and several instances have been listed by Meaney[88].

*Coffins*

There were no traces of the outline of the wood of coffins in the form of black dust or wood fragments as appeared in a rectangular shape round some of the skeletons and underneath them, at Holborough, Kent[89]. Nevertheless, there are other indications of some form of body container in some of the graves. At Holborough a single nail found at the foot of grave 18, but near the top of the fill, i.e. 1ft. 5in. (43.2cm) above the floor of the grave, might have been used in a coffin construction. This possibility is less likely for the single nail found at Dover on the left knee in grave 111, and the bent iron bar in grave 147 at the right foot, in view of their position near the floor. Connection with a coffin is more likely, however, for the disc-headed nail at the head of grave 162 which was lying 7.5cm above the floor of the grave. A fragment of iron sheet and bent ?nail in grave 163 to the right of the head cannot be identified for any particular function, and so may be considered as a possible coffin fitting.

There are three other types of iron object in the Dover graves which must have been used in connection with some kind of body container. One type occurred in grave 155 in the form of two iron bars with each end bent at right angles, one 12cm long and the other 7.8cm (Figure 60). The ends are not perfectly preserved, and no doubt originally came to a sharper point. They were found at diagonally opposite corners of the grave, one 7.5cm above the floor, and one 15cm above the floor. Traces of transverse wood grain on the inner surfaces, and on the outside of one of the terminals as well, show that they were hammered into wood to hold two butted planks together.

A second and different method of construction is evident in grave 135, where there were two clench bolts beside the body, one by the right elbow and one by the right femur (Figure 56). Except that they are smaller in size, they are identical in type to the clench bolts used for the clinker-built ships as at Sutton Hoo, i.e. a bolt with domed head and a diamond-shaped rove. They are used for joining two overlapping planks, and the bolts in grave 135 would have fastened together two planks each 2cm thick. As they were both on the same side of the grave and on the floor, it is not clear of what kind of construction they formed a part. It may have been some kind of bier or stretcher. Five more clench bolts, sturdier and designed to penetrate a 4.6cm thickness of wood, were found in the pit containing human bones, a knife fragment and medieval sherd, which apparently represents a reburial of disturbed grave contents in the medieval period (p 15 Figure 64, 1a, b). If this surmise is correct, the clench bolts would have come from an Anglo-Saxon grave. Their presence also in graves at Bifrons, Sarre and Ozingell[90] suggests that there, too, they were used in the construction of body containers. At the excavation at St. Peter's Church, Barton-upon-Humber, Humberside (Lincolnshire) five coffins with iron clenches and roves were found for which two distinctive shapes are proposed: a cross-section of a triangle or of a rectangle with incurved sides, and the use of barkwood is considered probable[91]. The bolts were perhaps more commonly used in boat-building, as in the ship-burial and Mound 2 at Sutton Hoo[92]. The same kind of clinker-built technique was also used on houses, for this type of rivet was found along the lines of the walls of Buildings A1(c) and A3(b) at Yeavering, dated to AD 651–c685, and on other settlement sites[93]. Later examples of Anglo-Saxon use of the technique survives on eleventh-century doors at Hadstock and Buttsbury, Essex[94].

The third type of iron fitting at Dover is an iron strip pierced by two rivets, seven of which were found in grave 41 (Figure 24). The rivets vary in length, the longest being 3.8cm, which suggests use either for joining very thick pieces of wood, or for fastening one plank lightly to another underneath. It would not be an efficient method for fastening overlapping planks as the clench bolt would be, but it would fasten together two thick, butted planks. All seven were at the top of the grave fill, 35cm above the floor of the grave, and all were apparently *in situ* except for 6a which was moved slightly in clearing the topsoil from the grave. They were lying parallel to the sides of the grave, five with the rivet shafts pointing more or less inwards, the other two downwards. As they were lying on a level with the surface of the chalk it is not possible to be sure that they had remained completely immune to disturbance by plough. If the angles of the position of these fittings had not altered, however, the suggestion made earlier[95] that they fastened together two horizontal butted planks is not likely to be right as they would have been set vertically for this purpose, and 35cm is rather wide for a single lower plank. There are two other more likely constructions. Short

---

88  Meaney 1981, 227–8
89  Evison 1956, 92, fig. 21
90  Brown 1915 III, 150, pl. XI, 6; Smith 1868, 165; Smith 1854, 17
91  Rodwell and Rodwell 1982, 291–2, fig. 5
92  Bruce-Mitford 1975a, 121, figs. 80 and 279
93  Hope-Taylor 1977, 193, fig. 91; Evison 1980a, 39, fig. 23, 28
94  Hewett 1978, 207, 211–14, fig. 11 and pls. I and II
95  Evison 1980b, 357

vertical planks could have been fastened together near the top. Alternatively if a lid were added, it could have been fastened to the plank sides by these fittings. The latter is not so convincing as the iron fittings have short rivets and are surely intended to make a flush joint with two planks.

Similar iron fittings have been found in other Anglo-Saxon graves, at Sarre, in Kent, for instance, where the positions are not known. A very thick coffin 'strengthened by eighteen pieces of iron, each having a strong rivet at each end and three iron staples' was noted in grave 172 at Sibertswold[96]. In grave 44 at Lyminge four of these strap fittings were found, apparently one in each corner[97]. The rivets were as much as 7cm long, and it is supposed that they passed through the side planks and into the end planks, presumably at the junction of an upper and lower horizontal plank, so that as a secondary function two planks were held together by the iron strip. From Broomfield in Essex whole and fragmentary fittings of this kind are preserved in the British Museum, amounting to five or six complete examples, all showing transverse wood grain on the inside, and one of them being as long as 17.5cm. The remains of about eight or nine similar fittings from the Taplow burial are also extant in the British Museum. On one of them is a substantial plank fragment with the original flat, planed surfaces of the wood preserved, so that it can be seen that a rivet 1.8cm long is embedded in a plank 2.3cm thick.

The positions of the Broomfield and Taplow fittings are not known, but the positions of the strips at Sutton Hoo show that they must have been fitted in a vertical position, and the shortness of the rivets shows that they penetrated a plank a minimum of 2.3cm thick, like that at Taplow, and so must have joined two horizontal planks. Although traces of a lid were noted at Lyminge, there is no definite evidence for a lid in the graves at Dover which have metal coffin fittings.

Even though iron fittings are present in some of the graves, it is evident that they alone would not have sufficed to hold a coffin together, and carpentry joins must have been used to a considerable extent, e.g. dove-tailing and wooden nails. The normal construction of the coffins at Barton-on-Humber involved pegging and dowelling[98]. In fact, in view of the almost complete absence of metal fittings found in connection with early Anglo-Saxon work in wood such as boxes and houses, it is clear that the major part of carpentry work was carried out without the aid of metal nails and fittings. It is quite likely, therefore, that there were wooden coffins in other graves at Dover as well, and there are some traces of wood which suggest this was so. Some wood fragments beside the skull position in grave 121 were not lying in the vicinity of any metal object and they have been identified as oak. There were two bronze bowls in the cemetery, and in both cases wood underneath them has been preserved to a certain extent. In grave 137 these fragments have been identified as oak, and in grave 20 as probably oak. In these three graves, therefore, there appears to have been partial preservation of an oak body container, and it seems probable that there were others of which no trace remains. The ten graves which have definite or possible indications of a coffin occur throughout the time in which the cemetery was in use, and belong to men, women and children.

*Wooden boxes with iron fittings* (distribution Figure 94)

Wooden boxes were identified by their iron fittings, many of which bore traces of wood. The approximate size can be estimated in some graves by the positions in which the fittings were found, and estimates suggest that the boxes were mostly rectangular in plan, about 32 × 20cm.

There are the remains of eight bolt-plates, each of the same basic type. The main part is a flat, sub-rectangular plate with turned-in edges, one end being square and the other slanting or narrowing. The middle of each end is extended in a rod, which passes freely through a looped staple embedded in wood. There is a slot in the middle of the plates 29/9, 35/8b, 55/5c,f, 59/4a, 60/6a and 81/1, (Figures 17, 21, 30, 33, 34 and 39) and two perforations, one in each corner of the square end, appear on 59/4a, 60/6a and 124/3f (Figures 33, 34 and 51).

The simplest form of this bolt-lock could be made completely in wood, where a key with two pins could be inserted in a slot to engage with two holes in the bolt, which could thereby be moved sideways in or out of the catch for the length of the slot. The Dover bolts make more use of iron, for the bolt itself is of iron, and the rod terminals would slide easily in the looped iron staples. There was no iron plate on the outside to protect the keyhole or slot in the box, although a brass plate which performed this function was found in grave 180 at Sibertswold, Kent[99].

A diagram section of the lid and side of a box with a shot bolt is shown in Text Figure 17a. The spring is down, engaged with the square end of the bolt, and a T-shaped key has been inserted in the lock. Text Figure 17b shows the bolt seen from inside the box. The key is then turned so that its pins fit in the two perforations, pulled upwards so that the spring lies flat and the bolt can then be drawn. A similar kind of spring lock, with a two-pronged key, was fitted on the front of the wooden box covered with ornamental bronze plates which was found in the woman's grave under Cologne cathedral[100].

---

96 Faussett 1856, 130
97 Warhurst 1955, 28; Evison 1979b, 123, fig. 6.1c
98 Rodwell and Rodwell 1982, 301, 310–12, fig. 11
99 Faussett 1856, 133, fig. 1. Only a fragment of this plate reached Liverpool Museum, and this was among the objects lost in 1941 (information Dr M Warhurst, Keeper of Antiquities, Liverpool Museum). Locks of this type from Scandinavia were discussed by Pitt-Rivers 1883, 14, pl. IV, figs. 1C, 2C, 3C, 4C and 5C.
100 Doppelfeld 1959, 68–71, Abb. 46, Taf. 7; Doppelfeld and Pirling 1966, Taf. 104

# GRAVE GOODS: DISCUSSION OF TYPES

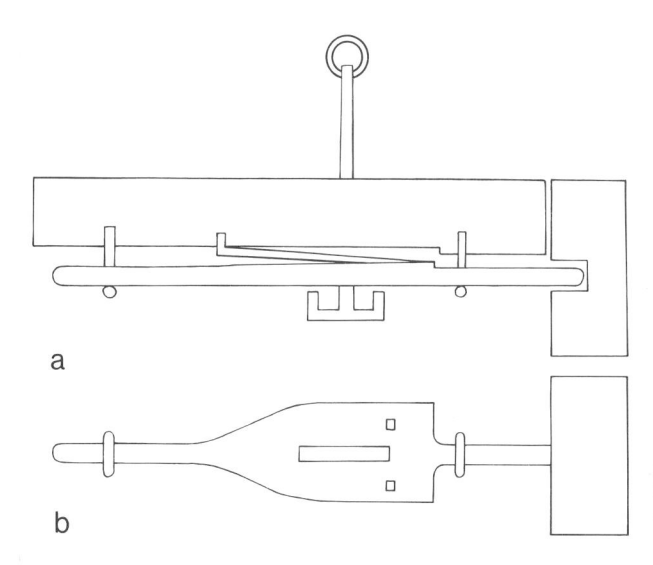

*Text Figure 17 a* Diagram of bolt plate in box lid, section of shot bolt with key inserted in lock
*b* View of bolt inside the box

Where there was a slot in the bolt-plate a symmetrical T-shaped key could be inserted and turned to engage its two pins in the pair of perforations (59/4a, 60/6a) (Table XVI). Where there was no slot in the bolt-plate (124/3f) a similar slot must have been cut in the wood of the box beside the bolt. An asymmetrical, L-shaped key with two pins could then have been inserted to engage with the two perforations in the plate at the side, as F/5, 29/9, 35/8b, 55/5c,f and 81/1. Where there are no perforations[101] the pins of the key could engage with the square shoulders of the bolt. Examples of T-shaped and L-shaped keys which could have performed this function may be seen in various graves: in one of the box graves, 35/7 (Figure 21) hanging at the hip of the occupant, and also 13/9, Figure 9 and 44/4a, Figure 26, and see p 116 below.

Found in a position close to some of the bolt-plates, there is an iron strip fixed into wood at one end, which must have functioned as a spring. One occurred in grave 32 without an iron bolt-plate, so that there the bolt was probably made of wood. This spring would have been attached to a recess on the inside of the lid, i.e. between the lid and the bolt-plate. It engaged with the turned-over square end of the bolt-plate when the bolt was shot, and when depressed by the key it would disengage from the plate edge into the recess so that the box could be opened by sliding sideways the key engaged with the bolt. Part of a key actually remains *in situ* in the slot of the bolt-plate 29/9. The spring 55/18a, and possibly also 124/3f, consists of a double strip.

Two boxes without locks were provided with alternative fastening devices. One ring-headed staple, 43/5b (Figure 25), still holds its corresponding hook fastener, and there was a second ring-headed staple nearby. Text Figure 18a is an attempted reconstruction. Item 143/1b (Figure 58), a hasp with pointed end, has a slot which fitted over an iron ring-staple as on a box in grave 48 at Shudy Camps in Cambridgeshire[102]. A pin through the ring would have secured the box. There is a difference in shape as the Shudy Camps hasp is straight, so that the top end was fixed in the edge of the lid and the loop-staple fastening on the side of the box. The Dover hasp, however, is curved. A ring-headed staple was found beside it which must have secured it to the top surface of the lid. The other end of the hasp was then pushed over the looped staple fixed on the side of the box, the curve in the hasp providing sufficient resilience for it to slide over the staple without breaking.

It is also likely that the curve in the hasp was to surmount a raised ridge of semi-circular section on the edge of the lid. This ridge would have continued on the top of the walls and at the opposite end. The latter would have formed a stop for the lid, and the front ridge would have functioned as a grip by which to pull the lid. The box at Köln functioned on hinges, but its lid was set in this way at a lower level within an upstanding rim. The two curved iron fittings may have been used to ornament the lid, as in the reconstruction Text Figure 18b.

Seven of the boxes have a rectangular handle, five of them occupying a central position within the extant fragments, so that they would appear to have been fixed in the middle of the lid. There is little evidence to suggest whether this was flat or convex like a chest, although the handle 55/5a seems, from the adhering wood traces, to have been lying on a flat surface. One box had a ring handle 143/1c (Figure 58), and this, too, was in a central position.

Only two have a hinge, and both consist of iron strips with interlocking ring ends. A single hinge, 35/8a (Figure 21), was found at the opposite side to the lock and lid lifter. In grave 43 (Figure 71), the rectangular handle takes a central position with a hinge on one side of it and the hook fasteners on the other. There was only one hinge in each of the graves 35 and 43, but presumably one had been lost from each box as they would hardly function well singly, and this simple type of hinge does occur in pairs in Kentish graves at Gilton and Kingston[103]. Unless it is to be assumed that a pair of hinges has been lost from all the other boxes, it must be assumed that their construction was different and the lid must have been removed in another way. One flimsy method would be for the lid to be swivelled sideways horizontally on a pivot. Alternatively, the lid could slide in channels cut in the side walls of the box as suggested for 143/1 (Figure 18b) where the hasp was found at one of the narrow ends of the box.

A number had corner fittings, plates, or rivets, (Table XVI). The bronze cleats 55/5b (Figure 30)

---

101 Because of the rusted condition of the iron there may have been some perforations which are not distinguishable. It has not been possible to obtain radiographs.

102 Lethbridge 1936, fig. 9, 2
103 Faussett 1856, 31, figs. 1 and 2, 48, fig. 3

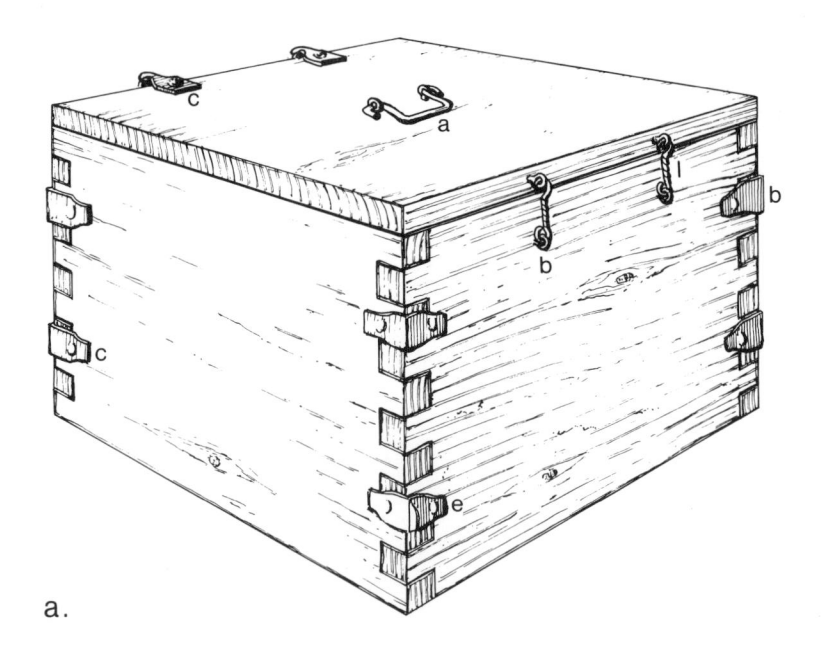

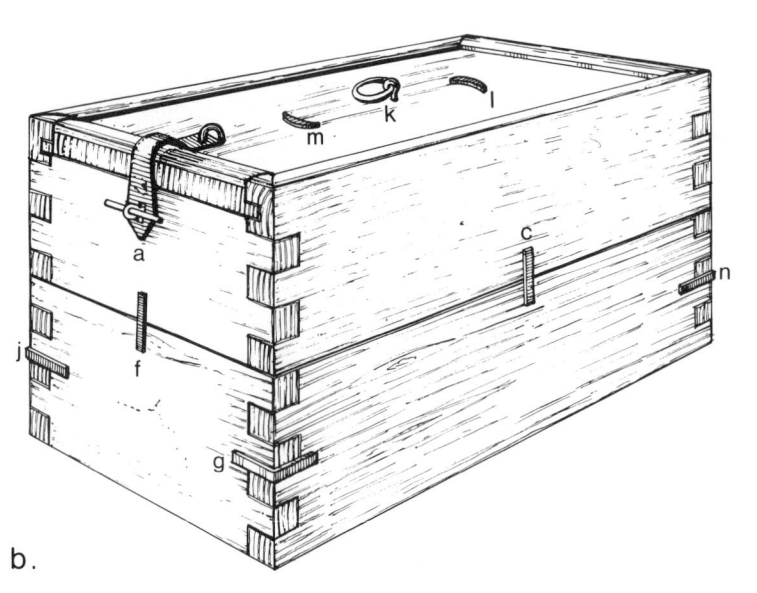

*Text Figure 18*   *a* Reconstruction of box, Dover grave 43
                   *b* Reconstruction of box, Dover grave 143

may have been part of the box or, more likely, of a wooden cup inside. The thickness of the walls of the boxes is indicated by the length of the shaft of some of the fittings: 32/8 (Figure 19) lid 1.3cm; 35/8 (Figure 21) hinge on wood 1.3cm; 43/5a handle (Figure 25) 1.2cm; 60/6d (Figure 34) rivets in wood 1.5cm; 124/3a (Figure 51) 1.3cm; 143/1c (Figure 58) ring handle 1.7cm. Wood fragments remaining from 124/3 and 143/1 have both been identified as beech, *Fagus sylvatica*.

Some of the fittings give an indication of the method of construction. On the inside of the corner fitting 43/5b the wood grain runs towards the corner on both sides, but on one of these sides a straight line marks a division and the beginning of end grain. This iron fitting must therefore have been strengthening a combing joint, (reconstruction Text Figure 18a). The same pattern of wood grain is visible on the inside of a corner fitting on box 143/1, so that a combing joint construction is again indicated, as in the reconstruction Text Figure 18b.[104] This kind of construction is visible in the extant wooden box in the woman's grave at Cologne[105], where dove-tailing in the middle section of the walls is combined with a mitre joint at top and bottom.

104  The reconstruction drawings Text Figures 18a and 18b are by Mr J Thorn, to whom I am indebted for discussion in this connection.

105  Doppelfeld 1959, Taf. 7, 3

TABLE XVI   IRON FITTINGS ON WOODEN BOXES

| Fitting | Grave number | | | | | | | | | | |
|---|---|---|---|---|---|---|---|---|---|---|---|
| | F | 29 | 32 | 35 | 43 | 55 | 59 | 60 | 81 | 124 | 143 |
| Bolt-plate | 1 | 1 | | 1 | | 1 | 1 | 1 | 1 | 1 | |
| Bolt-slot | | 1 | | 1 | | 1 | 1 | 1 | 1 | | |
| Bolt – 2 holes | | | | | | | 1 | 1 | | 1 | |
| Spring | 1 | 1 | 1 | | | | | | | 1 | |
| Key | | 1 | | | | | | | | | |
| Rectangular handle | 1 | | 1 | | 1 | 1 | 1 | 1 | | 1 | |
| Ring handle | | | | | | | | | | | 1 |
| Lid lifter | | | | 1 | | | | | | | |
| Hinge | | | | 1 | 1 | | | | | | |
| Latch | | | | | 1 | | | | | | |
| Iron strip | | | | 2 | 4 | | 7 | | | | |
| Corner fixture | | | | | 2 | 3 | | | | 4 | ?4 |
| Cleats | | | | | | 2 | | | | | ?6 |
| Rivets | | | | | | | 2 | 4 | | | |
| Looped staple | | | | | | | | 1 | | | |
| Ring-headed staple | | | | | | | | | | | 1 |

Although the traces of wood are minute, there is evidence to show that some of the boxes were ornamented. A narrow strip of wood 143/1e (Figure 58) is covered on one face with transverse hollow grooves. Corner fittings 124/3a, b (Figure 51) show traces of wood grain on the inner surfaces, and also raised parallel weals, transverse and diagonal on 3a and transverse and longitudinal on 3b. These appear to show that the surface of the box was ornamented, probably with strips of bone or metal inlaid in linear patterns. An example of the technique of silver strips inlaid in yew wood is to be seen on the Emly shrine, County Limerick, where step patterns and crosses are inlaid on the walls and roof of a house-shaped shrine of the seventh century[106]. The technique is therefore seen to be in contemporary use and may be compared with the technique of inlaying silver and other metals on iron which had a better chance of survival.

These boxes were all in the graves of women, except 143 which was a child and may have been female. They occur in plots B, D, E, H and I and in phases 3, 4, 6, and 7. Six out of the total of eleven belong to phase 3, and they are totally absent from phases 1 and 2. The box was at the foot in most graves, the space it took up affecting the position of the body in grave 43 where the skeleton was placed diagonally, and in grave 60 where the feet were crossed. In graves 29 and 81 where there was a lock fragment only, the unusual positions at the left hip in grave 29 and beside the skull in grave 81 suggest that possibly here the boxes were not complete when buried.

These iron box fittings are common in the graves of Anglo-Saxon women:– bolt plates: Chamberlains Barn, Leighton Buzzard, Bedfordshire[107], Kingston, Kent[108], Gilton, Ash, Kent[109], Sarre, Kent[110]; latch and handle: Shudy Camps, Cambridgeshire, grave 48[111]. A similar box in grave 621 at Mucking, Essex has a bolt-plate with two perforations, corner pieces, rivets, a rectangular handle, and a double strip spring[112].

*Bronze bowls* (distribution Figure 93)
Although the hemispherical bowl 137/1 (Figure 56) is a very simple shape, it is not a common one. From early Saxon contexts there is a similar bowl from Horton Kirby, Kent in Maidstone Museum, and fragments of another in grave 26, Howletts, Kent. This Howletts grave also contained an applied disc brooch with cruciform design, a bronze tube and dark blue translucent disc beads[113], all of which would fit a context at the very beginning of the fifth century. A bronze bowl which contained a cremation in the burial ground at Snape, Suffolk, (cremation 1), had similarly curving walls and simple, thickened rim, but it was rather larger, 31.5cm in diameter, and with a flat base[114]. On the Continent hemispherical bowls occur in fifth-century graves at Samson[115], and Haillot, Belgium[116]. At Rhenen, grave 503, containing a similar bowl, belongs to the beginning of the sixth century[117]. The rarity of this form of bowl, the fact that some of them are heavily patched, together with their early contexts at Howletts, Samson and Haillot, makes it seem likely that they were relics of the Roman past, although

---

106  Mitchell *et al*. 1977, 137, pl. 31
107  Hyslop 1963, 196, fig. 7, d
108  Douglas 1793, pl. 10, fig. 8
109  Faussett 1856, 19, fig.
110  Brent 1868, 314, fig., grave 238
111  Lethbridge 1936, fig. 9, 2 and 3
112  Unpublished. Excavators M U and W T Jones.
113  Evison 1978b, fig. 2, c-j
114  West and Owles 1973–5, fig. 19, 1
115  Dasnoy 1968, 312, fig. 14, 3
116  Breuer and Roosens 1957, 214, 255, fig. 11, 3
117  Glazema and Ypey 1956, pl. 23

grave 137 at Dover cannot have been dug before the second half of the seventh century. Another mended bowl in a later grave is reported at Foy-Marteau (Falaën)[118]. Silver bowls of similar shape found in the Sutton Hoo ship burial and elsewhere are related by shape and decoration to Byzantine products, and it seems probable that the hemispherical bronze bowls also, which may be dated to the period between the fourth and seventh centuries, were imported to the Germanic world from Mediterranean workshops[119]. The small piece of bronze in a phase 1 grave at Dover, 48/7 (Figure 27) must be part of the rim of a bowl of this kind, and it was in a woman's bag together with other small possessions, beads, a knife, and a fragment of Roman glass, and still another Roman object in the same grave was the dolphin buckle.

The bronze bowl in grave 20 (Figure 13, Plate 10b) has a beaded rim and foot-ring, and belongs to a series manufactured on the Continent. They occur mostly in the Rhine and Meuse valleys, with a few in Thuringia, France, England and elsewhere[120]. As analyses have shown that there is a large variation in the composition of their metal alloys it seems that they were manufactured by itinerant craftsmen who, in different localities, re-used scrap metal probably brought to them by prospective purchasers. Concentrations in areas distant from the manufacturing centres, such as England and Thuringia, may be the result of trade, or of a particularly long journey by an enterprising craftsman.

Distribution in England is scattered in north and east Kent, with one in Surrey and one in Sussex. Otherwise they occur in Anglian districts, near the Icknield Way, in Norfolk, Nottinghamshire and Leicestershire. None occur in the upper Thames valley or other Saxon areas. They were found in the graves of swordsmen at Sawston and Queniborough, but mostly with richly-endowed women. Grave 20 at Dover is also the grave of a rich female, but one under six years old, and, as the other bronze bowl of the cemetery was in the grave of a boy, it seems to have been the youth of the occupant rather than sex or wealth which determined the deposition of a bronze bowl here.

*Buckets* (distribution Figure 93)
The wood of the iron-bound bucket 53/7 (Figure 29, Plate 10d) had completely disappeared, but the handle, two attachment plates and three circumference bands remained. The diameter of these hoops shows that the bucket was slightly wider at the base than at the top. Iron-bound buckets were known in the Roman period, and continued in the Merovingian period on the Continent[121]. The plaques on these are often more complicated, branching off into lateral swan-neck extensions. In England few have been noted or adequately published. In grave 19 at Bergh Apton, Norfolk, the three lower bands of a bucket are double, with diameters larger than that of the top, wider hoop, which is surmounted by U-sectioned binding. No plates were preserved[122]. In grave 21 at Petersfinger, Wiltshire, an iron handle and one iron hoop only remained[123]. Others have been reported at: Ipswich, Suffolk, High Down and Alfriston, East Sussex, Broomfield, Essex[124], and the Sutton Hoo ship burial[125], so that they span the entire pagan period. Grave 53 at Dover was a woman's grave of phase 5.

The laboratory reconstruction of the bronze-bound bucket 28/1, Figure 16, Plate 10c, is not accurate as the height has been compressed. When measured *in situ* in the grave the height was 3.7in. (9.4cm), and, as it had no doubt collapsed a little, the original height must have been about 10cm. The more likely reconstruction is shown in Text Figure 19.[126] The projection of the upright above the rim shows that there must originally have been a handle, which, if broken, could have been replaced by a length of twine at the time of the burial.

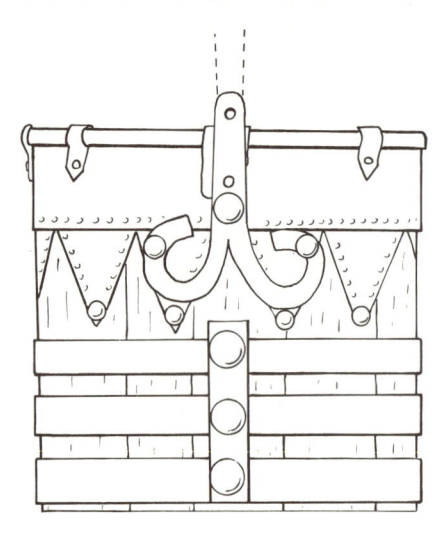

*Text Figure 19* Reconstruction of bronze-bound bucket, Dover 28/1. Scale 1/2

The bifurcating upright with curling terminals is related to the large family of bucket mounts with animal head terminals, of which the most elaborate versions are found in the sixth century in the Rhine and Meuse valleys with a few in northern France and Thuringia[127]. On this series of buckets the triangular

---

118  Breuer and Roosens 1957, 255
119  Bruce-Mitford 1983 III, 1, 69–124
120  Werner 1962b, 312–5, Abb. 4 and 5; Kennett 1968, 24–8; Kennett 1969b, 140–2
121  Pirling 1974 1, 111–12, Ibid 2, Taf. 75, 21a–d; Böhner 1958 1, 69–70, Abb. 3
122  Green and Rogerson 1978, 19, fig. 76, HJK
123  Evison 1965b, fig. 19a, b
124  Layard 1907, 342 (grave 52); Read 1895, 375–6 (grave 19); Griffith and Salzmann 1914, 43, pl. XV, 5, 5a; 47. pl. XV, 3 (graves 54, 70); Read 1893–5, 253
125  Bruce-Mitford 1975a, 442, items 117, 118, 119; East 1983
126  Reconstruction first suggested by Jean Cook.
127  Pirling 1974 1, 111–114, Abb. 6; Martin 1976, 117–121 Abb. 30

repoussé mounts are usually decorated with a human mask. Remnants of a few, not noted on the maps by Pirling and Martin, have been found in England[128], at Eastry, Howletts, and between Dover and Sandgate in Kent, and at Great Chesterford and Mucking in Essex, and there are also many other bronze-bound buckets in this country[129] which are closely related.

On the Dover bucket the curling terminals are not formed in the shape of an animal head, but a rivet (originally dome-headed) on each is positioned as it would be for the eye of an animal, so that the relationship is evident. The triangles, too, are undecorated save for a border of repoussé dots. Other buckets with the same kind of undecorated, bifurcating mounts were found in more northern counties, in grave 32, Luton, Bedfordshire, ?grave 56, Girton, Cambridgeshire, Fairford, Gloucestershire and North Luffenham, Leicestershire (Rutland)[130]. All these are old finds, and the contexts are either uncertain or unhelpful in dating. There are no triangular mounts on these four buckets, but they do occur on a number of others which have animal heads on the bifurcations, e.g. Brighthampton, grave 31[131].

The term 'bucket' is perhaps not suitable for a stave-built vessel held together by bronze bands, for, as they could not be shrunk on like iron hoops, the container would not be water-tight. They are found in both male and female graves, and here grave 28 belonged to a young woman of the middle of the sixth century who possessed a Frankish shield-on-tongue buckle with shoe-shaped rivets.

*Turned wooden vessels* (distribution Figure 94)
Turned wooden vessels must have been fairly common, but they have usually perished, and a trace only remains when a split in the wood had been mended with a bronze patch. A split rim was mended by a rectangle of sheet metal doubled over and fastened with two rivets as 90/2, in this case a mount of silver which still retains traces of the wood inside with the grain in transverse direction. The profile of the lip is similar to the rims of many earthenware pots of the period, and the shape of the vessel must have been somewhat similar, i.e. a slightly everted rim, hollow neck and globular body. In grave 150 the plates are of bronze with scalloped edges, and a thin bronze clip is wedged inside one, 150/3b. This makes it quite certain that three other similar clips in the grave, 150/3c, 3d must have been used to clamp together splits in the wooden vessel.

Bronze clips 55/5b may have been used on a wooden box, or on a cup inside the box. Two bronze bands riveted together with transverse wood grain in between, 19/1, must have been used to mend another such vessel, probably on the body rather than the rim.

Both mending plates and clips have been found in other cemeteries: Holywell Row, graves 31, 37, 23, 38, 29, 93[132], Shudy Camps, grave 36[133] and Kingston, Kent, graves 94, 113 and 137[134]. Similar bronze mending plates were found in graves and a hut at Mucking, Essex, and in two cases there a diameter of 13cm for the vessel rim was obtainable, one from the positions of two plates on opposite sides, and one from the stain of the rotted wood adjacent to the plate[135].

Iron clips of the same shape were found lying together in grave 16 at Alton, four inches above the floor of the grave, and were presumably used on a more robust wooden vessel of that height[136]. These graves, where dateable, range from the sixth to late seventh century, and although the two graves at Dover where the sex is identifiable are male, they occur in female graves elsewhere.

A more expensive type of turned wood vessel is that of the cups or bottles which had thinner walls, were finished off and ornamented at the rim by ring-shaped, U-sectioned mounts, often in silver, and probably usually fashioned in more expensive woods. A maplewood bottle from the Sutton Hoo ship burial is one of the more elaborate examples, the rim being held on by three riveted bands, and the neck covered in repoussé metal and ornamented vandykes spreading over the top half of the vessel[137]. The silver rim in Dover grave 32 is an example of the most simple version, with five fluted silver bands to fix it to the vessel. A pair like this was found in the grave of a swordsman of the seventh century at Alton[138]. The two cups, 29/12a and b are ornamented by birds' head plaques at the base of the holding strips, and these are related to the mushroom pendants worn on a necklace by the same woman (29/5, see p 56). Comparable rims have been found at Sarre, grave LIV, Sibertswold, grave 69, and Chartham Down, grave 48 and two of the small cups in the Sutton Hoo ship burial have similar rims and were made from walnut burr-wood[139]. Organic matter under the rim 32/7 was identified as probably a broad-leafed wood. The rim type seems to be confined to the late sixth or seventh century.

At Dover the earliest metal fitting on a turned vessel, a pair of bronze mending plates, 19/1 occur-

---

128 Evison 1969, 166; Evison 1973, 269–70
129 For fifth-century types: Evison 1965b, 22–3, Map 8
130 Austin *et al.* 1928, 183–4, 191, fig. 3, with spear and knife (pl. XXXV, 16 and 17), Luton Museum; Hollingworth and O'Reilly 1925, 9, pl. VI.2, Cambridge Museum; Wylie 1852, 20, pl. VIII.2; Crowther-Beynon 1901, 251, 255–6, fig. 5, BM Reg. No. 1946 7–5 5
131 Evison 1965b, fig. 11m
132 Lethbridge 1931, fig. 10B, 2, fig. 9, 5, fig. 14, J, K, fig. 13, E, F, where they were interpreted as shield bindings although their curvature would suit a vessel but not a shield.
133 Lethbridge 1936, fig. 7, 3
134 Faussett 1856, 57, 61 and fig. 3 on p 60, 65–6 and fig. 4 on p 65
135 Jones and Jones 1975, 178
136 Evison 1963, fig. 20, f-i
137 Bruce-Mitford 1975a, 202–6, figs. 133–7
138 Evison 1963, fig. 20d, e
139 Brent 1866, 167 with fig.; Faussett 1856, 113–14 with fig. and 174, pl. XVI, 7. Bruce-Mitford 1983 III, 1, figs. 267, 274

red in phase ?2, the silver rims in phase 3 and the clips and rim plates in phases 4 and 6.

*Bone-covered boxes*
In several graves there are remains of material which looks like bone and which are clearly not part of the human skeleton or animal bone from meat placed in the grave, but which have been worked and shaped. Some of these fragments have been identified by Dr J Clutton-Brock, British Museum (Natural History) as bone or antler, and some as possibly antler, as noted in the catalogue. Some small patches may be all that remain of combs, others, however, are larger, and probably represent facings to caskets, in graves 35, 141 and 150. Grave 35 contained a wooden box with iron fittings, 35/8a, b, c and the ?antler fragments $c$ 37 × 8cm were adjacent but presumably a separate box. The bone in grave 141 was mixed with black fragments of wood, probably oak, and measured $c$ 30cm × 10cm. In grave 150 the bone fragments on the lower legs (C) were in two lines $c$ 14cm apart and about 70cm long, and 7cm deep. Although somewhat long, this could have been a box, and two bronze plate fittings 3a and b on opposite sides may have functioned as mending plates in the same way that these plates were used on the edge of turned wooden bowls. Some bronze clips, 3c, 3d in the same area may have been used on the same box, but both plates and clips might alternatively indicate the presence of a bowl as well as a box. The bone fragments in the same grave by the skull are extensive enough to be another box, and the fragments at the right waist may have been a comb.

Bone-covered boxes, usually with overall geometric ornamentation, were in use at this time both in this country and on the Continent. Remnants of one were found at Sutton Hoo in Mound 3[140], there were well-preserved examples at Caistor-by-Norwich[141] and another on the outskirts of Dover, not far away at Old Park[142]. Grave 35 belonged to one of the row of rich women of phase 3, and 141 and 150 were near together in the middle of the cemetery (phase 6).

Miss Green has noted that these caskets were made in the fourth and fifth centuries, but as they occur in Merovingian[143] and later Anglo-Saxon graves, manufacture must have continued into the sixth and seventh centuries. There is no lack of evidence of even later occurrences, e.g. at Coppergate, York in a deposit probably of the tenth century[144].

*Bronze workbox*
When found, the workbox 107/4 had been squashed by the grave fill and had taken on an oval shape. It was removed from the grave *in situ* on the chalk base beneath it, and was excavated in the laboratory and reconstructed in the oval form it had assumed. Because of this deformity it has been cited as a unique workbox owing to its oval shape and lack of decoration on the end pieces, but neither of these statements are correct[145]. The quincunx decoration alone on the end discs shows that the shape was originally circular as with all other analagous boxes. The box, however, has passed through a number of accidents, mends and changes. The reconstruction from the front view, Text Figure 20a, shows how it functioned when first made, one side, the lid, opening by swivelling on one rivet, and shutting again by overlapping the middle band. At the time of burial, however, this side could not be opened because the original hole for this rivet was empty, and an additional rivet each side of the hole held the side rigidly to the middle plate, (Figure 48, back). The middle plate had been moved off centre, its original suspension tab had no doubt been broken and a new one fixed above the original holding rivet hole by two new rivets. An additional pair of rivet holes in the middle of the suspension plates near the junction with the cylinder would have helped to hold the box closed when they were occupied by rivets, but they are now empty. Riveted tabs on the suspension plates by the junction with the cylinder, and also on the disc ends, are no doubt mends.

The box, therefore, must have begun its life carrying out the normal functions of an openable container for needle-work materials, as testified by the cloth and thread caught in its suspension plates, and by the pin inside the cylinder. At the time of burial, however, the box was riveted permanently shut, the lid held unmoveable by the two rivets at the top, even if the pair of rivet holes in the middle by the cylinder were empty at the time of burial as they are now. As the box still contained a pin it seems likely that a much-used box was patched up to make it visually appropriate for burial although by then non-functional.

Anglo-Saxon bronze workboxes have received much attention, a major step forward in understanding them being taken by Leeds in 1936 when he included them among typical late objects in his survey of the final phase of pagan burials[146]. Although there is controversy about their purpose, many contain textile fragments and threads, and occasionally pins or needles[147]. It is an object type which does not make an appearance in Anglo-Saxon graves before the second half of the seventh century, and so must presumably owe its inspiration to foreign sources. At Vermand in northern Gaul, in Germanic graves of $c$ AD 400, bronze cylindrical boxes of two shapes were in use, a tall narrow

---

140 Bruce-Mitford 1975a, 114–115, figs. 63 and 69
141 Myres and Green 1973, 85–7, pls. XX, XXI
142 Kendrick 1937b, 448, pl. XCVII
143 cf Schoppa 1953, 44; Roes 1963, 79–80, pl. LXIII, 1–11; De Loë 1939, 162, fig. 132 from Maroeuil; Reliquary, St. Liudger's church, Essen-Werden, Hubert et al. 1967, 267 No. 294

144 Waterman 1959, 86, pl. XVII
145 Hawkes 1973, 197. The circular shape was confirmed by Mrs Sue Heaser when she was studying the fragments closely in order to make the drawing Text Figure 20.
146 Leeds 1936, chapter 6
147 Crowfoot 1973

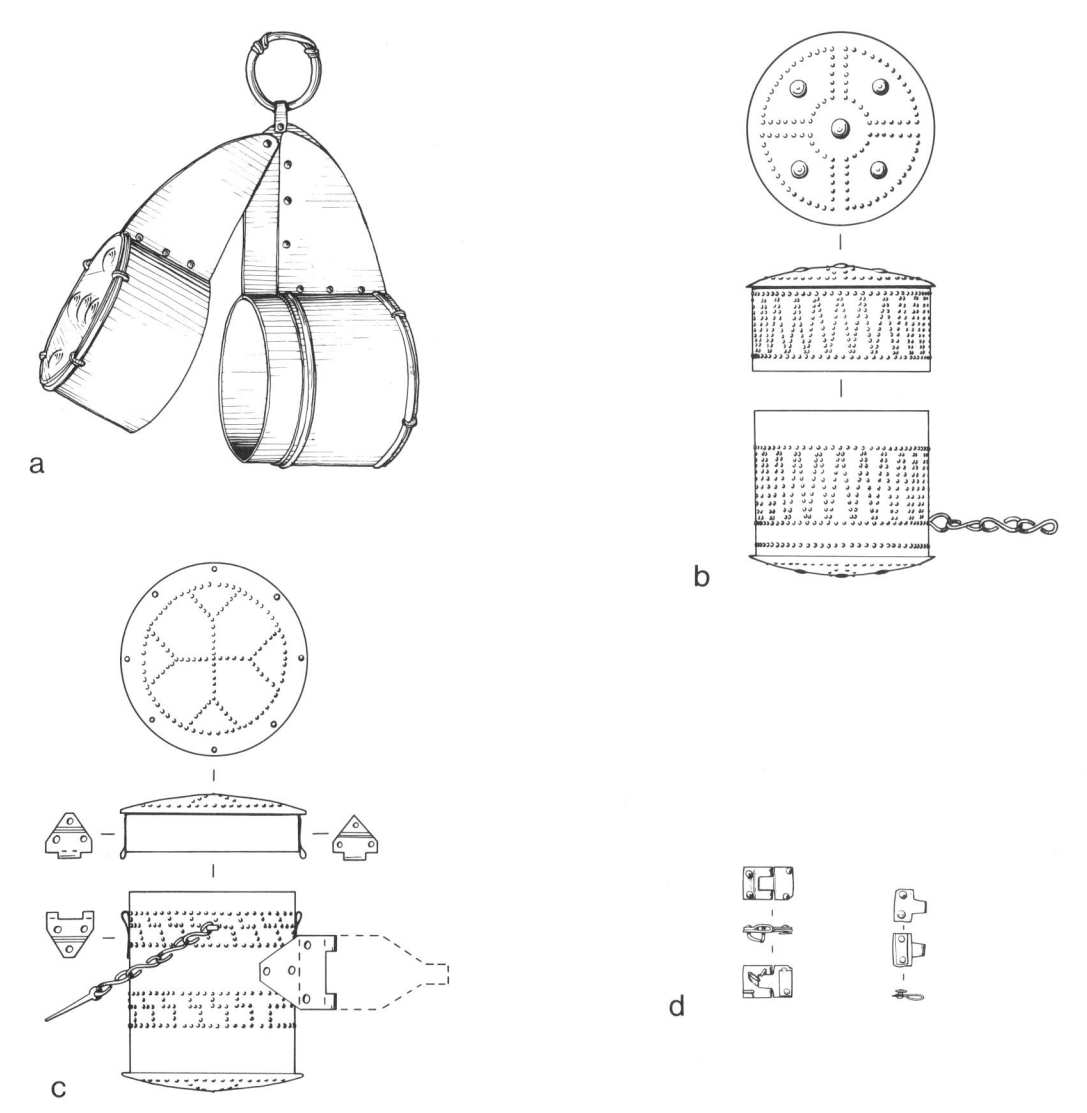

*Text Figure 20 a* Bronze workbox, Dover 107/4 before later alterations
*b* Bronze workbox from Hawnby, North Yorks
*c* Bronze workbox from Sibertswold, grave 60
*d* Bronze hinges, Dover 84/3. Scale 1/1

cylinder and a wide, flat cylinder[148]. Some of the flat shape have been noted in Scandinavia[149], and one of these contained threads. In Rhineland graves small cylindrical boxes and decorated spherical boxes often contained aromatic and other material, and are considered to be Christian amulet capsules[150]. Only a few of the continental examples are very close to the Anglo-Saxon series, e.g. Nocera Umbra, grave 87, which may well have had an unbroken development in Italy from the containers worn by Roman ladies. A connection with the Vermand type and Merovingian examples may be traced in one of the bronze boxes from Kingston grave 222[151], which is of slender cylindrical shape and has a bronze chain attached to each side and to the lid. This box is in turn related to the container to which the bone lid in grave 157 at Dover belonged (p 108). It seems very likely therefore, that the Roman custom was continued in diverse fashion in Italy and the Rhineland, and came to England along with many of the other imports in the wake of Christianity.

The majority of the Anglo-Saxon workboxes were suspended by bronze chains consisting of S-shaped loops. The Dover box, however, has suspension plates formed by an extension of the same sheet of bronze which forms the cylinder. Other boxes have similar, but not identical arrangements. The box decorated with zoomorphic interlace and story panels from Burwell, Cambridgeshire[152] has a suspension plate of similar shape and a smaller plate hinged to it for the lid. The box from North Leigh, Oxfordshire had a trefoil-shaped plate and a smaller plate for the lid. The box from grave 60 at Sibertswold, Kent[153], (Text Figure 20c) was fitted

---

148 Pilloy 1895, 247, pl. 13.5; Nenquin 1953, 78, fig. 16, G8, pl. XI, 11
149 Ørsnes-Christensen 1955, 75, fig. 5
150 Salin 1959, 112–18, distribution map fig. 24
151 Faussett 1856, pl. XIII. 7
152 Lethbridge 1931, 55–7, pl. III
153 Faussett 1856, pl. XIII. 8

with a projecting plate riveted to the middle of its body, and another plate with suspension loop was hinged with the projecting plate.

The construction of the Dover box is basically different from the others because it is in three pieces, consisting of a middle band to which are attached the box and the lid, both of equal size. The others are more flimsily constructed of two pieces only, usually a box and a shallow lid. Still of two-piece construction, but with lid and body of equal depth, is the example from Polhill[154].

These boxes do not appear until after the introduction of Christianity, and, although the needle and thread type of contents are work-a-day requisites, the cruciform decoration on the disc ends of the cylinders suggest that they may have had some Christian affinity. Some of the crosses on the end discs carried out in repoussé dots could simply have been a geometrical design, but some of the crosses are of shapes otherwise used as pectoral crosses and in manuscripts and sculpture, e.g. the cross with ring and boss centre, double line arms, and a boss between each arm from Hawnby, North Yorkshire (Text Figure 20b)[155], the Sibertswold cross with triangular terminals (Text Figure 20c), the double or Union Jack cross on the Garton Slack box[156], and the curved-arm cross with interlace in the spaces at North Leigh[157], so that a definite Christian intent is evident. Grave 107 at Dover is in the Christian part of the cemetery, and is not far from grave 110 which is coin-dated to after 660–70.

All the boxes mentioned above are in bronze, but one found at Krefeld Gellep is of iron[158], and there is evidence that there were identical boxes in perishable materials also, in wood, bone and leather. Any narrow cylindrical box in bone, such as the Merovingian box from Liège (p 109, Text Figure 21b), or the one indicated by the lid fragment in Dover grave 157 (Text Figure 21a), would have disappeared completely. Evidence for the existence of this narrow form in wood as well is forthcoming from Scandinavia[159] where one was found in a grave, and evidence of one in leather with bronze fittings comes from St. Denis in France[160].

Indications that boxes of similar shape and size in material other than bronze also existed in this country have been noted. Two bronze discs and three bronze bands riveted in circles were found at Haslingfield, Cambridgeshire, and had been restored in the form of a flat, cylindrical box. Each ring, however, has the same diameter, and must have been mounted on a cylindrical box of similar dimensions to the bronze versions but of perishable material, wood, bone or leather[161]. One other such box may be traced at Dover by comparison with the bronze box from grave 60, Sibertswold (Text Figure 20c). This drawing shows two small pairs of hinges connecting the lid with the body, one of which must have been permanently secured by a pin to act as a hinge. The other, on the opposite side of the box, could be fastened by the small pin attached to the box by a chain, as shown in the illustration by Faussett[162]. The hinges are triangular in shape, but one and a half pairs of square-shaped hinges, identical otherwise in design and size, were found by the hip of the young woman in grave 84 at Dover (Figure 40, 84/3). As the material accommodated by the rivets can only have been 1–2mm thick, they must have been mounted on a box of leather, and the metal parallel at Sibertswold suggests that this would have been cylindrical and of like size. Grave 84 is in the latest part of the cemetery.

The distribution map, (Figure 117, list p 269), shows a number in east Kent, but the rest, apart from a couple in Wiltshire, are north of the Thames, in the vicinity of the Icknield Way, in Derbyshire and north of the Humber, with none between the Humber and the Wash or in East Anglia and Essex.

It has been suggested that the bronze box found at Parfondeval, Seine Inférieure, may be an Anglo-Saxon export[163]. One other exported example may be detected at Domburg in Holland, where a sub-triangular bronze plate was found, decorated with small holes, presumably originally repoussé dots, and with a circular mending plate at the apex to which is riveted a looped tab with a bronze ring. The opposite end is stepped like a hinge. This was interpreted as a Viking necklace terminal, but the parallel offered was in cast, not sheet bronze[164]. This Domburg fragment matches closely the suspension plates of the Anglo-Saxon work-boxes, in particular the hinged plate on the Sibertswold box (Text Figure 20c), and must be another export.

Various possible functions of these boxes have been discussed by Meaney, who has suggested use as thread boxes, relic boxes, or first-aid boxes[165]. Whichever of these suggestions may be true, it seems likely that they were a symbol of the status of their owner.

*Bone lid*

A fragment of a bone ?lid, 157/6h (Figure 62), is ring-shaped with a hemispherical top and a rebate on the lower edge, and seems to be unique in Anglo-Saxon graves. Some bone objects found in Dutch terps, and at Dorestad and Southampton, are roughly comparable in form, with a narrower hole in the middle and steeper rebate. Two with the same

---

154 Hawkes 1973, fig. 53, 489
155 Leeds City Museum
156 Mortimer 1905, 248, 250, pl. LXXXIV. 643
157 Leeds 1939, 359, pl. XXVIII.i
158 Pirling 1974 2, Taf. 74, 13
159 Shetelig 1912, fig. 350
160 Salin 1959, 116
161 Ashmolean Museum 1909, 244. The restoration was visibly incorrect, and in answer to my enquiries David Brown kindly informed me of this result when the pieces were disentangled.
162 Faussett 1856, pl. XIII, 8
163 Hawkes 1973, 197; Cochet 1855, 310f. and fig.
164 Roes 1954b, pl. XIX. 83
165 Meaney 1981, 181–9

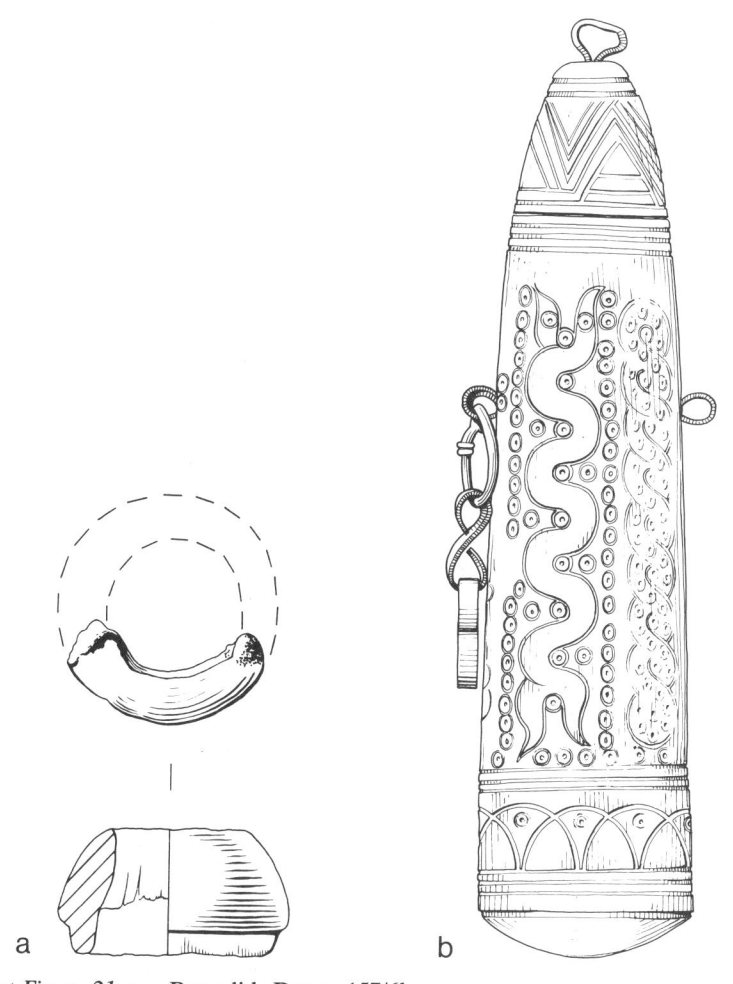

*Text Figure 21 a*  Bone lid, Dover 157/6h
               *b*  Bone box and lid, Sainte Walburge, Liège, Belgium. Scale 1/1

kind of dome-shaped top are decorated, and it has been suggested that they are knobs to canes[166]. If this is so, the central perforation does not seem to be necessary or functional. The rebated section of some are pierced by rivets, so that their function must differ from that of the Dover piece where the rebate is too narrow to accept rivets.

The Dover fragment is more likely to be the lid of a cylindrical box of bone, of which most had disintegrated except for this part of the lid which was in contact with the preservative properties of the bronze chain, as may be seen from the green staining on the bone. The bronze chain, 157/6c, was probably fastened to the sides of the cylinder as well as to the lid, the whole being suspended from the waist along with the keys. This may be deduced from a comparable box and lid, both decorated, from a Merovingian grave at Sainte Walburge at Liège, Belgium (Text Figure 21b)[167]. Another bone cylindrical box of this kind, also decorated, is in the Domschatz at Trier, Germany[168]. This one is considered to be a pyxis, and opinion differs as to whether it belongs to the Merovingian period or the tenth century, although, in view of the similarity of its decoration to the Liège example a Merovingian date is more likely. Earlier flasks in bronze or glass were used by Roman ladies to carry perfume or oil, and this type of container was sometimes fitted with a bronze chain attached to each side for suspension, and another bronze chain to retain the lid so that it could be worn on the person[169]. A smaller version in the lighter material of bone, as here, would make a suitable portable container for beauty cream or any other such personal requirement of small volume. The bronze knob with ring attachment for chain at the top would no doubt have expanded into a disc which would allow fitting into the bone lid. In the event of breakage of the lid the bronze fitting would be re-used on a new one. Cylindrical turned bone boxes without bronze fittings are present in Langobardic contexts[170].

A lid completely of bronze with chain attached was found in the cremation containing a francisca and limestone plaque in Mound 3 at Sutton Hoo[171], and its type of moulded casting suggests a Mediterranean origin where Roman traditions had

---

166  Roes 1965, 53, fig. 30, pl. XXIII, 171, 172; Roes 1963, 76, pl. LXI, 10, 13; Holdsworth 1976, 47, pl. VIB
167  Liège 1930, No. 735; Liège Museum, JB 45
168  Goldschmidt 1923, No. 158, pl. LII
169  Liversidge 1973, fig. 50, c
170  Werner 1935, 53 and note 3, Taf. 15, C, 3a
171  Bruce-Mitford 1975a, figs. 65 and 84

been continued. This is a male burial – but the lid was presumably a stopper to a flask probably of bronze, like those used in Roman times. In contrast, a cylindrical bronze box found in a woman's grave at Kingston, Kent, grave 222, was simply made, no doubt by an Anglo-Saxon craftsman, and this was furnished with side chains for suspension and one to the lid, and so is closely comparable to the Merovingian bone boxes (cf p 109)[172]. The woman in grave 157 at Dover, however, was buried with a Frankish pot, and the bone container she was wearing could also have come from across the Channel.

## Tools

### Sharpening steel

The occupant of grave 148 was male (according to the first bone report), and was buried with a knife, iron buckle and sharpening steel 148/2 (Figure 59) at the left waist. This form of iron bar, rounded at one end and with a tang at the other, has been found in other Anglo-Saxon graves. Others of straight-sided round-ended shape occurred at Polhill[1] in graves 38 (female), 102 and 56 (male), Winnall[2], Garton Slack, Humberside (Yorkshire)[3], Shudy Camps, Cambridgeshire[4] with squared end at Horndean, Hampshire[5] and Finglesham[6]. The sharpener 144/3 (Figure 59) has a semi-circular terminal which narrows in a rebate at each side to join the shaft. One with rebated sides from Kingston Down, Kent grave 8[7], is illustrated by Faussett, and as it was found with beads the grave must have belonged to a woman. These are seventh-century graves, and these forms of sharpener do not seem to occur outside this country.

### Awls

In grave 65, a man with a spear, seax, knife, buckle and tweezers, there were three other iron objects of somewhat similar size and appearance. One near the buckle at the right waist was looped at one end, pointed at the other, and was probably originally round in section (65/4, Figure 36). Two other bars were at the left waist with a knife and tweezers, and these, although looped at one end and pointed at the other, were square in section with wood traces on the sides (65/7, Figure 36). Similar shafts 9/2 were also at the left waist. These are objects of unknown use which are not common in England, but which occur frequently in northern France and Belgium. A number have been illustrated from the cemetery at Lavoye (Meuse)[8], most of them pointed, but two have chisel-shaped points, and in some the shaft is given a corkscrew twist in the middle, a trait which clearly makes them unsuitable for use as sharpeners. M Joffroy notes that these iron pins occur only in male graves, the direction in which they are pointing varies, but they are often contained in a purse. No overwhelmingly convincing function has been suggested, use as an awl being the most likely. The associated objects of seax and shield-on-tongue buckle make 65 a definite Frankish grave.

### ?Mattock

The fragment of a mattock or adze 145/3 (Figure 59) is not part of the deposited grave furniture, but it is certainly contemporary with it as it broke off while being used to dig the grave and remained stuck in the wall. It is a corner only, rather thicker than a carpenter's adze such as the tenth-century one from Thetford[9]. Judging from the shape of this fragment, it might be a corner of the iron shoe of a wooden spade[10], but such a tool would not have been strong enough to stand up to the resistance of the rock chalk the grave-digger had to contend with at Dover, and only a tool like a mattock or pick could have been used. A tool considered to be an adze was found in a sword grave at Sarre (grave 39)[11].

### Fire-steels (distribution Figure 95)

The attribution of the fire-steel or purse-mount 41/7, (Figure 24) to grave 41 is uncertain is it was returned from the laboratory with this grave number, but there is no record of this type of purse-mount being found in this or any other grave. It is probable that it was sent for conservation together with the knife or sword in a block of earth in unexcavated condition, and so was not visible for recording before treatment. It must originally have had a buckle on the middle strap extension, and the ends were turned over in long loops each expanding into the shape of an earless head with open jaws. In his collection of fire-steels and purse-mounts Brown[12] shows some related types: his fig. 18.1 from Oberflacht is a similar long, slim bar and the animal head with open jaws of the same shape also has an ear and an eye, but the tongue does not form a complete loop, as do shorter, broader versions from Lavoye[13]. The example from Oberflacht is considered by Brown to be a bird-head piece, which does not seem likely as the creature has a projecting ear, open jaws and extended curled tongue. In fact there seems to be no clear distinction between the form of bird head and horse-head varieties as suggested by Brown, for the difference is based on a subjective opinion as to which way up the bird and

---

172 Faussett 1856, pl. XIII, 7

1 Philp 1973a, fig. 57. 573, fig. 58. 599, fig. 57, 578. Fig. 583 is also quoted as a sharpening steel, but the drawing shows one edge thinner than the other and unequal steps to the tang, i.e. a knife.
2 Meaney and Hawkes 1970, fig. 12, grave 49.2
3 Mortimer 1905, grave 3, pl. LXXXIII fig. 625; grave 14, pl. LXXXVIII fig. 680
4 Lethbridge 1936, grave 57, fig. 1.A.4
5 Knocker 1956, fig. 10, grave S6, 4, fig. 11, grave 13, 1, fig. 15 location unknown
6 Swanton 1973, fig. 64, f
7 Faussett 1856, 44, pl. XV, 24
8 Joffroy 1974, 30–2, fig. 13
9 Wilson 1968b, 143, fig. 1, d
10 Wilson 1971, 76, fig. 14
11 Swanton 1973, 205, fig. 80e
12 Brown 1977b
13 Ibid, fig. 17.1 and 2; Joffroy 1974, fig. 20. 287 and 289

horse-heads should be. It is assumed that the bird-head turned upwards and the horse-head downwards. However, the bird-head pairs on square-headed brooches would often be seen sideways, and the horse on the foot of a cruciform brooch would face upwards, depending on the angle at which the brooch was pinned on the garment, and a modern opinion as to which way up the purse mounts look best is hardly a useful criterion. It does seem, however, that this buckled variety must have formed part of the tinder pouch besides functioning as a fire-steel, whichever way up it was attached. This particular type could easily have been sewn on by the looped ends.

Two other fire-steels are sub-triangular in shape with a straight back, convex curve on the opposite side and curled ends: 139/1 and 157/7 (Figures 57, 62). The fourth was somewhat similar, also with curled ends, but the back was curved and perforated by three rivet holes, 53/5 (Figure 29). This means that it could be attached to the tinder container by rivets or by thongs, although it would seem to be unnecessary in this case for it was found with an iron diamond inside an ivory ring (bag-holder) between the knees of a woman. Grave 157 also belonged to a woman and the fire-steel was found amongst her keys at the left knee. Grave 139 belonged to a male child, and the purse-mount was placed at its right waist together with the iron diamond to which it is still attached by rust. Similar fire-steels are fairly common in England, e.g. at Holborough, Kent,[14] Polhill, Kent, graves 68 and 85[15], Holywell Row, Cambridgeshire[16], Burwell, Cambridgeshire[17], Shudy Camps, Cambridgeshire[18], and Lowbury Hill, Oxfordshire (Berkshire)[19].

Grave 41 was near the north-western edge of the Dover cemetery, and belonged to phase 3. Graves 139 and 157 in plot G and grave 53 on the barrow were later, in phase 5. Signs of a container were evident in grave 53 (iron diamond and an ivory ring bag-holder), and grave 139 (iron diamond, see p 118) so that in these graves they could have been simply fire-steels, with no function as a purse-mount. In both women's graves they were suspended at knee-level, in grave 53 the direction was lengthwise in the grave, and in grave 157 it was lying at an angle. The position in the boy's grave was at the right waist, with the iron diamond, but because of their corroded condition they were removed in an unexcavated block, and the angle of original position is not known. No flints were found with any of the firesteels.

*Hones*
Although broken and discarded hones are quite frequent finds on early Saxon settlement sites, they are more rare as grave furniture. One fairly complete and the broken end of another were lying together in grave 162 which must have belonged to a child, judging from the small size of the grave. They seem to reflect a normal interest of the boy in knives, for two of these were also placed in the grave with him. Mr S E Ellis has shown[20] that in the pagan Anglo-Saxon period, as well as in Roman times, hones were made either from local stones or from others semi-remote, i.e. they were acquired from within a distance of less than 250 miles, while 'schist hones' from Norway were introduced by the Vikings about AD 900. The two Dover hones belong to the same general type of rock but are not identical, and amongst the many possible sources is the local Kentish Rag[21].

An element of pagan ritual has been established in connection with a few of the whetstone grave finds, e.g. the ornamented whetstone of the Sutton Hoo ship burial and the marked whetstone of comparable size from Uncleby, Humberside (Yorkshire), both of which must have been held upright in ceremonial fashion, one end resting on a knee, to function as a sceptre[22].

With one exception, the graves containing whetstones and which can be dated, are no earlier than the seventh century. The survival of a pagan whetstone in the Sutton Hoo grave is due to the conservation of traditional royal regalia. At Uncleby, Soham and elsewhere the whetstone may well have been included in a burial which represented a consciously determined pagan resistance to the new Christian religion. The relationship to this question of grave 162 and its neighbouring graves is discussed on p 136.

**Weaving equipment**

*Iron weaving battens* (distribution Figure 85)
Of the three weaving battens, 20/1 was the shortest and widest, 37.6 × 4.6cm (Figure 12), 38/11 was 41.1 × 4.2cm (Figure 23) and the longest was 46/1 at 62.3 × 4.3cm (Figure 26). The weaving sword in grave 46 was fitted with an iron ring at the top of the tang, so that it could be suspended, presumably on the loom or wall of the house. Pattern-welding is faintly indicated by radiograph on 38/11 (Figure 23), and on 46/1 (Figure 26). This technique has not been detected on a large number so far, probably because not all have been X-rayed[23], and Koch lists only four: Finglesham, Kent; Vieil-Aître (Meurthe-et-Moselle), Schretzheim grave 22 and Schretzheim grave 579.

The positions in which the weaving swords were placed in relation to the body at Dover were different each time; to the left of the skull pointing up in grave 20, to the right of the legs in the other two, but pointing up in grave 38 and down in grave 46. They were buried in phase 1 and phase 3.

On the Continent weaving swords belong mostly to women in Alamannic, Thuringian and Lan-

---

14  Evison 1956, fig. 16, 9
15  Philp 1973a, fig. 56, 551 and 556
16  Lethbridge 1931, fig. 18, A1, B1
17  Ibid, fig. 27, 7
18  Lethbridge 1936, fig. 1. A.5, B.2, fig. 2, 4
19  Evison 1963, fig. 27, k
20  Ellis 1969, 135–87; Evison 1975
21  Report p 197
22  Evison 1975, 79–83
23  Koch 1977 1, 93 Ibid 2, Taf. 9, 16 and Taf. 151, 9

gobardic graves, and not often in Frankish graves[24]. They are usually of the shorter lengths as in graves 20 and 38 here, but among the small number found in this country are some of the longest. Iron weaving blades also occur in Scandinavia, but they are of a different form, more like long spearheads[25]. To the list of English examples[26] already published may be added one at Barton, Humberside (Lincolnshire)[27], and a more recent find at Finglesham, Kent[28]. One other, which is the longest so far found, was lying outside the corner of Hall No. 7 at West Stow, Suffolk, the total length being 63cm (grip 16.8cm) without the terminal projection which was missing[29].

The graves containing these weaving swords are usually richly furnished, and although the occupants were not members of the highest ranks of nobility they must have been quite well up the social scale. The woman in her twenties in grave 38 fits well into this picture, but there were other women of the same phase who were equally well endowed who did not have a weaving sword, such as the row in plot B. However, there is probably additional special significance in the position of grave 38 at the very corner of the cemetery. The only two other weaving swords in the cemetery are in two graves side by side which do not correspond to the usual type of grave in which a weaving sword is included. The batten 20/1 was in the richly furnished grave of a girl under six years old, and 46/1 belonged to a woman in her twenties in the neighbouring grave who possessed only a knife and beads beside the weaving sword. If a weaving batten was a symbol of the lady of the house, or female head of the family, it is strange to find one with a child. It may be that the titular responsibility had devolved on a minor in grave 20, and that the occupant of grave 46 (relatively poorly endowed and who died in the same phase) was acting as a kind of family regent until the actual head should have become of age. There are other poorly-furnished graves with a weaving sword at Mitcham, London (Surrey), grave 49[30] with a pot, chatelaine and iron objects and possibly Ramsgate, Kent, grave 2[31]. The position is confused in this latter instance, however, as the evidence from inexpert finders attributed a male skeleton, the weaving sword and bronze-bound fragment of an ivory ?ring to this grave.

*Bone weaving pick*

Bone rods pointed at both ends at 75/5 (Figure 38) are interpreted as weaving picks. Hundreds of them have been found in the Frisian terps[32], and in England they occur both in the graves of women and in settlements. At Kingston, Kent, in grave 299, two were found in company with other objects useful in weaving, i.e. a bone tablet for tablet weaving, shears and spindle whorls[33]. Some were found in the houses at Sutton Courtenay, Oxfordshire (Berkshire) and West Stow, Suffolk[34].

*Bronze needle*

One bronze sewing needle, and a small iron pin of the sort used nowadays in dressmaking, were found together in a bag or pocket at the hip of the woman buried in grave 138, items 3 and 4 (Figure 57). Pins as small as this, and sewing needles, are rare in Anglo-Saxon graves, but it may be noted that a dressmaker's type of pin was also found in the bronze work-box at Dover, 107/5a. Amongst comparable needles the so-called 'bodkin' in grave 1 at Lyminge was apparently used as a pin to fasten cloth wrapping on a spearhead[35]. 'Two brass needles, gilt', were found in a cylindrical needle box at Kingston, Kent[36], grave 222, and another is recorded from Caistor-by-Norwich[37]. One was found associated with beads in a cremation pot at Spong Hill[38].

*Spindle whorls*

Two spindle whorls, together with other possessions, were contained in a wooden box at the feet of the woman in grave 60, one was made from the base of a Roman pot (60/9, Figure 34/9), and the other, a flat, discoid shape, possibly from oil shale (60/10, Figure 34/10). Another spindle whorl possibly of oil shale, 21/4 (Figure 14), was biconical in shape and decorated with turned grooves.[39] These two shale whorls belong to phases 3 and 1 respectively. Similar shale whorls are known from late Roman contexts e.g. Portchester and Shakenoak[40], and the Dover

---

24 Shetelig 1912, 95, 98, 177, fig. 220; Chadwick 1958, 11–18, 30–5, figs. 7 and 8; Werner 1962a, 34–5, 82, distribution map, Karte 2, Taf. 68, 2, Fundliste 2, 164–6; Koch 1969, 187–9, 193; Millard et al. 1969, 17–24; Koch 1977 1, 93–4
25 Petersen 1951, 285ff, figs. 155, 156
26 Chadwick 1958, 30, 31
27 Sheppard 1940, 38
28 Wilson 1968a, 158
29 West 1985 1, 139; 2, 21A, 13
30 Bidder and Morris 1959, 63, pls. XIX, XXI, fig. 17
31 Millard et al. 1969, 12–14, 17–24, fig. 2.4, 3.1
32 Roes 1963, 33–4, pl. XXXVI
33 Faussett 1856, 92–3 with figs.
34 Leeds 1923, 182–3, pl. XXVIII, fig. 2; West 1985 1, 140
35 Warhurst 1955, 7–8, fig. 4, 5
36 Faussett 1856, 81
37 Myres and Green 1973, fig. 20, N36, D
38 Hills and Penn 1981, 34, fig. 142.1799
39 The spindle whorls 21/4 and 60/10 are similar in appearance but investigation at the British Museum (Natural History) identified that from grave 21 as quartz and ?cassiterite and/or clay and that from grave 60 as amorphous. The objects were later examined by Mr B R Young of the Institute of Geological Sciences and X-ray powder diffraction patterns obtained. Although the whorls have a surface appearance similar to that of shale they do not give the normal pattern for shale, but could be made of an oil shale similar to that found at Kimmeridge. Mr Young considered that the material was possibly comparable to that of the Caergwrle bowl which is probably made of cannel coal from Clwyd (Flintshire) (Green et al. 1980). Identification as wood seemed unlikely in view of their excellent condition and the poor preservation of wood at Dover. More definite identification could not be obtained by a non-destructive method, and in view of the likelihood that the evidence would not be conclusive it was decided not to take further action involving an element of destruction.
40 Cunliffe 1975, 226, fig. 121, 127–32; Brodribb et al. 1968, 48, fig. 15, shale 1

specimens may be Roman survivals. One of hemispherical shape does, however, occur in a seventh-century context at Chamberlain's Barn, Leighton Buzzard, Bedfordshire[41].

A heavy whorl in the shape of a cone, 48/13, (Figure 27) consists of cassiterite and cerussite, and was therefore probably originally of lead, the material, if not the whorl itself, no doubt being of Roman origin. At the foot of the woman's skeleton in grave 6 (Figure 7), was a spindle whorl in calcareous material, flat based with a conical top turned with decorative grooves. This material has been identified as chalk containing iron oxides, possibly derived from pyrites. Lethbridge found a number of chalk whorls at Burwell, and suggested they might have been used as toggles[42]. He also noted some at Shudy Camps[43].

*Shears*

Shears were found in the graves of three women: in 110/2 (Figure 49) coin-dated to after 660–70, and in 75/2 (Figure 38) and 83/4 (Figure 39), both further east and later. On two, 75/2 and 110/2, the curved middle part is beaten out flat, while on 83/4 it is rounded in section. The woman in grave 75 wore a necklace, and possessed iron linked rods with an iron spoon and an ivory ring bag containing a weaving pick. The shears must be connected with her interest in weaving. In this grave and in 83 the shears were found by the left hip, points upwards, so that they do not appear to have been carried suspended by the bowed top as one might expect, but probably in a bag. The position of the shears in grave 110 is very unusual, for they were lying with the knife between the hands at the lower edge of the pelvis. As the woman was buried with an unborn foetus in the birth position, the placing of the knife and shears in such a position ready to hand must surely show that they were intended in this instance for midwifery function.

Shears occur mostly in seventh-century graves. At Shudy Camps, Cambridgeshire, grave 76, the woman's interest in spinning and weaving is again evident, for, apart from an iron, linked pot-hanger, she possessed three chalk spindle whorls and a spearhead, presumably for use as a weaving sword[44]. At Burwell, Cambridgeshire, grave 42 also contained the famous bronze workbox and a spindle whorl besides other objects[45]. Other shears were present at Burwell, Cambridgeshire, grave 2[46], and Polhill, Kent, grave 41[47].

**Personal equipment**

*Knives* (distribution Figure 96)

The knives in this cemetery total 131. Some, (42), are too disintegrated for identification, but the rest

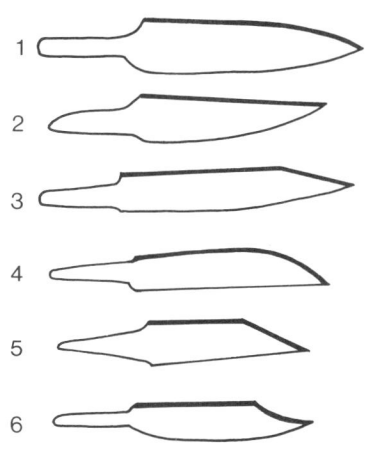

*Text Figure 22*    Knife types at Dover.

can, with a certain amount of confidence, be divided into six main types (Text Figure 22).

1. Curved back, curved cutting edge.
2. Straight back, curved cutting edge.
3. Angled back, curved cutting edge.
4. Curved back, straight cutting edge.
5. Angled back, straight cutting edge.
6. Straight back, incurved near tip.

The most numerous is type 1 (Table XVII), with a total of 39, and it occurs in all phases of the cemetery although not in plots J, L and M (distribution plan Figure 96). There are sixteen knives in type 3 and they also occur in all phases except 1, but not in plots, D, E, J, M or N. Type 5, also totalling 16, does not occur in plots A and B with the exception of grave 34, but it does occur in plots E, F, G, H and I, i.e. in phases 3–7. Type 4, totalling eight knives, occurs once in plot B (grave 44), and in plots G, H, I and N, i.e. in phases 4–7. Types 2 and 6 consist of five examples each. Type 2 occurs in plots A, D, F and H, i.e. from phase 1 to 6, and type 6 occurs in plots A, B and H, i.e. apparently in phases 1, 3 and 6, but see below.

The knives which are not in a good enough condition to be identified as any particular type are located throughout the cemetery, and so do not distort the distribution of the other types to any appreciable extent, although a considerable proportion in plots A and D are unidentifiable. Graves without knives are fairly evenly distributed, and there are rich graves without knives, e.g. graves 67, 92, 93 and 94b (Figures 37, 42, 43 and 44), and also poorly furnished graves without knives, e.g. graves 36, 76, 79 and 140 (Figures 20, 39, 39 and 57) There are five adult males without knives although one of these has a seax possibly accompanied by knives, 93/7 (Figure 43), but there are as many as twelve adult females without knives. In addition two adults, sex unknown, were without knives, apart from twelve unfurnished graves. No male child was without a knife, but two female children had no

---

41  Hyslop 1963, 179, fig. 12k
42  Lethbridge 1931, 76, fig. 37A
43  Lethbridge 1936, fig. 9, 8, fig. 11, 6 and 7
44  Ibid, fig. 11, 1, 2, 5

45  Lethbridge 1931, 53–7, figs. 26–8
46  Ibid, 48, fig. 22, 2, 8
47  Philp 1973a, 198, fig. 56.542

knife, and three children of unknown sex had no knife, apart from six unfurnished graves. It therefore seems to have been rather more important for a male to be provided with a knife than a female. No particular type was monopolised by either sex (Table XVII), unless such a claim might be made for the low numbers in types 2 and 6. Type 2 occurs in four sword graves and only once in a female grave. Type 6 occurs in three female graves, and there is one loose find and one in the fill of the male grave 91. There are two other knives which were found in the fill of a grave, one in 87 in plot A and one in 83 in plot I, both type 1. It is not known whether these represent accidental loss or deliberate deposition.

The length of the knives varies between 8.4cm and 31.2cm and the width of the blade from 1 to 3cm. The shapes are identical to those of some of the weapons known as seaxes, and the only difference is that of size. In fact, a large knife might be regarded either as a domestic utensil or an offensive weapon. The addition of a metal pommel could be regarded as more proper to a weapon, and there is one on each of the two seaxes discussed above. At an intermediate size the knife 64/1, type 1, is 24.1cm long and is provided with a suspension ring but no pommel, but would well have served as a weapon, this likelihood perhaps being increased by the proximity of the grave to grave 65 which contained a seax with pommel. Even larger is 56/2, type 3, length 31.2cm, with a welding line shown by X-ray along the middle of the blade, and the end of the tang beaten out into a disc. An indication that it should probably be regarded as a weapon is that it was found lying beside and parallel to the sword, possibly kept in a pocket on the scabbard.

Most of the knives consist of a simple blade and tang, with organic traces of a grip covering on the tang. On five knives which have been examined, the organic traces are probably horn: 38/8, 95/2, 96b/9, 117/1 and 120/1 (p 196 below). Some have a welding line revealed either by X-ray or by a visible split in the blade, which shows that the cutting edge, no doubt of better quality iron or steel, was welded on to the back section – UN/11, 50/2, 56/2, 130/1 and 156/2 (Figures 64, 28, 31, 53 and 61). These occur in plots A, K and G. A groove or grooves along the back of the blade are visible on 15/1, 10/3, 42/4 and 136/1 (plots A, B, C and F) which are types 1 and 3. In 33/3 (Figure 20) (type 3) a band of streaky iron, possibly pattern welding, is revealed by X-ray. Inlay of another metal is only visible on one knife fragment 98/5 (Figure 47) in a sword grave, where three parallel strips of bronze are inlaid along the back.

The tang of the knife 50/2 (Figure 28) has a raised ridge along the middle, on knife 56/2 (Figure 31) the end is flattened and shaped to a disc, and in grave 38 one knife 38/8 (Figure 22) has a tang which has a toothed outline at the end, all devices to provide a

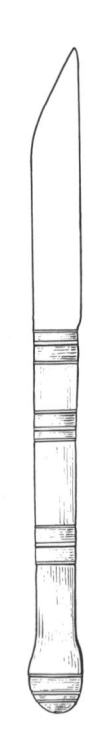

*Text Figure 23* Reconstruction of knife 158/2. Scale 1/2

more secure base to anchor the handle covering. A textile band at the junction of blade and tang in 64/1 (Figure 36) was no doubt inserted to make a loose handle firm, and this knife also has the remains of an iron guard plate. One knife has the remains of an ornamental handle, 158/2 (Figure 62 and Text Figure 23) of segments of different materials divided by iron plates. The three main sections are probably bone, between the iron tip and the first ?bone segment was a section of willow or poplar, and between the ?bone sections are the remains of some organic material that has been wound round the tang. A shaped wooden handle, segmented in this fashion, was fixed to a Roman knife at Great Chesterford, Essex[48]. A knife found in Clifford Street, York has a bone handle divided into segments by double incised lines which give the impression of being copied from a truly segmented type as at Dover. A suggested date for the York knife was eleventh century, but as it was found with two other knives of types 2 and 4, it probably belongs to an earlier period[49], i.e. seventh century. A handle with dividing metal plates was found in grave 48 at Lausanne, Bel-Air, Switzerland[50].

As knives have not received much attention, there are few records of decorative and other details such as grooves, welded cutting edges, and inlay of another metal or pattern-welding, and these are often only visible by X-ray. Grooves were present on a number of Polhill knives, according to the drawings, although they are not mentioned in the

---

48 Liversidge 1973, fig. 66a
49 Waterman 1959, 73, fig. 7, 3, 12, 13

50 Moosbrugger-Leu 1963–4, 1, fig. 1, CT424

description or discussion[51], and on one blade the draughtsman evidently saw some decoration which was presumably pattern-welding[52].

The method of suspension is evident for three knives as they were accompanied by an iron ring – 64/1, 127/2 and 150/2 (Figures 36, 52 and 60). A leather sheath was detected in grave 41 with impressed or openwork punched decoration, and lined with coarse textile (Figure 24). Line decoration is visible on the leather sheaths 134/6 and 142/3 (Figures 55 and 58). The presence of a leather sheath is indicated by two rows of small bronze rivets along the cutting edge of 145/1, and the edge of the sheath of 14/11 was bound by a U-sectioned bronze strip, 14/14, (Figures 59 and 10).

The position of the knife in the graves shows that it was usually worn at the waist by both male and female, about three quarters of these being found on the left side. 32 were found at the hip, two between the femurs, one at mid chest, four on the right of the body and twelve on the left. Eight females carried their knife in a bag, pocket or other container at the left hip – 1, 12, 23, 30, 32, 35, 38 and 44 (grave plan Figures 66, 67, 69, 69, 69, 70, 70 and 71). It could be that some people carried the knife either up the sleeve or strapped to their left forearm, but when the arm is bent across the body in the grave it is impossible to be sure whether the knife was attached to the arm or waist. However, in a number of graves the knife was close to, and parallel to the left forearm – 6, 33, 39, 46, 61, 71, 80, 87, 103, 114, 130, 145 and 146 (grave plan Figures 66, 70, 70, 71, 73, 74, 75, 76, 78, 79, 80, 82 and 82).

It may be noted that some of these types correspond to continental types noticed by Böhner in the Trier region: Type 1 is Böhner's type A[53] which was in use from 450–700. Type 2 is Böhner's type B[54] in use 450–600 and to a certain extent in the seventh century. Types 3, 4 and 5 seem to correspond to Böhner's type C which was only found in the seventh century[55]. Type 6 may correspond to one of Böhner's type D[56], but this is uncertain as there is no indication by drawn section or description as to which side of the blade is the cutting edge, and the description of 'sickle' blade suggests that, like the sickle, the cutting edge was on the inside curve, although this is hardly likely. The one example quoted at Eisenach belongs to the seventh century.

As type 1 at Dover is the most frequent and occurs throughout the cemetery, it must be as wide-ranging in date as the same kind at Trier i.e. fifth to seventh century (Table XVII). Type 3, of which there are 16 examples, was in use from phase 2 to 7. Type 2 is only represented by five knives, but makes an appearance in phases 1, 3, 4 and 6. There may be some significance in the fact that, in spite of its long time range, the graves in which it occurs are limited topographically to a narrow strip between graves 98 and 113. Type 5, more numerous with 16 examples, begins in phase ?3, and type 4 with 8 examples begins in phase 4, and both continue to the end of the cemetery, so corresponding fairly well with the seventh-century dating at Trier. Type 4 has already been noted as a form which was in use late in the pagan period at Portsdown in Hampshire[57], where one 20.9cm long, with a groove along the back and welded-on cutting edge was found in one of a group of graves of late date denoted by a conical 'sugar-loaf' shield boss. Similar eighth-century forms were noted from Frisia[58]. Since then other eighth-century type 4 forms have been published from the Continent[59]. A number also occurred in the Kentish cemetery at Polhill[60] which has been dated to the period from the middle of the seventh to the eighth century. Type 5 also occurs in the eighth-century continental graves[61] and in England at Polhill[62], Holborough[63], Horndean[64] and elsewhere.

Of the five knives of type 6, one was unassociated and two were in grave 95 and 141, both allocated to phase 6. This dating appears at first to be at variance with the find spots of the other two, one in grave 48 and one in the fill of grave 91 which belong to phase 1 and phase 3 respectively. However, as the knife was in the fill of grave 91 and not on the floor with the other grave goods it could have been a later intrusion, either an accidental one, or, if the occurrence of other knives in the fill of graves at Dover has any relevance, the insertion may have been deliberate. As to grave 48 it is undeniably one of the earliest graves on the site, but the knife differs somewhat from the others of type 6. They are fairly long, with the curve near the tip, while the knife in grave 48 is very short indeed, so that the curve takes up most of the length of the blade. The dating of type 6 may therefore be regarded as phase 6, with one possible early variant in phase 1. Type 6 occurs in seventh and eighth-century graves[65] and also as folding knives, on the Continent[66], and in England in late seventh to eighth-century contexts[67]. Two knives at Dover cannot be allocated to graves.[68]

---

51  Philp 1973a, fig. 57, 560, 563, 572, 576, 581; fig. 58, 585, 593, 601
52  Ibid, fig. 58, 590. It has not been possible to investigate these features as since publication these finds have not been available for inspection.
53  Böhner 1958 2, Taf. 60.1, 2
54  Ibid, Taf. 60.3, 4
55  Ibid, Taf. 60.5, 6
56  Ibid, Taf. 60.12
57  Evison 1967c, pl. IID
58  La Baume 1952–3, Taf. 1, 3; Schmid 1967, Abb. 4.4
59  Stein 1967, Taf. 33.27; 39.10
60  Philp 1973a, fig. 57.560, 561, 562, 567; 58.597
61  Stein 1967, Taf. 5, 8; 10, 9; 11, 4; 17, 16; 18, 14; 21, 7; 24, 14; 48, 16
62  Philp 1973a, fig. 57.572, 577, 580; fig. 58, 586, 592, 594, 598
63  Evison 1956, fig. 14, 1; 16, 4; 17, 3; 18, 3
64  Knocker 1956, fig. 11, S.17.
65  Werner 1953, Taf. 9, 6–9; Stein 1967, Taf. 7.6; 15.5; 17.11
66  Ibid. Taf. 14.10
67  Meaney and Hawkes 1970, fig. 11, gr. 15
68  Some confusion between knives at Dover arose when numbers became detached during laboratory treatment. One knife, (Figure 65, 20) type 4, was returned from the laboratory after conservation labelled 87/5, but the knife (Figure 65, 20) is complete and does not match the original

TABLE XVII  KNIFE TYPES IN RELATION TO PHASES

| Type | 1 | 1 or 2 | 2 | 3 | ?3 | 4 | ?4 | 5 | ?5 | 6 | ?6 | 7 | Unassociated |
|---|---|---|---|---|---|---|---|---|---|---|---|---|---|
| 1 | 21<br>87 | 17 | 14<br>15<br>23<br>50 | 1<br>30<br>32<br>35<br>38 (2)<br>57<br>91 | 115<br>123 | 18<br>64<br>65<br>66<br>96a | 54<br>135 | 6<br>129<br>137 (2)<br>156 | 9 | 138<br>149<br>150<br>160 | 105 | 74<br>82<br>83<br>145 | |
| 2 | 22 | | | 41 | | 71<br>96b | | | | 113 | | | |
| 3 | | | 28 | 33<br>56 | | 39<br>42<br>43 | 135<br>136 | 8<br>10<br>157 | | 108<br>148<br>161 | 111 | 117 | |
| 4 | | | | | | 44 | | | 130 | 110 | 142 | 80<br>83<br>120<br>146 | Un/20 |
| 5 | | | | 63 | | 34<br>55<br>131 | | 52<br>128<br>132<br>133<br>134 | | 103<br>124<br>158 | 106<br>109 | 77<br>85 | Un/21 |
| 6 | 48 | | | 91 | | | | | | 95<br>141 | | | Un/11 |
| Unknown | 12<br>13<br>20<br>46<br>87 | 16 | | C<br>F<br>29<br>60<br>61<br>98 | 5 | 27<br>58<br>62<br>90 | 97 | 53<br>139<br>155 | | 114<br>138<br>144<br>159<br>162 (2)<br>163 | 40<br>104<br>119<br>121<br>125<br>147 | 81<br>84<br>127 | Un/2<br>Un/12<br>Un/13<br>Un/18<br>Un/19 |

TABLE XVIII  KNIFE TYPES IN RELATION TO SEX

| Type | Male | Female | Ju | Unknown | Unassociated | Total |
|---|---|---|---|---|---|---|
| | | | | *Contexts* | | |
| 1 | 13 | 18 | 8 | – | – | 39 |
| 2 | 4 | 1 | – | – | – | 5 |
| 3 | 9 | 4 | 3 | – | – | 16 |
| 4 | 3 | 4 | – | 1 | – | 8 |
| 5 | 7 | 4 | 3 | 2 | – | 16 |
| 6 | 1 | 2 | 1 | – | 1 | 5 |
| Unidentified | 11 | 16 | 9 | 1 | 5 | 42 |

*Keys* (distribution Figure 97)
Keys occur in a large number of graves, all female, from child to old adult. In fact the number amounts to forty-five, so that only twenty-five female graves did not contain keys. They are mostly of iron, with only one in bronze (54/3, Figure 29). They generally range from about 10 to 14cm in length, attached in groups of two to four by a looped top to an iron ring. The shaft is usually circular in section, sometimes square, and, rarely, a twist is visible (30/8, 132/4e, Figures 18, 54), or the shaft becomes wider and flatter at the top (58/2b, 81/4a, Figures 32, 39). The end is usually hook-shaped, varying from wide and angular (38/9a, b Figure 22) or narrower and curled at the terminal like a shepherd's crook (29/11, Figure 17).

Some keys have L-shaped terminals, some with two prongs, and these tend to be large (53/3, 58/2a, 95/1a, 110/5, 1/10c, 44/4a, 55/3a, 142/2, 161/4a, Figures 28, 32, 44, 49, 5, 26, 30, 58, 63). A number of keys have T-shaped ends (54/2, 3, 58/2c, 60/6b, Figures 29, 32, 34) and these, too, are found in large sizes, (35/7, 160/5b, Figures 21, 62), and the three largest keys are 164/4, L.26.9cm (Figure 63) with L-shaped terminal, 95/1b, L.23.6cm (Figure 44) with

index card drawing or any of the other original drawings on index cards of Dover knives. The drawing (Figure 40, 87/5) matches the index card drawing, and so must be correct, but there is no matching knife extant. The knife (Figure 65, 21) type 5 was returned from the laboratory labelled 23/2. It does not match the original index card drawing, but it is fragmentary and when complete may have matched one of the index card drawings of Dover knives. There is no knife extant to match the drawing (Figure 15, 23/2).

bifurcating terminal[69], and 13/9, L.28cm (Figure 9) which has a T-shaped end on a plane forward from the shaft.

The keys were in a fragmentary condition, but it is clear from grave plans and drawings of exact positions in graves F and 6 (Figure 66) that a woman often wore more than one bunch of two to four keys, not all suspended from one ring but suspended in stages from left hip to knee, probably on separate, perishable, leather thongs or cords, or on the linked iron rods as 75/3b, 110/7, 113/5b, c, 132/4c, 134/7f (Figures 74, 78, 79, 81, 81). In fact the aim seems to have been to achieve the major display effect, so giving the impression that a greater number of keys had some significance. They were worn both by women in richly furnished graves and by others with few grave goods, and were in fashion from the beginning to the end of the time that the cemetery was in use (distribution Figure 97). The wearing of keys in numbers of more than two however did not begin before phase 3. Two of the largest keys were worn by old women (13/9 and 142/2). The function of these large keys was presumably to open the lock or lift the latch of a door, but the smaller keys were for casket locks, as we may see from grave 29/9 (Figure 17) where the key was still in place in the lock. With one exception the keys were of iron, and all capable of normal locking function. Even the one bronze exception, 54/3a, which was undecorated, was of the same T-shape as many of the iron keys, and would have been suitable to perform the same function. None of the women at Dover was wearing a purely decorative pair of keys incapable of mechanical function as found elsewhere in England and on the Continent[70], but the Dover keys, no less than the decorated variety, were for display, and probably registered a similar significance.

There is little doubt that the custom of Roman matrons to wear keys as an indication of their status was adopted and carried on by Germanic women. Credible suggestions as to other possible aspects of their symbolism include other heathen or Christian connotations[71], and a marital sexual parallel as indicated by two Anglo-Saxon riddles in the Exeter Book.

At Dover the women with keys were buried more or less in equal numbers in diverse parts of the cemetery which appear to be Christian or pagan. Six females under 18 were provided with keys, and seven women over 45, otherwise the women with keys were all between 18 and 45.

The short linked iron rods mentioned above, each incorporating a ring at each end, are not always accompanied by definite evidence of association with keys, i.e. graves 110, 132 and 134 contained keys, but graves 75, 113 and 121 did not. In grave 110 besides keys there was an iron spoon and a shaft embedded in a wooden object 110/4. A double row of this type of ring-ended rod occurred in grave 49 at Mitcham, London (Surrey), but there they were in bronze, hanging from a perforated plate in double lines but not actually linked together, and they were twisted with a strip of several layers of textile and some probable leather at the lower end[72]. Similar bronze ring-ended rods in a seventh-century grave, Burial 6a Painsthorpe Wold, Humberside (Yorkshire), appear to have been connected with a textile satchel[73].

In two graves there is another fitting connected with the suspension of the keys, a loop with ends flattened and riveted for attachment to a strap, (28/8, 134/7a, Figures 16, 55).

*Girdle hangers*

A variety of means were used to suspend articles from the girdle, amongst them loops with flattened ends for riveting to straps: 35/7, 110/8, 155/4b, 20/13a, 28/8 (Figures 21, 49, 60, 12, 16); a perforated bone 129/10d (Figure 53); and a tab looped over a ring: 35/7, 14/12, 58/2d (Figures 21, 10, 32). A more elaborate ring and tab, 164/2 (Figure 63), was in yellow metal and decorated. An S-shaped loop in iron 28/7 (Figure 16), and open-ended bronze S-loops 138/5d, e and 141/7a (Figures 57, 58), were no doubt also used for suspension. A similar pair of bronze S-loops were found with glass and amethyst beads near the neck of a skeleton in grave 121 at Kingston, Kent[74], so that this assemblage corresponds to the phase 6 date of graves 138 and 141 at Dover.

The woman in grave 129 possessed an ornamented bronze girdle hanger 129/10c (Figure 53) which was suspended from a bronze ring amongst iron keys. The lower end expands in trifoliate fashion, each lobe perforated, and a spatula hangs from one of the perforations. The girdle hanger itself is a yellow metal alloy, the spatula more red in colour, and by the right shoulder, perhaps in a bag or hanging on the necklace, was another spatula of bronze which was no doubt originally on the girdle hanger. Similar toilet implements of spatulate and other shapes occur on hangers in the graves of other Kentish women[75]. An ornamental plate very like the Dover girdle hanger was found at Ozengell[76], and there were others similar at Kingston and Gilton[77].

In grave 116, where the bone report is 'probably female 30–45', a bronze hook and peg on a bronze ring 116/1 (Figure 50) were lying on the left femur, and so were no doubt being used as a girdle hanger. As the shape and solidity of the casting suggests, however, they are of Roman origin, similar hooks being found at Colchester, Essex, and at Richborough, Kent[78]. There are two others from Anglo-Saxon graves, from Kempston, Bedfordshire,

---

69 cf Faussett 1856, pl. XV, 27
70 Steuer 1983, distribution map Abb. 10
71 Meaney 1981, 178–81; Steuer 1983
72 Bidder and Morris 1959, 110, fig. 17
73 Mortimer 1905, 117, fig. 281
74 Faussett 1856, 62
75 Ibid, pl. XII, 1, 3, 6 and 7
76 Smith 1854, pl. VI. 12
77 Faussett 1856, pl. XII, 2, 4 and 5
78 Colchester and Richborough Museums

and from Jordan's Hill, Dorset[79]. Hooks of this type form part of Roman weighing equipment, one being used above the rod to suspend the balance, and another underneath to hold the material being weighed, so that those found in Anglo-Saxon graves must be relics.[80]

*Tweezers*
Two flat fragmentary strips of iron, 107/1 (Figure 48), in a woman's grave are probably parts of a pair of tweezers. Iron tweezers in a more complete condition were found in the grave of a man with a spear, 156/4 (Figure 61). The other two tweezers are made of bronze, and the construction of each is different. Item 41/5 (Figure 24) is made in one piece with decorative moulding at the fold and ring-and-dot stamps. 65/8 (Figure 36) consists of two separate bands fastened together with two rivets at one end and decorated with triangular stamps. Each of the three complete tweezers were in a grave of a man with weapons, and this draws attention to the fact that tweezers are usually found with a man, often armed, e.g. in fifth-century graves at Petersfinger and Winterbourne Gunner, Wiltshire[81], and in a seax grave, probably of the seventh century at Sibertswold, Kent, grave 45[82]. This accords with the findings in Merovingian graves[83]. Iron seems to have been used more rarely than bronze for tweezers, although inferior survival chances may partly account for its absence. At Dover, however, the two graves containing iron tweezers are later than those containing bronze tweezers. In the same way, while bronze tweezers at Krefeld Gellep range from *Stufe* II to IV, the one iron pair belongs to *Stufe* IV[84]. It is possible that the iron tweezers may have been a seventh-century development.

*Spoons*
An iron spoon was suspended by the left femur with iron keys in three women's graves, 75/3c (Figure 38), 110/6 (Figure 49) and 127/3a (Figure 52). These are amongst the latest graves in the cemetery, and iron spoons in similar late contexts are fairly common: at Holborough, Kent, grave 11[85], Sibertswold, Kent, grave 60[86] and Burwell, Cambridgeshire, graves 83 and 90[87]. These were suspended from the waist along with keys, and their function may have been connected with cosmetics or table use.

The only spoon in bronze was the miniature type usually regarded as an ear scoop. This is a form which does appear in both male and female graves, where it often occurs at the waist, possibly with a knife[88], but in this particular grave the bronze spoon, 32/3 (Figure 19), acted as the centre piece of a necklace. Another occurrence on a necklace was in grave 55 at Shudy Camps, Cambridgeshire[89].

*Iron diamonds* (distribution Figure 95)
A rather enigmatic object is a flat piece of iron in the shape of a diamond with a perforation in the middle. There are fifteen altogether, all in graves of women except one, 139/2 (Figure 57), which is in a boy's grave. They seem to be a kind of washer, and resemble the roves found on ship rivets such as those in the Sutton Hoo ship burial[90], but are slightly smaller. In the perforation of one only 20/15, there is an iron rivet. The positions in which they were found were at the hip (12/2, 14/10, 20/14, 20/15, 48/9) or by the femurs (1/11, 38/9f, 38/9g, 53/4). One was in a box by the feet (60/8). In nine graves there were other small objects nearby, and some of these included purse mounts (53/5, 139/1), and ivory rings (38/10, 53/6), so that they are presumably connected with a bag and might have been used to hold a rivet attaching bag to belt.

Five occur in plot A and the rest on the barrow and graves of like date, so that the period of use (with the exception of two later children's graves, 74 and 139), was from the beginning of the cemetery to about 650. They probably often escaped notice in early excavations, but were noted at Bifrons, Kent, graves 29, 32 and 63[91].

*Ivory rings* (distribution Figures 95, 118)
An ivory ring, fairly complete or only fragmentary, was found in five graves, each one by the left femur or between the knees of a female, (1/8, 38/10, 53/6, 75/4, 160/7 Figures 5, 29, 38, 62). In each grave iron keys were either inside the ring or nearby. The ivory ring, diameter varying from 10.2cm to 14cm, must have functioned as a frame for the mouth of a bag, and the reconstruction suggested by Barbara Green is one which would provide the most convenient construction to give easy access for the hand without any danger of the contents spilling out[92]. Other objects found in close proximity, and which might also have had some part in the structure of the bag connected with suspension are: grave 1, iron and bronze ring 1/9, 1/12b and iron diamond 1/11 (Figure 5); grave 38, two iron diamonds 38/9f and g (Figure 22); grave 53, iron diamond 53/4 (Figure 29); grave 160, iron ring 160/5 (Figure 62). Some of the keys may have been carried in the bag, as well as a fire-steel 53/5 (Figure 29), a weaving pick 75/5 (Figure 38), and knives 38/7 and 8 (Figure 22).

In Frankish and Alamannic territory the mouth of the bag was often covered with an ornamental, openwork bronze disc[93]. At Caistor-by Norwich the

---

79  B.M. Reg. No. 1891, 6–24 161; B.M. Reg. No. 1912 5–28 16
80  Complete examples from Bernay, Eure and Cailly, Seine Inférieure are illustrated: Coutil 1898–1921, 57, fig. 15
81  Evison 1965b, fig. 18g, 20c
82  Faussett 1856, 110, pl. XII, 13
83  Böhner 1958 1, 219; Pirling 1974 1, 166
84  Ibid, 166
85  Evison 1956, fig. 18, 6
86  Faussett 1856, 112, pl. XII, 10
87  Lethbridge 1931, 62–6, fig. 33, 1; 66, fig. 30, 6
88  cf Faussett 1856, pl. XII, 1 and 3
89  Lethbridge 1936, fig. 4F, 2
90  Bruce-Mitford 1972, fig. 23
91  Godfrey-Faussett 1876, 309, 311; *idem*. 1880, 553
92  Myres and Green 1973, 100–3, text fig. 3
93  Vogt 1960, 85ff; Moosbrugger-Leu 1971A, 220–34; Renner 1970, 52–2

ivory rings occurred in fifth-century graves, but they are also known from sixth-century contexts and are not entirely absent from the seventh century. At Dover two of the graves may be dated to about 600, while the other three are later than the middle of the seventh century[94].

*Silver, bronze and iron rings*
Rings of various materials, and also other oddments found in a position on a skeleton which indicates the contents of a bag are regarded by D Brown[95] as being amulets. The hoarding of ring-shaped objects does not require such an explanation, however, for rings were widely used by both men and women for the suspension of objects from a belt, such as knives, keys, etc, and it is no wonder if a ring was kept against the day it would be needed.

At the cemetery of Dover the function of most of the rings is quite clear e.g. small bronze rings on pins 101/1, 147/1, an earscoop 32/3 and tweezers 41/5 were for suspension. Many graves contained keys (p 117) which were all kept on rings (e.g. 1/10a, 6/5, Figures 5, 7). A knife was suspended by a ring in graves 1/7, 12/3, 14/12, 62/1, 64/1, 109/2 and 150/2 (Figures 5, 8, 10, 35, 36, 49, 60) and a weaving batten in grave 46/1 (Figure 26). Of two iron rings in grave 28 one bore traces of a leather thong and both were associated with two iron diamonds situated under the belt buckle, and so must have functioned as part of a purse. In grave 92 a trench had cut away the grave near the rings 92/5 and 92/7 at the hip, so that suspended keys may have been lying in the missing part of the grave. A bronze or iron ring could be mounted on a spearshaft, see p 29. One plain silver ring, 29/3, and several silver wire slip knot rings were connected with beads, and are discussed on p 65: 29/4, 35/4, 107/7, 110/13, 157/2 (Figures 17, 21, 48, 49, 61).

The only rings which have no obvious purpose are a small iron loop bearing textile traces and possibly connected with a ?lyre 114/4 (Figure 50) and a bronze and iron ring in an ivory ring purse, 1/9 and 1/12 (Figure 5), but even these too could have been part of the purse fittings. There is therefore no evidence at Dover of the hoarding of rings as amulets.

*Combs*
There is little trace of combs at Dover as the bone did not survive well. Some flat bone fragments near the bronze workbox 107/3 presumably were part of a comb as the space available between the legs and the box is too small for anything larger than a comb.

Other small patches may be all that remain of combs, e.g. grave 20 under the bronze bowl, 113 R. of the femurs, 121 by R. pelvis, 144 L. of skull, 150 R. waist, 155 R. of feet. A rectangular patch of antler 15 × 7.5cm beside an iron-bound wooden box, 124/4 may also have been a comb or box. In another grave an iron rivet, 44/2 (Figure 26), fastened together three layers of bone, the two outer layers with grain running in the same direction, and the inner one with grain at right angles, i.e. presumably part of a composite comb or comb case.

The only two fairly well preserved combs owe their survival to the use of bronze in their make-up. 110/9 (Figure 49) is a double-sided comb of a type common throughout the pagan period, and with it are preserved parts of a double-sided comb-case. This is a quite complicated structure with the two sides hinging on a separate segment at the end,[96] and a bronze band attached to it by a chain to be slipped over the comb and case to keep them together (Text Figure 24). The ring-and-dot decorative pattern is one of the many variations to be found on combs of this period, and the strengthening bar in the middle is sometimes double as at Dover[97], or single as on the comb from Threadneedle Street[98]. This type of comb and case frequently occurs in Merovingian graves[99]. The Dover grave 110 comb is closely dated by its accompanying sceattas to the end of the seventh century.

Far more unusual is 30/1 (Figure 18). This is a single-sided composite comb, and it, too, has the double connecting plate, but there is a gap between the two bars which reveals a plate of bronze, one on each face. This would have increased the strength of the comb, but it was also decorative. As double-sided combs were the type in most general use at this period, consideration must be given to the possibility that the Dover comb had originally been double-sided but that after damage one side had been trimmed down. This possibility may be rejected, however, as the tooth plates extend some distance beyond the connecting plate at the plain edge and show no sign of saw cuts, nor are there any saw cuts on the side of the connecting plate made accidentally at the time the teeth were cut as happened along the opposite edge.

The use of two convex-topped connecting plates is very common, and occurs on the so-called 'Frisian' type of single-sided composite comb of the fifth century, of which a number have been found by C Hills at Spong Hill[100]. On this type of comb, however, they were placed close together, leaving no space for decoration in between. A zone of openwork decoration, however, is frequently found between these bars on double-sided combs extending at least from the fourth century to the thirteenth century.[101] The single-sided comb with these connecting plates is much less in evidence, and so is the use of bronze for ornament. A small bronze

---

94 Myres and Green 1973, 102
95 Brown 1977a
96 The terms used here and in the catalogue are adapted from those proposed for descriptions of combs by Galloway 1976.
97 cf Böhner 1958 2, Taf. 62.5 from Minden, grave 6
98 Wheeler 1935, 152, fig. 29
99 Behrens 1947, Abb. 12, 3; 15, 4; 27, 8; 120; Joffroy 1974, fig. 16; Glazema and Ypey 1956, 62 left, 63–4
100 Hills 1981
101 Roman: Keller 1971, 112–13, Taf. 33.2; a new ornate comb with openwork decoration and bronze plates was found in a late fourth century grave at Vron, N. France (grave exhibited in Boulogne Museum). Merovingian: Fingerlin 1971, 269, Taf. 82.10; medieval: Molaug 1975, 238, Abb. 17, 3.

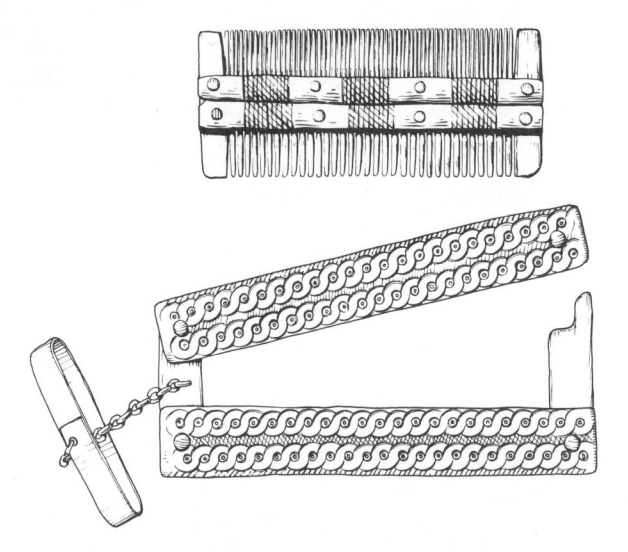

*Text Figure 24* Reconstruction of comb and case 110/9. Scale 1/2

plaque was fixed on one side of a triangular-shaped comb of about AD 400 at Landifay, Aisne[102]. In Northampton a single-sided comb was found which has a curved back with T-shaped perforations backed by a bronze sheet, and also with a bronze border strip and suspension ring[103], but there are no associations to provide a dated context. A smaller comb with animal decoration on the ends, apparently also with bronze-backed perforations, comes from Cheapside, London[104]. Another was found more recently at Clifford Street, York[105]. The general form of the Dover comb is rare, i.e. 9.5cm long, rectangular, with two convex-topped connecting plates, but one was found in a Dutch terp, a difference being that the connecting plates are close together, there is no bronze plate[106] and it is longer, 13.8cm. Two other combs from Holland, also of the longer variety, have two connecting plates, the top one being curved, and there is an ornamental row of perforations in between[107]. None of these comparable examples can be allocated to a definite date, and it is clear that some forms of comb continued with little change from the fourth to thirteenth centuries.

The Dover comb conforms to the small size of the combs in use from the fourth to seventh centuries, which were double-sided, or, if single-sided, of a different shape. The single-sided comb is not unknown, for one with a curved back does occur for instance in a sixth-century grave at Schwarzrheindorf[108], and the single-sided comb became more popular after the seventh century but with a considerable increase in length. The fairly close dating of grave 30 at Dover of *c* AD 600, therefore provides a useful dating point in connection with the study of this type of comb.

*Bronze balance*
The bronze balance in grave C (Figure 2) was found in a slight recess cut into one side of the grave, and was in 'some dark, peaty stuff'. We may assume from this that it was in some kind of container, probably a wooden box or leather satchel. A surviving wooden container of balance and square weights has been found at Lutlommel, Limburg, Belgium[109] and this one has been compared with balances from Byzantium, North Africa and Egypt. The balances found in Anglo-Saxon and Merovingian graves of the sixth to seventh centuries are for weighing light and small objects, probably coins only. With the Dover balance there was one blank bronze flan with some nicks in the edge (Figure 2, 2), twelve Roman coins of varying weights and sizes (four of these with nicked edges, Figure 2, 4 and 5, Figure 3, 11 and 12) and a large coin with a smaller one riveted to it (Figure 2, 3)[110]. These evidently functioned as weights, and the weight of some had been adjusted by addition or subtraction of metal.

A distribution map of these balances, and also of Merovingian mints, shows that they are largely mutually exclusive, the balances appearing on the fringes of the minting areas. It has been pointed out[111] that in areas where coins of regulated weight and gold content were in constant use, the coins could be accepted at face value and accepted as payment by number. In the non-minting area, however, coins were in circulation from diverse sources, and of varying weights and content. In these places it was necessary to test the gold by touchstone, and to check the weight. For this reason the distribution of balances is mainly confined to northern France and Belgium, the Rhineland, southern Germany and Switzerland[112]. They also occur in England, five in Kent, with four in the upper Thames area and six in counties north of the Thames as far north as Yorkshire (list p 270, Figure 119). None has yet been found in other counties south of the Thames. A recent find of a balance occurred in a swordsman's grave, No. 156, at Nouvion-en-Ponthieu, Somme[113], and in Kent in grave 76 at St. Peter's amongst the possessions of a woman wearing a gold pendant[114].

The man in grave C was clearly of high rank. He had a sword with silver pommel and scabbard fittings, an heirloom. An ornamented bow-headed rivet with interlocking ring had been added to the pommel, no doubt to signify the rank of its current owner who was probably a king's thegn or

---

102 Evison 1978a, pl. VI. 1, 1b
103 Brown 1915 IV, pl. LXXXVI, 2; Smith 1902, 233, 243, fig. 16; Cox 1897–9, 165, fig. on page 167
104 Brown 1915 IV, pl. LXXXVII. 1; Smith 1909, 164–5, fig. 27
105 MacGregor 1978, fig. 29, 4
106 Roes 1963, pl. XX.2
107 Ibid, pl. XXIII, 1 and 2
108 Behrens 1947, 25, Abb. 63, 2
109 van Bostraeten 1965, 81–4, 103–16, Afb. 18
110 p 180
111 Werner 1954
112 Werner 1962b, Abb. 15
113 Piton and Schuler 1981, pl. 9
114 Evison 1979a, fig. 36

companion[115]. These two significant items, the ring and the balance, suggest that he was the chief of the settlement in phase 3. Two richly endowed women were buried nearby in graves F and 1. Other contemporary sword bearers and rich women were buried in the Christian plot B, and his burial in plot D should indicate some radical difference, probably of religion.

*The ?lyre*
Tiny fragments of wood and bronze in grave 114 may be all that is left of a musical instrument. The wood of three of the pieces is about 4–5mm thick, and each consists of two separate pieces of wood, bevelled at 45° in a straight edge following the grain and butted together, being fastened by a bronze strip spanning the join on each side and gripped together by a pair of rivets, (Figure 50, 3a, b, c). On one fragment (Figure 50, 3c) there are two extra rivet holes which probably accommodated earlier rivets and strips which became broken. These three fragments were lying along the outside of the left femur, and a third bronze strip with two rivet heads but no wood was lying between the ankles. On the left ankle was an iron rivet which had pierced wood about 1.4cm thick. The distance from 3a to 3d was 2ft, (61cm).

The most common combination of wood with riveted bronze strips to be found in Saxon graves are interpreted as mending patches on turned wooden cups or bowls, but this cannot be the function of these pieces as there is no trace of curvature in either the wood or the bronze. Somewhat similar bronze strips have been found on the remains of lyres at Bergh Apton and Morning Thorpe in Norfolk where they are thought to have strengthened the uppermost extension of the sound-board[116]. This appears to have been about 5mm thick, and the type of wood was 'a diffuse-porous hardwood'. This compares with the use of other hardwoods, i.e. maple for the Sutton Hoo lyre, and yew in grave 114 at Dover. The length of the object in grave 114, about 2ft, corresponds with the estimated size of the Sutton Hoo lyre[117]. There are no decorative metal appliqués at Dover as exist on the joints of other lyres, and there is not sufficient of this object left to enable any reconstruction to be attempted. The only clue is that the three pieces by the top of the femur were lying more or less in a line about 7 ins. (c 18cm) long, and so may represent a single join in the sound box. However, because of the use of hardwood, because of the similarity of the bronze strips with those identified on lyres, because of the precise bevelling of the edges of the wood and because of the distance between the fragments, it seems highly likely that this is another Anglo-Saxon lyre to be added to those already noted at Sutton Hoo, Taplow, Abingdon, Bergh Apton, Morning Thorpe, as well as in graves in Germany[118]. The iron loop with textile impression found near 3b may have functioned on a suspension strap to the instrument.

Lawson has commented that Old English literature shows that the harp (as this instrument must have been called, O.E. *hearpe*) was played by nobles, professional bards (O.E. *scop*) and by any man so able to entertain his fellows. Royal and noble graves are indicated by the Sutton Hoo ship burial and the Taplow barrow, as well as by the German graves. Abingdon grave B42, and Morning Thorpe grave 97 which has not been published, are also well furnished. Grave B42 at Abingdon[119] was the grave of a man of sword-bearing rank, probably of the mid fifth century, and so belonged to an early period when burial of swords was customary. The comparative poverty of the Bergh Apton grave (bronze buckle, iron buckle, knife) Lawson attributes to 'the poor level of general preservation, and to the loss of one end of the grave through the action of tree roots.' The poor level of preservation can hardly be to blame, however, as wood and thin bronze sheet have survived in this grave. The head of the grave was, in fact, lost by quarrying, but the grave description makes no mention of tree roots[120], which, in any case, would have disturbed rather than destroyed the contents. The body in grave 22 was apparently buried on its left side with legs drawn up, judging from the position of the femurs which are all the bones that are left. It does not seem likely that a great deal of the grave was lost, and that was possibly an empty part. Most of the finds from this cemetery belong to the sixth century, but a nearby grave (18) contained a late floriate type of cruciform brooch. The bard in grave 22 was wearing a neat little bronze buckle with a rectangular plate bearing three rivets – a seventh-century type. The sparse grave furniture, therefore, is more likely to be a reflection of later and Christian custom and not an indication of poverty.

At Dover, grave 114 contained only a spearhead and knife beside the wood fragments. Its position in the cemetery shows that it must have been dug after AD 670, at a time when spears were no longer deposited as grave furniture, and this spearhead was placed in a unique position at the foot of the grave. Although without riches, therefore, this man was distinguished from his fellows. It seems to follow that at Bergh Apton and at Dover, we have the grave of a professional *scop*. The bejewelled lyres at Sutton Hoo and Taplow were the possessions of a king and noble, and it seems most likely that the common man might have temporary use of one or the other type when they were passed from hand to hand at a banquet, as related in the story of Caedmon.

*Amulets and keepsakes*
It is, of course, almost impossible to differentiate

---

115 Evison 1967a, 63
116 Lawson 1978, fig. 107
117 Bruce-Mitford and Bruce-Mitford 1970
118 Fremersdorf 1941–2
119 Evison 1965b, fig. 22
120 Green and Rogerson 1978, 21, 96

between these two categories. It is still a widespread human characteristic in the modern world to carry cherished oddments about, the man in his pockets and the woman in her handbag, or to keep them in a safe little box at home. The Anglo-Saxons were also prone to this sort of behaviour and whilst superstition plays a fairly small part in the modern habit in the form of lucky charms, etc, we may presumably attribute a more important role to superstition in the Anglo-Saxon world.

A comprehensive study of Anglo-Saxon amulets has recently been produced by Audrey Meaney[121], in which a great variety of objects are considered. Many of the types occur in this cemetery, and while the possible amuletic qualities of some of them are not denied, they are not all listed here under this heading, and in some cases the possibility of amuletic power would seem to be remote. References to Meaney's opinions are given in the appropriate sections of discussion. One element with such meaning must have been the cowrie shell[122], found only in the graves of women and thought to confer fertility. The distribution of graves with cowrie shells is shown on the map Figure 120, list p 270. They came mainly from the south of the Thames, Kent, Sussex, Surrey and Avon (Somerset) but also from Buckinghamshire, Bedfordshire, Leicestershire (Rutland) and Cambridgeshire. The graves are predominantly of the seventh century, but there is at least one of the sixth century[123].

The cowrie shell in the Dover grave 6/2 (Figure 7) is extraordinary as it has been sliced in half. It must have been sliced in this way so that use could be made of the thicker parts and serrated edge in order to manufacture beads like the beads 6/10a, 67/1b and c, 129/5a, 134/2a and 157/1a (Figures 7, 37, 53, 55 and 61) (p 59). These beads are also in graves of the seventh century. The thinner part of the shell would have been of little use to the jeweller, but obviously still had some notional value for the woman in grave 6. It was placed with other objects at her feet.[124]

Among personal possessions kept in a wooden box, such as spindle whorls and a bead, was a tooth of a large horse 60/12 (Figure 34). The surface is very weathered and the enamel all gone, so that it must have been exposed for a long time before burial, which means that it was probably found accidentally and kept by the woman.[125] A single horse tooth has made an appearance in a few other Anglo-Saxon graves, at Stapenhill, Staffordshire, Camerton, Avon (Somerset) and Winnall II, Hampshire[126].

Amongst other amulets or keepsakes are fossils e.g. 55/4, (Figure 30) *cyphosoma*, a cretaceous regular echinoid from the chalk, probably contained in an iron-bound wooden box, and a similar type seems to have been found by Douglas in grave XIX at Chatham Lines, Kent[127]. Another fossil, a porosphaera, was strung on a necklace with beads, 129/5h (Figure 53), and this custom has been followed in other Anglo-Saxon graves[128].

These fossils have also been noted in the sunken-featured buildings at West Stow, Suffolk, where they occur mainly in sixth-century contexts. The excavator thinks they were probably collected as gaming counters[129], but Meaney suggests that, like other holed stones, they may have been believed to keep away nightmares, which, one must agree, is a quality of even more practical value in a bedroom than in a grave[130].

Two lumps of iron ore or iron pyrites are not likely to be accidental inclusions in the grave fill as they were on the floor of the grave and very near the skeleton, in grave 67 by the feet, and in grave 131 with a spear by the skull. As these nodules occur naturally in chalk, they may have been overlooked in early excavations, but deliberate depositions have been noted at Holywell Row, Suffolk, Burwell, Cambridgeshire and Snell's Corner, Horndean, Hampshire[131].

Three small spherical pebbles were found in grave C (Figure 3), two of sandstone and one of chalk, but their positions are not known[132]. The spherical pebble in grave 11 (Figure 8), however, was placed on the left knee. A similar appearance was achieved by a baked clay globule from another, robbed grave (B, Figure 1). Other pebbles have been found in association with skeletons in graves[133]. One can only guess at their purpose, but a rather pretty, tartan-marked, disc-shaped pebble in a woman's bag at Dover, 147/4 Figure 59, has obvious visual attraction. It could have been used as a playing piece in a board game, and this was certainly the function of the plano-convex ?bone piece 14/8 Figure 10. In company with the latter in the woman's bag or pocket was a disc-headed stud from a shield – plainly a keepsake. Occasionally the bone counters have occurred elsewhere in numbers suitable for a board game, or with distinguishing marks or colours[134].

It is not necessary to imagine a superstitious reason for the hoarding of two Roman coins, 15/5 and 138/7, neither of which were perforated, both in a woman's bag with other items[135].

The category of amulets would also include objects marked with the Christian cross, i.e. pendants p 49, and a range of jewellery possibly endowed with magical power in both the jewels and the animal ornament.

---

121 Meaney 1981
122 Meaney and Hawkes 1970, 32; Meaney 1981, 123–7
123 Griffith and Salzmann 1914, 40, grave 43
124 Not at the waist as stated in Meaney 1981
125 I am grateful to Mr J Attridge, Birkbeck College for comment on this tooth.
126 Meaney 1981, 131–2
127 Ibid, 117
128 See p 60; Meaney 1981, 115–16
129 West, 1985 1, 70–71
130 Meaney 1981, 116
131 Ibid, 101
132 Ibid, 115 lists these as unperforated porosphaera.
133 Ibid, 88–9
134 Ibid, 261, fig. VII.o.1, 2, 4
135 Ibid, 213–16

# Chapter III

# Discussion

### Determination of Sex and Age

The sex of the body is stated in Table XIX, column 1 where this is evident from the grave goods. In most cases this determination accords with the final report on the bones by Miss R Powers and Mrs R Cullen of the British Museum (Natural History) (Column 3). Interim notes on the bones from all of the graves were kindly provided by them at an earlier stage and these notes are valid unless superseded by an alteration of opinion in the final report. In many cases where sex is not evident from the grave goods, the sex is determined by the bones. The information provided by the two bone reports, both interim and final, are included in Table XIX, and where these reports differ from the sex determination by grave goods, or where there are differences within the bone reports themselves, this is noted in the last column. Some assessments on bone evidence (seven) are tentative and are marked with a query (graves F, 4, 32, 75, 107, 141, 142). There are, however, eleven instances where the sexing according to bone evidence is definite and differs from the sexing by grave goods (graves 3, 14, 15, 30, 50, 54, 58, 61, 66, 87 and 94a), and there are four discrepancies within the final bone report itself (graves 29, 33, 93, 96b). Mr D Brothwell, then of the British Museum (Natural History), commented on this as follows:

'When the sexing according to grave groups differs from the anatomical sexing this is a fact of interest rather than a simple mistake. Both findings should be given, and distinguished. Reasons for confusion include: pelvic features in the female resembling the male form, double graves where one body has decayed, and a consistent proportion of individuals whose skeleton is genuinely intermediate in form between the sexes (around 5% to 10% even in well preserved series, unlike this series where decay has obscured several of the features that distinguish the sexes). The very young and the very old are not easily distinguishable either'.

Confusion arising from mixture of the bones of two bodies is not usually applicable in an excavation of this sort where each individual bone is visible and noted in its articulated position. The suggestion in the post-cranial pathology report, therefore, that an affected scapula in grave 33 might be from a second individual (p 199) is not actually possible, as the skeleton was recorded fairly complete, with no superfluous bones as large as a scapula (Figure 70, grave plan). For similar reasons 94b cannot be the same individual as 94a, as suggested in the post-cranial pathology report. In these two graves, moreover, the finds indicate a discrepancy in sex attribution.

From Brothwell's other comments it appears that bone differences between male and female can often be too slight to be used as conclusive evidence, particularly where, as here, the bones are generally partly decayed. Where, therefore, a skeleton is provided with grave goods exclusively attributable to one sex, e.g. brooches and beads for a woman and a sword or spear for a man, it is regarded reasonable here to assume that the grave goods are a true indication of sex, and that the bone evidence may indicate an intermediate stage not sufficiently marked to manifest itself to any perceptible extent in the life of the individual.

Table XIX records in the first column the sex judged from the grave-goods, in the second column are the sex, age and other details given in the preliminary bone report. In the third column are the sex and age given in the final bone report, and discrepancies between any of the first three columns are marked by a cross in the last column.

TABLE XIX   SEX ACCORDING TO GRAVE FINDS AND BONE REPORTS

| Grave No. | Grave finds | Preliminary bone report | Final bone report and later information | Discrepancy |
|---|---|---|---|---|
| B | F | – | | |
| C | M | – | | |
| D | Ju | – | | |
| E | – | – | | |
| F | F | M? | | X |
| 1 | F | F ?over 45 | F over 45 | |
| 2 | Ju? | Ju | | |
| 3 | M? | M ?25–35 | F 30–45 | X |
| 4 | M | F? Old? | | X |
| 5 | M | M | | |
| 6 | F | F ?20–25 | F 20–30 | |
| 7 | – | – | | |
| 8 | M | M? | | |
| 9 | M | M 20–25 | M 20–30 | |
| 10 | M | ? | | |
| 11 | ? | F? | F | |
| 12 | F | F? | | |
| 13 | F | ?Old | | |
| 14 | F | F? 20–25 | M 20–30 | X |
| 15 | F | M? | M 30–45 | X |
| 16 | Ju | – | | |
| 17 | Ju | – | | |
| 18 | F | F | | |
| 19 | ? | ? | | |

| Grave No. | Grave finds | Preliminary bone report | Final bone report and later information | Discrepancy | Grave No. | Grave finds | Preliminary bone report | Final bone report and later information | Discrepancy |
|---|---|---|---|---|---|---|---|---|---|
| 20 | F | Ju c 4yrs | 0–6 | | 73 | – | M? | | |
| 21 | F | Ju 6–9 | 6–12 | | 74 | F? | Ju c 5 | 0–6 | |
| 22 | M | ? | | | 75 | F | M? | | X |
| 23 | F | ? | 20–30 | | 76 | F Ju | – | | |
| 24 | Ju | Ju? | | | 77 | ? | Adult or sub-adult | | |
| 25 | – | F 20–35 | F 20–30 | | 78 | Ju | Ju c 10½ | Ju 6–12 | |
| 26 | – | Adolescent or F | | | 79 | ? | Adult or sub-adult | | |
| 27 | M | M ?45–55 | M over 45 | | 80 | ? | M ?18–25 | | |
| 28 | F | F? 25–35 | F 20–30 | | 81 | F | F | | |
| 29 | F | F? young adult | F Unsexable 20–30 Table XLVIII | | 82 | F | F | | |
| | | | | | 83 | F | F | | |
| 30 | F | M 35–40 | M 30–45 | X | 84 | F? | F ?15–18 | F | |
| 31 | – | – | | | 85 | Ju | – | | |
| 32 | F | ?M | 30–45 | X | 86 | – | – | | |
| 33 | M | M middle age. Fracture of left tibia possible, healed | M F over 45 Table XLVIII M Table LII | X | 87 | M | F | F | X |
| | | | | | 88 | – | ? | | |
| | | | | | 89 | – | Ju 6–9 | 6–12 | |
| | | | | | 90 | M | M over 40 | M over 45 | |
| 34 | Ju | Ju c 5½ | 0–6 | | 91 | M | Adult | 20–30 | |
| 35 | F | c 15yrs. | 12–18 | | 92 | F | F young adult | F 20–30 | |
| 36 | ? | M old | M over 45 | | 93 | M | F? | F 30–45 Table XLVIII M Table LII | X |
| 37 | F | F? c 20 | F 20–30 | | | | | | |
| 38 | F | F adult or sub-adult | F 20–30 | | 94a | F | M old osteoarthritis | M | X |
| 39 | M | M? | | | 94b | M | adult | | |
| 40 | Ju? | Ju? | | | 95 | F | F | | |
| 41 | M | ?adult | | | 96a | M | M | M ?over 40 | |
| 42 | F | F old | F over 45 | | 96b | M | ? | F 20–30 Table XLVIII M Table LII | X |
| 43 | F | Ju c 10 | 6–12 | | | | | | |
| 44 | F | F middle-aged | F over 45 | | 97 | ? | – | | |
| 45 | – | – | | | 98 | M | Adult | ?M | |
| 46 | F | F young adult | F 20–30 | | 99 | – | F 40–45. A minor anomaly of the lowest lumbar vertebra | F | |
| 47 | – | – | | | | | | | |
| 48 | F | F c 18 | 12–18 | | | | | | |
| 49 | F | middle-aged or old | ? | | | | | | |
| 50 | M | F | | X | 100 | F? | F | F | |
| 51 | – | – | | | 101 | F? | F | | |
| 52 | ? | M old | M over 45 | | 102 | – | Adult | | |
| 53 | F | F young adult | F 20–30 | | 103 | ? | M? | M 30–45 | |
| 54 | F | M 30–40 | M 30–45 | X | 104 | ? | M | | |
| 55 | F | Ju c 5 | 0–6 | | 105 | ? | Ju 10 | 6–12 | |
| 56 | M | M 25–35 | M 30–45 | | 106 | ? | M | | |
| 57 | M | Adult or sub-adult | | | 107 | F | M? | | X |
| 58 | F | M young adult | M 20–30 | X | 108 | Ju | – | | |
| 59 | F | F young adult | F 20–30 | | 109 | ? | Adult or ju | | |
| 60 | F | F | | | 110 | F unborn child | +F young adult and new-born infant or full-term foetus | F 20–30 + ju 0–6 | |
| 61 | M | F old | F over 45 | X | | | | | |
| 62 | F | F middle-aged | F over 45 | | | | | | |
| 63 | M | M young adult | M 30–45 | | 111 | M | | | |
| 64 | M | ?middle-aged | | | 112 | – | F old | F 30–45 | |
| 65 | M | M ?over 40 | M over 45 | | 113 | F | Adult or sub-adult | | |
| 66 | F | F 30–40 | M 30–45 | X | 114 | M | M young adult | M 20–30 | |
| 67 | F | F young adult | F 20–30 | | 115 | ? | F adult or adolescent | | |
| 68 | – | F young adult | | | 116 | F? | F? | 30–45 | |
| 69 | – | M preservation cf communal burial | | | 117 | ? | Ju 8 | 6–12 | |
| 70 | – | ? | | | 118 | Ju | – | | |
| 71 | M | M young adult. Similar preservation to 69 | M 20–30 | | 119 | ? | Ju 3 | 0–6 | |
| | | | | | 120 | ? | M over 45 | M | |
| 72 | – | young adult or adolescent | | | 121 | F | Over 45 | Over 45 | |
| | | | | | 122 | F Ju | – | | |

# DISCUSSION

| Grave No. | Grave finds | Preliminary bone report | Final bone report and later information | Discrepancy |
|---|---|---|---|---|
| 123 | Ju | – | | |
| 124 | F | Young adult or adolescent | 20–30 | |
| 125 | ? | M? over 45 | M over 45 | |
| 126 | F | Adult | | |
| 127 | F | Adult or ju | | |
| 128 | M | Adult | | |
| 129 | F | Young adult or adolescent | | |
| 130 | ? | Young adult or adolescent | 20–30 | |
| 131 | M | Young adult | | |
| 132 | F | F young adult | | |
| 133 | F | F ?middle-aged | | |
| 134 | F | ? | | |
| 135 | M | M ?25–35 | M adult | |
| 136 | ? | M old | | |
| 137 | M Ju | – | | |
| 138 | F | Young adult | 30–45 | |
| 139 | M Ju | – | | |
| 140 | Ju | Ju | 9–12 | |
| 141 | F | M? young adult | | X |
| 142 | F | M? old | | X |
| 143 | Ju? | Ju c 8 | | |
| 144 | ? | M? | | |
| 145 | ? | M | | |
| 146 | ? | M ?young adult | M 20–30 | |
| 147 | F? | ? over 30 | 30–45 | |
| 148 | ? | M | M adult | |
| 149 | ? | M ?over 60 | | |
| 150 | ? | M | | |
| 151 | ? | Adult, sub-adult or older ju | | |
| 152 | – | M ?35–45 | | |
| 153 | Ju | * | 6 12 | |
| 154 | Ju | – | | |
| 155 | F | – | | |
| 156 | M | M ?old | | |
| 157 | F | F young adult | | |
| 158 | ? | M? | | |
| 159 | Ju | Ju | | |
| 160 | F | ? middle-aged | over 45 | |
| 161 | F | – | | |
| 162 | M Ju | – | | |
| 163 | Ju | – | | |
| 164 | F | Adult or sub-adult | | |
| 165 | – | M Healed fracture of right wrist. | | |

Seven discrepancies where bone determination of sex is 'probable'. F, 4, 32, 75, 107, 141, 142. Eleven discrepancies where bone determination is definite. 3, 14, 15, 30, 50, 54, 58, 61, 66, 87, 94a. Four discrepancies within final bone report. 29, 33, 93, 96b.

* This grave probably contained two juveniles aged about 9 and 5 respectively, but may possibly be a single individual with anomalous tooth eruption.

---

Graves designated as male by the grave-goods and definitely female by the bones:
*Grave 3.* The grave-goods are fragments only of a shield boss. The grave, however, is a disturbed one, and at the time of excavation it was thought that the bones of two people were represented.
*Grave 50.* The grave-goods consist of a spearhead, knife, long iron pin and bronze buckle with two shoe-shaped rivets. The body was lying full-length in the grave and measured 5ft. 9 in. from top of skull to heel.
*Grave 61* contained a spearhead, knife and iron buckle and the remains of the skeleton was limited to skull, and main arm and leg bones.
*Grave 87.* A spearhead and ferrule give a length of spear of 6ft. 8½in., and there was also a knife and a pot. The body was supine and the measurement from top of skull to heel was 5ft. 10in.

Graves designated as male by the grave-goods and possibly female by the bones:
*Grave 4.* There must have been some disturbance in this grave, although a spearhead, tooth and femur were found in situ. Bones in the fill may have come from another grave.
*Graves 33, 93 and 96b* all contain a sword, spear and other objects, but appear in the final bone report as male in one part and female in another.

Graves designated as female by the grave-goods and definitely male by the bones:
*Grave 14* contained a disc brooch and beads at the neck as well as strapends and other objects. The grave floor rose in a shallow step to form a kind of pillow under the head. The position of the skeleton in the grave gave an impression of deformity which may be an illusion, a thick skull, right shoulder higher than the left, curving spine, long femurs.
*Grave 15.* A bracelet on the right forearm, buckle and shoe-shaped rivets, knife, beads and other oddments probably in a bag. Length of skeleton 5ft. 4in.
*Grave 30.* Disc brooch, pin, beads, buckle, etc. Length of skeleton 5ft.
*Grave 54.* Knife and keys, length of skeleton 5ft. 7in.
*Grave 58.* Knife and keys. This grave was superimposed on grave 59, which is also female. Length of skeleton 5ft. 2in.
*Grave 66.* Beads, knife and key. Length 5ft. 6in.
*Grave 94a.* Annular brooch, buckle loop.

Graves designated as female by the grave goods and possibly male by the bones:
*Grave F*. Disc brooch, pin, beads etc. Length ?*c* 5ft.
*Grave 32*. Disc brooch, pin, beads etc. Length 5ft.
*Grave 75*. Beads, shears, weaving pick, ivory ring etc. Length *c* 5ft. 4in.
*Grave 107*. Beads, keys, tweezers, workbox. Length *c* 5ft.
*Grave 141*. Bracelet, knife, pin, beads. Length *c* 5ft. 6in.
*Grave 142*. Pin, key, knife. Length *c* 5ft. 6in.

Two of the discrepancies are explained by disturbance of the graves. It cannot be known whether the occupant of grave 3 was a male owning a shield of which loose fragments were found, or a female who may have been one of two people whose disturbed bones were re-interred in this grave. The occupant of Grave 4 must have been a male as a tooth, femur and spearhead were found undisturbed and the female bones in the fill were no doubt from another grave.

Disturbances, however, cannot account for any of the other discrepancies. The length of the skeleton in the grave from top of skull to heel is noted in all cases where the body is outstretched and well enough preserved, and although it is realised that there are many factors which render this useless as a scientific measurement, it must give a reasonable idea of the height of the individual. It may be useful, for instance, in regard to graves 50 and 87, where two bodies, each with a spear, considered to be female on the bone evidence, are 5ft. 9in. and 5ft. 10in. long respectively, for Anglo-Saxon males are more likely to have achieved this height. It is, hovever, interesting to note that these two graves are placed side by side, and it is possible that the feminine peculiarity here is a family trait.

Of graves 33, 93 and 96b, which are considered to be both male and female in different parts of the final report, the contents make it certain that they are all male.

Of the 13 graves female according to grave-goods and certainly or possibly male according to the bone evidence, the heights range from 5ft. to 5ft. 7in., a normal stature for Anglo-Saxon women. All have possessions which must ordinarily be regarded as feminine. Keys always seem to be worn by women, so that it is not likely that even a skeleton with a knife and keys only might have been male, eg. Graves 54, 58 and 142.

The examination of the bones has not provided any particular physical feature which may be regarded as a family trait. In some cases the sex as indicated by the grave-goods is not confirmed by the sex according to the bone report, where the verdict varies from decisive to indecisive. It may be considered whether the fact that the female bone structure was rather masculine and vice versa may have been a family trait, a point which is suggested by the clustering of such individuals in some groups. In plot A, for instance, this applies to 14, 15, 50 and 87. In plot B, with its row of rich women, it is perhaps not surprising to find that two of them, 30 and 32 have masculine traits, while two males in adjacent graves, 33 and 93, have bones that are confusable with females. The female in grave F of plot D, who was connected with the plot B women by the brooch she wore, is likewise confusable with a male. Four other such bodies occur in the middle of the cemetery, in plots F and H, 96b, 107, 141 and 142, and a few more on the barrow in plot E; 54, 58, 61 and 66. These bodies where the bones tell a different story from the grave-goods, or where the bone report is self-contradictory, are therefore confined to specific areas of the cemetery, plots A, B, E, F and H.

In the only double grave, 96, a man of 40 was buried with a person of 20–30, identified by the bones once as female and once as male. There is no doubt from their weapons that they were both warriors of noble rank, and one wonders if there is more reason than identical time of death for their unique association together in one grave and the fact that they are the only swordsmen not laid out straight (p 129). If any significance at all can be accorded to the evidence regarding male-female bone similarity it raises the possibility that homosexuality was sufficiently socially acceptable to the Anglo-Saxons to allow for the provision of a double burial.

A similar combination of male and female characteristics has been noted in the skeleton found in a rich female grave at Lyminge, Kent[1]. Regarding the skeleton in grave 44, Dr J Joseph reported:

'These skeletal remains show certain peculiarities. The limb bones are small and suggest a female, height 5ft. 1in. (from a femur and a tibia). The innominate bone is female, as is the sacroiliac articulation, but the sacrum has certain male measurements. The frontal bone of the skull suggests male and the mastoid processes of the temporal bone could be male or female. The atlas is definitely female (transverse diameter 76mm). With regard to the age, the lower jar of the alveolus during life, and the remaining teeth show varying wear, some very worn and some not (40–45). The skull shows suture lines, including the metopic suture, suggesting age about 30. The skull is thicker than usual (10mm).'

There is some difficulty is differentiating between children and adults of small stature if the bone report is not definite. Examination of the bones has resulted in the following being identified as children or juveniles: (p 123).

| Years *c* 0–6 | Years *c* 6–12 | Years *c* 12–18 | Uncertain | In preliminary report only |
|---|---|---|---|---|
| 20 34 | 21 43 | 35 48 | 24 40 | 2 84 140 |
| 55 74 | 78 89 | 84 | | 143 159 |
| 110 119 | 105 117 | | | |
| | 140 143 | | | |
| | 153 | | | |

1 Warhurst 1955, 28, note 1

## DISCUSSION

With regard to the graves in the last two columns, the evidence of written records and drawn plans and photographs confirm the following as children:

- 2 Grave 5ft.4in. × 2ft.3in. (1.63m × 0.69m), no finds, 1 bone fragment, 1 tooth.
- 24 child's skull fragments.
- 40 Grave 6ft.4in. × 2ft.3in. (1.93m × 0.69m), but bone remains in top half of grave only suggest body height 3ft.6in. (1.07m), knife only.
- 140 child's skeleton 4ft. (1.22m) tall.
- 143 bone fragments and teeth, 3ft. (0.91m) tall
- 159 bone fragments – under 4ft. (1.22m) tall

The following graves are assumed to have belonged to children on the following evidence: (a) size of grave about 5ft. (1.52m) long or less, (b) no remains of bones (c) poor finds or none at all.

| Grave No. | Dimensions | Finds |
|---|---|---|
| D | Length 4ft.3in. (1.29m) | |
| 16 | 5ft.6in. × 1ft.9in. (1.68m × 0.53m) | knife |
| 17 | 4ft. × 2ft. (1.22m × 0.61m) | knife |
| 76 | 4ft. × 1ft.8in. (1.22m × 0.51m) | 2 beads |
| 85 | 5ft.× 2ft. (1.52m × 0.61m) | knife, buckle |
| 108 | 4ft.6in × 2ft. (1.37m × 0.61m) | knife, iron fragment |
| 118 | 3ft.4in. × 1ft.8in (1.02m × 0.51m) | no finds |
| 122 | 4ft.6in. × 2ft.3in. (1.37m × 0.69m) | keys, buckle |
| 123 | 3ft.10in. × 2ft.4in. (1.17m × 0.71m) | knife |
| 154 | 4ft.1in. × 1ft.11in. (1.24m × 0.58m) | no finds |
| 162 | 5ft.4in.× 2ft.4in. (1.63m × 0.71m) | 2 knives, whetstones and iron |
| 163 | 5ft.6in. × 2ft. 6in. shelving (1.68m × 0.76m) with middle pit 4ft.9in. × 1ft.6in. (1.47m × 0.46m) | knife, buckle |

The following graves are larger, but a child is indicated by the size and position, or complete absence of bones, and the positions and types of objects:

137 This grave is 7ft.10in. × 3ft.3in. (2.39m × 0.99m).
There are no bones, but a bronze bowl at the head and pottery bottle at the foot. Two knives and a buckle are near together at presumed waist position, and a small spearhead presumably at the right shoulder. A spear ferrule near the pot gives a length to the spear of only about 4ft. (1.22m), far too short for a man.

139 This grave is 6ft.3in. × 2ft.9in. (1.91m × 0.84m), and similar to 137. There are no bones, and a knife and pursemount presumably at the waist. A spearhead and pot were apparently beside the head, and animal bones towards the foot of the grave. Between there is a space for a body of less than 3ft. (0.92m). As in 137, something to drink was placed at the head of the grave, and something to eat at the foot.

Grave plans which show the size and position of bone fragments suggest that the following were under 5ft. (1.52m) tall. The preliminary bone report reads 'F young adult' for 132, but 147 is aged 30–45, and none of the bones in the other graves are judged to be juvenile, so that these must be adults of very small stature.

- 95 partly destroyed grave 1ft.9in. (0.53m) wide; knife and keys.
- 101 7ft.10in. × 2ft.9in. (2.39m × 0.84m); skull and femur fragments, pin at head.
- 130 edges of grave uncertain – bones indicate height of 4ft.6in. (1.37m); knife.
- 132 7ft. × 2ft.1in. (2.13m × 0.64m), bones indicate height of 4ft.6in. (1.37m); beads, pin, knife, keys.
- 147 8ft.9in. × 3ft.1in. (2.67m × 0.94m), bones indicate height of 4ft.9in. (1.45m); pin, knife and fragments.

The bone report gives little information regarding the state of health of the community except to confirm that these people must have experienced rheumatic pains like most of their Anglo-Saxon contemporaries for a number of skeletons exhibit bone deformity resulting from arthritis. Gross arthritic changes in cervical and lumbar vertebrae, and also of the sacrum and glenoid cavity are noted in grave 44. The awkward position of the skeleton, both legs slightly bent to the left, and a distinctly curving spine, possibly reflect a misshapen state of the woman's body at the time of her death at the age of over 45.

The woman between 20 and 30 who was buried ?alive in grave 67 seems to have had some illnesses in her young life. There was a small cavity in the left navicular, probably due to infection or arthritis, and the top sacral segment was unfixed in the mid line leaving a V-shaped cleft in the sacrum. Mr Brothwell informs me that the effect of the second anomaly on the individual is unknown. She may have been aware of having a 'weak back' with a tendency to ache, or she may have been lucky and had no symptoms.

In the interim report on the bones the preservation of the bones in graves 69 and 71 were said to be similar to those in the 'communal' burial. As the bones in grave 69 and the 'communal' burial had been disturbed and reburied probably in the medieval period, a similarity in the state of preservation between them, and a certain amount of difference from that of the undisturbed skeletons is understandable. Grave 71, however, was undisturbed, and there seems to be no reason for the similarity here.

### Age at Death

The categories of age allocated to the Dover skeletons have, of necessity, been varied in the range of precision, and the total results of all sexed adults and all juveniles are shown on Tables XX, XXI and XXII. Of the total of 54 males, the age can be assessed of only 31. Of these the age at death seems to be fairly well spread, for 16–17 died between the ages of 18 and 45, and 14–15 after the age of 45. This is a large proportion of survival after middle age. The women, however provide a definite contrast. Eighteen of a total of 66 are of unknown age. Of the remaining 48 it is probable that eleven of these died by the age of 18. Sixteen died in their twenties, and ten in their thirties. Only eleven seem to have been over 45. The early child-bearing period therefore took a considerable toll of the women, and survival to old age is less frequent than among the men. The total of juvenile deaths amounts to 35, only 17 of which can be aged at all, and fifteen died before the age of 12. The sex of only seven of these children is recognisable, and these are all female. Two more were female teenagers, and of the eighteen designated as juvenile without precision as to age, two were female, and three male. Out of a total of 161 persons who can be identified as adults or children, 35 died before the age of 18, i.e. about 22% or a proportion of 1:4.5. If the number of children is compared with the full total of graves, 172, the proportion is nearer 1:5. This compares closely with the proportion of children found at Polhill[2] where there were 30 children in a total of 125 (9 being indeterminate), i.e. c 1:4, and there, too, infant graves were absent. As there are no infant burials present, however, this cannot be regarded as the full tally of juvenile deaths which took place in that community.

With a cemetery of incomplete data such as at Dover, where a number of graves were destroyed, and where a definite age is assessable for only a proportion of the skeletons, no meaningful life expectancy figure can be produced. However, on the basis of the available figures, although infant deaths are unrecorded, about a fifth of the surviving juvenile population did not reach adulthood. Half of the males with assessable age managed to live to over 45, but only a quarter of the females. On the figures available, it is not possible to make any meaningful comparison with the figures for Saxon survival over the age of 50 given by Brothwell[3], 23 out of a total of 289, ie 7.9%. The total of females is slightly above the total of males (66:54), which does not accord with the normal slight predominance of male numbers noted by Brothwell[4] in Saxon and other early communities.

The women who were over 45 at death were evenly spaced over the time scale at one or two in each phase, while most of the men who died at this advanced age were buried in phases 3, 4 and 5 (Table XXIII). Juvenile deaths were pretty constant to begin with but increased considerably in the last two phases, these higher numbers being at least partially influenced by the increase in population. The highest numbers of male deaths under 45 occurred in phases 3, 4 and 7. The female deaths under 45 were lowest in phases 1, 4 and 7.

TABLE XX DOVER: AGE AT DEATH – MALE

| Age at Death | Grave No. |
| --- | --- |
| Adult or adolescent | 57 |
| 18–25 | 80 |
| young adult | 131 |
| 20–30 | 9, 71, 91, 96b*, 114, 146 |
| 25–45 | 3*, 56, 63, 93, 103, 135, 152 |
| over 40 | 96a |
| over 45 | 27, 33*, 36, 52, 61*, 65, 90, 120, 125 |
| middle-aged | 64 |
| over 60 | 149 |
| old | 4, 136, 156, |
| adult or ?adult age unknown | C, 5, 8?, 10, 22, 39, 41?, 50*, 69, 73, 87, 94b?, 98, 104?, 106, 111?, 128?, 144, 145, 148, 150, 158?, 165 |

TABLE XXI DOVER: AGE AT DEATH – FEMALE

| Age at Death | Grave No. |
| --- | --- |
| adult or juvenile | 127 |
| adult or adolescent | 26, 113, 115, 129, 164 |
| young adult | 68, 132, 141*, 157 |
| 15–18 | 84 |
| 20–30 | 6, 14*, 23, 25, 28, 29*, 37, 38, 46, 53, 58*, 59, 67, 92, 110, 124 |
| 30–45 | 15*, 30*, 32*, 54*, 66*, 99, 112, 116, 138, 147 |
| over 45 | 1, 42, 44, 62, 121, 160 |
| middle-aged | 133 |
| middle-aged or old | 49 |
| old | 13, 94a*, 142* |
| adult age unknown | B, F, 11, 12, 18, 60, 75*, 81, 82, 83, 95, 100, 101, 107*, 126, 134, 155, 161 |

*Sex given according to grave goods. Differs from bone report.

TABLE XXII DOVER: AGE AT DEATH – JUVENILE

| Age at Death | Grave No. |
| --- | --- |
| 0–6 years | 20 F, 34, 55 F, 74 F?, 110, 119 |
| 6–12 years | 21 F, 43 F, 78, 89, 105, 117, 140, 143 153 |
| 12–18 years | 35 F, 48 F, |
| juvenile | D, 2, 16, 17, 24, 40, 76 F, 85, 108, 118, 122 F, 123, 137 M, 139 M, 154, 159, 162 M, 163, |

2 Philp 1973a, 168–9
3 Brothwell 1972–3, table 26, 84

4 Ibid, table 24, 84–5

TABLE XXIII  NUMBER OF DEATHS UNDER AND OVER 45 IN THE SEVEN PHASES

|  | Male | Female | Juvenile |  |
|---|---|---|---|---|
| Under 45 |  |  |  |  |
| Phase |  |  |  |  |
| 1 | 0 | 1 | 3 | + 3 in |
| 2 | 0 | 5 | 0 | phase 1 or 2 |
| 3 | 6 | 8 | 5 |  |
| 4 | 4 | 4 | 3 |  |
| 5 | 1 | 7 | 3 |  |
| 6 | 2 | 8 | 11 |  |
| 7 | 3 | 4 | 7 |  |
| Totals | 16 | 37 | 35 |  |
| Over 45 |  |  |  |  |
| 1 | 0 | 1 |  |  |
| 2 | 0 | 1 |  |  |
| 3 | 3 | 2 |  |  |
| 4 | 5 | 3 |  |  |
| 5 | 3 | 1 |  |  |
| 6 | 2 | 3 |  |  |
| 7 | 1 | 0 |  |  |
| Totals | 14 | 11 |  |  |

Grave 96a, a man over 40, is included in the 'over 45' section, phase 4.

**Skeleton positions**

The approximate or precise positions of the limbs were recordable in 117 graves, (Tables XXIV, XXV). Of these the majority, i.e. 92, were laid on the back, with legs straight and feet together. A number (61) were sufficiently well preserved for the positions of the arms and hands to be certain. Other skeletons were defective (56), but there was sufficient evidence to show whether the legs were straight or bent, and sometimes the position of one of the arms. In thirty-one graves there was too little bone for the position of the skeleton to be discerned, four skeletons were disturbed, and in eighteen others there was either no bone at all or the grave was destroyed.

In the Tables XXIV, XXV skeletons are listed as complete if the bones are sufficiently well preserved for the positions of the legs and arms to be recognised, even if the skull might be fragmentary or missing. In a few graves the body was placed slightly on one side, and as an inevitable result one or both of the legs were slightly bent.

The most common position was supine, with the hands on the top of the femurs or in the pelvis (39 plus 14 defective skeletons)[5]. Five had one arm straight and the right arm only bent inwards[6], five had the left arm only bent inwards[7]. Skeletons supine with the arms straight down beside the body were more rare (6 plus 2 defective skeletons)[8] and of these six skulls were turned right, and two were facing upwards. Variant arm positions are: grave 12, right arm across body and left hand on left shoulder; 46, 102 and 115 left hand in pelvis and right arm across waist; 21, right arm straight, away from body. Five skeletons were placed with the knees bent to left or right[9], and five had one knee slightly bent[10].

The various positions do not seem to have specific reference to sex. The skull is turned to the right more often than to the left in the case of men, women and children: there are 22 male skulls turned right, 20 female and 4 juvenile, while 5 male skulls are turned left, 8 female and one juvenile. Variations from the normal position (arms and legs straight) occur fairly widespread throughout the cemetery, but there are not many variations in plots F, G and I. It may be noted that the four isolated graves 145, 146, 68 and 151 are variants (Figure 100). Of the complete skeletons, 42 have legs and arms straight, and 19 in other positions. Of the incomplete skeletons 44 had legs straight, 8 had both knees bent, 1 had 1 knee bent, five had one arm across the body and two were laid on the side.

Table XXVI lists the 23 male graves with 'complete' skeletons in the supine position, (legs straight and hands by the side, in the pelvis or on top of the femurs), the plot in which the grave is situated, and the main weapon deposited. Five of these are sword graves. Of the other sword graves which were undisturbed, the skeletons were slightly defective, but 22, 94, 93, 41 and 131 were lying with legs straight and the missing arms might also have been in normal positions. Only the double grave 96 deviated, with 96a inclined to the right with one knee and arm bent, and 96b with feet crossed. The straight supine position also continued into the later plots and weaponless graves, 36, 80, 103, 106, 120, 149, 150.

---

5  6, 9, 14, 15, 30, 33, 35, 36, 39, 42, 46, 49, 50, 54, 56, 58, 62, 63, 66, 71, 81, 82, 84, 87, 90, 91, 98, 102, 106, 110, 114, 115, 116, 120, 130, 135, 140, 150, 156 plus defective skeletons 18, 22, 29, 64, 73, 75, 92, 93, 95, 125, 128, 131, 133, 147.
6  6, 49, 98, 135, 140 plus defective skeletons 29, 75, 93, 95, 125, 133, 147.
7  9, 36, 56, 62, 71 plus defective skeletons 18, 22, 64, 73, 92, 128, 131.
8  27, 80, 99, 103, 138, 149 plus defective skeletons 38, 61.
9  25, 44, 129, 142, 148 plus defective skeletons 1, 48, 52, 68, 89, 101, 151, 160.
10  32, 65, 96a, 100, 145 plus defective skeleton 23.

TABLE XXIV  SKELETON POSITIONS, COMPLETE

**MALE**

| Grave No. | Legs straight | Knees bent | One knee bent | Feet crossed | Hands in pelvis | L. hand in pelvis | R. hand in pelvis | Arms straight | Arms across | L. arm across | R. arm across | L. arm on L. shoulder | R. arm outstretched | Prone | Body on L. side | Body on R. side | Skull to L. | Skull to R. |
|---|---|---|---|---|---|---|---|---|---|---|---|---|---|---|---|---|---|---|
| 9 | X | | | | | X | | X | | | | | | | | | X | X |
| 27 | X | | | | | | | X | | | | | | | | | | X |
| 33 | X | | | | X | | | | | | | | | | | | | X |
| 36 | X | | | | | X | | | | | | | | | | | X | X |
| 39 | X | | | | X | | | | | | | | | | | | | X |
| 50 | X | | | | X | | | | | | | | | | | | X | |
| 56 | X | | | | X | | | | | | | | | | | | X | |
| 57 | | | | | | | | | | | | | | X | | | | |
| 63 | X | | | | X | | | | | | | | | | | | | |
| 65 | | | X | | X | | | | | | | | | | | | | X |
| 71 | X | | | | | X | | | | | | | | | | | | X |
| 80 | X | | | | | | | X | | | | | | | | | | X |
| 87 | X | | | | | X | | | | | | | | | | | | |
| 90 | X | | | | X | | | | | | | | | | | | | |
| 91 | X | | | | X | | | | | | | | | | | | | |
| 96a | | | X | | | X | | | | | | | | | | | | X |
| 96b | | | | X | X | | | | | | | | | | | | | X |
| 98 | X | | | | | | X | | | | | | | | | | | |
| 103 | X | | | | | | | | X | | | | | | | | | X |
| 106 | X | | | | X | | | | | | | | | | | | | X |
| 114 | X | | | | X | | | | | | | | | | | | | X |
| 120 | X | | | | X | | | | | | | | | | | | | X |
| 135 | X | | | | | | | X | | | | | | | | | | |
| 145 | | | X | | X | | | | | | | | | | | | | X |
| 148 | | X | | | | | | | | | | X | | | | | X | |
| 149 | X | | | | | | | | X | | | | | | | | | X |
| 150 | X | | | | X | | | | | | | | | | | | | |
| 156 | X | | | | X | | | | | | | | | | | | | |

**FEMALE**

| Grave No. | Legs straight | Knees bent | One knee bent | Feet crossed | Hands in pelvis | L. hand in pelvis | R. hand in pelvis | Arms straight | Arms across | L. arm across | R. arm across | L. arm on L. shoulder | R. arm outstretched | Prone | Body on L. side | Body on R. side | Skull to L. | Skull to R. |
|---|---|---|---|---|---|---|---|---|---|---|---|---|---|---|---|---|---|---|
| 6 | X | | | | | | | X | | | | | | | | | | |
| 12 | X | | | | | | | | | X | X | | | | | | | X |
| 14 | X | | | | X | | | | | | | | | | | | X | X |
| 15 | X | | | | X | | | | | | | | | | | | | X |
| 25 | | X | | | | | | | X | | | | | | | | | |
| 30 | X | | | | X | | | | | | | | | | | | X | |
| 32 | | | X | | X | | | | | | | | | | | | | X |
| 42 | X | | | | X | | | | | | | | | | | | | X |
| 44 | | X | | | | X | | | | | | | | | | | X | |
| 46 | X | | | | | X | | | | | | X | | | | | | X |
| 49 | X | | | | | | X | | | | | | | | | | | |
| 54 | X | | | | X | | | | | | | | | | | | | X |
| 58 | X | | | | X | | | | | | | | | | | | | |
| 60 | | | | X | X | | | | | | | | | | | | | |
| 62 | X | | | | | X | | | | | | | | | | | | X |
| 66 | X | | | | X | | | | | | | | | | | | X | |
| 67 | | | | | | | | | | | | | | X | | | | |
| 81 | X | | | | X | | | | | | | | | | | | | X |
| 82 | X | | | | X | | | | | | | | | | | | X | |
| 84 | X | | | | X | | | | | | | | | | | | | X |
| 99 | X | | | | | | | X | | | | | | | | | | |

## TABLE XXIV CONTD.

### FEMALE

| Grave No. | Legs straight | Knees bent | One knee bent | Feet crossed | Hands in pelvis | L. hand in pelvis | R. hand in pelvis | Arms straight | Arms across | L. arm across | R. arm across | L. arm on L. shoulder | R. arm outstretched | Prone | Body on L. side | Body on R. side | Skull to L. | Skull to R. |
|---|---|---|---|---|---|---|---|---|---|---|---|---|---|---|---|---|---|---|
| 100 | | X | | | | | | X | | | | | | | | | | X |
| 110 | X | | | | X | | | | | | | | | | | | X | |
| 115 | X | | | | | X | | | | X | | | | | | | | |
| 116 | X | | | | X | | | | | | | | | | | | | |
| 129 | | X | | | | X | | | | X | | | | | | | | |
| 138 | X | | | | | | X | | | | | | | | | | | |
| 142 | | X | | | X | | | | | | | | | | | X | | |

### JUVENILE

| Grave No. | Legs straight | Knees bent | One knee bent | Feet crossed | Hands in pelvis | L. hand in pelvis | R. hand in pelvis | Arms straight | Arms across | L. arm across | R. arm across | L. arm on L. shoulder | R. arm outstretched | Prone | Body on L. side | Body on R. side | Skull to L. | Skull to R. |
|---|---|---|---|---|---|---|---|---|---|---|---|---|---|---|---|---|---|---|
| 21 | X | | | | | | | | | | | X | | | | | | |
| 35 | X | | | X | | | | | | | | | | | | | | X |
| 140 | X | | | | | X | | | | | | | | | | | | X |

### UNSEXED

| Grave No. | Legs straight | Knees bent | One knee bent | Feet crossed | Hands in pelvis | L. hand in pelvis | R. hand in pelvis | Arms straight | Arms across | L. arm across | R. arm across | L. arm on L. shoulder | R. arm outstretched | Prone | Body on L. side | Body on R. side | Skull to L. | Skull to R. |
|---|---|---|---|---|---|---|---|---|---|---|---|---|---|---|---|---|---|---|
| 102 | X | | | | | X | | | | X | | | | | | | | |
| 130 | X | | X | | | | | | | | | | | | | | | |

## TABLE XXV  SKELETON POSITIONS, DEFECTIVE

### MALE

| Grave No. | Legs straight | Knees bent | One knee bent | Feet crossed | Hands in pelvis | L. hand in pelvis | R. hand in pelvis | Arms straight | Arms across | L. arm across | R. arm across | L. arm on L. shoulder | R. arm outstretched | Prone | Body on L. side | Body on R. side | Skull to L. | Skull to R. |
|---|---|---|---|---|---|---|---|---|---|---|---|---|---|---|---|---|---|---|
| 8 | X | | | | | | | | | | | | | | | | | |
| 10 | X | | | | | | | | | | | | | | | | | |
| 22 | X | | | | | X | | | | | | | | | | | | |
| 41 | X | | | | | | | | | | | | | | | | | |
| 52 | | X | | | | | | | | | | | | | | | | X |
| 61 | X | | | | | | | | | | | | | | | | | X |
| 64 | X | | | | | X | | | | | | | | | | | | |
| 73 | X | | | | | X | | | | | | | | | | | | |
| 93 | X | | | | | | X | | | | | | | | | | | X |
| 94b | X | | | | | | | | | | | | | | | | | |
| 104 | X | | | | | | | | | | | | | | | | | |
| 111 | X | | | | | | | | | X | | | | | | | X | |
| 125 | X | | | | | X | | | | | | | | | | | | X |
| 128 | X | | | | X | | | | | | | | | | | | | |

## TABLE XXV CONTD.

### MALE

| Grave No. | Legs straight | Knees bent | One knee bent | Feet crossed | Hands in pelvis | L. hand in pelvis | R. hand in pelvis | Arms straight | Arms across | L. arm across | R. arm across | L. arm on L. shoulder | R. arm outstretched | Prone | Body on L. side | Body on R. side | Skull to L. | Skull to R. |
|---|---|---|---|---|---|---|---|---|---|---|---|---|---|---|---|---|---|---|
| 131 | X |   |   |   |   | X |   |   |   |   |   |   |   |   |   |   |   | X |
| 136 | X |   |   |   |   |   |   |   |   |   |   |   |   |   |   |   |   | X |
| 144 | X |   |   |   |   |   |   |   |   |   |   |   |   |   |   |   |   |   |
| 146 |   |   |   | X |   | X |   |   |   |   |   |   |   |   |   | X |   | X |
| 158 | X |   |   |   |   |   |   |   |   |   |   |   |   |   |   |   |   |   |
| 165 | X |   |   |   |   |   |   |   |   |   |   |   |   |   |   |   |   | X |

### FEMALE

| Grave No. | Legs straight | Knees bent | One knee bent | Feet crossed | Hands in pelvis | L. hand in pelvis | R. hand in pelvis | Arms straight | Arms across | L. arm across | R. arm across | L. arm on L. shoulder | R. arm outstretched | Prone | Body on L. side | Body on R. side | Skull to L. | Skull to R. |
|---|---|---|---|---|---|---|---|---|---|---|---|---|---|---|---|---|---|---|
| 1 |   | X |   |   |   |   |   |   | X |   |   |   |   |   |   |   |   | X |
| 11 | X |   |   |   |   |   |   |   |   |   |   |   |   |   |   |   |   |   |
| 13 |   |   |   |   |   |   |   |   |   |   |   |   |   |   |   |   |   | X |
| 18 | X |   |   |   |   | X |   |   |   |   |   |   |   |   |   |   |   |   |
| 23 |   |   | X |   |   |   |   |   |   |   |   |   |   |   |   |   |   |   |
| 28 | X |   |   |   |   |   |   |   |   |   |   |   |   |   |   |   |   |   |
| 29 | X |   |   |   |   |   | X |   |   |   |   |   |   |   |   |   |   | X |
| 37 | X |   |   |   |   |   |   |   |   |   |   |   |   |   |   |   |   |   |
| 38 | X |   |   |   |   |   |   |   |   |   |   |   |   |   |   |   |   | X |
| 53 | X |   |   |   |   |   |   |   |   |   |   |   |   |   |   |   |   | X |
| 59 |   |   |   |   |   |   |   |   |   |   |   |   |   |   |   |   |   | X |
| 68 |   | X |   |   |   |   |   |   |   |   |   |   |   |   |   |   |   | X |
| 75 | X |   |   |   |   |   | X |   |   |   |   |   |   |   |   |   |   |   |
| 83 | X |   |   |   |   |   |   |   |   |   |   |   |   |   |   |   |   |   |
| 92 | X |   |   |   |   | X |   |   |   |   |   |   |   |   |   |   |   |   |
| 94a | X |   |   |   |   |   |   |   |   |   |   |   |   |   |   |   |   |   |
| 95 |   |   |   |   |   |   | X |   |   | X |   |   |   |   |   |   |   |   |
| 101 |   | X |   |   |   |   |   |   |   |   |   |   |   |   |   |   |   | X |
| 107 | X |   |   |   |   |   |   |   |   |   |   |   |   |   |   |   |   |   |
| 112 |   |   |   |   |   |   |   |   |   |   |   |   |   |   | X | X |   |   |
| 127 | X |   |   |   |   |   |   |   |   | X |   |   |   |   |   |   |   |   |
| 133 | X |   |   |   |   |   | X |   |   |   |   |   |   |   |   |   | X |   |
| 141 | X |   |   |   |   |   |   |   |   |   |   | X |   |   |   |   |   | X |
| 147 | X |   |   |   |   |   | X |   |   |   |   |   |   |   |   |   |   |   |
| 157 | X |   |   |   |   |   |   |   |   |   |   |   |   |   |   |   |   |   |
| 160 |   | X |   |   |   |   |   |   |   |   |   |   |   |   |   |   |   |   |
| 164 | X |   |   |   |   |   |   |   |   |   |   |   |   |   |   |   |   |   |

### JUVENILE

| Grave No. | Legs straight | Knees bent | One knee bent | Feet crossed | Hands in pelvis | L. hand in pelvis | R. hand in pelvis | Arms straight | Arms across | L. arm across | R. arm across | L. arm on L. shoulder | R. arm outstretched | Prone | Body on L. side | Body on R. side | Skull to L. | Skull to R. |
|---|---|---|---|---|---|---|---|---|---|---|---|---|---|---|---|---|---|---|
| 34 | X |   |   |   |   |   |   |   |   |   |   |   |   |   |   |   |   |   |
| 43 | X |   |   |   |   |   |   |   |   |   |   |   |   |   |   |   |   |   |
| 48 |   | X |   |   |   |   |   |   |   |   |   |   |   |   |   |   |   | X |
| 78 | X |   |   |   |   |   |   |   |   |   |   |   |   |   |   |   | X |   |
| 89 |   | X |   |   |   |   |   |   |   |   |   |   |   |   |   |   |   |   |
| 117 | X |   |   |   |   |   |   |   |   |   |   |   |   |   |   |   |   | X |
| 159 | X |   |   |   |   |   |   |   |   |   |   |   |   |   |   |   |   |   |

### UNSEXED

| Grave No. | Legs straight | Knees bent | One knee bent | Feet crossed | Hands in pelvis | L. hand in pelvis | R. hand in pelvis | Arms straight | Arms across | L. arm across | R. arm across | L. arm on L. shoulder | R. arm outstretched | Prone | Body on L. side | Body on R. side | Skull to L. | Skull to R. |
|---|---|---|---|---|---|---|---|---|---|---|---|---|---|---|---|---|---|---|
| 19 | X |   |   |   |   |   |   |   |   |   |   |   |   |   |   |   |   |   |
| 77 | X |   |   |   |   |   |   |   |   |   |   |   |   |   |   |   |   |   |
| 79 | X |   |   |   |   |   |   |   |   |   |   |   |   |   |   |   |   |   |
| 151 |   |   | X |   |   |   |   |   |   |   |   |   |   |   |   |   |   |   |

TABLE XXVI MALE SKELETONS (complete enough to show positions of arms and legs) with legs straight and hands by the side, in the pelvis or on top of the femurs.

| Grave No. | Plot | Main weapon |
| --- | --- | --- |
| 9 | C | spear |
| 27 | B | sword |
| 33 | B | sword |
| 36 | J | weaponless |
| 39 | F | spear |
| 50 | A | spear |
| 56 | K | sword |
| 57 | K | spear |
| 63 | E | spear |
| 71 | F | sword |
| 80 | I | weaponless |
| 87 | A | spear |
| 90 | A | spear |
| 91 | B | spear |
| 98 | D | sword |
| 103 | I | weaponless |
| 106 | H | weaponless |
| 114 | H | spear |
| 120 | I | weaponless |
| 135 | F | spear |
| 149 | H | weaponless |
| 150 | H | weaponless |
| 156 | G | spear |

TABLE XXVII FEMALE SKELETONS (complete enough to show positions of arms and legs) with legs straight and hands by the side, in the pelvis or on top of the femurs.

| Grave No. | Plot | Class of grave goods |
| --- | --- | --- |
| 6 | C | Rich without brooch |
| 14 | A | Rich with brooch |
| 15 | A | Medium rich |
| 30 | B | Rich with brooch |
| 42 | B | Medium rich |
| 49 | A | ? Finds disturbed |
| 54 | E | Poor |
| 58 | E | Poor |
| 62 | E | Medium rich |
| 66 | E | Medium rich |
| 81 | I | Poor |
| 82 | I | Poor |
| 84 | I | Poor |
| 99 | I | Findless |
| 110 | H | Rich without brooch |
| 116 | D | Poor |
| 138 | H | Medium rich |
| *Juvenile* | | |
| 35 | B | Rich with brooch |

The 'complete' female skeletons in this straight position, including one juvenile, amount to 18 (Table XXVII), ranging from the richest graves to a findless one, and they are in both the earlier and later parts of the cemetery.

It therefore seems that often care was taken to lay out the body on the back with arms and legs straight, particularly in male sword graves. The variations from this position throughout the cemetery are mostly very slight, as there are no real crouched burials, and only one prone burial. Some of the bodies must have been displayed in the grave to onlookers, e.g. in 96 and 60 where the legs were crossed at the ankle in order to provide room for an object. It is not known whether all the bodies were viewed in the grave, however, and, where the body was lowered into the grave in a coffin or a shroud, it is possible that one or more limbs might have become slightly displaced during this operation. The isolated situations of the four graves 68, 145, 146 and 151, and the fact that they are all in variant bone positions suggests that there is some religious background governing these four burials which does not apply to other surrounding graves, except for four on the barrow. The other skeletons in variant positions are mainly confined to two plots, in plot A and scattered in plot H.

The range of positions of the bodies compare with the normal positions in Kentish cemeteries. At Lyminge[11] also most skeletons were supine, nineteen with arms straight, sixteen with arms across the pelvis, and three with crossed legs. Two children and one woman were on their sides with legs contracted.

Other examples of pregnant burials, as in grave 110, have been recorded, e.g. at Abingdon[12], grave 93, a girl of fifteen or sixteen years. Even a possible post-mortem birth has been discovered at Kingsworthy, Hampshire[13].

Prone burials, as in grave 67, are not common. A number of females have been noted in this position, at Standlake, Oxfordshire[14], and at Kingsworthy, Hampshire[15]. At Abingdon there were no less than three prone burials, in grave 51 a female child 12–13, in grave 1 a young adult female, and in 29 an adult female[16]. In grave 1 the arms were crossed, possibly bound. In both 29 and 51 the right hand was under the shoulder; in 29 the left hand was under the forehead, in 51 it was at the back of the neck and the excavators suggested the arm may have been dislocated before burial. In the last two burials the position of the right hand suggests that the girl was trying to raise herself up. In grave 7 at Droxford, Hampshire, a young woman was lying prone in an unfurnished grave[17].

It has been suggested that as only females are found prone, their positions often indicating maltreatment, this may be evidence of a means of

---

11  Warhurst 1955
12  Leeds and Harden 1936, 48–9
13  Hawkes and Wells 1975a
14  Dickinson 1973

15  Hawkes and Wells 1975b
16  Leeds and Harden 1936, 40–1, 31, 36
17  Aldsworth 1978, 114, figs. 13 and 15c

punishing sexual offenders. The young woman in grave 67 at Dover, and a young woman at Sewerby, Yorkshire[18] over another but normal female burial, were both thrust, living, into the grave, and so support this contention to a certain extent. However, another recent publication illustrates a prone male burial, where the arms were folded under the chest and the shield placed over the head[19]. According to the bone report this was an extremely powerful man, 5ft.11½in. tall. The fact that his hands were together under his chest may mean that they were tied together, but there is no evidence of struggle or movement after burial. Although the grave contained a shield, there was no offensive weapon. He was lying in the unusual orientation of E-W. The position is obviously meant to be ignominious, and must have been considered suitable as a punishment for some act of which the Anglo-Saxons disapproved, such as cowardice or treachery.

## Grouping according to grave finds

The plots A-N consist of groups of graves which have some elements in common, such as position, size, layout and orientation (see p 19–20, 174), and they provide a convenient division into integrated sections for systematic investigation. Other characteristics of the groups can be distinguished, mostly based on the grave goods, and comparisons will be made here to establish the dates of some of the graves and the general chronological relationship of one plot to another.

The plots will be considered in turn. Plot A is very distinctive, consisting mainly of women and children, the only exceptions being two spear graves, 50 and 87, one spear grave with a shield, 90, and two sword graves, 22 and 94b. Both of these two sword graves are superimposed by a female burial, 18 and 94a respectively. Affluence is suggested by the sword graves, of which 22 was provided with a glass vessel, and the sword with gold-topped rivets in the damaged grave 94b must have had a splendid pommel, possibly in gold. Both men were also armed with a spear ornamented with inlaid metal bands on the socket and tipped with a ferrule. Inlay is also traceable on the spearhead in graves 50 and 87, the latter also including a ferrule. There are no shields. The inlaid spears may be of Frankish origin, like the glass in 22 and the buckle in 50, but the handmade pot in 87 is of Anglian type and the disc-headed pin 50/3 and the mounts of the sword 94b/1 are Kentish.

Most of the graves of women or girls in plot A were richly furnished. Varieties of brooches present are: grave 13, two square-headed, one small-long, one annular; grave 20, two square-headed, one Frankish garnet disc; grave 48, one button, one saucer; grave 92, one Frankish garnet disc and one Kentish garnet disc; grave 23, one Frankish garnet disc; grave 14, one Kentish garnet disc.

These show Frankish, Saxon and Jutish or Danish connections. Others were less rich: ie 18, 15, 12, 21 and 46, although 46 as well as 20 possessed a weaving sword. 95 contained only a knife and large keys. Iron diamond plaques occurred in 12, 14, 20, 28 and 48. Most had beads of amber, and also glass, some of which were polychrome.

Plot B has well-defined differences. There are as many as four sword graves, three of which also possessed shield bosses, 27, 91 and 93. The warrior in 93 was especially distinguished by his shield ornamented with silvered appliqués, a seax, sword bead and spearhead inlaid with ring and swastika. Frankish connections are evident in the shield-on-tongue buckle 91/6, seax 93/7 and inlaid spearhead 93/3. Two shield bosses have disc-headed rivets, and two have knob-headed rivets.

The graves of the women and girls are more distinctive. The girls in 34 and 43, as well as the woman in 44, all on the periphery of the plot, had no jewellery except for a pin or strap end. The only type of brooch present in plot B are varieties of the Kentish disc-brooch, to be found in 29, 30, 32, 35 and 126. Each female had other jewellery in the form of pin or pendants. Beads were of amber and glass with some polychrome, millefiori, mosaic or reticella. Distinctive items are the wheel-thrown pot 43/4, the pendant 35/3 with Christian cross, possibly one also in 32, the garnet and gold pendants 29/6, 29/8 and the pendant 29/7 of a coin dated to c 560–70. Judging from the plan only it might seem that 42 and 27 might belong to plot G, but they are slightly further away from plot G and their orientation and alignment match better the graves of plot B. There is further affinity as to contents, for there are no sword graves or amber beads in plot G, and the reticella bead 42/1m matches the bead 93/1 in a sword grave. This plot had none of the square-headed and Frankish brooches of plot A, and the Kentish disc-brooches it contains range from the early type as in plot A, to later types. There are no iron diamond plaques, but the pendants, Christian cross and wheel-thrown pot are new.

The C plot to the south is well isolated from all others. It is known that about five graves were destroyed just north of grave 8, and those remaining were spaced well apart. Three were spear graves, 8, 9 and 10, grave 8 with a Frankish buckle and unusual, single-edged spear. The woman's grave contained amongst other things a Frankish glass tumbler, glass beads and one shell bead. This grave therefore differs from the plot B graves in having no brooch or amber beads, although the garnet pendant matches 29/6.

Plot D consists of five graves in the north-west of the cemetery, a number of graves known to have been destroyed to the south of them, of which grave D was the sole survivor on the high part of a cut-out

---

18 Laing and Laing 1979, 81–2, fig. 54, Hirst 1985, 40–43    19 Hills and Wade-Martins 1976, fig. 6

terrace, and a few graves remaining to the south of that. A space separates it from plot A and also from plot C. The destroyed graves must have included two sword graves and one or two rich females who wore a gold coin pendant and a square-headed brooch, for these unassociated objects came from that area (Unassociated 7, 8, 6 and 9, Figure 64). As only a strip of original land surface was left intact in the north, it is not possible to be certain that these graves are to be regarded as one group, and 115 and 116, for instance, may have been part of a separate group. The likelihood of this is increased by the fact that their contents contrast with the rest of the plot, being scanty, a knife only in 115 and Roman bronze objects re-used as a girdle-hanger in 116. Graves 41 and 98 were both sword graves, and the sword 98/1 belongs to a stage of development as late as the latest component of the sword C/1. In the south, besides graves of children, there were two sword graves, two others with shields, and two women, each with a Kentish disc-brooch, and amber and glass beads, one polychrome. There is therefore considerable affinity with plot B.

Plot E is situated on the eastern side of the barrow, and it is likely that there were more graves nearer the middle of the barrow which have been lost through erosion of the mound. There are both male and female graves. There were no swords, but three had spears 61, 63, 65, and one, 64, a large knife. The seax and shield-on-tongue buckle in 65 are Frankish. Of the women only one has a brooch, 59. Some have beads: amber beads occur in 55, 59, 60, 62, 66, while 53 and 67 have amethyst, and 67 shell also. There are also some polychrome and millefiori and mosaic glass beads, and metal beads, 67/5. Some connection with plots B and D, and even A, is shown by the early Kentish disc-brooch in grave 59, and the buckle in 61, while the disc pendants 67/3a, b, 4 are similar to those in graves 32 and 35 in plot B.

Some of the graves in this area, therefore belong to a later phase, and the women's graves may be divided preliminarily into an earlier phase, 55, 59, 60, 62, 66, and a later phase, 53, 58, 67, according to their contents of amber beads and one brooch in the first group, and amethyst, shell and metal beads and no brooches in the second group. Two phases are also indicated by the burial of 58 on top of 59, presumably because an elapse of time had obscured the earlier grave. Grave 61 contains a buckle with tinned bronze rivets similar to a buckle in 18, and both 61 and 63 contain D2 spears which appear from phases 2 to 4. The well-furnished male grave 65 has a buckle with shoe-shaped rivets as in grave 96a, and is no doubt earlier than 52 which has a small buckle with rectangular plate. The two groups indicated by difference in orientation are therefore confirmed by the grave goods, except that 55 and 66 have affinities with the northern group and must have been the earliest laid down in the southern group.

In plot F there are four sword graves, 131, 71 and 96a and b, and two spear graves near them, 39 and 135. There were also two poorly furnished graves, and one woman in a richly furnished grave, 38, who had a Kentish disc-brooch and amber beads. The woman, therefore, relates to those in plot B, but the contents of the men's graves indicate a later phase. The shield bosses with narrow flange and knob-headed rivets relate to the same forms in 27 and 90.

In plot G three graves were destroyed between 129 and 139. Comparison with plot F cannot be very close as the F graves were mostly male, and the G graves are mostly female. However, although there are no sword graves in G, spears appear in 128, 137 and 156. Buckles are small, with rectangular plates and three rivets, and there is a late kind of strap-end in 156. In the women's graves there are no brooches but pins occur, ie 132/1, 134/5, 155/1, 157/3, garnet and gold pendants 134/1, 3 and 4, silver rings 157/2 and necklaces of beads, including polychrome, glass, metal, shell and amethyst. The animal ornament on the pendant in grave 134 is in Style II. The plot is therefore quite distinct from plots A–F, and made even more so by the presence of five out of the seven wheel-thrown pots in the cemetery.

Plot H is a similarly spaced but larger group to the east. Only one man's grave contained any kind of weapon, a spearhead 114/2, the rest contained little more than a knife and sometimes an iron buckle, a pin, tag end or steel. The woman in 160 had expensive possessions, a silver pin, garnet pendant and glass palm cup. Grave 107 contained a bronze workbox, 110 a comb and two sceattas, 141 a bracelet and beads. Other jewellery was limited to a pin in 147, 138 and 142. Beads were scarce, consisting of glass beads in 107, 110, 141, a shell pendant in 141, and amethyst in 124. Graves 138 and 142 contained similar large iron keys, and bronze wire in S-shapes occurred in graves 141 and 138. Metal tag ends and very small buckles are late features. Possessions are therefore mostly different from those in plot G, and no doubt indicate a later date. Female graves in plot H to the east of grave 110 were sparsely furnished with only knife, keys, buckle or pin, and the male graves 103, 114 and 125 also contained very little. They are therefore more closely linked by contents to the graves in plot I than to the western part of plot H.

Plot I is distinctive because of the form and disposition of graves alone which are assembled in rows and are small, deep and narrow. Most are of women and children. Of the three male graves, 73 contained no finds, 80 a knife only and 103 a knife and fragmentary belt fittings. The graves of the children contained little more than a knife, if anything at all. The women's graves, too, were poorly furnished, containing a pin or knife. There were also shears in 75 and 83 and amethyst beads in 75 and 127.

The remaining plots J – N cover the more isolated graves along the northern border of the cemetery, but south of the barrow. Plot J consisted of one female and two male graves, two of them disturbed by modern machinery. The total contents were a small buckle and key fragments, neither useful for dating purposes. It may be that these graves should be regarded as part of plot G. Plot K consists of two graves near the barrrow, of which 56 is a sword grave and 57 a spear grave, probably related to each other and to similarly furnished graves in plot B. Plot L has more of the appearance of an integrated group. Grave 161 stood alone, obviously a woman of importance, with a garnet-decorated pin, and a larger ?pin with bronze helmeted head of Swedish origin. The other three graves were together, a woman with keys in 164, and children, 163 with a knife, and 162 with knives and whetstones. The hipped pin in 161 forms a link with a similar pin in grave 134 of plot G. Plot M is an isolated group of three, a man and two children without grave goods. N can hardly be described as a group, but the letter is used to cover the five remaining graves in isolated positions south and east of the barrow. Three contained no grave goods, and 145 and 146 were male graves with knife and buckle only.

## Relative and Absolute Chronology

The discussion of the grave finds above shows that, except for the very earliest and latest burials no one plot of any size was in exclusive use at any one time. The total period during which the cemetery was in use is divisible into seven phases. The relationship of the plots of graves to each other therefore appears to be as shown in Table XXVIII. The plots have proved each to have a certain amount of homogeneity within themselves so that they can be reckoned as useful entities for study. Nevertheless, they are not all chronologically homogeneous and there are relationships between some of the plots.

The sequence outlined in Table XXVIII shows that one single plot A contains the earliest graves. It is not known whether any graves earlier than this occurred in the destroyed sections. There is an indication of such a possibility, however, on the western extremity in grave 116, where part of a Roman balance is used as a girdle hanger, and so might indicate an early Anglo-Saxon grave. In the third phase part of plots B and D are contemporary with parts of E, F and K. In the fourth phase two further graves were added to A, and the eastern part of B is contemporary with the rest of F and some of E. In phase 5 plot C is contemporary with G and the rest of E. J is possibly contemporary with G. Phase 6 is the period of plot H, probably L, and one grave added to A. In the seventh and final phase burial seems to have been continuous in an easterly direction in the main body of graves in plot I and also in the isolated plots in the north, M and N.

The establishment of an absolute chronology for the cemetery is substantially assisted by coins which give a *terminus post quem* for graves in different locations. Very few of the individual graves can be accurately dated, and the few occurrences of Roman coins are of no value in this connection. However, there are four post-Roman coins which give useful location of dating points in the cemetery. The study of this site was based on the opinion on the date of these coins by the late Stuart Rigold in a report written in 1964. In view of the lapse of time between that report and publication it seemed prudent to seek an up-to-date opinion on the coins, and Dr J P C Kent of the British Museum kindly provided the report on p 180 in which a slightly earlier date is attributed to each coin. An unassociated find from the destroyed section in the west, probably just south of graves 98 and 41 in plot D, is a Visigothic coin dated by Rigold to AD 580–6, and by Kent to *c* 575. On either dating it is within the span attributed to phase 3 and plot D at Dover. The bronze-gilt imitation coin in grave 29 was considered by Rigold to belong probably to the late sixth century, *c* 590, but Kent considers that its most probable span is somewhere in the third quarter of the sixth century, *c* 560–70. This puts it slightly earlier than the beginning of phase 3 to which grave 29 belongs, but no doubt a few years should be added to the date of production to account for its travel from the place of origin (?east or north-west Gaul), conversion to use as a pendant by the addition of a loop, and wear by its owner. Similar reasoning could be applied to the sceattas which were found in grave 110 attributed to phases 6 at Dover, 675–700, for they were dated to 680–5 by Rigold, and to the third quarter of the seventh century, probably 660–70 by Kent. Starting with these dating points as a basis and by using every other means at our disposal, it is possible to establish a probable date for most graves.

The grave goods can be used for chronological indications, as many of the types have been well studied so that a sequence of development has been established, and by relating them to other find contexts, particularly continental contexts which are often coin-dated, a period of use can be discerned. Precision of less than fifty years by this method is not usually possible. It has been demonstrated that the distribution of one type of object in the cemetery often corresponds to grouping suggested by other means, and so assists in the chronological assessment.

In the earliest stages of the cemetery burials are not very numerous and may be limited to one family only, so that a small number of graves span a

TABLE XXVIII PLOTS A–N IN RELATION TO THE PHASES

| Phases | Plots | | | | | | | | | | | | |
|---|---|---|---|---|---|---|---|---|---|---|---|---|---|
| 1 | A | | | | | | | | | | | | |
| 2 | A | | | | | | | | | | | | |
| 3 | | B | | D | E | F | | | K | | | | |
| 4 | A | B | | | E | F | | | | | | | |
| 5 | | | C | | E | | G | | | ?J | | | |
| 6 | A | | | | | | | H | | | L | | |
| 7 | | | | | | | | | | I | | M | N |

considerable period. With the passing of time the number of people increases so that there are more burials in a shorter span of time. The number and variety of possessions deposited also increases. To begin with, therefore, the phases of the cemetery are envisaged as sequences of fifty years each. After phase 3, however, it does seem possible to distinguish phases of only twenty five years. By the time of the final phase, however, grave goods are scarce so that the longer period of 50 years is used again, and the exact date of the end of the cemetery is not determinable.

The list p 175 shows the graves which may be allocated to specific phases on the basis of the dating of the grave furniture, and the list p 176 indicates the phases to which the rest of the graves probably belong on the basis of less well-defined object dating and other evidence such as position in relation to other graves, size, shape, orientation etc. The only exception is phase 7 where there is very little grave furniture, and all graves in plots I, M and N are regarded as belonging to this phase. The allocation to phases is also shown in Figures 101–7. Text Figures 25–27 show the most important objects found in the graves of each of the phases 1–7. Where an object continued in existence through more than one phase, this is indicated by an arrow and the number of the phase to which it survived.

The earliest phase, represented only by plot A, must have begun by the second half of the fifth century, for the female grave in the middle, grave 48, contained fragments of a Roman glass vessel and bronze bowl, a buckle and lead spindle whorl current about AD 400, a spiral-decorated saucer brooch of the first half of the fifth century, and a button brooch which need not be much later than the middle of the fifth century. Other graves in the group are no doubt equally early.

If plot A is scrutinised more closely, two distinct major phases in its development can be discerned. A number of the graves were either placed over earlier graves or they disturbed earlier graves. The superimposition of 22 by 18 at a different angle suggests that the earlier grave was probably unmarked and forgotten by the time of the second burial. Grave 90 must have disturbed an earlier burial as there was a humerus in its fill. Grave 49 probably cut into both 46 and 48 although it was at the same angle. Grave 92 disturbed grave 70. Grave 94a was exactly on top of 94b, and so could have been a simultaneous burial or a later burial perhaps deliberately coincidental, but if the other superimpositions in this group are accidental it is probable that this also must be regarded as an accidental superimposition. In any case, two layers of graves are recognisably represented by 22, 46, 48, 70 and 94b below, and by 18, 49, 90, 92 and 94a on top.

The date of production of some of the finds in these graves has already been established by comparative studies, so that the division into two phases can be completed by this means. Graves which may be dated to the period 475–525 are 13, 21, 22, 20, 48, 87. These contain a variety of brooches: spiral-decorated saucer, button, small-long, early square-headed as well as a buckle with semi-circular plate, a Kempston-type glass cone beaker, a spearhead with inlaid bands, and a hand-made Anglo-Frisian pot. There is a buckle with shield-on-tongue and disc-headed rivets in grave 20, which also contained a Frankish disc brooch, square-headed brooches of a stage later than those in grave 13, and a gold D-bracteate, so that it must belong to the very end of phase 1[20]. Of these graves, 22 and 48 have already been allocated to the earlier phase by reason of superimposition. In addition, 46 has clear affinities with grave 20 beside it in a weaving sword and certain types of bead. Grave 12 is poorly furnished, but should probably be considered to be contemporary with the neighbouring graves 20 and 13 as, like 20, it contains an iron diamond plaque.

Several graves may be dated to 525–575. These include graves with Frankish brooches, 23 and 92, a Kentish disc brooch 14, and Frankish buckles with shoe-shaped rivets, 50, 15 and 28. Grave 92 is one of the upper layer of graves, and one of the other poorly furnished upper layer graves, 49, probably also belongs to phase 2. Grave 94b contains an inlaid spear, a type also found in 22, one of the other lower level graves, but one also occurs in grave 50 with a buckle of phase 2, and the sword in grave 94b should also belong to phase 2 or later.

The date of grave 18 is difficult to determine, although its position on top of 22 denotes a date no earlier than phase 2. It contains an iron buckle with silvered rivets on the plate as in grave 61 of phase 3, and it also has a pin which probably had a disc head, a bunch of small keys and polychrome beads, none of which begin before phase 3. There is also a single disc-shaped amber bead, and amber beads do not occur here after phase 4, but it also contains the distinctive biconical orange beads which do not occur here before phase 5. Grave 18 is therefore allocated to phase 4, although it might be later. Graves without finds or insufficient for dating evidence in this area are: 19, 88, 89 and 45.

It may be seen from the plan Figure 101 that the nine graves of phase 1 are laid out in two fairly regular rows within a small rectangular area. The graves of phase 2 are set partly in the same two rows, in between the earlier graves and extending the area northwards, the most northern grave 94b being rather isolated. The evidence of any extension southwards was destroyed by the road-cutting activities. A minor third row of more poorly furnished graves was laid down to the east, however, and a single grave lies outside the rectangular area on both the west and east side. The area available for burial was therefore clearly limited and marked out to begin with, and was only overstepped by two graves 19 and 45. As one of these was findless, and the other only contained a bronze strip, the date of the breaking of the bounds cannot be established.

---

20  Bakka 1981, 24

138                    THE BUCKLAND ANGLO-SAXON CEMETERY

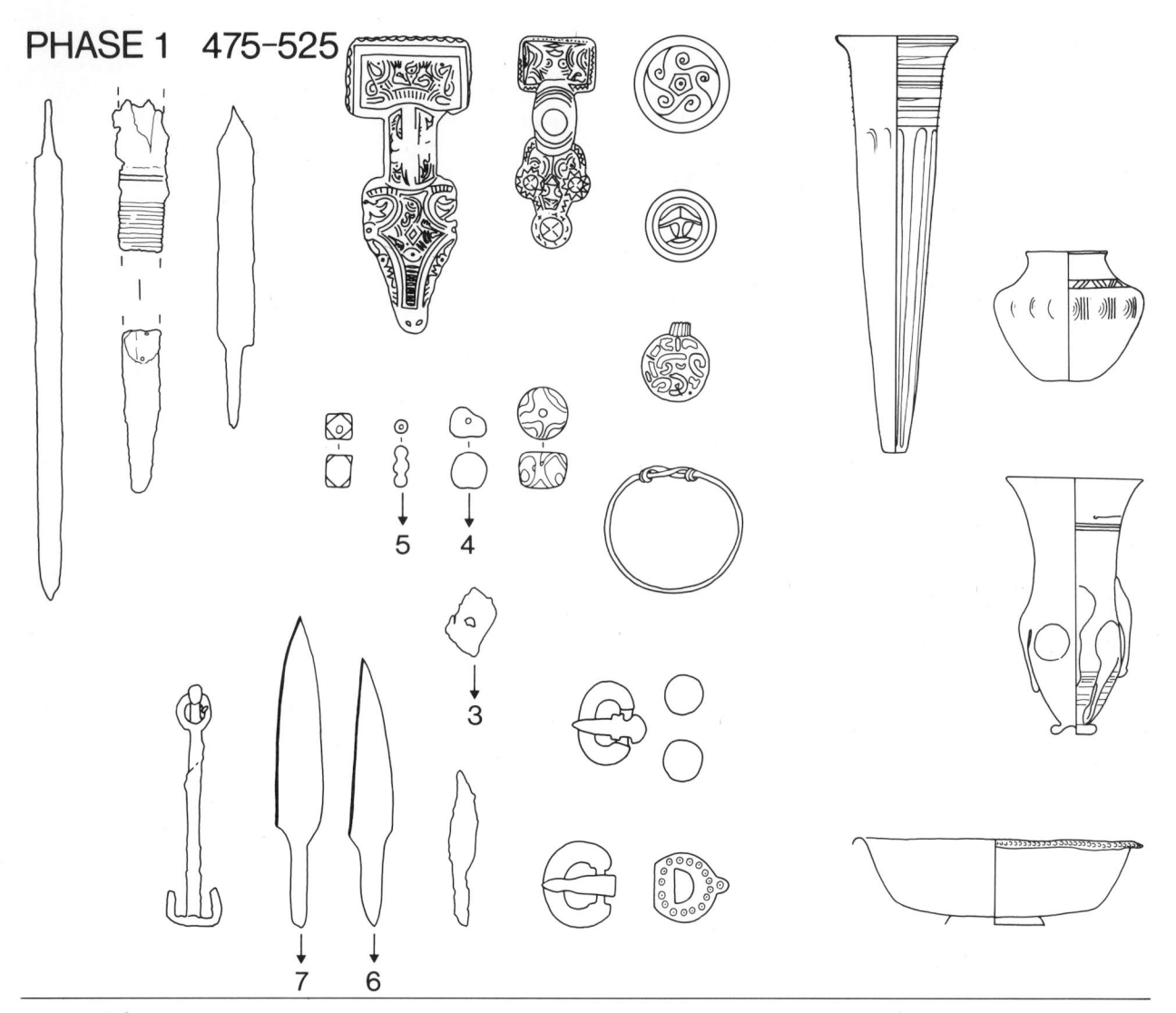

**PHASE 1   475–525**

**PHASE 2   525–575**

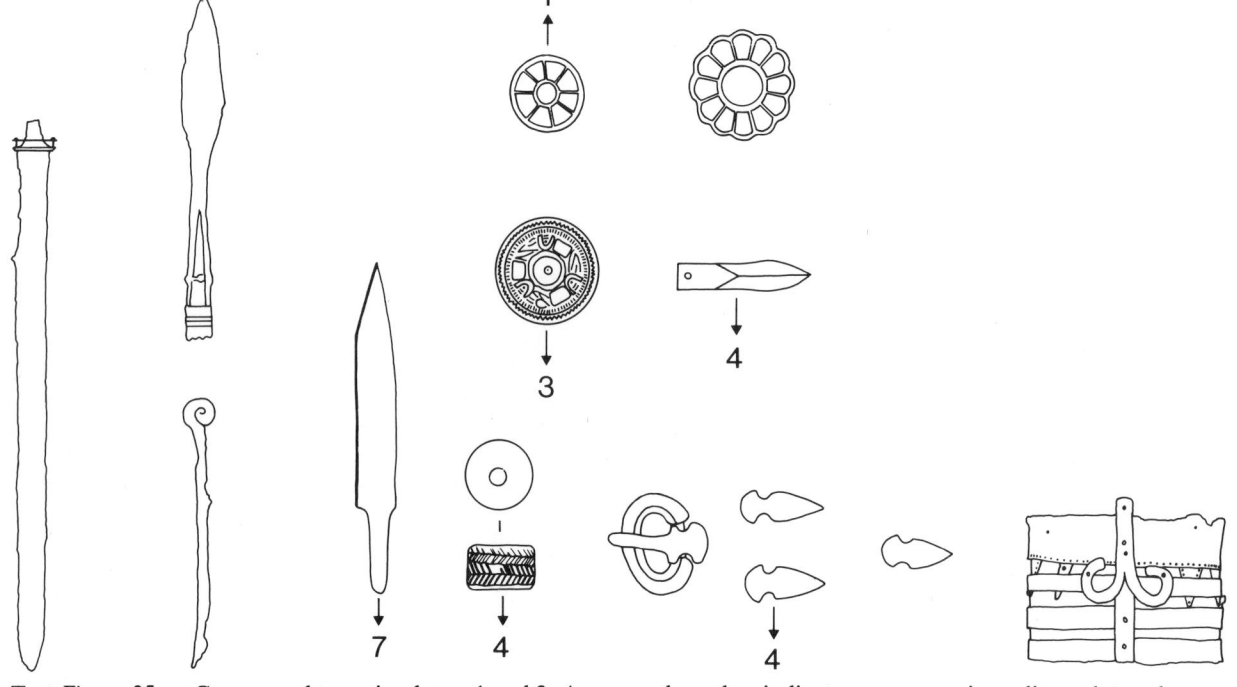

*Text Figure 25*   Grave good types in phases 1 and 2. Arrow and number indicate occurrence in earlier or later phase. Scale 1/2 except: spear (phase 1), pin (phase 2), bucket, knives, iron diamond: 1/4; glass 1/5; spear (phase 2), pot, bronze bowl, weaving batten, key 1/8; swords 1/12.

# DISCUSSION

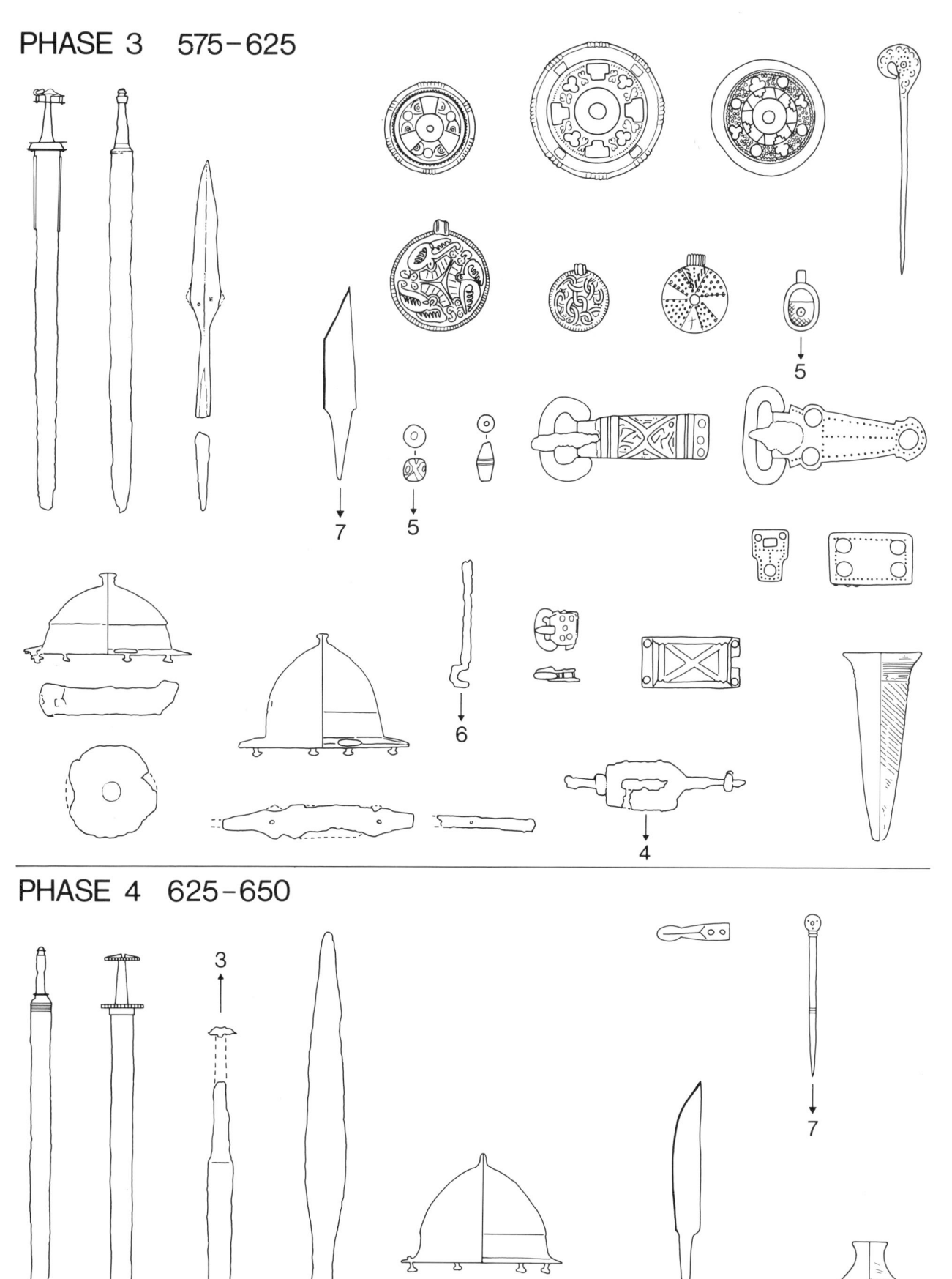

## PHASE 3  575–625

## PHASE 4  625–650

*Text Figure 26*  Grave good types in phases 3 and 4. Arrow and number indicate occurrence in earlier or later phase. Scale 1/2 except: spear (phase 4), small buckle, lock, knives, key 1/4; shield bosses and fittings, glass 1/5; spear (phase 3), seax, pot 1/8; swords 1/12

# THE BUCKLAND ANGLO-SAXON CEMETERY

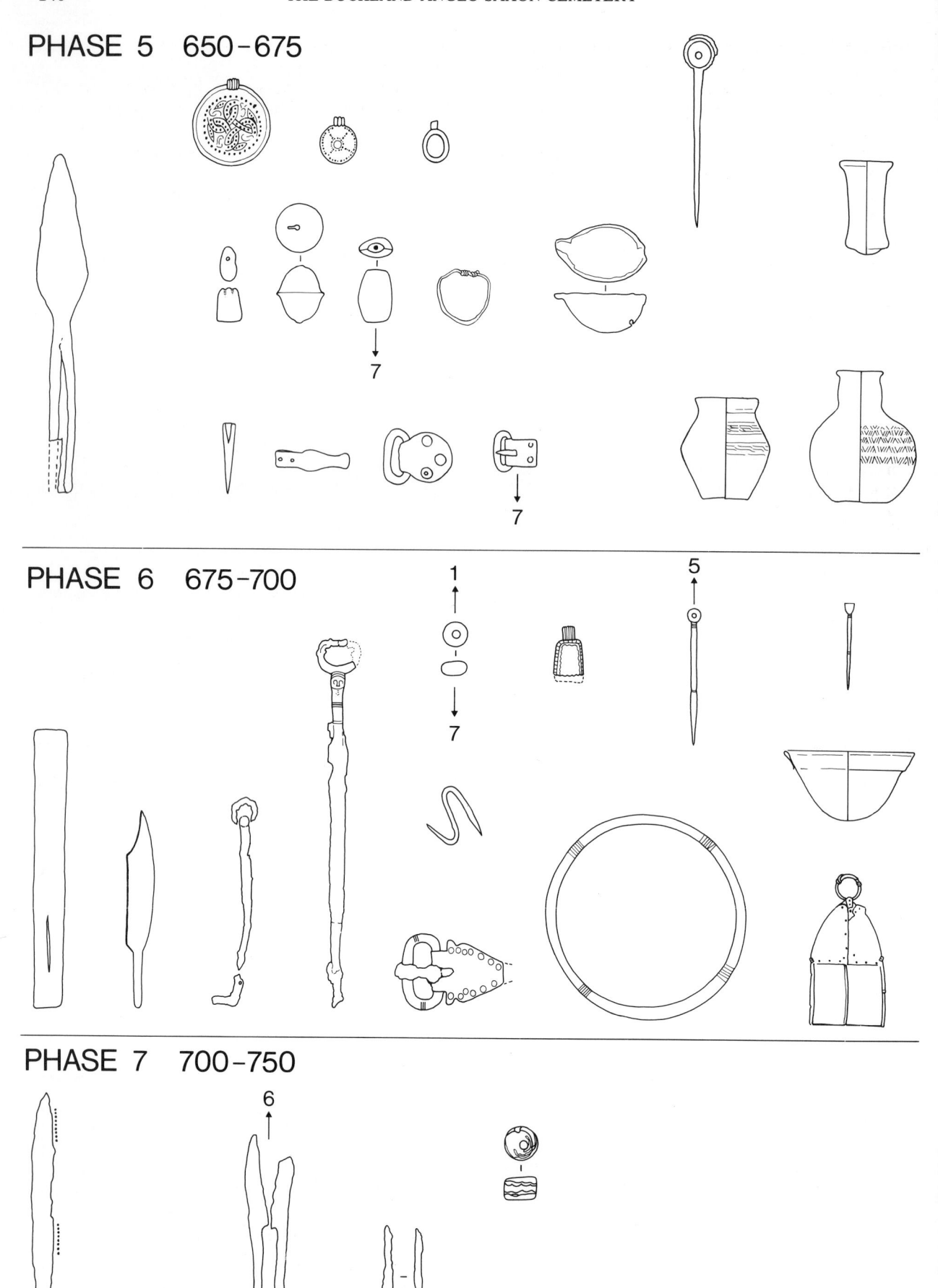

**PHASE 5  650-675**

**PHASE 6  675-700**

**PHASE 7  700-750**

*Text Figure 27*  Grave good types in phases 5, 6 and 7. Arrow and number indicate occurrence in earlier or later phase. Scale 1/2 except: spear, large buckle (phase 5), shoe-lace tag (phase 7), workbox, hone, shears, knives, spoon, shell 1/4; glass 1/5; pots; key 1/8

While superimposition may have been unwitting if markers were absent, it is also possible that there was a physical and inviolable limit to the area, and overburial was a necessity once the cemetery was full. In the north, graves 90 and 95 lie at different angles to the rows of graves which are fairly regularly orientated, and these anomalies will be discussed below.

The history of the cemetery continues straight on into plots in various parts of the cemetery with a different layout of the graves. An important link is the Kentish disc brooch, which occurs twice at early stages of development in plot A, then in plot B in stages which can be dated from 575–625, and in varying stages also in plots D, E and F. The differences between plots A and B are very striking, and although the earliest disc brooch in B is in a similar stage to those in A, the graves in B must be dated for the most part to the end of the sixth century. None of these graves in plot B appear to be earlier than 575, and there is homogeneity in the graves of brooch-wearing women, 29, 30, 32, 35 and 126, grave 29 containing the coin of c 560–70. As the male grave 33 is in the same row it is probably contemporary, and the male graves 91 and 93 immediately to the west may be judged to be contemporary also from their contents, which include shield bosses with disc-headed rivets. Grave 94a in plot A probably also belongs to phase 3.

The row of graves of women and children immediately to the east, 44, 43, 34 and 25, appear to be aligned to the row of rich women in plot B, but their contents, no brooch but pin and keys in 44, a wheel-thrown pot and keys in 43, and a late type of strapend in 34, show that they belong rather to the later period of 625–650, phase 4. The two graves to the east, 27 and 42, also belong to this later period: grave 42 is without a brooch, and grave 27 has a later type of shield boss.

The only well-furnished grave in the small group of plot C is 6, a woman without a brooch but fairly rich with imported glass vessel, garnet pendant and shell beads. The garnet pendant resembles one in grave 29. Sliced garnet pendants, however, also appear in grave 134 in plot G, and grave 6 is placed in the same category by the inclusion of shell beads on the necklace. The three furnished male graves contain spears but no swords. In grave 8 there is a Frankish buckle with circular plate, a type in use in the sixth and seventh centuries, and the disc-headed pin of grave 10 has a long life mostly concentrated in phase 6. Although the numbers are small, therefore, this section must have been in use when brooches and swords were no longer buried, and shell beads were in use, i.e. at the same time as plot G, phase 5.

In plot D, graves F and 1 must be assigned on the basis of late keystone disc brooches to the period about AD 600. Shield grips of early type in graves C and 3 are counter-balanced by a later form of strap grip in 5, and a later addition of a silver ring on the early sword pommel in C. A grave in the central destroyed area contained the Visigothic gold coin of about AD 575, phase 3, and the evidence of the strap grip in grave 5 is not enough to suggest continuation into phase 4.

The dates of the graves in the northern part of plot D are less certain. The re-use of a single Roman bronze object in 115 cannot be taken as indicating an early date. The sword grip with silver sleeve fittings in 98 is likely to be as late as the end of phase 3.

One of the most distinctive features of plot E is to be found in grave 59 which contains an early disc brooch of the period 525–575 along with a necklace which included amber beads. However, also on the necklace is a mosaic bead and polychrome beads which occur mostly in plots B and G, i.e. 575–675. The three mosaic beads in this cemetery occur in graves 30, 59 and 60. A wooden box with iron fittings as in grave 59 occurs in graves no earlier than plot B. Graves 59 and 60 are therefore placed in phase 3, 575–625. Graves 61 and 63 both contain a D2 spear, with a type 5 knife in 63 and a buckle similar to one in grave 18 in 61. They are tentatively allocated to phase 3 on account of their proximity and similar depth to 59 and 60. South of this group graves 55, 62 and 66 also have a few amber beads, but no brooch and no rich objects. Of two male graves, 65 contains a buckle with shoe-shaped rivets, seax, spear etc, and 64 a large knife. These last five graves are assigned to phase 4, AD 625–650. Grave 58, on top of 59, must be phase 4 or later. Female graves belonging to a later period still are graves containing amethyst, metal and shell beads, 53 and 67. Indicative also of this later period is the small bronze buckle with rectangular plate in 52. These are the latest graves in plot E, and may be compared with graves in plot G. The area of the barrow was therefore in use during phases 3, 4 and 5.

In plot F there is one woman only, in the richly furnished grave 38. The possessions include a gold finger-ring, disc brooch, buckle with degenerate Style I animal ornament, beads, a glass cone beaker, weaving sword and an iron diamond. Similar disc brooches belong to phase 3, weaving swords to phase 1, the only other grave with so many amber beads is 92 of phase 2, and the only two other graves containing a millefiori bead are 53 and 132 of phase 5. As, however, the woman was in her twenties at the time of death and the wearing of a Kentish disc brooch in the cemetery is almost exclusively limited to phase 3, this is regarded here as the time of deposition of grave 38.

There are four sword-graves in plot F, 131, 71 and 96a and b, and two spear graves, 39 and 135. The spearheads in these graves are rather long, the shield boss in 71/8 is a late type, and the sword 96a/4 is a Frankish type with inlaid guards which belongs to the period c 570–650. The female grave 38 is therefore earlier than the rest, and it must be considered whether grave 131 beside it is connected with it. These two graves are separated from the other graves in the group by a wider space, which suggests the possibility that they were husband and wife, and unconnected with the later male graves to the east. Their alignment probably related to the unoccupied space to the west. However, the shield discs in 131 are the same type as those in 27 and 39, and the grave should therefore be of similar date, i.e. phase 4, AD 625–650. Unless grave 38 is full of heirlooms therefore, and this is unlikely as it contains a woman in her twenties, it must be regarded as a single grave deposited in phase 3, while the rest of the plot belongs to phase 4. Confirmation is obtained from an analysis of the gold finger-ring which shows that its gold content is as high as 98.4% (p 86 above), a fineness which was not likely to occur after c 580.

The male graves in plot G show differences from the male graves in Plot F, i.e. there are no shields or swords, although two male adults and two boys have spears. Wheel-thrown pots occur with both male and female graves, and the buckles are small with rectangular plates and three rivets. The women have amethyst, shell and metal beads, garnet pendants, and a pendant in Style II animal ornament. A late type of strapend appears in grave 156, and a hipped pin compares with one in grave 161 in plot K.

The graves in plot G are a distinctive group as noted above (p 137), and may be allocated to phase 5. They immediately precede plot H, which may be regarded as dated to some time after AD 660–70, i.e. phase 6, by the sceattas on the necklace in grave 110. This area produced the bronze workbox, a bracelet, glass palm cup and cabochon garnet pendant. The beads are exclusively monochrome. There is a general trend towards more sparse grave furniture.

There can be no doubt that plot I is completely divorced from plot H. Although the lower limiting line continues south-eastwards, the graves are of slot type and grouped differently in close rows, more graves are empty of grave-goods, and the others are sparsely furnished. Although there are no objects that can be precisely dated, they include late objects such as shoe-lace tag ends and shears. The combination of these elements of evidence, particularly the general tendency of expansion in a south-easterly direction, suggests that the graves are all subsequent to plot H, and the number of graves involved shows that burial probably continued up to 750 (phase 7).

There is little evidence for the date of the graves in plot J, and it may perhaps be assumed that they are contemporary with the graves of plot G which they resemble in spacing, i.e. phase 5.

The two male graves in plot K are probably related to the barrow plot E, particularly as the orientation of 57 is peculiar and may be intentionally pointed towards the centre of the barrow. The Frankish belt set and spear in grave 56 belong to phase 3.

The only diagnostic features of plot L are the two pins in 161. One is a small hipped pin, similar to one in grave 134 in group G. The other is the helmeted pin of Scandinavian origin which cannot be exactly paralleled. The type of helmeted man is known from the sixth century, but this particular type of pin is not found before Viking contexts. The fact that this group of graves is fairly well furnished need not place it earlier in date than unfurnished graves if, as seems likely, its occupants were pagan. It is tentatively placed in the period phase 6, AD 675–700, but is possibly later.

There are no finds in plot M and very few in N, and the positioning, scattered and to the north and east, suggests they are to be dated after plot L. There are therefore considered to be contemporary with plot I, the latest in the cemetery.

### Interpretation of the Layout and Expansion of the Cemetery

Plot A contains the earliest settlers whose possessions suggest a mixture of Franks and Danes or Jutes, with perhaps an Angle and a Saxon. The earliest graves belong to the second half of the fifth century. As three of the women's graves in plot A are superimposed on another grave, two of which are definitely male, (18–22, 94a and b), the possibilities of suttee must be considered, i.e., the killing and burial of a wife on the death of her husband, or alternatively, the more civilized custom of the later re-opening of the man's grave on the subsequent death of his wife. The character of the female burials shows nothing extraordinary, the bodies were in normal positions, and had not been thrown in face downwards as in the case of a live burial on top of another burial at Sewerby[21]. The woman in grave 94a was old, and the woman in grave 92 was in her twenties, but the age of the woman in grave 18 is not known.

Grave 22 was the deepest sword grave (69cm), and 94b was also quite deep at 53 cm, so that it is possible that they were both dug with the knowledge that a second grave was to be placed on top. Nevertheless there are other graves in the area of a similar depth, 21, 23, 87 and 88. Although in 94a and b the outline of the grave corresponds in both cases, there was a distinct difference in orientation in 18–22. This latter suggests chance superimposition because of loss of surface indication of an earlier grave, and it has already been noted that there are other traces to show that there were, indeed, two phases of burials in this area. Grave 92 disturbed a shallow grave laid at a different angle to itself, and destroyed it except for the east end where foot bones were left articulated. Grave 90, a male grave, also must have disturbed another grave as there was a humerus in its fill. These are all in the same row but the group 46–48–49 (all female) shows that there was also a second row of earlier graves to the east. Here 46 and 48 were presumably contemporary, and either disturbed the earlier and shallower grave 49, or vice versa. The second possibility is more likely as 46 and 48 belong to phase 1.

Disappearance of traces of earlier graves on the land surface is a common reason for later intrusions, and it is certainly possible here as the period of use

---

21 Laing and Laing 1979, 81–2, fig. 54 Hirst 1985, 38–43

spans a century. Another possible explanation, however, suggests itself in this particular area. The graves, with the exception of 19 and 45, are closely confined, mostly in two rows, in a minimum amount of space. (Text Figure 2). The first period of deposition is from 475–525, a time when the invaders were struggling for a foothold in the country, and when the British gained the upper hand at Mount Badon. Dover was rather distant from the main Germanic settlements further north in Kent, although connected by the Roman roads, so that the settlers, for the time being, may have found themselves in a subservient position. It might be that a small enclosed space had been allocated by the Christian British to the foreign, pagan settlers for burial, and they therefore had no choice but to bury close together and, eventually, on top of earlier graves. The sword grave 94b belongs to phase 2 and was sited in an isolated position north of the close grave cluster but with similar orientation. This grave in the north, together with 19 and 45 outside the west and east borders, must have marked the beginning of a period of freedom to bury outside the original confines.

After about 575 some important change took place which resulted in a new cemetery being laid out in a different fashion, and adjoining it, to the north-east, (plot B), and by now a local Kentish jeweller was able to provide the brooches and other jewellery. As two of the graves here contained pendants bearing a Christian cross, and the date of the graves is between 575 and 625, it seems clear that in the new layout some of the people buried there were Christian. The beginning of this section was somewhat in advance of 597 when St. Augustine came to Kent, so that selection of a new plot of land is not apparently immediately connected with the results of his teaching. The fact that most early Germanic burials in Kent are inhumations and not cremations, and, moreover in a W–E direction, could be cited as evidence of some kind of contact with Christianity at a much earlier date. Further, if, as has been suggested, the settlement in phase 1 was initially under the control of the Britons, the invaders would have come into close contact with the British version of Christianity, for when Augustine arrived, some British churches were still repairable, and the British clergy was very much in evidence. A further significant point is that the artifacts in the graves show close contact in phases 1 and 2 with the Franks, who had already accepted Christianity under Clovis in AD 496. Moreover, Ethelbert's wife brought in a Frankish bishop, Liudhard, to Kent by about AD 580. There is therefore every likelihood that the wealthy families in the vicinity of Dover had become Christian at least by the last two decades of the sixth century and perhaps even before, if this is the significance of W–E burials in plot A. It must have been the increase in their fortunes, brought about by the growing power of Ethelbert, and reflected in the local production of sumptuous jewellery, which prompted the transfer of their cemetery to an adjacent, less restricted and newly consecrated plot rather than a dramatic change in religion.

Plot A had no doubt been sited next to a ?building plot in the area immediately to the south, where the excavation found a wide rectangular space between the graves but no traces in the chalk save for one posthole and a Roman pit. If there was a building here which was used in connection with the earliest burials whether pagan or Christian, it would no doubt have been consecrated and put to the same use by Ethelbert's Christians for the cemetery groups began to spread out round it, in plots B, D and F, and possibly in the north-west destroyed area also. Christian pendants appeared at the end of the period of use of plot B, so confirming the religion of the people in this coin-dated section of the cemetery. The orientation of the row of graves of rich women in plot B was related to this rectangular space, as was also the direction of the grave of the woman with similar jewellery in grave 38, plot F.

Graves F and 1 in plot D much further south were also next to a smaller space without graves on their east side, but because of destruction here immediately to the north the relationship of this space to the other to the north, if any, cannot be determined. One plot, E, does not fall in with this pattern, and one might suppose that while the other areas occupied at that time were consecrated ground, it is probable that the sides of a prehistoric barrow, separate and to the north, would be favoured by people who preferred to keep to their old gods. Some support can be found for this theory in grave 67. This young woman was wearing pendants probably marked with a Christian cross, but she had been thrown face down in the grave and apparently buried alive. Was this violent burial of an apparent Christian in a pagan area punishment for some unchristian act? As a small number of graves cover a long period of time in plot E, it appears to have accommodated a minority who retained paganism while the majority were buried further south, where two further plots, C and G, were subsequently laid down beside D and F.

Next the spread continued south-eastwards, following the straight line on the southern edge, the grave finds changing and becoming fewer, and dating of the middle part of the large plot H made certain (post 660–70) by the sceattas. Still following the spread in a south-eastern direction, plot I shows a complete change in grave shapes and layout and increasing scarcity of finds. Although, therefore, there is little here that is definitely dateable, an eighth-century date is certain from its relationship to group H and from the lack of grave furniture. The introduction of postholes is a new feature which occurs in similarly late context at St. Peter's, and these could have supported some kind of grave marker, if not a cross. They are not precisely aligned to graves, however, and other more likely functions are examined below.

The rest of the outlying grave plots J, K, L, M and N, must surely have been positioned where they are, at some distance from the others, for some special reason, the most likely of which is retention of paganism. The separateness of plot J is not without question, as the few grave goods are not dateable

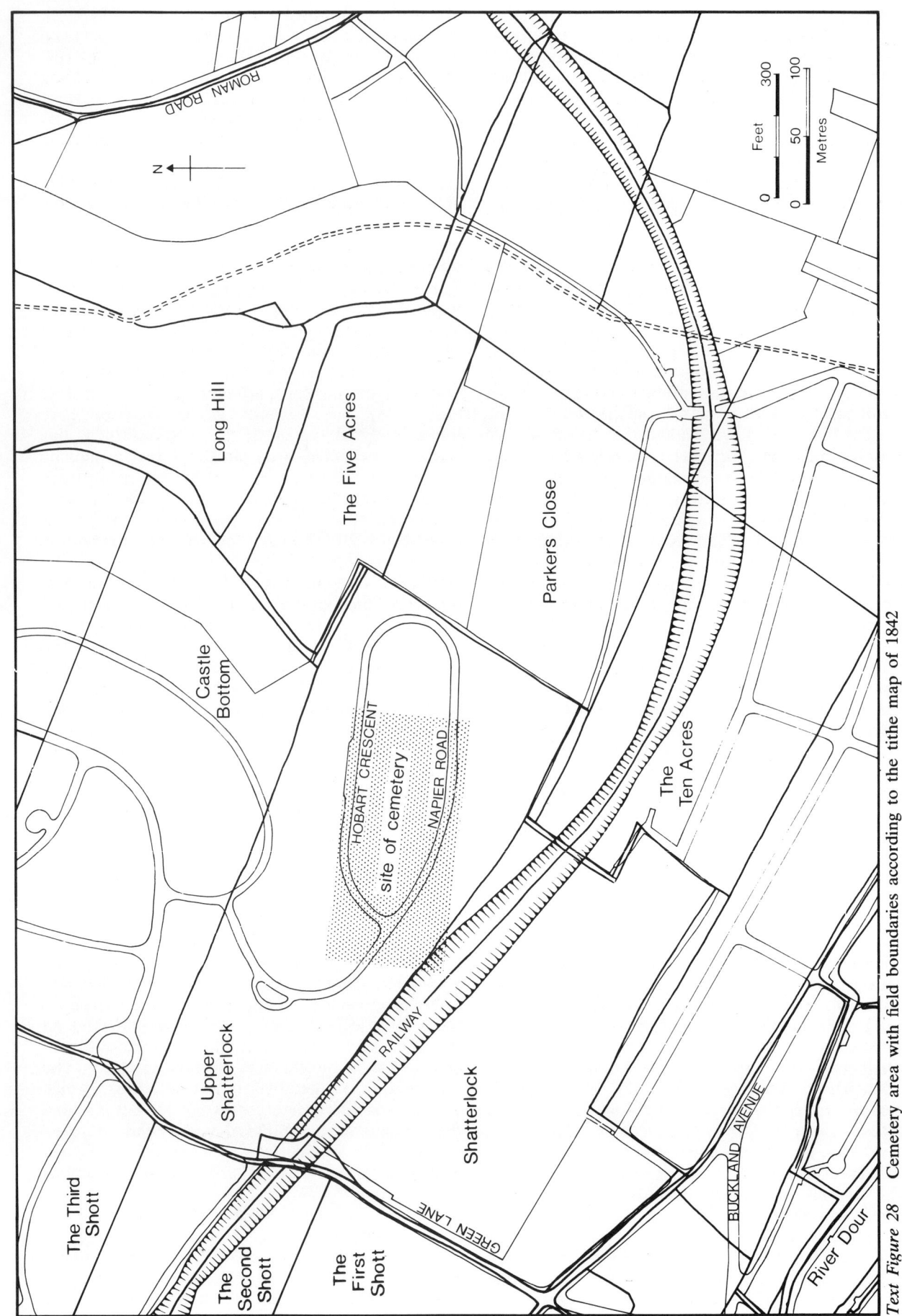

Text Figure 28   Cemetery area with field boundaries according to the tithe map of 1842

and it may constitute the northernmost edge of plot G. Of the two graves in plot K, 57 is orientated to the barrow. Grave 56 corresponds in date to graves in plots B, D and E, and so must also relate to the barrow. As to plot L, the probability of paganism is supported by the grave of the rich woman, 161, who was wearing a pin with the helmeted head presumed to be of Odin, and large flints were piled on top of her grave. The graves in plots M and N contained few grave goods, but their isolated positions would seem to set them apart from the other people.

Three graves which form the northern part of plot A demand special attention. Grave 94 is orientated in more or less the same direction as the rest of the group, although it is isolated, at an unusual distance from the rest, and not exactly in line with the two main rows. Its contents include a sword with gold on its hilt, so indicating a high rank. The space without graves surrounding it suggests that it may have been covered with a tumulus or fenced round. If the superimposed burial of an old woman was in fact the burial of a wife at her subsequent death, this marking of the grave would have facilitated identification of the original grave outline for the second interment. There are, however, two graves nearby at unique angles, 90 and 95. Grave 90 contains a man over 45 with a spear and a shield of phase 4. Grave 95 contains a woman with knife and two large iron keys. The only other comparable grave with a large key and little else is grave 164 which belongs to phase 6 or even perhaps 7, and the knife in grave 95 is type 6 which is limited to phase 6. Grave 94 was therefore positioned in impressive isolation, no doubt under a tumulus and probably in phase 2, and the two neighbouring graves with odd orientations were added much later, probably on the periphery of the tumulus. The angles of graves 90 and 95 (see below (p 156) suggest that they were not Christian, and this notion is reinforced to a certain extent by the similarity of the woman's keys to those in the pagan group of which 164 is a part. The suggestion here therefore, is that a tumulus remained as a monument to a swordbearing noble with pagan beliefs, and that at a fifty-year and a hundred-year interval pagan descendants elected to be buried in the same tumulus.

The straight line southern limit to plots A, F, H and I, with a graveless zone between them and plots D and C, indicates that there was probably a trackway leading along the side of the hill from the eastern slope to the western slope now occupied by Green Lane. This trackway would have run north of, and more or less parallel to the line shown on the 1842 tithe map of the parish of Buckland as the southern boundary of the field containing the cemetery known as Upper Shatterlock[22] (Text Figure 28). The track ran past the rectangular area in which there were no graves. An early Roman pit here, by grave 11, suggests that there may still have been traces of Roman occupation there in the Saxon period, such as the remains of a building, and there is one posthole (X) in the area. Immediately adjoining this space to the north the earliest pagan invaders of mixed race laid out their graves. This particular area and style of burial was abandoned in the sixth century, and another area of the cemetery begun.

It has been suggested that with the coming of Christianity, pagan cemetery sites in this country were completely abandoned and a new site consecrated. At Dover, however, the same cemetery continued in existence, although presumably the new areas which came into use were consecrated[23]. The prehistoric barrow, and the northern fringe of the cemetery as well, were no doubt consecrated to the pagan gods.

The opening of new graves continued to progress in a south-east direction, and the *terminus post quem* of the sceattas implies that all graves to the south-east of the area of grave 110 must belong to the late seventh – early eighth century. Although some of the graves do not contain dateable objects, therefore, they are all shown as belonging to phase 7 in Figure 107. The small number of objects in these graves and their types are in accord with an eighth century date, and the considerable number of thirty-one graves suggests use until about the middle of the century.

**Family Grouping**

Male, female and juvenile graves are scattered throughout the cemetery, but a certain amount of grouping according to sex and age can be distinguished. However, because of the overall intermingling of graves of men, women and children, the system of burial is evidently in family groups. At the beginning the head of the family can be recognised in the sword graves, and in phase 1 there is only one of these in plot A. At its foot there is a spear grave, but the rest of the burials which can be attributed to this phase are three women and three children. In the second phase there are seven women and a spear grave and no doubt some children also belong to this phase. At this time another sword grave was added to the north, which was later overlaid by a female grave. As the period covered is about a hundred years, this area probably represents one family.

In phase 3, plot B includes three sword graves, three women's graves and a teenage girl, the women and girl forming a row, with one of the men's graves ending the row and the other two men in a row to the west. Similar male and female grouping occurs in plot D (four swords) with children's graves in

---

22 In 1842 the owner of this field and an area on both sides of Green Lane to the west was the Archbishop of Canterbury. The name of the field, Upper Shatterlock, appears to mean 'an enclosed corner of land' from Old English *sceat*, *sceata* 'a corner of land, an angle, a projecting piece of land', and Old English *loc* which as a final element means 'a fold' or 'an enclosure'.

23 Meaney and Hawkes 1970, 53–5

between. The family or families were growing and were electing to be buried in separate plots, for a third set of people, or family, was now buried on or near the prehistoric barrow, a sword and a spear grave in plot K, and two women and two spear men on the barrow. The new plot F was begun with the single female grave 38.

In phase 4 the eastern part of plot B was laid down, and the rest of plot F which has an unusual juxtaposition of six male graves (one a double grave) with four swords. On the barrow three or four women, two men and a child were added, and in plot A a spearman and a woman. In phase 5 the whole of group G, and possibly J also, are contemporary, and here five women occupy the central position, while the men and children are on the outskirts. On the barrow a man and two women were added. A woman and two men with spears are in plot C. In plot H of phase 6, the male graves were strung along the northern and southern edges with graves of women and children in between. Plot L consisted of two women and two children. In phase 7 plots I, M and N are fairly evenly balanced between male, female and juvenile. Plot I, in particular, is divided into four small family groups, the male grave 80 being accompanied by two female and two juvenile graves, 120 with one female, two other adults and two children, 73 with a female, another adult and a child, but there are three women in 81, 82 and 83, accompanied by two children.

There was evidently some reason, which operated during both the pagan and Christian periods, why infants under five years of age were not buried with older children, adolescents and mature adults. In the whole cemetery there was only one child under 5, the girl in grave 21, and this burial was exceptional, because the head was placed at the east end of the grave. There must have been some very special reason which permitted departure from tradition in this sole instance. Infant mortality must have represented a considerable proportion of deaths in the Anglo-Saxon population, so that there may have been a different method of disposal, for which there is no evidence. If the infant graves were shallow and in the topsoil, however, all trace of them could have been lost. Comparison may be made with the Polhill cemetery[24], where there were no infant burials, but there were sixteen children under five years of age, out of a total of 125 burials. At Lyminge, out of 44 burials, there were only two children between 2 and 6 years, and one between 6–12 months[25]. At Finglesham in a total of 243 graves there were 23 under 5 years[26]. The evidence therefore varies at different cemeteries in the same county.

**Social Status**

To a certain extent possible pairs of high ranking male and female graves can be identified. In plot A the sword grave 22 cannot be matched by the female grave 18 above it. This latter had been partly destroyed and may have been richer than now appears, but it does belong to a much later time. Grave 23 with a Frankish brooch is nearby and accords with the Frankish connections in grave 22 of the glass and spear, but again, it is a young woman of a later phase. Grave 92 to the north also is later, but there must remain an enigma regarding the earlier grave 70 which it destroyed, and which might have contained a well-endowed spouse of grave 22. Either of graves 46 or 48 were suitably furnished, 46 a woman in her twenties with a weaving sword, and 48 a teenager with brooches. Both of these graves were nearer than 13, an old woman with brooches. The sword-bearing man in grave 94b may well be matched with the woman in her twenties nearby in grave 92, although the other young women of phase 2 further away in graves 23 and 14 were similarly wealthy.

In plot B four sword-bearing graves are ranged on the outskirts of the group, with a row of five bejewelled women in a row, and a row of lesser mortals at their feet, an old woman, a young woman without possessions, and two children. The two sword-graves, 91 and 93 are certainly in positions of prominence, as befits their rank, but the arrangement of the rest of the group, five richly endowed women side by side with subservient graves at their feet, and the other sword graves on the fringe of the cluster, creates an impression that here it was the company of five women that was all important. As with plot A, it is the rich women who dominate the area. Moreover, it is in plot B that the skeletons in the rich female graves have been pronounced as male, and two sword-bearers as female, evidence which could perhaps be regarded as supporting the impression of female dominance in this group.

In plot D destruction interferes with interpretation, but there are two rich female graves 1 and F, at the foot of the ring-sword grave C. In plot F the first two graves at the corner, side by side, are 38 a rich female, and 131 a swordsman, although they do appear to belong to different phases. The rest of the swordsmen were not buried near women. Two are close together in the destroyed part of plot D, 98 and 41, two are in grave 96 together, and 71 and 56 have spearmen for neighbours. Plot F, with its preponderance of male weapon graves, particularly with the double grave 96, could represent the fatal results of a military skirmish.

From the beginning of the existence of this cemetery, the inhabitants commanded a considerable amount of wealth. As the earlier plots, A, B, C, D, E, F, G and K appear to have been more or less fully furnished in the pagan tradition, their contents may be taken to reflect social status. With advance into the seventh century, however, it is not possible to assess how much restraint Christianity imposed on the grave contents, although it obviously had some effect.

---

24 Philp 1973a, 169
25 Warhurst 1955, 18 and 20

26 Hawkes 1976b, fig. 7

Statistical methods of analysis have been applied to cemeteries already excavated and published[27], most of them cemeteries only partially excavated and/or subjected to nineteenth-century standards of excavation and recording. In one case two methods of assessing the contents of the graves were used. In one a 'score' was given to each different type of object in a grave. In the other values were assigned to different types of object, but as a latch-lifter scored 28, a gold coin 19, and an iron ring and a sword both 16 each, this is a method which defies understanding or credibility[28]. Such methods, which are necessarily based on deficient cemetery records and which judge graves of all periods with the same yardsticks, would not appear to produce reliable data.

A method suggested by Professor Alcock[29] divides the graves into groups accorded marks of alpha, beta and gamma with possible quantifications of plus and minus. Amongst the male graves alpha signifies a sword grave, beta signifies spear graves and gamma signifies a knife grave. Amongst the female graves, gamma signifies a grave with knife, buckle and two or three beads. Alpha signifies a very rich grave with brooches and other rich objects, and the beta stratum is not so clear, but would seem to include a grave with a pair of brooches and beads. The cemeteries investigated were in the south of the country and contrasted with some in the north. Graves of the early and late periods are treated together.

The method used here is nearer to Alcock's method, although considerable advantage can here be derived from the fact that more reliable data is available, and the graves can be further examined in relation to the topographical groups of graves in the cemetery and the chronological development. It does seem possible to distinguish grades of rich, medium rich and poor, and an analysis of the grades of finds in the graves of men, women and children are given below. The divisions are as objective as possible, but there is a substantial element of subjectivity in distinguishing beween female medium rich and poor.

The male graves are divided into four types: graves which have a sword, graves with a spear but no sword, graves with grave-goods but no weapons, and graves without any kind of associated object, (Table XXIX). There are two male graves only without grave-goods, and these are in the later plots I and N. No male graves in plots A, B, C and D were without weapons and the two graves without weapons in the other two earlier groups, 52, plot E and 136, plot F belonged to old men who were presumably beyond their weapon-carrying time of life.

Grave 64, plot E, contained only a knife, but as this was 24cm long it might be considered as a weapon. The ages of the bodies in the findless graves 73, plot I and 165, plot N are not known, but the man in grave 165 had a healed fracture of the right wrist and may not have been able to wield a weapon.

Six other men without weapons were in the older age bracket. The age of nine others is not known, but two in plot I were of military age, one (80) was between 18–25 and one (103) between 30–45.

TABLE XXIX MALE GRAVES CLASSED ACCORDING TO GRAVE GOODS

| Plot | Sword | Spear only | Weaponless | Findless |
|---|---|---|---|---|
| A | 22<br>94b | 50<br>87<br>90 | | |
| B | 27<br>33<br>91<br>93 + seax | | | |
| C | | 8<br>9<br>10 | | |
| D | C<br>4<br>41<br>98<br>Unass.7<br>Unass.8 | 5 | | |
| E | seax<br>knife 24cm | 61<br>63<br>65 | 52<br>64 | |
| F | 71<br>96a<br>96b<br>131 | 39<br>135 | 136 | |
| G | | 128<br>156 | | |
| H | | 114 | 104<br>106<br>111<br>125<br>144<br>148<br>149<br>150<br>158 | |
| I | | | 80<br>103<br>120 | 73 |
| J | | | 36 | |
| K | 56 | 57 | | |
| N | | | 145<br>146 | 165 |

The following disturbed graves are excluded: D, 3, 7, 64, 69, 152.

27 Arnold 1980, 81–142
28 Ibid, table 4.5
29 Alcock 1981

### TABLE XXX  FEMALE GRAVES CLASSED ACCORDING TO GRAVE GOODS

| Plot | Rich with brooch | Rich without brooch | Medium Rich | Poor | Findless |
|---|---|---|---|---|---|
| A | 13<br>14<br>23<br>92 | | 15<br>28<br>46 | 12<br>95 | |
| B | 29<br>30<br>32<br>126 | | 42<br>44 | | 25 |
| C | | 6 | | | |
| D | F<br>1 | | 132 | 115<br>116<br>130 | |
| E | 59 | 67 | 53<br>60<br>62<br>66 | 54<br>58 | |
| F | 38 | | | | |
| G | | 129<br>134<br>155<br>157 | 133 | | |
| H | | 110<br>160 | 107<br>113<br>124<br>138<br>141 | 121<br>142<br>147 | 112 |
| I | | | 75<br>83<br>127 | 81<br>82<br>84<br>100<br>101 | 99 |
| J | | | | 37 | |
| L | | 161 | | 164 | |
| N | | | | | 68 |

The following disturbed graves are excluded: B, 11, 18, 26, 49, 94a.

### TABLE XXXI  JUVENILE GRAVES CLASSED ACCORDING TO GRAVE-GOODS

| Plot | Rich with brooches | Medium rich | Poor | Findless |
|---|---|---|---|---|
| A | 20 F<br>48 F | 21 F | 16<br>17 | 89 |
| B | 35 F | 43 | 34 | |
| C | | | | 24 |
| D | | 122 F<br>123 | | 2 |
| E | | 55 F | | |
| G | | 137 M<br>139 M | | |
| H | | | 40<br>105<br>108<br>119<br>140<br>143<br>159 | 118 |
| I | | | 74 ?F<br>76 F<br>78<br>85<br>117 | |
| L | | | 162 M<br>163 | |
| M | | | | 153<br>154 |

### TABLE XXXII  UNSEXED ADULT GRAVES CLASSED ACCORDING TO GRAVE-GOODS

| Plot | Bone report | Knife | Other finds | Disturbed | Findless |
|---|---|---|---|---|---|
| A | | | br. plates | 19<br>70<br>88 | 45 |
| B | | | | 31<br>47 | |
| C | | | | 7 | E |
| D | 20–30 | | 130 | | |
| F | | | 97 | | |

| Plot | Bone report | Knife | Other finds | Disturbed | Findless |
|---|---|---|---|---|---|
| H | Adult | | | | 102 |
| | Adult or ju. | 109 | iron ring pottery bottle | | |
| I | Young adult or adolescent | | | | 72 |
| | Adult or sub-adult | 77 | | | |
| | Adult or sub-adult | 79 | iron frag. | 86 | |
| N | Adult, sub-adult or ju. | | | | 151 |

The female graves are divided into rich graves with at least one brooch, rich graves without brooches, medium rich graves, poor graves and findless graves. The poor graves are those which contain a knife and/or keys and little else (Table XXX). The rich graves with brooches are in the earlier plots, and the rich graves without brooches must represent a corresponding rank in the later plots. As this grade is scarce in plot H, however, and absent in I and J, the corresponding rank in the latest phase must be represented by even less well furnished graves. Some are presumably to be found in the latest phase among the medium rich graves which appear in most groups. Poor graves occur in most groups, but there are more of them in plot I which has no rich graves. Only four female graves were findless, and, although the bone report is not definite on this point, the indications are that two of the occupants, 99 and 112, were fairly old. Of the other two, grave 25 was at the foot of the row of rich women, and 68 was the grave of a young woman in an isolated position.

As may be seen from Table XXXI, a higher proportion of children's graves were findless, (six). There are three rich female juvenile graves in plots A and B, all with brooches. The richest grave, 20, belonged to the youngest child, under six years. Four graves in the earlier plots, consisting of two male and two female, were medium rich, but the majority, nineteen, were poorly furnished. Of these seven had a knife only. Seven other graves had a knife and one or two other objects. Two small boys had two knives each, 137 and 162, the latter grave also containing whetstones. Knives, therefore, must have been important for boys, and it is interesting that the young prince buried under Cologne Cathedral had four in his grave[30]. Two of the pottery bottles were with boys, and three of the boxes and two spindle whorls with girls.

The interpretation of the social status on the basis of grave contents suggests that the rich graves in the earlier groups belong to the eorl or noble. In Wessex the equivalent rank of a *gesithcund man* carried a wergild six times as large as that of a ceorl, a freeman, but in Kent the ceorl's wergild was much larger in proportion so that the eorl's wergild was only three times as large[31]. Consequently there was not such a wide gap between the wergilds of the ceorl and eorl in Kent. If a parallel can be drawn between a wergild and grave furniture, this is borne out by the contents of the spear or medium rich male graves, such as 50, 87, 90 which usually contain other possessions such as a knife and shield or buckle, and which presumably represent the ceorl. Apart from the sword in the sword graves the difference in the contents of these two types of grave is often not very great.

A similar state of relative wealth is to be seen in the women's graves, the rich graves with brooch matching the sword graves, followed later by the rich graves without brooch matching spear graves in later groups. The medium rich and poor female graves must match the rest of the spear and weaponless graves in status. The poor female graves might represent poor relations in the free class, but not slaves, for most contain keys, and these may be taken to indicate the possession of precious articles normally locked up and not committed to the grave.

As the women's graves are more fully furnished than the men's graves in all periods, some opportunity is provided for establishing the status of a man by comparison with the contents of a nearby female grave which might have belonged to his partner in life. Grave 6 belonged to a woman without a brooch, but well-endowed with beads and garnet pendant, cowrie shell, spindle whorl, glass vessel, etc, and next to her was a man's grave, 10, with a spear, knife and pin. Two other spearmen's graves nearby were similarly furnished. Another rich woman without a brooch was in grave 67, next to a man's grave 65, with spear and seax. However, she was buried in a later phase, and there is a woman of less wealth in 66 nearby. Other women's graves of rich type were 129, 134, 155 and 157 in plot G, where two nearby male graves, 128 and 156 contained spear, knife and buckle, and 156 also contained a pot, tweezers and strapends. The spear in 156 was a superior type with inlaid decoration on the socket.

Two other women of this type were buried in plot H, one being grave 110 which had a male grave on either side, 111 and 125, both without weapons, and little or nothing else beside a knife. The woman in grave 160 with glass vessel, garnet pendant, silver pin etc was next to the male grave 150 which contained only a knife, wooden cup, pin and lace-tag. Only one grave in plot H, 114, contained a spear, but as it also seems to have contained a lyre, the man was presumably of high rank. Equidistant from this grave was 121 with only a knife and key link, and 113 another female grave with bronze

---

30  Doppelfeld 1964, 164–7, figs. 6 and 7, Taf. 40,1

31  Stenton 1947, 300

buckle and belt mount, knife and keys, so that 113 is more likely to have been the mate although 121 is noted as a deep grave. From this evidence it seems possible to conclude that the highest ranking woman in phases 5 and 6 was buried with necklace, pendants, glass vessel and other possessions, but that in phase 5 her husband would have been buried with little more than a spear, buckle and knife, and in phase 6 even the spear would normally be missing.

Other possible couples indicated by medium rich women's graves in plots H and I are: 107 or 124 matched with 106 knife only, 141 matched with 149 knife, two buckles and an awl and 127 matched with 73 no finds. Grave 124 is noted below as one of the deep graves. Two graves classified on the bone evidence as female juvenile 12–18 years old were rich with brooches, and the occupant may have been old enough to be a spouse to a nearby swordsman, 48 with 22 in plot A as noted above, and 35 with 91 in plot B. Judging from the consistent diminution in the grave goods in accordance with the passing of the phases, it seems that in phases 5 to 7 the highest rank was probably signified by the medium rich women's graves and men's graves with a knife and only one or two other objects or none at all.

Of the children's graves, a number are without grave goods, and only two are rich graves. As in the adult graves some are medium well furnished but most are poor. The well-furnished graves all belong to the early phases, and very little or nothing was placed in children's graves in the later phases.

Plot A therefore represents a rich family or families in phases 1 and 2. In phase 3 similar rich people were buried in plots B, D and E, in phase 4 in plot F, and in phase 5 in plots C, E and G. By phase 6 most burials were in plot H and included some rich and medium rich women and in phase 7 in plot I there are still some medium rich women. Christianity might have been the reason for W–E burial in plot A but the graves became larger and more regularly spaced in plot B under Ethelbert. After this phase the custom of burial of grave goods with the body gradually diminishes, but as the cemetery continued to spread in the fashion already begun, the men and women buried in poorly furnished or findless graves of the later phases must have been descendants of these rich families, and the lack of grave goods must reflect the influence of Christian custom rather than a change in their social status.

Apparently the same fairly rapid cessation of grave goods happened at Finglesham also, but there the interpretation put on it by the excavator is that the noble family moved away, leaving a lesser family in charge[32]. From the initial information available, it appears that, as at Dover, there is an absence of late swords and shields, late brooches and gold and garnet-set pendants. At Dover this seems to be the result of the early effect of Christianity rather than a change in the status of the resident families.

The number of undisturbed, unfurnished graves is surprisingly small. Apart from the six juvenile graves, there is one each in plots A, B and D (45, 25, E), two in H (102, 112), three in plot I (72, 73, 99) and three in plot N (68, 151, 165). This means that in the period when lavish grave goods were customary there were only three findless graves (in plots A, B and D). Of these grave 45 was outside the main cluster in plot A at the foot of the well-furnished graves, and grave 25 was at the feet of the row of rich women, both likely positions for slaves. Grave E was near a sword grave. The conclusion suggests itself that, with these possible exceptions, no slaves were buried in this cemetery. As most of the slave population in the later part of this period and in this county was no doubt British, a completely separate cemetery must have been in contemporary use.

**Depths of Graves**

Most of the graves were dug to depths in the chalk between 20 and 60cm (Table XXXIII, Figure 108). In the juvenile graves practically all were between these figures. In the male graves three were shallower, of which the shallowness of 98 was partly artificial due to surface skimming by machine. The deepest sword grave was 22, and 94b was also quite deep, nearly 55cm, both being overlaid by a female grave.

In the female graves the concentration is again in the 20 to 60cm bracket, but there are more shallow graves, particularly amongst those poorly furnished. The unsexed graves are almost all within the 20 to 60cm limits.

In her study of the Sewerby, Yorkshire, cemetery[33] Hirst compared depth of grave with number of objects in the grave, and concluded that 'some limited support can be given to the hypothesis that energy expended on grave digging is related to the status of the dead person, if the number of types of grave-goods is treated as an indicator of status.' There is little support for this point of view at Dover, where the main aim of the grave diggers seems to be a standard depth between 20 and 60cm. It is unfortunate that a relationship between depth and status cannot be established at this cemetery for it would have been a useful element in detecting status in the poorly-furnished late graves.

Consideration of the plan of the cemetery and the contents of the graves shows that no simple correlation can be found between the dimensions of the grave and the status of the individual. The dimensions of the graves obviously vary in this cemetery with the extension of the cemetery and the passing of time, and are probably mainly affected in plot A by the constrictions of the area available, and in plot I by current religion or custom.

A few rich graves are amongst the deepest, 1, 30 and 32. So, too, are 121, poor and 124, medium rich,

---

32  Hawkes 1976b, 36–7

33  Hirst 1980, 248, fig. 14. 5b

## TABLE XXXIII  DEPTH OF GRAVES IN RELATION TO CONTENTS

### MALE

| | 0 | 5 | 10 | 15 | 20 | 25 | 30 | 35 | 40 | 45 | 50 | 55 | 60 | 65 | 70 | 75 | 80 |
|---|---|---|---|---|---|---|---|---|---|---|---|---|---|---|---|---|---|
| Sword | | | 98 | | C 131 | 91 | 93 | 71 | 33 41 96 | 27 | 4 | 56 94b | | | | | |
| Spear only | | | 50 | | | 128 135 | 156 | 61 | 5 | 65 87 | 39 90 | 114 | 10 57 | 8 | 9 22 | | |
| Weaponless | | | | | | 80 52 104 111 106 | 136 | 146 148 | 36 | 103 125 149 145 | 120 144 | | 150 158 | | | | |
| Findless | | | | 73 | | | | | | | 165 | | | | | | |
| Disturbed | | | | | | 64 69 | | 152 | | | | | 3 | | | | |
| Depth in cm | 0 | 5 | 10 | 15 | 20 | 25 | 30 | 35 | 40 | 45 | 50 | 55 | 60 | 65 | 70 | 75 | 80 |

### FEMALE

| | 0 | 5 | 10 | 15 | 20 | 25 | 30 | 35 | 40 | 45 | 50 | 55 | 60 | 65 | 70 | 75 | 80 |
|---|---|---|---|---|---|---|---|---|---|---|---|---|---|---|---|---|---|
| Rich with brooch | | | | 14 38 | | F 92 59 | 13 | | | 23 29 | | 30 | | | 1 32 | | |
| Rich without brooch | 129 | | | | | | | | | 67 110 | | | | | | 6 | |
| Medium rich | | 107 | | | | 127 | | 155 161 | 160 | 53 | | 66 141 | | | | | |
| Poor | 95 | 37 116 | | 115 | 101 | 58 | 54 81 62 82 | 60 75 132 | 12 164 | 42 | 100 | 142 | 83 13 133 138 | 124 | | 121 | |
| Findless | | | | 28 44 | | | 68 | | 25 | 112 | | | 147 | | | | |
| Disturbed | | 49 | | | | 94a | | 11 | | B | | | 99 | | | | |
| Depth in cm | 0 | 5 | 10 | 15 | 20 | 25 | 30 | 35 | 40 | 45 | 50 | 55 | 60 | 65 | 70 | 75 | 80 |

### JUVENILE

| | 0 | 5 | 10 | 15 | 20 | 25 | 30 | 35 | 40 | 45 | 50 | 55 | 60 | 65 | 70 | 75 | 80 |
|---|---|---|---|---|---|---|---|---|---|---|---|---|---|---|---|---|---|
| Rich with brooch | | | | | | 20 48 | | | | | | 35 | | | | | |
| Medium rich | | | | | | 137 139 | | 55 | | 21 | | | | | | | |
| Poor | | | | | 16 122 | 40 123 | | 17 78 105 | 163 143 | 34 | 85 | 76 | | | | | |
| Findless | | | | | | 118 | | 2 | | | | | | | | | |
| Disturbed | | | | | 153 154 | 89 | D | | | | | | | | | | |
| Depth in cm | 0 | 5 | 10 | 15 | 20 | 25 | 30 | 35 | 40 | 45 | 50 | 55 | 60 | 65 | 70 | 75 | 80 |

### UNSEXED ADULT

| | 0 | 5 | 10 | 15 | 20 | 25 | 30 | 35 | 40 | 45 | 50 | 55 | 60 | 65 | 70 | 75 | 80 |
|---|---|---|---|---|---|---|---|---|---|---|---|---|---|---|---|---|---|
| Knife | | | | 130 | | | | 97 | | 77 109 | | | | | | | |
| Other finds | | | | | | | 79 | | | 109 | | | | | | | |
| Findless | | | 72 | 45 102 | | | E | | | 151 | | | | | | | |
| Disturbed | | | | | | | | | 88 | | | | | | | | |
| Depth in cm | 0 | 5 | 10 | 15 | 20 | 25 | 30 | 35 | 40 | 45 | 50 | 55 | 60 | 65 | 70 | 75 | 80 |

but as these two graves belong to phases 6 and 7 their depth and the space surrounding them may indicate high status in the period of less grave furniture. As noted above, the nearest male grave to 124 is 106, small and fairly deep with only a knife. The nearest male grave to 121 is 114 which is also small and fairly deep and more distinguished, with a knife, spear and the lyre. These are therefore probable coupled high-ranking graves of phases 6 and 7. The deep graves 8 and 9 are spear graves, but there is indication that the occupant of 8 may have had special status. On the other hand the shallowest graves occur sporadically from west to east of the cemetery, and include sword graves C and 98, rich graves with brooch 14 and 38, rich without brooch 129 and findless graves 72 and 73.

In reckoning the amount of energy expended on the digging of a grave the depth is not the only element to be considered. Length and breadth are also of potential significance, and energy expended would be more accurately assessed by calculating the volume of earth or rock removed. The comparative hardness of rock chalk, softer chalk and clay would also have been important at Dover, and of sand and gravel on other sites. Even so, other factors interfere with the validity of such mechanical results, for length and width and possibly depth are often controlled by the fact, for instance, that the occupant is a child, and a smaller grave is dug apparently without reference to class. A child, however, is not always given an extra small grave, and there are no doubt other unknown factors which play a part. The calculation of the volume of each grave has therefore not been carried out as it seems to be a fruitless exercise.

**Cemetery Layout and Orientation**

The graves in plots A, B and D appear not to be related in any way to the prehistoric barrow, their orientation and grouping being apparently governed by the adjoining rectangular space which was possibly occupied by a building (Figure 2). These graves belong to phases 1 and 2, continuing into phases 3 and 4. In phase 3, however, when the new major series of graves following the orientation of plots A, B and D was begun by the corner grave 38 of plot F, other burials with different orientations began on and near the barrow. The prehistoric barrow therefore has visible influence on the position, and also on the orientation, of this group of the graves. The earliest grave surviving in plot E (61) could be a little earlier than phase 3 to which it is attributed, but the latest graves in this plot are on the south-east border of the barrow, so that the spread in this vicinity was south-eastwards, and some of the earliest graves could have been placed near the centre of the barrow in the overburden of earth which had been eroded by the twentieth century. The buckle with unusual rivets in grave 61 matches one in grave 18 in plot A, so indicating that burials on the barrow may have started as early as the end of phase 2, and it is, of course, possible that some of the eradicated central graves might have been as early as phase 1. Most of the graves are lying in the roughly W–E direction normal on this site, but the angle is with the head slightly more to the north than the other graves. At first glance the layout seems to indicate division into two groups. The northern group consists of four graves with widely differing orientations, 59 (168°), 60 (81°), 61 (106°), and 63 (72.5°) (Figure 109). The grave which overlies 59, grave 58 (111°), should also be included, and possibly also 62 (104.5°) which is nearer in position to the southern group but with an orientation nearly identical to that of 61. The southern group consists of eight graves, all of almost identical orientation: 52 (123°), 53 (134°), 54 (137°), 55 (133°), 64 (141°), 65 (134°), 66 (141°) and 67 (142°). One of these graves (65) points directly to the centre of the barrow, and as it is a male grave with a seax, spear and Frankish buckle, and is one of the earliest in the group, it is likely to have been the first and major interment of these eight graves. The rest are more or less parallel to grave 65, and this may be regarded as being the main attraction, so that they have only a general orientation to the barrow rather than directly to the centre point.

Other points within the site which might have attracted orientation are few. The posthole Z, (diameter 50.8cm, depth 12.7cm, and lined with flints) at the south-eastern end of the cemetery is in direct line with the axis of grave 73 and also in the middle of the group 72, 73, 86, 127 so that it could have served as a marker for that group. The posthole Y to the east of grave 121, is not aligned with that grave, however, and has no immediately obvious purpose. It was of considerable size, with a maximum diameter of 45.7cm and a depth of 25.4cm. It is some distance from the nearest grave 121, and is not in line with its axis. A line drawn from posthole X to posthole Z could be regarded as forming a southern boundary to plots F, H and I. It does not lie at a uniform distance from the graves as does the line which has already been suggested for the track, but it does run to the south of all the graves except 77 and 81, and three other graves are to the south, three graves which are out of alignment with the rows of graves in plot I, 80, 79 and 86 (Figure 110).

If a line is drawn from posthole Y to the middle of the barrow (CC) and extended from the posthole south-eastwards through the rest of the graves, the resultant line appears to have significance and it is only 3° from true north. It does not pass through any grave, as almost any other line drawn radially from the centre of the barrow would do. The nearest graves to it on each side are at a fairly uniform, respectful distance and more or less at right angles to it, i.e. 145, 146, 162, 161, 121, 102, 101, 117, 100 and 99. Moreover, it exactly divides the widely spaced, larger, broader graves of plot H from the smaller, slot graves in rows of plot I. The centre of the barrow (CC) may well have been marked by a post in Anglo-Saxon times, as was the centre of the prehistoric western ring-ditch and eastern ring-ditch at Yeavering, both used for burial in this period[34]. This line could therefore represent the line of a boundary fence or other limiting mark dividing one section of the cemetery from another. It also seems feasible that another line could have run south-eastwards from posthole Y, parallel to the track, as this defines the northern limit of plot I, (Figure 110). Plot I is considered to be Christian on the evidence available, while plot E on the barrow, and plot L have been judged to be pagan, and dividing fences in these positions would have separated the Christian from the pagan burials in this part of the cemetery.

If the line defining the northern limit of plot I is extended from posthole Y westwards it crosses one grave, 141, which lies nearly in the same orientation, and graves 130 and 128 are close to and aligned with it. This, therefore, constitutes another possible division, although differences between the graves on each side of it are not so strongly marked as graves in other divisions. There is, in fact, what appears to be another kind of division just south of this line, a long, angled space between graves suitable for a track or wide pathway leading from between graves 128 and 131 at its western end, and 80 and 101 at the eastern end (Figure 110). Pathways are, of course, an essential part of cemeteries[35]. It may well be that although they are so near to each other, both the limiting line and the path existed at the same time, for only three graves lie in the space between them, and these are of little account, i.e. 118 a child with no possessions, 121 a woman over 45 with knife and ?key, and 125 a man over 45 with knife only.

As to differences between the graves on each side of the line westwards from Y, most of the graves in the middle on the northern side are arranged nearly in a circle with varied orientations: 158, 159, 160, 150, 149, 140, 147. Further, one type of object appears only south of the division and not to the north: wooden boxes with iron fittings in graves 143 and 124 (figure 94).

There is a probability that posthole X also was a single standard post and not part of a building. It was 22.8cm wide and 22.8cm deep, a similar depth to posthole Y. A line drawn between the centre of the barrow and posthole X does pass through one grave (137). However, orientation of some of the graves shows that there is a possibility that the line performs the same sort of function as the other line from Y to the barrow. Graves 27 and 42 of plot B are orientated at 121° and 126°, and graves 156 and 157 of plot G are similarly orientated at 126.5° and 125°, both being in the prevalent W–E direction. The graves between, in plots G and J which are contained between the posthole-X to centre-barrow (CC) line and a projection of the limiting eastern boundary of the unoccupied space by graves 38 and 131, are all orientated either directly to the barrow or much more closely in that direction than the graves in plots B and G adjacent to the north-west and south-east, except for grave 128. Grave 137 is crossed by the line, and grave 57 lies exactly parallel to it on its north-western side.

These barrow-orientated graves constitute plot J and part of plot G, i.e. graves 133, 134, 155, 132, 129, 139, 36, 37, 69, which are all between 87° and 106°. Graves 137 and 57 are also within these limits. Their general difference of position and orientation shows that they were different in some way from the Christians in plot B and from graves in plots F, H and the rest of G. It must be noticed that some of the graves in plots F, H and I have a similar orientation (e.g. 97, 118, 147, 82, 99) but these are isolated instances, not grouped together, and in consequence of their more south-easterly situations their axes do not point to the barrow.

The line drawn from the centre of the barrow to posthole X also focuses attention on the important and isolated positions of graves 38 and 131, a rich young woman and a swordsman, in this corner spot at the beginning of a new section of the cemetery. A border line from the centre of the barrow to posthole X would provide a rational justification for the peculiar orientation of the graves in the triangle on its northern side as opposed to those in the south. Further substance can be added to the existence of this line if it is extended westwards beyond posthole X across the destroyed area, for it skirts grave 11 and marks the limit of the cemetery just to the west of graves 5, 122 and D, which are all placed more or less equidistant from it. Graves 131, 156 and 56 further north are placed in a similar relationship to this line and at similar angles (128°, 126.5° and 131°). Projected still further, in the opposite direction from the centre of the barrow, this line divides two groups of graves in plot E. There does not seem to be any significance in projecting a line from CC to posthole Z, for such a line would intersect grave 164, and, although it is nearly at the east limit of the plot I graves, there are three to the east of it. However, a line projected from CC just to the east of these three graves, 72, 73 and 127, would also clear grave 164.

Some confirmation that these lines were carefully and precisely laid out may be inferred from the angles between them. The angle between the lines from X and Y to CC is about 76°, and so is the angle between the projection of the X–CC line and a line from CC to the end of plot I and the cemetery by grave 73. The function of post Z is discussed below.

As the line Y–CC is very nearly due N–S in direction, it should be considered whether any other N–S divisions were used in the Dover cemetery. Two are, in fact, possible, one dividing plot A from plot B and plot C from plot F on one side, and another dividing plots A and C from plot D on the other side (Figure 110). These must remain conjectural, however, as another line might appear to be equally reasonable: one running ENE from post X dividing plot A from plot B and continuing southwards, to skirt the west side of plot C.

The other graves nearest the periphery of the barrow do not point towards it, 56, 145, 146, 161, 162, 163, 164. However, they might be regarded as running roughly concentrically with the circum-

---

34 Hope-Taylor 1977, 112ff, figs 41, 50, 51, 52 and 83ff, fig.26      35  Rahtz 1978, 11

ference of the barrow. The respect shown by Anglo-Saxons for prehistoric barrows in burial ritual has long been known as they frequently dug their graves into an existing barrow[36]. For instance, Anglo-Saxon inhumations of the seventh century were placed to the north and east, and presumably originally also in the middle of a prehistoric barrow at Holborough, Kent[37], where the orientation of the graves, except for one infant, was more or less consistently W–E with little variation, quite uninfluenced by the relative position of the centre of the barrow.

Further light has been shed on this Anglo-Saxon custom by the evidence at Yeavering which shows that a tall post (BX) was erected at the centre of a ditched bowl barrow, probably between AD 300 and 500, and this post was used with post AX for the bearing of the axis of some graves (AX and BX1), and also for the middle axis of the great hall[38]. At the western end of the same site a post placed near the centre of a prehistoric stone circle provided a focal point for radially-set graves[39]. As the excavator points out, these practices must have been sanctioned by both the British and Anglo-Saxon inhabitants in the settlement. In addition to the alignment of the great hall with post BX, it is likely that points in the western part of the site were also established in relation to this line, i.e. posts D and E, and consequently, buildings D2 and E. Apart from the surveying practice of sighting in a straight line, the compass principle was used in the construction of the amphitheatre type of building[40]. In much the same way the layout of the cemetery at Dover also shows a sighting from two posts X and Y to the centre of a ring ditch to establish boundaries, a sighting from post Z to a second tumulus, (see below) and also a probable reference to the compass principle for the positioning and orientation of some of the graves surrounding the barrow. If some graves on the barrow have been obliterated, evidence regarding phases 1 and 2 in this area which might have existed, will have been lost. Otherwise, as matters stand, phases 1 and 2 are represented only by the severely confined plot A, and in phase 3 the beginning of the burial on the barrow and the setting out of the rest of the cemetery radiating from this centre point must be contemporary.

TABLE XXXIV  DOVER: ORIENTATIONS, CORRECT TO TRUE NORTH

| | MALE | | | | FEMALE | | |
|---|---|---|---|---|---|---|---|
| Grave No. | Orientation | Grave No. | Orientation | Grave No. | Orientation | Grave No. | Orientation |
| C | 131° | 91 | 116° | B | 109° | 81 | 138.5° |
| 3 | 113° | 93 | 117.5° | F | 107.5° | 82 | 74.5° |
| 4 | 129.5° | 94b | 118° | 1 | 113° | 83 | 93.5° |
| 5 | 122° | 96a+b | uncertain | 6 | 123.5° | 92 | 137.5° |
| 8 | 100.5° | 98 | 124° | 11 | 99.5° | 94a | 118° |
| 9 | 104° | 103 | 118° | 12 | 109.5° | 95 | 165.5° |
| 10 | 112° | 104 | 105.5° | 13 | 114.5° | 99 | 85.5° |
| 22 | 105.5° | 106 | 106° | 14 | 114° | 100 | 94.5° |
| 27 | 121° | 111 | 118° | 15 | 106.5° | 101 | 110.5° |
| 33 | 114.5° | 114 | 106° | 18 | 128° | 107 | 135° |
| * 36 | 94.5° | 120 | 109° | 23 | 118° | 110 | 104.5° |
| 39 | 133° | 125 | 102° | 25 | 124° | 112 | 108.5° |
| 41 | 118.5° | 128 | 119.5° | 28 | 118° | 113 | 117.5° |
| 50 | 122.5° | 131 | 128° | 29 | 115.5° | 115 | 120° |
| * 52 | 123° | 135 | 126° | 30 | 120° | 116 | 125° |
| * 56 | 131° | 136 | 110° | 32 | 121.5° | 121 | 99.5° |
| * 57 | 84° | 144 | 122.5° | * 37 | 94° | 124 | 106° |
| * 61 | 106° | * 145 | 106° | 38 | 116° | 126 | uncertain |
| * 63 | 72.5° | * 146 | 89° | 42 | 126° | 127 | 112° |
| * 64 | 141° | 148 | 107.5° | 44 | 125° | * 129 | 106° |
| * 65 | 134° | 149 | 126.5° | 46 | 112.5° | * 132 | 87° |
| * 69 | 101° | 150 | 114.5° | 49 | 117.5° | * 133 | 102° |
| 71 | 127° | * 152 | 117° | * 53 | 134° | * 134 | 105.5° |
| 73 | 95° | 156 | 126.5° | * 54 | 137° | 138 | 125° |
| 80 | 105.5° | 158 | 123.5° | * 58 | 111° | 141 | 107.5° |
| 87 | 107.5° | * 165 | 95° | * 59 | 168° | 142 | 113° |
| 90 | 53° | | | * 60 | 81° | 147 | 89° |
| | | | | * 62 | 104.5° | * 155 | 98° |
| | | | | * 66 | 141° | 157 | 125° |
| | | | | * 67 | 142° | 160 | 105° |
| | | | | * 68 | 104° | * 161 | 105° |
| | | | | 75 | 112.5° | * 164 | 89.5° |

\* Graves influenced by the barrow

36  Brown 1915 III, 132–5
37  Evison 1956, fig.3
38  Hope-Taylor 1977, figs. 62, 63
39  Ibid, 108ff, fig. 50
40  Ibid, fig. 63

## DISCUSSION

TABLE XXXV  DOVER: ORIENTATIONS, CORRECT TO TRUE NORTH

| | JUVENILE | | | UNKNOWN SEX | |
|---|---|---|---|---|---|
| Grave No. | Orientation | Grave No. | Orientation | Grave No. | Orientation |
| D | 130° | 89 | 115° | E | 123.5° |
| 2 | 93° | 105 | 107° | 7 | 104° |
| 16 | 120° | 108 | 107.5° | 19 | 123° |
| 17 | 123° | 117 | 96.5° | 26 | uncertain |
| 20 | 124° | 118 | 79.5° | 31 | destroyed |
| 21 | 290° | 119 | 97.5° | 45 | 122.5° |
| 24 | 105.5° | 122 | 127° | 47 | 146° |
| 34 | 104.5° | 123 | 127.5° | 51 | destroyed |
| 35 | 123.5° | * 137 | 104° | 70 | disturbed |
| 40 | 111° | * 139 | 92° | 72 | 96° |
| 43 | 108.5° | 140 | 99° | 77 | 119° |
| 48 | 121.5° | 143 | 119° | 79 | 120° |
| * 55 | 133° | 153 | 70° | 86 | 108° |
| 74 | 109° | 154 | 63° | 88 | 107° |
| 76 | 119° | 159 | 100° | 97 | 96.5° |
| 78 | 110° | 162 | 95° | 102 | 96.5° |
| 84 | 102° | 163 | 88° | 109 | 122.5° |
| 85 | 100° | | | 130 | 114.5° |
| | | | | * 151 | 104° |

*Graves influenced by the barrow

TABLE XXXVI  DOVER: ORIENTATIONS, CORRECT TO TRUE NORTH IN ORIENTATION ORDER

| Orientation | Grave No. | Orientation | Grave No. | Orientation | Grave No. |
|---|---|---|---|---|---|
| 53° | 90  Solstice | 107.5° | F,87,108,141,148 | 129.5° | 4 |
| | | 108° | 86 | 130° | D |
| 63° | 154* | 108.5° | 43,112 | 131° | C,56* |
| 70° | 153* | 109° | B,74,120 | 133° | 39,55* |
| 72.5° | 63* | 109.5° | 12 | 134° | 53*,65* |
| 74.5° | 82 | 110° | 78,136 | 135° | 107 |
| 79.5° | 118 | 110.5° | 101 | 137° | 54* |
| 81° | 60* | 111° | 40,58* | 137.5° | 92 |
| 84° | 57* | 112° | 10,127 | 138.5° | 81 |
| 85.5° | 99 | 112.5° | 46,75 | 141° | 64*,66* |
| 87° | 132* | 113° | 1,3,142 | 142° | 67 |
| 88° | 163* | 114° | 14 | 146° | 47 |
| 89° | 146*,147 | 114.5° | 13,33,130,150 | 165.5° | 95 |
| 89.5° | 164* | 115° | 89 | 168° | 59* |
| 92° | 139* | 115.5° | 29 | 290° | 21 |
| 93° | 2 | 116° | 38,91 | Orientation | 31,51,70,96a, |
| 93.5° | 83 | 117° | 152 | unknown | 96b,126 |
| 94° | 37* | 117.5° | 49,93,113 | | |
| 94.5° | 36*,100 | 118° | 23,28,94a,94b,103,111 | | |
| 95° | 73,162*,165* | 118.5° | 41 | | |
| 96° | 72 | 119° | 76,77,143 | | |
| 96.5° | 97,102,117 | 119.5° | 128 | | |
| 97.5° | 119 | 120° | 16,30,79,115 | | |
| 98° | 155* | 121° | 27 | | |
| 99° | 140 | 121.5° | 32,48 | | |
| 99.5° | 11,121 | 122° | 5 | | |
| 100° | 85,159 | 122.5° | 45,50,109,144 | | |
| 100.5° | 8 | 123° | 17,19,52* | | |
| 101° | 69 | 123.5° | E,6,35,158 | | |
| 102° | 84,125,133* | 124° | 20,25,98 | | |
| 104° | 7,9,68*,137*,151* | 125° | 44,116,138,157 | | |
| 104.5° | 34,62*,110 | 126° | 42,135 | | |
| 105° | 160*,161* | 126.5° | 149,156 | | |
| 105.5° | 22,24,80,104,134* | 127° | 71,122 | | |
| 106° | 61*,106,114,124 129*,145* | 127.5° | 123 | | |
| | | 128° | 18,131  Solstice | | |
| 106.5° | 15 | | | | |
| 107° | 88,105 | | | | |

* Graves influenced by the barrow

Interpretation of the archaeological evidence at Dover to indicate the use of surveying methods provides a reasonable explanation for varying orientations and groupings of graves. Further, with the exception of posthole Z, postholes X and Y are the only others detected on the site, and depth was sufficiently important for their function for digging to continue into the rock chalk. The top of the barrow at Dover had been ploughed away, but, as this did not happen at Yeavering, evidence is now available there of the use of a central post on a prehistoric barrow for alignments by the British and the Anglo-Saxons. Aligning the posts X and Y with the centre of the barrow at Dover therefore seems a reasonable analogous exercise.

The orientations of all the graves are shown on the diagram Text Figure 29. The orientations which appear to have been influenced by the barrow, i.e. plots E, J, K, L, M, N and the north-west part of G, are shown on the diagrams Text Figure 30a–d where they are separated into male, female, juvenile and unsexed graves. These are graves numbers 36, 37, 52, 53, 54, 55, 56, 57, 58, 59, 60, 61, 62, 63, 64, 65, 66, 67, 68, 69, 129, 132, 133, 134, 137, 139, 145, 146, 151, 152, 153, 154, 161, 162, 163, 164, 165. A second set of diagrams Text Figure 31a–d shows the variation in orientation of those graves not apparently influenced by the barrow. Most of the orientations on Text Figure 29 are within the same narrow range south of east, but two diverge considerably from the rest. Grave 90 is angled much further north than the other male graves, and grave 95 points much further south than the other female graves. This suggests that, in spite of their position in plot A, they belong to the non-Christian northern series with diverse orientations, and this point is discussed above p 145.

The orientations of the rest of the graves not influenced by the barrow are narrowly constricted, mostly in a direction just south of east and within the solstice angles of 60.5° and 128.5°. Males graves are between 95° and 133° (Text Figure 31a). Female graves are between 93.5° and 138.5° (Text Figure 31b), with three exceptions pointing further north, 147 at 89°, 99 at 85.5° and 82 at 74.5°. Juvenile graves are between 93° and 127.5° (Text Figure 31c), with the exception of the small grave 118 at 79.5°, and the one E–W burial, grave 21 at 290°. The graves of unknown sex are between 93.5° and 123.5° (Text Figure 31d), with the exception of grave 47 which was at the south-western edge of plot B and may, like graves 90 and 95 nearby, belong to the series of oddly orientated graves.

From these figures and from the list in orientation order Table XXXVI, it may be seen that the northern limits are much the same for all graves, one only being north of the solstice, and only twelve north of 90°. The juvenile and unknown-sex directions extend slightly less to the south. There is therefore a fairly universal conformity with the erratic exceptions of the graves of three females and one child, 147 and 118 in plot H and 99 and 82 in plot I, two of them without finds and two poorly furnished. Further comment will be made on these four graves below.

During the early Anglo-Saxon period there were two landmarks clearly visible from the site, the pair of Roman lighthouses standing on the two hills overlooking the harbour. The northern and nearer one on Castle Hill still stands adjoining the church of St. Mary-in-Castro, which may have been built between 616 and 640. There is every possibility that the church could have been preceded by a pagan temple on this plot or even an earlier church, and any of these buildings might have attracted orientations of graves in successive periods. The angle of direction from the site to the northern lighthouse coincides with the angle of a number of graves: $c$ 127.5°, and is near the southern limit of the spread. If all the graves were aligned to this visible and constant point, however, much less variation would have ensued, and the range would have run further south. Although the pharos on the Western Heights was mostly removed in the nineteenth century, its position is known[41]. The angle in respect of the cemetery is 165°, much further south than all the graves, except for 59 (168°) and 95 (165.5°), so that it appears to have exerted no influence unless it was on these two graves.

It may be suspected that the validity of the results obtained from a severely mathematical approach to a study of the orientation of Anglo-Saxon graves is rather doubtful. Calculation of the medial axis of a grave is not always capable of precision as the graves are cut to various uneven shapes. It is also sometimes doubtful, where the alignment of the skeleton varies from that of the medial axis of the grave, as to which direction is the operative one. Further, in common with the situation in most Anglo-Saxon cemeteries, no great care was exercised in the digging of the graves at Dover. The rock chalk is resistant, and is likely to break away in fault lines, but, if accurate orientation had been considered vitally important far greater precision could have been achieved in obtaining straight and vertical sides and flat floors to the graves. It seems reasonable to suppose, therefore, that a similar lack of care would have been exercised in fixing the orientation of the graves as in their digging. Other factors contribute to uncertainty. Where there are rows of graves, it may be that orientation was accurately noted for the first, and others were laid out roughly parallel. When the sky was overcast an element of guesswork may have entered into the establishment of the sunrise angle. The skyline may have been heightened consistently or intermittently by trees, and the view from the cemetery differs greatly according to whether the standpoint is at its west, east, north or south limits, for there is considerable variation in distance between them and in the height above sea-level.

Much thought has been given recently to the

---

41 Philp 1981, fig 2

# DISCUSSION

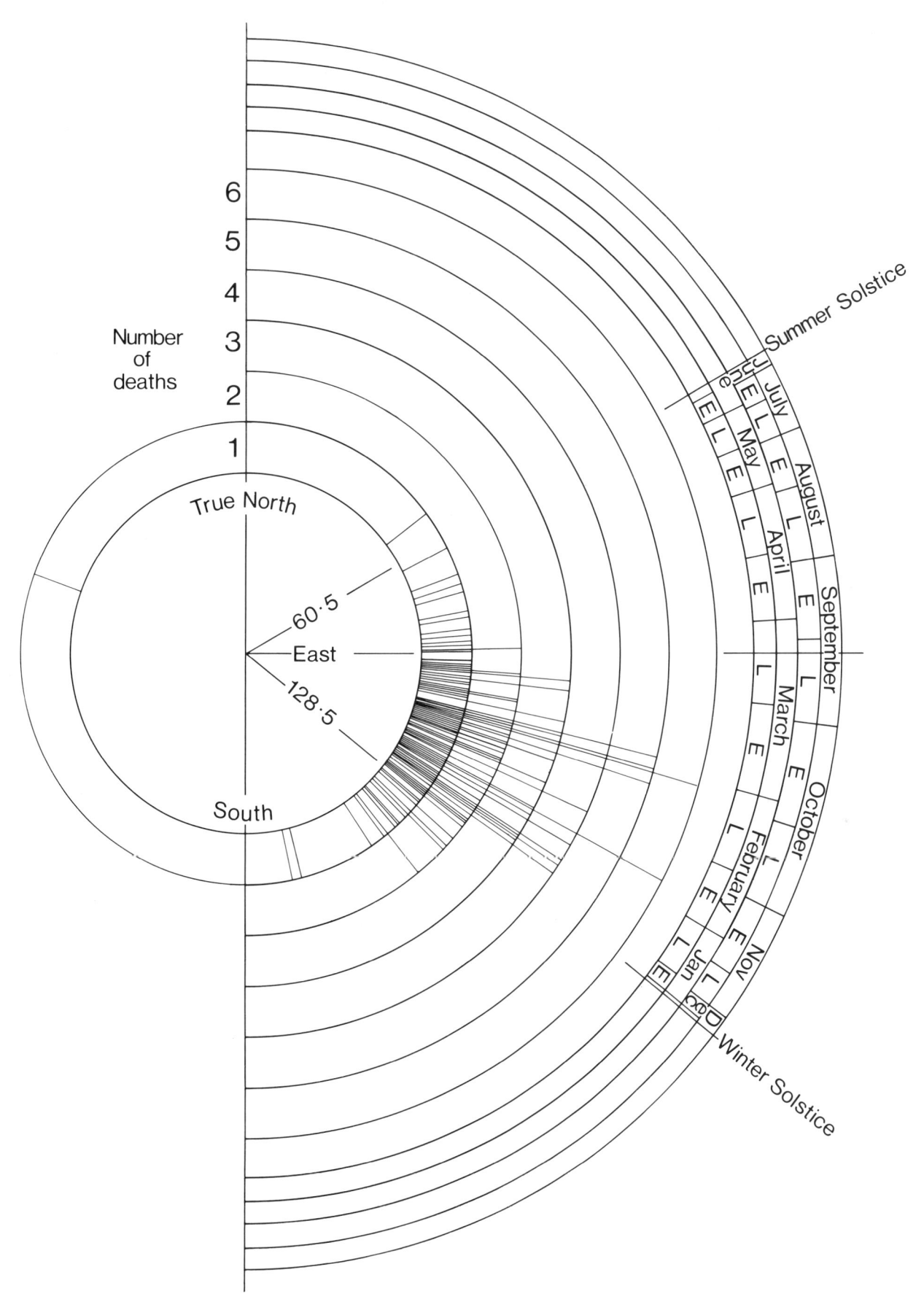

*Text Figure 29* Orientation. All graves

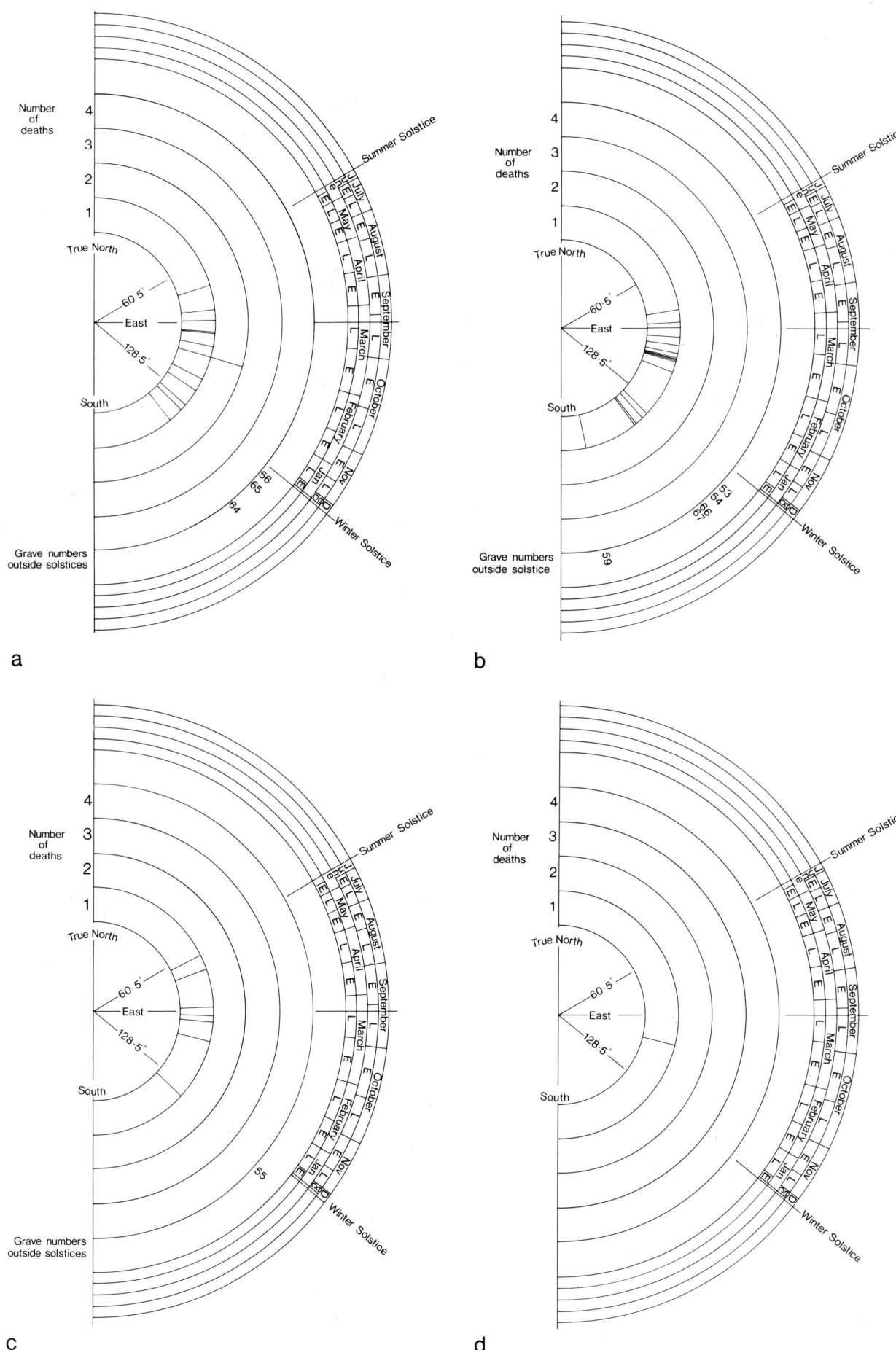

*Text Figure 30*  Orientation. Graves influenced by barrow. a. male, b. female, c. juvenile, d. unknown sex.

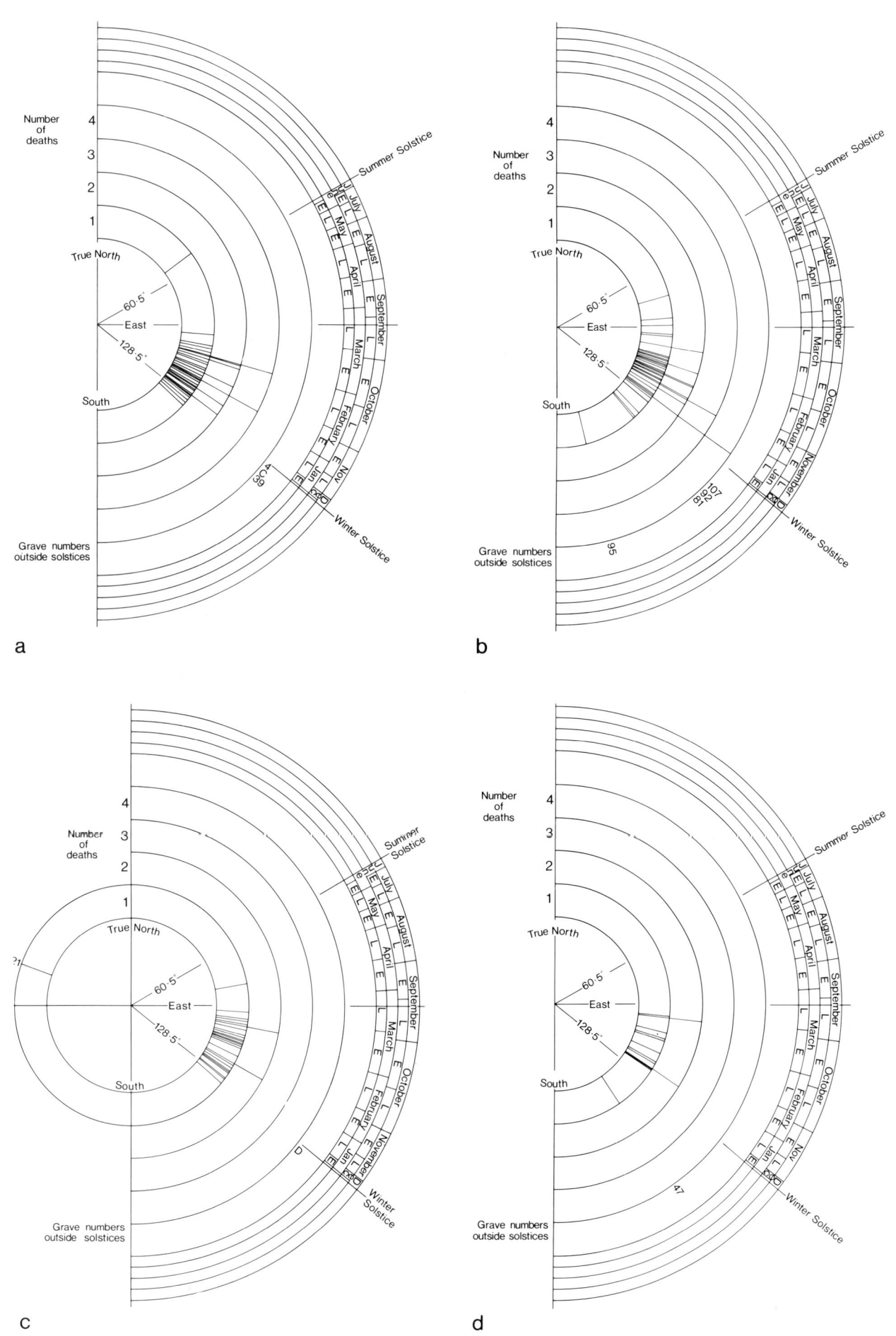

# DISCUSSION

*Text Figure 31*   Orientation. Graves not influenced by barrow. a. male, b. female, c. juvenile, d. unknown sex.

subject of grave orientations,[42] with particular interest in the effect of the position of the sun at sunrise throughout the year. At Finglesham the earlier, and presumed pagan, graves are aligned NE to NNE, 23° to 40°, while the seventh and eighth-century graves are clustered between N.50°.559 and N.129°.441, the positions of the summer and winter solstices. It seems likely, therefore, that, as at Dover, there is a difference of orientation between the pagan and Christian graves. There are differences beween the practice in the two cemeteries, however, as the pagan graves at Dover are affected by the barrow. Most of them (Figures 30a–d) nevertheless, are orientated between 90° and 141° in the same way as the Christian graves, but also three graves, one each of male, female and juvenile or unknown sex, have bearings north of east up to 63°. Only grave 59 overshoots the winter solstice and approaches the south point at 168°.

At Dover the Christian graves cover an arc from 93° to 138.5°, a span of only 45.5° as opposed to 79° at Finglesham. Moreover, the arc is centred almost exclusively south of east instead of the general orientation at Finglesham of slightly more north-east than south-east.

The interpretation suggested for the Finglesham burials is that the Christian graves were dug on sunrise bearings, and that the maximum number of deaths occurred at the periods considered to be the most unhealthy. This orientation is 67°–112°, corresponding to sunrise bearings from the last three weeks in February, the whole of March and April, and the last three weeks in August and all September and October. The span, however, covers orientations about 40° both north and south of east, and might be regarded as simply representing the amount of accuracy possible on cloudy days in deciding the direction of the east. Nevertheless, this is not so likely at Dover, where the arc is narrower, and ranges, not with the emphasis north of east, but almost exclusively south of east.

It has been noted that at Dover the west-east orientation is present from the beginning of the cemetery in plots A and B, in phases 1, 2 and 3, and that it is not before phase 3 that graves with other orientations appear. It has been suggested above that the west-east orientation of the plot A burials may have been influenced by the British church, and also possibly by the constraint of Frankish Christian immigrants. Ethelbert's reign had a visible effect in the beginning of a new part of the cemetery with larger graves more widely spaced. At the same time burials with variant orientations began on the barrow. With the establishment of Christianity, and a climate of religious consciousness, it looks as though some people made a resolute decision in favour of a non-Christian religion, and the northern part of the cemetery was used to accommodate these people, and also to include a Christian woman apparently being punished for some crime. If the sunrise-bearing theory were applied to the Dover Christian burials, there would have been no deaths in the summer months. There must, therefore, be some other reason for this narrowly WNW–ESE orientation. A reason which might be suggested is that a more-or-less W–E orientation was required for Christian reasons, and the graves were dug in this general direction as most convenient to the slope of the hillside.

However, the view of the horizon is not unimpeded. It may be seen from the contours on the map, Figure 2, that the majority of the graves are situated south-west of the barrow, which was near the highest point of the hill, so that they are at a comparatively lower level. Moreover, land over 400ft high intervenes between the 250ft height of Long Hill and the sea in a north-easterly direction. The summer sunrise would therefore not be visible from the cemetery until the sun had moved higher in the sky and further south, so skirting the higher land. Text Figure 29 shows the orientation of all graves, Text Figures 30a–d show the orientation of all graves which appear to be influenced by the barrow, and Text Figures 31a–d show the orientation of graves not influenced by the barrow[43].

With few exceptions the orientation of the graves could have been fixed by reference to the rising sun. Grave 90 points north of the solar arc and contains a male with shield, spear, knife and bronze mend to a wooden bowl, of phase 4. If the rising sun was the guiding factor the only other deaths in the months of April, May, June, July, August and early September, (i.e. north of 90°) (excluding graves influenced by the barrow ) would have been 82, 99, 118 and 147 (see p 156). These consist of three females and a juvenile of phases 6 and 7, buried with only a knife and other fragments, or no finds at all. It may be seen from the plan, Figure 110, that a line drawn eastwards from grave 90 passes through all of these graves, except 99 which is nevertheless near, and, moreover, if extended, the line ends at posthole Z. Strange though this may seem, it does suggest that these graves of phases 6 and 7 were deliberately set on a line taken from the grave of a phase 4 spearman to posthole Z. It may be noted that in plot H this line partly coincides with part of the pathway already suggested in view of the space between graves (p 153, Figure 110). As grave 90 presumably shared a tumulus raised over grave 94 in phase 2, and no doubt caused it to be enlarged, the sighting in phase 6 or 7, when the other graves on the line were put down, could have been to a post marker on the tumulus which had been placed over grave 90.

These graves are orientated north of 90°, an arbitrarily selected point of the compass, and it may be that other graves which point slightly further south may be related. On the distribution plan (Figure 109) these graves may be distinguished from those orientated between 90° and 102°. There are a number of other graves in the 0–90° range, all

---

42 e.g. Wells and Green 1973, Hawkes 1976b, Rahtz 1978, Clarke 1975

43 These figures have been prepared with the kind help of Dr I Reid and Dr P Trent, Birkbeck College.

influenced by the barrow, i.e. 57, 60, 63, 146, 163, 164, 153, 154. Some of the graves in the next category, 90°–102°, occur on or near the line from grave 90 to Z: 140, 125, 121, 117, 100, the 83–85 group and 72–73. Of the rest of this category, (90°–102°), many are in the segment north of the X–CC line (36, 37, 69, 132, 133, 139, 155), and two, 162 and 165, are amongst the barrow-influenced group. Not obviously connected with these are grave 159 at the north edge of plot H, and 119 and 102 at the southern edge. Graves 2, 8 and 11 are also on outer fringes, but grave 97 is in the middle of plot F. Amongst the graves of the next category, 104°–120°, some are near to the orientations of the previous group, within 104°–106°, and of these two are in the sector north of the X–CC line, 129, 134, grave 137 is crossed by it, and others are barrow-influenced: 160, 145, 161, 68 and 151. There are also exceptions in the 104°–106° group, but the most striking result of this examination is that fifteen graves, of an almost identical orientation unusual in this cemetery, are associated with the 90–posthole Z line, and a number of other graves with this orientation are in specifically heathen localities.

As to wanderers in the opposite direction, some graves are orientated to points south of the azimuth. Of those some are very close to 128.5°, eg 4, D, C and 56, and their variation may be due to minor error. One group is on the south-east side of the barrow: 59, 53, 54, 55, 64, 65, 60, 67. Three are on the southernmost limit of the cemetery at different points: graves 4, 39, 107 and 81. Grave 47 lies between plots A and B. Grave 21 is the only E–W burial, but its reverse orientation is within the azimuth. The direction of grave 95 has been discussed above and related to grave 94 in a possible tumulus. The angle of 92 may have been diverted as the diggers encountered and disturbed an earlier burial.

Graves orientated between 121°–128° occur in all parts of the cemetery except during the latest phases in the south-east, i.e. plot I, the south-eastern part of plot H, and plots L, M and N. It is the only sector of the compass which does not attract graves in this area.

It may be seen, therefore, that most of the burials in the cemetery are limited to between the angles of 94.5° and 128°. Burials which are outside the azimuth to the south, and those which lie at an angle of less than 90° or 95° seem to be distinguished from other graves in various ways and some connections between them can be established. If, however, the remaining main body of the burials were orientated to the rising sun, this would mean that the majority of deaths were in the winter months of late September to mid March and that there were hardly any at all in the summer. Although it is credible that the harsher conditions of winter would have been responsible for more deaths, summer immunity to this extent seems excessive. The orientation of the majority of the graves contrasts strongly with that at Finglesham, where it is north of east. There is a closer similarity to the orientation at Cannington, although there the limitations of the orientation of the majority are a few degrees further north, so leaving a period of few deaths in late November to early January, and showing a substantial number in late March-early April and in the middle of September. The apparent absence of deaths in summer at Dover would, if true, indicate an absence of plague or other infectious diseases which flourish in higher temperatures, and a small measure of support arises from the fact that, with one exception, there are no double or multiple graves, and no sudden occurrence of a large number of contemporary graves. No trace in fact, for instance, of the pestilence of AD 664 which took off Eorcenberht.

At the beginning of the study of the layout of this cemetery, it had every appearance of being a rather unorganised conglomeration of graves, with some indication of grouping, and a general aim at a roughly west-east orientation of casually cut graves. During close examination it has, however, gradually become clear that the layout was executed with geometrical precision, employing compass work and a combination of straight lines and carefully calculated angles probably based on a north point. The majority of graves are, indeed, orientated within the azimuth, but only within a section of it south of east, so that unless people who died in the summer were buried elsewhere, orientation to the rising sun is not a convincing proposition. Most of the rest of the graves, with the orientations further north or further south appear to have heathen connections, whereas the conforming majority are Christian. The first impression of casual or haphazard arrangement proves, therefore to be quite wrong, and there can be no doubt but that the position and orientation of each grave was selected and executed with extreme care, and that there was a reason for each decision. Unfortunately we cannot go very far in divining these reasons. We can see some divisions between Christians and heathens, but we cannot know why some heathen graves pointed further south-east and some further north-east, and why no Christian graves were orientated between 60.5° and 92°, unless this direction was studiously avoided because it was customary for pagans.

To a certain extent it is now possible to visualise the physical appearance of the cemetery at the end of its period of use. Most of the graves must have been distinguished by a mound or small tumulus. The hillside was dominated by the prehistoric tumulus on a false crest surmounted by a substantial wooden post, no doubt carved in an Anglo-Saxon animal style in the manner of a totem pole. From this radiated divisions in the form of fences or hedges, and other boundaries followed the tracks and pathways which crossed the site. Other carved posts stood at three widely spaced points, X, Y and Z, and a fourth surmounted the tumulus over graves 94 and 90. There were probably buildings in the space between plots A and F, and the whole cemetery, silhouetted on the false crest of Long Hill, must have been an impressive sight from the settlement in the valley below, and visible for a long stretch to travellers along the road to Canterbury.

## Comparable Cemetery Plans

Not many Kentish Anglo-Saxon cemeteries have been excavated in recent years and well published, so that it is difficult to make accurate comparisons. However, the cemetery at Lyminge, Kent has been partially excavated and published, and may be used for this purpose to a certain extent[44]. A further excavation took place on this site, and some of the finds from this are in Maidstone Museum, but the additions to the plan are not yet available[45].

The cemetery plan of the earlier excavation (Text Figure 32) shows that the area investigated was in a central part of the cemetery, no borders being discernible. Out of the total of 44 bodies 19 were male, 19 were female and 6 were children, of whom two were identifiable as female. The graves were fairly well spaced in irregular rows, mostly of W–E orientation, although the orientation of some was attracted to two rectangular gullies. Except for six graves, all were within the solstice angles of 60.5° and 128.5° (Table XXXVII) and of these six graves four contained nothing and the other two were poorly furnished. Although the children's graves were interspersed among the adults, the male graves tended to bunch together, and the female graves together (Text Figure 32a). The period of burial in this part of the cemetery extends from about AD 425–550, and is therefore well within the earlier period at Dover when fully-furnished burials were the rule. Nevertheless, there are no sword graves here, although there are five spear graves, one of which also contained an axe, and there was also a grave with an axe only. Eight men (four of them 45 or over) were without weapons, and six, (five of them over 40, and one disturbed) without finds. Six of the women wore brooches, another four might be classed as medium rich, two women over 40 had few possessions, and five, two of them over 50, were without finds. The children were evenly spread between the classes, one rich, one medium rich, three poor and two without finds, (Table XXXVIII)[46].

TABLE XXXVII  LYMINGE ORIENTATIONS

| Orientation °E of N | Grave No. | Orientation °E of N | Grave No. |
|---|---|---|---|
| 28.5° | 20 | 90° | 2 |
| 32° | 42 | 90.5° | 4,40 |
| 39° | 18 | 91° | 30 |
| 48° | 24 | 93.5° | 21 |
| 56° | 32 | 94° | 43 |
| 58° | 19 | 96° | 25,29 |
| 70° |  | 96.5° | 14 |
| 73.5° | 23 | 97° | 16,28 |
| 77° | 15 | 98° | 1 |
| 78° | 22 | 98.5° | 3 |
| 80° | 9, 34 | 100.5° | 27 |
| 80.5° | 13 | 102.5° | 44 |
| 82° | 10 | 106° | 7 |
| 83° | 12 | 109° | 31,41 |
| 84° | 26,35 | 119° | 36 |
| 86° | 6,17 | 121° | 33,37 |
| 86.5° | 11 | 125° | 39 |
|  | 5 | 128° | 38 |

(Based on the published plans, Grid North).

TABLE XXXVIII  CLASSIFICATION OF GRAVES AT LYMINGE WITH AGE AT DEATH

**Male**

| Sword | Spear | Weaponless | Findless |
|---|---|---|---|
|  | 1 + axe (50yrs) | 12 (45 yrs) | 2 (40–45yrs) |
|  | 4 (adult) | 15 (55yrs) | 8 (45–50yrs) |
|  | 5 (20–25yrs) | 22 (35–40yrs) | 20 (40–45yrs) |
|  | 6 (30yrs) | 23 (60yrs) | 21 (45–50yrs) |
|  | 7 axe (no spear) | 30 (20yrs) | 34 (40yrs) |
|  | 31 (40–45yrs) | 32 (15–20yrs) | 40 (25–30yrs) |
|  |  | 36 (55–60yrs) | Disturbed |

**Female**

| Rich + brooch | Medium rich | Poor | Findless |
|---|---|---|---|
| 10 (over 60) | 3 (60yrs) | 9 (over 60) | 11 (30yrs) |
| 16 | 13 (20yrs) | 17 (40–45yrs) | 14 (35–40yrs) |
| 25 (30 yrs) | 29 (55–60yrs) | 28 (50–55yrs) | 18 (55–60yrs) |
| 33 (50yrs) | 41 (25yrs) |  | 19 (30–35yrs) |
| 39 (60yrs) |  |  |  |
| 44 (40–45yrs) |  |  | 43 (50–60yrs) |

**Children** (f or unknown)

| Rich + brooch | Medium rich | Poor | Findless |
|---|---|---|---|
| 24 (5yrs) | 27 (2–6yrs) | 35 (12yrs) | 26 (15yrs) |
|  |  | 37 (10–11yrs) | 38 (12yrs) |
|  |  | 42 (6–12 months) |  |

Except for the lack of sword graves, therefore, the class structure in this part of the cemetery is similar to the structure in the earlier groups at Dover, although the proportion of findless graves is greater[47].

---

44  Warhurst 1955

45  Mr A Warhurst informs me that some of the documentation was destroyed by a bomb in Belfast

46  This estimate differs from that of the excavator which was that most of the finds were being buried during the middle and latter part of the sixth century AD. Warhurst 1955, 39.

47  When considering the report on the bones in the cemetery of Lyminge by Dr J Joseph it should be kept in mind that the estimated ages are far in excess of the normal age at death of an Anglo-Saxon. The population is said to have reached a ripe old age, for out of forty-four individuals, fifteen are said to have been over forty-five, some of them even over 60.

DISCUSSION 163

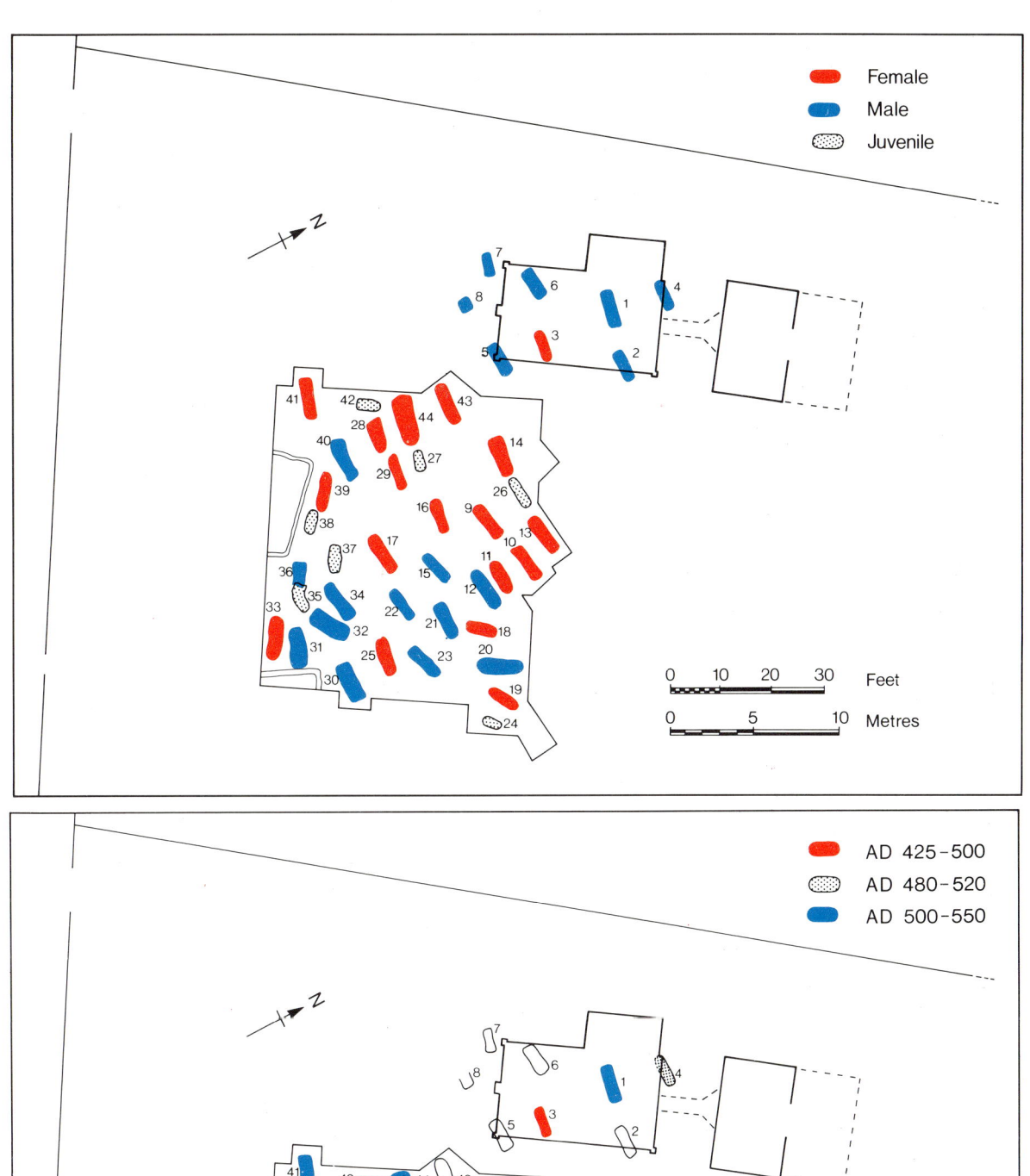

*Text Figure 32a*    Cemetery at Lyminge, Kent: sex
        *b*    Cemetery at Lyminge, Kent: chronology

With regard to the chronology at Lyminge, some graves may be allocated to AD 425–500, (3, 10, 12, 22, 29, 4 2), some to 480–520 (4, 9, 13, 17, 24, 25, 27, 32, 33, 36), and some to 500–550 (1, 16, 39, 41, 44) (Text Figure 32b). The graves of the earliest phase were situated at well-spaced intervals in the middle of the excavated area. The second phase graves were scattered between and around the earliest graves. The latest were also between the others, but more to the west, and some of the graves of the middle and latest phases assumed a different orientation, aligned with, and adjacent to the rectangular gullies (39, 36, 33), Text Figure 32b. From the small area excavated it appears that later graves were intermingled with earlier ones more generally than at Dover, although there is an indication of a westward spread in the sixth century.

The depth of the graves at Lyminge were fairly regularly between 1ft.2in. and 2ft.6in., 36cm and 76cm, with the exception of 34, 35 and 36 which were between 2ft.8in. and 3ft.2in, 81cm and 97cm, and the rich female grave 44, the deepest at 4ft.3in., 129cm. The graves are therefore deeper than at Dover, but it is likely that the reason for the difference is that at Dover the hillside suffered more from erosion, rather than that the custom of digging was different.

The earliest graves at Lyminge contained quoit brooch style metalwork, and a metal-inlaid Frankish buckle and spear, followed in the middle phase by other Frankish buckles, purse-mount and glass, with applied disc brooches ultimately of Saxon origin. One pot is Anglo-Frisian in decoration, and the other plain hand-made. Kentish-made disc and square-headed brooches make their appearance in the sixth century, as well as a Scandinavian bracteate, button brooch of Saxon origin, and Frankish brooch and perforated spoon and crystal. The Frankish connection therefore started earlier in the fifth century than at Dover, and was even stronger about AD 500, Just as at Dover, however, there is the sprinkling of individual items which can be attributed to various origins, Saxon, Anglian and Scandinavian.

The section of the cemetery excavated at Orpington, Kent, provides an interesting plan (Text Figure 33a)[48]. Although only part of the cemetery was excavated at the time of the second report, the northern and western limits appear to have been reached, and the eastern section, which contains most of the graves, respects the limit of a Roman ditch in the southern part. Although there are three female graves actually on the ditch and others further west, all the male graves are situated to the east of the ditch. The orientation is mostly west-east, with a few south-north, and one each in the opposite direction, north-south (62) and east-west (65). There is a superimposition of three S-N graves by W-E graves (24–25, 66–67, 2–3) and of one of the W-E graves by a N-S grave (60–62), and one W-E grave by a S-N grave (44–40) so that the W–E orientation cannot be regarded as exclusively the latest.

There are ten graves recognisable as male, of which eight are W–E and two S–N, 26 and 23. Grave 23 is in a rather isolated position, the other male graves lying round it in a near-circle, with a gap in the south-east. There are only four children's graves in between. The spacing therefore suggests that grave 23 was under a tumulus, the male graves being placed on the perimeter, and the children on the overburden. The impression that, although without grave goods, grave 23 contained a man of importance, is further sustained by the fact that, at 50 years, he died at a greater age than any of the other men whose ages range from 20+ to 40. He was 5ft.10in. tall, was buried without any grave goods, and has the distinction of being the only man in the cemetery without weapons. In fact, nine of the men are equipped in a uniform manner (Table XXXIX), each with a shield-boss, eight with a spear, eight with a knife, with slight variations only in that some had different kinds of belt fittings, and some of the shields had decorative studs. Two shield bosses had silvered rivets (3 and 7), and one man (36) possessed a sword instead of a spear. Otherwise the uniformity of this group is impressive and they have every appearance of being men of a regularly equipped army, the minor differences no doubt indicating grades of rank.

TABLE XXXIX ORPINGTON: CONTENTS OF MALE GRAVES

| Grave No. | Spear | Shield boss | Shield studs | Knife | Belt Mounts |
| --- | --- | --- | --- | --- | --- |
| 3 | 1 | 1 (silver studs) | 4 ?on grip | 1 | iron buckle |
| 5 | 1 | 1 | | 1 | |
| 7 | 1 | 1 (silver studs) | 2 on grip | 1 | |
| 25 | 1 | 1 | 4 | 1 | iron buckle ?strapend. |
| 26 | 1 | 1 | 3 2 bronze plates | 1 | |
| 36 | (sword) | 1 | | 1 | bronze buckle |
| 37 | 1 | 1 | | 1 | |
| 38 | 1 | 1 | | 1 | |
| 42 | 1 | 1 | 3 | | bronze ring + rectangular plates |
| 23 | – | – | – | – | – |

On the distribution plan, Text Figure 33b, the graves which can be allocated to the fifth century by the objects contained in them are indicated, and also graves which could belong either to the fifth or sixth century. This shows that the first group of graves are

---

48 Tester 1968; Tester 1969. Further excavation has been conducted by Mrs S Palmer who informs me that the report is in progress, and that there is a possibility of further continuance of excavation.

DISCUSSION

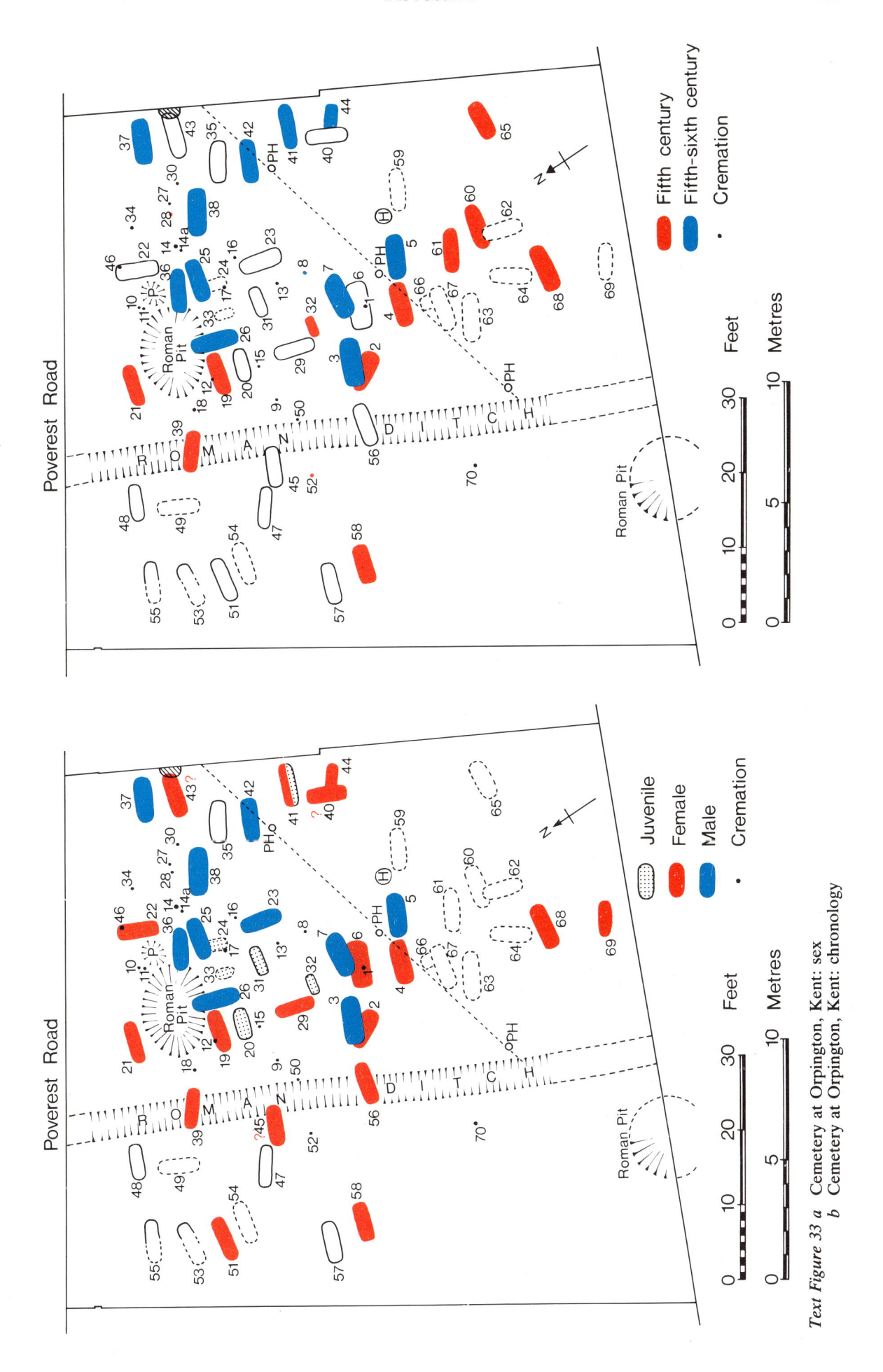

Text Figure 33 a  Cemetery at Orpington, Kent: sex
            b  Cemetery at Orpington, Kent: chronology

on the south-west side of the cemetery, and the others to the north-east. This picture however, is distorted by the fact that most of the fifth–sixth century graves are male, for it is not possible to allocate the shield boss and spear types precisely within the time span, so that all the male graves could belong either to the fifth century or early sixth century. There is, however, one girl's grave at the eastern edge which contains a button brooch and square-headed brooch which are not likely to be earlier than AD 500. It is possible, therefore, that all of the people in this excavated part of the cemetery died by about AD 500. A comparatively late date for three of the male graves is shown by the superimposition of 3 and 7 on the female graves 2 and 6 respectively, and of 25 on the juvenile grave 4. There is no burial stratified above a male grave. Amongst the contents of grave 3 was a shield boss with silver rivets, and the grave it cut contained a knife and late Roman glass bracelet. Grave 7 also contained a boss with silver studs and the grave it cut contained a woman without possessions. This arrangement suggests two men of the same rank, each buried near his wife who had died earlier. Other male-female pairs could be 4 and 5 which are end to end, 19 and 26 and also 36 and 22 which are at right angles to each other.

It could be that further excavations may alter the picture of the arrangement of the graves, but on the present information consideration should be given to the possibility that, not only may this be the burial of a lord and his retainers, but that it could illustrate the Anglo-Saxon ideal of retainers fighting to the death with their lord, for their deaths could all have occurred at the same time.

As nothing is known about the sex or age of the ashes in the cremation pots no conclusions can be drawn regarding their relationship with inhumed individuals, although some relationship, possibly of a child and its mother, might be indicated by a cremation actually in the fill of a female inhumation as cremation 46 in grave 22.

There is a posthole towards the south of the site immediately east of the Roman ditch, and two others which lie to the north-east enable a line to be drawn connecting them diagonally from the ditch across the cemetery. It is not respected in any way by the placing of the graves, in fact, it cuts graves 4 and 42, but it appears to form the southern limit for the cremations, as all are north of this line, mostly within the triangle it forms with the Roman ditch, except for two cremations precisely situated on the western side of the ditch and equidistant from it (52 and 70).

When the possessions of the women are examined for ethnic pointers, it may be noted that three graves contain Romano-British objects: 2, 39 and 67. There are also two objects of quoit brooch style, a buckle and a D-sectioned tube, and two Frankish buckles. Pottery is Anglian and Saxon in type. Three varieties of brooch are Saxon, a button brooch, saucer and applied brooches. Except for one square-headed brooch of Kentish origin, the rest are disc brooches, a type which evolved mainly in England as another variant of the circular brooch favoured by the Saxons.

Turning to the cemetery of Bergh Apton in Norfolk[49], there the sexing of graves depends on grave goods alone as only a few fragments of bone remained. Of a total of 62 graves, 18 were male, 26 female, 6 unknown, and 12 probably children, (Text Figure 34a). The male graves seem to have been placed with some kind of plan in mind, in two diagonal lines in the middle, for instance, and a number of them are larger than the other graves. The women and children fill the spaces between in no regular fashion. This leads to a certain degree of segregation of the sexes as at Dover.

The standard of living was below that enjoyed by the inhabitants of Dover. Amongst the male graves there was one swordsman in a large grave (19), and of the twelve spearmen three were distinguished in some way, 71 by a large grave containing a coffin, 26 by mounts in the shape of griffins on the shield, and 50 by a bronze necklet. Grave 73 was weaponless but with a shield, and 22 weaponless with a lyre. Of six graves where the sex is unknown, five are weaponless 17, 32, 43, 51, 63, and one, 58, is findless.

Among the 26 female graves 20 wore brooches, usually a pair of annular brooches, with a few cruciform and small long brooches. All were in bronze, only two square-headed and one floriate cruciform brooch being gilded. These represent the most expensive items in the cemetery, with the exception of a silver disc pendant in grave 21. This latter grave is near two of the graves with gilded brooches, 7 and 18.

The ditch which traverses the cemetery from north to south is cut by a number of graves, and does not seem to have any effect on spacing. The graves are close to each other, but some spacing which may indicate deliberate divisions may be noted. The group of three graves in the north, 66, 12, 77, is distanced from the others. Further, there appears to be a narrow space across the cemetery from between 53 and 19 on the west and 28 and 49 on the east. A few postholes and pits were excavated, and of these three, 48, 49 and 79, were of similar size and depth, and were equidistant and in line. A line drawn through these three (Text Figure 34a) and projected further each way runs mainly between graves, touched by graves 10, 17 and 32, but, more significantly, just south of the line of male graves 19, 16, 26 and 2. If a line is drawn parallel to this along the space already noted above, the resulting strip contains, beside these male graves, the female graves 9, 15, 29–36–35 and two juvenile graves 4 and 28. It seems to be a possible family plot. The lines are also parallel to the lines of male graves 27, 8, 40 and 13, 71, 41 to the north. A further parallel line in the northern part of the cemetery would divide the three graves, 66, 12 and 77, from the rest.

---

49   Green and Rogerson 1978

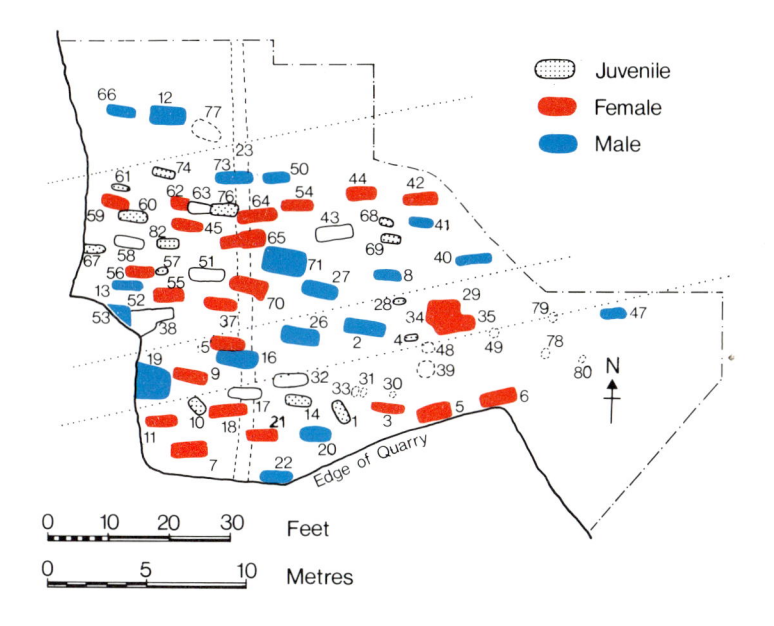

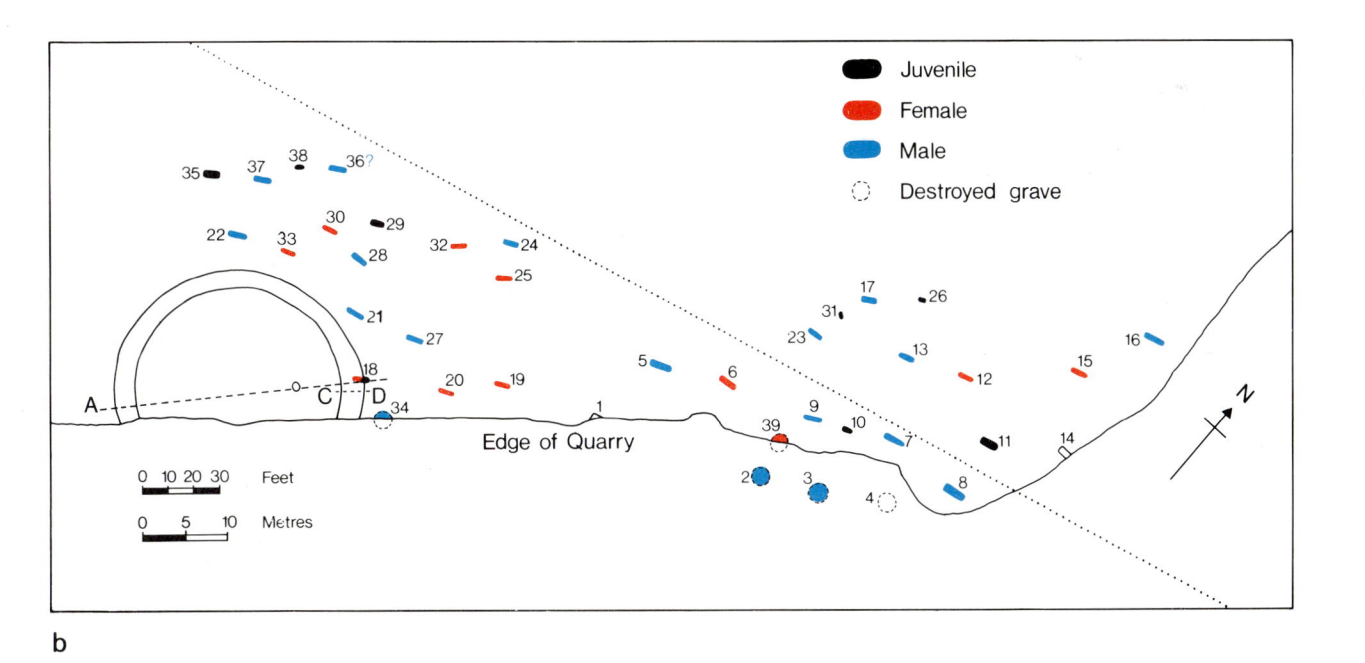

*Text Figure 34 a* Cemetery at Bergh Apton, Norfolk: sex
*b* Cemetery at Holborough, Kent: sex

Holborough differs from Dover, Lyminge and Orpington in that the only part excavated is exclusively late, belonging to the seventh century or later[50]. The arrangement of the graves is much more spacious, (Text Figure 34b), the considerable space between each grave no doubt indicating that they were each covered by a small, individual tumulus. The orientations are all roughly W–E with the exception of one N–S infant grave. Except for six graves orientation is within the solstice angles, (Table XL). Male, female and juvenile graves were intermingled. There were no postholes at all in the area of chalk searched. Some of the spacing might be interpreted as indicating family groups, 24, 25 and 32, for example, and a wide space north of grave 1 might indicate the separation of the cemetery into a western and an eastern group.

The placing of postholes at Bergh Apton and Orpington to form a line seems at first to be arbitrary, and, although the wide spacing of the postholes at Orpington shows clearly that they must have been used for some kind of fence, some doubt must be attached to the purpose of the three postholes at Bergh Apton as they are close enough to have functioned as part of a building. However, comparison between the published plans shows that at both sites the angle of the line formed by the postholes is 76.5° from Grid North. This suggests that the angle was one deliberately chosen. There is no evidence of such a line at Lyminge, although there the graves are aligned side by side with some attempt at regularity in the N–S rows. At Dover the angle of the line X–CC joining posthole X and the centre of the barrow is 79° from Grid North, and 78° from the nearly north line Y–CC from posthole Y to the centre of the barrow. It might be considered that these angles are sufficiently close to have been identical in intention. The barrow at Dover was not excavated, and the circular ditch drawn on the plan was deduced from what traces were available in the chalk. The centre point of the barrow could therefore have been slightly differently placed, perhaps sufficiently for the N–S line Y–CC to be accurately due north, and for the line X–CC to be 76.5°.

At Holborough a line drawn at 76.5° could be placed with some meaning as shown in Text Figure 34b where it forms a boundary at the north of the western group of graves, and divides the eastern group into two sections, the southern section containing some graves which are larger than those north of the line. There is little evidence to support this imaginary limit produced on analogy with other sites where there are postholes, but the result is worth recording.

In each of these three cemeteries therefore, the position of each grave was carefully selected, and in two, as at Dover, there is some structural evidence of divisions within the cemetery.

TABLE XL  HOLBOROUGH ORIENTATIONS

| Orientation °E of N | Grave No. |
|---|---|
| 46° | 32 |
| 52° | 35 |
| 53° | 25 |
| 56° | 38 |
| 58° | 36 |
| 58.5° | 37 |
| 60.5° | 18 |
| 61° | 17,22 |
| 62° | 24 |
| 63° | 9,29 |
| 64° | 19 |
| 65.5° | 20 |
| 66.5° | 27 |
| 67° | 5 |
| 70° | 12 |
| 70.5° | 33 |
| 71° | 10,30 |
| 72° | 15,26 |
| 74° | 16 |
| 75° | 13 |
| 76° | 7 |
| 77° | 11 |
| 78° | 8,21 |
| 80° | 6 |
| 86° | 23 |
| 88° | 28 |
| 90° | 14 |
| 133° | 31 |

Based on the published plans, Grid North

**Anglo-Saxon Dover**

As Dover is situated at the nearest point of land to the Continent, and also lies at the mouth of the only river for a distance of some miles which provides an inlet through the chalk cliffs, the value of its position as a port was not lost on the Romans. A site on the west bank, some way inland from the present silted-up coastline, was chosen for a fort of the *Classis Britannica*, and an adjacent and overlapping site served for the later Saxon Shore fort[51]. There is evidence to suggest that the associated settlement area extended further to an area of about 12½ acres, small finds ranging from the first to fourth centuries, but with a main concentration in the second century[52]. There appears to have been little settlement on the eastern bank (Text Figure 35).

Three Roman roads converge at Dover, their main lines being certain, but their exact positions and junctions in the immediate vicinity of the port are still not precisely located. The map Text Figure 36 shows the routes suggested by Margary[53] as follows. The road from London, Rochester and Canterbury, Watling Street, joined the road from

50  Evison 1956
51  Philp 1981, fig. 3; Philp undated fig. 5
52  Philp 1981, 11
53  Margary 1955, 29–31, 33–4, 43–4

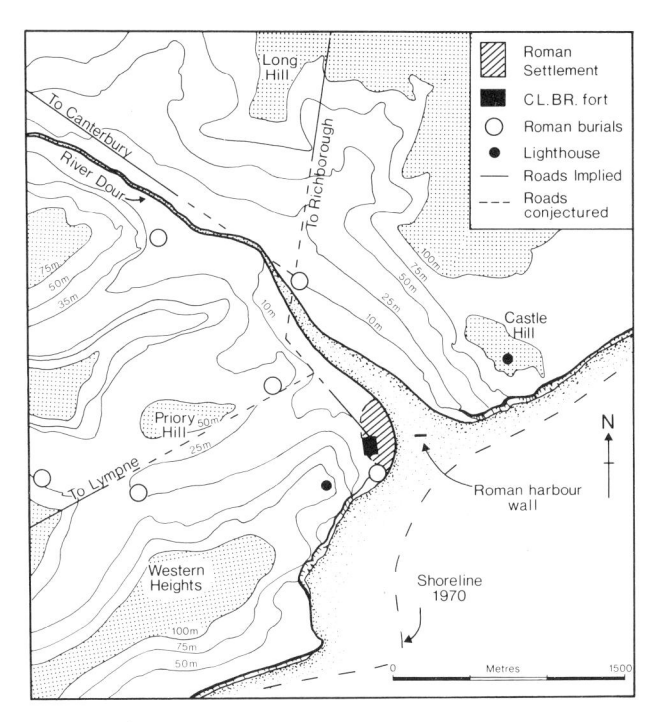

*Text Figure 35*  The Dover area in the Roman period (after Philp)

Richborough, which crossed the Dour in the region of Bridge Street, in the area of the present High Street, the line of the Canterbury road continuing southwards along the valley to the Dover fort and settlement, and the Richborough road taking a northern by-pass route via Tower Hamlets Road over the Downs to join the road westwards to Lympne. The road from Lympne also continued in an alternative and more direct approach into the Dover settlement. More accurate information may come to light in the course of the present excavations at Dover, a hope stimulated by the notion, put forward by Philp, that if the certain, straight line of the Richborough road is projected across the valley it strikes the newly-discovered *Classis Britannica* fort[54], and if this was in fact the original route, a lower crossing point would have been used.

A find of two penannular brooches and two buckles just to the west of the shore fort at Durham Hill suggests the possible position of Anglo-Saxon graves or a cemetery (Text Figure 36, No. 17). Apart from these all other Saxon finds in this shore fort area are part of the occupational debris of the settlement produced mainly in the current excavations. A stray sherd of a Frankish pottery bottle at Yewdens Court was the first find, and its rouletted pattern matched that of the five-strand interlace on the bottles in graves 109 and 157. Further sherds of imported continental pots were found in Market Square in 1972 (Text Figures 36, 15b),[55] i.e. bottles, spouted pitchers, biconical and globular bowls, with various rouletted patterns, chevron, cable, undulating, and the five-strand interlace. Also from Market Square were glass fragments, and a gold finger-ring of the sixth century set with a garnet and filigree-collared gold granules. A *Grubenhaus* cut through a wall of the 'Painted House' contained loomweights, pottery and a bronze workbox of the type found in grave 107. Further pottery and glass of the seventh to ninth centuries associated with a rectangular wooden structure in Queen Street may represent part of the monastery of St. Martin which was probably transferred to the town at the end of the seventh century from the Castle Hill site (Text Figures 36, 15d, 21).

It is evident that the type of wheel-thrown pottery which was imported from northern France from about AD 550 onwards and was deposited in some graves at Buckland, was also in everyday use in the town houses of the port. No pottery from the settlement of the earlier part of the pagan period has yet been published. However, the hand-made pot of about AD 500 from grave 87 is duplicated by sherds of exact replicas found in the town. This is important evidence as substantial signs of town occupation at this date have not before come to light. Other signs of occupation in the neighbourhood are to be read in some of the single finds, a pottery bottle with undulating rouletting at the meeting of St. Radigund's Road and the Roman road to Canterbury, and three Merovingian gold coins found 'near Dover', 'possibly Dover' and 'Sutton-by-Dover' (see p 170, Text Figure 36).

Otherwise all evidence for pagan Saxons in this vicinity is in the form of burials, or of finds which by reason of their completeness or number must come from burials. The jewelled disc brooch found on Priory Hill indicates a rich cemetery on the west bank of the river, possibly connected with the Roman cemetery in this area[56]. A short distance

---

54  Philp 1981, 12
55  Evison 1979a, 18

56  Philp 1981, 11

170    THE BUCKLAND ANGLO-SAXON CEMETERY

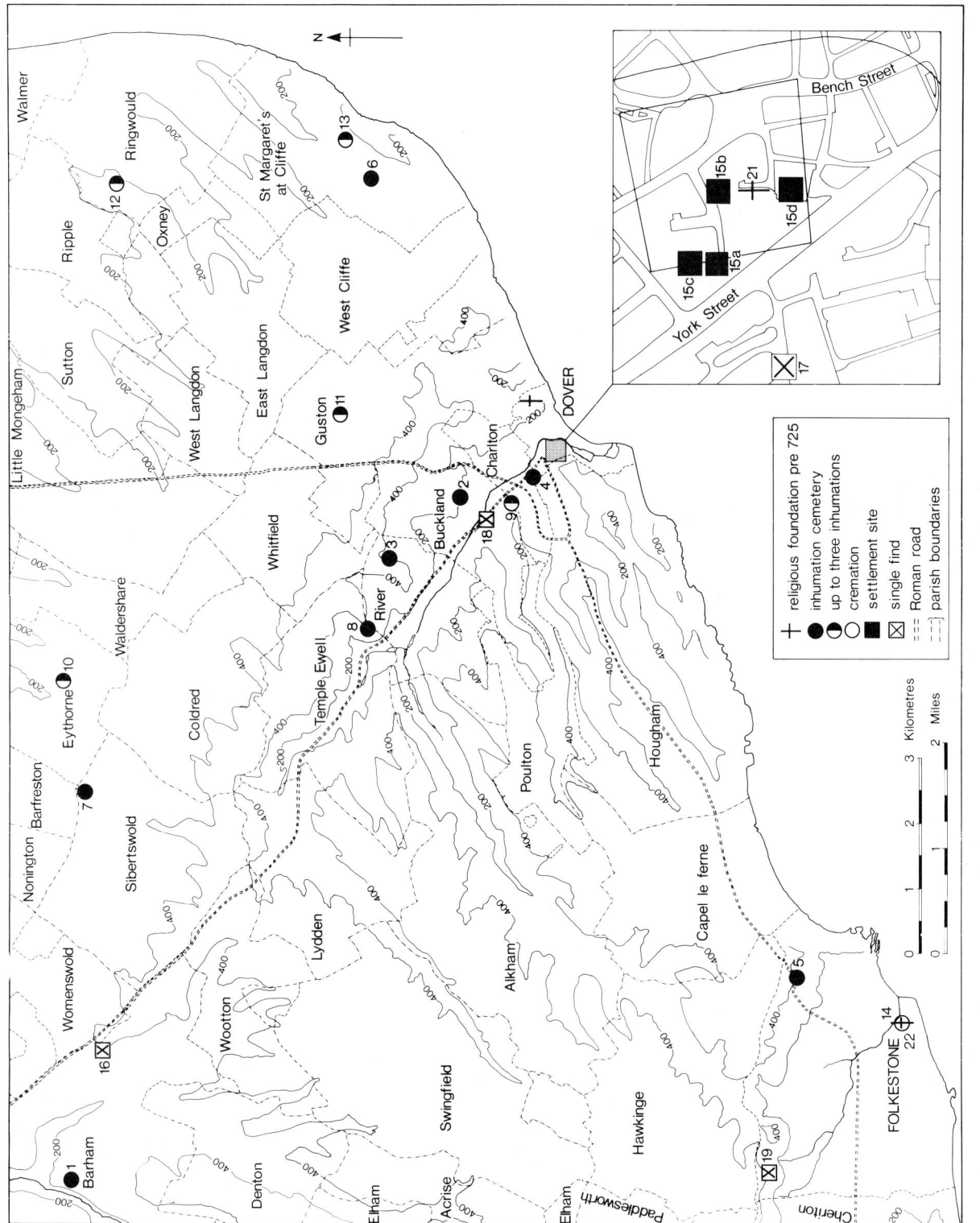

Text Figure 36   Anglo-Saxon sites in the Dover area: – – – parish boundaries as at 1876 ––––– as at 1946

further north on the western slope of the valley, the single seventh-century grave at High Meadow, may indicate another cemetery or possibly even a continuation of the same one. Three more cemeteries are indicated on the eastern hillsides further north, the first being that on Buckland Estate, Long Hill, the subject of this report. Green Lane, probably a prehistoric track, runs eastwards from the Dour valley along the side of a valley separating Long Hill from the next hill further north, Old Park. From the top of Old Park have come some rich finds which must indicate a cemetery:- escutcheons and appliqués from a hanging bowl, the ornamented silver gilt mount of a cup, and ivory plaques from a casket. Still on the eastern hills of the Dour valley, further north, some tumuli were opened at Temple Ewell at the end of the eighteenth century, each revealing a skeleton with sword and spear. All these were ranged along the sides of the valley of the Dour, and there appears to have been another cemetery on the hills of the parish of Guston further to the north-east.

Further away, but within the area covered by the map, (Text Figure 36) there are finds in the Folkestone district, i.e. an inhumation cemetery, a possible secondary burial in a barrow, and a cremation, unique in this area. In the opposite direction, tumuli at St. Margaret-at-Cliffe indicate a cemetery, and a burial and other finds suggest another half a mile away. Further north at Ringwould finds reveal that there must have been another cemetery there. In the north of the area is the southern fringe of a group of cemeteries which border the Roman road to Canterbury, i.e. Barham, Sibertswold-Barfriston and Eythorne.

It is the comparative absence of Anglo-Saxon finds in the vicinity of Dover which is more striking. Although the Roman road from Dover to Canterbury is bordered by Anglo-Saxon cemeteries along its course from Barham to Canterbury, the stretch from Barham to Temple Ewell is quite blank. Similar unoccupied stretches occur along the Roman roads from Dover to Richborough, and Dover to Folkestone. Further, although there are cemeteries on the hill slopes each side of the Dour valley just north of the town, there is no record of any Anglo-Saxon finds on the two hills overlooking the harbour, and on which the pair of Roman lighthouses were still standing in the early Saxon period.

Most of the finds in this area were made years ago and were not efficiently recorded. Nevertheless, it may be recognised that Anglo-Saxon objects of high value from the middle to late sixth century are in evidence, e.g. the Kentish jewelled disc brooches from Folkestone, Dover and Guston. Somewhat later, from the end of the sixth century or the seventh century, are the cup mount and hanging bowl from Old Park, and the gold pendant from High Meadow. The most significant find in regard to the Buckland cemetery, however, is the large sherd of a wheel-thrown pottery bottle found at the junction of St. Radigund's Road and London Road (Text Figure 36, 18)[57]. It bears a rouletted pattern of triple rows of small squares in waves with a rectangular grid in the upper valleys. As it was a single find of a sherd it is more likely to be an indication of occupation material than an object from a grave, and the position in which it was found, near the west bank of the river and directly opposite the cemetery site on Long Hill, is the most logical position for the related settlement. It could also have been the position of the river crossing of the Roman London Road, rather than at Bridge Street further south.

The roulette pattern on the bottle is lightly impressed so that only half is visible, and the whole pattern may therefore have been the same as the undulating pattern with a grid on one side and a rosette on the other which ornaments the cut-down bottle of no provenance in Canterbury Museum, 7644[58]. Similar patterns are to be seen on a sherd from Mucking, on the biconical bowl from Arques, N. France, and the bossed bowl from Sint Joris Winge, Belgium[59]. Similar triple undulated patterns are noted from Boulogne and Wierre Effroy. Undulating roulette patterns in general were fairly widely distributed in France and Belgium, but the main concentration was in the Pas-de-Calais[60]. Although the St. Radigund's Road motif cannot be exactly matched in the Buckland cemetery, the bottle is of similar date and provenance to the bottles found there, and sherds with undulating roulettes were found in settlement material in the Saxon short fort.

Historical information on the immediate post-Roman period is lacking and it is not possible to be certain at what point in the fifth or sixth century the control of the Dover area passed from the Britons to the Anglo-Saxons because of the present fragmentary nature of the data. It is worth noting that, in common with other river names in this county and elsewhere, the Celtic name of the Dour (which means 'water') has persisted to the present day. It is more remarkable that the British name of the town, Dover, also survived the arrival of the Anglo-Saxons, and in a form which has been regarded as evidence of intercourse between the two peoples:

'(O.E. Dofras, R.B Dubris, British Dubrás, Late British Dobrás) which implies that the Anglo-Saxons who adopted it could recognize Celtic plurals in oblique cases'[61].

Traces of the earliest arrival of Germanic people in the fifth century do not seem to be present although a great deal of evidence is available regarding the presence of Germanic people in the fifth century in the whole of the rest of the area south of the Thames, and particularly in east Kent. A considerable amount of inlaid metalwork, for

---

57  Evison 1979a, 84–5, fig. 37
58  Ibid, 1e16, fig. 6e, fig. 23f. pl. VII, C
59  Ibid, fig. 19d, 37, fig. 30i and fig. 32c
60  Ibid, 110–12, map 4
61  Wainwright 1962, 62

instance, was brought in from areas settled by the Franks in northern France, Belgium and Germany, and this type of metalwork is intimately connected with the insular products in quoit brooch style[62]. Other imports such as swords, buckles, buckets and glassware[63] came in from the Meuse valley and northern France. In Kent this material occurs plentifully in the cemeteries of the Thanet area, and in the cemeteries to the south-east of Canterbury such as Howletts and Bifrons which are situated near the road from Dover. Inlaid metalwork, an early glass and a quoit brooch have also been found not far away from Dover to the west at Lyminge. Nothing as early as this, however, appears to have been found in the cemetery at Folkestone or at any of the sites in and around Dover, where evidence of the fifth century is almost entirely missing. This is possibly due to the fact that, with few exceptions, all the finds are accidental and not the result of supervised excavation. It is to be hoped that information regarding the fifth century will be forthcoming from the results of the current excavations in the town of Dover.

As to the Buckland Estate cemetery itself, the earliest date that can be definitely assigned to any of the graves is about AD 475, although one or two could be earlier. A large area was destroyed, however, adjoining and to the south of plot A, in just the place where fifth-century graves would have been situated if they existed. Some of the graves contained early material, such as fragments and objects of the Romano-British era in grave 48, where, as well as a dolphin buckle, the woman had a lead spindle whorl and a fragment of Roman glass. Apart from the few Roman coins, Roman objects do not occur to any extent in later phases.

If the objects are examined for traces of relationships with other countries, the earliest grave in phase 1, which could have been 22, contained a Kempston-type cone-beaker, a pattern-welded sword and a spear with metal inlay, that is, an assemblage appropriate to the grave of a Frankish man. Closely following this in date was the woman with Saxon saucer and button brooches in grave 48, and then the spearman with an Anglian pot in grave 87, and the woman with square-headed brooches of south Scandinavian origin in grave 13. At the end of phase 1 there is the girl in grave 20 with a brooch, buckle and bronze bowl from the Rhineland, a gold bracteate of south Scandinavian origin, and a pair of square-headed brooches and glass claw-beaker made by Kentish craftsmen. This earliest phase, therefore, shows a wide variety of foreign connections with the Angles and Saxons and south Scandinavians, but mostly with the Franks.

In phase 2, AD 525–575, there were still two Frankish garnet brooches, but the Kentish jewellers were by then in full production with keystone garnet disc brooches. Frankish buckles, two with shoe-shaped rivets, were in evidence, also Frankish spearheads with inlaid metal bands, and a bronze bowl.

By phase 3, the jewellery of the women was exclusively Kentish and included a bracteate in Style II, but connections with the Franks were still to be seen in the seax, buckles, a glass vessel, and the swords. A glass pendant probably came from Syria, perhaps along with some of the glass beads. In phase 4 Frankish buckles and swords continued, but brooches were no longer worn and the first pottery bottle from the Continent appeared. By phase 5 amethyst and shell beads began to come in from eastern sources via the Continent, and wheel-thrown pots were imported from northern France and Belgium, as well as a glass tumbler from the Rhine or Meuse valley. In phase 6 a glass palm cup was the only probable import from France or Germany, and shell and amethyst beads continued to be imported. The anthropomorphic pin in grave 161 made an unexpected appearance as an import from Sweden. By phase 7 grave goods were very sparse, and there were no foreign articles save amethyst and glass beads.

It may be seen, therefore, that from the very beginning of the cemetery in the fifth century to its end, connections with Frankish territory in France, Belgium and the Rhineland were the most important. None of the female graves contains exclusively Frankish goods, but it is not possible to distinguish some of the male graves from those of Franks, eg 22, 56, 65 and 91. Apart from imported objects, there are other traces of Frankish influence such as in the style of the jewellery, in the custom of writing runes on the back of a brooch and in the reversed position of a spearhead in a grave. Anglian, Saxon, Jutish and Swedish elements, therefore, merely put in an appearance in a material culture which is mainly Kentish and Frankish throughout.

The information gained from an intensive study of this cemetery cannot be regarded as exactly reflecting the condition of the whole of Kent at this period, and many more intensive studies of other cemeteries excavated by archaeologists will be required before such general conclusions can be drawn. It is, however, a beginning, and should be enough to show how slight the possibly Jutish elements are in relation to the Frankish elements, even from the fifth century. Although there was once much resistance to the notion of early Frankish presence there seems to be little now as subsequent discoveries have added substantially to the supporting evidence. One point which was brought forward against the presence of Franks in the fifth century was the absence of their wheel-thrown pottery in graves, and the fact that Frankish wheel-thrown pottery did not appear in Anglo-Saxon graves before AD 550 has been used in an attempt to argue that 'It must be seen as a not very substantial element in the later cultural impact of Merovingian prosperity on the Kentish people that is typified in

---

62 Evison 1965b and 1968

63 Evison 1981a

other ways by, for example, the growth of the gold and garnet jewellery industry and eventually by the coming of Christianity with St. Augustine in 597'[64]. Even though graves of the first half of the fifth century are not present at Dover, the presence of Franks is more marked than that of any other people in phases 1 and 2, and from phase 3 Frankish influence increased with the Augustine mission.

It can clearly be seen how futile it is to base conclusions on pottery alone. Here very little pottery was deposited in graves, most of the pots were limited to a small area and short time span, and, although many Frankish objects were deposited before AD 575, there was at that time only one deposition of a single pot and that was Anglian. It was obviously not the custom of this community to put pots in graves at all at this period, and even if some wheel-thrown pots had been brought in from abroad, they would have been a scarce commodity as they were not replaceable, when broken, from kilns in this country. The earliest grave in which a wheel-thrown pot was deposited was grave 43 in phase 4, i.e. between AD 625 and 650. Theories built on the numbers of hand-made pots of the fifth-century which were used for cremations north of the Thames can have no relevance to a cemetery such as Dover where inhumation without pottery was the ritual in use. Comparison with the published part of Lyminge cemetery shows that this same custom was followed there, for there were only two pots, and these were hand-made and in the graves of children.[65] It remains to be seen how far evidence will be increased by the pottery data in the settlement site excavations in Kent, unpublished to date.

A connection with Sussex is evident in the button brooch in phase 1, but on the whole internal connections are mainly with other parts of Kent, mostly to the north, e.g. a square-headed brooch by the same maker of Unassociated 9 at Howletts, similar small-long brooches at Broadstairs and Howletts, the same die for a gold bracteate at Wingham, and similar claw-beakers at Sarre and Lyminge. There are also some connections with areas north of the Thames in the annular brooches, and the fish symbols on the shields which were paralleled in the Thames at Barnes, in Essex, Bedfordshire and Norfolk. At this period the goods manufactured in Kent were sent into other counties of England, but as the flow of goods in the opposite direction was no doubt mainly in raw materials and other perishables and untraceable commodities such as slaves, little evidence can be expected in grave furniture.

In the other direction, however, Kentish exports have been noted in northern France, and the numbers have been increased by recent excavations.

Kentish square-headed brooches are represented by one burnt fragment at Waben[66], and others complete in the inhumation cemeteries at Vron and Giberville[67]. The keystone garnet disc brooches were appreciated and also copied on the Continent, as well as button brooches[68]. Silver cocked-hat sword pommels with ring-knobs produced by Kentish craftsmen also found their way abroad, to Grenay, Pas-de-Calais, Fèrebrianges, Marne and Langenenslingen, Germany[69]. Some glass claw-beakers especially those with tooled trail decoration, seem to have been exported[70]. All of these goods were high quality Kentish products of the sixth century which well deserved the high esteem in which they were obviously held on the Continent, but the two-way flow of trade seems to have turned into more of a one-way flow into England by the seventh century, at least as far as non-perishable goods can be traced.

Comments made on the contents of this cemetery and that of Sarre have emphasised the high proportion of weapons found in male graves at these two sites, and it has been suggested that they represent military establishments of the King's port reeves[71]. This is, of course, possible. However, like most general conclusions which it is the custom to draw from early records of finds of this period, it is likely to be inaccurate because of the deficient nature of the evidence available. The proportion of weapons recovered from any Anglo-Saxon cemetery cannot be reliably calculated as not one complete cemetery has been excavated and adequately recorded. The two most important reasons for any absence of weapons are that the part of the cemetery in question containing them may have been destroyed, or that the graves belong to a period when the practice of depositing swords had ceased. If these sword-bearing men at Buckland were directly connected with the business of the port they would have been living in or near the town, and would have been buried in one of the nearer cemeteries on Priory Hill or High Meadow, or possibly in an undiscovered cemetery on one of the lighthouse hills overlooking the town. The Buckland cemetery is stationed on the false crest of Long Hill when viewed from the Dour valley, and the probability is that the settlement to which it belonged was immediately at the foot of Long Hill. The swordsmen would have had a mile to run or gallop to reach the sea front in the event of trouble at the port. Nevertheless, the river was probably navigable nearly up to this point below Long Hill (Text Figure 36), and their duties may have been to guard the river crossing of the Canterbury and Richborough roads.

Although the cemetery at Buckland continued in use throughout the period of pagan tradition of

---

64 Myres 1980
65 One was not wheel-thrown as described in the report Warhurst 1955, 18; Myres 1977 2, fig.95.3094.
66 St. Germain museum, 8N; Bellanger and Seillier 1982, pl. XXVII, 2
67 Information M. Cl. Seillier. Pilet 1979, Taf. IV, 14, 15

68 Ibid, Taf. IV, 11–13; Avent 1975 ii, pl. 77, No. 189; Avent and Evison 1982, pl. XVIII, 37.1 and a–d; Bellanger and Seillier 1982, 17–18, fig. 2
69 Evison 1979c; Pilet 1979
70 Evison 1982, pl. VIb
71 Hawkes 1969, 191–2

burial with grave goods, it shows evidence of the co-existence of Christianity. There is no sign amongst the earliest burials of pagan practices such as cremations or of south-north inhumations as there are at some other cemeteries of the period in Kent. Burial is by inhumation only in W–E graves right from the beginning, and this could have been due to the influence of Christianity practised by many people at this time, even if the Germanic inhabitants destined for these graves had not fully accepted this Mediterranean religion. The first recorded event which registers the re-establishment of the faith in Kent is the grant of a chapel to Liudhard the Frankish Bishop of Bertha, Ethelbert's wife before AD 588, i.e. more than a decade before the arrival of St. Augustine. The way in which the graves emerged from the close confines of plot A about 575 and changed into larger and more widely separated graves in plot B which was Christian, plots C and D well distanced but of unknown faith, and plot E situated on a prehistoric barrow, apparently heathen, all this deliberate dispersal seems to show a self-conscious declaration of religion. Most of the recognisable signs of Christianity, cruciform designs on pendants, and probably also the fish symbol on a shield, occurred during phase 3 in the reign of Ethelbert. These signs do not continue into phase 4, when burial of both heathens and Christians apparently continued on the same site, although in separate plots.

The archaeological evidence is not inconsistent with what we know of the progress of Christianity in the immediate vicinity. After the first flush of Christianity under Ethelbert, some discouragement must have been experienced at the beginning of Eadbald's reign when the King himself was pagan, which may be reflected in the use of separate plots by the end of phase 3 and in the absence of any object specifically Christian in phase 4. Later in his reign Eadbald is said to have founded the monastery at Folkestone for his daughter Eanswith about AD 630[72]. The destruction of the church has been variously attributed to the sea and the Danes[73].

During the life of the cemetery a number of churches were founded in Kent: St. Mary's, St. Augustine's St. Martin's, St. Pancras and Christ church cathedral at Canterbury, St. Andrew's at Rochester, St. Mary's at Reculver, St. Mary's at Lyminge[74], Minster in Sheppey, Minster at Hoo, Minster in Thanet, St. Peter's in Thanet[75], and possibly Stone-by-Faversham and Richborough[76]. Even nearer to Long Hill was the foundation of the monastery at Dover. There are two traditions about its foundation, both post-Conquest in their existing forms. The fourteenth-century tradition of the Priory Church of St. Martin, Dover was that it was founded by Eadbald (d.640) who ordained 22 canons to serve God in the chapel of St. Mary in the castle of Dover[77]. In 696 Wihtred removed them from the castle to the church of St. Martin in the town. The other tradition is recorded by Florence of Worcester and the *Liber Vitae* of Hyde Monastery to the effect that the monastery was founded *c* 700 as St. Martin's in the town of Dover. Archaeological evidence of structural remains of the seventh to ninth centuries has been found near the site of St. Martin's in the town, as noted on p 169. Taylor and Taylor state that the church of St. Mary-in-Castro, while using the Roman lighthouse as a western annexe, is a complete church of the period AD 950–1000[78].

Close connections between Kent in general with the areas of the Continent under Frankish rule have been discussed elsewhere in connection with the import of wheel-thrown pottery[79]. The relationship was particularly intimate in the royal family for two members of it had a Frankish name, Hlothere and Eorcengota, two kings, Ethelbert and Eadbald took a Frankish wife, while Eorcengota became a nun at Farmoutiers in northern France.

Dover had a long history of connection with Boulogne in the Roman period, and this probably continued for a while to a certain extent as, although the mouth of the Liane on which Boulogne stands was becoming silted up, there is archaeological evidence that Boulogne continued to be occupied during the sixth and seventh centuries[80]. In addition,

---

72  Livett 1926, 12
73  According to Fowler 1926, 236 the life of St. Eanswith in the *Nova Legenda Angliae* states that the site of the church was swallowed up by the sea while, in a charter of AD 927, it was described as the place where there was formerly an abbey where St. Eanswith was buried, which had been destroyed by the Danes.
74  Fletcher 1965
75  A list of seven religious establishments appears in the grant of privileges to the churches and monasteries of Kent by King Wihtred at a Council at Baccancelde in AD 696, which was confirmed at a Council at Cloveshoh in AD 716. The churches were Upmynster, Raculf (Reculver), Suthmynster, Dofras (Dover), Folcanstan (Folkestone), Limming (Lyminge), Scepeis (Sheppey) and Hoe (Hoo), Livett 1926, 12. Minster in Sheppey was founded by Sexburga, the widow of Erconbert of Kent *c* 670 Fowler 1926, 149 and contains masonry of the period AD 650–700; Taylor and Taylor 1965 I, 429–30. Stenton 1933, 323–4 suggested that Minster at Hoo was founded in the late seventh century as a colony from Medehamstede. Suthmynster has been identified as Minster in Thanet (Livett 1926, 12) and a charter of Wihtred dated AD 696 confirming its privileges is probably authentic,

Sawyer 1968, 75, no. 17. According to Elmham Egbert of Kent gave the land to Domneva for the foundation of a monastery and she was consecrated abbess by Theodore, Archbishop of Canterbury AD 669–90, Fowler 1926, 151. Upmynster has been identified as St. Peter's in Thanet (Livett 1926, 12), but the earliest charters for this minster seem to be dated AD 748 and 761 (Sawyer 1968, 94, no.91 and 78–9, no.29) and refer to a monastery dedicated in AD 741 or later by Archbishop Cuthbert, Fowler 1926, 151.
76  Excavations at Stone-by-Faversham have indicated that the western part of the chancel was a mausoleum or martyrium of about the fourth century AD. There was also evidence for an Anglo-Saxon wooden nave. Taylor 1978, 1084. A tradition of a chapel built at Richborough after St. Augustine's arrival was recorded by Thorne in the fourteenth century (Livett 1926, 4) and excavations have revealed a chapel in the Anglo-Saxon cemetery at Richborough Castle, Taylor 1978, 752.
77  Fowler 1926, 133
78  Taylor and Taylor 1965 I, 214–7
79  Evison 1979a, chapter 4
80  Ibid, 62

it might have been possible for landfalls to have been made in the mouth of the Aa further north, and certainly it was possible to the south, to Quentovic on the Canche, and also to the mouth of the river Authie. At these points traders and travellers could gather for the crossing, led there by the Roman roads which crossed France from Atlantic and Mediterranean coasts and from the Rhineland and beyond. The traffic through Dover already covered a number of commercial commodities during the sixth century, but it must have increased a great deal during the seventh century because of the activity involved in the Christian religion. The number of travellers was increased by pilgrims and ecclesiastics about their business, and products of the Mediterranean and Near East, some of which, such as wine and oil, silks and jewels, may have been brought in at first for Christian ritual and no doubt created a substantial commercial demand among the richer secular customers in Kent and further inland.

During the fifth and sixth centuries many of the types of expensive items found in Kentish graves also occurred in graves in the upper Thames, Sussex, Hampshire and the Isle of Wight. In the fifth century the material consists of the brooches, bronze belt mounts and inlaid ironwork connected with the quoit brooch style, as well as early glass vessels. In the middle of the sixth century the square-headed brooches appear in Sussex and the Isle of Wight as well as in Kent, but glass vessels by this time were already absent from Sussex, Hampshire and the Isle of Wight. In connection with Sussex a reason for the sixth-century phenomenon of low quality burial furniture has been suggested: 'A sudden absence of gold, silver and bronze objects in graves might be explained in terms of tribute payment to rival overlords and perhaps this apparent impoverishment reflects the campaigns involving Ceawlin, the West Saxon king, and Aethelbert of Kent recorded in the *Anglo-Saxon Chronicle*.'[81]

Developing that line of thought, it is apparent that the affluence of the region south of the Thames in the fifth century must have arisen, in the first place, from the payments by the British to the Germanic mercenaries, and, in the second place, from the requisitioning of much wealth by the Germanic mercenaries and their relatives when they later decided to settle. The first wealthy period of Sussex was no doubt contemporary with the Bretwaldaship of Aelle. The next known Bretwalda was Ceawlin of the West Saxons, who was superseded by Ethelbert of Kent. The wealth of Kent, mirrored in phase 3 of the Buckland cemetery, rose to a peak during his tenure. After his death in 616 in phase 4 of the Buckland cemetery, as in the last quarter of the sixth century in Sussex, Dover graves were bereft of brooches and other jewellery, but the men were well armed. It can be no coincidence that the grave of the next Bretwalda, Redwald, contained the most splendid gold jewellery and varied possessions of the period. In fact it vividly brings to mind the story of Weland, or Volund[82], a master smith who refused to work for a Swedish king, but was hamstrung and transported to an island so that he had no alternative but to comply. It is likely that in a Germanic society the court jeweller and his craftsmen would be given an offer by the new Bretwalda that he could not refuse, so that the best Kentish workshop moved to Suffolk. This kind of transaction would also account for the appearance and continuity later of Kentish type gold and silver jewellery in Yorkshire when Edwin became the next Bretwalda in the seventh century. During such vicissitudes the tribute-paying areas were less wealthy, but as Kent was in the south-eastern corner of the country most favourably placed for trade with the Continent, its inhabitants were able to retrieve some of their fortunes, and expensive items once more appeared sporadically in graves at Buckland from phase 5 onwards.

While many similarities are to be detected between the cemetery at Buckland and other Kentish cemeteries, there are also many unexplained differences in layout, orientation and contents. Useful comparisons cannot be made until other recently excavated cemeteries are studied and published, Finglesham, St. Peters, Broadstairs and Ozingell.

### List of graves in each plot

|  |  |
|---|---|
| Plot A | 12 13 14 15 16 17 18 19 20 21 22 23 28 45 46 48 49 50 70 87 88 89 90 92 94 95. |
| Plot B | 25 27 29 30 31 32 33 34 35 42 43 44 47 91 93 126. |
| Plot C | 6 7 8 9 10 11 24. |
| Plot D | B C D E F 1 2 3 4 5 26 41 98 115 116 122 123. |
| Plot E | 52 53 54 55 58 59 60 61 62 63 64 65 66 67. |
| Plot F | 38 49 71 96 97 131 135 136. |
| Plot G | 128 129 130 132 133 134 137 139 155 156 157. |
| Plot H | 40 101 102 103 104 105 106 107 108 109 110 111 112 113 114 118 119 121 124 125 138 140 141 142 143 144 147 148 149 150 158 159 160. |
| Plot I | 72 73 74 75 76 77 78 79 80 81 82 83 84 85 86 99 100 117 120 127. |
| Plot J | 36 37 69. |
| Plot K | 56 57. |
| Plot L | 161 162 163 164. |
| Plot M | 152 153 154. |
| Plot N | 68 145 146 151 165. |

### Graves allocated to specific phases

|  |  |
|---|---|
| Phase 1 | 12 13 20 21 22 46 48 70 87. |
| Phase 2 | 14 15 23 28 49 50 92 94b. |
| Phase 3 | C D F 1 3 4 29 30 32 33 35 38 41 56 57 59 60 61 63 91 93 94a 98 126. |
| Phase 4 | 18 27 34 39 42 43 44 55 58 62 64 65 66 71 90 96ab 131. |
| Phase 5 | 6 8 10 52 53 67 128 129 132 133 134 137 139 155 156 157. |
| Phase 6 | 95 101 103 107 108 110 113 114 124 138 141 144 148 149 150 158 159 160 161 162 163 164. |

---

81 Welch 1980, 282

82 Auden and Taylor 1981, 3–8

Phase 7     68 72 73 74 75 76 77 78 79 80 81 82 83 84 85 86 99 100 117 120 127 145 146 151 152 153 154 165.

**Graves presumed to belong to specific phases**

Phase 1 or 2   16 17 19 45 88 89.
Phase 3        B E 2 5 26 115 116 122 123.
Phase 4        25 54 97 135 136.
Phase 5        7 9 24 36 37 69 130.
Phase 6        40 102 104 105 106 109 111 112 118 119 121 125 140 142 143 147.

The dating of the graves is based firstly on the coins found in the cemetery which give a firm date *post quem* for three distinct sections. Next, dates are allocated to specific objects on the basis of comparison with similar objects found in dated continental and English graves. The distribution of objects, the positions and orientations of graves in relation to each other and the cemetery as a whole and the sizes and shapes of the graves are also considered. There are some graves disturbed, with no finds, or too few for diagnosis, but other factors strongly suggest the phase of deposition. If there are no graves of another period in the immediate area, e.g in plot I, these graves are presumed to belong to the same phase as their neighbours. They are reckoned as belonging to the designated phase in assessments, e.g. Tables XII–XV. This is not possible in plot A, however, where a number of phases are represented.

**Early Anglo-Saxon finds in the Dover area** (Text Figure 36)

*Inhumation cemetery*

1. *Barham, Breach Downs.*. TR 20674900 (O.S. record cards TR 24 NW1). Tumuli excavated c 1809, Smith 1908a, 348–9; 1841, Conyngham 1844a; c 1843, Smith 1848, 7–8, pl.VI 11–15; *Proc Soc Antiq* ser.1, 3 (1853–6) 137–8; Bartlett 1845; 1844, *Archaeol J* 1 (1844) 271; Croker 1844; Meaney 1964, 111; Willson 1984. British Museum, British Museum (Natural History).
2. *Dover, Buckland Estate.* TR 310430 (O.S. *Britain in the Dark Ages*). Present Report. Meaney 1964, 117, where wrongly identified as Old Park. British Museum. 1879, composite brooch, beads, silver wire ring and silver wire bangle, provenance uncertain, possibly Buckland, see p 46. Rigold and Webster 1970, 10, 13–17; Avent 1975 ii, pl.64 No.174. British Museum.
3. *Dover Old Park.* TR 3044 (O.S. record cards TR 34 SW 49). 1861, discs, escutcheons and a flat ring from hanging bowls, *Proc Soc Antiq*, ser 2, 22 (1907–9) 77–8. Before 1915, a late sixth century silver-gilt mount, Kendrick 1937a. Before 1915, thirteen ivory mounts from a casket, Kendrick 1937b; Meaney 1964, 117. British Museum, Dover Museum.
4. *Dover, Priory Hill.* TR 31454175 (O.S. record cards TR34 SW6). 1883 Disc brooch, (lost) Kendrick 1933b; Rigold and Webster 1970, 1–2, 8–12; Avent 1975 ii, pl.53 No. 154. See above p 00. Before 1889, Anglo-Saxon interments found on Priory Hill, Payne 1889, 205; Payne 1893, 199. Dover Museum.
5. *Folkestone, Dover Hill.* TR 23803759 (O.S. record cards TR23 NW7). Before 1848, gilt bronze radiate brooch, *J Brit Archaeol Ass* 4 (1848) 159. c 1889, 9 Anglo-Saxon graves, Payne 1889, 205; Payne 1893, 199. 1907, c38 Anglo-Saxon graves. *Archaeol Cantiana* 28 (1909) lxxiv. 1910, 4 Anglo-Saxon graves, Parsons 1911, 102–3; Meaney 1964, 120–1. Finds from 1907 are in Folkestone Museum. Finds from earlier excavations were in Dover Museum and were destroyed in the war 1939–45. O.S record cards.
6. *St. Margaret's at Cliffe.* TR 360443 (O.S. record cards TR34 SE6, TR 34 SE11). 1775 and 1782, tumuli, Douglas 1793, 119–20. Three Anglo-Saxon shield bosses, a knife, an Anglo-Saxon spearhead and fragments of a brooch, probably from the same cemetery (O.S. record cards TR 34 SE11). Meaney 1964, 135. Dover Museum.
7. *Sibertswold-Barfriston.* TR 265488. (O.S. record cards TR24 NE2). 1772–3, c 239 graves. Faussett 1856, 101–43; Meaney 1964, 136. Liverpool Museum.
8. *Temple Ewell.* TR 29064428, TR 29144435, TR 29164436. (O.S. record cards TR24 SE14). Before 1799, several tumuli excavated, skeletons each with sword and spear, Hasted 1799, 42. In Lousyberry Wood are three tumuli which are probably those referred to (O.S. record cards TR24 SE14), Meaney 1964, 139.

*Inhumation burials up to 3 in number*

9. *Dover, High Meadow.* TR 31014197 (O.S. record cards TR34 SW76). 1956 Anglo-Saxon grave, gold and garnet disc pendant, bronze ring and glass bead. Evison 1967b; Meaney 1964, 117, Dover Museum.
10. *Eythorne.* TR 2749 (O.S. record cards TR24 NE17). 1828, Anglo-Saxon objects including three spearheads, part of a knife and fragments of shield bosses dug up at Eythorne were presented to the predecessor of the Beaney Institute and Royal Museum, Canterbury. The finds are not at present traceable. O.S. record cards TR24 NE17. Maidstone Museum Archaeological Gazetteer; Meaney 1964, 118.
11. *Guston.* TR 3244. (O.S. record cards TR34 SW59). 1864, a silver-gilt and garnet disc brooch, probably found with a shield boss and spearhead in the parish of Guston, *Archaeol J* 21 (1864) 101; Avent 1975 ii, no.129, 33, pl.42; Meaney 1964, 122–3. Leeds Museum.

12. *Ringwould*. TR 35914832. (O.S. record cards TR34 NE8, TR34 NE18). *c* 1852, 2 skeletons found with two spearheads, single-edged iron 'coutel', spear ferrule L. 6in., bronze buckle and gilt metal belt plate set with ?garnets. Poynter 1852; Meaney 1964, 133. British Museum. Disc brooch found in an isolated grave near Ringwould village, probably from same group. O.S. record cards TR34 NE18. Stebbing MS. Deal Library. The brooch is not at present traceable.
13. *St Margaret's at Cliffe*. TR 36584468 (O.S. record cards TR34 SE5). *c* 1930, Saxon burial with iron spearhead and glass beads found whilst digging foundations for a house called 'Ballygange' now 'Wave Hill' in Salisbury Road, St. Margaret's Bay. Finds probably retained by the late Col. Cavenagh, a local historian, who investigated this site. O.S. record cards TR34 SE5.

*Cremation burial*
14. *Folkestone, The Bayle*. TR 231359. (O.S. record cards TR23 NW19). 1850. Anglo-Saxon spearhead found with fragments of an urn which had been filled with calcined bone. Wright 1849–53a, 175; Meaney 1964, 120.

*Settlement*
Several traces have been found of a Saxon settlement in the centre of Dover, within and near the third-century Saxon Shore fort, including:
15a. *Yewdens Court*. A handmade, black, carinated rim-sherd and a Frankish wheel-made sherd of grey ware with rouletting decoration, Dunning 1957, fig. 14.2 and 3; Evison 1979a, 71, group1f3.
  b. *Market Street*. TR 318415. 1972. Deep deposit of occupation rubbish over and under a metalled area. Finds included imported pottery of sixth-seventh century, fragments of glass vessels, decorated bone objects and a gold finger-ring set with a garnet. Webster 1973, 145; Philp 1973b.
  c. *Market Square*. TR 319414. 1975. A *Grubenhaus* had cut through the north wall of room 3 of the 'Painted House', and in it were found about thirty clay loomweights, pottery and a bronze workbox of the eighth century. Webster 1976, 164.
  d. *Queen Street*. TR318413. 1977. A section of a large wooden structure of Anglo-Saxon date was excavated on the site of the Bacon Factory. It was rectangular, on an E–W axis and of at least six periods, one with a stone floor. Webster 1978, 147. Pottery and glass from the area suggest dates in the seventh-ninth centuries. May have been part of the monastery of St. Martin cf no.21 below. Philp 1978; Webster 1979, 240–1; *idem*. 1980, 227.

*Single finds*
16. *Barham*. TR 22634852, (O.S. record cards TR24 NW13). *c* 1855, silver spoon, Brown 1913–14; Brown 1915 IV, pl. XCV.1.
17. *Dover, Durham Hill*. TR 317413. (O.S. record cards TR34 SW50). Before 1939, 2 Anglo-Saxon penannular brooches and 2 Anglo-Saxon buckles. O.S. record cards TR34 SW50. Dover Museum Accessions Book; Meaney 1964, 118. Dover Museum.
18. *Dover, St. Radigund's Road*. 1860–70, wheelthrown bottle sherd. Evison 1979a, 84–5, fig.37. Dover Museum.
19. *Folkestone, Cherry Garden Hill*. TR 20833801 (O.S. record cards TR23 NW 25). ?Secondary burial in barrow. Some pieces of a Frankish jug with a fowl's spur and some bones of the foot. Smith 1852, 219.

*Minsters or other religious foundations founded before AD 725*
20. *Dover*. Church of 22 canons founded by Eadbald (616–640) in the chapel of St. Mary in Castro. B.M. Cott. Vesp. B.xi. fol. 73. Fowler 1926, 133.
21. *St Martin's, Dover*. In 696 Wihtraed transferred the canons from the castle to the church of St. Martin in the town (see 15d above). B.M. Cott. Jul. D.V. Fowler 1926, 133.
22. *Folkestone*. Priory founded by Eadbald *c* 630 for his daughter Eanswith. B.M. Cott. MS. Tib. A.ii.fol.12b. Fowler 1926, 236. Rigold 1972, 35.

*Finds not marked on map, exact location not recorded*

*Barham Downs*. Possible cremation burial excavated sixteenth century; burials excavated 1759, 1944. Meaney 1964, 108.
*Near Dover*. Before 1847, gold tremissis, London mint, 'Derivative Legend'. Smith 1848, pl.XXII, 9; Rigold 1975, 675. no.123. Ashmolean Museum.
*Folkestone, Martello Dairy Farm*. Kentish silve-gilt jewelled disc brooch (Leeds class 1, a, Avent class 2.10). Webster 1972, 157; Avent 1975 ii, no.71, 19, pl.14.
*Folkestone*. Merovingian tremissis, LOCO SANCTO. (Lieusaint-en-Brie, Seine-et-Marne). Moneyer: Dacoaldus. Rigold 1975, 672, no.79.
*Folkestone*. 1899. Merovingian tremissis, LOCO SANCTO. Moneyer: Dacoaldus. Rigold 1975, 672, no.80.
*Folkestone*. Apparently similar tremissis. Rigold 1975, 672, no.81.
*Between Sandgate and Dover*. Bronze triangular bucket mount. *Archaeol J* 8 (1851) 177. British Museum.
*Sutton-by-Dover*. Before 1841, 'Alemannic' tremissis. Evans 1942, 39, pl.I.10. Rigold 1975, 667, no. 44.

*Doubtful finds not marked on the map*

*Inhumation cemetery*

    *Barham Downs.* TR 22264884 (O.S. record cards TR24 NW21). 1969, 5 inhumantion burials. A green bead and several sherds, one eight-ninth century. Bradshaw 1969, 235. O.S. record cards TR24 NW21. Royal Museum, Canterbury.

    *St. Margaret's at Cliffe, Bay Hill.* TR 36414449 (O.S. record cards TR34 SE2). 1920, 6 graves in a round barrow. No finds. O.S. record cards TR34 SE2. Meaney 1964, 135. British Museum (Natural History).

*Inhumation burials up to 3 in number*

    *Lydden* 1760. Two skeletons with a dagger beside them. Gough 1786, xv; O.S. record cards TR24 NE12.

    *Ringwould, Mill Service Station.* TR 36474935. Spear and shield in isolated grave. Parfitt 1981, 111

*Single finds*

    *Dover, Cannon Street.* TR 319415. (O.S. record cards. TR34 SW48). 1880. Bone comb. Smith 1908a, 384; Meaney 1964, 117. Dover Museum, missing.

    *Possibly Dover.* Before 1920, Merovingian tremissis MARCILIACO, (Marcilly-en-Gault, Loire-et-Cher). Moneyer: Odmundus. Rigold 1975, 672, no.84. British Museum.

    *Possibly Dover.* Before 1819, saucer brooch. Smith 1908b, 102. British Museum OA 6740.

    *Possibly Dover or near Dover* 1984. Two button brooches, Bury St Edmunds Museum. Information K. East.

# Chapter IV

# Specialist Reports

**The Sherds of Prehistoric Pottery** *by Paul Ashbee*

Small burned and abraded sherds of Later Neolithic and Earlier Bronze Age pottery are often found associated with round barrows[1] and the so-called 'ring-ditches' which are so often all that remains of them. Such sherds are often associated with occupation debris, dark soil, pieces of charcoal, broken flint artefacts, knapping debris and pieces of bone. Material of this kind was regularly incorporated into long barrows[2]. In these the deposition of occupation debris was clearly intentional but intent cannot be demonstrated for many round barrows[3].

Presumably the ring-ditch, associated with the Buckland Anglo-Saxon cemetery marks the site of a round barrow, of which there are numbers in the vicinity[4]. This would account for the scatter of prehistoric sherds. As the sherds were found in the infill of the Anglo-Saxon graves, it is possible that the barrow was razed at an early juncture. Alternatively, the sherds were present in the top-soil, for occupation debris was used for manuring fields[5]. Observation of the Overton Down Experimental Earthwork has shown the dangers of dating works and ditches by the uncritical use of what is clearly incidental material[6].

*List of the pottery sherds*

Grave 66  Abraded sherd of ?rusticated beaker, with finger-nail and finger tip and nail ornament, containing flint grits.

Grave 113 (a) A hard, dark-faced sherd, containing water-worn flint grits, bearing a design of close-set, round-bottomed, hatching. It could well be a fragment of a globular vessel of a general Deverel-Rimbury tradition.

(b) Three plain, thick, sherds abundantly gritted might well be from a bucket-form urn.

Grave 114  A small dark-faced sherd, with traces of sooting and mica inclusions among its fine grits. ?Early Neolithic or Iron Age.

Grave 125  An abraded rim sherd of dark-faced ware, flint gritted and bearing shallow grooving. It has been burned.

Grave 128  Three black, refired sherds with traces of line ornament. Organic temper has been burned from one of them. ?Grooved ware.

Grave 151  An abraded red-faced sherd with abundant flint grits.

Grave 156  A broken sherd of ?organically tempered ware with traces of finger-tip and finger nail ornament. ?Rusticated or grooved ware.

**The petrology of the Anglo-Saxon pottery** *by I C Freestone (British Museum Research Laboratory)*

Eight sherds were examined in thin section. The hand-made pot (87/3) is characterised by inclusions of quartz, glauconite, calcite and fragments of ferruginous sandstone and sandy glauconitic limestone, up to about 1mm. This assemblage is consistent with a derivation from Kentish sediments, for example the Lower Greensand, which outcrops as a strip, a few miles wide, running inland from Folkestone through Maidstone and Sevenoaks.

In the wheel-made pottery, the predominant inclusion is quartz, with minor amount of glauconite and muscovite mica in some cases. The ubiquity of these minerals in sedimentary deposits does not allow the provenancing of the pottery. However, it is possible to group the pottery on the basis of the occurrence and amount of glauconite and muscovite and on the size, sorting and proportion of the quartz grains. Such subdivision must be regarded as tentative, subject to confirmation, as the variability in output of a single workshop is unknown. However, the suggestion is that at least three fabrics are represented. Of these, no.156/6 stands out most clearly as a distinctive fabric type, containing very abundant, closely packed, very fine glauconitic sand and coarse silt. Interestingly, this sherd is chemically distinct from the other Dover sherds and from the 'Continental' group[7], and a Kentish source has been suggested[8]. The petrology is consistent with these

1  Ashbee 1960, 55
2  Ashbee 1978, 76–80
3  Ashbee 1979–80, 31
4  Ashbee and Dunning 1960
5  Phillips 1980, 228
6  Jewell and Dimbleby, 1966, 340–1
7  Cowell 1979
8  Evison 1979a, 58

conclusions; similar fabrics have been observed in the Kentish pottery of the pre-Roman Iron Age[9]. Another distinctive fabric is that of the biconical bowl, 139/4, which has a very fine fabric lacking the quartz sand component characteristic of the bottles. The remaining five bottles contain varying amounts of quartz sand typically around 0.25mm diameter. The significance of the differences between these sherds, for example in the sand/clay ratio and the presence/absence of minor glauconite is uncertain, so they have not been subdivided.

In conclusion, it is emphasised that no petrological proof of provenance has been forthcoming. However the subdivision of the fabrics that has been possible shows an encouraging concordance with chemistry and typology.

**The coins** by *J P C Kent, British Museum*
[all weights quoted are after cleaning]

*Roman Coins*

*Grave C*

An associated group of Roman coins used as weights, found with a pair of scales, to right of body.

C/3b1 Sestertius, Faustina II (under Antoninus Pius, *c* 160). Reverse, apparently Spes, as *BMC* 2200, but obverse belongs to a different issue, *BMC* 2167. Very worn, with slight traces of filing on edge and surface. Weight 21.11 g.

C/3b2 Sestertius, 2nd century, fabric suggests Hadrian (117–138). The types have been completely obliterated by filing. Six nicks have been cut into one edge. Weight, 18.59 g.

C/3b3 Sestertius, Antoninus Pius (138–161). Reverse, standing figure. Very worn, with traces of filing. A bronze disc, perhaps a coin, has been riveted to the centre of the obverse. There is a large notch on the obverse edge, and a punch-mark on the reverse. Weight, 17.70 g.

C/3b4 Dupondius, Antoninus Pius (138–161). Reverse, standing figure. Very worn, and filed on both sides. There are four notches on the obverse edge. Weight, 12.31 g.

C/3b5 As, Caracalla (211–217). Reverse, PM TRP XX COS IIII PP, Radiate lion to left, with thunderbolt in mouth (AD 217), *BMC* 311. One notch on obverse edge, three punched dots on obverse. Weight, 9.10 g.

C/3b6 As, Caligula (37–41). Reverse (filed flat), head of Germanicus to left. *RIC* 44 or 45. Weight, 8.83 g.

C/3b7 Antoninianus, Allectus (293–296). Reverse, PAX AVG $\frac{S|A}{M L}$ *RIC* 33. Some filing on high spots, perhaps two punch-marks on reverse. Weight, 4.06 g.

C/3b8 Antoninianus, Carausius (286–293). Reverse, PAX AVGGG $\frac{S|P}{M L X X I}$. *RIC* 141. Corroded; there are possible punch-marks on both sides. Weight, 3.41 g.

C/3b9 Antoninianus, Tetricus I (270–274). Reverse, HILARITAS AVGG. *RIC* 76. Filed on both sides and on edge, one punched dot on obverse. Weight, 3.03 g.

C3b10 Antoninianus, Claudius II (268–270). Reverse, PROVIDENT AVG $\underline{|S|}$ *RIC* 91 or 92. Filed on edge and both sides, perhaps some slight punch-marking. Weight, 2.95 g.

C/3b11 Antoninianus, Tetricus I (270–274). As no. 9, but no filing or punch-marks. Weight 2.61 g.

C/3b12 False Antoninianus ('barbarous radiate'), Carausius (286–293). Reverse, Pax standing. One notch in edge. Weight 2.53 g.

C/3b13 Antoninianus, Claudius II (269–270). Reverse FIDES EXERCI *RIC* 35. Heavily corroded. Weight, 2.15 g.

C/3b14 Centenionalis, Constantine I (306–337). Reverse uncertain, but obverse suggests a date *c* 320. Filed on both sides, severely corroded and chipped. Weight, 0.89 g. The original weight of this series is around 3.00 g.

A note on the record card suggests that there may have been two or three more coins.

Comparable sets of weights have been found in four other Kentish graves:-
a) Guilton (Ash), grave 66: seventeen weights, including two very heavy ones, scales and touchstone[10].
b) Ozingell (Ramsgate): fifteen weights[11].
c) Sarre, grave xxvi: fifteen weights[12].
d) Ash sand-pit, to be distinguished from (a), which was found eight years previously: a mass of weights, piled in descending order of size, at least two of which were coins; there were also scales and a touchstone[13].

It appears that more than one weight system was in use, but corrosion and damage make it difficult to establish it in detail. The principal system appears to be based on a unity of slightly over 3.00 g. for which notched or punch-marked weights, generally adapted from Roman coins, have been noted from Guilton, Ozingell and Sarre. Marked weights corresponding to 1, 3, 4, 5, 6, and 7 units are known. The Romano-Byzantine solidus, around 4.50 g., also furnished a standard. At Guilton were found two Byzantine weights, one for 2 solidi (marked NB and two pellets, weight 8.04 g.), the other for a tremissis of 8 siliquae, about 1.50 g. The latter is clearly for a full-weight coin, and in spite of its present defective weight, the former must originally have denoted two

---

9 Freestone and Rigby, work in progress
10 Faussett 1856, 73, pl. xvii
11 Smith, 1854, 12, pl. iv
12 Brent 1866, 161
13 Douglas 1793, 51, pl.xii, 8, 9

full solidi. The numerous coins all unrelated and generally inferior to the 3.00+g. standard are presumably multiples of a subsidiary unit. The Guilton tremissis weight is indicated in siliquae (carats), but there is no certainty about the Anglo-Saxon sub-multiple unit.

In any event, it is notoriously impossible to define a weight-standard from surviving base metal weights. Not merely are there incalculable losses (and occasional gains), from natural causes, but even in its pristine state, the pieces may have incorporated some charge or discount. The extensive filing plainly indicates that care was taken over the conversion of coin to weight. How unmarked pieces were used is not at all clear; perhaps they were counters rather than weights.

*Grave 14*
14/2   Centenionalis, probably Constantine II. Reverse VIRTVS EXERCIT, date 319/20. *RIC* (London) 190 or 197/8. Pierced and very worn.

*Grave 15*
15/5   Antoninianus, Carausius (286–293). Reverse, PAX AVGGG $\frac{S|P}{MLXXI}$. *RIC* 138.

*Grave 129*
129/3  Antoninianus, Valerian I (253–260). Reverse, SECVRIT PERPET. *RIC* 256. Pierced.

*Grave 138*
138/7  Æ 3. Constans. Reverse FEL TEMP REPARATIO, Phoenix on globe, date 348–350. *RIC* (Trier) 232/4/6.

*Grave 141*
141/3  Denarius, Clodius Albinus (193–196). Reverse ROMAE AETERNAE. *RIC* 11. Pierced.

*Post-Roman Coins*
Unassociated; washed out of bank, October 1951.
Unass. 6   Tremissis, period of Leovigild, King of the Visigoths (568–586), the so-called CVRRV series, date *c* 575. Tomasini no. 581. A three-fluted gold loop has been soldered above the bust. Weight, including mount, 1.44 g.
   This series, which derives its characteristic legend from barbarised pieces naming the Byzantine emperor Justinian (527–565), is directly ancestral to the earliest issues incribed with Leovigild's name. It is likely that these in turn gave way to Leovigild's second type (cross on steps) *c* 580, and a date *c* 575 for the latest CVRRV issues seems likely. This is the latest in date of several Visigothic tremisses found in eastern England[14].

*Grave 29*
29/7   Bronze gilt imitation of a tremissis. Weight, including three-fluted silver loop, 0.73 g. The legend is completely barbarised, but the types are ultimately derived from tremisses struck for Justinian I in Italy after about 540. Rigold attributes this piece to east or north-west Gaul[15].

*Grave 110*
110/10  Silver 'sceatta' i.e. penny, related to PADA series. Kentish, late 7th century. Rigold class PIIB. Weight, excluding six-fluted silver loop, 1.08 g.
110/11  Silver 'sceatta' ie penny. Kentish, inscribed PADA (runic), late 7th century. Rigold class P III. Weight, excluding six-fluted silver loop, 1.22 g.

The place of these coins in the early Anglo-Saxon silver coinage has been discussed by S E Rigold[16]. Analysis shows a substantial and rather unexpected admixture of copper (12% 110/10, 24% 110/11) in their alloy, and their appearance confirms their relative baseness. No.110/10 remains unique, but there are several examples similar to 110/11.

**Gold Analyses** by *M Cowell, British Museum Research Laboratory*

*Five Gold Bracteates*
The bracteates were all analysed by XRF and, additionally, the specific gravity (SG) of each was measured for comparison. The XRF determination was carried out on areas abraded and polished on the back surfaces of the objects. However, because the areas were rather smaller than usual due to the nature of the surface design, the accuracy of the analysis may not be as good as could be achieved under ideal circumstances. The XRF results given in Table XLI for the major elements are only therefore quoted to the nearest whole percent. From the XRF analysis it is possible to calculate the approximate SG of the article and this can be compared with the actual measured SG.

TABLE XLI  XRF RESULTS FOR FIVE GOLD BRACTEATES

| Object No. | %Gold | %Silver | %Copper | SG (calc) | SG (meas.) |
|---|---|---|---|---|---|
| 1/1 | 73 | 24 | 3.1 | 15.5 | 14.97 |
| 20/4 | 87 | 11 | 1.8 | 17.1 | 16.91 |
| 29/8 | 63 | 34 | 2.5 | 14.5 | 13.86 |
| 134/1 | 59 | 39 | 2.3 | 14.1 | 13.89 |
| Unassociated 6 | 95 | 3.9 | 1.1 | 18.3 | 18.13 |

The agreement between SG and XRF is on the whole fairly good considering that these are composite objects with loop suspenders and rims which may be of a different composition from the main body of the bracteate. The SG results will therefore

---

14  Rigold 1975, 667, No. 43
15  Ibid, 666, No. 35

16  Rigold 1960–1, 14, 15, 31, 32, 53

be averages for the whole object whereas the XRF results apply only to the main body.

The similarity of 29/8 and 134/1 in terms of XRF and SG suggests a common origin for these two bracteates. The other items however, do not seem to show similarities.

*Gold finger-ring from grave 38.*
The ring was analysed by XRF on a small area which had been lightly abraded to remove any possible surface enrichment or corrosion. The following results were obtained.

| Object No. | %Gold | %Silver | %Copper |
|---|---|---|---|
| 38/6 | 98.4 | 1.5 | 0.2 |

**Qualitative analyses of some of the beads** by *Justine Bayley, Ancient Monuments Laboratory*

A selection of beads from the cemetery were kindly made available for analysis by Mrs L Webster of the Medieval and Later Antiquities Department of the British Museum. All were examined under a low power microscope and analysed by energy dispersive X-ray fluorescence. For some of the polychrome beads more than one area was analysed in an attempt to separate the different colours. This separation was not complete as the area being analysed was often as large as the bead itself but the variations detected were recorded (see Table XLV).

*Analytical technique and presentation of results*
The beads were analysed by X-ray fluorescence (XRF) using an energy dispersive system. The primary radiation source was an X-ray tube with a rhodium target run at 35 kv; the sample chamber was evacuated to allow detection of elements below atomic number 19 and the fluorescent X-rays were detected by a Si(Li) detector run for a live time of 20 seconds with a photon flux of about 5–10 Kcps.

Sodium, magnesium and aluminium were not detectable though the first of these elements was almost certainly present in most if not all of the beads and the other two were probably also present in minor amounts. Other elements detected but not appearing in Tables XLIV and XLV include potassium, calcium, strontium and silicon. As the beads were not prepared in any way for analysis it was thought that the potassium levels were not likely to be significant. The figures obtained show small but relatively constant amounts detected so the figures would not have been diagnostic even if they had been meaningful. The calcium figures could not be used as many of the beads had varying amounts of chalk stuck in surface irregularities or in the perforation, ie not all the calcium detected was in the glass.

As the beads were of very variable size, shape and surface texture the absolute peak heights recorded could not usefully be directly compared. To allow approximate comparisons to be made, the readings were normalised by dividing each by the corresponding silicon reading. As a first approximation the proportion of silicon in each bead is constant so this is the most sensible element of those available to use in this way. The only cases where this approximation is less good is where the glass contains major amounts of lead. The colours particularly affected by this are greens and opaque yellows, where the lead figures are enhanced by the way the data has been treated; it does not however materially affect the interpretation given.

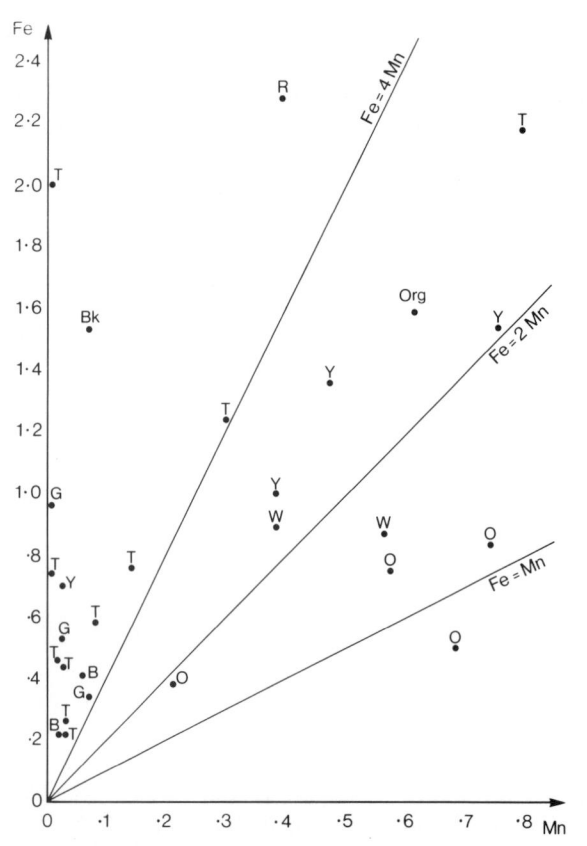

*Text Figure 37* Plot of analytical results for monochrome beads; iron (Fe) v. manganese (Mn.) The symbols on Text Figures 37–42 refer to different colours (see Table XLII)

The individual peak heights bear no direct relationship to the proportion of that element present as different elements are excited more or less efficiently by the primary X-rays, e.g. tin is excited far less than copper so the figures given in Tables XLIV and XLV are consistently lower even when the amounts involved are similar. A constant proportion of one element will also give signals of varying strength depending on the composition of the matrix in which it is present.

The figures given in Tables XLIV and XLV should be treated as approximate values as they result from a single measurement of one part of the object only. For this reason divisions based on fine distinctions have been avoided as they would be illusory; however, broad divisions into groups can be made on the basis of absence or presence of a particular element. Sometimes the division can be refined by recording absence, presence or abundance. The elements recorded in Tables XLIV and XLV are titanium (Ti), manganese (Mn), iron (Fe), cobalt (Co), copper (Cu), zinc (Zn), lead (Pb), arsenic (As), tin (Sn) and antimony (Sb). The peak measured was the $K_\alpha$ peak except for lead where the $L_\alpha$

peak was used. Peak heights (normalised to silicon) are given for all elements except cobalt. This is recorded only as detected/not detected as the peak overlaps with the iron $K_\beta$ peak (which is universally present) and is itself very small as the quantities of cobalt necessary to produce a deep colour are minute[17]. Most of the elements recorded have an effect on the colour or opacity of the glass, exceptions being titanium, which is found in small amounts in much glass, and zinc. It has been suggested that the variations in the amount of titanium present may indicate different sources of silica, one of the glass-making raw materials, as titania is found as an impurity in sand (silica)[18]. The zinc appears to have entered these glasses with the copper (see discussion below).

It has been possible to calibrate approximately some of the XRF ratios by comparing XRF and neutron activation analyses (NAA) for a group of Anglian beads from Sewerby[19]. The elements common to both programmes of analyses were manganese, copper, tin and antimony. The factors by which the XRF ratios have to be multiplied to give approximate percentage compositions are respectively unity or just under, ½–1, 2–5 and 2. The conversion is not completely constant for any one element but it should be remembered that XRF analyses only the surface and NAA the bulk glass so some variation is to be expected. It is likely that a multiplication factor of just under one would also be appropriate for the iron and zinc ratios as their positions in the XRF spectrum are close to those of manganese and copper respectively. No calibration is available for the lead ratios but comparison with Roman enamel analyses[20] suggests that the ratios are of the right order of magnitude and that the lead contents of the beads probably range from under one percent up to around 20%. This would correspond to a multiplication factor of 1–2.

The comparison of XRF and NAA results also allowed an estimate to be made of detection limits. These seem to be about 0.1% for copper and around 0.2% for tin and antimony.

*Discussion of results*

The normalised peak heights are tabulated in Tables XLIV and XLV. The results for the monochrome beads, where the analytical data relate to a single colour of glass, are considered first and presented visually in Text Figures 37–42. The data from the polychrome beads do not lend themselves to the same sort of presentation as the analyses were not usually of a small enough area to isolate the individual colours, so Table XLV gives an average for the two or more colours present. This makes interpretation more complex and the conclusions reached necessarily more tentative.

*The monochrome beads*

A total of 27 beads and one vessel sherd were

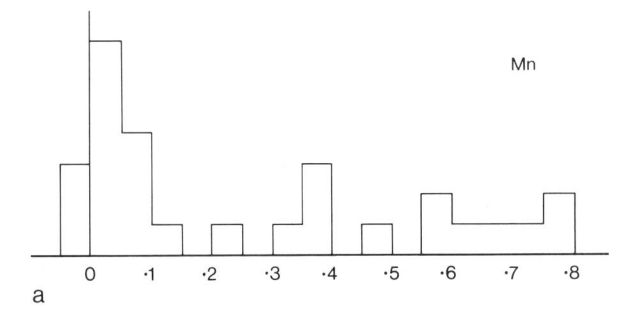

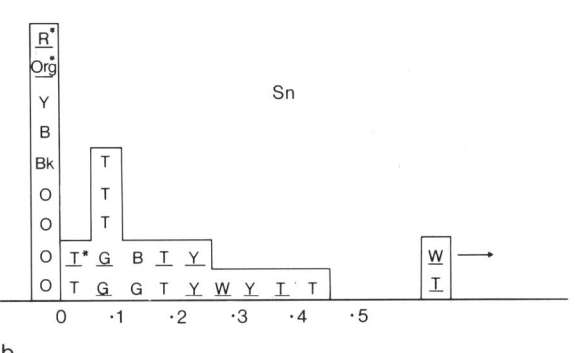

*Text Figure 38* Histograms of analytical results for manganese (Mn) and tin (Sn). The vertical axes are frequency (number of examples). Columns to the left of the zero line represent objects where the element was not detectable.

analysed. These can be grouped into 9 colours, some of which are found as both translucent and opaque glass. A general discussion of the composition of coloured glass and the colouring and opacifying effects of individual elements can be found in Bayley[21].

TABLE XLII    THE MONOCHROME BEADS

| Colour (symbol used in figures) | Opaque | Translucent | Total |
|---|---|---|---|
| Red (R) | 1 | | 1 |
| Orange (Org) | 1 | | 1 |
| Yellow (Y) | 3 | 1 | 4 |
| Green (G) | 2 | 1 | 3 |
| Blue/Green and Turquoise (T) | 3 | 6 | 9 |
| Blue (B) | | 2 | 2 |
| White (W) | 2 | | 2 |
| Black (Bk) | | 1 | 1 |
| 'Colourless' (O) | | 4 | 4 |

The beads described as blue/green and turquoise were of a range of colours. There is no hard and fast division between these and the green beads, a point which shows up in the Figures. There is also no rigid distinction between opaque and translucent colours as the degree of transparency depends on the

17  Phillips 1941
18  Spitzer-Aronson 1979
19  Biek *et al.*, 1985

20  Bateson and Hedges 1975; Biek *et al.*, 1980
21  Bayley, forthcoming a

thickness of the object, the depth of colour and the presence of bubbles and opaque inclusions. Many beads which appear opaque in the hand are seen to be translucent with opaque inclusions when examined at low magnifications; this is true of most of the opaque blue and green beads and also, to a lesser extent, the whites and yellows.

With the exception of the vessel sherd 59/3q, which is of a unique composition and is discussed below, three general points can be made about the analyses. Firstly, antimony was not detected in any of the monochrome beads; secondly, decolourisation was due to the presence of manganese and finally, opacity was due to copper compounds (red and orange) or tin compounds (other colours). The lack of antimony is to be expected in a post-Roman context. It does however suggest that none of the beads are re-used Roman ones and that they are not made of re-used Roman glass. This, however, can really only be taken to apply to the beads where antimony might reasonably be expected, i.e. the opaque whites, yellows, blues and greens and the transparent 'colourless' beads. It also assumes an absolute correspondence of antimony with Roman and earlier, and lack of antimony with post-Roman glass. While this assumption is generally sound exceptions do exist[22].

All the glass contained detectable amounts of iron. Where the colour this imparted to the glass was not going to be masked by another colourant, its effect was neutralised by adding manganese. This is particularly noticeable (see Text Figure 37) for the 'colourless' and white glass (manganese values greater than half the iron values: $Mn > \frac{1}{2} Fe$) when compared with e.g. the greens and turquoises (iron values greater than four times the manganese values: $Fe > 4 Mn$). Composition is not the only variable here as changing the furnace atmosphere can also affect the colour[23]. The frequency distribution of manganese values (see Text Figure 38a) suggests that the low values (up to about 0.1 or 0.2) represent accidental inclusions, occurring naturally in the glass-making raw materials, while the higher values are most probably deliberate additions made to the glass.

The presence of tin as an opacifying agent, like the absence of antimony discussed above, is to be expected in post-Roman glass[24]. The presence of small amounts of tin does not usually impart opacity (see Text Figure 38b); higher levels of tin may also be found in translucent glass (e.g. 35/5f). The opacity of the objects marked with an asterisk in Text Figure 38b is not due to tin; the two without detectable tin are copper opacified (see below) and the one with very low tin was the vessel sherd which was antimony and/or arsenic opacified. The two low tin opaque beads are both greens and both contain far more lead than the other green bead which may be the reason for the difference in appearance.

Text Figure 39, a plot of tin v. copper values,

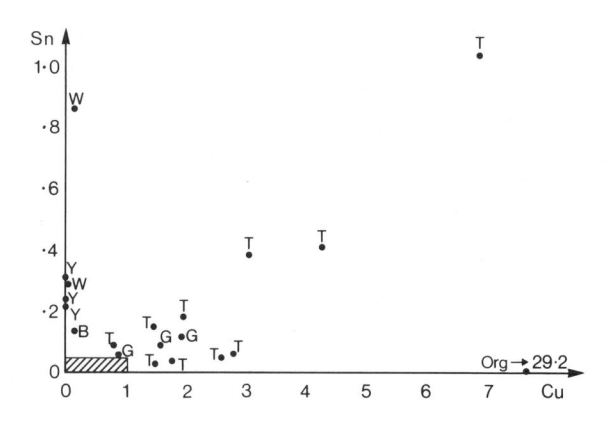

*Text Figure 39* Plot of analytical results for monochrome beads; tin (Sn) v. copper (Cu). Points in the shaded area have been omitted for clarity; none contained any detectable tin

shows three distinct groups of beads. The first are the opaque whites and yellows which have high tin values and zero or virtually zero copper values. The high tin is to be expected as the colour and opacity are due to the presence of lead-tin oxide (yellow) or tin oxide (white). The second group is the greens and blue-greens. Here there seems to be some correlation between the tin and copper suggesting that the tin may have entered the glass along with the copper if the latter was added as an alloy rather than as pure copper. Whether the glass ended up opaque or translucent may have been chance, depending on the overall level of additions. The third group is the glass with low levels of copper and no detectable tin which comprises the black, red and 'colourless' beads as well as the transparent yellow (which should be considered as high-iron 'colourless' rather than as yellow).

The copper v. zinc plot (Text Figure 40) shows positive correlation which suggests the zinc entered the glass with the copper. The relative values of the copper and zinc ratios indicate alloys containing about 15–20% zinc. There are a few beads which contain copper but no detectable zinc (62/4h, 6/10d, 38/4d, 59/3q, 35/5f), while in some there are significant amounts of both tin and zinc present which suggests pure copper, brass, bronze and gunmetals were all being used to impart 'copper' colours. There is not yet enough data available on the use of the different copper alloys in the Saxon period to allow any conclusions to be drawn from this observation.

Text Figure 41 (lead plotted v. copper) shows three groups of points. The first is the opaque yellows with high lead and no detectable copper, the second the points with significant amounts of copper and variable lead levels, and the final group comprises those glasses with very low levels of both copper and lead, the whites, blues, black and 'colourless' beads. The opaque yellows contain very much more lead than the whites which are otherwise

---

22 Biek 1983, 309; Biek and Bayley 1979, 9f; Sayre 1963; Henderson and Warren 1983, 169

23 Newton 1978
24 Biek and Bayley 1979; Biek 1983

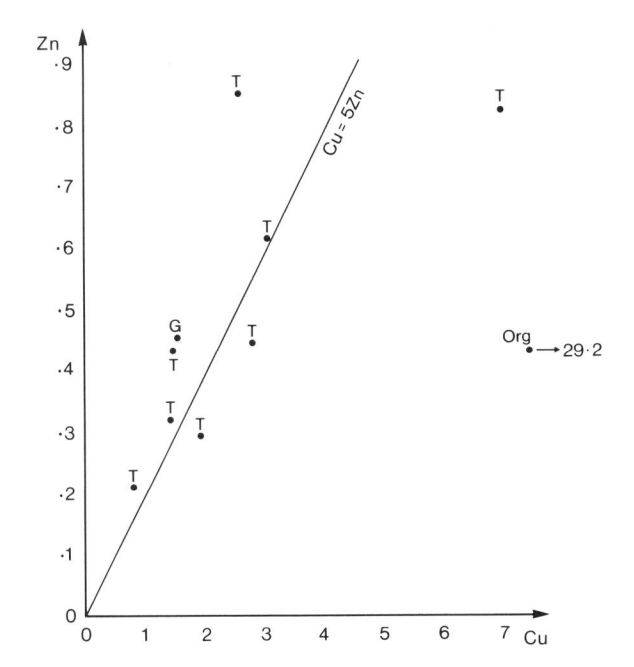

*Text Figure 40* Plot of analytical results for monochrome beads; zinc (Zn) v. copper (Cu). Points with zinc values below 0.2 have been omitted

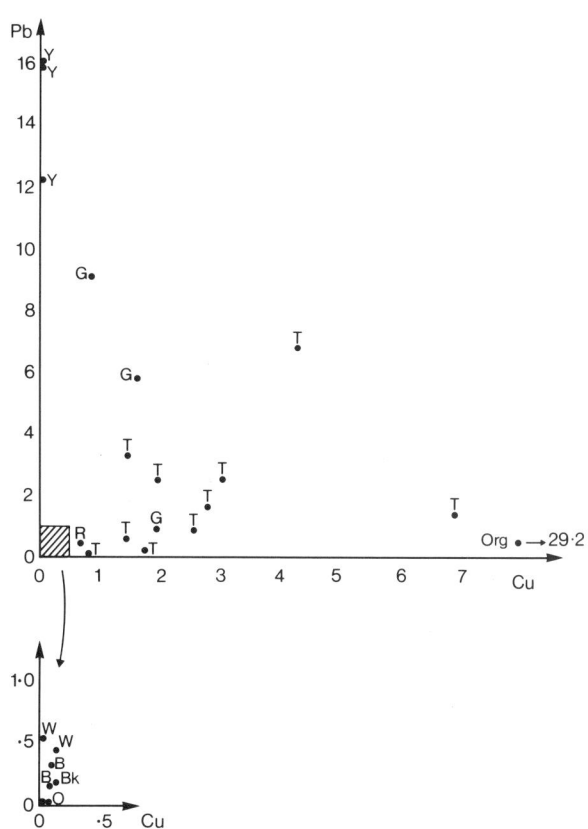

*Text Figure 41* Plot of analytical results for monochrome beads; lead (Pb) v. copper (Cu). Four beads (3 colourless and 1 yellow) containing no detectable lead are omitted from the figure

similar to them in composition. This suggests that the whites and yellows were made separately although white tin oxide is produced irreversibly if yellow lead tin oxide ('PbSnO$_3$') is heated above 900°[25]. This indicates precise control by the beadmakers as no overheated yellows were noted.

The copper containing colours are the red, orange, blue/greens and greens. The opaque reduced colours (red and orange) are low in lead. The orange contains far more copper than the red but is otherwise very similar. The low lead/low copper red is probably comparable to Hughes'[26] 'less brilliantly coloured' reds where the colour is thought to be due to finely divided metallic copper rather than cuprous oxide though Bateson and Hedges[27] saw cuprous oxide crystals even in their low copper red enamels. The colour of red seen depends on the atmosphere in which the glass was heated. A true, bright red is produced under fully reducing conditions while heating in contact with air gives rise to dull, brick red, chestnut brown or even black[28]. The high level of copper in the orange bead is in agreement with the findings of Biek *et al.* and Bateson and Hedges[29] for orange enamels.

The oxidised copper colours (blue/green and green) contain significant amounts of iron (Text Figure 42). There seems to be some correlation between the copper and iron, as though more copper was added to glass containing higher levels of iron to ensure a good colour. In alkali glass copper gives a turquoise-blue colour but in a lead glass it gives a true green[30]. It is not surprising therefore that the copper-containing glasses with higher lead levels are greens (see Text Figure 41). The low lead green 6/10d is relatively high in iron so it is probably this element that is dominant in producing the colour noted.

The low copper levels of the blue beads (as compared with the blue/greens) is unexpected as the results obtained by Bateson and Hedges and Biek *et al.*[31] showed that most blue Roman enamels contain significant amounts of copper though they appear a true 'cobalt blue' colour. Here the two blue beads 30/4d and 30/4e contain only very low levels of cobalt, but they contain virtually no copper so their colour is unlikely to be affected by it.

The black glass is not, as might be supposed, all the left-overs melted up together. Apart from its high iron content, which produces the colour, its composition is closest to that of the 'colourless' glass. The 'colourless', the transparent yellow and the black can best be seen as a progression containing increasing amounts of iron though otherwise of similar composition.

The vessel sherd 59/3q was in many ways of a typical composition for its colour. However, there were two quite atypical elements detected. One was antimony and the other arsenic. The tin present was

25 Rooksby 1964, 21
26 Hughes 1972
27 Bateson and Hedges 1975
28 Brill 1970, 119ff

29 Biek *et al.* 1980; Bateson and Hedges 1975
30 Sayre and Smith 1974
31 Bateson and Hedges 1975; Biek *et al* 1980

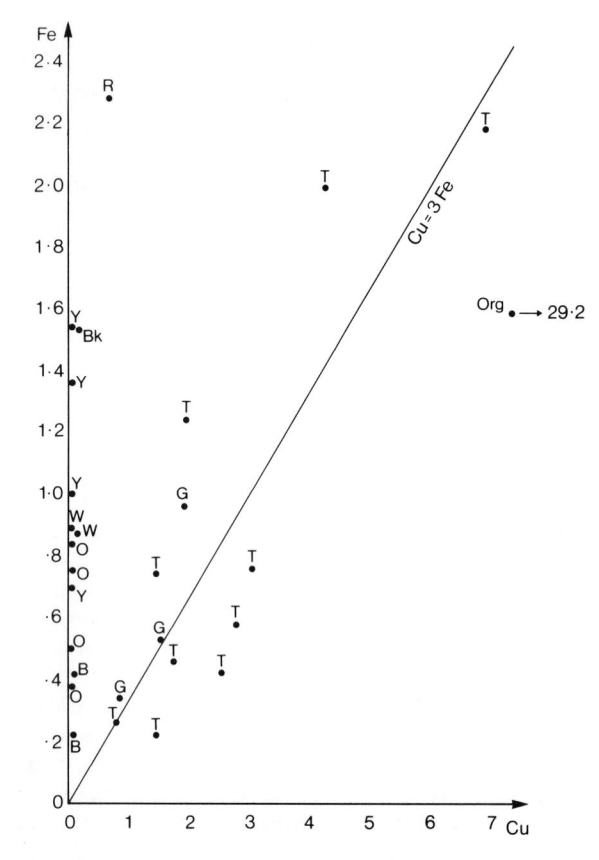

*Text Figure 42* Plot of analytical results for monochrome beads; iron (Fe) v. copper (Cu)

not there in sufficient quantities to produce the opacity noted so this must be due to the antimony and/or arsenic. Antimony is a well known opacifying agent in Roman and earlier times but arsenic is far less commonly reported; Turner and Rooksby[32], have noted it, but only in seventeenth century AD and later glass.

### The polychrome beads

The analytical data for these has been processed in the same way as that from the monochrome beads. However it cannot be so simply interpreted as most of the analyses include more than one colour of glass (see Table XLV for details). In most cases the figures are what would be expected from a mixture of the two (or more) colours present, based on a consideration of the results for the monochrome beads.

The most striking difference between the monochrome and polychrome beads is the detection of significant amounts of antimony in some of the latter. With the possible exception of 92/3d, all the opaque yellows are tin opacified as would be expected from comparison with the monochrome beads. It is some of the whites which appear to be antimony opacified e.g. 59/3g and 133/1c, but this is not a universal trend as tin-opacified whites were also detected among the polychrome beads e.g. 42/1k, 18/2h, 1/4x and 60/3q. This variety of composition strongly suggests multiple sources for

TABLE XLIII   COMPARISON OF OPACIFYING AND DECOLOURISING AGENTS

|  | Dover | Portway | Sewerby |
|---|---|---|---|
| *Monochrome beads* | | | |
| Antimony detected | 0 of 27 | 4 of 16 | 8 of 26 |
| Opaque colours containing antimony | None | white | white |
|  |  | red* | blue |
|  |  |  | green/turquoise |
| Antimony decolourisation | No | Yes | Yes |
| Tin detected | 18 of 27 | 6 of 16 | 12 of 26 |
| Tin opacified colours | yellow | red* | yellow |
|  | white | black* | white |
|  | green/turquoise |  | green/turquoise |
|  |  |  | red* |
| Manganese decolourisation | Yes | Yes | Yes |
| *Polychrome beads* | | | |
| Antimony detected | 4 of 37 | 0 of 22 | 0 of 0 |
| Tin detected | 34 of 37 | 20 of 22 | 0 of 0 |

Note:- * = opacity is mainly due to copper and/or iron but antimony or tin (as appropriate) were also detected.

---

32  Turner and Rooksby 1959

the beads. Those containing antimony are more likely to have come from craftsmen working in a Roman or Mediterranean tradition while those opacified with tin probably have a more northerly, Germanic inspiration[33]. There are no hard or fast geographical or chronological boundaries but the broad division suggested is supported by the few relevant analyses that are available[34].

A few of the polychrome beads, especially 30/4s and 30/4t, contain very high levels of manganese relative to iron. In 30/4s this is responsible for the pink/purple colour of the 'colourless' glass; it is the complimentary effect to the yellow that is produced by high iron. These high manganese levels may have been due to naturally occurring impurities in the raw materials used by a particular workshop or may have been deliberate additions to the glass melts; either way their composition singles them out from the rest of the beads and suggests a separate origin. It is not only compositional variation that suggests multiple origins for this group of beads. The polychrome beads appear to be made in several different traditions. There are wound beads comparable to the monochrome ones which were then decorated with trails and/or spots of other colours; there are beads produced by rolling up slabs of glass formed by fusing together strips of monochrome glass or slices of millefiori rods and there are twisted composite rods laid side by side round a core. Most of the beads were marvered, producing a variety of shapes within each manufacturing tradition.

*Comparison of results and conclusions*

A number of beads from the Saxon cemetery at Portway, Andover, Hampshire[35] and the Anglian cemetery at Sewerby, Yorkshire[36] have been analysed in the same way as those from Dover. The results are broadly similar with the same colours having approximately the same compositions. However, there is less homogeneity in the use of decolourising and opacifying agents though it should be noted that the range and relative proportions of colours from the individual sites varied so the figures are not strictly comparable, e.g. there was only one white monochrome bead from Dover but two from Portway and five from Sewerby. The results are summarised in Table XLIII.

These analyses are only the beginnings of investigations on the composition of glass beads. A more extensive programme of work might be able to confirm some of the suggestions made above and would show whether inter-site differences such as those demonstrated in Table XLIII are meaningful. The untapped potential of this type of work has been summarised by Hirst and Biek[37] who state that scientific examination and analysis '. . . allows precise associations of similar glasses and separation of superficially similar though technically very different glasses both within one assemblage and between different assemblages. Eventually this information may be used not only to document manufacturing techniques but to suggest trading patterns, different centres of bead-making and finer relative dating by more precise associations'.

TABLE XLIV XRF PEAK HEIGHTS NORMALISED TO SILICON FOR MONOCHROME BEADS

| Bead No. | Type No. | Ti | Mn | Fe | Co | Cu | Zn | Pb | Sn | Sb | Colour |
|---|---|---|---|---|---|---|---|---|---|---|---|
| 62/4h | B09 | ? | .39 | 2.28 | | .66 | | .46 | ? | | Red (O) |
| 62/4i | B21 | ? | .38 | 1.00 | | | | 12.21 | .22 | | Yellow (O) |
| 1/4f | B10 | .20 | .61 | 1.59 | | 29.20 | .43 | .48 | | | Orange (O) |
| 157/1b | B22 | | ? | .70 | | | | | | | Yellow (T) |
| 83/1 | B23 | .04 | .21 | .38 | | .06 | | | | | 'Colourless' (T) |
| 6/10d | B26 | .17 | | .96 | | 1.90 | | .87 | .12 | | Green (T) |
| 133/2d | B25 | .12 | .79 | 2.18 | | 6.88 | .82 | 1.42 | 1.02 | | Blue/green (O) |
| 75/1f | B29 | .11 | ? | .53 | | 1.52 | .45 | 5.82 | .09 | | Green (O) |
| 129/5e | B33 | .06 | .08 | .58 | | 2.77 | .44 | 1.66 | .06 | | Blue/green (T) |
| 32/4e | B34 | .15 | | .74 | | 1.43 | .43 | 3.29 | .15 | | Blue/green (T) |
| 38/4d | B37 | ? | .07 | .34 | | .83 | | 9.08 | .06 | | Green (O) |
| 55/1g | B38 | .04 | ? | .42 | | 2.53 | .85 | .85 | .05 | | Blue/green (T) |
| Un/5 | B39 | ? | .14 | .76 | | 3.03 | .61 | 2.55 | .38 | | Blue/green (O) |
| 1/4c | B40 | .10 | .30 | 1.24 | | 1.92 | .29 | 2.52 | .18 | | Blue/green (O) |
| 132/2c | B41 | .03 | .03 | .26 | | .79 | .21 | .17 | .09 | | Blue/green (T) |
| 129/5f | B44 | .03 | .03 | .22 | | 1.43 | .32 | .62 | .03 | | Blue/green (T) |
| 30/4d | B45 | ? | .06 | .41 | ? | .11 | | .33 | .14 | | Blue (T) |
| 30/4e | B48 | ? | ? | .22 | + | .09 | | .15 | | | Blue (T) |
| 62/4c | B52 | .12 | .56 | .87 | | .13 | .12 | .46 | | .86 | White (O) |

33 Biek 1983, 309
34 Guido *et al.*, forthcoming
35 Bayley, forthcoming, b
36 Biek *et al.* 1985
37 Hirst and Biek 1981, 139

| Bead No. | Type No. | Ti | Mn | Fe | Co | Cu | Zn | Pb | Sn | Sb | Colour |
|---|---|---|---|---|---|---|---|---|---|---|---|
| 62/4k | B60 | .05 | .38 | .89 | | .03 | | .54 | .29 | | White (O) |
| 30/4g | B61 | ? | .07 | 1.53 | | .13 | | .18 | | | Black (T) |
| 20/5f | B64 | ? | .68 | .50 | | | | | | | 'Colourless' (T) |
| 59/3q | vessel sherd | .03 | ? | .46 | | 1.73 | | .22 | .04 | .14 (As = .2) | Blue/green (O) |
| 32/4c | B15 | ? | .75 | 1.54 | | | | 15.83 | .24 | | Yellow (O) |
| 35/5f | B34 | ? | | 1.99 | | 4.25 | | 6.82 | .40 | | Blue/green (T) |
| 46/3c | B15 | .19 | .47 | 1.36 | | | | 15.88 | .31 | | Yellow (O) |
| 48/4g | C08 | .04 | .57 | .75 | | | | | | | 'Colourless' (T) |
| 48/4k | C09 | .06 | .74 | .84 | | | | | | | 'Colourless' (T) |

Key to Tables XLIV and XLV.
O = opaque
T = translucent
? = uncertain
– = no figure available
+ = detected

TABLE XLV   XRF PEAK HEIGHTS NORMALISED TO SILICON FOR POLYCHROME BEADS

| Bead No. | Type No. | Ti | Mn | Fe | Co | Cu | Zn | Pb | Sn | Sb | Colours |
|---|---|---|---|---|---|---|---|---|---|---|---|
| 59/3g | D01 | .04 | .25 | .72 | | .07 | | .11 | | .09 | Mainly White (O) |
| | | .03 | .12 | 1.25 | + | 0.15 | | .21 | .07 | .07 | White (O) + Blue (T) |
| 59/3h | D02 | .19 | .45 | 2.66 | | .51 | .22 | 8.55 | .17 | | Red (O) + Yellow (O) |
| 133/2e | D07 | .05 | .48 | 1.87 | | .09 | | .19 | .23 | ? | Mainly Black (O) |
| | | .10 | .82 | 4.82 | | .22 | | .25 | .28 | ? | Black (O) + White (O) |
| 30/4k | D06 | .10 | .47 | 3.53 | | .85 | .22 | 4.56 | .16 | | Red (O) + Yellow (O) |
| 133/1c | D08 | .08 | .51 | .84 | + | .20 | | .21 | | .09 | Blue (T) + some White (O) |
| | | .04 | .22 | .42 | | .10 | | .12 | | .05 | White (O) + some Blue (T) |
| 1/4t | D10 | .17 | .41 | 1.35 | | 4.53 | .40 | 9.72 | .71 | | Green (O) + Yellow (O) |
| 1/4u | D16 | .11 | .54 | 2.68 | | .72 | .15 | 2.13 | .28 | | Red (O) + White (O) |
| 76/1b | D13 | .18 | | 8.09 | | .21 | .20 | 5.08 | .27 | | Black (O) + Yellow (O) |
| | | .12 | | 2.59 | | ? | ? | 5.02 | .33 | | Black (O) + Yellow (O) + White (O) |
| | | .13 | | .94 | | ? | ? | 7.10 | .41 | | Mainly Yellow (O) + White (O) |
| 30/4m | D21 | ? | .68 | 2.59 | | .54 | .32 | 3.86 | .11 | | Yellow (O) + Red (O) |
| | | ? | .68 | – | | ? | ? | 8.01 | .62 | | Mainly Yellow (O) |
| 55/1h | D36 | .19 | .31 | 1.31 | ? | .23 | | .54 | .66 | | White (O) + Blue (T) |
| 42/1k | D23 | .04 | .23 | .89 | | .07 | | .48 | .28 | | White (O) + Blue (T) |
| | | | .46 | – | | | | .96 | .94 | | White only |
| 18/2h | D35 | .11 | .15 | .69 | | 3.19 | 1.04 | 2.23 | .52 | | White (O) + Turquoise (O) |
| 59/3l | D38 | .18 | .42 | 2.45 | | .65 | .16 | 6.06 | .11 | | Red (O) + Yellow (O) |
| 1/4z | D37 | .13 | .29 | 2.15 | | .60 | | 1.11 | .37 | | Red (O) + White (O) |
| 13/3h | D43 | .10 | .58 | 1.04 | | .20 | .14 | .22 | ? | ? | 'Colourless' (T) + Blue (T) |
| | | .13 | .46 | 1.36 | | .41 | | .58 | | ? | 'Colourless' (T) + Blue (T) + Red (O) |
| 35/5k | D50 | .10 | .32 | 1.02 | | .36 | ? | 3.78 | .12 | | 'Colourless'/Turquoise (T) + some Yellow (O) |
| 129/5h | D53 | ? | .79 | 5.03 | | .47 | ? | .77 | .24 | | Mainly Black (T) |
| | | .07 | .56 | 2.99 | | .65 | .13 | 1.20 | .15 | | Black (T) + White (O) + Red (O) |
| 157/1f | D56 | | .27 | 1.01 | ? | .34 | .16 | .52 | | .14 | Mainly Blue (T) |
| | | .11 | .39 | 1.78 | | .67 | .16 | 2.03 | | .18 | Blue (T) + Red (O) |

*TABLE XLV (Cont.)*

| Bead No. | Type No. | Ti | Mn | Fe | Co | Cu | Zn | Pb | Sn | Sb | Colours |
|---|---|---|---|---|---|---|---|---|---|---|---|
| 30/4s | D57 |  | .94 | – |  | ? | ? |  |  |  | 'Colourless'/Pink (T) |
|  |  | .04 | .74 | .56 |  | .21 | .14 | .64 | .13 |  | 'Colourless'/Pink (T) + White (O) + Red (O) |
| 30/4t | D58 | .21 | .81 | 1.48 |  | 2.02 | .39 | .83 |  |  | Turquoise (T) |
|  |  | .05 | .53 | .66 |  | 1.26 | .26 | .88 | .17 |  | Turquoise (T) + Red (O) + White (O) |
| 59/3p | D59 | .09 | ? | .66 |  | 1.24 | .28 | 4.36 | .17 |  | Mainly Green (O) + Blue (T) |
|  |  | .05 | .08 | .59 |  | .68 | .14 | 2.12 | .10 |  | Mainly Blue (T) + Green (O) |
| 60/3t | D60 | .28 |  | .67 |  | 1.07 | .62 | 3.07 | .12 |  | Green (O) |
|  |  | ? | .65 | 1.07 |  | .65 | .76 | 5.85 | .19 |  | Yellow (O) + some Green (O) |
| 38/4g | D62 | .06 | .19 | .68 |  | .49 | .12 | .99 | .14 |  | Blue (T) + White (T) + Red (O) |
| 132/2f | D65 | ? | .58 | 1.39 |  | 1.67 | .84 | 2.05 | .19 |  | Red (O) |
|  |  | .08 | .36 | .67 |  | 1.65 | .14 | 1.16 | .15 |  | Mainly Blue (T) + White (O) |
|  |  | .07 | .50 | .69 |  | 1.00 | .16 | .169 | .12 |  | Mainly Green (T) + Yellow (O) |
| 42/1t | D66 |  | .48 | 2.66 |  | 1.55 | .27 | 2.38 | .55 |  | Red (O) + 'White'(T) |
|  |  | .24 | .98 | 3.66 |  | 2.63 | .49 | 5.85 | .26 |  | Mainly Red (O) + Yellow (O) |
| 92/3d | D67 | .08 | .37 | 6.12 |  | 1.98 | .24 | 2.43 | .08 | .04 | Mainly Red (O) + Yellow (O) |
|  |  | .10 | .25 | 2.83 |  | 2.13 | .37 | 3.64 | .07 | .03 | Red (O) + Yellow (O) + Black (O) |
| 93/1 | D68 | .19 | 2.29 | 4.43 |  | 1.33 | .46 | 2.27 |  |  | Mainly Red/Brown (O) + 'Colourless' (T) |
|  |  | .14 | 1.54 | 2.75 |  | .97 | .33 | 3.56 | .11 |  | Red (O) + Yellow (O) + 'Colourless' (T) |
| 129/5i | D61 | ? | .11 | 1.41 |  | .14 |  |  |  |  | Yellow (T) |
|  |  | .09 | .24 | .86 | + | .30 |  | .34 | .07 |  | Yellow (T) + Blue (T) |
| 1/4v | D18 | .11 | .76 | 4.67 |  | 1.30 | .34 | 2.14 | .35 |  | Red (O) + White (O) |
| 1/4w | D20 | .07 | .20 | 2.15 |  | .63 | .33 | 2.69 | .35 |  | Red (O) + White (O) |
| 1/4x | D26 | .08 | .49 | 1.66 | ? | .20 |  | 1.67 | 1.26 |  | White (O) + Blue (T) |
| 1/4z[1] | D46 | .12 | .16 | 2.18 |  | 1.04 | .39 | 7.17 | .24 |  | Red (O) + Yellow (O) |
| 30/4n | D30 | .13 | .54 | 2.61 |  | .76 | .15 | 4.86 | .16 |  | Red (O) + Yellow (O) |
| 53/1c | D63 | .12 | .85 | 1.22 |  | 1.26 | .42 | 1.56 | .16 |  | Mainly 'Colourless' (T) + Red (O) |
|  |  | .13 | 1.00 | 1.20 |  | 1.81 | .20 | 2.41 | .19 |  | Mainly Green (T) + Yellow (O) |
| 60/3q | D26 | .10 | .14 | 1.04 | ? | .27 |  | .80 | .61 |  | White (O) + Blue (T) |
| 132/2e | D64 | .09 | .38 | .90 |  | .93 | .44 | 1.74 | .13 |  | Red (O) + White (O) + Blue (T) |
|  |  | .10 | .58 | 1.03 |  | 1.25 | .49 | 2.93 | .19 |  | Yellow (O) + Green (T) + Red (O) |
| 59/3j | D14 | .06 | .43 | 1.81 |  | .69 | .08 | 4.01 | .07 |  | Red (O) + Yellow (O) |

# THE BUCKLAND ANGLO-SAXON CEMETERY

## The Textiles by Elisabeth Crowfoot

### TABLE XLVI CATALOGUE

Note: The abbreviation 'replaced' is used to indicate 'fibres replaced by metal oxides'. The spinning direction of yarns is indicated by the letters Z and S, the probable warp thread being placed first. The overall measurements of best fragments are given in cms, and weave counts in threads per 1 cm, except where otherwise stated.

| Grave | Sex | No. | Object | Position | Fibre | Spin | Weave | Count | Measurement | Comments |
|---|---|---|---|---|---|---|---|---|---|---|
| 1 | F | 2 | disc brooch | back | replaced | Z/Z | tabby | c 16/16 | 1.0 × 0.7 | and smaller fragments |
| 4 | M | 1 | spearhead | underside | replaced | ?Sply/Z | tabby, decorated ?soumak | 8/14 | c 1.8 × 1.8<br>2.3 × 1.8 | (Plate 11d, Text Figure 43, ii, p. 194 two areas at right angles; on both holes left by thick thread, wrapped or embroidered pattern; warps grouped alternate 2 and 1 by pattern thread, 5 throws tabby between 2 pattern rows. |
| 5 | M | 4 | spearhead | socket | replaced | Z/Z | tabby | – | 3.0 × 1.5 | medium weave, surface poor |
| 8 | M | 3 | iron buckle | | replaced | Z/S | 2/2 twill | – | 3.5 × 2.3 | fine, deteriorated |
| 9 | M | 2 | iron shaft and loop | on length<br>on loop | replaced<br>replaced | Z/<br>Z/Z | ?pile, fringe<br>?twill | –<br>– | c 3.0 × 1.0<br>– | threads lying parallel<br>coarse |
| 10 | M | 2 | spearhead | socket | replaced | Z/Z | tabby | 7/5 on 5 mm | 5.0 × 2.0 | |
| 13 | F | 5 | small-long brooch | back (a) | replaced | Z/Z | tabby | c 35/9, (7 2mm/4-5 5mm) | 0.8 × 0.2 | ?braid or border, warp face |
| | | 5 | iron pin | pinhead (b) | replaced | Z/S | 2/2 twill | – | – | and smaller fragments |
| | | 6 | ring brooch | pin, ring (b) | replaced | Z/S | 2/2 twill | c 16/14 | 1.5 × 0.8 | |
| | | 9 | large key and ring | all surface (b) | replaced | Z/S | 2/2 twill, broken diamond | c 14/12 | 2.0 × 1.0 | all probably same twill reverses both systems |
| 14 | F | 1 | disc brooch with garnets | detached from back | wool | Z/Z | tabby | 9/8 on 5 mm | – | wool bright brown, close weave, smaller scraps replaced |
| 20 | FC | 1 | ?weaving batten | both sides (a) | replaced | Z/Z | tabby | c 18/14 | – | in folds |
| | | 6 | squarehead brooch | pinhead (b) | deteriorated | Z/S | 2/2 twill | – | c 1.5 × 0.9 | lump |
| 22 | M | 5 | spearhead | socket, one side | replaced | ?S | – | – | – | long wavy fibres, occasional S, but probably fleece, not pile |
| | | | | other side | replaced | ?/Z | ?tabby | est. 6/18-20 or 18-20/6 | 0.5 × 1.5 | ?weft face mat, or warp face braid (see p 194 |
| 27 | M | 4 | iron buckle | underside | replaced | S,Zply/S,Zply | ?2–hole tablet weave | c 18/12 | c 1.0 × 1.0 | (p 195 and Unass. 7) diagonals meeting centre of band; belt-end leather, under pin |
| 28 | F | 3 | iron ring | impression | – | Z/S | 2/2 twill, broken diamond | c 16/16 | c 1.5 × 0.6 | centre as in Text Figure 43.iii |

| Grave | Sex | No. | Object | Position | Condition | Spin | Weave | Count | Size (cm) | Notes |
|---|---|---|---|---|---|---|---|---|---|---|
| 29 | F | 9 | ?lock | both sides, round bar | replaced | Z/Z | tabby | 20/12 | 2.8 × 2.0 | ?warp very regular, much finer than ?weft, so both visible; one side, coarse Z ?sewing thread where weave goes round coarser threads |
| 34 | C | 2 | iron buckle | on leather on iron | impression | Z | tabby | 9/7 on 5 mm | 0.6 × 0.4 | patches |
| 35 | F | 7<br>2 | keys<br>pin | on loop<br>along shaft round pin | replaced<br>replaced | Z/Z<br>Z/Z | tabby<br>tabby | 16/16<br>— | 5.0 × 1.0<br>— | appearance ?flax; pulled similar, pulled diagonally |
| 36 | F | 1 | iron buckle | underneath<br>on top side | replaced<br>replaced | Z/Z<br>Z | tabby<br>— | 14/13<br>— | 2.5 × 3.0<br>— | irregular spinning coarser threads |
| 41 | M | 3<br>4<br>7 | sword<br>knife<br>purse mount | ?from scabbard<br>in leather sheath one side<br>other side | replaced<br>replaced<br>impression | —<br>?Z/Z<br>Z/S | —<br>—<br>twill | —<br>—<br>— | —<br>0.7 × 0.5<br>1.5 × 0.7 | ?fleece fibres, with wood weave uncertain, threads damaged weave and spin not clear |
| 43 | FC | 3 | keys | all over shafts (a) | replaced | Z/Z | tabby | 16/12 | c 2.0 × 1.0 | two layers in curved folds, regular spin and weave fine, probably flax |
| 44 | F | 3 | knife | under (a) on iron (b) | replaced | Z/Z | tabby | 14/12 on 5 mm | 1.0 × 0.8 | probably flax |
| 48 | F | 3 | iron chain | on most pieces (a) | replaced | Z/Z | 2/2 twill, broken diamond | 11/11 on 5 mm<br>14–16/10–12 | c 0.8 × 0.6<br>1.0 × 1.7, 1.7 × 1.5 | (see Text Figure 43, iii, but remains suggest repeat on more threads) |
|  |  | 1 | button brooch | two pieces front | replaced<br>replaced | Z/Z<br>Z/Z | tabby<br>tabby | c 16/12 | — | twisted scraps. as on chain |
| 53 | F | 7 | bucket | in chalk fill | impression | ?Z/Z | tabby | 6/6 on 5 mm | — | spin not very clear |
| 54 | F | 3 | keys | bronze key<br>iron key | replaced<br>replaced | Z/Z<br>Z/S | tabby<br>— | c 12/12 | 1.0 × 0.4 | traces |
| 55 | FC | 5 | iron and wood fragment |  | replaced | Z/Z | tabby | 14/13 | c 1.7 × 1.5 | fragment |
| 56 | M | 6<br>7–11<br>2 | bronze buckle<br>strap mounts<br>knife | back<br>most pieces | replaced<br>replaced<br>replaced | Z/Z<br>Z/Z<br>Z/Z | tabby<br>tabby<br>— | 8/6 on 5 mm | — | traces; on one count as on 6 textile, deteriorated |
| 57 | M | 4c | buckle |  | replaced | Z/Z | tabby | 18/16 | c 2.8 × 1.0 | fine weave, in folds |
| 59 | F | 2 | iron pin |  | replaced | Z/S | 2/2 twill | 6 on 5 mm ? | 1.5 × 0.8 | coarser threads end of piece |
| 61 | M | 3 | buckle | under plate front | replaced<br>replaced | Z/Z | tabby | 14–16/16 | 2.3 × 2.7 | folds, fine, appearance ?flax coarse fibres |
| 62 | F | 3 | keys |  | replaced | Z/Z | tabby | est. 20/14 | — | traces, fine threads |
| 65 | M | 1 | spearhead |  | replaced | Z/S | 2/2 twill, broken diamond | 8/8 | c 2.5 × 1.5 | probably same type as Text Figure 43, iii, but too damaged to draw |
| 66 | F | 2 | iron ring |  | replaced | Z/Z | tabby | 7/5 on 5 mm | — | fragment |
| 75 | F | 3 | keys | on shafts and on piece with bronze link | replaced | Z/Z | tabby | est. c 18/14 | 1.0 × 0.5 | one system threads uneven |
| 82 | F | 2 | keys |  | replaced | Z/Z | tabby | 7/5 on 5 mm | 1.5 × 0.7 |  |

| Grave | Sex | No. | Object | Position | Fibre | Spin | Weave | Count | Measurement | Comments |
|---|---|---|---|---|---|---|---|---|---|---|
| 92 | F | 7 | iron rings | areas round ring | replaced | Z/S | 2/2 twill, ?broken diamond twill | 7/8 on 5 mm | 2.2 × 0.8 | and other areas; threads seem to reverse both systems |
| 94b | M | 1 | disc brooch | on pinhead | replaced | Z/? | | | – | threads one system |
| | | 3 | spearhead, copper bands | on ferrule (a) | replaced | Z/S | 2/2 twill, broken diamond | c 12/10 | 4.0 × 2.3 | diamond pattern not clear |
| | | | | other side (b) from spear | replaced replaced | Z/Z Z/Z | tabby tabby | c 20/16 20/16 | 2.0 × 1.0 4.3 × 1.5 | in folds, and detached fragment similar |
| 96a | M | 2 | iron fragment | from pin (a) | replaced | Z/S | 2/2 twill ?chevron or diamond | – | 1.0 × 0.5 | diagonals reverse, but surface deteriorated |
| 96b | M | 6a | shield boss | over surface (b) | replaced | Z/Z | tabby | 17/16 | c 1.5 × 1.8 | and smaller fragments, open weave |
| | | 7 | spearhead | socket (a) | replaced | Z/Z | 2/2 twill broken diamond | 11/9 | 2.8 × 1.4 | (Plate 11. Text Figure 43. iii) |
| 98 | M | 9 | knife | | replaced | Z/Z | tabby | c 16/16 | 1.3 × 1.3 | fine |
| | | 3b | shield grip | (b) | replaced | Z/S | 2/2 twill chevron or diamond | 9/9–10 | 3.0 × 1.0 | and other patches; diagonals reverse half way across piece |
| 107 | F | 1 | tweezers | patch and folds near tip (a) | replaced | Z/Z | tabby | 10/8 on 5 mm | 2.5 × 1.0 | fine, uneven, probably flax |
| | | 4 | workbox | under (a) inside | replaced ?flax | Z/? Z/ | ?twill – | – – | – – | showing longer threads below fine fibres, flattened threads Z, weave not clear, breaking up |
| 113 | F | 5 | keys | all over piece | replaced | Z/Z | tabby | 20/20 | L.3.5 cm | (Plate 11b) in folds, fine showing part of seam, run and fell or double hemmed, coarse Zply thread, stitches c 3 mm apart, c 3 mm long showing from other side of seam |
| 114 | M | 4 | iron loop | on ring | replaced | Z/Z | tabby | 12/10 on 5 mm | 0.9 × 0.8 | coarse Z, Sply threads tied round ring under another patch same tabby, deteriorated |
| 122 | F | 1 | keys | on fragments | replaced | Z/Z | tabby | 12/10, 11/6 5 mm (22–24/12–20) | 0.4 × 1.0, 0.7 × 0.8 | variable counts, appearance suggests flax |
| 124 | F | 3 | wooden box fittings | lying on top | replaced | Z/Z*S | tabby | est 16/16 | 2.8 × 1.0 | in folds over area, ?finer than Gr.122 tabby |
| 127 | F | 2 | knife | all along back (a) | replaced | Z/Z | tabby | 9/7 on 5 mm | 1.0 × 0.8 | fragments, ?warp-faced band or weft face on plyed warp; no edges visible |
| | | 3b | iron ring | (b) | replaced | Z/S or Sply | tabby | 28/8 on 5 mm (i.e. c 56/16) | 2.5 × 0.7 (area) | |
| | | 3c | key shafts | on two pieces | replaced impressions | Z/S or Sply | tabby | – | c 1.0 × 1.7 c 4.0 × 1.5 | scattered scraps. ?warp round piece, as on edge of 3b; breaks make it impossible to see if lines of tape or continuous fine fabric |

* Further examination by Dr Lise Bender-Jørgensen and the author indicate that one thread system in this weave includes Z and S-spun threads, but they do not give a clear pattern.

# SPECIALIST REPORTS

| | | | | | | | | | |
|---|---|---|---|---|---|---|---|---|---|
| 129 | F | 10a | key shafts | | (a) replaced | Z/S | 2/2 twill ?chevron or broken diamond | c 12/10 | c 2.0 × 0.5 | surface deteriorated |
| | | 10c | manicure set | head piece back | (a) replaced | Z/S | 2/2 twill | 7/7 on 5 mm | 1.0 × 0.6 | probably same medium fine, many broken threads |
| | | 10b | iron buckle | | (b) replaced | Z/Z | ?tabby | | 1.8 × 1.2 | |
| 132 | F | 4 | keys | on fragments | replaced | Z/Z | tabby | 18/14  16/12 | 3.0 × 1.5 | in patches over area |
| 137 | M | 3 | spearhead | on socket | replaced | Z/S | tabby | 12/10 | 2.0 × 2.0 | fine very regular thread (p00) |
| 139 | MC | 1 | purse mount | over one side | replaced | Z/Z | ?tabby ?with pile | — | — | very damaged, but ?parallel lines Z and some S threads across: ?pile seen from back of weave |
| 142 | ?F | 2 | large single key | | replaced | ?Z/Z | tabby | 30/15 (warp 15 on 5 mm) | 3.0 × 0.5 | fragments over area, spinning not clear |
| 148 | M | 2 | sharpening steel | | replaced | Z/Z | tabby | est.c 20/16 | 1.0 × 0.8 | folds; threads packed one side, ?selvedge, but no loops preserved ?better preserved piece of same weave |
| | | 3 | iron buckle | underneath | replaced | Z/Z | tabby | 14/9 on 5 mm (28/18) | 2.5 × 1.5 | |
| 155 | F | 4 | keys | | replaced | Z/Z | tabby | 17/10 on 5 mm (34/20) | 1.2 × 1.0 | appearance suggests flax |
| 156 | M | 1 | spearhead | all round socket | replaced | Z/S | 2/2 twill broken chevron or diamond | est.22/18 | 4.0 × 2.5 | surface deteriorated, reverses |
| 157 | F | 6 | keys | one surface other side and areas | (a) replaced (a) (b) replaced | Z/Z Z/Z | tabby tabby | 9/8 on 5 mm 5/4 on 5 mm | c 0.8 × 0.5, c 2.5 × 2.5 — | traces same small areas, coarse, very open; some coarse Z threads lying across |
| 160 | F | 5a | iron ring | | replaced | Z/Z | ?twill | est.c 20/20 | — | tiny scraps, spin suggests flax |
| 161 | F | 4b | key | detached | replaced | Z/Z | tabby | 9/8 on 5 mm | 0.8 × 0.5 | spinning uneven |
| | | 3 | pin, bronze head | | replaced | Z/Z | tabby | 20/20 (10 on 5 mm) | 1.6 × 0.6 | Probably same fabric, ?flax |
| C | M | 6 | buckle loop | against ?wood | replaced | Z/S | 2/2 twill, ?broken diamond | — | 2.0 × 1.2 | in folds, but reverses suggest broken diamond |
| F | F | 1 | inlaid brooch | round pin | replaced | Z/Z | ?2/1 twill | — | — | possibly three-shed, but not clear |
| Unass. | | 16 | brooch pin | pin head | replaced | Z/? | 2/2 twill, broken diamond | est.18/14 | — | same type weave as Text Fig. 43, iii; one system only preserved (Plate IIc) |
| Unass. | | 7 | Scabbard fragment | one side under ?bitumen ?round top | replaced | Z/? | tablet weave, ?2-hole | twists c 16, wefts c 12 | w. ?0.7 cm | ?braid would round top of scabbard two layers with 0.5–0.6 cm exposed; small fragment, 0.7, possibly full width, lying across pattern of meeting diagonals. |

Note: very deteriorated remains of Z/Z tabby weaves 38/9 and 131/4, unidentifiable weaves with Z spinning 39/1, 50/4, 63/1 and 85/2, and with Z/S spinning 79/1; possible fibres from fleece with wood 91/5 sword.

*Discussion*

Most of the textile remains from the cemetery are preserved on iron objects, and the fibres have been completely replaced by metal oxides, leaving a cast, often very clear and detailed, of a small part of the fabric; the only exceptions are a few fragments of wool protected by a brooch, and tiny thread scraps from a work-box. An impression of textile has also survived in the chalk fill of a bucket.

No selvedges or other borders have been preserved, but in the catalogue the closer thread count has normally been placed first, in the warp position, since in Anglo-Saxon textiles, woven on the warp-weighted loom, the warp count is normally the higher.

*Fibres*

The scraps of wool preserved by the garnet-decorated brooch in Grave 14 are bright brown, with glossy fibres, used for a fine tabby weave. The tiny pieces of thread from the work-box in Grave 107 have been identified by H M Appleyard, F T I, as poorly preserved vegetable fibre, i.e. probably flax.

*Tabby weaves*

The proportion of tabby (plain) weaves (Text Figure 34, ia) in the cemetery is unusually high, more than two-thirds of the total textiles, a characteristic noted in two other Kentish cemeteries, Finglesham and Updown, perhaps a southern taste for less weighty fabrics than the twills of eastern and northern sites. The majority of these tabbies are very similar in count, spinning and weaving to the Grave 14 woollen fragments, and are also likely to have been of wool, but the appearance of some pieces with slightly higher counts, uneven yarn and soft folds, 43/3, 44/3, 107/1, 122/1, 142/2, 148/3 and 161/3, suggests that these may have been of linen.

One interesting tabby is 137/3, a very regular piece of weaving with Z spinning in one system and S in the other, a combination used occasionally in Roman material and frequently in good quality medieval tabbies, but rare in those of Anglo-Saxon date. There are, however, certain Anglo-Saxon tabbies and twills in which probable coloured stripes and checks can be identified by the use of groups of threads of different spinning directions in warp and weft,[38] and with only small fragments surviving it is possible that this tabby comes from a fabric of this type, and what is preserved is part of a wide stripe.

On one side of a spearhead socket (22/5) is a tiny fragment of tabby in which only one system of close-packed threads is visible; this could come from a weft-face weave such as a mat – finer similar fragments on metalwork at Sutton Hoo suggested possibly mats of the *kilim* type laid on the floor of the burial-chamber[39], and a replaced fragment from Kingston has a type of selvedge frequently found on rugs. Alternatively it may be from a warp-face braid used as a binding, or a wrist-loop. There are two other possible remains of warp-face tabby braids or tapes at Dover, a scrap on the back of a brooch (13/5), and very fine remains suggesting a flax tape wound round an iron ring, perhaps tying keys to it (127/3b,c); the quality of this, estimated at *c* 56/16 threads to the cm, is not far from that of tapes wound round the top of scabbards at Sutton Hoo (62–64/23 per cm) and Broomfield Barrow (60/16)[40].

*Patterned or embroidered weave*

One textile on a spearhead (4/1) is of considerable interest. Two fragments are preserved, lying at right angles to each other, from a tabby weave which must

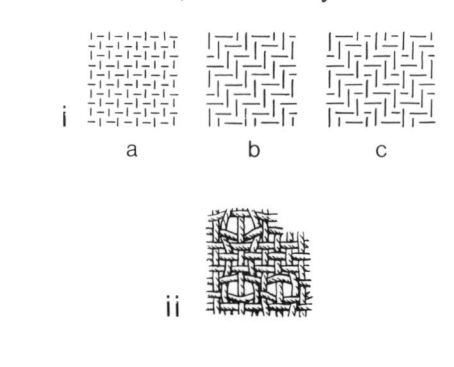

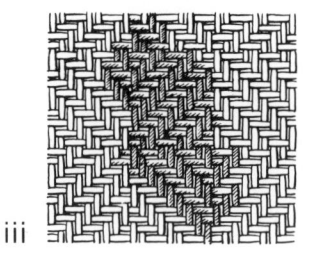

Text Figure 43    Textiles:
*i a* Tabby weave, *b* 2/2 (four-shed) twill, *c* Four-shed chevron twill
*ii* Diagram of ground weave, pattern threads missing, from spearhead 4/1
*iii* Diagram of broken diamond twill weave, (shaded threads as preserved on 96b/7)

have had some form of decoration in heavy thread, either embroidered or in a wrapped (soumak) technique. The pattern thread must have disintegrated before oxidisation, but the pairs of holes opened by its passage between ?warp threads, grouped alternately one and two, are clear on both pieces (Plate IId, Text Figure 43, ii). This appearance at once suggests the grouped warps and holes of the replaced textile with soumak decoration, SH 7, on chainmail in the Sutton Hoo ship[41], a feature that can also be seen where the

---

38  Updown, Kent. Graves 14, 29; Finglesham, Kent. Graves 8, 169; Worthy Park, Hampshire. Grave 75. Mucking, Essex. Graves 448, 975; Crowfoot 1985b, 15–16
39  Crowfoot 1983, SH 17, 18, 444, fig. 316
40  Ibid, 449–450, 473, figs. 320, 335
41  Ibid, 433–8, 476, figs. 309, 337

pattern thread has decayed on fragments of tabby with soumak decoration from Taplow Barrow (purple wool on white linen) and Valsgärde in Sweden (probably undyed wool on blue linen)[42]. Later examples in this technique from the Oseberg Ship (Viking)[43] and from Skog[44] and Överhogdal, Norway (medieval)[45] may have been used as hangings; the Sutton Hoo cloth seems to have been folded, and was obviously also a large piece. With so little of the Dover textile remaining it is however possible that the holes were caused by some form of embroidered decoration; H-J Hundt has suggested Persian stitch, a form of herringbone, as the cause of very similar holes on a much earlier silk fragment from Athens[46]. At any rate it is clear that some form of decorated cloth lay across the spearhead.

*Twill weaves*
Most of the twills preserved are lightweight four-shed weaves. The spinning in all but two is Z and S; from the evidence on sites where selvedges or borders have been preserved, the Z system is likely to be the warp. At this period the use of different spinning directions in warp and weft often indicates good quality twills, though after the late 7th century Z spinning in both systems becomes the rule even for very fine fine woollens. It is possible that the two completely Z spun twills here (48/3, 160/5a) were of flax. There are indications that most of the Dover twills, whether light or medium weight, had 2/2 four-shed patterns, either chevrons (Text Figure 43, ic) or broken diamonds (Text Figure 43, iii, from Grave 96b), types found in many Anglo Saxon cemeteries[47]. There seem to have been none of the coarser simple 2/2 twills (Text Figure 43ib), but with such small fragments preserved it is possible that outer layers of heavier fabrics may have been lost.

*Tablet weaves*
In two cases (Grave 27/4, Unassociated 7) remains of braids suggest a type made with 2-hole tablets to produce a fairly coarse twilled effect; in the first case this may have been a border to some garment, in the other a narrow braid used as binding for the top of a scabbard. Insufficient was present in either case to be satisfactorily drawn, but they can be recognised as of a type found both in England and Norway[48].

*?Pile weaves*
On one side of the spearhead from Grave 22 long fibres are replaced, whose wavy appearance suggests a sheep's fleece; they seem to be unspun, but while possibly simply sheepskin, they could also have come from a pile weave, since a fragment from Banstead Down was decorated with pile rows of silky unspun locks[49]. One other object (139/1) has a fabric with parallel lines of thread which, though they could be stitching, also suggest the appearance of the locks passing on the reverse of a pile weave.

*Garments and furnishings*
Most of the textiles are suitable garment fabrics, woollen or linen tabbies and twills for tunics, trousers, gowns and head-coverings, preserved on the metal objects that fastened them or lay against them. In one case a stitched seam is preserved on keys in a woman's grave (113/5, Pl.IIb), either the side seam of her skirt, or perhaps the seam of a bag or purse also hanging from her belt.

The presence of good quality fabrics on spearheads and in the chalk filling of the bucket (53/7) does suggest perhaps that a light cloak or blanket may have been laid over the whole contents of graves, but so far it is difficult to say if this practice, general in Scandinavian burials of much earlier periods, continued in Anglo-Saxon cemeteries. A grave at Eriswell, Suffolk, was described by its US Air Force excavators as having had 'heavy fabrics over the entire body'[50] but this may simply have been the women's clothing, since nothing described as from this layer was presented for examination. Decorated fabrics have in several cases been associated with weapons – the patterned or embroidered tabby on the Grave 4 spearhead here, on one from Mucking, Essex (Grave 961) and another, more heavily patterned (Grave 939), and a shield-boss from Wakerley, Northamptonshire (Grave 85) – but these may perhaps indicate a special wrapping rather than a furnishing covering the whole burial.

The general impression that emerges from the remains from Buckland is of good workmanship, a high standard both of spinning and weaving, and a uniformity that suggests either a strong local tradition, or perhaps the presence of some professional weavers in the community.


**Wood** *by D F Cutler, Jodrell Laboratory, Royal Botanic Gardens, Kew*

The samples are in a very varied state of preservation from very decayed wood to partly or wholly carbonised. Many appear to have undergone considerable compression or withering before carbonisation. Two samples are so compressed that there are no recognisable characters remaining.

Some of the identifications (marked with*) are rather tentative since there are not always enough diagnostic characters remaining in the sample to be

---

42 Arwidsson 1942, 87ff., pl.40
43 Hougen 1940, Abb.2–4
44 Arwidsson 1942, figs. 69, 70
45 Hoffmann 1964, 171–2, figs. 82, 83
46 Hundt 1969, 69, pl. 15
47 Crowfoot 1983, 418–424, 469, figs. 297–9, 326–7; Crowfoot 1967, fig. 7; Crowfoot 1969, 51; Crowfoot 1976a, fig. 12a, b; Crowfoot 1978, fig. 110.1; Crowfoot *et al.* 1981, fig. 31a, b; Crowfoot 1984, fig. 7; Crowfoot 1985a, 52, fig. 19.1b; and unpublished
48 Dedekam 1924–5, 42–5 figs. 21, 22; Wakerley, Northamptonshire. Grave 78
49 Crowfoot 1976b, 69
50 Hutchinson 1966, 12

positive. The samples are similar in structure to our reference material as shown in Table XLVII.

TABLE XLVII  WOOD IDENTIFICATIONS

| Grave | Object | Sample | |
|---|---|---|---|
| C | Scabbard | 1 | *Field maple, *Acer campestre* |
| 143 | Box | 2 | Beech, *Fagus sylvatica* |
| 94b | Spear | 3 | *Field maple, *Acer campestre* |
| 124 | Ironbound box | 4 | Beech *Fagus sylvatica* |
| 138 | Iron F | 5 | Hazel, *Corylus avellana* |
| 34 | At foot of grave | 6 | *Family Rosaceae which includes the subfamilies Prunoideae, (*Prunus* spp. wild cherry, blackthorn, bird cherry) and Pomoideae (*Sorbus* spp. mountain ash, whitebeam), *Crataegus* sp. hawthorn, *Pyrus* sp. pear, *Malus* sp. apple |
| 28 | Bucket | 7 | Too compressed |
| 137 | Under bronze bowl | 8a | Oak, *Quercus* sp. |
|  |  | b | Black material under bowl, too compressed |
| 20 |  | 9a | Black material under bowl – *oak, *Quercus* sp. |
|  |  | b | Wood sample – *oak, *Quercus* sp. |
| 141 | Patch under skull | 10 | *Oak, *Quercus* sp. |
| 6 | By centre of pelvis | 11 | Lime, *Tilia* sp. |
| 121 | To left of skull | 12 | Oak, *Quercus* sp. |

Since the samples are pre-fifteenth century, it is assumed that no other *Acer* species would be represented.

**Organic material associated with metal objects** *by Jacqui Watson, Ancient Monuments Laboratory*

*Object No.*
C/1  Preserved organic material on ring-sword: scabbard – wood is *Populus* sp (Poplar) or *Salix* sp. (Willow). There are also the remains of a fleece lining and the possibility of leather overlying the wood.
Hilt – lower guard appears to be a mixture of random fragments of organic material, generally lying with grain perpendicular to the tang. Wood fragments are *Populus* sp or *Salix* sp, so they could come from the scabbard.
Grip has organic material with grain lying along the tang, this is probably horn.
Organic material between the pommel bars also appears to be horn, probably cattle, with grain direction perpendicular to the tang, (Plate 12a).
Black fragments (near waist) appear to be very small pieces of charcoal rather than leather.

8/1  Mineral preserved wood in spearhead socket: *Fraxinus* sp (Ash) from mature timber.

38/8  Mineral preserved organic on knife tang: probably horn.

48/14  Preserved wood on reverse of copper alloy buckle *Tilia* sp (Lime), (Plate 12b).

91/6  Fragments of organic material associated with buckle are mainly textile, and some pieces are possibly leather.

93/7  Preserved organic material associated with seax: the handles of all three 'knives' appear to be horn.
The seax has traces of a wooden scabbard, probably *Salix* sp or *Populus* sp. However, the two smaller 'knives' have only animal fur preserved on their blades. Possibly the seax scabbard was held together with the animal skin, and the two smaller 'knives' slotted between the wood and the skin? (Plate 12c).

93/6  Preserved organic material associated with sword: organic material lying directly beneath pommel bar and with grain direction perpendicular to tang, is possibly ivory, (Plate 12d).
Grip is also ivory, but the grain lies along the tang.
Lower guard, with grain perpendicular to tang, is possibly ivory, (Plate 12e)
Scabbard has fleece lining, but none of the wood has been preserved.

94b/2+3  Mineral preserved wood from spearhead and ferrule: both are *Fraxinus* sp from mature timber.

95/2  Mineral preserved organic on knife tang is probably horn. Traces of a possible leather sheath on blade.

96b/9  Mineral preserved organic on knife tang is probably horn.

96b/10b  Wood corresponding to copper alloy tag with sword: ring porous wood, possibly *Quercus* sp (Oak) or *Fraxinus* sp (Ash).

107/3  Fragments of organic from above copper alloy box are bone or antler.

117/1  Mineral preserved organic on knife tang is probably horn.

120/1  Mineral preserved organic on knife tang is probably horn.

158/2  Knife with composite handle. The three main sections are probably bone. The lower one had wood packed between the iron tang and the bone: *Salix* sp or *Populus* sp.
Between the bone sections are the remains of some organic material that has been wound round the tang.

**The wooden belt from grave 20** *by Professor K Wilson*

The fragments were too friable to cut, until embedded in wax. They show a black tarry-looking deposit on one side. The fragments were immersed in pure alcohol until saturated, and then transferred, through mixtures, to benzene. Paraffin wax was added, and the benzene evaporated off, the last stages being done at 56°C so that only pure liquid wax, now permeating the material, remained. This was then allowed to cool and harden. Sections for microscopic examination, cut parallel to the flat surface of the fragments, show wood structure corresponding in appearance to that of a radial plane in the tree. Appropriate directions of cutting could thus be found to show transverse and tangential planes.

The structure of the wood was partially decayed, but sufficient remains to enable it to be identified as willow. The black deposit on the surface is a layer of spores, presumed fungal, but not identified. The belt therefore apparently consisted of a thin strip of willow wood, sawn or cleaved from a radial plane in a log.

Willow wood is noted for its pliability when cut thin, and has been widely used for 'chip' baskets for fruit. It can be fastened with wire staples without readily splitting. Modern 'chip' baskets were made from veneers 'peeled' off a log by rotating it against a slowly advancing knife. The flat surface of the veneer thus corresponded to a tangential plane in the tree. Old fashioned 'chips' were however cut radially (before the adoption of veneer-peeling machinery) as the belt must have been[51]. There is no doubt that a strip of willow-wood would make an effective belt.

## The hones from grave 162 *by S E Ellis*

Both hones are arenaceous limestones in which coarse angular quartz silt, amounting to about 40% of the stone, is cemented by calcite of similar grain-size. They are described petrographically in an account of Saxon and medieval English honestones[52].

Hone 162/4, BM (NH) 1964, 727 (1); Ellis, type IVA (3) has a grain size about 0.5mm and contains abundant fragments of indeterminable ostracod shells and a little oxidised glauconite.

Hone 162/5, BM (NH) 1964, 727 (2); Ellis, type IVC (5) is coarser, ranging from 0.06 to 0.10mm grain-size, and is devoid of fossils but contains abundant rounded glauconite grains, both green (fresh) and brown (oxidised).

It is not possible to be positive as to provenance. The nearest sandy or silty limestones are in the Hythe Beds of the Lower Greensand, typically developed as 'Kentish Rag' between Sevenoaks and Ashford. These honestones are not typical of the Kentish Rag, which usually shows lustre-mottling due to large calcite grains enclosing smaller quartz-grains, but they may be from some other part of the Hythe Beds. However, 162/4 resembles ostracod limestone hones found at Hamwih (Southampton) which have been traced mostly to the Purbeck Beds of the Dorset coast but in one case to the lower part of the Lincolnshire Limestone or equivalent beds in the Humber area. Ostracod limestones derived from this region are common as erratics in the East Anglian drift and are found as hones on some sites; e.g. West Stow. 162/5 is so like 162/4 in texture that it is probably from an ostracod-free bed in the same series. Although a local source cannot be ruled out, the possible provenance is therefore very wide, ranging from Dorset to Yorkshire and probably also to the neighbouring part of France.

## Seed analysis *by Professor G W Dimbleby*

*Sample from Anglo-Saxon grave; Dover, grave 13*
Sample  (a) foot of grave
        (b) left pelvis
        (c) top left shoulder

All three samples contained a quantity of uncarbonised seeds, mostly in a fragmentary condition. There was no apparent difference between the three samples. The few intact specimens of seeds were of the family *Chenopodiaceae*, probably the genus *Chenopodium* (goosefoot) itself.

These samples are from a highly calcareous freely-drained site, that is a condition under which decompositon of organic matter would be rapid. It is difficult to believe that uncarbonised seeds could have survived in the soil for over a thousand years.

It has been shown[53] that uncarbonised seeds occurring in aerobic conditions at relatively shallow depth must be regarded as natural contamination from modern vegetation. The *Chenopodiaceae* in particular are mentioned as coming into this category. There are several possible agencies which could introduce seeds in this way, the most important being earthworm action. Earthworms are abundant in calcareous soils such as these.

## The human skeletal remains *by Rosemary Powers, British Museum (Natural History), London and Rachel Cullen, Somerville College, Oxford*

### General Remarks

*Preservation*
The majority of the skeletal material from this site was very severely eroded: the only fairly complete skulls were numbers 9, 30, 62, 135 and 136, and some others were represented only by crumbling, almost unidentifiable fragments. This erosion, presumably due to alkaline solution in the chalky matrix, obscured the surface features of the skull, and in many cases the dental enamel was also too eroded to show surface morphology. A result of pseudo-caries due to post-mortem erosion, especially at the dentine-enamel junction on the outer

---

51  Edlin 1949
52  Ellis 1969

53  Keepax 1977

surface of the jaws, was that only the largest caries cavities could be diagnosed: hence the incidence of caries (see Table LIII) is probably too low. Enamel hypoplasia and cribra orbitalia, osteitis and minor healed wounds would have been disguised by the same cause. The teeth of several individuals, notably numbers 91 and 92, had been deeply stained a brown colour, and reduced to a fragile shell of enamel through preferential dissolution of the dentine. Areas such as teeth roots, where dentine had at one time been covered by bone, were better preserved than areas which had not; this explains the good preservation of unerupted juvenile teeth, and is probably the reason why they show a high incidence of Carabelli's cusp, which cannot be detected in the adult teeth, exposed as they were to attrition and erosion. Post-cranial bones too suffered very severely from this alkaline erosion, so that even the few bones measured probably gave slightly smaller measurements than were correct.

Indications of grave goods

*Green metal stains*: Five skulls showed green stains due to contact with a copper or bronze object, three of these being stained on the mandible. In number 1 the stain was to the left of the symphysis, in number 92 to the right, both on the lower margin of the jaw. In number 30 the stain was on the inner surface of the mandible on both sides, though deeper on the left. Number 62 had green staining on the root of an isolated third molar, probably an upper one; number 28 had green stains on the left temporal and the lower forepart of the parietal. Three of these stained skulls were female, and the other two were probably female. Bronze stains were present on the post-cranial skeleton in ten cases, four of which, on the arm just below the elbow, were probably due to bracelets. These were: 1, a female, the top of whose left ulna was stained; 15, of indeterminate sex, with staining at the top of the right radius and ulna; 91, of unknown sex, both left forearm bones stained; and 98, probably a male, with staining on the left ulna. Number 14, a female, apparently wore a ring on her right hand, probably on the middle phalanx of the third finger, and a brooch slightly to the right of the manubrium sterni. A similarly positioned stain on number 100 also indicates the wearing of a brooch: the left leg bones of number 53, a female, were deeply stained just below the knee. Number 21, a child, showed staining on the inner side of the sacrum and the right ilium, perhaps from a belt ornament, while there was a similar stain on number 148, an adult male and another adult male, number 135, had a green stain on the outer side of the left innominate, above the *acetabulum*.

*Iron and red stains*: Flakes of iron were found in Grave 3 'Bones under others' and Grave 5 'Bones loose in top fill'. Number 22 showed iron stains on the head of the right femur, and there was a trace of similar staining on number 37, near lambda. Number 56, a male, had iron stains all up the right forearm, and there were stains also on the right forearm of a female, number 81.

*Possible artefacts*: Among loose teeth of number 55, a juvenile, was found a rough stone bead (possibly a naturally perforated pebble). It was roughly cylindrical, with a pitted surface, 10mm broad by 11mm long, the hole being about 3mm in diameter throughout and circular in section.

*Morphology*
Morphology
Two cases of tori mandibulares were observed (nos. 27 and 81). No cases of tori maxillares were seen, but few palates were sufficiently complete to show this feature. The incidence of persistent metopic suture was 8.2% (sample size 61). Wormian bones along the lambdoid suture were visible in one skull (no.39), but as with the other discontinuous traits of the skull, the very poor preservation of the bones probably prevented identification in a number of cases.

A resumé of osteometric measurements and stature estimates is given in Tables L to LII. A more detailed analysis of the individual measurements, in comparison with other Saxon data, is being undertaken, but will not be completed for some time yet. There is no evidence to suggest that this Dover group was especially distinctive.

Dental Morphology
No striking dental anomalies were found. No supernumaries, retained deciduous teeth, or missing lateral incisors were observed; molarised premolars and double-rooted canines were looked for and not found. Apparent lack of third molars was frequent, although not confirmed by radiography. One case of a deeply embedded, horizontally impacted third molar was seen (no. 61). The upper molars frequently showed reduction to the triangular, 3-cusped form (Table LIV), and there were also 2 third molars of much wrinkled pattern. In addition, 13 M1's showed some indication of Carabelli's cusp in slight or moderate development, and 4 juveniles also showed it on Pm2. No paramolar or other extra cusps were seen, with the exception of a well-marked lingual tubercle on the canine of no.57, and a cusp centrally placed on the lingual surface of the canine of no. 124. The lingual surface of upper incisors varied in form from featureless to a very slight shovel shape. A high proportion of upper lateral incisors showed lateral grooves on either mesial or distal surfaces, and no. 55 was peculiar in that both teeth showed the character, one on the mesial and one on the distal surface. No. 103 was symmetrical for this feature, and nine other skulls showed it on one side only. Of 34 individuals, 11 were affected. Absence of the lower third molars appeared present in 9 individuals out of 46 examined, while two cases were certainly unilateral and three other, imperfect specimens, probably so.

*Pathology*

Oral Pathology
Of sixty adults whose teeth could be examined, seventeen had one or more carious teeth; in

addition, no. 42 was practically edentulous, and no.'s 1 and 61 were partially edentulous. No.61 showed an unusually deeply embedded horizontally impacted left lower third molar; there was an irregular cementum deposit on the root of the second molar where the occlusal surface of the impacted tooth pressed against it. The mandible was incomplete, so it was not possible to determine whether the condition was bilateral. Of the juveniles, no.117 (aged about 8 years) showed an interproximal caries of a deciduous molar which had not advanced very far; no.55 (aged about 5 years) showed symmetrical caries cavities on the dorsal neck region of both lower deciduous first molars.

Cranial pathology
'Osteophytes' were noted on the inner table of the frontal bone in three skulls. They were small projections and distributed on either side of the midline. No.36 had several, no.10 had less and smaller ones, while no.1 showed the earliest stage in this development. All three had missing and decayed teeth, and no.1 also had osteo-arthritis of the cervical vertebrae, so the hyperostosis is probably a sign of late middle-age. No.42 had a small, dense, smooth osteophyte on the inner table of the skull just inside the temporo-mandibular joint area, but this skull was fragmentary and it was not possible to determine whether other such structures were present. No.44 showed arthritic deformation of the left mandibular condyle, in conjunction with decayed teeth and considerable post-cranial osteo-arthritis. No.37 showed a small circular depression penetrating to the diploe in the hinder part of the right parietal. The surface was eroded by root marks, and the feature may have been due to post-mortem erosion or to an old injury in life. There was no sign of trauma on the inner table below it.

Post-cranial pathology
*Osteo-arthritis*: Bone deformity resulting from arthritis was noted in as much detail as the remains permitted. Owing to bone fragmentation and erosion, a detailed account of the frequency of osteo-arthritis was not possible. However, it would seem worthwhile indicating which skeletons showed evidence of the disease, in order to give a general impression of its commonness. The individuals affected were:-

1 Female
O.A. changes on lumbar vertebrae, hip and tarsals.
25 Female
Slight changes on the inter-vertebral disc area.
29 Female
Slight changes on the inter-vertebral disc area.
33 Male
O.A. changes at elbow and wrist, and on tarsals; affected scapula may come from a second individual.

44 Female
Gross arthritic changes in cervical and lumbar vertebrae, sacrum and glenoid cavity.
49 Uncertain sex
Arthritic changes at left elbow.
61 Female
O.A. changes of cervical vertebrae.
65 Male
O.A. changes of cervical and lumbar vertebrae.
87 Female
Vertebral O.A.
94A Male
O.A. of lumbar vertebrae.
94B Probably same individual as 94A
Slight O.A. changes in disc area.
96A ?Uncertain
Arthritic changes in cervical vertebrae.
99 Female
Arthritic changes to thoracic vertebrae.
120 Male
Arthritis of lumbar vertebrae and right scaphoid
125 Male
O.A. of lumbar vertebrae and sacrum.

*Anomalies of the spine*
67 Female
Top sacral segment unfused in the midline, leaving v-shaped cleft in sacrum.
84 Female
Similar mid-line defect. Cleft is nearly closed.
99 Female
Detached arch of fourth lumbar vertebra (spondylolisthesis).
100 Female
Lack of fusion between arch of first two sacral segments.

Other post-cranial pathology includes:
56 Male
Exostosis on outer side of right tibia shaft, probably the result of an old healed inflammation.
67 Female
Small cavity in left navicular, probably due to infection or arthritis.
78 Juvenile
Right femur is grossly thickened and 'spongy'. Some of affected leg is missing, but rest of skeleton, including left femur is normal.
90 Male
Periostitis on central front surface of both femur shafts.
99 Female
Cartilage defect of one acetabulum.
145 ?Uncertain
Signs of disease in articulation of right femur head.

## TABLE XLVIII  AGE AND SEX DISTRIBUTION OF ADULTS

| Sex | Specimens – age in years (approx) | | |
|---|---|---|---|
| | 20–30 | 30–45 | Over 45 |
| MALES* (39%) | 9, 14, 58, 71, 114, 146 | 15, 30, 54, 56, 63, 66, 103 | 27, 36, 52, 65, 90, 125 |
| FEMALES* (30%) | 6, 25, 28, 37, 38, 46, 53, 59, 67, 92, 96B, 110 | 3, 93, 112 | 1, 33, 42, 44, 61, 62 |
| UNSEXABLE Age estimate only | 23, 29, 91, 124, 130 | 32, 116, 138, 147 | 121, 160 |
| Age groups as % of total | 22% | 13% | 13% |

*These are percentages based only on skeletons complete enough for estimates of age or sex to be formed.

## TABLE XLIX  AGE DISTRIBUTION OF JUVENILES*

| Specimens – age in years (approx) | | |
|---|---|---|
| 0–6 | 6–12 | 12–18 |
| 20, 34, 55, 74, 110, 119 | 21, 43, 78, 89, 105, 117, 153 | 35, 48 |

* In a few instances, an age could not even be established tentatively.

## TABLE L  POST CRANIAL MEANS

| | $FeL_1$ | $FeL_2$ | $FeD_1$ | $FeD_2$ | $TiL_1$ | $TiD_1$ | $TiD_2$ | $HuL_1$ | $HuD_1$ | $HuD_2$ | $RaL_1$ | $UlL_1$ |
|---|---|---|---|---|---|---|---|---|---|---|---|---|
| ♂ | 488 (3) | 466 (7) | 26.5 (7) | 34 (7) | 379 (6) | 37.5 (6) | 24 (6) | 340 (3) | 22.5 (4) | 18 (4) | 254 (2) | 286 (2) |
| ♀ | 465 (2) | 454 (3) | 26 (4) | 30.7 (4) | 364 (8) | 32 (6) | 23 (6) | 316.5 (4) | 22 (4) | 15 (4) | 238 (4) | 256 (2) |

## TABLE LIA  CRANIAL MEANS

| Measurement | Biometric Symbol | Males | Females |
|---|---|---|---|
| Glabello-occipital length | L | 179(8) | 186(9) |
| Biparietal breadth | B | 141(4) | 135(8) |
| Minimum frontal breadth | B' | 97(17) | 95(12) |
| Maximum frontal breadth | B'' | 117(9) | 115(10) |
| Nasion – bregma arc | $S_1$ | 127(14) | 125(18) |
| Nasion – bregma chord | $S'1$ | 110(16) | 108(19) |
| Bregma-lambda arc | $S_2$ | 125(8) | 127(14) |
| Bregma-lambda chord | $S'2$ | 117(9) | 114(13) |
| Lambda-opisthion arc | $S_3$ | 124(2) | 121(7) |
| Lambda-opisthion chord | $S'_3$ | 105(2) | 97(7) |
| Lambda-asterion arc | $0_7$ | 96(6) | 99(9) |
| Lambda-asterion chord | | 84(4) | 88(9) |

## TABLE LIB  FACIAL AND MANDIBULAR MEANS

| Measurement | Biometric Symbol | Males | Females |
|---|---|---|---|
| Palate length | G'1 | 38(4) | 36(7) |
| Palate breadth | $G_2$ | 40(7) | 35(6) |
| Maximum zygomatic breadth | J | 80(3) | 86(2) |
| Nasal breadth | NB | 24(2) | 22(5) |
| Bicondylar breadth | $W_1$ | 123(2) | 117(5) |
| Bigonial breadth | GoGo | 106(2) | 97(4) |
| Symphyseal height | $H_1$ | 33(17) | 30.5(16) |
| Minimum ramus breadth | RB' | 33(16) | 31(15) |
| Bimental breadth | ZZ | 44(15) | 43(9) |

All numbers in parentheses indicate sample sizes.

TABLE LII  ESTIMATED MAXIMUM STATURE FROM LONGBONES

| | MALES | | | FEMALES | |
|---|---|---|---|---|---|
| Specimen | Estimated stature | | Specimen | Estimated stature | |
| | from combined femur & tibia lengths (cm) | from tibia length alone (cm) | | from combined femur & tibia lengths (cm) | from tibia length alone (cm) |
| 9 | 182 | | 1 | | 171 |
| 33 | | 173 | 6 | | 161 |
| 36 | | 169 | 11 | | 164.5 |
| 56 | | 169 | 46 | | 164.5 |
| 93 | 178 | | 62 | | 165 |
| 96B | 175.5 | | 67 | 171 | |
| | | | 87 | | 165 |
| | | | 99 | 171 | |

TABLE LIII  DENTAL PATHOLOGY

| | Size of tooth group | Total caries | % | Abscess | % | A.M. loss | % |
|---|---|---|---|---|---|---|---|
| MOLARS | 587 | 51 | 8.7 | 9 | 1.5 | 43 (excepting no.42) | 7.1 |
| PREMOLARS | 440 | 13 | 2.9 | 5 | 1.1 | 14 | 3.2 |
| CANINES | 224 | 1 | 0.4 | 2 or 3 | 0.8 + | 0 | 0 |
| INCISORS | 330 | 2 or 3 | 6.0 + | 3 or 4 | 1.3 + | 1 | 0.3 |

TABLE LIV  REDUCTION OF UPPER MOLARS

| | Number of individuals | 4-cusped | 3-cusped | 2-cusped | Much reduced |
|---|---|---|---|---|---|
| M1 | 41 | 41 | 0 | 0 | 0 |
| M2 | 35 | 13 | 22 | 0 | 0 |
| M3 | 27 | 2 | 21 | 1 | 1 |

# Bibliography

**Åberg N 1926** *The Anglo-Saxons in England*, Uppsala.
**Abbott G W 1920** Further discoveries in Anglo-Saxon cemeteries at Woodston, Hunts., *Précis of the 49th annual report of the Peterborough Natural History, Scientific and Archaeological Society*, 34–40.
**Adams B 1982** *The Anglo-Saxon cemetery at Wakerley, Northamptonshire*, M Phil thesis, Birkbeck College, University of London.
**Addyman P V 1964** A dark-age settlement at Maxey, Northants., *Medieval Archaeol* 8, 20–73.
**Addyman P V and Hill D H 1969** Saxon Southampton: a review of the evidence, part II : industry, trade and everyday life, *Proc Hampshire Fld Clb Archaeol Soc* 26, 61–96.
**Addyman P V, Leigh D and Hughes M J 1972** Anglo-Saxon houses at Chalton, Hampshire, *Medieval Archaeol* 16, 13–31.
**Ahrens C (ed) 1978** *Sachsen und Angelsachsen*, Veröffentlichungen des Helms-Museums 32, Hamburg.
**Akerman J Y 1860** Second report of researches in a cemetery of the Anglo-Saxon period at Brighthampton, Oxon., *Archaeologia* 38, 84–97.
**Akerman J Y 1862** Report on researches in an Anglo-Saxon cemetery at Long Wittenham, Berkshire, in 1859, *Archaeologia* 38, 2, 327–52.
**Alcock L 1981** Quantity or quality: the Anglian graves of Bernicia, in Evison 1981b, 168–86.
**Aldsworth F R 1978** The Droxford Anglo-Saxon cemetery, Soberton, Hampshire, *Proc Hampshire Fld Clb Archaeol Soc* 35, 93–182.
**Alénus-Lecerf J 1975** *Le Cimetière Mérovingien de Hamoir I Catalogue*, Archaeologia Belgica 181, Bruxelles.
**Alénus-Lecerf J 1978** *Le Cimetière Mérovingien de Hamoir II Étude*, Archaeologia Belgica 201, Bruxelles.
**Alénus-Lecerf J 1981** Découverte d'un cimetière des V$^e$–VI$^e$ siècles à Vieuxville, *Conspectus MCMLXXX*, Archaeologia Belgica 238, Bruxelles, 59–63.
**Alföldi A 1935** Ein spätrömisches Schildzeichen keltischer oder germanischer Herkunft, *Germania* 19, 324–8.
**Almgren B 1948** Romerska drag i nordisk figurkonst från folkvandringstiden, *Tor* 1, 81–103.
**Ament H 1976** *Die fränkischen Grabfunde aus Mayen und der Pellenz*, Germanische Denkmäler der Völkerwanderungszeit ser B, 9, Berlin.
**Arbman H 1937** *Schweden und das Karolingische Reich*, Kungl. Vitterhets Historie och Antikvitets Akadamiens Handlingar 43, Stockholm.
**Arbman H 1943** *Birka* I, 2 vols., Uppsala.
**Arnold C 1980** Wealth and social structure: a matter of life and death, in Rahtz *et al.* 1980, 81–142.
**Arnold C J 1982** *The Anglo-Saxon cemeteries of the Isle of Wight*, London.
**Arntz H and Zeiss H 1939** *Die einheimischen Runendenkmäler des Festlandes*, Gesamtaugabe der älteren Runendenkmäler 1, Leipzig.
**Arrhenius B 1971** *Granatschmuck und Gemmen aus nordischen Funden des frühen Mittelalters*, Acta Universitatis Stockholmiensis, Studies in North-European Archaeology ser. B, 3, Stockholm.
**L'Art Mérovingien 1954**, Brussels.
**Arwidsson G 1942** *Die Gräberfunde von Valsgärde I Valsgärde 6*, Uppsala.
**Arwidsson G 1954** *Die Gräberfunde von Valsgärde II Valsgärde 8*, Uppsala.
**Ashbee P 1960** *The Bronze Age round barrow in Britain*, London.
**Ashbee P 1978** *The ancient British*, Norwich.
**Ashbee P 1979–80** Amesbury barrow 39: Excavations 1960, *Wiltshire Archaeol Natur Hist Mag* 74/75, 3–34.
**Ashbee P and Dunning G C 1960** The round barrows of east Kent, *Archaeol Cantiana* 74, 48–57.
**Aspinall A and Warren S E (ed) 1983** *Proceedings of the 22nd. symposium on archaeometry held at the university of Bradford, Bradford, U.K. 30th March – 3rd April 1982*, Bradford.
**Auden W H and Taylor P B 1981** *Norse poems*, London.
**Austin W, Bagshawe T W and Parsons F G 1928** A Saxon cemetery at Luton, Beds., *Antiq J* 8, 177–92.
**Avent R 1973** An Anglo-Saxon variant of a Merovingian rounded-plaque buckle, *Medieval Archaeol* 17, 126–8.
**Avent R 1975** *Anglo-Saxon garnet inlaid disc and composite brooches*, Brit Archaeol Rep British Ser 11, i and ii, Oxford.
**Avent R and Evison V I 1982** Anglo-Saxon button brooches, *Archaeologia* 107, 77–124.
**Avent R and Leigh D 1977** A study of cross-hatched gold foils in Anglo-Saxon jewellery, *Medieval Archaeol* 21, 1–46.
**Axboe M 1981** The Scandinavian gold bracteates, *Acta Archaeologica* 52, 1–100.

**Bagshawe T W 1931** A Saxon burial at Luton, Bedfordshire, *Antiq J* 11, 282–4.
**Baker R S 1880** On the discovery of the Anglo-Saxon remains at Desborough, Northamptonshire, *Archaeologia* 45, 2, 466–71.
**Baker R S 1881–3** Notes on archaeological discoveries at Irchester, Islip, Twigwell, Cransley, *Proc Soc Antiq* 9, 85–95.
**Bakka E 1958** *On the beginning of Salin's Style I in England*, Historisk-antikvarisk rekke 3, Universitetet i Bergen Årbok.
**Bakka E 1970** Scandinavian trade relations with the Continent and the British Isles in pre-Viking times, *Early Medieval Studies* 3, Antikvariskt Archiv 40, Stockholm, 37–51.
**Bakka E 1981** Scandinavian-type gold bracteates in Kentish and continental grave-finds, in Evison 1981b, 11–38.
**Barfoot J F and Price Williams D 1976** The Saxon barrow at Gally Hills, Banstead Down, Surrey, *Res Vol Surrey Archaeol Soc* 3, Guildford, 59–76.

**Bartlett J P 1845** An ornamental bronze pin, *J Brit Archaeol Ass* 1, 316–17.

**Bateman T 1848** *Vestiges of the antiquities of Derbyshire*, London.

**Bateman T 1861** *Ten years' diggings in Celtic and Saxon grave hills*, London.

**Bateson J D and Hedges R E M 1975** The scientific analysis of a group of Roman-age enamelled brooches, *Archaeometry* 17, 177–90.

**Battiscombe C F (ed) 1956** *The relics of St. Cuthbert*, Oxford.

**La Baume P 1952–3** Die Wikingerzeit auf den Nordfriesischen Inseln, *Jahrbuch des Nordfriesischen Vereins für Heimatkunde und Heimatliebe* 29, 5–185.

**De Baye J 1893** *The industrial arts of the Anglo-Saxons*, London.

**Bayley J forthcoming a** Notes on the compositon of coloured glass, in Campbell *et al.*

**Bayley J forthcoming b** Analyses of the glass beads, in Cook and Dacre.

**Behmer E 1939** *Das zweischneidige Schwert der germanischen Völkerwanderungszeit*, Stockholm.

**Behrens G 1947** Merovingerzeit, *Römisch-Germanisches Zentralmuseum zu Mainz Katalog* 13, Mainz.

**Bellanger G and Seillier C 1982** *Répertoire des cimetières mérovingiens du Pas-de-Calais*, Bulletin de la Commission d'Histoire et d'Archéologie du Pas-de-Calais, Numéro spécial, Arras.

**Besteman J C 1974** Carolingian Medemblik, *Berichten van de Rijksdienst voor het Oudheidkundig Bodemonderzoek* 24, 43–106.

**Bidder H F and Morris J 1959** The Anglo-Saxon cemetery at Mitcham, *Surrey Archaeol Collect* 56, 51–131.

**Biddle M 1970** Excavations at Winchester, 1969: eighth interim report, *Antiq J* 50, 277–326.

**Biddle M 1975** Excavations at Winchester, 1971 tenth and final interim report: Part I, *Antiq J* 55, 96–126.

**Biek L 1983** The ethnic factor in archaeotechnology, in Aspinall and Warren 1983, 303–15.

**Biek L and Bayley J 1979** Glass and other vitreous materials, *World Archaeol* 11, 1, 1–25.

**Biek L, Butcher S A, Carruthers T G, Rooksby H P, Warren S E, Crummett J G, Hedges R E M and Kaczmarczyk A 1980** Enamels and glass pastes on Roman-period 'bronzes' found at Nornour, Isles of Scilly, in Slater and Tate 1980, 50–79.

**Biek L, Bayley J and Gilmore G 1985** Scientific examination of the glass beads, in Hirst 1985, 77–85.

**Bishay A (ed) 1974** *Recent advances in the science and technology of materials* 3, New York.

**Bjørn A 1929** *Bronsekar og glassbegre fra folkevandringstiden i Norge*, Det kgl. norske videnskabers selskabs skrifter 6, Trondhjem.

**Bloemers J H F, Louwe Kooijams L P and Sarfatij H 1981** *Verleden Land*, Amsterdam.

**Böhme H W 1974** *Germanische Grabfunde des 4.bis 5.Jahrhunderts zwischen unterer Elbe und Loire*, Münchner Beiträge zur Vor und Frühgeschichte 19, 2 vols., München.

**Böhner K 1958** *Die Fränkischen Altertümer des Trierer Landes*, Germanische Denkmäler der Völkerwanderungszeit ser B, 1, 1 and 2, Berlin.

**Boon G C 1966** Gilt glass beads from Caerleon and elsewhere, *Bull Board Celtic Stud* 22, I, 104–9.

**Boon G C 1977** Gold-in-glass beads from the ancient world, *Britannia* 8, 193–207.

**van Bostraeten H C 1965** *De Merovingische begraafplaats te Lutlommel*, Archaeologia Belgica 86, Bruxelles.

**Bradshaw J 1969** Ashford and Area Archaeological Group, *Archaeol Cantiana* 84, 234–6.

**Brent J 1866** Account of the society's researches in the Anglo-Saxon cemetery at Sarr, *Archaeol Cantiana* 6, 157–85.

**Brent J 1868** Account of the society's researches in the Anglo-Saxon cemetery at Sarr, *Archaeol Cantiana* 7, 307–21.

**Breuer J and Roosens H 1957** *Le cimetière franc de Haillot*, Archaeologia Belgica 34, Bruxelles.

**Brill R H 1970** The chemical interpretation of the texts, in Oppenheim *et al.* 1970, 105–28.

**Brodribb A C C, Hands A R and Walker D R 1968** *Excavations at Shakenoak* I, Oxford.

**Brodribb A C C, Hands A R and Walker D R 1971** *Excavations of Shakenoak* II, Oxford.

**Brothwell D 1972–3** Palaeodemography and earlier British populations, *World Archaeol* 4, 75–87.

**Brown G B 1913–14** An early spoon found in Kent, *Burlington Mag.* 24, 99–100.

**Brown G B 1915** *Saxon art and industry in the pagan period The arts in early England* III and IV, London.

**Brown P D C 1977a** The significance of the Londesborough ring brooch, *Antiq J* 57, 95–7.

**Brown P D C 1977b** Firesteels and pursemounts again, *Bonner Jahrbücher* 177, 451–77.

**Brown P D C 1981** Swastika patterns, in Evison 1981b, 227–40.

**Brown P D C and Schweitzer F 1973** X-ray fluorescent analysis of Anglo Saxon jewellery, *Archaeometry* 15, 175–92.

**Brown P D C, Campbell J and Hawkes S C 1981** *Anglo-Saxon Studies in Archaeology and History* 2, Brit Archaeol Rep British Ser 92, Oxford.

**Bruce-Mitford R 1949–51** The Sutton Hoo ship-burial, *Proc Suffolk Inst Archaeol* 25, 1–78.

**Bruce-Mitford R L S 1956** The pectoral cross, in Battiscombe 1956, 308–25.

**Bruce-Mitford R 1971–2** The Sutton Hoo helmet: a new reconstruction, *Brit Mus Quart* 36, 120–30.

**Bruce-Mitford R 1972** *The Sutton Hoo ship-burial* 2nd edition, London.

**Bruce-Mitford R 1974** *Aspects of Anglo-Saxon archaeology*, London.

**Bruce-Mitford R 1975a** *The Sutton Hoo ship-burial* 1, London.

**Bruce-Mitford R (ed) 1975b** *Recent archaeological excavations in Europe*, London and Boston.

**Bruce-Mitford R 1978** *The Sutton Hoo ship-burial* 2, London.

**Bruce-Mitford R 1979** *The Sutton Hoo ship-burial A handbook* 3rd edition, London.

**Bruce-Mitford R 1983** *The Sutton Hoo ship-burial* 3, I and II, London.

**Bruce-Mitford R and Bruce-Mitford M 1970** The Sutton Hoo lyre, *Beowulf*, and the origins of the frame harp, *Antiquity* 44, 7–13.

**Brulet R 1970** *Catalogue du matériel mérovingien conservé au Musée Archéologique de Charleroi*, Répertoires Archéologiques ser. B, V, Brussels.

**Bushe-Fox J P 1926** *First report on the excavation of the Roman fort at Richborough, Kent*, Rep Res Comm Soc Antiq London VI, London.

**Callmer J 1977** *Trade beads and bead trade in Scandinavia ca. 800–1000 AD*, Acta Archaeologica Lundensia ser. in 4°, 11, Lund and Bonn.

**Campbell J, John E and Wormald P 1982** *The Anglo-Saxons*, Oxford.

**Campbell S et al. forthcoming** *The 'Aula Nova', Almonry Chapel and Lanfranc's Dormitory, Excavations in the cathedral precincts 1, The archaeology of Canterbury III*, Maidstone.

**Capelle T 1976** *Die frühgeschichtlichen Metallfunde von Domburg auf Walcheren*, Nederlandse Oudheden 5, 1 and 2.

**Capelle T and Vierck H 1971** Modeln der Merowinger- und Wikingerzeit, *Frühmittelalterliche Studien* 5, 42-100.

**Carpenter A 1874–9** On the skeletons discovered at Park Farm, Beddington, in 1871 and 1875, *Surrey Archaeol Collect* 7, xxxvii-xxxix.

**Chadwick S E 1958** The Anglo-Saxon cemetery at Finglesham, Kent: a reconsideration, *Medieval Archaeol* 2, 1–71.

**Chalvignac J and Lemant J-P 1978** La sépulture n° 87 de la nécropole mérovingienne de Barbaise-Ardennes, *Bulletin de la Societé archéologique champenoise*, n° 4, 65–70.

**Christlein R 1979** *Kleinfunde der frühgeschichtlichen Perioden aus den Plangrabungen 1967–1972, Der Runde Berg bei Urach III*, Heidelberger Akademie der Wissenschaften Kommission für Alamannische Altertumskunde Schriften 4, Heidelberg.

**Clark J 1980** A Saxon knife and a shield-mount from the Thames foreshore, *Antiq J* 60, 348–9.

**Clarke E D 1817** Observations upon some Celtic remains, lately discovered by the public road leading from London to Cambridge near the village of Sawston, distant seven miles from the university, *Archaeologia* 18, 340–3.

**Clarke G 1970** Lankhills School, in Biddle 1970, 292–8.

**Clarke G 1975** Lankhills School, in Biddle 1975, 121–6.

**Clarke G 1979** *The Roman cemetery at Lankhills Pre-Roman and Roman Winchester II*, Winchester Studies 3, Oxford.

**Claus M, Haarnagel W and Raddatz K (ed) 1968** *Studien zur europäischen Vor- und Frühgeschichte*, Neumünster.

**Clough T H McK, Dornier A and Rutland R A 1975** *Anglo-Saxon and Viking Leicestershire including Rutland*, Leicester.

**Cochet J B D 1855** *La Normandie souterraine ou notices sur des cimetières romains et des cimetières francs explorés en Normandie*, 2nd edition, Dieppe.

**Cocks A H 1909** Anglo-Saxon burials at Ellesborough, *Rec Buckinghamshire* 9, 425–30.

**Conyngham A 1844a** An account of the opening and examination of a considerable number of tumuli on Breach Downs, in the county of Kent, *Archaeologia* 30, 47–56.

**Conyngham A 1844b** Account of the opening of some Anglo-Saxon graves at Wingham in Kent, *Archaeologia* 30, 550–51.

**Cook A M 1981** *The Anglo-Saxon cemetery at Fonaby, Lincolnshire*, Sleaford.

**Cook A M and Dacre M W forthcoming** *The Saxon cemetery at Portway, Andover*, Oxford Monograph Series.

**Corney A, Ashbee P, Evison V I and Brothwell D 1967** A Prehistoric and Anglo-Saxon burial ground, Ports Down, Portsmouth, *Proc Hampshire Fld Clb Archaeol Soc* 24, 20–41.

**Cosack E 1982** *Das sächsische Gräberfeld bei Liebenau*, Germanische Denkmäler der Völkerwanderungszeit ser. A, 15, Berlin.

**Coutil L 1898–1921** *Arrondissement de Bernay Archéologie Gauloise, Gallo-Romaine, Franque et Carolingienne III*, Évreux.

**Cowell M R 1979** Report on the analysis of some sixth- and seventh-century pottery from sites in southern Britain and northern Europe, in Evison 1979a, 96–7.

**Cox J 1897–9** A Saxon or Danish comb found in Fish Street, Northampton, *Proc Soc Antiq* ser. 2, 17, 165, fig. on 167.

**Croker T C 1844** An account of further excavations of barrows on Breach Downs, *Archaeol J* 1, 379–80.

**Crowfoot E 1967** The textiles, in Davidson and Webster 1967, 37–9.

**Crowfoot E 1969** Textiles, in Tester 1969, 50–3.

**Crowfoot E 1973** Textile fragments from Polhill, in Philp 1973a, 202–3.

**Crowfoot E 1976a** The textile remains, in Hills and Wade-Martins 1976, 29–32.

**Crowfoot E 1976b** The textiles and leather, in Barfoot and Price Williams 1976, 68–71.

**Crowfoot E 1978** The textiles, in Green and Rogerson 1978, 98–106.

**Crowfoot 1983** The Textiles in Bruce-Mitford 1983 3 I, 409–479.

**Crowfoot 1984** The Textiles in C Hills, K Penn and R Rickett, *The Anglo-Saxon Cemetery at Spong Hill, North Elmham. Pt 3. East Anglian Archaeol, Report No. 21*, 17–28.

**Crowfoot 1985a** The Textiles in Hirst 1985 48–54

**Crowfoot 1985b** Textiles in J D Hedges and D G Buckley, Anglo-Saxon Burials and Later Features excavated at Orsett, Essex, 1975. *Medieval Archaeol* XXIX, 15–16.

**Crowfoot E, Henshall A S and Appleyard H M 1981** The textiles, in Cook 1981, 89–101.

**Crowther-Beynon V B 1901** Anglo-Saxon remains found at North Luffenham, in the County of Rutland, *Associated Architectural Societies' Reports and Papers* 26, 246–59.

**Crummy P 1981** *Aspects of Anglo-Saxon and Norman Colchester*, Colchester Archaeological Report 1, Counc Brit Archaeol Res Rep 39, London.

**Cunliffe B 1975** *Excavations at Portchester Castle I: Roman*, Rep Res Comm Soc Antiq London XXXII, London.

**Cunnington M E and Goddard E H 1934** *Catalogue of antiquities in the Museum of the Wiltshire Archaeological and Natural History Society at Devizes: part II*, Devizes.

**Dasnoy A 1955** Quelques tombes de la région namuroise datées par des monnaies (V$^e$–VI$^e$ siècles), *Annales de la Société Archéologique de Namur* 48, 1, 5–40.

**Dasnoy A 1968** La nécropole de Samson (IV$^e$–VI$^e$ siècles),

*Annales de la Société Archéologique de Namur* 54 277–333.

**Davidson H R E and Webster L 1967** The Anglo-Saxon burial at Coombe (Woodnesborough), Kent, *Medieval Archaeol* 11, 1–41.

**Dedekam H 1924–5** *To tekstilfund fra folkevandringstiden*, Historisk-antikvarisk raekke 3, Bergens Museums Aarbok.

**Denny H 1859–68** Notice of early British tumuli on the Hambleton Hills near Thirsk, *Proc Geol Soc West Riding Yorkshire* 4, 488–502.

**Dickinson T M 1973** Excavations at Standlake Down in 1954: the Anglo-Saxon graves, *Oxoniensia* 38, 239–57.

**Dickinson T M 1979** On the origin and chronology of the early Anglo-Saxon disc brooch, in Hawkes *et al.* 1979, 39–80.

**Doppelfeld O 1959** Die Domgrabung XI. Das fränkische Frauengrab, *Kölner Domblatt* 16/17, 41–78.

**Doppelfeld O 1964** Das fränkische Knabengrab unter dem Chor des Kölner Domes, *Germania* 42, 156–88.

**Doppelfeld O and Pirling R 1966** *Fränkische Fürsten im Rheinland Schriften des Rheinischen Landesmuseums Bonn* 2, Düsseldorf.

**Douglas J 1793** *Nenia Britannica*, London.

**Drury P J and Wickenden N P 1982** An early Saxon settlement within the Romano-British small town at Heybridge, Essex, *Medieval Archaeol* 26, 1–40.

**Dryden H 1849** An account of a discovery of early Saxon remains at Barrow Furlong, on the Hill Farm, in the parish of Marston St. Lawrence, in the county of Northampton, *Archaeologia* 33, 326–34.

**Dryden H 1885** Excavation of an ancient burial ground at Marston St. Lawrence, co. Northampton, *Archaeologia* 48, 327–39.

**Dunning G C 1957** Saxon and medieval pottery, in Threipland 1957, 36–7.

**Dunning G C and Evison V I 1961** The Palace of Westminster sword, *Archaeologia* 98, 123–58.

**Eagles B N 1979** *The Anglo-Saxon settlement of Humberside*, Brit Archaeol Rep British Ser 68, i and ii, Oxford.

**Eagles B N and Evison V I 1970** Excavations at Harrold, Bedfordshire, 1951–53, *Bedfordshire Archaeol J* 5, 17–55.

**East K 1983** The tub and the buckets, in Bruce-Mitford 1983 II, 554–96.

**Edlin H L 1949** *Woodland crafts in Britain*, London.

**Edwards J G, Galbraith V H and Jacob E F (ed) 1933** *Historical essays in honour of James Tait*, Manchester.

**Ellis S E 1969** The petrography and provenance of Anglo-Saxon and medieval English honestones, with notes on some other hones, *Bull British Museum (Natur Hist) Mineralogy* 2, 3, 133–87.

**Van Es W A and Verwers W J H 1980** *Excavations at Dorestad 1 The harbour: Hoogstraat I* Nederlandse Oudheden 9, Kromme Rijn Projekt 1, 2 vols, Amersfoort.

**Evans A 1942** Notes on early Anglo-Saxon gold coins, *Numismatic Chronicle* ser. 6, 2, 19–41.

**Evison V I 1951** The white material in Kentish disc brooches, *Antiq J* 31, 197–200.

**Evison V I 1955** Early Anglo-Saxon inlaid metalwork, *Antiq J* 35, 20–45.

**Evison V I 1956** An Anglo-Saxon cemetery at Holborough, Kent, *Archaeol Cantiana* 70, 84–141.

**Evison V I 1958** Further Anglo-Saxon inlay, *Antiq J* 38, 240–4.

**Evison V I 1961** The Saxon objects, in Hurst 1961, 226–30.

**Evison V I 1962** An Anglo-Saxon disc brooch from Northamptonshire, *Antiq J* 42, 53–6.

**Evison V I 1963** Sugar-loaf shield bosses, *Antiq J* 43, 38–96.

**Evison V I 1964** The Dover rune brooch, *Antiq J* 44, 242–5.

**Evison V I 1965a** The Dover, Breach Downs and Birka men, *Antiquity* 39, 214–17.

**Evison V I 1965b** *The fifth-century invasions south of the Thames*, London.

**Evison V I 1967a** The Dover ring-sword and other sword-rings and beads, *Archaeologia* 101, 63–118.

**Evison V I 1967b** Anglo-Saxon grave, Dover, *Archaeol Cantiana* 82, 283–4.

**Evison V I 1967c** The Saxon finds, in Corney *et al.* 1967, 33–6.

**Evison V I 1968** Quoit brooch style buckles, *Antiq J* 48, 231–49.

**Evison V I 1969** Five Anglo-Saxon inhumation graves containing pots at Great Chesterford, Essex, *Berichten van de Rijksdienst voor het Oudheidkundig Bodemonderzoek* 19, 157–73.

**Evison V I 1972** Glass cone beakers of the 'Kempston' type, *J Glass Stud* 14, 48–66.

**Evison V I 1973** Anglo-Saxon grave-goods from Mucking, Essex, *Antiq J* 53, 269–70.

**Evison V I 1974** The Asthall type of bottle, in Evison *et al.* 1974, 77–94.

**Evison V I 1975** Pagan Saxon whetstones, *Antiq J* 55, 70–85.

**Evison V I 1976** Sword rings and beads, *Archaeologia* 105, 303–15.

**Evison V I 1977** An enamelled disc from Great Saxham, *Proc Suffolk Inst. Archaeol* 34, 1, 1–13.

**Evison V I 1978a** La tombe de guerrier de Landifay (France, Aisne), in Fleury and Périn 1978, 39–44.

**Evison V I 1978b** Early Anglo-Saxon applied disc brooches. Part II: in England, *Antiq J* 58, 260–78.

**Evison V I 1979a** *A corpus of wheel-thrown pottery in Anglo-Saxon graves*, Roy Archaeol Inst Monogr Ser, London.

**Evison V I 1979b** The body in the ship at Sutton Hoo, in Hawkes *et al.* 1979, 121–38.

**Evison V I 1979c** A sword pommel with ring-knob at Grenay, Pas-de-Calais, *Septentrion* 9, 37–9.

**Evison V I 1980a** Iron objects, in Haslam *et al.* 1980, 35–9.

**Evison V I 1980b** The Sutton Hoo coffin, in Rahtz *et al.* 1980, 357–61.

**Evison V I 1980c** Review of: *The Sutton Hoo Ship-Burial. Volume 2 Arms, Armour and Regalia* by Rupert Bruce-Mitford, *Antiq J* 60, 124–7.

**Evison V I 1981a** Distribution maps and England in the first two phases, in Evison 1981b, 126–67.

**Evison V I (ed) 1981b** *Angles, Saxons, and Jutes*, Oxford.

**Evison V I 1982** Anglo-Saxon glass claw-beakers, *Archaeologia* 107, 43–76.

**Evison V I 1983a** Bichrome glass vessels of the seventh and eighth centuries, in Hässler 1983, 7–21.

**Evison V I 1983b** Some distinctive glass vessels of the post-Roman period, *J Glass Stud* 25, 87–93.

**Evison V I 1985** The glass, in West 1985, 75–6.

**Evison V I and Cooper V 1985** The beads, in West 1985, 71–5.

**Evison V I, Hodges H and Hurst J G (ed) 1974** *Medieval pottery from excavations*, London.

**Faider-Feytmans G 1970** *Les Collections d'Archéologie Régionale du Musée de Mariemont II Les Nécropoles Mérovingiennes*, 1 and 2, Morlanwelz-Mariemont.

**Faussett B 1856** *Inventorium Sepulchrale*, London.

**Fennell K R 1969** The Loveden Man, *Frühmittelalterliche Studien* 3, 211–5.

**Fingerlin G 1971** *Die Alamannischen Gräberfelder von Güttingen und Merdingen in Südbaden* Germanische Denkmäler der Völkerwanderungszeit ser. A, 12, 2 vols., Berlin.

**Fingerlin G 1977** *Neue alamannische Grabfunde aus Hüfingen Texte zu einer Ausstellung*, Freiburg.

**Fitch S E 1863–4** Discovery of Saxon remains at Kempston, *Reports of the Associated Architectural Societies* 7, 269–99.

**Fletcher E 1965** Early Kentish churches, *Medieval Archaeol* 9, 16–31.

**Fleury M and Périn P 1978** *Problèmes de chronologie relative et absolue concernant les cimetières mérovingiens d'entre Loire et Rhin*, Actes due II$^e$ colloque archaéologique de la IV$^e$ Section de l'École pratique des Hautes Études (Paris, 1973), Bibliothèque de l'École des Hautes Études IV$^e$ Section – Sciences historiques et philologiques – 326, Paris.

**Forssander J E 1936–7** Provinzialrömisches und Germanisches, *Kungl. Humanistiska Vetenskapssamfundets i Lund Årberättelse 1936–7 VII, Meddelanden från Lunds Universitets historiska museum*, 11–100.

**Foster W K 1880–4** Account of the excavation of an Anglo-Saxon cemetery at Barrington, Cambridgeshire, *Cambridge Antiq Soc Communications* 5, 5–32.

**Fowler R C 1926** Religious Houses, in *The Victoria history of the counties of England: A history of Kent II*, London, 112–242.

**Fox C 1923** *The archaeology of the Cambridge region*, Cambridge.

**Fremersdorf F 1941–2** Zwei wichtige Frankengräber aus Köln, *IPEK* 15–16, 124–39.

**Van Friezen Franken en Saksen 350–750 1959–60** *Van Friezen Franken en Saksen 350–750*, Leeuwarden, 1959 and Den Haag, 1960.

**Galloway P 1976** Note on descriptions of bone and antler combs, *Medieval Archaeol* 20, 154–6.

**Gebers W, Hinz H and Drenhaus U 1977** Ein Körpergrab der Völkerwanderungszeit aus Bosan, Kreis Ostholstein, *Offa* 34, 5–39.

**Genrich A 1951** Über Schmuckgegenstände der Völkerwanderungszeit im nordöstlichen Niedersachsen, *Neues Archiv für Niedersachsen* 23, 251–81.

**Genrich A 1967** Einheimische und importierte Schmuckstücke des gemischtbelegten Friedhofes von Liebenau, Kr. Nienburg, *Nachrichten aus Niedersachsens Urgeschichte* 36, 75–96.

**Genrich A 1975** Die Friedhof bei Liebenau in Niedersachsen, *Ausgrabungen in Deutschland Gefördert von der Deutschen Forschungsgemeinschaft 1950–1975, Frühmittelalter II, Archäologie und Naturwissenschaften Katalog. Karten und Modelle*, Römisch-Germanisches Zentralmuseum zu Mainz Forschungsinstitut für Vor- und Frühgeschichte Monographien 1, 3, Mainz, 17–40.

**Genrich A 1981** A remarkable inhumation grave from Liebenau, Nienburg, Germany, in Evison 1981b, 59–71.

**Gingell C J 1975–6** The excavation of an early Anglo-Saxon cemetery at Collingbourne Ducis, *Wiltshire Archaeol Mag* 70–1, 61–98.

**Glass in London 1970** *Glass in London*, London Museum exhibition catalogue.

**Glazema P and Ypey J 1955** *Kunst en Schoonheid uit de vroege middeleeuwen, De Merovingische grafvelden van Alphen, Rhenen en Maastricht*, Amersfoort.

**Glazema P and Ypey J 1956** *Merovingische Ambachtskunst*, Baarn.

**Godfrey-Faussett T G 1876** The Saxon cemetery at Bifrons, *Archaeol Cantiana* 10, 298–315.

**Godfrey-Faussett T G 1880** The Saxon cemetery at Bifrons, *Archaeol Cantiana* 13, 552–6.

**Göldner H and Sippel K 1980** *Kirchberg, Gde. Niederstein, Schwalm-Ederkreis Grabfunde des 8.–17. Jahrhunderts*, Archäologische Denkmäler in Hessen 12.

**Goldschmidt A 1923** *Die Elfenbeinskulpturen aus der Romanischen Zeit* III, Berlin.

**Gough R 1786** *Sepulchral monuments in Great Britain* I, London.

**Green B and Rogerson A 1978** *The Anglo-Saxon cemetery at Bergh Apton, Norfolk*, East Anglian Archaeol, Report No. 7, Norfolk, Gressenhall.

**Green H S, Smith A H V, Young B R and Harrison R K 1980** *The Caergwrle Bowl: its composition, geological source and archaeological significance*, Institute of Geological Sciences Report 80/1, London.

**Griffith A F 1915** An Anglo-Saxon cemetery at Alfriston, Sussex, *Sussex Archaeol Collect* 57, 197–210.

**Griffith A F and Salzmann L F 1914** An Anglo-Saxon cemetery at Alfriston, Sussex, *Sussex Archaeol Collect* 56, 16–53.

**Grimes W F (ed) 1951** *Aspects of archaeology in Britain and beyond*, London.

**Grohne E 1953** *Mahndorf*, Bremen-Horn.

**Guido M 1978** *The glass beads of the prehistoric and Roman periods in Britain and Ireland*, Rep Res Comm Soc Antiq London XXXV, London.

**Guido M 1981** The beads, in Crummy 1981, 11–12.

**Guido M, Bayley J and Biek L forthcoming** The coloured glass, in Woodward.

**Haberey W 1942** Spätantike Gläser aus Gräbern von Mayen, *Bonner Jahrbücher* 147, 249–84.

**Härke H 1981** Anglo-Saxon laminated shields at Petersfinger – a myth, *Medieval Archaeol* 25, 141–4.

**Hässler H-J 1981** Inlaid metalwork of the late migration period and the Merovingian period from Lower Saxony, in Evison 1981b, 72–95.

**Hässler H-J (ed) 1983** *Studien zur Sachsenforschung* 3 *Veröffentlichungen der urgeschichtlichen*, Sammlungen des Landesmuseums zu Hannover 27, Hildesheim.

**Haevernick T E and von Saldern A 1976** *Festschrift für Waldemar Haberey*, Mainz/Rhein.

**Hagberg U E 1976** Fundort und Fundgebiet der Modeln aus Torslunda, *Frühmittelalterliche Studien* 10, 323–49.

**Haigneré D 1866** Quatres cimetières mérovingiens du Boulonnais, *Mémoires Soc Acad Boulogne-sur-mer* 1, 5–76. Lafitte Reprints, Marseilles, 1977.

**Hall R A 1978** *Viking age York and the north*, Counc Brit Archaeol Rep 27, London.

**Harden D B 1956a** Glass vessels in Britain and Ireland, A.D. 400–1000, in Harden 1956b, 132–67.

**Harden D B (ed) 1956b** *Dark-Age Britain*, London.

**Harden D B 1971** Glass, in Brodribb *et al.* 1971, 98–108.

**Harden D B 1982** Glass, in Drury and Wickenden 1982, 28.

**Haseloff G 1974** Salin's Style I, *Medieval Archaeol* 18, 1–15.

**Haseloff G 1981** *Die germanische Tierornamentik der Völkerwanderungszeit*, Vorgeschichtliche Forschungen 17, I, II and III, Berlin.

**Haslam J, Biek L and Tylecote R F 1980** A middle Saxon smelting site at Ramsbury, Wiltshire, *Medieval Archaeol* 24, 1–68.

**Hasted E 1799** *The history and topographical survey of the county of Kent* IV, Canterbury.

**Hauck K 1970** *Goldbrakteaten aus Sievern*, Münstersche Mittelalter – Schriften 1, München.

**Hawkes S C 1969** Early Anglo-Saxon Kent, *Archaeol J* 126, 186–92.

**Hawkes S C 1973** The dating and social significance of the burials in the Polhill cemetery, in Philp 1973a, 186–201.

**Hawkes S C 1974** Some recent finds of late Roman buckles, *Britannia* 5, 386–93.

**Hawkes S C 1976a** Interim report by Mrs S C Hawkes, MA, FSA, on the excavations at Eastry, *Archaeol Cantiana* 92, 247–8.

**Hawkes S C 1976b** Orientation at Finglesham: sunrise dating of death and burial in an Anglo-Saxon cemetery in east Kent, *Archaeol Cantiana* 92, 33–51.

**Hawkes S C 1979** Eastry in Anglo-Saxon Kent: its importance, and a newly-found grave, in Hawkes *et al.* 1979, 81–113.

**Hawkes S C 1982** The archaeology of conversion: cemeteries, in Campbell *et al.* 1982, 48–9.

**Hawkes S C and Dunning G C 1961** Soldiers and settlers in Britain, fourth to fifth century: with a catalogue of animal-ornamented buckles and related belt-fittings, *Medieval Archaeol* 5, 1–70.

**Hawkes S C and Hogarth A C 1974** The Anglo-Saxon cemetery at Monkton, Thanet, *Archaeol Cantiana* 89, 49–89.

**Hawkes S C and Pollard M 1981** The gold bracteates from sixth-century Anglo-Saxon graves in Kent in the light of a new find from Finglesham, *Frühmittelalterliche Studien* 15, 316–70.

**Hawkes S C and Wells C 1975a** An Anglo-Saxon obstetric calamity from Kingsworthy, Hampshire, *Medical and Biological Illustration* 25, 47–51.

**Hawkes S C and Wells C 1975b** Crime and punishment in an Anglo-Saxon cemetery?, *Antiquity* 49, 118–22.

**Hawkes S C, Ellis Davidson H R and Hawkes C 1965** The Finglesham man, *Antiquity* 39, 17–32.

**Hawkes S C, Merrick J M and Metcalf D M 1966** X-ray fluorescent analysis of some dark age coins and jewellery, *Archaeometry* 9, 98–138.

**Hawkes S C, Brown D and Campbell J 1979** *Anglo-Saxon Studies in Archaeology and History* 1, Brit Archaeol Rep British ser 72, Oxford.

**Henderson J and Warren S E 1983** Analysis of prehistoric lead glass, in Aspinall and Warren 1983, 168–80.

**Hewett C A 1978** Anglo-Saxon carpentry, *Anglo-Saxon England* 7, 205–29.

**Hillier G 1856** *The history and antiquities of the Isle of Wight* I, London.

**Hills C 1977a** *The Anglo-Saxon cemetery at Spong Hill, North Elmham, Part I*, East Anglian Archaeol, Report No. 6, Norfolk, Gressenhall.

**Hills C 1977b** A chamber grave from Spong Hill, North Elmham, Norfolk, *Medieval Archaeol* 21, 167–76.

**Hills C 1981** Barred zoomorphic combs of the migration period, in Evison 1981b, 96–125.

**Hills C and Penn K 1981** *The Anglo-Saxon cemetery at Spong Hill, North Elmham, Part II*, East Anglian Archaeol, Report No. 11, Norfolk, Gressenhall.

**Hills C and Wade-Martins P 1976** The Anglo-Saxon cemetery at the Paddocks, Swaffham, *East Anglian Archaeol, Report No. 2, Norfolk*, Gressenhall, 1–44.

**Hirst S 1980** Some aspects of the analysis and publication of an inhumation cemetery, in Rahtz *et al.* 1980, 239–52.

**Hirst S 1985** *An Anglo-Saxon inhumation cemetery at Sewerby, Yorkshire*, York Univ Arch. Publications 4, York.

**Hirst S M and Biek L 1981** Investigation of a glass bead assemblage from an Anglo-Saxon cemetery near York, *Revue d'Archéometrie* (Supplément 1981), 139–46.

**Hoare R C 1812** *The ancient history of south Wiltshire* London.

**Hoffmann M 1964** *The warp-weighted loom*, Studia Norvegica 14, Oslo.

**Hogarth A C 1973** Structural features in Anglo-Saxon graves, *Archaeol J* 130, 104–19.

**Holden E W 1969** Anglo-Saxon burials at Crane Down, Jevington, *Sussex Archaeol Collect* 107, 126–34.

**Holdsworth P 1976** Saxon Southampton; a new review, *Medieval Archaeol* 20, 26–61.

**Hollingworth E J and O'Reilly M M 1925** *The Anglo-Saxon cemetery at Girton College, Cambridge*, Cambridge.

**Holmqvist W 1951** *Tauschierte Metallarbeiten des Nordens aus Römerzeit und Völkerwanderung*, Stockholm.

**Holmqvist W (ed) 1961** *Excavations at Helgö* I, Stockholm, 1961.

**Holmqvist W (ed) 1970** *Excavations at Helgö* III, Stockholm.

**Holmqvist W and Arrhenius B (ed) 1964** *Excavations at Helgö* II, Stockholm.

**Hope-Taylor B 1950** Excavations on Farthing Down, Coulsdon, Surrey, *Archaeol News Letter* 2, 10 (March) 170.

**Hope-Taylor B 1977** *Yeavering. An Anglo-British centre of early Northumbria*, Archaeol Rep 7, London.

**Horne Very Rev Prior 1933** Anglo-Saxon cemetery at Camerton, Somerset, Part II, *Proc Somerset Archaeol Natur Hist Soc* 79, 39–63.

**Hornell J 1914** *The sacred chank of India: a monograph of the Indian conch (Turbinella pyrum)*, Madras Fisheries Bureau Bulletin 7, Madras.

**Hornell J 1942** The chank shell cult of India, *Antiquity* 16, 113–33.

**Horsfield T W 1824** *The history and antiquities of Lewes and its vicinity*, Lewes.

**Hougen B 1940** Osebergfunnets billedvev, *Viking* 4, 85–124.

**Hubert J, Porcher J and Volbach W F 1967** *L'Europe des invasions*, Paris.
**Hübener W 1969** *Absatzgebiete frühgeschichtlicher Töpfereien in der Zone nördlich der Alpen*, Antiquitas ser. 3, 6, 2 vols., Bonn.
**Huggins P J 1976** The excavation of an 11th-century Viking hall and 14th-century rooms at Waltham Abbey, Essex, 1969–71, *Medieval Archaeol* 20, 75–133.
**Hughes M J 1972** A technical study of opaque red glass of the Iron Age in Britain, *Proc Prehist Soc* 38, 98–107.
**Humphreys J, Ryland J W, Barnard E A B, Wellstood F C and Barnett T G 1923** An Anglo-Saxon cemetery at Bidford-on-Avon, Warwickshire, *Archaeologia* 73, 89–116.
**Hundt H-J 1969** Über vorgeschichtliche Seidenfunde, *Jahrbuch des Römisch-Germanischen Zentralmuseums Mainz* 16, 59–71.
**Hunter J R 1977** *Scandinavian glass of the Ist millenium A.D. – a typological and physical examination*, unpublished Ph D thesis, University of Durham.
**Hunter J and Sanderson D 1982** The Snartemo/Kempston problem, *Fornvännen* 77, 22–9.
**Hurd H 1913** *Some notes on recent archaeological discoveries at Broadstairs*, Broadstairs.
**Hurst J G 1961** The kitchen area of Northolt Manor, Middlesex, *Medieval Archaeol* 5, 211–99.
**Hutchins A B 1844** An account of the opening of a barrow, situated seven miles to the east of Sarum, near Winterslow Hut Inn inclosures, *Archaeol J* 1, 156–7.
**Hutchinson P 1966** The Anglo-Saxon cemetery at Little Eriswell, Suffolk, *Proc Cambridge Antiq Soc* 59, 1–32.
**Hyslop M 1963** Two Anglo-Saxon cemeteries at Chamberlains Barn, Leighton Buzzard, Bedfordshire, *Archaeol J* 120, 161–200.

**Janssen W 1972** *Issendorf ein Urnenfriedhof der späten Kaiserzeit und der Völkerwanderungszeit, 1: Die Ergebnisse der Ausgrabung 1967*, Materialhefte zur Ur- und Frühgeschichte Niedersachsens 6, Hildesheim.
**Jessup R 1950** *Anglo-Saxon jewellery*, London.
**Jewell P A and Dimbleby G W (ed) 1966** The experimental earthwork on Overton Down, Wiltshire, England: the first four years, *Proc Prehist Soc* 32, 313–42.
**Jewitt L 1870** *Grave-mounds and their contents*, London.
**Joffroy R 1974** *Le cimetière de Lavoye*, Paris, 1974.
**Jones M U and Jones W T 1975** The crop-mark sites at Mucking, Essex, England, in Bruce-Mitford 1975b, 133–87.

**Keepax C 1977** Contamination of archaeological deposits by seeds of modern origin with particular reference to the use of flotation machines, *J Archaeol Sci* 4, 221–9.
**Keller E 1971** *Die Spätrömischen Grabfunde in Südbayern* Münchner Beiträge zur Vor- und Frühgeschichte 14 Veröffentlichungen der Kommission zur Archäologischen Erforschung des Spätrömischen Raetien, Der Bayerischen Akademie der Wissenschaften 8, München.
**Kendrick T D 1933a** Polychrome jewellery in Kent, *Antiquity* 7, 429–52.
**Kendrick T D 1933b** The Dover post-Roman circular brooch, *Dover Museum Bulletin* 3 (Jan 1933) front page and back page.
**Kendrick T D 1934** Style in early Anglo-Saxon ornament, *IPEK* 9, 66–76.
**Kendrick T D 1937a** A Jutish fragment from Kent, *Antiq J* 17, 76–7.
**Kendrick T D 1937b** Ivory mounts from a casket, *Antiq J* 17, 448.
**Kennett D H 1968** The Irchester bowls, *J Northampton Mus* 4, 5–39.
**Kennett D H 1969a** The Anglo-Saxon grave from Battle Edge, near Burford, Oxfordshire, *Oxoniensia* 34, 111–15.
**Kennett D H 1969b** Late Roman bronze vessel hoards in Britain, *Jahrbuch des Römisch-Germanischen Zentralmuseums Mainz* 16, 123–48.
**Kennett D H 1971** Graves with swords at Little Wilbraham and Linton Heath, *Proc Cambridge Antiq Soc* 63, 9–26.
**Kennett D H 1974** Some decorative aspects of the Anglo-Saxon shield, *Bedfordshire Archaeol J* 9, 55–70.
**Kessler P T 1940** Fürstengrab von Planig, *Mainzer Zeitschrift* 35, 1–12.
**Knocker G M 1956** Early burials and an Anglo-Saxon cemetery at Snell's Corner, near Horndean, Hampshire, *Proc Hampshire Fld Club Archaeol Soc* 19, 2, 117–70.
**Knorr R 1912** Die Terra Sigillata Gefässe von Aislingen, *Jahrbuch des historischen Vereins in Dillingen* 25.
**Koch U 1969** Alamannische Gräber der ersten Hälfte des 6. Jahrhunderts in Südbayern, *Bayerische Vorgeschichtsblätter* 34, 162–93.
**Koch U 1974a** Probleme merowingerzeitlicher Glasperlen aus Süddeutschland, *Annales du 6ᵉ Congrès International d'Étude Historique du Verre Cologne 1–7 juillet 1973*, Liège, 131–42.
**Koch U 1974b** Mediterrane und fränkische Glasperlen des 6. und 7. Jahrhunderts aus Finnland, in Kossack and Ulbert 1974, II, 495–520.
**Koch U 1977** *Das Reihengräberfeld bei Schretzheim*, Germanische Denkmäler der Völkerwanderungszeit ser. A, 13, 1 and 2, Berlin.
**Kossack G and Ulbert G 1974** *Studien zur Vor- und Frühgeschichtlichen Archäologie*, Münchner Beiträge zur Vor- und Frühgeschichte Ergänzungsband 1, I and II, Munich.
**Krause W and Jankuhn H 1966** *Die Runeninschriften im älteren Futhark*, Abhandlungen der Akademie der Wissenschaften in Göttingen Philologisch – Historische Klasse ser. 3, 65, I and II, Göttingen.

**Lafaurie J, Jansen B and Zadoks-Josephus Jitta A 1961** Le trésor de Wieuwerd, *Oudheidkundige Mededelingen* 42, 78–107.
**Laing L 1975** *The archaeology of late Celtic Britain and Ireland c 400–1200 A.D.*, London.
**Laing L and Laing J 1979** *Anglo-Saxon England*, London.
**Lawson G 1978** The lyre from grave 22, in Green and Rogerson 1978, 87–97.
**Layard N F 1907** An Anglo-Saxon cemetery in Ipswich, *Archaeologia* 60, 2, 325–52.
**Leeds E T 1912** The distribution of the Anglo-Saxon saucer brooch in relation to the battle of Bedford, A.D. 571, *Archaeologia* 63, 159–202.
**Leeds E T 1913** *The archaeology of the Anglo-Saxon settlements*, Oxford.
**Leeds E T 1916–17** An Anglo-Saxon cemetery at

Wheatley, Oxfordshire, *Proc Soc Antiq* ser. 2, 29, 48–65.

**Leeds E T 1923** A Saxon village near Sutton Courtenay, Berkshire, *Archaeologia* 73, 147–92.

**Leeds E T 1936** *Early Anglo-Saxon art and archaeology*, Oxford.

**Leeds E T 1939** Anglo-Saxon remains, in *The Victoria history of the counties of England: A history of Oxfordshire I*, London, 346–72.

**Leeds E T 1940** Two Saxon cemeteries in north Oxfordshire, *Oxoniensia* 5, 21–30.

**Leeds E T 1945** The distribution of the Angles and Saxons archaeologically considered, *Archaeologia* 91, 1–106.

**Leeds E T 1946** Denmark and early England, *Antiq J* 26, 22–37.

**Leeds E T and Atkinson R J C 1944** An Anglo-Saxon cemetery at Nassington, Northants., *Antiq J* 24, 100–28.

**Leeds E T and Harden D B 1936** *The Anglo-Saxon cemetery at Abingdon, Berkshire*, Oxford.

**Leeds E T and Riley M 1942** Two early Saxon cemeteries at Cassington, Oxon., *Oxoniensia* 7, 61–70.

**Leeds E T and Shortt H de S 1953** *An Anglo-Saxon cemetery at Petersfinger, near Salisbury, Wilts*, Salisbury.

**Leigh D 1984** Ambiguity in Anglo-Saxon Style I Art. *Antiq J* LXIV, 34–42.

**Lethbridge T C 1926–7** The Anglo-Saxon cemetery at Burwell, Cambs. Part III, *Proc Cambridge Antiq Soc* 29, 84–94.

**Lethbridge T C 1927** An Anglo-Saxon hut on the Car Dyke, at Waterbeach, *Antiq J* 7, 141–6.

**Lethbridge T C 1931** *Recent excavations in Anglo-Saxon cemeteries in Cambridgeshire and Suffolk*, Cambridge Antiquarian Society Quarto Publications new ser. 3, Cambridge.

**Lethbridge T C 1931–2** Anglo-Saxon burials at Soham, Cambridgeshire, *Proc Cambridge Antiq Soc* 33, 152–63.

**Lethbridge T C 1936** *A cemetery at Shudy Camps, Cambridgeshire* Cambridge Antiquarian Society Quarto Publications new ser. 5, Cambridge.

**Lethbridge T C 1951** *A cemetery at Lackford, Suffolk*, Cambridge Antiquarian Society Quarto Publications new ser. 6, Cambridge.

**Liège 1930** *Catalogue de l'exposition de l'art de l'ancien pays de Liège*, Liège.

**Lindqvist S 1936** *Uppsala Högar och Ottarshögen*, Kungl. Vitterhets Historie och Antikvitets Akademien Arkeologiska Monografier 23, Stockholm.

**Liversidge J 1973** *Britain in the Roman Empire*, London.

**Livett G M 1926** Ecclesiastical history: Part I (to death of Lanfranc), in *The Victoria history of the counties of England: A history of Kent II*, London, 1–25.

**De Loë 1939** *La Période Franque*, Belgique Ancienne IV, Brussels.

**Lundström A 1970** Beads, in Holmqvist 1970, 78–9.

**Lundström A 1976** *Bead making in Scandinavia in the early middle ages*, Early Medieval Studies 9, Antikvariskt Archiv 61, Stockholm.

**Lundström A 1981** Survey of the glass from Helgö, in Lundström *et al.* 1981, 1–38.

**Lundström A and Lindeberg I 1964** Beads, in Holmqvist and Arrhenius 1964, 133–6.

**Lundström A, Werner G, Knape A, Brinch Madsen H and Reisborg S 1981** *Excavations at Helgö* VII, Stockholm.

**Lundström P 1961** Beads, in Holmqvist 1961, 160–3.

**Mac Dermott M 1955** The Kells crosier, *Archaeologia* 96, 59–113.

**MacGregor A 1978** Industry and commerce in Anglo-Scandinavian York, in Hall 1978, 37–57.

**Mackeprang M B 1952** *De Nordiske Guldbrakteater* Jysk Arkaeologisk Selskabs Skrifter II, Aarhus.

**Margary I D 1955** *Roman roads in Britain I*, London.

**Martin M 1967** Zwei spätrömische Gürtel aus Augst/BL, *Römerhaus und Museum Augst Jahresbericht*, 3–20.

**Martin M 1976** *Das fränksiche Gräberfeld von Basel-Bernerring*, Basel.

**Matson F R and Rindone G E (eds) 1963** *Advances in glass technology* 2, New York.

**Matthews C L 1962** The Anglo-Saxon cemetery at Marina Drive, Dunstable, *Bedfordshire Archaeol J* 1, 25–47.

**Meaney A 1964** *A gazetteer of early Anglo-Saxon burial sites*, London.

**Meaney A L 1981** *Anglo-Saxon amulets and curing stones*, Brit Archaeol Rep British ser 96, Oxford.

**Meaney A L and Hawkes S C 1970** *Two Anglo-Saxon cemeteries at Winnall*, Soc Medieval Archaeol Monogr Ser 4, London.

**Mellinkoff R 1970** *The horned Moses in medieval art and thought*, Los Angeles and London.

**Menghin W 1973** Aufhängevorrichtung und Trageweise zweischneidiger Langschwerter aus germanischen Gräbern des 5. bis 7. Jahrhunderts, *Anzeiger des germanischen Nationalmuseums*, 7–56.

**Merewether J 1851** Diary of the examination of barrows and other earthworks in the neighbourhood of Silbury Hill and Avebury in July and August 1849, in *Memoirs illustrative of the history and antiquities of Wiltshire and the city of Salisbury, communicated to the annual meeting of the Archaeological Institute of Great Britain and Ireland, held at Salisbury, July 1849*, London, 82–107.

**Miket R 1974** 'Undoubted Anglian burials' from Hepple, Northumberland, *Archaeol Aeliana* ser. 5, 2, 275–80.

**Millard L, Jarman S and Hawkes S C 1969** Anglo-Saxon burials near The Lord of the Manor, Ramsgate. New light on the site of Ozengell?, *Archaeol Cantiana* 84, 9–30.

**Mitchell G F, Harbison P, de Paor L, de Paor M and Stalley R A 1977** *Treasures of Irish Art 1500BC–1500AD*, New York.

**Moir J R 1921** The excavation of two tumuli on Brightwell Heath, Suffolk, *J Ipswich Dist Fld Club* 6, 1–14.

**Molaug P B 1975** Oslo im Mittelalter. Ergebnisse der neuen archäologischen Ausgrabungen, *Zeitschrift für Archäologie des Mittelalters* 3, 217–60.

**Moore J W 1963–6** An Anglo-Saxon settlement at Wykeham, North Yorkshire, *Yorkshire Archaeol J* 41, 403–44.

**Moosbrugger-Leu R 1963–4** Le scramasax décoré de Lausanne, Bel-Air (tombe 48), *Zeitschrift für Schweizerische Archäologie und Kunstgeschichte* 23, 10–21.

**Moosbrugger-Leu R 1971** *Die Schweiz zur Merowingerzeit*, A and B, Bern.

**Mortimer J R 1905** *Forty years' researches in British and Saxon burial mounds of East Yorkshire*, London.

**Moss A A 1953a** Niello, *Stud. Conservation* 1, 2, 49–62.

**Moss A A 1953b** Niello, *Antiq J* 33, 75–7.

**Moss A A 1955** Report on the composition of the niello inlays, in Mac Dermott 1955, 100.

**Musty J 1969** The excavation of two barrows, one of Saxon date, at Ford, Laverstock, near Salisbury, Wiltshire, *Antiq J* 49, 98–117.

**Myres J N L 1969** *Anglo-Saxon pottery and the settlement of England*, Oxford.

**Myres J N L 1977** *A corpus of Anglo-Saxon pottery of the pagan period*, 1 and 2, Cambridge.

**Myres J N L 1980** Review of: *A Corpus of Wheel-thrown Pottery in Anglo-Saxon Graves* by Vera I. Evison, *Antiq J* 60, 389–91.

**Myres J N L and Green B 1973** *The Anglo-Saxon cemeteries of Caistor-by-Norwich and Markshall, Norfolk* Rep Res Comm Soc Antiq London XXX, London.

**Myres J N L and Southern W H 1973** *The Anglo-Saxon cremation cemetery at Sancton, East Yorkshire*, Hull Museum Publications 218.

**Nenquin J A E 1953** *La nécropole de Furfooz*, Dissertationes Archaeologicae Gandenses I, Bruges.

**Nerman B 1935** *Die Völkerwanderungszeit Gotlands*, Stockholm.

**Neumann H 1981** Jutish burials in the Roman Iron Age, in Evison 1981b, 1–10.

**Neville R C 1854** Anglo-Saxon cemetery on Linton Heath, Cambridgeshire, *Archaeol J* 11, 95–115.

**Newton R G 1978** Colouring agents used by medieval glassmakers, *Glass Technology* 19, 59–60.

**Nichols J 1807** *The history and antiquities of the county of Leicester* IV part I, London.

**Nichols J 1815** *The history and antiquities of the county of Leicester* I part II *Appendix to the history of Leicestershire Additions and corrections in Vol. III*, London.

**Norris N E S 1956** Miscellaneous researches, 1949–56, *Sussex Archaeol Collect* 94, 1–12.

**Nowothnig W 1970** Einige frühgeschichtliche Funde aus Niedersachsen, *Nachrichten aus Niedersachsens Urgeschichte* 39, 126–43.

**Oakley K 1965** Folklore of fossils: Part I, *Antiquity* 39, 9–16.

**Odenstedt B 1981** The Gilton runic inscription, in Brown *et al.* 1981, 37–48.

**Ørsnes-Christensen M 1955** Kyndby. Ein seelandischer Grabplatz aus dem 7.–8. Jahrhundert nach Christus, *Acta Archaeologica* 26, 69–162.

**Olsen P 1949–51** Ett vendeltida nyckelskaft, *Tor* 116–24.

**Oppenheim A L, Brill R H, Barag D and von Saldern A 1970** *Glass and glassmaking in ancient Mesopotamia*, The Corning Museum of Glass Monograph 3, Corning, New York.

**Oswald F and Pryce T D 1920** *An introduction to the study of Terra Sigillata*, London

**Page R I 1973** *An Introduction to English Runes*, London.

**Parfitt K 1981** The Ringwould water main, 1980/81. *Kent Archaeological Review* 65 (Autumn), 107–111.

**Parsons F G 1911** On some Saxon bones from Folkestone, *J Roy Anthrop Inst* 41, 101–29.

**Paulsen P 1967** *Alamannische Adelsgräber von Niederstotzingen*, Veröffentlichungen des Staatlichen Amtes für Denkmalpflege Stuttgart Reihe A, Heft 12/1, Stuttgart.

**Payne G 1889** On a Roman statue and other remains at Dover Museum, *Archaeol Cantiana* 18, 202–5.

**Payne G 1893** *Collectanea Cantiana*, London.

**Payne G 1893–5** Anglo-Saxon remains found at Dover, *Proc Soc Antiq* ser. 2, 15, 178–83.

**Peake H and Hooton E A 1915** Saxon graveyard at East Shefford, Berks., *J Roy Anthrop Inst* 45, 92–130.

**Peers C and Radford C A R 1943** The Saxon monastery of Whitby, *Archaeologia* 89, 27–88.

**Périn P 1972** Typologie et chronologie des verreries provenant des sépultures mérovingiennes de la region Ardennoise (V$^e$ – VIII$^e$ siècles), *Congresso internazionale del vetro: atti* 9, 2, 11–50.

**Périn P 1980** *La datation des tombes mérovingiennes*, Centre de recherches d'histoire et de philologie de la IV$^e$ section de l'école pratique de des hautes études V Hautes études médiévales et modernes 39, Geneva.

**Petersen J 1951** *Vikingetidens redskaper Skrifter utgitt av det Norske Videnskaps-Akademi i Oslo*, II Historisk-Filosofisk Klasse 2, No. 4.

**Phillips C J 1941** *Glass: the miracle-maker, its history, technology and applications*, New York.

**Phillips P 1980** *The prehistory of Europe*, London.

**Philp B undated** *Buried Dover*, Dover.

**Philp B 1973a** *Excavations in west Kent 1960–1970*, Dover.

**Philp B 1973b** Saxon gold ring found at Dover, *Kent Archaeological Review* 31 (Spring 1973), 10.

**Philp B 1978** Major Saxon building discovered at Dover, *Kent Archaeological Review* 53 (Autumn 1978), 64–5.

**Philp B 1981** *The excavation of the Roman forts of the Classis Britannica at Dover 1970–1977*, Dover.

**Pilet C 1979** Quelques témoignages de la présence Anglo-Saxonne dans le Calvados, Basse-Normandie (France), *Frühmittelalterliche Studien* 13, 357–81.

**Pilet C, Lemiere J and Alduc-Le-Bagousse d'A 1981** *Les nécropoles de Giberville*, Publication du Musée de Normandie 1, Caen.

**Pilloy J 1895** *Études sur d'anciens lieux de sépultures dans l'Aisne* 2, Paris.

**Pirling R 1966** *Das Römisch-Fränkische Gräberfeld von Krefeld-Gellep*, Germanische Denkmäler der Völkerwanderungszeit ser. B, 2, 1 and 2, Berlin.

**Pirling R 1974** *Das Römisch-Fränkische Gräberfeld von Krefeld-Gellep 1960–1963*, Germanische Denkmäler der Völkwerwanderungszeit ser. B, 8, 1 and 2, Berlin.

**Piton D and Schuler R 1981** La nécropole de Nouvion-en-Ponthieu (Somme) IV$^e$ – VII$^e$ siècle, *Cahiers Archéologiques de Picardie* 8, 217–83.

**Pitt-Rivers A H L F 1883** *On the development and distribution of primitive locks and keys*, London.

**Pollitt Mr 1931** Further Anglo-Saxon remains in Essex, *Antiq J* 11, 61–2.

**Pownall A 1864–7** Anglo-Saxon antiquities discovered at Glen Parva in Leicestershire, *Proc Soc Antiq* ser. 2, 3, 344–6.

**Poynter A 1852** Several relics of the Anglo-Saxon period, *Archaeol J* 9, 304–5.

**Rademacher F 1942** Fränkische Gläser aus dem Rheinland, *Bonner Jahrbücher* 147, 285–344.

**Rahtz P 1978** Grave orientation, *Archaeol J* 135, 1–14.

**Rahtz P 1979** *The Saxon and medieval palaces at Cheddar*, Brit Archaeol Rep British ser 65, Oxford.

**Rahtz P, Dickinson T and Watts L (ed) 1980** *Anglo-Saxon cemeteries 1979*, Brit Archaeol Rep British Ser 82, Oxford.

**Rau H G 1976** Konische Glasbecher mit schrägen Wandrillen als Beleg frühfränkischer Glasproduktion, in Haevernick and von Saldern 1976, 111–20.

**Read C H 1893–5** Account of the exploration of a Saxon grave at Broomfield, Essex, *Proc Soc Antiq* ser. 2, 15, 250–5.

**Read C H 1895** On excavations in a cemetery of South Saxons on High Down, Sussex, *Archaeologia* 54, 2, 369–82.

**Reinerth H 1940** *Vorgeschichte der deutschen Stämme* I, II and III, Leipzig.

**Renner D 1970** *Die durchbrochenen Zierscheiben der Merowingerzeit*, Römisch-Germanisches Zentralmuseum zu Mainz Kataloge vor- und frühgeschichtlicher Altertümer 18, Mainz.

**Rice R G 1923** An Anglo-Saxon bronze bowl from Mitcham, *Antiq J* 3, 70–1.

**Rigold S E 1960–1** The two primary series of sceattas, *Brit Numis J* 30, 6–53.

**Rigold S E 1972** Roman Folkestone reconsidered, *Archaeol Cantiana* 87, 31–41.

**Rigold S E 1975** The Sutton Hoo coins in the light of the contemporary background of coinage in England, in Bruce-Mitford 1975a, 653–77.

**Rigold S E and Webster L E 1970** Three Anglo-Saxon disc brooches, *Archaeol Cantiana* 85, 1–18.

**Ringquist P-O 1969** Två vikingatida uppländska människofigurer i brons, *Fornvännen* 64, 287–96.

**Robinson H R 1975** *The armour of Imperial Rome*, London.

**Rodwell W and Rodwell K 1982** St. Peter's church, Barton-upon-Humber: excavation and structural study, 1978–81, *Antiq J* 62, 283–315.

**Roeder F 1927** *Die sächsische Schalenfibel der Völkerwanderungszeit*, Göttingen.

**Roes A 1954a** Les trouvailles de Dombourg (Zélande), *Berichten van de Rijksdienst voor het Oudheidkundig Bodemonderzoek* 5, 65–9.

**Roes A 1954b** A travers les collections archaéologiques de la Hollande, *Berichten van de Rijksdienst voor het Oudheidkundig Bodemonderzoek* 5, 62–4.

**Roes A 1963** *Bone and antler objects from the Frisian terp-mounds*, Haarlem.

**Roes A 1965** *Vondsten van Dorestad*, Archaeologica Traiectina 7 Groningen.

**Rooksby H P 1964** A yellow cubic lead tin oxide opacifier in ancient glasses, *Physics and Chemistry of Glasses* 5, 20–5.

**Roosens H 1973** Glas, *Archéologie*, 47.

**Rupp H 1937** *Die Herkunft der Zelleneinlage und die Almandin-Scheibenfibeln im Rheinland*, Rheinische Forschungen zur Vorgeschichte II, Bonn, 1937.

**Rygh O 1880** *Norske Oldsager* 1, Christiania.

**Salin E 1939** *Le haut moyen-age en Lorraine*, Paris.

**Salin E 1959** *La civilisation Mérovingienne* 4, Paris.

**Sawyer J 1892** Important discovery of Anglo-Saxon remains at Kingston, Lewes, *Sussex Archaeol Collect* 38, 177–83.

**Sawyer P H 1968** *Anglo-Saxon Charters*, Royal Historical Society Guides and Handbooks 8, London.

**Sayre E V 1963** The intentional use of antimony and manganese in ancient glasses, in Matson and Rindone 1963, 263–82.

**Sayre E V and Smith R W 1974** Analytical studies of ancient Egyptian glass, in Bishay 1974, 47–70.

**Schmid P 1967** Das frühmittelalterliche Gräberfeld von Dunum, Kr. Wittmund (Ostfr.), *Nachrichten aus Niedersachsens Urgeschichte* 36, 39–60.

**Schoppa H 1953** Ein fränkisches Holzkästchen aus Weilbach, *Germania* 31, 44–50.

**Schröter Th A and Gummel H 1957** Der Goldbrakteatenfund von Sievern, *Die Kunde* new ser. 8, 3–24.

**Sheppard T 1913** The Anglo-Saxon cemetery at Hornsea, *Trans Hull Sci Fld Natur Club* 4, 5, 258–72.

**Sheppard T 1938** Anglo-Saxon cemeteries in east Yorkshire, *The Naturalist*, 1–23.

**Sheppard T 1939** Saxon relics from Barton, Lincs. *The Naturalist*, 257–62.

**Sheppard T 1940** Saxon relics from Barton, Lincs., Part II, *The Naturalist*, 37–49.

**Shetelig H 1912** *Vestlandske graver fra jernalderen*, Bergens Museums Skrifter new ser. 2, 1, Bergen.

**Shetelig H 1925** *Norges Forhistorie*, Instituttet for Sammenlignende Kulturforskning ser. A, Va, Oslo.

**Sirat J 1967** Le cimetière mérovingien de Rueil, *Bulletin Arch. du Vexin français* 3, 113–22.

**Slater E A and Tate J O (ed) 1980** *Proceedings of the 16th international symposium on archaeometry and archaeological prospection, Edinburgh 1976*, Edinburgh.

**Smith C R 1844** An account of some antiquities found in the neighbourhood of Sandwich, in the county of Kent, *Archaeologia* 30, 132–6.

**Smith C R 1846** On some Anglo-Saxon remains, discovered at Stowting, in the county of Kent, *Archaeologia* 31, 398–403.

**Smith C R 1848** *Collectanea Antiqua* I, London.

**Smith C R 1852** *Collectanea Antiqua* II, London.

**Smith C R 1854** *Collectanea Antiqua* III, London.

**Smith C R 1868** *Collectanea Antiqua* VI, London.

**Smith H E 1884** An ancient cemetery at Saffron Walden, *Trans Essex Archaeol Soc* new ser. 2, 311–34.

**Smith R 1911–12** An Anglo-Saxon cemetery at Uncleby, East Riding of Yorkshire, *Proc Soc Antiq* ser. 2, 24, 146–58.

**Smith R A 1902** Anglo-Saxon remains, in *The Victoria history of the counties of England: A history of the county of Northampton I*, Westminster, 223–56.

**Smith R A 1906** Anglo-Saxon remains, in *The Victoria history of the counties of England: A history of Berkshire I*, London, 229–49.

**Smith R A 1908a** Anglo-Saxon remains, in *The Victoria history of the counties of England: A history of Kent I*, London, 339–87.

**Smith R A 1908b** Anglo-Saxon remains, in *The Victoria history of the counties of England: A history of Rutland I*, London, 95–106.

**Smith R A 1909** Anglo-Saxon remains, in *The Victoria history of the counties of England: A history of London I*, London, 147–70.

**Smith R A 1911** Anglo-Saxon remains, in *The Victoria history of the counties of England: A history of Suffolk I*, London, 325–55.

**Smith R A 1912** Anglo-Saxon remains, in *The Victoria history of the counties of England: A history of Yorkshire II*, 73–108.

**Smith R A 1917–18a** Prehistoric and Anglo-Saxon remains discovered by Captain L Moysey at Howletts, near Bridge, Kent, *Proc Soc Antiq* ser. 2, 30, 102–13.

**Smith R A 1917–18b** Anglo-Saxon antiquities discovered at Islip, Northants., *Proc Soc Antiq* ser. 2, 30, 113–20.

**Smith R A 1923** *A guide to the Anglo-Saxon and foreign teutonic antiquities in the Department of British and Mediaeval Antiquities*, London.

**Speake G 1980** *Anglo-Saxon animal art and its Germanic background*, Oxford.

**Spitzer-Aronson M 1979** Titanium, possible indicator for medieval archaeology owing to exactness of a new method for the study of the old-stained glasses, *Archaeo-Physika* 10, 286.

**Stead L 1969** Verulamium 1966–8, *Antiquity* 43, 45–52.

**Stein F 1967** *Adelsgräber des Achten Jahrhunderts in Deutschland*, Germanische Denkmäler der Völkerwanderungszeit ser. A, 9, 2 vols., Berlin.

**Stenton F M 1933** Medehamstede and its colonies, in Edwards *et al.* 1933, 313–26.

**Stenton F M 1947** *Anglo-Saxon England*, Oxford.

**Steuer H 1983** Schlüsselpaare in frühgeschichtlichen Gräbern. – Zur Deutung einer Amulett-Beigabe, in Hässler 1983, 185–247.

**Stevenson R B K 1955** Pins and the chronology of brochs, *Proc Prehist Soc* 21, 282–94.

**Stolpe H and Arne T J 1927** *La Nécropole de Vendel Kungl. Vitterhets Historie och Antikvitetsakadamien, Monografiserien* 17, Stockholm.

**Stone S 1856–9** Account of certain (supposed) British and Saxon remains, recently discovered at Standlake, in the county of Oxford, *Proc Soc Antiq* ser. 1, 4, 92–100.

**Swanton M J 1973** *The spearheads of the Anglo-Saxon settlements*, London.

**Swanton M J 1974** *A corpus of pagan Anglo-Saxon spear types*, Brit Archaeol Rep 7, Oxford.

**Taylor H M 1978** *Anglo-Saxon architecture* III, Cambridge.

**Taylor H M and Taylor J 1965** *Anglo-Saxon architecture* I and II, Cambridge.

**Tester P J 1968** An Anglo-Saxon cemetery at Orpington, *Archaeol Cantiana* 83, 125–50.

**Tester P J 1969** Excavations at Fordcroft, Orpington, *Archaeol Cantiana* 84, 39–77.

**Thomas G W 1887** On excavations in an Anglo-Saxon cemetery at Sleaford, in Lincolnshire, *Archaeologia* 50, 383–406.

**Thorvildsen E 1972** Dankirke, *Nationalmuseets Arbejdsmark*, 47–60.

**Threipland L M 1957** Excavations in Dover, *Archaeol Cantiana* 71, 14–37.

**Turner W E S and Rooksby H P 1959** A study of the opalising agents in ancient glasses throughout three thousand four hundred years, *Glastechnische Berichte* 32K, 8, 17–28.

**Vierck H 1978a** Religion, Rang und Herrschaft im Spiegel der Tracht, in Ahrens 1978, 271–83.

**Vierck H E F 1978b** La "chemise de Sainte Bathilde" à Chelles et l'influence byzantine sur l'art de cour mérovingien au VII$^e$ siècle, in *Centenaire de l'abbé Cochet – 1975 Actes du Colloque International d'Archéologie Rouen 3–4–5 Juillet 1975*, Rouen, 521–70.

**Vierck H 1981** *Imitatio imperii* und *Interpretatio Germanica* vor der wikingerzeit, in Zeitler 1981, 64–113.

**Vierck H 1983** Ein Schmiedeplatz aus Alt-Ladoga und der präurbane Handel zur Ostsee vor der Wikingerzeit, *Münstersche Beiträge zur antiken Handelsgeschichte* II, 2, 3–64.

**Vogt E 1960** Interpretation und museale Auswertung alamannischer Grabfunde, *Zeitschrift für Schweizerische Archäologie und Kunstgeschichte* 20, 70–90.

**Voss O 1954** The Høstentorp silver hoard and its period, *Acta Archaeologica* 25, 171–219.

**Wainwright F T 1962** *Archaeology and place-names and history*, London.

**Warhurst A 1955** The Jutish cemetery at Lyminge, *Archaeol Cantiana* 69, 1–40.

**Warmington E H 1974** *The commerce between the Roman Empire and India*, London.

**Waterman D M 1959** Late Saxon, Viking and early medieval finds from York, *Archaeologia* 97, 59–105.

**Webster L E 1972** Medieval Britain in 1971: I, Pre-Conquest, *Medieval Archaeol* 16, 147–70.

**Webster L E 1973** Medieval Britain in 1972: I, Pre-Conquest, *Medieval Archaeol* 17, 138–52.

**Webster L E 1974** Medieval Britain in 1973: I, Pre-Conquest, *Medieval Archaeol* 18, 174–87.

**Webster L E 1975** Medieval Britain in 1974: I, Pre-Conquest, *Medieval Archaeol* 19, 220–32.

**Webster L E 1976** Medieval Britain in 1975: I, Pre-Conquest, *Medieval Archaeol* 20, 158–76.

**Webster L E 1978** Medieval Britain in 1977: I, Pre-Conquest, *Medieval Archaeol* 22, 142–55.

**Webster L E 1979** Medieval Britain in 1978: I, Pre-Conquest, *Medieval Archaeol* 23, 234–8.

**Webster L E 1980** Medieval Britain in 1979: I, Pre-Conquest, *Medieval Archaeol* 24, 218–36.

**Welch M 1980** The Saxon cemeteries of Sussex, in Rahtz *et al.* 1980, 255–83.

**Welch M 1983** *Early Anglo-Saxon Sussex*, Brit Archaeol Rep Brit Ser 112, i and ii, Oxford.

**Wells C and Green C 1973** Sunrise dating of death and burial, *Norfolk Archaeol* 35, 435–42.

**Werner J 1935** *Munzdatierte Austrasische Grabfunde* Germanische Denkmäler der Völkerwanderungszeit 3, Berlin and Leipzig.

**Werner J 1953** *Das Alamannische Gräberfeld von Bülach*, Monographien zu Ur- und Frühgeschichte der Schweiz 9, Basel.

**Werner J 1954** Waage und Geld in der Merowingerzeit, *Sitzungberichte der Philosophisch-historischen Klasse der Bayerischen Akademie der Wissenschaftern zu München* 1954, 1, München.

**Werner J 1955a** Bügelfibeln des 6 Jahrhunderts aus Domburg, Zeeland, *Berichten van de Rijksdienst voor het Oudheidkundig Bodemonderzoek* 6, 75–7.

**Werner J 1955b** *Das Alamannische Gräberfeld von Mindelheim*, Materialhefte zur Bayerische Vorgeschichte 6, Kallmünz/Opf.

**Werner J 1961** *Katalog der Sammlung Diergardt* 1, Römisch-Germanisches Museum Köln, Berlin.

**Werner J 1962a** *Die Langobarden in Pannonien*, Bayerische Adademie der Wissenschaften Philosophisch-Historische Klasse Abhandlungen new ser. 55, A and B, Munich.

**Werner J 1962b** Fernhandel und Naturalwirtschaft im östlichen Merowingerreich nach archäologischen und numismatischen Zeugnissen, *Bericht der Römisch-Germanischen Kommission* 42, 307–46.

**West S E 1985** *West Stow. The Anglo-Saxon Village* East Anglian Archaeol, Report No. 24, 1 and 2, Ipswich.

**West S E and Owles 1973–5** Anglo-Saxon cremation burials from Snape, *Proc Suffolk Inst Archaeol* 33, 47–57.

**Wheeler R E M 1935** *London and the Saxons*, London Museum Catalogues: No. 6, London.

**Wheeler R E M 1951** Roman contact with India, Pakistan and Afghanistan, in Grimes 1951, 345–81.

**Wilkins E P, Kell E and Locke J 1860** Account of the examination of the largest barrow in the Anglo-Saxon cemetery on Bowcombe Down, Isle of Wight, *J Brit Archaeol Ass* 16, 253–61.

**Willson J 1984** Further Saxon burials from Breach Down, Barham. *Kent Archaeological Review* 76 (Summer), 125–130.

**Wilson A E N.D.** *A guide to the Anglo-Saxon collection*, Worthing Museum Publications 1, 2nd edition.

**Wilson D M 1955** The initial excavation of an Anglo-Saxon cemetery at Melbourn, Cambridgeshire, *Proc Cambridge Antiq Soc* 49, 29–41.

**Wilson D M 1956** An Anglo-Saxon grave near Dartford, Kent, *Archaeol Cantiana* 70, 187–91.

**Wilson D M 1960** Medieval Britain in 1959: I, Pre-Conquest, *Medieval Archaeol* 4, 134–9.

**Wilson D M 1964** *Anglo-Saxon ornamental metalwork 700–1100*, Catalogue of the antiquities of the later Saxon period I, London.

**Wilson D M 1967** Medieval Britain in 1966: I, Pre-Conquest, *Medieval Archaeol* 11, 262–72.

**Wilson D M 1968a** Medieval Britain in 1967: I, Pre-Conquest, *Medieval Archaeol* 12, 155–64.

**Wilson D M 1968b** Anglo-Saxon carpenter's tools, in Claus *et al.* 1968, 143–50.

**Wilson D M 1969** Medieval Britain in 1968: I, Pre-Conquest, *Medieval Archaeol* 13, 230–43.

**Wilson D M 1970** Medieval Britain in 1969: I, Pre-Conquest, *Medieval Archaeol* 14, 155–65.

**Wilson D M 1971** *The Anglo-Saxons*, Harmondsworth.

**Woodward P J forthcoming** *The excavation of a late Iron Age trading settlement and Romano-British BB1 pottery production site at Ower, Dorset*, Dorset Natur Hist Archaeol Soc Monogr Series.

**Wrench F 1845** *A brief account of the parish of Stowting in the county of Kent, and of the antiquities lately discovered there*, London.

**Wright T 1846** On recent discoveries of Anglo-Saxon antiquities, *J Brit Archaeol Ass* 2, 50–9.

**Wright T 1849–53a** Fragments of Roman and Saxon pottery, recently found in the neighbourhood of Folkestone, *Proc Soc Antiq* ser. 1, 2, 174–6.

**Wright T 1849–53b** Three Saxon weapons, *Proc Soc Antiq* ser. 1, 2, 255.

**Wylie W M 1852** *Fairford graves*, Oxford.

**Ypey J 1968** Vroeg-middeleeuws glas, *Antiek* 2, 8, 376–86.

**Ypey J 1980** A sword with damascened blade from Dorestad, Hoogstraat I, in Van Es and Verwers 1980, 190–206.

**Ypey J 1983** Twee saxen uit frankische graven op het Volkhof te Nijmegen (ca. 620–680), *Rijksdienst voor het Oudheidkundig Bodemonderzoek* 30, 32–5.

**Zeitler R (ed) 1981** *Les Pays du Nord et Byzance*, Acta Universitatis Upsaliensis Figura new ser. 19, Stockholm.

**Zouhdi B 1978** Medaillons 'pendentifs' en verre du musée national de Damas, *Annales du 7ᵉ Congrès de l'Association Internationale pour l'Histoire du Verre Berlin-Leipzig 15–21 août 1977*, 51–65, Liège.

# Chapter V

# Grave Catalogue

The graves are irregular in shape, and the measurements given are the maximum length, width and depth. Because of the generally N–S slope of the hill and the more or less W–E orientation of most of the graves, the northern edge of the grave was usually deeper than the southern edge, and the deeper measurement is given.
M = male, F = female, Ju = juvenile.
Position of skeleton is normally supine with legs straight and arms fairly straight with hands on top of femur or in pelvis. Any divergent position is noted.

GRAVE B (Figure 1) F. 109°.
5ft 4in × 1ft 8 in × 1ft 7in (1.63m × 0.51m × 0.48m)
This grave had already been excavated. Mr Stebbing searched it later and found:
1. *Yellow glass disc bead.*
2. Baked *clay globule*, diam 1.5cm.

GRAVE C (Figure 1–3, 66) M. 131°
8ft 3in × 2ft 8in × 8in (2.51m × 0.81m × 0.2m)
This grave was excavated by Mr Stebbing. The skeleton was said to be decomposed. The grave was refilled and was later re-excavated by VE, when the foot of the grave was found to be undisturbed and it contained a spear ferrule (Figure 1, 2b) in the north-east corner. The plan (Figure 66) is reconstructed from the description, photographs and second excavation. The positions of the objects shown are approximate and the positions of items 6 and 7 are not known.
1. *Ring sword* (Plate 5a). Silver-gilt cocked hat pommel fastened by a pair of rivets in tall collars at each end which penetrated a wooden guard 1.1cm thick, sandwiched between two silver-gilt oval plates. The pommel (Figure 1, 1b) is worn, especially at the top, and gilding remains in the two lenticular depressions on the sides and in the beading along the lower edge of the front. Three nielloed ring-and-dot motifs (analysis p 45) on the front are joined by curving lines, and in the middle is a carelessly scratched chevron decoration. A dot at the top of the pommel is probably all that remains of a worn-off ring-and-dot stamp. The back is undecorated except for two scratched lines.

    The upper plate of the upper guard is thin, the lower thicker with upturned edge (Figure 1, 1b, d, e). The outer rivets have domed heads. The inner pairs are served by a joint washer and three of the inner rivet shafts have square sections, while the fourth is round. Organic material remains p 196.

    One of the outer rivets has a ring head (Figure 1, 1b, 1c) which completes about two-thirds of a circle and is cut to fit on the edge of the pommel between the two rivet collars. A complete ring is linked in this and fits tightly so that it can be moved sideways only and cannot be swivelled over away from the pommel. Its continual rubbing on the side of the pommel has worn a depression there. The two rings are inlaid on the circumference by a zig-zag niello line bounded by two lines of niello triangles. Each side surface has a V-shaped depression which is gilt, the top and the front respectively being beaded.

    An oval, silver-gilt beaded strip (Figure 1, 1f) encircled the grip adjoining one of the guards, and there was originally a second one for the other end of the grip. (A second ring was found but was not with the sword fragments by the time they reached London). The lower guard is similar to the upper, but wider (Figure 1, 1e).

    The blade is pattern-welded, probably in three zones, the lines of the pattern being longitudinal and diagonal. At the top each side of the scabbard was protected by a silver U-section binding 16cm long with four zones of moulding at each end and fastened in position by two rivets at each end. This shows signs of wear at the back. There are rows of binding cord at the top of the scabbard. There are traces of fur on the blade, and by the silver edging it is possible to see that leather covered the wooden scabbard so that the scabbard must have consisted of three layers i.e. leather-covered wood outside with fur lining (Figure 1, 1g). The scabbard is made of hardwood, probably field maple, *Acer campestre* or poplar or willow (p 196).
    Total length 91.4cm width of blade 5.1cm.
2a. *Spearhead*, angular blade split socket, L. 52.8cm
 b. *Spear ferrule*, conical, L 14.2cm.
3a. *Bronze balance.* The doubled looped support is moulded near the looped end and at the other fastened by a rivet to a projecting tongue in the middle of the arm; the arm is broken and 10.8cm long, but judging from the fact that the end of the longer half is widening for the terminal, it seems that the original width was *c* 14.4cm. There are two bronze dishes, diam 4.2cm, one bearing many scratches inside possibly made to equalise its weight with the other; each has three perforations, in some of which there still remains a bronze ringlet. One of these bore traces of the flax thread which suspended it from the arm.
 b. Fourteen *bronze Roman coins* used as weights.

(Description p 180). Some have notches cut in the edge (2, 4, 5, 12), and a smaller coin is riveted to no. 3.
4. *Knife*, tip broken, L 15cm.
5a. *Shield-boss*, fragment of button top and convex dome.
  b. Two *tinned bronze disc-headed iron studs* with leather adhering probably belong to this boss, diam 2cm.
  c. *Grip*, ends missing, incurved sides. L. 13.2 cm.
  d. Three pieces of flat *iron strip*, one with a spatulate end. May have been applied to the shield – said to have been found by the head, L 7.9cm, 4.6cm, 3.6cm.
6. *Iron buckle* loop and tongue, width 2.4cm. Traces of textile and leather strap. Frag. of wood with textile impressions (see p193) on one side.
7. Two spherical sandstone *pebbles*, diam 3cm, 1.8cm. One spherical chalk *pebble*, diam 1.5cm. These may be natural. (One only illustrated).
8. *Shield boss*, button top, conical convex dome, definite waist, wide flange with ?four disc-headed rivets. Diam 16.3cm, ht 10.7cm. This boss is also attributed to this grave, but probably belongs to another, such as D.

From notes and a photograph supplied by Mr Stebbing, it is evident that the skeleton was decomposed. The sword was lying along the left side of the body, the spear to the left of it, almost touching, and the knife was under the middle of the sword blade. The shield boss was near the head, and the scales and coins with 'some dark peaty stuff' were in a slight recess in the wall of the other side of the grave, nearer the foot.

GRAVE D (Figure 3) Ju, ?M. 130°.
4ft 3in × 1ft 10in × 10in (1.29m × 0.56m × 0.25m)
This grave had been sliced diagonally by the terracing excavations, and emptied. It probably contained the following objects as they were accompanied by a note from Mr Stebbing, dated 6 September 1951, stating that they came from a grave only partly excavated to the north of the grave with coins etc. (i.e. Grave C). The possible attribution of this buckle and rivet to Grave C in Evison (1967) 86 was based on my record of a conversation with Mr Stebbing. The note referred to above, however, predates this conversation by some weeks, and must therefore take precedence.
1. *Tinned bronze buckle*, oval loop, surface shelving and decorated by groups of three transverse grooves; tongue with quadrangular-shaped base with cavity for stone setting. Width 3.8cm.
2. *Tinned bronze shoe-shaped rivet*, L 3.3cm.

GRAVE E 123.5°.
7ft 8in × 3ft 4in × 1ft (2.34m × 1.02m × 0.31m)
The fill of this grave was undisturbed, but it contained nothing.

GRAVE F (Figure 4, 66) F, (see p 123). 107.5°.
9ft 6in × 2ft 10in × 9in (2.89m × 0.86m × 0.23m)
This grave had been dug into in the middle of the north side, but luckily this interference had not gone far enough to disturb any objects. There were a number of large flints round the edge of the grave, on the floor. There was no trace of the skeleton, except for one or two teeth amongst the beads.
1. *Silver disc brooch* (plate 6i). A worn 'light and shade' border surrounds a band of reserved silver and niello zig-zag. The centre of the brooch is covered by a gold plate secured by four rivets and with a beaded filigree border. A central cabochon shell holds a central sliced garnet with filigree collar. Four step-shaped garnets set alternately between four discs of shell in a zone covered untidily by beaded filigree in annulets and a few C or S shapes. The four shell discs cover the rivets. The foil backing to the garnets is impressed with a fine grid, and its silver colour gives a dark tone to the garnets (Avent 1977, No. 69, standard foil.) Pin-holder and catch at back and iron pin. Diam 4.2cm.
2. *Bronze pin*, flat disc head, zone of girth moulding in middle of shaft, L 4.3cm.
3. *Silver wire finger ring*, wire coiled into a flat disc bezel. Diam 2.2cm.
4. *Beads*:
   Amber a. 5 roughly-shaped.
   Glass b. 1 large annular dark blue streaky translucent.
   1 to 4 at neck position
5. *Iron fittings to wooden box*:
   *Lock*, the middle slotted part, 2.6cm wide, extends in two narrower rods which pass through two iron loops. A narrow iron band with right-angled point covers the slot. L 13.8cm. Part of a right-angled *iron handle*, one end hooked into a ring-headed rivet. At the foot.
6. Bunch of fragmentary *iron keys*. A ring at the top, round-sectioned shafts and hooked wards. Total length of group c 20cm. Illustrated in position found. At left hip.
7. *Iron key fragment*, L 3.4cm. In a dark patch of earth at right waist.
8. Part of *knife*, L 4.8cm. Left waist

GRAVE 1 (Figures 4, 5, 66) F over 45. 113°.
8ft × 2ft 6in × 2ft 3in (2.44m × 0.76m × 0.69m)
Skull turned right, left arm bent across body, right forearm missing, knees slightly flexed.
1. Reddish *gold bracteate* (Text Figure 10g, h, Plate 7f); loop fluted at the sides; *repoussé* symmetrical design of two serpentine forms in double bands; a beaded filigree border soldered on the front edge. The disc is battered and split near the loop, and bears a mending patch on the back. There is a right-angled frame behind the eye of each animal; in front are three dots adjoining long, looped jaws, the end of the lower jaw crossing the upper jaw; the body loops and passes under its own neck, returning through the jaws to loop once more and finish in a tail. Diam 2.1cm (Gold Analysis p 181).

2. *Silver gilt disc brooch* (Colour Plate IIb), 'light and shade' border of sets of eight beads alternating with three, and inner rim of reserved silver and niello zig-zag; central circular garnet in shell cabochon with filigree border; three keystone garnets with trellis pattern foil background (Avent 1977, No. 160, special boxed type, 16 squares) and three flat-topped shell discs are spaced alternately in the lower field of gilt, chip-carved animal heads. Pin-catch and spring holder on back with remains of iron pin. Diam 3.3cm.
3. *Bronze pin*, made of rolled bronze sheet; girth moulding at head. L 5.3cm.
4. *Beads*:
   Amber a. 2 disc (not illustrated)
   b. 4 roughly-shaped
   Glass c. 1 disc green-blue with rust red streaks (Colour Plate III B40 1/4c)
   d. 1 disc white
   e. 4 globular yellow
   f. 1 barrel orange (smooth surface) (Colour Plate III B10 1/4f)
   g. 1 biconical rust red
   h. 1 biconical yellow
   i. 4 short cylinder rust red
   j. 2 short cylinder yellow
   k. 27 small, short cylinder blue-green
   l. 12 small, short cylinder blue-green (double)
   m. 3 small, short cylinder blue-green (triple)
   n. 3 short cylinder blue
   o. 5 short cylinder blue-white
   p. 17 cylinder yellow
   q. 1 pentagonal cylinder blue
   r. 1 flat pendant light green
   s. 13 globular very light green translucent drawn
   t. 2 biconical light green, yellow zig-zag trail (Colour Plate III D10 1/4t)
   u. 2 cylinder rust red, white combed trails (Colour Plate III D16 1/4u)
   v. 2 disc rust red, white crossing trails
   w. 1 disc rust red, white crossing trails (double)
   x. 1 disc white, blue translucent crossing trails
   y. 2 disc white, crossing trails missing (not illustrated)
   z. 2 disc rust red, white crossing trails and circumference trail (Colour Plate IV D37 1/4z)
   $z^1$. 3 barrel rust red, yellow crossing trails and dots (Colour Plate IV D46 $1/4z^1$)
   $z^2$. 4 barrel rust red, white crossing trails and dots (Colour Plate IV D48 $1/4z^2$)
   1–4 at neck.
5. *Bronze wire bracelet*, two slip-knots on opposite sides, diam 7.6cm.
   On left forearm.
6. *Knife*, both sides curving to point. L 13.2cm.
   To left of pelvis.
7. Half an *iron-ring*, diam 2.8cm.
   Inside top left femur.
8. *Ivory ring*, diam c 14cm. Outside left femur.
9. *Bronze ring*, round in section but flattened on inner side, diam 3cm.
10a. Two *iron key fragments*, attached to an iron ring. L c 11cm.
10b. *Iron key shaft*, L 8.9cm.
10c. *Iron key*, with remains of two-pronged ward, L 13.5cm.
11. Flat piece of *iron* in diamond-shape with central perforation, L 4.3cm.
12. Fragmentary *iron ring*, diam 2.8cm and two small fragments.
   The bronze ring and iron diamond, 9 and 11, were lying close together, touching the outside of the ivory ring, 8. The keys, 10, 12 were inside and beside the ring, one passing under the femur.
   Black fragments near the waist are probably charcoal (p 196).

GRAVE 2    Ju. 93°.
5ft 4in × 2ft 3in × 1ft 1in (1.63m × 0.69m × 0.33m)
Only a tooth and minute bone fragments remained of the skeleton. No finds.

GRAVE 3 (Figures 6, 66) M, 30–45, (see p 123). 113°.
9ft × 4ft × 2ft (2.74m × 1.22m × 0.61m)
Disturbed grave. Bones and objects in disorder.
1. Fragments of *iron shield grip* with expanded end and upturned edge. L 5.5cm.
2. An *iron disc-headed stud* with bronze plating, diam 1.8cm.

GRAVE 4 (Figures 6, 66) M ?old, (see p 123). 129.5°.
8ft 2in × 2ft 9in × 1ft 6in (2.49m × 0.84m × 0.46m)
The grave partially disturbed and one tooth and bone fragment only were found. The sword tang remaining shows that the rest of a sword must have been removed, but the excavation did not reach the spearhead which was *in situ*. The buckle was overlooked and shovelled back in the fill.
1. *Spearhead*; flat, angular blade, split socket; L 28.7cm. Coarse textile on blade. Right of head position, apparently not disturbed.
2. Iron fragment of *sword tang*, with wood adhering; L 3.3cm. By right femur – disturbed position.
3. *Silvered bronze buckle* with shield-on-tongue, width 3.3cm. In fill.

GRAVE 5 (Figures 6, 66) M. 122°.
9ft × 3ft × 1ft 2in (2.74m × 0.91m × 0.36m)
Disturbed: all the objects displaced and lying near middle of grave. Some bones in the fill, but right arm bones *in situ*.
1. *Iron buckle loop* fragment, width c 2.5cm.
2. Two fragments of *shield grip*, narrow in the middle and widening at each end. Total L 11.2cm.
3. *Knife* fragments. L 4.7cm.

4. *Spearhead socket*, L 7.4cm. (Textile impression).

GRAVE 6 (Figures 7, 66) F, 20–30. 123.5°.
9ft 4in × 2ft 8in × 2ft 6in (2.84m × 0.81m × 0.76m)
Large flints in the top part of the fill. Skull turned slightly right and tilted as if pillowed; right arm bent with hand in pelvis, left arm straight. Charcoal fragments in pelvis identified as lime, *Tilia* sp.
1. *Glass bell-beaker* (Plate 9a); unevenly blown, constriction in body, domed base with circular indentation and well-defined carination; punty mark on base; rim everted and rolled over inwards; light greenish-amber, iridescent, very bubbly and blown thin. Ht 8.4cm, diam mouth 4.8cm.
2. *Cowrie shell*; sawn across so that toothed edges are missing, and parts of the dome are broken and missing. L 6.9cm.
3. *Spindle whorl*, turned calcareous material, flat base with one circular groove, conical top with three grooves; diam 2.5cm.
4. *Iron pin*, L 3.8cm.
  1–4 were grouped together below the feet, the spindle whorl lying under the cowrie shell.
5. *Iron keys* with hooked wards, three separate bunches, each on a ring. One key shaft is twisted. Illustrated in position. Found at left hip. Total length of bunch 30.5cm.
6. *Knife*, both edges curved. L 13.7cm. Inside left forearm.
7. *Iron shaft*, L 8.1cm, on ring – ?key. With knife.
8a. *Pendant fragments;* semi-circular piece of light amber glass, smaller disc of shell and remains of bronze backing and rim. Bronze backing has impressed pattern of pellets in grid. At neck.
8b. Reconstruction of 8a on the analogy of pendant 29/6.
9. *Iron pin*, globular head, L 4.3cm.
10. *Beads*:
    Shell  a. 1 corrugated edge
    Glass  b. 18 disc yellow
            c. 5 disc yellow (double)
            d. 1 disc light green translucent (Colour Plate III B26 6/10d)
            e. 1 disc white
            f. 7 cylinder rust red
            g. 1 globular very light green translucent drawn
            h. 2 globular colourless gilt drawn (Colour Plate III C10 6/10h)
    8–10 at neck.

GRAVE 7    104°.
9ft × 4ft (2.74m × 1.22m)
Disturbed and empty except for minute bone fragments and fragment of a clay pipe, the grave outline probably enlarged when rifled.

GRAVE 8 (Text Figure 4a, Figures 8, 66) M. 100.5°.
8ft 6in × 3ft 5in × 2ft (2.59m × 1.04m × 0.61m)
Fragments of skull and leg bones only. Large flints on floor of grave packed round the body or coffin. Inside these flints was fine white hard chalk, outside the flints and above the body was the usual loose mixed chalk and earth.
1. *Spearhead*, asymmetrical curved tip, one cutting edge only, split socket; L 31.3cm. Position about 13cm above floor level to left of skull; in line with it towards the foot of the grave was a streak of black wood fragments, the line continuing as an oval-shaped hollow in the chalk fill – representing the space left by the decayed shaft of the spear. The black wood fragments are identified as *acer* (maple), and the wood in the socket as ash (p 196).
2. *Knife*, angled back, L 15.5cm. Left waist.
3. *Iron buckle*, oval loop, circular plate with three bronze dome-headed rivets and filigree collars; L 4.8cm. Mid-waist. (Fragmentary, drawing made from X-ray).
4. Thin *iron binding* round oval-shaped wood shaft; at feet. Diam 2.8cm. Found near the middle of the foot of the grave (see p 27).

GRAVE 9 (Figures 8, 67) M, 20–30. 104°.
7ft × 2ft 8in × 2ft 2in (2.13m × 0.81m × 0.66m)
Partly cut away by excavating machine on south side, but contents undisturbed. Skeleton well preserved, skull pillowed, inclined left, left hand in pelvis.
1. *Spearhead*, split socket with transverse rivet, blade leaf-shaped, defective, half missing. L 18cm. Left of skull, 13cm above floor.
2. *Iron shafts*: a. one broken, with looped end, L 5.3cm. b. One with looped end and twisted shaft, L 8.6cm. Two end in a point, c. L 6.6cm and d. 3.4cm, e. one fragment with wood adhering to one side and textile traces on the other, L 8cm. Lying with loops downwards at left waist.
3. *Iron buckle* loop and tongue, width 2.8cm (lost). Mid waist.
4. *Knife*, both sides curve to point, L 13.6cm. At left hip.
5. *Bronze buckle* loop and tongue, width 1.3cm. By knife, probably for attaching knife sheath to belt.

GRAVE 10 (Figures 8, 67) M.    112°.
7ft 9in × 2ft 6in × 1ft 10in (2.36m × 0.76m × 0.56m)
Many large flints in the fill. Teeth and leg fragments only.
1. *Bronze pin*, flat disc head with moulded neck; L 3.9cm.
2. *Spearhead*, long, leaf-shaped blade, open socket, L 38.1cm. To right of skull, the pin under its blade. Textile impressions on socket.
3. *Knife*, angled back, groove along back; remains of wooden grip 1.6cm wide. L 14.9cm. Left waist.

GRAVE 11 (Figures 8, 67) F.    99.5°.
3ft 6in × 2ft 6in × 1ft 2in (1.07m × 0.76m × 0.36m)
The head of this grave had been completely cut away in the making of the road; only the legs remained.
1. Small spherical *pebble* on left knee, diam 1.3cm. The south side was cut through a circu-

lar pit, diam 2ft 9in (83cm) depth 2ft (61cm), containing *Romano-British pottery*. (p 15).

GRAVE 12 (Figures 8, 67) F.      109.5°.
8ft 3in × 2ft 9in × 1ft 2in (2.51m × 0.84m × 0.36m)
Large flints in fill. Skull right, right forearm bent at right-angles across body, left hand on left shoulder.
1. *Knife* fragment, L 11.2cm.
2. *Iron diamond* with perforated centre, L 4.3cm.
3. *Iron ring*, diam 3.6cm.
4. Kidney-shaped *iron loop*, L 6.4cm.
   1–4 together at left hip.
5. *Iron buckle* loop and tongue, width 2.9cm. In pelvis.
6. Rust red glass disc *bead*, white combed trails. Near head.

GRAVE 13 (Figures 9, 67) F, ?old. 114.5°.
7ft 9in × 2ft 6in × 1ft (2.36m × 0.76m × 0.31m)
A later trench cut across the grave at right angles, taking with it the lower leg bones, but leaving the upper part undisturbed. Remains of skull facing right, left humerus and femur, as well as the bones of the feet which were found earlier as an isolated feature and removed before the grave plan was drawn.
1. *Silver-gilt square-headed brooch* (Text Figure 6a, Plate 6b, Colour Plate Ia); the casting is thin, with perforations in the shallower parts so that the design on the head is almost completely *à jour*. The brooch is very worn, but gilding is preserved in the recesses. The rectangular head has an outer border of arcs in relief remaining on two sides, with a plain, raised inner border. In the middle at the top of the rectangular panel is an eye with profile angular head contour, each side of which is a bent arm with projecting cuff, three fingers and thumb extended. In each top corner is a pear-shaped thigh with bent leg and two-toed claw curled under, to extend in a double arc framing the thigh. A pellet above each thigh and one below the eye are space-fillers, but the pellet below the thigh must represent the eye of a human head, the double element in the corner a mouth, and the ribbing in the middle the animal bodies.

   The bow is very worn, but is carinated and divided into two vertical panels. On the left a leg and claw, two bars and an obliterated shape are visible at the top, and an eye with double-arc frame, possibly a second eye and another worn shape at the bottom. The right hand panel was divided into two halves, a leg and claw, two bars and worn patch at the top, and a worn patch, double arc and human foot with 'cuff' at the bottom.

   The foot is undivided, with ring-and-dot lateral lobes and animal head finial of which only the lenticular eyes remain. The downward-biting animal heads at the top have a right-angled eye frame, open jaws, the upper one curled back on itself, and a straight tongue. (The right-hand one is partly missing).

   The necks of these animals and the lower part of the foot are filled with chip-carved transverse bars. Round the lozenge centre are dismembered animal limbs, an eye at top and bottom, a thigh, leg and claw each side, a leg with curled claw above. The head of a downward crawling border animal each side of the foot has been worn away, leaving only a faint front haunch and claw, two transverse bars for the body, a ring-and-dot haunch and tail. At the back a bronze pin-catch was soldered to the back of the foot and a bent bronze band was soldered to the back of the head to hold the coils of the iron pin. Both are presumably mends. L 8.6cm.

2. *Silver-gilt square-headed brooch* (Text Figure 6b, Plate 6c, Colour Plate Ic), rectangular head, border worn, but there are indications of division into panels at the side and top, and the irregularity of the remaining traces suggests animal ornament. There is a row of tooled beading along the lower edge. The head is divided into five rectangular panels, each containing a schematic, but articulated, whole or part Style I animal. In the centre panel the head and front leg of an animal facing left are identifiable, with the body and leg above; in each side panel is the head, foreleg and probable hind leg of a creature crawling upwards: in the top panels are two complete *couchant* animals facing each other, each foreleg having a 'cuff', the one on the left with a number of small toes, the one on the right with two. The hollow bow swells slightly in the middle where there are traces of a circle, the design inside worn away. Ornamental grooves concentric with this figure on the lower parts of the bow.

   On top of the foot are pendent animal or bird's heads with grooved neck, curved helmet and curling beak. On the left-hand side which is more complete, the eye of the bird also doubles as the eye of a human profile with nose, mouth and beard, the lines on the neck of the bird also functioning as the man's hair or helmet. A lozenge surrounded by a zone of chip-carved transverse bars occupies the middle of the foot; a profile head faces downwards in each lateral lobe, and in the finial lobe there is another type of profile head. This finial lobe is gripped by the snout of an animal head, worn, but with the nostrils clearly recognisable. Each side of this is part of an openwork human-headed animal crawling upwards with a thick helmet, and forearm with cuff and two fingers. Framing lines to the head panels of the brooch, the foot lobes and central diamond are coloured black. On the back a bronze pin-catch was soldered as a mend to the back of the foot. Behind the head a pair of lugs were cast with the brooch to hold the iron spring of the pin. Textile impressions behind the head. L 9.4 cm.

3. *Beads*:
   Amber a. 3 roughly-shaped

Jet  b. 1 faceted (Colour Plate III A07 13/3b)
Glass  c. 1 globular colourless gilt drawn (double)
d. 6 globular colourless gilt drawn (triple)
e. 3 cylinder dark blue translucent drawn
f. 1 cylinder dark blue translucent drawn beaded
g. 1 cylinder dark blue translucent drawn twisted
h. 1 disc light blue, blue translucent crossing rails and rust red dots (Colour Plate IV D43 13/3h).

4. Fragment: *iron rivet*, hollow round shaft, embedded in wood, with curved bronze washer.
The two square-headed brooches were placed sideways on the breast, one above the other, the beads running from the head of one to the head of the other.

5. *Small-long silvered bronze brooch*, square head, oval foot with bi-lobed terminal: stamped ring-and-dot ornament on head and foot. Iron pin remains at back. L 5.3cm.

6. *Bronze ring brooch* with iron pin, diam 3.3cm.

7. *Knife*, L 13.5cm.
5–7 by the left humerus.

8. Bent fragment of *iron rod*, L 4.3cm, outside left femur.

9. Large *iron key*, T-shaped end projecting from plane of shaft, the other end looped over iron ring. L 28cm. At left pelvis position, the ringed end downwards.

## GRAVE 14 (Figures 10, 67) F, 20–30 (see p 123). 114°.
4ft × 1ft 9in × 5in (1.22m × 0.53m × 0.13m)
Damaged. The mechanical scraper had recently sliced off the top of this grave, reducing its depth to a maximum of 5in (13cm) and taking with it the top of the skull. In addition, the foot of the grave, below the knees of the skeleton, had been dug away when the trench passed through it at right angles. Skull pillowed on shallow step in floor and turned slightly right; right arm bent with hand in pelvis, left arm slightly bent with hand inside left femur.

1. *Silver-gilt disc brooch* (Text Figure 7, Colour Plate Ie): outer border of reserved silver zig-zag and niello and an inner beaded border. An inner zone of three wide keystone garnets with grid pattern foil backing (Avent 1977, No 12, standard pattern) interspersed with three chip-carved Style I animals consisting of head and one leg; a central flat disc setting of shell with incised ring-and-dot. The brooch is thin and all the ornament on one plane. Pin-holder and catch at back and remains of iron pin. Diam 2.9cm.

2. Bronze perforated *Roman coin*, very worn, diam 1.8cm. (p 181)

3. *Beads*:
Amber  a. 4 small roughly-shaped (not illustrated)
b. 23 roughly-shaped
White composition  c. 1 large short cylinder (magnesium carbonate) diam 2cm
Glass  d. 6 globular colourless drawn (Colour Plate III C05 14/3d)
e. 5 globular colourless drawn (double).

1, 2 and 3 were at the neck.

4, 5. Two *bronze strap-ends*, median rib, pointed tip slightly up-curved, split at the other end for attachment with one rivet to strap. L 3.7cm. Outside right pelvis and femur.

6. *Iron shaft* fragments, one with looped end, L 3.6cm, ?keys.

7. *Bronze wire* twisted into a loop, L 4.3cm.

8. Semi-spherical *?bone playing piece*, diam 2cm.

9. *Bronze stud* with applied silver disc, diam 1.9cm.
6–9 were probably in a bag inside top left femur.

10. *Iron diamond* with central perforation. L 3.4cm. Under left pelvis.

11. *Knife*, both sides curved, L 20.2cm. Outside left elbow.

12. *Bronze ring* with slip-knot, with a tab folded over it and fastened on itself by two rivets, extra perforation shows re-use. Total L 3.4cm. With knife – probably attached knife sheath to belt.

13. *Iron buckle* loop and tongue, width 2.7cm. At waist.

14. *Bronze fragments* of U-section binding, possibly of knife sheath, the largest L 2.2cm. Outside left hip.

## GRAVE 15 (Figures 10, 11, 67) F, 30–45 (see p 123). 106.5°.
7ft 5in × 3ft × 1ft (2.26m × 0.91m × 0.31m)
West end slightly damaged. Skull right, both forearms bent in.

1. *Knife*, both sides curving, groove along back, L 16cm. At left waist.

2. *Iron buckle* plated with silver, shield-on-tongue, width 3.7cm, two *shoe-shaped rivets*, L 1.8cm, one pointing away from loop, one towards it as illustrated. Mid waist.

3. Fragmentary *bronze wire bracelet*, slip-knot fastening diam c 6.4cm. On right forearm.

4. Curved fragment of thick, light blue-green *glass*, 2cm × 2.2cm, the inside of the curve showing wear – the outside of the vessel.

5. *Roman bronze coin* (p 181).

6. *Bronze band* fragment with perforation, L 2cm.

7. *Beads*:
Glass  a. 1 cylinder black coiled
b. 6 cylinder dark blue translucent drawn
c. 1 cylinder dark blue translucent drawn twisted.

4–7 probably all contained in a purse worn at left hip.

GRAVE 16 (Figures 11, 67) Ju.   120°.
5ft 6in × 1ft 9in × 8in (1.68m × 0.53m × 0.2m)
No skeleton.
1. *Knife*, tip missing, L 12.7cm. At waist position.

GRAVE 17 (Figures 11, 68) Ju.   123°.
4ft × 2ft × 1ft 2in (1.22m × 0.61m × 0.36m)
Flints along south side at top of grave. No skeleton.
1. *Knife* fragment, both edges curving, L 6.4cm. Mid grave.

GRAVE 18 (Figures 11, 68) F. 128°.
The head of this grave had been sliced away by the scraper, so that the skull was missing and the beads disturbed. Probable length 8ft × 2ft 6in × 1ft 1in (2.44m × 0.76m × 0.33m). It had been dug partly into the fill of Grave 22 below. The fill was mostly of earth with little chalk. The modern ditch crossed its foot, removing the legs below the knee. Some of the middle part of the skeleton remained, the left forearm was in the pelvis and the right arm was straight.
1. Oval *iron loop* and tongue, rectangular iron plate with three rows of three copper rivets each with a tinned bronze disc head. 4.5cm × 3.3cm. Mid waist.
2. *Beads*:
   Amber a. 1 disc
   Glass b. 5 barrel rust red
   c. 2 barrel orange
   d. 2 barrel green-blue
   e. 4 short cylinder rust red, yellow crossing trails (Colour Plate IV D32 18/2e)
   f. 1 short cylinder rust red, yellow crossing trails (double)
   g. 2 short cylinder rust red, white crossing trails (Colour Plate IV D34 18/2g)
   h. 2 short cylinder blue-white, green-blue translucent crossing trails (Colour Plate IV D35 18/2h).
3. *Bronze pin*, transverse scoring near head and middle of shaft, has probably lost head. L 3.3cm. With the beads at neck.
4. *Knife*, both edges curving, L 9.9cm. Left waist.
5. *Two iron rings*, diam 4.1cm and 2.8cm with five to seven pendant *keys* with hooked wards. Outside left hip.

GRAVE 19 (Figures 11, 68) Sex indeterminate. 123°.
Head half cut away – about 4ft remaining × 2ft 6in (1.22m × 0.76m). Leg bone fragments.
1. Two *bronze plates*, slightly curved, riveted together at each end 5mm apart, remains of wood sandwiched between, with grain transverse. L 3.6cm, width 9mm. To right of foot position.

GRAVE 20 (Figures 12–13, 69, Plate 3c) F, Ju, 0–6. 124°.
5ft 2in × 2ft 3in (1.57m × 0.69m)
Remains of skull only.
1. *Iron weaving batten*, L 37.6cm, width 4.6cm. No pattern-welding visible on radiograph. Left of skull.
2. *Disc brooch* (Plate 6m): six keystone garnets (no backing visible) set in bronze round a central elliptical cell – empty; the base plate and outer rim of iron 2mm thick decorated by inlaid transverse copper strips, with a narrow strip of copper round the edge of the back. Iron rust at back. Diam 1.8cm.
3. *Silver pin*, ring-shaped head with terminal knob. L 6.1cm.
4. *Gold bracteate* (Text Figure 10d, e, f, Plate 7e); Class D; *repoussé* design of animal in double bands, a hind and fore-leg interlacing with the body. Beaded border, fluted suspension loop. Diam 2.1cm. (Gold Analysis p 181).
5. *Beads*:
   Amber a. 15 small roughly-shaped (not illustrated)
   b. 6 roughly-shaped
   Glass c. 1 disc yellow
   d. 1 disc green
   e. 2 disc black (1 small, not illustrated)
   f. 1 annular colourless
   g. 1 cylinder green and other fragments
   h. 1 cylinder dark blue translucent
   i. 1 cylinder decomposed (not illustrated)
   j. 8 globular colourless gilt drawn
   k. 8 globular colourless gilt drawn (double)
   l. 4 globular colourless gilt drawn (triple)
   m. 1 globular colourless gilt drawn (quadruple)
   n. 4 cylinder dark blue translucent drawn.
   2–5 at neck.
6. *Silver-gilt square-headed brooch* (Plate 6d), foot broken off, one mending rivet remaining and two empty rivet holes. Inverted mask in middle of head with, on each side, a descending Style I animal consisting of head, body and hind leg with two toes. Outer border of reserved silver zig-zag and niello triangles. The middle of the bow is set with a disc of shell (calcite and aragonite) with a central silver ring also holding remains of shell. Transverse moulding at each end of the bow. On the foot are part of a central mask and two lateral discs each scored with a diagonal cross. From these discs spring the curving necks of a pair of birds' heads, each with a curved, divided beak. The borders of the lateral discs, the neck and back head line of the birds are all deep grooves which probably once contained niello. All edges are much worn. Remains of a double pin-holder, mended with an additional plate on one side, catch and iron pin remains at the back. L 4.8cm.

7. *Silver wire bracelet*; slip-knot fastening, diam 4.3cm.
Waist position, probably on left forearm.
8. *Silver-gilt square-headed brooch* (Text Figure 6d, Plate 6e, Colour Plate Ib): inverted mask in middle of head with, on each side, a descending Style I animal consisting of head, body and hind leg (one three-toed, the other two-toed). The bow is inset with a flat disc garnet with foil grid backing; from this radiate zig-zag lines and there is transverse moulding at the joins with head and foot. A mask occupies the centre of the foot and the lateral disc terminals are ornamented with a diagonal cross. From these discs spring the curving necks of a pair of birds' heads. All the borders were left ungilded, reserved silver zig-zag with niello triangles enclosing the head and foot. The two lateral disc borders are scored with zig-zag lines, and the terminal disc with Y-shapes presumably in imitation of plait. These two latter borders and the zig-zags on the bow show black in the recesses but they bear no traces of actual niello inlay like the triangles on the head and foot. Two projections behind the head held the iron spring and a short catch is behind the foot. L 6.1cm. These two brooches, 6 and 8, were placed one below the other (the broken one at the top) between the lower part of the chest and the waist, with the feet pointing left and slightly upwards – a cloak fastening?
9. *Bronze buckle* with shield-on-tongue, width 2.4cm, two disc-headed *rivets*, diam 1.2cm. Mid waist.
10. *Bronze wire bracelet*, slip-knot fastening, diam 4.6cm. Right waist, probably on right forearm.
11. *Knife*, L 14cm. Left waist.
12. *Iron ?key* fragments:
  a. Shank flattening towards ringed end. L 7.2cm.
  b. Rod curving at end and riveted in wood, L 5.4cm.
  c. Similar rod, round in section with curved rivet terminal.
13a. Fragments of *iron riveted loop*, L 3.4cm.
  b. *?Key shafts* and terminal with washer.
14. *Iron diamond*, L 2.9cm.
15. *Iron diamond* L 3cm.
12–15 were together at left hip.
16. *Brown glass claw-beaker* (Plate 8a), fragmentary. Tall, slender bell beaker with everted and thickened rim, the end pushed in with a pointed tool and folded to form a foot ring which enables the vessel to stand. A fine trail was dropped on below the rim and wound downwards seven times, but this has disappeared, leaving only the scar. Another trail was dropped on near the base and given ten turns upwards, and this trail remains. There are eight claws in two rows of four each spaced alternately, the top row beginning nearly half-way down the vessel and the tips of the lower claws stopping short of the foot. The marks of the tool are clear on each claw, and these are flat and close to the side of the vessel. The metal contains a few small bubbles, and is streaky and iridescent, and the vessel has been blown extremely thin with careless shaping of rim and foot. Ht 18.8cm, diam mouth 9.3–9.8cm, diam foot 2.9cm.
17. *Spun bronze bowl* (Plate 10b) with everted beaded rim and ring foot; the wall joins the base at an angle; incised concentric circles in five zones on inner surface of base. Ht 9.9cm, diam 34.3cm. Black wood under the bowl is probably oak (p 196). Over the feet, the claw-beaker (16) between the bowl and the keys.
18. *Large cylindrical bead*, white material (apatite), diam 1.9cm.
19. *Wooden belt* (Plate 10a), three lengths:
  a. Roughly pointed at one end, broken off at the other. A series of pairs of holes along the middle spaced at intervals of 1.3cm to 2.5cm, in one case there are three holes. This is followed by a length decorated by impressed line ornament divided into panels, at the end of each of which is a pair of perforations. 33.2cm × 1.6cm.
  b. Broken off at each end, undecorated but pairs of perforations at intervals. 20cm × 2.8cm.
  c. With one end squared off, *c* 4.8cm × 2.8cm. The spacing between the perforations on b corresponds to the spacing between the perforations on the decorated zone of a. The decorated front of the belt, a, was placed over the other end of the belt, b, and the two were laced together by means of a strong thread, some of which remains in the holes. The end of the thread would be attached to the large bead (Text Figure 16). This belt and the bead (18) were underneath the inverted bronze bowl, as well as fragments of textile and wood and flat fragments of bone with parallel grooves, probably antler. (Report on belt material p 196).

GRAVE 21 (Figures 14, 69) F, Ju, 6–12. 290°.
6ft × 3ft × 1ft 4in (1.83m × 0.91m × 0.41m)
This is the only grave in which the head was to the east and the feet to the west. Remains of skull, but this and the chest had been disturbed by the trench crossing transversely. The lower half of the body from mid spine, including forearms, remained.
1. *Bronze buckle* (Plate 5c) with tongue, width 2.5cm; gilt plate in shape of a major circle segment with projection at end to hold a rivet; two other rivets through plate with remains of washers on lower extremities. Semi-circular garnet in centre, no foil backing; decoration by ring-and-dot stamps. Lower spine.
2. *Knife*, both sides curving, L 12.9cm. Under body, left waist.
3. Remains of *iron chain*, a double row of links. Remains of leather on underside. Outside left knee.
4. *Spindle-whorl* (probably shale, p 112), disc-shaped with carination and moulded rim to perforation. Diam 3.3cm. To right of right tibia.

GRAVE 22 (Figures 14, 68) M. 105.5°.
8ft × 3ft × 2ft 3in (2.44m × 0.91m × 0.69m)
Grave 18 was partly dug into the top fill of this grave, apparently not disturbing its contents, except perhaps, the spearhead. Modern slicing by the scraping machine at the west end had removed most of the skull and broken and scattered the glass beaker. The fill was mostly of chalk, in contrast to the fill of grave 18 above, which was mostly of earth. Only the lower jaw remained, left forearm bent in, and the more solid leg bones.
1. *Glass cone beaker* (Plate 8b); very light green, thickened and everted cupped rim, flattened tip; zone of self-coloured horizontal trails at rim, eleven vertical loops below; in fragments. Streaky with a few bubbles. L 30.5cm, diam mouth 9.4cm. Right of skull.
2. *Knife*, straight back, tip missing, L 13.7cm. Top, mid chest.
3. *Sword*, traces of wooden scabbard and lower cross-guard. Pattern-welding, lines longitudinal and diagonal, probably in three zones. Probable traces of a circular impression in the middle of the blade which appears slightly denser on a radiograph, diam *c* 2cm at a distance of 6.5cm from tang, 87.6cm × 5.1cm. Lying on left side of body with hilt at the head.
4. Small oval *bronze ring*, maximum diam 1.5cm.
5. *Spearhead socket*, gripped by iron band inlaid with bronze strip, ribbing or iron wire binding below. L 8.6cm.
6. *Spear ferrule*, conical with flat bronze disc, probably covering join, L 9.4cm. The spear was laid along the left side of the body, and the bronze ring (4) which was about equidistant from head (5) and ferrule (6), may have marked the middle gripping position on the shaft.

GRAVE 23 (Figures 15, 69) F, 20–30. 118°.
7ft 8in × 2ft 10in × 1ft 6in (2.34m × 0.86m × 0.46m)
Modern trench cut across the foot. Remains of lower jaw and leg bones only.
1. *Silver disc brooch* (Plate 6l) with scalloped edges; circular cell in centre empty, surrounded by twelve keystone garnets set on foil backing with grid pattern; an outer filigree edge, very worn. Mended by application of silver spring-holder and bronze pin-catch at back; remains of iron pin. Diam 2.8cm. At neck.
2. *Knife* fragment, L 9.4cm.
3a. *Iron key* with suspension loop, L 8.4cm.
 b. *Iron key* with suspension loop, L 7.9cm.
 c. Part *iron ring*, diam 3.6cm.
4. *Beads*:
    Amber a. 1 small roughly-shaped
    Glass b. 2 disc yellow
           c. 1 disc green
           d. 1 disc yellow, traces of dot inlay.
    2–4 together at waist.

GRAVE 24 Ju. 105.5°
Very shallow with edges ill-defined. At west end, fragments of child's skull.

GRAVE 25 (Figure 69) F, 20–30. 124°.
5ft 7in × 1ft 8in × 1ft 4in (1.7m × 0.51m × 0.41m)
Skull propped up by edge of grave, hands folded at waist, left over right; both knees drawn up to the right. No finds.

GRAVE 26 Adolescent or F. 93.5°.
Discovered by blasting operations. Mostly destroyed; a few bones salvaged.

GRAVE 27 (Figures 15, 69) M over 45. 121°.
8ft × 3ft × 1ft 4in (2.44m × 0.91m × 0.41m).
Skull half right.
1. *Spearhead*, leaf-shaped blade, split socket, L 29.9cm.
2. *Spear ferrule*, conical, L 8.1cm. As the spearhead was outside the left shoulder and the butt outside the left hip pointing to the spearhead, the shaft must have been broken before deposition.
3. *Sword*, small iron pommel, traces of iron scabbard rim or lower guard on the blade. Inlaid circle of another metal on top part of blade to one side and 7cm below the guard. Pattern-welding in four zones of straight and diagonal lines seems to continue to the point so that the unusual shortness of this blade may have been caused by breakage and cutting down. A radiograph shows a slightly denser ring mark consisting of an outer ring diam 2.1cm and an inner ring 6cm diam in the middle of the blade 2cm below the guard which may indicate the position of a scabbard button. 65.6cm × 5.1cm. Text Figure 3b. Along left side of body, hilt at shoulder.
4. *Iron buckle*, flattened oval, tongue and remains of folded plate. Width 4.6cm. Mid waist.
5. *Knife*, L 15.2cm. Left waist.
6. Small *iron buckle*, loop and tongue, width 3.2cm. Between femurs.
7a. *Shield boss* fragments; top missing, conical with slight carination, diam 13.2cm. Four knob headed rivets in narrow flange;
 b. Fragmentary *strap grip*, L 14.2cm.
8. Two *iron discs* with knob in centre, width 4.3cm, one each side of the boss – shield appliqués. Shield placed over legs, boss on left tibia.

GRAVE 28 (Figures 16, 69, Text Figure 44) F, 20–30. 118°.
6ft × 2ft × 6in (1.83m × 0.61m × 0.15m)
Remains of skull, one humerus and leg bones.
1. *Bronze-bound wooden bucket* (Text Figure 19, Plate 10c). There are four bronze hoops, the three lowest equidistant and diminishing in width upwards, the lowest being 1.2cm wide, the next 1cm, the next 0.9cm. The top one, nearly 2.5cm wide and decorated with a row of *repoussé* dots on the lower edge, is bound by a U-shaped rim overlapped by six riveted tabs at intervals. From this band five triangles

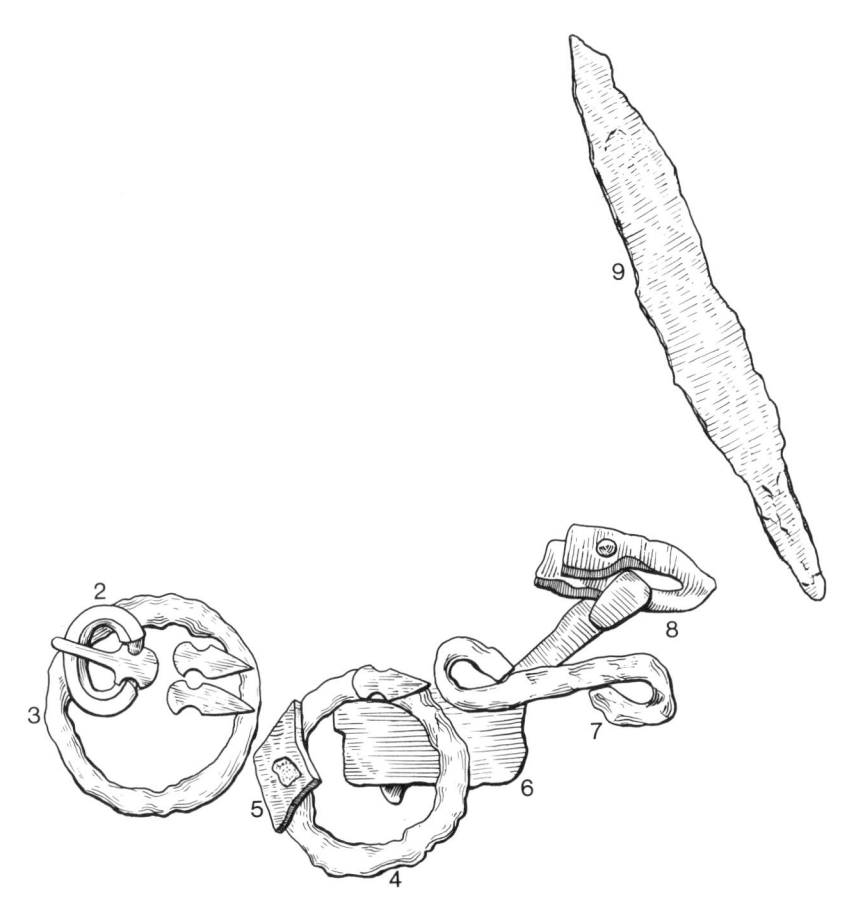

*Text Figure 44* Grave 28, objects at waist. Scale 1/2

decorated by *repoussé* dots are pendant each side, passing under the third hoop from the bottom and being riveted to the wood between the second and third hoops. At opposite sides the three lower hoops are riveted to a vertical bronze upright. Above this a separate bronze upright bifurcates into a pair of curling ends. The top of this upright is riveted to a strengthening band folded over the rim and projects above the rim of the bucket and presumably a handle was riveted to it. The opposite member is missing. Some of the wooden staves are preserved but the wood is not identifiable. Ht *c* 10cm, diam *c* 10.2cm. Touching left side of skull.

2. *Bronze buckle* with shield-on-tongue, width 2.6cm; three *shoe-shaped rivets*, L 2.1cm, two placed together near the buckle and the third 5cm away, all pointing away from the loop.
3. *Iron ring*, square section, diam 5.8cm. Remains of leather suspension thong.
4. *Iron ring*, diam 5.1cm.
5. *Iron diamond* with centre perforation, L 3.7cm.
6a. *Iron diamond* L 4cm, with iron ring, diam 2.7cm, rusted to one face, and b. fragment of an *iron square* (?diamond) with centre perforation, L 2.5cm.
7. *Iron S-shaped rod*, L 6.6cm.
8. *Iron key*, L 9.4cm, the looped top passes through a doubled iron loop with flattened terminals suitable for attaching to a belt or strap.
9. *Knife*, angled back, L 16.1cm.
2–9 were all lying together at the waist, with the buckle and rivets lying on top.

GRAVE 29 (Figures 17, 69, Plate 3b) F, 20–30 (see p 124). 115.5°.
8ft 3in × 3ft 4in × 1ft 6in (2.51m × 1.02m × 0.46m)
Skull slightly right, remains of right arm only and both legs.

1. *Silver disc brooch* (Colour Plate IId), central shell boss surmounted by flat garnet, each with filigree collar; four step-shaped garnets with four tri-lobed flat shell inlays in between, in a field of double loops in gilt chip-carving; round this a keyed pattern of niello on silver with four oblong garnets at quarter points; 'light and shade' outer border. All the garnets have the same foil backing (trellis with squares 4 × 4) except the centre one which is squared but not trellised. (Also noted by Avent 1977, No. 158, 'standard' and 'special boxed' foil.) Pin-holder and catch at back and remains of iron pin. Diam 4.8cm.
2. *Beads*:
Amber a. 1 small roughly-shaped (not illustrated)
Glass b. 2 roughly shaped
c. 1 disc rust red
d. 58 disc yellow
e. 11 disc yellow (double)

f. 2 small disc blue
g. 1 short cylinder rust red (double)
h. 4 short cylinder yellow
i. 2 short cylinder green (double)
j. 3 small short cylinder blue-green
k. 1 short cylinder blue
l. 1 short cylinder white
m. 2 globular very light green translucent drawn
n. 2 globular colourless drawn
o. 1 cylinder colourless drawn beaded
p. 1 short cylinder rust red, random yellow trailing
q. 1 disc light blue, blue translucent crossing trails and rust red dots.
r. 1 barrel rust red, white crossing trails and dots.

3. *Silver-ring*, diam 1.6cm.
4. *Expanding silver wire ring* fragment, L 1.5cm.
5a–c. Fragments of three mushroom-shaped *silver pendants* with fluted suspension loops, the largest, a, (Plate 7i) bearing a scratched semi-circular design, width 1.8cm.
6. *Oval silver pendant* (Plate 7j) with fluted suspension loop and filigree border. The oval is divided into two unequal sections by a horizontal bar. The lower half is set with a garnet on trellis-impressed gold foil (Avent 1977, No. 161, 'special boxed, 16 squares) and in the middle of this was set a disc of material, now brown (?bone), probably originally with a silver rim. The top half contains remains of pale blue glass. L 2.3cm.
7. *Gilt bronze pendant* (Plate 7b) coin imitation with fluted silver loop, diam 1.5cm (see p 181).
8. *Gold disc pendant* (Text Figure 10k, Plate 7g), fluted loop. A beaded filigree wire is soldered to the front edge, and reflected by an inner border of *repoussé* beading. A *repoussé* design of three identical animals placed with their backs touching in the centre. Each has a ring-and-dot eye and curving beak with a similar ring-and-dot rump. The body is ornamented by transverse lines alternately plain and beaded; the two limbs spring from pear-shaped joints, and sweep to a feathery six-toed foot in a fine curve broken only by a transverse band. Diam 3.7cm. All these ornaments, 1–8, were on the right upper part of the chest. Positions indicate that the two small rings held the ends of the necklace, the pendants were interspersed amongst the beads, the gold pendant forming the middle piece at the lowest point. (Gold analysis p 181).
9. *Iron fragments*; lock with slot in middle and key fragment inserted. Textile impressions on both sides. L 9.4cm. At left hip.
10. *Knife* fragments, L 14cm.
11. *Iron keys* including three with wards, one of which is attached to a shaft 8.4cm long; suspension ring, diam 2.8cm.
10 and 11 outside left femur.
12a. *Silver rim*, U-section, with three fluted silver bands folded over it at regular intervals and fastened together through the vessel by means of two rivets. Each lower rivet also held a decorative silver plate in the shape of a pair of birds' heads, the eyes and beak being indicated by stamped dots. Diam 5.1cm.
b. *Silver rim* (part) as above, with one birds' head mount, slightly smaller. Diam 4.8cm. Both 12a and 12b placed by the feet.

GRAVE 30 (Figure 18, 69) F, 30–45 (see p 124). 120°.
8ft 3in × 3ft 6in × 2ft (2.51m × 1.07m × 0.61m)
Skull turned left.
1. Single-sided composite *bone comb*; segments of tooth plate, slightly graduated at each end, are sandwiched between two pairs of semi-circular sectioned bone ribs or connecting plates, each fastened through with four iron rivets. A gap between the connecting plates reveals a bronze strip 1cm wide each side. Transverse lines decorate the bone ribs on one face. L 9.6cm. Under top of skull.
2. *Silver-gilt disc brooch* (Plate 6g), the central cell is empty with scratch marks. In the field three keystone cells, two still holding cracked garnets, apparently without foil backing, with schematic Style I animal in chip-carving between each on a slightly lower plane; zig-zag reserved silver and niello border. On the back is an ornamental border of two rows of stamped triangles, no niello visible. Stump of pin-catch remaining, with rectangular patch of a solder which had fixed a replacement catch. Iron spring. Diam 2.8cm.
3. *Silver pin*, flat head in shape of bird's head with curving beak, one side ornamented with stamped ring-and-dot for eye and pattern of dots and arcs, the other side with arc stamps only. L 8.4cm.
4. *Beads*:
Amber a. 14 roughly-shaped
Glass b. 12 disc rust red
c. 12 disc yellow
d. 7 disc blue (Colour Plate III B45 30/4d)
e. 8 disc dark blue translucent (Colour Plate III B48 30/4e)
f. 6 disc blue-white
g. 1 disc black (Colour Plate III B61 30/4g)
h. 1 biconical dark green
i. 1 cylinder green
j. 1 cylinder dark blue translucent
k. 1 disc rust red, yellow zig-zag trail (Colour Plate III D06 30/4k)
l. 2 disc rust red, white crossing trails (double)
m. 1 disc yellow, rust red crossing trails (Colour Plate IV D21 30/4m)
n. 1 barrel rust red, yellow crossing trails (Colour Plate IV D30 30/4n)
o. 1 barrel rust red, yellow crossing

o. 1 barrel rust red, yellow crossing trails and circumference trail
p. 3 disc rust red, yellow crossing trails and dots (Colour Plate IV D40 30/4p)
q. 4 disc rust red, yellow crossing trails and dots (double)
r. 2 barrel rust red, white crossing trails and dots unmarvered (1 with trails and dots marvered, not illustrated)
s. 3 folded mosaic, biconical purple translucent with rust red and white band round middle (one of these is folded longitudinally, not illustrated) (Colour Plate IV D57 30/4s)
t. 1 folded mosaic, biconical dark green translucent with rust red and white band round middle (Colour Plate IV D58 30/4t).

5. *Silver pendant*, elongated oval shape with end bent over to form loop. Decoration by row of dots longitudinally, three of which have pierced the metal, and three dots transversely. L 2.4cm.
2–5 were at the neck.
6. *Rectangular buckle* of white metal, ?pewter, with bevelled surface and zig-zag line decoration; iron tongue. Width 3.3cm. At waist.
7. *Knife*, both sides curved, L 14.7cm.
8. *Iron keys*; remains of at least three, suspension loops at top, one hooked ward, two with twisted shafts.
7 and 8 under left hip.

## GRAVE 31
Only the rough position of this grave is known for it was obliterated by excavating machines.

## GRAVE 32 (Figures 19, 69) F, 30–45 (see p 124). 121.5°.
8ft 1in × 3ft × 2ft 4in (2.46m × 0.91m × 0.71m)
Skull turned right
1. *Silver-gilt disc brooch* (Plate 6f), central boss of shell with garnet centre. In the surrounding field three garnets of elongated wedge shape (trellis foil backing) with three intervening flat discs of white material, possibly shell; simple loop motif chip-carved in between, surrounded by narrow reserved silver zig-zag with niello and a 'light and shade' border. Bronze pin-catch and iron pin at the back. Diam 2.9cm.
2. *Iron pin*, curled-over head, L 5.3cm.
3. *Bronze ear-scoop*, perforated swelling towards head, through which passes a slip-knot ring; transverse mouldings on head. L 8.1cm.
4. *Beads*:
    Glass
    a. 49 disc yellow
    b. 9 disc yellow (double)
    c. 14 globular yellow
    d. 1 short cylinder yellow
    e. 46 small, short cylinder blue-green (Colour Plate III B34 32/4e)
    f. 10 small, short cylinder blue-green (double)
    g. 1 small, short cylinder blue-green (triple)
    h. 1 short cylinder blue
    i. 24 globular very light green translucent drawn
    j. 27 globular colourless gilt drawn
    k. 1 disc white, blue translucent crossing trails (Colour Plate IV D17 32/4k)
    l. 1 disc white, blue translucent crossing trails (Colour Plate IV D25 32/4l)
    m. 4 disc white, blue translucent crossing trails
    n. 3 short cylinder rust red, yellow crossing trails
    o. 2 short cylinder white, blue translucent crossing trails
    p. Fragments of silver disc pendant with lines of punched dots.
1 and 2 were at the neck, 3 mid-chest and the beads, (4), were on the chest from neck to mid-chest.
5. *Knife*, curving back, L 13.7cm. Inside top left femur.
6a. Fragments of *three iron keys* with hooked wards; L 7.8cm. On top of knife.
6b. *Key fragments* and part of *iron ring*; diam 3.6cm. Below knife.
7. *Silver rim*, U-section, gripped by five fluted silver bands, each fastened with two rivets to a wooden vessel. Diam 5.8cm. Organic material below the rim is probably a broad-leafed wood (Professor K Wilson).
8a. *Iron box handle*, linked in looped rivets with shank passing through lid 1.3cm thick. L 9.4cm.
b. *Iron lock fragments*; flat iron band, tapering off and bent into a rivet at one end L 8.2cm, 2cm.
7 and 8 were by the left foot.

## GRAVE 33 (Figures 20, 70) M, over 45 (see p 124). 114.5°.
7ft 9in × 3ft 4in × 1ft 2in (2.36m × 1.02m × 0.36m)
Skull tipped forward, arms slightly bent with hands on top of femurs.
1. *Spearhead*, straight-edged, angular join to split socket; transverse rivet. L 47cm. Left of skull.
2. *Sword*, tang, 11.3cm long, narrowing at the end where the upper guard, 1.5cm wide, was fixed. Traces of lower guard. A boat-shaped iron pommel, 5.3cm wide, with a rectangular hole for the tang. Pattern-welding, three zones of zig-zag revealed by X-ray. Traces of fur on the blade. Total length 89.4cm, width 5.5cm. Along left side of body, reaching from humerus to knee.
3. *Knife*, angled back. A strip of streaky iron, possibly pattern-welding, is revealed by X-ray along the back. L 17 cm.
4. *Iron pin*, disc head with moulding below, L 6cm.
3 and 4 at left hip.

5. *Iron buckle*, tongue and oval loop; rectangular plate doubled over and fixed by the remains of three bronze rivets in a row. An X-ray shows a wider dense area at each rivet, indicating that there were originally disc or dome-heads in a denser metal than iron. L 4.6cm. As this was under the sacrum it must have been worn at the back.

GRAVE 34 (Figures 20, 70) Ju, 0–6. 104.5°.
5ft 5in × 2ft × 1ft 6in (1.65m × 0.61m × 0.46m)
Fragments of skull, arm and legs only.
1. *Knife*, point broken, L 10.2cm. At waist.
2. *Iron buckle* loop and tongue, width 2.3cm. Remains of doubled-over plate. Right waist.
3. *Bronze strap-end*, oval-shaped terminal, median ridge, two rivets in line longitudinally. L 2.7cm. Near right arm. Black wood fragments at foot of grave, identified tentatively as family *Rosaceae* which includes the subfamilies *Prunoideae* (*Prunus* sp, wild cherry, blackthorn, bird cherry) and *Pomoideae* (*Sorbus* sp, mountain ash, whitebeam, *Crataegus* sp, hawthorn, *Pyrus* sp, pear, *Malus* sp, apple) (p 196).

GRAVE 35 (Figures 21, 70) F, 12–18. 123.5°
8ft 6in × 3ft 9in × 1ft 10in (2.59m × 1.14m × 0.56m)
Skull tipped forward and slightly right, both arms bent, right hand on femur, left hand in pelvis.
1. *Silver-gilt disc brooch* (Colour Plate IIc), reserved silver and niello zig-zag border inside gilt 'light and shade' rim on which long stretches of beading alternate with short stretches; three keystone garnets backed by foil with an impressed trellis pattern containing ring-and-dot in each square (Avent 1977, No. 167); in between these three small bosses of shell each flanked by addorsed Style I animal heads in chip-carving; a large central boss of shell within a beaded border and surmounted by a small disc of blue glass also in a beaded border. The pin, spring and catch on the back are preserved. Diam 3.3cm.
2. *Iron pin* fragments, coiled head. L 3cm.
3. *Silver-gilt disc pendant* (Colour Plate Id), central hollow boss from which spring four triangular arms of a cross; these are gilded, the top one is stamped with a cable ornament and a few rings; one side arm bears the beginnings of a different cable ornament and there is a scratched cross in the lowest segment. The spaces between are ungilded and heavily ring-stamped – in this way the smooth shining gilt surface of the cross stands out well against the stamped silver background. The tubular loop is fluted. Diam 2.4cm.
4. *Silver wire ring* with slip-knot, diam 1.5cm.
5. *Beads*:
   Amber a. 1 small roughly-shaped (not illustrated)
   b. 1 roughly-shaped
   Glass c. 4 disc yellow
   d. 1 disc yellow (double)
   e. 1 disc white
   f. 1 small short cylinder blue-green
   g. 1 short cylinder blue-white
   h. 2 short cylinder white
   i. 22 globular very light green translucent drawn
   j. 30 globular colourless gilt drawn
   k. 1 barrel dark green, yellow crossing trails and dots (Colour Plate IV D50 35/5k).
   1–5 at neck
6. *Knife*, tip missing, L 11.4cm.
7. *Iron keys*; a. one T-shaped, L 13cm, looped on to iron ring; b. others with thinner shafts and hooked wards, c. A bronze looped tab riveted through two pieces of leather and holding an iron ring. L 1.7cm.
6 and 7 outside left femur.
8. *Iron box fittings*:
   a. *Iron hinge* consisting of two looped tabs, L 5.3cm and 5.8cm interlocked each with two rivets; transverse wood grain on underside, with rivet showing wood to be 1.3cm thick.
   b. Remains *iron lock*, L 13.6cm. Oblong centre with slot, one end squared the other narrowing to a rod and both fastened by staples; two triangular clamps.
   c. *Iron latch* with spiral grip linked to a looped staple, L 7.1cm.
   These iron fittings were by the left foot. Considerable traces of material identified as possibly antler stretched along the side of the lower leg, but although these were near 8a there were no such traces near 8b and 8c. It is not likely therefore that these were traces of the body of this box, but of another one nearby in antler without metal fittings.

GRAVE 36 (Figures 20, 70) M, over 45. 94.5°
6ft × 2ft × 1ft 2in (1.84m × 0.61m × 0.36m)
Skull half right, left hand on right pelvis.
1. *Oval iron buckle loop*, tongue and double iron plate fixed with rivet. Textile impression on back. L 3.8cm. At right waist.

GRAVE 37 (Figures 20, 70) F, 20–30. 94°.
7ft 4in × 1ft 10in × 3in (2.24m × 0.56m × 0.08m)
Remains only of skull and legs; partly disturbed by passage of mechanical scraper.
1. Fragments of hollow *iron shafts of ?keys* with looped ends. At left waist.

GRAVE 38 (Figures 22–3, 70 Text Figure 45) F, 20–30. 116°.
7ft 7in × 3ft (2.31m × 0.91m)
Skull turned right, remains of arms and legs only.
1. *Silver gilt-disc brooch* (Colour Plate IIa); flat centre setting of white material (shell) with a scored ring which possibly contained a metal ring inset; round this are three triangular garnets, with grid pattern foil backing (Avent 1977, No.25, standard pattern), each separated by a chip-carving design of Style I animal on a lower plane, head and one leg only; outer border of reserved zig-zag silver and niello;

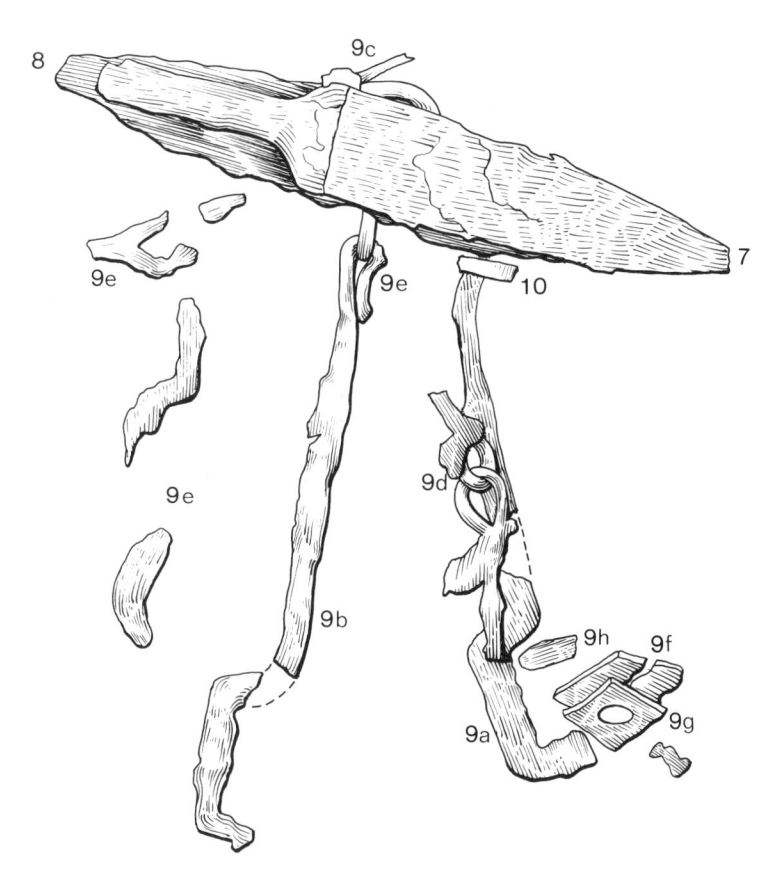

*Text Figure 45*     Grave 38, iron objects between femurs. Scale 1/2

remains of pin-holder and catch on back. Diam 2.8cm.
2. *Bronze pin*; at the head a bronze saucer with scalloped edge is joined to the shaft, and no doubt once contained a jewel or bead. L 7.9cm.
3. Fragments of a *silver disc*, ?pendant, with raised central boss decorated with radial rows of stamped triangles. Diam 1.5cm.
4. *Beads:*
   Amber a. 70 roughly-shaped
   Glass  b. 1 disc rust red
   c. 2 large disc dark blue translucent (Colour Plate III B48 38/4c)
   d. 1 flat hexagonal blue-green (Colour Plate III B37 38/4d)
   e. 1 cylinder dark blue translucent drawn
   f. 1 disc yellow, rust red crossing trails
   g. 1 large globular millefiori, dark blue translucent with rust red dots in white rings (Colour Plate IV D62 38/4g).

1–3 were at the neck, with the beads, (4), on the chest from neck to waist.
5. *Bronze buckle* (Plate 5d), oval loop with iron tongue. The plate is raised and semi-cylindrical in section, divided by a diagonal cross into four triangular fields, each containing a different chip-carving design in Style I. At the end away from the loop three rivets fasten the front plate to the back. The other end is also fastened to the back plate, and one side of this back plate has been mended by the addition of a further riveted plate. The zoomorphic features are formalised and hardly recognisable. In the side panels one profile head and two legs, one profile head in a top panel and other limbs. L 8.4cm. Mid waist.
6. *Red gold finger ring,* a plain band, width 4mm at one end, diminishing to 2mm at the other. These two ends are slightly overlapped, but not fastened. Diam 2cm. Mid pelvis position – ?on left hand.
7. *Knife*, broad blade, both sides curving, L 18.3cm.
8. *Knife*, broad blade, both sides curving, spikes at end of tang, L 17cm. Organic material on tang probably horn (p 196)
9a. *Iron key* fragments, hooked end, L 14cm; near left femur.
  b. *Iron key* fragments, hooked end, L c16.5cm. Near right femur.
  c. *Bronze ring* at junction of keys, oval and worn, diam 3cm.
  d. Two interlinked *iron loops*, total L 3cm.
  e. Fragments of thin *iron shafts* ?keys.
  f. *Iron diamond* with central depression, L 3.3cm.
  g. Fragments of a second *iron diamond*.
  h. Small *iron fragment*.
10. Fragments of *ivory ring*, no illustration, under knives.

7–10 were together between the femurs.

11. *Iron weaving batten*, no pattern-welding visible on radiograph, L 41.1cm, width 4.2cm. Outside right leg, pointing towards head.
12. *Glass cone beaker* (Plate 8c), restored, nearly complete. Rim everted and thickened, tip flattened, with punty mark. Spiral moulding. Light green bubbly glass. A white unmarvered tail was dropped on below the rim turned once downwards, then crossed itself and turned five times towards the rim. Ht 16.8cm, mouth diam 7.3cm. Outside right foot.
13. Small *bronze tab*, with one side extended in a ring which has been pendant and is worn; decorated by dot and dash stamps. L 1.5cm. At back of skull, presumably hair ornament.

GRAVE 39 (Figure 23, 70) M. 133°.
9ft 7in × 2ft 10in × 1ft 6in (2.92m × 0.86m × 0.46m)
Skull turned right.
1. *Spearhead*, leaf-shaped blade, angular join to solid shaft and split socket, L 36.4cm. Left of skull.
2. a. *Shield boss*; sloping flange, slight carination, convex conical dome, small knobhead rivets, diam 13.1cm. b. *strap grip*, one original end squared with two rivets. On underside longitudinal wood impressions in middle, leather at each end. On upper surface marks of irregular binding with coarse twine, L 13.2cm. c. Three *iron convex disc-headed rivets*, knob top, diam 4cm, to pierce first leather then wood 1.2cm thick. The boss was lying on its side above the skull together with one of the rivets. The other two rivets were on either side at a distance of 43.2cm from each other and 15cm above the floor of the grave.
3. *Knife* angled back, L 15.5cm. At left hip.
4. *Iron buckle*, tongue, oval loop, doubled rectangular plate – broken, radiograph shows 3 rivets in a row, L 3.6cm. At left hip.

GRAVE 40 (Figures 23, 70) Ju.   111°.
6ft 4in × 2ft 3in × 11in (1.93m × 0.69m × 0.28m)
Roughly cut. Remains of skull, right humerus and femur only.
1. *Knife* fragment, L 6.9cm, at left waist.

GRAVE 41 (Figures 24, 71) M.   118.5°.
9ft 7in × 2ft 10in × 1ft 2in (2.92m × 0.86m × 0.36m)
Fragments of skull and legs only.
1. *Spearhead*, leaf-shaped, solid shank, split socket, L 22.9cm.
2. Conical *ferrule*, L 5.3cm. Wood in socket identified as probably ash. Spearhead to right of skull and ferrule at foot of grave, 2.03m away from spearhead.
3. *Sword*, tang 11.4cm, no pommel. Traces of longitudinal wood grain of scabbard and transverse grain of lower guard. Traces of fur on scabbard. Pattern-welding, probably three zones, alternately diagonal and straight. 87.7cm × 5.1cm. Along left side of body with hilt near skull.
4. *Knife*, straight back. Fragments of leather sheath with impressed or openwork punched decoration, lined with coarse textile. L 16.5cm.
5. *Bronze tweezers*, decorated by notches at top, scored transverse and border lines and two ring-and-dot stamps. End looped on bronze ring with remains of leather strap. L 7.1cm.
4 and 5 at mid waist.
6. *Iron coffin fittings*; seven iron bands each pierced by two disc-headed nails with circular shafts, maximum length of shaft 3.8cm. All show transverse grain of wood on underside between the rivet shafts. b only illustrated.
   a. 8.6 × 2.5cm.
   b. 8.5 × 2.1cm, the longest rivet 3.8cm covered with transverse wood grain.
   c. 8.6 × 2.1cm, widening to 2.4cm at ends.
   d. 8.7 × 2.2cm, 2.6cm at ends.
   e. 9 × 2.3cm, 2.7cm at ends.
   f. 8.5 × 2.5cm.
   g. 9.4 × 2.3cm.
   The position of a at the head of the grave is not precise as it was moved slightly in clearing the topsoil. All were 35.5cm above the floor of the grave on a level with the present chalk surface and within a few inches of the side of the grave. b and c were opposite each other near the head position, d and e by the top of the femurs, and f and g below the foot position.
7. *Purse mount* fragment looped at each end with middle strap-like projection. Bird's head decoration revealed by X-ray. L 13.2cm. The presence and position of this object was not noted in the grave, and it must have been found in the laboratory in the unexcavated earth surrounding the sword or knife.

GRAVE 42 (Figures 24–5, 71) F over 45.   126°.
7ft 6in × 2ft 9in × 1ft 4in (2.29m × 0.84m × 0.41m)
Remains of skull to right, no teeth remaining in the jaw, arms bent slightly in.
1. *Beads*:
   Amber a. 17 roughly-drawn
   Glass  b. 7 disc yellow
          c. 1 annular yellow with square perforation (double)
          d. 1 short cylinder white
          e. 1 barrel rust red, striped with yellow trails
          f. 1 cylinder rust red, striped with decomposed yellow trails
          g. 3 cylinder rust red, striped with white trails (Colour Plate III D05 42/1g)
          h. 5 cylinder rust red, longitudinal white zig-zag trail (Colour Plate III D11 42/1h).
          i. 2 cylinder rust red, yellow combed trails
          j. 1 disc rust red, white crossing trails (Colour Plate IV D19 42/1j)
          k. 2 disc light blue, blue translucent crossing trails (Colour Plate IV D23 42/1k)

l. 1 annular blue-white, crossing trails missing
  m. 2 barrel blue-white, crossing trails missing
  n. 1 disc rust red, yellow crossing trails and dots
  o. 3 barrel rust red, yellow crossing trails and dots
  p. 3 barrel rust red, white crossing trails and dots
  q. 1 barrel blue-white crossing trails and dots missing
  r. 1 barrel white, rust red crossing trails and dots (Colour Plate IV D52 42/1r)
  s. 1 short cylinder rust red, yellow crossing trails and dots (Colour Plate IV D54 42/1s)
  t. 1 large short cylinder reticella, three zones, the outer blue-white and rust red thickly twisted, the middle rust red and yellow reticella (Colour Plate IV D66 42/1t).
2. *Bronze pin*, flat, spatulate head with perforation in centre L 7.6cm. With beads at neck.
3. *Bronze buckle loop* with shield-on-tongue, width 2.5cm. At left waist.
4. *Knife*, angled back with groove, L 14.7cm. Outside left hip.

GRAVE 43 (Figures 25, 71) F, Ju, 6–12. 108.5°.
6ft 6in × 2ft 3in × 1ft 6in (1.98m × 0.69m × 0.46m)
Remains of skull, right side near grave wall, left humerus and leg bones pointing towards opposite corner, i.e. the body was placed diagonally in the grave.
1. *Iron pin* fragment, L 2.5cm. Right chest.
2. *Knife*, L 13.2cm.
3. *Iron keys*, shafts of at least three and a linked shaft in three sections. With knife at left waist.
4. *Squat pottery bottle*, wheel-thrown with girth grooves, wide, concave base, slight carination, short, hollow neck, everted rim rounded on top; rouletting on upper half of rhomboid shapes zig-zag fashion giving the impression of a schematic fern-leaf design. Reddish buff core with black, partially burnished surface. Ht 18.5cm, maximum diam 15cm, diam mouth 5.7cm, diam base 8.5cm. At foot of grave.
5. *Iron fittings to wooden box*; (reconstruction Text Figure 18a)
  a. Rectangular *handle* swivelled in ring-headed rivets, one of which remains and shows the lid to have been c 1.2cm thick. Remains of wood adheres to one side of the handle.
  b. To right of handle, *iron plate corner fitting*, a *loop-and-hook fastening*, a *looped staple* and a *rivet*.
  c. On opposite side of handle, fragments of *rivets* and *iron plates*, swivelling looped *hinge* and *corner fitting*.
  d. Plate and rivet *fitting* under the pot.
  e. Small *iron fragment* with rivet nearer foot of grave. The size of the box was c 35cm × 35cm × minimum depth of 5cm, with wood thickness c1.2cm. At foot of grave with pot.

GRAVE 44 (Figures 26, 71) F over 45. 125°.
6ft 9in × 2ft 6in × 6in (2.06m × 0.76m × 0.15m)
Skull slightly left, left hand on top left femur; both knees slightly flexed to the left.
1. *Silver pin*, flat disc head with centre perforation surrounded by three ring-and-dot stamps on each side; moulding below head and further moulding at hip. L 5.8cm. At neck.
2. *Iron rivet* sandwiching three layers of bone grain running the same way on the outer pieces and at right angles on the inner piece – probably the remains of a *comb*. Right waist.
3. *Knife*, straight cutting edge, curved back. L 15.5cm.
4. *Iron keys*:
  a. One flat-shafted with two-pronged ward, L 13.6cm, and fragments of a second.
  b. Fragments of a shaft with link at each end L 7.4cm.
  c. Iron ring and shaft fragment.
  3 and 4 at left hip.

GRAVE 45 122.5°.
6ft 3in × 2ft 7in × 7in (1.91m × 0.79m × 0.18m)
No remains or finds.

GRAVE 46 (Figures 26, 71) F, 20–30. 112.5°.
7ft × 2ft 6in × 1ft (2.13m × 0.76m × 0.31m)
Skull half right, right forearm across body.
1. *Weaving batten*, tapering to a long point. X-ray shows longitudinal and diagonal lines of probable pattern-welding. L 62.3cm, width 4.3cm. An iron ring diam 3.3cm near top of tang was in a vertical position. Lying beside right leg, pointing to foot of grave.
2. *Knife*, L 12.7cm, at left hip.
3. *Beads*:
  Glass a. 39 disc yellow
  b. 10 disc yellow (double)
  c. 4 globular yellow
  d. 79 small short cylinder blue-green
  e. 9 small short cylinder blue-green (double)
  f. 14 globular very light green translucent drawn
  g. 24 globular colourless gilt drawn.
  At neck

GRAVE 47 146°.
6ft × 2ft 6in (1.83m × 0.76m)
Destroyed

GRAVE 48 (Figures 27, 71, Text Figure 46) F, Ju, 12–18. 121.5°.
6ft 6in × 2ft 6in × 11in (1.98m × 0.76m × 0.28m)
Skull inclined down and half right, remains of right humerus but no other bones except legs slightly drawn up to right.
1. *Button brooch* (Plate 6k), gilt bronze, mask

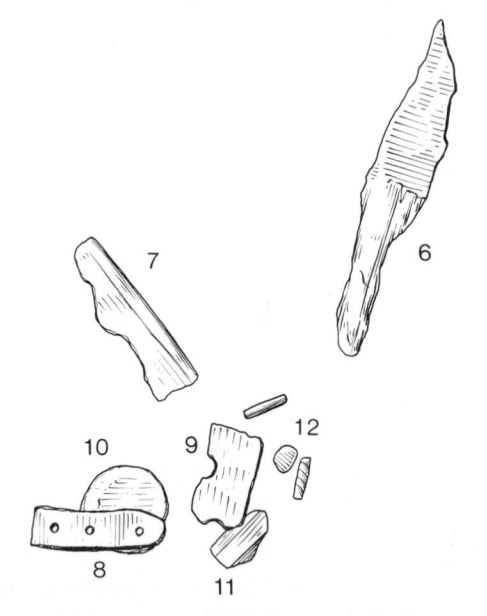

*Text Figure 46* Grave 48, objects at left hip

design in chip-carving; pin-holder and catch at back with remains of iron pin. Diam 2cm.
2. *Saucer brooch* (Plate 6j), gilt bronze, chip-carving design of five spirals round central circle-and-dot. Notching to simulate beading on outer ridge. Pin-holder and catch on back and iron pin. Diam 2.8cm.
3. *Iron chain* consisting of circular links, diam 1.3cm, fragments of textile and leather adhering. The length was approximately 30.5cm. Textile impressions on the rings (p 195).
4. *Beads:*
Amber a. 1 wedge
b. 1 small roughly-shaped (not illustrated)
c. 5 roughly-shaped and fragments
Glass d. 2 4-sided cylinder very light green translucent
e. 2 globular colourless drawn
f. 2 globular colourless drawn (triple)
g. 1 globular colourless drawn (quadruple)
h. 1 globular colourless gilt drawn (double)
i. 3 cylinder dark blue translucent drawn
j. 1 cylinder dark blue translucent drawn beaded
k. 1 cylinder colourless drawn beaded.

The button brooch was at the neck and the saucer brooch a few inches below it in the middle of the chest; the iron chain, together with the string of beads was looped from one brooch to the other.

5. *Oval bronze buckle loop*, remains of iron tongue. Width 3cm. Mid waist.
6. *Knife*, back incurved near tip. L 8.9cm.
7. *Bronze fragment* of ?bowl rim, L 4.7cm.
8. *Bronze strip*, squared at one end, rounded at the other, three perforations along middle. L 3.6cm.
9. Part of *iron diamond* with perforated centre, L 2.5cm.
10. *Iron disc*, width 2.3cm.
11. *Glass fragment*, light green, part of folded lip or base of Roman vessel. Wear on the flat surface.
12. *Beads*:
Amber a. 1 roughly-shaped
Glass b. 1 cylinder dark blue translucent drawn
c. 1 cylinder dark blue translucent drawn twisted.

6–12 were together at the left hip, probably contained in a bag.

13. *Spindle whorl* fragments; in shape of a truncated cone, probably lead and tin composition as it consists of cassiterite and cerussite (Report by W G Couper, Dept. of Mineralogy, British Museum (Natural History)). Diam 3cm.
14. *Bronze buckle* consisting of two dolphins with curling tails, a diamond shape between their jaws. Two looped projections from the tails accommodate a bar on which pivots an iron tongue. At the back is a thin fragment of wood (lime) shaped to follow the curve of the tail. Width 3.8cm

13 and 14 by the left knee.

GRAVE 49 (Figures 28, 71) F, middle-aged or old. 117.5°.
Remains of this skeleton were lying on the surface of the chalk in between graves 46 and 48. A few inches of the grave edge at the foot was distinguishable. This appears to have been laid down after 46 and 48 but as it was only about 7cm below ground level there was no stratification to decide which was the earlier. The skull was missing and the rest of the bones in a powdery state.
  a. 1 roughly-shaped amber *bead* and fragments.
  b. A fragment of colourless *glass* with bright blue streaks (Colour Plate IV 49/1b). L 1.3cm.
  At neck.

GRAVE 50 (Figures 28, 71) M (see p 124). 122.5°.
7ft 3in × 2ft × 4in (2.21m × 0.61m × 0.1m)
Skull turned left.
1. *Spearhead*, leaf-shaped blade, solid shank, split socket, rivet across socket; iron band with three inlaid bronze strips and iron wire below binding end of socket, L 36.1cm. Left of skull.
2. *Knife*, both sides curved, X-ray shows a cutting edge welded on separately. Raised mid rib along tang. L 15.5cm.
3. *Iron pin* with coiled head L 14.2cm. With knife at left waist.
4. *?Tinned bronze buckle* with shield-on-tongue, width 3.3cm, (cloth impression on back). Two *shoe-shaped rivets*, L 3cm. Mid waist.

GRAVE 51.
Destroyed.

GRAVE 52 (Figures 28, 71) M over 45. 123°.
8ft 3in × 3ft × 10in (2.51m × 0.91m × 0.25m)

Remains of skull turned right, pelvis and legs.
1. *Knife*, slender, L 6.4cm.
2. Small *bronze buckle* with double plate attached by two rivets. L1.7cm. Both objects by pelvis.

GRAVE 53 (Figures 28–9, 72) F, 20–30.    134°.
8ft × 2ft 9in × 1ft 6in (2.44m × 0.84m × 0.46m)
Skull turned right, remains of arms and legs.
1. *Beads*:
   Amethyst a. 3 large almond-shaped (Colour Plate III A06 53/1a)
   Glass    b. 4 barrel orange
            c. 1 large globular colourless millefiori, yellow flowers on green translucent, white flowers on dark blue translucent, rust red border trails (Colour Plate IV D63 53/1c).
   At neck
2. *Knife*, fragments, L 6.9cm. At left hip.
3. Number of *iron keys* with hooked wards on iron ring, one complete with L-shaped ward L 12.7cm.
4. *Iron diamond*, centre perforation, L 3.6cm.
5. *Iron purse mount*, curved back and curling ends, L 7.6cm. Three rivet holes along the back revealed by X-ray.
6. *Ivory ring*, diam c 10.2cm.
   4, 5 and 6 inside the left femur, and the keys (3) extending from hip to knee.
7. *Iron bound wooden bucket* (Plate 10d): three iron hoops; the lowest 1.3cm wide, ending in two meeting points. Two upper hoops, c 1.7cm wide, are complete rings. The handle is hooked at the ends, and the sides curved upwards in semi-tubular shape in the middle. A pair of sub-triangular mounts fastened by two rivets to the top hoop and side of the bucket, with a perforation to accommodate the handle. Ht c 19.5cm, diam base 21.5cm. There was an impression of cloth on the chalk which filled with bucket (p 195). At left foot.
   The left leg bones were deeply stained green just below the knee, but there was no trace of a bronze object in this area.

GRAVE 54 (Figures 29, 72) F, 30–45 (see p 124). 137°.
7ft 6in × 2ft 8in × 1ft (2.29m × 0.81m × 0.31m)
Skull right, left hand on top of left femur.
1. *Knife*, curved back, L 13.6cm. At left hip, under wrist.
2. *Iron keys*, T-shaped (L 12.5cm) and three hooked terminals (one L 9.8), under left femur;
   a. upper half of bunch
   b. lower half
3. *Bronze key*, T-shaped, adhering to an iron key, L 9.4cm, part of key complex.

GRAVE 55 (Figures 30, 72) F, Ju, 0–6.    133°
6ft 4in × 2ft 7in × 1ft 2in (1.93m × 0.79m × 0.36m)
Remains of skull only.
1. *Beads*:
   Amber a. 2 roughly-shaped

   Stone b. 1 large disc white, marbled grey (Colour Plate III A09 55/1b)
         c. 1 cup coral (probable identification by Mr J Attridge, Zoology Department, Birkbeck College.)
   Glass d. 1 disc yellow
         e. 1 globular dark green
         f. 1 biconical orange
         g. 1 cylinder dark blue-green (Colour Plate III B38 55/1g)
         h. 1 short cylinder white, blue translucent crossing trails (Colour Plate IV D36 55/1h)
         i. 1 short cylinder rust red, yellow crossing trails and dots.
   At neck, the large bead extreme right and probably centre piece.
2. *Knife*, angled back. L 11.2cm.
3. *Iron keys*:
   a. one with flat shaft and two-pronged ward, L 10.7cm, others attached to ring;
   b. fragments of spoon, L 11.4cm.
   2 and 3 at waist position.
4. *Fossil*, Cyphosoma, cretaceous regular echinoid from the chalk.
5. *Fittings to wooden box*:
   a. Rectangular iron handle, hooked into a pair of staples. L 6.9cm.
   b. Two bronze clips, L 1.5cm, 2.3cm.
   c. *Part of lock-plate*, L 3.2cm.
   d. *Corner fitting*, L 3.2cm.
   e. *Corner fitting*.
   f. *Part of lock-plate*, L 8.2cm.
   g. *Corner fitting*; iron band with rivet.
   The positions of three corner fittings, 5d, 5e and 5g suggest that the box shape may be reconstructed as in the grave plan, (Figure 72) the handle in the middle, size c 38cm × 22cm. The fossil (4) was nearby and may have been in the box.

GRAVE 56 (Figures 31, 72) M, 30–45.    131°.
9ft 3in × 2ft 7in × 1ft 9in (2.82m × 0.79m × 0.53m)
Skull, left, right hand on top of right femur, left forearm across body with hand in pelvis.
1. *Sword*, traces of upper and lower guard at each end of tang. Traces of wood and fur on blade. Pattern-welding, three zones diagonal and straight. 87cm × 5cm, tang L 12cm.
2. Large *knife*, slightly angular back, traces of wooden handle, end of tang flattened to a disc. X-ray shows probable welding line for separate cutting edge. L 31.2cm. The sword was along the left side of the body with hilt on shoulder; the knife was beside and parallel to it, and the left forearm across both blades.
3. *Spearhead*, long, straight-sided triangular blade with mid-rib, short split socket pierced by bronze rivet. L 46cm. Right of skull.
4. *Spear ferrule*, conical, split, L 9.5cm. By right foot. Total length of spear 2.23m.
5a. *Shield boss* fragments, straight-sided dome, vertical waist, wide flange, disc-headed rivets

which pierced a shield 6mm thick. Diam 15.5cm, ht 7.5cm.
b. *Strap grip* with splayed ends, L 12.7cm. 5 a and b at edge of grave by right shoulder, the grip on top and 23cm above the floor.
c. *Three iron disc-headed rivets* diam 1.6cm lying together about 7.5cm away from the boss.
6. *Tinned bronze buckle* (Text Figure 15a), oval loop, iron tongue, long triangular plate with shield-shaped end, fastened by three dome-headed rivets to a thin back plate; decorated by border of impressed dots, with a further row along the middle. L 6.8cm.
7. *Tinned bronze belt mount*, nearly rectangular but narrowing towards one end by curved steps on two sides. A large dome-headed rivet at the narrow end and two smaller ones in the corners of the wide end fasten it to a thin back plate which bears a textile impression. There is a rectangular perforation in the plates between the smaller rivets. (Not cleaned, probably decorated). 1.9cm × 1.5cm.
8. *Rectangular tinned bronze belt mount*; bevelled edges, punched dotted border, traces of ring-and-dot stamping in centre; dome-headed rivet in each corner attaches a fragmentary back plate. 3cm × 1.8cm.
9. *Tinned bronze belt mount*, shape as 7, decorative border of stamped dots.
10. *Silver rectangular plate*, dome-headed rivet in each corner attached to two strips of bronze at the back. (Re-used metal: a row of circular punch marks on back). 2cm × 1.3cm. Probably slightly displaced in excavation.
11a. *Tinned bronze plate* with bevelled edges, nearly rectangular, narrowing with curved sides at one end; dome-headed rivet in each corner fastened to two bronze washers at the back. Three rectangular perforations in the plate and decoration by lines of impressed dots. 2.3cm × 1.8cm.
b. *Disc-shaped mount* with projection; one dome-headed rivet: silvered and dotted decoration. L 1.7cm. Possibly part of zoomorphic plaque. 11a and b under the knife, in line with 7 and 8. The buckle, 6, was at mid waist and the plates, 7, 8, 9 and 11, spaced at fairly regular intervals along the waist line. An animal bone by the feet, a sheep-sized rib.

GRAVE 57 (Figures 32, 72) M. ?Adolescent. 84°.
9ft 3in × 2ft 7in × 1ft 10in (2.82m × 0.79m × 0.56m)
Remains of skull, arms and legs, the body probably on its left side.
1. *Spearhead*, long narrow leaf-shaped blade, socket defective. L 27.9cm. Left of skull.
2. *Knife*, L 12.7cm.
3. *Iron spike*, ?arrow. Traces of lengthwise wood grain for 3.6cm from one end where the section is rectangular. L 6.1cm.
4a. Piece of a similar *spike*, L 3.8cm.
b. Thin *iron fragment* with wood grain transversely on one side. Two inlaid yellow metal rings, ?part of belt mount. L 2.3cm.
c. *Iron buckle* with two bronze rivets fastening remains of thin rectangular iron plate, L 2cm (sketch of radiograph beside illustration). 3 and 4 were found to right and ahead of skull.
5a. *Iron spike* fragment, rectangular section, surfaces showing longitudinal wood grain, L 2.5cm.
b. *Iron fragment*, flat transverse wood grain on one side. L 2.4cm. Perhaps a flat blade to ?arrow 5a. Amongst the teeth. The right humerus and the knife by it were 15cm above the floor of the grave.

GRAVE 58 (Figures 32, 72) F, 20–30 (see p 124) 111°.
The dimensions of this grave cannot be determined precisely for it was dug into and across an earlier grave, 59; the result is a shallow excavation for both of maximum depth 23cm, maximum diameter 2.7m and of rather quatrefoil shape (see p 124). Grave 58 was c 6ft 6in long and 3ft wide (1.98m × 0.91m). Skull tipped forward, both forearms bent in.
1. *Knife*, L 14cm.
2a. *Iron key* with hooked ward and looped terminal, L 12.2cm.
b. *Iron key shaft* with ring, L 13.6cm, and fragment of a second shaft L 5.4cm.
c. *Two key wards*, one L-shaped, one T-shaped. L 2.2cm.
d. *Bronze tab* with two rivets, L 1.8cm, on iron ring. Knife and keys were under the left forearm but on top of the right humerus of Grave 59.

GRAVE 59 (Figures 33, 72) F, 20–30. 168°.
6ft 10in × 3ft 6in (2.08m × 1.07m)
Skull right, left and right humerus, but the rest of the larger bones of the skeleton, with the exception of the right tibia, must have been removed when Grave 58 was dug.
1. *Silver-gilt disc brooch* (Colour Plate If), worn beaded outer border, zone of reserved silver and niello zig-zag within; in central field three keystone garnets without foil backing, each separated by schematic Style I animal consisting of head and one leg in gilded chip carving on a slightly lower plane; central white setting of shell, decomposed, but probably originally flat, set in a silver filigree collar. Remains of bronze catch and spring base at back, diam 3.1cm.
2. *Iron pin*, L 5.3cm.
3. *Beads*:
   Amber a. 3 roughly-shaped
   Glass b. 6 disc rust red
   c. 9 disc yellow
   d. 8 disc blue
   e. 2 disc dark blue translucent
   f. 3 disc blue-white
   g. 1 disc white striped with dark blue translucent trails (Colour Plate III D01 59/3g)
   h. 1 barrel rust red, striped with

yellow trails (Colour Plate III D02 59/3h)
i. 1 cylinder rust red, striped with white trails
j. 3 cylinder rust red, yellow combed trails (Colour Plate III D14 59/3j)
k. 1 cylinder rust red, yellow combed trails (Colour Plate III D15 59/3k)
l. 1 barrel rust red, yellow crossing trails and circumference trail (Colour Plate IV D38 59/3l)
m. 1 disc rust red, white crossing trails and dots (Colour Plate IV D42 59/3m)
n. 2 barrel rust red, yellow crossing trails and dots
o. 1 barrel rust red, white crossing trails and dots
p. 1 oval green, dark blue translucent end (Colour Plate D59 IV 59/3p)
q. 1 curved fragment of bright green-blue glass containing sand fragments (Colour Plate IV 59/3q). 1.5mm thick.

Most of these beads were lying in one continuous line, and they were picked up and threaded in their original position (Colour Plate IV). The brooch and pin (1 and 2) and large blue and white beads were at the neck, with the string of beads hanging down the chest.

4. *Iron fittings to wooden box*:
   a. *Lock-plate*, rectangular iron sheet with incurved edges and slot in middle and perforation each side at one end; a bar extends from each narrower end and passes through a looped rivet, L 11.7cm.
   b. *Triangular fixture*, L 3.3cm.
   c. *Handle* fragments, fitted into two loops, L 6.5cm.
   d. *Triangular fixture*, L 3.6cm.
   e. *Flat band* fragments, one with rivets. L 5.4cm and 3cm.
   f. *Pin* fragment, L 2.7cm.
   g. Fragments of two *triangular fixtures* and shaft. L 2cm, 3cm and 2.2cm.
   If these iron fittings were undisturbed, the box must have been quite large, about 61cm × 30.5cm. It is presumed to belong to grave 59 because (a) it extends beyond the probable south wall of grave 58, and (b) fittings g were found underneath the right tibia of grave 58.

GRAVE 60 (Figures 34, 73) F. 81°.
7ft 3in × 3ft 3in × 1ft 2in (2.21m × 0.99m × 0.36m)
The grave was very shallow at the head and the skull almost entirely missing; both arms slightly bent in with hands on top of femurs; left foot crossed over right.
1. *Iron pin*, fragment L 2.8cm, at neck.
2. *Beads*:
   Amber a. 5 roughly-shaped
   Glass b. 1 small disc yellow
   c. 1 short cylinder dark blue translucent

At neck
3. *Beads*:
   Amber a. 1 roughly-shaped
   Glass b. 4 disc yellow and fragments (2 small, not illustrated)
   c. 1 disc dark blue translucent
   d. 1 disc blue-white
   e. 2 small disc black
   f. 8 short cylinder rust red (2 small, not illustrated)
   g. 4 short cylinder yellow
   h. 1 short cylinder blue
   i. 3 short cylinder dark blue translucent
   j. 3 short cylinder blue-white
   k. 1 cylinder black
   l. 1 globular colourless drawn
   m. 1 globular colourless drawn (double)
   n. 2 cylinder dark blue translucent drawn
   o. 1 disc yellow, rust red crossing trails (Colour Plate IV D22 60/3o)
   p. 3 disc blue/white, blue translucent crossing trails
   q. 1 disc white, blue translucent crossing trails (Colour Plate IV D26 60/3q)
   r. 1 disc white, crossing trails missing (not illustrated)
   s. 1 barrel rust red, white crossing trails and dots
   t. 2 oval green, yellow end (Colour Plate IV D60 60/3t).
   Also a tiny bronze loop (missing).
   In line down left side of chest.
4. *Knife*, L 9.4cm, left pelvis.
5a. *Flat iron bar* fragment, L 3.6cm, to left of pelvis;
  b. another *iron bar fragment*, slightly curved, L 4.3cm, in pelvis; both fragments show wood grain running across the narrow edges.
6. Fragments of *iron fittings to wooden box*;
   a. Rectangular *lock-plate* with slot in middle and two holes at one end, rod terminals in looped staples, total length 9cm.
   b. *Handle*, L 7.8cm.
   c. *Looped staple*.
   d. Two *rivets* to penetrate wood 1.5cm thick.
   e. Two *rivets*.
7a. *Key*, L 10cm.
  b. *Looped ?key shaft* on ring fragment
  c. *Iron ?key shaft* fragment, L 2.8cm.
8. *Iron diamond*, perforated centre, L 3.8cm.
9. *Spindle whorl*, flat disc. Roman pottery, grey core, red surfaces. Diam 4.1cm.
10. *Spindle whorl*, disc-shaped, ?shale (p 112), diam 3.3cm.
11. 1 roughly-shaped *amber bead*.
12. *Animal tooth*, second lower premolar of right hand side of a large horse.
    7–12 were contained in the wooden box to the right of the feet.
    Iron Age sherd in fill.

GRAVE 61 (Figures 35, 73) M over 45 (see p 124). 106°.
7ft 1in × 1ft 10in (2.16m × 0.56m)
Skull inclined right, remains of arms and legs.
1. *Spearhead*, flat, leaf-shaped blade, split socket, L 30.4cm. Outside right hip, pointing towards head of grave.
2. *Knife* fragments, L 6.4cm and 3cm.
3. *Iron buckle and plate* (Plate 5b), oval loop with tongue, rectangular doubled plate with five disc-headed rivets in quincunx. Copper rivets with tinned, sweated bronze caps giving the appearance of silver. L 3.2cm.
2 and 3 at left waist.

GRAVE 62 (Figures 35, 73) F over 45 104.5°.
7ft 6in × 2ft 9in × 1ft (2.29m × 0.84m × 0.31m)
The head of the grave overlapped the barrow ditch. Skull turned right, left arm bent with hand in pelvis.
1. Half an *iron ring*, diam 3.6cm.
2. *Knife*, fragments, L 16.6cm.
3. *Iron keys*: three keys with hooked wards suspended from an iron ring. L 14.7cm.
1–3 at left pelvis.
4. *Beads*:
   Amber a. 3 roughly shaped
   Glass  b. 3 disc yellow and fragment
          c. 1 disc blue-white (Colour Plate III B52 62/4c)
          d. 1 disc black
          e. 1 barrel yellow
          f. 2 short cylinder rust red
          g. 1 cylinder blue-white
          h. 1 4-sided cylinder rust red with square perforation (Colour Plate III B09 62/4h)
          i. 6 pentagonal cylinder yellow (Colour Plate III B21 62/4i)
          j. 4 pentagonal cylinder blue
          k. 2 pentagonal cylinder white (Colour Plate III B60 62/4k)
          l. 1 cylinder rust red striped with yellow trails unmarvered (Colour Plate III D04 62/41).
   At neck.
5. *Bronze pin*, consisting of wire twisted in a single loop to form head. L 4.7cm. Under chin.

GRAVE 63 (Figures 36, 73) M, 30–45. 72.5°.
7ft × 2ft (2.13m × 0.61m)
Skull partly displaced, hands on top of femurs.
1. *Spearhead*, leaf-shaped blade, solid shaft, split socket, L 34cm. Left of skull.
2. *Knife*, angled back, remains of wooden grip, L 16.2cm. At left hip.
3. Oval *iron buckle loop* with tongue, width 3.8cm. Mid waist.
4. Two shapeless *iron rust lumps*. Outside left knee.

GRAVE 64 (Figures 36, 73) M, middle-aged. 141°.
6ft × 3ft × 9in (1.83m × 0.91m × 0.23m)
The grave was shallow, the top half being over the barrow ditch; the surface had been scraped by machine and as a result only the lower half of the body remained, right humerus, left radius, part of pelvis, and both legs together.
1. *Knife*, long narrow blade, both sides curved, with traces of iron ring on handle before lifting. Remains of iron guard, band of textile impression 1.5cm wide between guard and wood remains of grip. L 24.1cm. At right waist.

GRAVE 65 (Figures 36, 73) M over 45. 134°.
10ft 6in × 2ft 10in × 1ft 4in (3.2m × 0.86m × 0.41m)
Skull right, right arm missing, both hands on top of femurs, right knee slightly bent.
1. *Spearhead*, long leaf-shaped blade, angled at base, solid shank, split socket, L 45.7cm. Textile on socket. Along left humerus.
2. *Spear ferrule*, conical L 7.1cm, by left knee, pointing towards spearhead, i.e. shaft broken before deposition.
3. *Seax*, angled back, curved cutting edge, iron boat-shaped pommel and upper guard, L 41.2cm. Width of blade 4cm. The pommel was found about 7.5cm away from the tang. Lying diagonally across the middle of the body.
4. *Iron shaft*, pointed tip, ring head, L 11.8cm. Possibly a sharpening steel; right waist.
5. *Tinned bronze or iron buckle* with shield-on-tongue, width 3.8cm, remains of leather strap 2cm wide. Three *tinned bronze shoe-shaped rivets*, L 2.4cm, one with a bronze staple threaded through perforation. Right waist.
6. *Knife*, broad blade, curved cutting edge, L 17.8cm.
7. Two *iron shafts* with suspension loop; one L 12.7cm is square in section and ends in a point, the other broken off at 7.6cm.
8. *Bronze tweezers*, stamped ring and triangle decoration, perforation at narrow end where two rivets fasten together the two separate strips.
6, 7 and 8 together at left waist.

GRAVE 66 (Figures 37, 73) F, 30–45 (see p 124). 141°.
7ft × 2ft × 1ft 8in (2.13m × 0.61m × 0.51m)
Skull half left, hands on top of femurs.
1. 7 roughly-shaped amber *beads*, at neck.
2. *Iron ring* fragment, diam 3.3cm.
3. *Knife*, curved back, L 10.2cm.
4. *Iron key*, hooked ward, L 6cm.
2–4 outside left femur
Small sherd with finger impressions in fill (p 179).

GRAVE 67 (Figures 37, 73. Plate 3d) F, 20–30. 142°.
8ft × 3ft 3in × 1ft 6in × (2.44m × 0.99m × 0.46m)
Skeleton well-preserved and in a very contorted position: the body, including the pelvis was lying face downward in the grave, but the skull was twisted sideways to the left and upwards; the right arm passed under the skull and was bent back with the hand over the left shoulder; the left arm was

down by the side of the body and bent in with the hand under the pelvis; the left leg was extended, the right drawn up with the right foot under the left knee.
1. Beads:
   Amethyst a. 3 small almond-shaped
   Shell b. 2 with corrugated edge
   c. 4 roughly rectangular
   Glass d. 1 annular dark blue translucent
   e. 3 barrel rust red
   f. 4 barrel orange
   g. 1 short cylinder blue-white.
2. Small rectangular *gold pendant* (Plate 7k) with fluted loop, a semi-cylindrical garnet with goldfoil backing in grid pattern of oblong appearance, possibly due to distortion caused by the curved surface of the garnet. L 1.2cm.
3a, b. Two *silver-gilt disc pendants*: central boss, impressed borders and cruciform dot ornament, fluted loop. Diam 1.4cm.
4. Fragments of a larger *silver-gilt disc* with boss centre and radial lines of *repoussé* dots, diam 1.8cm. Other fragments.
5. Three conical *bronze bead halves*, diam 1cm. 1.5 under the skull.
6. *Bronze wire bracelet* with clumsy slip-knot, diam 6.4cm. Between the skull and the north side of the grave.
*Lump of iron pyrites* by left foot.

GRAVE 68 (Figure 74) F, young adult. 104°.
7ft 10in × 2ft 3in × 1ft (2.39m × 0.69m × 0.31m)
Remains only of skull and legs. No finds.

GRAVE 69 (Figure 74) M 101°.
4ft 1in × 2ft 9in × 9in (1.24m × 0.84m × 0.23m)
Damaged by vehicles. Fragments of left forearm and ribs at east end grave. A re-burial? (see p 127). No finds.

GRAVE 70 (Figure 74).
*c* 2ft 6in × 2ft 6in (*c* 0.76m × 0.76m).
Shallow cut. Adjacent to Grave 92, and disturbed by it and the modern trench; containing part of an articulated foot, and displaced skull and pelvis fragments.

GRAVE 71 (Figures 38, 74) M, 20–30. 127°.
8ft × 2ft 5in × 1ft (2.44m × 0.74m × 0.31m)
Skull half right, left forearm across body with hand at right pelvis.
1. *Sword*, long iron pommel, wooden grip, traces of lower guard. Pattern-welding, two-zone herring-bone in the middle and a longitudinal zone each side. 88.8cm × 5.6cm. Along right side of body, pommel on right shoulder.
2. *Spearhead*, angular blade, split socket, L 36.8cm. Outside left humerus.
3. *Bronze ring* consisting of band 8mm wide bent in a circle, the folded edges being fixed by a rivet which extends the entire diameter. Diam 1cm. Found 30cm from the sword pommel, under the blade; probably the terminal of the 'sword knot'.
4. *Bronze band*, bent at right angle; broken each end, one of which shows a perforation; two decorative lines scored along each edge, width 8mm. Lying under spearhead socket.
5. *Knife*, L 12cm. At left waist, under left radius.
6. *Iron buckle* with doubled rectangular plate fixed by three rivets, L 4.8cm. Right waist.
7. *Iron ring*, diam 2.8cm. Outside left femur. Probably marked the middle point of the spear shaft.
8a. *Shield boss*, conical with narrow flange, slight carination, convex dome and spike terminal; diam 14.5cm, ht 9.7cm.
  b. *Strap grip*, narrow, L 14.2cm.
  c. *Shield appliqués*, iron, one each side of the boss, consist of a pair of disc-headed rivets with the heads joined, the boss touching right tibia, one pair of rivets nearly touching it, the other pair on the opposite side, outside the left tibia. The shield could not have been laid flat in the grave as one edge of the boss is only a few inches from the edge of the grave. Presumably it was placed diagonally with one edge on the floor outside the left leg and the other leaning against the opposite wall of the grave. The two outer rivets would then sink to their final position near the boss.

GRAVE 72 (Figure 74) Sex indeterminate, young adult. 96°.
7ft 3in × 2ft × 6in (2.21m × 0.61m × 0.15m)
Flints packed in top fill. Remains of skull, teeth and right humerus only. No finds.

GRAVE 73 (Figure 74) M? 95°.
7ft 9in × 2ft 3in × 5in (2.36m × 0.69m × 0.13m)
Remains of skull turned right, right arm missing, left arm bent, and leg bones. No finds.

GRAVE 74 (Figures 38, 74) F, Ju, 0–6. 109°.
4ft 9in × 2ft × 9in (1.45m × 0.61m × 0.23m)
Skull fragments and teeth only.
1. Fragment of *iron diamond* with perforated centre, L 3cm. Near teeth.
2. *Knife*, slender, both sides curved, L 13.6cm. Left waist.

GRAVE 75 (Figures 38, 74, Plate 3e) F (see p 124). 112.5°.
6ft 6in × 2ft × 1ft 3in (1.98m × 0.61m × 0.38m)
A rabbit hole in the head of the grave accounts for the disturbance of the skull and the displacement of the left humerus to near the right humerus. The rest of the bones are undisturbed; right arm bent in.
1. Beads:
   Amethyst a. 1 small almond-shaped (not illustrated)
   b. 3 large almond-shaped
   Shell c. 1 hemispherical with central perforation
   Glass d. 2 disc rust red
   e. 1 globular green
   f. 2 short cylinder green (Colour Plate III B29 75/1f)

At neck.
2. *Pair of shears*, L 15.7cm, outside left hip.
3. *Iron keys*:
   a. iron shaft attached to an *S-shaped bronze link*; L 7.6cm.
   b. other *shafts* with ring ends;
   c. *iron spoon*, L 8.1cm.
   Extending along the inside of the left femur.
4. *Ivory ring*, diam *c* 12.7cm.
5. *Bone weaving pick*; pointed at both ends, L 9.7cm.
   4 and 5 between the knees.

GRAVE 76 (Figures 39, 74) F, Ju. 119°.
4ft × 1ft 8in × 1ft 10in (1.22m × 0.51m × 0.56m)
No bone remains.
1. *Beads*:
   Glass  a. 1 short cylinder yellow
   b. 2 short cylinder dark grey, combed white trails and yellow trails (Colour Plate III D13 76/1b)
   At head position.

GRAVE 77 (Figures 39, 75) Adult or sub-adult. 119°.
8ft × 2ft 7in × 1ft 6in ( 2.44m × 0.79m × 0.46m)
Fragments of leg bones only.
1. *Knife*, angled back, L 11.2cm. By right tibia.

GRAVE 78 (Figures 39, 75) Ju, 6–12. 110°.
5ft 4in × 1ft 4in +? × 1ft 2in (1.63m × 0.41m × 0.36m)
The south side of this grave had been cut away by the scraper so that the original width is not known. Right arm and part of right leg missing, skull turned left.
1. *Bronze pin*, flattened disc head, moulded neck, L 3.3cm. Right neck.
2. *Bronze wire* coiled in a ring, diam 1.8cm. Left hip.

GRAVE 79 (Figures 39, 75) Adult or sub-adult. 120°.
8ft 3in × 2ft 3in × 1ft 1in (2.51m × 0.69m × 0.33m)
Fragments of one femur and two tibia only.
1. *Iron fragment*, flat on one side, convex on the other, oval-shaped, L 3cm. In left femur position.

GRAVE 80 (Figures 39, 75) M? 18–25. 105.5°.
5ft 6in × 1ft 7in × 9in (1.68m × 0.48m × 0.23m)
Skull right and pillowed on rising floor of the grave.
1. *Knife*, curved back, L 15.7cm. Lying close to left forearm.

GRAVE 81 (Figures 39, 75) F. 138.5°.
6ft 3in × 2ft × 1ft 1in (1.91m × 0.61m × 0.33m)
Skull tilted right, jaw displaced at left shoulder; both hands bent in to lower pelvis.
1. *Iron lock*, part, L 7.4cm, left of skull.
2. *Knife*, L 13.6cm.
3. *Iron shaft*, flattening and widening at one end, L 8.2cm.
   2 and 3 at left pelvis.

4. *Iron keys* fragments:
   a. flat shaft with loop terminal on a ring, L 10.8cm;
   b. S-shaped links.
   Inside left femur.

GRAVE 82 (Figures 39, 75) F. 74.5°.
6ft 9in × 2ft × 1ft (2.06m × 0.61m × 0.31m)
Skull half left, both arms slightly bent.
1. *Knife*, slender, L 15cm.
2. Fragments of *iron key* with flat shaft.
   1 and 2 under left forearm.
   Iron lump (not illustrated). By right femur.

GRAVE 83 (Figures 39, 75) F. 93.5°.
8ft 6in × 2ft × 1ft 10in (2.59m × 0.61m × 0.56m)
Fragments of skull and legs only.
1. Very light green translucent glass disc *bead* (Colour Plate III, B23 83/1) diam 2.2cm.
2. *Bronze pin*, knob head with moulding on neck, L 5cm.
   1 and 2 at neck.
3. *Knife*, curved back, radiograph shows possible groove along the back, L 14.4cm. At waist
4. *Iron shears* fragmentary, L 14.7cm. At left pelvis.
5. *Iron bar* fragment, L 6.4cm, and part iron ring. By knife, but possibly part of shears.
6. *Knife*, slender, L 10.4cm. In top fill.

GRAVE 84 (Figures 40, 75) F, 15–18. 102°.
7ft × 2ft 5in × 1ft 5in (2.13m × 0.74m × 0.43m)
Skull inclined right, both arms bent.
1. *Knife*, narrow blade, tip missing, L 13cm.
2. *Iron link*, rod with looped ends, L 5.6cm; two other fragments, one with doubled-back spring end.
   1 and 2 at left waist.
3. *Bronze hinge* (Text Figure 20d), L 1.3cm, doubled sheet bronze, T-shaped part fitting into recess in rectangular part; the T-shaped part fitted into a strap 1mm thick, and the rectangular part to a strap 2mm thick. T-shaped part of a second hinge. Beside left pelvis and femur.

GRAVE 85 (Figures 40, 75) Ju. 100°.
5ft × 2ft × 1ft 8in (1.52m × 0.61m × 0.51m)
No skeletal remains.
1. *Knife*, angled back, L 10.7cm.
2. *Iron buckle* loop and tongue. Width 3.3cm.
   Together near middle of grave.

GRAVE 86  108°.
9ft 3in × 3ft (2.82m × 0.91m)
Destroyed.

GRAVE 87 (Figures 40, 76) M (see p 124). 107.5°.
7ft 9in × 2ft 7in × 1ft 4in (2.36m × 0.79m × 0.41m)
Left hand in pelvis.
1. *Spearhead*, diamond-shaped blade, tip missing, solid shaft, split socket, L 19.1cm. (X-ray shows thin dense line across socket which seems to be too fine to represent inlaid metal).

Left of skull.
2. *Spear ferrule*, conical and split, L 9.4cm. At left foot. Total length of spear 2.08m.
3. Hand-made, high-shouldered *pot* (Plate 9d) with narrow neck and slightly everted rim; shoulder carination emphasised by thirteen vertical bosses each separated by three vertical grooves, with a zone of slanting lines in sets of three chevron-wise above; brown fabric with fine grits; black polished surface; ht 15.2cm, maximum diam 18.8cm, diam mouth 10.2cm. On top of spearhead.
4. *Knife*, point missing, angled, L 9.1cm. Under left forearm.
   In the top of fill of this grave were found a ?humerus and a
5. *Knife*, both sides curved, L 13cm.

GRAVE 88 (Figure 76) 107°.
6ft 3in × 3ft 6in × 1ft 8in (1.91m × 1.07m × 0.51m)
One only fragmentary bone, humerus, and body stain. The fill was loose – probably rifled.

GRAVE 89 (Figure 76) Ju, 6–12. 115°.
6ft 1in × 2ft 6in × 9in (1.85m × 0.76m × 0.23m)
Fragments of skull, arms and legs only, knees drawn up slightly to right.

GRAVE 90 (Figures 40, 76) M over 45. 53°.
8ft × 3ft × 1ft 7in (2.44m × 0.91m × 0.48m)
Skull slightly left.
1. *Spearhead*, small blunt-nosed oval blade, solid shaft, split socket, L 16.5cm. Left of skull, lying at an angle pointing upwards with the end of the socket 13cm above the floor.
2. *Silver band*, width 1cm, doubled over and fastened by two rivets, L 0.5cm. Edging to a wooden bowl. Wood inside – grain transverse. Left of skull.
3a. *Shield boss* fragments, narrow flange, vertical waist, carination, knob-headed rivets, diam *c* 12.7cm;
  b. *Strap grip*, expanding at ends, broken at one end, L 10.9cm.. At edge of grave by left arm, projecting slightly above the chalk edge.
4. *Knife*, broad blade, tip missing, L 9.9cm. Right pelvis. Brown stain between top of femurs.

GRAVE 91 (Figures 41, 76) M, 20–30. 116°.
8ft 6in × 3ft 6in × 10in (2.59m × 1.07m × 0.25m)
Skull fragments, forearms bent in.
1a. *Shield boss*; convex dome with only slight waist, wide flange with disc-headed rivets, one with textile impressions on the underside; small disc knob; diam 15.7cm, ht *c* 10.2cm.
  b. *Grip* with upturned edges extending into lozenge shape where the rivets fixed it to the shield, and a long bar extension. At head of grave near skull, 18cm above the floor of the grave.
2. *Knife* blade, both sides curving, L 12.7cm. By right elbow.
3. *Spearhead*, angular blade, solid shank, split socket, L 41.9cm.
4. Conical, split *ferrule*, L 11.9cm. Spearhead to right of skull, ferrule at feet, length of spear 1.98m.
5. *Sword*, traces of guard and pommel. Pattern-welding, three zones, diagonal and straight lines alternating. Wood and fur remains, some textile under the fur. L 89.4cm × 5.1cm. Along left side of body, hilt at shoulder.
6. *Bronze buckle* with shield-on-tongue, line decoration at base of tongue, width 3.8cm. (Textile and possibly leather nearby, p 196). Three *shoe-shaped rivets*, L 2.3cm, found in position (Figure 41). Left pelvis.
7. *Knife* blade, back curving at tip, L 10.4cm. In top fill.

GRAVE 92 (Figures 42, 76) F, 20–30. 137.5°.
7ft 10in × 2ft 10in × 10in (2.39m × 0.86m × 0.25m)
Remains of skull, right humerus, left arm with forearm bent in, both tibias. A trench cut across the middle of the grave, taking the femurs.
1. *Silver-gilt disc brooch* (Plate 6h), flat central disc of bone (apatite) with greenish staining, surrounded by a zone of three keystone garnets and simplified Style I animals in chip-carving; border of reserved silver zig-zag and niello. There is no gold foil at the back of the garnets, instead crumbly white material, stained dark at the edges. Pin-holder, catch and remains of iron pin at the back. Diam 3.1cm. At neck.
2. *Garnet disc brooch* (Plate 6n), eight keystone garnets set round a circular garnet in silver *cloisons*; back plate of iron 5mm thick with inlaid transverse bands of yellow metal on edge; remains of catch and pin at back. The action of rust has caused the garnets to rise from their cells in the middle. Diam 1.9cm. About 15cm below brooch 1 in the middle of the chest.
3. *Large beads*:
   Amber a. 47 roughly-shaped and fragment
   Jet b. 1 disc with nicked decoration
   Glass c. 1 cylinder dark blue translucent drawn
   d. 1 large short cylinder rust red with five reticella trails round the body, two rust red and yellow, one green and yellow, one rust red, green and yellow with preponderance of green, one rust red, green and yellow with preponderance of rust red (Colour Plate IV D67 92/3d).

*Small beads*:
Amber e. 1 small roughly-shaped (not illustrated)
f. 26 roughly-shaped
Glass g. 2 globular colourless drawn
h. 2 globular colourless drawn (double)
i. 1 globular colourless drawn (triple)
j. 1 globular colourless drawn (quadruple)

k. 1 cylinder dark blue translucent drawn
l. 1 cylinder colourless drawn beaded.
The smaller amber and glass beads, 3e–k, were lying between the two brooches; a double row of larger amber beads with a multi-coloured glass one at the bottom, 3a–d, hung straight down from 2, the Frankish brooch.
4. *Oval buckle loop*, cast white metal, flat surface with bevelled edges, diam 2.8cm; dome-headed *rivet*, diam 0.8cm and fragments of another. Left waist.
5. *Bronze ring*, diamond-shaped section, diam 3.8cm.
6. *Bronze band*, bent into a flattened tube and originally fastened together by two rivets. Width 1.5cm.
7. Fragments of three *iron rings*, one circular, diam 3.3cm, one oval, diam 3.9cm and one fragment. 5, 6 and 7 at left pelvis.

GRAVE 93 (Figures 43, 76, Text Figure 5, Plate 4b) M, 30–45 (see p 124). 117.5°.
8ft 7in × 3ft × 11in (2.62m × 0.91m × 0.28m)
Skull right, right forearm bent in.
1. Large, short cylindrical glass *bead*, consisting of a double band of reticella threads in the middle, rust red, with yellow opaque and light green translucent threads, and a single band at each side of the rust red opaque and light green translucent (Colour Plate IV D68 93/1). Diam 1.9cm.
2. *Iron rod* bent nearly into a triangle; longest side L 3.3cm.
1 and 2 to left of skull.
3. *Spearhead*, angular blade on two levels, split socket. On one side of the lower blade a small circle inlaid in wire of a denser metal, and on the other a swastika. L 37.2cm.
4. *Spear ferrule*, L 11.7cm. The shaft was broken before deposition as the spearhead was to the left of the skull and the ferrule outside the right elbow.
5a. *Bronze band*, bent and with iron rivet in unbroken end, width *c* 8mm, L 3.3cm. Outside right humerus.
b. *Bronze band* fragments, remains of iron rivet in two end pieces, one bearing wood fibres in transverse direction on inner side. L 3.4cm. Inside right humerus.
6. *Sword*, small iron pommel with thin base plate; traces of material of upper and lower guards, probably ivory (p 196). Traces of wood and fur of scabbard and two cords across the blade *c* 9cm from the tang. Clear pattern-welding, two zones, herring-bone. The radiograph indicates faintly a circular mark 2.2cm diam surrounding a circle 7mm diam of less density, in the middle of the blade 18.5cm from the guard, and this can also be detected visually on the surface of the blade. 86.8cm × 4.3cm. Along left side of body resting on the edge of the blade.
7. *Seax*, with curve in back near point; iron pommel with narrow, slightly curved guard sandwiched between iron plates. Lower iron guard inlaid with two copper wires. On each side of the blade and 8mm away from it was an iron bar, lenticular in section at the top half, and rusted but apparently flat on the side near the blade and rounded on the other on the lower half. Nevertheless the tang of the seax and the tangs of these two strips were probably covered with horn, and they may have been knives (p 31) L 39cm, width of blade 3.5cm. Parallel to the sword.
8. Iron fragments, probably of *buckle* loop. Mid waist.
9. *Bronze ring*, diam 3.2cm. Outside right hip. This may have been on the part of the spear shaft attached to the ferrule.
10a. *Shield boss*, convex conical dome, wide flange, five disc-headed rivets, small button top, diam 15.2cm, ht 7.6cm. On feet.
b. Fragments of *strap grip*, L 13.4cm.
c. Flat *iron strap appliqué*, broken at one end, forked at the other and covered there with silver plate; strap widens at middle, and is ornamented with two silver rivets, one diamond-shaped and one disc-shaped. The underside bears wood grain longitudinally; the rivets pierce wood 1cm thick, and are fastened by diamond-shaped bronze washers. L 10.4cm. On right ankle.
d. Fragments of *iron strap appliqué*; two rivets in widest part, one has silver lozenge-shaped head, one a disc-shaped head, both with bronze washers at other side. Silver plating on the forked end and fragment of silver plating at the other end. L 11.2cm. These appliqués were on opposite sides on the boss, 35.5cm apart.

GRAVE 94a (Figures 44, 77) F, old (see p 124). 118°.
9ft × 3ft × 10in (2.74m × 0.91m × 0.25m)
The trench passed across the head of this grave. The skeleton was incomplete, but *in situ* were lower vertebrae, right pelvis and femur.
1. *Iron fragments*, ?buckle loop, at waist.
2. *Bronze annular brooch*, oval section, pin missing, transverse scoring on face. Diam 4.3cm. At foot, but probably not in original position.

GRAVE 94b (Figures 44, 77) M adult. 118°.
9ft × 3ft × 1ft 9in (2.74m × 0.91m × 0.53m)
Directly below Grave 94a. The trench crossed the head of this grave also, taking with it any skull bones, the spear blade and sword pommel. The top half of the body was disturbed, but fragmentary leg bones were in position.
1. *Sword*, pommel and upper guard missing, but lower silver guard with bronze upper plate and two silver rivets with gold dome heads and filigree collars remaining. Pattern-welded blade, three zones of zig-zag. Traces of four rows of twisted cord immediately below guard. Traces of fur on blade. 87.5cm × 4.8cm. Along left side of body.

2. *Spearhead*, blade missing, socket only remains, diam 1.6cm, with five bands of yellow metal each 2mm wide, inlaid round shaft, stopping short of the split in the socket. Wood in the socket may be field maple, (*Acer campestre*) or ash (p 196). Right shoulder position.
3. Conical *ferrule*, split. Six copper bands inlaid round the top. L 9.7cm. Traces of two textiles on the ferrule (p 192). Right of feet, the shaft of the spear being 1.6m long. Wood fragments probably ash (p 196).
4. *Bronze strip*, with two rivets, L 3.3cm. To right of right tibia, possibly on spear shaft.

GRAVE 95 (Figures 44, 77) F.  165.5°.
Very shallow so that length not ascertainable; 1ft 9in wide and 2in deep (0.53m × 0.05m)
Remains only of left arm bent across under right forearm, vertebrae, pelvis and left femur.
1. *Two iron keys*:
   a. L-shaped with rolled suspension terminal, L 20.8cm.
   b. Bifurcated, with rolled suspension terminal on bronze ring; L 23.6cm.
2. *Knife*, back curves in at tip, L 11.4cm. Organic material on grip probably horn.
1 and 2 at left hip.

GRAVE 96a and 96b (Figure 77, Plate 4a).
Exact orientation uncertain.
7ft 6in × 3ft 9in × 1ft 2in (2.29m × 1.14m × 0.36m)
A double grave with the bodies placed side by side.

GRAVE 96a (Figure 45) M? over 40.
Skull right, left arm and right leg slightly bent.
1. *Spearhead*, leaf-shaped blade, solid shank, split socket with transverse rivet, L 27.6cm.
2. *Iron pin*, coiled head, tip missing, L 10.7cm.
1 and 2 to right of skull.
3. Silver plated *buckle loop*, with bevelled surface; shield-on-tongue decorated by stamped dots and nicked edge. Width 3.6cm. Three *shoe-shaped rivets*, L 2cm, decorated in the same way. Mid waist.
4. *Sword*, guard each end of hilt with small iron pommel fastened to upper guard by two rivets. The guards are wood, oval in section, with an outer face of a thin iron band ornamented with transverse bronze strips: a rivet at each end presumably fastened two thin iron encasing plates no longer existing. Bronze band, width 1.3cm, at scabbard mouth overlapping at back. Pattern-welded blade – two zones herring-bone with possibly some curling patterns. 90.2cm × 4.8cm. Along left side of body.
5. *Knife*, both edges curve to point, L 13.5cm. Left waist.
6a. *Shield boss*, low convex dome, point missing, wide flange with bronze disc-headed rivets; diam 16.8cm, ht 6.6cm.
  b. *Grip*, sides folded in middle and containing wood grain longitudinally for 6.4cm, transverse grain as grip becomes flat and extends in bars fastened at end by bronze disc-headed rivets. L 43cm. On feet.

GRAVE 96b (Figure 46) M, 20–30 (see p 124).
Skull right, both arms straight with hands on top of femurs; right foot crossed over left.
7. *Spearhead*, long narrow leaf-shaped blade, solid shank, split socket, L 41cm. By left shoulder.
8. *Iron pin*, coiled head, L 8.4cm. At neck.
9. *Knife*, straight back, curved blade, L 11.4cm. Organic material on tag probably horn (p 196). Left waist.
10. *Sword*, traces of upper and lower wooden cross guards, the tang beaten slightly flat at end. Gilt bronze strip, (Figure 46, 10b) 5.5cm wide, round scabbard top, ribbed and roughly beaded in horizontal direction. A bronze plaque with perforated projection (now separate) was originally soldered over the join at the back (Figure 46, 10c). A fragment of wood probably oak or ash, (p 196) identical in shape to this plaque was preserved. Pattern-welded blade, two zones of herring-bone. 91cm × 4.3cm. Along left side of body, parallel to 4.

GRAVE 97 (Figure 46) 96.5°.
8ft 5in × 3ft 2in × 1ft 1in (2.57m × 0.97m × 0.33m)
1. Fragment of *knife blade*, L 5.8cm.

GRAVE 98 (Figures 46, 77) M, adult 124°.
Very shallow, edges not discernible except at foot, width 2ft 10in (0.86m). Depth 4in (0.1m). Bones fragmentary, right arm slightly bent.
1. *Sword*, tang with remnants of iron pommel, L 13cm. Silver sleeve at each end of grip adjoining position of wooden guards. The surface of the sleeve narrows in a curve to lie flush with the original wooden grip. The upper band is plain, but the lower one has an upper border of niello zig-zag cable pattern and a lower border of a simplified version of this. The blade has two zones of diagonal pattern-welding. Traces of leather covering to both grip and wooden scabbard. 91.4cm × 5.1cm. Along left side of body.
2. Split *socket* of a spearhead, blade missing, fastened by three rivets across shaft, each with a knob head at each side. L 8.9cm. Outside left humerus.
3a. *Shield boss*, low convex dome, small button top, disc-headed rivets, diam 15.5cm, ht 7.6cm.
  b. *Strap grip* transverse wood grain at one end, longitudinal in middle, textile on other side. L 13cm.
  c–f Four *iron discs* with central knobs, slightly convex: traces of bronze on centre of underside of two. Diam 8.6cm. Mid chest, with pair of discs on either side, giving minimum width to shield of 50.8cm. The top of boss has been broken off (?by ploughing) and was near the skull.
4a. Rectangular tinned bronze *belt mount* (Text Figure 15b), at each corner is a dome-headed rivet fastening the front plate to a thin bronze back plate; the rectangular field of the top plate is raised and divided by a diagonal cross

of moulded beading which continues along the shorter edges. 3.6cm × 1.8cm. Under right forearm.
- b. Tinned bronze *belt mount*, as above, but without beading. Middle of one long side recessed for passage of strap at right angles to belt. 3.7cm × 1.8cm. Mid waist, face down, and so probably fixed to back of belt.
- c. Tinned bronze *belt mount*, as 4a. Rectangular piece cut out of one short side, probably to admit passage of tongue of an original buckle loop now lost. Face up, mid waist.
5. *Knife* fragment, broad blade, radiograph and bronze traces indicate three strips of bronze inlay along back. L 7.6cm. Mid waist.
6. *Bronze strap end*, pointed tongue shape with bevelled surface, the butt end is split, fastened with one rivet, and decorated with transverse grooves and side facets: slight parallel scratches on one side of tongue. L 5.6cm. On left pelvis.

GRAVE 99 (Figure 77) F, 40–45. 85.5°.
6ft 10in × 1ft 9in × 1ft 11in (2.08m × 0.53m × 0.58m)
Well preserved skeleton lying perfectly straight. No finds.

GRAVE 100 (Figures 48, 77) F. 94.5°.
6ft 4in × 1ft 10in × 1ft 7in (1.93m × 0.56m × 0.48m)
Skull half right, right leg slightly bent.
1. *Bronze pin*, slight constriction to form neck, L 3.6cm. At neck.

GRAVE 101 (Figures 48, 77) F. 110.5°.
7ft 10in × 2ft 9in × 8in (2.39m × 0.84m × 0.2m)
Remains of skull only, turned right and femurs drawn up to right.
1. *Bronze pin*, flat disc head with centre perforation, through which passes a bronze slip-knot ring; moulding at neck. Total L 6.1cm. At neck.

GRAVE 102 (Figure 77) Adult. 96.5°.
6ft 6in × 2ft 1in × 8in (1.98m × 0.64m × 0.2m)
Remains of lower jaw, right arm across body, left arm slightly bent in. No finds.

GRAVE 103 (Figures 48, 78) M, 30–45. 118°.
8ft × 2ft 10in × 1ft 4in (2.44m × 0.86m × 0.41m)
Skull right.
1. *Knife*, angled back, L 16cm. Left waist.
2. *Bronze belt mount*, sub-triangular shape with rivet in each corner and semi-circular perforation. L 1.7cm.
3. Fragment of rectangular *bronze* sheet, rivet in each corner. L 3cm.
2 and 3 mid waist.

GRAVE 104 (Figures 48, 78) M. 105.5°.
7ft 9in × 2ft 10in × 9in (2.36m × 0.86m × 0.23m)
Fragments of skull and legs.
1. *Knife*, curved back, L 12.7cm. Left hip.

GRAVE 105 (Figures 48, 78) Ju, 6–12. 107°.
5ft 9in × 2ft × 1ft 2in (1.75m × 0.61m × 0.36m)
One tooth only.
1. *Knife*, long, slender, both sides curve to point, L 19.8cm. Left waist.

GRAVE 106 (Figures 48, 78) M. 106°.
7ft × 2ft 7in × 9in (2.13m × 0.79m × 0.23m)
Skull right, hands on top of femurs.
1. *Knife*, angled back, L 14.7cm. Left waist.

GRAVE 107 (Figures 48, 78) F (see p 124). 135°
6ft 6in × 2ft 6in × 2in (1.98m × 0.76m × 0.05m)
Skeleton fragmentary.
1. *Iron fragments* ?tweezers, L 6.2cm. By left forearm.
2. Fragments *iron key shafts*. Each side of left femur.
3. *Bone* or antler (p 196) fragments, flat ?comb (not illustrated). Between femurs.
4. *Bronze workbox*: a cylindrical box with a sub-triangular suspension plate. The back is shown in Figure 48. The front is shown in the reconstruction Text Figure 20a. A bronze band 1.9cm wide forms the basic middle part of the suspension plate and cylinder. To this is riveted the right hand side of the double suspension plates and the right hand side of the cylinder. The left hand sides were fastened to the middle band at the top only by one rivet. When closed the left side of the cylinder covers half the middle band and meets the right side. A bronze wire is soldered to the right side round this edge and another bronze wire at each end of the cylinder. The circular ends are decorated with a quincunx of *repoussé* knobs. The remains of two mending bronze bands are riveted to each end disc, and there is a similar riveted tab mend at each side of the suspension plate where it joins the cylinder. A tab and wire slip-knot suspension loop is fixed to the top of the plate. One bronze wire claw, out of an original four on each end, remains gripping the border wire. A fragment of the box was found by the left hip, displaced from the rest of the box which was between the knees.

The box must originally have opened by swivelling the left half on one rivet at the top. There are now, however, two rivets fixing it rigid at the top with the original rivet hole left empty, and the underlying middle band is asymmetrically placed. The suspension tab is fixed by two rivets above the original empty rivet hole in the middle band. Further, there are two rivet holes, empty, one on each side of the join near the cylinder, and if these were fastened with rivets the box would be even more firmly sealed shut. There are three further rivet holes at the back of the fixed side, one with a rivet, which have no corresponding holes in the opposing layer, and these must presumably indicate a mistake in the original spacing of the holes.

Pieces of cloth and thread were caught between the left suspension plate and the middle band. (Textile report p 192). Total length 12cm, diam of end discs 4.9cm.
5a. *Knob-headed bronze pin*, grooves at neck, point missing, L 2.4cm.
  b. One *bronze rivet*, possibly part of workbox (not illustrated). Pin and rivet inside the workbox.
6. *Beads*:
   Glass   a. 1 disc yellow
           b. 1 short cylinder rust red.
   At neck.
7. *Silver wire ring* fragment, at neck.

GRAVE 108 (Figures 48, 78) Ju. 107.5°.
4ft 6in × 2ft × 1ft 1in (1.37m × 0.61m × 0.33m)
No skeleton.
1. *Knife* fragment, angled back, L 7.6cm.
2. Small *iron buckle* with tongue and remains of double iron plate with two silver rivets; total L 2cm.
   Together in middle of grave.

GRAVE 109 (Figures 49, 78) Adult or Ju. 122.5°.
7ft 6in × 2ft 7in × 1ft 6in (2.29m × 0.79m × 0.46m)
Fragments of legs only.
1. *Knife*, angled back, L 12.7cm.
2. *Iron penannular ring* with upturned terminals, diam 3.5cm.
   1 and 2 together at left hip.
3. *Pottery bottle* (Plate 9e), squat, ovoid body, short incurved neck, everted rim rounded on top, rouletting on upper half of a wide band of five-strand interlace of notched rows. Reddish buff sandy fabric, black surface, slightly burnished. Ht 20cm, maximum diam 16cm, diam mouth 7.2cm, diam base 8.5cm. At foot.

GRAVE 110 (Figures 49, 78, Plate 4c) F, 20–30 and Ju, 0–6.   104.5°.
7ft 1in × 2ft 10in × 1ft 7in (2.16m × 0.86m × 0.48m)
Skull left, hands on top of femurs. Skeleton of unborn child in pelvis of adult, head downwards.
1. *Bronze bracelet*, widening and flattening at one end, overlaid by the other end in the shape of a pointed snake's head with moulded neck. Maximum diam 6.9cm. On left forearm.
2. *Pair of shears*, with fragments of *iron wire*, probably suspension loop. L 18.3cm. Lying across between the hands at lower part of pelvis.
3. *Knife*, curved back, L 11.7cm. With the shears.
4. *Iron ?key shaft* fragments including one shaft, L 6.9cm, with a shaft at right angles which had been embedded in wood to a depth of 3cm. Between top femurs and knees.
5. *Iron key*, L-shaped ward, shaft flattened and widened towards top where it is attached to a ring. L 18.8cm.
6. *Iron spoon*, L 11.7cm.
7. *Linked iron shafts*, including one iron suspension ring and wards of two keys.
8. Small *bronze loop* with flattened ends fastened by a rivet, L 1.4cm.
   5–8 between the knees.
9. *Bone comb and case* fragments. A double-sided comb with two parallel convex-topped connecting plates each fixed to the middle of each side of the row of tooth segments by four rivets, the connecting plates decorated with panels of criss-cross lines at intervals between the rivets. Of the case some of the decorated plates and two iron rivets remain. These rivets pass through three layers of bone, showing that the decorated lengthwise strips were riveted one on each side of separator segments at the ends. The tops of the lengthwise strips were decorated with two rows of geometric cables, and the under face with a single cable bordered by small ring-and-dot motifs. A short bronze chain was riveted to the middle of one end separator segment and connected with a bronze band which encircled the comb and case. To use the comb the bronze band would slide off the top end of the case so that one lengthwise strip could be swung open. Dimensions from the position of the end rivets in the grave, 12cm × 5cm. (Reconstruction Text Figure 24). Between the middle part of the femurs.
10. *Silver coin pendant* (Plate 7c); fluted silver loop fastened on with an iron rivet. The metal of the coin seems to be baser than that of the loop for the coin was green when found. Obv. male profile to right, Rev. three semicircles of dots with a row of lettering between the second and third rows, eccentrically placed. Diam 1.3cm.
11. *Silver coin pendant* (Plate 7d), with silver loop riveted on as above. Obv. male profile to right including shoulders. Rev. beaded circle containing cross with ringlet between each arm; eccentric, surrounded by lettering and beaded outer border (p 181).
12. *Beads*:
    Glass   a. 6 short cylinder rust red
            b. 2 short cylinder green
            c. 2 short cylinder green-blue
            d. 3 short cylinder blue-white
13. *Silver wire slip-knot ring*, diam 2.3cm.
    10–13 between lower legs.

GRAVE 111 (Figures 50, 79) M. 118°.
8ft 4in × 3ft 3in × 10in (2.54m × 0.99m × 0.25m)
Skull left, left forearm across body.
1. *Knife*, angled back, L 12.2cm. Left hip.
2. *Square-sectioned headless nail*, L 5.8cm. Right knee.

GRAVE 112 (Figure 79) F, 30–45. 108.5°.
6ft 7in × 3ft 6in × 1ft 6in (2.01m × 1.07m × 0.46m)
The head rested on a step 10cm deep in one corner. Remains of skull turned left, one arm and legs only. Body probably on left side as legs are close together. No finds.

GRAVE 113 (Figures 50, 79) F adult or sub-adult. 117.5°.
9ft 6in × 3ft 9in × 1ft 10in (2.9m × 1.14m × 0.56m)
Traces only of skull and femurs.
1. *Bronze buckle* loop and tongue, width 2.4cm, double bronze plate folded over loop and riveted together by means of three dome-headed rivets; line decoration on plate, loop and tongue. Mid waist.
2. *Bronze belt mount*, triangular, with rivet in each corner and semi-circular perforation in centre; a bronze washer strip was attached to the back. L 1.6cm. With knife and keys at left waist.
3. *Iron Fragment*, roughly semi-circular, L 3cm. To left of skull.
4. *Knife*, straight back, L 14cm.
5. Fragments of hollow *iron shafts* ?keys:
   a. Two fragments, one linked to a loose ring. (Textile impression). L 3.2cm
   b. Two interlinked shafts, L 12.5cm.
   c. Two sets of interlinked shafts and one linked to a loose ring.
   2, 4 and 5 at left waist position.
6. *Iron shoelace tag*, split at one end, L 1.8cm. Right foot.
7. *Iron shaft* with ring end, probably part of key links, L 6.1cm. Right chest position. Sherds in fill (p 179). There were fragments of antler or bone to the right of the femurs, possibly a comb.

GRAVE 114 (Figures 50, 79) M 20–30. 106°.
7ft 6in × 2ft 6in × 1ft 9in (2.29m × 0.76m × 0.53m)
Skull right, hands on top of femurs.
1. *Knife*, point missing, L 11.4cm. Left waist.
2. *Spearhead*, narrow, spike blade, split socket, L 18.8cm. By left foot, pointing to foot of grave.
3. *Wood fragments* with *bronze tabs*: a, b and c: two flat pieces of wood (yew p 121) 4mm–5mm thick, are fastened together at a straight bevelled edge by means of a small rivet through each, connected on either side through a rectangular bronze washer of lengths varying from 1cm to 1.8cm. Of d the washer only remains. Three of these fragments were in a line outside the left femur; the fourth, a bronze strip without wood, was between the ankles.
   e. *Iron rivet*, end bent at right-angles, its shaft bearing traces of wood grain transversely for its complete length, i.e. the wood was c 1.4cm thick. On left ankle.
4. *Iron oval loop*, width 2cm, (textile). By left femur. 3a–e and 4 possibly part of a lyre (p 121).
   Prehistoric sherd on backbone (p 179).

GRAVE 115 (Figures 50, 79) F adult or adolescent. 120°.
Length about 6ft 9in (2.06m), but outline doubtful as grave was very shallow. Remains of left arm, right forearm across body, pelvis and legs.
1. *Knife* ?both edges curved, L 13.2cm. At left hip.

GRAVE 116 (Figures 50, 79) F 30–45. 125°.
Very shallow, edges not discernible. Remains of lower jaw, arms, spine, pelvis and legs.
1. *Bronze ?girdle hanger*; wire ring with each end thickly coiled on itself, diam 2cm. From this are pendent two bronze objects; a *hook* with flat shaft, ring terminal and line decoration, L 8.6cm, and a moulded *baluster-like object* with ring terminal, dividing at the other end into two prongs each with a perforation. The object looks rather like a clothes peg and was no doubt fastened to a wooden shaft by means of a rivet through the perforated limbs (p 117). L 6.9cm. Top left femur.

GRAVE 117 (Figures 50, 79, Plate 4d) Ju 6–12. 96.5°.
4ft 8in × 1ft × 1ft (1.42m × 0.3m × 0.3m)
Remains of skull turned right, arms and legs.
1. *Knife*, angled back, L 13.2cm. Organic material on tang probably horn. Right hip.

GRAVE 118 Ju. 79.5°.
3ft 4in × 1ft 8in × 11in (1.02m × 0.51m × 0.28m)
No skeletal remains or finds.

GRAVE 119 (Figures 50, 79) Ju, 0–6. 97.5°.
5ft 6in × 1ft 10in × 1ft (1.68m × 0.56m × 0.31m)
Remains of skull and femurs.
1. *Knife*, fragments, L 9.4cm and 1.8cm. At left hip.

GRAVE 120 (Figures 51, 80) M over 45. 109°.
7ft × 1ft 10in × 1ft 7in (2.13m × 0.56m × 0.48m)
Skeleton fairly well preserved, skull half right.
1. *Knife*, large, back curved near point, L 22.4cm. Organic material on tang probably horn. At left waist.
2. *Iron shoe-lace tag*, cylindrical with bifurcation at one end, L 2.3cm. On left ankle.
   Animal bone in top fill, mid chest: fragment of tibia of largish animal, ?shin of beef.

GRAVE 121 (Figures 51, 79) F over 45. 99.5°.
9ft 1in × 3ft 6in × 2ft 5in (2.77m × 1.07m × 0.74m)
Teeth only.
1. *Knife*, point missing, L 10.9cm.
2. *Iron shaft* with loop at each end, L 7.9cm.
   1 and 2 at left waist.
   Bone or antler fragments by R. pelvis, possibly a comb. To the left of the skull were remains of oak (p 196).

GRAVE 122 (Figures 51, 80) F, Ju. 127°.
4ft 6in × 2ft 3in × 8in (1.37m × 0.69m × 0.2m)
No skeletal remains.
1. Fragments of *iron ?key shafts*, two on a ring, L 7cm. Middle of grave, ?knee position.

GRAVE 123 (Figures 51, 80) Ju. 127.5°.
3ft 10in × 2ft 4in × 11in (1.17m × 0.71m × 0.28m)
No skeletal remains.
1. *Knife*, short, both sides curving, L 10.7cm. Middle of grave, ?waist position.

GRAVE 124 (Figures 51, 80) F, 20–30. 106°.
8ft × 2ft 10in × 2ft (2.44m × 0.86m × 0.61m)
Minute bone fragments in west end, femurs in usual position but some teeth in position of lower legs. It is not known whether this peculiar position is because of an original displacement or subsequent animal disturbance.
1. Two large almond-shaped amethyst *beads*; left of feet postion.
2. *Knife*, angled back, L 13cm. At left waist.
3. *Iron fittings to wooden box*:
   a. Right angled *iron band corner strengthening*; the wood grain on the inside runs longitudinally along one side, and at the end of the other side, showing a thickness of wood of 1.3cm. On the first side there are transverse ridges and on the second side there are also raised diagonal lines presumably formed by iron wires.
   b. *Corner piece* as above, a rivet through each side, and longitudinal ridges on one side and transverse parallel ridges on the other.
   c. *Corner piece* fragment with longitudinal ridges on one side.
   d. *Corner piece*.
   e. Rectangular *handle*, hooked into a pair of looped staples which penetrated wood 1.3cm thick. It was lying flat on wood with grain longitudinal. L 10.2cm.
   f. *Lock* fragments. Flat iron plate narrowing to a bar at each end, two perforations at one end, a looped staple on the bar at the other. A separate smaller iron bar with rivet end underneath and under surface covered with transverse wood grain, L 9cm.
   g. *Iron fragment*, L 2.8cm, rectangular section, sandwiched between fabric on one side and leather on the other. The corner pieces indicate that the wooden box was c 33cm × 20.3cm with the handle and lock in the middle. The wood is identified as beech, *Fagus sylvatica*, (p 196). At the feet.
4. Rectangular patch of *antler*, 15cm × 7.5cm, beside the wooden box to the left, but separate from it, possibly a comb or another box.

GRAVE 125 (Figures 51, 80) M over 45. 102°.
7ft × 2ft 9in × 1ft 5in (2.13m × 0.84m × 0.43m)
Rectangular, with projections at each corner.
Skull right, right hand on top femur.
1. *Knife*, long slender blade, broken, L 14cm. Left waist.
Sherds in fill (p 179).

GRAVE 126 (Figure 52) F adult.
This grave was cut through by the mechanical digger in January, 1952, bones disturbed and a brooch retrieved by a workman. This was not reported until the following April, when a few bones were found nearby and the brooch recovered.
1. *Silver disc brooch* (Colour Plate IIe), light-and-shade border with long and short stretches of beading on the worn rim; silver zig-zag and niello within; central sunken field covered with a gold plate fastened by four rivets to the back plate, and bearing on the outer zone a border of beaded filigree with four circular cells and four trefoil cells arranged alternately in a field of gold filigree beaded annulets; three of these cells are now empty, but two opposite round ones contain yellow translucent *cabochon* glass; and another opaque light blue *cabochon* glass. Two of the trefoil cells still retain flat shell. It is these trefoil cells which shield the rivets. Within this is a zone of *cloisonné*, surrounding white shell *en cabochon* with a central *cabochon* garnet in a gold collar. Two stones are missing from the *cloisonné* zone, but all those remaining are garnet with the exception of one triangular cell of white material. The arrangement is cruciform, four triangular cells with four step cells in between. The two opposed triangular cells and the step cells hold garnets more orange in tone than the others; the backing to the step cells is a fine, lozenge-shaped trellis different from the boxed pattern backing the intervening cells.* At the back are the remains of pin catch and spring holder. Diam 4.2cm.
A runic inscription of six symbols (Text Figure 9) is placed centrally in one half between two framing lines running parallel to the catch and holder, the uprights of the two end characters closing the frame. A separate inscription, in much lighter scratches, appears in the opposite half, again contained in a frame, but not aligned to the axis of the brooch. One of the shorter ends forms part of a character, and the other end is a single long stroke continued far beyond the frame and may be intended solely as a border or as the letter i. Between this border and the other character is another symbol.

GRAVE 127 (Figures 52, 80) F adult or Ju. 112°.
6ft 7in × 2ft × 10in (2.01m × 0.61m × 0.25m)
Remains only of left arm across body, and legs.
1. *Beads*:
   Amethyst   a. 2 small almond-shaped
   Glass      b. 2 short cylinder rust red
              c. 2 short cylinder rust red streaky
              d. 1 short cylinder green
              e. 1 short cylinder blue-white.
   At neck except for one rust red bead, (c), near mid waist.
2. *Knife*, with fragment of iron ring, L 11.2cm. Left waist.
3. Complex of *iron fragments* including:
   a. *spoon* with oval bowl, L 8.1cm;
   b. *ring*, diam 2.5cm, and fragments of two others;
   c. broken shafts of ?*keys* round and flat in section.
4. *Bronze annular brooch*, diam 3.1cm, semicircular section, transverse moulding at

---

*Avent 1977, p 26, No. 168, 'Most of the foils appear to be of the boxed type, although they are not clear enough to be read, but one is of the standard type with grooves set at 40°/135°, thus producing a lozenge-shaped pattern with the reading given in the table (pl.II.C; Fig. 1.h).'

intervals; a constriction for attachment of pin opposite a nick in the other side for the passage of the point. 3 and 4 on top of left femur. Minute fragments of prehistoric pot in the fill.

GRAVE 128 (Figures 52, 80) M adult. 119.5°.
7ft 6in × 2ft 6in × 10in (2.29m × 0.76m × 0.25m)
Remains of skull, left arm bent in, and legs.
1. *Spearhead*, angled blade, long split socket, L 24.9cm. Right of skull.
2. *Knife*, angled back, L 14.5cm. Inside left humerus.
3. *Iron buckle* loop and tongue, double rectangular iron plate with three bronze dome-headed rivets. Width 2.8cm. At left waist near knife. Fragmentary sherds from mid to left waist. (p 179).

GRAVE 129 (Figures 53, 80, Text Figure 47) F young adult or adolescent. 106°.
Outline uncertain because of shallowness. Remains of skull, left forearm across body, right arm bent in, legs half drawn up to left.
1. *Pottery bottle* fragment; wheel-thrown, ovoid body, incurved base, wall remains to a height of 9.2cm, no decoration. Light grey sandy ware. Maximum diam 15cm, diam base 7.9cm. By right foot.
2. *Bronze bracelet*, knotted wire, diam 5.8cm.
3. *Roman coin*, perforated; diam 2.3cm (p 181).
4. *Bronze thong tag*, sheet bronze rolled in a cone, slit at the wide end where a rivet passes through its diameter; decorative scored lines near edge. L 2.5cm.
5. Beads:
   Shell a. 1 small pendant and fragment
   Fossil b. 1 *porosphaera*
   Glass c. 1 disc blue-white
   d. 1 melon dark green-blue
   e. 1 biconical dark green (Colour Plate III B33 129/5e)
   f. 1 biconical dark green-blue (Colour Plate III B44 129/5f)
   g. 1 biconical blue-white
   h. 1 barrel black, white crossing trails and rust red dots (Colour Plate IV D53 129/5h)
   i. 1 disc light olive translucent, dark blue translucent blob (Colour Plate IV D61 129/5i)
6a. *Bronze beads*: flat bronze fragment circular with perforated centre diam 1cm, fragments of a second and piece of tubular bronze, probably parts of biconical bronze beads.
   b. Reconstruction of 6a.
7. Fragments of biconical *bronze bead*, (not illustrated).
8. *Bronze spatula* with end looped for suspension, L 5.1cm.
   2–8 all together at right shoulder.
9. *Knife* fragments, curved back, L *c* 12.7cm. Under right femur.
10a. Two *iron shafts*, one of which ends in a point, ?keys.

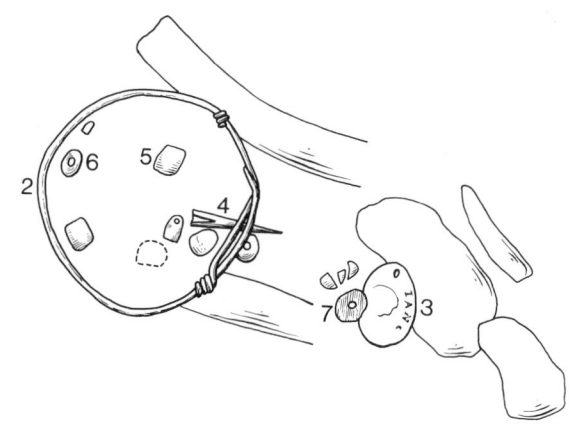

*Text Figure 47* Grave 129, objects at right shoulder. Scale 1/2

b. *Iron buckle* loop and tongue, diam 2cm; remains of double iron plate.
c. Complex of two or three *iron key shafts* with cloth impression on under surface; on top a yellow *bronze girdle-hanger* L 4.4cm hanging on a bronze loop, the lower end expands into three perforated lobes and is decorated with punched ring-and-dot ornament; from one of the perforations hangs a copper spatula. Below the top end of this complex was a naturally *perforated bone* (d), probably functioning as a suspension ring. Left waist.

GRAVE 130 (Figures 53, 80) Sex indeterminate 20–30. 114.5°.
Shallow grave, edges uncertain *c* 5ft 10in × 2 ft × 6in (1.7m × 0.61m × 0.15m). Fragmentary skull, arms bent in, and legs.
1. *Knife*, broad, L 19.8cm. X-ray shows that the tang and back are in one piece with the blade welded on separately. Right waist.

GRAVE 131 (Figures 54, 81) M young adult. 128°.
8ft 6in × 3ft × 8in (2.59m × 0.91m × 0.2m)
Skull right, left arm bent in.
1. *Spearhead*, long, narrow, pointed leaf-shaped blade, socket fragmentary, L 31.8cm. Right of skull.
2. *Sword*, remains of small pommel, traces of wooden cross guard adjacent to it and remains of lower guard with iron frame (or strengthening band on the mouth of the scabbard) along the top of the blade. Pattern-welded, three zones of diagonal and straight lines, probably double-sided as a longitudinal welding line appears along the middle of the middle zone. Longitudinal wood grain of scabbard on blade. 88.9cm × 4.6cm. Left side of body.
3. *Knife*, tip missing, angled back, straight cutting edge, L 15.2cm. Under left forearm.
4. *Oval iron buckle* loop and tongue, width 2.5cm; mid waist.
5a. *Iron rivet* with disc head diam 4.3cm.
   b. Fragments of a second *disc-headed rivet* with bronze traces at back. Together at right waist. These presumably belonged to a shield, the

boss of which may have protruded above the edge of the grave and been ploughed away. To right of waist.
6. *Iron buckle loop*, nearly circular, and tongue, width 2.5cm; under discs. Fragment of iron ore by spear.

GRAVE 132 (Figures 54, 81) F young adult. 87°.
7ft × 2ft 1in × 1ft 3in (2.13m × 0.64m × 0.38m)
Fragments only of skull, arms and legs.
1. *Bronze pin*, flat disc head, transverse moulding in middle of shaft. L 4.2cm.
2. *Beads*:
   Amethyst a. 6 small almond-shaped
   Glass    b. 2 barrel orange
            c. 2 barrel green-blue
            d. 1 disc light blue, blue translucent crossing trails and rust red dots now decomposed
            e. 1 large globular millefiori rust red, green translucent/yellow flowers and white ring, rust red dot and dark blue translucent background (Colour Plate IV D64 132/2e)
            f. 1 cylinder millefiori green translucent and yellow spirals, dark blue translucent and white flowers, rust red band (Colour Plate IV D65 132/2f).
   1 and 2 at neck.
3. *Knife*, angled back, straight cutting edge, L 11.4cm. Left waist.
4. *Key complex*; fragments of numerous iron keys, reaching from left waist to right knee.
   a. Looped shaft with textile adhering, L 7cm.
   b. Looped shaft, L 4.6cm.
   c. Iron shafts linked together, L 15.6cm.
   d. Key shafts, one looped link.
   e. Three keys with twisted shafts and hooked wards on a ring, each L 11.6cm.

GRAVE 133 (Figures 55, 81) F ?Middle-aged. 102°.
9ft × 3ft 6in × 1ft 10in (2.74m × 1.07m × 0.56m)
Skull left, remains of arms and legs.
1. *Beads*:
   Silver a. 2 halves of large biconical bead, with key-hole-shaped perforation at each end; half of another bead.
          b. 1 barrel orange
          c. 1 annular dark blue translucent, white zig-zag trail (Colour Plate III D08 133/1c)
   At head of grave.
2. Amethyst a. 2 large almond-shaped
   Glass    b. 4 barrel orange
            c. 1 4-sided cylinder rust red
            d. 1 pentagonal cylinder light green (Colour Plate III B25 133/2d)
            e. 1 disc black, white zig-zag trail (Colour Plate III D07 133/2e).
   At neck.
3. *Iron* fragment with three bronze rivets, L 1cm. At foot of grave.
4. *Knife*, angled back, straight cutting edge, L 18.5cm. Left waist.
   Animal bones by feet: fragments of vertebrae of ?sheep.

GRAVE 134 (Figures 55, 81, Text Figure 48) F. 105.5°
8ft 3in × 2ft 6in × 11in (2.52m × 0.76m × 0.28m)
Fragment only of left femur.
1. *Yellow gold disc pendant* (Text Figure 10j, Plate 7h), fluted loop attached flat to the back. *Repoussé* design of four interlaced serpents, each with forward-tipped ear and upper jaw curling over the lower jaw; the bodies consist of two outer bands with a middle row of dots. The border is an angular cable design, alternately plain and dotted. A thick filigree wire is soldered round the edge on the front. Diam 3cm. (Gold Analysis p 181).
2. *Beads*:
   Shell a. 2 4-sided cylinder
   Glass b. 1 disc yellow
         c. 1 disc very light green translucent
         d. 2 disc green
         e. 2 barrel orange
         f. 1 fragment disc white, blue translucent crossing trails.
3. *Pendant*, oval sliced garnet with bevelled edge, silver plate backing with suspension loop, L 1.5cm.
4. *Pendant*, flat oval garnet with bevelled edged and hollow cut at back, with silver plate backing and suspension loop. This garnet is much darker than the garnet above which is sliced. L 1.5cm
5. *Silver pin*, hollow, rounded cube head with cabochon garnet set at apex, a hole in each of the four sides, moulding below the head and in the middle of shaft, below which the shaft swells, to taper in facets to the point. L 3cm.
   All these ornaments, 1–5, at neck.
6. *Knife*, angled back, fragment of line-decorated leather sheath adhering to blade. L 11.5cm. Mid waist.
7. Complex of *keys*: (See Text Figure 48b)
   a. *Iron ring* with small *bronze loop* with flattened and widened ends fastened together by two rivets. L 2.3cm.
   b. *Three keys* with hooked wards, L 16cm, 8cm and 3.4cm.
   c. *Shaft fragments*.
   d. *Key shaft* with looped end and part iron ring rusted to it. L 7.4cm.
   e. *Two keys* with hooked ends, L 13.6cm.
   f. *Shaft* linked to another. Other shafts attached to a ring or looped together.
   g. Two *key shafts*, one with looped and twisted wire terminal, L 7cm.
   These keys extended from knife at waist down left side of body.

GRAVE 135 (Figures 56, 81) M, 25–35. 126°.
7ft × 2ft 9in × 10in (2.13m × 0.84m × 0.25m)
Skull tipped forward by rising floor, right arm bent

246 THE BUCKLAND ANGLO-SAXON CEMETERY

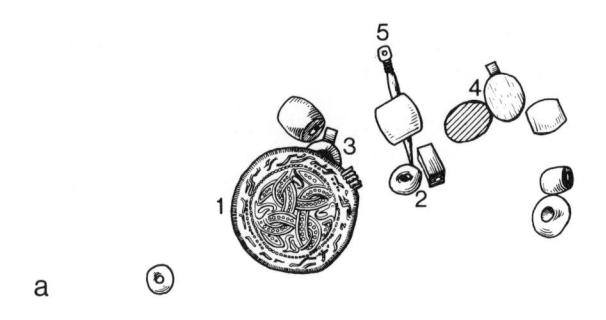

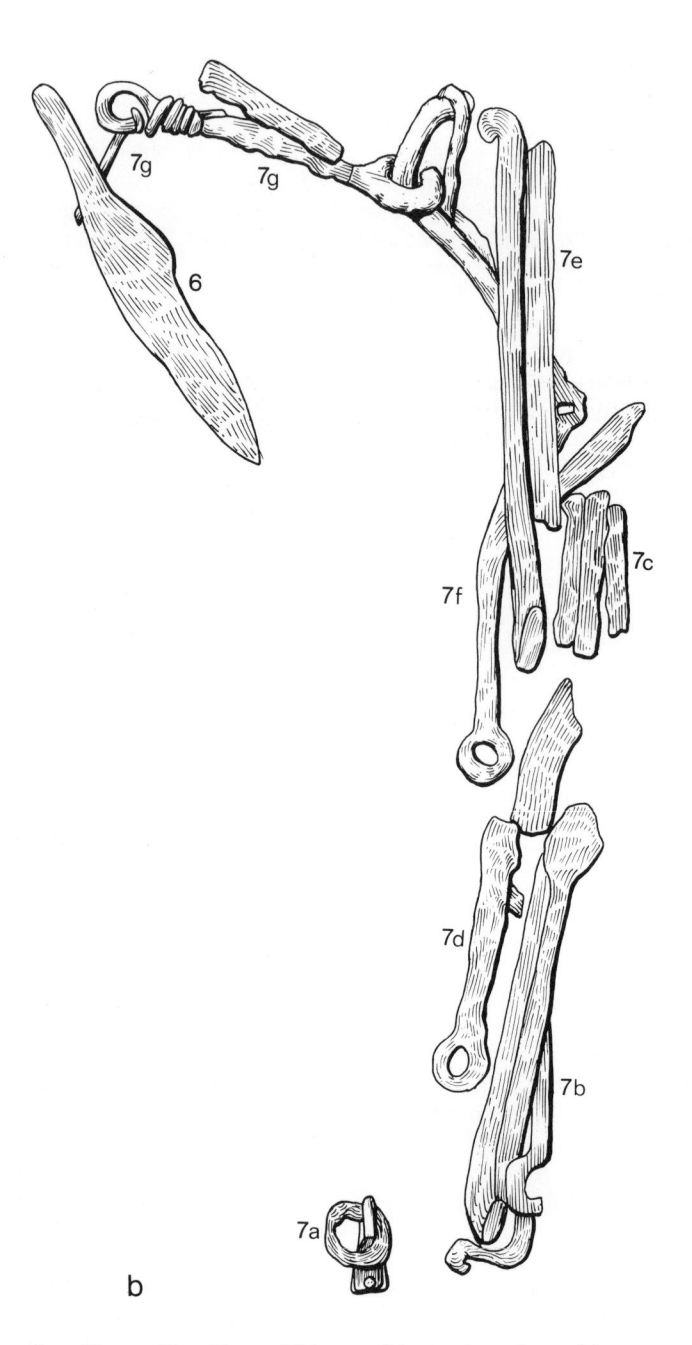

*Text Figure 48*   Grave 134   *a*   objects at neck position
                                *b*   objects at left hip. Scale 1/2

towards pelvis, but only one finger bone remained there, the rest of the hand being by the right knee. Probably a disturbance by animals soon after burial.
1. *Spearhead*, small, narrow blade with relatively long, split socket transfixed by a rivet, encircled by an iron band and extending in two prongs. L 30.5cm. At right shoulder.
2. Large *knife*, back and cutting edge curved, L 23.3cm.
3. *Knife*, angled back, L 12.7cm. 2 and 3 together at left waist.
4. *Iron buckle*, long triangular plate with bronze rivet in each corner; remains of bronze backplate. L 5cm. Mid waist.
5. *Iron bolt* with dome head, diamond rove, to pierce wood, 4cm thick. L 5.6cm.
6. *Iron bolt* as 5 but defective. 5 and 6 at right side of body, by elbow and femur; probably coffin fittings.
7. A tiny *iron fragment* by the skull. Not illustrated.

GRAVE 136 (Figures 56, 81) M old. 110°.
110°.
8ft 4in × 2ft 6in × 11in (2.54m × 0.76m × 0.28m)
Skull half right, remains of arms and legs.
1. *Knife*, angled back, groove along back on one side, L 15.4cm. At left waist.
2. *Iron pin*, knob head, point missing, L 3.6cm. Under skull. In the fill by the head was a lump of iron pyrites.
3. Above the grave a piece of *bronze*, 5.3cm × 1.3cm, pierced by two rivets and a ?human ankle bone indicating a disturbed grave in the vicinity.

GRAVE 137 (Figures 56, 81) M Ju. 104°.
7ft 10in × 3ft 3in × 9in (2.39m × 0.99m × 0.23m)
Roughly cut, large chalk lumps in fill. Although no bones remained, it may be concluded that this was the grave of a small body. The spear is very small, and was placed to the right of the head or chest. Nearby were the buckle and two knives, no doubt at the waist.
1. *Bronze bowl*, semi-spherical with slightly thickened rim; the rim was mended at one point by means of a bronze band 8.1cm × 1.8cm riveted on the outside with a small band on the inside; another square patch on the body held by eight staples. Ht 7cm, diam c 19.6cm. At head of grave.
2. *Bronze buckle* loop and tongue, moulding on tongue; remains of rectangular bronze sheet plate with scored line decoration, fastened by a row of three dome-headed rivets to a back plate. Width 1.5cm. Mid waist position.
3. Small *spearhead*, leaf-shaped blade, triangular section at junction with socket, L 14.7cm. Right ?chest.
4. *Spear ferrule*, L 9.9cm; the conical tip is 3.8cm long, then merges into four-sided conical spike with lengthwise traces of wood grain on all sides. At foot. Length of spear 1.22m.
5. *Knife*, slender, curving back and cutting edge, L 11.6cm.
6. Small *knife* fragments, L 8.4cm. 5 and 6 at left waist.
7. *Pottery bottle*, wheel-thrown ovoid body, narrow incurved base, neck and rim missing; three turns of a roulette band, maximum width 2cm, of small square impressions. Light red core, light grey surfaces, sandy texture. Ht 16cm, maximum diam 17cm, diam base 6cm. At foot, near spear ferrule.

There were traces of black wood 7–13mm thick under the bronze bowl, identified as oak, *Quercus* sp (p 196) and fragments of some large twigs.

GRAVE 138 (Figures 57, 81, Text Figure 49) F, 30–45. 125°.
9ft × 3ft 3in × 1ft 10in (2.7m × 0.99m × 0.56m)
Remains of skull, arms and legs.

*Text Figure 49*  Grave 138, objects at left hip. Scale 1/2

1. *Iron pin*, flat head, L 4.3cm. At neck.
2. *Bronze pin*, spatulate head with moulding at junction with shaft and half way down. L 3.2cm.
3. *Bronze needle*, L 3.3cm.
4. *Iron pin*, L 2.3cm.
5. Two *bronze S-shaped hooks*, L 2cm.
6. *Bronze tab*, doubled and fastened with iron rivet, L 1cm.
7. *Bronze Roman coin*, (p 181).
8. *Bronze band* fragments, 0.5cm wide and curved, double at end where riveted together, L 2.5cm.
9. *Knife*, both sides curving, L 14.7cm.
10. *Iron shaft* with longitudinal wood grain on outside, ?knife tang, L 2.7cm.

11. Small fragmentary *iron looped rods*.
    2–11 at left hip.
12. *Iron key*, right-angled ward, suspended on iron ring, diam 2.5cm. L16.8cm.
13. *Iron key* fragments, with iron ring, total L 16cm.
    12 and 13 outside left femur.
    Animal bones in fill: fragments of scapula and rib of ?sheep.

GRAVE 139 (Figures 57, 82) M Ju. 92°.
6ft 3in × 2ft 9in × 10in (1.91m × 0.84m × 0.25m)
No skeletal remains, but probably a child because of disappearance of bones and small size of spear. Assuming that the pot and spearhead were beside the head and the joint of meat was beyond the feet, the skeleton would have been of a child about 3ft tall and the other iron objects would have been at waist level.
1. *Iron purse mount*, straight back, coiled terminals, L 6.6cm.
2. *Iron diamond* with circular perforation in centre, L 3.8cm.
   Rusted to 1. Right waist.
3. *Knife* fragments, slender blade, L 12.4cm. Left waist.
4. Tall, biconical, wheel-thrown *bowl* (Plate 9c), slightly everted straight rim, concave base. One band of rouletted key pattern between two limiting grooves on the carination, and one above. Red ware, surfaces blackened and burnished. Ht 15cm, maximum diam 14.5cm, diam mouth 9.5cm, diam base 7cm.
5. Small *?toy spearhead* or arrow; leaf-shaped blade, remains of wood in closed socket, L 8.9cm. 4 and 5 at head.
6. Fragments of thin *horseshoe*, two rectangular nail holes, width 2.5cm, narrowing towards middle and end. This was at the foot of the grave, above the animal bones, and although some inches above the floor of the grave, yet it was in the grave fill, well below the level of the chalk edge. As it is a shallow grave, it may be an intrusion.
   Animal bones at foot, right humerus of young ox (*cf 'Bos longifrons'*).

GRAVE 140 (Figures 57, 82) Ju 9–12. 99°.
5ft 3in × 1ft 10in × 1ft 3in (1.6m × 0.56m × 0.38m)
Large flints in fill round edge. Skull right, right hand on top femur.
1. *Iron pin*, L 6.9cm. Left neck.

GRAVE 141 (Figures 58, 82, Text Figure 50) F (see p 125.) 107.5°.
9ft 1in × 3ft × 1ft 9in (2.77m × 0.91m × 0.53m)
Skull half right, right forearm across body.
1. *Bronze bracelet*, round section, ornamented by zones of transverse scoring at four equidistant points. Diam 7.6cm. Possibly on left forearm, but the bones were missing.
2. *Knife*, with angled back incurved at the point, L 14cm.

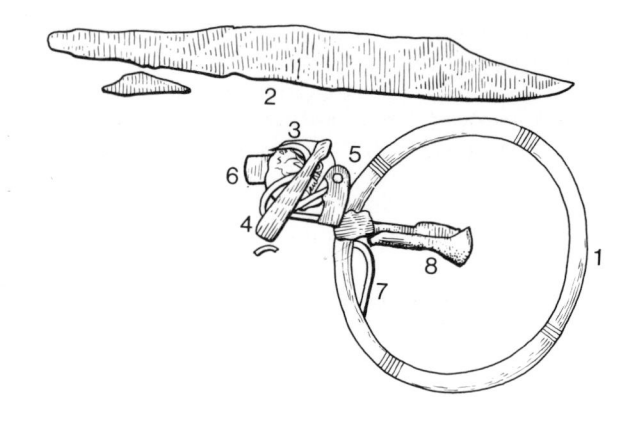

*Text Figure 50*   Grave 141, objects at left waist. Scale 1/2

3. Perforated *Roman silvered bronze coin*, diam 1.6cm (see p 181).
4. *S-shaped bronze wire* and *iron pin* fragment, adhering to 3. L 2.9cm.
5. Perforated *shell pendant*, L 1.6cm.
6. *Beads:*
   Glass  a. 1 disc rust red
          b. 1 melon dark green-blue.
7. *Bronze S-hook* and remains of a second.
   *Iron pin* rusted to above, L 3.8cm.
8. Fragments of *iron pins*, one L 5cm.
   2–8 at left waist.
9. ?Box between skull and head of grave; a rectangular area *c* 30.5cm × 10cm of black ?oak and ?antler fragments, (p 196).

GRAVE 142 (Figures 58, 82) F old, (see p 125). 113°.
8ft 7in × 2ft 9in × 1ft 9in (2.62m × 0.84m × 0.53m)
Skull left, hands together in pelvis, legs slightly bent to left.
1. *Bronze pin*, perforated disc head, moulded neck, L 4.3cm.
   At right neck.
2. *Iron key*, ward broken but presumably two-pronged, other end bent over iron ring. L 22.4cm.
3. *Knife*, curved back, straight edge, leather sheath fragment with parallel line decoration. L 14cm. 2 and 3 between femurs.

GRAVE 143 (Figure 58, 82) Ju 8. 119°.
7ft 4in × 2ft 7in × 1ft 5in (2.24m × 0.79m × 0.43m)
Traces only of skull, teeth, one arm and legs.
1. *Iron fittings to wooden box*: (reconstruction Text Figure 18b)
   a. Fragments of about eight similar *clamps* with each end bent at right angles, the middle part flat, the ends with circular section. Two others are similar, but with a crescentic curve. Transverse wood grain on inner side of flat part. On some the wood grain runs in the other direction and on one there is longitudinal and end grain, indicating a dovetail joint. L 3.8cm, two only illustrated.
   b. *Hasp*, a curved band with a rectangular hole in the wider and pointed end. L 5.2cm.

c. *Ring handle*, diam 3.2cm, linked to a staple piercing wood 1.7cm thick.
d. Remains of another *staple*.
e. *Wood fragment* decorated on one surface with grooves, L 2.8cm, and two fragments of *clamps*.

The ring handle was in the middle of the clamps, the positions of which indicate a box size of 38cm × 20cm. The wood is identified as beech, *Fagus sylvatica*, (p 196). At the foot of the grave.

GRAVE 144 (Figures 59, 82) M? 122.5°.
8ft 10in × 3ft × 1ft 7in (2.69m × 0.91m × 0.48m)
Remains of skull, arms and legs.
1. *Iron buckle*, long strap plate with rounded end, L 4.8cm.
2. *Knife* fragment, traces of wooden handle, L 11.4cm.
3. *Iron ?sharpener*, pointed at top and rounded in section, becoming flatter lower down and ending in a semi-circular terminal, L *c* 16.5cm.
4. *Bronze buckle* with double rectangular plate fastened by two rivets; three line decoration at base of tongue. L 2.3cm.
5. *Bronze conical thong terminal*, L 1.3cm and fragments of a second. 1–5 at left waist.
6. *Iron fragment, ?shoe-lace tag*, by right foot. L 1cm. Antler fragments left of skull, ?a comb.

GRAVE 145 (Figures 59, 82) M. 106°.
7ft 3in × 2ft 9in × 1ft 5in (2.21m × 0.84m × 0.43m)
Skull right, right knee slightly bent out.
1. Long *knife*, back curved down to the point, small *bronze rivets* in rows at two positions along the blade edge fastened the leather sheath, L 18cm. At left waist.
2. *Iron* fragments with double rectangular plate, ?buckle, L 5.4cm. Right waist.
3. *Iron adze* fragment, L 6.4cm. At edge of grave in wall to right of head.

GRAVE 146 (Figures 59, 82) M, 20–30. 89°.
8ft 3in × 3ft × 1ft (2.51m × 0.91m × 0.31m)
Body placed on its right side; skull right, left arm slightly bent, left foot on top of right foot.
1. *Bronze buckle* with folded rectangular plate fastened by three rivets; decorative lines on tongue. L 2.5cm. Right hip.
2. *Knife*, curved back, L 15cm. Left hip.

GRAVE 147 (Figures 59, 83) F 30–45. 89°.
8ft 9in × 3ft 1in × 1ft 10in (2.67m × 0.94m × 0.56m)
Remains of skull, right forearm bent in, and legs.
1. *Bronze pin*, perforated disc head threaded with slip knot wire ring, moulded neck, tip broken, L 5.8cm. At neck.
2. *Knife* fragments, L 11.9cm.
3. *Iron pin* fragment, L 1.9cm.
4. *Disc-shaped pebble*, dull red with white streaks. Diam. 2.2cm.
2–4 at left hip.
5. *Iron* square-sectioned shaft with right-angled bend, flat at one end, tapering to a point. L 4.3cm. At foot

GRAVE 148 (Figures 59, 83, Plate 4e) M. 107.5°.
6ft 9in × 3ft 1in × 1ft 1in (2.06m × 0.94m × 0.33m)
Skull left, right forearm across body, knees slightly flexed to left.
1. *Knife*, angled back. L 17.3cm.
2. *Sharpening steel*, flat iron bar with one rounded end and narrowing to a tang at the other, 10.4cm × 1.3cm.
3. *Iron buckle* with doubled rectangular plate, textile on back, L 3.3cm.
1–3 at left waist.

GRAVE 149 (Figures 60, 83) M ?over 60 126.5°
8ft 4in × 2ft 4in × 1ft 4in (2.54m × 0.71m × 0.41m)
The skeleton was lying a few inches above the floor of the grave, and in parts, e.g. right shoulder, resting on some of the large flints packed around it. Skull right. Large flints and chalk lumps in fill.
1. *Knife*, back curved, L 19.5cm.
2. *Iron buckle* with triangular plate, double and fastened by three bronze rivets, L 4.8cm.
1 and 2 at left hip.
3. *Iron spike* ?arrow or awl, 3cm of which has been embedded in wood, longitudinal grain, L 6.4cm. Under left forearm.
4. *Small iron buckle* with riveted plate, width 1.5cm. Under left pelvis.

GRAVE 150 (Figures 60, 83) M. 114.5°.
8ft × 2ft 9in × 1ft 10in (2.44m × 0.84m × 0.56m)
Remains of skull, left arm bent in, right hand on top femur, and legs.
1. *Iron pin* fragments, widening head, flat on top, L 2.8cm.
At neck.
2. Slender *knife*, curved back, L 14.8cm, with *iron ring* with traces of leather suspension strap, diam 3.3cm. Left waist.
3a. *Bronze plate fitting*, doubled-over edge of turned wooden bowl and fastened with two rivets; the bronze plate is scalloped at the lower outside edge and the lip of the vessel is slightly everted. The transverse grain inside is 2.5mm thick. 1.9cm × 1.3cm.
b. Similar *bronze plate*, two rivets, scalloped edge, and a clip wedged inside. 1.5cm × 1.5cm.
c. *Bronze clip*, L 1.3cm
d. Two very thin *bronze clips*. One illustrated.
4. *Bronze tag end*, conical with transverse rivet, L 2.2cm.
Nos. 3 and 4 together at feet.
Three sets of ?antler fragments (see Figure 83 A, B and C) each 5cm to 7cm deep, right side of skull, by right waist and over the lower legs. The fragments C were in two parallel lines about 14cm apart, presumably the ?antler-covered sides of a box. The bronze plates and clips (3a–d) are usually fixed to a wooden bowl

but as the bronze plates were found at the edges of the ?antler fragments and in line with them, they may be connected with the ?antler ?box.

GRAVE 151 (Figure 83) Adult, sub-adult or older Ju. 104°.
8ft 1in × 2ft 10in × 1ft 6in (2.46m × 0.86m × 0.46m)
Remains of two femurs only.
Sherd in fill (p 179). Medieval sherd in fill.

GRAVE 152 M, 35–45. 117°
6ft 6in × 3ft 10in × 1ft 1in (1.98m × 1.17m × 0.33m)
Rifled by local children; said to contain nothing but bones.

GRAVE 153 Ju 6–12. 70°.
4ft 3in × 2ft 8in × 7in (1.29m × 0.81m × 0.18m)
Rifled by local children; a few teeth.

GRAVE 154 Ju. 63°.
4ft 1in × 1ft 11in × 8in (1.24m × 0.58m × 0.2m)
Contained nothing.

GRAVE 155 (Figures 60, 83) F. 98°.
8ft 9in × 3ft 6in × 1ft 3in (2.67m × 1.07m × 0.38m)
No bones.
1. *Silver pin*, disc head, gold collar surrounded by filigree containing white material, probably composition, *en cabochon* with garnet centre. L 7.1cm.
2. *Beads*:
    Glass   a. 2 disc rust red
            b. 2 disc green
            c. 1 short 4-sided cylinder rust red
            d. Rust red fragments.
    1 and 2 at neck position.
3. *Knife* fragment, L 8.6cm.
4a. *Iron key* fragments, shafts with ring terminals on a ring. L 5.6cm, 5.7cm, 2.2cm and 1.8cm.
  b. *Bronze loop* with flattened ends riveted together, transverse line decoration.
    3 and 4 at left waist.
5. *Iron bar*, square-sectioned and bent at each end, grain of wood transversely on inside for complete length, and on outside of one end as well. L 7.6cm.
6. *Iron bar*, square-sectioned and each end bent at right angle, transverse grain of wood on ends and in middle, L 12cm. At diagonally opposite corners of the grave, item 5 at the head right corner, 7.5cm above the floor; item 6 at the foot, 15cm above the floor; probably coffin or bier fittings.
?Bone fragments by right foot.

GRAVE 156 (Figures 61, 83) M old. 126.5°.
9ft 3in × 2ft 9in × 11in (2.82m × 0.84m × 0.28m)
Little left of top half of body except skull fragments; hands on top of femurs.
1. *Spearhead*, lozenge-shaped blade, long split socket. An X-ray shows horizontal strips of a denser metal on the socket, L 23.6cm. At left hip, 11cm above floor.
2. *Knife*, X-ray shows a dense core with rounded end 3cm from the point – i.e. probably a thick core with thinner cutting edge welded on, L 21.1cm.
3. *Bronze buckle* loop, width 1.4cm.
4. *Iron shaft*, ?arrow or awl, point missing, square-sectioned with traces of wood on one end, L 5.6cm. Adhering to *iron tweezers*, L 9.4cm.
Items 2–4 at left waist.
5. *Two bronze ?shoe-lace tags*; double plates of key-hole shape, three rivets at squared end of one, two rivets on the other, L 2.8cm. At ankles.
6. *Pottery bottle*, wheel-thrown, irregular globular body, concave base, wide tubular neck, everted rim, four rows of chevron rouletting on the body. Grey fabric with large grits, buff exterior discoloured patchy red and black. Ht 19.5cm, diam mouth 7cm, diam base 7.5cm, maximum diam 15cm. At the foot.
Prehistoric sherd, R of chest.

GRAVE 157 (Figures 61–2, 83) F young adult. 125°.
7ft 6in × 2ft 6in × 11in (2.29m × 0.76m × 0.25m)
Remains of skull, arms and legs.
1. *Beads*:
    Shell   a. 1 corrugated edge.
    Glass   b. 1 disc yellow translucent (Colour Plate III B22 157/1b)
            c. 1 disc very light green translucent
            d. 1 disc black
            e. 2 biconical orange
            f. 1 disc blue, rust red marvered dots (Colour Plate IV D56 157/1f)
Fragment of glass bead and of two shell beads.
2. Three *silver slip-knot rings*, one fragmentary, diam 2cm.
3. *Iron pin*, spherical head of colourless glass with circumference groove. L 4.1cm.
1–3 at neck.
4. *Knife*, angled back, L 11.9cm.
5. Fragments of *iron key shaft*, L 7.4cm.
4 and 5 at left waist.
6a. *Iron key* fragments, hooked rod and looped shaft.
  b. Flat piece of *iron*, L 6.1cm ?key shaft.
  c. Three *iron key shafts* rusted together, L 7.6cm, with *bronze chain* and iron chain of S-shaped links. *Iron rod* inserted in looped rivet.
  d. *Key* with hooked ward, L 11cm.
  e. *Iron shaft*, with an S-looped terminal, L 8.4cm, and bone fragments.
  f. Four *iron keys* etc rusted together pendent from iron ring. Total L 12.5cm.
  g. *Iron key* fragment with looped end, L 5.7cm.
  h. Remains of hollow, *bone dome-shaped object* (Text Figure 21a), with edge at widest part recessed externally, i.e. a bone lid to a small cylindrical box. Maximum diam 3cm. The outside is stained green.
7. *Iron purse mount*, one edge straight, curved on opposite side with curling ends. X-ray shows no inlay. L 8.9cm.

6 and 7 along and under left femur.
8. *Pottery bottle*, wheel-thrown, squat, shouldered, girth grooves, narrow concave base, short straight neck, everted rim rounded on top; rouletting on upper part of a wide band of five-strand interlace of notched rows. Red ware, grey surfaces. Ht 22.5cm, maximum diam 16.5cm, diam mouth 6.2cm, diam base 7.3cm.
By left foot.

GRAVE 158 (Figures 62, 84) M? 123.5°.
8ft 3in × 3ft 3in × 1ft 10in (2.51m × 0.99m × 0.56m)
Remains of skull, arms and legs.
1. *Bronze buckle* loop and plate with iron tongue, the loop is oval with transverse scoring at intervals; the plate is triangular, tip missing, folded over and fastened on itself by two small dome-headed rivets; ring-and-dot punched border. Total L 4.1cm. Mid waist.
2. *Knife* angled back, tip missing. The long iron tang was covered with a segmented handle. The three major segments consist of bone. Thin iron plates limit the intervening double segments which were filled with other organic material wound round the tang. There is a thin lining of willow or poplar between the tang and its bone covering in the end segment (p 158). L 16.5cm. (Reconstruction Text Figure 23).
3. *Bronze pin* with flat disc head and adjacent moulding: L 4.3cm.
4. *Bronze buckle* loop and tongue, width 1.2cm, with remains of tiny plate and two rivets.
2–4 at left waist.

GRAVE 159 (Figures 62, 84) Ju. 100°.
6ft 3in × 2ft 1in × 9in (1.91m × 0.64m × 0.23m)
Remains of one arm and legs only.
1. *Knife*, tip broken, L 11.4cm. Left waist.
2. *Iron buckle* with doubled-over plate, two rivets, total L 2.5cm.
Mid waist.
3. Fragmentary *iron shaft* ?key; L 9.4cm. Right waist.

GRAVE 160 (Figures 62, 84) F over 45. 105°.
9ft 5in × 3ft 6in × 1ft 5in (2.87m × 1.07m × 0.43m)
Large flints and chalk lumps round edge of grave. Remains of skull, right arm and legs bent to right.
1. *Silver pin*, with double axe-shaped head, L 3.3cm.
2. *Beads*:
    Glass   a. 1 short cylinder rust red
            b. 3 short cylinder green
            c. 2 short cylinder white.
3. *Cabochon garnet pendant* of tapering rectangular shape with a serrated silver collar and remains of an outer frame of silver filigree wire. Silver back plate and fluted loop. L 1.8cm.
1–3 at neck.
4. *Knife*, curved back, L 12.2cm. Left waist.
5a. *Iron ring*, diam 2.5cm, with three broken key shafts pendent from it.
 b. *T-shaped iron key*, L 15cm, with iron ring at top containing small bronze ring.
 c. *Iron ring*, diam 2.5cm, with piece of the ivory ring (7) attached, and textile impressions. Iron shaft fragments.
 d. *Iron buckle loop*, circular with tongue, diam 2cm.
 e. *Iron rod* fragments, L 2.5cm, under femur.
Fragments 5a–e stretched from the knife downwards along the left femur.
6. *Small iron fragment*, triangular section, pointed at one end ?shoe-lace tag. L 1.6cm. On right foot.
7. *Ivory ring* fragments, diam c 10.2cm. By left knee.
8. *Glass palm cup* (Plate 9b) nearly complete, light blue-green, rim folded over outwards unevenly to depth of 1.8cm to 2.2cm, touching the vessel wall except at the rim where it is rolled and hollow and projects inwards. Punty mark on outside of base. Thick base, irregular ripple in wall. Small bubbles. Outside of wall surface more extensively weathered than inside. Ht 6.4cm, diam 12.2cm.
At foot.

GRAVE 161 (Figures 63, 84) F. 105°.
8ft 6in × 3ft × 1ft 3in (2.59m × 0.91m × 0.38m)
Entirely covered with large number of big flints. No bones.
1. *Silver pin*, head spherical with two slightly flattened sides in the centre of which are set two roughly cut garnets. Shaft is moulded below the head and swells about two-thirds of the way towards the tip, L 4.9cm. Mid chest position.
2. *Knife* fragment, angled back, L 12.2cm.
3. *Bronze and iron pin* (Plate 5e); a thin shaft of iron, covered with wood, the grain running lengthwise, and textile impression on the tip. Into the other end of this is fitted the hollow end of a cast bronze shaft decorated with girth moulding, ending in a human head with prominent chin, wearing a helmet with back neckguard in one with the crown. A curving line across the upper lip may be either a moustache or the lower edge of a visor. The helmet is surmounted by a pair of inward-curving horns with birds' head terminals. These were joined by a shaped bar with flat under surface suitable for suspension on a strap. A radiograph (Text Figure 14a) shows that the iron shaft is inlaid with two strips of a denser metal, probably silver or bronze, twisting spirally. A narrower shaft may be seen immediately below the bronze shaft, inserted in a socket in the main iron shaft. The textile fragment remains, but the tip of the pin has been lost. The object was lying in fragments in the grave, and was reconstructed with the help of a sketch made at the time of finding. The drawing Figure 63 was made at this early stage, and is a reliable

record of its original appearance. Original length 12.8cm.
2 and 3 at left waist.
4a. *Iron key* with two projections to ward, L 7.5cm.
  b. Iron shaft with looped end, key fragment, L 4.3cm.
  At right waist.
5. Dark blue translucent glass disc *bead*. By left femur position.
Fragment of animal bone above position of skull; radius of sheep – forehock of mutton?

GRAVE 162 (Figures 63, 84) M Ju. 95°.
5ft 4in × 2ft 4in × 1ft 1in (1.63m × 0.71m × 0.33m)
No bones – child.
1. *Iron nail*, disc head, L 2.3cm. At head of grave, 7.5cm above floor.
2. *Knife*, slender blade, curved back, L 12.4cm
3. *Knife*, back curved at tip, wide tang L 10.2cm.
2 and 3 at mid waist position.
4. *Whetstone*, square-sectioned bar, narrowing slightly to one end, a groove in one face. Cream in colour. 20.3cm × 2.5cm × 2.3cm (p 197). At left leg position.
5. *Whetstone*, broken end haunch-shaped, cream 5.1cm × 2.8cm × 1.8cm (p 197).
6. *Iron spike*, ?nail, arrow or awl, L 4.8cm.
5 and 6 at left foot position.
7. Small *iron ring* fragment, L 2cm. Near 4.

GRAVE 163 (Figures 63, 84) Ju. 88°.
5ft 6in × 2ft 6in × 1ft 4in (1.68m × 0.76m × 0.41m)
A rough ledge was left round the edge of the grave about 15cm wide and 7cm above the floor. No bones.
1. *Iron plate* and fragments, ?coffin fitting, 6cm × 4cm, and *nail shaft* or buckle tongue, L 2.4cm. Right of head.
2. *Knife*, curved back, L 15cm. Left waist.

GRAVE 164 (Figures 63, 84) F adult or sub-adult. 89.5°.
7ft 9in × 2ft 9in × 1ft 3in (2.36m × 0.84m × 0.38m)
Remains of legs only.
1. *Iron ring*, with remains of double piece of twine, diam 3.6cm.
2. *Yellow metal ring*, flat section, ring-and-dot stamps on both sides; a twist of yarn wound round at one point; diam 1.8cm; also a *yellow metal tab*, folded through the ring and the two ends joined by two rivets; the flattened parts decorated on the outer sides by a row of ring-and-dot stamps and the end nicked, L 2cm.
3. *Bronze double loop*, in shape of an 8, showing suspension wear at one end, and looped to an iron shaft at the other. Total L 2.7cm.
Small iron lump with trace of bronze, not illustrated.
4. *Iron key*, L-shaped ward, top folded over iron ring, L 26.9cm.
1–3 at top end of key (4) at left hip.

GRAVE 165 (Figure 84) M. 95°.
7ft 8in × 2ft 6in × 1ft 7in (2.34m × 0.76m × 0.48m)
Skull right, arms and legs. There were signs of animal occupation in this grave, which no doubt accounts for the position of some of the teeth in the pelvic region. No finds.

# Unassociated objects

**A reburial** (Figure 64, 1–3, 84)

Some bones from the disturbed burials reinterred in a small, roughly circular hole about 60cm in diameter in the disturbed area east of grave 129. These bones represent a minimum of six individuals, as follows: a. male aged over 35; b. female; c. new-born or full-term foetus, left forearm; d, e and f, shafts of long bones of three adults. There are also some fragments of cremated long bone, not necessarily human.
1. a and b. Five *clinch bolts* with disc head and diamond-shaped rove: (two illustrated). L of shank 4.6cm.
2. *Knife* fragment, L 6.9cm.
3. *Sherd*, fragment of strap handle with pierced holes, width 4.6cm. Probably medieval and indicative of date of reburial.

**Finds made before the beginning of the excavation.** (Figure 64)
4. Rust red glass disc *bead*.
5. Light green-blue glass barrel-shaped *bead* (Colour Plate III B39UN/5).
6. *Gold Visigothic coin pendant* (Plate 7a) coin transformed into a pendant by the addition of a fluted loop. Diam 1.8cm. (Gold analysis and coin report p 181).
7. *Sword*, traces of upper and lower guard. Pattern-welded, two zones herringbone. 87cm × 5cm. (p 25).
8. *Sword* traces of upper and lower guard. Pattern-welded, straight and diagonal lines, but the number of zones is not clear. L 90.9cm × 5cm.
9. *Silver-gilt square-headed brooch* (Text Figure 6c, Plate 6a), on the head an outer border of stamped ring-and-dot, except for the lower edge where there is a row of small stamped dots. Inside an inner beaded border there is another border of transverse ridges in pairs with a square garnet in each upper corner. A further border of reserved silver zig-zag and niello triangles frames a central panel of two ascending Style I animals in chip carving, each with a human head, above a circular garnet between a pair of triangular garnets. A disc-shaped garnet is inset on each lobe of the foot and a lozenge-shaped one in the centre: a mask is set above the central garnet, with a downward-curving bird's head with curling beak on each side. An outer border and an

inner border, together with the outline of the birds' heads, are marked with a single line of niello triangles in silver, one of the bird's head borders sweeping round further than the other. Further decorative moulding on the bow is hidden by the disc-on-bow which is a replica of a disc brooch and is fixed on by a rivet. On this disc a border of reserved silver zig-zag and niello encloses a field of three chip-carved animals consisting of a head and one limb, separated by three keystone garnets round a central disc of white material with a impressed circular channel which may have held a metal ring. The backing foil to the garnets is impressed with a fine grid (Avent 1977, No. 162, special boxed foils, 20 and 16 squares). The bronze pin at the back has a shield-shaped head to cover the iron spring. Cloth impression. L 9.5cm.
10. *Spear* fragment, parallel-sided blade, L 16cm.
11. *Knife* fragment, curve at back of tip.
After cleaning a join appeared along the middle of the blade indicating a separate welding on of the cutting edge. L 10.9cm.
12. *Knife* tip, L 4.3cm.

**Finds from the area where five graves were destroyed between graves 8 and 38** (Figure 65).

13. *Knife* tang, L 4.6cm.
14. *Sheet bronze belt fitting*; sub-triangular with slot near base; rivet in each corner, L 1.9cm.
15. Rust red glass biconical *bead*, yellow zig-zag trail (Colour Plate IV D09 UN/15).

**Loose finds in topsoil** (Figure 65).
16. *Bronze annular brooch*, perforation for pin, decoration by a few transverse grooves at pin hole and opposite, and borders of stamped triangles. Worn thin on two opposite sides halfway between the transverse lines. Diam 5.3cm.
17. Conical *spear ferrule*, unwelded, L 12.2cm.
18. *Knife*, back curving at tip, L 7.8cm.
19. *Knife* blade fragment, L 7.9cm.

*Unidentified knives* (Figure 65)
20. *Knife*, L 13.1cm.
21. *Knife*, L 12 cm.

# Concordance: Dover catalogue numbers and British Museum accession numbers

| Grave no. | Cat. no. | B.M. accession no. | Grave no. | Cat. no. | B.M. accession no. |
|---|---|---|---|---|---|
| B | 1 | 1963 11–8 744A | | 9 | 35 |
| | 2 | 744B | | 10 | 36–8 |
| C | 1 | 751 | 8 | 1 | 39 |
| | 2 | 747 | | 2 | 40 |
| | 3a | 752 | | 3 | 41 |
| | 3b | 750 | | 4 | not extant |
| | 4 | 748 | 9 | 1 | 42 |
| | 5a | 754A | | 2 | 43 |
| | 5b | 754B, 767A, B | | 3 | lost |
| | | | | 4 | 44 |
| | 5c | 753 | | 5 | 45 |
| | 5d | 756 | | | |
| | 6 | 749 | 10 | 1 | 47 |
| | 7 | 746 | | 2 | 46 |
| | | | | 3 | 48 |
| ?C?D | 8 | 755 | 11 | 1 | 49 |
| D | 1 | 757 | 12 | 1 | 50 |
| | 2 | 757 | | 2 | 53 |
| F | 1 | 758 | | 3 | 51 |
| | 2 | 760 | | 4 | 52 |
| | 3 | 759 | | 5 | 54 |
| | 4 | 761 | | 6 | 55 |
| | 5 | 764 | | | |
| | 6 | 765 | 13 | 1 | 806 |
| | 7 | 762 | | 2 | 807 |
| | 8 | 763 | | 3 | 58 |
| | | | | 4 | 57 |
| 1 | 1 | 145 | | 5 | 59 |
| | 2 | 2 | | 6 | 60 |
| | 3 | 3 | | 7 | 61 |
| | 4 | 4, 5 | | 8 | 62 |
| | 5 | 6 | | 9 | 56 |
| | 6 | 7 | | | |
| | 7 | 8 | 14 | 1 | 78 |
| | 8 | 9 | | 2 | 64A |
| | 9 | 10 | | 3 | 64–8 |
| | 10a, b | 11–13 | | 4 | 69 |
| | 10c | 15 | | 5 | 70 |
| | 11 | 14 | | 6 | 71 |
| | 12 | 14 | | 7 | 72 |
| | | | | 8 | 808 |
| 3 | 1 | 16 | | 9 | 73 |
| | 2 | 16 | | 10 | 74 |
| 4 | 1 | 17 | | 11 | 76 |
| | 2 | 18 | | 12 | 75 |
| | 3 | 769 | | 13 | 77 |
| 5 | 1 | 19 | | 14 | 79 |
| | 2 | 20, 22 | 15 | 1 | 80 |
| | 3 | 21 | | 2 | 81 |
| | 4 | 23 | | 3 | 82 |
| 6 | 1 | 24 | | 4 | 83 |
| | 2 | 25 | | 5 | 803 |
| | 3 | 26 | | 6 | 85 |
| | 4 | 27 | | 7 | 84 |
| | 5 | 28, 30–1 | 16 | 1 | 86 |
| | 6 | 32 | 17 | 1 | lost |
| | 7 | 33 | | | |
| | 8a | 34 | 18 | 1 | 809 |

## GRAVE CATALOGUE

| Grave no. | Cat. no. | B.M. accession no. | Grave no. | Cat. no. | B.M. accession no. |
|---|---|---|---|---|---|
|  | 2 | 87 |  | 9 | 146, 148 |
|  | 3 | 88 |  | 10 | 147 |
|  | 4 | 89 |  | 11 | 149 |
|  | 5 | 90–6 |  | 12 | 150 |
| 19 | 1 | 97 | 30 | 1 | 155 |
| 20 | 1 | 98 |  | 2 | 156 |
|  | 2 | 99 |  | 3 | 157 |
|  | 3 | 100 |  | 4 | 158 |
|  | 4 | 1 |  | 5 | 159 |
|  | 5 | 102 |  | 6 | 160 |
|  | 6 | 811 |  | 7 | 161 |
|  | 7 | 103 |  | 8 | 162 |
|  | 8 | 104 | 32 | 1 | 163 |
|  | 9 | 105 |  | 2 | 164 |
|  | 10 | 106 |  | 3 | 165 |
|  | 11 | 107 |  | 4 | 166 |
|  | 12a, b | 113 |  | 5 | 167 |
|  | 12c | 108 |  | 6a | 168 |
|  | 13 | 113 |  | 6b | 172 |
|  | 14 | 112 |  | 7 | 169 |
|  | 15 | 111 |  | 8a | 171 |
|  | 16 | 109 |  | 8b | 170 |
|  | 17 | 115 | 33 | 1 | 173 |
|  | 18 | 110 |  | 2 | 174 |
|  | 19 | 114 |  | 3 | 175 |
| 21 | 1 | 116 |  | 4 | 176 |
|  | 2 | 117 |  | 5 | 177 |
|  | 3 | 118 | 34 | 1 | 813 |
|  | 4 | 812 |  | 2 | 179 |
| 22 | 1 | 119 |  | 3 | 180 |
|  | 2 | 120 | 35 | 1 | 181 |
|  | 3 | 124 |  | 2 | 182 |
|  | 4 | 121 |  | 3 | 183 |
|  | 5 | 122 |  | 4 | 184 |
|  | 6 | 123 |  | 5 | 185 |
| 23 | 1 | 125 |  | 6 | 186 |
|  | 2 | lost |  | 7a | 189 |
|  | 3 | 126 |  | 7b | 188 |
|  | 4 | 127 |  | 7c | lost |
| 27 | 1 | 129 |  | 8 | 187 |
|  | 2 | 130 | 36 | 1 | 190 |
|  | 3 | 128 | 37 | 1 | 191 |
|  | 4 | 131 | 38 | 1 | 192 |
|  | 5 | 132 |  | 2 | 193 |
|  | 6 | 133 |  | 3 | 194 |
|  | 7 | 800 |  | 4 | 194 |
|  | 8 | 799 |  | 5 | 195 |
| 28 | 1 | 801 |  | 6 | 197 |
|  | 2 | 802 |  | 7 | 198 |
|  | 3 | 134 |  | 8 | 196 |
|  | 4 | 135 |  | 9a, b | 199–200 |
|  | 5 | 136 |  | 9c | 201 |
|  | 6 | 137 |  | 9d | 202 |
|  | 7 | 138 |  | 9e | 206 |
|  | 8 | 139 |  | 9f | 204 |
|  | 9 | 140 |  | 9g | 205 |
| 29 | 1 | 141 |  | 9h | 200 |
|  | 2 | 142 |  | 10 | 203 |
|  | 3 | 143 |  | 11 | 207 |
|  | 4 | 142 |  | 12 | 269 |
|  | 5 | 151 |  | 13 | 208 |
|  | 6 | 144 | 39 | 1 | 270 |
|  | 7 | 153 |  | 2 | 271 |
|  | 8 | 101 |  | 3 | 272 |

| Grave no. | Cat. no. | B.M. accession no. | Grave no. | Cat. no. | B.M. accession no. |
|---|---|---|---|---|---|
|    | 4  | 273 |    | 3   | 333 |
| 40 | 1  | 274 |    | 4   | 334 |
|    |    |     |    | 5a  | 335 |
| 41 | 1  | 275 |    | 5b  | 336 |
|    | 2  | 275 |    | 5c  | 337 |
|    | 3  | 281 |    | 5d  | 337 |
|    | 4  | 276 |    | 5e  | 339 |
|    | 5  | 277 |    | 5f  | 339 |
|    | 6  | 278 |    | 5g  | 338 |
|    |    | a = G, b = D, c = F, d = E, e = B, f = A, g = C. | 56 | 1 | 340 |
|    |    |     |    | 2   | 341 |
|    |    |     |    | 3   | 342 |
|    | 7  | 279 |    | 4   | 343 |
| 42 | 1  | 280 |    | 5a, b | 344 |
|    | 2  | 283 |    | 5c  | 488 |
|    | 3  | 282 |    | 6   | 345 |
|    | 4  | 284 |    | 7   | 350 |
|    |    |     |    | 8   | 347 |
| 43 | 1  | 288 |    | 9   | 349 |
|    | 2  | 815 |    | 10  | 348 |
|    | 3  | 285 |    | 11a | 350 |
|    | 4  | 286 |    | 11b | 346 |
|    | 5  | 287 | 57 | 1   | 351 |
|    |    |     |    | 2   | 352 |
| 44 | 1  | 289 |    | 3   | 353 |
|    | 2  | 291 |    | 4a  | 354 |
|    | 3  | 290 |    | 4b  | 355 |
|    | 4  | 292 |    | 4c  | 356 |
|    |    |     |    | 5a  | 357 |
| 46 | 1  | 293 |    | 5b  | 357 |
|    | 2  | 816 | 58 | 1   | 358 |
|    | 3  | 295 |    | 2a, b | 359–60 |
| 48 | 1  | 296 |    | 2c  | 361 |
|    | 2  | 297 |    | 2d  | 362 |
|    | 3  | 300 |    |     |     |
|    | 4  | 298 | 59 | 1   | 364A |
|    | 5  | 301 |    | 2   | 364B |
|    | 6  | 302 |    | 3   | 819 |
|    | 7  | 303 |    | 4   | 365–70 |
|    | 8  | 304 |    |     |     |
|    | 9  | 305 | 60 | 1   | 371 |
|    | 10 | 306 |    | 2   | 372 |
|    | 11 | 307 |    | 3   | 373 |
|    | 12 | 299 |    | 4   | 374 |
|    | 13 | 817 |    | 5a  | 375 |
|    | 14 | 308 |    | 5b  | 376 |
| 49 | 1  | 309 |    | 6, 7 | 377–82 |
|    |    |     |    | 8   | 383 |
| 50 | 1  | 310 |    | 9   | 384 |
|    | 2  | 311 |    | 10  | 820 |
|    | 3  | 312 |    | 11  | 385 |
|    | 4  | 313 |    | 12  | 821 |
| 52 | 1  | 314 | 61 | 1   | 386 |
|    | 2  | 315 |    | 2   | 387 |
|    |    |     |    | 3   | 822 |
| 53 | 1  | 316 |    |     |     |
|    | 2  | 317 | 62 | 1   | 388 |
|    | 3  | 318 |    | 2   | 389–90 |
|    | 4  | 319 |    | 3   | 391 |
|    | 5  | 320 |    | 4   | 392 |
|    | 6  | 322 |    | 5   | 393 |
|    | 7  | 321 | 63 | 1   | 394 |
| 54 | 1  | 326 |    | 2   | 395 |
|    | 2  | 328 |    | 3   | 396 |
|    | 3  | 329 |    | 4   | 397 |
| 55 | 1  | 330–1 | 64 | 1 | 398 |
|    | 2  | 332 |    |     |     |

# GRAVE CATALOGUE

| Grave no. | Cat. no. | B.M. accession no. | Grave no. | Cat. no. | B.M. accession no. |
|---|---|---|---|---|---|
| 65 | 1 | 399 | | 4 | 459 |
| | 2 | 400 | | 5 | lost |
| | 3 | 401, 407 | 90 | 1 | 460 |
| | 4 | 402 | | 2 | 461 |
| | 5 | 405 | | 3 | 462 |
| | 6 | 403 | | 4 | 463 |
| | 7 | 404 | | | |
| | 8 | 406 | 91 | 1 | 464 |
| | | | | 2 | 465 |
| 66 | 1 | 408 | | 3 | 468A |
| | 2 | 409 | | 4 | 468B |
| | 3 | 410 | | 5 | 469 |
| | 4 | 411 | | 6 | 467 |
| | | | | 7 | 466 |
| 67 | 1 | 824 | | | |
| | 2 | 412 | 92 | 1 | 826 |
| | 3 | 413 | | 2 | 470 |
| | 4 | 413 | | 3 | 471–3 |
| | 5 | 414 | | 4 | 474 |
| | 6 | 415 | | 5 | 475 |
| | | | | 6 | 476 |
| 71 | 1 | 416 | | 7 | 477 |
| | 2 | 417 | | | |
| | 3 | 418 | 93 | 1 | 478 |
| | 4 | 419 | | 2 | 479 |
| | 5 | 420 | | 3 | lost |
| | 6 | 421 | | 4 | 480 |
| | 7 | 422 | | 5a | 481 |
| | 8 | 423, 766 | | 5b | 482 |
| | | | | 6 | 483 |
| 74 | 1 | 424 | | 7 | 484 |
| | 2 | 425 | | 8 | 490 |
| | | | | 9 | 489 |
| 75 | 1 | 426 | | 10a, b | 485 |
| | 2 | 427 | | 10c | 486 |
| | 3 | 428–30 | | 10d | 487 |
| | 4 | 431 | | | |
| | 5 | 432 | 94a | 1 | 491 |
| | | | | 2 | 492 |
| 76 | 1 | 433 | | | |
| | | | 94b | 1 | 493 |
| 77 | 1 | 434 | | 2 | 494 |
| | | | | 3 | 495 |
| 78 | 1 | 435 | | 4 | 496 |
| | 2 | 436 | | | |
| | | | 95 | 1 | 497 |
| 79 | 1 | 437 | | 2 | 498 |
| 80 | 1 | 438 | | | |
| | | | 96a | 1 | 499 |
| 81 | 1 | 439 | | 2 | 500 |
| | 2 | 440A | | 3 | 501 |
| | 3 | 440B | | 4 | 502 |
| | 4a | 441A | | 5 | 503 |
| | 4b | 441B | | 6 | 504 |
| 82 | 1 | 442 | | | |
| | 2 | 443 | 96b | 7 | 506 |
| | | | | 8 | 507 |
| 83 | 1 | 445 | | 9 | 508 |
| | 2 | 447 | | 10 | 509 |
| | 3 | 446 | | | |
| | 4 | 448 | 97 | 1 | 510 |
| | 5 | 449 | 98 | 1 | 511 |
| | 6 | 450 | | 2 | 512 |
| | | | | 3 | 513 |
| 84 | 1 | 451 | | 4a | 514 |
| | 2 | 452 | | 4b | 515 |
| | 3 | 453–4 | | 4c | 516 |
| | | | | 5 | 517 |
| 85 | 1 | 294 | | 6 | 518 |
| | 2 | 455 | | | |
| | | | 100 | 1 | 519 |
| 87 | 1 | 456 | | | |
| | 2 | 457 | 101 | 1 | 520 |
| | 3 | 458 | | | |

| Grave no. | Cat. no. | B.M. accession no. | Grave no. | Cat. no. | B.M. accession no. |
|---|---|---|---|---|---|
| 103 | 1 | 521 | 124 | 1 | 579 |
|  | 2 | 522 |  | 2 | 580 |
|  | 3 | 522 |  | 3 | 581 |
| 104 | 1 | 523 |  | 4 | 831 |
| 105 | 1 | 524 | 125 | 1 | 582 |
| 106 | 1 | 525 | 126 | 1 | 583 |
| 107 | 1 | 526 | 127 | 1 | 584 |
|  | 2 | 528–31 |  | 2 | 585 |
|  | 3 | lost |  | 3a | 586c |
|  | 4 | 527, 534 |  | 3b | 586a |
|  | 5a | 534 |  | 3c | 586b |
|  | 5b | 534 |  | 4 | 587 |
|  | 6 | 532 | 128 | 1 | 588 |
|  | 7 | 533 |  | 2 | 589 |
| 108 | 1 | 536 |  | 3 | 590 |
|  | 2 | 535 | 129 | 1 | 608 |
| 109 | 1 | 537 |  | 2 | 591 |
|  | 2 | 538 |  | 3 | 834 |
|  | 3 | 539 |  | 4 | 592 |
| 110 | 1 | 540 |  | 5 | 593 |
|  | 2 | 541 |  | 6 | 594 |
|  | 3 | 542 |  | 7 | 595 |
|  | 4 | 543 |  | 8 | 596 |
|  | 5 | 545A |  | 9 | 597 |
|  | 6 | 544 |  | 10a | 598 |
|  | 7 | 546 |  | 10b | 600 |
|  | 8 | 545B |  | 10c | 327 |
|  | 9 | 547 |  | 10d | 599 |
|  | 10 | 788 | 130 | 1 | 601 |
|  | 11 | 789 | 131 | 1 | 602 |
|  | 12 | 548 |  | 2 | 603 |
|  | 13 | 549 |  | 3 | 604 |
| 111 | 1 | 550 |  | 4 | 606 |
|  | 2 | 551 |  | 5a | 605A |
|  |  |  |  | 5b | 605B |
| 113 | 1 | 552 |  | 6 | 607 |
|  | 2 | 553 | 132 | 1 | 609 |
|  | 3 | 554 |  | 2 | 610 |
|  | 4 | 555 |  | 3 | 611 |
|  | 5 | 556–8 |  | 4 | 612 |
|  | 6 | 559 | 133 | 1a | 613 |
|  | 7 | 560 |  | 1b, c | 614 |
| 114 | 1 | 561 |  | 2 | 614 |
|  | 2 | 562 |  | 3 | 615 |
|  | 3a | 563 |  | 4 | 616 |
|  | 3b | 564 | 134 | 1 | 617 |
|  | 3c | 565 |  | 2 | 618 |
|  | 3d | 566 |  | 3 | 619 |
|  | 3e | 567 |  | 4 | 620 |
|  | 4 | 568 |  | 5 | 621 |
| 115 | 1 | 569 |  | 6 | 622 |
| 116 | 1 | 570 |  | 7 | 623 |
| 117 | 1 | 571 | 135 | 1 | 624 |
| 119 | 1 | 572 |  | 2 | 625 |
|  |  |  |  | 3 | 626 |
| 120 | 1 | 574 |  | 4 | 627 |
|  | 2 | 573 |  | 5 | 628 |
| 121 | 1 | 575 |  | 6 | 629 |
|  | 2 | 576 |  | 7 | 630 |
| 122 | 1 | 577 | 136 | 1 | 631 |
|  |  |  |  | 2 | 632 |
| 123 | 1 | 578 |  | 3 | 633 |

# GRAVE CATALOGUE

| Grave no. | Cat. no. | B.M. accession no. | Grave no. | Cat. no. | B.M. accession no. |
|---|---|---|---|---|---|
| 137 | 1 | 640 | 150 | 1 | 685 |
|  | 2 | 635 |  | 2 | 686 |
|  | 3 | 636 |  | 3a | 687b |
|  | 4 | 639 |  | 3b | 687a |
|  | 5 | 637 |  | 3c | 687c |
|  | 6 | 638 |  | 3d | 687c |
|  | 7 | 641 |  | 4 | 688 |
| 138 | 1 | 643 | 155 | 1 | 689 |
|  | 2 | 642A |  | 2 | 690 |
|  | 3 | 642B |  | 3 | 691 |
|  | 4 | 642 |  | 4a | 692A, 693 |
|  | 5 | 642E, F |  | 4b | 692B |
|  | 6 | 642C |  | 5 | 694 |
|  | 7 | 657B |  | 6 | 695 |
|  | 8 | 642D | 156 | 1 | 697 |
|  | 9 | 642u |  | 2 | 698 |
|  | 10 | 642b |  | 3 | 699 |
|  | 11 | 642e, k, o, q, v. |  | 4 | 700 |
|  | 12 | 644 |  | 5 | 701–2 |
|  | 13 | 645 |  | 6 | 696 |
| 139 | 1 | 647 | 157 | 1 | 704 |
|  | 2 | 647 |  | 2 | 705 |
|  | 3 | 648 |  | 3 | 706 |
|  | 4 | 651 |  | 4 | 707 |
|  | 5 | 646 |  | 5 | 708 |
|  | 6 | 649 |  | 6a-g | 709 |
| 140 | 1 | 650 |  | 6h | 843 |
| 141 | 1 | 652 |  | 7 | 710 |
|  | 2 | 653 |  | 8 | 703 |
|  | 3 | 657A | 158 | 1 | 712 |
|  | 4 | 656b |  | 2 | 713 |
|  | 5 | 654 |  | 3 | 714 |
|  | 6 | 655 |  | 4 | 715 |
|  | 7 | 656a | 159 | 1 | 716 |
|  | 8 | 657 |  | 2 | 717 |
| 142 | 1 | 658 |  | 3 | 718 |
|  | 2 | 659 | 160 | 1 | 720 |
|  | 3 | 660 |  | 2 | 721 |
| 143 | 1 | 661 |  | 3 | 722–3 |
| 144 | 1 | 662 |  | 4 | 724 |
|  | 2 | 663 |  | 5a | 725B |
|  | 3 | 664 |  | 5b | 725C |
|  | 4 | 665 |  | 5c | 725F |
|  | 5 | 666 |  | 5d | 725A |
|  | 6 | 667 |  | 5e | 725D |
| 145 | 1 | 668 |  | 6 | 726 |
|  | 2 | 669 |  | 7 | 727 |
|  | 3 | 670 |  | 8 | 728 |
| 146 | 1 | 671 | 161 | 1 | 729 |
|  | 2 | 672 |  | 2 | 730 |
| 147 | 1 | 673 |  | 3 | 733 |
|  | 2 | 674 |  | 4 | 731 |
|  | 3 | 675 |  | 5 | 732 |
|  | 4 | 676 | 162 | 1 | 734 |
|  | 5 | 677 |  | 2 | 735 |
| 148 | 1 | 678 |  | 3 | 736 |
|  | 2 | 679 |  | 4 | 739 |
|  | 3 | 680 |  | 5 | 740 |
| 149 | 1 | 681 |  | 6 | 737 |
|  | 2 | 682 |  | 7 | 738 |
|  | 3 | 683 | 163 | 1 | 741 |
|  | 4 | 684 |  | 2 | 742 |
|  |  |  | 164 | 1 | 743B |

| Grave no. | Cat. no. | B.M. accession no. | Grave no. | Cat. no. | B.M. accession no. |
|---|---|---|---|---|---|
|  | 2, 3 | 743D |  | 10 | 768 |
|  | 4 | 743A, C |  | 11 | 770 |
| Reburial | 1 | 745 |  | 12 | 771 |
|  | 2 | 780 |  | 13 | 775A |
|  | 3 | lost |  | 14 | 775B |
|  |  |  |  | 15 | 775C |
| Unassociated | 4 | 767 |  | 16 | 773 |
|  | 5 | 767 |  | 17 | 777 |
|  | 6 | 790 |  | 18 | 779 |
|  | 7 | 782 |  | 19 | 778 |
|  | 8 | 783 |  | 20 | 846 |
|  | 9 | 776 |  | 21 | 847 |

TABLE LV GRAVE CONTENTS

| Grave number | B | C | D | E | F | 1 | 2 | 3 | 4 | 5 | 6 | 7 | 8 | 9 | 10 | 11 | 12 | 13 | 14 | 15 | 16 | 17 | 18 | 19 | 20 | 21 | 22 | 23 | 24 | 25 | 26 | 27 | 28 | 29 |
|---|---|---|---|---|---|---|---|---|---|---|---|---|---|---|---|---|---|---|---|---|---|---|---|---|---|---|---|---|---|---|---|---|---|---|
| Sword |  | X |  |  |  |  |  |  | X |  |  |  |  |  |  |  |  |  |  |  |  |  |  |  | X |  | X |  |  |  |  |  |  |  |
| Spearhead |  | X |  |  |  |  |  |  | X | X |  |  | X | X | X |  |  |  |  |  |  |  |  |  | X |  | X |  |  |  |  |  |  |  |
| Ferrule |  | X |  |  |  |  |  |  |  |  |  |  |  |  |  |  |  |  |  |  |  |  |  |  | X |  | X |  |  |  |  |  |  |  |
| Arrow |  |  |  |  |  |  |  |  |  |  |  |  |  |  |  |  |  |  |  |  |  |  |  |  |  |  |  |  |  |  |  |  |  |  |
| Seax |  |  |  |  |  |  |  |  |  |  |  |  |  |  |  |  |  |  |  |  |  |  |  |  |  |  |  |  |  |  |  |  |  |  |
| Shield |  | X |  |  |  |  |  | X |  | X |  |  |  |  |  |  |  |  |  |  |  |  |  |  |  |  |  |  |  |  |  | X |  |  |
| Square-headed brooch |  |  |  |  |  |  |  |  |  |  |  |  |  |  |  |  |  | X |  |  |  |  |  |  | X |  |  |  |  |  |  |  |  |  |
| Small-long brooch |  |  |  |  |  |  |  |  |  |  |  |  |  |  |  |  |  | X |  |  |  |  |  |  |  |  |  |  |  |  |  |  |  |  |
| Kentish disc brooch |  |  |  | X | X |  |  |  |  |  |  |  |  |  |  |  |  |  | X |  |  |  |  |  |  |  |  |  |  |  |  |  |  | X |
| Frankish disc brooch |  |  |  |  |  |  |  |  |  |  |  |  |  |  |  |  |  |  |  |  |  |  |  | X |  |  | X |  |  |  |  |  |  |  |
| Saucer brooch |  |  |  |  |  |  |  |  |  |  |  |  |  |  |  |  |  |  |  |  |  |  |  |  |  |  |  |  |  |  |  |  |  |  |
| Button brooch |  |  |  |  |  |  |  |  |  |  |  |  |  |  |  |  |  |  |  |  |  |  |  |  |  |  |  |  |  |  |  |  |  |  |
| Annular brooch |  |  |  |  |  |  |  |  |  |  |  |  |  |  |  |  | X |  | X |  |  |  |  |  |  |  |  |  |  |  |  |  |  |  |
| Coin Pendant |  |  |  |  |  |  |  |  |  |  |  |  |  |  |  |  |  |  |  |  |  |  |  |  |  |  |  |  |  |  |  |  |  | X |
| Au bracteate |  |  |  |  | X |  |  |  |  |  |  |  |  |  |  |  |  |  |  |  |  |  |  |  | X |  |  |  |  |  |  |  |  | X |
| Ag disc pendant |  |  |  |  |  |  |  |  |  |  |  |  |  |  |  |  |  |  |  |  |  |  |  |  |  |  |  |  |  |  |  |  |  |  |
| Ag misc. pendant |  |  |  |  |  |  |  |  |  |  |  |  |  |  |  |  |  |  |  |  |  |  |  |  |  |  |  |  |  |  |  |  |  | X |
| Garnet pendant |  |  |  |  |  |  |  |  |  |  | X |  |  |  |  |  |  |  |  |  |  |  |  |  |  |  |  |  |  |  |  |  |  | X |
| Misc. pendant |  |  |  |  | X |  |  |  |  |  |  |  |  |  |  |  |  |  |  |  |  |  |  |  |  |  |  |  |  |  |  |  |  |  |
| Beads | X |  |  | X | X |  |  |  |  |  | X |  |  |  |  |  | X | X | X | X |  | X |  |  | X |  | X | X |  |  |  |  |  | X |
| Pin |  |  |  | X | X |  |  |  |  |  | X |  |  | X |  |  |  |  |  |  |  | X |  |  | X |  |  |  |  |  |  |  |  |  |
| Bracelet |  |  |  |  | X |  |  |  |  |  |  |  |  |  |  |  |  |  |  | X |  |  |  |  | X |  |  |  |  |  |  |  |  |  |
| Finger ring |  |  |  | X |  |  |  |  |  |  |  |  |  |  |  |  |  |  |  |  |  |  |  |  |  |  |  |  |  |  |  |  |  |  |
| Ae buckle shield-on-tongue |  | X |  |  |  |  |  |  | X |  |  |  |  |  |  |  |  |  | X |  |  |  |  |  | X |  |  |  |  |  | X |  |  |  |
| Ae buckle small |  |  |  |  |  |  |  |  |  |  |  |  | X |  |  |  |  |  |  |  |  |  |  |  |  | X |  |  |  |  |  |  |  |  |
| Ae buckle misc. |  |  |  |  |  |  |  |  |  |  |  |  |  |  |  |  |  |  |  |  |  |  |  |  |  |  |  |  |  |  |  |  |  |  |
| Fe buckle |  | X |  |  |  |  |  |  |  |  | X |  | X | X |  | X |  | X |  |  | X |  |  |  |  |  | X |  |  |  |  |  |  |  |
| Belt or strap mount |  |  |  |  |  |  |  |  |  |  |  |  |  |  |  |  |  | X |  |  |  |  |  |  |  |  |  |  |  |  |  |  |  |  |
| Lace tag |  |  |  |  |  |  |  |  |  |  |  |  |  |  |  |  |  |  |  |  |  |  |  |  |  |  |  |  |  |  |  |  |  |  |
| Wooden belt |  |  |  |  |  |  |  |  |  |  |  |  |  |  |  |  |  |  |  | X |  |  |  |  |  |  |  |  |  |  |  |  |  |  |
| Pottery |  |  |  |  |  |  |  |  |  |  |  |  |  |  |  |  |  |  |  |  |  |  |  |  |  |  |  |  |  |  |  |  |  |  |
| Glass |  |  |  |  |  |  |  |  |  |  | X |  |  |  |  |  |  |  |  | X |  |  |  |  | X |  | X |  |  |  |  |  |  |  |
| Coffin |  |  |  |  |  |  |  |  |  |  |  |  |  |  |  |  |  |  |  |  |  |  |  |  | X |  |  |  |  |  |  |  |  |  |
| Wooden box |  |  |  | X |  |  |  |  |  |  |  |  |  |  |  |  |  |  |  |  |  |  |  |  | X |  |  |  |  |  |  |  |  | X |
| Ae bowl |  |  |  |  |  |  |  |  |  |  |  |  |  |  |  |  |  |  |  |  |  |  |  |  |  |  |  |  |  |  |  |  |  |  |
| Bucket |  |  |  |  |  |  |  |  |  |  |  |  |  |  |  |  |  |  |  |  |  |  |  |  |  |  |  |  |  |  |  | X |  |  |
| Wood vessel |  |  |  |  |  |  |  |  |  |  |  |  |  |  |  |  |  |  |  |  |  |  | X |  |  |  |  |  |  |  |  |  |  | X |
| Bone box |  |  |  |  |  |  |  |  |  |  |  |  |  |  |  |  |  |  |  |  |  |  |  |  |  |  |  |  |  |  |  |  |  |  |
| Ae work box |  |  |  |  |  |  |  |  |  |  |  |  |  |  |  |  |  |  |  |  |  |  |  |  |  |  |  |  |  |  |  |  |  |  |
| Bone lid |  |  |  |  |  |  |  |  |  |  |  |  |  |  |  |  |  |  |  |  |  |  |  |  |  |  |  |  |  |  |  |  |  |  |
| Sharpening steel |  |  |  |  |  |  |  |  |  |  |  |  |  |  |  |  |  |  |  |  |  |  |  |  |  |  |  |  |  |  |  |  |  |  |
| Awl |  |  |  |  |  |  |  |  |  |  |  |  | X |  |  |  |  |  |  |  |  |  |  |  |  |  |  |  |  |  |  |  |  |  |
| ?Mattock |  |  |  |  |  |  |  |  |  |  |  |  |  |  |  |  |  |  |  |  |  |  |  |  |  |  |  |  |  |  |  |  |  |  |
| Fire-steel |  |  |  |  |  |  |  |  |  |  |  |  |  |  |  |  |  |  |  |  |  |  |  |  |  |  |  |  |  |  |  |  |  |  |
| Hone |  |  |  |  |  |  |  |  |  |  |  |  |  |  |  |  |  |  |  |  |  |  |  |  |  |  |  |  |  |  |  |  |  |  |
| Fe weaving batten |  |  |  |  |  |  |  |  |  |  |  |  |  |  |  |  |  |  |  |  |  |  |  |  | X |  |  |  |  |  |  |  |  |  |
| Weaving pick |  |  |  |  |  |  |  |  |  |  |  |  |  |  |  |  |  |  |  |  |  |  |  |  |  |  |  |  |  |  |  |  |  |  |
| Ae needle |  |  |  |  |  |  |  |  |  |  |  |  |  |  |  |  |  |  |  |  |  |  |  |  |  |  |  |  |  |  |  |  |  |  |
| Spindle whorl |  |  |  |  |  |  |  |  |  |  | X |  |  |  |  |  |  |  |  |  |  |  |  |  | X |  |  |  |  |  |  |  |  |  |
| Shears |  |  |  |  |  |  |  |  |  |  |  |  |  |  |  |  |  |  |  |  |  |  |  |  |  |  |  |  |  |  |  |  |  |  |
| Knife |  | X |  | X |  |  |  |  | X | X |  | X | X | X |  | X | X | X | X | X | X | X |  |  | X | X | X | X |  |  |  | X | X | X |
| Key |  |  |  | X | X |  |  |  |  |  | X |  |  |  |  |  |  | X | X |  |  | X |  |  | X |  | X |  |  |  |  | X | X |  |
| Girdle-hanger |  |  |  |  |  |  |  |  |  |  |  |  |  |  |  |  |  |  | X |  |  |  |  |  | X |  |  |  |  |  |  | X |  |  |
| Tweezers |  |  |  |  |  |  |  |  |  |  |  |  |  |  |  |  |  |  |  |  |  |  |  |  |  |  |  |  |  |  |  |  |  |  |
| Spoon |  |  |  |  |  |  |  |  |  |  |  |  |  |  |  |  |  |  |  |  |  |  |  |  |  |  |  |  |  |  |  |  |  |  |
| Fe diamond |  |  |  | X |  |  |  |  |  |  |  |  |  |  |  | X |  | X |  |  |  |  |  |  | X |  |  |  |  |  |  | X |  |  |
| Ivory ring |  |  |  | X |  |  |  |  |  |  |  |  |  |  |  |  |  |  |  |  |  |  |  |  |  |  |  |  |  |  |  |  |  |  |
| Ag ring |  |  |  |  |  |  |  |  |  |  |  |  |  |  |  |  |  |  |  |  |  |  |  |  |  |  |  |  |  |  |  |  |  | X |
| Comb |  |  |  |  |  |  |  |  |  |  |  |  |  |  |  |  |  |  |  |  |  |  |  |  | X |  |  |  |  |  |  |  |  |  |
| Ae balance |  | X |  |  |  |  |  |  |  |  |  |  |  |  |  |  |  |  |  |  |  |  |  |  |  |  |  |  |  |  |  |  |  |  |
| ?Lyre |  |  |  |  |  |  |  |  |  |  |  |  |  |  |  |  |  |  |  |  |  |  |  |  |  |  |  |  |  |  |  |  |  |  |
| Amulet etc. | X | X |  |  |  |  |  |  |  |  | X |  |  |  | X |  |  |  | X | X |  |  |  |  |  |  |  |  |  |  |  |  |  |  |
| Ae misc |  |  |  |  |  |  |  |  |  |  |  |  |  |  |  |  |  |  |  | X |  |  |  |  |  |  |  |  |  |  |  |  |  |  |
| Fe misc |  |  |  |  |  |  |  |  |  | X |  |  |  |  | X |  |  |  |  |  |  |  |  | X |  |  |  |  |  |  |  |  |  |  |
| Misc. |  |  |  |  |  |  |  |  |  |  |  |  |  |  |  |  |  |  |  |  |  |  |  |  |  |  |  |  |  |  |  |  |  |  |
| Misc. (Fill) |  |  |  |  |  |  |  |  |  |  |  |  |  |  |  |  |  |  |  |  |  |  |  |  |  |  |  |  |  |  |  |  |  |  |

TABLE LV GRAVE CONTENTS

| | Grave number | 30 | 31 | 32 | 33 | 34 | 35 | 36 | 37 | 38 | 39 | 40 | 41 | 42 | 43 | 44 | 45 | 46 | 47 | 48 | 49 | 50 | 51 | 52 | 53 | 54 | 55 | 56 | 57 | 58 | 59 |
|---|---|---|---|---|---|---|---|---|---|---|---|---|---|---|---|---|---|---|---|---|---|---|---|---|---|---|---|---|---|---|---|
| Weapons | Sword | | | X | | | | | | | | | X | | | | | | | | | | | | | | | X | | | |
| | Spearhead | | | X | | | | | | | X | | X | | | | | | | X | | | | | | | | X | X | | |
| | Ferrule | | | | | | | | | | | | X | | | | | | | | | | | | | | | X | | | |
| | Arrow | | | | | | | | | | | | | | | | | | | | | | | | | | | | X | | |
| | Seax | | | | | | | | | | | | | | | | | | | | | | | | | | | | | | |
| | Shield | | | | | | | | | X | | | | | | | | | | | | | | | | | | X | | | |
| Jewellery | Square-headed brooch | | | | | | | | | | | | | | | | | | | | | | | | | | | | | | |
| | Small-long brooch | | | | | | | | | | | | | | | | | | | | | | | | | | | | | | |
| | Kentish disc brooch | X | | X | | | X | | | X | | | | | | | | | | | | | | | | | | | | | X |
| | Frankish disc brooch | | | | | | | | | | | | | | | | | | | | | | | | | | | | | | |
| | Saucer brooch | | | | | | | | | | | | | | | | | | | X | | | | | | | | | | | |
| | Button brooch | | | | | | | | | | | | | | | | | | | X | | | | | | | | | | | |
| | Annular brooch | | | | | | | | | | | | | | | | | | | | | | | | | | | | | | |
| | Coin Pendant | | | | | | | | | | | | | | | | | | | | | | | | | | | | | | |
| | Au bracteate | | | | | | | | | | | | | | | | | | | | | | | | | | | | | | |
| | Ag disc pendant | | | X | | | X | | | X | | | | | | | | | | | | | | | | | | | | | |
| | Ag misc. pendant | X | | | | | | | | | | | | | | | | | | | | | | | | | | | | | |
| | Garnet pendant | | | | | | | | | | | | | | | | | | | | | | | | | | | | | | |
| | Misc. pendant | | | | | | | | | X | | | | | | | | | | | | | | | | | | | | | |
| | Beads | X | | X | | | X | | | X | | | | X | | | X | | | X X | | | X | | X | | | | | | X |
| | Pin | X | | X | X | | X | | | X | | | | X | X | X | | | | | X | | | | | | | | | | X |
| | Bracelet | | | | | | | | | | | | | | | | | | | | | | | | | | | | | | |
| | Finger ring | | | | | | | | | X | | | | | | | | | | | | | | | | | | | | | |
| Belt mounts | Ae buckle shield-on-tongue | | | | | | | | | | | | | X | | | | | | | X | | | | | | | | | | |
| | Ae buckle small | | | | | | | | | | | | | | | | | | | | | X | | | | | | | | | |
| | Ae buckle misc. | X | | | | | | | | X | | | X | | | | | | | X | | | | | | | X | | | | |
| | Fe buckle | | | | X | X | | X | | X | | | | | | | | | | | | | | | | | | X | | | |
| | Belt or strap mount | | | | X | | | | | | | | | | | | | | | | | | | | | | | X | X | | |
| | Lace tag | | | | | | | | | | | | | | | | | | | | | | | | | | | | | | |
| | Wooden belt | | | | | | | | | | | | | | | | | | | | | | | | | | | | | | |
| Containers | Pottery | | | | | | | | | | | | | | X | | | | | | | | | | | | | | | | |
| | Glass | | | | | | | | | | X | | | | | | | | | X X | | | | | | | | | | | X |
| | Coffin | | | | | | | | | | | X | | | | | | | | | | | | | | | | | | | |
| | Wooden box | | | X | | | X | | | | | | | | X | | | | | X | | | | | | | X | | | | X |
| | Ae bowl | | | | | | | | | | | | | | | | | | | | | | | | | | | | | | |
| | Bucket | | | | | | | | | | | | | | | | | | | | | | | X | | | | | | | |
| | Wood vessel | | | X | | | | | | X | | | | | | | | | | | | | | | | | | | | | |
| | Bone box | | | | | | | | | | | | | | | | | | | | | | | | | | | | | | |
| | Ae work box | | | | | | | | | | | | | | | | | | | | | | | | | | | | | | |
| | Bone lid | | | | | | | | | | | | | | | | | | | | | | | | | | | | | | |
| Tools | Sharpening steel | | | | | | | | | | | | | | | | | | | | | | | | | | | | | | |
| | Awl | | | | | | | | | | | | | | | | | | | | | | | | | | | | | | |
| | ?Mattock | | | | | | | | | | | | | | | | | | | | | | | | | | | | | | |
| | Fire-steel | | | | | | | | | | | | | | X | | | | | | | | | | X | | | | | | |
| | Hone | | | | | | | | | | | | | | | | | | | | | | | | | | | | | | |
| Weaving equipment | Fe weaving batten | | | | | | | | | X | | | | | | | | | X | | | | | | | | | | | | |
| | Weaving pick | | | | | | | | | | | | | | | | | | | | | | | | | | | | | | |
| | Ae needle | | | | | | | | | | | | | | | | | | | | | | | | | | | | | | |
| | Spindle whorl | | | | | | | | | | | | | | | | | | | X | | | | | | | | | | | |
| | Shears | | | | | | | | | | | | | | | | | | | | | | | | | | | | | | |
| Personal equipment | Knife | X | | X X X X | | | X X X X X X X | X | X | X | | | | X X X X X X X |
| | Key | X | | X | | | X | | X X | | | | | X X | | | | | | | | | | X X X | | | | X |
| | Girdle-hanger | | | | | | X | | | | | | | | | | | | | | | | | | | | | | | | X |
| | Tweezers | | | | | | | | | | | X | | | | | | | | | | | | | | | | | | | |
| | Spoon | | | X | | | | | | | | | | | | | | | | | | | | | | | X | | | | |
| | Fe diamond | | | | | | | | | X | | | | | | | | | | X | | | | | X | | | | | | |
| | Ivory ring | | | | | | | | | X | | | | | | | | | | | | | | | X | | | | | | |
| | Ag ring | | | | | | X | | | | | | | | | | | | | | | | | | | | | | | | |
| | Comb | X | | | | | | | | | | | | | | X | | | | | | | | | | | | | | | |
| | Ae balance | | | | | | | | | | | | | | | | | | | | | | | | | | | | | | |
| | ?Lyre | | | | | | | | | | | | | | | | | | | | | | | | | | | | | | |
| Misc. | Amulet etc. | | | | | | | | | | | | | | | | | | | | | | | | | X | | | | | |
| | Ae misc | | | | | | | | | | | | | | | | | | | X | | | | | | | | | | | |
| | Fe misc | | | | | | | | | X | | | | | | | | | | X | | | | | | | | | | | |
| | Misc. | | | | | | | | | | | | | | | | | | | | | | | | | X | | | | | |
| Fill | Misc. | | | | | | | | | | | | | | | | | | | | | | | | | | | | | | |

| | 60 | 61 | 62 | 63 | 64 | 65 | 66 | 67 | 68 | 69 | 70 | 71 | 72 | 73 | 74 | 75 | 76 | 77 | 78 | 79 | 80 | 81 | 82 | 83 | 84 | 85 | 86 | 87 | 88 | 89 | 90 | 91 | 92 | 93 | 94a | 94b | 95 |
|---|---|---|---|---|---|---|---|---|---|---|---|---|---|---|---|---|---|---|---|---|---|---|---|---|---|---|---|---|---|---|---|---|---|---|---|---|---|
| | | x | | x | x | | | | | | | x | | | | | | | | | | | | | | | | | | | | x | x | x | x | x | x |
| | | | | | x | | | | | | | x | | | | | | | | | | | | | | | | x | | | x | x | x | x | x | x | |
| | | | | | | x | | | | | | | | | | | | | | | | | | | | | | | | | | | x | | | | |
| | | | | | | | | | | | | x | | | | | | | | | | | | | | | | | | | x | x | | x | | | x |
| | | | | | | | | | | | | | | | | | | | | | | | | | | | | | | | | x | | | | | |
| | | | | | | | | | | | | | | | | | | | | | | | | | | | | | | | | | | x | | | |
| | | | | | | | | x | | | | | | | | | | | | | | | | | | | | | | | | | | | | | |
| | | | | | | | | x | | | | | | | | | | | | | | | | | | | | | | | | | | | | | |
| | x | | x | | | | x | x | | | | | | | x | x | | | | | | x | | x | | | | | | | | x | x | | | | x |
| | x | | x | | | | | | | | | | | | | | | | | | | | | | | | | | | | | | | | | | x |
| | | | | | | | x | | | | | | | | | | | | | | | | | | | | | | | | | | | | | | |
| | | | | | | x | | | | | | | | | | | | | | | | | | | | | | | | | x | | | | | | x |
| | | x | | x | | | | | | | | | | x | | | | | | | | | | x | | | | | | | | x | | | | | |
| | | | | | | | | | | | | | | | | | | | | | | | | | | | | | | | | | x | | | | |
| | x | | | | | | | | | | | | | | | | | | x | | | | | | | | | | | | | | | | | | |
| | | | | | | | | | | | | | | | | | | | | | | | x | | | | | | | | | | | | | | |
| | | | | | | | | | | | | | | | | | | | | | | | | | | | | x | | | | | | | | | |
| | | | | | | | | | | | | | | | | | | | | | | x | | | | | | | | | | | | | | | |
| | | | | x | | | | | | | | | | | | | | | | | | | | | | | | | | | | | | | | | |
| | | | | x | | | | | | | | | | | | | | | | | | | | | | | | | | | | | | | | | |
| | | | | | | | | | | | | | | | x | | | | | | | | | | | | | | | | | | | | | | |
| | x | | | | | | | | | | | | | | | x | | | | | | | x | | | | | | | | | | | | | | |
| | x | x | x | x | x | x | x | | | | | x | | x | x | x | | x | | | x | x | x | x | x | x | | x | x | | | x | x | | | x | x |
| | x | | x | | | | | x | | | | | | | x | | | | | | | | | | | | | | | | | | | | | x | |
| | | | | | | x | | | | | | | | | x | | | | | | | | | | | | | | | | | | | | | | |
| | x | | | | | | | | | | | | | | x | | | | | | | | | | | | | | | | | | | | | | |
| | x | | | | | | | x | | | | | | | | | | | | | | | | | | | | | | | | x | x | | | | |
| | x | | | x | | | | | | | | | | x | | | | x | | | | | | | | | | | | | | x | | | x | x | |
| | x | | | | | | | | | | | | | | | | | | x | x | | x | | | | | | | | | | x | | | | | |
| | x | | | x | | | | | | | | | | | | | | | | | | x | | | x | | | x | | | | | | | | | |

TABLE LV GRAVE CONTENTS

| Category | Grave number | 96b | 97 | 98 | 99 | 100 | 101 | 102 | 103 | 104 | 105 | 106 | 107 | 108 | 109 | 110 | 111 | 112 | 113 | 114 | 115 | 116 | 117 | 118 | 119 | 120 | 121 | 122 | 123 | 124 | 125 | 126 |
|---|---|---|---|---|---|---|---|---|---|---|---|---|---|---|---|---|---|---|---|---|---|---|---|---|---|---|---|---|---|---|---|---|
| Weapons | Sword | X |  | X |  |  |  |  |  |  |  |  |  |  |  |  |  |  |  |  |  |  |  |  |  |  |  |  |  |  |  |  |
|  | Spearhead | X |  | X |  |  |  |  |  |  |  |  |  |  |  |  |  |  |  | X |  |  |  |  |  |  |  |  |  |  |  |  |
|  | Ferrule |  |  |  |  |  |  |  |  |  |  |  |  |  |  |  |  |  |  |  |  |  |  |  |  |  |  |  |  |  |  |  |
|  | Arrow |  |  |  |  |  |  |  |  |  |  |  |  |  |  |  |  |  |  |  |  |  |  |  |  |  |  |  |  |  |  |  |
|  | Seax |  |  |  |  |  |  |  |  |  |  |  |  |  |  |  |  |  |  |  |  |  |  |  |  |  |  |  |  |  |  |  |
|  | Shield |  |  | X |  |  |  |  |  |  |  |  |  |  |  |  |  |  |  |  |  |  |  |  |  |  |  |  |  |  |  |  |
| Jewellery | Square-headed brooch |  |  |  |  |  |  |  |  |  |  |  |  |  |  |  |  |  |  |  |  |  |  |  |  |  |  |  |  |  |  |  |
|  | Small-long brooch |  |  |  |  |  |  |  |  |  |  |  |  |  |  |  |  |  |  |  |  |  |  |  |  |  |  |  |  |  |  |  |
|  | Kentish disc brooch |  |  |  |  |  |  |  |  |  |  |  |  |  |  |  |  |  |  |  |  |  |  |  |  |  |  |  |  |  |  | X |
|  | Frankish disc brooch |  |  |  |  |  |  |  |  |  |  |  |  |  |  |  |  |  |  |  |  |  |  |  |  |  |  |  |  |  |  |  |
|  | Saucer brooch |  |  |  |  |  |  |  |  |  |  |  |  |  |  |  |  |  |  |  |  |  |  |  |  |  |  |  |  |  |  |  |
|  | Button brooch |  |  |  |  |  |  |  |  |  |  |  |  |  |  |  |  |  |  |  |  |  |  |  |  |  |  |  |  |  |  |  |
|  | Annular brooch |  |  |  |  |  |  |  |  |  |  |  |  |  |  |  |  |  |  |  |  |  |  |  |  |  |  |  |  |  |  |  |
|  | Coin Pendant |  |  |  |  |  |  |  |  |  |  |  |  |  | X |  |  |  |  |  |  |  |  |  |  |  |  |  |  |  |  |  |
|  | Au bracteate |  |  |  |  |  |  |  |  |  |  |  |  |  |  |  |  |  |  |  |  |  |  |  |  |  |  |  |  |  |  |  |
|  | Ag disc pendant |  |  |  |  |  |  |  |  |  |  |  |  |  |  |  |  |  |  |  |  |  |  |  |  |  |  |  |  |  |  |  |
|  | Ag. misc. pendant |  |  |  |  |  |  |  |  |  |  |  |  |  |  |  |  |  |  |  |  |  |  |  |  |  |  |  |  |  |  |  |
|  | Garnet pendant |  |  |  |  |  |  |  |  |  |  |  |  |  |  |  |  |  |  |  |  |  |  |  |  |  |  |  |  |  |  |  |
|  | Misc. pendant |  |  |  |  |  |  |  |  |  |  |  |  |  |  |  |  |  |  |  |  |  |  |  |  |  |  |  |  |  |  |  |
|  | Beads |  |  |  |  |  |  |  |  |  |  |  | X |  |  | X |  |  |  |  |  |  |  |  |  |  |  |  |  |  |  |  |
|  | Pin | X |  |  |  | X | X |  |  |  |  |  | X |  |  |  |  |  |  |  |  |  |  |  |  |  |  |  | X |  |  |  |
|  | Bracelet |  |  |  |  |  |  |  |  |  |  |  |  |  |  | X |  |  |  |  |  |  |  |  |  |  |  |  |  |  |  |  |
|  | Finger ring |  |  |  |  |  |  |  |  |  |  |  |  |  |  |  |  |  |  |  |  |  |  |  |  |  |  |  |  |  |  |  |
| Belt mounts | Ae buckle shield-on-tongue |  |  |  |  |  |  |  |  |  |  |  |  |  |  |  |  |  |  |  |  |  |  |  |  |  |  |  |  |  |  |  |
|  | Ae buckle small |  |  |  |  |  |  |  |  |  |  |  |  |  |  |  |  |  |  |  |  |  |  |  |  |  |  |  |  |  |  |  |
|  | Ae buckle misc. |  |  |  |  |  |  |  |  |  |  |  |  |  |  |  |  |  | X |  |  |  |  |  |  |  |  |  |  |  |  |  |
|  | Fe buckle |  |  |  |  |  |  |  |  |  |  |  |  | X |  |  |  |  |  |  |  |  |  |  |  |  |  |  |  |  |  |  |
|  | Belt or strap mount |  |  | X |  |  |  |  | X |  |  |  |  |  |  |  |  |  | X |  |  |  |  |  |  |  |  |  |  |  |  |  |
|  | Lace tag |  |  |  |  |  |  |  |  |  |  |  |  |  |  |  |  |  | X |  |  |  |  |  |  |  |  |  |  |  |  |  |
|  | Wooden belt |  |  |  |  |  |  |  |  |  |  |  |  |  |  |  |  |  |  |  |  |  |  | X |  |  |  |  |  |  |  |  |
| Containers | Pottery |  |  |  |  |  |  |  |  |  |  |  |  | X |  |  |  |  |  |  |  |  |  |  |  |  |  |  |  |  |  |  |
|  | Glass |  |  |  |  |  |  |  |  |  |  |  |  |  |  |  |  |  |  |  |  |  |  |  |  |  |  |  |  |  |  |  |
|  | Coffin |  |  |  |  |  |  |  |  |  |  |  |  |  |  |  |  |  |  |  |  |  |  |  |  |  |  |  |  |  |  |  |
|  | Wooden box |  |  |  |  |  |  |  |  |  |  |  |  |  |  |  |  |  |  |  |  |  |  |  |  | X |  |  | X |  |  |  |
|  | Ae bowl |  |  |  |  |  |  |  |  |  |  |  |  |  |  |  |  |  |  |  |  |  |  |  |  |  |  |  |  |  |  |  |
|  | Bucket |  |  |  |  |  |  |  |  |  |  |  |  |  |  |  |  |  |  |  |  |  |  |  |  |  |  |  |  |  |  |  |
|  | Wood vessel |  |  |  |  |  |  |  |  |  |  |  |  |  |  |  |  |  |  |  |  |  |  |  |  |  |  |  |  |  |  |  |
|  | Bone box |  |  |  |  |  |  |  |  |  |  |  |  |  |  |  |  |  |  |  |  |  |  |  |  |  |  |  |  |  |  |  |
|  | Ae work box |  |  |  |  |  |  |  |  |  |  |  | X |  |  |  |  |  |  |  |  |  |  |  |  |  |  |  |  |  |  |  |
|  | Bone lid |  |  |  |  |  |  |  |  |  |  |  |  |  |  |  |  |  |  |  |  |  |  |  |  |  |  |  |  |  |  |  |
| Tools | Sharpening steel |  |  |  |  |  |  |  |  |  |  |  |  |  |  |  |  |  |  |  |  |  |  |  |  |  |  |  |  |  |  |  |
|  | Awl |  |  |  |  |  |  |  |  |  |  |  |  |  |  |  |  |  |  |  |  |  |  |  |  |  |  |  |  |  |  |  |
|  | ?Mattock |  |  |  |  |  |  |  |  |  |  |  |  |  |  |  |  |  |  |  |  |  |  |  |  |  |  |  |  |  |  |  |
|  | Fire-steel |  |  |  |  |  |  |  |  |  |  |  |  |  |  |  |  |  |  |  |  |  |  |  |  |  |  |  |  |  |  |  |
|  | Hone |  |  |  |  |  |  |  |  |  |  |  |  |  |  |  |  |  |  |  |  |  |  |  |  |  |  |  |  |  |  |  |
| Weaving equipment | Fe weaving batten |  |  |  |  |  |  |  |  |  |  |  |  |  |  |  |  |  |  |  |  |  |  |  |  |  |  |  |  |  |  |  |
|  | Weaving pick |  |  |  |  |  |  |  |  |  |  |  |  |  |  |  |  |  |  |  |  |  |  |  |  |  |  |  |  |  |  |  |
|  | Ae needle |  |  |  |  |  |  |  |  |  |  |  |  |  |  |  |  |  |  |  |  |  |  |  |  |  |  |  |  |  |  |  |
|  | Spindle whorl |  |  |  |  |  |  |  |  |  |  |  |  |  |  |  |  |  |  |  |  |  |  |  |  |  |  |  |  |  |  |  |
|  | Shears |  |  |  |  |  |  |  |  |  |  |  |  |  | X |  |  |  |  |  |  |  |  |  |  |  |  |  |  |  |  |  |
| Personal equipment | Knife | X | X | X |  |  |  |  | X | X | X | X |  | X | X | X | X |  | X | X | X |  | X |  | X | X | X | X |  | X | X | X |
|  | Key |  |  |  |  |  |  |  |  |  |  |  | X |  |  | X |  |  | X |  |  |  |  |  |  |  | X |  |  |  |  |  |
|  | Girdle-hanger |  |  |  |  |  |  |  |  |  |  |  |  |  |  | X |  |  |  |  |  | X |  |  |  |  |  |  |  |  |  |  |
|  | Tweezers |  |  |  |  |  |  |  |  |  |  |  | X |  |  |  |  |  |  |  |  |  |  |  |  |  |  |  |  |  |  |  |
|  | Spoon |  |  |  |  |  |  |  |  |  |  |  |  |  |  | X |  |  |  |  |  |  |  |  |  |  |  |  |  |  |  |  |
|  | Fe diamond |  |  |  |  |  |  |  |  |  |  |  |  |  |  |  |  |  |  |  |  |  |  |  |  |  |  |  |  |  |  |  |
|  | Ivory ring |  |  |  |  |  |  |  |  |  |  |  |  |  |  |  |  |  |  |  |  |  |  |  |  |  |  |  |  |  |  |  |
|  | Ag ring |  |  |  |  |  |  |  |  |  |  |  | X |  |  | X |  |  |  |  |  |  |  |  |  |  |  |  |  |  |  |  |
|  | Comb |  |  |  |  |  |  |  |  |  |  |  | X |  |  | X |  |  |  |  |  |  |  |  |  |  |  |  |  |  |  |  |
|  | Ae balance |  |  |  |  |  |  |  |  |  |  |  |  |  |  |  |  |  | X |  |  |  |  |  |  |  | X |  | X |  | X |  |
|  | ?Lyre |  |  |  |  |  |  |  |  |  |  |  |  |  |  | X |  |  |  |  |  |  |  |  |  |  |  |  |  |  |  |  |
| Misc. | Amulet etc. |  |  |  |  |  |  |  |  |  |  |  |  |  |  |  |  |  |  |  |  |  |  |  |  |  |  |  |  |  |  |  |
|  | Ae misc |  |  |  |  |  |  |  |  |  |  |  |  |  |  |  |  |  |  |  |  |  |  |  |  |  |  |  |  |  |  |  |
|  | Fe misc |  |  |  |  |  |  |  |  |  |  |  |  | X |  | X |  |  |  |  |  |  |  |  |  |  | X |  |  |  |  |  |
|  | Misc. |  |  |  |  |  |  |  |  |  |  |  |  |  |  | X |  |  |  |  |  |  |  |  |  |  |  |  |  |  |  |  |
| Fill | Misc. |  |  |  |  |  |  |  |  |  |  |  |  |  |  | X |  |  |  |  |  |  |  |  |  |  |  | X |  |  | X |  |

# GRAVE CATALOGUE

| | 127 | 128 | 129 | 130 | 131 | 132 | 133 | 134 | 135 | 136 | 137 | 138 | 139 | 140 | 141 | 142 | 143 | 144 | 145 | 146 | 147 | 148 | 149 | 150 | 151 | 152 | 153 | 154 | 155 | 156 | 157 | 158 | 159 | 160 | 161 | 162 | 163 | 164 | 165 | UN |
|---|---|---|---|---|---|---|---|---|---|---|---|---|---|---|---|---|---|---|---|---|---|---|---|---|---|---|---|---|---|---|---|---|---|---|---|---|---|---|---|---|
| | | x | | | x x | | | | | x | x x | x | | | | | | | | | | | | | | | | | | x | | | | | | | | | | x x x |
| | | | | | x | | | | | | | | | | | | | | | | | | | | | | | | | | | | | | | | | | | |
| | | | | | | | | | | | | | | | | | | | | | | | | | | | | | | | | | | | | | | | | x |
| | x | x | | | | | | | x | | | | | x | | | | | | | | | | | | | | | | | | | | | | | | | | x x |
| | x | x x x | | | x x x | x | x | | | | x | | x | x x x x | | x | | | | | x | | x | | | | x x | x | x x | | x x | x x | | | x |
| | | x x | | x | | | x | | | x | | | | | x x | x | | x | | x x | | x x | | | | | | | x | x x | | x x | | | | | x |
| | | x | | | | | | | x | x | x | | | | | | | | x | | | | | | | | | x x | | x | | | | x x | | | x |
| | | | | | | | | | | | x | | | | | | | x | | | | x x | | | | | | | x | | | | | | | | | | |
| | | | | | | | | | | | | | | | | | | | | | | | | | | | | | | x | | | | | | | | | | |
| | | | | | | | | | | | | | x | | | | | | | | | | | | | | | | | | | | | | | | | | | |
| x x x | x | x x x x | x | x x x | x | x x | x x | x x x | x | x x x | x | | x x | x x | x | x x x x x x x | | | | | | | | | x x x | x x | x x x x | x | x x x x | x | | x |
| x | x x | | | | | | x | x | | | | x | | | | | | | | | | | | | | | | | | x | x | | | | | | | | | |
| | | | | | | | | | | | | | | | | | | | | x | | x | | | | | x | x | x | | | | | | | | | | |
| | x | x | | | x x x | x | x | x x | x | | x | | x | | | | | | | | x | | | | | | | x x | | | | | x x | | x | | | |
| | | | | | | | | x | x x | | | | | | | | | | | | | | | | x | | x | | | | | | | | | | | x |

# Numerical keys to sites shown on the distribution maps (Figures 111–120)

### Figure 111: Button brooches Class B (Avent and Evison 1982, 106–9, 117)

*Class Bi.*
1. Alfriston, East Sussex.
2. Chessell Down, Isle of Wight, grave 5.
3. Droxford, Hampshire.
4. Howletts, Kent, grave 29.
5. Mucking, Essex, grave 281.
6. Oakley Down, Dorset, barrow 1.
7. Petersfinger, Wiltshire, 3 examples, grave 25.
8. South Cadbury, Somerset.

*Class Bii.*
9. Alfriston, East Sussex, 3 examples, grave C (1), unassociated (2).
10. Dover (Buckland), Kent, grave 48.
11. High Down, West Sussex, 2 examples.
12. Worthy Park, King's Worthy, Hampshire, grave 80.

*Class B Miscellaneous.*
13. Chatham Lines, Kent, tumulus II.
14. Droxford, Hampshire.
15. Harnham Hill, Wiltshire, grave 40.
16. Lyminge, Kent, grave 16.
17. Orpington, London (Kent), grave 41.
18. Petersfinger area, Wiltshire.
19. Herpes, Charente, France.
20. Marchélepot, Somme, France.
21. Nouvion-en-Ponthieu, Somme, France, grave 143.

### Figure 112: Saucer brooches decorated with five spirals

(Dash lines indicate Roman roads, dot line the Icknield Way)

1. Abingdon, Oxfordshire (Berkshire), 2 examples, grave 60 (1) Leeds and Harden 1936, 43, pl.XII; Welch 1983 i, 44; grave 100 (1) Leeds and Harden 1936, 50, pl.XVII.
2. Alfriston, East Sussex, 9 examples, grave 46 (2) Griffith and Salzmann 1914, 41, pl.VII, 1, 1A; Welch 1983 i, 44; ii, 362, fig.22a; grave 60 (2) Griffith and Salzmann 1914, 44, pl.VII, 3, 3A; Welch 1983 i, 45; ii, 366, fig.28A; grave 65 (1) Griffith and Salzmann 1914, 45, pl.VII, 4; Welch 1983 i, 45; ii, 368, fig.30a; grave 87 (2) Griffith 1915, 204, pl.XXIII, 1, 1A; Welch 1983 i, 45; ii, 374, fig. 36a; unstratified (2) Griffith and Salzmann 1914, 50; Welch 1983 i, 45–6; ii, 383.
3. Alton, Hampshire, 2 examples, cremation 1. Excavation V I Evison.
4. Beckford A, Hereford and Worcester (Worcestershire), grave 12. Excavation V I Evison.
5. Beddington, London (Surrey), 2 examples. Meaney 1964, 237.
6. Berinsfield, Oxfordshire, 4 examples, grave 22 (2), grave 73 (2). Excavation D Miles and P D C Brown; Welch 1983 i, 45.
7. Caistor-by-Norwich, Norfolk. Myres and Green 1973, 90, text fig.2, 207, fig.60, 1, pl.XIX,c; Welch 1983 i, 42, 44.
8. Cassington (Purwell Farm), Oxfordshire, 2 examples, grave II. Leeds and Riley 1942, 65, pl.V,C.
9. Dover (Buckland), Kent, grave 48. Present report Figure 27.
10. Droxford, Hampshire. Aldsworth 1978, 136, fig.31.5, British Museum 1902 7–22 5.
11. Duston, Northamptonshire. Brown 1915 III, xxxii, pl.LIX, 3.
12. East Shefford, Berkshire, grave 18. Peake and Hooton 1915, 117, pl.III.
13. Great Chesterford, Essex, 4 examples, grave 2 (2), grave 126 (2). Excavation V I Evison. British Museum.
14. ?Hastings, East Sussex. Welch 1983 i, 44; ii, 506, fig.1a.
15. High Down, West Sussex, 4 examples, grave 2 (2) Wilson N.D., 4, pl.3,3; Welch 1983 i, 46; ii, 463, fig.87a, Worthing Museum 3406, 3407; unstratified (2) Welch 1983 i, 46; ii, fig. 113a, Worthing Museum 3413, 3414.
16. Hornton, Oxfordshire, 2 examples. Meaney 1964, 209. British Museum 1836 3–23 11 and 12.
17. Kempston, Bedfordshire. British Museum 91 6–24 245.
18. Leighton Buzzard, Bedfordshire. British Museum 82 8–24 1.
19. Lewes (Malling Hill), East Sussex. Norris 1956, 11; Welch 1983 i, 46; ii, 405, fig. 65a.
20. Long Wittenham, Oxfordshire (Berkshire), 2 examples, grave 111. Akerman 1862, 347. British Museum 75 3–10 290 and 291.
21. Marston St. Lawrence, Northamptonshire, grave 13. Dryden 1885, 329, pl.XXIII, 13.
22. Mitcham, London (Surrey), 2 examples, grave 66. Bidder and Morris 1959, 64, pl.VIII; Welch 1983 i, 44.
23. Orpington, London (Kent), 2 examples, grave 75. Excavation Mrs Palmer, Orpington Museum.
24. Pewsey, Wiltshire, 2 examples, grave 104. Welch 1983 i, 44.
25. Reading, Berkshire. Smith 1906, 241.
26. Spong Hill, North Elmham, Norfolk, 2 examples, cremation 2376. Excavation C Hills; Welch 1983 i, 43.
27. Welbeck Hill, Humberside (Lincolnshire). Wilson 1967, 267; Welch 1983 i, 42.
28. Wheatley, Oxfordshire, grave 20. Leeds 1916–17, 53, fig.2, 20.
29. Woodston, Peterborough, Cambridgeshire (Huntingdonshire). Abbott 1920, pl. opp.40, No.4; Welch 1983 i, 44.
30. ?Bury St. Edmunds, Suffolk. Moyses Hall Museum Reg. No. 1982–369. Information E J Owles.

### Figure 113: Dolphin buckle loops with tails

*Variant a[1]*
1. Caerwent, Gwent (Monmouth). Hawkes and Dunning 1961, 51, fig.17,b.

2. Dover (Buckland) Kent, grave 48. Present report.
3. Dragonby, Humberside (Lincolnshire), Hawkes 1974, 387, fig.3,4; Eagles 1979, i, 61, ii, fig.111,3.
4. Leicester, Leicestershire. Hawkes and Dunning 1961, 52, fig.17,i.
5. Lincoln, Lincolnshire. Hawkes 1974, 387, fig.3,5; Eagles 1979, i, 61, ii, fig.111,1.
6. Lullingstone, Kent. Hawkes and Dunning 1961, 52, fig.17,j.
7. Lydney, Gloucestershire. Ibid, 52, fig.17,k.
8. St. Albans, Hertfordshire. Ibid, 55, fig.18,d.
9. Silchester, Hampshire. Ibid, 55, fig.18,g.
10. Water Newton, Cambridgeshire (Huntingdonshire). Ibid, 55, fig.18,h.
11. Winchester, Hampshire, grave 443. Clarke 1979, 89, fig.100,603.

*Variant a$^2$*
12. Caistor-by-Norwich, Norfolk. Hawkes and Dunning 1961, 51, fig.17,c.
13. Duston, Northamptonshire. Ibid, 52, fig.17,f.
14. Lakenheath, Suffolk. Ibid, 57, fig.18,j.
15. Mitcham, London (Surrey), grave 38. Ibid, 55, fig.18,f.
16. Mucking, Essex, grave 989. Evison 1981a, fig.5,a.
17. North Wraxhall, Wiltshire. Hawkes and Dunning 1961, 52, fig.18,b.
18. Winchester, Hampshire, grave 37. Clarke 1970, 295, fig.4,92.

### Figure 114: Kempston-type glass cone-beakers

(Numbers in brackets preceded by E refer to the numbers given to the cones in Evison 1972)

*England*
1. Kempston, Bedfordshire, light green ht.26.2cm, d.m. (diameter of mouth) 9cm (E No.1, fig.8).
2. Alfriston, East Sussex, a. grave 39, light green, ht. 29cm d.m.10cm (E No.2); b. grave 43, light green, nearly colourless, ht.27.5cm, d.m.9.5cm (E No.3); c. light green, ht.22.5cm. d.m.8cm (E No.4).
3. High Down, West Sussex, grave 27, light green, ht. 29cm, d.m.7.5cm (E No.5, fig.9).
4. Guildown, Surrey, a. grave 56, light olive green ht. 23.5cm d.m.11.8cm (E No.6, figs.2,16); b. grave 109, light green, ht.25cm, d.m.9cm (E No.7, figs.3,17).
5. Mitcham, London (Surrey), grave 201, light green, ht.26.4cm, d.m.9.2cm (E No.8).
6. Ozingell, Kent, light green, ht.21.5cm, d.m.8.4cm (E No.9).
7. Westbere, Kent, light green, ht.28cm, d.m.9.8cm (E No.10).
8. Howletts, Kent, a. grave 18, light green, fragments, d.m.8.6cm (E No.11); b. grave 30, light green, ht. 27.5cm, d.m.9.3cm (E No.12, fig.10).
9. Chessell Down, Isle of Wight, amber, ht.c.22cm, d.m.10.5cm (E No.13, fig.15).
10. Cassington (Smith's Pit II), Oxfordshire, light green, nearly colourless, ht.22.5cm, d.m.9.6cm (E No.14, fig.1).
11. East Shefford, Berkshire, a. grave 24, light green, ht. 26cm, d.m.9.2cm (E No.15); b. light green, ht. 25cm, d.m.8.7cm (E No.16, fig.12).
12. Longbridge, Warwickshire, base fragment, light green, ht.11cm (E No.17).
13. Lyminge, Kent, grave 63, light green, nearly colourless, ht.17.2cm, d.m.9.7 × 9.4cm, base 3.8cm, Maidstone Museum.
14. Dover (Buckland), Kent, grave 22, light green, ht. 30.5cm, d.m.9.4cm (E No.19, fig.11).
15. Faversham, Kent, light olive green, ht.19cm, d.m.9.7cm (E No.20, fig.6).
16. Wye Down, Kent, light green, ht.19cm, d.m.9cm (E No.21, fig.7).
17. Acklam, North Yorkshire, light olive green, ht. 23.5cm, d.m.9.8cm (E No.22, figs.4–5).
18. Wigston Magna, Leicestershire, fragments, Nichols 1807, 377, pl.LV, 18 (E p.55).
19. Barrington, A, Cambridgeshire, light green fragment, Cambridge Museum (E p.55).
20. Rivenhall, Essex, olive green fragments (E p.56, fig.18).
21. Mucking, Essex, a.grave 924, light green, ht.28.3cm, d.m.9.3cm; b. settlement glass fragment No.40, light olive green; c. settlement glass fragment No.256, well 7, brown. Excavation M U and W T Jones.
22. Spong Hill, North Elmham, Norfolk, a. 1058/1 light green, Hills 1977, 41, fig.128; b. 1602/1, light green, ibid 62, fig.128; c. 1911/2, light blue-green, Hills and Penn 1981, 41–2 fig.164; d. 2526/3 light green; e.2737/4 light green; f. 3222/1 light green, and other possible fragments, excavation C Hills.
23. Heybridge, Essex, light green fragment, Drury and Wickenden 1982, 28, fig.12.26.
24. No provenance, Canterbury Museum, light green, rim only to depth of 9cm, d.m.8.5cm (E No.18).

*Germany*
25. Krefeld-Stratum, light green, ht.24.5cm (E No.23).
26. Rill, Mörs, ht.c25cm (E No.24).
27. Schwarzrheindorf, grave 10 ht.28.5cm, d.m.8.3cm (E No.25).
28. Rittersdorf, grave 125, light green, ht.26.5cm, d.m. 8.5cm (E No.26).
29. Monsheim, Rheinhessen, 'Weissem Glas', ht. 27.3cm (E No.27).
30. Wenigumstadt, Obernburg, grave I, light green, ht. 21.6cm (E No.28).
31. Eick, Mörs, grave 75, light olive green, ht.21cm (E No.29).
32. Mühlhausen, Kepplersche Sandgrube, ht.26cm (E No.30).
33. Weimar, Nordfriedhof, grave 31, ht.29.4cm (E No.31).
34. Entringen II, ht.c.20cm (E No.32).
35. Wurmlingen, Tuttlingen, ht.23.5cm (E No.33).
36. Hailfingen, Rottenburg, grave 269, ht.25cm and 28cm (E No.34).
37. Sindlingen a. M, ht.27cm (E No.35).
38. Weisbaden, a. Dotzheimerstr., light green (E No.36); b. Schierstein, light green ht.24cm, d.m. 8.5cm (E No.37); c. Dotzheimerstr., ht.25.5cm, d.m.8.5cm (E No.38).
39. Düsseldorf-Oberkassel, grave 4 (E No.39).
40. Beckum, Westphalia, grave 13 (E No.40).
41. Quedlinburg, Bochshornshanze, grave 41 (E No.41).
42. Krefeld-Gellep, grave 1850, olive green, ht.24.2cm. Pirling 1974, Taf.59.23.
43. Pommerhof, Plaidt, Mayen-Koblenz, colourless, ht.17cm, d.m.8.7cm, Ament 1976, Taf.59.34.
44. Liebenau, Niedersachsen, a. Fläche VIII/19, Genrich 1975, Abb.2,9; b. J10, cremation B1, green fragments, Cosack 1982, 51, Taf.45,5c,d.
45. Hüfingen, Schwarzwald, yellowish, nearly colourless, Fingerlin 1977, front cover.

46. Runde Berg bei Urach, a-e. Nos. 589, 590, 593, 594, 596, Christlein 1979, Taf.26.13, 14, 17, 18, 19, 20, light green; f. No.592, Ibid, Taf.26.16, light green-yellow; g, h. No. 591, 599, Ibid, Taf.26.15, 23, light green – colourless. (Other possible fragments, Ibid, Taf.26.).
47. No provenance, Völkerkunde Museum, Berlin (E No.42).

*Belgium*
48. Sint Gillis bij Dendermonde, yellowish, nearly colourless, ht.21.5cm, d.m.8cm (E No.43, fig.21).
49. Pry, yellowish, nearly colourless, ht.22cm, d.m. 8.5cm (E No.44, fig.20).
50. Samson, light green, ht.22.7cm, d.m.8.5cm (E No.45, fig.19).
51. Anderlecht, light yellow, ht.21cm. Roosens 1973, 47.
52. Vieuxville, a. yellow, Alénus-Lecerf 1981, fig.26 (top); b. yellow, fragmentary (information Alénus-Lecerf).

*Holland*
53. Aalden, Zweeloo, ht.25.7cm, d.m.9.7cm (E No.46).
54. Maastricht, St. Servaaskerk, grave 72, light olive green, ht.12.5cm, d.m.6.7cm (E No.47).

*France*
55. Herpes, Charente, light green, ht.20cm, d.m.8.5cm (E No.48, fig.13).
56. Marchélepot, 'verre blanc', ht.22.5cm (E No.49).
57. St. Nicolas, Arras (E No.50).
58. No provenance, Troyes Museum 4583, yellowish, nearly colourless, ht.25cm, d.m.9.6cm (E No.51, fig.22).

*Czechoslovakia*
59. Veleslavin, Prague, grave 3, greenish, lost (E No.52).
60. Kobylisy, Prague, a. grave IV, yellow-green, ht. 27.5cm, d.m.9.7cm (E No.53); b. brownish fragments (E No.65).
61. Certova-ruha, Masov, near Turnov, greenish fragments (E No.65).

*Denmark*
62. Dankirke, Ribe, blue with white trails, ht.c.23cm, Thorvildsen 1972, colour plate opp.48.

*Sweden*
63. Helgö, Stockholm, 1320 K15, light olive fragment, Historical Museum, Stockholm.

*Scandinavia*
64. No provenance, ht.24cm, d.m.7.9cm (E No.66), American Swedish Institute, Minneapolis.


**Figure 115 a and b: Claw-beakers (Evison 1982, 61–70)**

*Type 1*
1. Mucking, Essex, grave 843.

*Type 2a*
2. Castle Eden, Durham.
3. Chatteris, Isle of Ely, Cambridgeshire.
4. Eastry, Kent.

*Type 2b*
5. Broadstairs (Valetta House), Kent.

6. Faversham, Kent. British Museum 1336a '70.
7. Reculver (Broomfield), Kent.

*Type 3a*
8. Lyminge, Kent, grave 41.
9. Sarre, Kent, grave 60.
10. Dover (Buckland), Kent, grave 20.

*Type 3b*
11. Finglesham, Kent, grave D3.
12. Howletts, Kent, grave 7.
13. Howletts, Kent, grave 14.
14. Faversham, Kent. British Museum 1337 '70.

*Type 3c*
15. Snape, Suffolk.
16. Cambridgeshire.
17. Howletts, Kent, grave 37.
18. Asgarby, Lincolnshire.
19. Sittingbourne (Bexhill Marsh), Kent.
20. Pitsford, Northamptonshire.
21. Dinas Powys, South Glamorgan.
22. West Stow, Suffolk, hut 50.
23. Loveden Hill, Lincolnshire, cremation 280.
24. Loveden Hill, Lincolnshire, cremation 842.
25. Mucking, Essex, hut 166.
26. Spong Hill, North Elmham, Norfolk, cremation 1087.
27. Spong Hill, North Elmham, Norfolk, cremation 1133.
28. Spong Hill, North Elmham, Norfolk, cremation 1641.
29. Spong Hill, North Elmham, Norfolk, cremation 1745.
30. Westbere, Kent.
31. Newport Pagnell, Buckinghamshire.
32. Great Chesterford, Essex, grave 122.
33. Mucking, Essex, grave 92.
34. Fairford, Gloucestershire.
35. East Shefford, Berkshire.
36. Croydon, London (Surrey).
37. Islip, Northamptonshire.
38. Loveden Hill, Lincolnshire, cremation 781.
39. Spong Hill, North Elmham, Norfolk, cremation 1376.

*Type 3d*
40. Bifrons, Kent.
41. ?Micheldever, Hampshire.
42. Loveden Hill, Lincolnshire, cremation 920.
43. Spong Hill, North Elmham, Norfolk, cremation 1890/1891.

*Type 3e*
44. Coombe, Kent.

*Type 4a*
45. Taplow, Buckinghamshire. British Museum 83 12–14 13.
46. Taplow, Buckinghamshire. British Museum 83 12–14 14.

*Type 4b*
47. Taplow, Buckinghamshire. British Museum 83 12–14 15.
48. Taplow, Buckinghamshire. British Museum 83 12–14 16.
49. Ashford, Kent.
50. Gilton, Ash, Kent, grave 83.

*Type 4c*
51. Wickhambreux, Kent.
52. Faversham, Kent. British Museum 1336b '70.
53. Faversham, Kent, 1 claw.
54. Loveden Hill, Lincolnshire, unstratified.

*Type 5*
55. Sarre, Kent, grave 168.

*Additions not shown on map*
   Broadstairs, Kent, grave 42, contemporary with type 1. Evison 1982, 75, note 23.
   Finglesham, Kent, grave 204, type 2b. Ibid, 71.
   Ozingell, Kent, type 3a or b. Ibid, 60.
   West Stow, Suffolk, type 3c. Ibid, 60.
   Brandon, Suffolk, 3 examples, ?type 4e. Ibid, 60.
   Northampton, claw fragments. Ibid, 71.
   Spong Hill, North Elmham, Norfolk, small finds 1617 and 1656, cremations 2928/3, 2948/3, 2998/2. Excavator C Hills.

**Figure 116: Bronze bowls with beaded rim**

1. Alfriston, East Sussex, grave 28. Griffith and Salzmann 1914, 35, pl.XIII,1.
2. Baginton, Warwickshire. Herbert Museum, Coventry.
3. Bifrons, Kent, grave 21. Godfrey-Faussett 1876, 307.
4. Broughton Lodge, Willoughby-on-the-Wolds, Nottinghamshire. Information from M Dean.
5. Darenth and Stone Hospital, near Dartford, Kent. Wilson 1956, 191.
6. Dover (Buckland) Kent, grave 20. Present report.
7. Gilton, Ash, Kent. Smith 1844, 133–4. Fig. on 133.
8. Great Chesterford, Essex. Excavation V I Evison. British Museum Accession no.: 1964 7–2 577.
9. Holywell Row, Suffolk, grave 11. Lethbridge 1931, 8.
10. Lackford, Suffolk, cremation 50, 172A. Lethbridge 1951, 20, fig.24.
11. Mitcham, London (Surrey), grave 230. Rice 1923; Bidder and Morris 1959, 75–6, 104–5, pl.XXIII,a.
12. Morningthorpe, Norfolk. Webster 1975, 224.
13. North Luffenham, Leicestershire (Rutland). Kennett 1969b, 142.
14. Queniborough, Leicestershire. Nichols 1815, 136, pl.L,1.
15. Sawston, Cambridgeshire. Clarke 1817, 341–2, pls. XXIV and XXV, 9.
16. Spong Hill, North Elmham, Norfolk, cremation 1871. Hills and Penn 1981, 39, fig.144.
17. Stowting, Kent. Wrench 1845, 9, 11, pl.III.9; Smith 1846, 399–401; Brown 1915 IV, 472, pl.CXVI, 3.

**Figure 117: Bronze workboxes**

1. Aldborough, North Yorkshire. Roman Town and Museum, Aldborough.
2. Barrington, Cambridgeshire. University Museum of Archaeology and Anthropology, Cambridge 22.689A.C.A., 22.689C.C.A.
3. Barton-upon-Humber, Humberside (Lincolnshire), 2 examples, graves 1 and 2. Sheppard 1939, 258, 260; *Idem* 1940, 46–8, fig.18.
4. Bidford-on-Avon, Warwickshire, grave 100. Humphreys *et al.* 1923, 101, fig.5.
5. Burwell, Cambridgeshire, 2 examples, graves 42 and 121. Lethbridge 1926–7, 86, 88, fig.A, pl.II; *Idem* 1931, 70, fig.36,1.
6. Cransley, Northamptonshire. Baker 1881–3, 94.
7. Dover (Buckland), Kent, 2 examples, graves 84 and 107. Present report figs. 40 and 48.
8. Dover (Market Square), Kent. Webster 1976, 164.
9. Eastry (Updown), Kent. Hawkes 1976a, 248, Hawkes 1982, 49, fig.4.
10. Finglesham, Northbourne, Kent, grave 8. Wilson 1960, 135; Meaney 1981, 140.
11. Garton II, Humberside (Yorkshire), grave 7. Mortimer 1905, 248, 250, fig.643.
12. Haslingfield, Cambridgeshire. Ashmolean Museum, Oxford 1909.244.
13. Hawnby, North Yorkshire. Denny 1859–68, 498–9.
14. Hepple, Northumberland. Miket 1974, 279–80, fig.3.11.
15. Hurdlow, Derbyshire. Bateman 1861, 53–4; Jewitt 1870, 284–5, fig.466.
16. Kempston, Bedfordshire, 2 examples. Fitch 1863–4, 289, 291–2, pl.V,3.
17. Kingston Down, Kent, 2 examples, graves 96 and 222. Faussett 1856, 58, 81, pl.XIII, 7 and 11.
18. North Leigh, Oxfordshire. Leeds 1940, 21–2, pl.VI, C and D.
19. Painsthorpe Wold I, Humberside (Yorkshire), barrow 4, grave 6a. Mortimer 1905, 117, fig.279.
20. Polhill, Kent, grave 43. Philp 1973a, 177, 205, fig.53, 488–9.
21. St. Albans, Hertfordshire, 2 examples. Stead 1969, 47.
22. Sibertswold, Kent, grave 60. Faussett 1856, 112, pl.XIII,8.
23. Standlake, Oxfordshire. Stone 1856–9, 93.
24. Standlow, Derbyshire. Bateman 1848, 74–5.
25. Totternhoe (Marina Drive), Bedfordshire, 2 examples, graves B3, B4 and E1, E2. Matthews 1962, 28, 31, fig.4,8.
26. Uncleby, Humberside (Yorkshire), 5 examples, graves 1, 3, 29 and 31 (2). Smith 1911–2, 149, 151, fig.2.
27. Yatesbury, Wiltshire. Merewether 1851, 96.
28. Hambleton Moor, North Yorkshire. Exact provenance uncertain. Smith 1912, 96.
29. No provenance. Ashmolean Museum, Oxford 1909.568.
30. No provenance. British Museum OA5623.

**Figure 118: Ivory rings**

(figures in brackets refer to corpus nos. in Myres 1977)

1. Abingdon, Oxfordshire (Berkshire), 3 examples, cremations 55 and 73, grave 29. Leeds and Harden 1936, 20, 22, 36, pl.VIII.
2. Alfriston, East Sussex, grave 68. Griffith and Salzmann, 1914, 46.
3. Barrington A, Cambridgeshire. Myres and Green 1973, 101.
4. Barrington B, Cambridgeshire, 2 examples, graves 7 and 75. Foster 1880–4, 15, 24.
5. Bidford-on-Avon, Warwickshire, Humphreys *et al.* 1923, 104.
6. Brighthampton, Oxfordshire, 2 examples, graves 22 and 49. Akerman 1860, 86, 89.
7. Brightwell Heath, Suffolk, tumulus 3. Moir 1921, 13, fig. 28.
8. Burton-Stather, Humberside (Lincolnshire). Meaney 1964, 152.

9. Caister-by-Norwich, Norfolk, 5 examples, cremations N52 (1542), P12 (1709), P25 (1621), P53 (1544) and stray find 2. Myres and Green 1973, 158, 171, 173, 178, 207, figs.1, 22, 11, 60; Myres 1977 1, 322, 296, 307, 225.
10. Castle Acre, Norfolk. Myres and Green 1973, 101.
11. Chatham Lines, Kent, 2 examples, tumuli II and XVIII. Douglas 1793, 6, 64 pl.2, fig.6 and pl.15, fig.2.
12. Cheesecake Hill, Driffield, Humberside (Yorkshire), barrow C44, grave 11. Mortimer 1905, 293, pl.CXIV, fig.892.
13. Devizes, Wiltshire. Myres and Green 1973, 101.
14. Dover (Buckland), Kent, 5 examples, graves 1, 38, 53, 75 and 160. Present report.
15. Driffield, Humberside (Yorkshire), barrow C38, grave 18. Mortimer 1905, 279.
16. Eye, Cambridgeshire (Northamptonshire). Meaney 1964, 189.
17. Fairford, Gloucestershire. Wylie, 1852, 15.
18. Girton, Cambridgeshire. Hollingworth and O'Reilly 1925, 11.
19. Glen Parva, Leicestershire. Pownall 1864–7, 345.
20. Harnham Hill, Wiltshire. Smith 1923, 75.
21. Holdenby, Northamptonshire. *J Northamptonshire Natur Hist Soc Fld Club* 11 (1901–2) 7.
22. Holywell Row, Suffolk, grave 43. Lethbridge 1931, 23.
23. Hornsea, Humberside (Yorkshire), skeleton 9. Sheppard 1913, 271, pl.XXIII, fig.XXI.
24. Howletts, Kent. Myres and Green 1973, 101.
25. Illington, Norfolk, 7 examples, cremations 42 (2174), 43 (2221), 69 (2110), 102 (2124), 151 (2251) and 168 (2178). Myres 1977 1, 165, 328, 311, 356, 347, 344, 155.
26. Kempston, Bedfordshire. Fitch 1863–4, 286.
27. Kingston, Kent, 2 examples, graves 20 and 142. Faussett 1856, 47, 67–8.
28. Kirton-in-Lindsey, Humberside (Lincolnshire). Myres and Green 1973, 101.
29. Lackford, Suffolk, 13 examples, including cremations 49, 24/UDY 73 (2636), 49, 25A/WDY 16 (899), 50, 71/HG91 (914), 50, 85A/TDY 39 (975), 49, 585 (869) and 50, 122a/UDY 38 (2866). Lethbridge 1951, 17, 18, 16–17, figs.14 and 5; Myres 1977 1, 341, 265, 134, 165, 322, 292; Ibid 2, fig.15.
30. Limbury, Leagrave, Bedfordshire. Austin *et al*. 1928, 178.
31. Little Eriswell, Suffolk, grave 28. Hutchinson 1966, 11.
32. Lord of the Manor, Ramsgate, Kent. Millard *et al*. 1969, 12–14, fig.3, 1.
33. Loveden Hill, Lincolnshire, 4 examples, cremations, A2/242 (1424), A3/243 (1403), A21/261 (1402) and 61/248 (1408); Myres 1977 1, 153, 175, 273, 302.
34. Luton, Bedfordshire. Myres and Green 1973, 101.
35. Markshall, Norfolk, cremation IX. Myres and Green 1973, 249, fig.16,E.
36. Mitcham, London (Surrey), grave 221. Bidder and Morris 1959, 74, pl.XVII.
37. Nassington, Northamptonshire, 2 examples, graves 31 and A. Leeds and Atkinson 1944, 110, 112, pl.XXX.
38. Newark, Nottinghamshire, cremation 353 (3915). Myres 1977 1, 220; Ibid 2, fig.163.
39. Petersfinger, Wiltshire, grave XLVIII. Leeds and Shortt 1953, 30, pl.VII.
40. Pewsey, Wiltshire, 2 examples. Wilson 1970, 164; Webster 1974, 184.
41. Ruskington, Lincolnshire. Webster 1976, 165.
42. Sancton, Humberside (Yorkshire), 4 examples, cremations 2012, 3732, 3734 and 3753. Myres and Southern 1973, 34, 48, 74, 60; Myres 1977 1, 128, 153, 292, 225.
43. Shudy Camps, Cambridgeshire, grave 19. Lethbridge 1936, 6.
44. Sleaford, Lincolnshire, 5 examples, graves 78, 86, 143, 151 and 207. Thomas 1887, 393, 398, 399, 402.
45. Soham, Cambridgeshire, grave 7. Lethbridge 1931–2, 158.
46. Spong Hill, North Elmham, Norfolk, at least 5 examples, including cremations 1187, 1739, 1755, 2017 and 2067. Hills 1977a, 46, fig.138; Hills and Penn 1981, 30, 32, 48, 50, 52, fig.180.
47. Staxton, North Yorkshire, Sheppard 1938, 10, fig.9.
48. Sutton Courtenay, Oxfordshire (Berkshire), house IV. Leeds 1923, 158, pl.XXVIII, fig.1,H.
49. Waterbeach, Cambridgeshire. Lethbridge 1927, 145, fig.4, 8.
50. Willoughby-on-the-Wolds, Nottinghamshire. Myres and Green 1973, 101.
51. Woodston, Cambridgeshire (Huntingdonshire), grave 7. Abbot 1920, 36.
52. Woodyates, Dorset. Hoare 1812, 235, pl.XXXII.

## Figure 119: Bronze balances

1. Abingdon, Oxfordshire (Berkshire), grave 118. Leeds and Harden 1936, 54, pl.XVII.
2. Barton-upon-Humber, Humberside (Lincolnshire), grave 1. Sheppard 1940, 38–42, pl. on 37.
3. Broadstairs (St. Peter's), Kent, grave 76. Evison 1974, 88, fig.5a.
4. Desborough, Northamptonshire. Baker 1880, 468.
5. Dover (Buckland), Kent, grave C. Present report fig.2.
6. Gilton, Ash, Kent, 2 examples, grave 66. Faussett 1856, 22–3, pl.XVII; Tumulus XV Douglas 1793, 51, pl.12, 6, 7, 8, 9 and 10.
7. Icklingham, Suffolk. Ashmolean Museum, Oxford, Reg. No. 1909.467.
8. Long Wittenham, Oxfordshire (Berkshire), grave 80. Akerman 1862, 344, fig. on 344.
9. Ozingell, Kent. Smith 1854, 12–14, pl.IV.
10. Sarre, Kent, grave 26. Brent 1866, 161–3. pl. facing 61.
11. Shrivenham, Oxfordshire (Berkshire). Information from C J Scull, Oxford Unit.
12. Wheatley, Oxfordshire, grave 34. Leeds 1916–17, 56.
13. Wykeham, North Yorkshire, 2 examples, sites 11 and 17. Moore 1963–6, 418, 424, pl.I, fig.7, 3 and 6.

## Figure 120: Cowrie shells

1. Alfriston, East Sussex, grave 43. Griffith and Salzmann 1914, 40.
2. Breach Downs, Kent. Bagshawe 1931, 283.
3. Burwell, Cambridgeshire, grave 42. Lethbridge 1926–7, 86, fig.2, 2.
4. Camerton, Avon (Somerset), grave 100. Horne 1933, 61, fig.2.
5. Dover (Buckland), Kent, grave 6. Present report fig.7
6. Ellesborough, Buckinghamshire. Cocks 1909, 427–8, pl.I.
7. Empingham, Leicestershire (Rutland). Wilson 1970, 162.

8. Farthingdown, Coulsdon, London (Surrey). Hope-Taylor 1950.
9. Haslingfield, Cambridgeshire. Brown 1915 IV, 450, pl.CVII,1.
10. Kingston Down, Kent, 2 examples, graves 142 and 299. Faussett 1856, 68, 92.
11. Linton Heath, Cambridgeshire, grave 73. Neville 1854, 109.
12. Luton (Dallow Road), Bedfordshire. Bagshawe 1931, 282–3.
13. Sarre, Kent, grave 238. Brent 1868, 314.
14. Shudy Camps, Cambridgeshire, 2 examples, graves 48 and 91. Lethbridge 1936, 17, 24, fig.9, 4 and 5.
15. Sibertswold, Kent, grave 180. Faussett 1856, 133.
16. Staxton, North Yorkshire, grave 1. Sheppard 1938, 12, pl.I, fig.12.
17. West Stow, Suffolk. Information from S.E. West.
18. Wingham, Kent, 2 examples. Conyngham 1844b, 551; Bagshawe 1931, 283.

Doubtful Examples
19. Chatham Lines, Kent. Douglas 1793, 85–6; Åberg 1926, 105, 208.[1]
20. Dunstable (Puddlehill), Bedfordshire, hut 6. Meaney 1981, 303, note 44.[2]
21. Totternhoe (Marina Drive), Bedfordshire, 3 examples, graves B2, E3 and F2. Matthews 1962, 28, 32.[3]

---

[1] The reference in Douglas is to fragments of a shell and a cowrie shell bead. Åberg refers to a cowrie shell in this grave but there is no indication of whether he himself had seen the shell at the Ashmolean Museum or was referring to the report in Douglas.

[2] The reference given in Meaney's note is for the cowrie at Empingham. No report of the find at Puddlehill has been located.

[3] These shells are referred to in Meaney 1981, 28 and 124 but not in her list of cowries 303, note 44. They may be the small native *Cyprea europa* as at Cheesecake Hill, Humberside (Yorkshire), rather than the larger *Cyprea pantherina* or *Cyprea arabica* which was obtained from sources no nearer to Britain than the Red Sea.

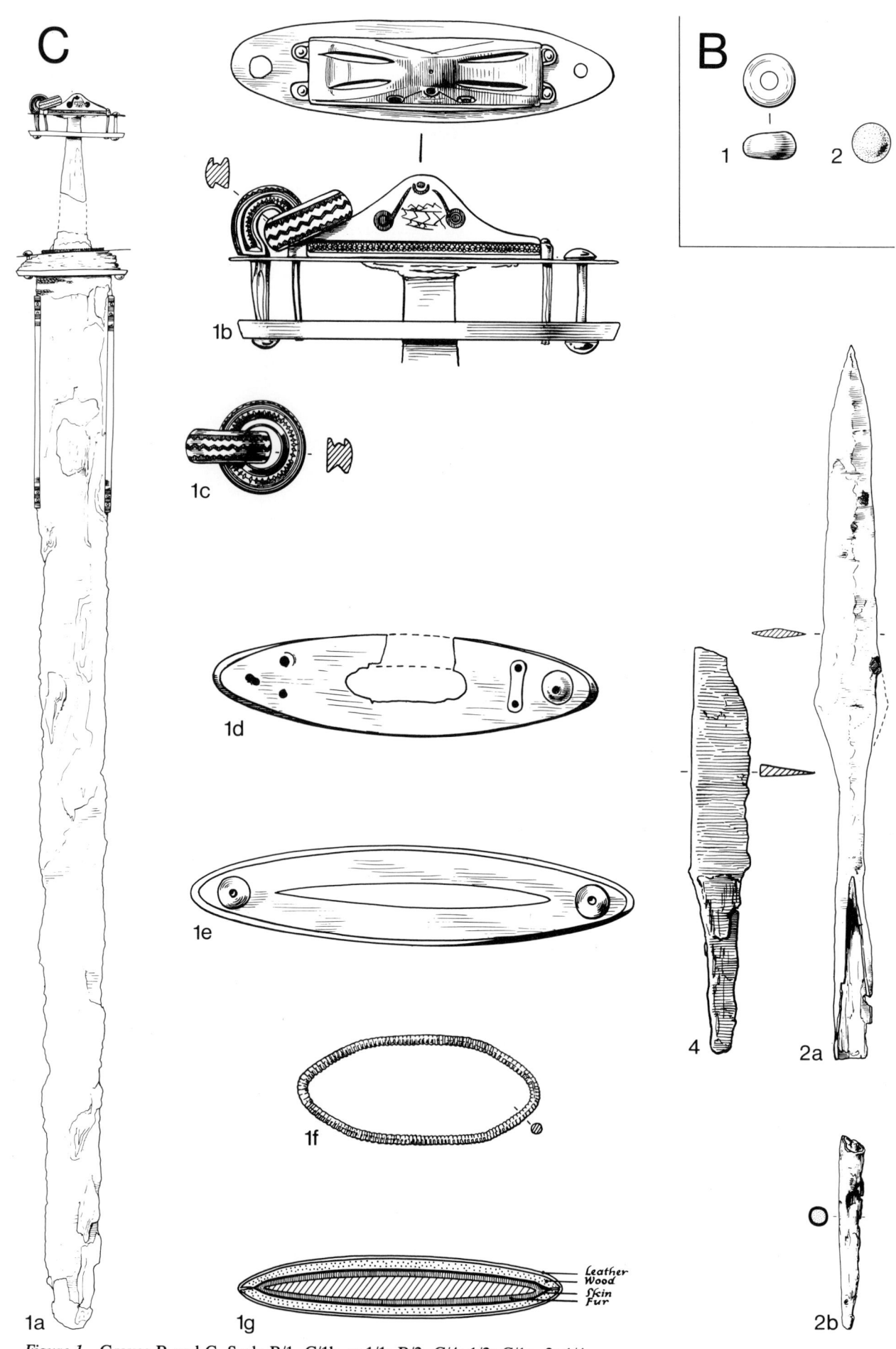

*Figure 1* Graves B and C. Scale B/1, C/1b–g: 1/1: B/2, C/4: 1/2; C/1a, 2: 1/4

GRAVE CATALOGUE 273

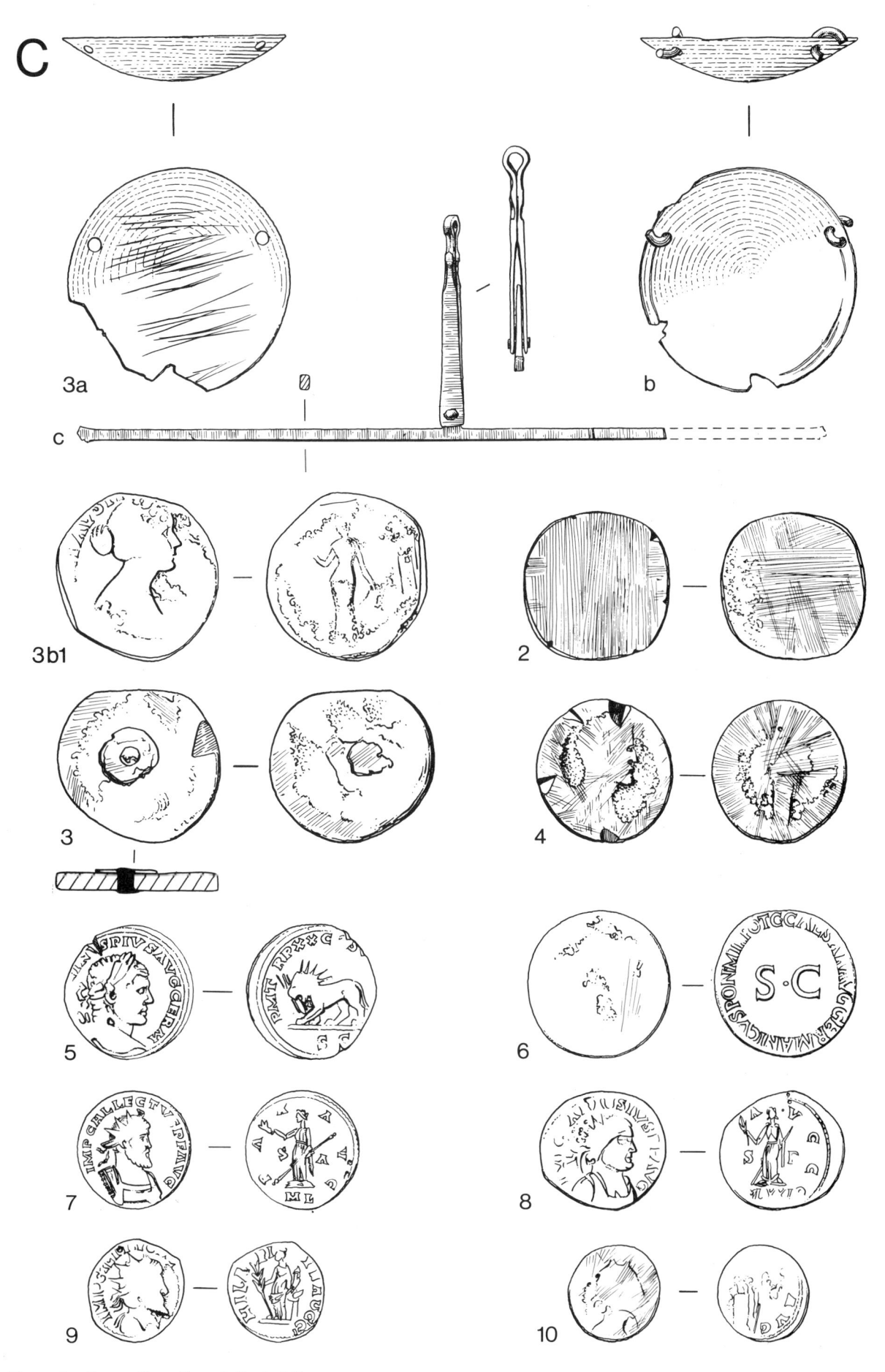

*Figure 2* Grave C continued. Scale 1/1

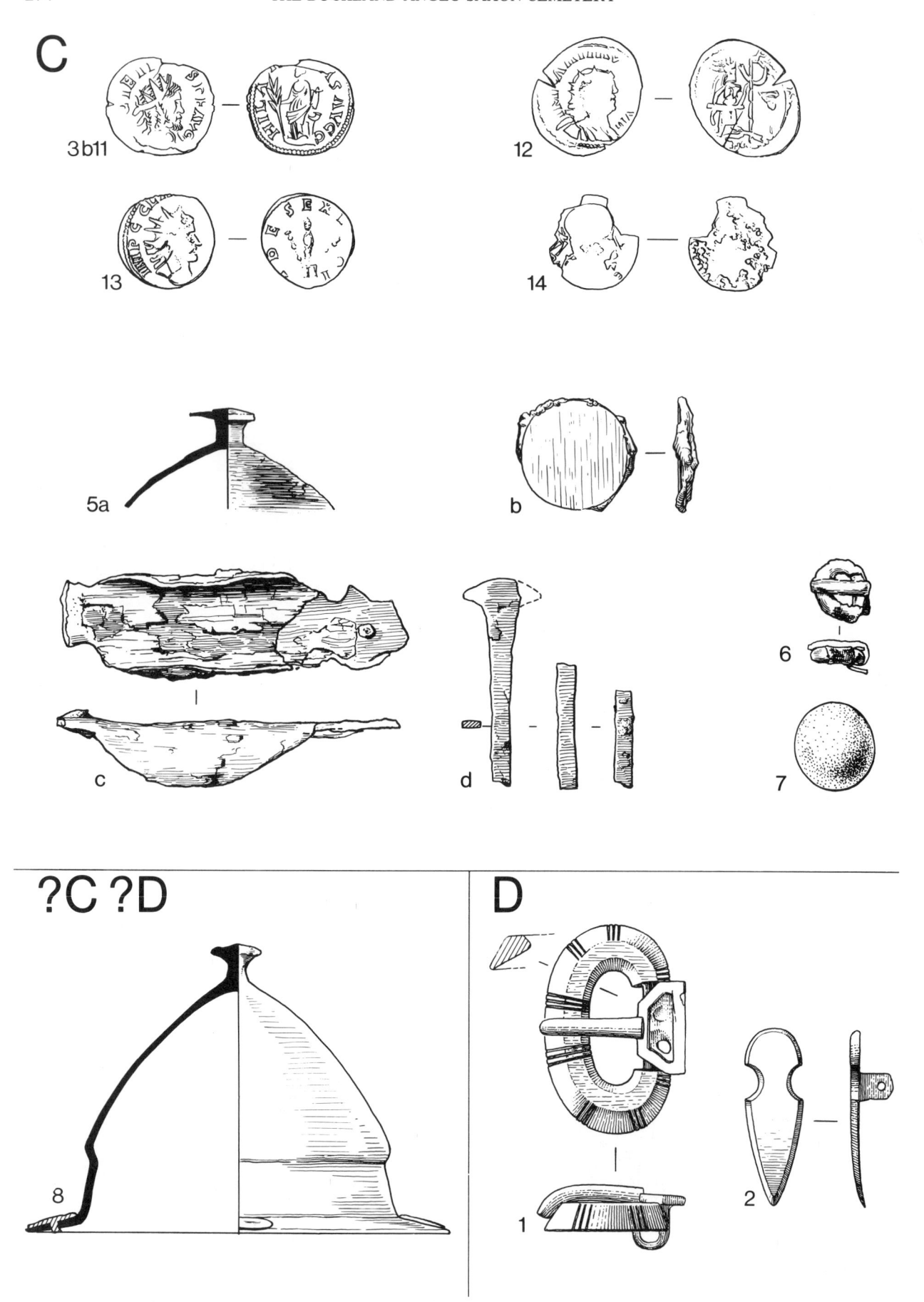

*Figure 3* Grave C continued, grave C or D and grave D. Scale C/3, 5b, 7, D/1–2: 1/1; C/5a, c–d, 6, ?C?D/8: 1/2

GRAVE CATALOGUE 275

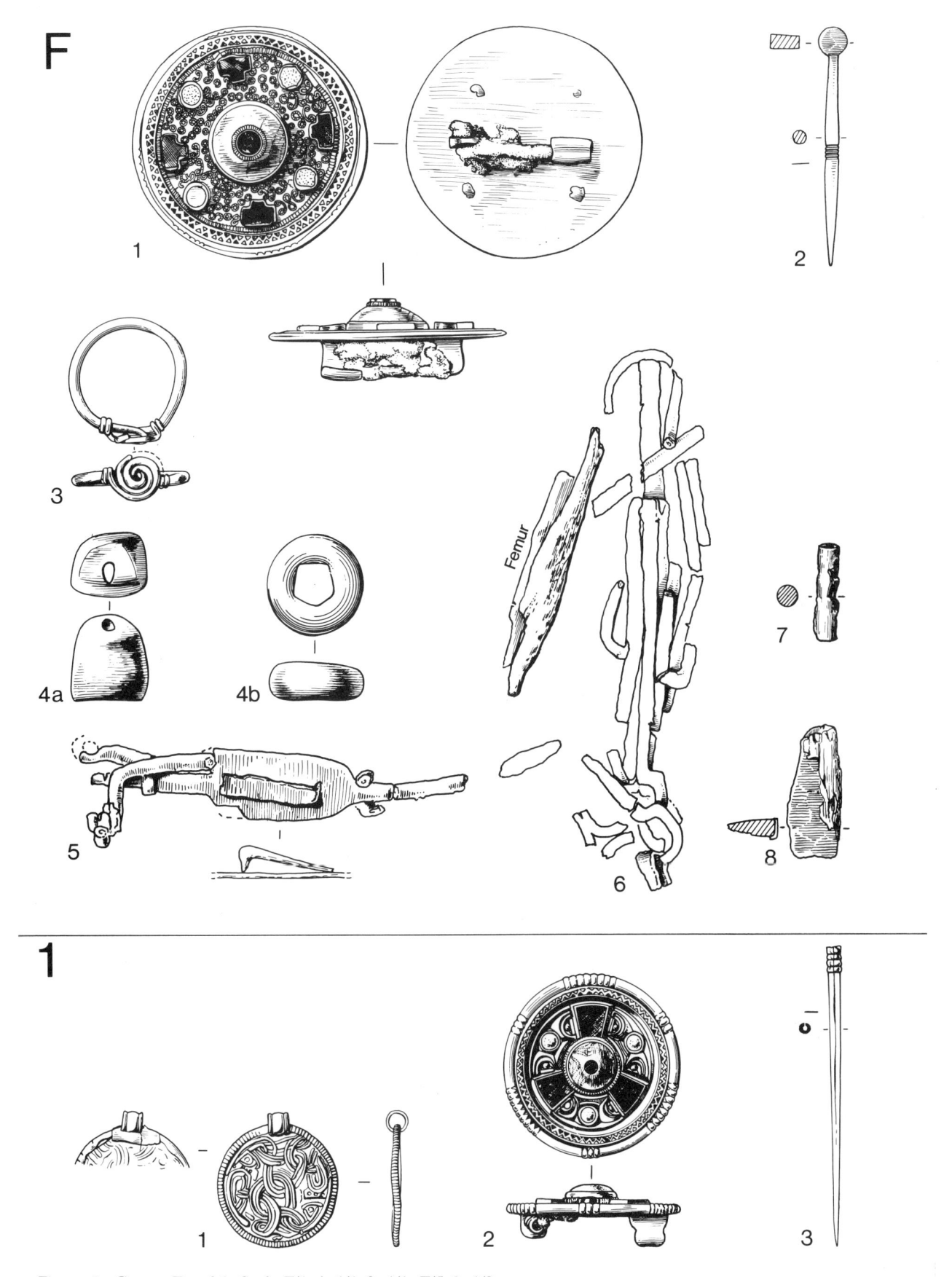

*Figure 4* Graves F and 1. Scale F/1–4, 1/1–3: 1/1; F/5–8: 1/2

276       THE BUCKLAND ANGLO-SAXON CEMETERY

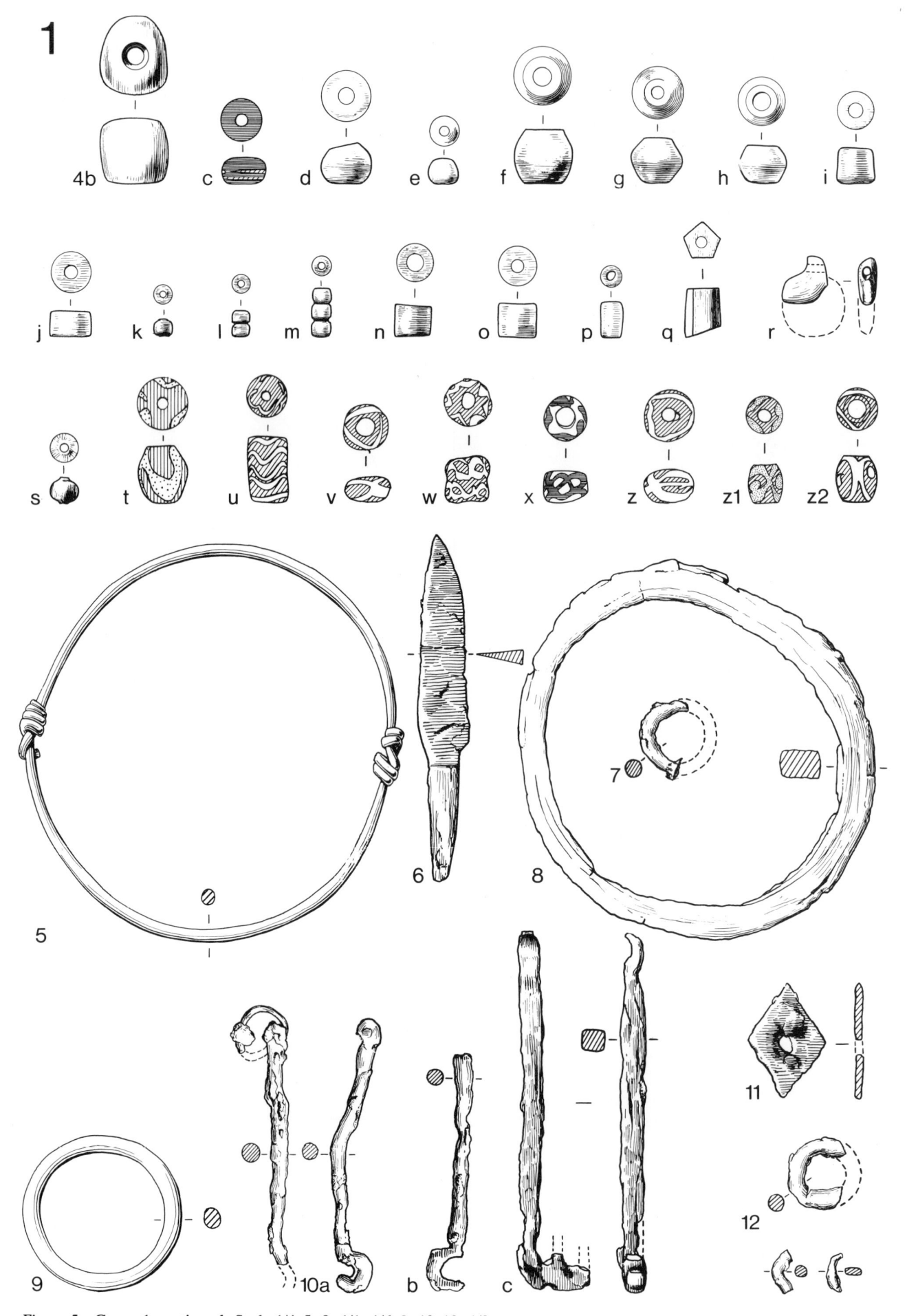

*Figure 5*  Grave 1 continued. Scale 1/4–5, 9; 1/1: 1/6–8, 10–12: 1/2

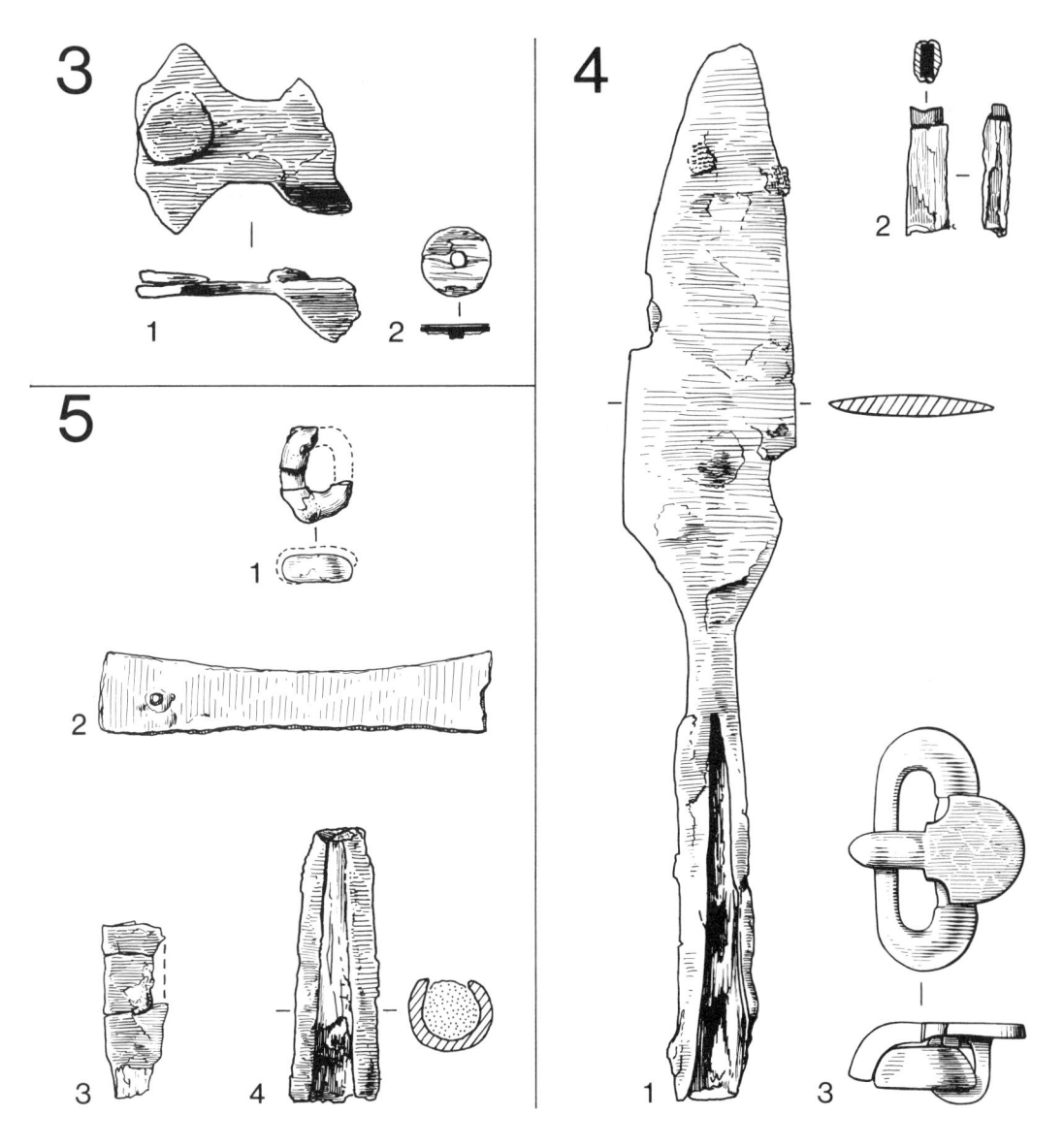

*Figure 6* Graves 3, 4 and 5. Scale 4/3: 1/1; 3/1–2, 4/1–2, 5/1–4: 1/2

278    THE BUCKLAND ANGLO-SAXON CEMETERY

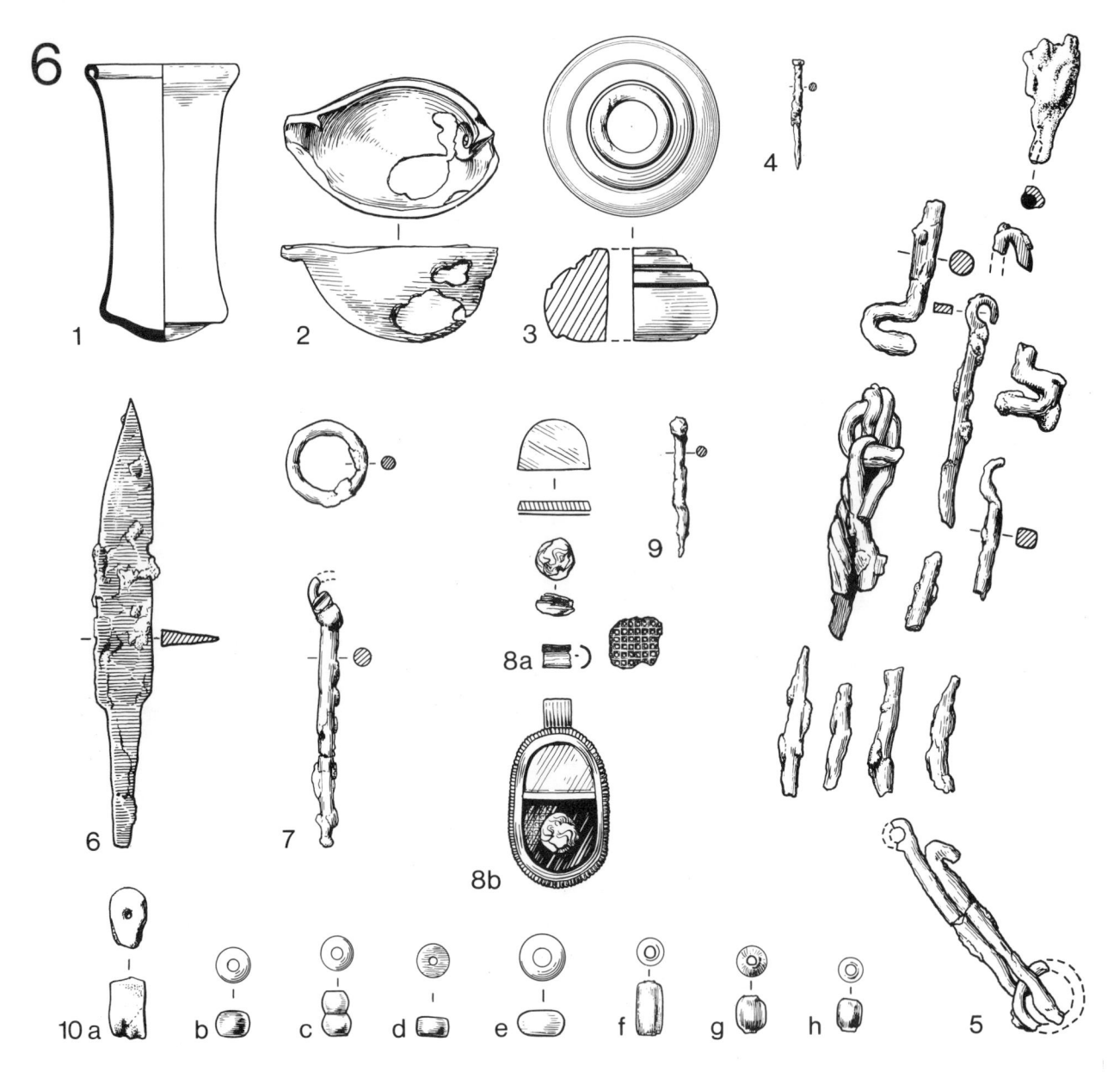

*Figure 7*   Grave 6. Scale 6/3, 8, 10: 1/1; 6/1–2, 4–7, 9: 1/2

GRAVE CATALOGUE                                                             279

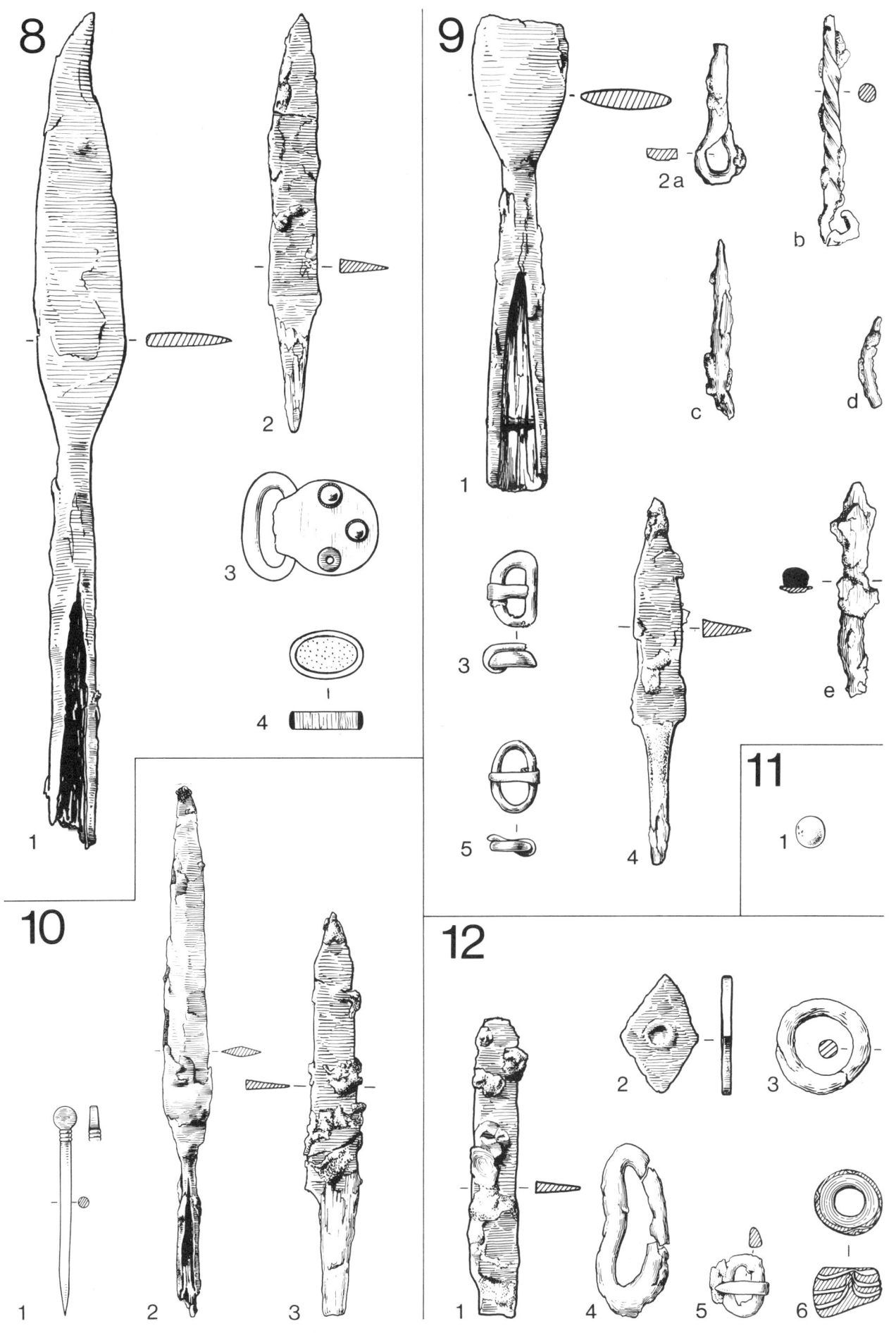

*Figure 8*   Graves 8, 9, 10, 11 and 12. Scale 9/5, 10/1, 12/6: 1/1; 8/1–4, 9/1–4, 10/3, 11/1, 12/1–5: 1/2; 10/2: 1/4

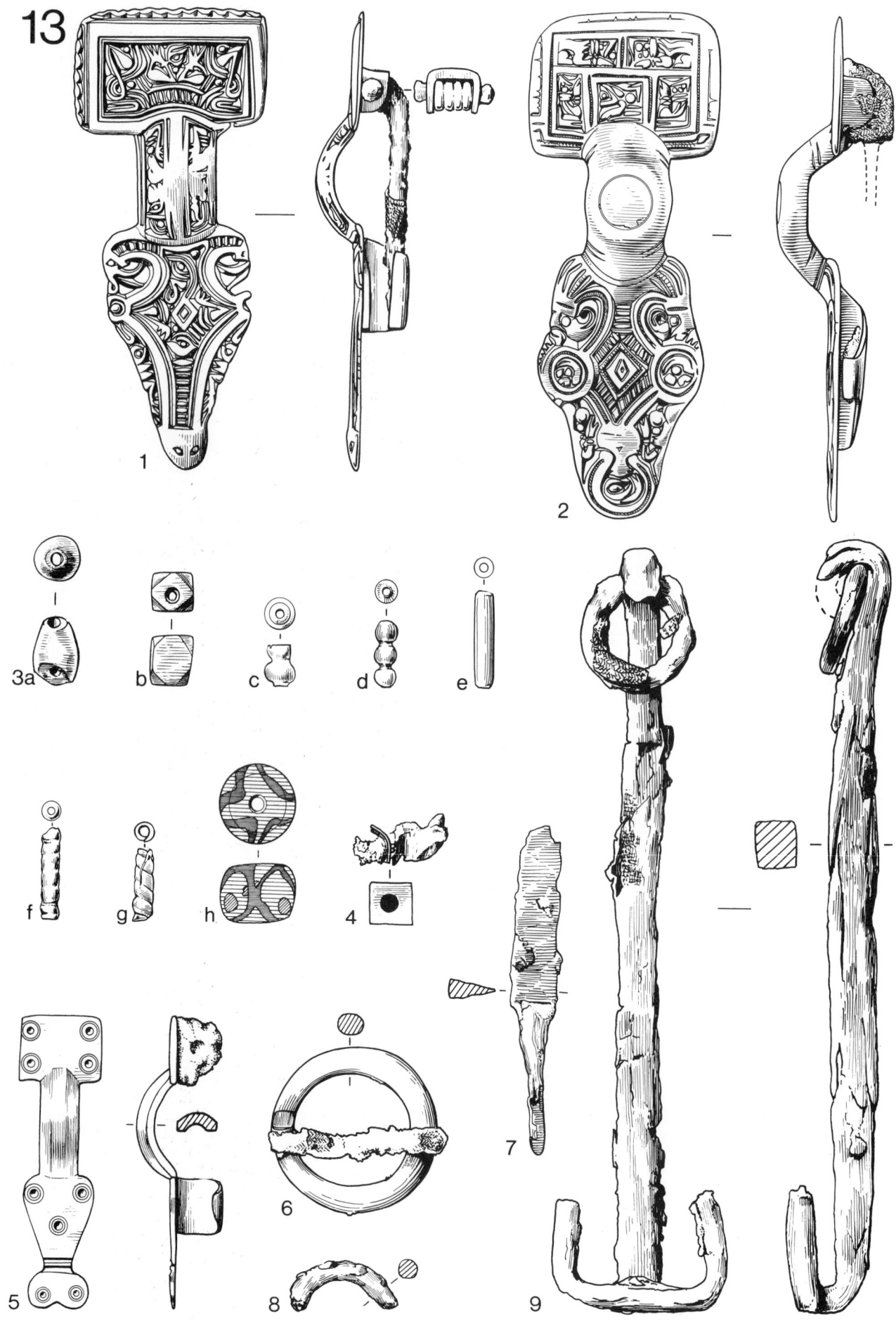

*Figure 9*  Grave 13. Scale 13/1–6: 1/1; 7–9: 1/2

GRAVE CATALOGUE 281

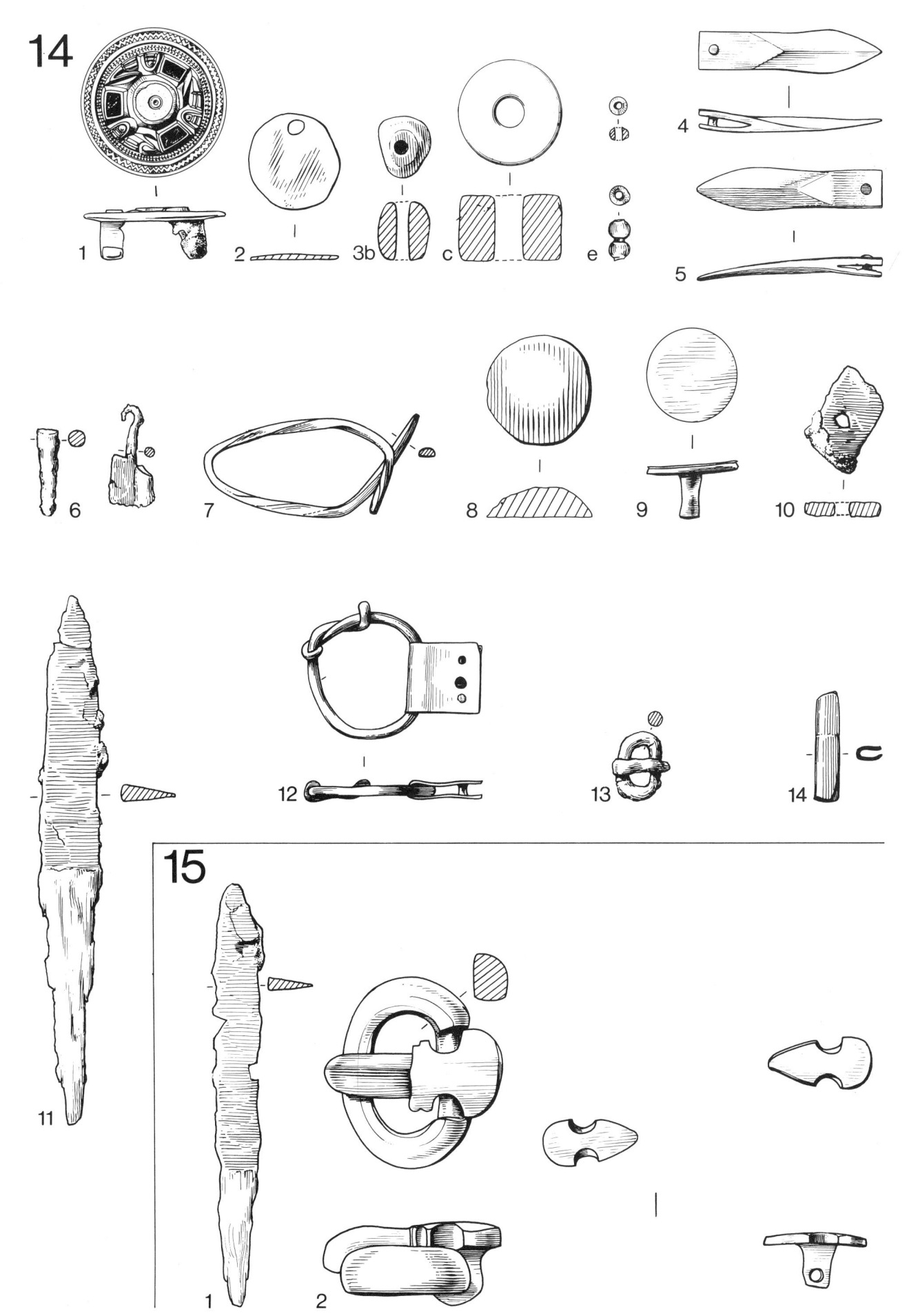

*Figure 10*  Graves 14 and 15. Scale 14/1, 3–5, 7–9, 12, 14, 15/2: 1/1; 14/2, 6, 10–11, 13, 15/1: 1/2

282

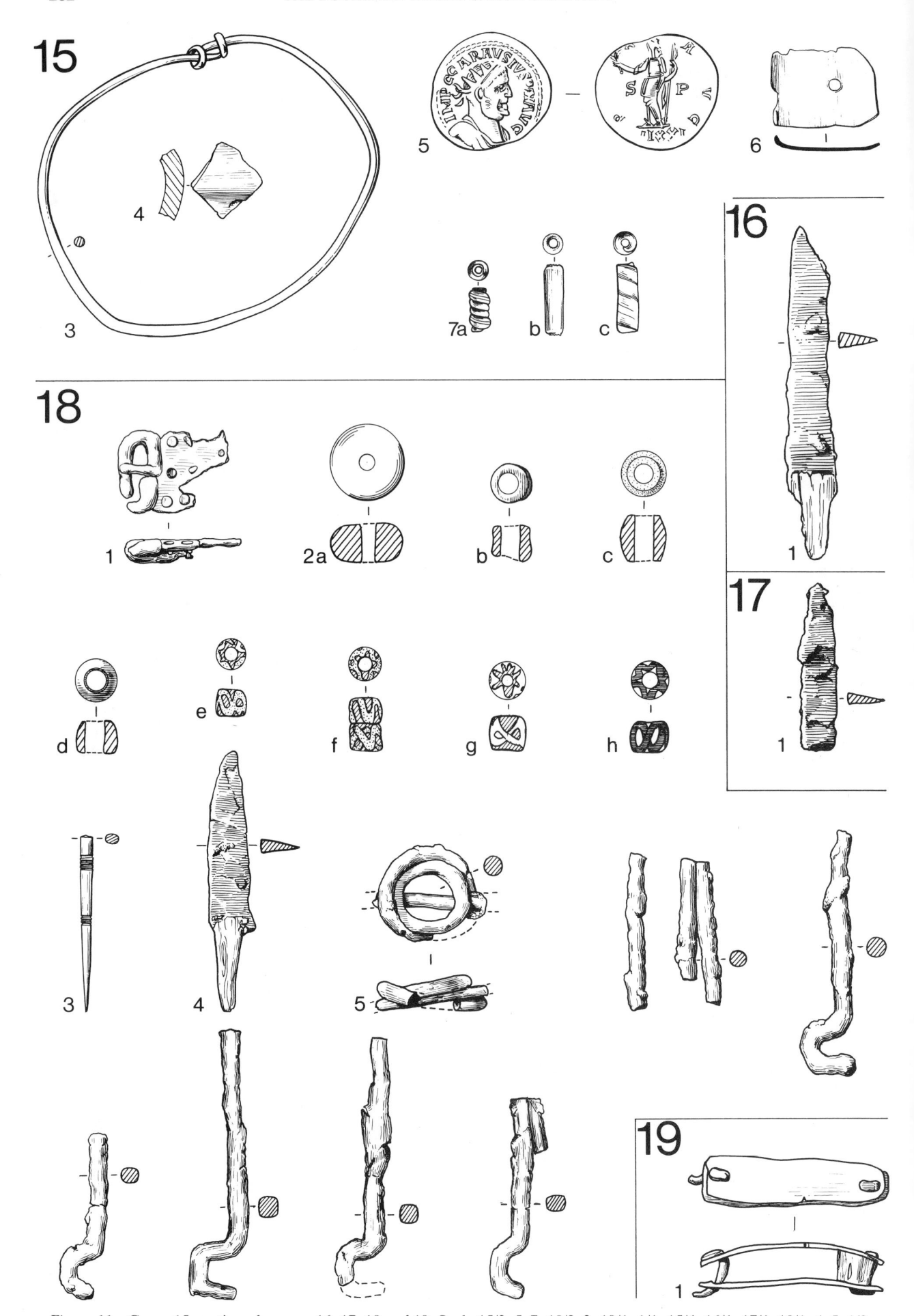

*Figure 11* Grave 15 continued, graves 16, 17, 18 and 19. Scale 15/3, 5–7, 18/2–3, 19/1: 1/1; 15/4, 16/1, 17/1, 18/1, 4–5: 1/2

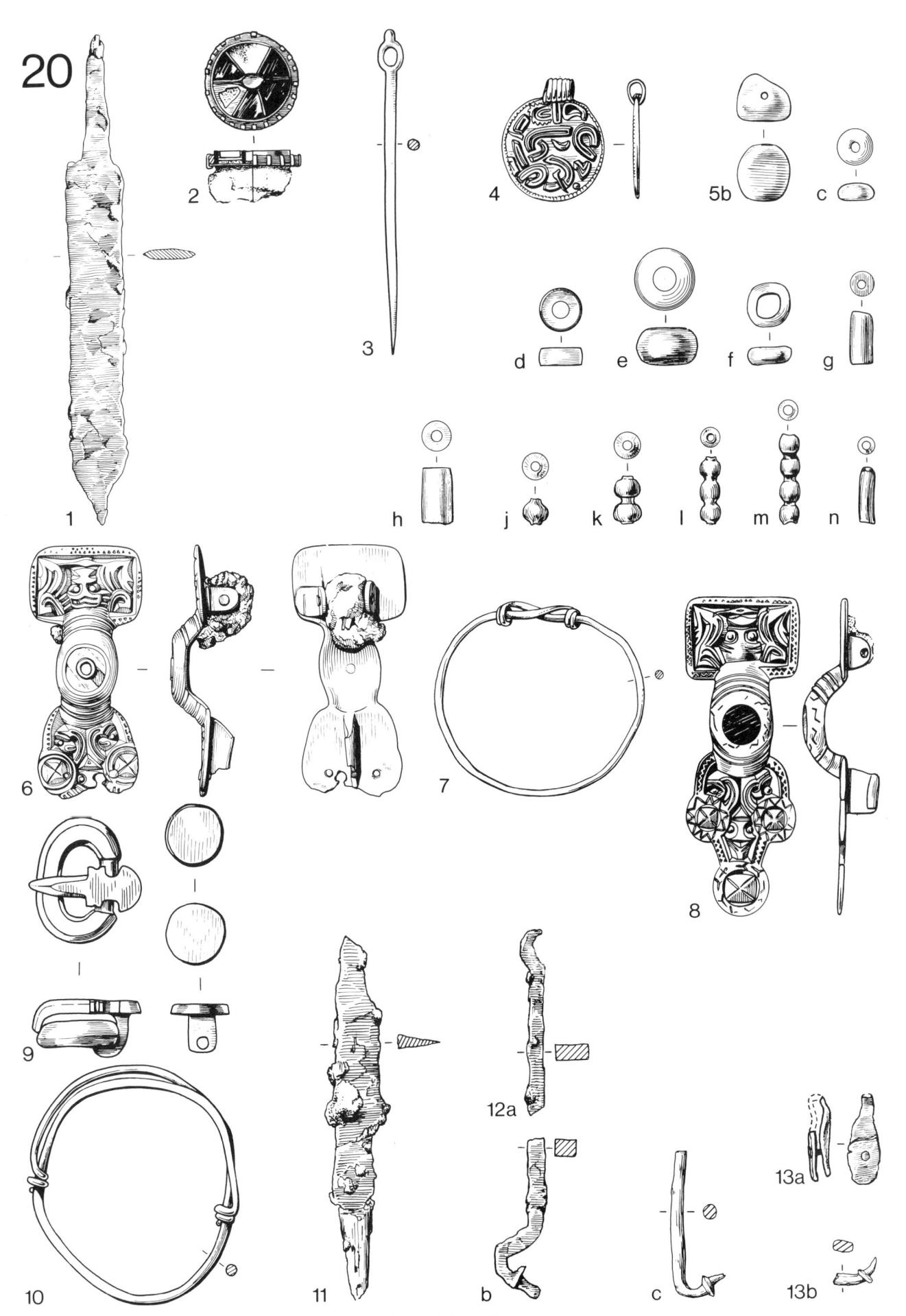

*Figure 12* Grave 20. Scale 20/2–10: 1/1; 20/11–13: 1/2; 20/1: 1/4

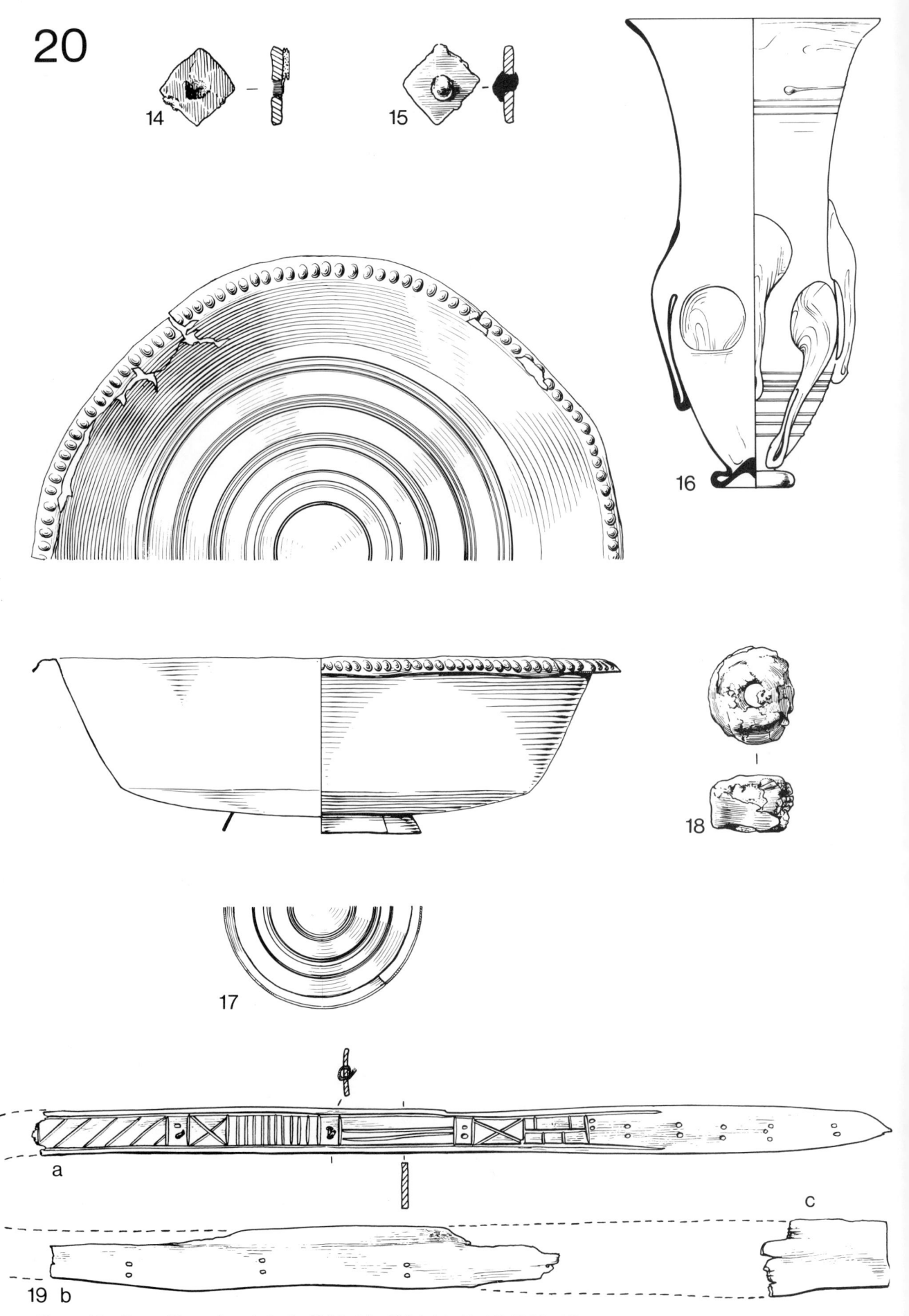

*Figure 13* Grave 20 continued. Scale 20/18: 1/1; 20/14–16, 19: 1/2 20/17: 1/3

# GRAVE CATALOGUE

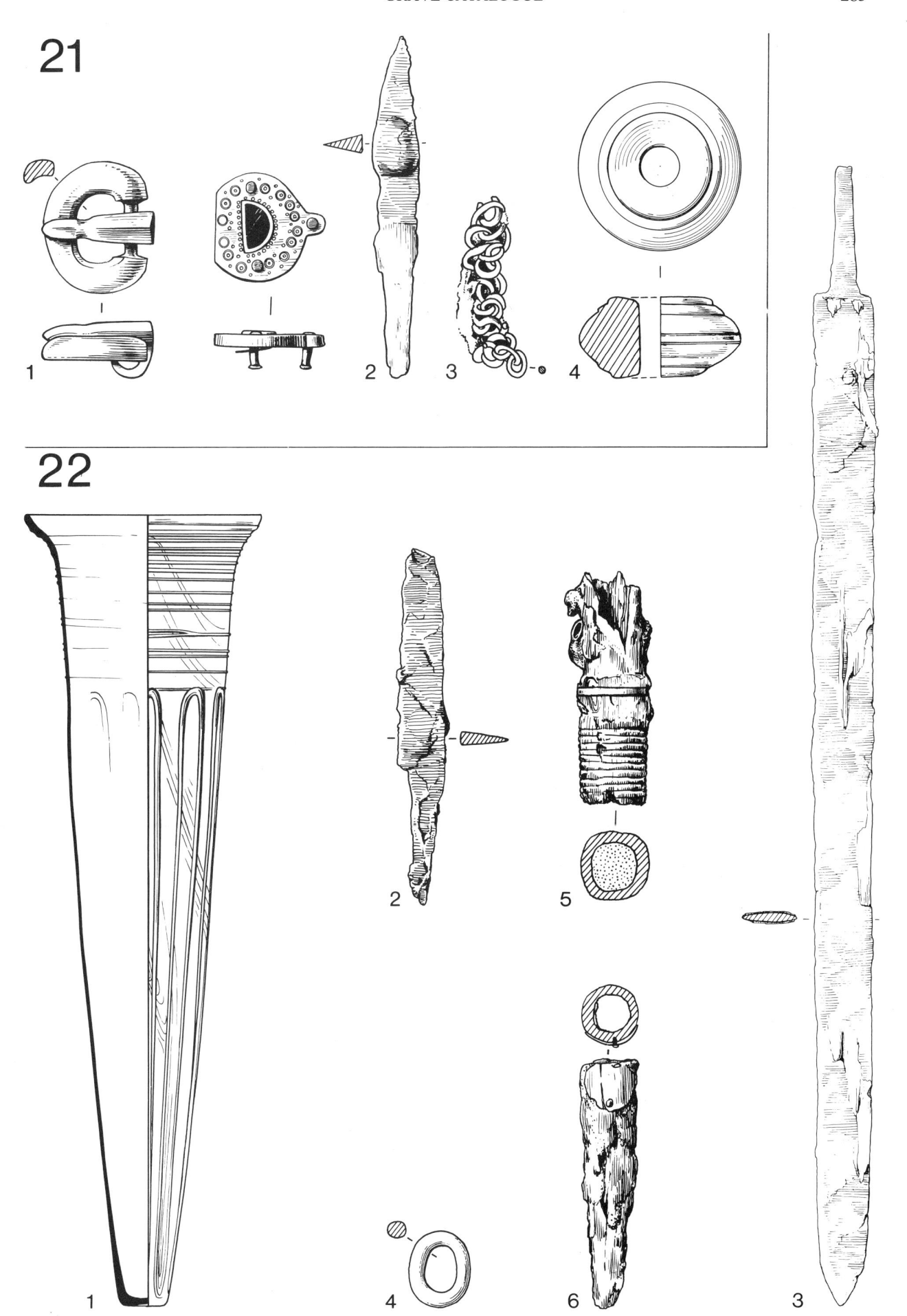

*Figure 14* Graves 21 and 22. Scale 21/1, 4, 22/4: 1/1; 21/2–3, 22/1–2, 5–6: 1/2; 22/3: 1/4

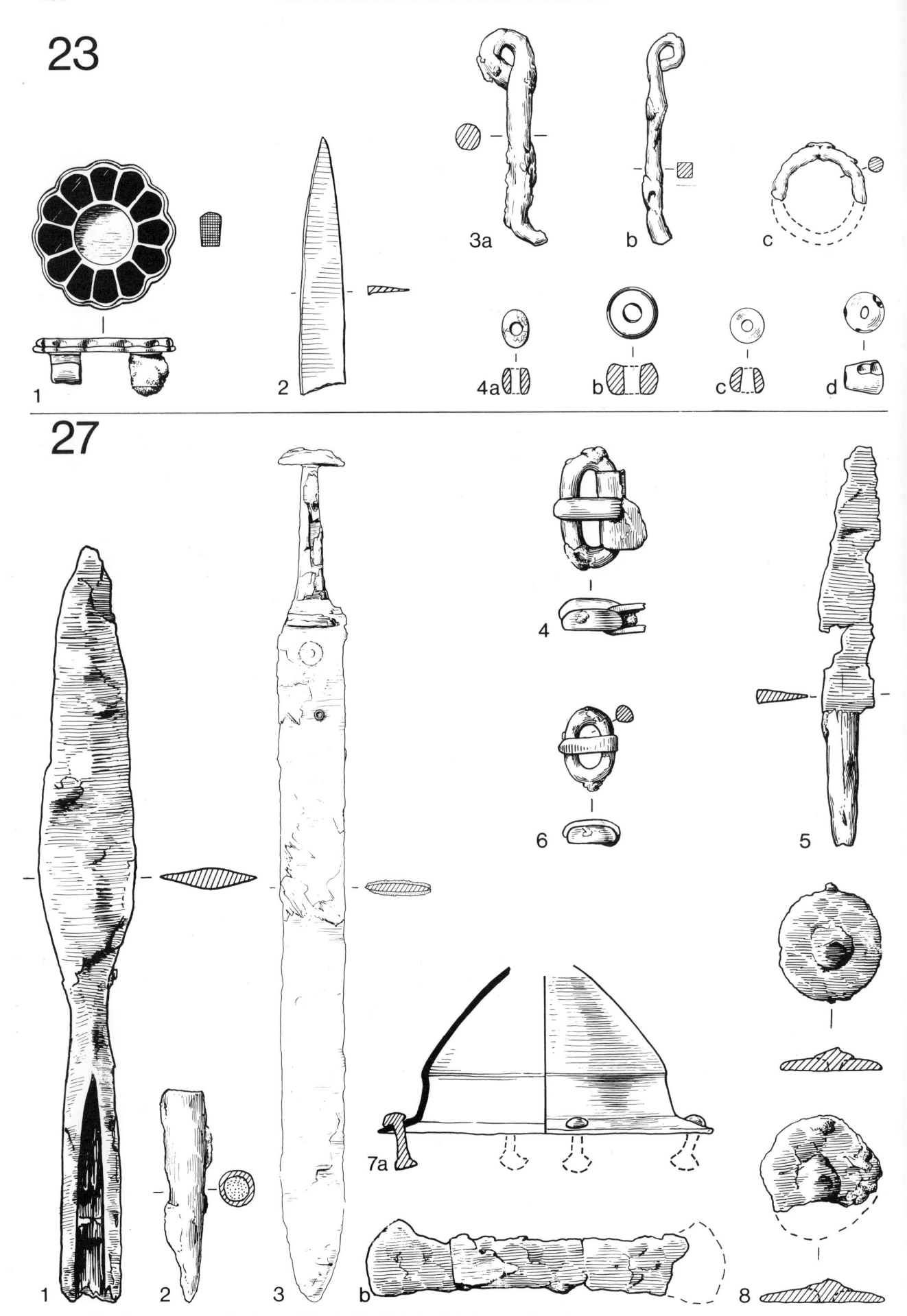

*Figure 15* Graves 23 and 27. Scale 23/1, 4: 1/1; 23/2–3, 27/1–2, 4–8: 1/2; 27/3:1/4

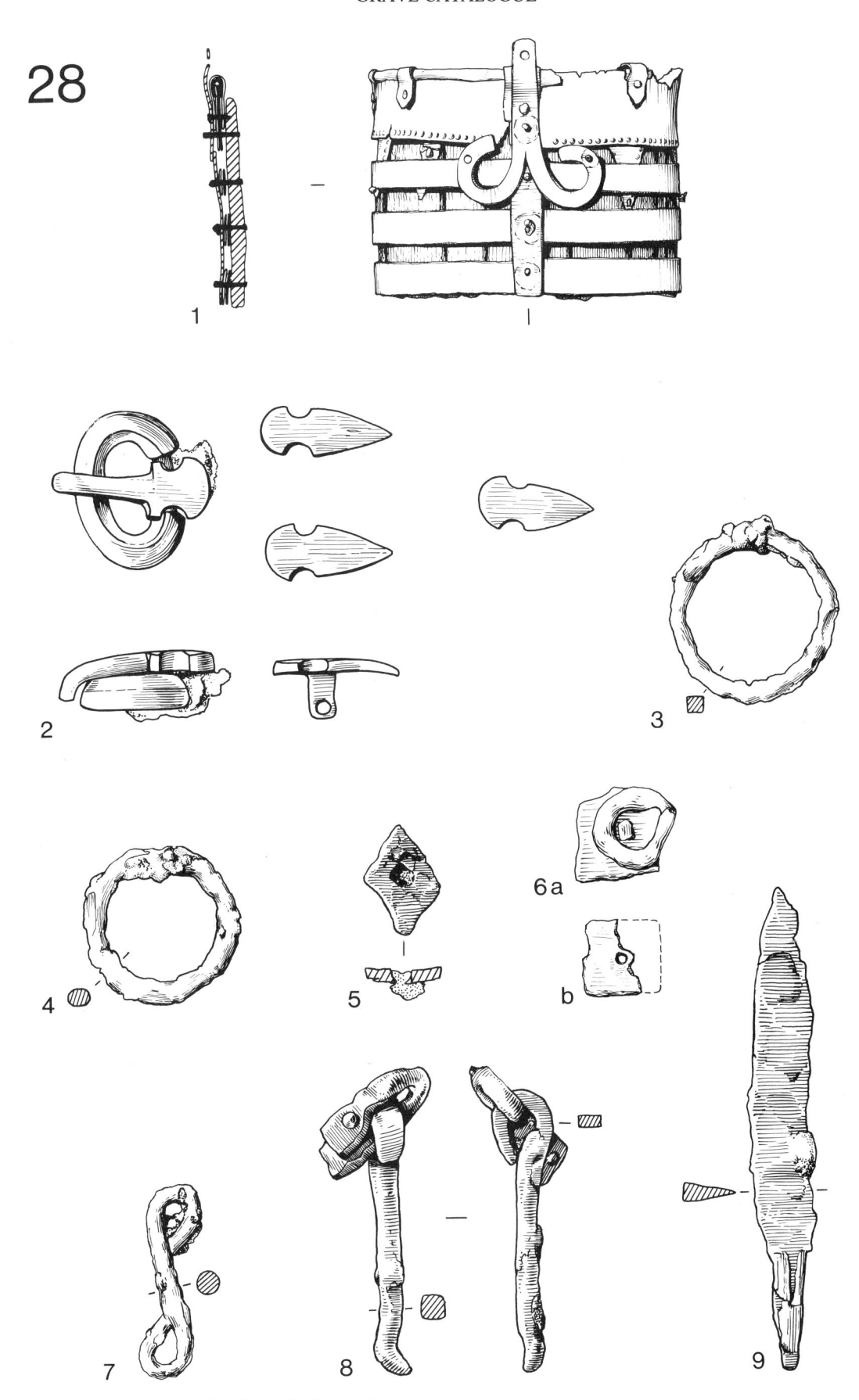

*Figure 16* Grave 28. Scale 28/2: 1/1; 28/1, 3–9: 1/2

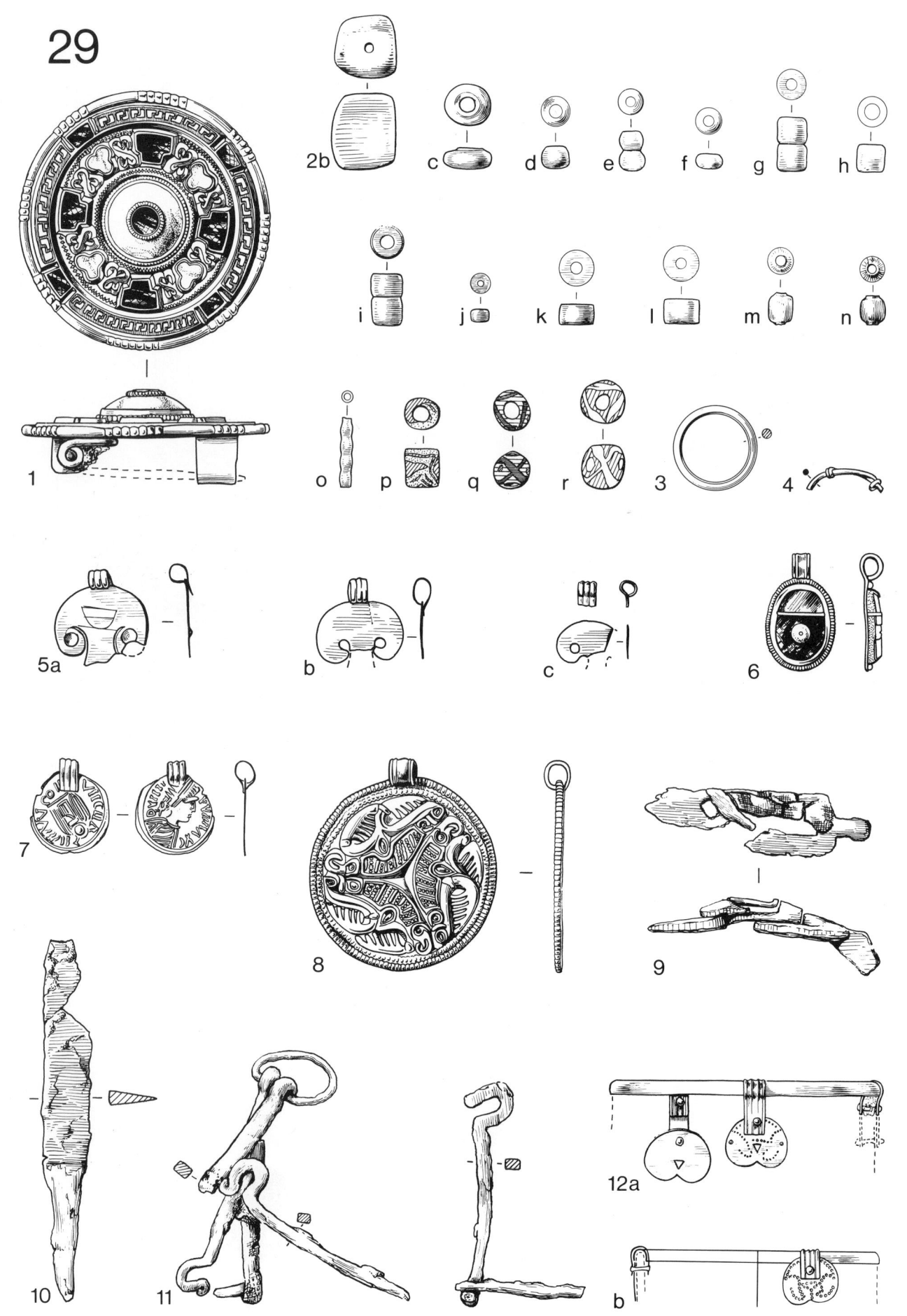

*Figure 17* Grave 29. Scale 29/1–8, 12: 1/1; 29/9–11: 1/2

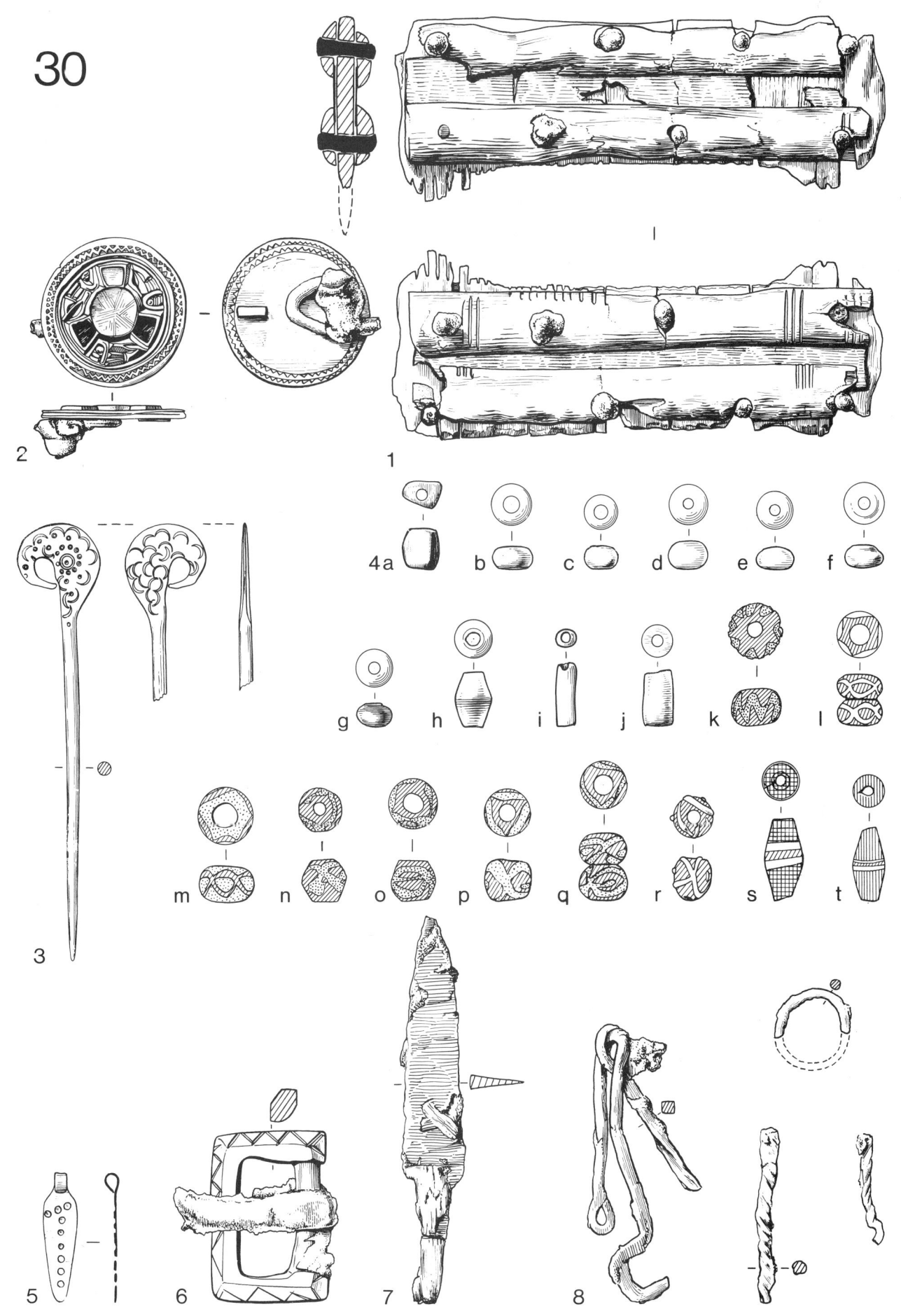

*Figure 18* Grave 30. Scale 30/1–6: 1/1; 30/7–8: 1/2

290

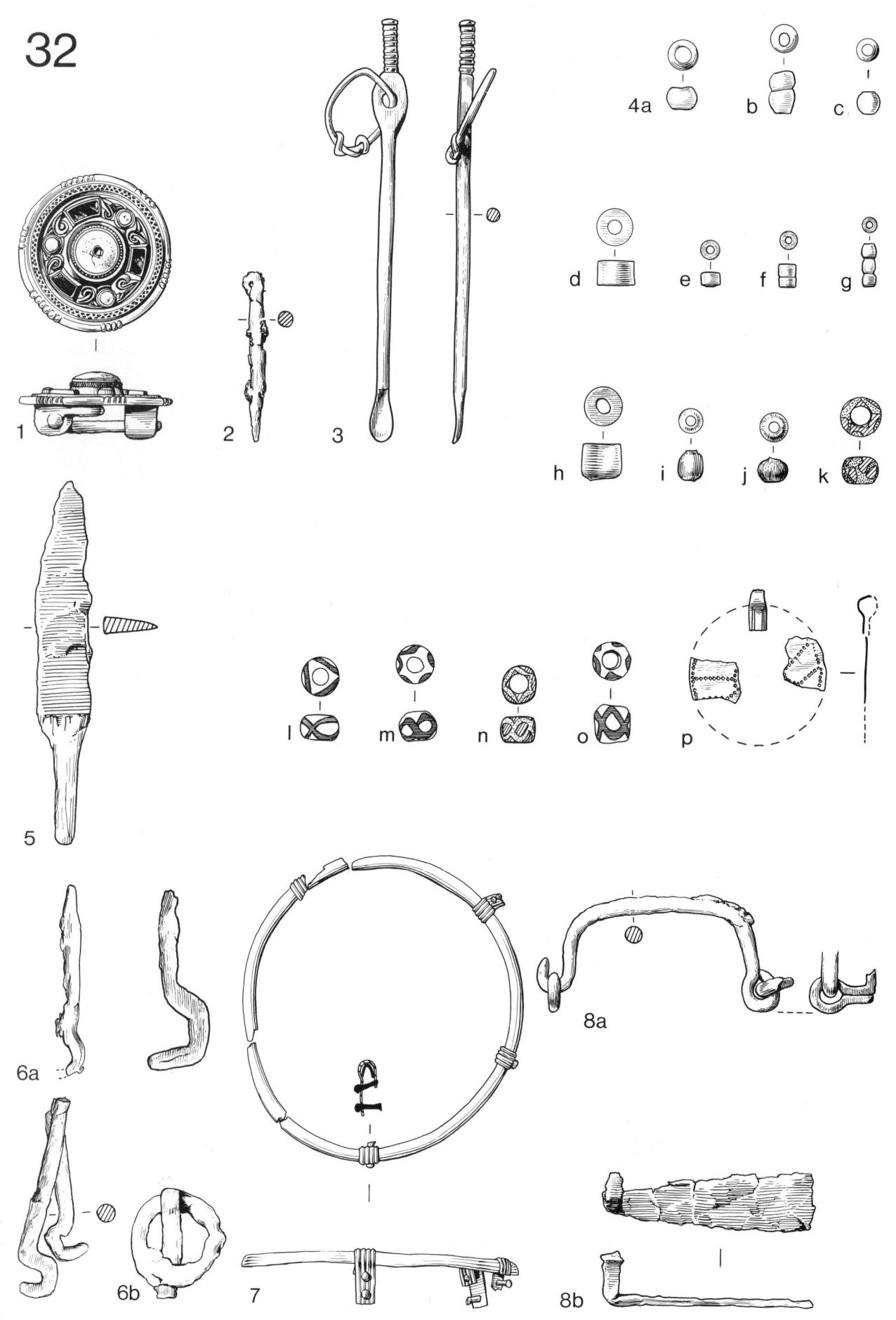

**32**

*Figure 19* Grave 32. Scale 32/1, 3–4, 7: 1/1; 32/2, 5–6, 8: 1/2

GRAVE CATALOGUE

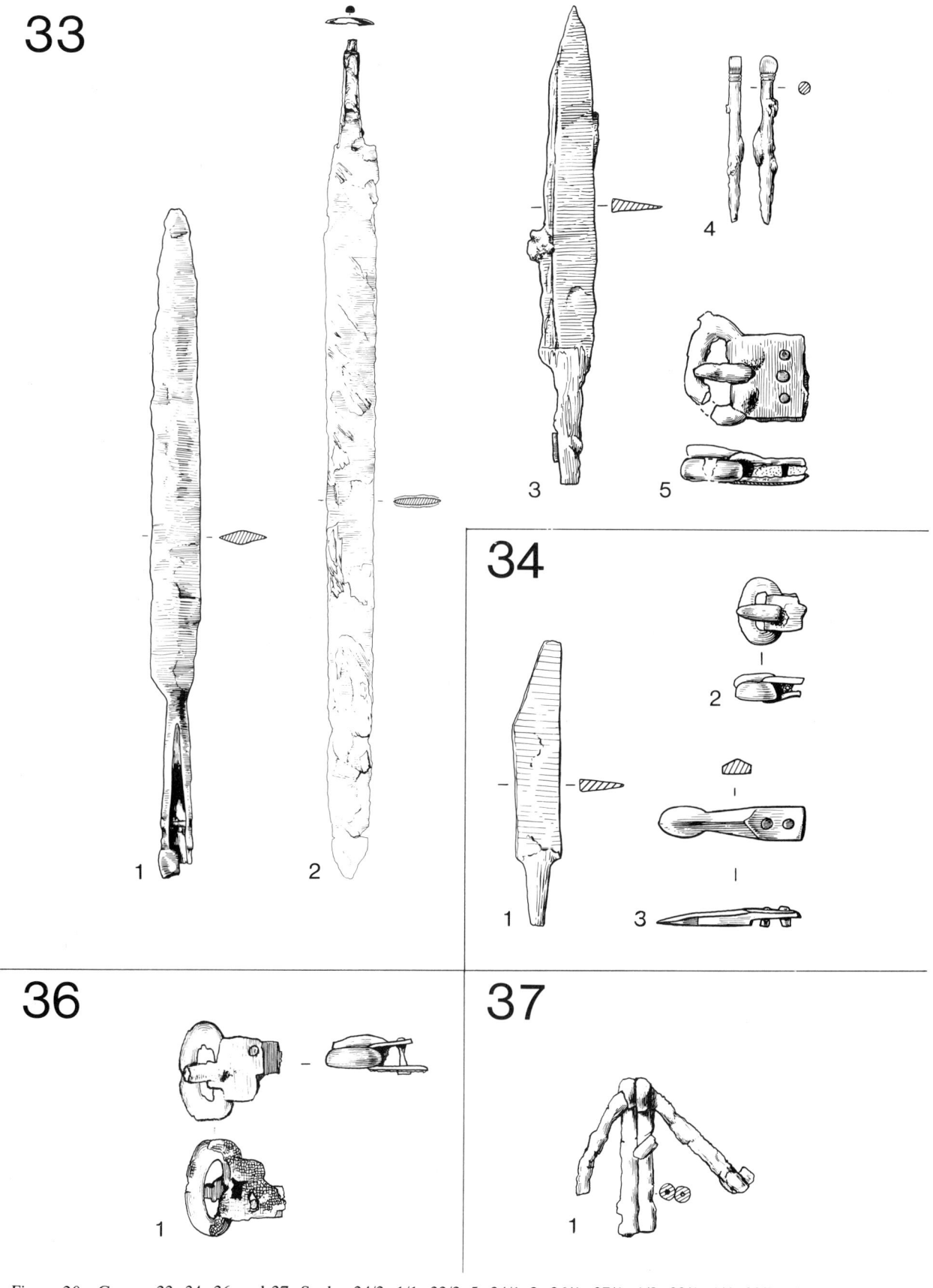

*Figure 20* Graves 33, 34, 36 and 37. Scales 34/3: 1/1; 33/3–5, 34/1–2, 36/1, 37/1: 1/2; 33/1: 1/4; 33/2: 1/6

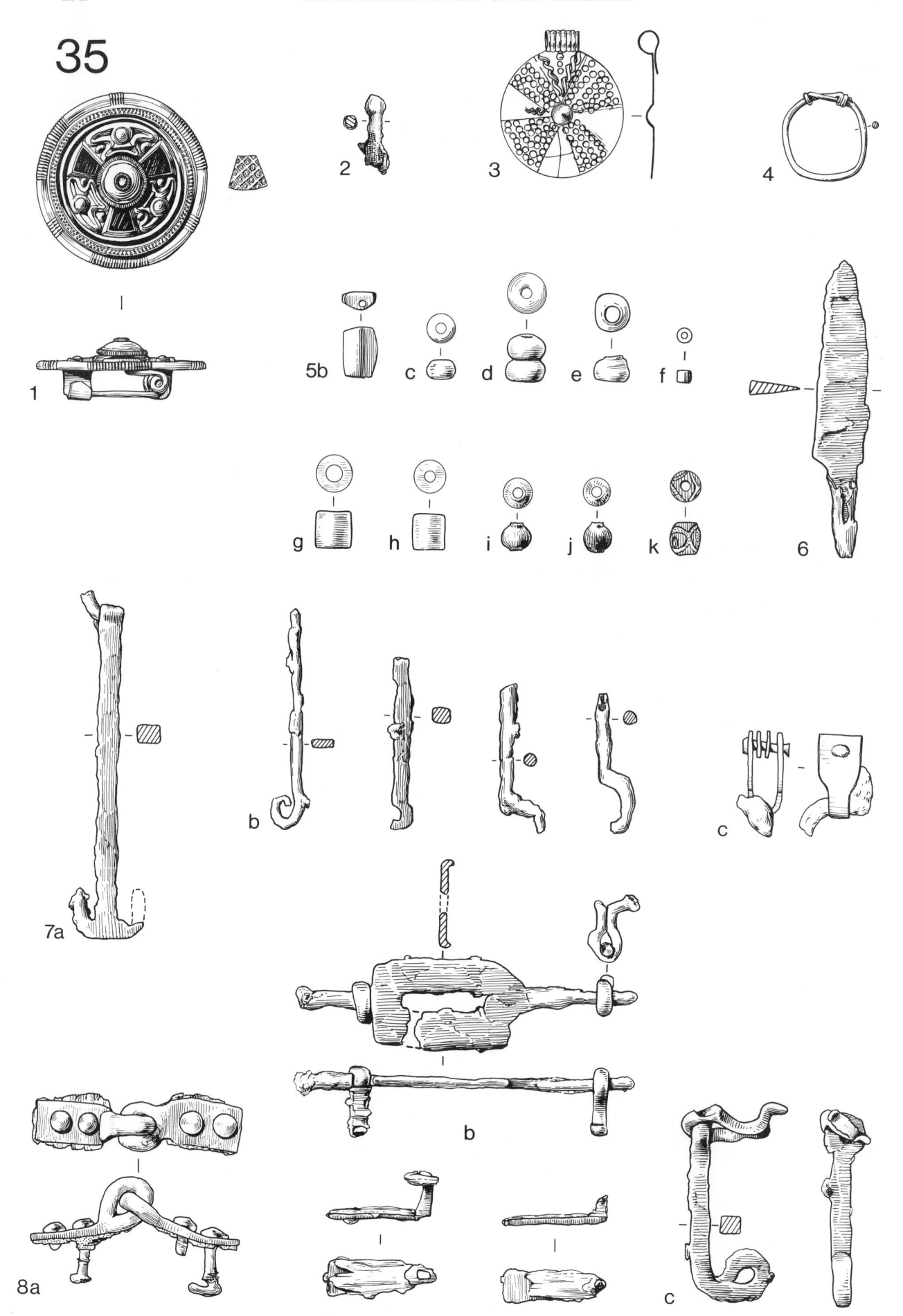

*Figure 21* Grave 35. Scale 35/1, 3–5, 7c: 1/1; 35/2, 6, 7a, b, 8: 1/2

GRAVE CATALOGUE 293

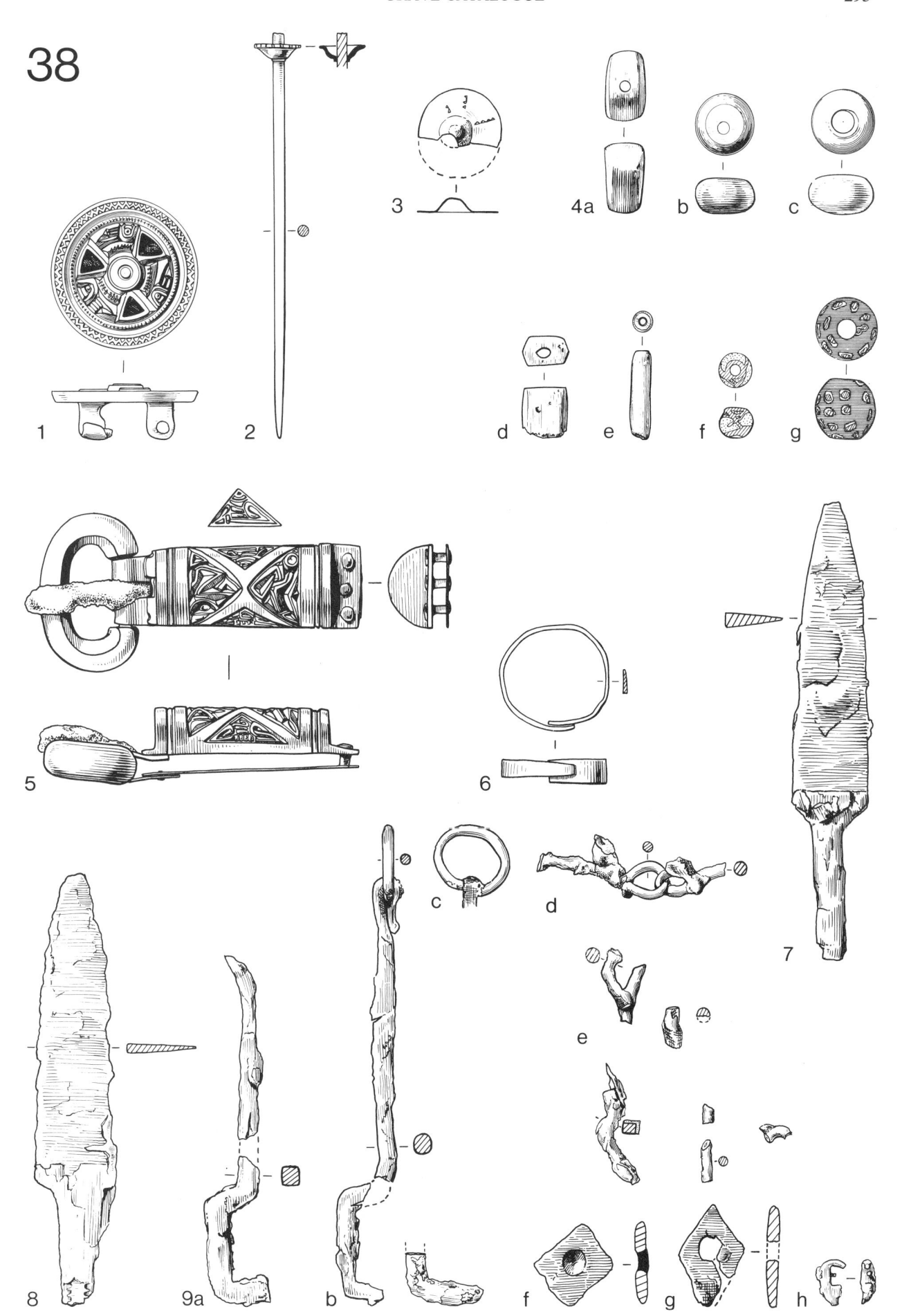

*Figure 22*  Grave 38. Scale 38/1–6: 1/1; 38/7–9: 1/2

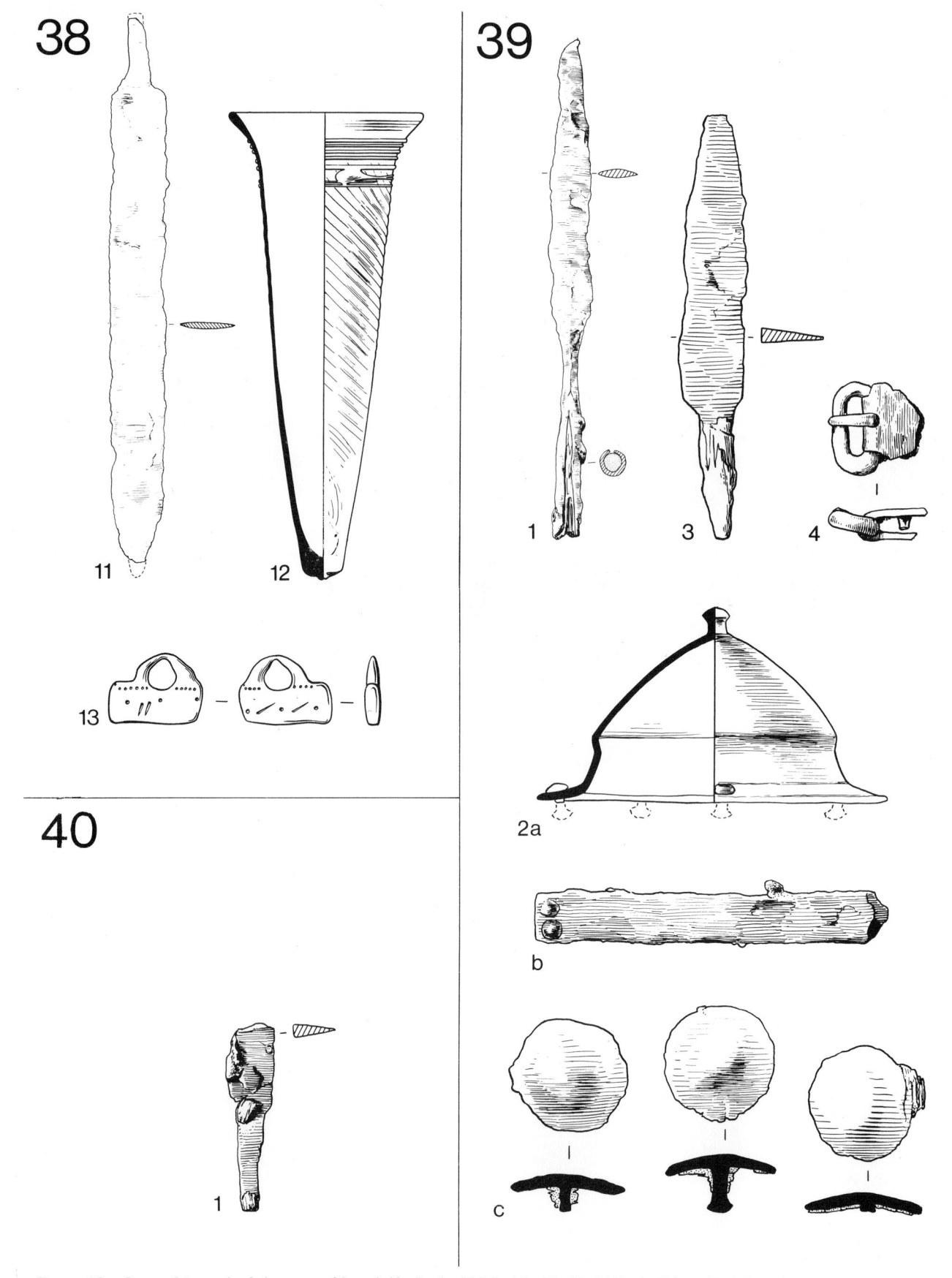

*Figure 23* Grave 38 continued, graves 39 and 40. Scale 38/13: 1/1; 38–12, 39/2–4, 40/1: 1/2; 38/11, 39/1: 1/4

GRAVE CATALOGUE 295

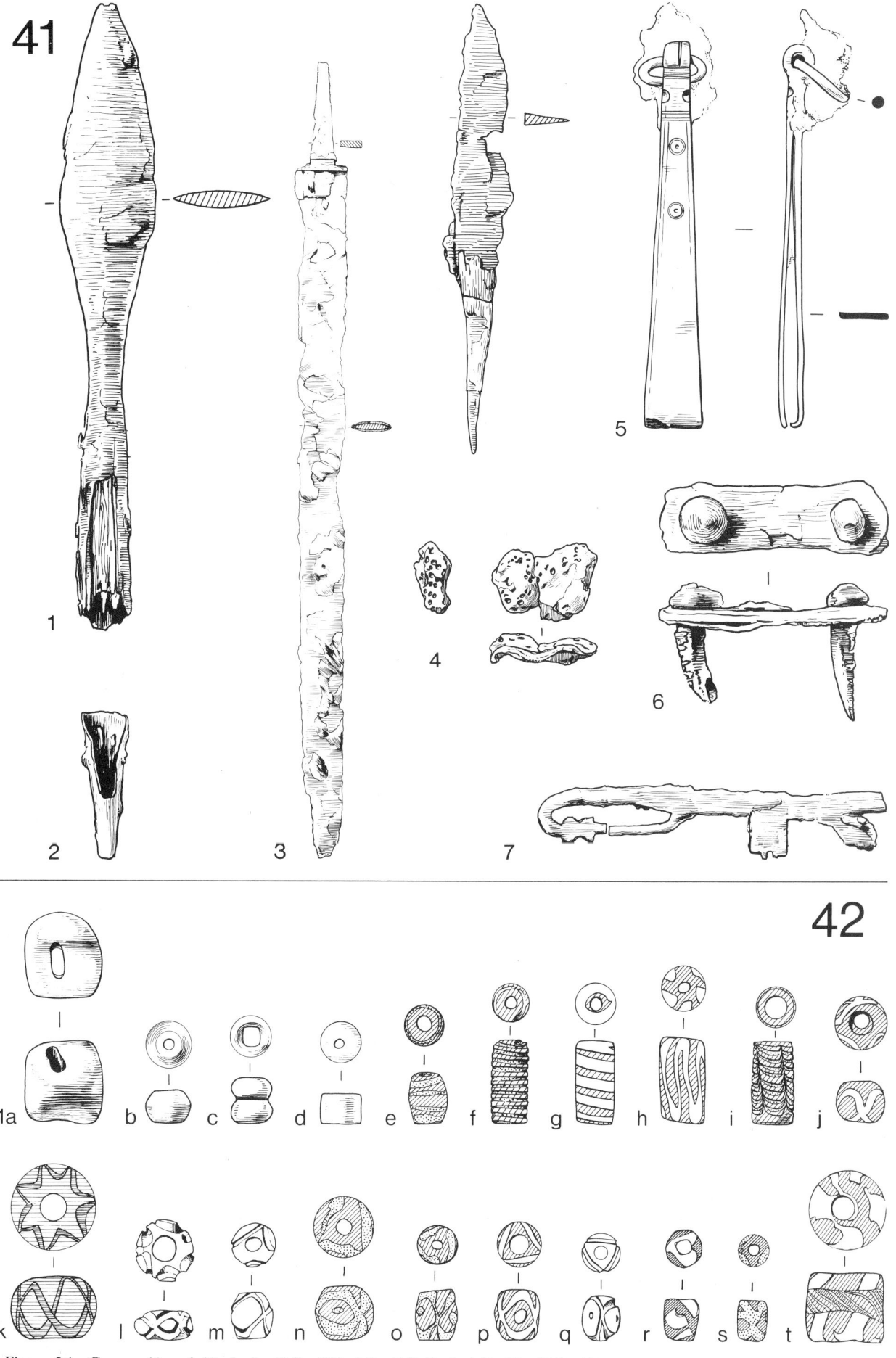

*Figure 24* Graves 41 and 42. Scale 41/5, 42/1: 1/1; 41/1–2, 4, 6–7: 1/2; 41/3: 1/6.

296    THE BUCKLAND ANGLO-SAXON CEMETERY

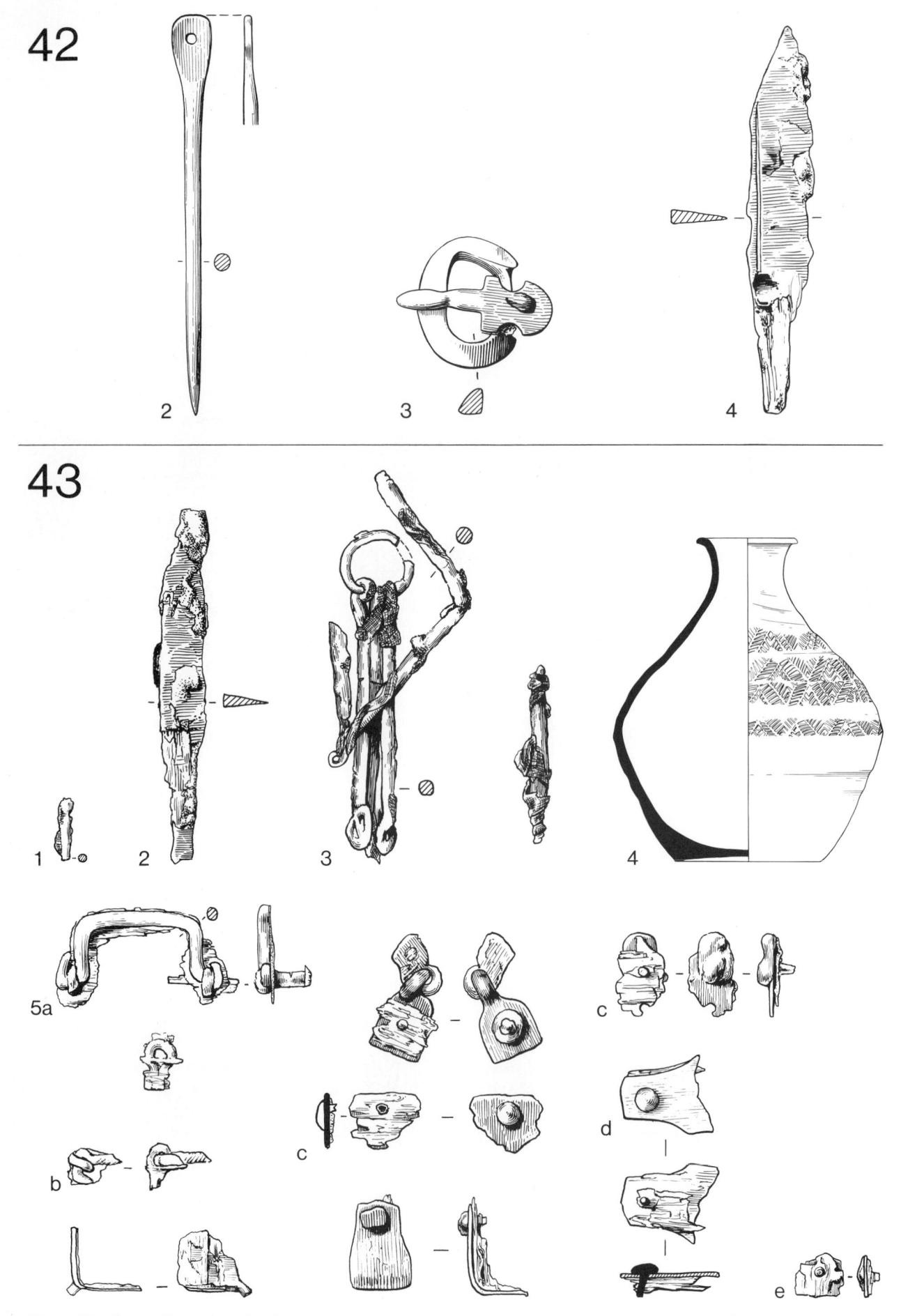

*Figure 25*   Grave 42 continued and grave 43. Scale 42/2–3: 1/1; 42/4, 43/1–3, 5: 1/2; 43/4: 1/3

# GRAVE CATALOGUE

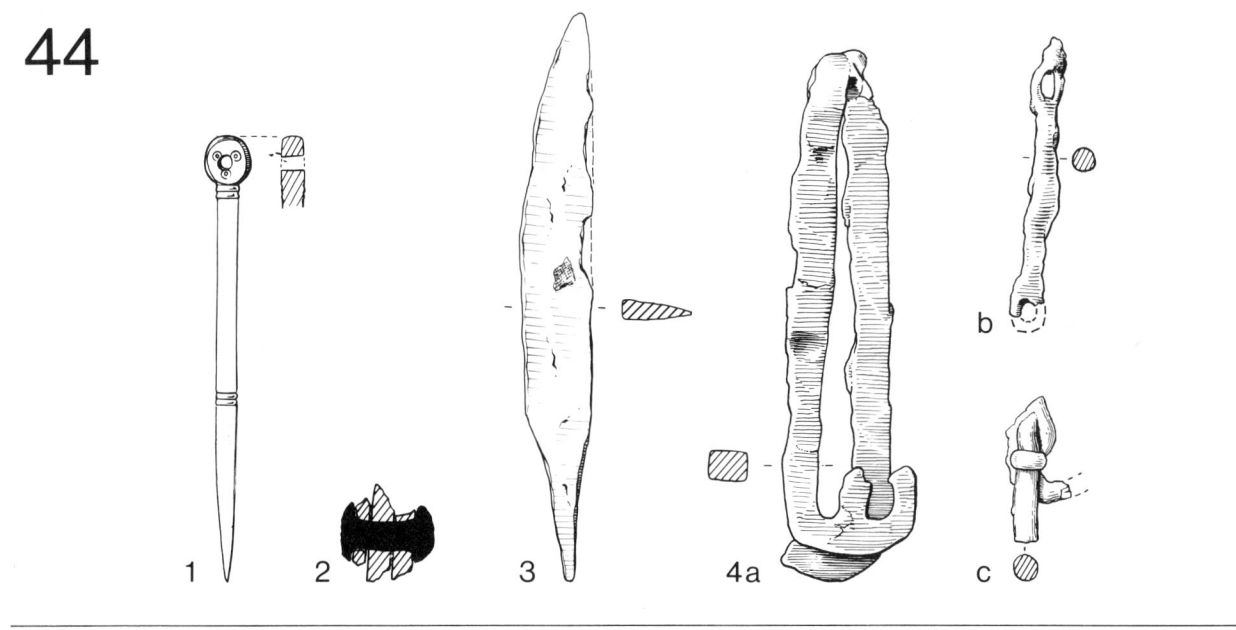

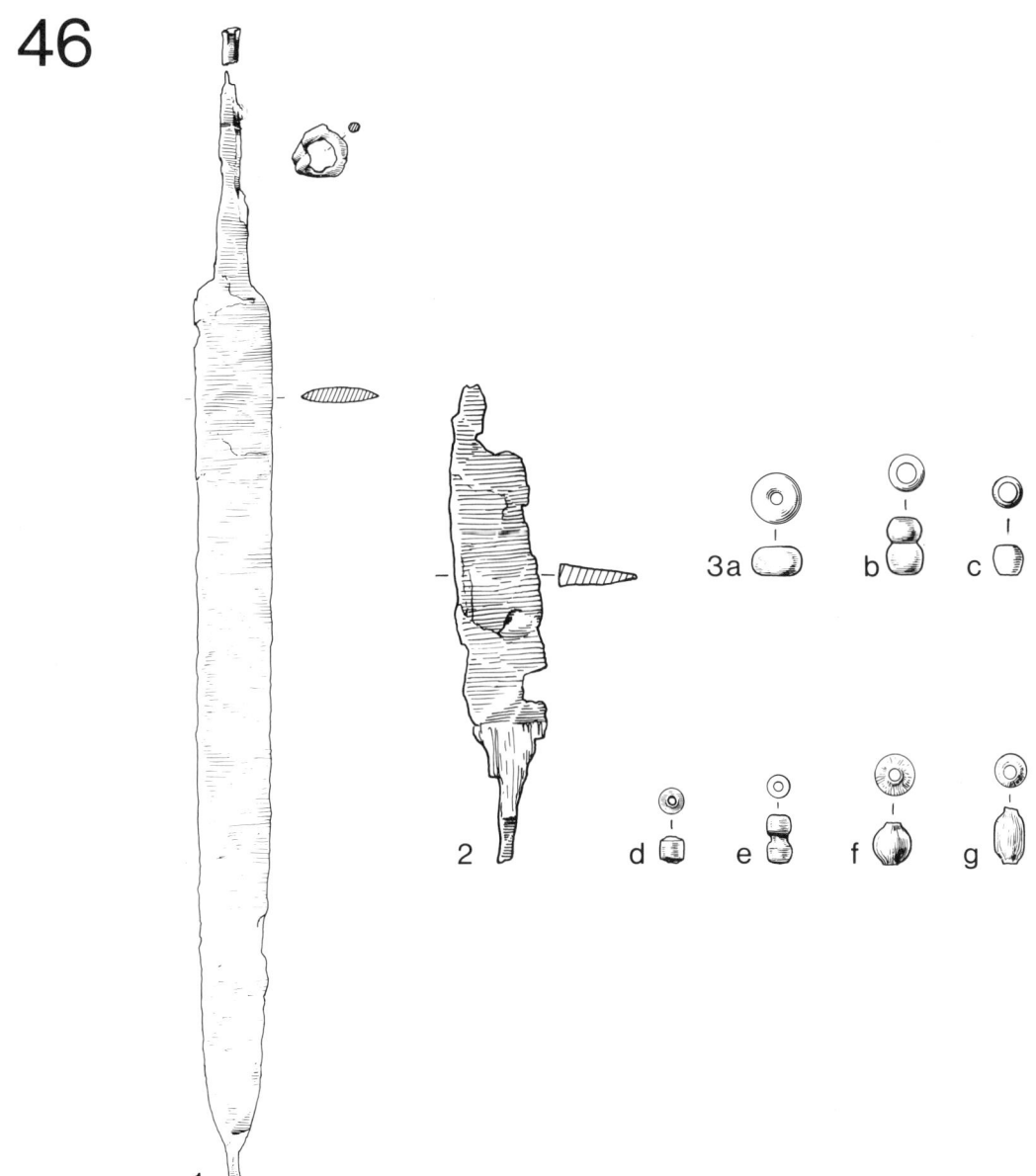

*Figure 26* Graves 44 and 46. Scale 44/1–2, 46/3: 1/1; 44/3–4, 46/2: 1/2; 46/1: 1/4

298

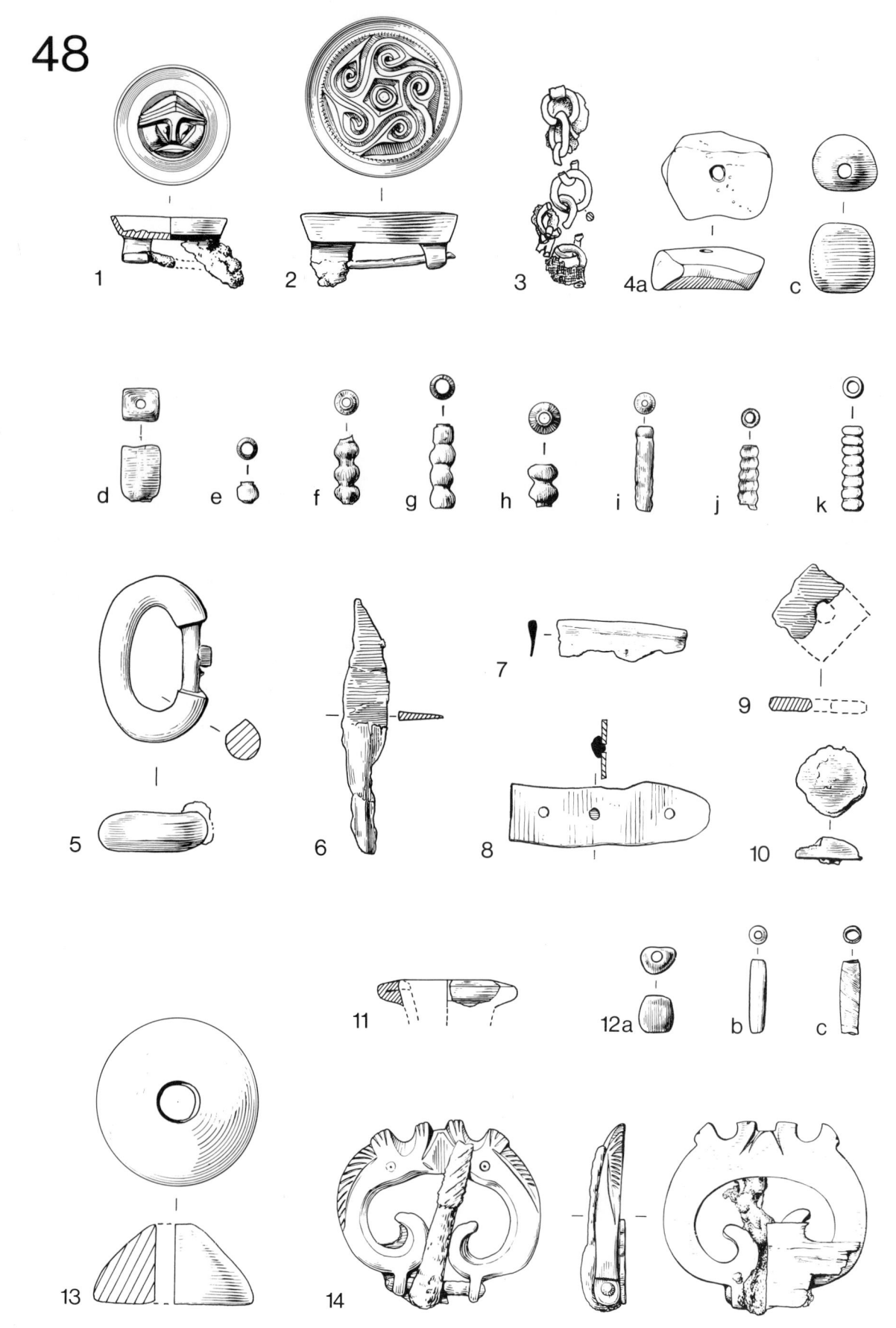

*Figure 27* Grave 48. Scale 48/1–2, 4–5, 8, 12–14: 1/1; 48/3, 6–7, 9–11: 1/2

GRAVE CATALOGUE 299

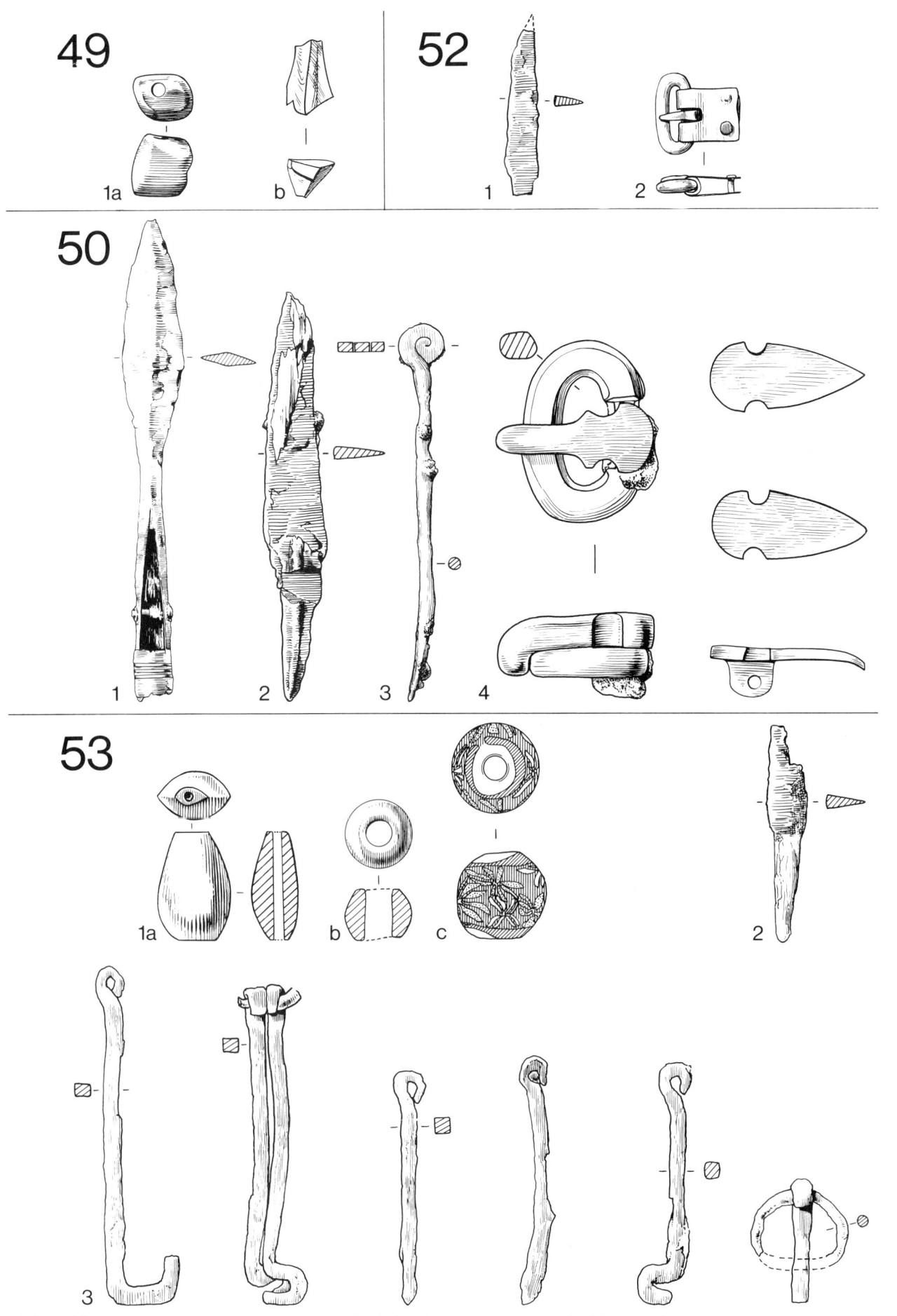

*Figure 28* Graves 49, 50, 52 and 53. Scale 49/1, 50/4, 52/2, 53/1: 1/1; 50/2–3, 52/1, 53/2–3: 1/2; 50/1: 1/4

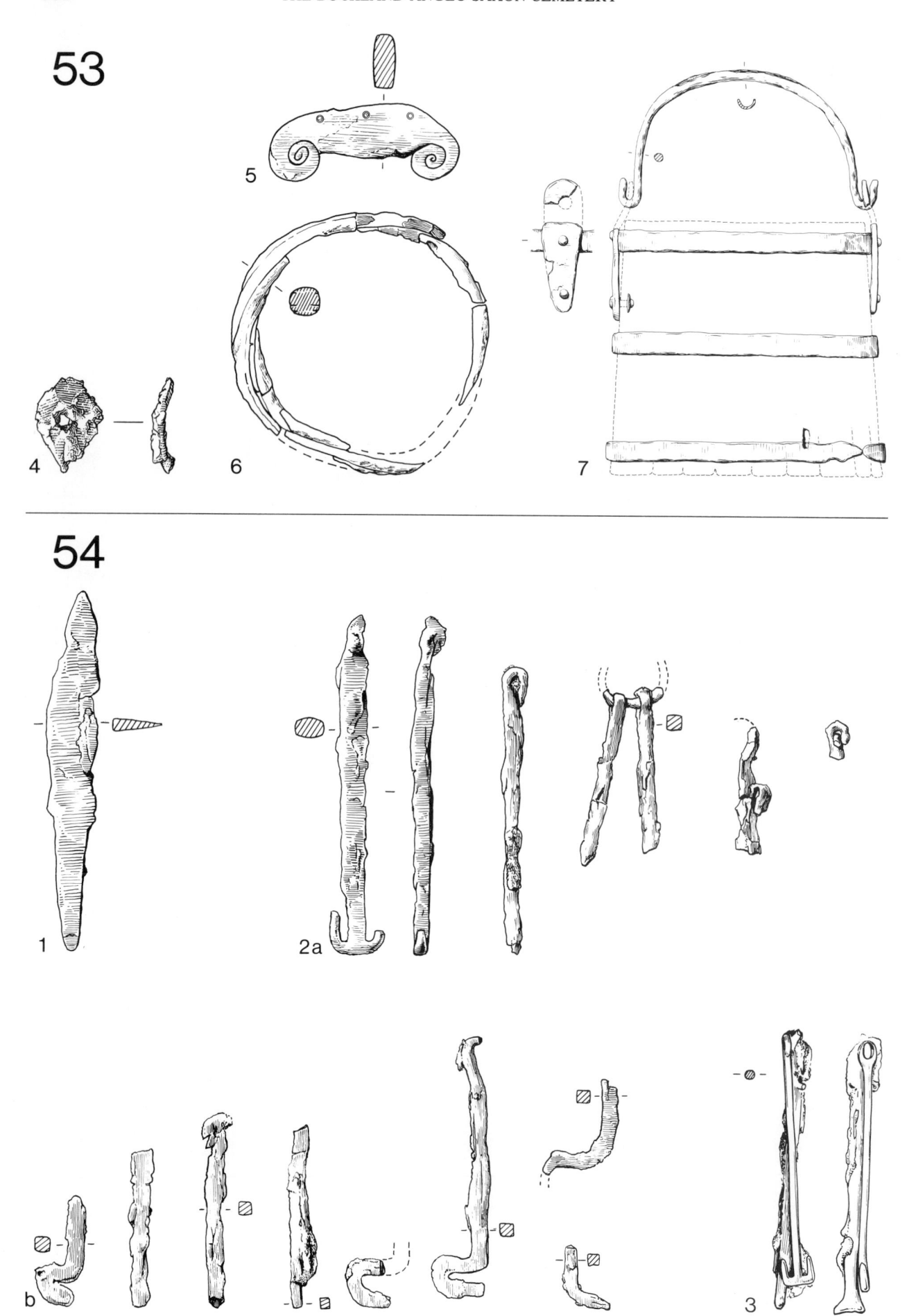

*Figure 29* Grave 53 continued and grave 54. Scale 53/4–6, 54/1–3:1/2; 53/7: 1/4

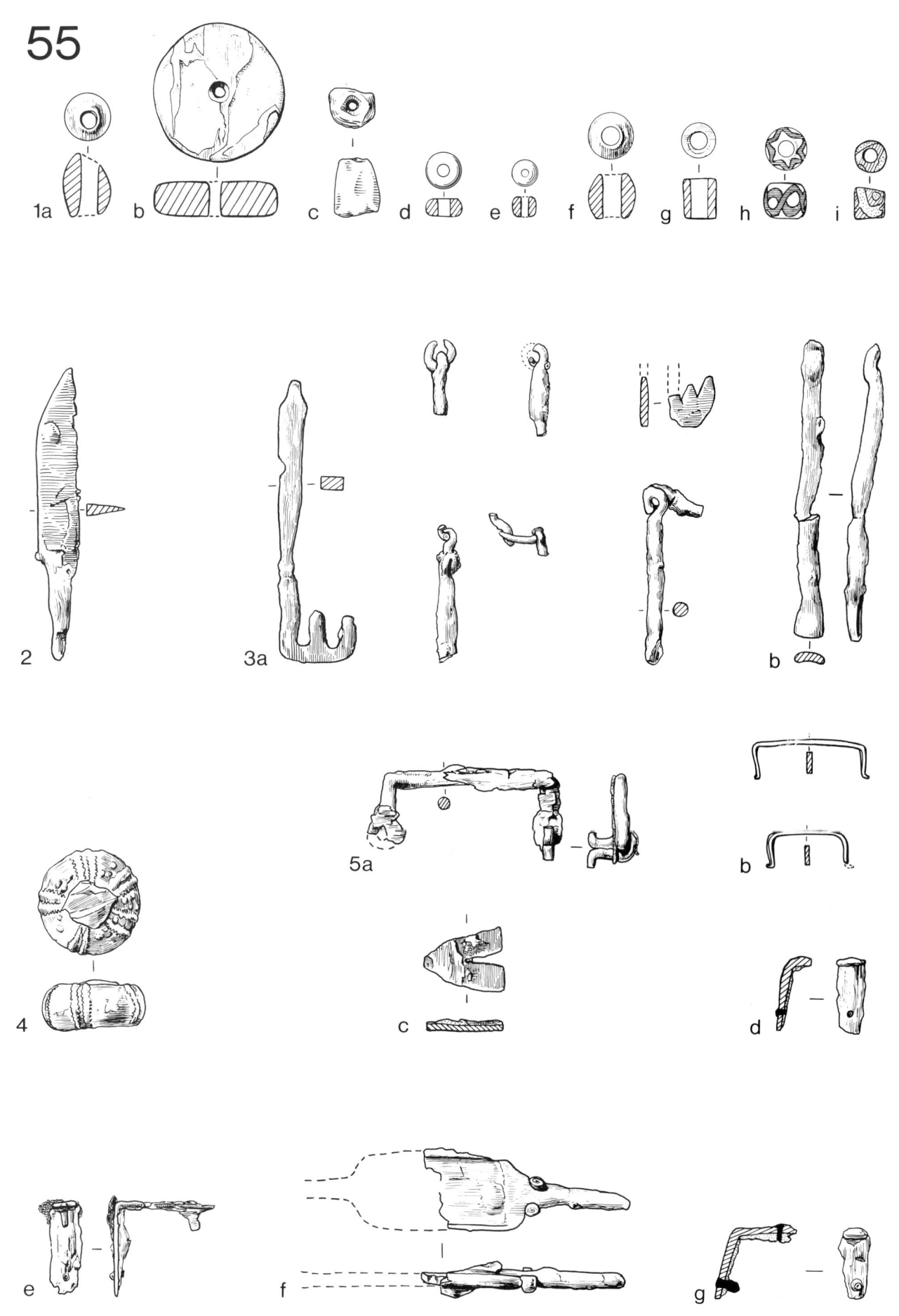

*Figure 30* Grave 55. Scale 55/1, 4, 5b: 1/1; 55/2–3, 5a, c–g: 1/2

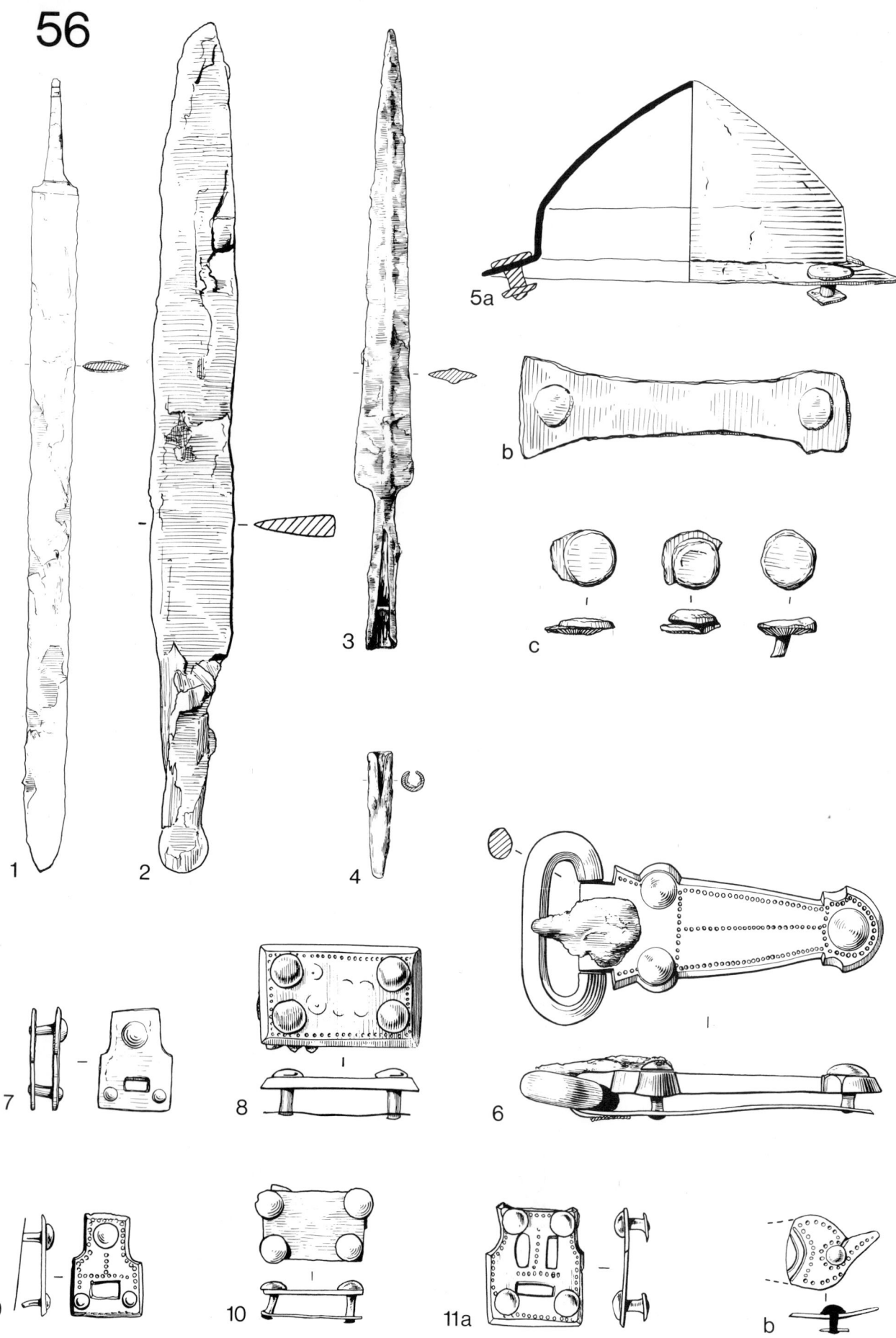

*Figure 31*  Grave 56. Scale 56/6–11: 1/1; 56/2, 5: 1/2; 56/3–4: 1/4; 56/1: 1/6

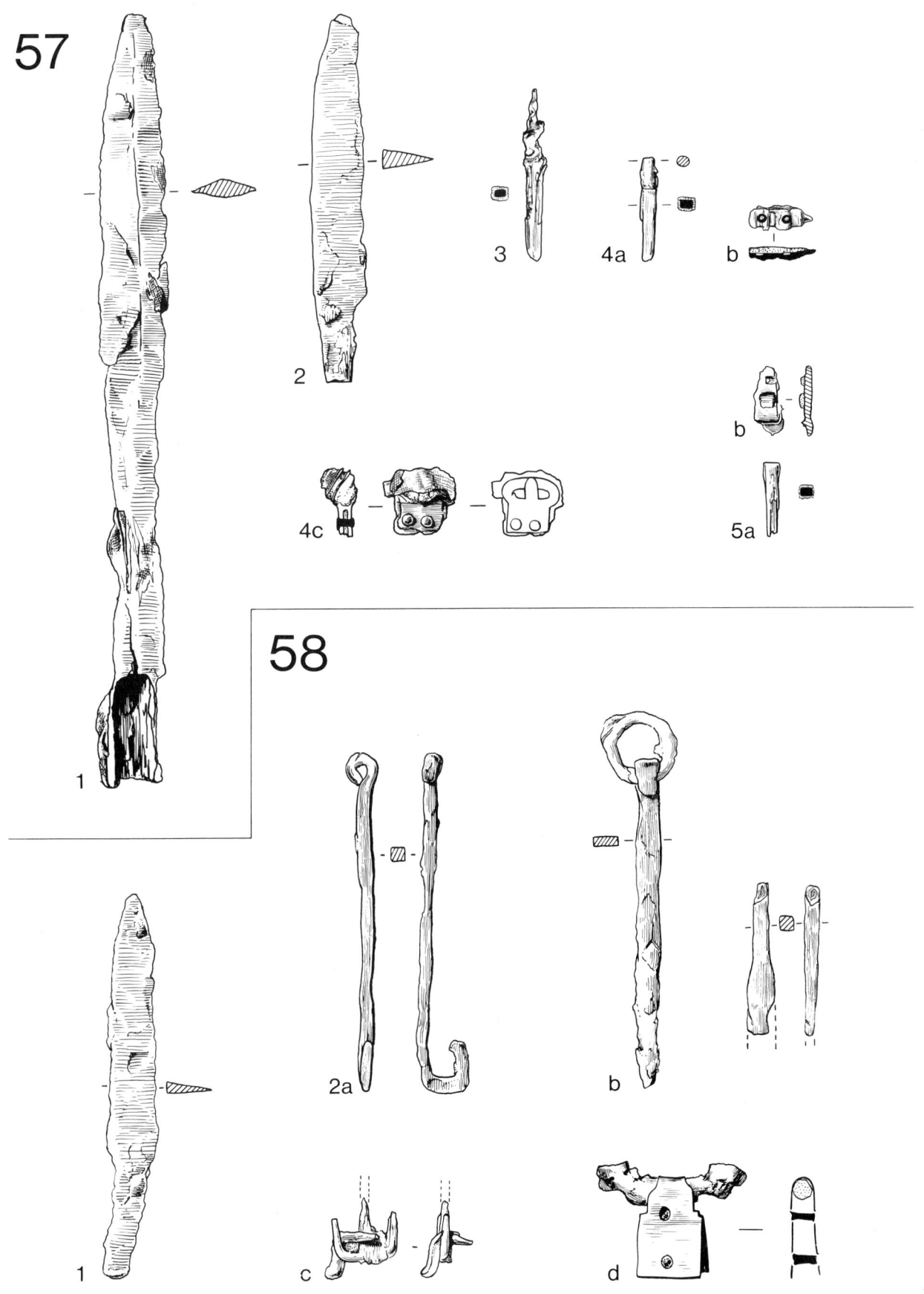

*Figure 32* Graves 57 and 58. Scale 58/2d: 1/1; 57/1–5, 58/1–2a–c: 1/2

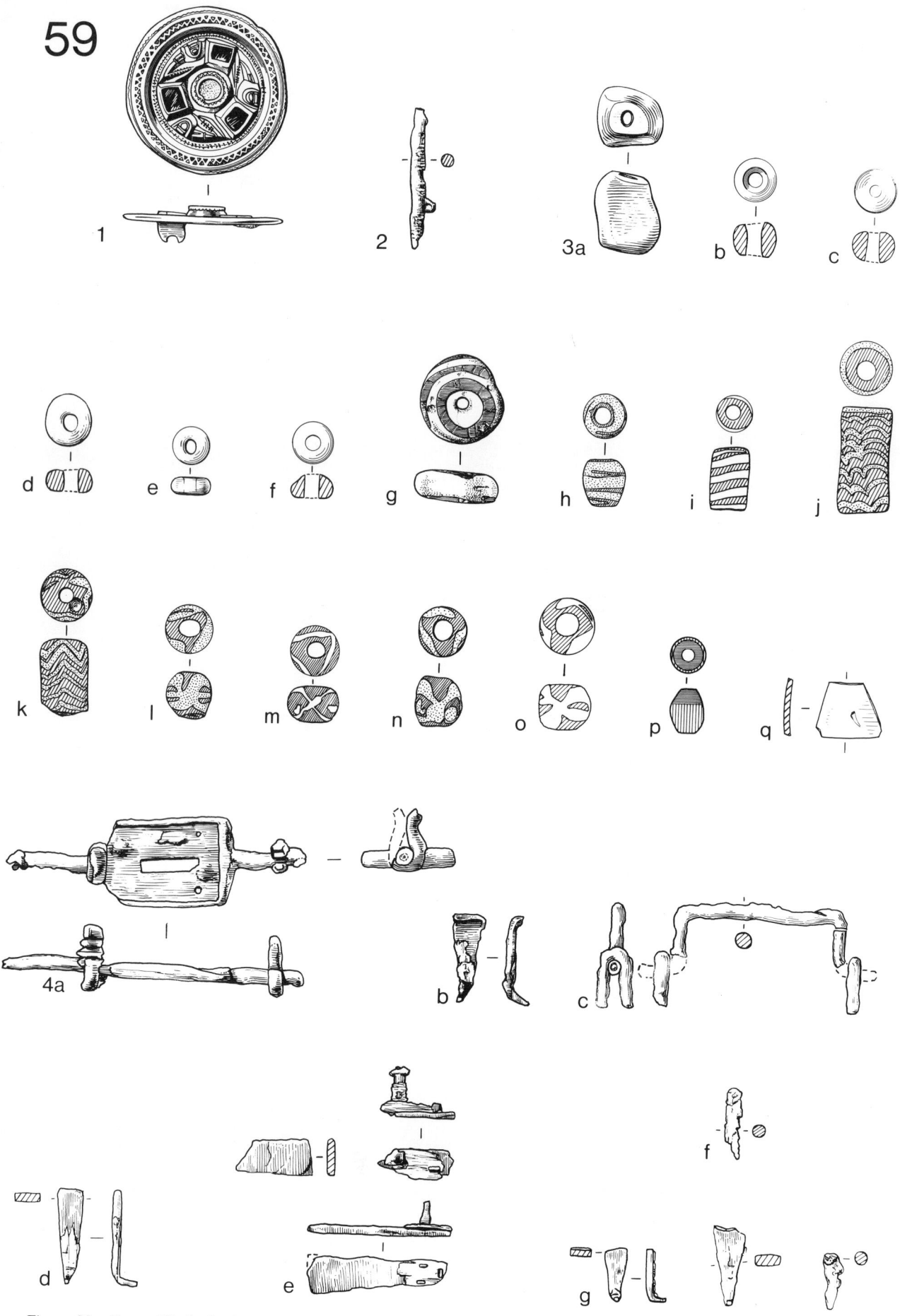

*Figure 33* Grave 59. Scale 59/1, 3: 1/1; 59/2, 4: 1/2

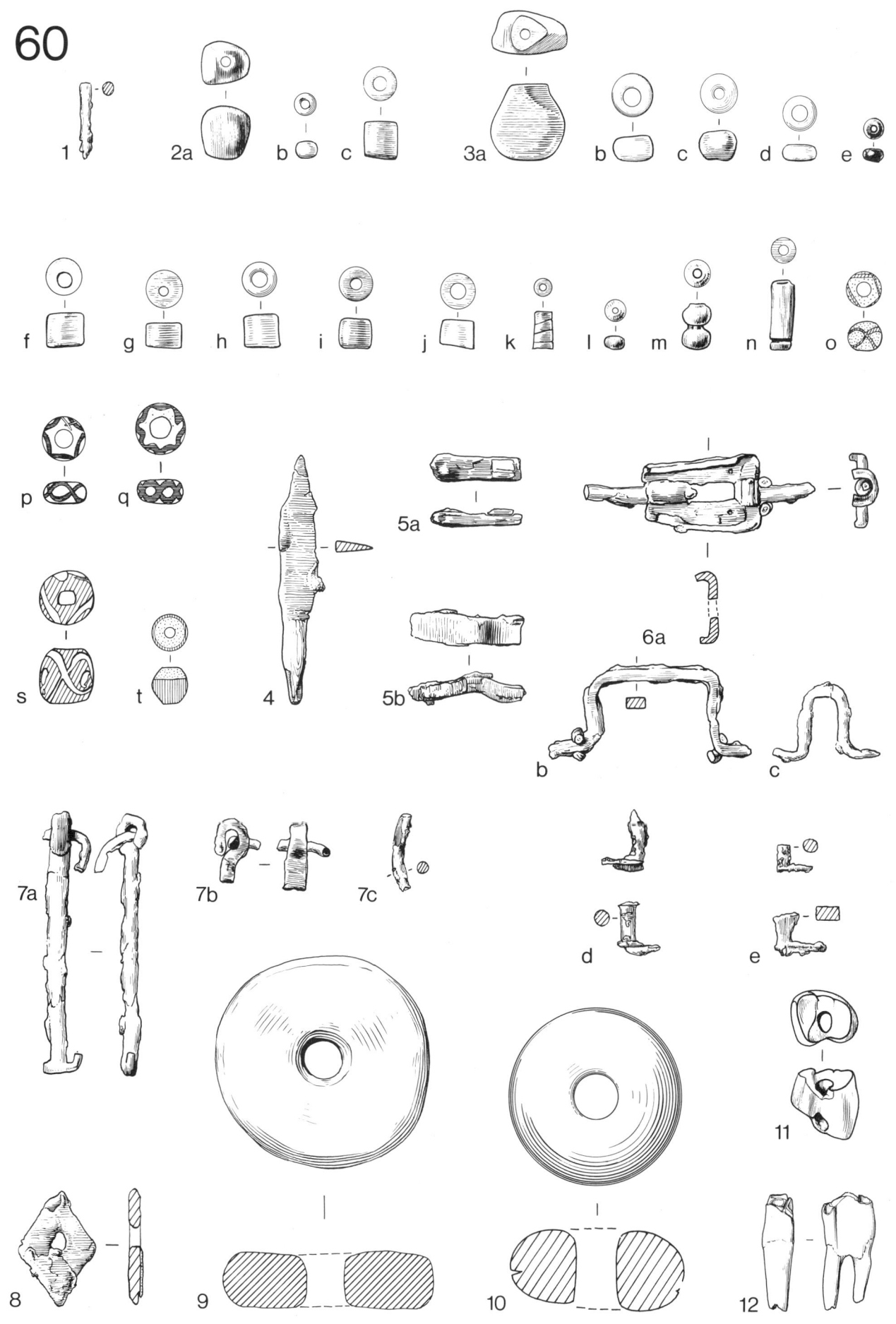

*Figure 34* Grave 60. Scale 60/2–3, 9–11: 1/1; 60/1, 4–8, 12: 1/2

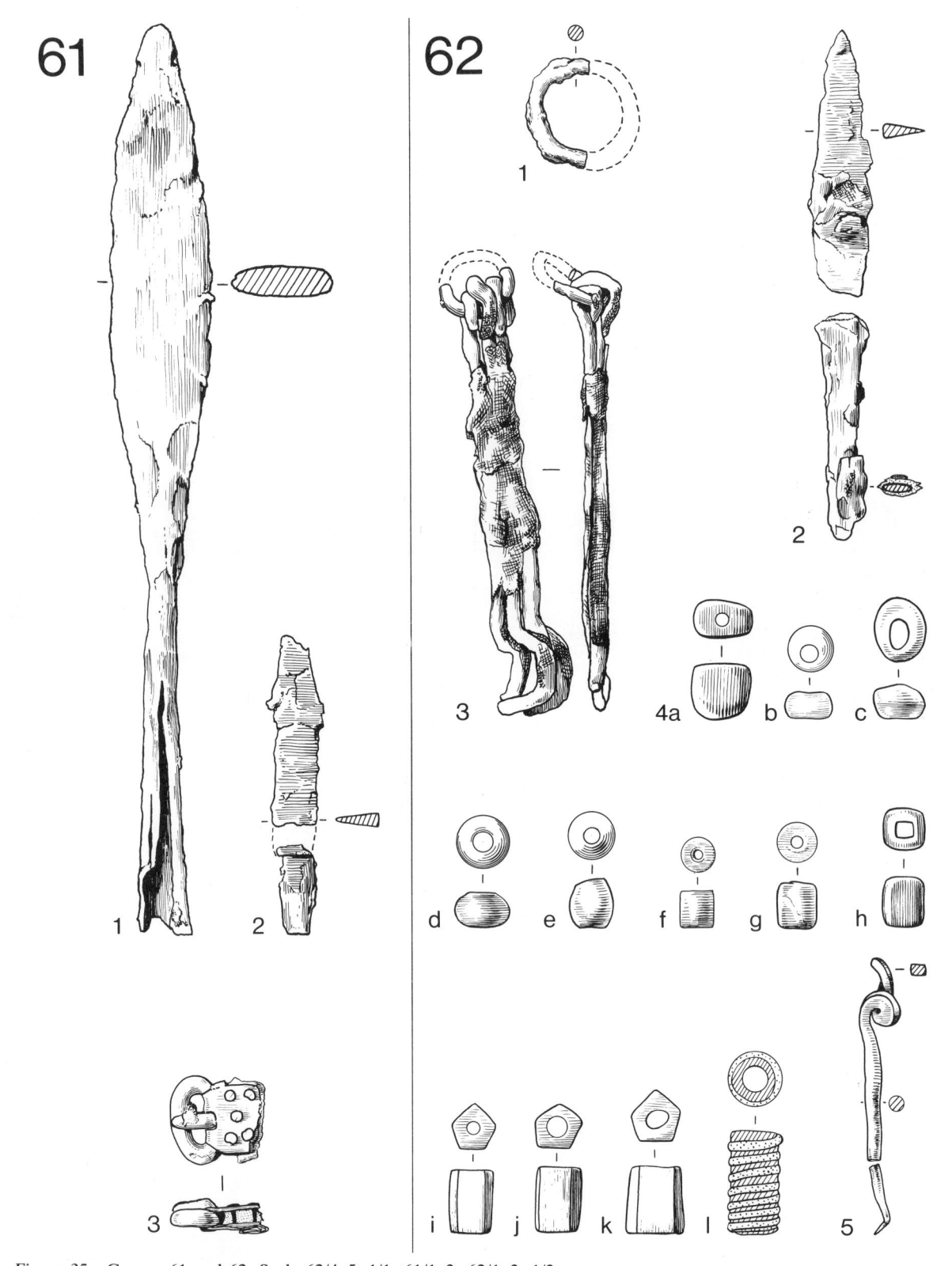

*Figure 35* Graves 61 and 62. Scale 62/4–5: 1/1; 61/1–3, 62/1–3: 1/2

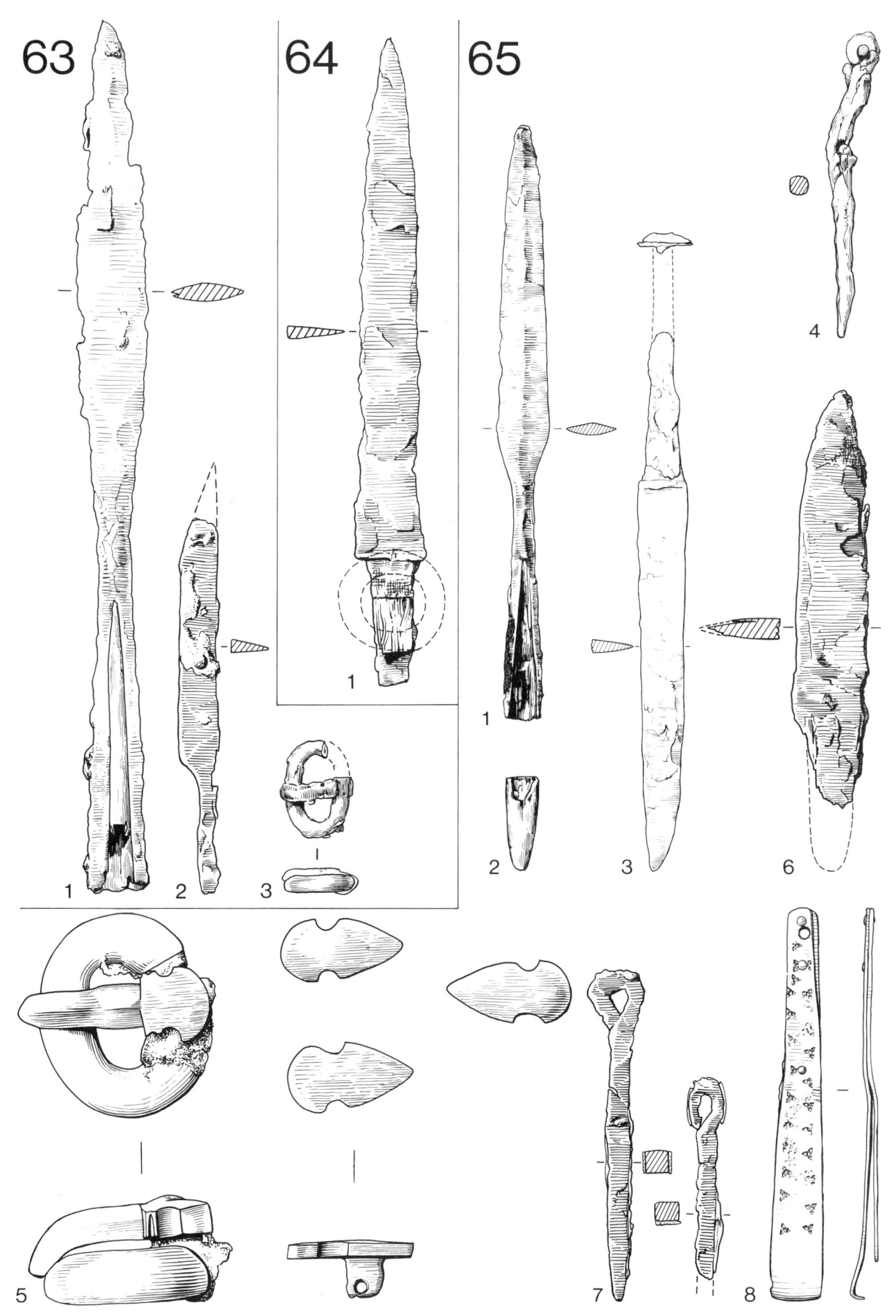

*Figure 36* Graves 63, 64 and 65. Scale 65/5, 8: 1/1; 63/1–3, 64/1, 65/4, 6–7: 1/2; 65/1–3: 1/4

**66**

1  2  3  4

**67**

1a  b  c  d  e  f  g

2  3a  b  4

5  6

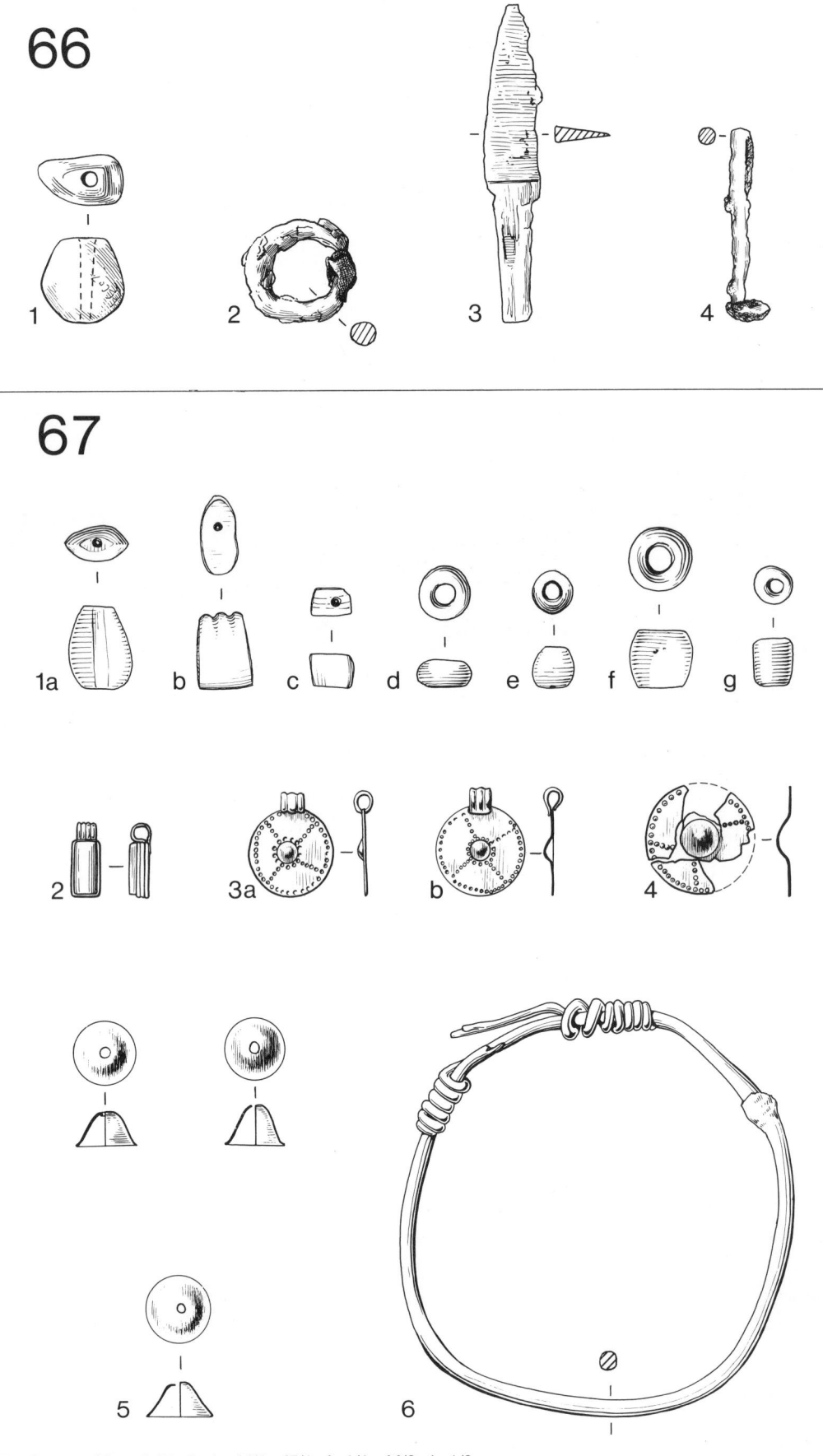

*Figure 37* Graves 66 and 67. Scale 66/1, 67/1–6: 1/1; 66/2–4: 1/2

GRAVE CATALOGUE

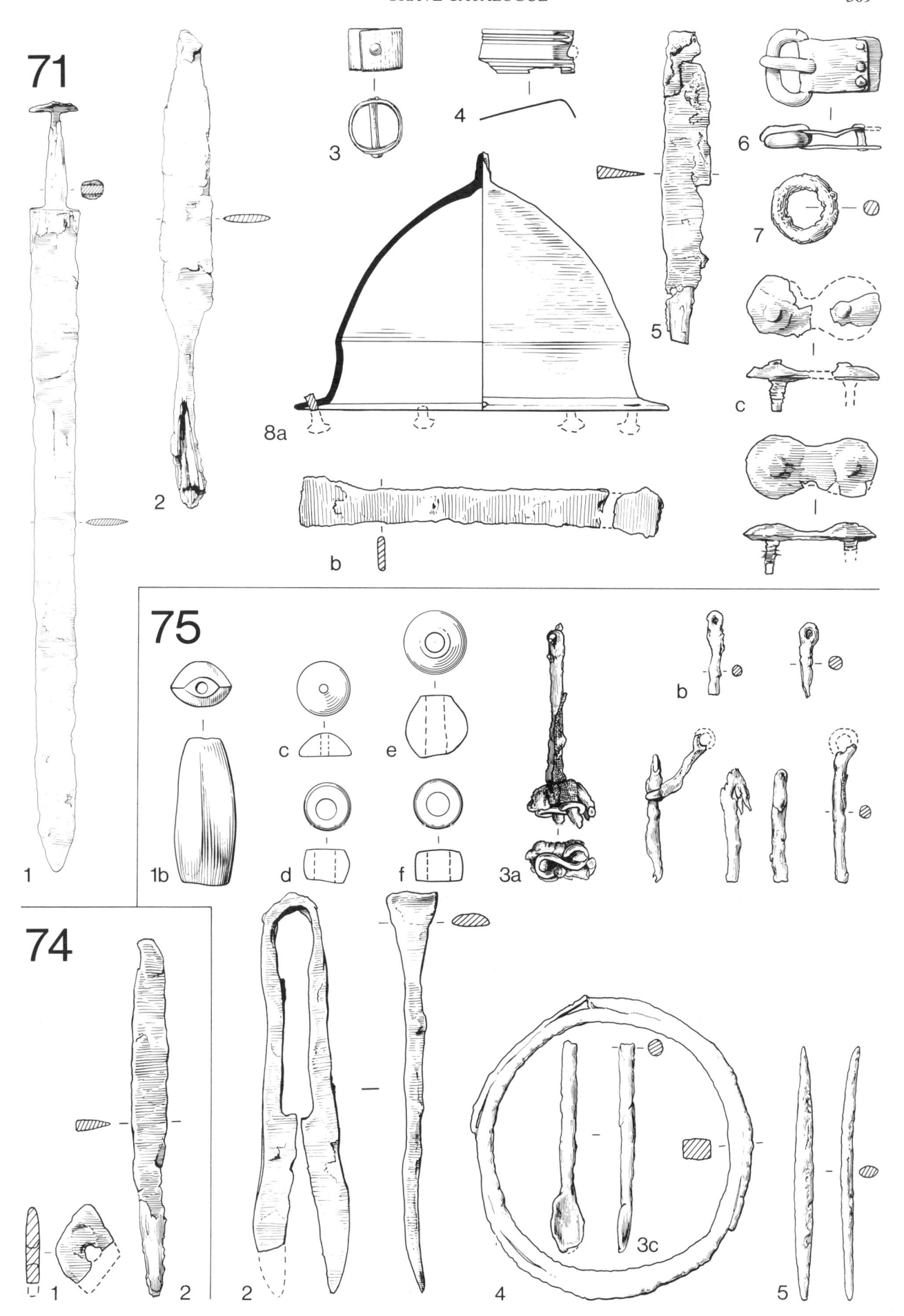

*Figure 38* Graves 71, 74 and 75. Scale 71/3–4, 75/1: 1/1; 71/5–8, 74/1–2, 75/2–5: 1/2; 71/2: 1/4; 71/1: 1/6

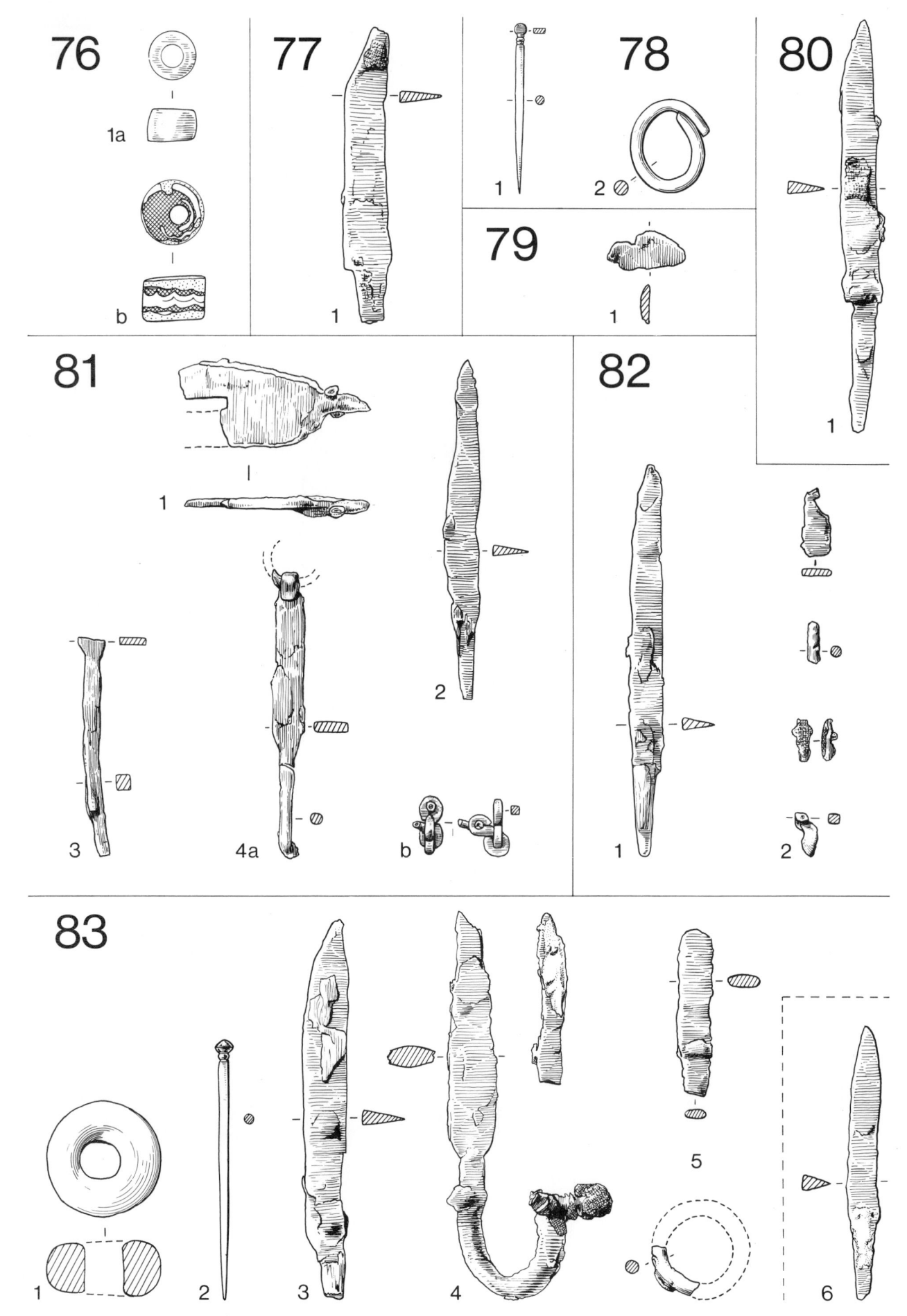

*Figure 39* Graves 76, 77, 78, 79, 80, 81, 82 and 83. Scale 76/1, 78/1–2, 83/1–2: 1/1; 77/1, 79/1, 80/1, 81/1–4, 82/1–2, 83/3–6: 1/2

GRAVE CATALOGUE 311

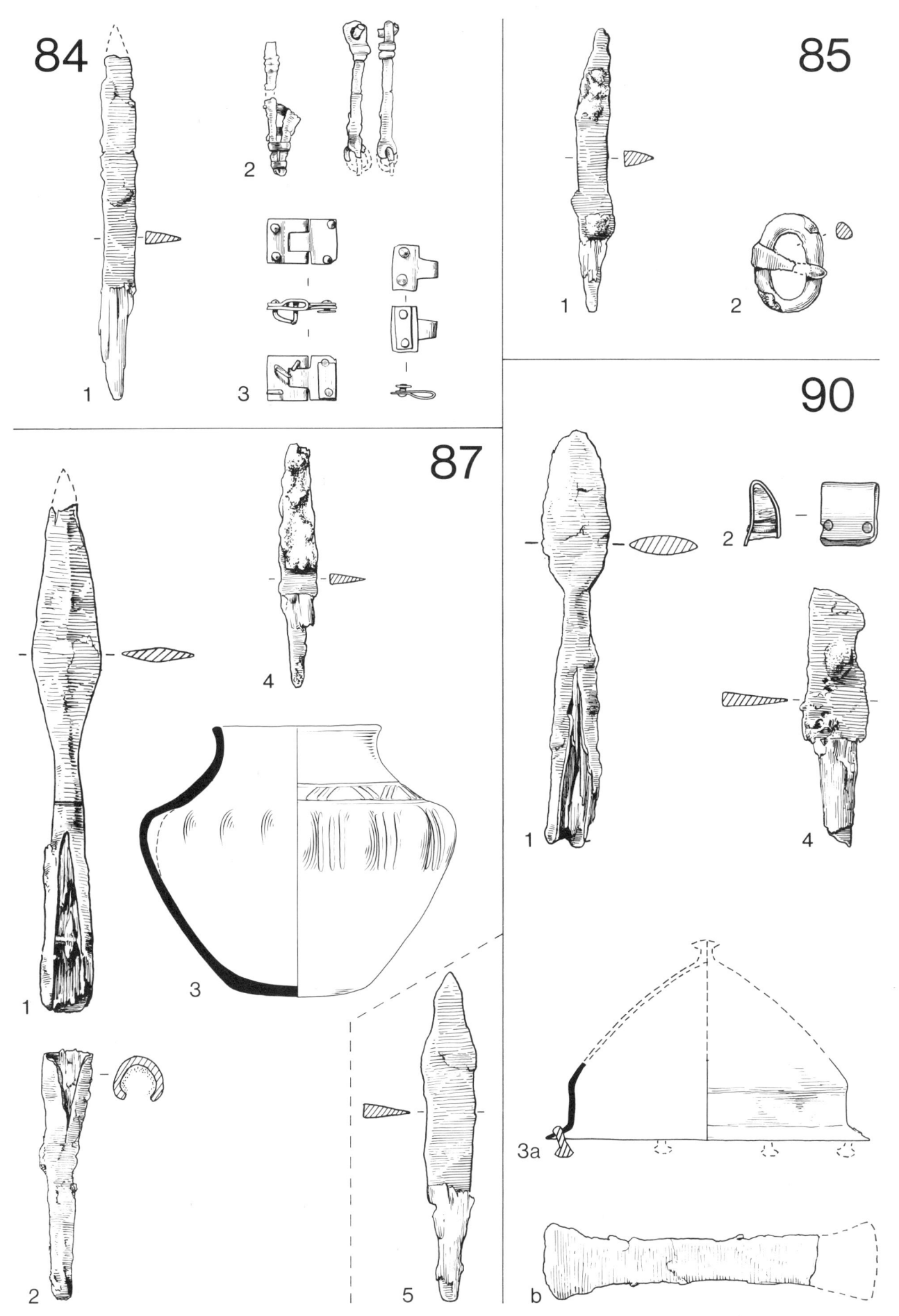

*Figure 40* Graves 84, 85, 87 and 90. Scale 84/3, 90/2: 1/1; 84/1–2, 85/1–2, 87/1–2, 4–5, 90/1, 3–4: 1/2; 87/3: 1/3

91

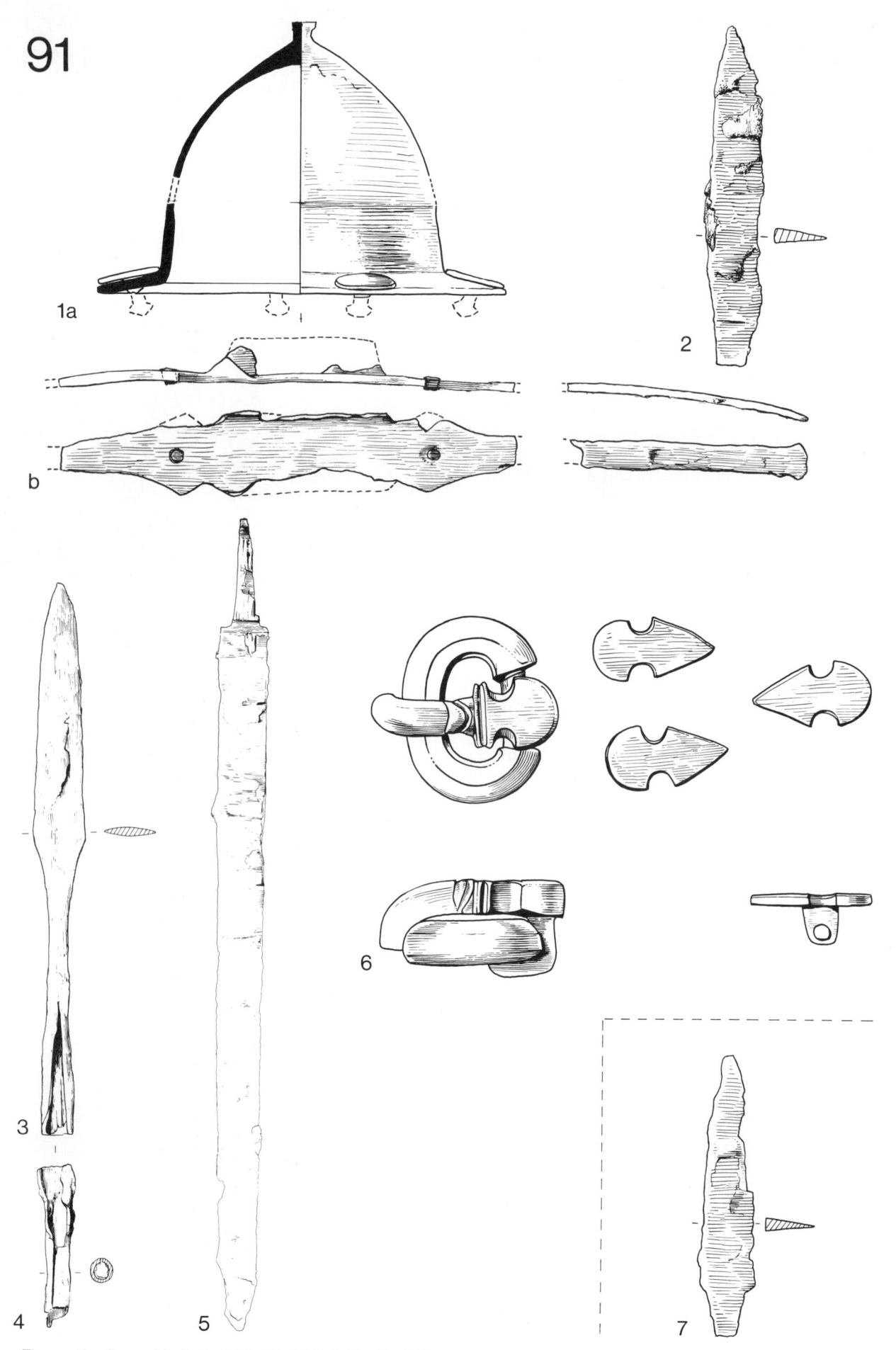

*Figure 41* Grave 91. Scale 91/6: 1/1; 91/1–2, 7: 1/2; 91/3–4: 1/4; 91/5: 1/6

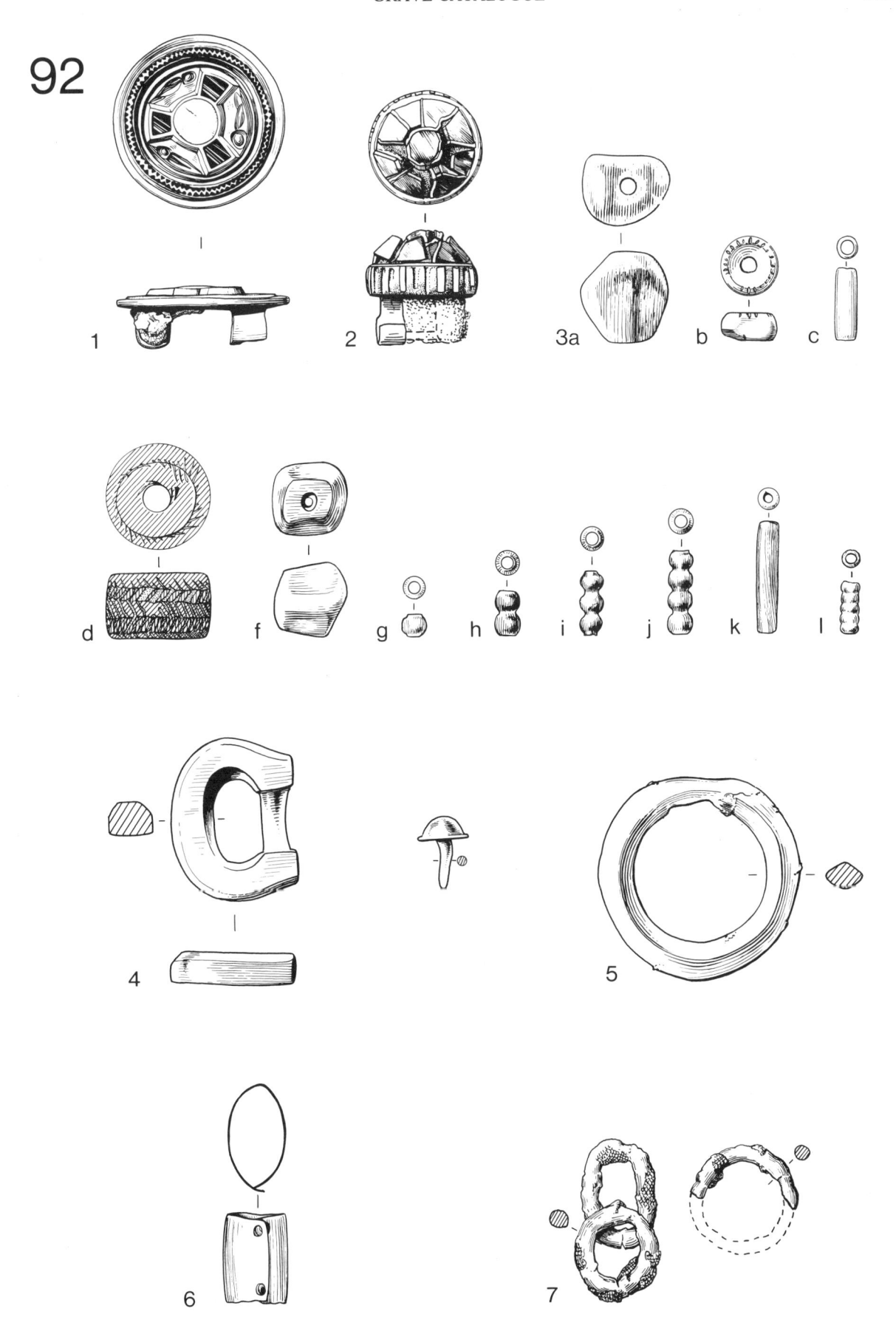

*Figure 42* Grave 92. Scale 92/1–6: 1/1; 92/7: 1/2

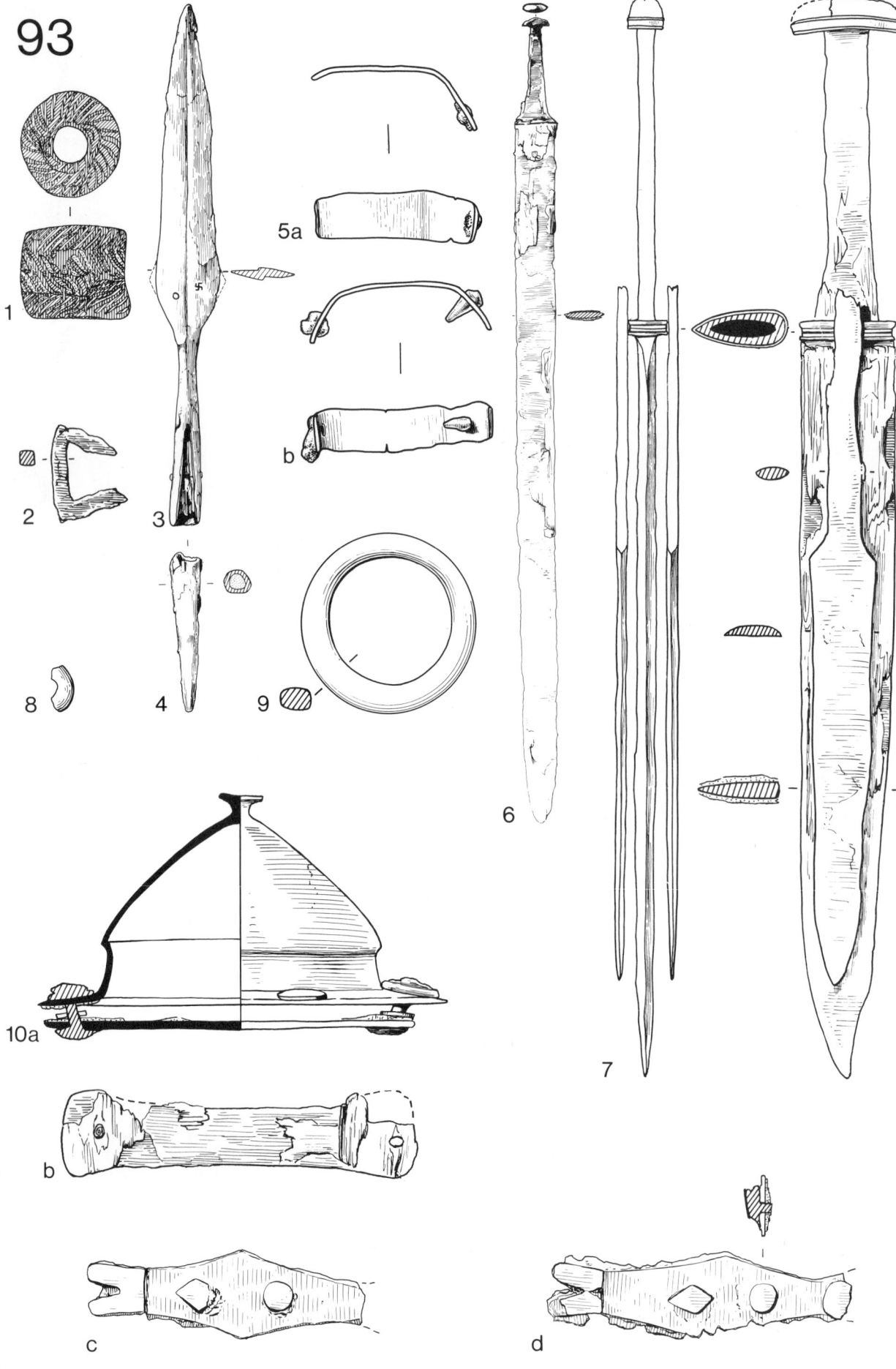

*Figure 43*    Grave 93. Scale 93/1, 5, 9: 1/1; 93/2, 7–8, 10: 1/2; 93/3–4: 1/4; 93/6: 1/6

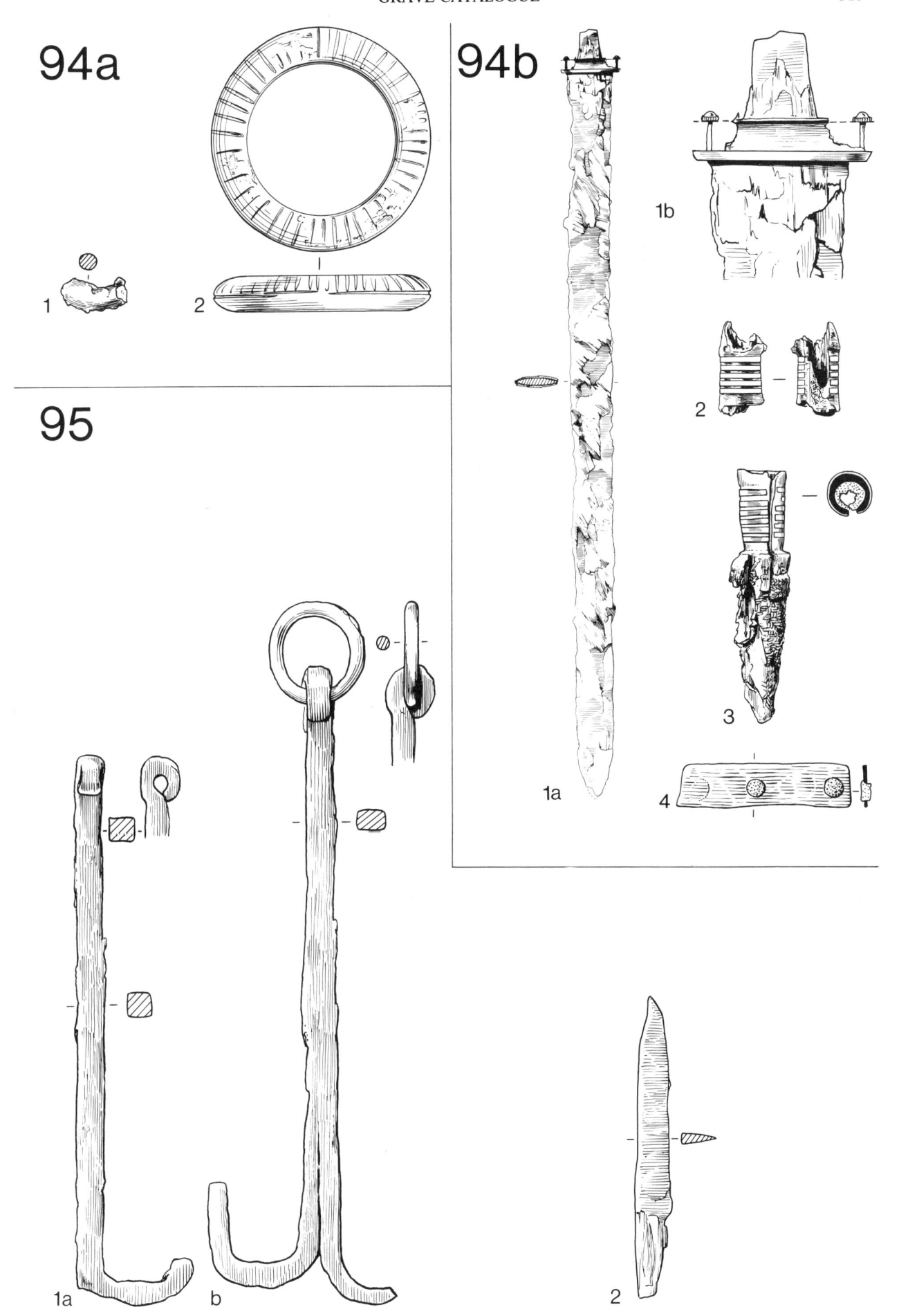

*Figure 44* Graves 94a, 94b and 95. Scale 94a/2, 94b/4: 1/1; 94a/1, 94b/1b, 2–3, 95/1–2: 1/2; 94b/1a: 1/6

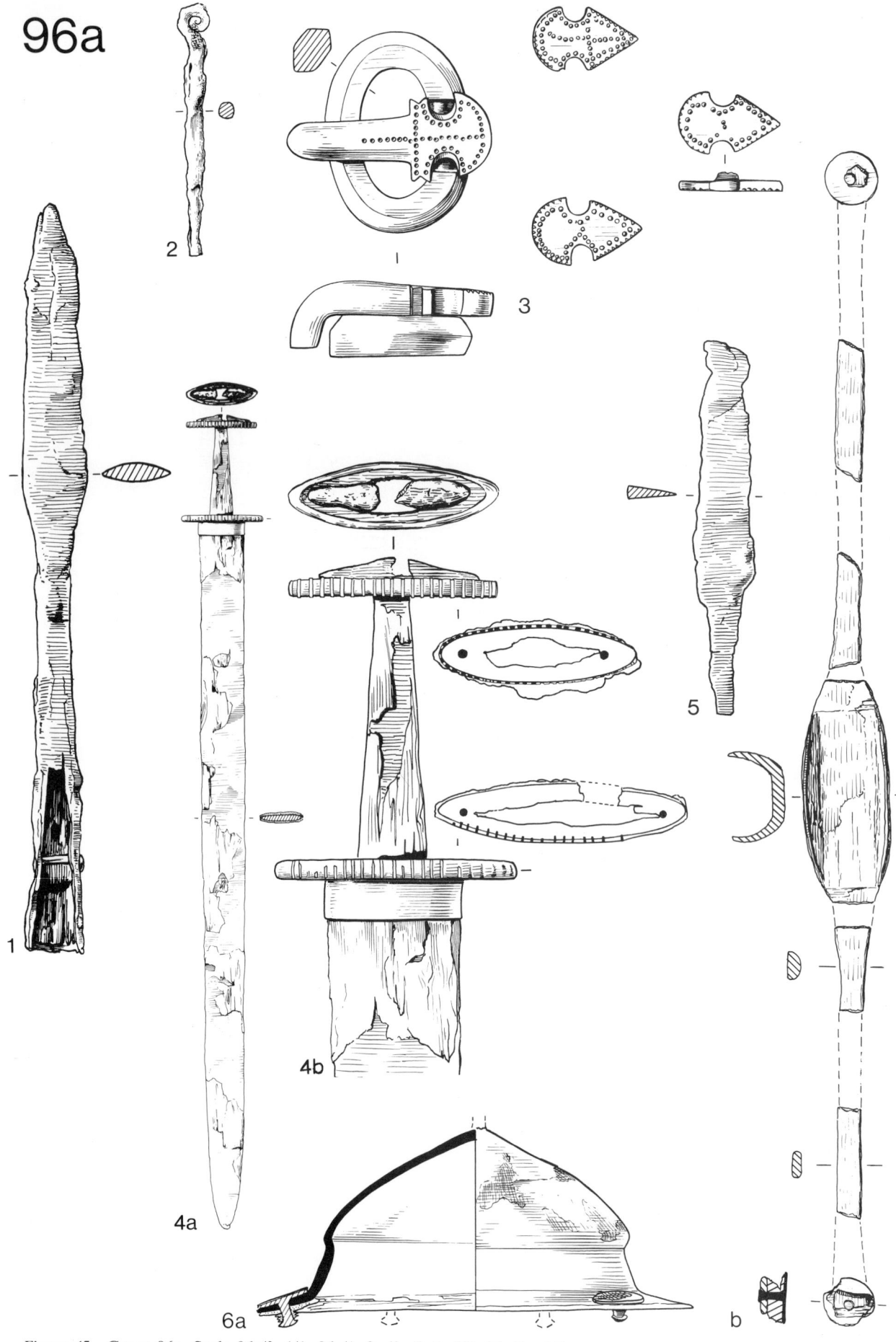

*Figure 45* Grave 96a. Scale 96a/3: 1/1; 96a/1, 2, 4b, 5, 6: 1/2; 96a/4a: 1/6

# GRAVE CATALOGUE

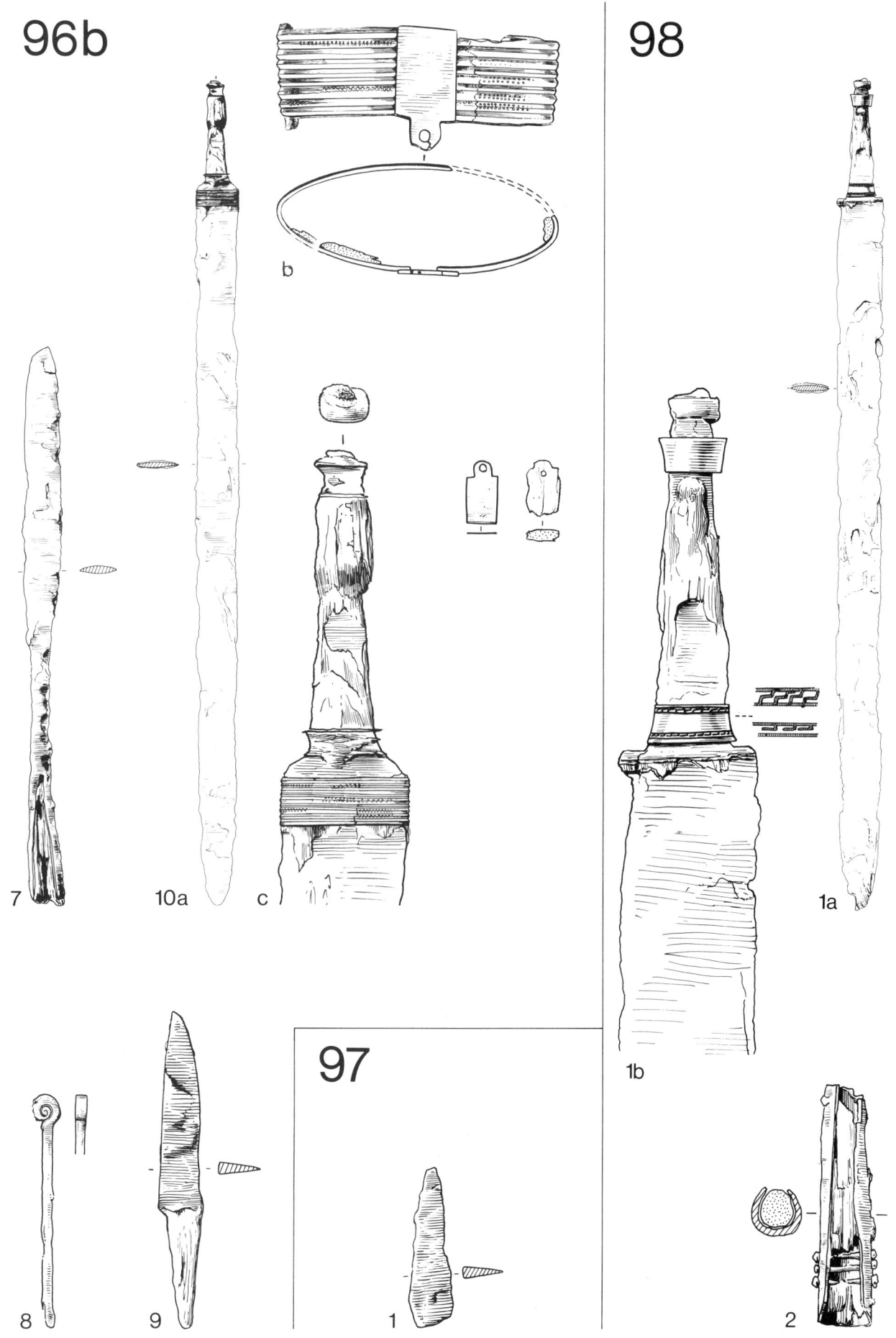

**96b**

**98**

**97**

*Figure 46* Graves 96b, 97 and 98. Scale 96b/10b: 1/1; 96b/8–9, 10c, 97/1, 98/1b, 2: 1/2; 96b/7: 1/4; 96b/10a, 98/1a: 1/6

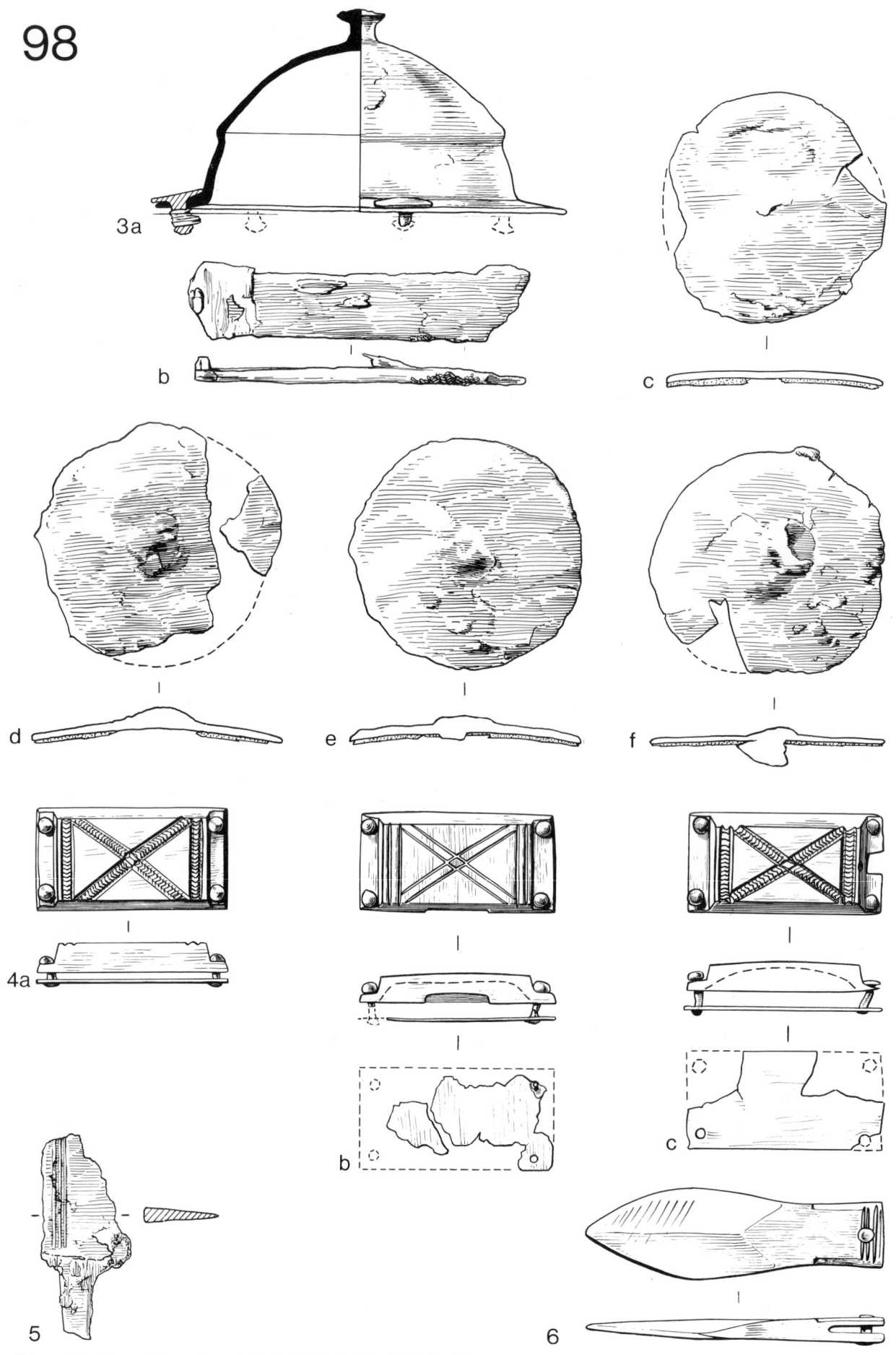

*Figure 47* Grave 98 continued. Scale 98/4, 6: 1/1; 98/3, 5: 1/2.

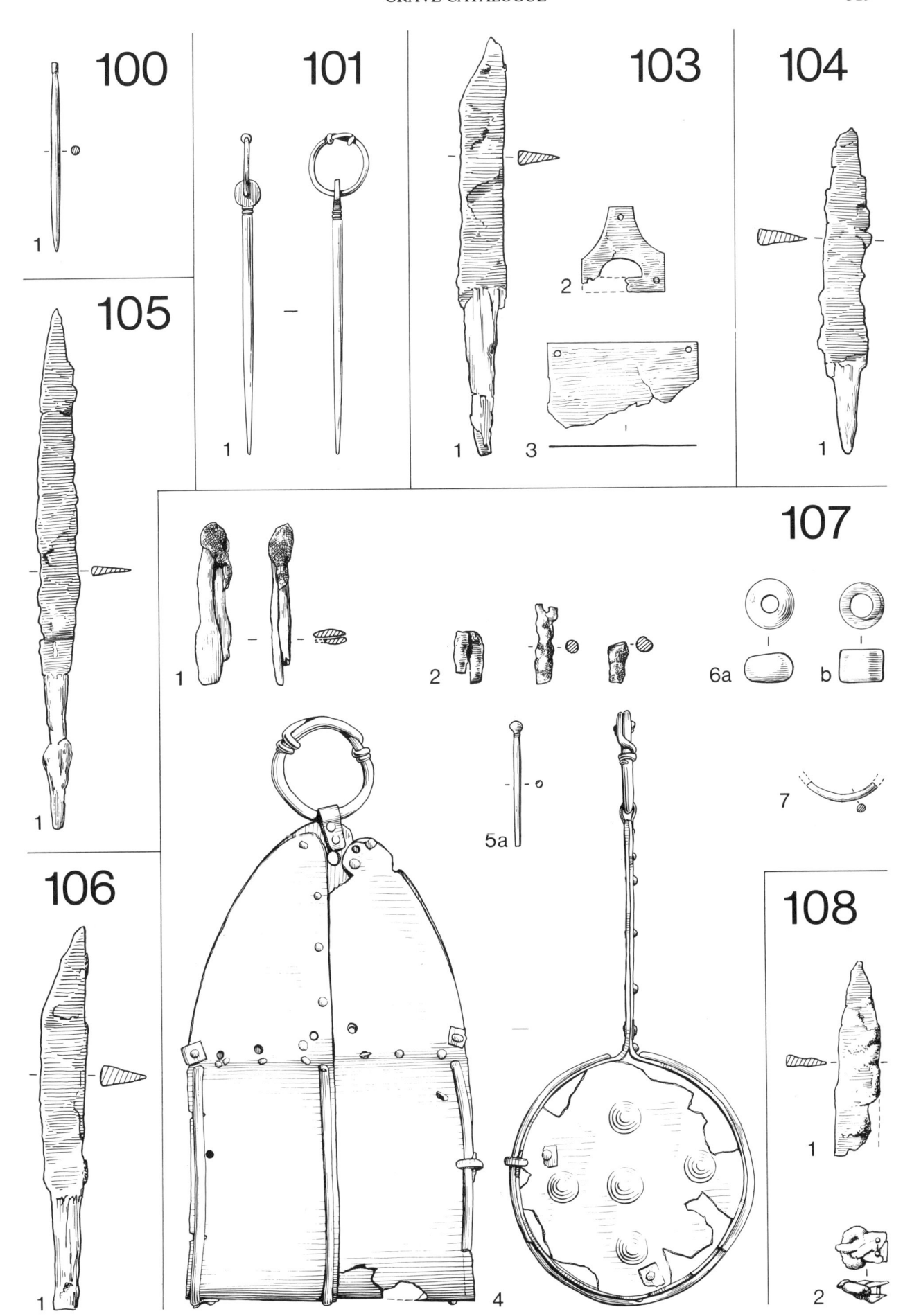

*Figure 48* Graves 100, 101, 103, 104, 105, 106, 107 and 108. Scale 100/1, 101/1, 103/2–3, 107/4, 5a, 6, 7: 1/1; 103/1, 104/1, 105/1, 106/1, 107/1–2, 108/1–2: 1/2

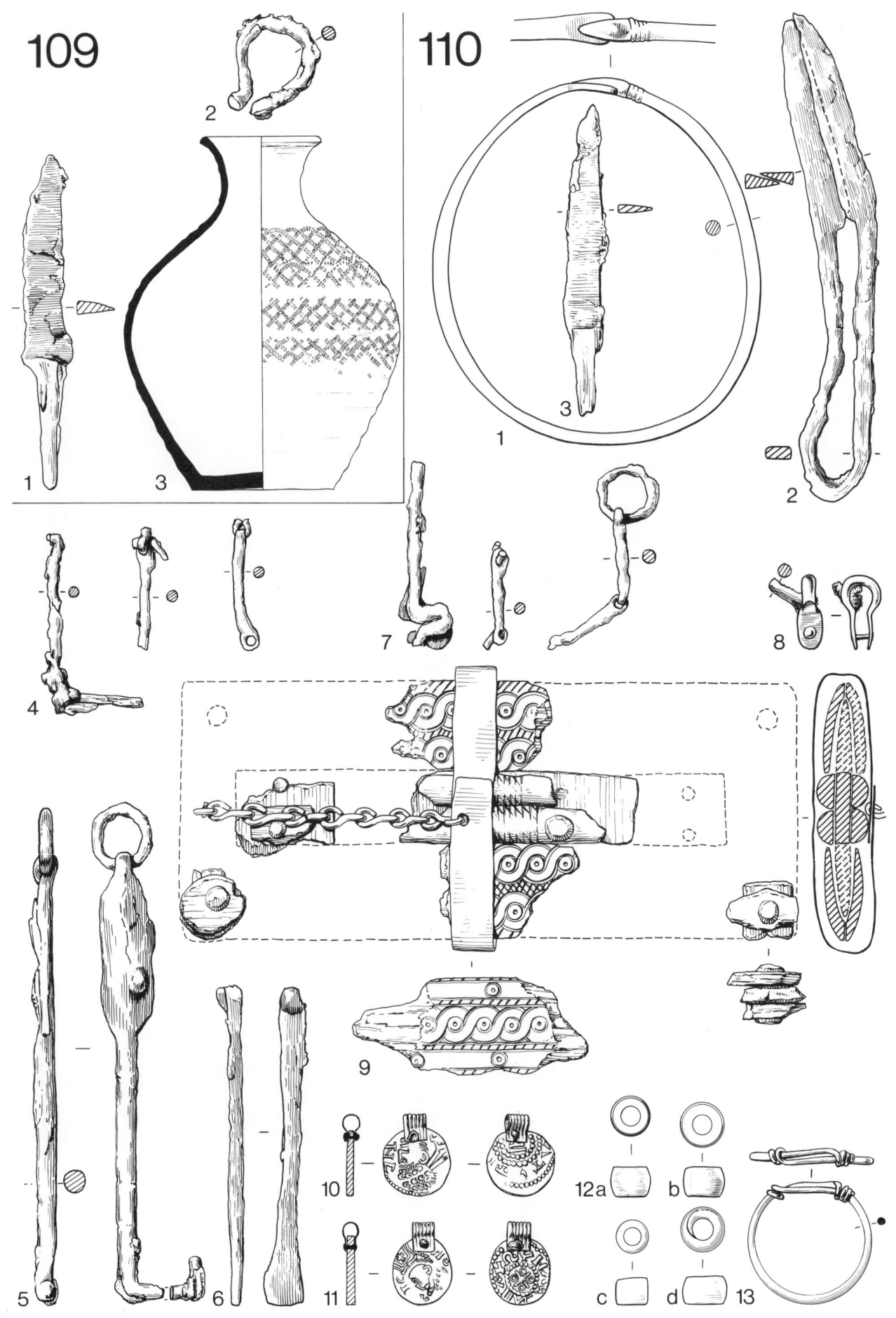

*Figure 49* Graves 109 and 110. Scale 110/1, 8–13: 1/1; 109/1–2, 110/2–7: 1/2; 109/3: 1/3

GRAVE CATALOGUE

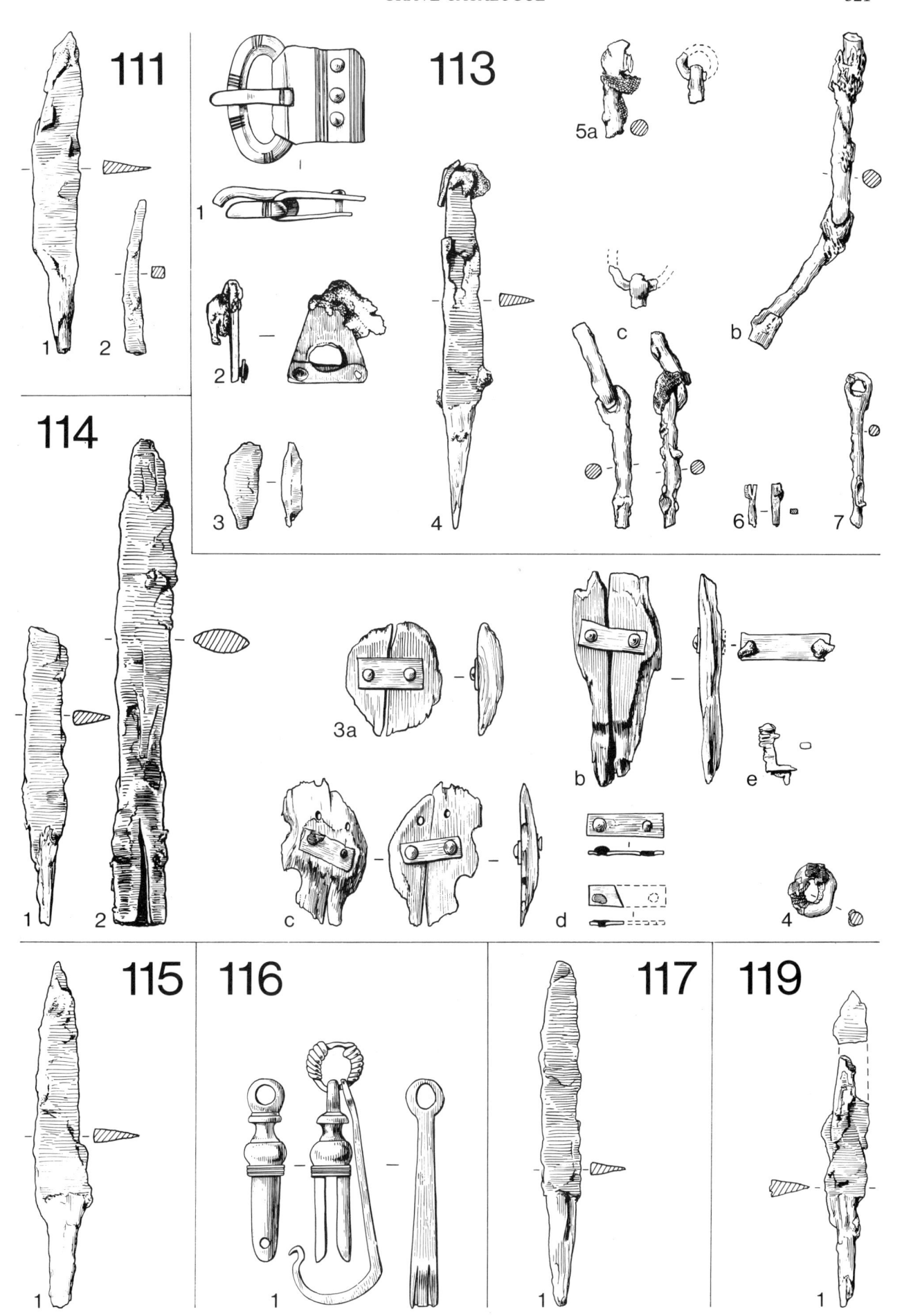

*Figure 50* Graves 111, 113, 114, 115, 116, 117 and 119. Scale 113/1–2, 114/3a–d: 1/1; 111/1–2, 113/3–7, 114/1–2, 3e, 4, 115/1, 116/1, 117/1, 118/1: 1/2

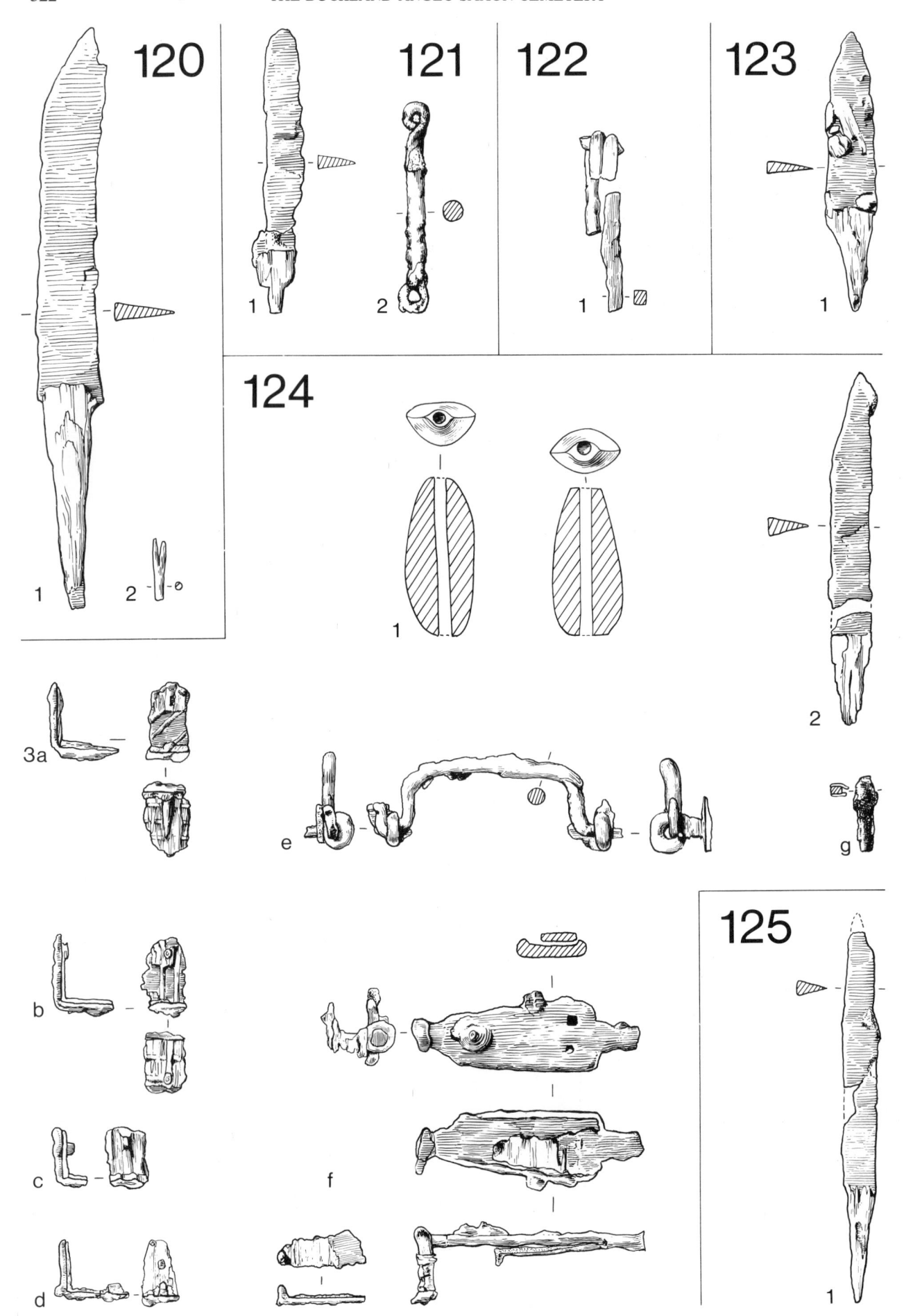

*Figure 51* Graves 120, 121, 122, 123, 124 and 125. Scale 124/1: 1/1; 120/1–2, 121/1–2, 122/1, 123/1, 124/2–3, 125/1: 1/2

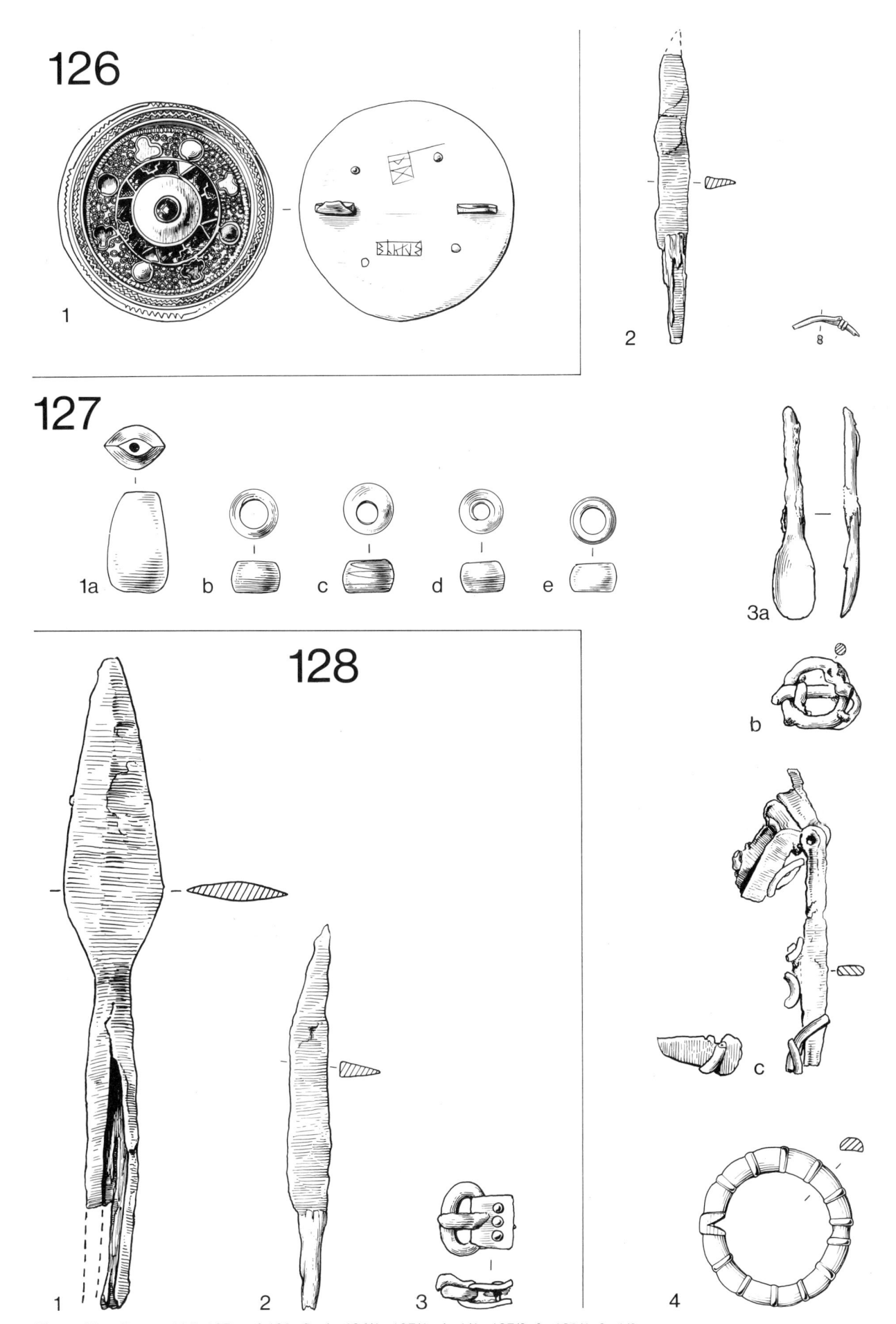

*Figure 52* Graves 126, 127 and 128. Scale 126/1, 127/1, 4: 1/1; 127/2–3, 128/1–3: 1/2

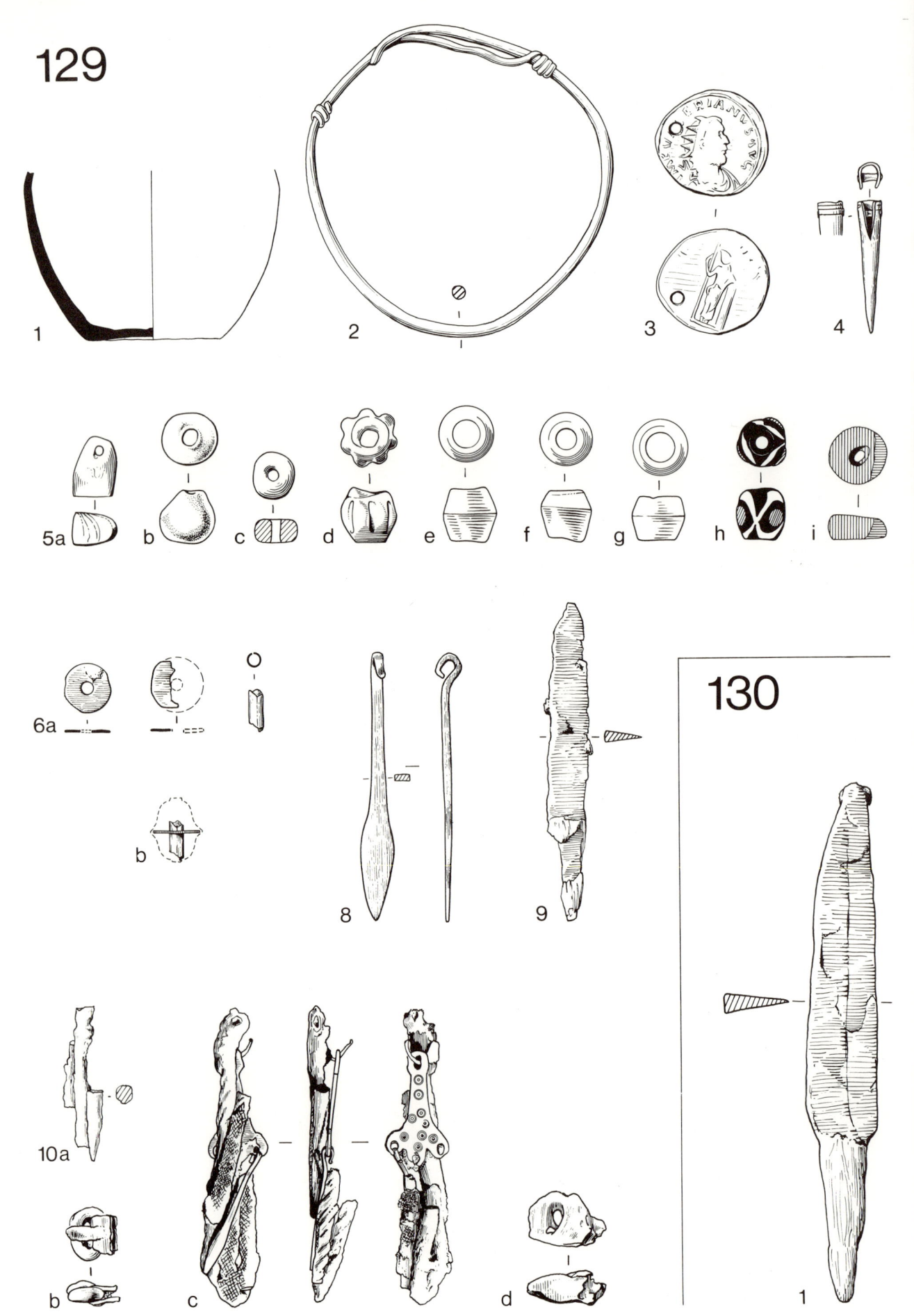

*Figure 53* Graves 129 and 130. Scale 129/2–6, 8: 1/1; 129/9–10, 130/1: 1/2; 129/1: 1/3

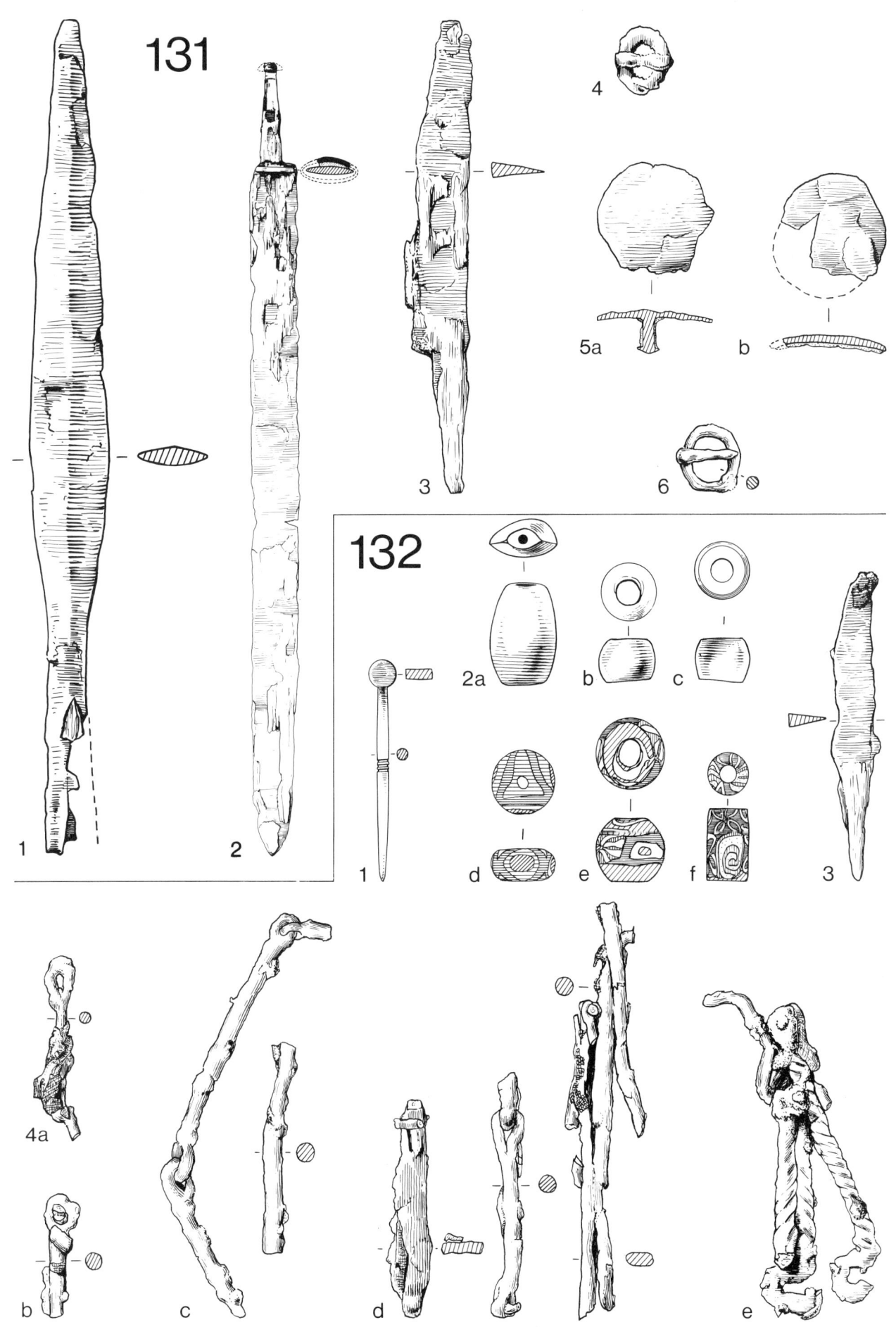

*Figure 54*  Graves 131 and 132. Scale 132/1–2: 1/1; 131/1, 3–6, 132/3–4: 1/2; 131/2: 1/6

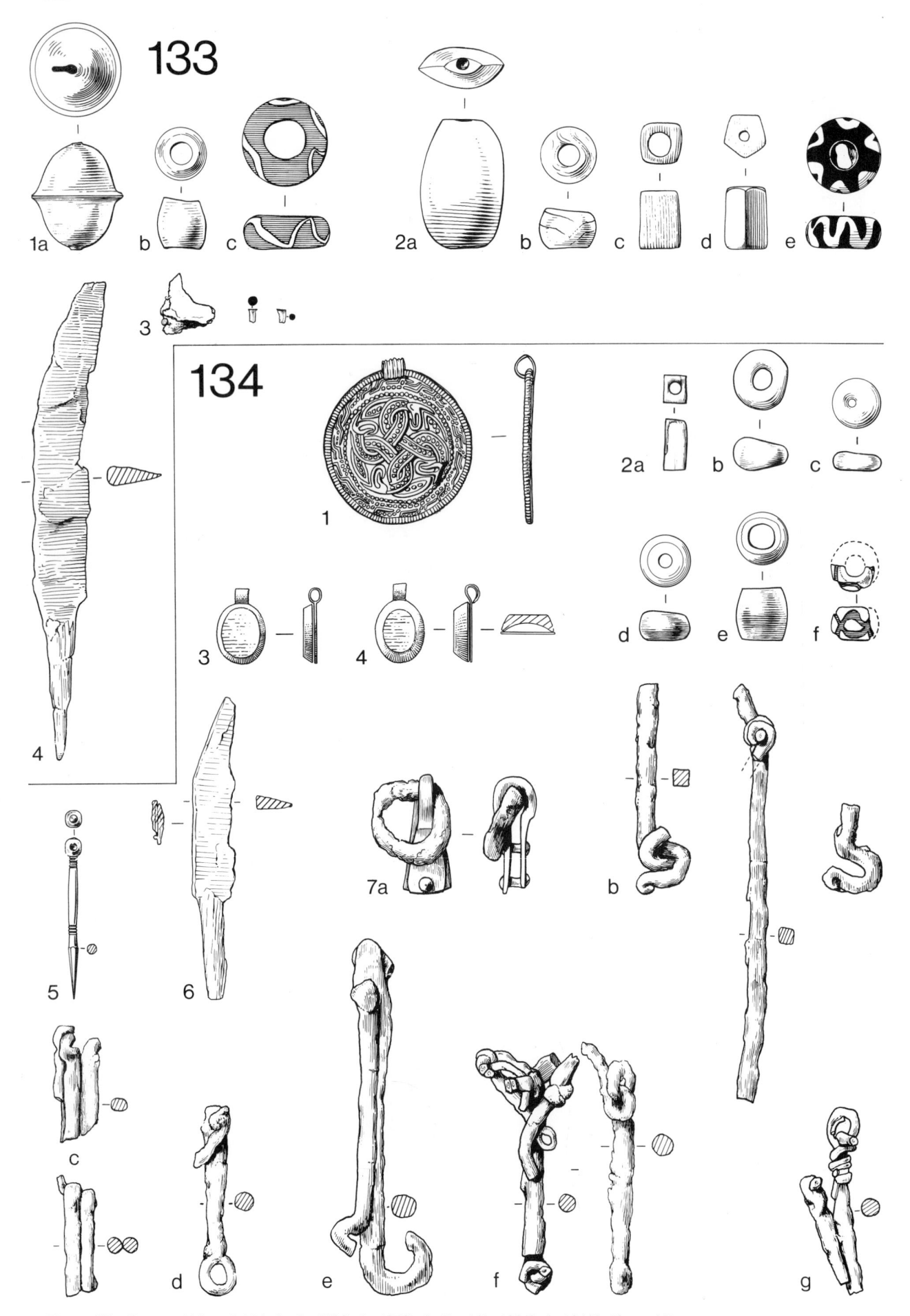

*Figure 55* Graves 133 and 134. Scale 133/1–2, 134/1–5, 7a: 1/1; 133/3–4, 134/6, 7b–g: 1/2

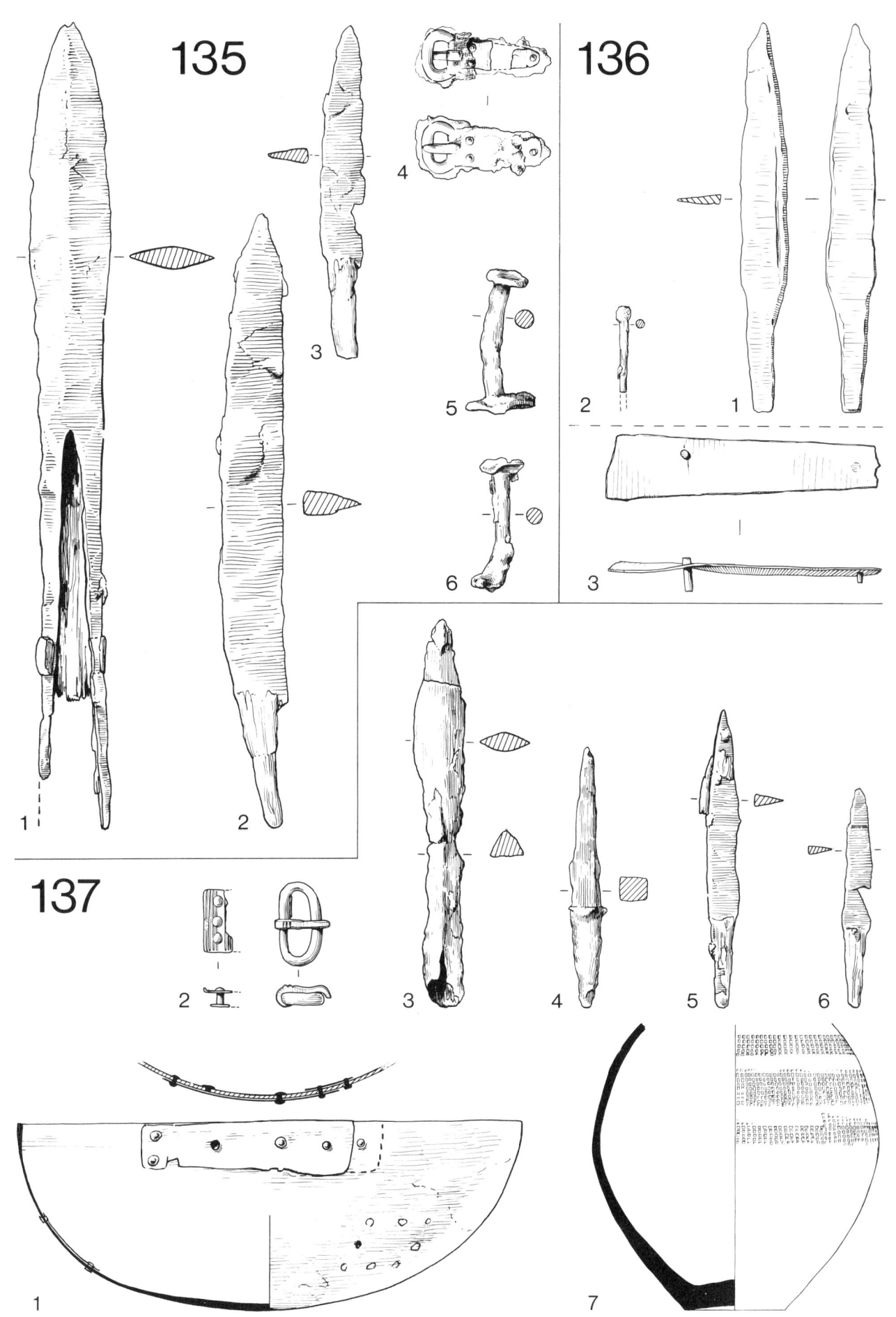

*Figure 56* Graves 135, 136 and 137. Scale 136/3, 137/2: 1/1; 135/1–6, 136/1–2, 137/1, 3–6: 1/2; 137/7: 1/3

328                THE BUCKLAND ANGLO-SAXON CEMETERY

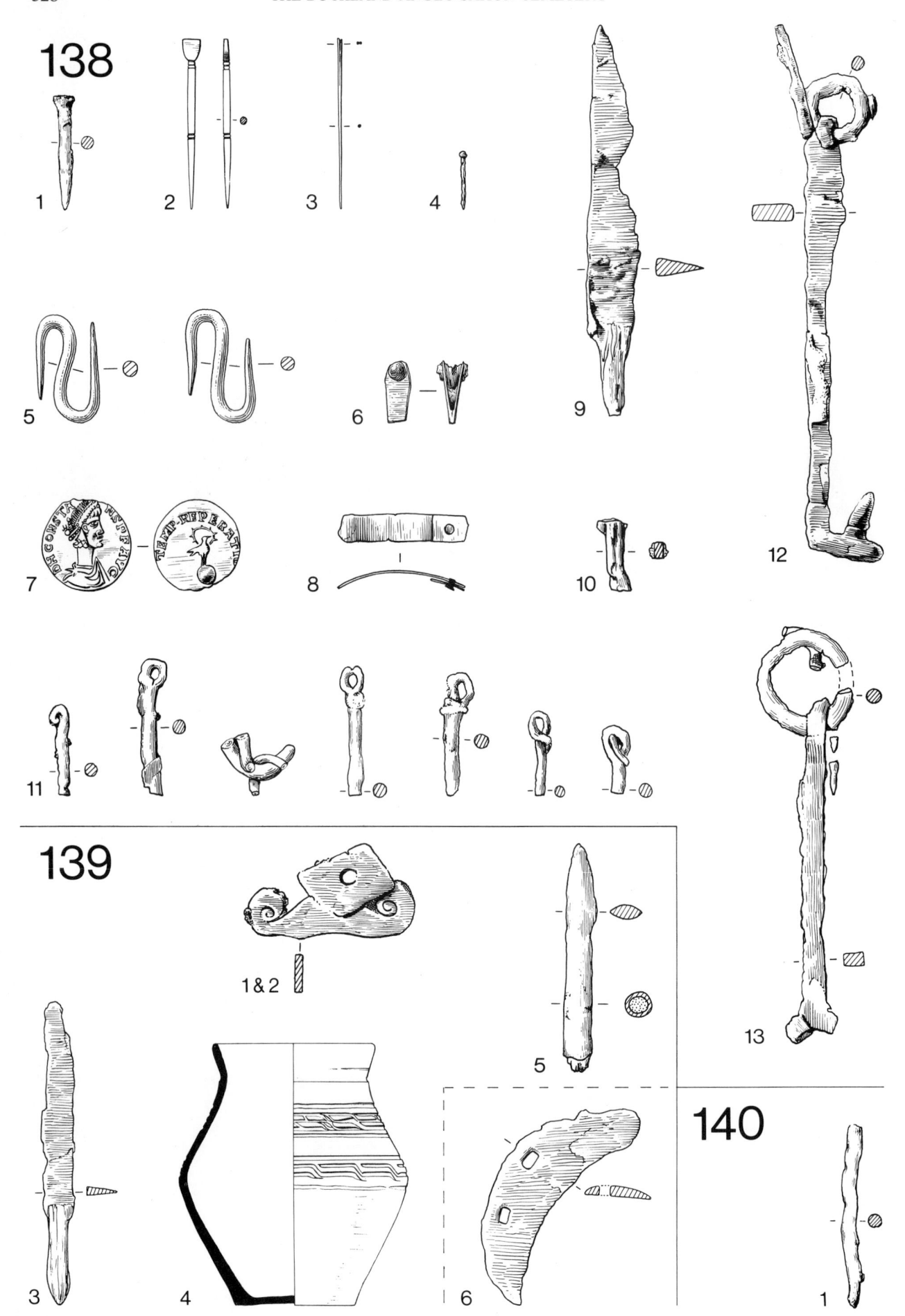

*Figure 57*   Graves 138, 139 and 140. Scale 138/2–3, 5–8: 1/1; 138/1, 4, 9–13, 139/1–3, 5–6, 140/1: 1/2; 139/4: 1/3

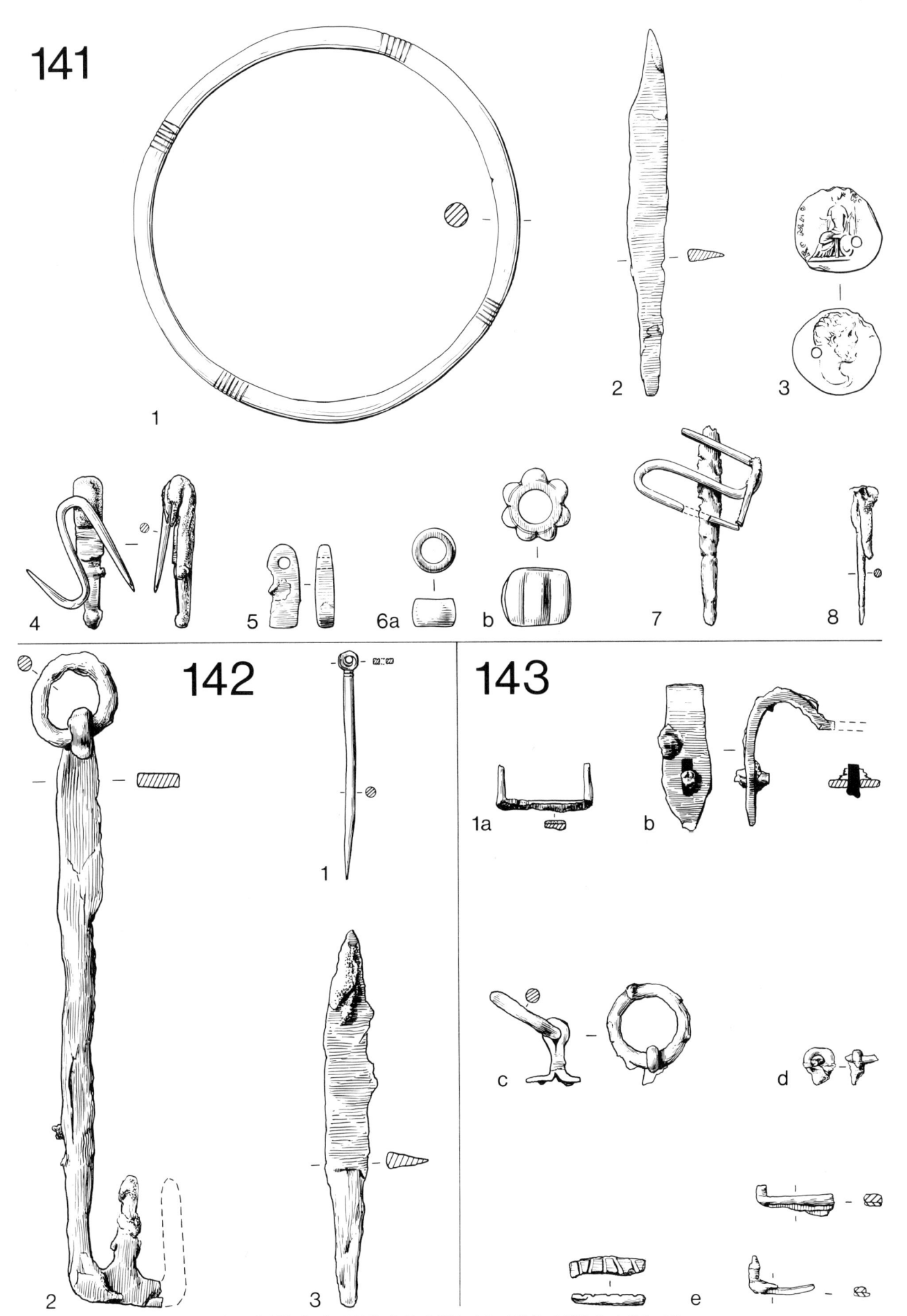

*Figure 58*   Graves 141, 142 and 143. Scale 141/1, 3–7, 142/1: 1/1; 141/8, 142/2–3, 143/1: 1/2

330   THE BUCKLAND ANGLO-SAXON CEMETERY

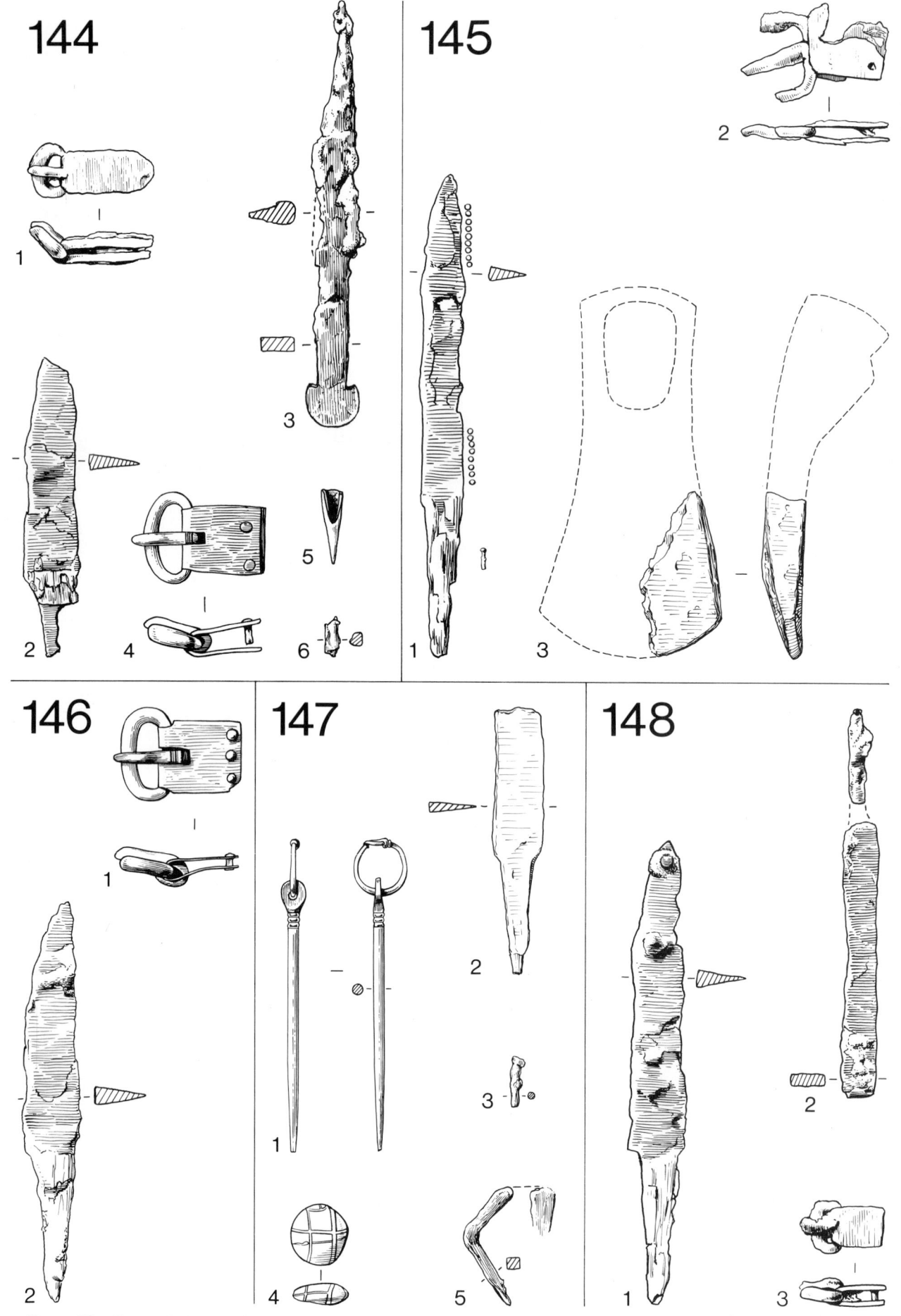

*Figure 59*   Graves 144, 145, 146, 147 and 148. Scale 144/4–5, 146/1, 147/1: 1/1; 144/1–3, 6, 145/1–3, 146/2, 147/2–5, 148/1–3: 1/2

GRAVE CATALOGUE 331

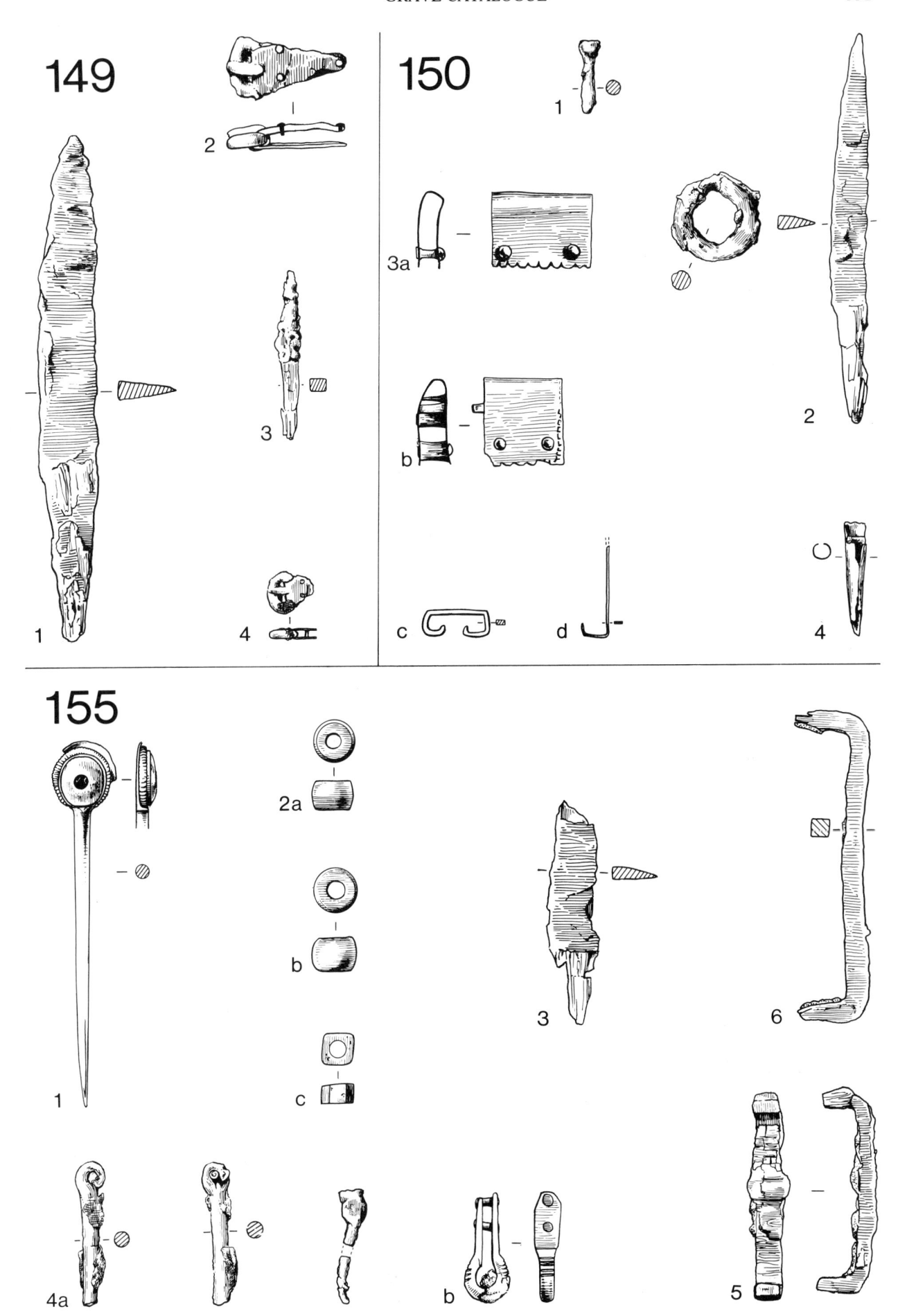

*Figure 60* Graves 149, 150 and 155. Scale 150/3–4, 155/1–2, 4b: 1/1; 149/1–4, 150/1–2, 155/3–4a, 5–6: 1/2

332    THE BUCKLAND ANGLO-SAXON CEMETERY

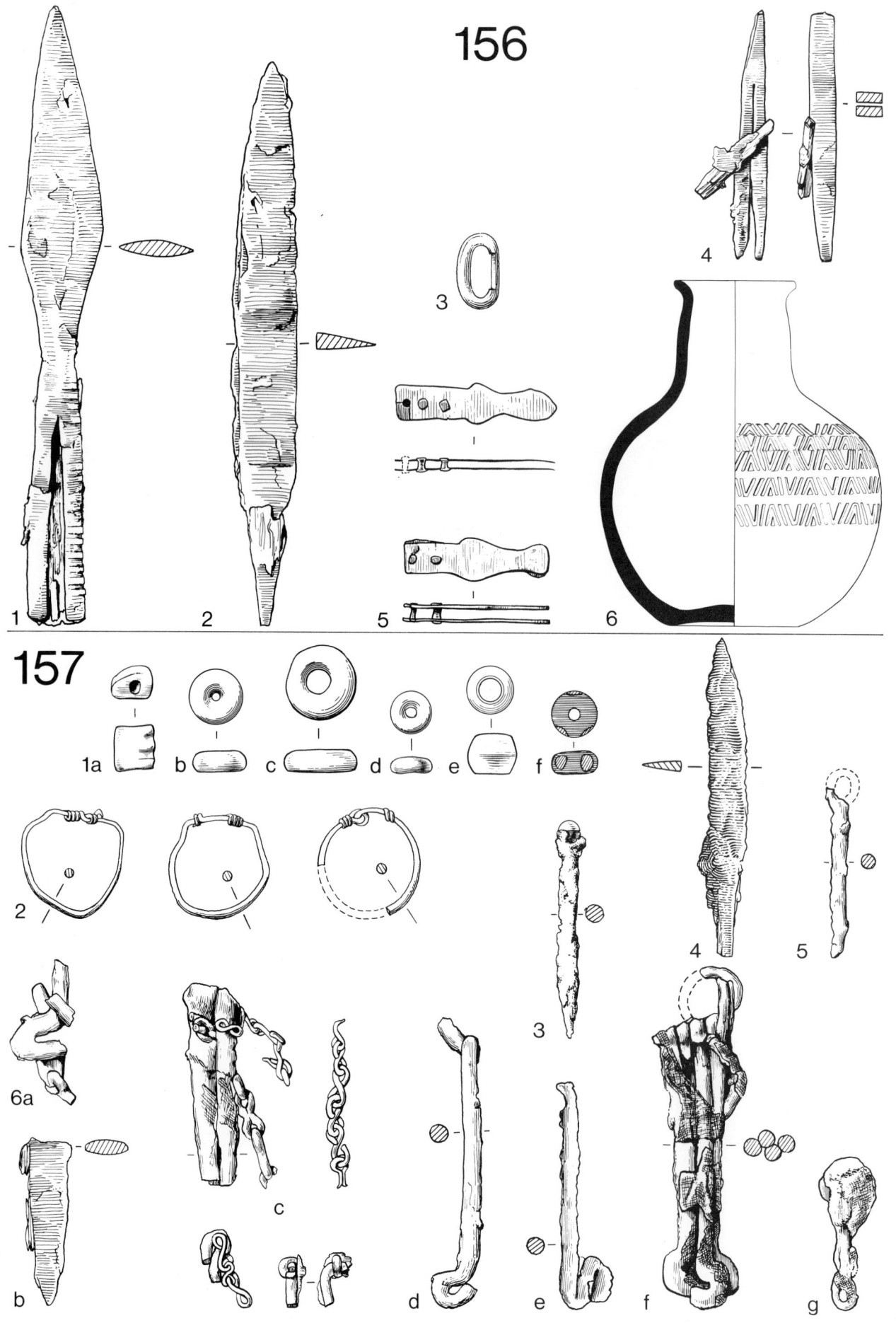

## 156

## 157

*Figure 61*   Graves 156 and 157. Scale 156/3, 5, 157/1–3: 1/1; 156/1–2, 4, 157/4–6: 1/2; 156/6: 1/3

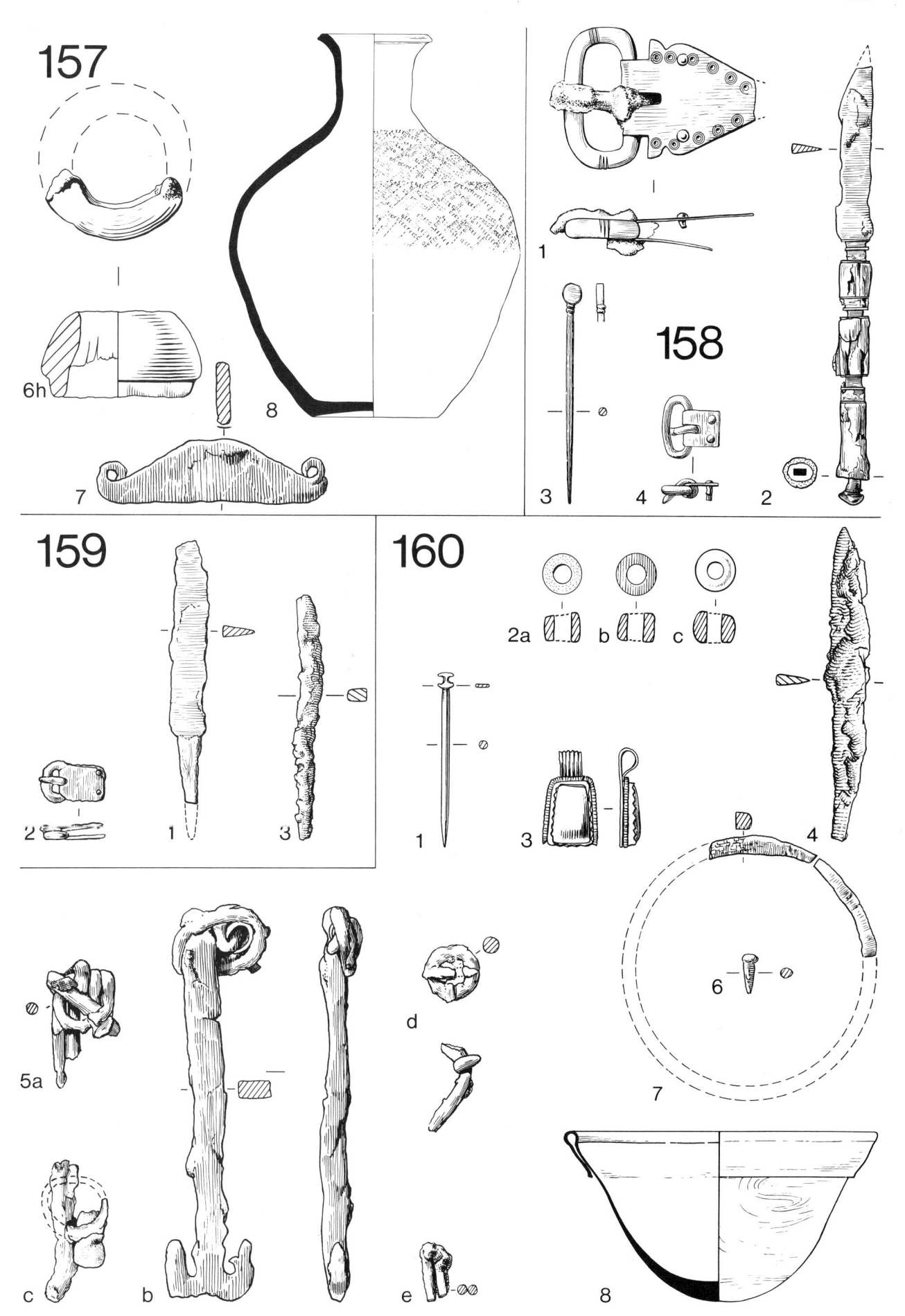

*Figure 62* Grave 157 continued, graves 158, 159 and 160. Scale 157/6b, 158/1, 3–4, 160/1–3: 1/1; 157/7, 158/2, 159/1–3, 160/4–8: 1/2; 157/8: 1/3

334   THE BUCKLAND ANGLO-SAXON CEMETERY

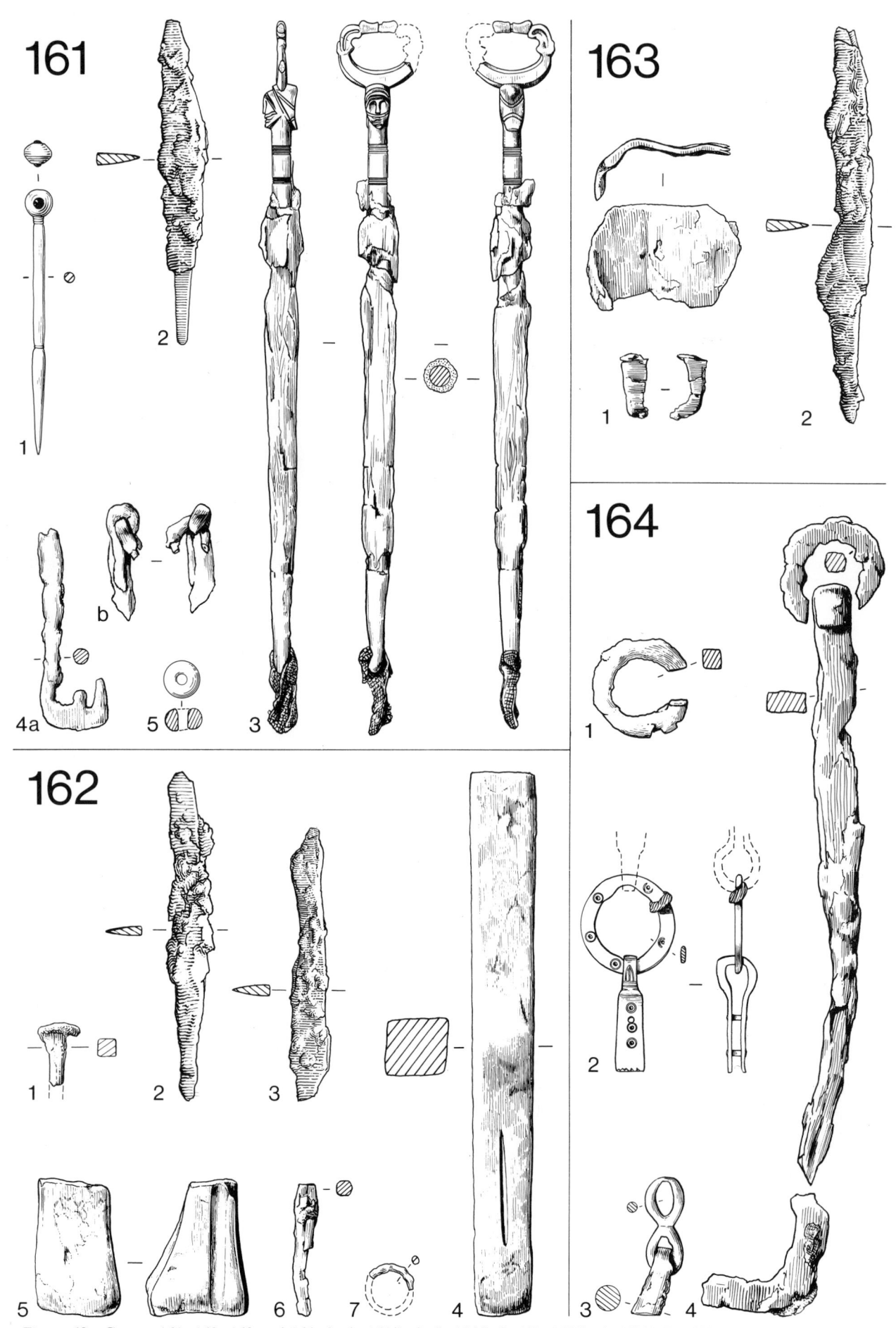

*Figure 63*   Graves 161, 162, 163 and 164. Scale 161/1, 3, 5, 164/2–3: 1/1; 161/2, 4, 162/1–7, 163/1–2, 164/1, 4: 1/2.

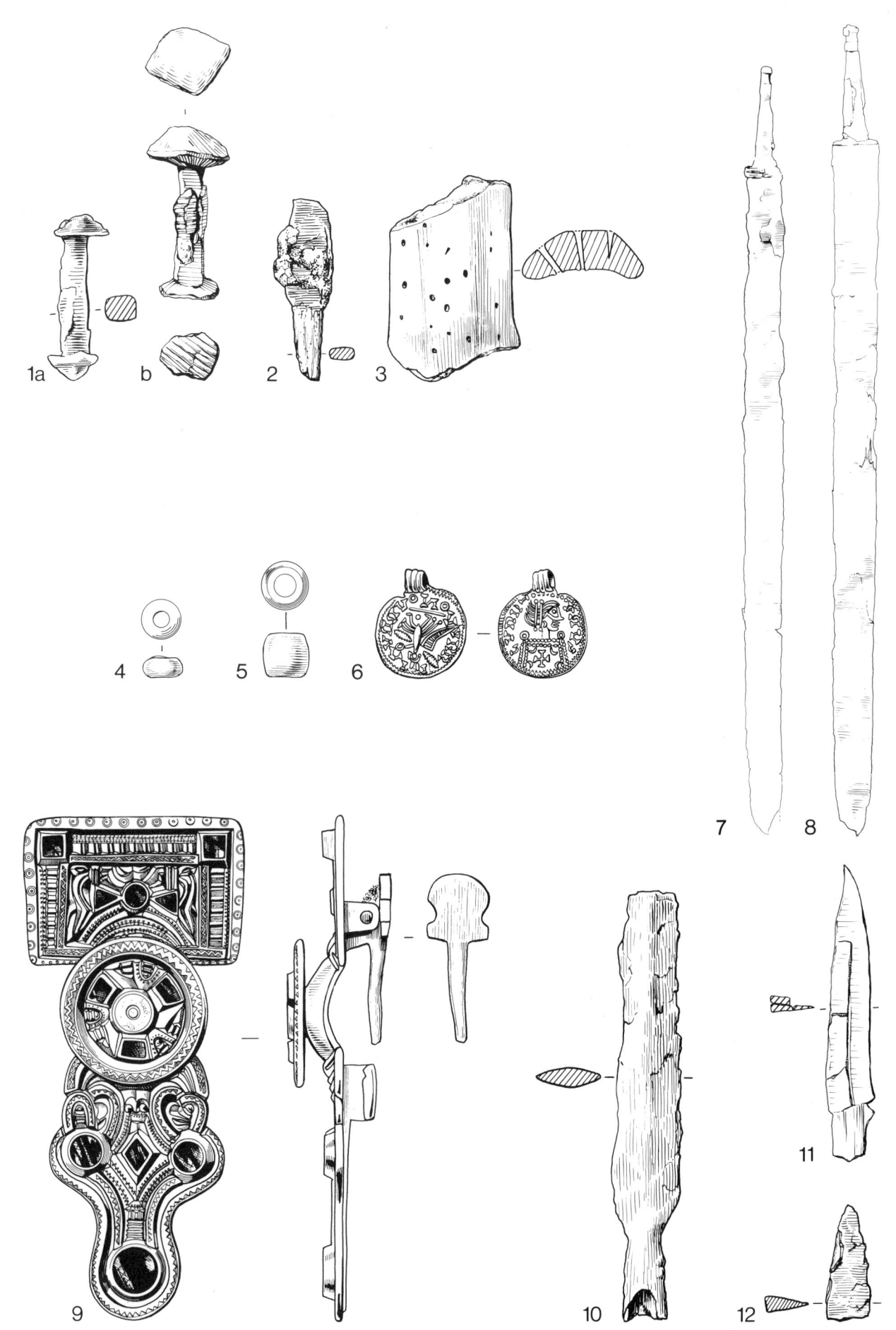

*Figure 64* Unassociated objects. 1–3 A reburial. 4–12 Finds made before the beginning of the excavation. Scale 4–6, 9: 1/1; 1–3, 10–12: 1/2; 7–8: 1/6

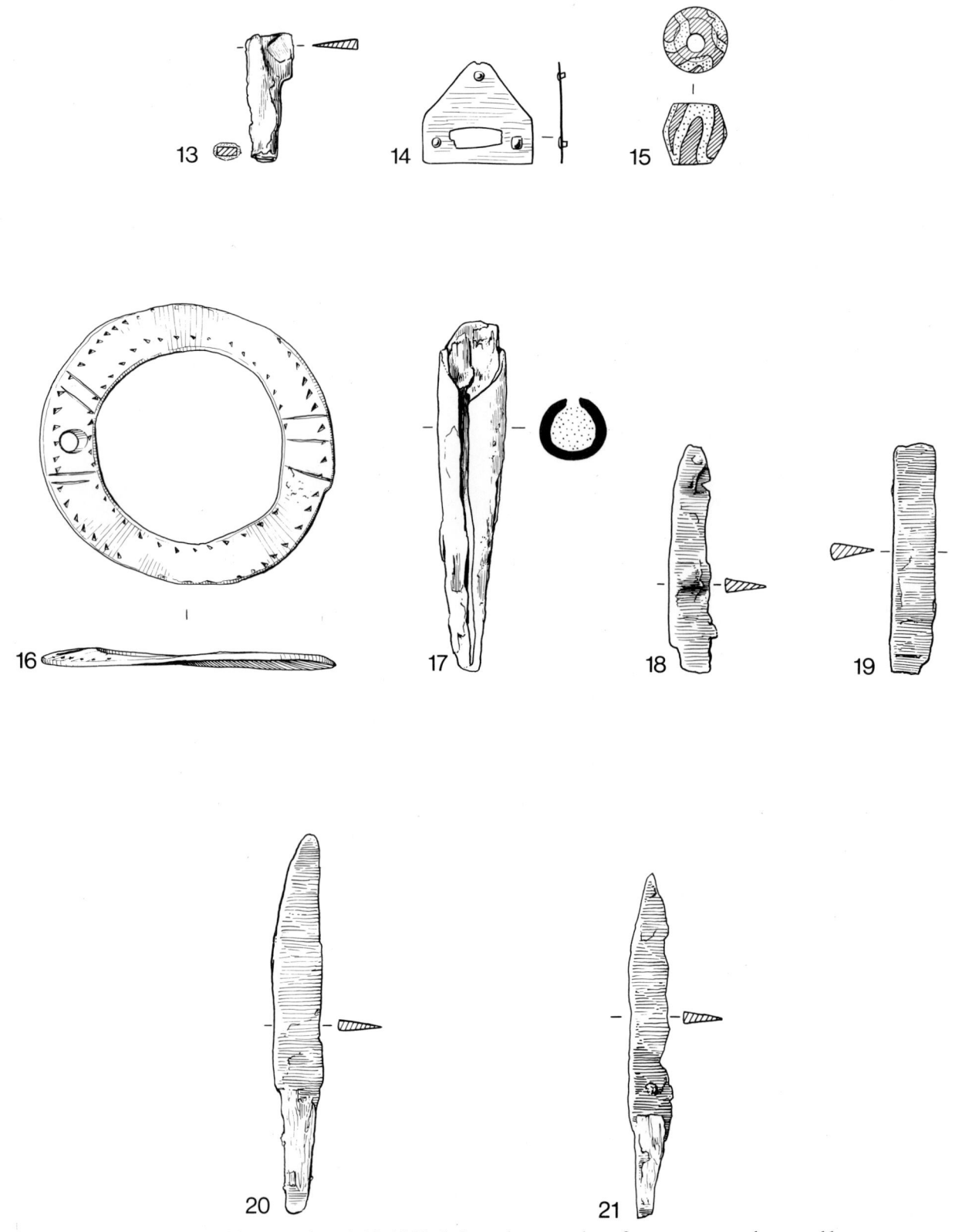

*Figure 65* Unassociated objects continued. 13–15 Finds from the area where five graves were destroyed between graves 8 and 38. 16–19 Loose finds in topsoil. 20–21 Unidentified knives. Scale 14–16: 1/1; 13, 17–21: 1/2

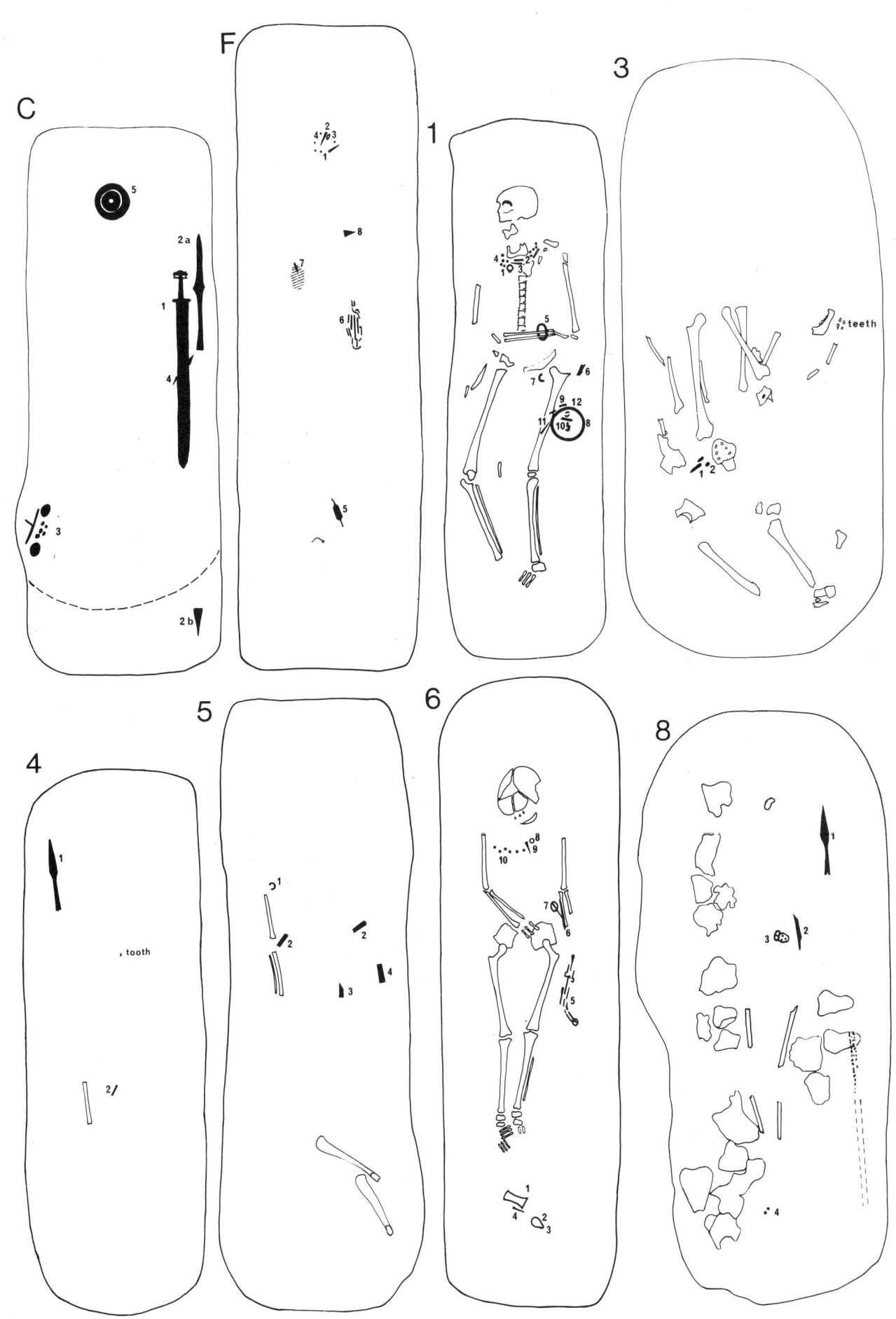

*Figure 66* Grave plans. Scale 1:24

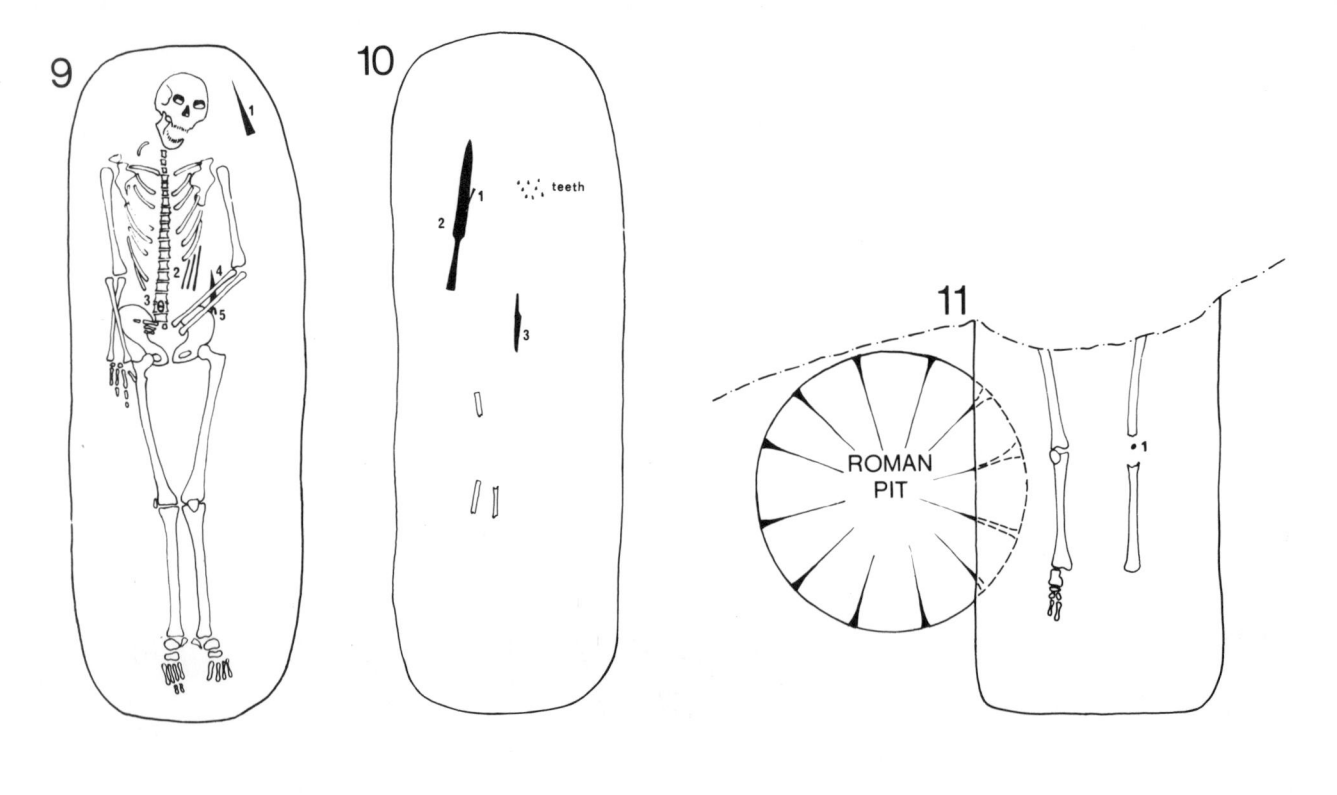

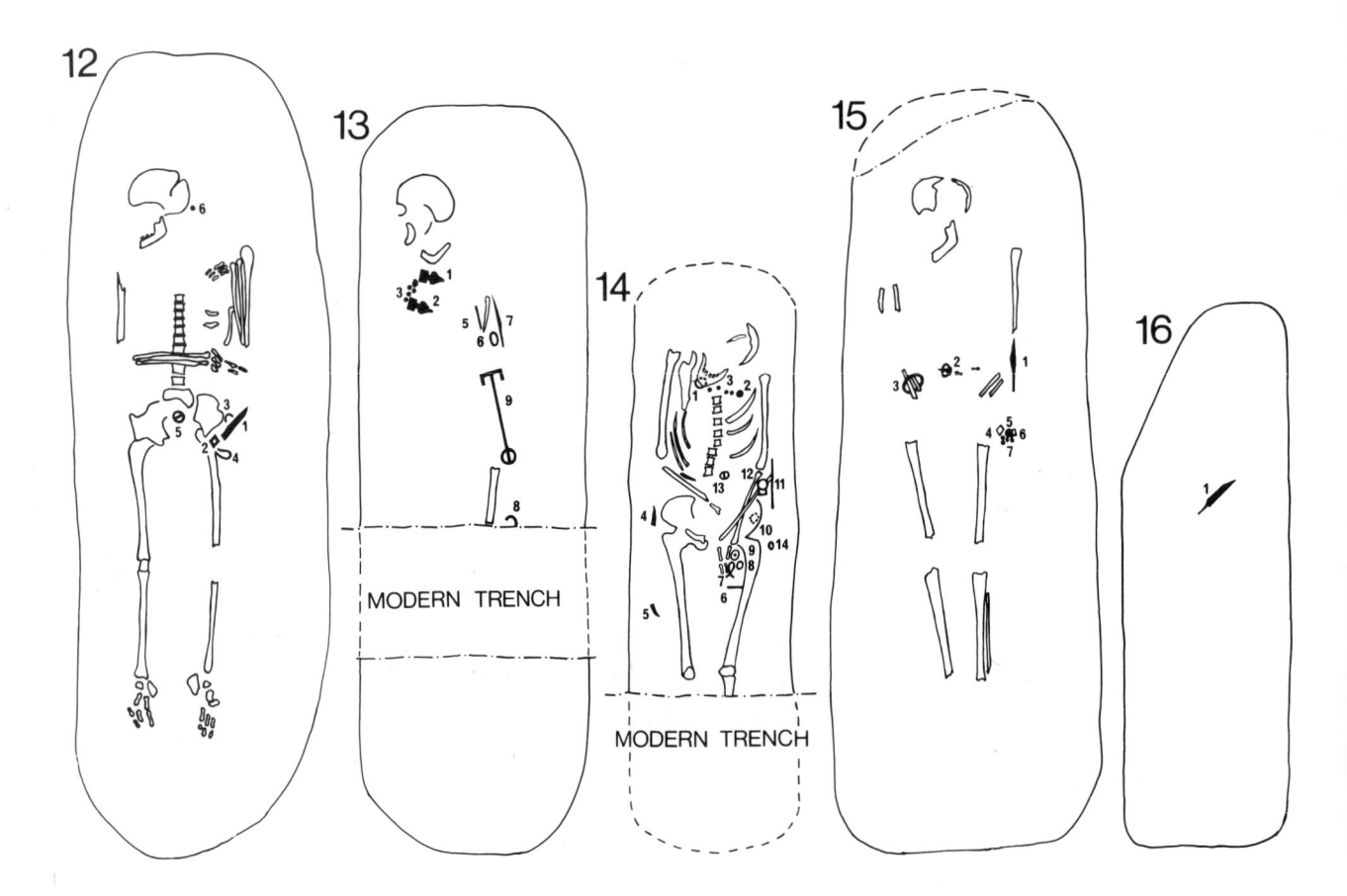

*Figure 67* Grave plans. Scale 1:24

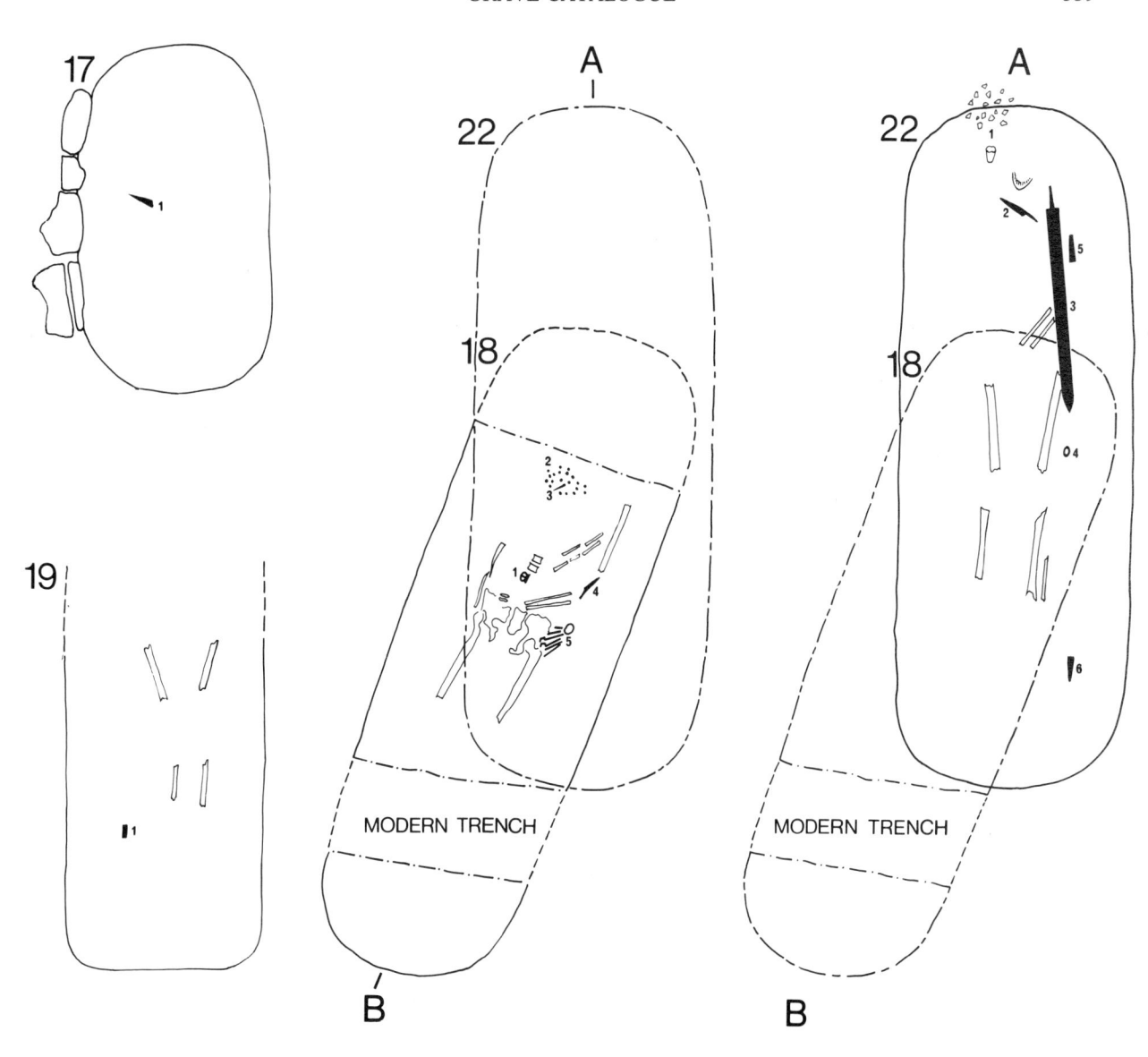

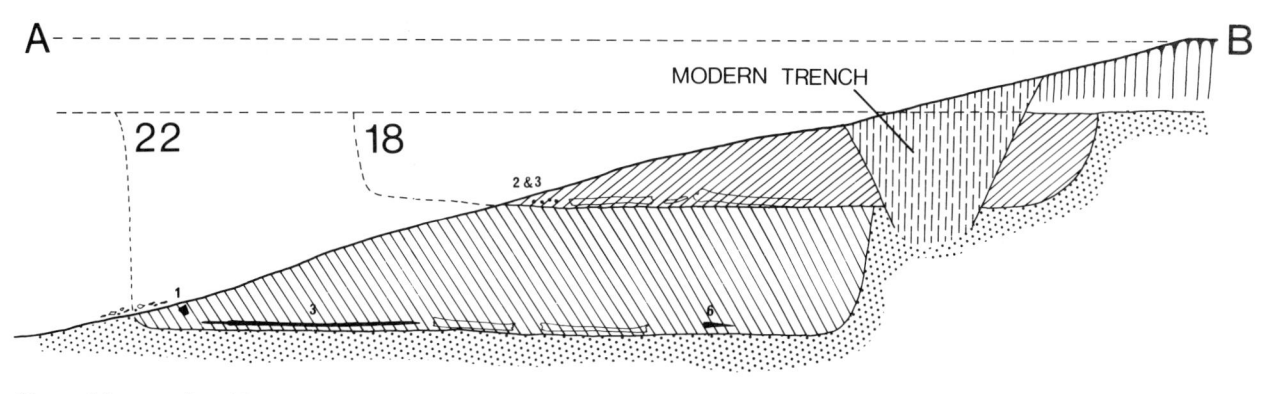

GRAVE CATALOGUE 339

Section A–B

*Figure 68* Grave plans. Scale 1:24

340  THE BUCKLAND ANGLO-SAXON CEMETERY

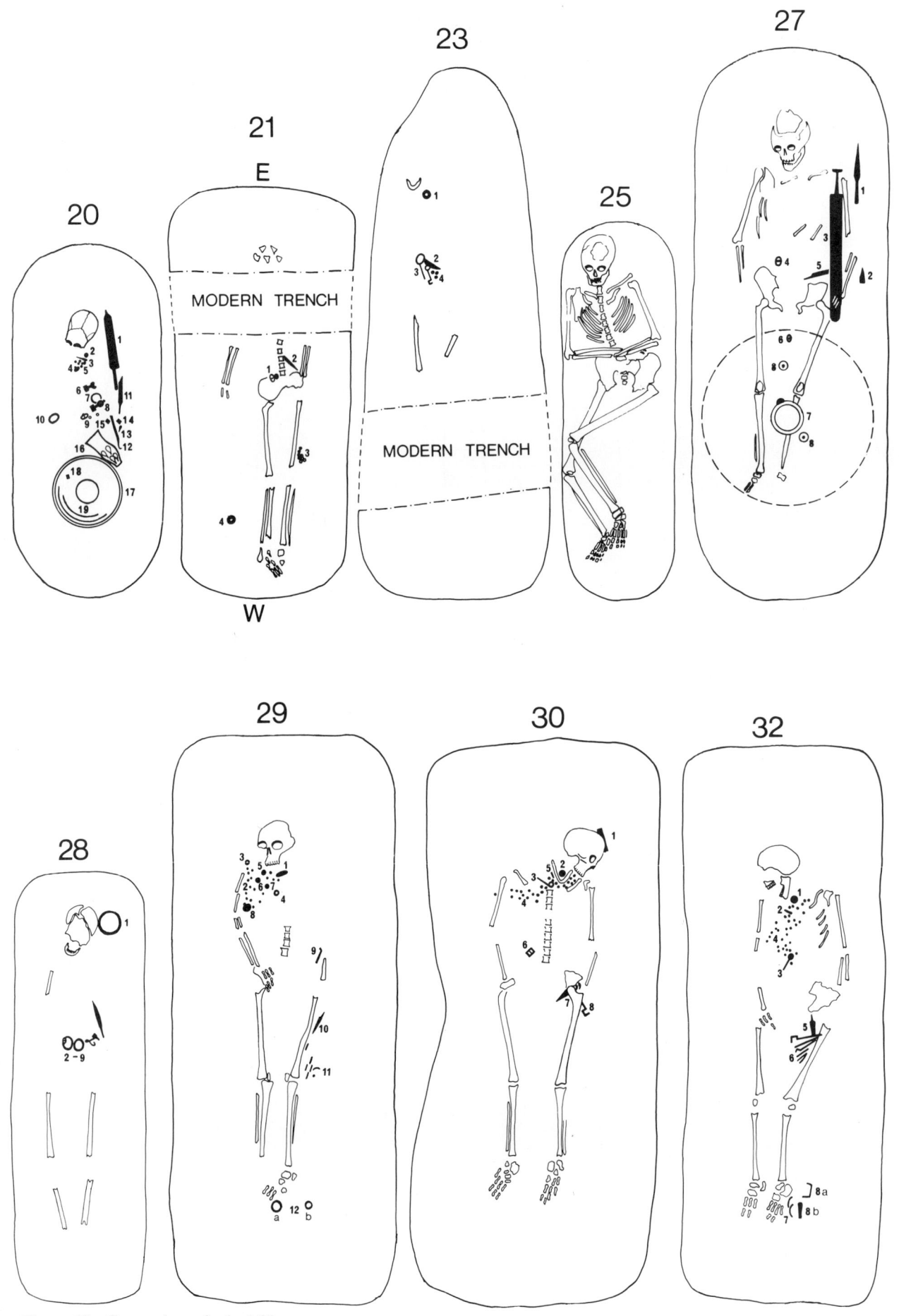

*Figure 69* Grave plans. Scale 1:24

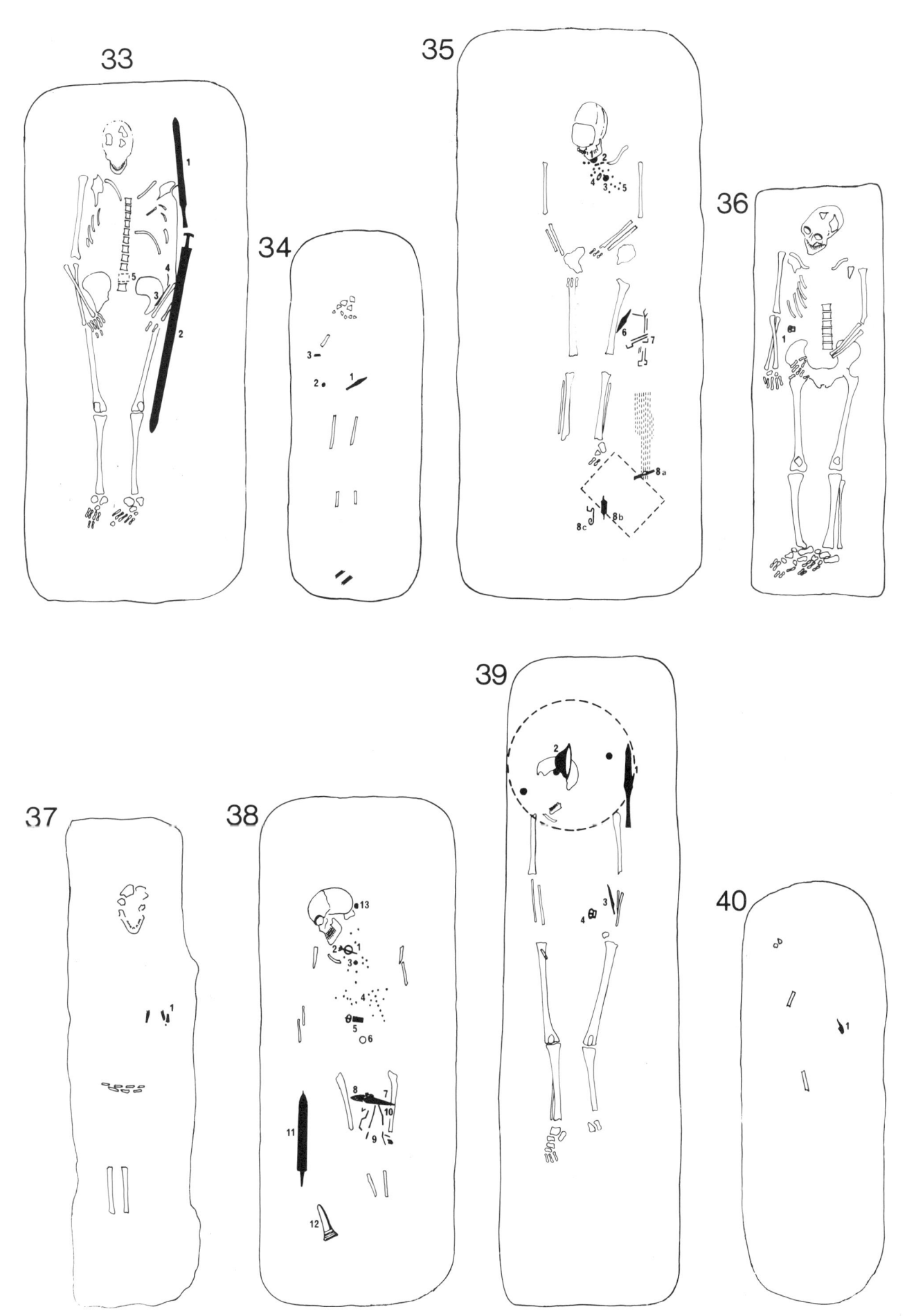

*Figure 70* Grave plans. Scale 1:24

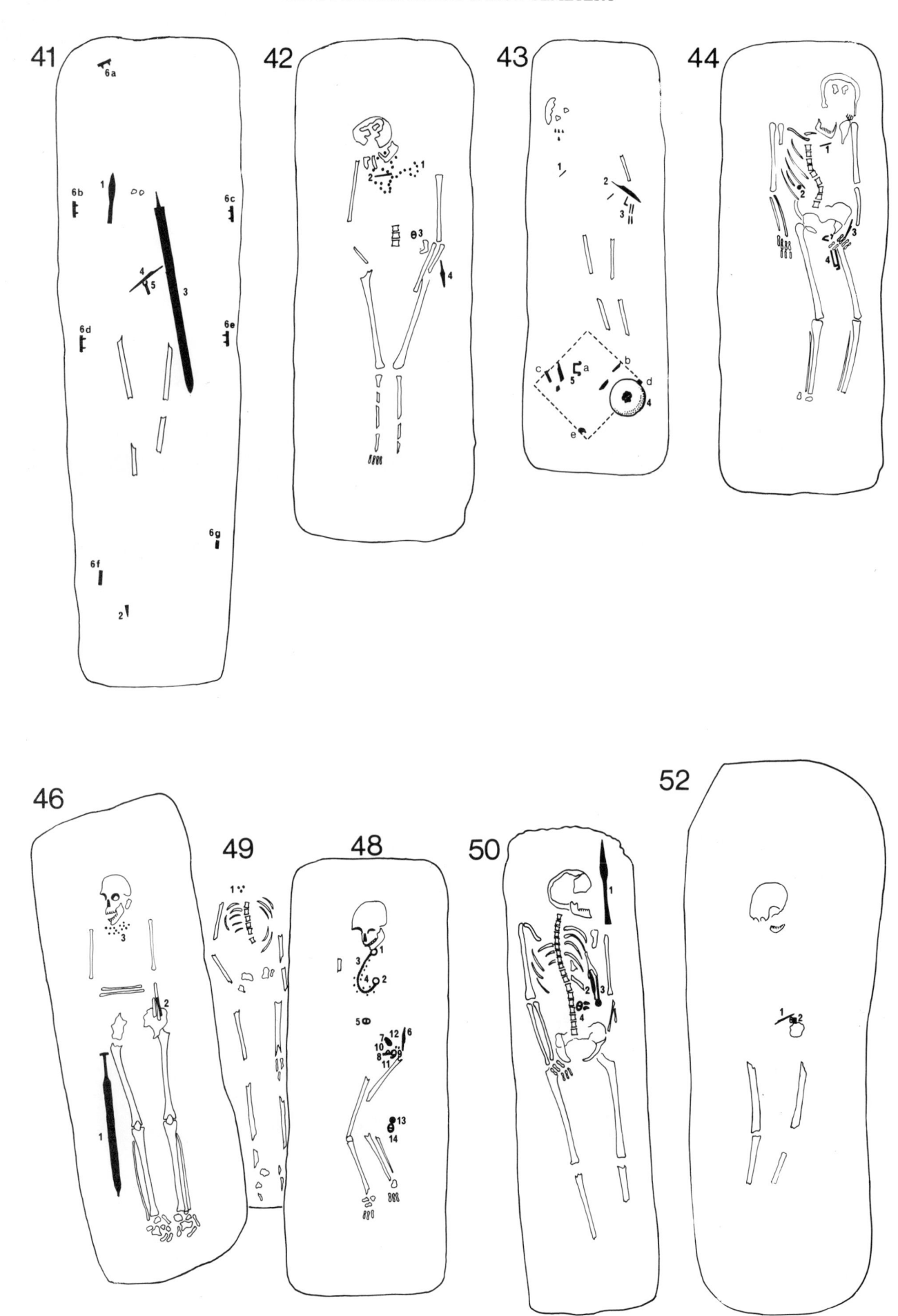

*Figure 71* Grave plans. Scale 1:24

343

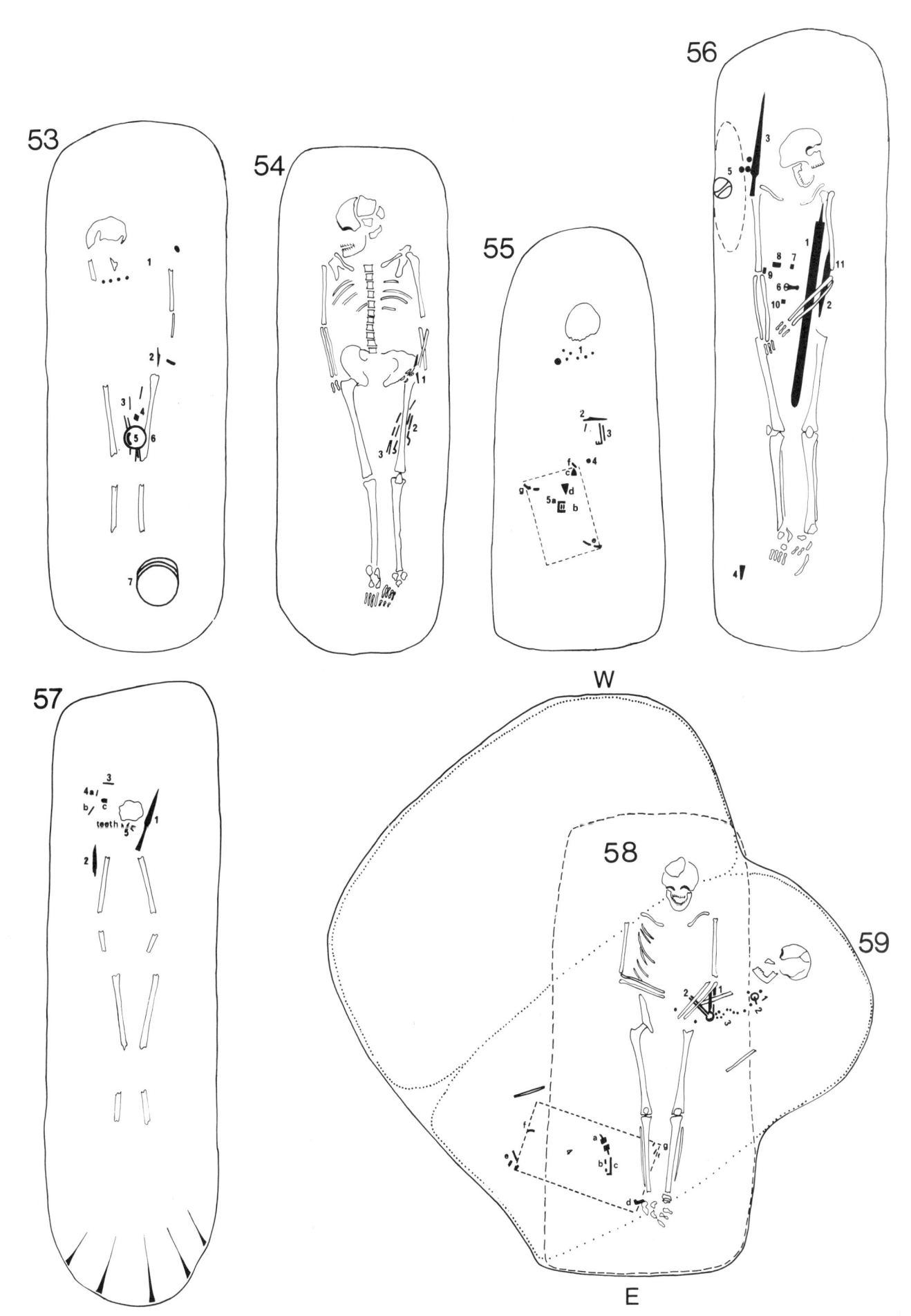

*Figure 72* Grave plans. Scale 1:24

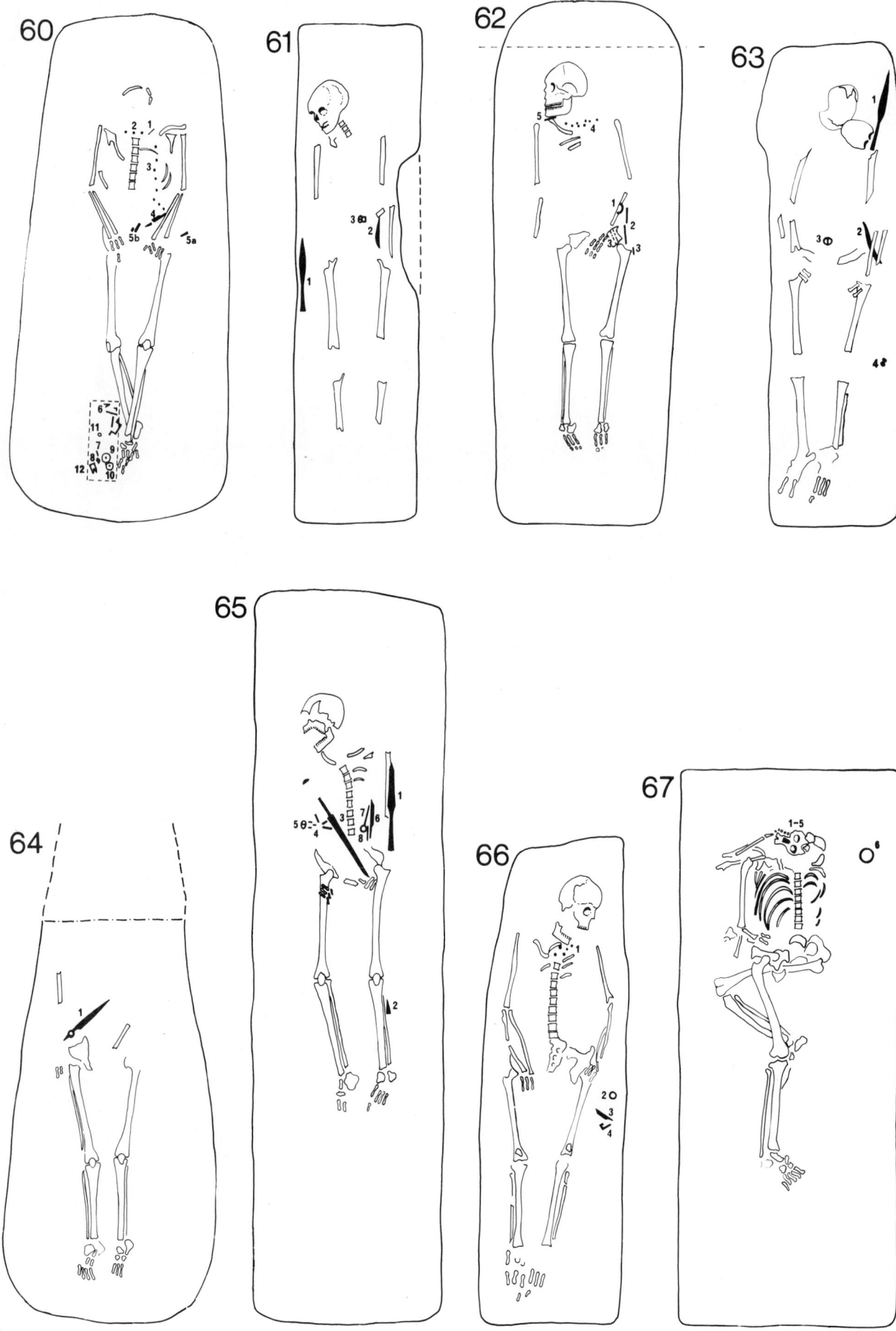

*Figure 73* Grave plans. Scale 1:24

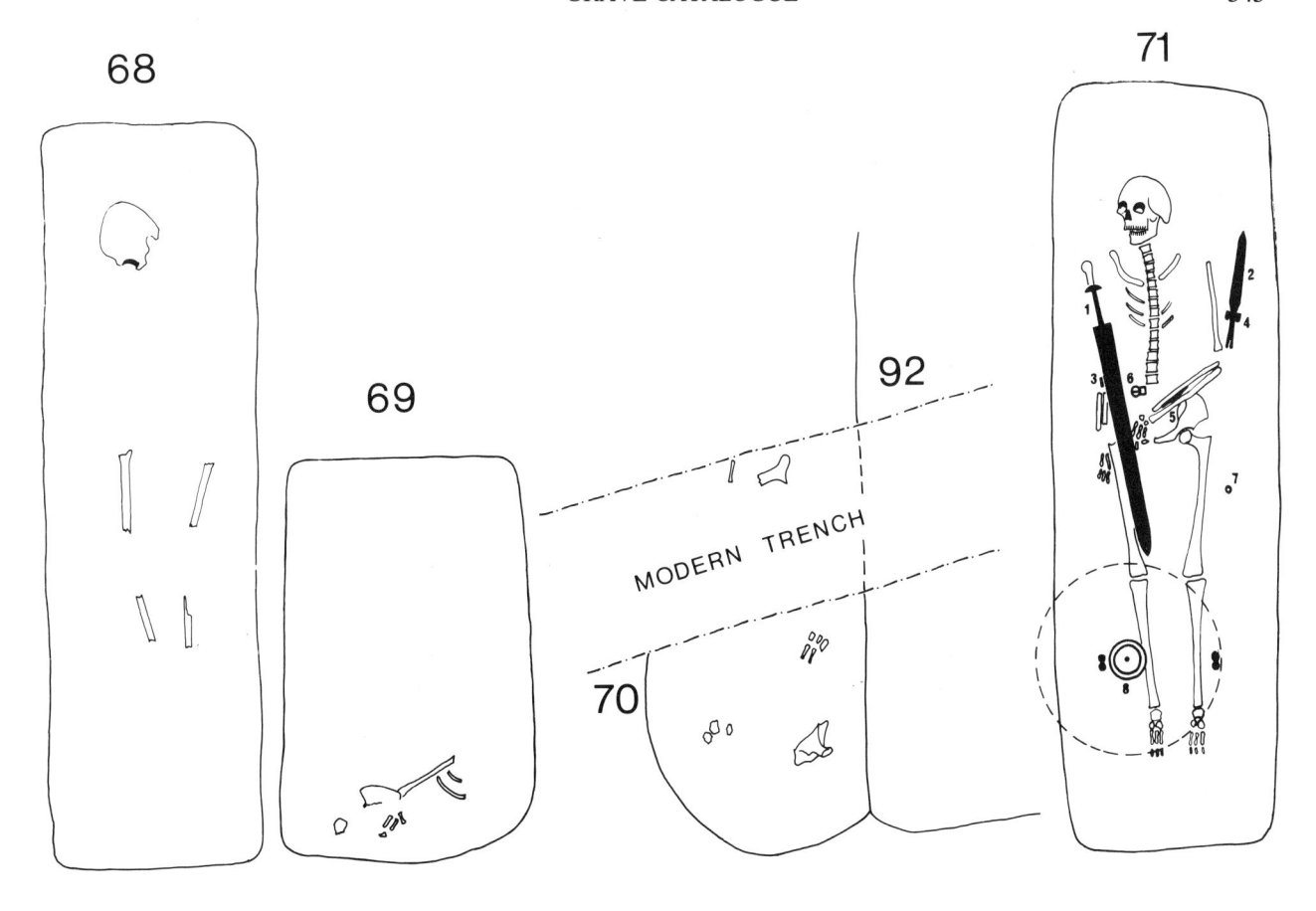

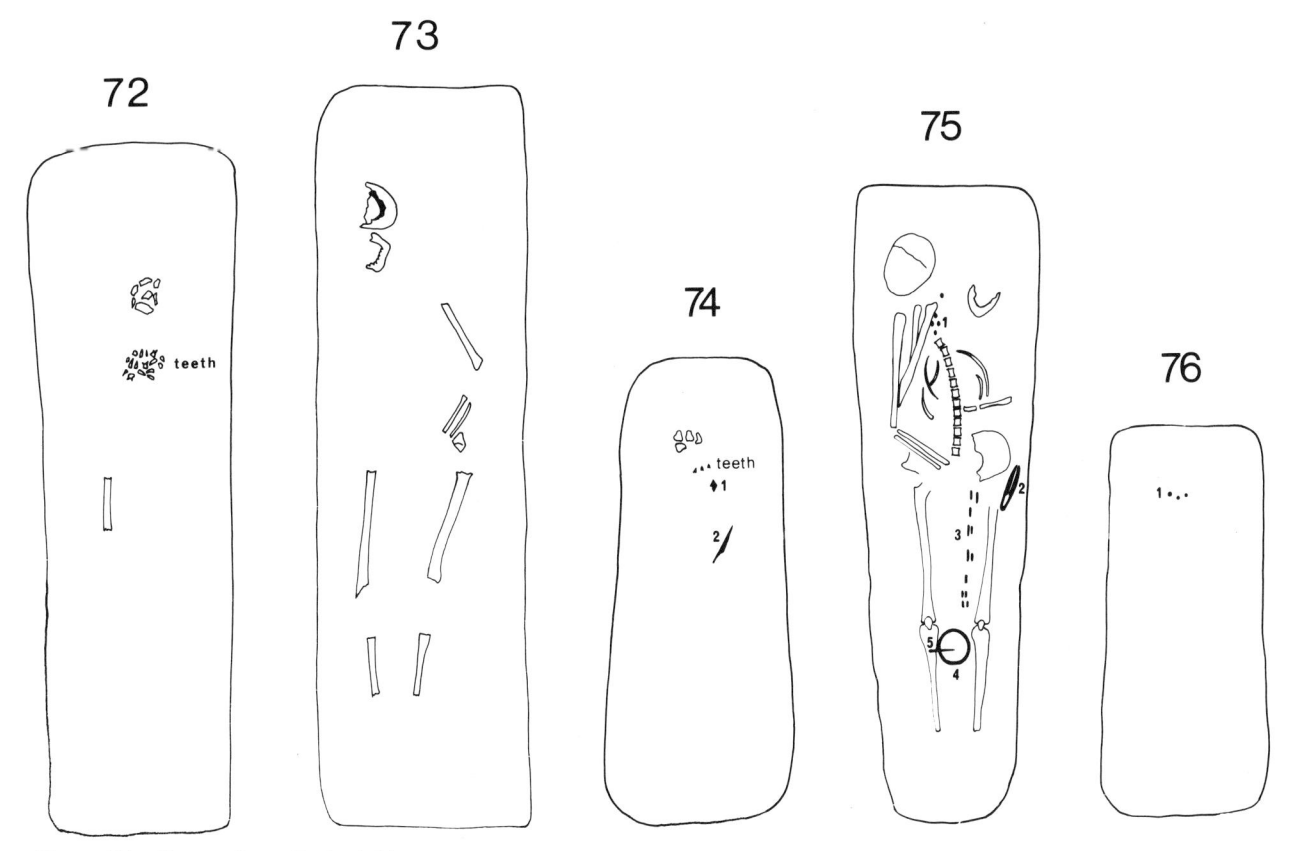

*Figure 74* Grave plans. Scale 1:24

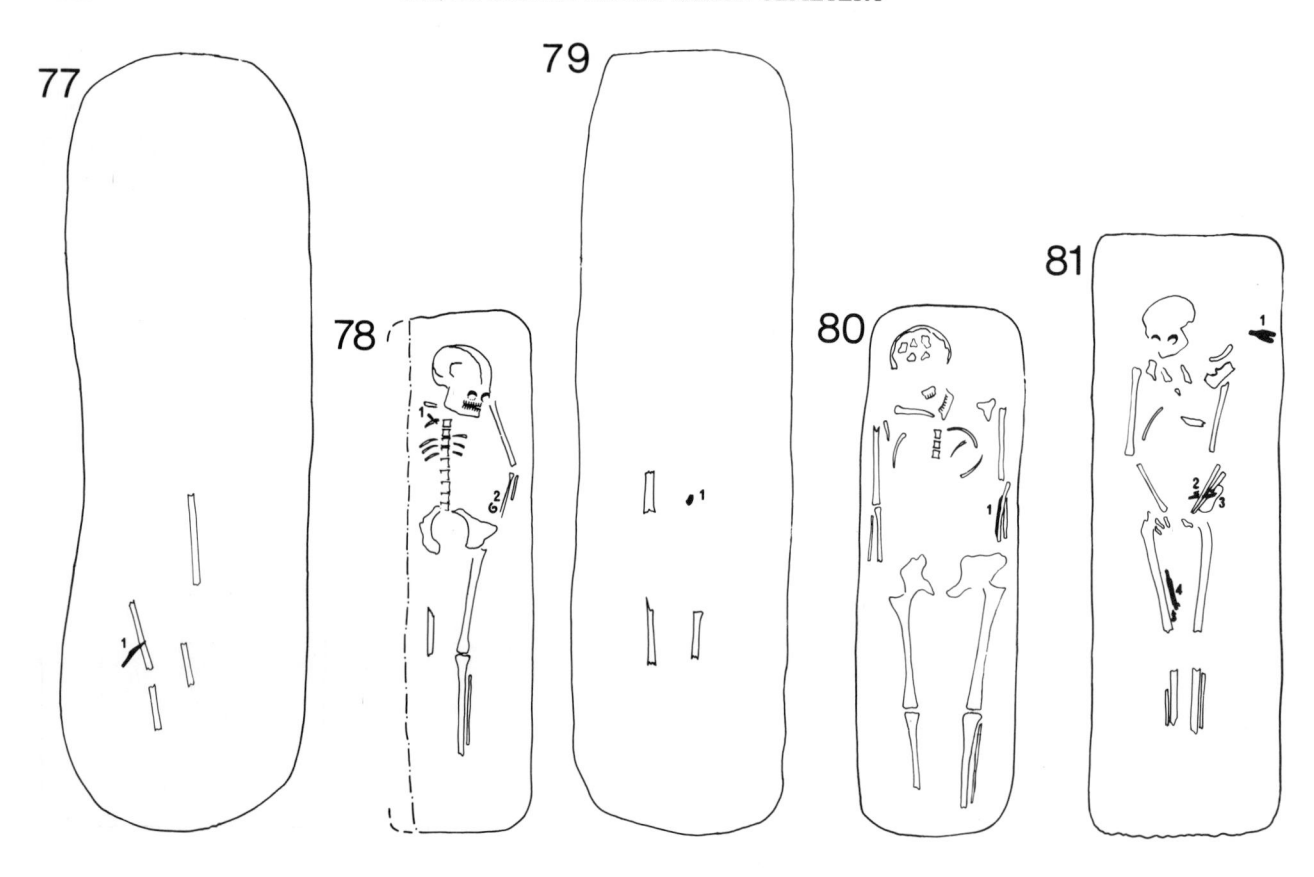

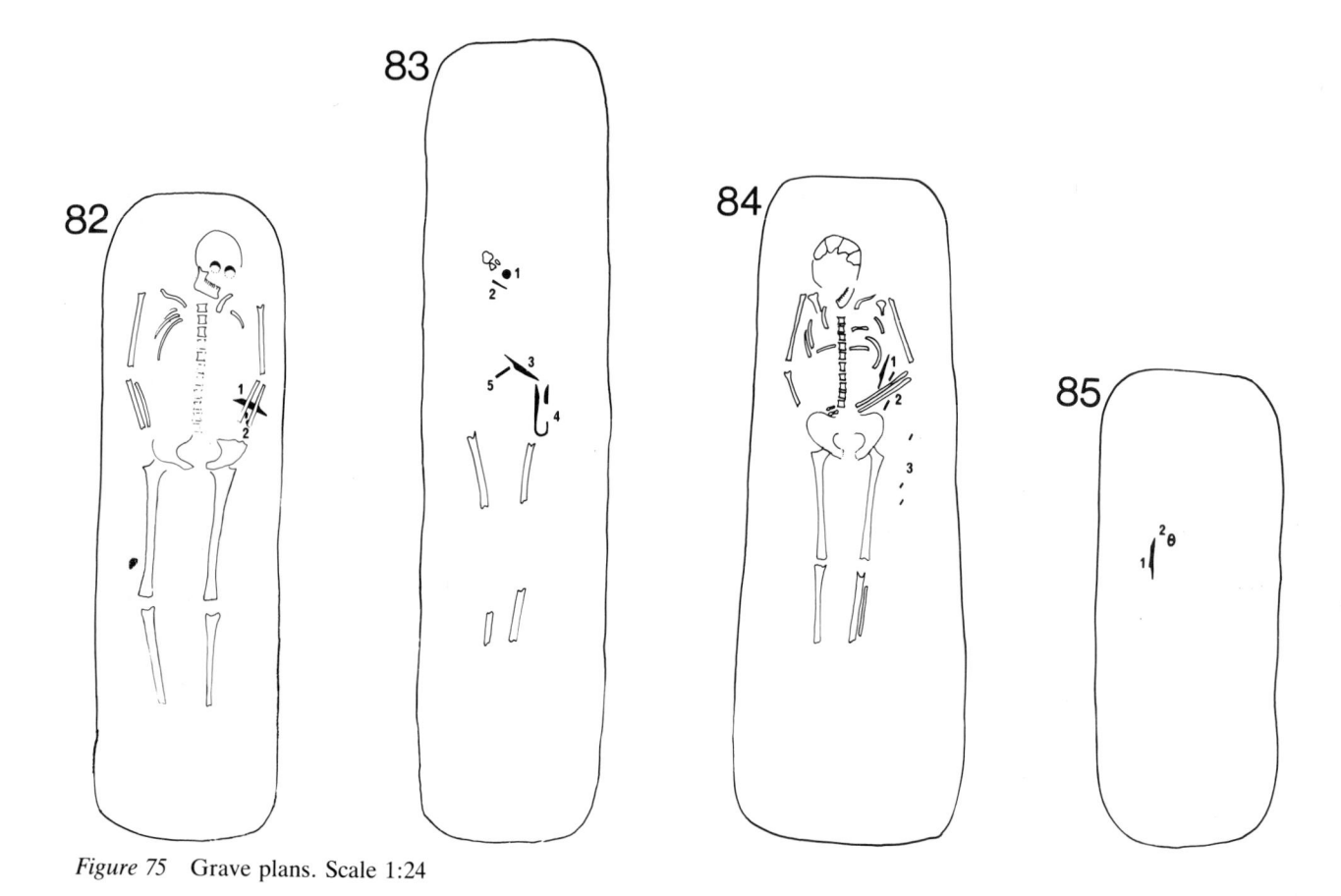

*Figure 75* Grave plans. Scale 1:24

GRAVE CATALOGUE 347

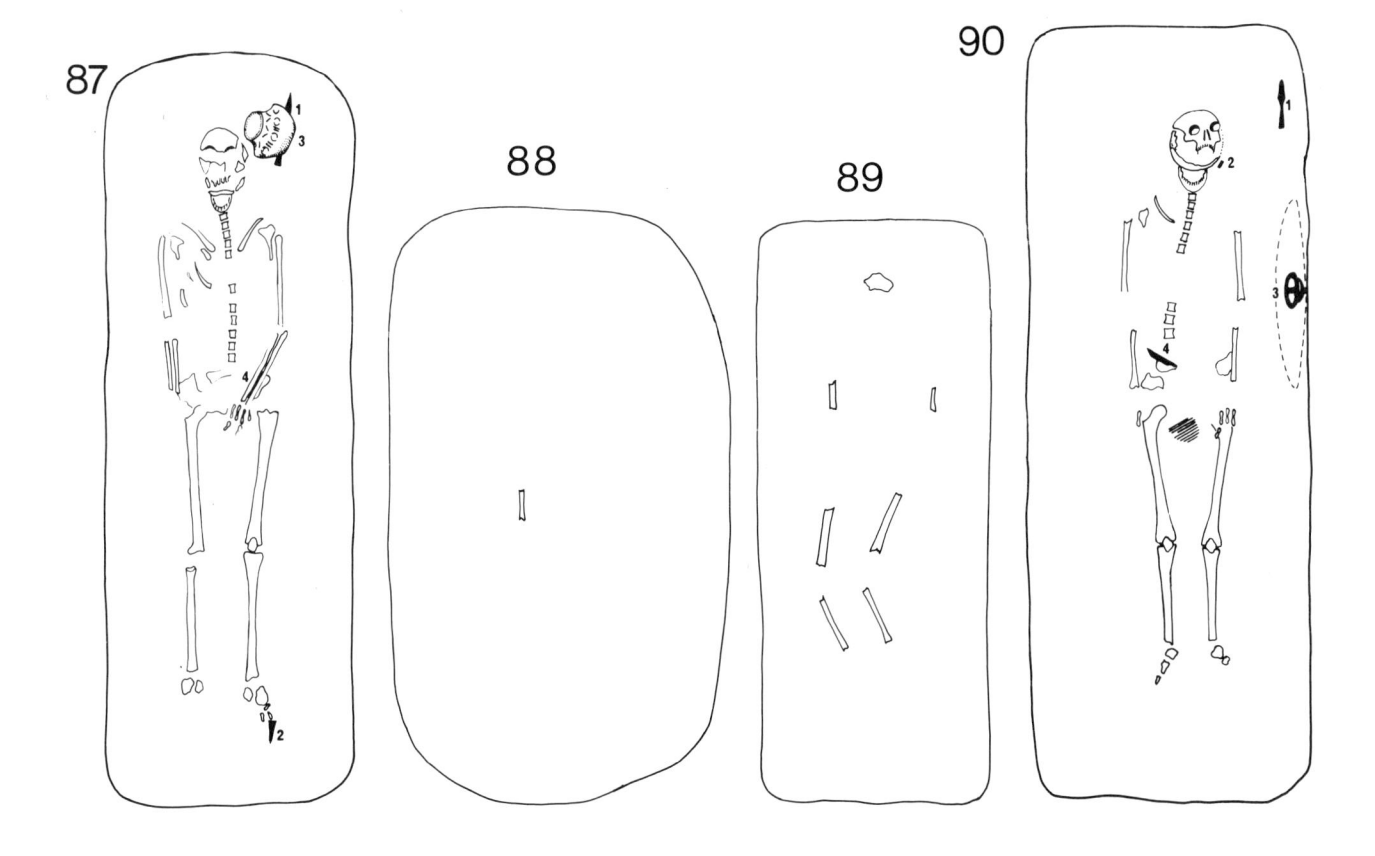

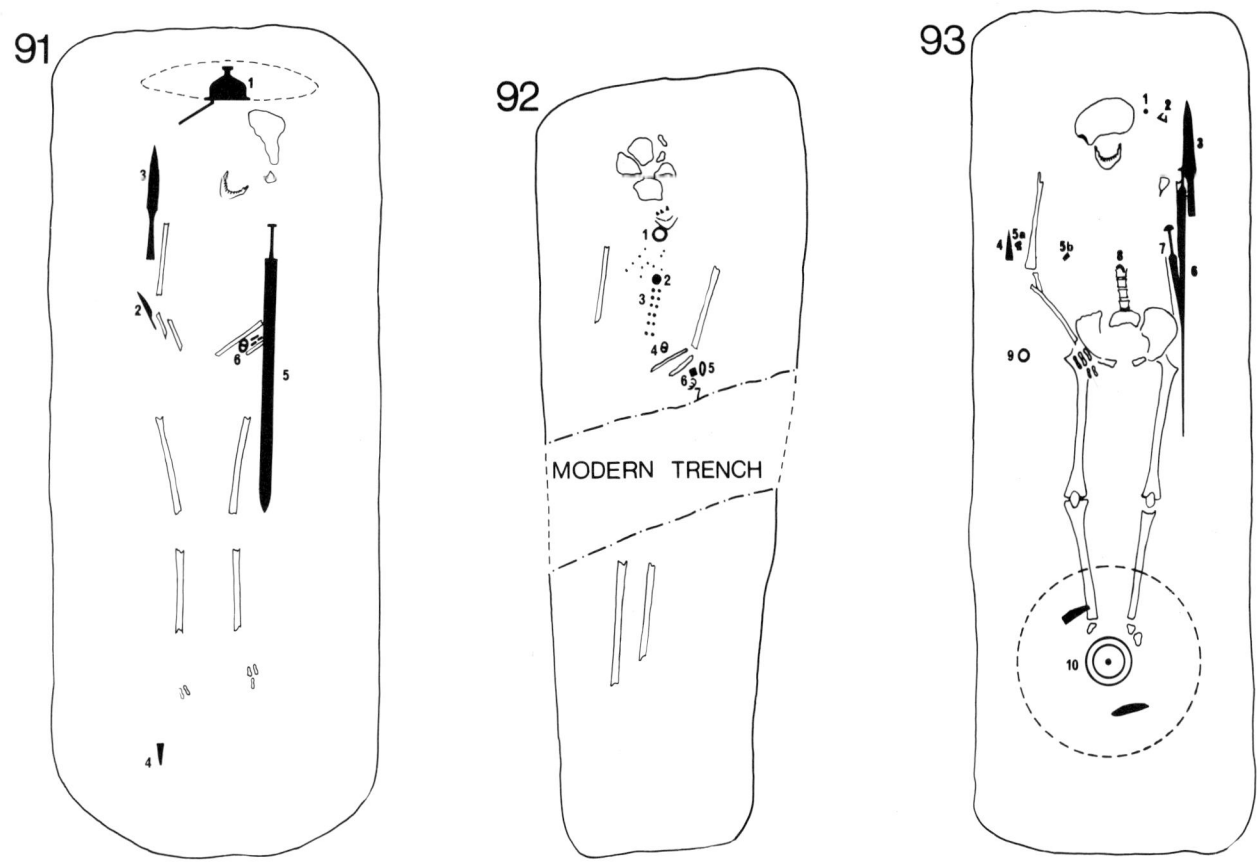

*Figure 76* Grave plans. Scale 1:24

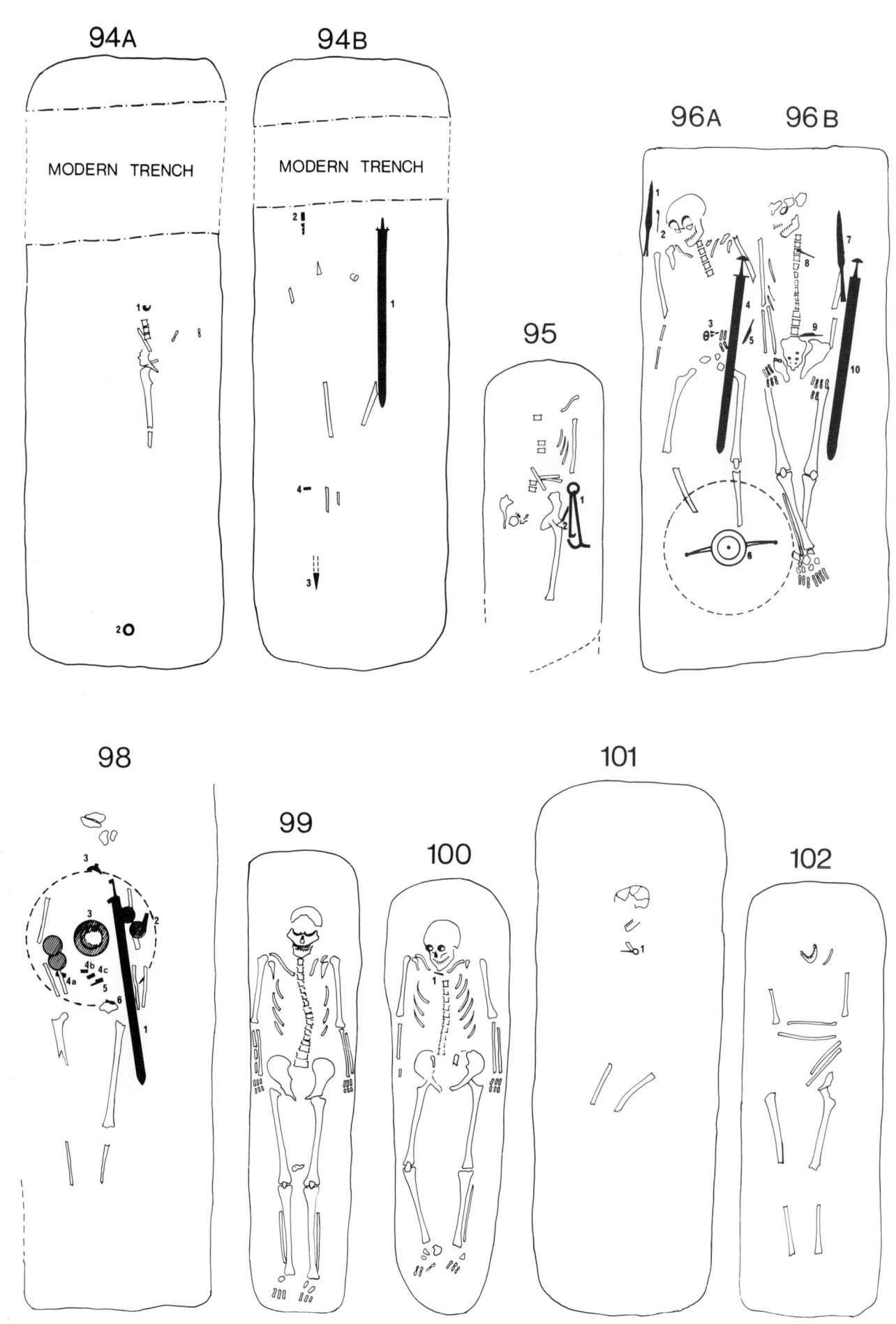

*Figure 77* Grave plans. Scale 1:24

GRAVE CATALOGUE 349

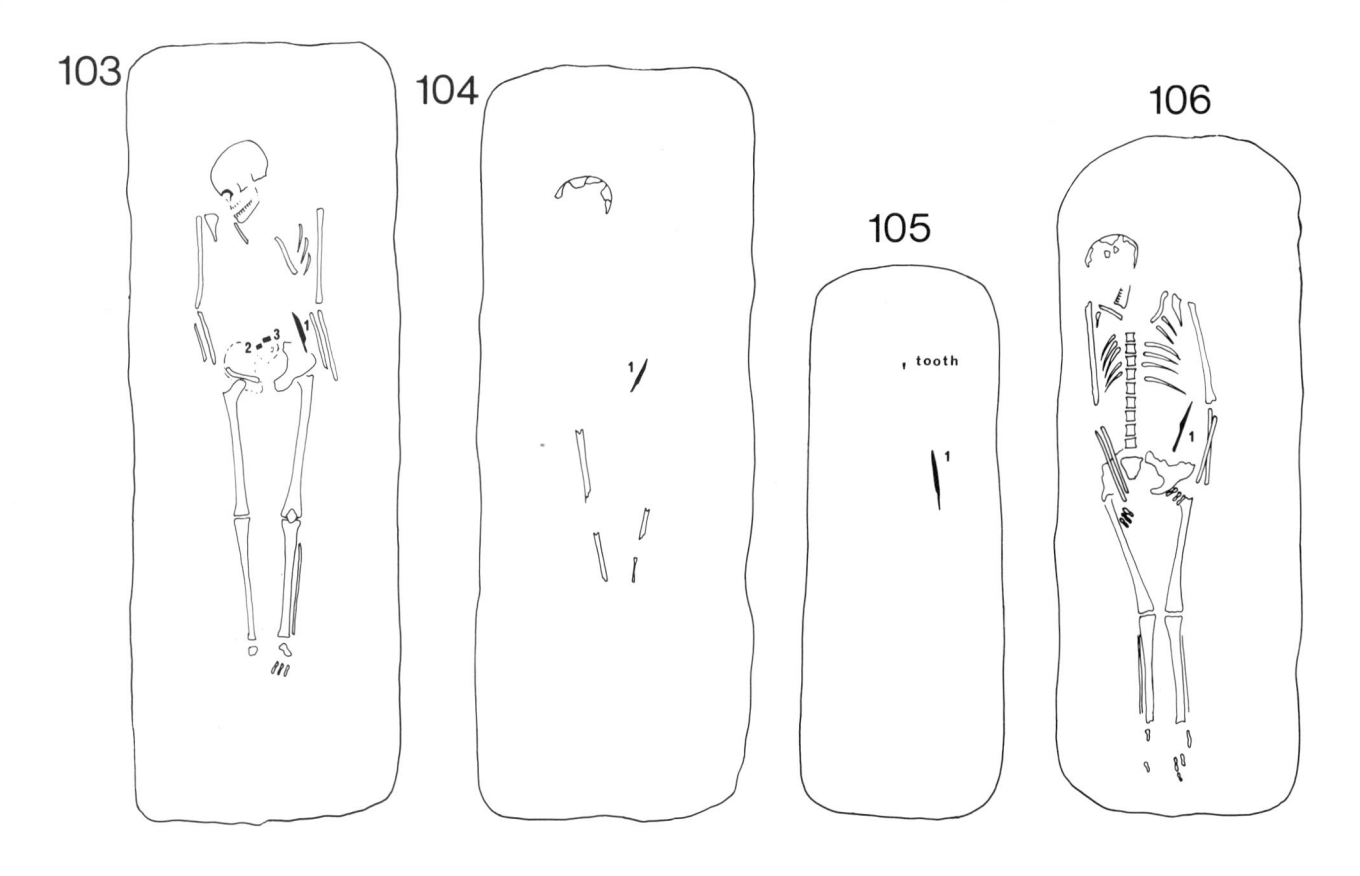

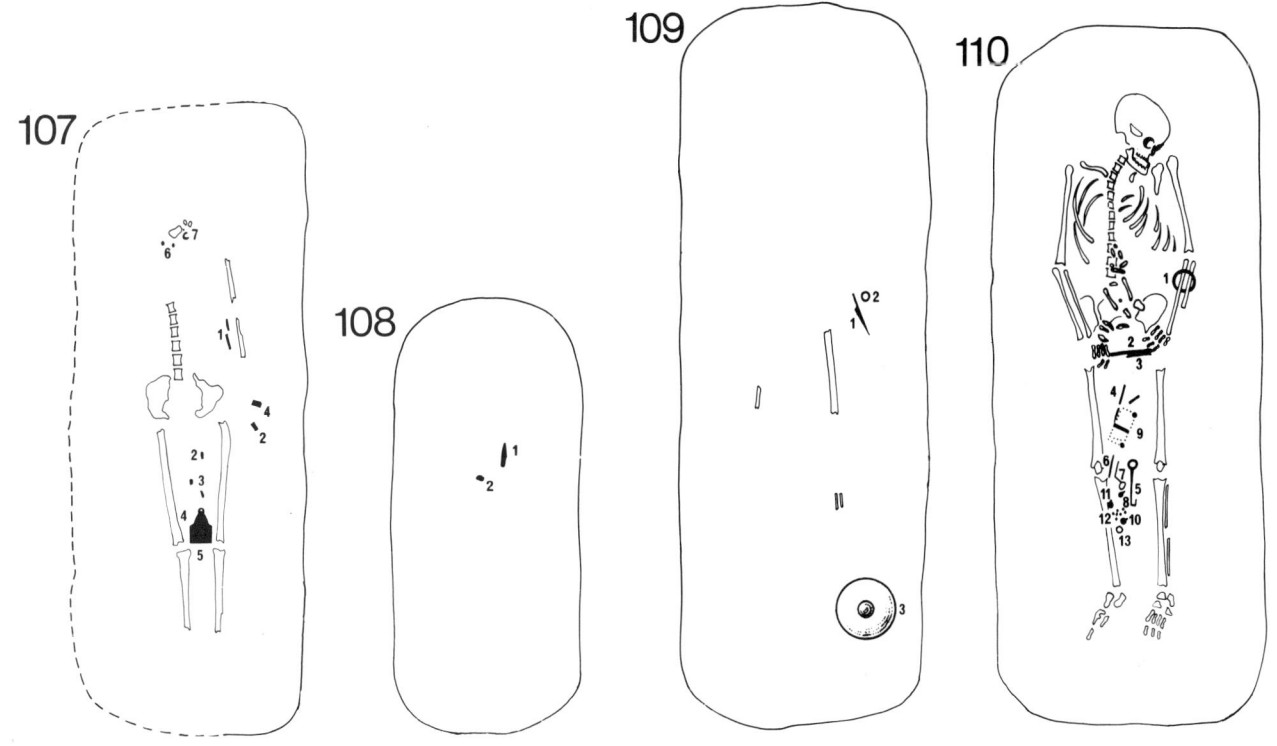

*Figure 78* Grave plans. Scale 1:24

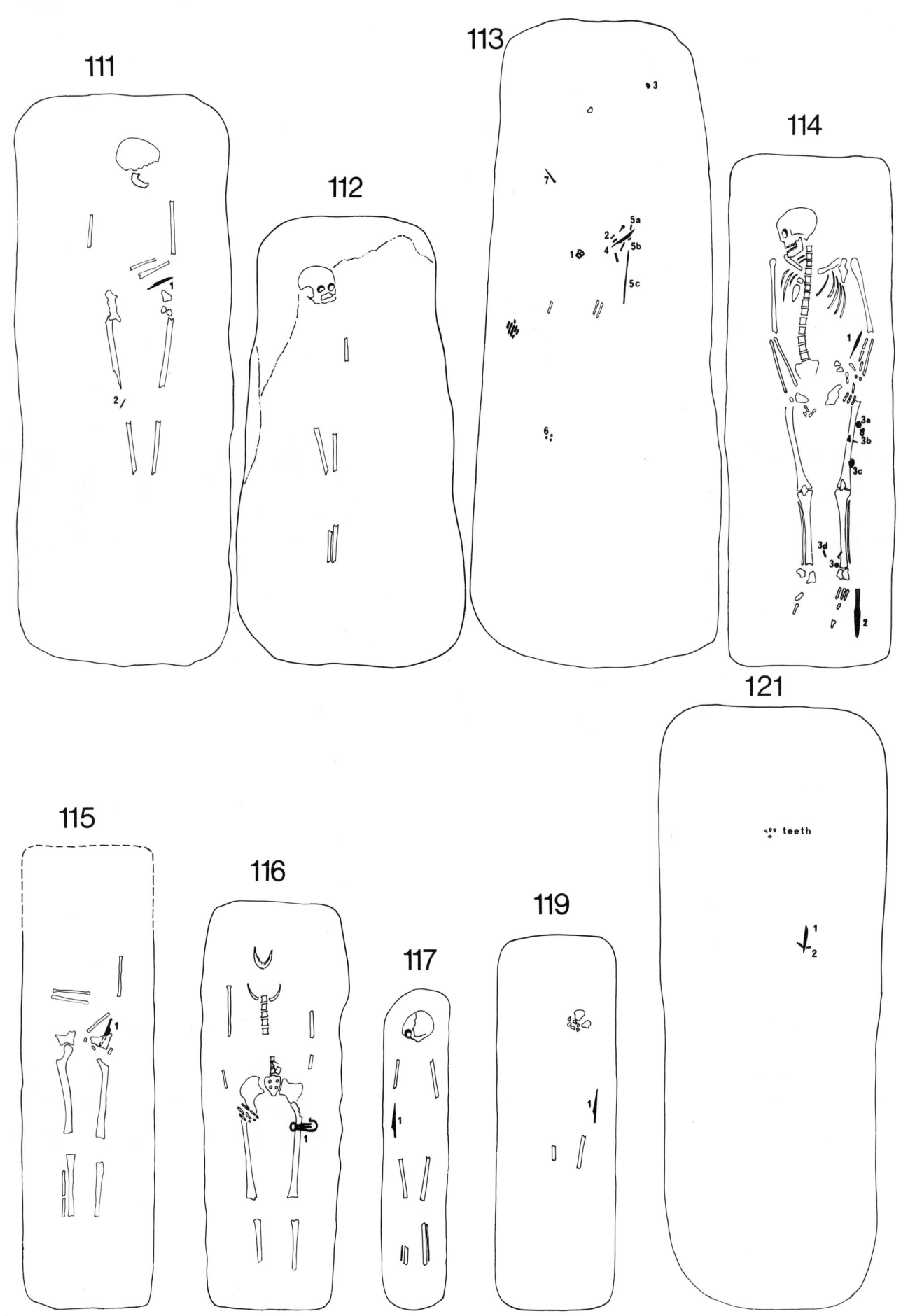

*Figure 79* Grave plans. Scale 1:24

GRAVE CATALOGUE 351

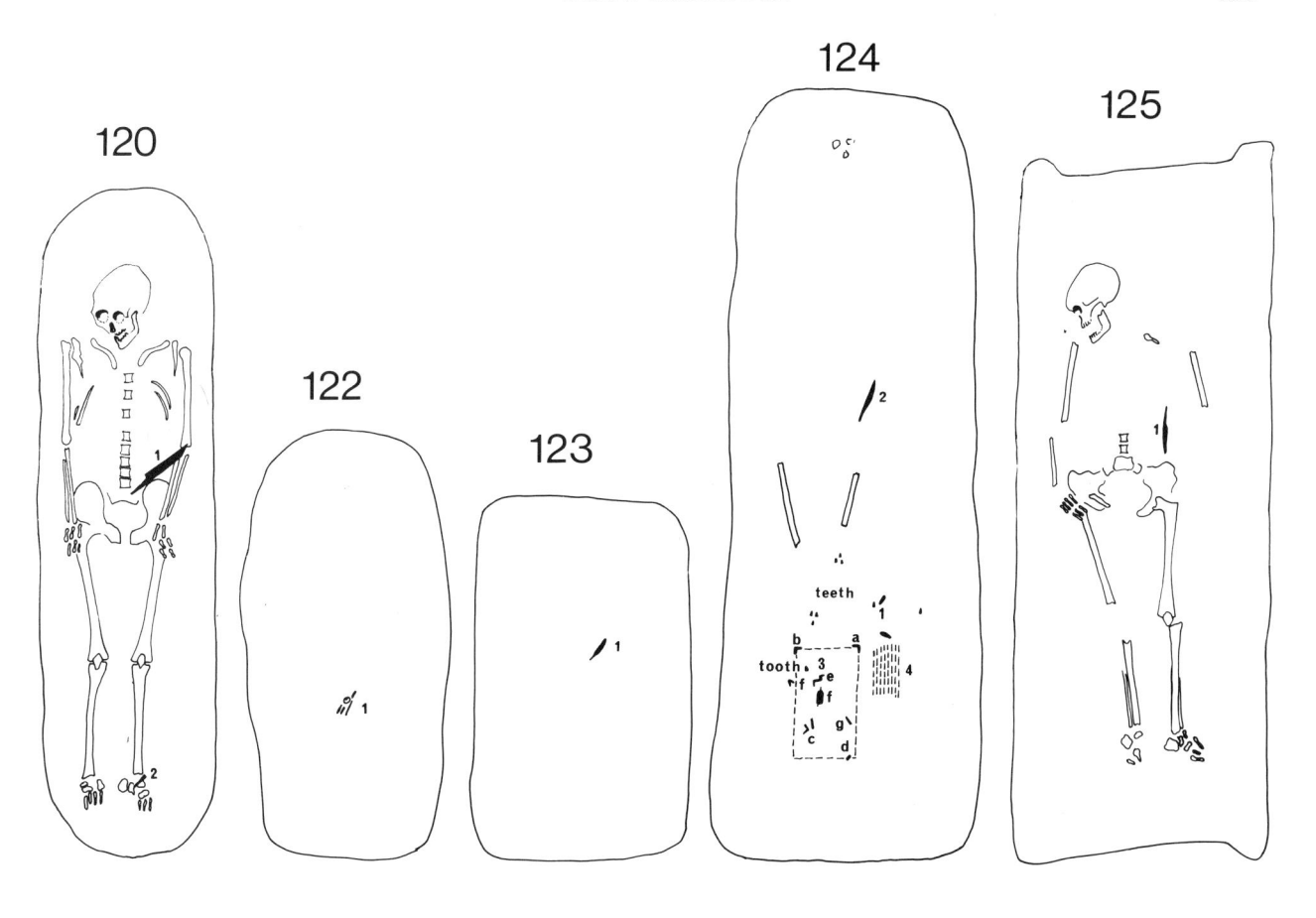

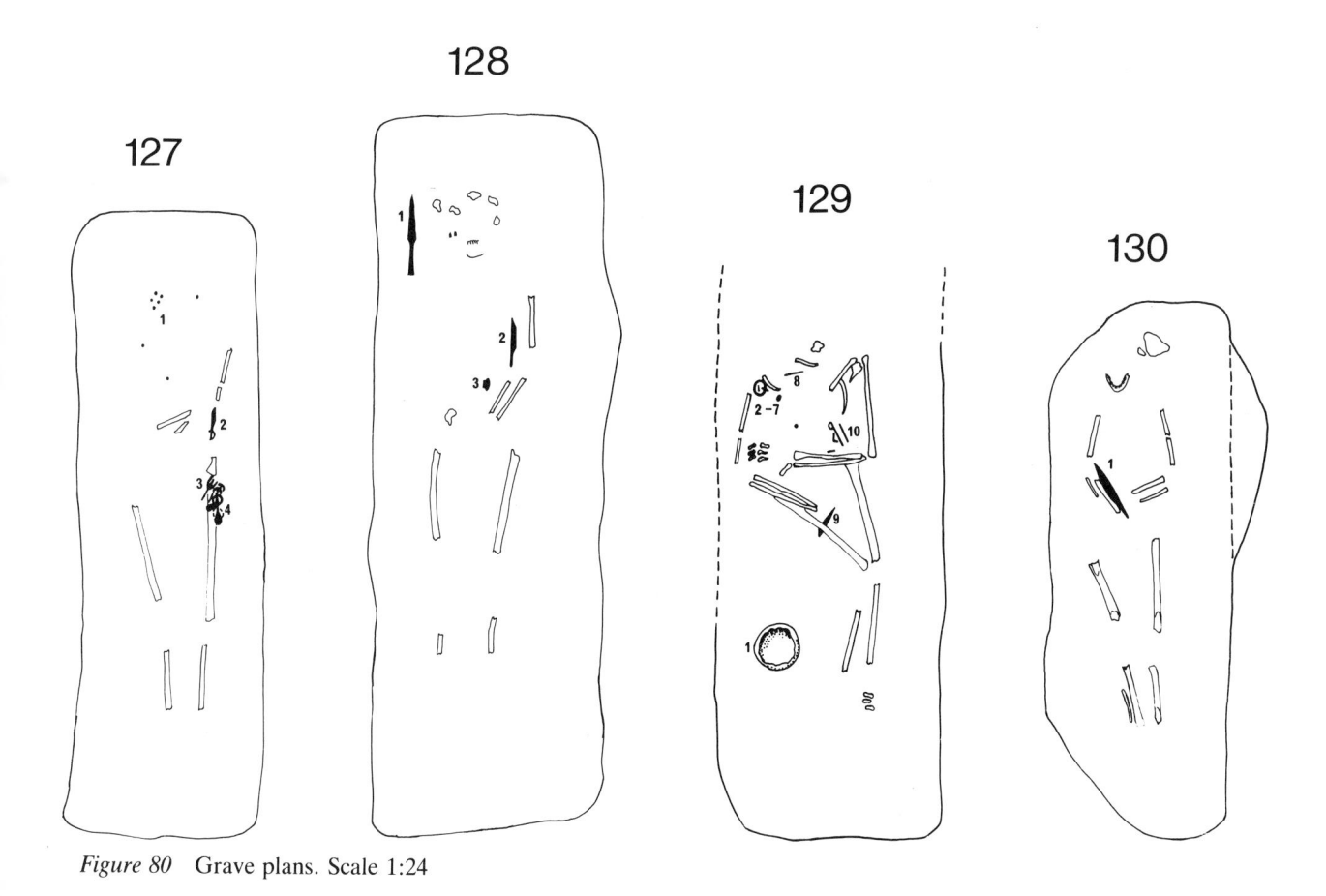

*Figure 80* Grave plans. Scale 1:24

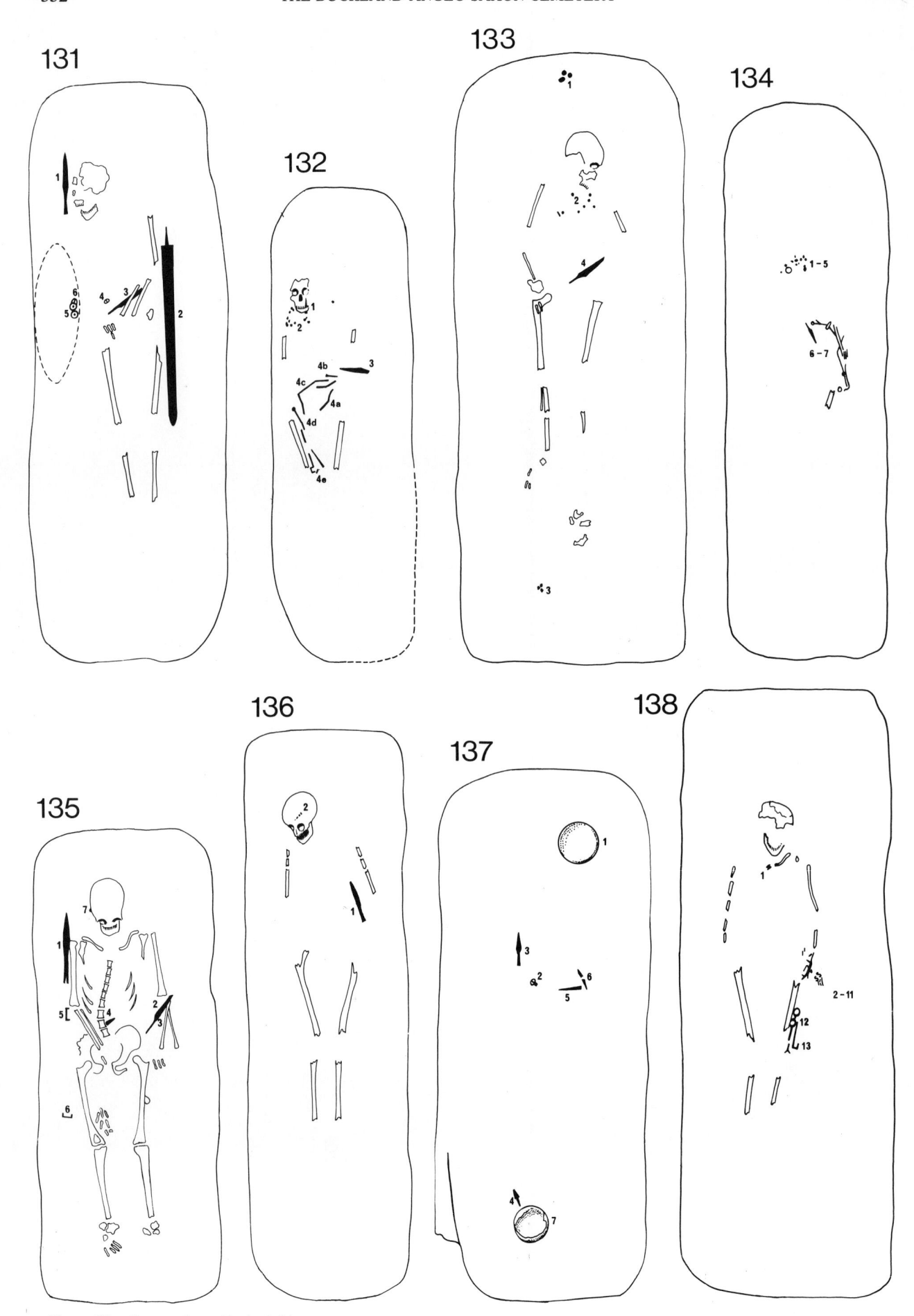

*Figure 81* Grave plans. Scale 1:24

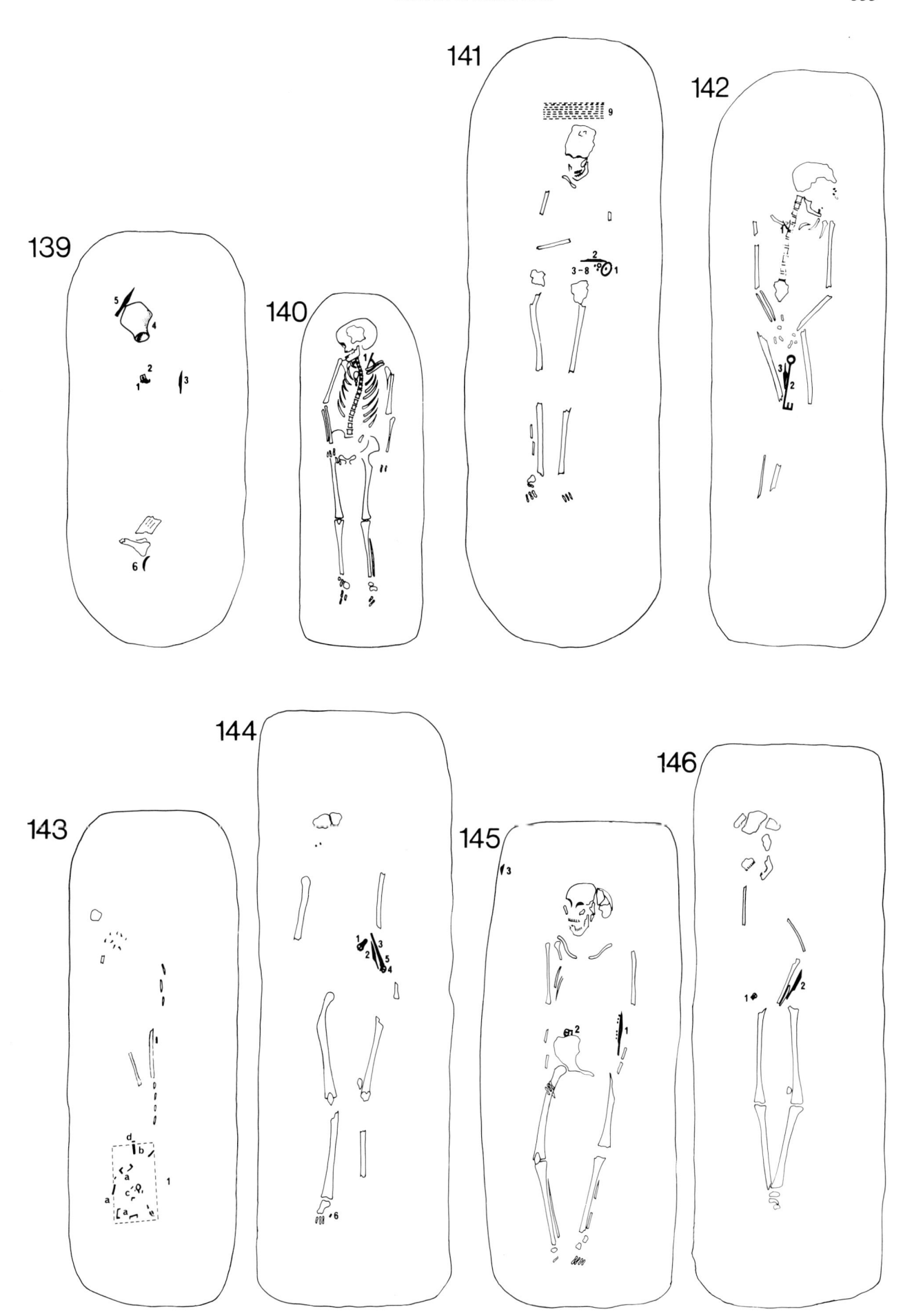

*Figure 82* Grave plans. Scale 1:24

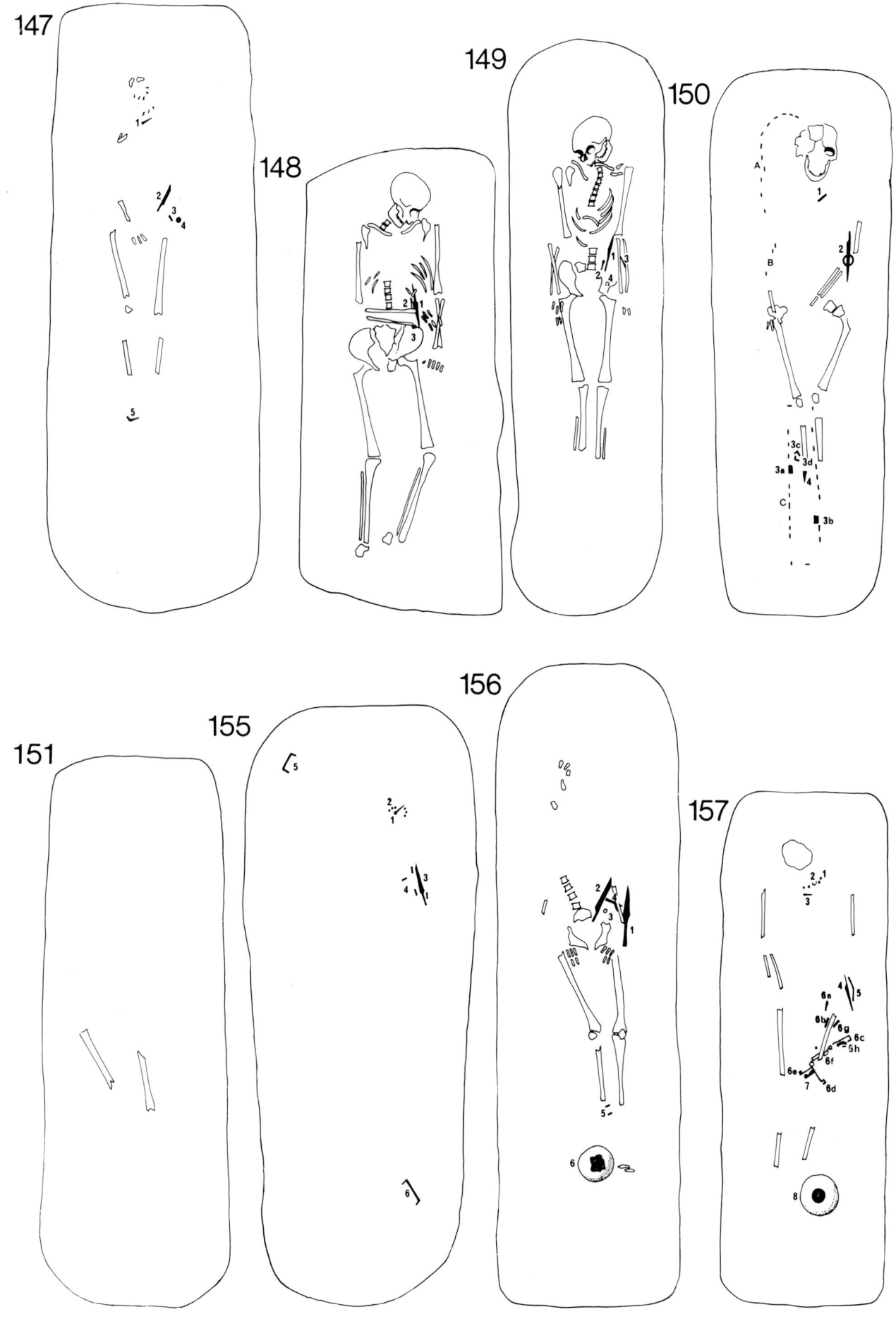

*Figure 83*  Grave plans. Scale 1:24

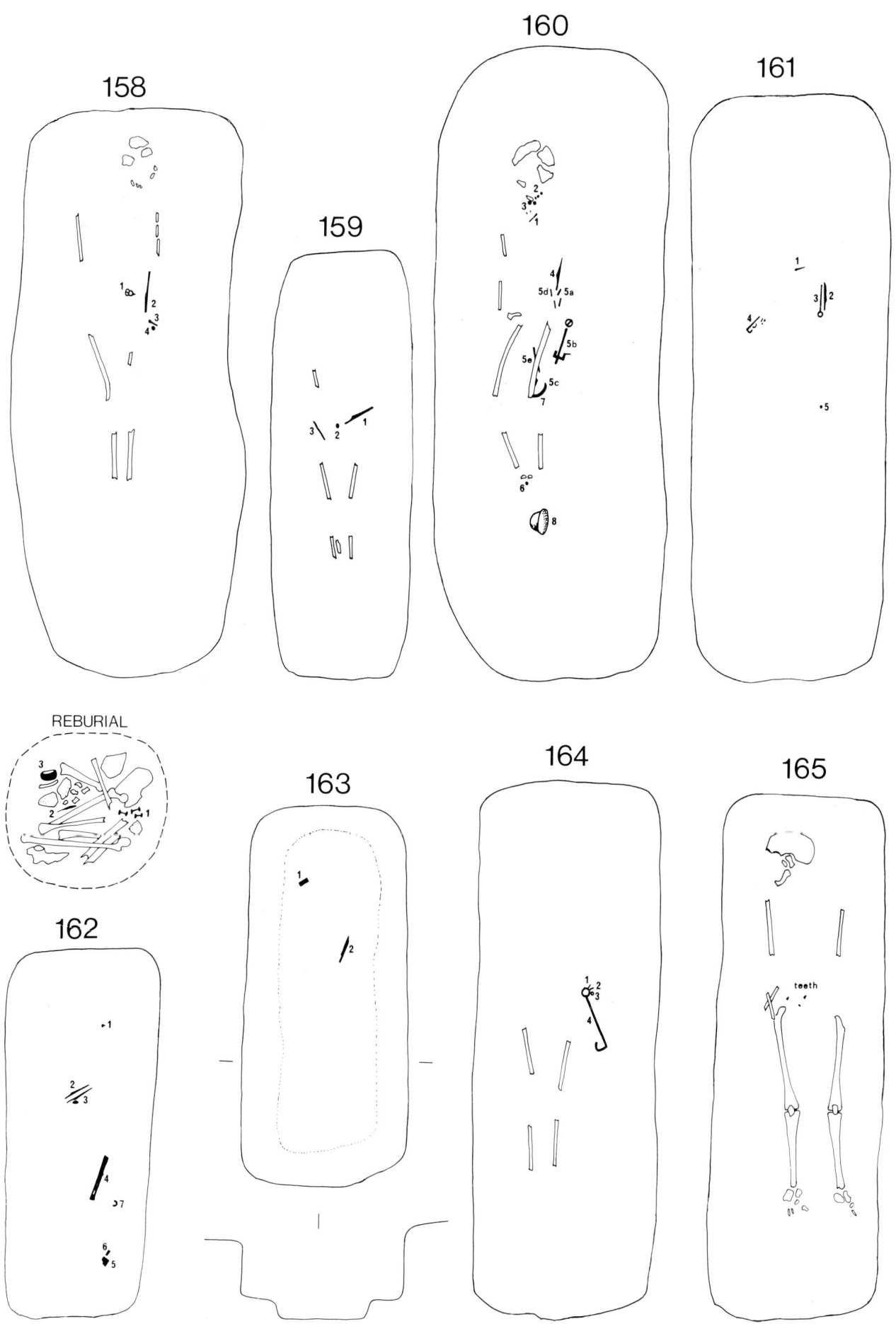

*Figure 84* Grave plans. Scale 1:24

## THE BUCKLAND ANGLO-SAXON CEMETERY

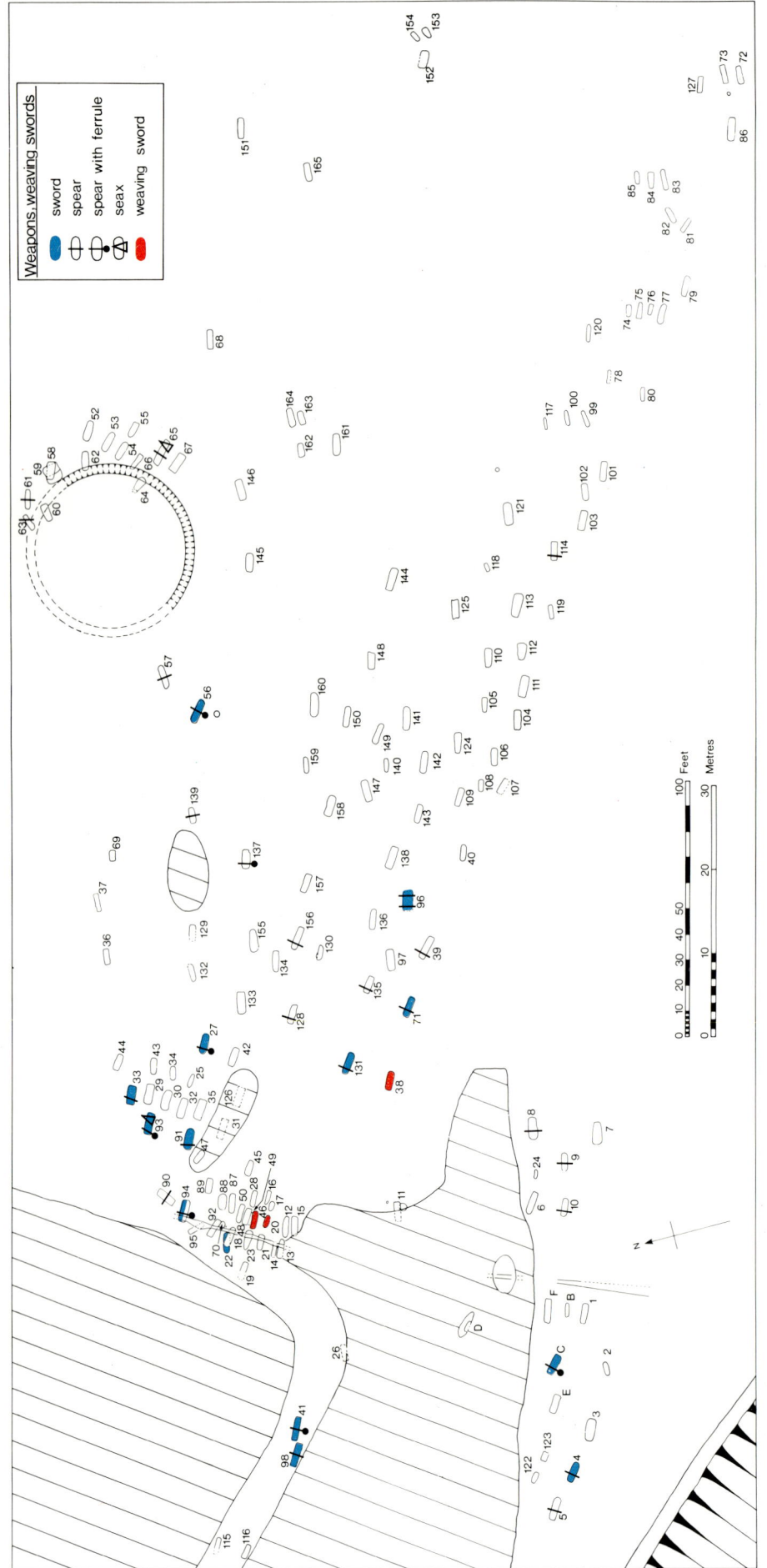

*Figure 85* Distribution. Weapons and weaving swords

GRAVE CATALOGUE 357

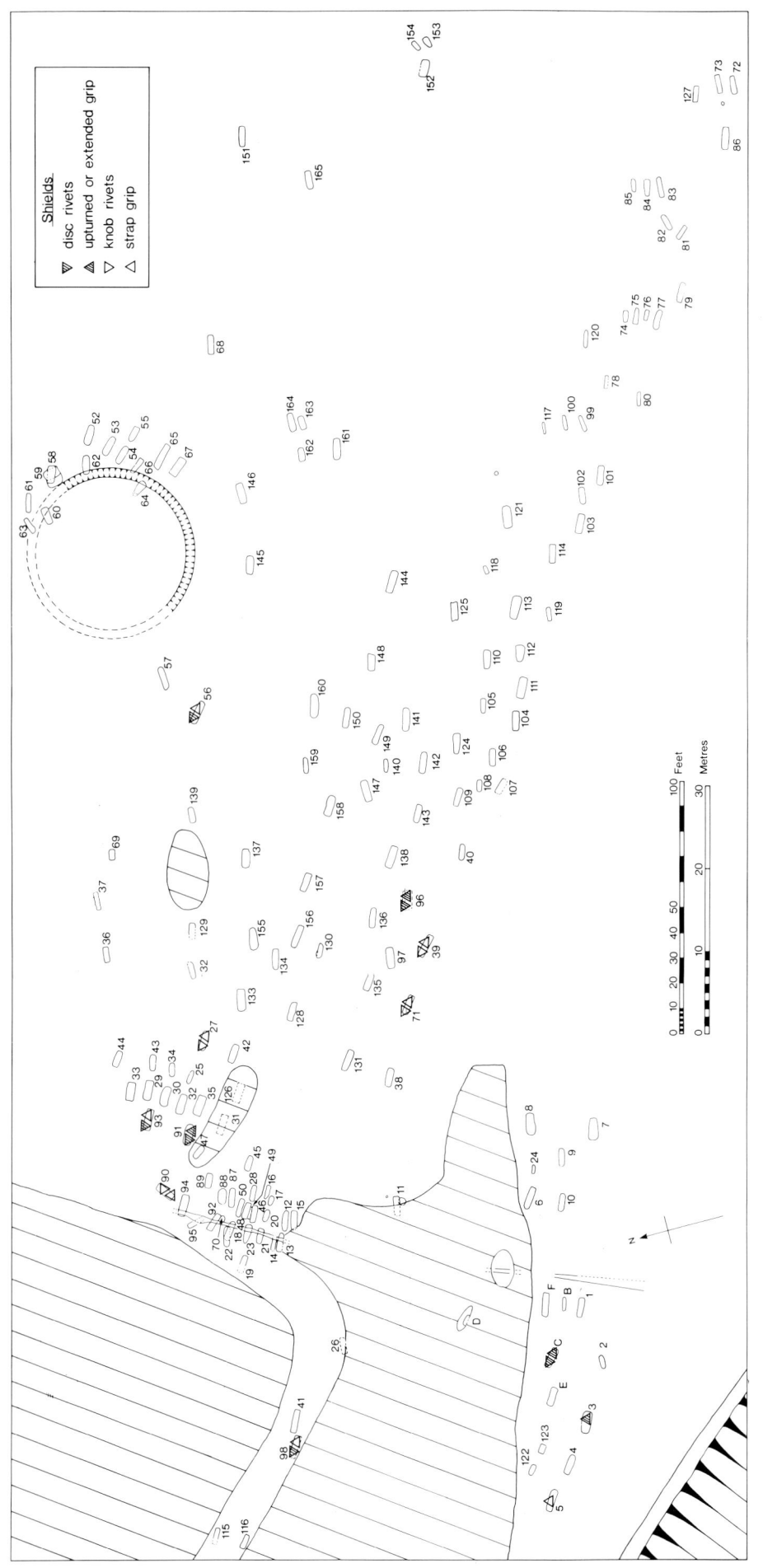

*Figure 86* Distribution. Shields

358

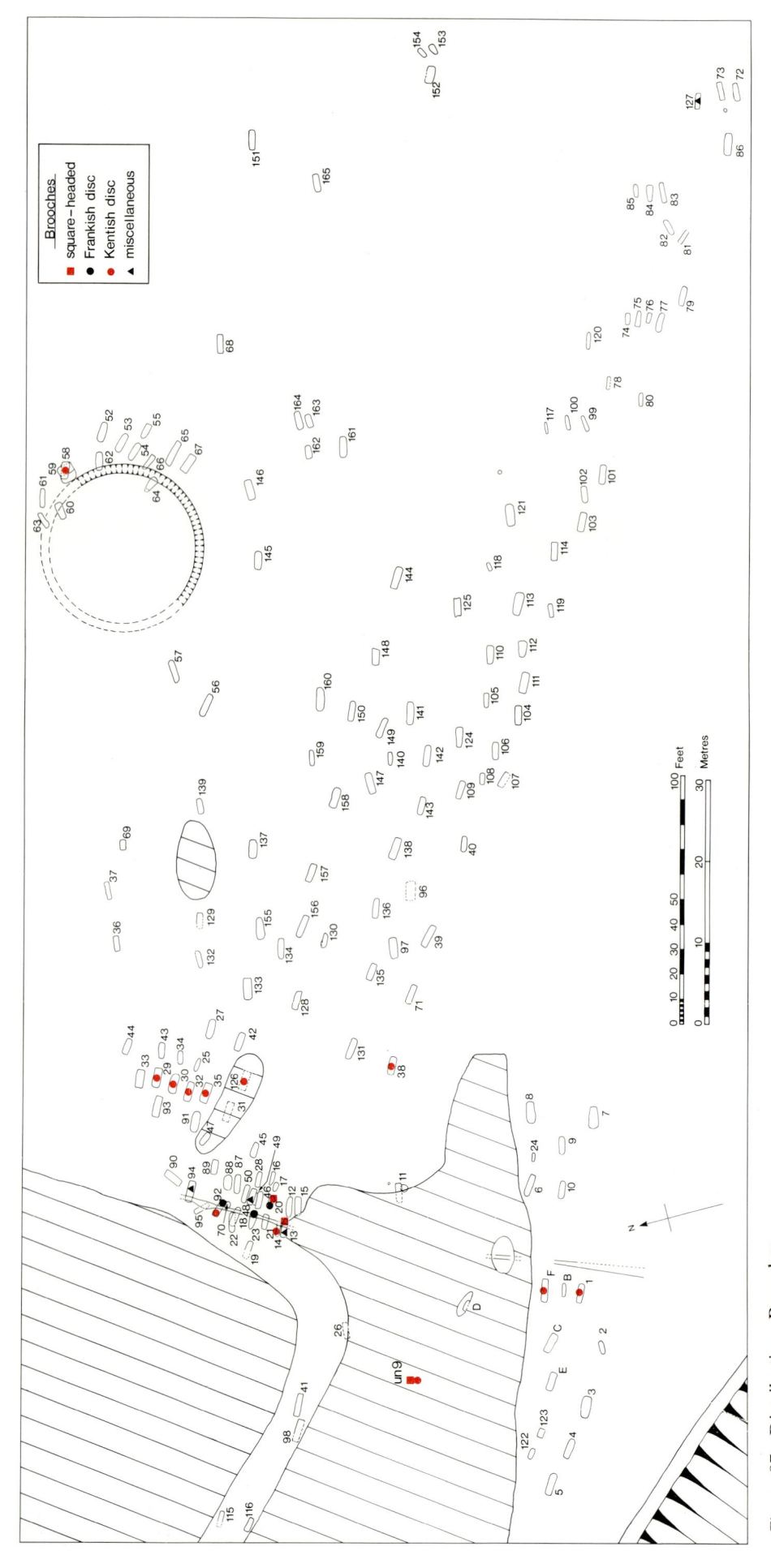

THE BUCKLAND ANGLO-SAXON CEMETERY

*Figure 87* Distribution. Brooches

GRAVE CATALOGUE

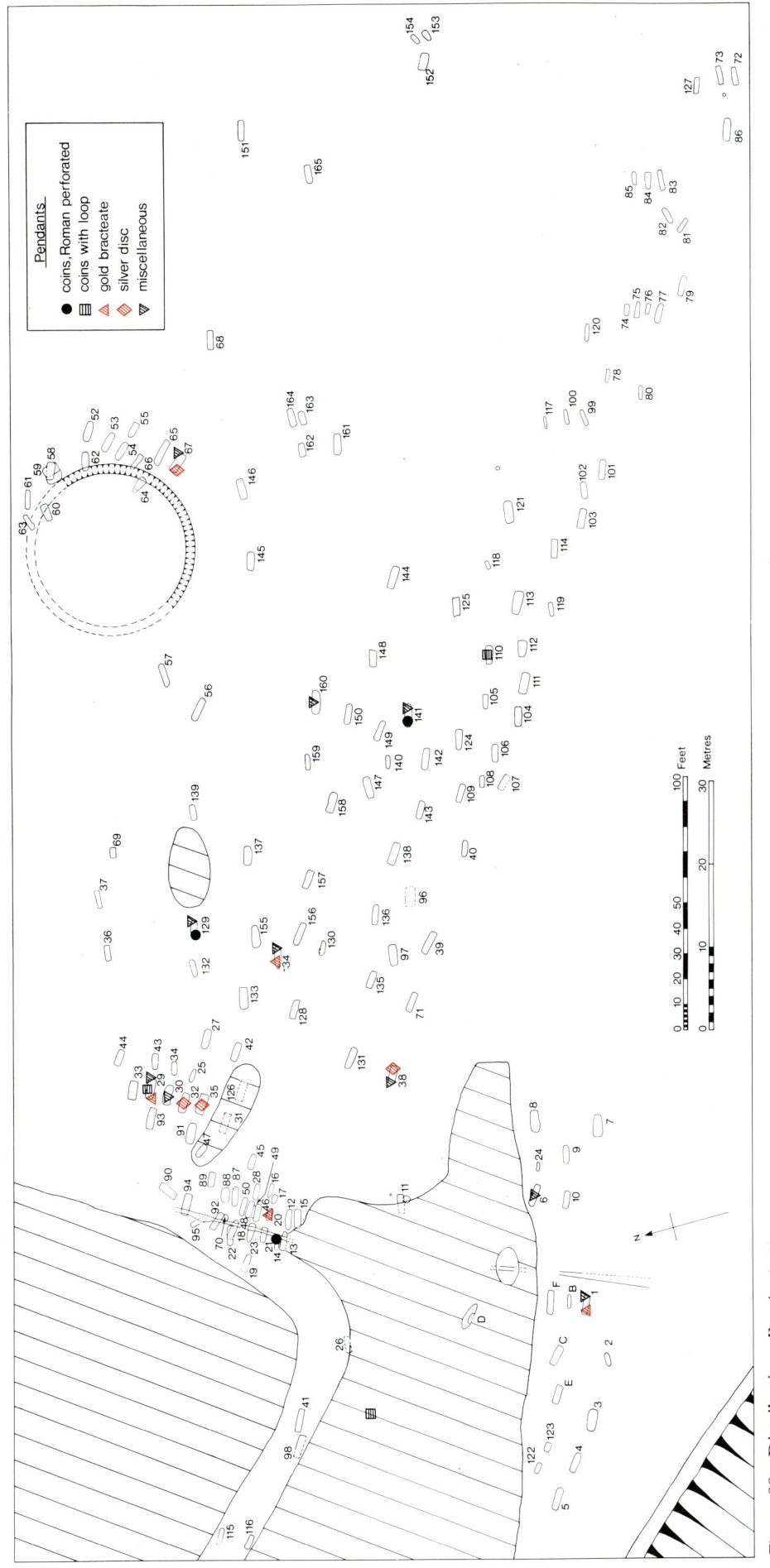

*Figure 88* Distribution. Pendants

360

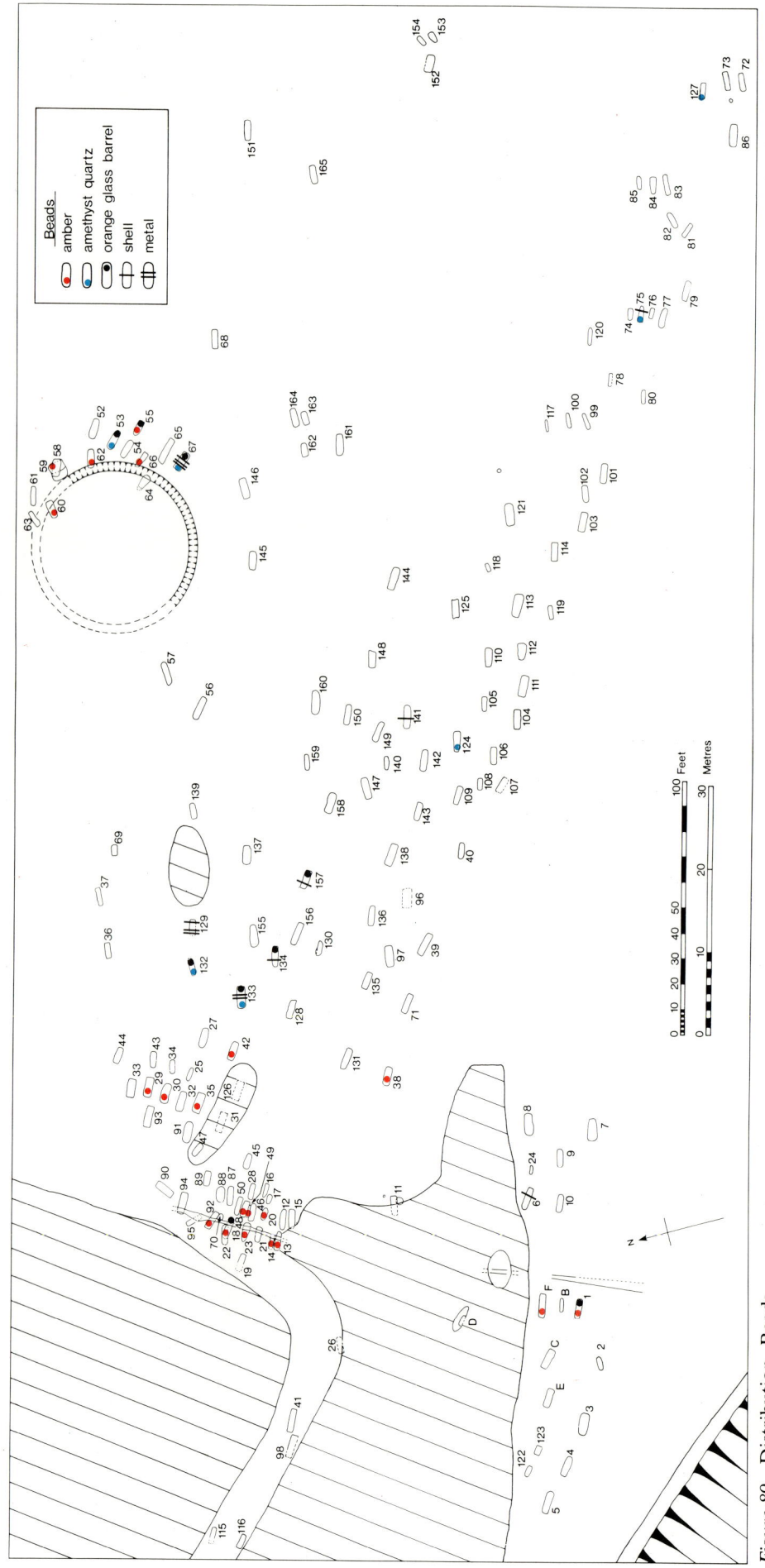

THE BUCKLAND ANGLO-SAXON CEMETERY

*Figure 89* Distribution. Beads

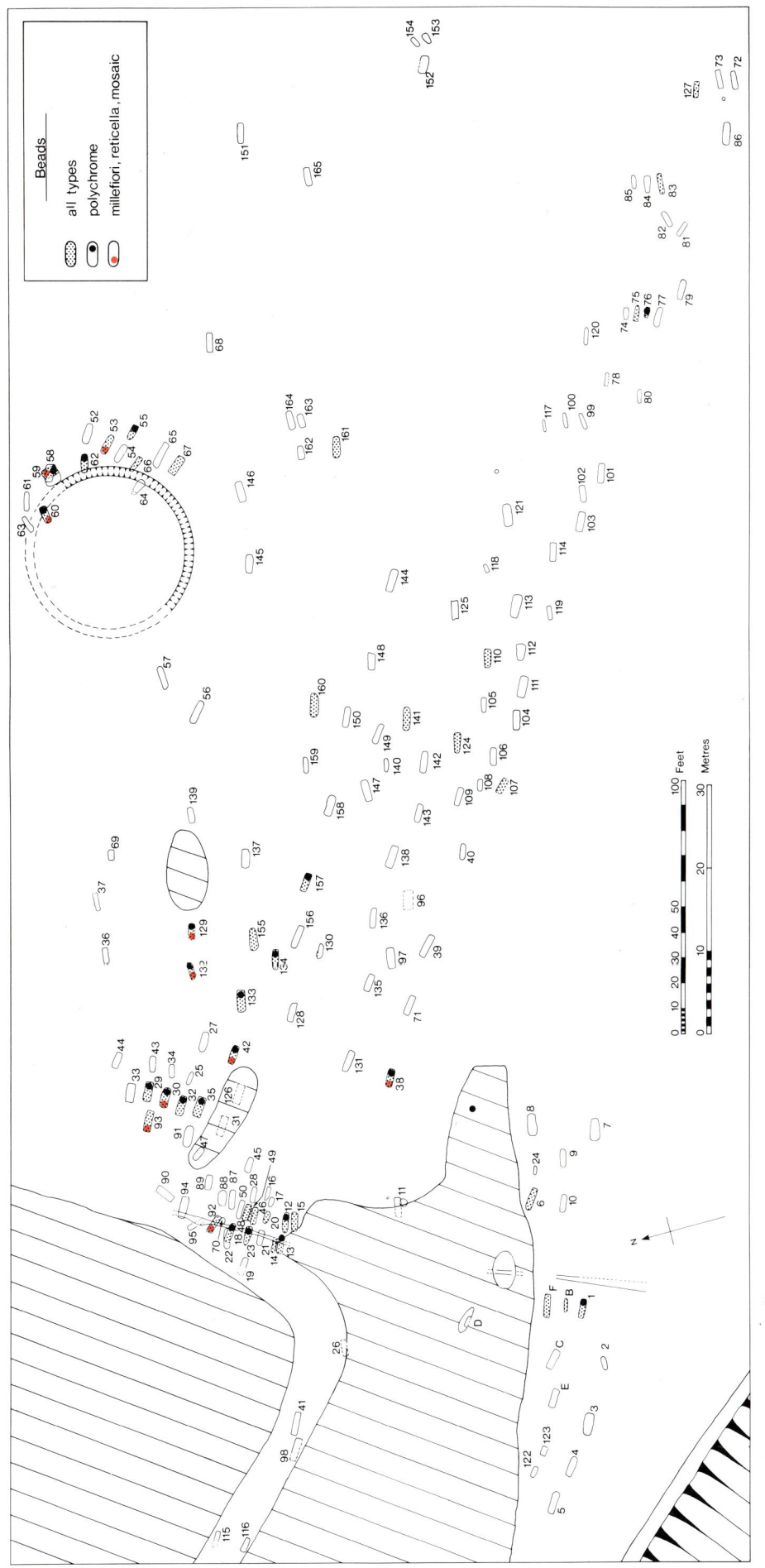

*Figure 90* Distribution. Beads

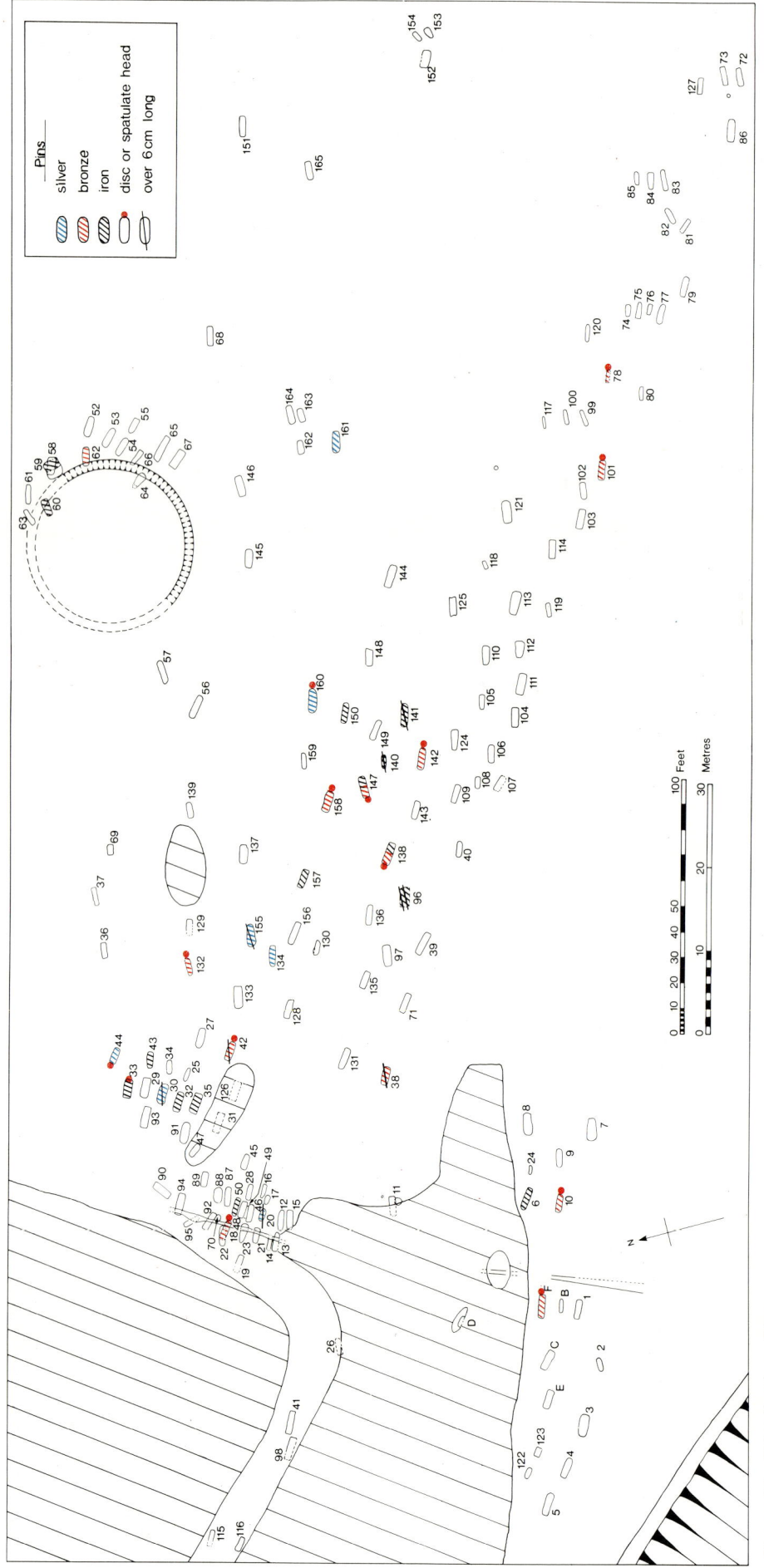

Figure 91  Distribution. Pins

# GRAVE CATALOGUE

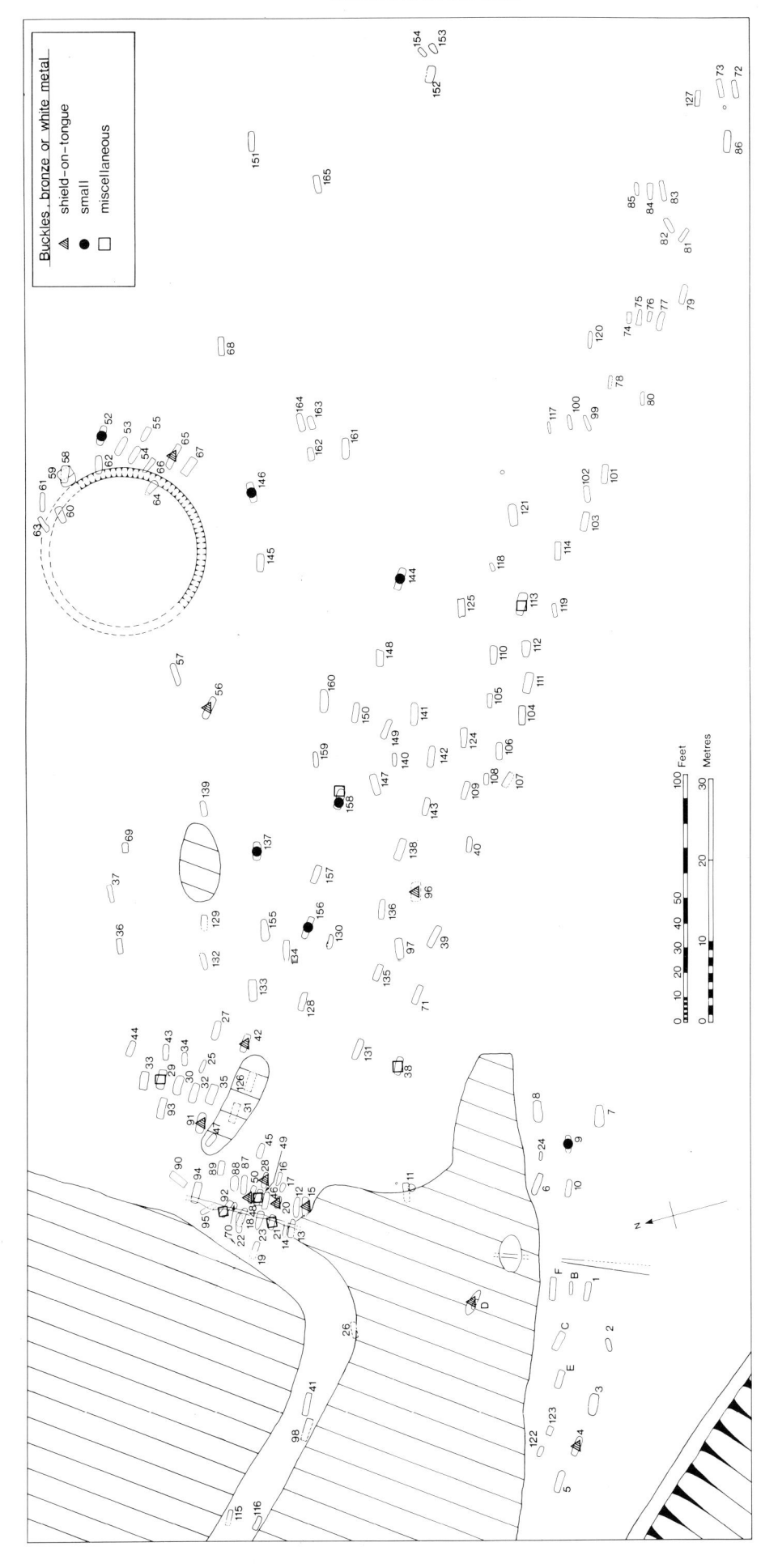

*Figure 92* Distribution. Buckles, bronze or white metal

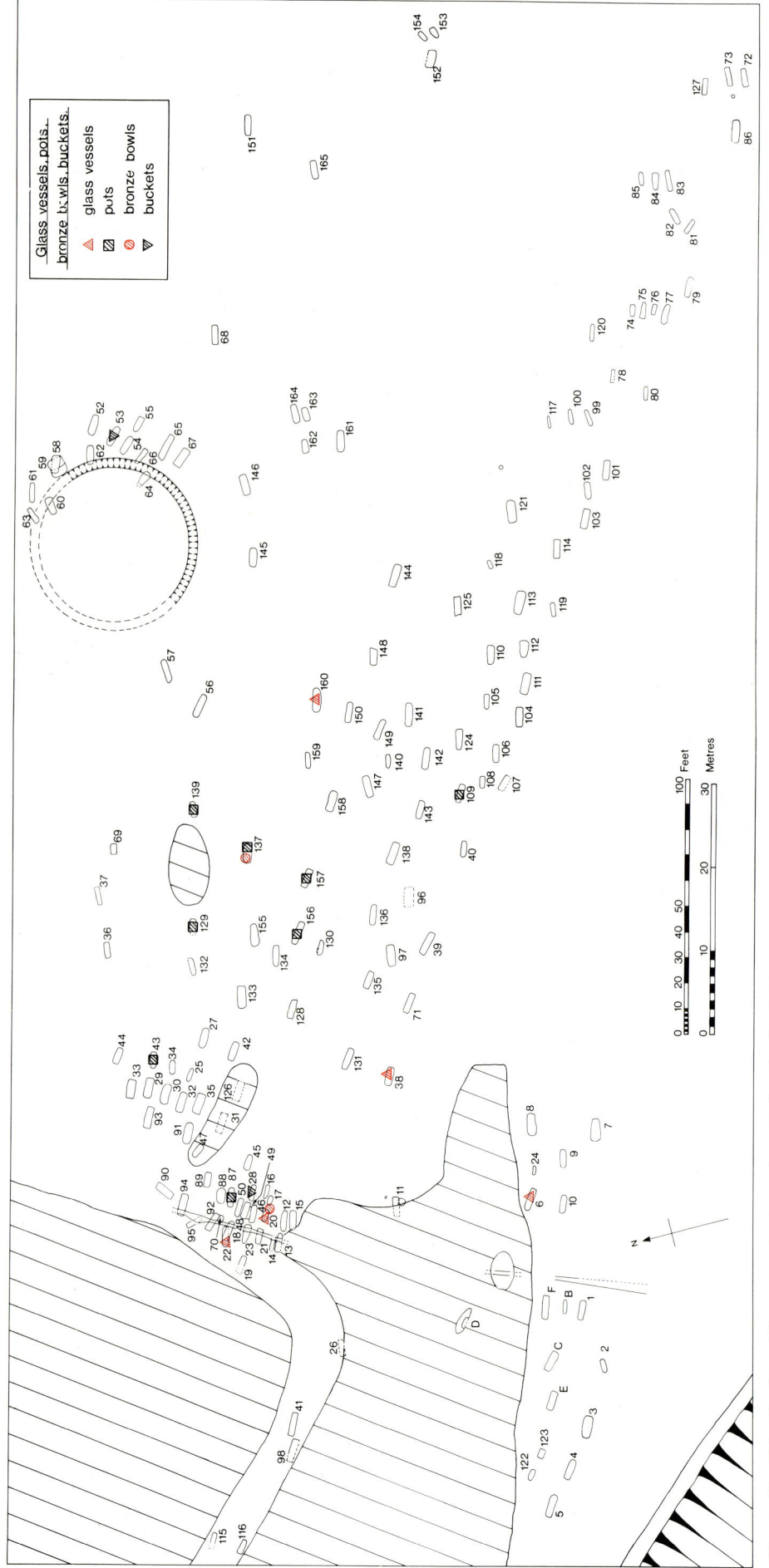

*Figure 93* Distribution. Glass vessels, pots, bronze bowls, buckets

GRAVE CATALOGUE 365

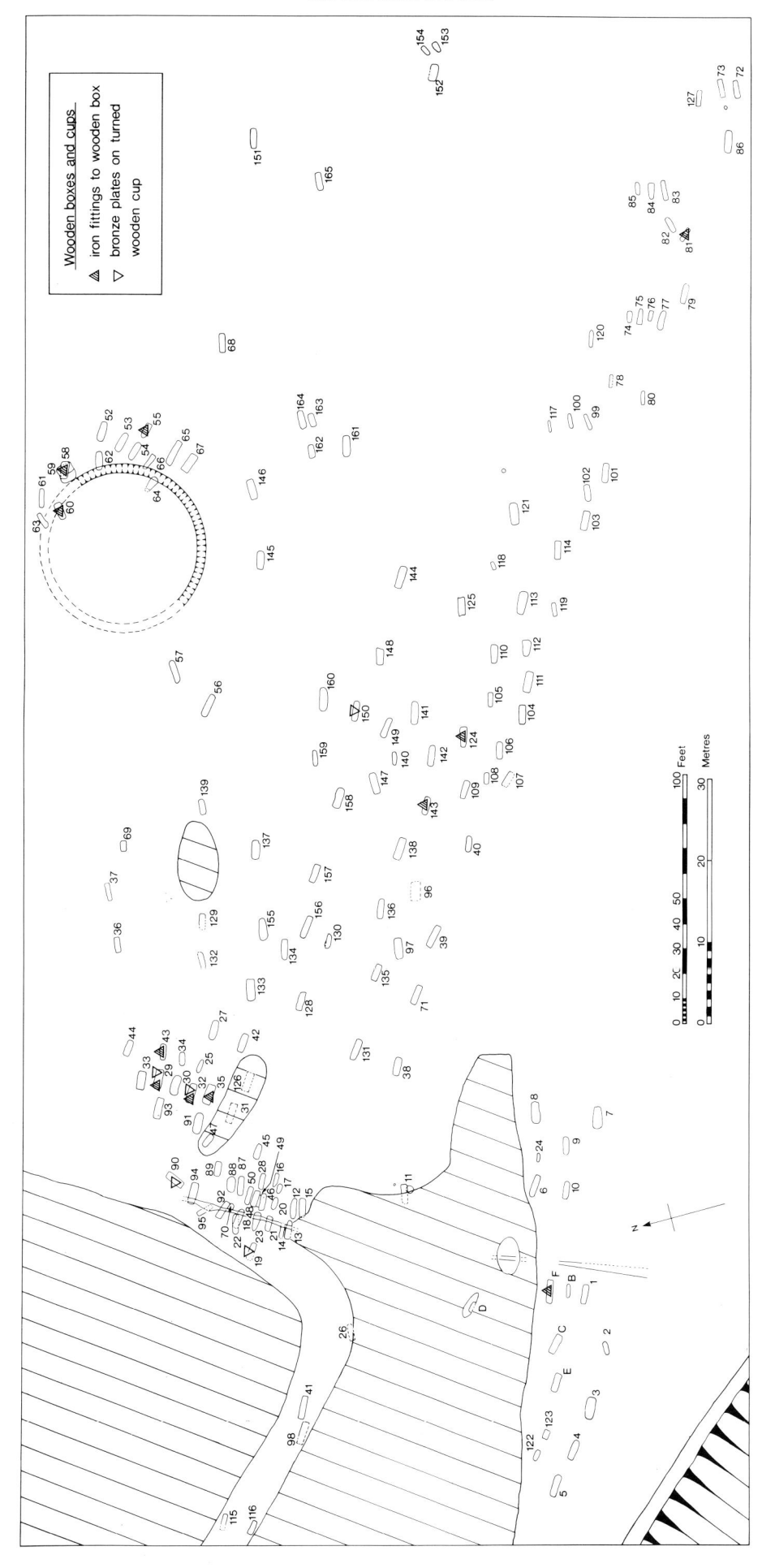

*Figure 94* Distribution. Wooden boxes and cups.

366 THE BUCKLAND ANGLO-SAXON CEMETERY

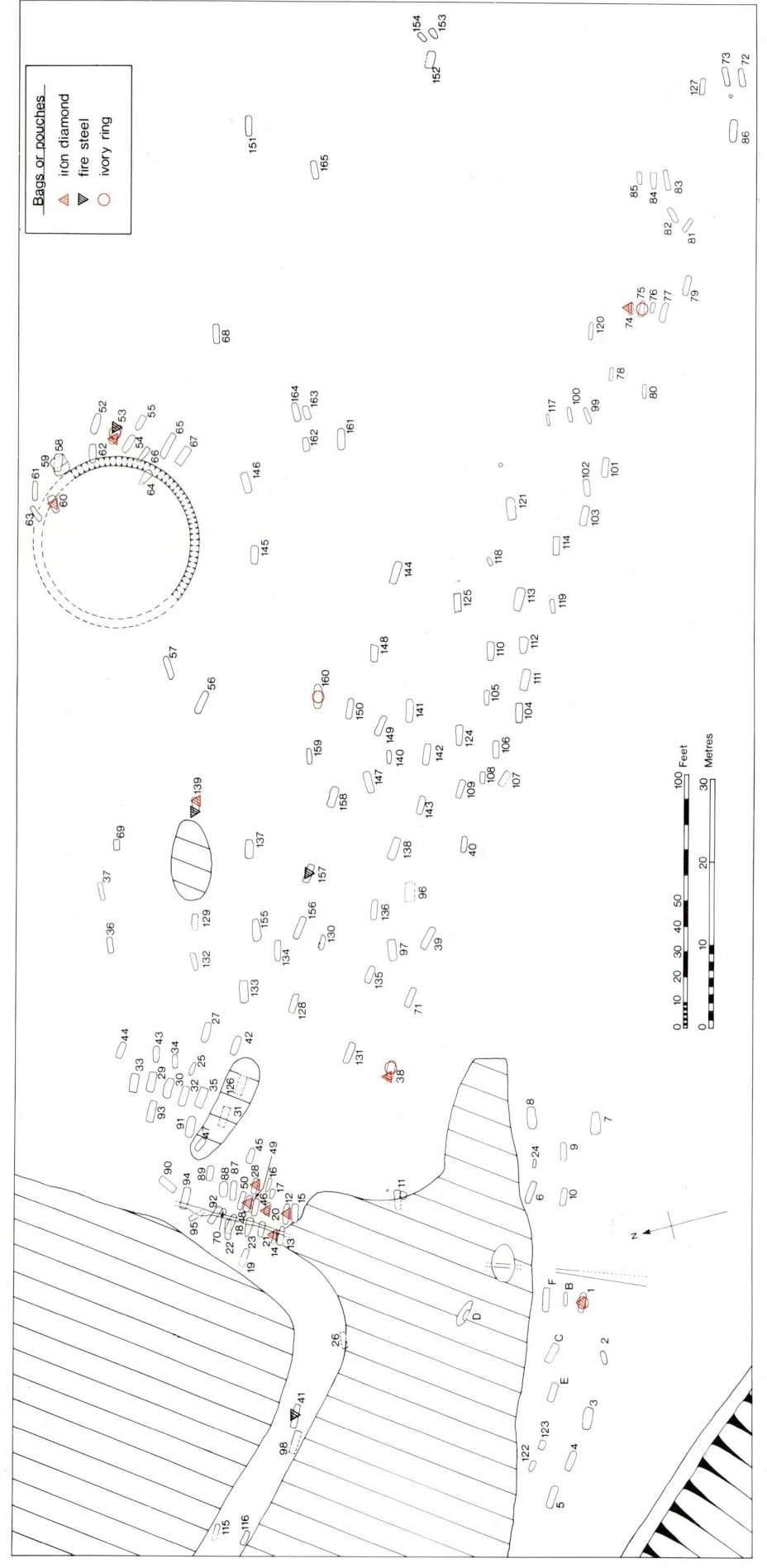

Figure 95 Distribution. Bags or pouches. Iron diamonds, fire-steels, ivory rings

# GRAVE CATALOGUE

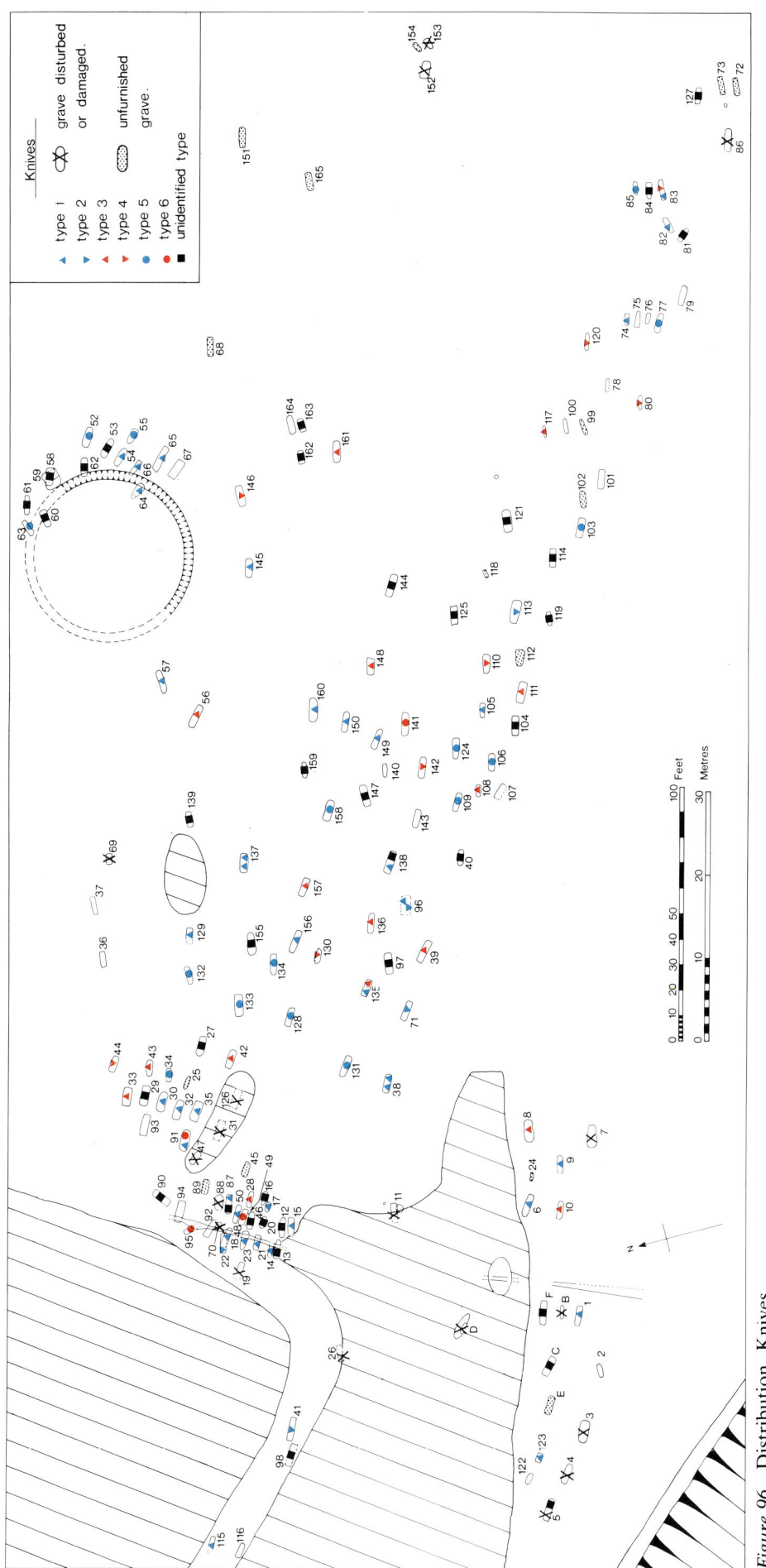

*Figure 96* Distribution. Knives

368 THE BUCKLAND ANGLO-SAXON CEMETERY

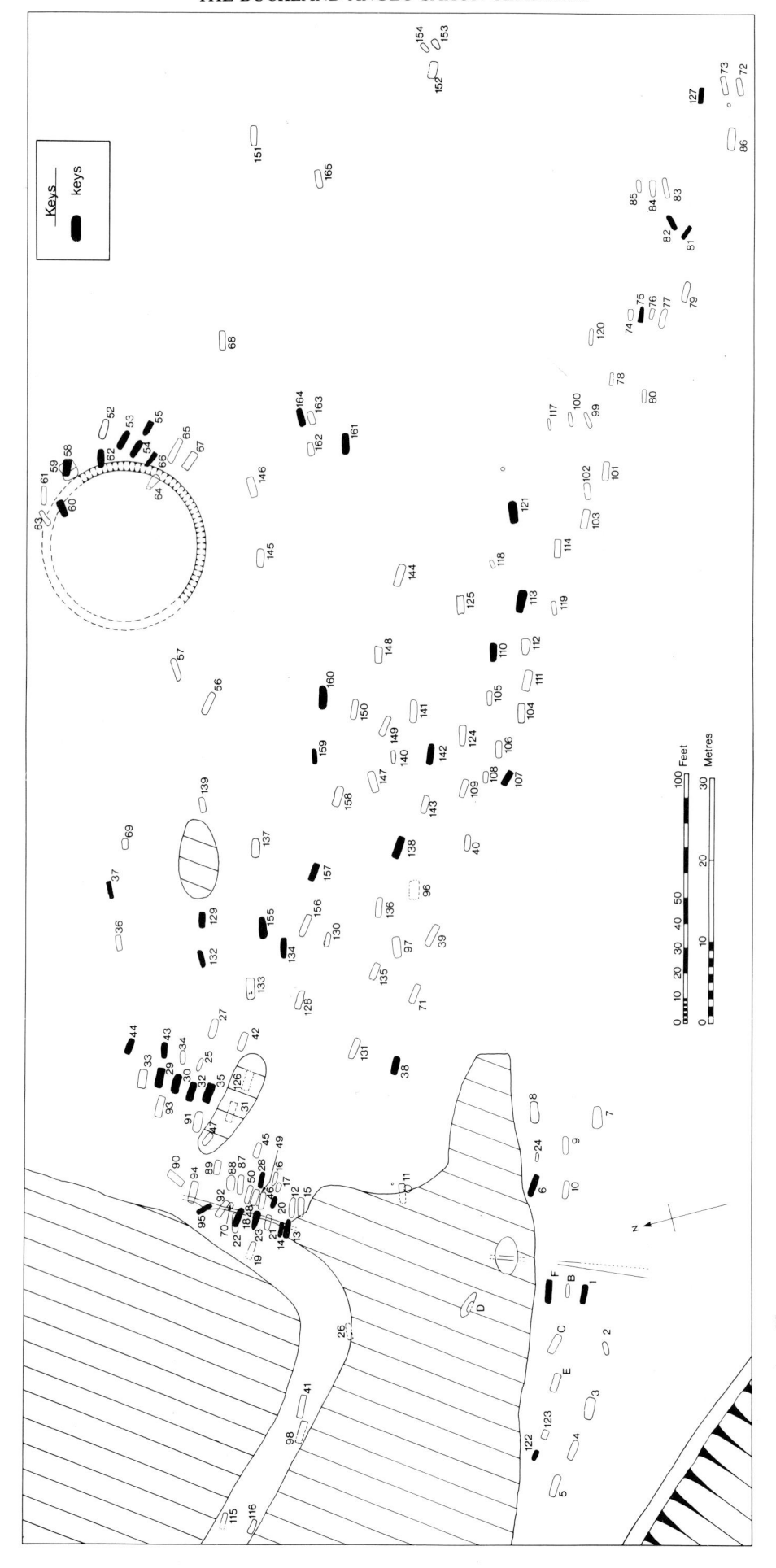

*Figure 97* Distribution. Keys

# GRAVE CATALOGUE

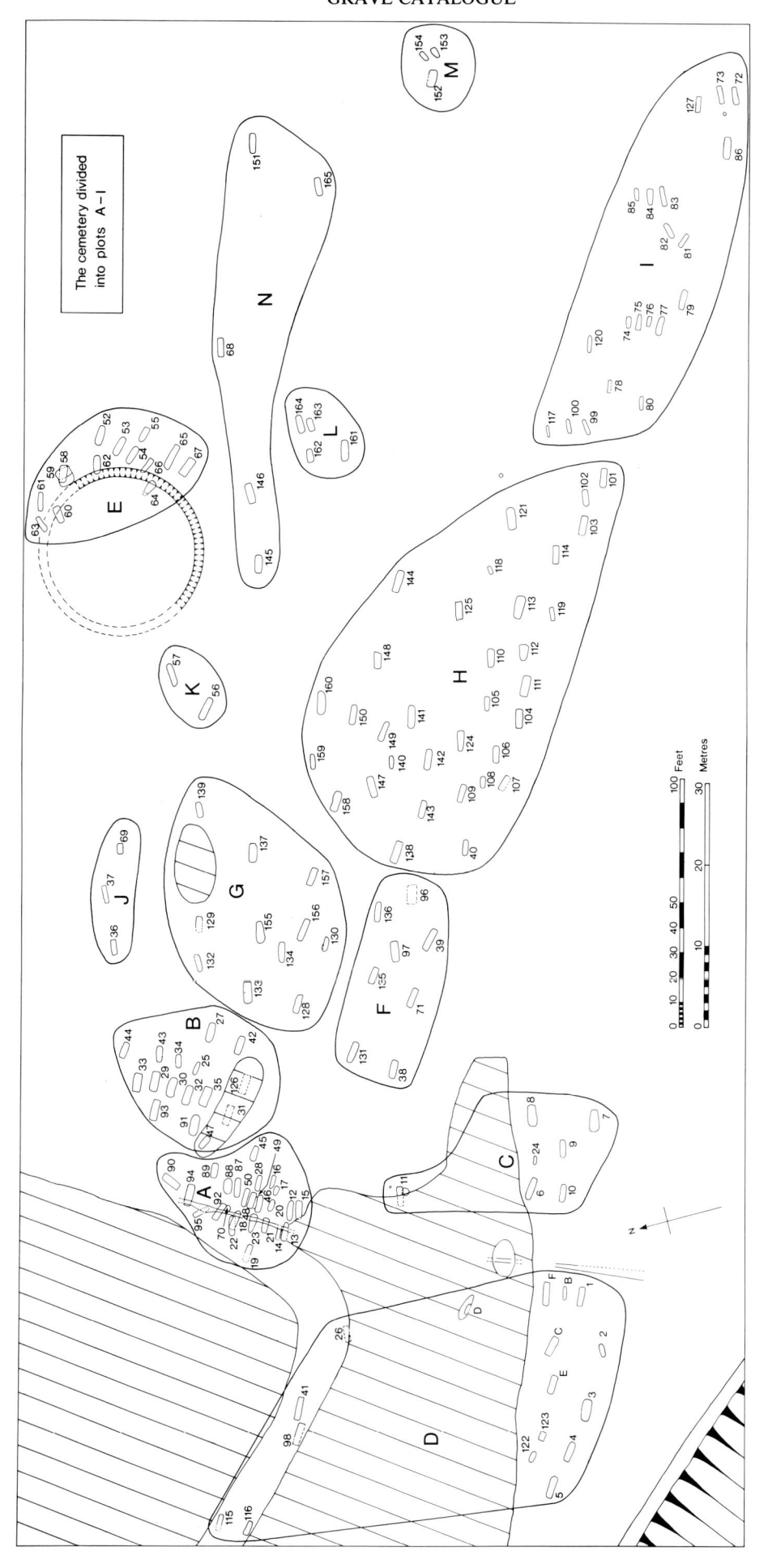

*Figure 98* The cemetery divided into plots A–I

370                    THE BUCKLAND ANGLO-SAXON CEMETERY

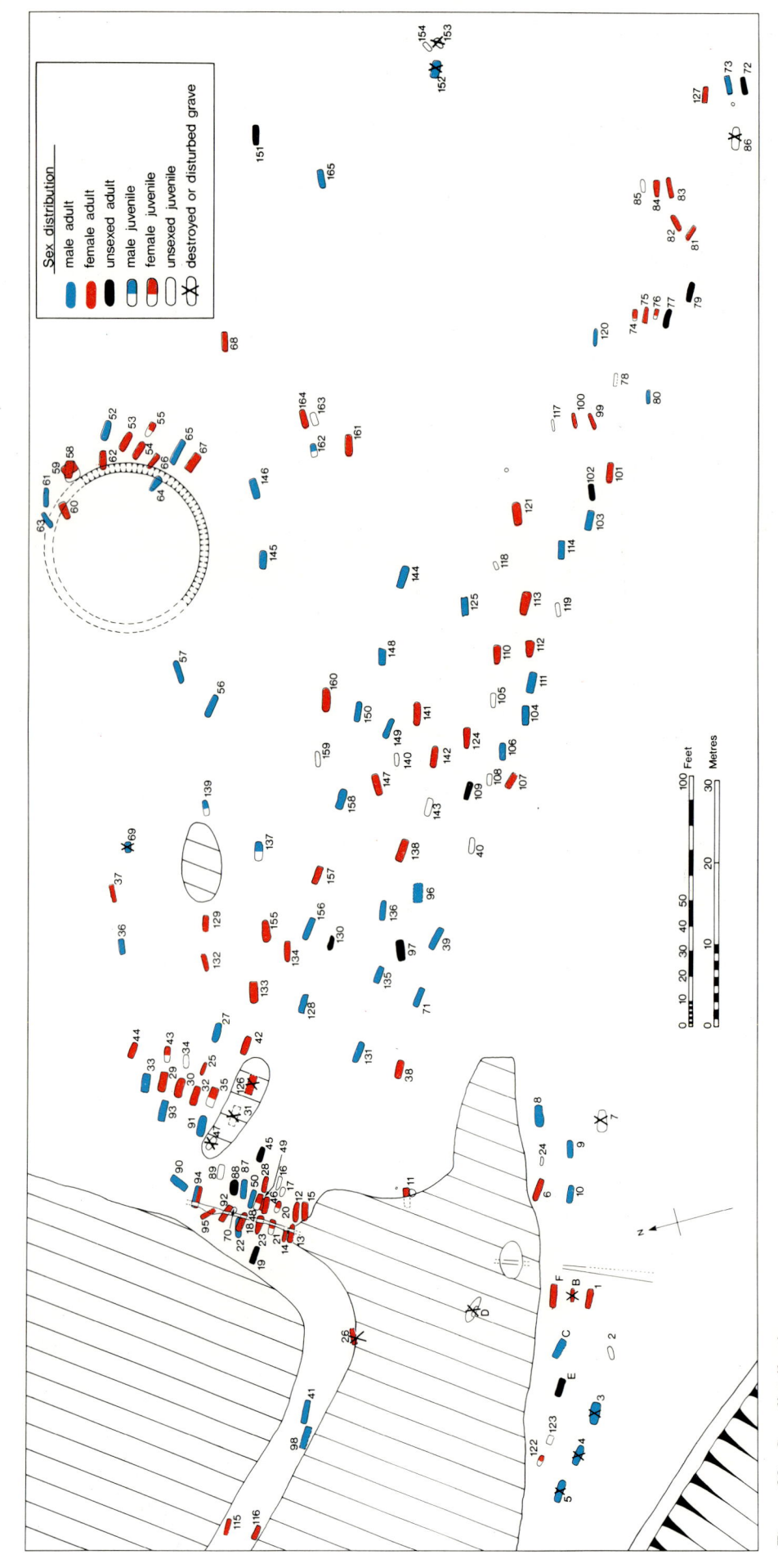

*Figure 99* Sex distribution

GRAVE CATALOGUE 371

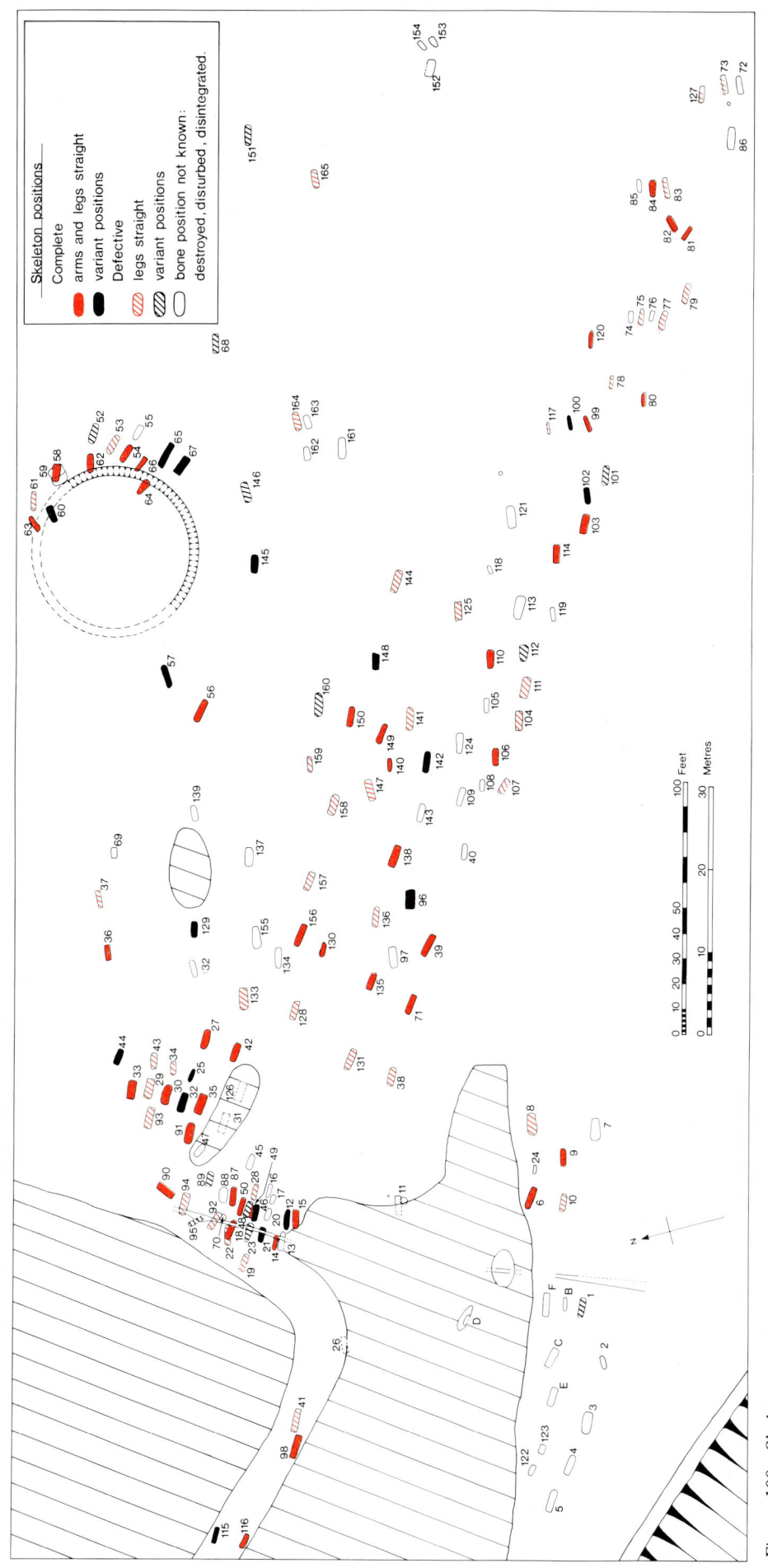

*Figure 100* Skeleton positions

372 THE BUCKLAND ANGLO-SAXON CEMETERY

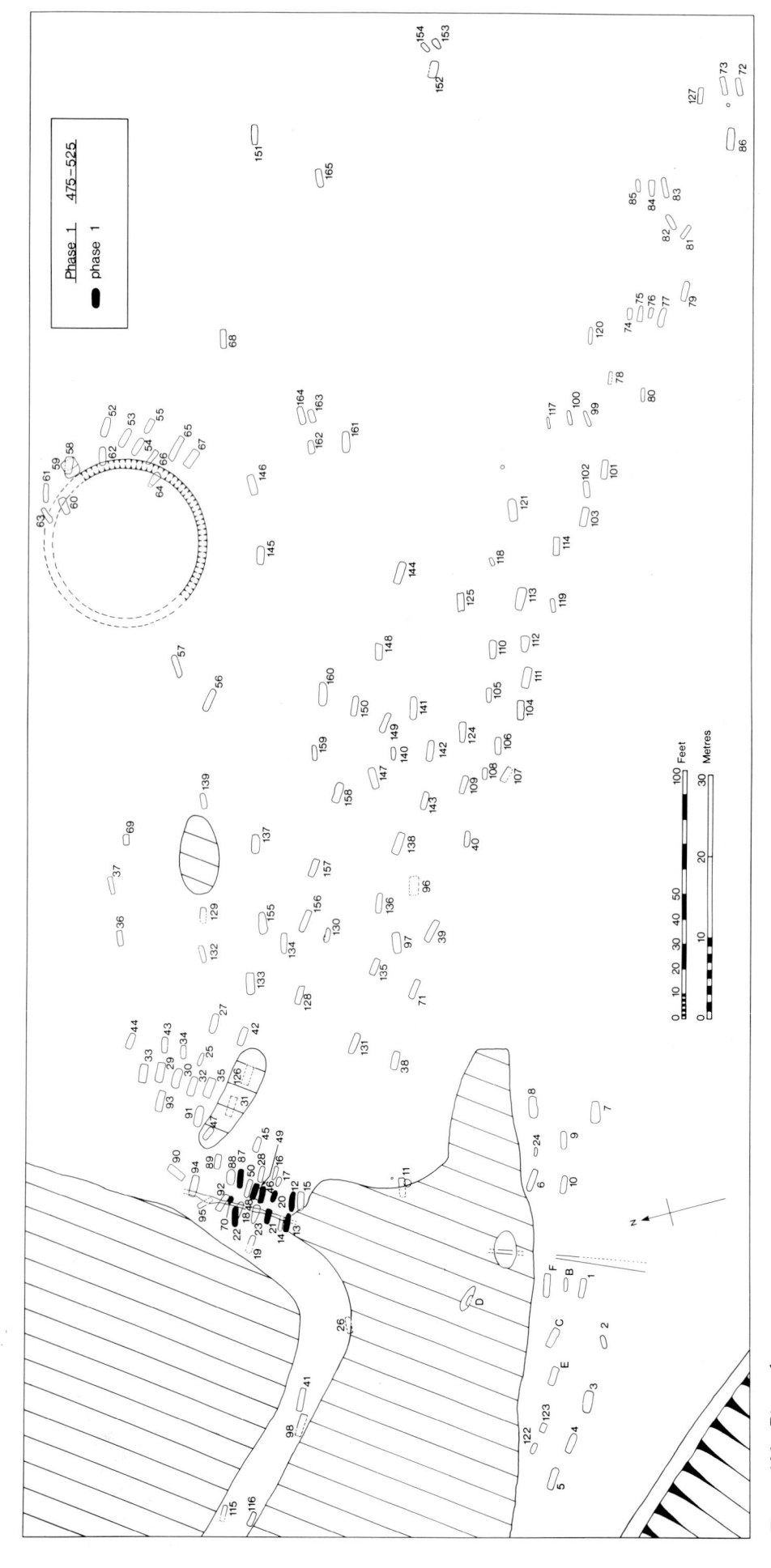

*Figure 101* Phase 1

# GRAVE CATALOGUE

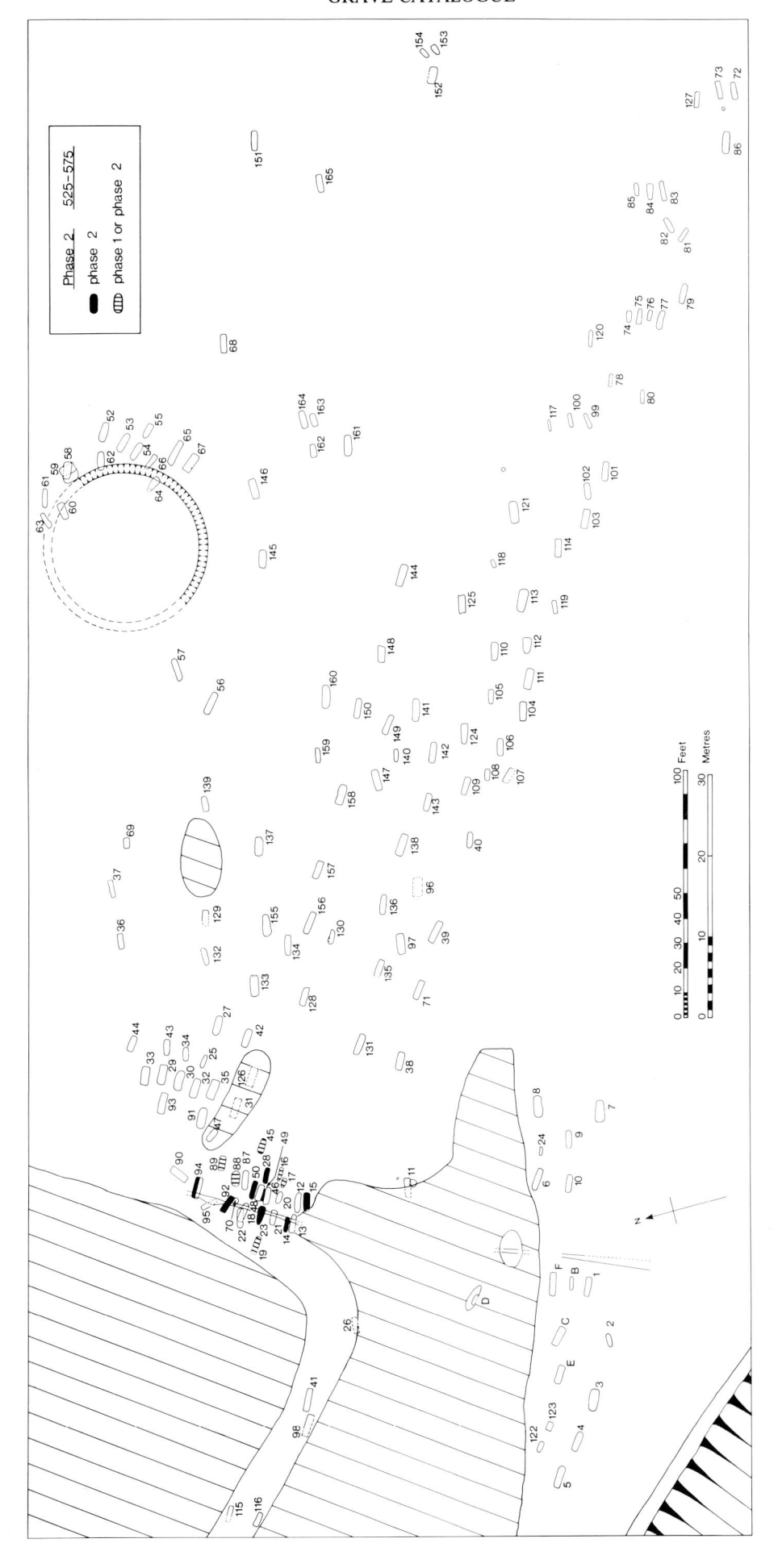

*Figure 102* Phase 2

374 THE BUCKLAND ANGLO-SAXON CEMETERY

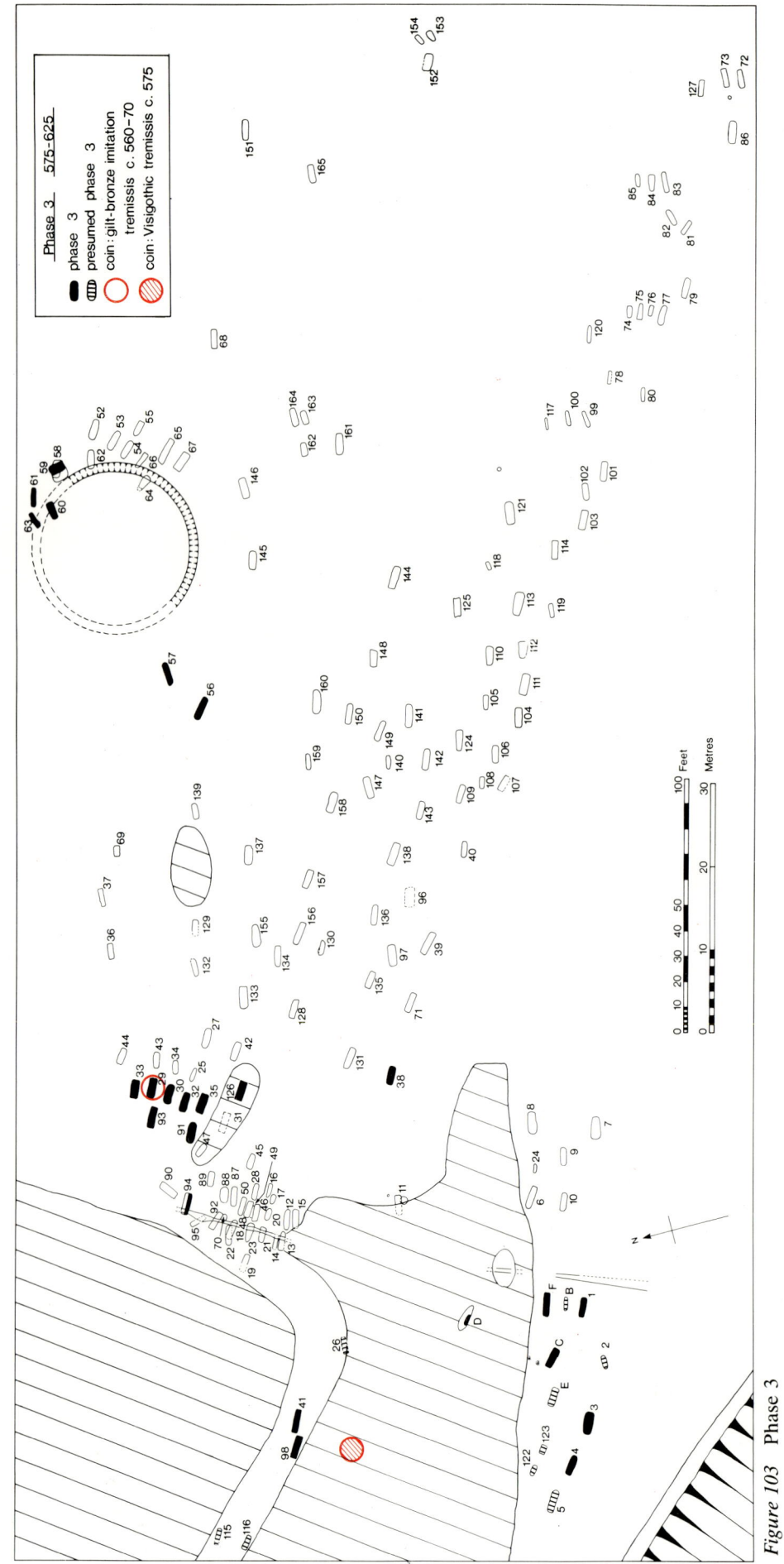

*Figure 103* Phase 3

GRAVE CATALOGUE

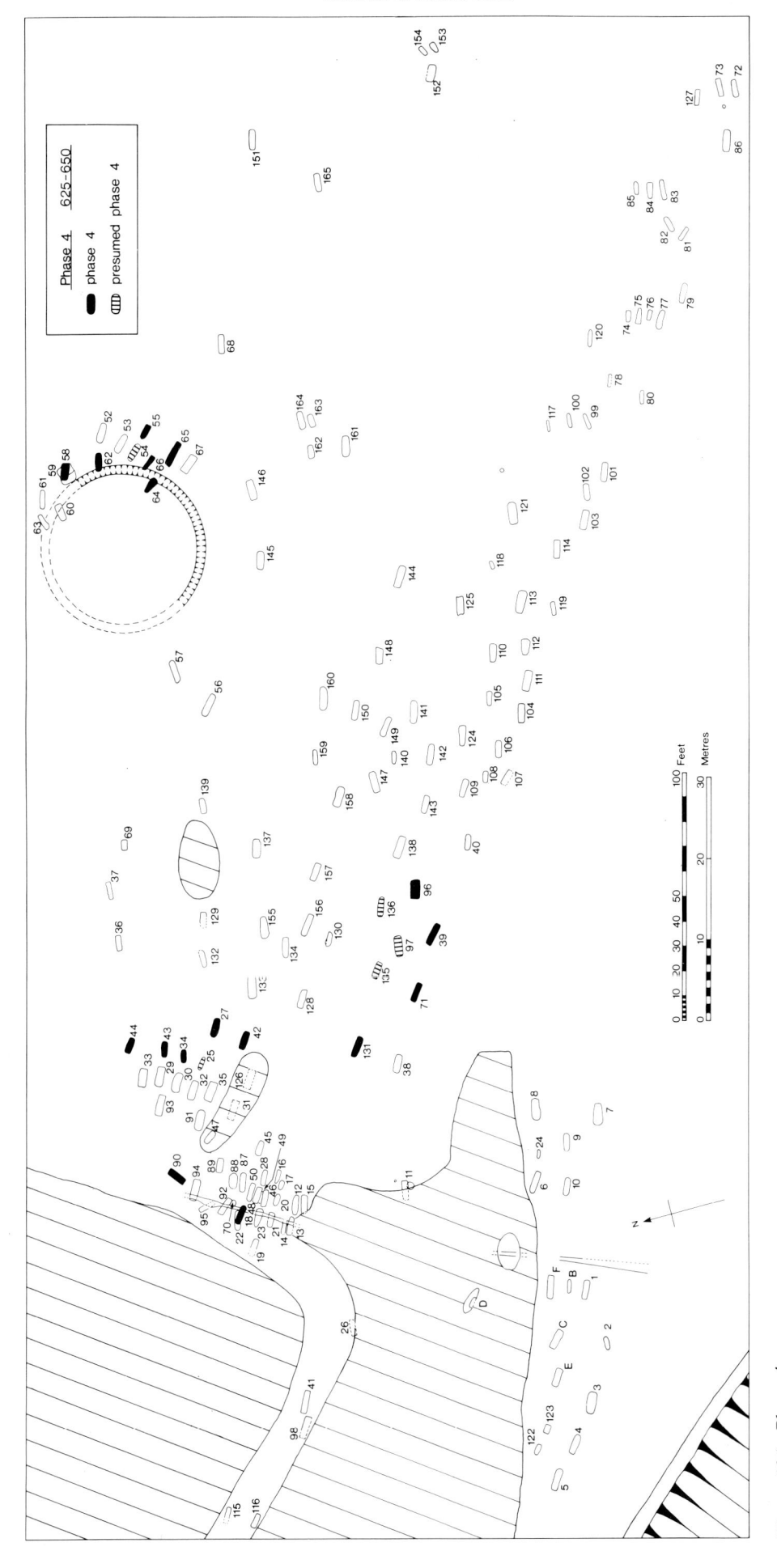

*Figure 104* Phase 4

376                          THE BUCKLAND ANGLO-SAXON CEMETERY

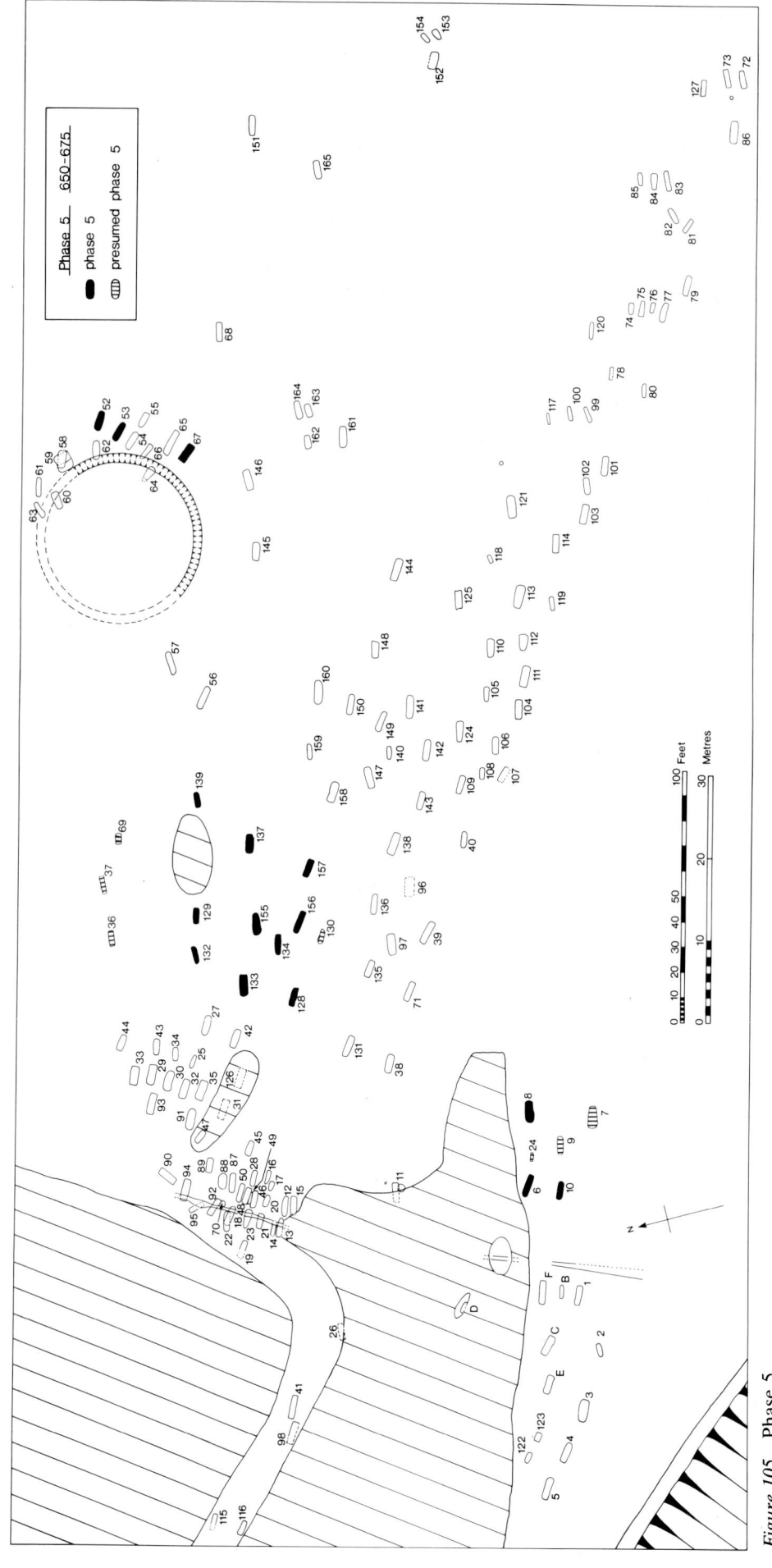

*Figure 105* Phase 5

GRAVE CATALOGUE 377

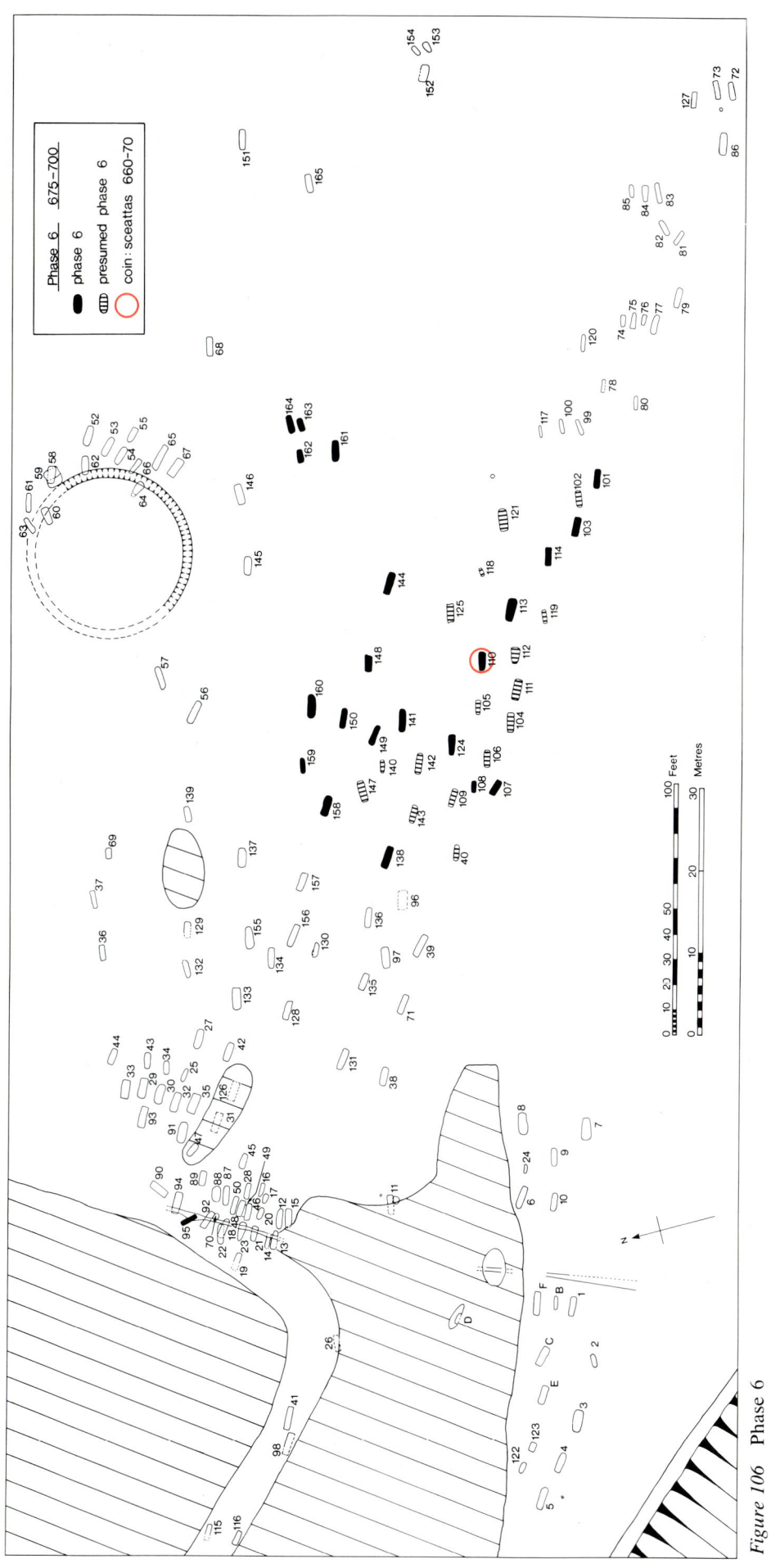

*Figure 106* Phase 6

378 THE BUCKLAND ANGLO-SAXON CEMETERY

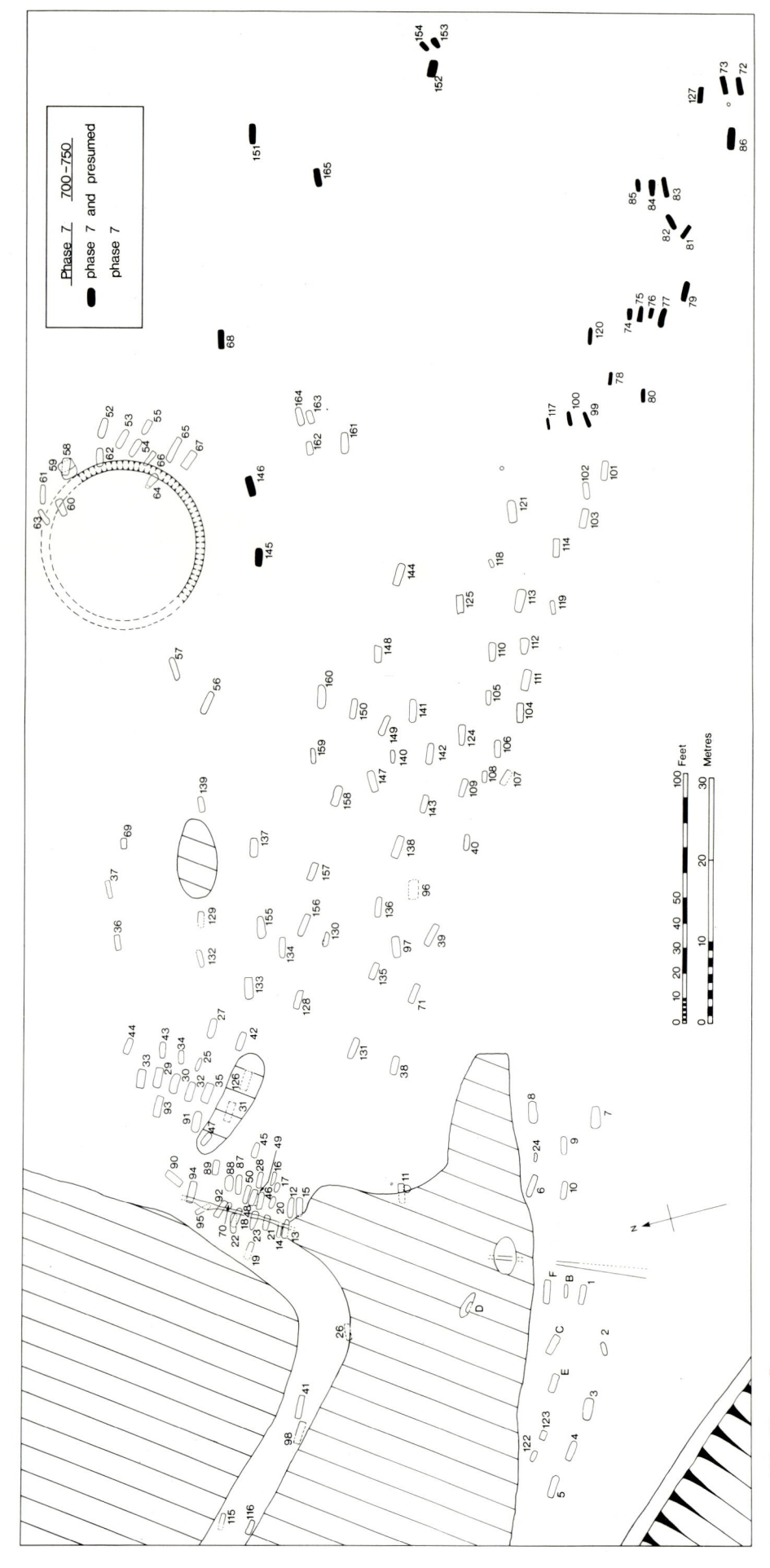

*Figure 107* Phase 7

# GRAVE CATALOGUE

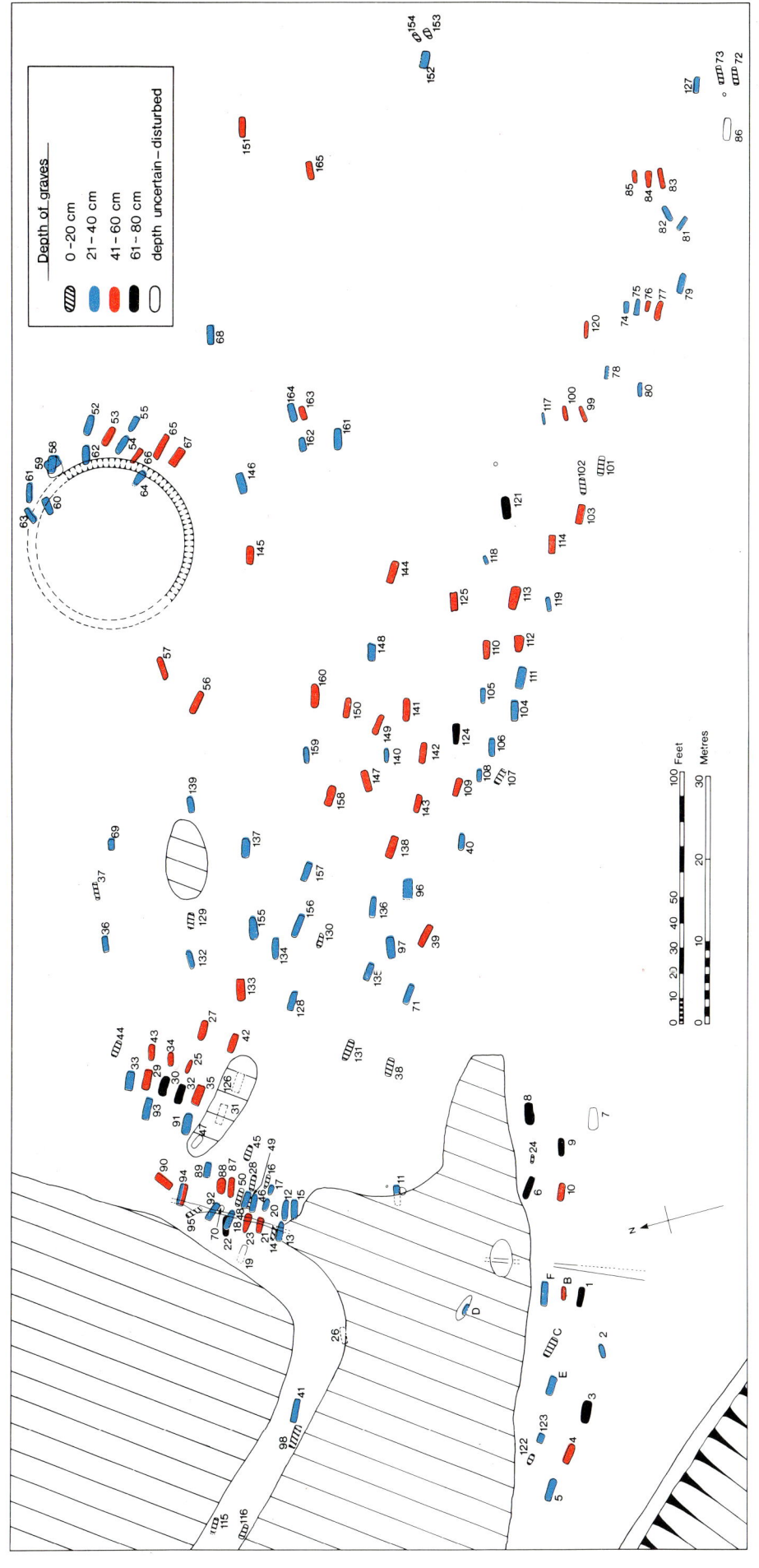

*Figure 108* Depth of graves

380                    THE BUCKLAND ANGLO-SAXON CEMETERY

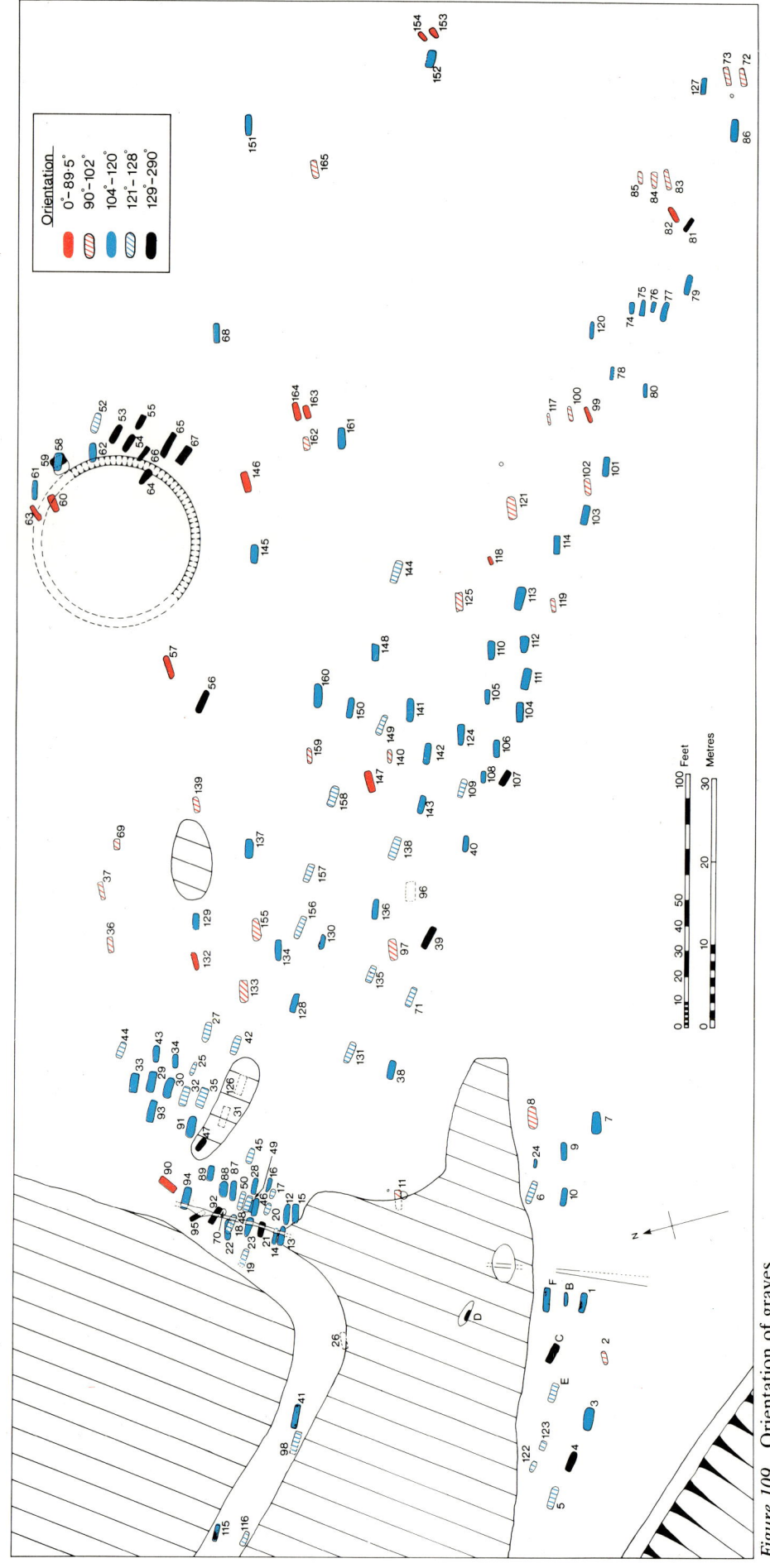

Figure 109  Orientation of graves

GRAVE CATALOGUE 381

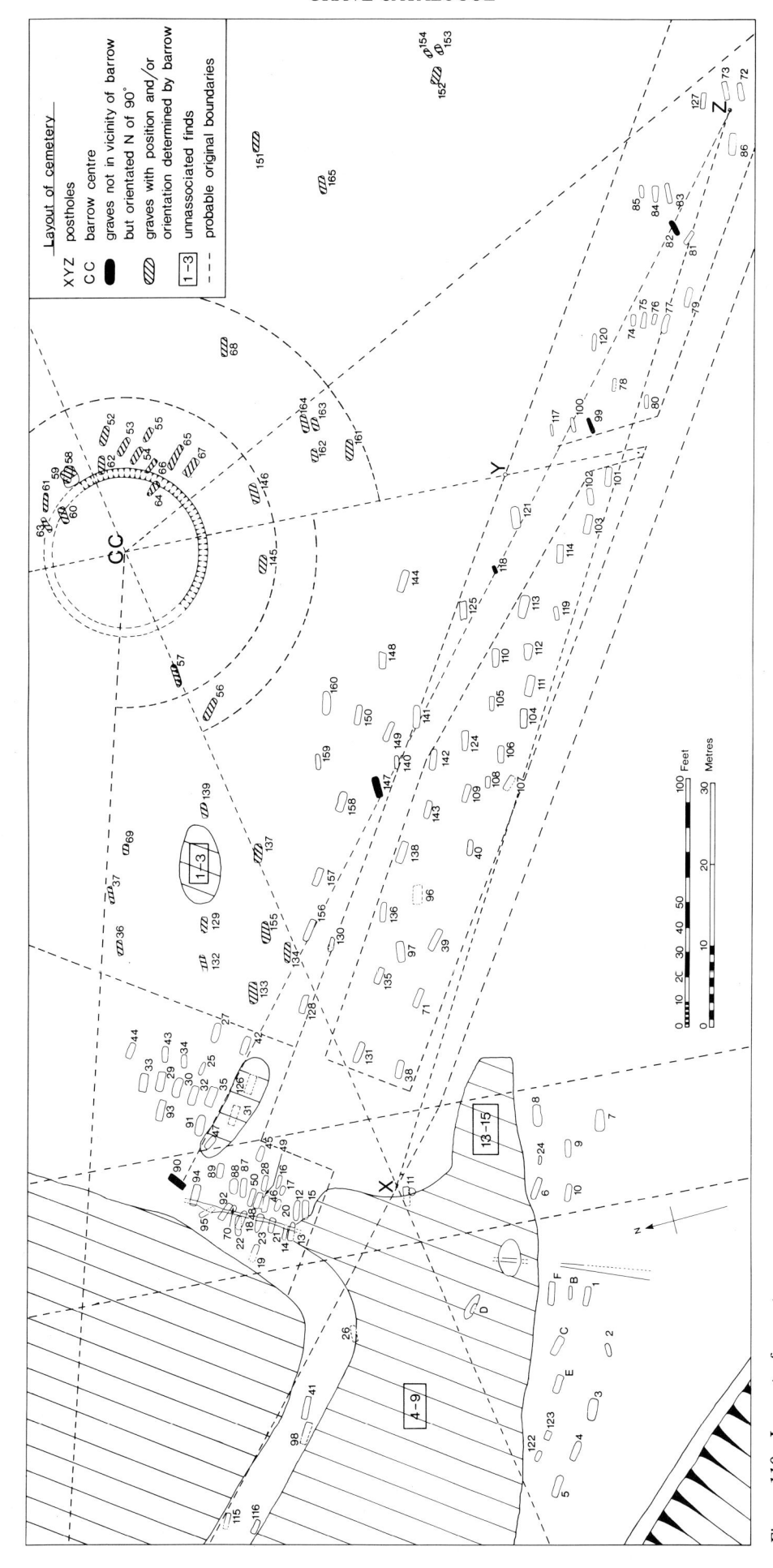

*Figure 110* Layout of cemetery

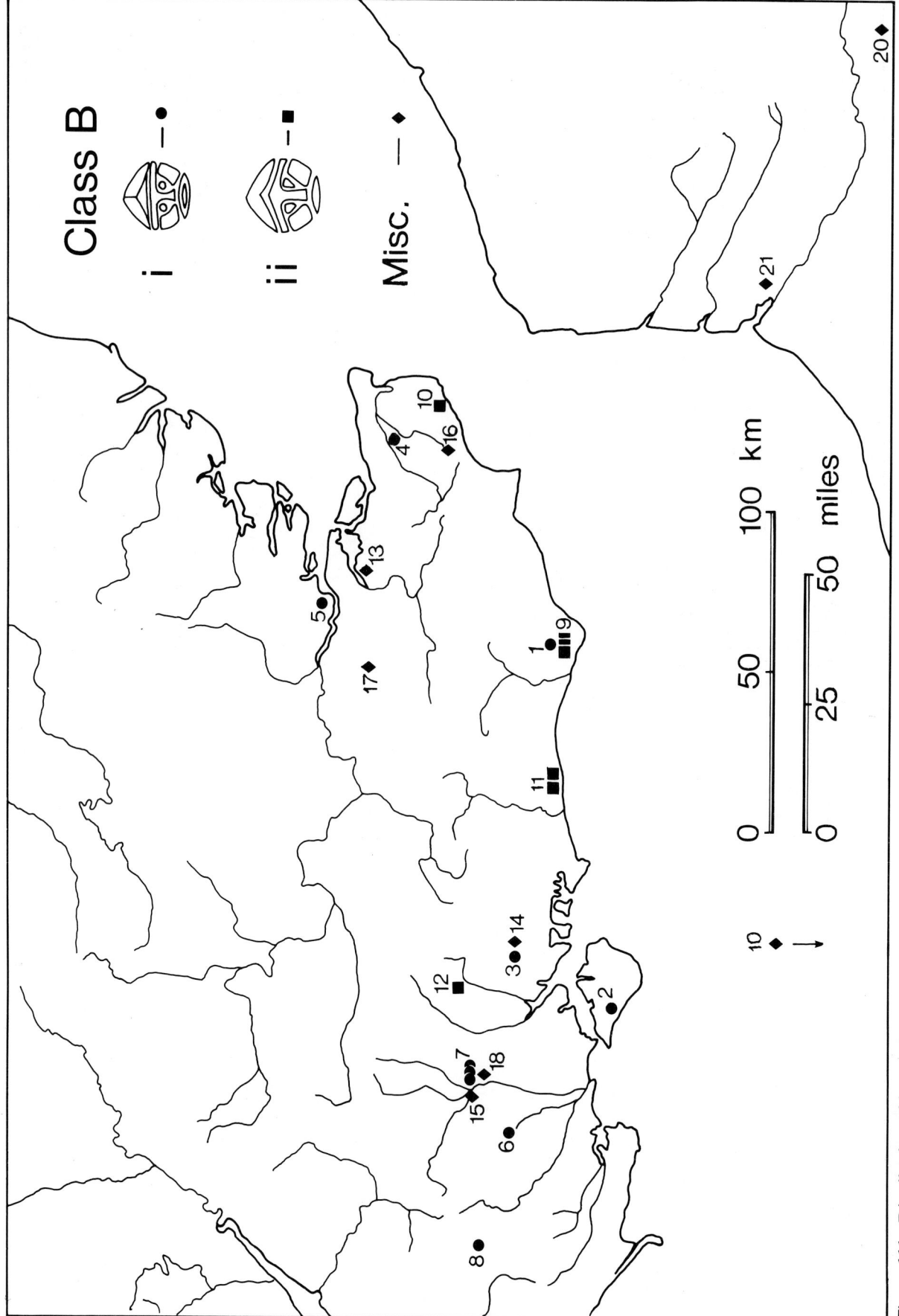

*Figure 111* Distribution of button brooches, class B

GRAVE CATALOGUE 383

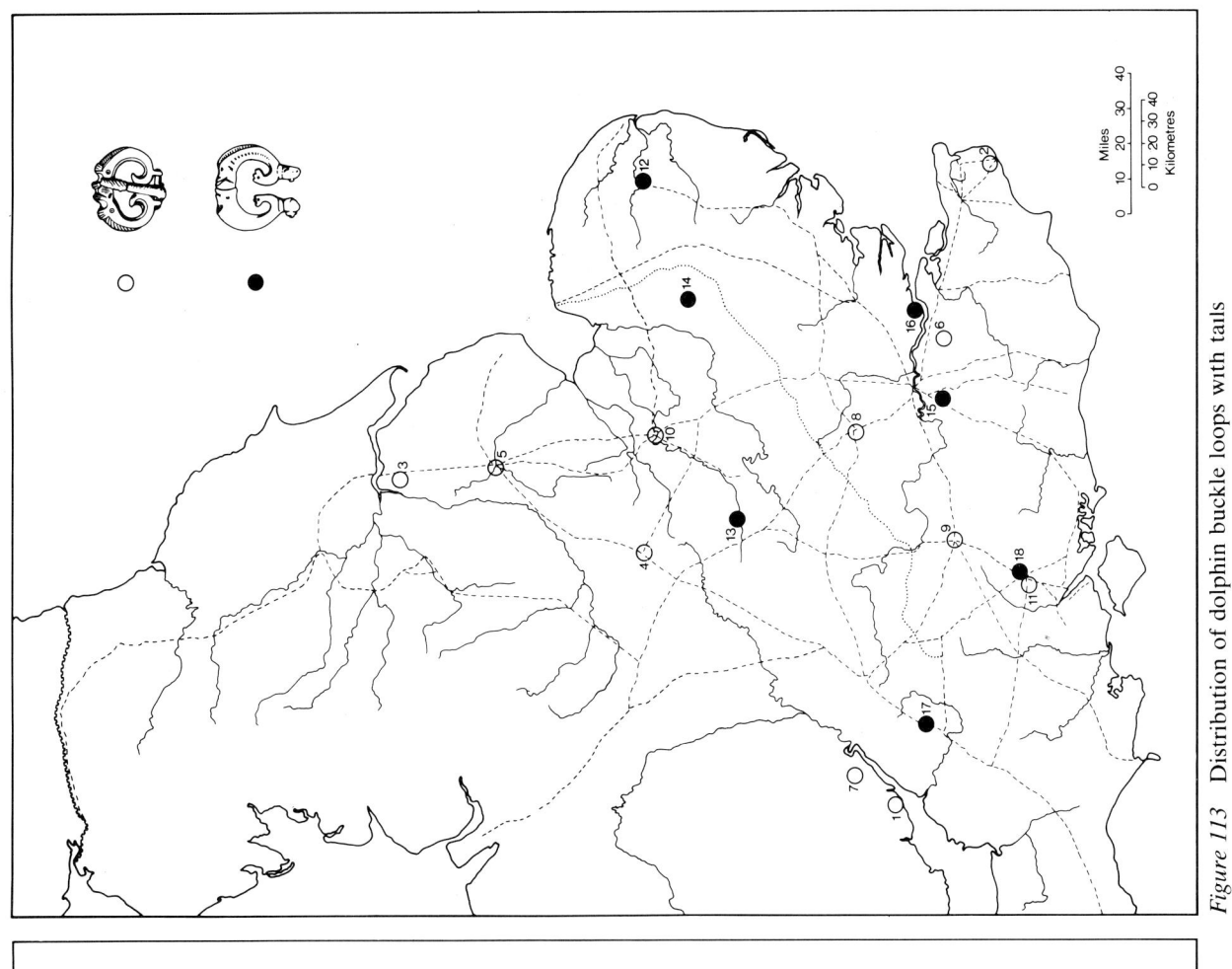

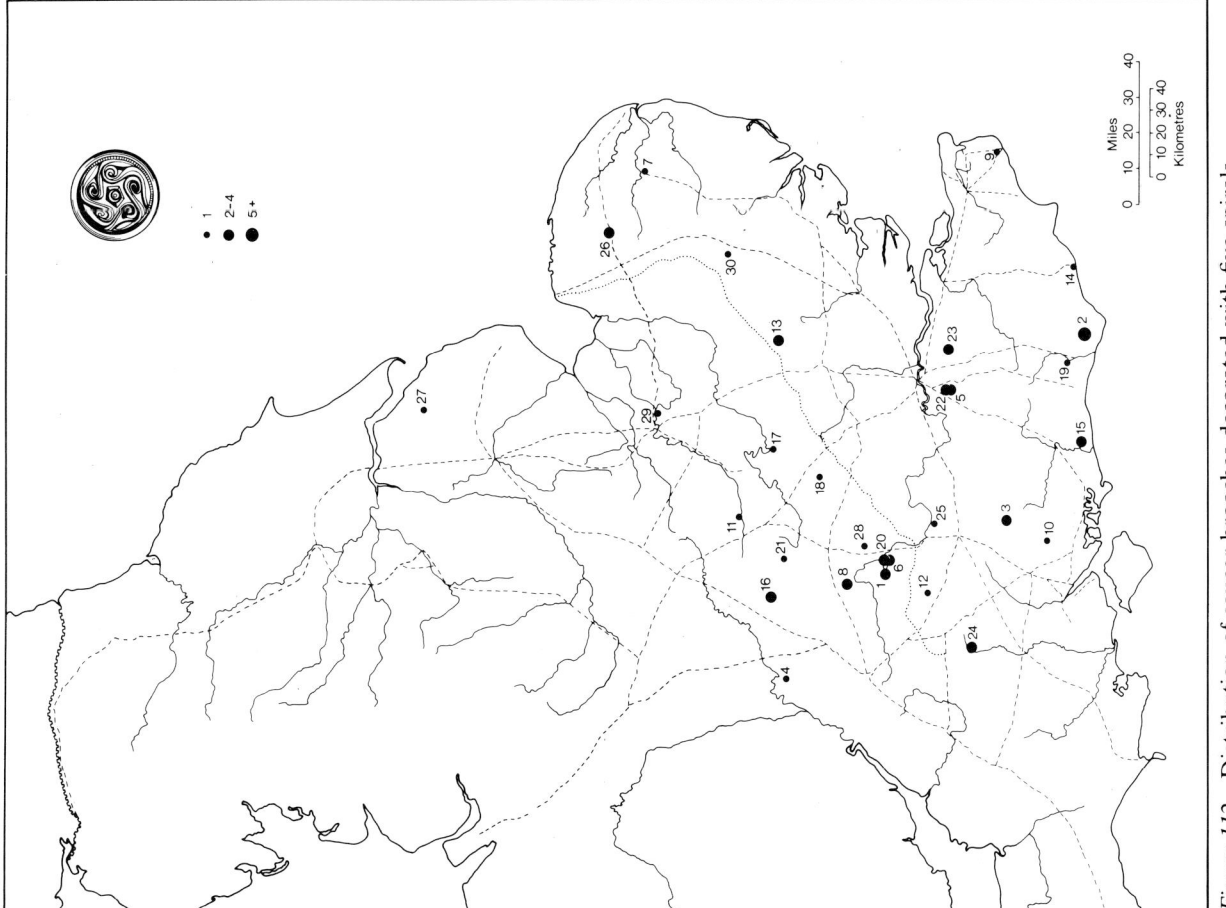

*Figure 113* Distribution of dolphin buckle loops with tails

*Figure 112* Distribution of saucer brooches decorated with five spirals

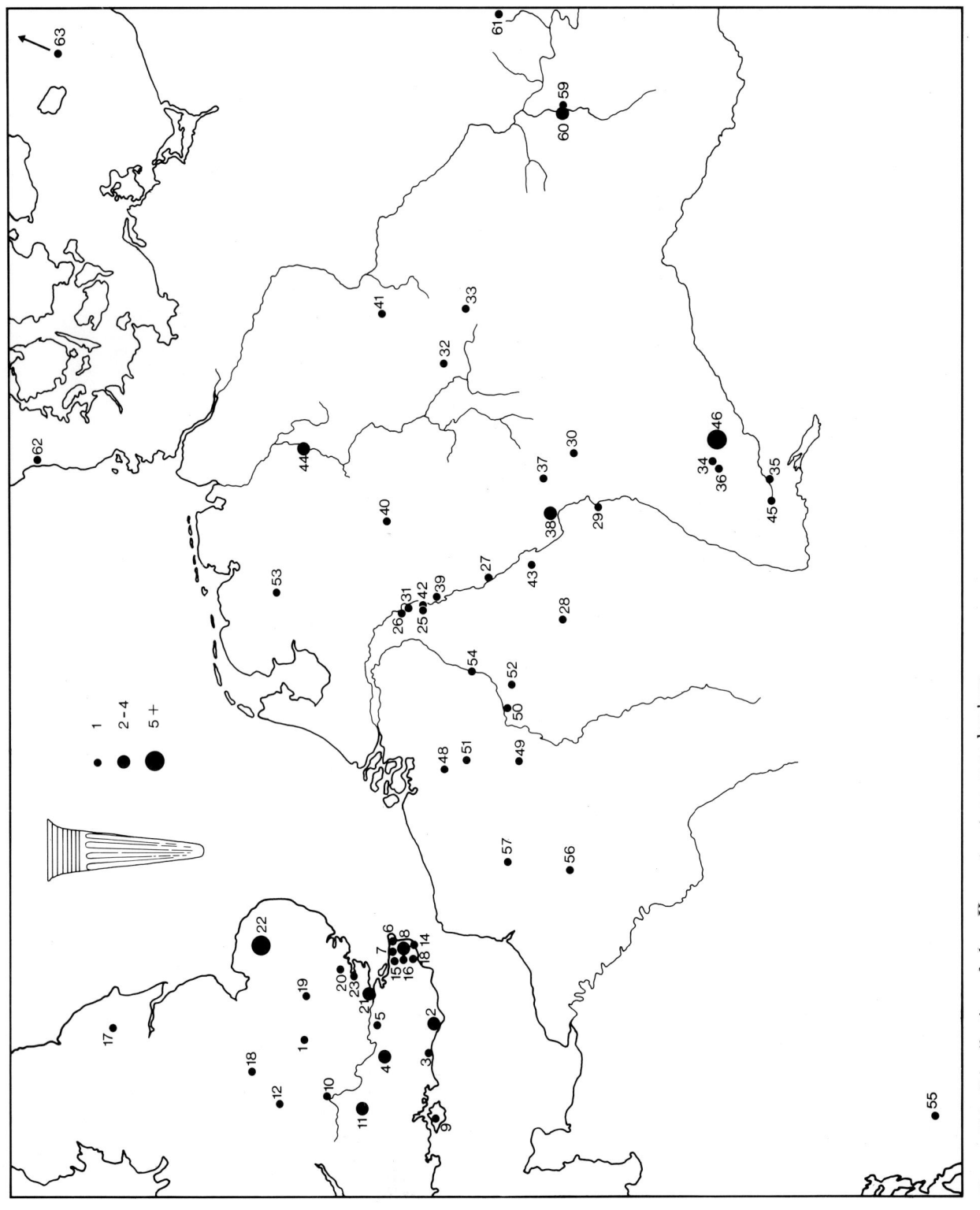

*Figure 114* Distribution of glass Kempston-type cone beakers

GRAVE CATALOGUE                                                                                                              385

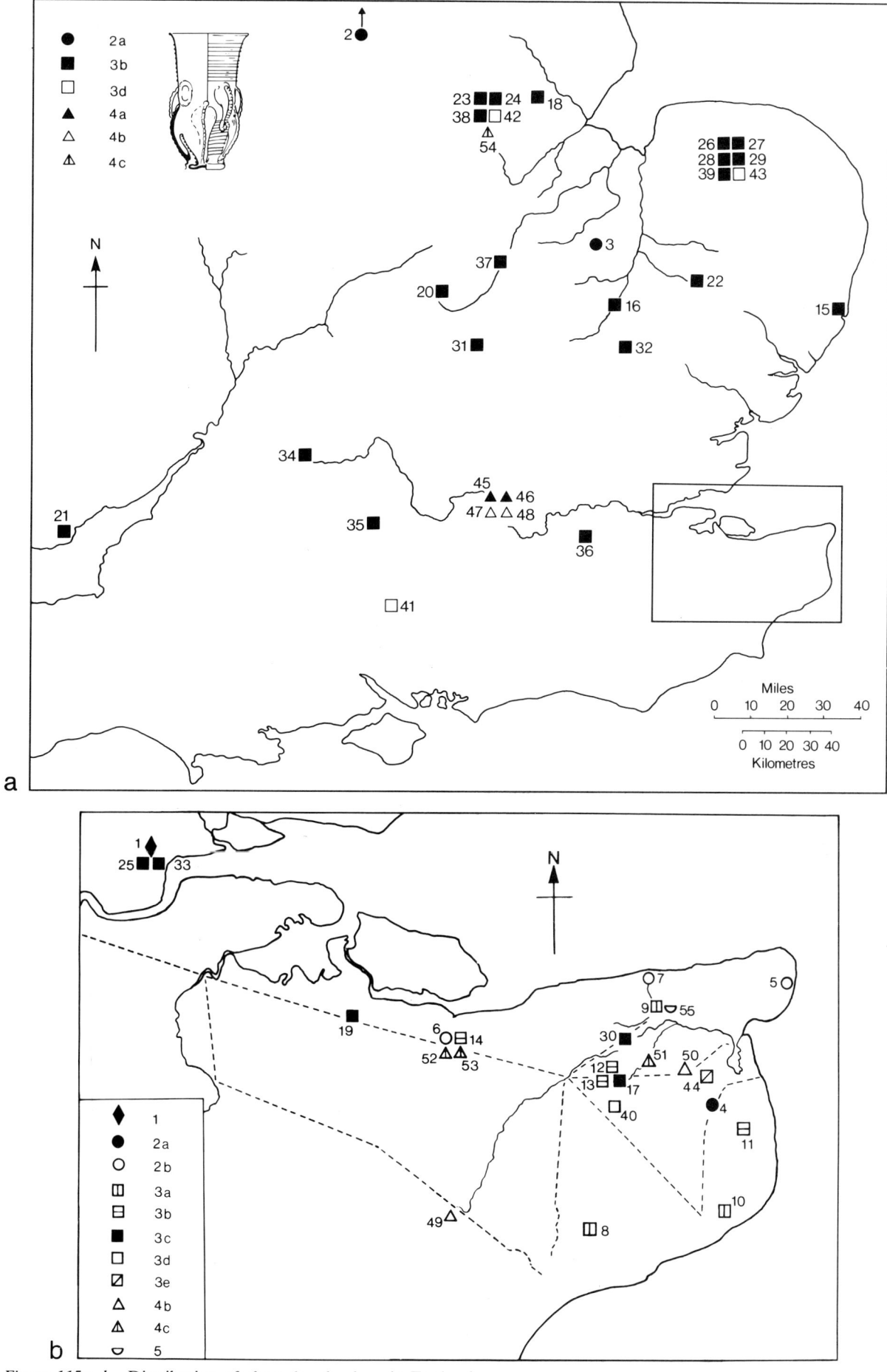

*Figure 115a, b*   Distribution of glass claw-beakers in England

386 THE BUCKLAND ANGLO-SAXON CEMETERY

Figure 117  Distribution of bronze workboxes

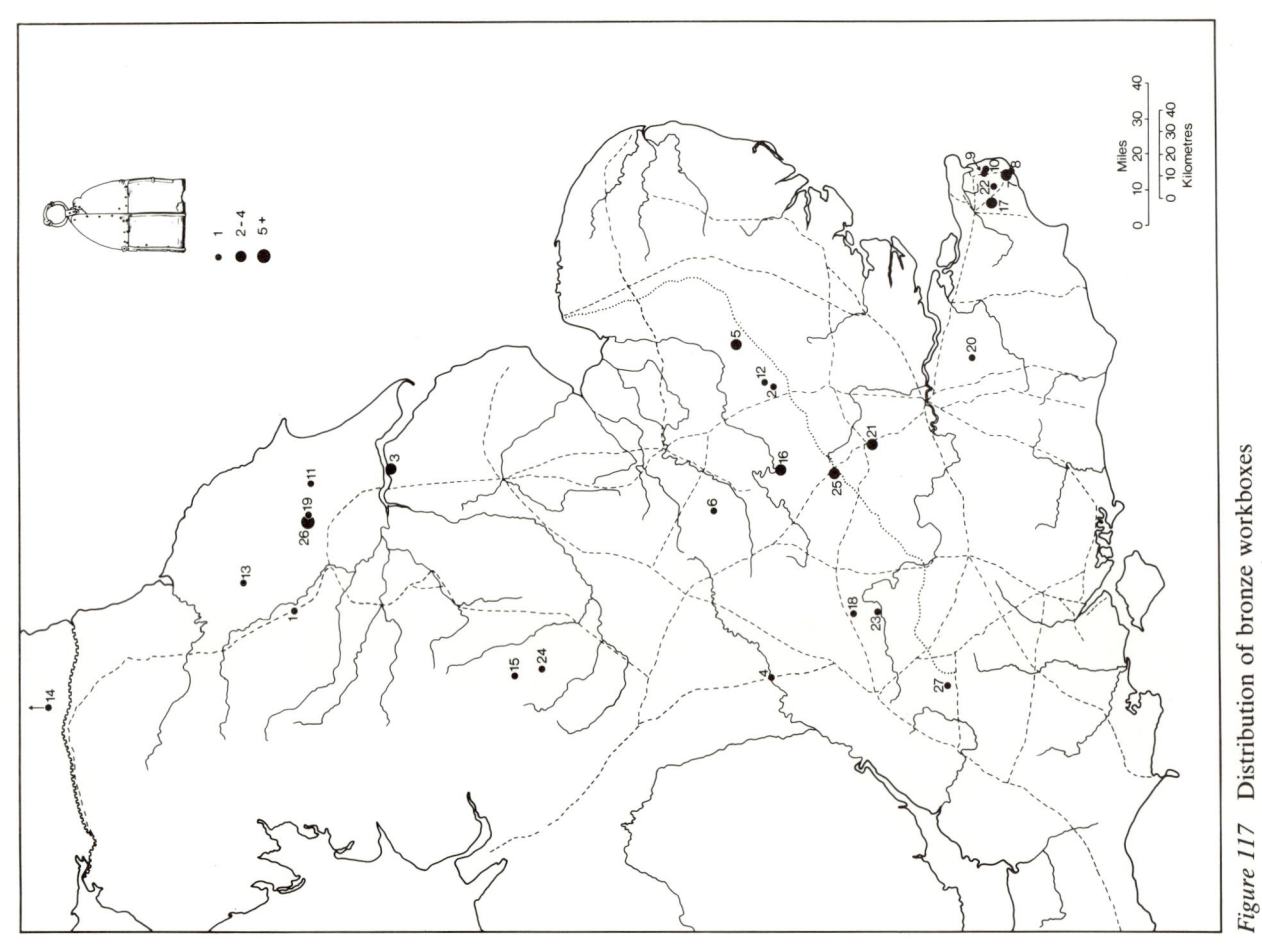

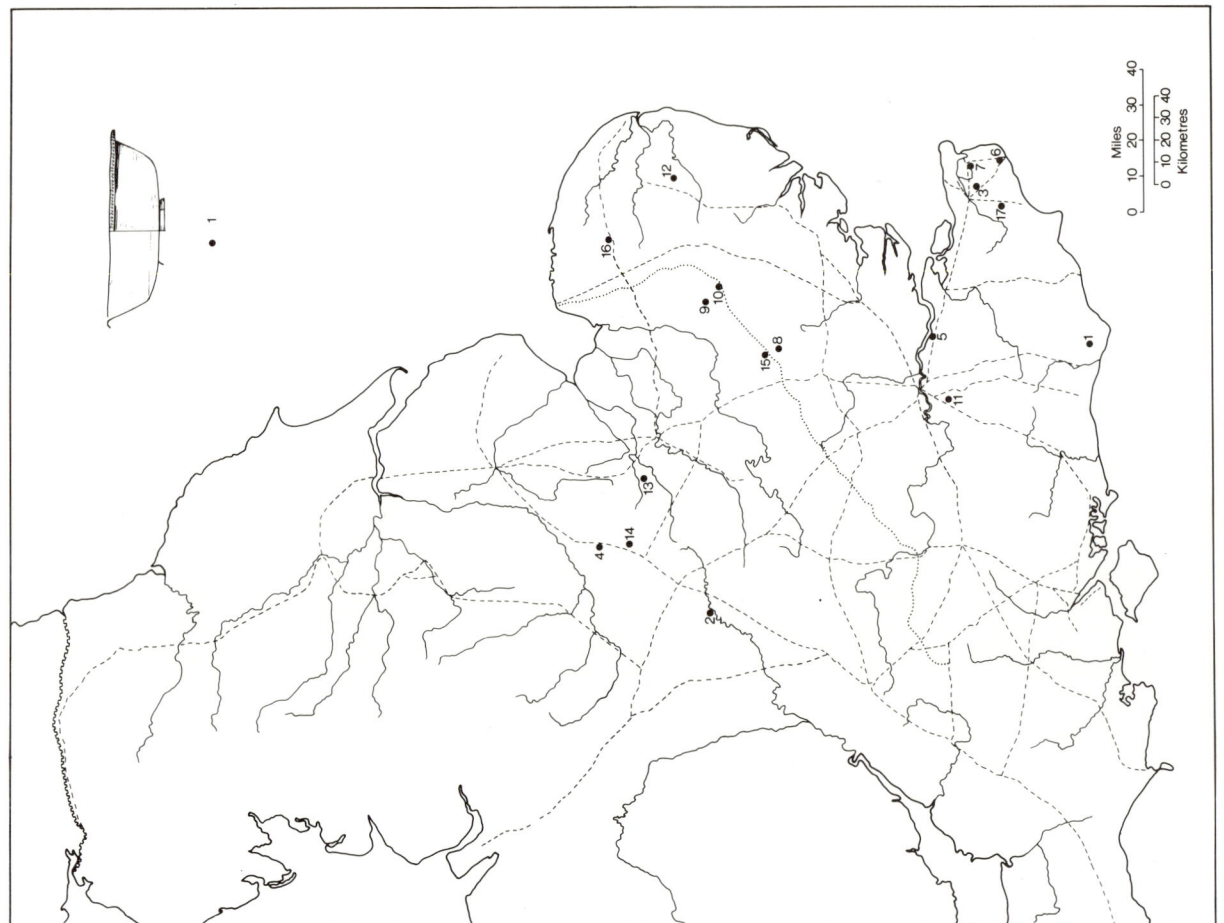

Figure 116  Distribution of bronze bowls with beaded rim

387

*Figure 119* Distribution of bronze balances

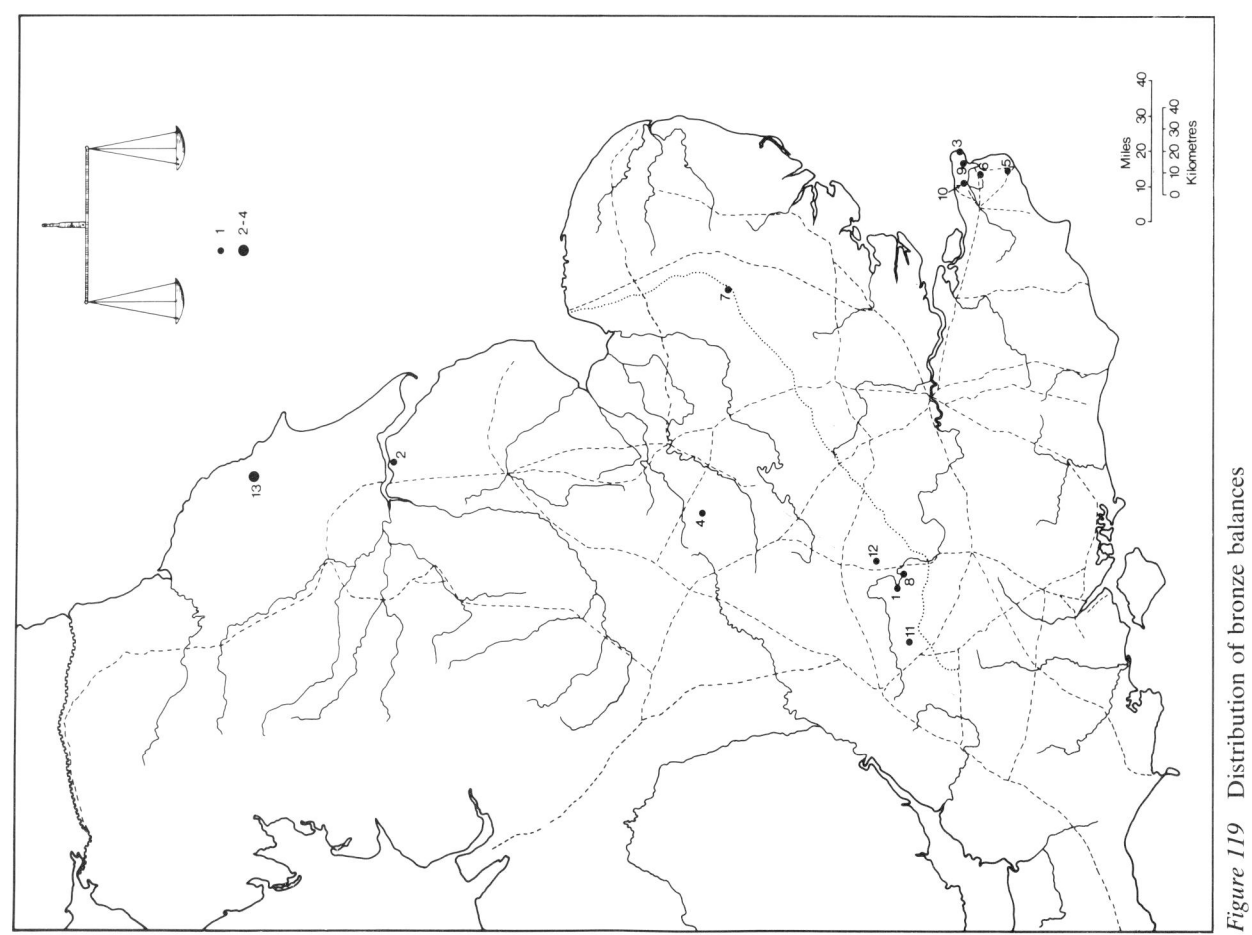

*Figure 118* Distribution of ivory rings

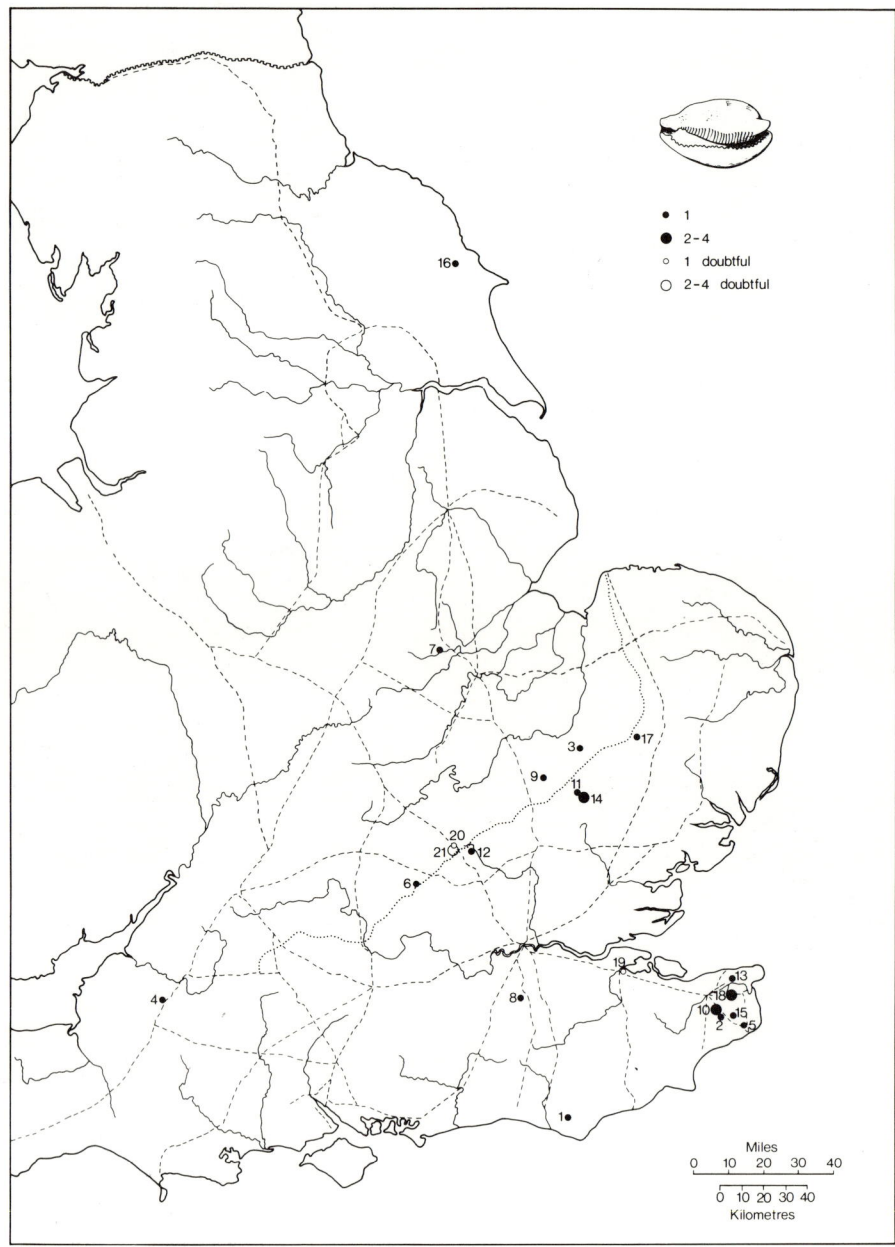

*Figure 120* Distribution of cowrie shells

*Colour Plate 1* Brooches and pendant
a 13/1, b 20/8, c 13/2, d 35/3, e 14/1, f 59/1
(Scale 3/2)

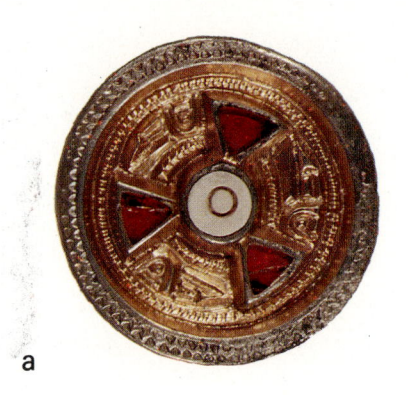

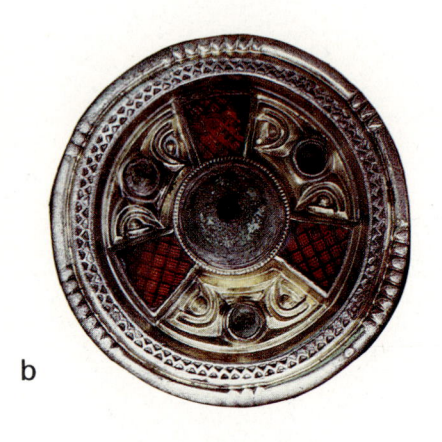

*Colour Plate II*  Brooches
     a 38/1, b 1/2, c 35/1, d 29/1, e 126/1 (Scale 3/2)

PLATES

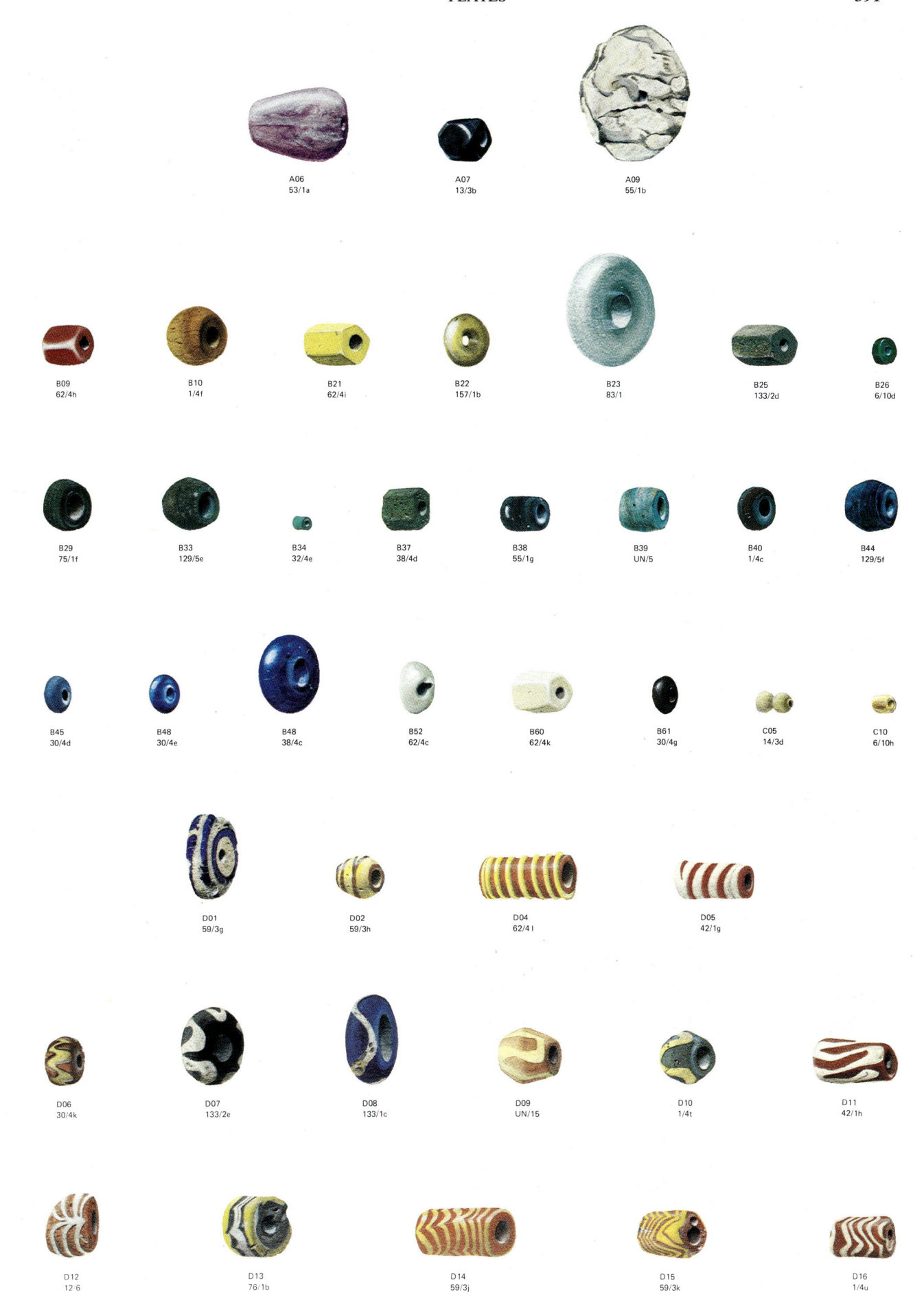

| | | |
|---|---|---|
| A06 53/1a | A07 13/3b | A09 55/1b |

| B09 62/4h | B10 1/4f | B21 62/4i | B22 157/1b | B23 83/1 | B25 133/2d | B26 6/10d |
|---|---|---|---|---|---|---|

| B29 75/1f | B33 129/5e | B34 32/4e | B37 38/4d | B38 55/1g | B39 UN/5 | B40 1/4c | B44 129/5f |
|---|---|---|---|---|---|---|---|

| B45 30/4d | B48 30/4e | B48 38/4c | B52 62/4c | B60 62/4k | B61 30/4g | C05 14/3d | C10 6/10h |
|---|---|---|---|---|---|---|---|

| D01 59/3g | D02 59/3h | D04 62/4l | D05 42/1g |
|---|---|---|---|

| D06 30/4k | D07 133/2e | D08 133/1c | D09 UN/15 | D10 1/4t | D11 42/1h |
|---|---|---|---|---|---|

| D12 12/6 | D13 76/1b | D14 59/3j | D15 59/3k | D16 1/4u |
|---|---|---|---|---|

*Colour Plate III* Non-glass beads, monochrome and polychrome glass beads (Scale 1/1)

392                THE BUCKLAND ANGLO-SAXON CEMETERY

| D17 32/4k | D19 42/1j | D21 30/4m | D22 60/3o | D23 42/1k | D25 32/4 l |
| D26 60/3q | D30 30/4n | D32 18/2e | D34 18/2g | D35 18/2h | D36 55/1h |
| D37 1/4z | D38 59/3 l | D40 30/4p | D42 59/3m | D43 13/3h | D46 1/4z¹ |
| D48 1/4z² | D50 35/5k | D52 42/1r | D53 129/5h | D54 42/1s | D56 157/1f |
| D57 30/4s | D58 30/4t | D59 59/3p | D60 60/3t | D61 129/5i | |
| D62 38/4g | D63 53/1c | D64 132/2e | D65 132/2f | | |
| D66 42/1t | D67 92/3d | D68 93/1 | 49/1b | 59/3q | 59/3 |

*Colour Plate IV*   Polychrome glass beads, part necklace 59/3 in original order, glass fragments (Scale 1/1)

*Plate 1*   *a* Air view of cemetery site in 1947 (top left), Dover town left and Dover Castle right
  *b* Dover harbour from cemetery site

Plate 2  *a* Cemetery site from the west in 1951
*b* Excavating grave 56

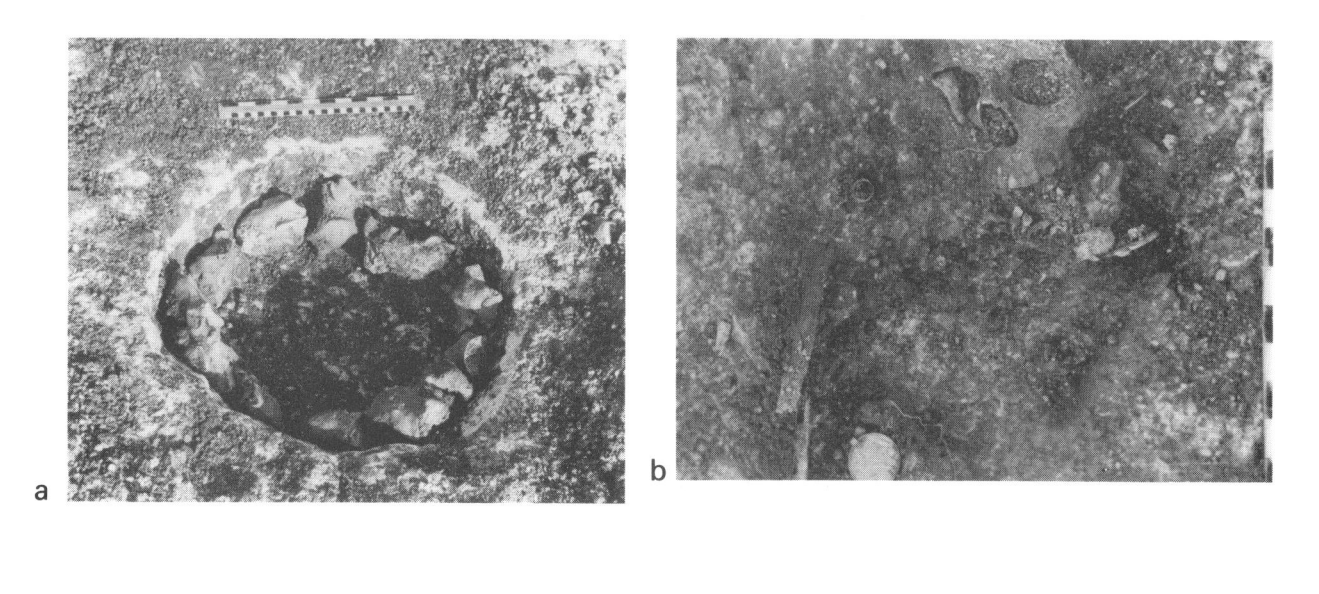

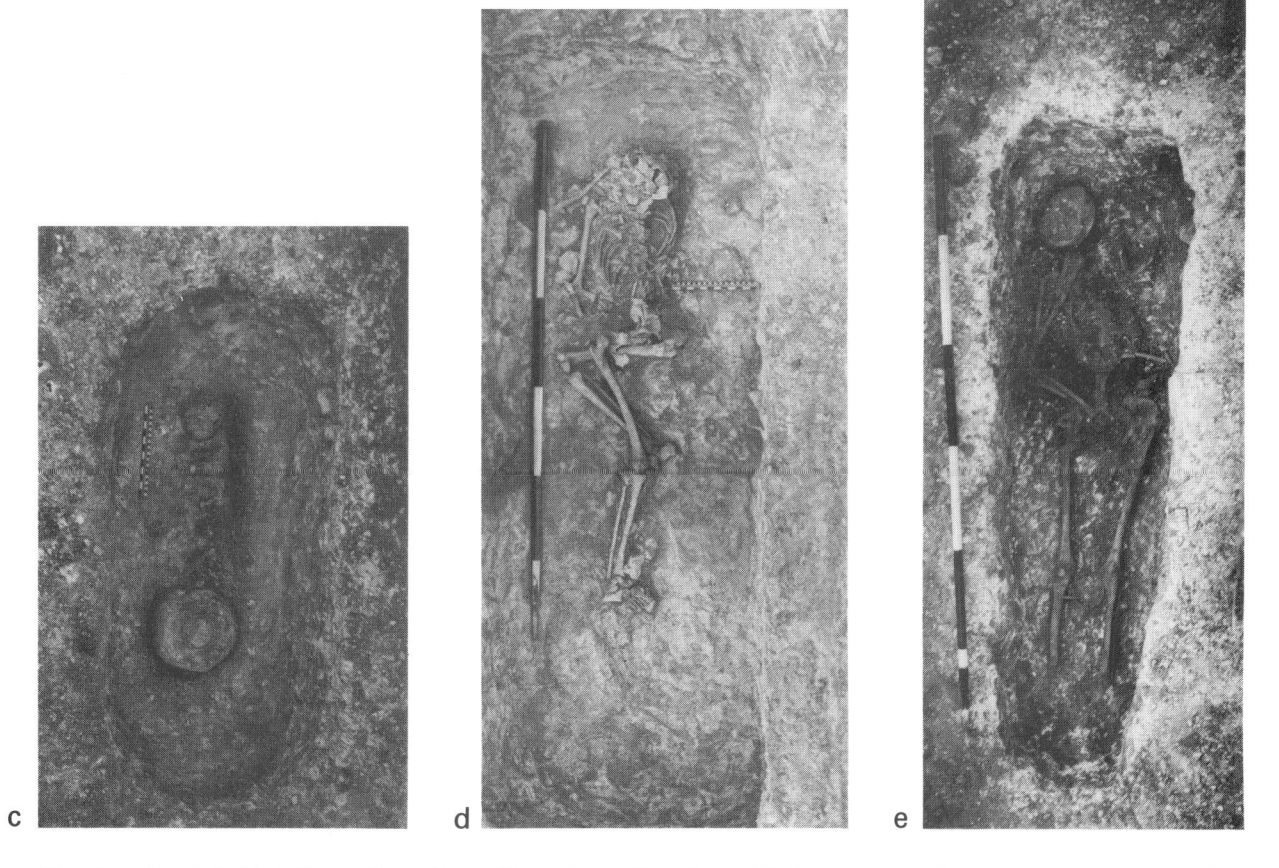

*Plate 3*    *a* Posthole Z, *b* Grave 29, *c* Grave 20, *d* Grave 67, *e* Grave 75 (Scale *c–e* 1–24)

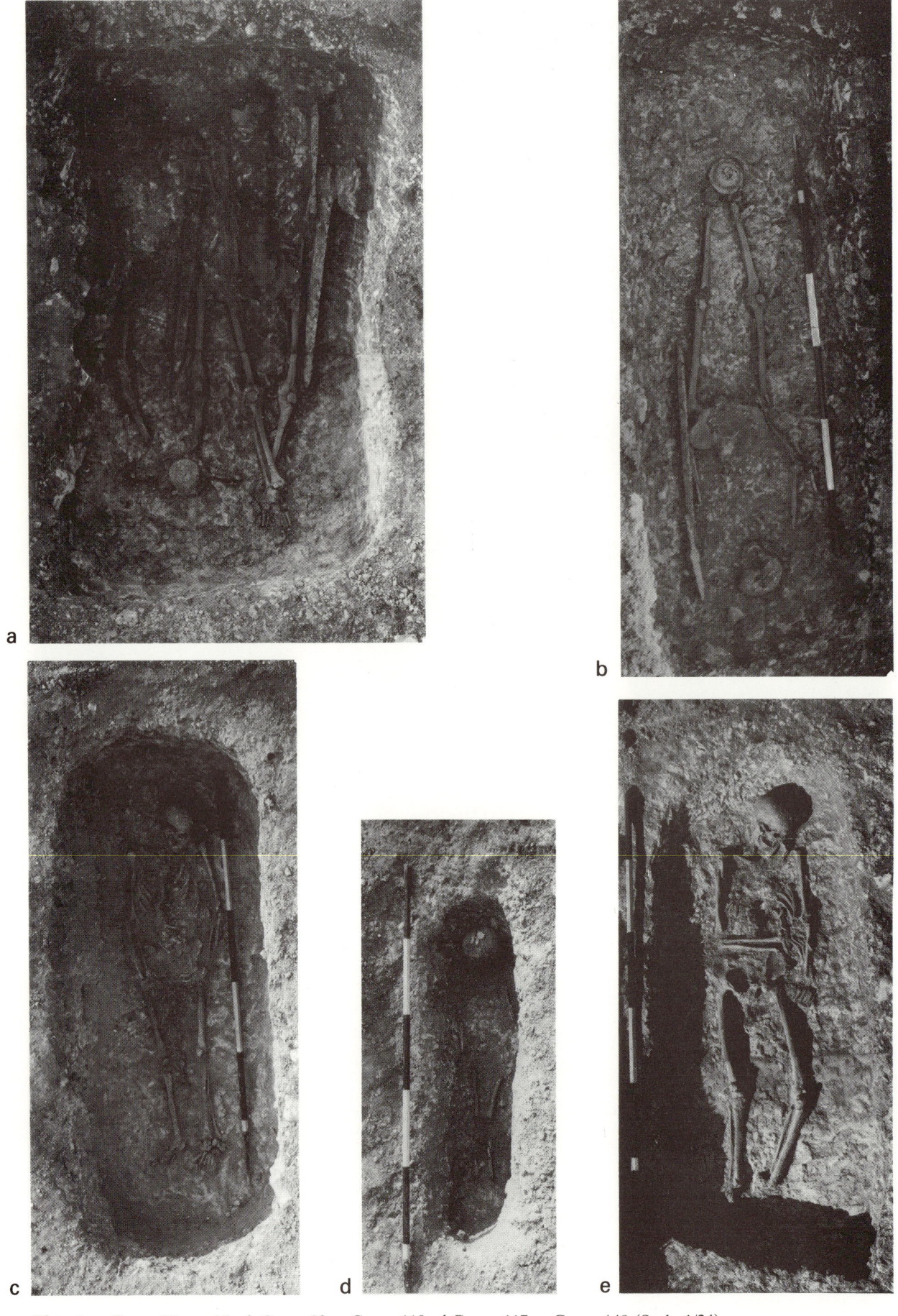

*Plate 4* *a* Grave 96a and b, *b* Grave 93, *c* Grave 110, *d* Grave 117, *e* Grave 148 (Scale 1/24)

PLATES 397

*Plate 5* Sword, buckles and pin. *a* C31, *b* 61/3, *c* 21/1, *d* 38/5, *e*, 161/3 (Scale *a–d* 1/1, *e* 2/1)

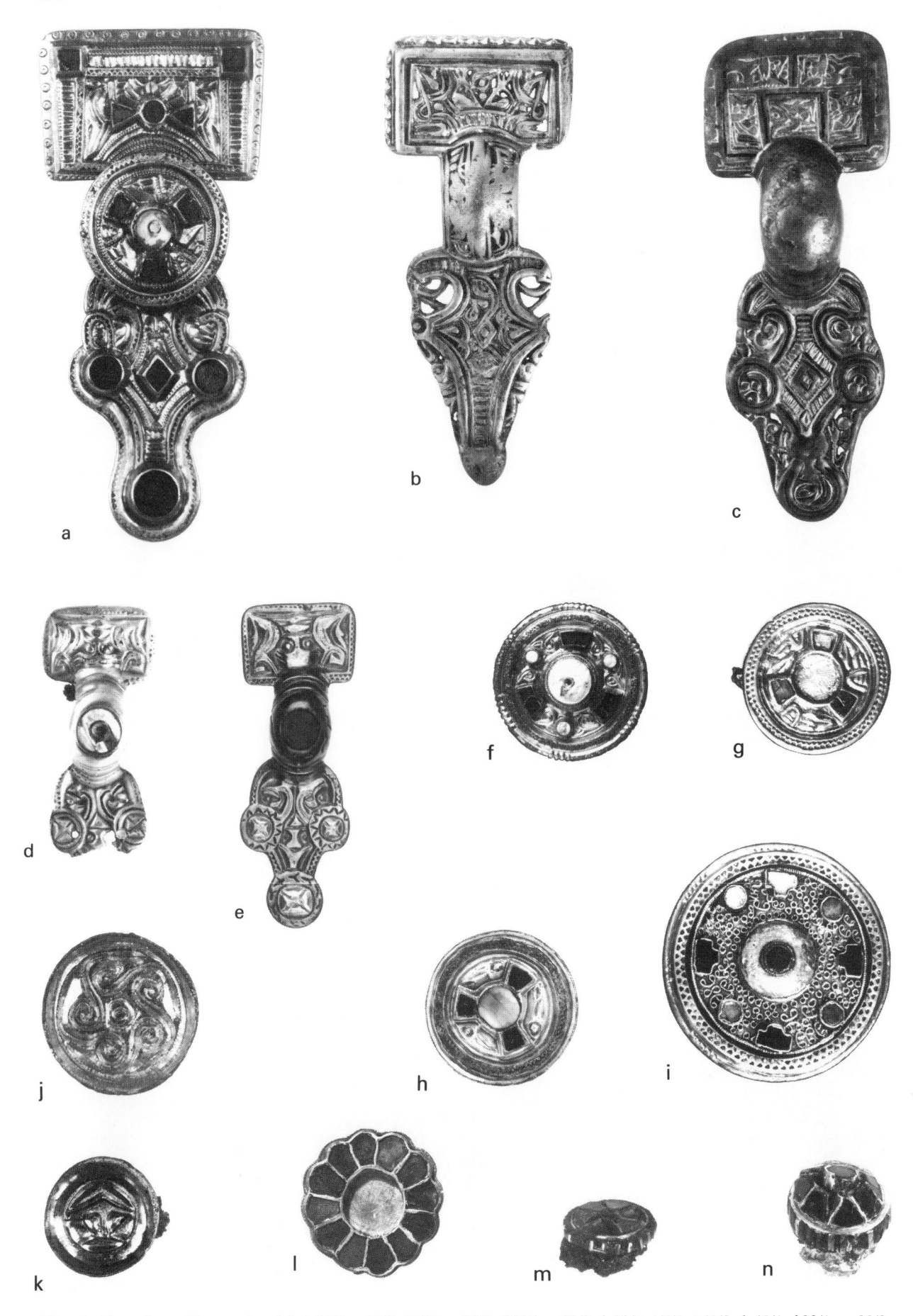

*Plate 6* Brooches *a* Unassociated 9, *b* 13/1, *c* 13/2 *d* 20/6, *e* 20/8, *f* 32/1, *g* 30/2, *h* 92/1, *i* F/1, *j* 48/2, *k* 48/1, *l* 23/1, *m* 20/2, *n* 92/2 (Scale 1/1)

*Plate 7* Pendants *a* Unassociated 6, *b* 29/7, *c* 110/10, *d* 110/11, *e* 20/4, *f* 1/1, *g* 29/8, *h* 134/1, *i* 29/5a, *j* 29/6, *k* 67/2 (Scale 2/1)

400 THE BUCKLAND ANGLO-SAXON CEMETERY

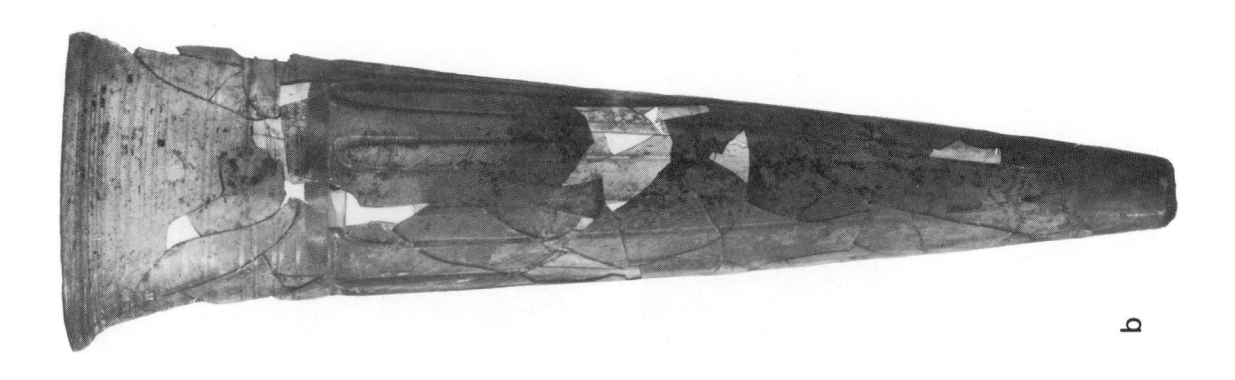

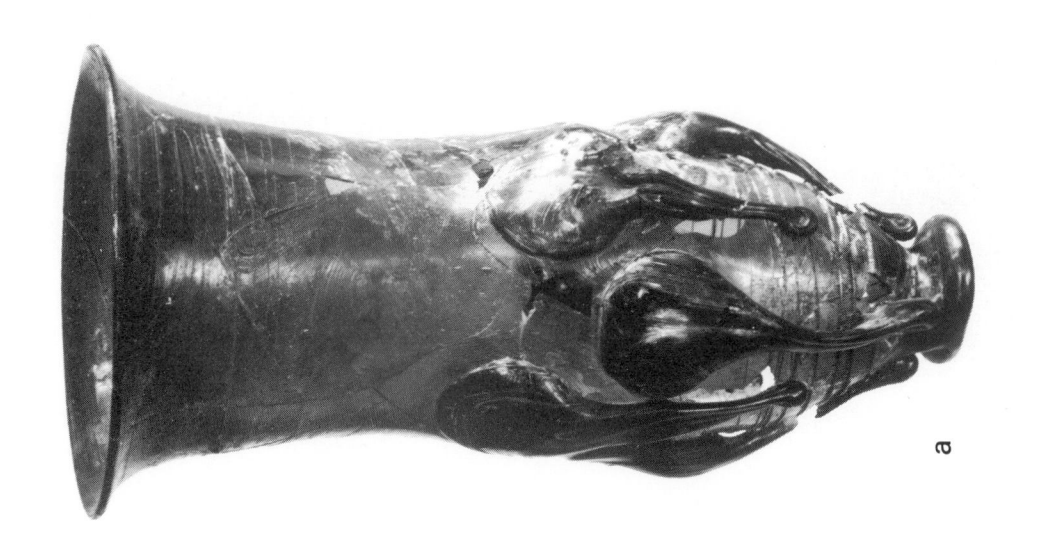

*Plate 8* Glass vessels *a* 20/16, *b* 22/1, *c* 38/12. (Scale a,c 2/3, b 1/2)

*Plate 9* Glass and pottery vessels
 *a* 6/1, *b* 160/8, *c* 139/4, *d* 87/3, *e* 109/3 (Scale *a* 1/1, *b* 2/3, *c–e* 1/3)

402                    THE BUCKLAND ANGLO-SAXON CEMETERY

*Plate 10*   Belt, bronze bowl and buckets.
             *a* 20/19, *b* 20/17, *c* 28/1, *d* 53/7 (Scale *a* 1/2, *b*,*d* 1/3, *c* 2/3)

*Plate 11* Textile impressions: *a* 96b/7, *b* 113/5, *c* Unassociated 16, *d* 4/1 (Scale enlarged)

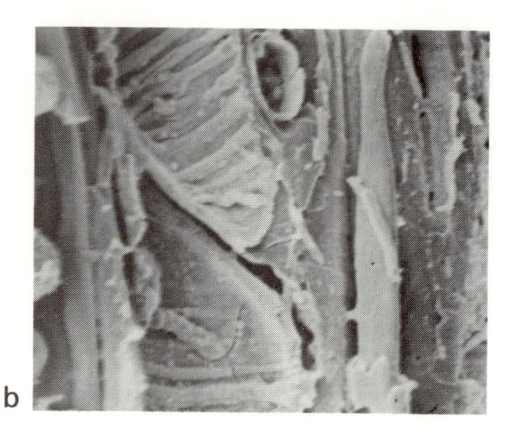

*Plate 12*   *a* Preserved cattle horn from pommel of ring-sword C/1 (Magnified *c* 100x)
   *b* Copper alloy preserved wood from reverse of buckle 48/14 (Magnified *c* 1000x)
   *c* Preserved animal fur from 'knife' blade associated with seax 93/7 (Magnified *c* 300x)
   *d* Preserved organic material from pommel 93/6, possibly ivory (Magnified *c* 1000x)
   *e* Preserved ivory from lower guard of sword hilt 93/6 (Magnified *c* 1000x)

# Index

**compiled by Elizabeth Fowler**

adze-blade 17, 100, 249, *330*
aescas (A – S spearshaft) 27

amber beads 57, *58*, 59, 60, 67, 71, 134, 135, 137, 141, 215, 216, 222, 224, 227, 228, 230, 233, 234, *275*, *276*, *286*, *293*, *298*, *299*
   dist. by graves 67
   set in bone pin head 83
amethyst quartz beads 49, 57, *58*, 59, 60, 66, 67, 69, 70, 71, 142, 171, 231, 235, 243
amulets 121–2
Angles 142, 171
angons 28, 29
animal bone, *see* bones 16
   disturbance of graves 16
   ornament *see* ornament
antimony 63, 70, 185–6
antler 106, 119, 196, 221, 243, 249–50
apatite, objects made from 25, 60, 70, 71, 221, 237, *284*
arrowheads 29, 30–1, 90, 232, *303*
   list of in A – S graves 30–1
arsenic 70, 155–6
arthritis 127, 199
   list of skeletons with 199
ash (*Fraxinus* sp.) 27, 196, 217, 228
Athalaric 47
awls 30, 90, 110, 150, 217, 249, 250, *279*

bag (also pouch) 98, 104, 112, 113, 122, 125, 216, 219, 230
   dist. in cem. 366
   *see also* ivory, purse
balance, bronze 120–1, 180, 214, 273
   distribution map 270, 387
baldric, leather 23–4
barrow, prehistoric 13, *14*, 15, 16, 20, 126, 145, 146, 152–4
   graves orientated on 153, 160, 161
   incorporated in Plot E 133, 135, 141, 143, 173
   line from mid barrow to posthole Y 152–3, 168
   to posthole X 153, 168
   possible post in centre 152
bars, iron 99
   *see also* coffin fittings
beads 18–19, 49, 57–82, 125, 126
   analysis of 70
   biconical bronze *58*, 59, 61, 71, 135, 142, 235, 244, *308*, *324*
   bone 23
   dist. of in cem. 360
   fossil *58*, 59, 60, 66, 71, 122
   glass *see* sep. entry
   horn 23
   jet 57, *58*, 59, 60–1, 71
   magical properties of 66–7
   metal 57, 66, 71
   non-glass illust. of *58*, 71 (Table VIII), colour pl. III
   in phases 79 (Table XII)
   shell 45, 53, 57, *58*, 59, 60, 66, 67, 71, 122, 134, 135, 141, 142, 171, 217, 235, 244, *278*
   silver *58*, 59, 61, 71, 245, *326*
   source of 66
   stone *58*, 59, 60, 71, 198
   sword *see* swords
   types of *58*, 64
   in graves 59 (Table VII)
   white composition 24, 24–5, 57, *58*, 59, 60–1, 66, 67, 71
bed 17
beech (*Fagus sylvatica*) 102, 196, 243, 249
bell-beakers (tumblers), glass 97–8, 134, 171, 217, *278*
belts
   appliqué mounts for 87
   imitation of - with metal plaques 91
   - mounts 39, 87, 150, 174
   - plate 21, 39
   reconstructions of 88
   rectangular mounts 87, 240, *319*
   sub-rect. - mounts 87
   tinned bronze - mounts 239–40, *318*
   triangular - mounts 87, 240, 242, *319*, *321*
   wooden - 70, 91, 221, *284*
Beowulf 28
Bertha, Queen 174
bier 17, 19, 99
binding, U-section *see* strips
birds
   headed 51, 83
   heads as mounts 56, 105
   as ornament 32, 37, 39, 54, 55, 218, 220, 221, 228
   silver plaques on cups 105, 224, *288*
bolt-plates 100, *101*
bone
   beads *see* beads
   covers for boxes 106
   discs 23
   knife handle 114
   lid 107, 250, *333*
   perforated 117, 244, *324*
   playing piece 122, 219, *281*
   sword beads 23
   weaving picks *see* weaving equipment
   workbox 108, 196
bones, animal 127, 248, 252
   foetus 18, 113, 241
   human *see also* skeletons 11, 13, 15, 16, 197–201
bottles, pottery 92–3, 126, 149, 170, 171, 229, 241, 244, 247, 250, 251, *296*, *320*, *324*, *327*, *332*, *333*
   wooden with silver rims 105
boxes, antler-covered 249
   bone *109*, 109–10
   bone-covered 106
   wooden 17, 18, 19, 100–103, *102*, 112, 119, 120, 122, 149, 153, 196
   wooden, bronze cleats for 101–2
   dist. in cem. 365
   iron fittings for 100–103, 106, 196, 215, 226, 229, 231, 233, 243, 248–9, *275*, *292*, *296*, *301*, *304*, *305*, *321*, *329*
   ornamented with bone or metal inlays 103
bracelets
   bronze 18, 67, 86, 235, 248, *308*, *329*
   silver 85, 221, *283*
   slip-knot, bronze wire 18, 85–6, 125, 126, 135, 216, 219, 221, 244, *276*, *282*, *283*, *244*, *324*
   snake's head 86, 241, *320*
bracteates *50*, 51–5, 57, 67, 69
   gold 43, 51–3, 86, 137, 171, 172, 215, 220, 224, 245, *275*, *283*, *326*
   metal content 52, 53, 55, 86, 181–2
braid 69
Bretwaldas 175
bronze, *see* beads, bowls, pins etc
   inlay on pin 84
   staining on skeletons 198
brooches 17, 18, 19, 35–49, 137
   annular 48–9, 125, 134, 172, 219, 238, 243–4, 253, *280*, *315*, *323*, *336*
   button 48, 67, 69, 134, 171, 172, 229–30, 266, *298*
   dist. of 382
   disc 11, 22, 37, 38, 39–47, 53, 55, 56, 57, 67, 69, 96, 125, 126
   direction of pin 46
   Frankish 47, 53, 134, 137, 146, 164, 171, 215–6, 237, *275*, *313*
   inlaid metal technique 47
   Kentish 141, 171, 172, 190, 194, 215, 219, 220, 222, 224, 225, 226, 227, 232, 237, 243, *275*, *281*, *283*, *286*, *289*, *290*, *292*, *293*, *304*, *313*, *323*
   keystone garnet 141, 171, 172, 190, 194, 215, 219, 220, 222, 224, 225, 226, 226–7, 232, 237, 243, *275*, *281*, *283*, *286*, *289*, *290*, *292*, *293*, *304*, *313*, *323*
   runic inscription on 11, 46–7, 171, 243, *323*
   saucer 47–8, 67, 134, 171, 230, *298*
   composite 48
   dist. of 266, 383
   number of spirals 48, 137
   repoussé sheet 48
   small-long 39, 67, 134, 172, 219, *280*
   square-headed 11, 35–8, *38*, 39, 45–6, 67, 69, 137, 174, 176, 218, 220, 221, *280*, *283*
   Kentish exported 172
   Jutland Group 35–6, 37
   South Scaninavian 171
buckets 16, 19, 104–5
   bronze bound 104, *104*, 222–3, *287*
   dist. in cem. 364
   iron bound 104, 231, *300*
   mounts with animal head terminals 104–5
Buckland Estate, Dover 11, 12, 169, 171, 172, 175, *176*
buckles 15, 19, 28, 30, 86–90, 96, 110, 127, 150
   confronted dolphins 86–7, 104, 137, 230, *298*
   dist. of 266, 383
   cylindrical mounts 89
   Frankish 28, 47, 53, 87, 105, 134, 137, 141, 152, 166, 171, 217, 221, *285*
   iron 16, 32, 35, 89–90, 125, 135, 137, 215, 217, 218, 219, 220, 222, 225, 226, 228, 234, 235, 236, 238, 244,

245, 247, 249, 251, *274, 279, 281, 283, 286, 291, 294, 306, 307, 309, 311, 323, 324, 325, 327, 330, 333*
matching belt plates 21
shield-buckle *see* shields
shield-on-tongue 87, 105, 134, 135, 137, 216, 217, 219, 221, 223, 229, 230, 230, 234, 237, 239, *277, 279, 281, 283, 287, 296, 299, 307, 312, 316*
shoe-shaped rivets 87, 89, 105, 125, 135, 137, 215, 219, 223, 230, 234, 237, 239, *274, 281, 287, 299, 312, 316*
silvered bronze and mounts 87, 232, *302*
small bronze, rect. plate 89, 135, 141, 142, 231, 242, 247, 249, 250, 251, *299, 321, 327, 330, 332, 333*
small iron 90, 222, 232, 241, 249, *286, 303, 319, 330, 331*
stamped ornament on 39
Style I ornament on 89–90, 141, 227, *293*
triangular plates for 21, 247, 249, 251, *327, 331, 330*
white metal 87, 225, 238, *289, 313*
burials 13, 18, 123–78
abnormal 133
double male 86, 126
family grouping 145–6
female 17, 18, 57, 60, 82, 89, 103, 104, 106, 111, 134, 135
male 82, 89, 111, 118
pagan/Christian 172–3
pregnant 18, 110, 113, 133
related to grave depth 150–2
richly furnished 112, 119–20, 133, 134, 141, 143, 146
sex dist. in cem. 370
social status 146–50
spearman 16, 134
sword bearer 87, 129, 134
warrior 17, 126
young people 94, 104, 127
buttons, *see* swords
Byzantine fashions 57, 69

carpentry 100
clinker-building techniques 99
casket, ivory mounts for 170
cassiterite and cerussite, spindle whorl 112
cemetery, Buckland
Anglo-Saxon 15
appearance of 11, 160
'building' within 143, 152, 161
comparable ones 162–8
fences in 153
Kentish 11
lay-out and expansion of 142–5
limits of *14*, 20
orientation and lay-out 152–61, 381
phases of 136–42
plan of *14*, 19–20, 381
plots within 19–20, 126, 134–6, 174–5, 369
small mounds over graves 160, 161
track through *144*, 145, 161
*see also* phases and plots
chain
bronze with comb-case 119, *120*
bronze with keys 250, *332*
bronze with workbox 109
iron 221, 250, *285*
iron with beads 67, 69, 230, *298*
chalk 11, 13
lumps in graves 17
pebbles 122, 215
spindle whorl 112–3

chank shell (*Xancus pyrum*), in jewellery 44–5
charcoal 19, 196, 216
Christianity 18, 33, 51, 121, 143, 150, 153, 160, 171, 173, 174
symbols, cross 122, 134
others 33, 34, 42, 43, 46, 55, 56, 108, 173, 226, 235, 239, 240, 243
churches, founding of 173, 177
claw-beakers 11, 53, 96–7, 171, 172, 221, 268, *284*, 385
colours 97
dating 97
distribution 97
clench bolts, iron 15, 99, 247, *327*
clothing 69, 82, 84, 90–91, 195
Clovis 143
coffins 17, 19, 27, 99–100
bars, iron 99, 250, *331*
clamps 19, 99
fittings 11, 99–100, 228, 252, *295, 334*
strip and rivets, iron 99–100
coins 22, 39, 41, 47, 55, 136, 143
deposition in graves 51
Merovingian gold 169
mounted with loop 49, 51, 241, *320*
perforated Roman 49, 57, 181, 219, 244, 248, *281, 324, 329*
post-Roman dating 136
Roman 99, 120, 122, 136, 171, 180–1, 219, *282*
report on coins 180–1
sceattas 135, 142, 143, 145, 181, 241, *320*
used as weights 120, 180, 272, *273, 274*
combs, bone 106, 119–20, 229, 240, *297*
bronze plate on 119
and case 119, *120*, 135, 241, *320*
composite 119, 224, *289*
composition, white, objects made from *58*, 59, 60–1, 62, 66, 67
*see also* apatite, cristobalite, magnesium carbonate, meerschaum
cone-beakers 11, 94, 96, 98, 134, 141
dating 96
imported 96
Kempston-type 11, 94, 98, 137, 171, 222, 228, 267, *285, 294*, 384
analysis of K-type 95–6
dist. of 94–5
colours 94–5
production of 94–5
Snartemo types 95–6
copper, use of
bracteates 52, 53
staining on skulls 198
coral bead *58*, 60, 71, 231, *301*
cord
on sword 238
lacing on belt 91
on scabbard mouths 22–3
suspension of keys 117
cowrie shell 122, 149, 217, *278*
dist. of 270, 388
cristobalite, objects made from 25, 60
cruciform *see* Christianity and ornament
cups, wooden 102, 149
dist. in cem. 365
silver-gilt mount for 170
U-sect. mounts for rim 105, 224, 225, *288, 290*
cushion 29

Danes 142
decoration, types of
beading 22, 38, 43, 214
bone 44

boxed zigzags 43
cabochon 42, 43, 44, 46
cloisonné 43, 44, 46
filigree 46
foil backing 38, 43, 44
garnet *see* sep. entry
inlay 22, 83, 84, 103 *see also* metalwork inlaid
niello *see* sep. entry
shell 38, 41, 42, 43, 44
silver zigzag 38, 39, 46, 219
trefoil cell 43, 46
use of stamps *see* ornament
white paste 38
diamond, iron 118, 119, 134, 137, 141, 216, 217, 218, 219, 221, 223, 227, 230, 231, 233, 235, 248, *276, 279, 281, 284, 287, 293, 298, 300, 305, 328*
dist. in cem. 366
ditches, barrow 13, 15, 179
penannular 17
r. Dour 11, 168, 169, 170, 172
Dover 168–78, *169*
Anglo-Saxon finds in area 175–8, *176*
grave slab with runic inscription 47
monastery at 173, 177
town excavations 92, 169, 170, 171, 177
traffic between – and Continent 174
survival of town name 170

Eadbald 174
Eanswith 174
earscoop, bronze 67, 69, 119
on necklace 118, 225, *290*
earthworms 16
Ethelbert of Kent 143, 160
excavation of cemetery 11–20

finger-rings 86
gold 86, 96, 141, 142, 169, 227, *293*
silver wire 86, 215, *275*
fire-steels, *see* purse-mounts
fish
appliqués on shields 32–4, 172, 173
as Christian symbols 33–4
flax 192, 194, 195, 214
flint, flakes 15
lumps or nodules 17, 18, 19, 27, 145, 215, 217
footwear 90–1
fossils, *cyphosoma* 122, 231, *301*
*porosphaera* *58*, 59, 60, 66, 71, 122
Franks 142, 143, 171–2
Frankish influence/origins 21, 28, 31, 42, 43, 47, 87, 110, 134, 135, 141, 146, 164, 169, 171–2
royal connections 174
fur, animal 31, 196, 225, 228, 231, 237, 238

gaming-counters 122
garnet, use of 35, 38, 41, 43, 44
cabochon 56
cut 56, 141, 215
keystone 42, 43, 47
pendants 53, 56
on pins 83
reused 56
T-shaped 42–3
triangular 41–2
used with glass/shell 56
girdle hangers 39, 117–8
bronze hook and peg on ring 117, 219, *281*
ornamented bronze 117, 244, *324*
Roman balance reused as 135, 136, 243, *321*

INDEX 407

*see also* loops
glass beads   60–7, 135
  amber inset   56
  dist. in cem.   361
  dist. in graves   59
  drawn monochrome   *58*, 62, 66, 75
  Frankish   28
  manufacture of   59, 62, 66
  millefiori   57, 63, 65, 66, 70, 78, 135, 141, 231, *290*
  monochrome   *58*, 61–3, 66, 72–5, 142, 182, 183, *184*, *185*, 187–8
  mosaic   63, *64*, 65, 70, 77, 135, 141
  opacifying agents in   183, 186
  other Anglo-Saxon glass beads   187
  in phases   79–80, 82
  polychrome   63–6, *64*, 69, 76–8, 134, 135, 137, 141, 182–3, 189
  qualitative analyses   182–9
  reticella   23, 33, 57, 59, 60, 62, 65, 66, 67, 69, 70, 78, 134, 238, *314*
  Roman glass *see* Roman survivals
  spherical on pin   84
  sword-bead *see* swords
  types of   *58*, 59, 61
glass vessels   94–9, 134, 149, 174, 219, 230, *282*, *298*
  dist. in cem.   364
*see also* bell, claw and cone-beakers
gold, use of   22, 38, 51–2, 56
  analysis of   181
  content in bracteates   52–3
  in finger-ring   142, 182
graves in cemetery   11, 13, 15, 16
  catalogue   214–53
  chronology and dating   136–42, 143
  classified according to grave-goods   147–50
  content   261–5
  depth   150–2
  destruction of   171
  digging of   152, 156
  discrepancies grave-goods and sex   125–6
  distribution   379
  disturbance   125, 126, 127, 135, 150
  double   17, 126, 146
  figures of grave-goods   272–336
  figures of graves   337–55
  fill of   17–18
  - goods   21–122
  grouping acc. to grave-goods   134–6
  inhumation   17, 143, 173
  isolated   129, 133
  marking of 1   17, 160, 161
  numbering during excavations   13
  orientation of   16, 20, 142, 143, 150, 152–60, *157*, *158*, *159*, 380
  plots *see* cemetery and plots
  positions of grave furniture   18–19, 21
  related to social status   150–2
  shape of   16–17, 135
  superimposed   17, 20, 125, 135, 137, 142
Grave B   214, *272*
Grave C   11, 13, *14*, 22, 23–4, *24*, 25, 27, 28, 31, 32, 34, 45, 90, 120–1, 122, 123, 135, 146, 152, 180, 193, 196, 214–5, *272*, *273*, *274*, *337*, date of 141
Grave D   13, *14*, 15, 87, 123, 134, 153, 215, *274*
Grave E   *14*, 150, 215
Grave F   13, *14*, 17, 18, 39, *40*, 43–4, 45, 62, 67, *68*, 69, 83, 86, 101, 117, 121, 123, 126, 143, 146, 193, 215, *275*, *337*, date of 141
Grave 1   *14*, 15, 39, *40*, 41, 42, 43, 44, *50*, 52, 53, 55, 56, 61, 62, 67, *68*, 69, 83, 85, 116, 118, 119, 121, 123, 143, 146, 150, 181, 190, 198, 215–6, *275*, *276*, *337*, date of 141
Grave 2   *14*, 216
Grave 3   *14*, 15, 34, 123, 125, 198, 216, *277*, *337*, date of 141
Grave 4   *14*, 15, 27, 29, 90, 123, 153, 190, 198, 216–7, *277*, *337*
Grave 6   13, *14*, 18, 56, 60, 62, 84, 97–8, 112, 116, 119, 122, 123, 149, 196, 217, *278*, *337*, date of 141
Grave 7   13, *14*, 15, 16, 217
Grave 8   13, *14*, 17, 18, 19, 27, *28*, 29, 89, 123, 134, 152, 190, 196, 217, *279*, *337*, date of 141
Grave 9   13, *14*, 19, 26, 28, 29, 89, 90, 123, 134, 152, 190, 197, 217, *279*, 338
Grave 10   13, *14*, 17, 20, 26, 28, 29, 82, 83, 114, 123, 134, 149, 190, 217, *279*, 338, date of 141
Grave 11   13, *14*, 15, 20, 122, 123, 145, 153, 217, *279*, 338
Grave 12   *14*, 17, 18, 62, 63, 90, 118, 119, 123, 134, 137, 218, *279*, 338, date of 137
Grave 13   13, *14*, 15, 16, 19, 20, 35–7, 39, 45–6, 49, 60, 63, 67, *68*, 69, 70, 101, 117, 123, 134, 146, 171, 190, 194, 218, *280*, 338, date of 137
Grave 14   *14*, 15, 25, 34, 37–8, 39, *40*, 41, 44, 45, 49, 60, 62, 67, *68*, 69, 90, 115, 117, 118, 119, 122, 123, 125, 126, 146, 152, 190, 198, 219, *281*, *338*, date of 137
Grave 15   *14*, 19, 20, 27, 85, 87, 89, 99, 114, 122, 123, 125, 126, 134, 198, 219–20, *281*, *282*, *338*, date of 137
Grave 16   *14*, 18, 123, 220, *282*, 338
Grave 17   *14*, 17, 18, 123, 220, *282*, *339*
Grave 18   *14*, 15, 19, 62, 83, 90, 123, 134, 137, 142, 146, 152, 220, *282*, *339*, date of 137
Grave 19   *14*, 19, 20, 105, 137, 142, 220, *282*, *339*
Grave 20   11, *14*, 25, *36*, 38–9, 43, 47, *50*, 51, 53, 60, 67, *68*, 69, 83, 85, 87, 89, 91, *91*, 97, 100, 111, 112, 117, 118, 119, 124, 137, 142, 149, 171, 181, 190, 196, 220–1, *283*, *284*, *340*, date of 137
Grave 21   *14*, 15, 16, 39, 89, 112, 124, 134, 137, 142, 146, 160, 198, 221, *285*, *340*, date of 137
Grave 22   11, *14*, 19, 21, 24, 25, 27, 28, 29, 94, 124, 129, 134, 137, 142, 146, 150, 171, 190, 194, 195, 198, 222, *285*, *340*, date of 137
Grave 23   *14*, 15, 17, 47, 63, 124, 142, 146, 222, *286*, *340*, date of 137
Grave 24   *14*, 124, 222
Grave 25   *14*, 20, 124, 149, 150, 222, *340*, date of 141
Grave 26   13, *14*, 20, 124, 222
Grave 27   *14*, 15, 20, 23, 24, *24*, 25, 26, 28, 31, 32, 35, 90, 124, 134, 153, 190, 195, 222, *286*, *340*, date of 141
Grave 28   *14*, 16, 89, 104, 117, 119, 124, 190, 196, 198, 222–3, *223*, *287*, *340*, date of 137
Grave 29   *14*, 22, 39, *40*, 42–3, 44, 45, 49, *50*, 53, 54, 55, 56, 62, 65, 67, *68*, 69, 98, 100, 101, 103, 105, 116, 117, 119, 123, 124, 134, 136, 141, 181, 191, 223–4, *288*, *340*, date of 141
Grave 30   *14*, 39, *40*, 41, 44, 45, 56, 62, 63, 67, *68*, 69, 70, 83, 87, 89, 116, 119, 120, 123, 124, 125, 126, 134, 141, 150, 197, 198, 224–5, *289*, *340*, date of 141
date of 141
Grave 31   13, *14*, 16, 20, 225
Grave 32   *14*, 16, 39, *40*, 41, 43, 44, 55, 62, 67, 84, 101, 102, 105, 118, 119, 123, 124, 134, 135, 150, 225, *390*, *340*, date of 141
Grave 33   *14*, 19, 21, 25, 27, 28, 82, 90, 114, 123, 124, 125, 126, 225–6, *291*, *341*, date of 141
Grave 34   *14*, 19, 124, 134, 191, 196, 226, *291*, *341*, date of 141
Grave 35   *14*, 19, 39, *40*, 41, 42, 43, 44, 55, 56, 65, 67, *68*, 69, 84, 98, 100, 101, 102, 106, 116, 117, 124, 134, 135, 150, 191, 226, *292*, *341*, date of 141
Grave 36   *14*, 20, 124, 129, 153, 191, 226, *291*, 341
Grave 37   *14*, 20, 43, 124, 153, 198, 226, *291*, 341
Grave 38   *14*, 20, 39, *40*, 41, 42, 44, 45, 55, 62, 65, 67, *68*, 83, 86, 89, 96, 111, 112, 114, 116, 118, 124, 135, 143, 146, 152, 153, 182, 196, 226–7, *227*, *293*, *294*, *341*, date of 141
Grave 39   *14*, 20, 27, 28, 29, 31, 32, 35, 124, 135, 228, *294*, *341*, date of 141
Grave 40   *14*, 16, 124, 228, *294*, *341*
Grave 41   11, 13, *14*, 20, 21, 25, 26, 27, 28, 39, 99, 110, 115, 118, 119, 124, 129, 135, 146, 191, 228, *295*, 342
Grave 42   *14*, 20, 23, 65, 67, *68*, 70, 83, 87, 89, 114, 124, 153, 222–9, *295*, *296*, *342*, date of 141
Grave 43   11, *14*, 18, 84, 92–3, 94, 101, *102*, 102, 103, 124, 134, 172, 191, 194, 229, *296*, *342*, date of 141
Grave 44   *14*, 16, 20, 39, 83, 101, 116, 119, 124, 127, 134, 191, 194, 229, *297*, *342*, date of 141
Grave 45   *14*, 19, 137, 143, 150, 229
Grave 46   *14*, 19, 62, 65, 111, 112, 119, 124, 134, 137, 142, 146, 229, *297*, *342*
Grave 47   13, *14*, 16, 229
Grave 48   *14*, 19, 47–8, 62, 67, *68*, 69, 86, 92, 98–9, 104, 112, 115, 118, 124, 137, 142, 146, 150, 171, 191, 195, 196, 229–30, *298*, *342*, date of 137
Grave 49   *14*, 16, 19, 62, 99, 124, 137, 142, 230, *299*, *342*, date of 137
Grave 50   *14*, 26, 28, 82, 89, 114, 123, 124, 125, 126, 134, 149, 230, *299*, *342*, date of 137
Grave 51   13, *14*, 16, 230
Grave 52   *14*, 20, 89, 124, 135, 147, 152, 230–1, *299*, *342*, date of 141
Grave 53   *14*, 20, 60, 62, 65, 104, 111, 116, 118, 124, 135, 152, 191, 195, 198, 231, *299*, *300*, *343*, date of 141
Grave 54   *14*, 20, 116, 117, 123, 124, 125, 126, 152, 191, 231, *300*, *343*
Grave 55   *14*, 20, 60, 62, 67, *68*, 69, 100, 101, 105, 116, 122, 124, 135, 152, 191, 198, 231, *301*, *343*, date of 141
Grave 56   *14*, 21, 25, 26, 28, 29, 31, 32, 35, 39, 87, *88*, 114, 124, 146, 153, 171, 191, 198, 231–3, *302*, *343*, date of 142
Grave 57   *14*, 17, 26, 28, 29, 30, 90, 124, 153, 191, 232, *303*, *343*, date of 142
Grave 58   *14*, 17, 20, 116, 117, 123, 124, 125, 126, 135, 152, 232, *303*, *343*, date of 141
Grave 59   *14*, 17, 20, 39, *40*, 41, 44, 45, 63, 67, *68*, 69, 70, 84, 98, 100, 101, 124, 135, 141, 152, 191, 232–3, *304*, *343*, date of 141
Grave 60   *14*, 15, 16, 17, 18, 20, 65, 67,

408                                                                INDEX

68, 69, 84, 100, 101, 102, 103, 112, 116, 118, 122, 124, 133, 135, 141, 152, 233, *305, 344*, date of 141

Grave 61   *14*, 20, 26, 28, 90, 123, 124, 125, 126, 135, 137, 152, 191, 233–4, *306, 344*, date of 141

Grave 62   *14*, 16, 20, 62, 67, *68*, 69, 83, 119, 124, 135, 152, 191, 197, 198, 234, *306, 344*, date of 141

Grave 63   *14*, 20, 26, 28, 90, 124, 135, 152, 234, *307, 344*, date of 141

Grave 64   *14*, 15, 16, 20, 114, 115, 119, 124, 135, 147, 152, 234, *307, 344*, date of 141

Grave 65   11, *14*, 16–17, 20, 26, 28, 29, 31, 39, 87, 110, 114, 118, 124, 135, 149, 152, 171, 191, 234, *307, 344*, date of 141

Grave 66   *14*, 15, 62, 123, 124, 125, 126, 135, 149, 152, 191, 234, *308, 344*, date of 141

Grave 67   *14*, 18, 20, 55, 60, 61, 62, 69–70, 85, 122, 124, 127, 133, 135, 143, 149, 152, 234–5, *308, 344*, date of 141

Grave 68   *14*, 124, 129, 133, 149, 150, 235, *345*

Grave 69   *14*, 15, 124, 127, 153, 235, *345*

Grave 70   *14*, 19, 137, 146, 235, *345*

Grave 71   *14*, 20, 21, 23, 25, 26, 28, 29, 31, 32, 33, 35, 124, 127, 135, 146, 235, *305, 345*, date of 141

Grave 72   *14*, 15, 20, 124, 150, 152, 153, 235, *345*

Grave 73   *14*, 5, 20, 124, 135, 146, 147, 150, 152, 153, 235, *345*

Grave 74   *14*, 124, 235, *309, 345*

Grave 75   *14*, 16, 45, 60, 112, 113, 117, 118, 123, 124, 126, 135, 191, 235–6, *309, 345*

Grave 76   *14*, 124, 236, *310, 345*

Grave 77   *14*, 124, 152, 236, *310, 346*

Grave 78   *14*, 82, 83, 124, 236, *310, 346*

Grave 79   *14*, 124, 152, 236, *310, 346*

Grave 80   *14*, 124, 129, 135, 146, 147, 152, 236, *310, 346*

Grave 81   *14*, 19, 100, 101, 103, 116, 124, 146, 152, 198, 236, *310, 346*

Grave 82   *14*, 124, 146, 153, 160, 191, 236, *310, 346*

Grave 83   *14*, 19, 62, 63, 70, 83, 124, 135, 146, 236, *310, 346*

Grave 84   *14*, 107, 108, 113, 124, 236, *311, 346*

Grave 85   *14*, 18, 90, 124, 236, *311, 346*

Grave 86   13, *14*, 15, 16, 20, 152, 236

Grave 87   *14*, 19, 27, 28, 29, 92, 93, 94, 123, 124, 125, 126, 134, 137, 142, 149, 171, 179, 236–7, *311, 347*, date of 137

Grave 88   *14*, 15, 19, 124, 137, 142, 237, *347*

Grave 89   *14*, 124, 137, 237, *347*

Grave 90   *14*, 19, 26, 28, 29, 32, 35, 105, 124, 134, 137, 141, 145, 149, 160, 237, *311, 347*

Grave 91   *14*, 19, 20, 21, 25, 26, 28, 32, 33, 34, 35, 87, 89, 115, 124, 134, 146, 150, 171, 196, 237, *312, 347*

Grave 92   *14*, 15, 19, *40*, 14, 44, 47, 60, 62, 63, 65, 67, *68*, 69, 70, 87, 119, 124, 137, 142, 146, 192, 198, 237–8, *313, 347*, date of 137

Grave 93   11, *14*, 20, 21, 23, 24, 25, 26, 27, 28, 29, 31, 32, *33*, 34, 35, 65, 70, 90, 123, 124, 125, 126, 129, 134, 146, 196, 238, *314, 347*, date of 141

Grave 94a   *14*, 15, 19, 22, 49, 190, 123, 124, 125, 134, 137, 142, 145, 238, *315, 348*, date of 141

Grave 94b   *14*, 15, 21, 22, 25, 27, 28, 28, 123, 124, 129, 134, 137, 142, 145, 146, 150, 160, 192, 196, 238–9, *315, 348*, date of 137

Grave 95   *14*, 15, 19, 114, 115, 116, 124, 141, 145, 196, 239, *315, 348*

Grave 96   *14*, 17, 18, 146

  96a   21, 22, 23, 25, 26, 28, 29, 32, 34, 35, 39, 82, 87, 89, 124, 129, 133, 135, 192, 239, *316, 348*, date of 141

  96b   21, 23, 24, 25, 26, 28, 29, 82, 114, 124, 125, 126, 129, 133, 135, 192, *194*, 195, 196, 239, *317, 348*, date of 141

Grave 97   *14*, 153, 239, *317*

Grave 98   13, *14*, 21, 22, 25, 27, 32, 35, 45, 87, *88*, 90, 114, 124, 135, 141, 146, 150, 152, 192, 198, 239–40, *317, 318, 348*

Grave 99   *14*, 124, 149, 150, 152, 153, 160, 240, *348*

Grave 100   *14*, 82, 83, 124, 152, 198, 240, *319, 348*

Grave 101   *14*, 20, 82, 83, 119, 124, 152, 240, *319, 348*

Grave 102   *14*, 124, 150, 240, *348*

Grave 103   *14*, 87, 124, 129, 135, 147, 240, *319, 349*

Grave 104   *14*, 124, 240, *319, 349*

Grave 105   *14*, 124, 240, *319, 349*

Grave 106   *14*, 124, 129, 150, 152, 240, *319, 349*

Grave 107   13, *14*, 66, 82, 83, 84, 106, *107*, 108, 112, 118, 119, 123, 124, 126, 135, 150, 169, 192, 194, 196, 240–1, *319, 349*

Grave 108   *14*, 18, 90, 124, 241, *319, 349*

Grave 109   11, *14*, 92, 93, 94, 119, 124, 169, 241, *320, 349*

Grave 110   *14*, 18, 49, 66, 86, 108, 113, 116, 117, 118, 119, *120*, 124, 133, 135, 136, 149, 241, *320, 349*, date of 142

Grave 111   *14*, 99, 124, 149, 241, *321, 350*

Grave 112   *14*, 124, 149, 150, 241, *350*

Grave 113   *14*, 15, 87, 89, 91, 117, 119, 125, 149–50, 192, 195, 241–2, *321, 350*

Grave 114   *14*, 15, 26, 28, 29, 119, 121, 125, 135, 149, 152, 192, 242, *321, 350*

Grave 115   13, *14*, 20, 125, 135, 141, 242, *321, 350*

Grave 116   13, *14*, 20, 117, 125, 135, 136, 242, *321, 350*

Grave 117   *14*, 114, 125, 152, 196, 242, *321, 350*

Grave 118   *14*, 17, 18, 125, 153, 160, 242

Grave 119   *14*, 124, 242, *321, 350*

Grave 120   *14*, 91, 114, 125, 129, 146, 196, 242, *322, 351*

Grave 121   *14*, 15, 16, 20, 100, 117, 119, 125, 149–50, 152, 196, 242, *322, 350*

Grave 122   *14*, 18, 125, 153, 192, 194, 242, *322, 351*

Grave 123   *14*, 18, 125, 242, *322, 351*

Grave 124   *14*, 16, 60, 62, 100, 101, 103, 119, 125, 135, 150, 152, 153, 192, 243, *322, 351*

Grave 125   *14*, 15, 17, 125, 135, 149, 153, 243, *325, 351*

Grave 126   11, *14*, 16, 20, 39, *40*, 43, 44, 45, 46, 125, 134, *323*, date of 141

Grave 127   *14*, 15, 20, 49, 60, 67, *68*, 69, 115, 118, 125, 135, 150, 152, 153, 192, 194, 243, *323, 351*

Grave 128   *14*, 15, 20, 26, 28, 90, 125, 135, 149, 153, 244, *323, 351*

Grave 129   11, *14*, 15, 39, 49, 56, 60, 61, 62, 65, 67, *68*, 69, 85, 90, 91, 93, 117, 122, 125, 135, 149, 152, 153, 193, 244, *324, 351*

Grave 130   *14*, 20, 114, 125, 153, 244, *324, 351*

Grave 131   *14*, 20, 21, 23, 25, 26, 28, 32, 35, 90, 122, 125, 129, 135, 146, 153, 244–5, *325, 352*, date of 141

Grave 132   *14*, 16, 20, 60, 65, 83, 116, 117, 125, 135, 153, 193, 245, *325, 352*

Grave 133   *14*, 20, 60, 61, 62, 70, 125, 153, 245, *326, 352*

Grave 134   *14*, 43, *50*, 53, 54, 55, 56, 60, 62, 67, *68*, 69, 83, 115, 117, 122, 125, 135, 149, 153, 181, 197, 245, *246, 326, 352*

Grave 135   *14*, 16, 17, 20, 26, 28, 90, 99, 125, 135, 197, 198, 245, 246, *327, 352*, date of 141

Grave 136   *14*, 20, 82, 94, 114, 125, 147, 247, *327, 352*

Grave 137   11, *14*, 19, 20, 26, 28, 29, 89, 93, 93, 100, 103–4, 125, 135, 149, 153, 193, 194, 196, 247, *327, 352*

Grave 138   *14*, 82, 83, 84, 112, 117, 122, 125, 135, 196, 247–8, *238, 352*

Grave 139   11, *14*, 19, 27, 28, 30, 93, 94, 111, 118, 125, 135, 153, 180, 193, 195, 248, *328, 353*

Grave 140   *14*, 18, 82, 84, 125, 153, 248, *328, 353*

Grave 141   *14*, 17, 49, 56, 60, 62, 84, 86, 106, 115, 117, 123, 125, 126, 135, 150, 153, 196, 248, *329, 353*

Grave 142   *14*, 83, 115, 116, 117, 123, 125, 126, 135, 193, 194, 248, *329, 353*

Grave 143   *14*, 101, *102*, 102, 103, 125, 153, 196, 248–9, *329, 353*

Grave 144   *14*, 89, 91, 110, 119, 125, 249, *330, 353*

Grave 145   *14*, 17, 110, 115, 125, 129, 133, 135, 152, 153, 249, *330, 353*

Grave 146   *14*, 16, 89, 125, 129, 133, 135, 152, 153, 249, *330, 353*

Grave 147   *14*, 17, 83, 84, 99, 119, 122, 125, 135, 153, 160, 249, *330, 353*

Grave 148   *14*, 90, 110, 125, 193, 194, 198, 249, *330, 354*

Grave 149   *14*, 17, 19, 30, 90, 125, 129, 150, 153, 249, *331, 354*

Grave 150   *14*, 17, 82, 91, 105, 106, 115, 119, 125, 129, 149, 153, 249, *331, 354*

Grave 151   13, *14*, 15, 18, 125, 129, 133, 150, 250, *354*

Grave 152   13, *14*, 16, 125, 250

Grave 153   13, *14*, 16, 125, 250

Grave 154   13, *14*, 16, 18, 125, 250

Grave 155   *14*, 19, 45, 62, 63, 83, 99, 117, 119, 125, 135, 149, 153, 193, 250, *331, 354*

Grave 156   11, *14*, 15, 20, 27, 28, 29, 30, 89, 90, 92, 93, 94, 114, 118, 125, 135, 149, 153, 179, 193, 250, *332, 354*, date of 142

Grave 157   11, *14*, 20, 60, 62, 66, 70, 84, 92, 93, 94, 107, 108, *109*, 110, 111, 119, 122, 125, 135, 149, 153, 169, 193, 250–1, *332, 333, 354*

Grave 158   *14*, 39, 82, 83, 89, 114, 125, 153, 196, 251, *333, 355*

Grave 159   *14*, 90, 125, 153, 251, *333, 355*

Grave 160   *14*, 17, 18, 56, 83, 90, 98, 116, 118, 125, 135, 149, 153, 193, 195, 251, *333, 355*

Grave 161 11, *14*, 17, 18, 63, 83, 84–5, 116, 125, 136, 142, 152, 153, 193, 194, 251–2, *334, 355*, date of 142
Grave 162 11, *14*, 18, 30, 99, 111, 125, 149, 152, 153, 197, 252, *334, 355*
Grave 163 *14*, 17, 18, 19, 125, 136, 153, 352, *334, 355*
Grave 164 *14*, 39, 116, 117, 125, 136, 145, 153, 252, *334, 355*
Grave 165 *14*, 16, 125, 147, 150, 252, *355*
graves, loose finds, annular brooch 16, 49, 253, *336*
graves, unassociated grave-goods
    gold coin pendant 6 49, 134, 136, 141, 181, 252, *335*
    square-headed brooch 9 36, 37–8, 39, *40*, 41, 44, 56, 135, 172, 252–3, *335*
    swords 7 and 8 21, 25, 193, 252, *335*
Grettis-saga 28

hair ornament, bronze pendant 57, 96, 228, *294*
handles
    buckets 104
    wooden boxes 101, 225, 229, 231, 233, 243, 249, *290, 296, 301, 304, 305, 321, 329*
hazel (*Corylus avellana*) 27, 196
helmets, portrayal of 85
hinges, bronze 108, 236, *311*
    iron strips 101
hilts *see* swords
horn, knife grips 114
    knife tangs 196, 239
    seax grips 31
    sword grips 21, 196
hones, *see* whetstones
horse, tooth as keepsake 122, 233, *305*
horseshoe 19, 248, *325*
housing estate, Buckland 11

inlay 22
(*see also* metalwork, niello and various grave-goods)
inscription, runic on brooch 11, *46*, 46–7, 171, 243, *323*
iron, bindings on spear shafts 27, 217, *279*
    diamonds *see* diamonds
    inlay with bronze 22
    shafts, *see also* arrows, awls, rods 234
    staining on skeletons 198
ivory, mounts for casket 170
    rings (bag mouths) 111, 118–9, 125, 126, 227, 231, 236, 251, *276, 293, 300, 309, 333*
    dist. in cem. 366
    list of and map 269–70, 387
    sword guard/grip 21, 196, 238

jewellery, arrangement on body 67–70
    discussion of types 35–92
    gold and garnet – industry 171, 172
    Kentish–workshop 174
    *see under* beads, brooches, bracelets, bracteates, buckles, finger-rings, pendants, pins
Jutes 142, 171
Jutland 17

keepsakes 121–2
Kentish Rag stone 111, 197
keys 111, 116–7, 125, 126, 127, 134, 135, 149
    associated with ivory rings 118
    bronze 116, 231, *300*
    dist. in cem. 368

L-shaped 101, 116, 145
    suspension of 49, 90, 119, 223
    T-shaped 100, 101, 116–7
    textile impression (stitched seam) 195, 242
knives 15, 19, 29, 30, 82, 84, 95, 104, 110, 111, *113*, 113–16, 118, 121, 125, 126, 127, 134, 135, 145, 149, 150, 160
    bronze inlay on 114, 239, *318*
    dating of 115
    dist. in cem. 113, 367
    dist. by sex 116
    iron guard plate 114
    knife sheaths 89, 90, 115, 228, 248, 249
    organic covering on tang 114
    ornamental handle 114, 196, 251, *333*
    position of – in grave 115, *223*
    suspension of 115, 249
    types of 113, *113*, 115
    welding line on 114, 253

lead 70, 112
leather 23, 196, 221, 243
    containers 90
    key suspension 117, 223
    scabbard covering 239
    sheaths for knives 87, 115, 228, 245, 248
    seaxes 31
    shield covering 35
    strap for knife 249
    thongs 119
    workbox 108
Leovigild, gold tremissis 49, 181
lid, bone 107, 108–110, *109*
lighthouse, Roman 170
    used for grave orientation 156, *169*
lime (*Tilia* sp.) 86, 196
linen cloth 194
Liudhard, Bishop 143, 174
locks 100–1, *101, 102*
    iron 19, 215, 224, 225, 226, 233, 236, 243, *275, 288, 290, 292, 305, 310, 321*
Long Hill, Buckland, Dover 11, *12*, 161, *162*, 170, 172, *176*, 173–4
loomweights 169, 177
loops, S-shaped
    bronze 117, 135, 241, 247, 248, 252, *320, 328, 329, 334*
    iron 117, 223, 236, *287, 310*
    textile impression on 121
lyre fragments, bronze 29, 119, 121, 149, 152, 242, *321*

magnesite 25
magnesium carbonate, objects made from 25, 60, 71
manganese 70
maple (*Acer campestre*) 22, 27, 105, 121, 196, 214, 217, 238
?mattock 110
meerschaum 25, 61
mercenaries 174
Merovingian coins 169, 177
metal, white 87
metal, yellow 117
metalwork, inlaid 170–1, 174
midwifery 113
monastery, founding 173
Mount Badon 143

nails, disc-headed 99, 241, 252, *334*
necklaces 15, 17, 18, 25, 45, 49, 57, 98, 113, 122, (216, 217, 218–19, 219, 220, 223–4, 224, 225, 226, 228–9, 229, 230, 231, 232–3, 233, 234, 235, 237, 241, 243, 244, 245, 250, *276,

*278, 280, 281, 283, 288, 289, 290, 292, 295, 297, 298, 301, 304, 305, 306, 308, 309, 313, 320, 323, 324, 325, 326, 332*)
    bronze miniature spoon on 118
    found in container 66
    make-up 65–6
    position on body 67–70
    white beads in 25
needles 106
    bronze sewing 112, 247, *328*
niello 22, 38, 39, 43, 45–6, 214, 215, 216, 219, 220, 221, 223
    acanthite (silver sulphide) 45
    galena (lead) 45
    jalpaite 22
    stromeyerite (sulphides of silver and copper) 45

oak (*Quercus* sp.) 27, 100, 106, 196, 242, 247
Odin 85, 145
Old Park, Dover, probable cemetery *12*, 170, 175, *176*
organic materials,
    associated with iron 196
ornament, animal 35–7, *36*, 38, *50*, 51–5, 89, 218, 230, 224, *283, 287*
    beaded bodies 53, 224
    on bracteates 51–5
    human masks in 35, 36, 37, 38–9, 48, 54–5, 218
    Quoit Brooch style 54, 164, 171, 174
    Style I 35, 41, 53, 54, 89, 141, 219, 220, 221, 226, 232, 237, 252
    Style II 42, 43, 53, 135, 142, 171
ornament designs/patterns
    chip-carved 41, 43, 47–8, 89, 219, 224, 225, 226, 227, 230, 237
    cross/cruciform 33, 34, 42, 43, 46, *46*, 51, 55, 56, 108, 173, 232
    key 22
    punched 55, 56, 232
    repoussé dots 105, 223, 224, 235, 240
    ring and dot 29, 39, 54, 83, 87, 118, 119, 214, 219, 224, 229, 232, 241, 244, 251, 252, *289, 297*
    spirals 47–8
    use of stamps 39, 83, 87, 224, 227, 232, 238
    zigzags, niello 22, 38, 39, 43, 46, 215, 216, 219, 220, 221, 225, 226, 232, 239, 243, 232–3

paganism 85, 142, 143, 145, 153, 172
palm cups, glass 98, 135, 142, 171, 251, *333*
pattern-welding,
    knife 114
    weaving battens 111
    *see also* swords
paste, white, use of 38
pelta motif 56
pendants
    animal ornament on *see* bracteates
    bar - 57, 235, *308*
    bronze 57, 224
    coin loops for 49, 51, 57, 241, *320*
    Christian cross 55–6, 57, 70, 135, 343, 173, 235, *308*
    disc-shaped, silver 55–6, 57, 70, 227, *293*
    dist. in cem. 359
    garnet 18, 53, 55, 56, 57, 67, 70, 98, 134, 135, 141, 142, 149, 224, 245, *288, 326*
    garnet cabochon 142, 251, *333*
    glass 57, 171, 217, *278*

gold   67, 170, 224, *288, 335*
mushroom-shaped, silver   67, 105, 224, *288*
perforated coins   49, 57, 67, 134, 181
shell   56–7, 135, 248, *329*
like shields   55–6
silver   56, 225, 235, *289*
silver-gilt   18, 67
stamped ornament on   39
phases within cemetery   136–75
   graves assigned to specific phases   175
   phase 1   137, *138*, 143, 145, 150, 152, 154, 160, 171, 172, plan 372
   phase 2   137, *138*, 143, 145, 150, 152, 154, 160, 171, 172, plan 373
   phase 3   *139*, 141, 142, 143, 145–6, 150, 152, 154, 160, 171, 172, 173, 174, plan 374
   phase 4   *139*, 141, 142, 146, 150, 152, 160, 171, 173, 174, plan 375
   phase 5   *140*, 141, 142, 146, 150, 171, 174, plan 376
   phase 6   141, 142, 146, 150, 152, 160, 171, plan 377
   phase 7   *140*, 142, 145, 146, 150, 152, 160, 171, plan 378
pins,
   anthropomorphic (helmeted)   11, 84–5, *84*, 136, 142, 171, 251, *334*
   bone   84
   bronze   67, 82, 215, 220, 227, 229, 234, 247, 306, *275, 282, 293, 296, 328*
   decorated iron   84, 125
   dist. in cem.   362
   dressmaking   84, 106, 112, 247, *328*
   in female graves   82
   flat disc head, bronze   83, 141, 235, 217, 236, 240, 245, 248, 249, *275, 279, 310, 319, 325, 329, 330*
   iron   225, *291*
   with glass head   250, *332*
   'hipped' pin shafts   83
   hipped silver   53, 136, 142
   iron   66, 84, 217, 229, 232, 233, 247, 248, 249, *278, 296, 304, 305, 327, 328, 329, 330, 331*
   iron, coiled head   82, 134, 225, 226, 230, 239, *290, 292, 299, 316, 317*
   knobbed head   83–4, 236, 240, 241, *310, 319*
   in male graves   82
   position of – on body   82
   silver   67, 82, 83, 135, 149, 230, *283*
   silver, bird's head   224, *289*
   silver, double axe-head   83, 251, *355*
   silver with garnets   83, 245, 251, *326, 334*
   silver with shell and garnet cabochon   83, 136, 250, *331*
   stamped ornament on   39, 83, 229, *297*
pipe, clay   16, 217
pit, medieval reburial   99
   Romano-British   15, 20, 145, 217–18, *338*
'Plots' within cemetery   19–20, 134–6, 369
   list of graves within each plot   174–5
   in relation to phases   136–42
   Plot A   17, 18, 19, 20, 57, 63, 85, 114, 118, 126, 134, 136, 137, 141, 142–3, 145, 149, 150, 152, 154, 160, 171, 173
   Plot B   19–20, 57, 63, 94, 103, 114, 121, 126, 134, 136, 141, 143, 145, 146, 149, 150, 152, 153, 160, 173
   Plot C   18, 20, 60, 114, 134, 136, 141, 143, 145, 146, 150, 173

Plot D   18, 20, 57, 62, 63, 103, 121, 126, 134–5, 136, 141, 143, 145, 145–6, 150, 152, 173
Plot E   20, 57, 60, 62, 63, 103, 126, 135, 136, 141, 143, 146, 147, 150, 152, 153, 173
Plot F   20, 57, 62, 63, 114, 126, 129, 135, 136, 141, 143, 146, 147, 150, 152, 153
Plot G   20, 60, 62, 63, 85, 94, 111, 114, 129, 135, 136, 141, 142, 145, 149, 150, 153
Plot H   18, 20, 60, 62, 63, 86, 94, 103, 126, 135, 136, 142, 143, 146, 149, 150, 152, 161
Plot I   17, 18, 20, 60, 63, 135, 136, 137, 142, 143, 145, 146, 147, 149, 150, 152, 153, 161
Plot J and K   20, 103, 114, 129, 135–6, 142, 143, 145, 146, 149, 153
Plot L   18, 20, 63, 136, 142, 143, 144, 146, 153, 161
Plot M and N   20, 136, 137, 142, 143, 144, 146, 147, 161
pommels, *see* swords
poplar (*Populus* sp.)   22, 31, 114, 196
post-holes   15, 143
   orientation of cemetery on   152–3
   p-h X   15, 20, 145, 152, 156, 161, 168
   p-h Y   15, 20, 152, 156, 161, 168
   p-h Z   15, 20, 152, 154, 156, 160, 161
pottery, Anglo-Saxon   92–4, 172
   analysis of   93–4
   Anglian   134, 171, 172
   biconical   43
   biconical bowl   93
   bottles   92–3
   dating   94
   designs on   92
   dist. in cem.   364
   domestic or funerary   94
   fabric   92, 93–4
   Frankish wheelthrown   169, 171–2
   hand-made   92, 134, 137, 169, 179, 236–7, *311*
   imported   94, 169, 171
   petrology   179–80
   wheel-thrown   11, 92–4, 134, 135, 142, 169, 172, 179–80
pottery, medieval   15, 18, 94, 250, 252
   prehistoric   15, 18, 179, 242, 250
   Romano-British   15, 218
   spindle whorl made from   112, 233
Priory Hill, Dover   *12*, 169, *169*, 172, 175, *176*
purse *see also* bags   98, 119
purse-mounts (fire-steels)   110–11, 119, 127, 228, 231, 248, *250, 295, 300, 328, 332*
   dist. in cem.   366
pyrites, iron   18, 122

quiver   30

radiography, use of   24–6, 111
railway cutting   11, *12*, 15
reticella, *see* glass beads
rings   19, 69
   bronze   119, 216, 222, 236, 238, *276, 285, 310, 313*
   finger-rings *see* finger-rings
   iron   119, 216, 218, 223, *223*, 238, 243, 252, *276, 279, 287, 313, 323, 334*
   iron with bronze tab   232, *303*
   penannular   241, 320
   silver   67, 119, 135
   slip-knot, bronze   219, *281*
   slip-knot, silver with beads   65–6, 67, 94, 119, 224, 226, 241, 250, *288, 292, 320, 332*
   on swords *see* swords
   yellow metal with tab   252, *334*
ring-and-dot motif on
   belt mounts   232
   brooch   219, 252
   buckles   251
   comb-case   119, 241
   girdle hanger   244
   suspension ring and tab   252
   sword pommel   214
   tweezers   118, 228, 229, *289, 297*
ring-and-swastika motif
   inlay on spear blade   29, 134
ring sword, *see* swords
rivets,
   assoc. with iron diamond   118
   bronze on leather sheath   115
   disc-headed   32, 87
   dome-headed   21
   dome-headed, gold   22
   fastening bronze strip   121
   iron with bronze washer   219, *280*
   iron with bone   119
   shoe-shaped, *see* buckles
   silvered   22, 137
roads, Roman   161, 168–9, 170
rods   238, *314*
   iron, linked   113, 242, *322*
   for key suspension   117, 223, *223*, 245, *246*, 248, 250, *287, 325, 326, 328, 332*
Roman, survival of objects   49, 60, 62, 70, 171, 230
   bowl, bronze   103
   glass   98–9, 104, 137, 219, 230, *298*
   glass-making tradition   95, 96
   hook and peg (weighing equipment)   117–18, 141, 242, *321*
   pot   112, 233
   spindle whorl   112, 230
fam. *Rosaceae*   196, 226
runes   11, 26, 46–7, 171

St. Augustine   143, 171, 173
St Cuthbert's pectoral cross   45, 83
satchel, leather   120
Saxons   142, 169–70, 171
scabbards   22–4
   Anglo-Saxon mount types   23
   binding strips   23
   buttons and beads on   *24*, 24–5, 222, 238, *286*
   lined with fur   22, 196, 214, 238
   metal bindings   23, *24*, 214, 239, *317*
   mouths   22–3, 238
   wooden   22, 196, 222, 228, 238, 239, 244
scale, *see* balance
sceattas, mounted as pendants, *see* coins and pendants
seaxes   11, 28, 29, 31, 110, 113, 114, 134, 135, *139*, 149, 152, 171, 234, 238, *307, 314*
   dist. in cem.   356
   inlaid guard   238, *314*
   pommel   30, 234
   sheath   31
seeds   16, 197
settlement, Germanic peoples   170–1
shale   112
sharpening steels   110, 234, 249, *307, 330*
shears   113, 126, 135, 142, 235, 236, 241, *309, 310, 320*
sheaths, *see* knives, seaxes, scabbards, swords
shell, beads *see* beads

use in jewellery 38, 44, 56–7, 59, 60, 66, 67, 215, 219, 220
sherds, *see* pottery
shields 18, 29, 31–5, 134, 135, 345, 360
   appliqués, iron 32, *33*, 172, 222, 235, 238, *286*, *309*, *311*
   appliqués, silver plating on 32–3, 134, 238, *311*
   boss 11, 15, 19, 31–2, 35, 125, 134, 135, 214, 216, 222, 228, 231–3, 235, 237, 238, 239, *274*, *277*, *286*, *294*, *302*, *309*, *311*, *312*, *314*, *316*, *318*
   buckles 32, 35, 90
   construction 34–5
   decoration on 32–4
   diameters 35
   discs, iron 32, 239, *318*
   disc-headed rivets, bronze 34
      iron 32, 141, 214, 228, 244, *274*
   dist. in cem. 357
   grips 34, 141, 215, 216, 237, 239, *274*, *277*, *312*, *316*
   leather covering 35
   position in grave 32, 35, 222
   strap-grips 32, 141, 222, 228, 232, 235, 237, 239, *302*, *309*, *311*, *318*
   thickness 34–5
shoe laces, strap tags 90, 135, 142, 149, 242, 249, 250, 251, *321*, *322*, *330*, *331*, *333*
silver,
   analysis of in sceattas 56, 181
   beads *see* beads
   content in bracteates 52, 53
   gilt 21, 22, 35, 37
   inlay on pin 85
skeletons 11, 13, 15, 16, 197–201
   adult or child 126–7
   age at death 127–8, 129
   analysis of graves BCDEF 1–19 123
      20–112 124
      113–165 125
   arthritis 199
   complete 130–1
   defective 131–2
   discrepancies sex/grave-goods 125–6
   female 130–1, 132, 133
   graves figured 337–55
   health of 127
   height 126–7, 200
   infant mortality 146
   juvenile 131, 132, 133
   male 130, 131, 133
   morphology 198
   pathology 199
   position of bones 18, 127, 129–34, 371
   prone 133–4
   sex 123–5, 200, 370
   skull staining by metal 198
   state of preservation 15, 123, 127, 197–8, 237, *338*
   supine 129, 133
   variant positions 129, 133
slaves 150
spatulas, bronze 117, 244, *324*
spears/spearheads 11, 15, 17, 19, 26–30, 110, 125, 127, 135, 145, 149, 150, 152, 160, 196, 214, 216, 217, 222, 225, 228, 230, 231, 232, 234, 235, 236, 237, 239, 243, 244, 247, 250, *272*, *277*, *279*, *286*, *291*, *294*, *295*, *299*, *302*, *303*, *306*, *307*, *309*, *311*, *312*, *316*, *317*, *321*, *323*, *325*, *327*, *332*
   dating 39–40
   decorated 21
   as display weapons 37–8, *28*
   dist. in cem. 356

ferrules 19, 95, 125, 127, 134
   hollow conical 28, 214, 222, 228, 231, 234, 236, 237, 238, 253, *272*, *285*, *286*, *295*, *302*, *307*, *311*, *312*, *336*
   ferrules, solid conical 28, 247, *327*
   inlay on blade 26, 29, 134, 137, 171, 238, *314*
   on ferrule 29, 239, *315*
   on socket 28–9, 95, 222, *285*
   length 28
   in phases of cem. 29–30
   position in graves 28, 121, 171, 217
   sockets 16, 28–9, 95, 124, 149, 171, 217, 230, 238, *277*, *299*, *315*
   shaft binding 239, *317*
   shafts broken 28
   shaft rings 29, 119, 222, 235, 238, *309*
   small, in juvenile graves 27, 248, *325*
   textile impressions on 29, 82, 194, 216
   types of 26–7
   wrapped in cloth 82–3, 194–5
spindle whorls 112–13, 122, 149, 217, 221, 233, *278*, *285*, *305*
   lead 112, 137, 171, 230, *298*
spoons 118
   miniature *see* earscoop
   iron 113, 117, 118, 236, 241, 243, *309*, *320*, *323*
staples, ring-headed 101, *102*
Stebbing, W P B 11
stone
   beads *see* beads
   fossils *see* fossils
   pebbles, disc-shaped 122, 249, *330*
   sandstone 122, 215, *274*
straps 23, 30, 117
   ends 87, 125, 135, 142, 149
   keeled 90, 219, 226, 240, *281*, *291*, *318*
   keyhole-shaped 90–1, 94
   mounts 90, 231, *303*
   legging tags 90
stretcher 19, 99
strips, bronze
   fastenings for lyre 121
   flat 230, 239, *298*, *315*
   for sheaths 115, 219, *281*
stud, bronze with silver disc 219, *281*
Sussex 172, 174
swords 15, 19, 21–6, 29, 95, 171, 222, 225, 228, 231, 235, 237, 238, 239, 244, *285*, *291*, *295*, *302*, *309*, *312*, *314*, *315*, *316*, *317*, *325*
   beads 23, 70, 134, 238, *314*
   belts 21, 25
   buckles 90
   buttons on *24*, 24–5, 61
   fittings, bronze 21, 235, 238, *309*, *314*
   iron 22
   silver 238, 239
   silver gilt 21
   graves 29, 35, 125
   grips 21, 45
   gold-topped rivets on 22, 134, 145
   guards 21–2, 238, 239, 244
   hilts 15
   inlaid rings on guards 25–6, 28, 45, 141
   Kentish 22
   loops 22
   measurements 21
   parallels 22
   pattern-welding 25, 171, 222, 225, 231, 235, 237, 238, 239, 244
   plates, silver gilt 21
   pommels, bronze 22, 23
   cocked-hat 22, 23, 172, 214, *272*

   decorated 21, 45
   iron 21, 22, 222, 225, 235, 238, 239
   Kentish cocked-hat series 22
   ring 141
   ring sword 3, 11, 22, 45, 141, 146, 214, *272*
   sleeve bands 22, 141, 239, *317*
   suspension of 25
   tang 15, 21, 216, *277*

tag-ends, *see* shoe-laces and straps
teeth, animal 122
teeth, human 16
   caries 198–9, 201
   morphology 198
   pathology 201
   preservation 197–8
   staining 198
textiles 190–5
   braids 194
   container 90
   impressions on awl 217
   band on knife 114
   buckle 193, 215, 232
   chalk in bucket 231
   impressions on 'chatelaine' 244
      iron loop 119
      lining of leather sheath 115, 228
      lock 224
      pins 82, 84
      shield grips 35, 237
      spears 29, 82, 216, 217, 234
      workbox 106, 194, 240
   pile weaves 195
   tabby-weave 194–5
   tablet weaves 194
   twill-weaves 194
thong terminals, bronze 91, 244, 249, *324*, *330*
   leather 117, 119
   single iron 91
tinder pouch, *see* purse-mount/firesteel 111
toggles 69
   white bead 70, 91
toilet instrument sets 84
tools 110–11
tweezers 84–5, 110, 118, 119, 126, 149
   bronze 118, 228, 234, *295*, *307*
   iron 23, 118, 240, 250, *319*, *332*
   in male weapon graves 118
   stamped ornament on 39, 118, 234
twine 35, 252

vessel, turned wooden 105–6
   mending plates, metal 105

weapons, dist. in cem. 356
*see* spears, swords etc
weaving equipment 111–13
   battens, iron 19, 96, 111–12, 119, 134, 141, 220, 228, 229, *283*, *294*, *297*
   dist. in cem. 356
   pick, bone 112, 113, 118, 126, 236, *309*
weights 11, 120, 180, 214, *273*, *274*
   Roman coins used as 120, 180
wergild 149
Wessex 149, 174
whetstones (hones) 11, 30, 111, 149, 197, 252, *334*
willow (*Salix* sp.) 22, 31
   belt 91, 196, 197
   knife handle 114
wood 195–7
   arrow shaft 30
   backing for buckle loop 86, 230
   belt 70, 91–2, 196–7

bowl 91
box 17, 18, 19, 91
coffins 190
inlay 103
lyre 121

sheath for pin 84
traces of – grain on 99, 102, 105, 110
used for scabbards, shields, spear shafts and sword grips 21, 22, 27, 31, 35, 196, 217

vessels 56, 105–6, 224, 225
wool, preserved on brooch 194

yew 121